EXODUS
19–40

VOLUME 2A

THE ANCHOR BIBLE is a fresh approach to the world's greatest classic. Its object is to make the Bible accessible to the modern reader; its method is to arrive at the meaning of biblical literature through exact translation and extended exposition, and to reconstruct the ancient setting of the biblical story, as well as the circumstances of its transcription and the characteristics of its transcribers.

THE ANCHOR BIBLE is a project of international and interfaith scope: Protestant, Catholic, and Jewish scholars from many countries contribute individual volumes. The project is not sponsored by any ecclesiastical organization and is not intended to reflect any particular theological doctrine. Prepared under our joint supervision, THE ANCHOR BIBLE is an effort to make available all the significant historical and linguistic knowledge which bears on the interpretation of the biblical record.

THE ANCHOR BIBLE is aimed at the general reader with no special formal training in biblical studies; yet it is written with the most exacting standards of scholarship, reflecting the highest technical accomplishment.

This project marks the beginning of a new era of cooperation among scholars in biblical research, thus forming a common body of knowledge to be shared by all.

William Foxwell Albright
David Noel Freedman
GENERAL EDITORS

THE ANCHOR BIBLE

EXODUS
19–40

◆

A New Translation
with Introduction and Commentary

WILLIAM H. C. PROPP

THE ANCHOR BIBLE
Doubleday
New York   London   Toronto   Sydney   Auckland

THE ANCHOR BIBLE
PUBLISHED BY DOUBLEDAY
a division of Random House, Inc.
1745 Broadway, New York, New York 10019

THE ANCHOR BIBLE, DOUBLEDAY, and the portrayal of an anchor
with the letters A and B are registered trademarks of Doubleday,
a division of Random House, Inc.

LIBRARY OF CONGRESS CATALOGING-IN-PUBLICATION DATA
is on file at the Library of Congress

ISBN 0-385-24693-5

For lovers of the Bible

ACKNOWLEDGMENTS

◆

I wish to thank Louis Bookheim, Andrew Corbin, Anna Propp Covici, Antonin Dvořák, Richard Elliot Friedman, W. Randall Garr, Ronald S. Hendel, Janice Dempsey, Elizabeth W. Goldstein, David Goodblatt, David G. Gutierrez, John Kaltner, Thomas E. Levy, the late Laurel J. Mannen, Alden Mosshammer, Shawna Dolansky Overton, Saul B. Propp, Jonah P. Propp, Miriam Sherman, Donald F. Tuzin and Laura M. Zucconi for their various contributions. Above all, I owe a debt to series editor David Noel Freedman, who entrusted the privilege of writing this commentary to a (then) very young scholar. Even more than the many improvements that he has suggested, I am grateful for his confidence in me and in this work.

W. H. C. P.

CONTENTS

◆

FIGURES AND MAPS

◆

All illustrations are by the author

LIST OF ABBREVIATIONS AND TERMS

◆

I. SYMBOLS, ABBREVIATIONS AND TERMS

. . .	omitted or unreadable words
(?)	reading uncertain
[ ]	reconstructed or restored text
*	reconstructed, unattested form
<	develops out of
>	develops into
< >	text lost by parablepsis
†	original reading in doubt; translation follows *BHS*
††	translation does not follow *BHS*
I	first dictionary definition
I-	first radical (pe' of tri-literal root)
1	first person
1 Chr	1 Chronicles
1 Cor	1 Corinthians
1 Esdr	1 Esdras
1 Kgs	1 Kings
1 Macc	1 Maccabees
1 Pet	1 Peter
1QpHab	DSS *Pesher on Habbakuk* (Cross et al. 1972: 149–63)
1QS	DSS *1QSerek* (Burrows 1950–51)
1QSb	Appendix B *(Blessings)* to 1QS
1 Sam	1 Samuel
1 Thess	1 Thessalonians
1 Tim	1 Timothy
II	second dictionary definition
II-	second radical ('ayin of tri-literal root)
2	second person
2 Chr	2 Chronicles
2 Cor	2 Corinthians
2 Esdr	2 Esdras
2 Kgs	2 Kings
2 Pet	2 Peter
2QExod[b]	DSS Exod (DJD 3.52–56)
2 Sam	2 Samuel

2 Thess	2 Thessalonians
2 Tim	2 Timothy
III-	third radical (lamedh of tri-literal root)
3	third person
3 Macc	3 Maccabees
4Q554	DSS New Jerusalem Text (forthcoming in DJD 37)
4QBibPar	DSS periphrastic Torah (DJD 5.1–6)
4QDeut[i]	DSS Deuteronomy (Duncan 1992; DJD 14.75–91)
4QDeut[n]	DSS Deuteronomy (White 1990)
4QExod-Lev[f]	DSS Exodus-Leviticus (DJD 12.133–43)
4QMezA-G	DSS Mezuzah (DJD 6.80–85)
4QpaleoExod[m]	DSS Exodus (DJD 9.53–130)
4QpaleoGen-Exod[l]	DSS Genesis-Exodus (DJD 9.17–50)
4QParaphrase of Genesis and Exodus	DSS periphrastic Torah (DJD 13.417–41)
4QPhylA-R	DSS phylactery (DJD 6.48–77)
4QReworked Pentateuch[b]	DSS periphrastic Torah (DJD 13.197–254)
4QReworked Pentateuch[c]	DSS periphrastic Torah (DJD 13.255–318)
4QReworked Pentateuch[d]	DSS periphrastic Torah (DJD 13.335–43)
4QSam[a]	DSS Samuel. Readings from McCarter (1980, 1984)
4QShirShabb[d]	DSS Songs of the Sabbath Sacrifice (Strugnell 1960)
4QTestim	DSS 4QTestimonia, (DJD 5.57–60)
4QtgLev	DSS Targum to Leviticus (DJD 6.86–87)
8QPhyl	DSS phylactery (DJD 3.149–56)
11QPs[a]	DSS Psalms (DJD 4.19–49)
11QTemple	DSS Temple Scroll (Yadin 1983)
a	first half of verse
Abarbanel	Isaac ben Judah Abarbanel, Iberian Jewish philosopher, commentator, 1437–1508 C.E.
abecedary	practice alphabet
ʿAbod. Zar.	tractate ʿAboda Zara
absolute state	base form of Aramaic noun
Abst.	Porphry, *de Abstinentia*
adyton	most sacred place
a fortiori	how much more so
AHI	G. I. Davies, *Ancient Hebrew Inscriptions* (Cambridge: Cambridge University, 1991)
AHw	W. von Soden, *Akkadisches Handwörterbuch* (Wiesbaden: Harrassowitz, 1965–1981)
aʾīlu	see *awīlu*
Akhenaten	pharaoh, r. c. 1363–1347 B.C.E.
Akkadian	Mesopotamian Semitic language; main dialects Assyrian (north) and Babylonian (south)
ʾaleph	first letter of the Hebrew alphabet
alloform	alternative form
alpha	in a position of social dominance
ʾal tiqrê	"Do not read"; interpretation technique based on wordplay
Amarna	Egyptian site yielding tablets containing Egyptian diplomatic correspondence (fourteenth century B.C.E.); capital of Akhenaten
Amenophis IV	see Akhenaten
Amun(-Re)	Chief god of New Kingdom Egypt

ʿAnatu	Ugaritic goddess of passion
ANEP	J. B. Pritchard, ed. *The Ancient Near East in Pictures Relating to the Old Testament* (Princeton, N.J.: Princeton University, 1969)
ANET	J. B. Pritchard, ed. *Ancient Near Eastern Texts Relating to the Old Testament* (Princeton, N.J.: Princeton University, 1950)
ANET³	ANET, third edition with Supplement (1969)
aniconic	without images
Ant.	Josephus, *Antiquities*
anthropomorphism	imputing human traits to nonhuman beings
Ap.	Josephus, *Against Apion*
ʾAphʿel	causative conjugation of the Aramaic verb
apodictic	law phrased as direct command
apodosis	"then" clause in a conditional sentence
apud	cited at secondhand from
Aquila	Jewish translator of Bible into Greek, c. 125 C.E.
Arabic	Semitic language; also, daughter translation of LXX
ʿArak.	tractate *ʿArakin*
Aramaic	Northwest Semitic language of ancient Syria
Arch of Titus	Roman triumphal monument depicting the spoils of the Second Temple (70 C.E.)
archaic	old-fashioned
archaistic	artificially made to look old-fashioned
ʿārōb	fourth plague, likely an insect (NOTE to 8:17)
Ascending-offering	burnt offering, holocaust (*ʿōlâ*)
Asherah	sacred wooden pole or tree; also a goddess
assimilation	becoming similar or identical
asyndeton	omission of conjunctions
ʾAṯiratu	Ugaritic chief goddess
autograph	original MS
AV	Authorized (King James) Version
awīlu	Akkadian for "(free)man" (Assyrian *aʾīlu*)
ʿayin	sixteenth letter of the Hebrew alphabet
b	second half of a verse
b.	Babylonian Talmud
baetyl	sacred pillar
bailee	one who receives goods on deposit
bailor	one who deposits goods
B. Bat.	tractate *Baba Batra*
B.C.E.	Before the Common Era (= B.C.)
BDB	F. Brown, S. R. Driver, C. A. Briggs, *A Hebrew and English Lexicon of the Old Testament* (Boston/New York: Houghton Mifflin, 1907)
Bek.	tractate *Bekorot*
Bekhor Shor	Joseph ben Isaac Bekhor Shor, French Jewish exegete, twelfth century C.E.
Bel	Bel and the Dragon
Ber.	tractate *Berakot*
beth	second letter of the Hebrew alphabet
BHS	*Biblia Hebraica Stuttgartensia* (Stuttgart: Deutsche Bibelgesellschaft, 1983)
Bib. Ant.	Pseudo-Philo, *Biblical Antiquities*, c. 50 C.E. (OTP 2.304–77)

Bikk.	tractate *Bikkurim*
B. Meṣ.	tractate *Baba Meṣi'a*
B. Qam.	tractate *Baba Qamma*
byform	alternate form
C	consonant
c.	approximately *(circa)*
ca.	approximately *(circa)*
CAD	*The Assyrian Dictionary of the Oriental Institute of the University of Chicago (Chicago Assyrian Dictionary)* (Chicago: Oriental Institute, 1956–)
Cairo Genizah	repository for discarded scrolls in Ezra Synagogue of Cairo (since eighth century C.E.)
Calvin	John Calvin, protestant reformer and Bible commentator, 1509–1564 C.E.
Cant	Canticles, Song of Songs
cantillation	Massoretic musical/accentual/syntactic notation (trope)
Cant. Rab.	*Canticles Rabba*, midrashic compendium
case ending	declined suffixes on nominal forms in some Semitic languages and in proto-Semitic
casuistic	law phrased as a condition ("if . . . then")
CAT	M. Dietrich, O. Loretz, J. Sanmartín, *The Cuneiform Alphabetic Texts* (Münster: Ugarit-Verlag, 1995)
C.E.	Common Era (= A.D.)
cf.	compare *(confer)*
chiasm	symmetrical ABB'A' structure
Chronicler	anonymous author of 1–2 Chronicles
Clear, Clearing	(obtain) purification, atonement *(kpr)*
cognate	etymologically related
Col	Colossians
common gender	either masculine or feminine
composite text	Torah composed of JEDP sources
Concluding-offering	eaten sacrifice *(šelem)*
conflation	combination
conjectural emendation	emendation without textual basis
continous writing	omitting divisions between words
Congr.	Philo, *De Congressu Eruditionis gratia*
cubit	measure, c. 1.5 feet/50 cm.
D	source of Deuteronomy
daghesh	point placed inside letter to indicate doubling or, in *bgdkpt*, plosive pronunciation
Dan	Daniel
Debhir	the Temple's inner chamber
Decal.	Philo, *De Decalogo*
Decalog	Ten Commandments
defective	written without *matres lectionis*
Deity	translation for *'ĕlōhîm* 'God' (NOTE to 1:17)
denominative	derived from a noun
Deut	Deuteronomy
Deuteronomistic	pertaining to the editorial stratum of the Deuteronomistic History
Deuteronom(ist)ic	pertaining to either D or Dtr

Deuteronomistic History   Deuteronomy through 2 Kings
direct object marker   preposition 'ēt
dittography   accidental double writing
DJD   Discoveries in the Judaean Desert (Oxford: Clarendon Press)
Documentary Hypothesis   theory that the Torah is composed of several sources
Donation   consecrated contribution (tərûmâ)
DSS   Dead Sea Scroll(s)
D-stem   verbal conjugation with doubled middle radical; Hebrew Piʻel
Dtr   Deuteronomistic History
Dtr²   exilic, second edition of Dtr
D(tr)   Deuteronom(ist)ic
dual   noun form indicating a pair (e.g., yādayim 'two hands')
E   Elohistic source
Eccl   Ecclesiastes, Qohelet
Eighteenth Dynasty   Egypt c. 1558–1303 B.C.E.
eisegesis   reading into a text
Elevation   sacred donation (tənûpâ)
ellipsis   omission of a word or words that are nevertheless to be understood
Elohist   author of E
emphatic state   definite form of Aramaic noun terminating in -ā'
Eph   Ephesians
eponymous   that for which something or someone is named
'Erub.   tractate 'Erubin
Eshnunna   Mesopotamian city; lawcode from c. 1770 B.C.E.
Esth   Esther
Ethiopic   Geʻez, classical Semitic language of Ethiopia; also, daughter
    translation of LXX
etiology   explanation of origins
Eusebius   Eusebius of Caesarea, Christian theologian and historian,
    c. 260–339 C.E.
exegesis   interpretation
exilic   pertaining to the Jews' Babylonian exile, 587–539 B.C.E.
Exod   Exodus
Exod. Rab.   Exodus Rabba, midrashic compendium
expansion   scribal addition
Ezek   Ezekiel
f.   feminine
Faro edition (1487)   early printed edition of Pentateuch
felix culpa   "fortunate sin," Christian term for the Fall of Man
fem.   feminine
fig.   figure
Filling   The consecration offering (millū'îm)
First Code   Exod 20:22[19]–23:33
first hand   the original text of a MS, later altered
First Isaiah   Isaiah chaps. 1–33, 36–39
Fragmentary Targum   imperfectly preserved Palestinian Targum(s) (Klein 1980)
g.   gram
Gal   Galatians
Gen   Genesis
Genizah   see Cairo Genizah

Gen. Rab.	*Genesis Rabba,* midrashic compendium
Gersonides	R. Levi ben Gershom, French Jewish philosopher and commentator, 1288–1344 C.E.
gimel	third letter of the Hebrew alphabet
Giṭ.	tractate *Giṭṭin*
GKC	*Gesenius' Hebräische Grammatik,* 28th ed., ed. E. Kautzsch, trans. A. E. Cowley (Oxford: Clarendon, 1910)
gloss	explanatory textual insertion
Greater J	supposed Yahwistic document present in Genesis through 1 Kings (Friedman 1998)
Guide	Maimonides, *Guide of the Perplexed*
guttural	fricative consonant pronounced in back of throat; in Hebrew, 'aleph, he', ḥeth, 'ayin
Hab	Habakkuk
Ḥag.	tractate *Ḥagiga*
Halakhah	Rabbinic law
HALOT	L. Koehler and W. Baumgartner, revised W. Baumgartner and J. J. Stamm et al.; translated and edited M. E. J. Richardson, *Hebrew and Aramaic Lexicon of the Old Testament* (Leiden/Boston: Brill, 2001)
Hammurapi	Babylonian king, r. c. 1792–1750 B.C.E.
hapax legomenon	term occurring only once
haplography	accidental omission due to sequence of similar letters or words
harmonize	resolve a contradiction
he'	fifth letter of the Hebrew alphabet
Heb	Hebrews
hendiadys	two coordinated words conveying a single concept
ḥeth	eighth letter of the Hebrew alphabet
Hex	Hexapla
Hexapla	Origen's compilation of Hebrew and Greek versions of the Bible
High Place	Israelite local temple *(bāmâ)*
Hiphʿil	causative conjugation of the Hebrew verb
Hithpaʿel	reflexive conjugation of the Hebrew verb
Hittite(s)	dominant civilization in Anatolia, c. 1600–1200 B.C.E.
Hittite Laws	legal compendia from ca. 1650–1500 and ca. 1400–1180 B.C.E.
Ḥizquni	Hezekiah ben Manoah, French Jewish commentator, mid-thirteenth century C.E.
hollow root	verbal root with middle waw or yodh
homoioarkton	consecutive words or phrases with same initial letter(s)
homoioteleuton	consecutive words or phrases with same final letter(s)
Hophʿal	passive-causative conjugation of the Hebrew verb
Hor.	tractate *Horayot*
Hos	Hosea
Ḥul.	tractate *Ḥullin*
hypercorrection	conforming a minor anomaly to the norm
hypostasis	personified attribute of a god
hysteron proteron	events narrated in reverse order
ibn Ezra	Abraham ibn Ezra, itinerant Jewish commentator and poet, 1089–1164 C.E.

ibn Janaḥ	Jonah ibn Janaḥ, Spanish Jewish grammarian and lexicographer, eleventh century C.E.
iconolatry	worship of images
ille locus	"that place," primordial, mythic space
illud tempus	"that time," primordial, mythic time
imitatio dei	imitation of a god
imperative	command
imperfect	Hebrew prefix conjugation of verb *(yiktōb)*
inclusio	framing through repitition of words or phrases
incongruence	grammatical nonagreement (e.g., in number or gender)
in loco parentis	in place of a parent
inner-Greek	within the transmission of LXX
inverted syntax	in Hebrew, subject before verb
Isa	Isaiah
Israel's Sons	the nation of Israel *(bənê yiśrā'ēl)*
Ixar Bible (1490)	early printed Torah
J	Yahwistic source
Japheth ben Ali	Qara'ite commentator (tenth cent. C.E.)
Jas	James
Jdt	Judith
JE	combination of J and E
Jer	Jeremiah
Jerome	Christian theologian, translator of Vg, c. 347–419 C.E.
Johannine	pertaining to the apostle John and works attributed to him
Josephus	Flavius Josephus, Jewish soldier and historian, c. 37–95 C.E.
Josh	Joshua
Jub	Jubilees
Judg	Judges
jussive	third-person command
KAI	H. Donner and W. Röllig, *Kanaanäische und aramäische Inschriften* (Wiesbaden: Harrassowitz, 1962)
kaph	eleventh letter of the Hebrew alphabet
KB	L. Köhler and W. Baumgartner, *Lexikon in Veteris Testamenti libros* (Leiden: Brill, 1958)
Kenn	MS collated by B. Kennicott (1776–80)
Ker.	tractate *Keritot*
kerygma	gospel, preaching
Kethibh	written (but not pronounced) (scribal annotation)
Ketub.	tractate *Ketubot*
kg.	kilogram
KJV	King James Version (= AV)
KTU	M. Dietrich, O. Loretz, J. Sanmartín, *Die keilalphabetischen Texte aus Ugarit* (Neukirchen-Vluyn: Neukirchener Verlag, 1976)
kur	Mesopotamian measure, c. 300 ltr.
L	Leningrad Codex
l.	line
lb.	pound
Lam	Lamentations
lamedh	twelfth letter of the Hebrew alphabet

LB	Late Bronze Age c. 1550–1200 B.C.E.
LCMAM	*Law Collections from Mesopotamia and Asia Minor*, ed. M. T. Roth (SBLWAWS 6; Atlanta: Scholars Press, 1995)
lectio brevior	shorter reading
lectio difficilior	more difficult reading
lectio facilior	easier reading
Leitwort	theme word
Leningrad Codex	St. Petersburg Museum biblical MS B 19a, written 1009 C.E.
Lev	Leviticus
Lev. Rab.	*Leviticus Rabba*, midrashic compendium
lex talionis	law of retribution, "eye for eye . . ."
Lipit-Ishtar	king of Isin c. 1930 B.C.E., promulgated law code in Sumerian
ltr.	liter
Luzzatto	Samuel David Luzzatto, Italian Jewish philosopher, commentator, 1800–65 C.E.
LXX	Septuagint, Greek Pentateuch
LXX^A	codex Alexandrinus
LXX^B	codex Vaticanus
LXX^F	codex Ambrosianus
LXX^M	codex Coislinianus
m.	masculine, meter
m.	Mishnah
Maimonides	R. Moses Maimonides (Rambam), Spanish-Egyptian Jewish theologian, 1135–1204 C.E.
Mak.	tractate *Makkot*
Mal	Malachi
marg.	margin
masc.	masculine
Massoretes	scribes who established MT, c. 700–900 C.E.
Massoretic Text	canonical Jewish Hebrew Bible
mater (pl. *matres*) *lectionis*	nonpronounced he', waw and yodh (*'ēm qərî'â*)
Matt	Matthew
mechanical	accidental, predictable scribal error
Mek.	*Mekilta*, midrashic compendium on Exodus
Mel. Mišk.	*Bāraytā' dimle(')ket hammiškān* (Kirschner 1992)
mem	thirteenth letter of the Hebrew alphabet
Menaḥ.	tractate *Menaḥot*
merism	expression of totality by naming the extremes
Merneptah	pharaoh, r. c. 1212–1202 B.C.E.
metathesis	reversal
metonymy	the whole named for a constituent or related object or concept
Mic	Micah
Mid.	tractate *Middot*
Middle Assyrian Laws	legal compendium, eleventh cent. B.C.E.
Middle Bronze Age	2000–1550 B.C.E.
Middle Kingdom	Egypt c. 2040–1633 B.C.E.
midrash	parabiblical Jewish legend
Mig.	Philo, *De Migratione Abrahami*
minus	missing text

minuscule	MS written in lowercase latters
Moʿed Qat.	tractate *Moʿed Qatan*
Mosaic	pertaining to Moses
Moses	Philo, *De Vita Mosis*
MS(S)	manuscript(s)
MT	Massoretic Text
Mut.	Philo, *De Mutatione Nominum*
mutatis mutandis	changing what must be changed, analogously
n.	note
Nah	Nahum
naos	temple's inner shrine
naptaru	acquaintance (Akkadian)
Nash Papyrus	Hebrew MS c. 100 B.C.E. containing Exod 20:2–17 and Deut 6:4–5 harmonized (Cooke 1903).
NEB	*New English Bible*
Ned.	tractate *Nedarim*
Neh	Nehemiah
Neo-Babylonian Laws	legal collection from Sippar, c. 700 B.C.E.
New Kingdom	Egypt c. 1558–1085 B.C.E.
Nineteenth Dynasty	Egypt c. 1303–1200 B.C.E.
Niphʿal	passive-reflexive conjugation of Hebrew verb
non sequitur	that which does not follow logically
Northwest Semitic	Amorite, Ugaritic, Aramaic, Phoenician, Canaanite, Moabite, Ammonite, Edomite, Hebrew
Num	Numbers
Num. Rab.	*Numbers Rabba*, midrashic compendium
nun	fourteenth letter of the Hebrew alphabet
Obad	Obadiah
OG	Old Greek; the Greek Old Testament
Ohol.	tractate *Oholot*
Old Kingdom	Egypt c. 2686–2160 B.C.E.
omphalus mundi	World Navel, center of earth, link to Heaven
ostracon	(inscribed) potsherd
OTP	J. H. Charlesworth, ed. *The Old Testament Pseudepigrapha* (2 vols.; Garden City, N.Y.: Doubleday, 1985)
oxymoron	self-contradictory figure of speech
oz.	ounce
P	the Priestly source
p.	page, plural
pace	in respectful dissent with
paleo-Hebrew script	the original, preexilic form of the Hebrew alphabet
parablepsis	skip of the eye
paragogic nun	archaic suffix attached to 2 m.p. and 3 m.p. imperfect verbs (e.g., *yiktōbûn*)
paronomasia	wordplay
pars pro toto	the part for the whole
participle	adjectival form of Hebrew verb (e.g., *kōtēb*)
passim	here and there
patronymic	identification by father's name

pausal	special form of word used at major syntactic breaks
pe'	seventeenth letter of the Hebrew alphabet
Pentateuch	Torah
perfect	Hebrew suffix conjugation of the verb (e.g., *kātab*)
pericope	section of text
Pesaḥ	Israelite festival/sacrifice antecedent to Jewish Passover
Pesaḥ.	tractate *Pesaḥim*
Pesiq. Rab Kah.	*Pesiqta deRab Kahana*
Phil	Philippians
Philo	Philo of Alexandria, Hellenistic Jewish writer and philosopher, c. 20 B.C.E.–50 C.E.
Philo of Byblos	author of *Phoenician History*, c. 70–160 C.E.
Phlm	Philemon
Pi'el	Hebrew verbal conjugation with doubled middle radical
Pirqe R. El.	*Pirqe Rabbi Eliezer*
pl.	plural, plate
plene	full use of *matres lectionis*
plus	a longer text
pointing	the Hebrew vocalization, *niqqûd*
postexilic	after 539 B.C.E.
praeferenda est	must be preferred
Praep. evangelica	Eusebius, *Praeparatio evangelica*
preexilic	before 587 B.C.E.
Priestly	pertaining to the P source or its author
Priestly Writer	author of P
privately	personal communication
protasis	"if" clause in a conditional sentence
proto-MT	standard Jewish Bible prior to c. 700 C.E.
Proto-Semitic	ancestor of the Semitic languages
Prov	Proverbs
PRU	*le Palais royal d'Ugarit*
Ps	Psalm(s)
PS	Proto-Semitic
ps.	pseudo
pseudo-Lucian	author of *The Syrian Goddess*
Pu'al	passive of Pi'el conjugation
Qal	base form of Hebrew verb (Pa'al)
Qal Passive	internal passive of the Qal
Qara'ites	literalistic Jewish sect, c. 765 C.E. to present
Qere	pronounced (though not written) (scribal annotation)
Qidd.	tractate *Qiddušin*
Qimḥi	David Qimḥi, Provençal Jewish commentator and grammarian, c. 1160–1235 C.E.
Qoh. Rab.	*Qohelet Rabba*, midrashic compendium
qoph	nineteenth letter of the Hebrew alphabet
Quaest. in Exod.	Philo, *Quaestiones in Exodum*
Quis Her.	Philo, *Quis rerum divinarum Heres sit*
R	Redactorial stratum of Torah
r.	reigned
R.	Rabbi

Rabbanite	Jews upholding the validity of Talmudic law
radical	root letter/consonant
Rahlfs	A. Rahlfs, *Verzeichnis der griechischen Handschriften des Alten Testaments* (MSU 2; Berlin: Weidmann, 1914).
Ramban	R. Moses ben Nachman (Nachmanides), Spanish Jewish commentator, 1194–1270 C.E.
Ramesses II	pharaoh, r. c. 1279–1212 B.C.E.
Ramesses III	pharaoh, r. c. 1182–1151 B.C.E.
Rashbam	R. Samuel ben Meir, French Jewish commentator on Bible and Talmud, c. 1080–1174 C.E.
Rashi	R. Solomon ben Isaac, French Jewish commentator on Bible and Talmud, 1040–1105 C.E.
Ravad	R. Avraham ben David. French Jewish legal commentator, 1125–1198 C.E.
received text	MT
Redactor	final editor of Torah
Redactor[JE]	editor who produced JE
redivivus	returned to life
resh	twentieth letter of the Hebrew alphabet
resumptive repetition	repetition framing a digression (epanalepsis, *Wiederaufnahme*)
Rev	Revelation
Rom	Romans
Roš Haš.	tractate *Roš Haššana*
Rossi	MS collated by J. B. de Rossi (1784–85)
Saadiah	Saadiah ben Joseph Gaon, Babylonian Jewish scholar, 882–942 C.E.
Šabb.	tractate *Šabbat*
Sabbatical	year of release from certain legal obligations and agricultural activity every seven years
Sahidic	dialect of Coptic; also, daughter translation of LXX
Saite period	Twenty-sixth Dynasty Egypt, 664–525 B.C.E.
Sam	Samaritan Torah
Samaritans	sect/community of Jews from middle first millennium B.C.E. until present
Samaritan Tg.	translation of Torah into Samaritan Aramaic
samekh	fifteenth letter of the Hebrew alphabet
sanctum	holy thing, place
Sanh.	tractate *Sanhedrin*
ṣāraʿat	skin disease; "leprosy"
Šeb.	tractate *Šebiʿit*
Sebhirin	tentative marginal correction or scruple, "one might think" (scribal annotation)
Šebu.	tractate *Šebuʿot*
secondary	added later
Second Code	Exod 34:11–26
Second Isaiah	Isaiah 34–35, 40–66
sekretu	class of set-apart women (Akkadian)
Šeqal.	tractate *Šeqalim*
Septuagint	Greek Torah (third century B.C.E.)
Sforno	Obadiah ben Jacob Sforno, Italian Jewish commentator, c. 1470–1550 C.E.

Shalmaneser III	Assyrian king, r. c. 858–823 B.C.E.
shekel	unit of weight, c. 11.4 g.
shin	twenty-first letter of the Hebrew alphabet
Sifra	midrashic compendium to Leviticus
sila	Mesopotamian measure, c. 1 ltr.
sin	alternative pronunciation of the twenty-first letter of the Hebrew alphabet
Sin-offering	purifying, atoning sacrifice (*ḥaṭṭā[']t*)
Sir	Wisdom of Jesus ben Sira
Soncino Bible (1488)	first printed Hebrew Bible
Spec. Leg.	Philo, *De Specialibus Legibus*
Spinoza	Baruch (Benedict) Spinoza, Dutch Jewish philosopher, 1632–77 C.E.
square script	Aramaic alphabet used for Hebrew writing since c. 400 B.C.E.
Sukk.	tractate *Sukka*
Sumerian	dominant civilization of Mesopotamia c. 3000–2000 B.C.E.
Sumerian Laws about Rented Oxen	legal text from Nippur, c. 1800 B.C.E.
Sumerian Laws Exercise Tablet	legal text, c. 1800 B.C.E.
superlinear	inserted above the line
syllabic orthography	special use of hieroglyphics to write foreign names
Symmachus	Jewish reviser of LXX to proto-MT (c. 200 C.E.)
synecdoche	part for the whole
Syr	Syriac Bible
SyrHex	Syro-Hexapla
Syro-Hexapla	translation of Hexapla into Syriac
t.	Tosephta
Taʿan.	tractate *Taʿanit*
talent	unit of weight, c. 30 kg.
talion	retribution
Tanḥ.	*Midraš Tanḥuma*
Targum	Jewish Aramaic Bible translation
taw	twenty-second letter of the Hebrew alphabet
Ten Words	Ten Commandments, Decalog
teth	ninth letter of the Hebrew alphabet
Tetragrammaton	divine name *yhwh*
Tg.	Targum
Tg. Neofiti I	Palestinian Targum to the Torah
Tg. Onqelos	literalistic Targum to the Torah
Tg. Ps.-Jonathan	midrashic Palestinian Targum to the Torah
theodicy	theological speculation about divine justice
Theodotion	Jewish revision of LXX to proto-MT (c. 50 B.C.E.)
theophany	divine manifestation
theriomorphism	imputing animal traits to non-animal entities
Three, the	Symmachus, Aquila, Theodotion
Ṭohar.	tractate *Ṭoharot*
Torah	first five books of Bible
tractate	division of the Talmud
Tract. theolog.-pol.	Spinoza, *Tractatus theologico-politicus*
Tribute-offering	grain offering (*minḥâ*)
trope	cantillation

Twelve Tables	ancient Roman legal text
Twentieth Dynasty	Egypt c. 1200–1085 B.C.E.
type	model; prefiguration
Ugarit	city in N. Syria, flourished c. 1400–1200 B.C.E.
Ur-Namma	king of Ur, r. c. 2112–2095 B.C.E.
v	verse
Version(s)	suriving witness(es) to biblical text
Vetus Latina	early Latin translation of LXX
Vg	Vulgate
Virt.	Philo, *De Virtute*
vocalization	Hebrew vowel points *(niqqûd)*
Vorlage	Hebrew text underlying translation
vs.	versus
Vulgate	translation of Bible into Latin by Jerome
War	Josephus, *Jewish War*
waw	sixth letter of the Hebrew alphabet
Wiederaufnahme	resumptive repetition, epanalepsis
Wis	Wisdom of Solomon
witness	any biblical MS or translation
y.	Palestinian/Jerusalem Talmud
Yahweh	God's name
Yahwism	Israelite religion
Yahwist	author of J
Yebam.	tractate *Yebamot*
yodh	tenth letter of the Hebrew alphabet
Zadokite	descendant of Zadok, high priest under King Solomon
zayin	seventh letter of the Hebrew alphabet
Zebaḥ.	tractate *Zebaḥim*
Zech	Zechariah
zeugma	incongruous attachment of a single modifier to two incompatible antecedents

II. BIBLIOGRAPHICAL ABBREVIATIONS

AB	Anchor Bible
ABD	*Anchor Bible Dictionary*
ABRL	Anchor Bible Reference Library
AGJU	Arbeiten zur Geschichte des antiken Judentums und des Urchristentums
AJSL	*American Journal of Semitic Languages and Literature*
AL	Orientalia Lovaniensia analecta
ALUOS	*Annual of the Leeds University Oriental Society*
AnBib	Analecta biblica
AOAT	Alter Orient und Altes Testament
AOS	American Oriental Society
ASOR	American Schools of Oriental Research
ASORDS	ASOR Dissertation Series
ASTI	*Annual of the Swedish Theological Institute*
AUSS	*Andrews University Seminary Studies*
BA	*Biblical Archaeologist*

BARev	Biblical Archaeology Review
BASOR	Bulletin of the American Schools of Oriental Research
BASORSup	BASOR, Supplements
BBB	Bonner biblische Beiträge
Bib	*Biblica*
BibB	Biblische Beiträge
BibOr	Biblica et orientalia
BN	*Biblische Notizen*
BRev	*Bible Review*
BS	*Bibliotheca Sacra*
BZ	*Biblische Zeitschrift*
BZAW	Beihefte zur ZAW
CahRB	Cahiers de la *Revue biblique*
CBQ	*Catholic Biblical Quarterly*
CBQMS	CBQ Monograph Series
ConBOT	Coniectanea biblica, Old Testament
CRAIBL	*Comptes rendus de l'Académie des inscriptions et belles-lettres*
diss.	dissertation
DJD	Discoveries in the Judaean Desert
ed.	edited by
EM	'Enṣiqlôpedyâ miqrā'ît
EncJud	*Encyclopedia Judaica*
ErIsr	Eretz Israel
et al.	and others (*et alii*)
FRLANT	Forschungen zur Religion und Literatur des Alten und Neuen Testaments
Fs.	Festschrift
HAR	*Hebrew Annual Review*
HKAT	Handkommentar zum Alten Testament
HSM	Harvard Semitic Monographs
HSS	Harvard Semitic Studies
HTR	*Harvard Theological Review*
HUCA	*Hebrew Union College Annual*
IDB	*Interpreter's Dictionary of the Bible*
IEJ	*Israel Exploration Journal*
IKZ	*Internationale katholische Zeitschrift*
Int	*Interpretation*
JA	*Journal asiatique*
JANES	Journal of the Ancient Near Eastern Society
JARCE	Journal of the American Research Center in Egypt
JAOS	Journal of the American Oriental Society
JBL	Journal of Biblical Literature
JBLMS	JBL Monograph Series
JBQ	Jewish Biblical Quarterly
JCS	Journal of Cuneiform Studies
JEA	Journal of Egyptian Archaeology
JFA	Journal of Field Archaeology
JJS	Journal of Jewish Studies
JNES	Journal of Near Eastern Studies

JNSL	*Journal of Northwest Semitic Languages*
JQR	*Jewish Quarterly Review*
JPS	Jewish Publication Society
JSOT	*Journal for the Study of the Old Testament*
JSOTSup	*JSOT,* Supplements
JSS	*Journal of Semitic Studies*
JTS	*Journal of Theological Studies*
LCL	Loeb Classical Library
Leš	*Lešonénu*
MSU	Mitteilungen des Septuaginta-Unternehmens
N.A.B.U.	*Nouvelles Assyriologiques Brèves et Utilitaires.*
NIV	New International Version
OBO	Orbis biblicus et orientalis
OLA	*Orientalia Lovaniensia Analecta*
Or	*Orientalia*
orig.	original edition
OTL	Old Testament Library
OTS	*Oudtestamentische Studiën*
PEQ	*Palestine Exploration Quarterly*
pub.	published
Qad	*Qadmoniyot*
RB	*Revue biblique*
RHR	*Revue de l'histoire des religions*
RlA	*Reallexikon der Asssyriologie*
SBLDS	SBL Dissertation Series
SBLSCS	SBL Septuagint and Cognate Studies
SBLTT	SBL Texts and Translations
SBLWAW	SBL Writings from the Ancient World
SBT	Studies in Biblical Theology
ScrHier	Scripta hierosolymitana
SJOT	*Scandinavian Journal of the Old Testament*
SSN	Studia Semitica Neerlandica
STDJ	Studies on the Texts of the Desert of Judah
TA	*Tel Aviv*
TDOT	*Theological Dictionary of the Old Testament*
UF	*Ugarit-Forschungen*
Ug	*Ugaritica*
VT	*Vetus Testamentum*
VTSup	*VT,* Supplements
WBC	Word Biblical Commentary
WMANT	Wissenschaftliche Monographien zum Alten und Neuen Testament
WO	*Die Welt des Orients*
ZABR	*Zeitschrift für Altorientalische und Biblische Rechtsgeschichte*
ZAH	*Zeitschrift für Althebräistik*
ZAW	*Zeitschrift für die alttestamentliche Wissenschaft*
ZDMG	*Zeitschrift der deutschen morgenländischen Gesellschaft*
ZDPV	*Zeitschrift des deutschen Palästina-Vereins*

TRANSLITERATION SYSTEM

◆

My Hebrew transliteration slightly modifies a system familiar to scholars, though fairly inscrutable to the uninitiated. Its advantage is a near one-to-one correspondence to Massoretic symbols. It probably does not, however, reflect the Massoretes' actual pronunciation, still less the ancient Israelites'.

I do not generally indicate a "weak" dagesh in *bgdkpt*; when necessary, however, I show spirantization by over- or underlining. *Matres lectionis* are indicated either by circumflex *(â, î, ê, ô, û)* or by a letter in parentheses *(h or y)*. Quiescent 'aleph retained by historical spelling is often put within parentheses, e.g., *rō(')š* 'head.' Parenthetical shewa—(ə)—indicates a shewa that might or might not have been vocalic in Massoretic Hebrew. Like other grammarians, I consider so-called lamedh-he' roots to be lamedh-yodh (e.g., the root "to build" is *bny*, not *bnh*). Here are the alphabetic consonants and vowel points:

HEBREW TRANSLITERATION

	Consonants				Vowel Points		
	Medial	Final					
Letter	Position	Position	Transliteration		Vowel	Pointing	Transliteration
'aleph	א		'		vocal šəwā'	אְ	ə
beth	ב		b		qāmeṣ	אָ	ā
gimel	ג		g		pataḥ	אַ	a
daleth	ד		d		ḥātēp pataḥ	אֲ	ă
he	ה		h		ḥîreq	אִ	i*
waw	ו		w		ḥîreq yôd	אִי	î
zayin	ז		z		ṣērê	אֵ	ē
ḥeth	ח		ḥ		ṣērê yôd	אֵי	ê
teth	ט		ṭ		səgōl	אֶ	e
yodh	י		y		ḥātēp səgōl	אֱ	ě
kaph	כ	ך	k		ḥōlem	אֹ	ō

* ḥîreq—rarely ī long ḥîreq

lamedh	ל		l		ḥōlem wāw	וֹ	ô
mem	מ	ם	m		qāmeṣ qāṭôn	אָ	o
nun	נ	ן	n		ḥatēp qāmeṣ	אֳ	ŏ
samekh	ס		s		qibbûṣ	אֻ	u**
ʿayin	ע		ʿ		šûreq	וּ	û
pe	פ	ך	p				
ṣadhe	צ	ץ	ṣ				
qoph	ק		q				
resh	ר		r				
shin	שׁ		š				
sin	שׂ		ś				
taw	ת		t				

** qibbûs—rarely ū long qibbûṣ

And here is the last verse of MT Exodus in transliteration: *kî ʿănan yahwe(h) ʿal-hammiškān yômām wəʾēš tihye(h) laylâ bô ləʿênê kol-bêt-yiśrāʾēl bəkol-masʿêhem.*

Exodus 19–40
A Translation

◆

PART IV. THE FIRST COVENANT (EXODUS 19–24)

XVIII. *All that Yahweh spoke we will do and heed* (19:1–24:18)*

19 ¹ In the third month of Israel's Sons going out from the land of Egypt, on this day, they came to the Sinai Wilderness. ²And they set forth from Rephidim and came to the Sinai Wilderness and camped in the wilderness. And Israel camped there, opposite the mountain, ³but Moses, he ascended to the Deity.

And Yahweh called to him from the mountain, saying: "Thus you will say to Jacob's house, and tell to Israel's Sons: ⁴'You, you saw what I did to Egypt, and I carried you on vultures' wings and brought you to me. ⁵And now, if you will listen, listen to my voice and keep my Covenant, then you will become for me a treasure beyond all the peoples, for mine is all the earth. ⁶And you, you will become for me a priests' kingdom and a holy nation.' These are the words that you will speak to Israel's Sons."

⁷And Moses came and called to the people's elders and put before them all these words that Yahweh commanded him. ⁸And all the people answered as one and said, "All that Yahweh spoke we will do." And Moses brought the people's words back to Yahweh.

⁹And Yahweh said to Moses, "See: I am coming to you in the nimbus cloud, so that the people may hear during my speaking with you, and also in you they may trust to eternity." And Moses told the people's words to Yahweh.

¹⁰And Yahweh said to Moses, "Go to the people, and you shall sanctify them today and tomorrow, and they shall wash their robes. ¹¹And they must be ready for the third day, for on the third day Yahweh will descend in all the people's *eyes* onto Mount Sinai. ¹²And you shall restrict the people all around, saying, "Guard yourselves (from) ascending on the mountain and infringing upon its edge. Any infringing upon the mountain must be put to death, death. ¹³A hand must not touch him; but he must be stoned, stoned or shot, shot: whether animal whether man, he shall not live. When the *ram pulls*, they, they shall ascend on the mountain."

¹⁴And Moses descended from the mountain to the people and sanctified the people, and they washed their robes. ¹⁵And he said to the people, "Be ready for three days; don't come near to a woman."

Note: The translation of Exodus 19–40 is based upon a reconstructed Hebrew text diverging from that found in printed Bibles. All differences are explained under TEXTUAL NOTES. Special idioms and untranslated Hebrew terms are italicized; these are explained under NOTES. On the hyperliteral style, see vol. I, pp. 40, 41; below, pp. 805–6.

* Printed editions of the Hebrew Bible vary in their verse enumeration for chap. 20 after v 13 (see NOTE to 20:1). This edition follows *BHS*, supplying in parentheses the alternative numbering. Untranslated Hebrew terms and literally rendered idioms are italicized; capitalization indicates a proper noun or a technical expression.

¹⁶And it happened on the third day at morning's happening, and there were *sounds* and lightnings and a heavy cloud on the mountain and a horn's sound, very strong. And all the people who were in the camp quaked. ¹⁷And Moses took the people out to meet the Deity from the camp, and they stationed themselves at the mountain's bottom. ¹⁸And Mount Sinai, it smoked, all of it, forasmuch as Yahweh had descended upon it in fire, and its smoke ascended like furnace smoke, and all the mountain quaked greatly. ¹⁹And the horn's sound was *going and strengthening* greatly; Moses, he would speak, and the Deity, he would answer him with sound. ²⁰And Yahweh descended onto Mount Sinai, to the mountain's head, and Yahweh called Moses to the mountain's head. And Moses ascended.

²¹But Yahweh said to Moses, "Descend, warn the people, lest they break through to Yahweh to see, and many of it fall. ²²And also the priests approaching to Yahweh, they must sanctify themselves, lest Yahweh erupt against them."

²³But Moses said to Yahweh, "The people will not be able to ascend to Mount Sinai, for you, you warned us, saying, 'Restrict the mountain, and you shall sanctify it.' "

²⁴And Yahweh said to him, "Go, descend, and you shall ascend, you and Aaron with you; but the priests and the people, they must not break through to ascend to Yahweh, lest he erupt against them."

²⁵So Moses descended to the people and said to them—

20 ¹And Deity spoke all these words, saying: ²"I am Yahweh your deity who took you out from the land of Egypt, from a slaves' house.

³"There shall be for you no other gods before my face.

⁴"Don't make for yourself a statue or any image, what is in the heavens above or what is in the earth below or what is in the waters below the earth. ⁵Don't bow to them or serve them, for I am Yahweh your deity, a jealous deity, reckoning fathers' sin upon sons, upon a third and upon a fourth (generation) for my haters, ⁶but doing fidelity to a thousandth (generation) for my lovers and my command-keepers.

⁷"Don't raise Yahweh's name for nothing, for Yahweh will not clear whoever raises his name for nothing.

⁸"Remember the Sabbath day, to sanctify it. ⁹Six days you may work and do your every task, ¹⁰but the seventh day is Sabbath for Yahweh your deity. Don't do any task, you or your son or your daughter, your manservant or your maidservant or your animal or your sojourner who is in your gates. ¹¹For (in) six days Yahweh made the heavens and the earth, the sea and all that is in them, but he rested on the seventh day. Therefore Yahweh blessed the Sabbath day and sanctified it.

¹²"Honor your father and your mother, so that your days may lengthen upon the soil that Yahweh your deity is giving to you.

¹³"Don't murder.

¹⁴(13)"Don't commit adultery.

¹⁵(13)"Don't steal.

¹⁶(13)"Don't testify against your fellow as a false witness.

¹⁷(14)"Don't covet your fellow's house; don't covet your fellow's wife or his manservant or his maidservant or his bull or his ass or anything of your fellow."

18(15) And all the people were seeing the *sounds* and the *torches* and the horn's sound and the mountain smoking, and the people feared and recoiled and stood from afar. 19(16) And they said to Moses, "Speak you with us, that we may hear; but Deity must not speak with us, lest we die."

20(17) And Moses said to the people, "Don't fear; because for the sake of testing you has the Deity come, and for the sake of his fear will be *upon your face*, so that you won't sin."

21(18) And the people stood from afar, but Moses, he approached to the dark-cloud where the Deity was there.

22(19) And Yahweh said to Moses, "Thus you will say to Israel's Sons: 'You, you saw that from the sky I spoke with you. 23(20) Don't make along with me silver gods, and gold gods don't make for yourselves. 24(21) An earthen altar you may make for me, and you will sacrifice on it your Ascending-offerings and your Concluding-offerings, your flock and your herd; in any place where I announce my name, I will come to you and bless you. 25(22) But if an altar of stones you make for me, don't build them *cutstone*, for your blade you shall have lifted against it and profaned it. 26(23) And don't ascend by steps up to my altar, at which your nudity must not be revealed.'

21   1 "These are the case-laws that you shall set before them:

2 'When you buy a Hebrew manservant, six years he shall serve, and in the seventh he shall depart as a freeman, gratis. 3 If with his *gap* he enters, with his *gap* he shall depart; if he is a woman's husband, then his woman shall depart with him. 4 If his master gives him a woman and she bears him sons or daughters, then the woman and her children, she shall belong to her master, and he, he shall depart with his *gap*.

5 'If the manservant should say, say, "I love my master, my woman and my sons; I will not depart a freeman," 6 then his master shall bring him to the Deity and bring him to the door or to the doorpost. And his master shall drill his ear with a drill, and he must serve him forever.

7 'And when a man sells his daughter as a maidservant, she shall not depart as the manservants' departing. 8 If she is bad in her master's eyes, who did not engage for her, then he must let her be ransomed; to alien kin he is not entitled to sell her, for his breach of contract with her. 9 And if for his son he engages for her, according to the daughters' case he shall do with her. 10 If another (woman) he takes for himself, her flesh, her covering and her 'ōnâ he may not stint. 11 And if these three he does not do for her, then she may depart gratis; there is no silver.

12 'Whoever strikes a man and he dies must be put to death, death. 13 But the one who did not lie in wait, but the Deity by happenstance brought it to his hand, then I will set for you a place whither he may flee. 14 But when a man presumes against his fellow to kill him by premeditation, from beside my altar you may take him to die.

15 'Whoever strikes his father or his mother must be put to death, death. 16 And whoever steals a man—and he sells him and/or he/it is found *in his hand*—must be put to death, death.

17 'And whoever curses his father or his mother must be put to death, death.

18 'And when men contend, and a man strikes his fellow with a stone or with a fist, and he does not die, but falls to bed, 19 if he gets up and walks about outside upon his cane, then the striker is cleared; only (for?) his sitting idle he must give, and he must heal, heal.

20 'And when a man strikes his manservant or his maidservant with the rod, and he dies under his hand, he must be avenged, avenged. 21 However, if a day or two days he *stands*, he shall not be avenged, for he is his silver.

22 'And when men fight, and they strike a pregnant woman, and her child comes out, and there is no injury, he must be fined, fined, as the woman's husband may stipulate against him, and he shall give what is fair. 23 But if injury there is, then you must give — life for life, 24 eye for eye, tooth for tooth, arm for arm, leg for leg, 25 burn for burn, wound for wound, stripe for stripe.

26 'And when a man strikes his manservant's eye or his maidservant's eye and ruins it, as a freeman he must release him for his eye. 27 And if his manservant's tooth or his maidservant's tooth he makes fall out, as a freeman he must release him for his tooth.

28 'And when a bull gores a man or woman and he dies, the bull must be stoned, stoned, and its meat may not be eaten; but the bull's owner is clear. 29 But if it was a gorer bull *from yesterday-the day before*, and it was warned about to its owner, but he did not guard it, and it caused a man or a woman to die, the bull shall be stoned, and also its owner must be put to death. 30 If a ransom is imposed upon him, then he must give his life's redemption, as whatever is imposed upon him. 31 Whether a son it gores or a daughter it gores, according to this case shall be done to it. 32 If a manservant the bull gores or a maidservant, silver, thirty shekels, he must give to his master, and the bull must be stoned.

33 'And when a man opens a pit or when a man digs a pit and does not cover it, and a bull or an ass falls therein, 34 the pit's owner must reimburse; silver he must restore to its owner, and the dead shall be his.

35 'And when a man's bull injures his fellow's bull, and it dies, then they shall sell the living bull and divide its silver, and also the dead they shall divide. 36 Or (if) it was known that it was a gorer bull *from yesterday-the day before*, and its owner did not guard it, he must reimburse, reimburse, bull for bull, and the dead shall be his.

37 'When a man steals a bull or a sheep and slaughters it or sells it, five large cattle for the bull he must reimburse, or four small cattle for the sheep. 22 1 If in breaking in the thief is found, and he strikes him and he dies, there is no *bloodiness* for him. 2 If the sun shone upon him, there is *bloodiness* for him; he must pay, pay. If he has nothing, then he shall be sold for his theft. 3 If the theft, from bull to ass to sheep, is found, found in his hand alive, twofold he must pay.

4 'When a man clears a field or vineyard, and he releases his cattle, and it clears in another's field, he shall pay, pay from his field according to its yield; and if the entire field it clears, his field's best and his vineyard's best he shall pay. 5 If fire goes out and reaches briars, and stacked grain or the standing grain or the field is consumed, the fire-setter must pay, pay for the burning.

6 'When a man gives to his fellow silver or objects to keep, and it is stolen from

the man's house, if the thief is found, he shall pay twofold. [7] If the thief is not found, then the house owner shall approach to the Deity: if he did not send his hand against his fellow's property. . . . [8] In any crime case about a bull, about an ass, about a sheep, about a robe, about anything lost concerning which one says that, "That's it," unto the Deity the case of the two of them shall come. Whomever Deity finds guilty shall pay twofold to his fellow.

[9] 'When a man gives to his fellow an ass or a bull or a sheep or any animal to keep, and it dies or suffers a break or is raided without one seeing, [10] an oath by Yahweh will be between the two of them: if he did not send his hand against his fellow's property. . . . And its owner shall accept, and he shall not pay. [11] If it is stolen, stolen from with him, he must pay its owner. [12] If it is torn, torn, let him bring it, evidence of the tearing; he shall not pay.

[13] 'And when a man borrows from his fellow, and it suffers a break or dies, its owner not with it, he must pay, pay. [14] If its owner is with it, he shall not pay. If it is hired, it came in its payment.

[15] 'And when a man seduces a virgin who was not betrothed and lies with her, he must pay, pay her bride-price as a wife to him. [16] If her father refuses, refuses to give her to him, silver he must weigh out, according to the virgins' bride-price.

[17] 'A sorceress don't let live.

[18] 'Everyone who lies with an animal must be put to death, death.

[19] 'Whoever sacrifices to other gods must be destroyed.

[20] 'And a sojourner, don't afflict and don't oppress him, for sojourners you were in the land of Egypt. [21] Any widow or orphan don't oppress. [22] If you oppress, oppress him—for if he should cry out, cry out to me, I shall hear, hear his cry—[23] then my *nose* will flare, and I shall kill you by the sword, and your wives will be widows and your sons orphans.

[24] 'If silver you lend my people, the poor man with you, don't be to him as a creditor; don't lay *bite* upon him. [25] If you accept, accept as collateral your fellow's robe, by the sun's *entry* return it to him. [26] For it alone is his covering, it is his robe for his skin: in what will he lie down? And it will happen, when he cries out to me, then I will hear, for I am gracious.

[27] 'Deity don't curse, and a leader among your people don't execrate.

[28] 'Your fullness and your *dema'* don't postpone. The firstborn of your sons you must give to me. [29] You must do likewise for your bull, for your flock: seven days it will be with its mother; on the eighth day you must give it to me.

[30] And Holiness men you must become for me, and *torn meat* don't eat; to the dog you must throw it.

23   [1] 'Don't carry a false rumor. Don't set your hand with a wicked man to be a criminal witness. [2] Don't be consorting after a multitude, and don't testify about a dispute inclining after a multitude in order to influence. [3] And a pauper don't exalt in his lawsuit.

[4] 'When you encounter your enemy's bull or his ass astray, return, return it to him. [5] When you see your adversary's ass recumbent under its burden and would refrain from leaving (it) to him, you must leave, leave (it) with him.

[6] 'Don't influence your pauper's verdict in his lawsuit. [7] From a false *word* keep

distant, and an innocent or righteous one don't kill; for I shall not vindicate a guilty one. ⁸And a bribe don't take; for the bribe, it blinds the sighted and perverts the righteous's words.

⁹'And a sojourner don't oppress; for you, you have known the sojourner's soul, for sojourners you were in the land of Egypt.

¹⁰'And six years you may sow your land and gather its harvest. ¹¹But the seventh, abandon it and leave it alone, that your people's paupers may eat, and their leftovers the field animal may eat. So you will do for your vineyard, for your *olive.*

¹²'Six days you may do your doings, but on the seventh day you will cease, so that your bull and your ass may rest, and your maidservant's son and the sojourner may catch breath.

¹³'And through all that I have said to you, you will *keep* yourselves, and the name of other gods' don't mention. It shall not be heard upon your mouth.

¹⁴'Three *feet* you must celebrate to me in the year. ¹⁵The Unleavened Bread Festival you must keep: seven days you must eat unleavened bread as I commanded you, on the occasion of the New Grain Month, for on it you went out from Egypt. And my Face must not be seen emptily. ¹⁶And the Harvest Festival, the firstfruits of your produce that you sow in the field, and the Ingathering Festival at the year's *departure,* in your ingathering your produce from the field. ¹⁷Three times in the year all your malehood must appear to the Lord Yahweh's Face.

¹⁸'Don't offer with leavened food my Slaughter-offering blood, and my *festival* fat must not linger until morning.

¹⁹'Your soil's first firstfruits you shall bring to Yahweh your deity's House.

'Don't cook a kid in its mother's milk.

²⁰'See: I am sending a Messenger before you to guard you on the way and to bring you to the place that I have prepared. ²¹ Guard yourself from his *face* and heed his voice; don't rebel against him, for he will not *lift* your offense, for my Name will be within him. ²²But if you heed, heed his voice and do all that I speak, then I will oppose your opponents and attack your attackers.

²³'For my Messenger will go before you and bring you to the Amorite and the Hittite and the Perizzite and the Canaanite and the Hivvite and the Jebusite, and I will eradicate him. ²⁴Don't bow to their gods and don't serve them and don't do like their deeds. Rather, you must destroy, destroy them and smash, smash their pillars.

²⁵'And you shall serve Yahweh your deity, and he will bless your bread and your water, and I will remove illness from your midst. ²⁶There will not be a bereft or barren (female) in your land; your days' number I will make full.

²⁷'My terror I will release before you and discomfit all the peoples that you come against them, and I will set all your enemies *with the back of the neck toward you.* ²⁸And I will send the ṣirʿâ before you, and it will expel the Hivvite, the Canaanite and the Hittite from before you. ²⁹I will not expel him before you in one year, lest the land become a waste and the field animals multiply against you. ³⁰Little by little I will expel him before you, until that you bear fruit and acquire the land. ³¹And I will set your border from the Suph Sea and to the Philistines'

Sea, and from Desert to the River, for I will give into your hand the land's inhabitants, and you will expel them before you.

³² Don't *cut* with them or with their gods a covenant. ³³ They may not dwell in your land, lest they cause you to sin against me; when you serve their gods, indeed it will become for you as a snare.' "

24 ¹ But to Moses he said, "Ascend to Yahweh, you and Aaron, Nadab and Abihu, and seventy from Israel's elders, and you shall bow down from afar. ² And Moses alone will approach to Yahweh, but they, they may not approach, and the people, they may not ascend with him."

³ And Moses came and recounted to the people all Yahweh's words and all the case-laws. And the people answered in one voice and said, "All the words that Yahweh spoke we will do." ⁴ And Moses wrote down all Yahweh's words.

And he got up early in the morning and built an altar *under* the mountain and twelve pillar for Israel's twelve tribes. ⁵ And he sent the youths of Israel's Sons, and they *sent up* Ascending-offerings and *slaughtered* Slaughter-offerings, Concluding-offerings to Yahweh, bulls. ⁶ And Moses took half the blood and put in the bowls, and half the blood he cast against the altar. ⁷ And he took the Covenant Document and read in the people's ears. And they said, "All that Yahweh spoke we will do and heed."

⁸ Then Moses took the blood and cast upon the people and said, "See: the Covenant blood that Yahweh has *cut* with you by all these words."

⁹ Then Moses and Aaron, Nadab and Abihu and seventy from Israel's elders ascended ¹⁰ and saw Israel's deity. And under his feet: like lapis lazuli brickwork, and like the heavens' *bone* for clarity. ¹¹ And against the elite of Israel's Sons he did not send forth his arm, but they beheld the Deity and ate and drank.

¹² And Yahweh said to Moses, "Ascend to me to the mountain and be there, that I may give you the stone tablets, the Direction and the command that I have written to direct them."

¹³ So Moses and Joshua his attendant got up, and Moses ascended to the Deity's mountain. ¹⁴ But to the elders he had said, "Stay for us in this (place) until when we return to you. See: Aaron and Hur are with you; whoever has *words*, let him approach to them. ¹⁵ And Moses ascended to the mountain, and the cloud covered the mountain. ¹⁶ And Yahweh's Glory settled upon Mount Sinai, and the cloud covered it six days.

And he called to Moses on the seventh day from inside the cloud. ¹⁷ Now, the appearance of Yahweh's Glory was like a consuming fire on the mountain's head to the eyes of Israel's Sons. ¹⁸ And Moses came inside the cloud, and he ascended to the mountain. And Moses was on the mountain forty day and forty night.

Part V. THE TABERNACLE DIRECTIONS
(EXODUS 25–31)

XIX. *Take for me a Donation-offering* (25:1–31:18)

25 ¹And Yahweh spoke to Moses, saying: ²"Speak to Israel's Sons, and they shall take for me a Donation-offering. From every man whose heart ennobles him you shall take my Donation-offering. ³And this is the Donation-offering that you shall take from them: gold, silver and bronze, ⁴blue and purple and worm-crimson and linen and *goats* ⁵and reddened ram skins and beaded skins and acacia wood, ⁶oil for illumination, fragrances for the Ointment Oil and for the Spice Incense, ⁷carnelian stones and *filling* stones for the Ephod and for the *ḥōšen.* ⁸And they shall make for me a Sanctum, and I will tent in your midst. ⁹According to all that I am making you see, the Tabernacle's model and the model of all its implements, so you shall make.

¹⁰"And you shall make a chest, acacia wood: two cubits and a half its length and a cubit and a half its breadth and a cubit and a half its height. ¹¹And you shall plate it pure gold, from inside and from outside you shall plate it. And you shall make atop it a gold *zēr* around. ¹²And you shall cast four gold rings for it, and you shall set on its four *feet*, and two rings on its one flank and two rings on its second flank. ¹³And you shall make acacia wood poles and plate them gold. ¹⁴And you shall insert the poles into the rings on the Chest's flanks for carrying the Chest by them. ¹⁵In the Chest's rings the poles shall be; they shall not be removed from it. ¹⁶And you shall set into the Chest the Testimony that I will give you.

¹⁷"And you shall make a pure gold *kappōret*: two cubits and a half its length and a cubit and a half its breadth. ¹⁸And you shall make two Griffins, gold: *miqšâ* you shall make them; on the *kappōret*'s two ends ¹⁹they shall be made; one Griffin on this end here and one Griffin on this end here; on the *kappōret* you shall make the Griffins on its two ends, ²⁰so that the Griffins will be spreading wings above, screening over the *kappōret* with their wings, and their faces (each) *man toward his brother,* toward the *kappōret* the Griffins' faces shall be. ²¹And you shall set the *kappōret* on the Chest, above, and into the Chest you shall set the Testimony. ²²And I will be meetable for you there, and I shall speak with you from atop the *kappōret*—from between the two Griffins that are on the Testimony Chest— everything that I shall command you for Israel's Sons.

²³"And you shall make a table, acacia wood: two cubits its length and a cubit its breadth and a cubit and a half its height. ²⁴And you shall plate it pure gold. And you shall make for it a gold *zēr* around. ²⁵And you shall make for it a handbreadth's frame around. And you shall make a gold *zēr* for its frame around. ²⁶And you shall make four gold rings for it and set the rings on the four corners which are of its four legs. ²⁷Aligned with the frame the rings shall be, housings for poles for carrying the Table. ²⁸And you shall make the poles, acacia wood, and plate them gold; and the Table shall be carried by them. ²⁹And you shall make its bowls and its spoons and its dippers and its rinsers from which may be poured; pure gold you

shall make them. [30]And you shall set on the Table *Face Bread* before my face continually.

[31]"And you shall make a pure gold lampstand: *miqšâ* the Lampstand shall be made, its *thigh* and its *reeds*, its cups, its *kaptōrîm* and its *flowers*, they shall be from it. [32]And six *reeds* going out from its sides—three Lampstand *reeds* from its one side and three Lampstand *reeds* from its second side—[33]three 'almondized' cups on the one *reed—kaptōr* and *flower*—and three 'almondized' cups on the one *reed—kaptōr* and *flower*—thus for the six *reeds* going out from the Lampstand. [34]And on the Lampstand four 'almondized' cups—its *kaptōrîm* and its *flowers*—[35]and a *kaptōr* under the two *reeds* from it, and a *kaptōr* under the two *reeds* from it, and a *kaptōr* under the two *reeds* from it, for the six *reeds* going out from the Lampstand. [36]Their *kaptōrîm* and their *reeds*, they shall be from it, all of it one *miqšâ*, pure gold. [37]And you shall make its lamps seven, and one shall *raise* its lamps and illumine opposite its front; [38]and its tweezers and its fire-pans, pure gold. [39]A talent, pure gold one shall make it, along with all these implements. [40]And see and make by their model that you are being made to see on the mountain.

26 [1]"And the Tabernacle you shall make, ten curtains: twisted linen, blue and purple and worm-crimson, Griffins, webster's work you shall make them. [2]The one curtain's length eight-and-twenty by the cubit, and breadth four by the cubit, the one curtain. One measure for all the curtains. [3]Five of the curtains, they shall be fastening (each) *woman to her sister*, and five curtains fastening (each) *woman to her sister*. [4]And you shall make blue loops on the one curtain's *lip*, on the edge on the *fastening*, and so you shall make on the outer curtain's *lip*, on the second *fastening*. [5]Fifty loops you shall make on the one curtain, and fifty loops you shall make on the edge of the curtain that is on the second *fastening*, the loops aligning (each) *woman to her sister*. [6]And you shall make fifty gold clasps and fasten the curtains (each) *woman to her sister* with the clasps, so that the Tabernacle shall be one.

[7]"And you shall make *goat* curtains to tent over the Tabernacle: eleven curtains you shall make them. [8]The one curtain's length thirty by the cubit, and breadth four by the cubit the one curtain. One measure for the eleven curtains. [9]And you shall fasten the five curtains separate and the six curtains separate. And you shall double the sixth curtain against the Tent's front. [10]And you shall make loops fifty on the one curtain's *lip*, the outermost on the *fastening*, and fifty loops on the *lip* of the curtain, the second *fastening*. [11]And you shall make bronze clasps, fifty, and bring the clasps into the loops and fasten the Tent, so that it shall be one. [12]And the superfluous overhang of the Tent's curtains: half of the superfluous curtain shall hang over the Tent's back; [13]and the cubit on this (side) and the cubit on this (side) as the superfluity along the Tent curtains' length shall be overhung on the Tabernacle's sides, on this (side) and on this (side) to cover it. [14]And you shall make a cover for the Tent: reddened ram skins, and a beaded skins cover above.

[15]"And you shall make the *qərāšîm* for the Tabernacle: standing acacia wood, [16]ten cubits the *qereš*'s length, a cubit and a half-cubit the one *qereš*'s breadth, [17]two *arms* for the one *qereš*, pegged (each) *woman to her sister*; so you shall make

for all the Tabernacle's *qərāšîm*. ¹⁸And you shall make the *qərāšîm* for the Tabernacle: twenty *qereš* for the austral, southward side. ¹⁹And forty silver bases you shall make under the twenty *qereš*, two bases under the one *qereš* for its two *arms*, and two bases under the one *qereš* for its two *arms*. ²⁰And for the Tabernacle's second flank, for the north side, twenty *qereš* ²¹ and their forty bases, silver, two bases under the one *qereš* and two bases under the one *qereš*. ²²And for the Tabernacle's *seaward* backparts you shall make six *qərāšîm*. ²³And two *qərāšîm* you shall make for the Tabernacle's corners at the backparts. ²⁴And they shall be twinning from below; together they shall be whole up to its *head*, to the one ring. So shall it be for the two of them, for the two corners they shall be. ²⁵And there shall be eight *qərāšîm* and their bases, silver; sixteen bases, two bases under the one *qereš*, and two bases under the one *qereš*. ²⁶And you shall make crossbars, acacia wood: five for the *qərāšîm* of the Tabernacle's one flank ²⁷ and five crossbars for the *qərāšîm* of the Tabernacle's second flank and five crossbars for the Tabernacle's *qərāšîm* at the *seaward* backparts, ²⁸and the inner crossbar amid the *qərāšîm* barring from end to end. ²⁹And the *qərāšîm* you shall plate gold; and their rings you shall make gold, housings for the crossbars; and you shall plate the crossbars gold. ³⁰And you shall erect the Tabernacle according to its rule that you were made to see on the mountain.

³¹ "And you shall make a veil: blue and purple and worm-crimson and twisted linen; webster's work one shall make it, Griffins. ³²And you shall set it on four gold-plated acacia posts, their Y-brackets gold, on four silver bases. ³³And you shall set the Veil under the clasps, and you shall insert there, inside the Veil, the Testimony Chest, so that the Veil will separate for you between the Holiness and between the Holiness of Holinesses. ³⁴And you shall set the *kappōret* on the Testimony Chest in the Holiness of Holinesses. ³⁵And you shall put the Table outside the Veil, and the Lampstand opposite the Table by the Tabernacle's flank southward, and the Table you shall set by the north flank.

³⁶"And you shall make a screen for the Tent Opening, blue and purple and worm-crimson and twisted linen, embroiderer's work. ³⁷And you shall make for the Screen five acacia posts and plate them gold, their Y-brackets gold, and you shall cast for them five bronze bases.

27   ¹"And you shall make the Altar, acacia wood: five cubits length and five cubits breadth—foursquare the Altar shall be—and three cubits its height. ²And you shall make its *horns* on its four corners—from it its *horns* shall be—and you shall plate it bronze. ³And you shall make its pots for de-ashing it and its shovels and its bowls and its forks and its fire-pans—in short, all its implements you shall make bronze. ⁴And you shall make for it a mesh, lattice work, bronze; and you shall make on the lattice four bronze rings on its four corners. ⁵And you shall set it under the Altar's rim beneath, and the lattice shall as be far as half the Altar. ⁶And you shall make poles for the Altar, acacia-wood poles, and plate them bronze. ⁷And its poles shall be inserted into the rings, so that the poles will be on the Altar's two flanks in carrying it. ⁸Hollow-planked you shall make it. As he made you see on the mountain, so they shall make.

⁹"And you shall make the Tabernacle's Plaza: on the austral, southward side,

sheets for the Plaza, twisted linen, length one hundred by the cubit on the one side, [10]and its posts twenty and their bases twenty, bronze; their Y-brackets and their *ḥăšūqîm*, silver. [11]And likewise on the north side in length: sheets, one hundred by the cubit, and its posts twenty and their bases twenty, bronze; their Y-brackets and their *ḥăšūqîm*, silver. [12]And the Plaza's breadth on the sea side: sheets, fifty cubit, their posts ten and their bases ten. [13]And the Plaza's breadth on the *forward, sunrise* side: fifty cubit. [14]Fifteen cubit, sheets for the *shoulder*, their posts three and their bases three. [15]And for the second *shoulder*, fifteen sheets, their posts three and their bases three. [16]And for the Plaza gate a screen, twenty cubit, blue and purple and worm-crimson and twisted linen, embroiderer's work, its posts four and their bases four. [17]All the Plaza's posts around, *məḥuššāqîm* silver, their Y-brackets, silver, and their bases, bronze—[18]the Plaza's length one hundred upon one hundred, and breadth fifty upon fifty, and height five cubits, twisted linen—and their bases, bronze—[19]in short, all the Tabernacle's implements in all its Work and all its tent-pegs and all the Plaza's tent-pegs, bronze.

[20]"And you, you shall command Israel's Sons: and they shall take to you pure, crushed olive oil for illumination, to *raise* a continual lamp [21]in Meeting Tent, outside the Veil that is before the Testimony. Let Aaron and his sons arrange it from evening till morning before Yahweh. An eternal rule *for their ages* from Israel's Sons.

28 [1]"And you, Bring Near to yourself Aaron your brother and his sons with him from the midst of Israel's Sons to priest for me: Aaron, Nadab and Abihu, Eleazar and Ithamar, Aaron's sons. [2]And you shall make Holiness Garments for Aaron your brother for glory and for splendor. [3]And you, you shall speak to all wised-hearted whom I have filled (with) wisdom's spirit, and they shall make Aaron's garments, to make him holy to priest for me. [4]And these are the garments that they shall make: a *ḥōšen* and an ephod and a robe and a woven shift, a turban and a sash; and they shall make Holiness garments for Aaron and for his sons to priest for me. [5]And they, they shall take the gold and the blue and the purple and the worm-crimson and the linen.

[6]"And they shall make the Ephod: gold, blue and purple, worm-crimson and twisted linen, webster's work. [7]Two fastening shoulder-pieces, it shall be for it; at its two sides it shall be fastened. [8]And the woven-band for its ephod-binding that is on it, like its work, from it shall it be: gold, blue and purple and worm-crimson and twisted linen. [9]And you shall take two carnelian stones and engrave on them the names of Israel's sons: [10]six of their names on the one stone and the names of the remaining six on the second stone, according to their genealogy. [11]Stone-cutter's work, seal engravings, one shall engrave the two stones by the names of Israel's sons; set in gold plait-rings you shall make them. [12]And you shall put the two stones on the Ephod's shoulder-pieces, Memorial stones for Israel's Sons, so that Aaron may bear their names before Yahweh on his two shoulder-pieces as a Memorial.

[13]"And you shall make gold plait-rings. [14]And two pure gold chains: *migbālōt* you shall make them, rope work. And you shall set the rope chains on the plait-rings.

¹⁵ "And you shall make the Judgment *ḥōšen*, webster's work, like an ephod's work you shall make it, gold; blue and purple and worm-crimson and twisted linen you shall make it. ¹⁶ Foursquare it shall be, doubled; a span its length and a span its breadth. ¹⁷ And you shall *fill* in it stone *filling*, four rows, stone. A row: *'ōdem, piṭdâ* and emerald, the one row; ¹⁸ and the second row: turquoise, lapis lazuli and *yāhǎlōm*; ¹⁹ and the third row: *lešem, šǝbô* and jasper; ²⁰ and the fourth row: *taršîš*, carnelian and jade. Plait-ringed in gold they shall be in their *fillings*. ²¹ And the stones, they shall be by the names of Israel's sons, twelve by their names, seal engravings, (each) *man* by his name they shall be, for twelve tribe. ²² And you shall make upon the *ḥōšen gablūt* chains, rope work, pure gold. ²³ And you shall make upon the *ḥōšen* two gold rings, and you shall set the rings on the *ḥōšen's* edges. ²⁴ And you shall set the two gold ropes on the two rings on the *ḥōšen's* edges. ²⁵ And the two ropes' two ends you shall set on the two plait-rings; and you shall set on the Ephod's shoulder-pieces, against its front. ²⁶ And you shall make two gold rings and put them on the *ḥōšen's* two edges, at its *lip* that is against the Ephod inside. ²⁷ And you shall make two gold rings and set them on the Ephod's two shoulder-pieces below, against its front, opposite its fastening, above the Ephod's woven-band. ²⁸ And they must tie the *ḥōšen* by its rings to the Ephod's rings with blue cord for being over the Ephod's woven-band, so the *ḥōšen* will not slip from upon the Ephod. ²⁹ And Aaron shall bear the names of Israel's sons in the Judgment *ḥōšen* over his heart in his coming into the Holiness as a Memorial before Yahweh continually. ³⁰ And you shall set into the Judgment *ḥōšen* the Urim and the Thummim, so that they will be over Aaron's heart in his coming before Yahweh. And Aaron shall bear the Judgment of Israel's Sons over his heart before Yahweh continually.

³¹ "And you shall make the Ephod's Robe: completely blue. ³² And its *head mouth* shall be in its midst; a *lip* will be for its *mouth* around, weaver's work, like an anus *mouth* will be for it; it will not be torn. ³³ And you shall make on its skirts pomegranates of blue and purple and worm-crimson on its skirts around, and gold bells in their midst around — ³⁴ a gold bell and a pomegranate, a gold bell and a pomegranate — on the Robe's skirts around. ³⁵ And it shall be upon Aaron for attending, so that his sound will be heard in his coming into the Holiness before Yahweh and in his leaving, and he shall not die.

³⁶ "And you shall make a pure gold blossom and engrave on it seal engravings: 'a Holiness of Yahweh.' ³⁷ And you shall put it on blue cord, and it shall be on the Turban; against the Turban's front it shall be. ³⁸ And it shall be upon Aaron's forehead, and Aaron shall Bear the Transgression of the Holinesses that Israel's Sons shall make holy, for all their holy gifts; and it shall be upon his forehead continually, for favor for them before Yahweh.

³⁹ "And you shall plait the Shift, linen, and make a linen Turban, and a Sash you shall make, embroiderer's work.

⁴⁰ "And for Aaron's sons you shall make shifts, and you shall make sashes for them, and hats you shall make for them, for glory and for splendor. ⁴¹ And you shall make Aaron your brother and his sons with him wear them, and you shall anoint them and *fill their hand* and make them holy, so that they may priest for me.

⁴²"And make for them linen underpants to cover naked *flesh*; from hips and to thighs they shall be. ⁴³And they shall be on Aaron and on his sons in their coming into Meeting Tent or in their approaching to the Altar to attend in the Holiness, lest they Bear Transgression and die. An eternal rule for him and for his *seed* after him.

29 ¹"And this is the thing that you shall do to them to make them holy to priest for me: take one bull, cattle's son, and rams, two, perfect, ²and bread, unleavened bread, and unleavened *ḥallōt* saturated with oil and unleavened bread wafers anointed with oil, wheat bran you shall make them. ³And you shall set them on one basket and Bring them Near in the basket, and the bull and the two rams, ⁴and Aaron and his sons you shall Bring Near to Meeting Tent Opening and wash them with water. ⁵And you shall take the garments and make Aaron wear the Shift and the Ephod's Robe and the Ephod and the *ḥōšen*, and you shall "ephod" to him with the Ephod's *woven-band*. ⁶And you shall set the Turban on his head and put the Holiness Crown on the Turban. ⁷And you shall take the Ointment Oil and pour on his head and anoint him. ⁸And his sons you shall Bring Near and make them wear shifts ⁹and gird them with a sash, Aaron and his sons, and bind hats for them. And priesthood shall be for them as an eternal rule.

"And you shall *fill* Aaron's *hand* and his sons' *hand*. ¹⁰And you shall Bring Near the bull before Meeting Tent, and Aaron and his sons shall press their hands on the bull's head. ¹¹And you shall slaughter the bull before Yahweh (at) Meeting Tent Opening. ¹²And you shall take from the bull's blood and apply on the Altar's *horns* with your finger, and all the blood you shall pour toward the Altar's fundament. ¹³And you shall take all the fat covering the entrails and all the excrescence on the liver and the two kidneys and the fat that is on them and *smoke* them on the Altar. ¹⁴And the bull's meat and his skin and his dung you shall burn with fire outside the camp. He is a Sin-offering.

¹⁵"And the one ram you shall take, and Aaron and his sons shall press their hands on the ram's head. ¹⁶And you shall slaughter the ram and take his blood and dash it against the Altar around. ¹⁷And the ram you shall dismember into his members, and wash his entrails and his shanks and set with his members and with his head. ¹⁸And you shall *smoke* the entire ram on the Altar. He is an Ascending-offering for Yahweh; a Soothing Scent, a Gift for Yahweh is he.

¹⁹"And you shall take the second ram, and Aaron and his sons shall press their hands on the ram's head. ²⁰And you shall slaughter the ram and take from his blood and apply on Aaron's earlobe and on his sons' right earlobe and on their right hand-thumb and on their right *foot-thumb*, and you shall dash the blood against the Altar around. ²¹And you shall take from the blood that is against the Altar and from the Ointment Oil and sprinkle upon Aaron and upon his garments and upon his sons and upon his sons' garments with him. And he and his garments and his sons and his sons' garments with him shall become holy. ²²And you shall take from the ram the fat: the fat-tail and the fat covering the entrails and the liver's excrescence and the two kidneys and the fat that is on them and the right thigh—for he is a *Filling* Ram—²³and one bread loaf and one oil bread *ḥallâ* and one wafer from the unleavened bread basket that is before Yahweh. ²⁴And you shall put the whole on Aaron's palms and his sons' palms, and you shall elevate

them (as) an Elevation-offering before Yahweh. 25 And you shall take them from their hand and *smoke* on the Altar in addition to the Ascending-offering as a Soothing Scent before Yahweh. It is a Gift to Yahweh.

26 "And you shall take the breast from the *Filling* Ram that is Aaron's and elevate it (as) an Elevation-offering before Yahweh, and it will be as a portion for you. 27 And you shall make holy the Elevation breast and the Donation thigh, that is elevated and that is donated from the *Filling* Ram, from what is Aaron's and from what is his sons', 28 and he shall be for Aaron and for his sons as an eternal rule from Israel's Sons. For it is a Donation-offering, and a Donation-offering he will be from Israel's Sons from their Concluding Slaughter-offerings, their Donation-offering for Yahweh.

29 "And the Holiness Garments that are Aaron's will be for his sons after him, for being anointed in them and for *filling their hand* in them. 30 Seven days the priest replacing him, from his sons, who will come into Meeting Tent to attend in the Holiness, must wear them.

31 "And the *Filling* ram you shall take and boil his meat in a holy place. 32 And Aaron and his sons shall eat the ram's meat and the bread that is in the basket (at) Meeting Tent Opening. 33 They must eat them by which Clearing was effected, for *filling their hand* for making them holy. But an outsider may not eat, for they are Holiness. 34 And if (any) of the *Filling* meat or of the bread is left over until the morning, then you shall burn the leftover in fire. It may not be eaten, for it is Holiness. 35 And you shall do for Aaron and for his sons likewise, as all that I have commanded you; seven days you shall *fill their hand.*

36 "And a Sin bull you shall do (each) day concerning the Clearing. And you shall Un-sin upon the Altar in your effecting Clearing upon it. And you shall anoint it to make it holy. 37 Seven days you shall effect Clearing upon the Altar and make it holy. And the Altar shall be Holiness of Holinesses; any touching the Altar becomes holy.

38 "And this is what you must do upon the Altar: lambs, *sons of* a year, two per day (as a) Continual-offering. 39 The one lamb you shall do in the morning, and the second lamb you shall do *between the two evenings,* 40 and a tenth of bran saturated with a quarter-hin crushed oil, and a quarter-hin wine libation, for the one lamb. 41 And the second lamb you shall do *between the two evenings;* like the morning Tribute-offering and like its libation you shall do for it, a Soothing Scent, a Gift for Yahweh, 42 a Continual Ascending-offering *for your ages* (at) Meeting Tent Opening before Yahweh, where I will be meetable for you to speak to you there.

43 "And I will be inquirable there for Israel's Sons, and it/one will be made holy by my Glory. 44 And I will make holy Meeting Tent and the Altar, and Aaron and his sons I will make holy to priest for me. 45 And I will tent in Israel's Sons' midst, and I will be for them as a deity, 46 and they will know that I am Yahweh their deity who took them out from the land of Egypt by my tenting among them—I am Yahweh their deity.

30   1 "And you shall make an altar, an incense censer: acacia wood you shall make it, 2 a cubit its length and a cubit its breadth—foursquare it shall be—and

two cubits its height; from it its *horns*. [3] And you shall plate it pure gold: its *roof* and its *walls* around and its *horns*. And you shall make for it a gold *zēr* around. [4] And two gold rings you shall make for it beneath its *zēr* on its two flanks, you shall make on its two sides, and they shall be as housings for poles for carrying it with them. [5] And you shall make the poles, acacia wood, and plate them gold. [6] And you shall set it before the Veil that is before the Testimony Chest, where I will be meetable for you there. [7] And Aaron shall cense on it Spice Incense by morning by morning, in his adjusting the lamps let him cense it; [8] and in Aaron's *raising* the lamps *between the two evenings* let him cense it, continual incense before Yahweh *for your ages*. [9] Do not *send up* on it alien incense or an Ascending-offering or a Tribute-offering, and a libation do not libate on it. [10] And Aaron shall effect Clearing on its *horns* once in the year from the blood of the Clearing Sin-offering, once in the year he shall effect Clearing on it *for your ages*. It is a Holiness of Holinesses for Yahweh."

[11] And Yahweh spoke to Moses, saying: [12] "When you *lift the head* of Israel's Sons in their accountings, then (each) man shall give to Yahweh his *soul's* ransom in their being accounted, lest there be harm against them in accounting them. [13] This they must give, each passing over the accountings: the half-shekel by the Holiness Shekel—twenty gerah the shekel—the half-shekel (as) a Donation-offering for Yahweh. [14] Each *passing over* the accountings, from the *son of* twenty year and upward, must give Yahweh's Donation-offering. [15] The rich may not (give) more and the poor may not (give) less than than the half-shekel, to give Yahweh's Donation-offering to effect Clearing for your *souls*. [16] And you shall take the Clearing Silver from Israel's Sons and give it toward the Meeting Tent Work, so that it will be for Israel's Sons as a Memorial before Yahweh, to effect Clearing for your *souls*."

[17] And Yahweh spoke to Moses, saying: [18] "And you shall make a basin, bronze, and its stand, bronze, for washing, and you shall set it between Meeting Tent and between the Altar, and set there water. [19] And Aaron and his sons shall wash their hands and their feet from it; [20] in their coming into Meeting Tent they must wash with water, lest they die; or in their approaching to the Altar to attend, to *smoke* a Gift to Yahweh, [21] they must wash their hands and their feet, lest they die. And it will be for them an eternal rule, for him and for his *seed for their ages*."

[22] And Yahweh spoke to Moses, saying: [23] "And you, take for yourself fragrances: *head* of *dərôr* myrrh, five hundred; and fragrant cinnamon half as much, fifty and two hundred; and fragrant cane, fifty and two hundred; [24] and *qiddâ*, five hundred by the Holiness Shekel; and olive oil, a hin. [25] And you shall make it (into) Holiness Ointment Oil, a compounding compound, compounder's work; Holiness Ointment it shall be. [26] And you shall anoint with it Meeting Tent and the Testimony Chest, [27] the Table and all its implements, the Lamp and all its implements, the Incense Altar [28] and the Ascending-offering Altar and all its implements, the Basin and its Stand. [29] And you shall make them holy, and they shall be a Holiness of Holinesses. Any touching them becomes holy. [30] And Aaron and his sons you shall anoint, and you shall make them holy to priest for me. [31] And to Israel's Sons you shall speak, saying: 'Holiness Ointment Oil this shall be for me *for your ages*.

³²On a human's flesh it must not be poured, and in its composition you shall not make its like. It is a Holiness; a Holiness shall it be for you. ³³A man who compounds its like or who puts (any) of it on an outsider, then he shall be Cut Off from his kin.' "

³⁴And Yahweh said to Moses, "Take for yourself spices—gumdrop and *šəḥēlet* and galbanum—spices and pure frankincense, part for part it shall be. ³⁵And you shall make it (into) incense, a compound, compounder's work, salted, pure, Holiness. ³⁶And you shall pulverize (some) of it fine and set (some) of it before the Testimony in Meeting Tent, where I will be meetable for you there. A Holiness of Holinesses it shall be for you. ³⁷And the incense that you make, in its composition you shall not make for yourselves. A Holiness for Yahweh it shall be for you. ³⁸A man who makes its like to smell it, then he shall be Cut Off from his kin."

31 ¹And Yahweh spoke to Moses, saying: ²"See, I have called by name Bezalel son of Uri son of Hur from the tribe of Judah ³and filled him with a divine spirit in wisdom and in understanding and in knowledge and in every task, ⁴for planning plans, to make in gold and in silver and in bronze ⁵and in stone carving for *filling* and in wood carving, to do every task. ⁶And I, see: I have given with him Oholiab son of Ahisamach from the tribe of Dan, and into the heart of every wisehearted I have set wisdom.

"And they shall make all that I commanded you: ⁷Meeting Tent and the Chest for the Testimony and the *kappōret* that is over it and all the Tent's implements, ⁸the Table and its implements, the pure Lampstand and all its implements, the Incense Altar ⁹and the Ascending-offering Altar and all its implements, the Basin and its stand, ¹⁰the Textile Garments and the Holiness Garments for Aaron the priest and his sons' garments for priesting, ¹¹the Ointment Oil and the Spice Incense for the Holiness. As all that I commanded you they shall make."

¹²And Yahweh said to Moses, saying: ¹³"And you, speak to Israel's Sons, saying: 'Nevertheless, my Sabbaths you must keep. For it is a sign between me and between you *for your ages*, to know that I, Yahweh, am your sanctifier. ¹⁴And you shall observe the Sabbath, for it is a Holiness for you. Its desecrater must be put to death, death; for any doing a task on it—then that *soul* shall be Cut Off from its kinfolks' midst. ¹⁵Six days a task may be done. But on the seventh day: a Sabbatical Sabbath, a Holiness of Yahweh. Anyone doing a task on the Sabbath day must be put to death, death. ¹⁶And Israel's Sons shall observe the Sabbath, doing the Sabbath *for their ages*, an eternal covenant. ¹⁷Between me and between Israel's Sons it is a sign for eternity: for six days Yahweh made the heavens and the earth, but on the seventh day he ceased and caught his breath."

¹⁸And he gave to Moses, as he concluded speaking with him at Mount Sinai, the two Testimony Tablets, stone tablets, written by Deity's finger.

PART VI. THE COVENANT BROKEN AND RESTORED (EXODUS 32–34)

XX. *These are your deity, Israel* (32:1–35)

32 ¹And the people saw that Moses had delayed to descend from the mountain, and the people assembled around Aaron and said to him, "Get up, make us deity that they may go before us, for this one, Moses, the man who took us up from the land of Egypt, we do not know what happened to him."

²So Aaron said to them, "Strip off the gold rings that are in your *women's*, sons' and daughters' ears, and bring to me." ³And all the people stripped off from themselves the gold rings that were in their ears and brought to Aaron. ⁴And he took from their hand and bound it in the bag and made it a metal calf. And they said, "These are your deity, Israel, who took you up from the land of Egypt."

⁵And Aaron saw/feared and built an altar before it, and Aaron called and said, "Tomorrow is a festival for Yahweh."

⁶And they got up early the next day and *sent up* Ascending-offerings and presented Concluding-offerings. And the people sat down to eat and drink, and they got up to revel.

⁷And Yahweh spoke to Moses, saying, "Descend, for your people whom you took up from the land of Egypt has corrupted, ⁸they have quickly departed from the way that I commanded them. They have made themselves a metal calf and bowed to it and sacrificed to it and said, 'These are your deity, Israel, who took you up from the land of Egypt.' "

⁹And Yahweh said to Moses, "I have seen this people, and, see: it is a hard-necked people. ¹⁰And now leave me alone, that my *nose* may flare against them and I may finish them off and make you into a great nation."

¹¹But Moses placated Yahweh his deity's *face*, and he said, "Why, Yahweh, should your *nose* flare against your people whom you took out from Egypt with great strength and with a strong limb? ¹²Why should Egypt say, saying, 'For bad he took them out, to kill them in the mountains and to finish them off from the earth's surface'? Turn back from your *nose* flaring and repent about the bad to your people. ¹³Remember for Abraham, for Isaac and for Israel, your slaves, to whom you swore by yourself and spoke to them: 'I will mutiply your *seed* like the heavens' stars, and all this land that I said, "I will give to your *seed*," and they will possess to eternity.' "

¹⁴And Yahweh repented concerning the bad that he spoke to do to his people.

¹⁵Then Moses turned and descended from the mountain, and the two Testimony Tablets in his hands, tablets written from their two sides, *on here and on here* they were written; ¹⁶and the tablets, they were Deity's work; and the writing, it was Deity's writing engraved on the tablets.

¹⁷And Joshua heard the people's sound in its shouting, and he said to Moses, "A *sound*: war in the camp."

¹⁸ And he said, "Not the sound of ʿănôt of strength, nor the sound of ʿănôt of conquest; the sound of ʿannôt I am hearing."

¹⁹ And it happened, as he approached to the camp and saw the calf and dances, then Moses' *nose* flared, and he threw the tablets from his hands and smashed them at the mountain's bottom. ²⁰ And he took the calf that they had made, and he burned with fire and ground till fine and sprinkled onto the waters' surface and made Israel's Sons drink.

²¹ And Moses said to Aaron, "What did this people do to you that you brought upon it a great sin?"

²² And Aaron said, "My lord's *nose* should not flare. You, you know the people, that it is in bad; ²³ and they said to me, 'Make us deity that they (cf. 32:1) may go before us, for this one, Moses, the man who took us up from the land of Egypt, we do not know what happened to him.' ²⁴ So I said to them, 'Whoever has gold, strip it off yourself,' and they gave to me; and I threw it into the fire, and this calf came out."

²⁵ And Moses saw the people, that it was wild—for Aaron had made them wild, for contempt among their *uprisers*—²⁶ and Moses stood at the camp's gate and said, "Whoever is for Yahweh, to me!" And all Levi's Sons gathered to him.

²⁷ And he said to them, "Thus has Yahweh Israel's deity said: Put, (each) man his sword upon his thigh, and cross and return from gate to gate in the camp and kill, (each) man his brother and (each) man his fellow and (each) man his relative." ²⁸ And Levi's Sons did according to Moses' word. And about three thousand man of the people fell on that day. ²⁹ And Moses said, "Today, your *hand has been filled* for Yahweh, indeed (each) man through his son and through his brother, even to place a blessing on yourselves today."

³⁰ And it happened on the next day, and Moses said to the people, "You, you have sinned a great sin. And now, I will ascend to Yahweh; perhaps I can Clear for your sin."

³¹ And Moses returned to Yahweh and said, "Ah now, this people has sinned a great sin, and they made for themselves a gold deity. ³² And now, if you will *lift* their sin . . . but if not, erase me then from your Document that you have written."

³³ And Yahweh said to Moses, "Whoever has sinned against me, I will erase him from my Document. ³⁴ But now go, lead the people to where I spoke to you. See: my Messenger, he will go before you. And in the day of my accounting, then I will account their sin against them."

³⁵ And Yahweh harmed the people, inasmuch as they had made the calf that Aaron made.

XXI. *This nation is your people* (33:1–34:35)

33   ¹ And Yahweh spoke to Moses, saying: "Go, go up from here, you and the people that you took up from the land of Egypt, to the land that I swore to Abraham, to Isaac and to Jacob, saying, 'To your *seed* I will give it'—² and I shall send before you a Messenger, and I will expel the Canaanite, the Amorite and the Hittite and the Perizzite, the Hivvite and the Jebusite—³ to a land flowing of milk and

honey—although I will not go up in your midst, for you are a hard-necked people, lest I finish you off on the way."

⁴And the people heard this bad word and mourned, and they did not put, (each) man his finery, on himself. ⁵And Yahweh said to Moses, "Say to Israel's Sons, 'A hard-necked people are you; (if) one instant I go up in your midst, then I will finish you off. And now, lay down your finery from on you, and I will know what I will do with you.' " ⁶So Israel's Sons stripped themselves their finery from Mount Horeb.

⁷And Moses, he would take the tent and pitch it/for him outside the camp, far from the camp, and he would call it "Meeting Tent." And it would happen, any seeking Yahweh would go out to Meeting Tent that was outside the camp. ⁸And it would happen, as Moses' going out to the Tent, all the people would stand up and station themselves, (each) man at his tent's opening, and gaze after Moses until his entering into the Tent. ⁹And it would happen, as Moses' entering into the Tent, the Cloud Pillar would descend and stand at the Tent's Opening, and he would speak with Moses. ¹⁰And all the people would see the Cloud Pillar standing at the Tent's Opening, and all the people would *stand* and bow down, (each) man at his tent's opening. ¹¹And Yahweh would speak to Moses face to face, as a man might speak to his friend, and he would return to the camp. But his attendant, Joshua son of Nun, was a youth; he would not depart from inside the Tent.

¹²And Moses said to Yahweh, "See, you are saying to me, 'Take up this people,' but you, you have not let me know whom/what you will send with me,' yet you, you said, 'I know you by name, and also you have found favor in my eyes.' ¹³And now, if indeed I have found favor in your eyes, let me know your ways that I may know you, so that I may find favor in your eyes. And see, that this nation is your people."

¹⁴Then he said, "My Face, it will go, and I will make rest for you."

¹⁵And he said to him, "If your Face is not going, do not make us go up from here. ¹⁶And by what, then, will it be known that I have found favor in your eyes, I and your people? Is it not by your going with us? Then I and your people will be distinguished from all peoples that are on the earth's surface."

¹⁷And Yahweh said to Moses, "Even this thing that you have spoken I will do, for you have found favor in my eyes, and I have known you by name."

¹⁸And he said, "Show me then your Glory."

¹⁹And he said, "I, I shall make all my splendor pass before your face, and I shall call Yahweh's name before you: for I shall favor whom I favor, and love whom I love."

²⁰And he said, "You may not see my Face, for Man may not see me and live." ²¹And Yahweh said, "See: a place by me; and you will station yourself on the mountain. ²²And it will happen, in my Glory's passing, then I will put you in the mountain's crevice, and I will shelter my hand/skirt over you during my passing. ²³Then I will remove my hand/skirt, and you will see my backparts. But my Face may not be seen."

34 ¹And Yahweh said to Moses, "Carve for yourself two stone tablets like the first, that I may write on the tablets the words that were on the tablets that you

smashed, ²and be ready for the morning. And you shall ascend in the morning to Mount Sinai, and you shall station yourself before me there on the mountain's head. ³But no man may ascend with you; and also a man may not be seen in all the mountain. Also, the flock and the herd must not graze opposite that mountain."

⁴So he carved two stone tablets like the first, and Moses got up early in the morning and ascended to Mount Sinai, as Yahweh commanded him, and he took in his hand two stone tablets. ⁵And Yahweh descended in the cloud. And he stationed himself by him there, and he called upon Yahweh's name.

⁶And Yahweh passed before his face, and he called, "Yahweh, Yahweh, a merciful and benevolent god, *long-faced* and great in trust and reliability, ⁷conserving fidelity to a thousandth (generation), *bearing* transgression and crime and sin— although he does not acquit, acquit, reckoning fathers' sins upon sons and upon sons' sons, upon a third and upon a fourth (generation)."

⁸And Moses hurried and prostrated himself on the ground and bowed down. ⁹And he said, "If indeed I have found favor in your eyes, my Lordship, let my Lordship go in our midst, although it is a hard-necked people, yet may you pardon our transgression and our sin and possess us."

¹⁰And he said, "See: me *cutting* a covenant. Before all your people I will work wonders that have not been created in all the world or among all the nations, so that all the people in whose midst you are will see Yahweh's deed, that it is so dreadful, what I am going to do with you.

¹¹"Keep for yourself what I am commanding you today. See: me expelling from before you the Amorite and the Canaanite and the Hittite and the Perizzite and the Hivvite and the Jebusite. ¹²Be careful for yourself, lest you *cut* a covenant with the inhabitant of the land upon which you are coming, lest he become a snare in your midst—¹³rather, their altars you must break, and their pillars you must smash, and his Asherim you must cut down; ¹⁴for you must not bow down to another god, for Jealous Yahweh is his name; he is a jealous god—¹⁵lest you *cut* a covenant with the land's inhabitant, and they *whore* after their gods and sacrifice to their gods, and he call you and you eat of his sacrifice, ¹⁶and you take from his daughters for your sons, and his daughters *whore* after their gods, and they make your sons *whore* after their gods.

¹⁷"Metal gods don't make for yourself.

¹⁸"The Unleavened Bread Festival you must keep. Seven days you shall eat unleavened bread, which I commanded you at the occasion of the New Grain Month, for in the New Grain Month you went out from Egypt.

¹⁹"Every *loosening* the womb is mine, and all your cattle you must 'male,' *loosening* of a bull or a sheep, ²⁰but an ass's *loosening* you shall redeem with a sheep/goat, or if you do not redeem, then you shall 'neck' it. Every firstborn of your sons you must redeem.

And my *Face must not be seen emptily*.

²¹"Six days you shall work, but on the seventh day you must cease; in plowing and in harvest you must cease.

²²"And a Festival of Weeks you shall make for yourself, the firstfruits of the

wheat harvest, and the Ingathering Festival (at) the year's *revolution.* ²³Three times in the year all your malehood must appear to the Face of the Lord Yahweh, Israel's deity. ²⁴Because I shall dispossess nations from before you and widen your border, then not *any man* will covet your land in your going up to appear to Yahweh your deity three times in the year.

²⁵"Don't slaughter my Slaughter-offering blood with leavened food, and the *Pesaḥ* festival Slaughter-offering must not abide till the morning.

²⁶"The first of your soil's firstfruits you must bring to Yahweh your deity's House.
"Don't cook a kid in its mother's milk."

²⁷And Yahweh said to Moses, "Write for yourself these words, for *by the mouth of* these words I have *cut* a covenant with you and with Israel."

²⁸So he was there with Yahweh forty day and forty night; bread he did not eat, and water he did not drink. And he wrote upon the tablets the Covenant words, the Ten Words.

²⁹And it happened, in Moses' descending from Mount Sinai, and the two Testimony Tablets in Moses' hand in his descending from the mountain, and Moses did not know that his face skin had "horned" in his speaking with him. ³⁰And Aaron and all Israel's Sons saw Moses and, see: his face skin had "horned," and they were too frightened to approach him. ³¹But Moses called to them, and Aaron and all the leaders in the congregation returned to him, and Moses spoke to them. ³²And afterwards all Israel's Sons approached, and he commanded them all that Yahweh spoke with him on Mount Sinai.

³³And Moses finished speaking with them, and he put a veil on his face.

³⁴And in Moses' entering before Yahweh to speak with him, he would remove the veil until his going out, and he would go out and speak to Israel's Sons what he would be commanded. ³⁵And Israel's Sons would see Moses' face, that Moses' face skin "horned," and he would return the veil over his face, until his entering to speak with him.

PART VII. BUILDING THE TABERNACLE
(EXODUS 35–40)

XXII. *And Moses completed the Task* (35:1–40:38)

35   ¹And Moses assembled all the congregation of Israel's Sons and said to them, "These are the *words* that Yahweh commanded to do them. ²Six days a task may be done. But on the seventh day a Holiness shall be for you, a sabbatical Sabbath for Yahweh. Anyone doing a task on it must be put to death. ³Do not burn fire in all your dwellings on the Sabbath day."

⁴And Moses said to all the congregation of Israel's Sons, saying, "This is the *word* that Yahweh commanded, saying: ⁵'Take from with you a Donation-offering for Yahweh. Everyone noble-hearted shall bring it, Yahweh's Donation: gold, silver and bronze, ⁶blue and purple and worm-crimson and linen and *goats* ⁷and

reddened ram skins and beaded skins and acacia wood [8] and oil for illumination and fragrances for the Ointment Oil and for the Spice Incense [9] and carnelian stones and *filling* stones for the Ephod and for the *ḥōšen*.

[10] 'And every wise-hearted among you, they shall come and make all that Yahweh commanded: [11] the Tabernacle, its Tent and its cover, its clasps and its *qərāšîm*, its crossbars, its posts and its bases, [12] the Chest and its poles, the *kappōret* and the Veil screen, [13] the Table and its poles and all its implements and the *Face Bread* [14] and the Illumination Lampstand and its implements and its lamps and the Illumination Oil [15] and the Incense Altar and its poles and the Ointment Oil and the Spice Incense and the Opening Screen for the Tabernacle Opening, [16] the Ascending-offering Altar and the bronze mesh that is its, its poles and all its implements, the Basin and its Stand, [17] the Plaza's sheets and its posts and its bases and the Screen of the Plaza's gate, [18] the Tabernacle's tent-pegs and the Plaza's tent-pegs and their cords, [19] the Textile Garments for attending in the Holiness: the Holiness Garments for Aaron the priest and his sons' garments for priesting.' "

[20] And all the congregation of Israel's Sons went out from before Moses. [21] And every man whose heart ennobled him came, and everyone whose spirit ennobled him, they brought Yahweh's Donation-offering for the Meeting Tent Task and for all its Work and for the Holiness Garments. [22] And the men came in addition to the women. Everyone noble-hearted brought nose-ring and earring and finger-ring and *kûmāz*, any gold item, and every man that elevated a gold Elevation-offering for Yahweh. [23] And everyone with whom was found blue and purple and worm-crimson and linen and *goats* and reddened ram skins and beaded skins, they brought. [24] Each donor of a silver or bronze Donation-offering, they brought Yahweh's Donation-offering. And everyone with whom was found acacia wood, for the Task of the Work they brought.

[25] And every wise-hearted woman, with her hands they spun. And they brought spinning-stuff: the blue and the purple, the worm-crimson and the linen. [26] And all the women whose heart uplifted them, with wisdom they spun the *goats*.

[27] And the chieftains, they brought the carnelian stones and the *filling* stones for the Ephod and for the *ḥōšen* [28] and the fragrance and the oil, for illumination and for the Ointment Oil and for the Spice Incense. [29] Every man and woman whose heart ennobled them to bring for all the Task that Yahweh commanded to do by Moses' *hand*, Israel's Sons brought largesse for Yahweh.

[30] And Moses said to Israel's Sons, "See, Yahweh has called by name Bezalel son of Uri son of Hur from the tribe of Judah [31] and filled him with a divine spirit in wisdom, in understanding and in knowledge and in every task, [32] and for planning plans, to make in gold and in silver and in bronze [33] and in stone carving for *fillings* and in wood carving, to do every planning task; [34] and to direct he has set in his heart. Him and Oholiab son of Ahisamach from the tribe of Dan, [35] he has filled them with heart-wisdom to do every task of carver and of webster and of embroiderer—in the blue and in the purple, in the worm-crimson and in the linen—and of weaver, doers of every task and planners of plans. 36 [1] And Bezalel and Oholiab will make, and every wise-hearted man in whom Yahweh set wisdom and understanding, to know (how) to do all the Holiness Work Task, for all that Yahweh commanded."

² So Moses called Bezalel and Oholiab and every wise-hearted man, in whose heart Yahweh set wisdom, everyone whose heart uplifted him, to approach to the Task to do it. ³ And they took from before Moses all the Donation-offering that Israel's Sons brought for the Holiness Work Task to do it. But they, they brought him still more largesse *by morning by morning.*

⁴ And all the wise doing all the Holiness Task came, *man (by) man* from his task that they were doing, ⁵ and they said to Moses, saying: "The people are bringing more than enough for the Work in respect of the Task that Yahweh commanded to do it."

⁶ So Moses commanded, and they *made a voice pass* in the camp, saying: "Man and woman must not do any more Task for the Holiness Donation-offering." And the people were restrained from giving. ⁷ And the Task was enough for them for all the Task for doing it—and more!

⁸ And every wise-hearted among those doing the Task made the Tabernacle, ten curtains: twisted linen, blue and purple and worm-crimson, Griffins, webster's work he made them. ⁹ The one curtain's length eight-and-twenty by the cubit, and breadth four by the cubit, the one curtain. One measure for all the curtains. ¹⁰ And he fastened five of the curtains one to one, and five curtains he fastened, one to one. ¹¹ And he made blue loops on the one curtain's *lip*, on the edge on the *fastening*; so he made on the outer curtain's *lip*, on the second *fastening*. ¹² Fifty loops he made on the one curtain, and fifty loops he made on the edge of the curtain that was on the second *fastening*, the loops aligning one to one. ¹³ And he made fifty gold clasps and fastened the curtains one to one with the clasps, so that the Tabernacle was one.

¹⁴ And he made *goat* curtains to tent over the Tabernacle: eleven curtains he made them. ¹⁵ The one curtain's length thirty by the cubit, and four cubits the one curtain's breadth. One measure for the eleven curtains. ¹⁶ And he fastened the five curtains separate and the six curtains separate. ¹⁷ And he made loops fifty on the *lip* of the curtain outermost on the *fastening*, and fifty loops he made on the *lip* of the curtain, the second *fastening*. ¹⁸ And he made bronze clasps, fifty, to fasten the Tent, to be one.

¹⁹ And he made a cover for the Tent: reddened ram skins and a beaded skins cover above.

²⁰ And he made the *qərāšîm* for the Tabernacle: standing acacia wood, ²¹ ten cubits the *qereš*'s length, a cubit and a half-cubit the one *qereš*'s breadth, ²² two *arms* for the one *qereš*, pegged one to one; so he made for all the Tabernacle's *qərāšîm*. ²³ And he made the *qərāšîm* for the Tabernacle, twenty *qərāšîm* for the austral, southward side. ²⁴ And forty silver bases he made under the twenty *qərāšîm*, two bases under the one *qereš* for its two *arms*, and two bases under the one *qereš* for its two *arms*. ²⁵ And for the Tabernacle's second flank, for the north side, he made twenty *qərāšîm* ²⁶ and their forty bases, silver, two bases under the one *qereš* and two bases under the one *qereš*. ²⁷ And for the Tabernacle's *seaward* backparts he made six *qərāšîm*. ²⁸ And two *qərāšîm* he made for the Tabernacle's corners at the backparts. ²⁹ And they shall be twinning from below; together they shall be whole to its *head*, to the one ring. So he made for the two of them, for the two corners. ³⁰ And there shall be eight *qərāšîm* and their bases, silver: sixteen bases, two

bases, two bases under the one *qereš.* ³¹ And he made acacia-wood crossbars: five for the *qərāšîm* of the Tabernacle's one flank ³² and five crossbars for the *qərāšîm* of the Tabernacle's second flank and five crossbars for the Tabernacle's *qərāšîm* at the *seaward* backparts. ³³ And he made the inner crossbar to bar amid the *qərāšîm* from end to end. ³⁴ And the *qərāšîm* he plated gold; and their rings he made gold, housings for the crossbars; and he plated the crossbars gold.

³⁵ And he made the Veil: blue and purple and worm-crimson and twisted linen, webster's work he made it, Griffins. ³⁶ And he made for it four acacia-wood posts and plated them gold, their Y-brackets gold, and he cast for them four silver bases.

³⁷ And he made a screen for the Tent Opening: blue and purple and worm-crimson and twisted linen, embroiderer's work, ³⁸ its posts, five, and their Y-brackets, and he will plate their *heads* and their *ḥăšūqîm* gold, and their bases, five, bronze.

37   ¹ And Bezalel made the Chest, acacia wood: two cubits and a half its length and a cubit and a half its breadth and a cubit and a half its height. ² And he plated it pure gold from inside and from outside. And he made for it a gold *zēr* around. ³ And he cast four gold rings for it on its four *feet*, and two rings on its one flank and two rings on its second flank. ⁴ And he made acacia-wood poles and plated them gold. ⁵ And he inserted the poles into the rings on the Chest's flanks for carrying the Chest.

⁶ And he made a pure gold *kappōret*: two cubits and a half its length and a cubit and a half its breadth. ⁷ And he made two Griffins, gold: *miqšâ* he made them on the *kappōret*'s two ends; ⁸ one Griffin on this end here and one Griffin on this end here; on the *kappōret* he made the Griffins on its two ends, ⁹ so that the Griffins will be spreading wings above, screening over the *kappōret* with their wings, and their faces *one to one*, toward the *kappōret* the Griffins' faces were.

¹⁰ And he made the Table, acacia wood: two cubits its length and a cubit its breadth and a cubit and a half its height. ¹¹ And he plated it pure gold. And he made for it a gold *zēr* around. ¹² And he made for it a handbreadth's frame around. And he made a gold *zēr* for its frame around. ¹³ And he cast four gold rings and set the rings on the four corners that belonged to its four legs. ¹⁴ Aligned with the frame the rings were, housings for the poles for carrying the Table. ¹⁵ And he made the poles, acacia wood, and plated them gold, for carrying the Table. ¹⁶ And he made the implements that were on the Table: its bowls and its spoons and its rinsers and the dippers from which may be poured, pure gold.

¹⁷ And he made the Lampstand, pure gold: *miqšâ* he made the Lampstand, its *thigh* and its *reeds,* its cups, its *kaptōrîm* and its *flowers,* they were from it. ¹⁸ And six *reeds* going out from its sides—three Lampstand *reeds* from its one side and three Lampstand *reeds* from its second side—¹⁹ three "almondized" cups on the one *reed—kaptōr* and *flower*—and three "almondized" cups on the one *reed—kaptōr* and *flower*—so for the six *reeds* going out from the Lampstand. ²⁰ And on the Lampstand four "almondized" cups—its *kaptōrîm* and its *flowers*—²¹ and a *kaptōr* under the two *reeds* from it, and a *kaptōr* under the two *reeds* from it, and a *kaptōr* under the two *reeds* from it, for the six *reeds* going out from it. ²² Their *kaptōrîm* and their *reeds,* they were from it, all of it one *miqšâ,* pure gold. ²³ And he made its

lamps seven and its tweezers and its fire-pans, pure gold. ²⁴A talent, pure gold he made it and all its implements.

²⁵And he made the Incense Altar, acacia wood: a cubit its length and a cubit its breadth—foursquare—and two cubits its height; from it its *horns* were. ²⁶And he plated it pure gold: its *roof* and its *walls* around and its *horns*. And he made for it a gold *zēr* around. ²⁷And two gold rings he made for it beneath its *zēr* on its two flanks on its two sides as housings for poles for carrying it with them. ²⁸And he made the poles, acacia wood, and plated them gold.

²⁹And he made the Ointment Oil, a Holiness, and the Herb Incense, pure, compounder's work.

38   ¹And he made the Ascending-offering Altar, acacia wood: five cubits its length and five cubits its breadth—foursquare—and three cubits its height. ²And he made its *horns* on its four corners—from it its *horns* were—and he plated it bronze. ³And he made all the Altar's implements: the pots and the shovels and the bowls, the forks and the fire-pans—all its implements he made bronze. ⁴And he made for the Altar a mesh, lattice work, bronze, under its rim as far as its half. ⁵And he cast four rings at the four corners for the bronze mesh, housings for the poles. ⁶And he made the poles, acacia wood, and plated them bronze. ⁷And he inserted the poles into the rings on the Altar's flanks to carry it with them. Hollow-planked he made it.

⁸And he made the Basin, bronze, and its Stand, bronze, out of the mirrors of the *ṣōbə'ōt*-women who *ṣābā(')*-ed (at) the Meeting Tent Opening.

⁹And he made the Plaza: on the austral, southward side, the Plaza's sheets, twisted linen, one hundred by the cubit, ¹⁰their posts twenty and their bases twenty, bronze; the posts' Y-brackets and their *ḥăšūqîm*, silver. ¹¹And on the north side: one hundred by the cubit, their posts twenty and their bases twenty, bronze; the posts' Y-brackets and their *ḥăšūqîm*, silver. ¹²And on the *sea* side: sheets, fifty by the cubit, their posts ten and their bases ten, the posts' Y-brackets and their *ḥăšūqîm*, silver. ¹³And on the *forward, sunrise* side: fifty cubit. ¹⁴Sheets, fifteen cubit, for the *shoulder*, their posts three and their bases three. ¹⁵And for the second *shoulder*, from this (side) and from this (side) for the Plaza's gate, sheets, fifteen cubit, their posts three and their bases three. ¹⁶All the Plaza's sheets around, twisted linen; ¹⁷and the bases for the posts, bronze, the posts' Y-brackets and their *ḥăšūqîm*, silver, and their *heads'* plating, silver, for they were *məhuššāqîm* silver, all the Plaza's posts. ¹⁸And the Plaza's gate Screen, embroiderer's work, blue and purple and worm-crimson and twisted linen; and twenty cubit length, and height by breadth five cubit, corresponding to the Plaza's sheets. ¹⁹And their posts four and their bases four, bronze, their Y-brackets, silver, and their *heads'* plating and their *ḥăšūqîm*, silver; ²⁰and all the tent-pegs for the Tabernacle and for the Plaza around, bronze.

²¹These are the accountings of the Tabernacle, the Testimony Tabernacle, that were accounted at Moses' *mouth* (as) the Levites' Work, *by the hand of* Ithamar Aaron's son, the priest. ²²And Bezalel son of Uri son of Hur from the tribe of Judah had made all that Yahweh commanded Moses, ²³and with him Oholiab son of Ahisamach from the tribe of Dan, a cutter and webster and embroiderer in

the blue and in the purple and in the worm-crimson and in the linen. 24 All the gold worked for the Task in all the Holiness Task: and the Elevation-offering gold was nine-and-twenty talent and seven hundred and thirty shekel by the Holiness Shekel. 25 And the silver of the community's accountings: one hundred talent and one thousand and seven hundred, five-and-seventy shekel. 26 A beka per *skull*, the half-shekel by the Holiness Shekel, for each passing over the accountings, from the *son of* twenty year and upward, for six hundred thousand and three thousand and five hundred and fifty. 27 And the one hundred talent of silver was for casting the Holiness's bases and the Veil's bases: the one hundred bases for the one hundred talent, a talent per base. 28 And the one thousand and seven hundred and five-and-seventy he made Y-brackets for the posts. And he will plate their *heads* and *ḥiššaq* them. 29 And the Elevation-offering bronze: seventy talent and two thousand and four hundred shekel. 30 And he made with it the bases of the Meeting Tent Opening and the Bronze Altar and the bronze mesh that pertained to it and all the Altar's implements 31 and the Plaza's bases around and the bases of the Plaza's gate and all the Tabernacle's tent-pegs and all the Plaza's tent-pegs around.

39   1 And from the blue and the purple and the worm-crimson they made Textile Garments for attending in the Holiness, and they made the Holiness Garments that were Aaron's—as Yahweh commanded Moses.

2 And he made the Ephod: gold, blue and purple and worm-crimson and twisted linen. 3 And they beat out the gold plates and cut threads to work amid the blue and amid the purple and amid the worm-crimson and amid the linen, webster's work. 4 Shoulder-pieces they made for it, fastening; at its two sides it was fastened. 5 And the woven-band for its ephod-binding that was on it, it was from it, like its work: gold, blue and purple and worm-crimson and twisted linen—as Yahweh commanded Moses.

6 And they made the carnelian stones, set in gold plait-rings, engraved (with) seal engravings, by the names of Israel's sons. 7 And he put them on the Ephod's shoulder-pieces, Memorial stones for Israel's Sons—as Yahweh commanded Moses.

8 And he made the *ḥōšen*, webster's work, like an ephod's work: gold, blue and purple and worm-crimson and twisted linen. 9 It was foursquare, doubled they made the *ḥōšen*; a span its length and a span its breadth, doubled. 10 And they *filled* in it four rows of stone—a row: *'ōdem, piṭdâ* and *bāreqet,* the one row; 11 and the second row: *nōpek, sappîr* and *yāhǎlōm;* 12 and the third row: *lešem, šəbô* and *'aḥlāmâ;* 13 and the fourth row: *taršîš,* carnelian and jade; plait-ringed in gold in their *fillings.* 14 And the stones, they were by the names of Israel's sons, twelve by their names, seal engravings, (each) *man* by his name, for twelve tribe. 15 And they made upon the *ḥōšen gablūt* chains, rope work, pure gold. 16 And they made two gold plait-rings and two gold rings, and they set the two rings on the *ḥōšen's* two edges. 17 And they set the two gold ropes on the two rings on the *ḥōšen's* edges. 18 And the two ropes' two ends they set on the two plait-rings; and they set them on the Ephod's shoulder-pieces, against its front. 19 And they made two gold rings and put on the *ḥōšen's* two edges, at its *lip* that is against the Ephod inside. 20 And they

made two gold rings and set them on the Ephod's two shoulder-pieces, below, against its front, opposite its fastening, above the Ephod's woven-band. ²¹And they tied the ḥōšen by its rings to the Ephod's rings with blue cord for being over the Ephod's woven-band, so the ḥōšen would not slip from upon the Ephod—as Yahweh commanded Moses.

²²And he made the Robe, weaver's work: completely blue; ²³and the Robe's *mouth* in its midst like an anus *mouth*, a *lip* for its *mouth* around; it would not be torn. ²⁴And they made on the Robe's skirts pomegranates of blue and purple and worm-crimson. ²⁵And they made pure gold bells and set the bells amid the pomegranates on the Robe's skirts around amid the pomegranates—²⁶a bell and a pomegranate, a bell and a pomegranate—on the Robe's skirts around, for attending—as Yahweh commanded Moses.

²⁷And they made the shifts: linen, weaver's work, for Aaron and for his sons, ²⁸and the Turban, linen, and the hump-hats, linen splendor-hats, and the linen underpants, twisted linen, ²⁹and the Sash, twisted linen, blue and purple and worm-crimson, embroiderer's work—as Yahweh commanded Moses. ³⁰And they made the Holiness Crown's Blossom, pure gold, and wrote on it seal-engraving writing: "a Holiness of Yahweh." ³¹And they set on it blue cord to set on the Turban above—as Yahweh commanded Moses.

³²And all the Work of the Meeting Tent Tabernacle was completed. And Israel's Sons did, as all that Yahweh commanded Moses, so they did. ³³And they brought the Tabernacle to Moses: the Tent and all its implements, its clasps, its *qərāšîm*, its crossbars and its posts and its bases ³⁴and the reddened skins cover and the beaded skins cover and the Veil Screen, ³⁵the Testimony Chest and its poles and the *kappōret*, ³⁶the Table, all its implements and the *Face Bread*, ³⁷the pure Lampstand, its lamps—the arrangement lamps—and all its implements and the Illumination Oil, ³⁸and the Golden Altar and the Ointment Oil and the Spice Incense and the Tent Opening Screen, ³⁹the Bronze Altar and the bronze mesh that pertained to it, its poles and all its implements, the Basin and its Stand, ⁴⁰the Plaza's sheets, its posts and its bases and the Screen for the Plaza's gate, its cords and its tent-pegs and all the implements of the Tabernacle Work for Meeting Tent, ⁴¹the Textile Garments for attending in the Holiness: the Holiness Garments for Aaron the priest and his sons' garments for priesting—⁴²as all that Yahweh commanded Moses, so Israel's Sons did all the Work.

⁴³And Moses saw all the Task, and, see: they did it—as Yahweh commanded Moses, so they did. And Moses blessed them.

40   ¹And Yahweh spoke to Moses, saying: ²"On the day of the first new moon, on the first of the month, you shall erect the Meeting Tent Tabernacle; ³and you shall put there the Testimony Chest, and you shall screen the Veil before the Chest, ⁴and you shall bring the Table and arrange its arrangement, and you shall bring the Lampstand and *raise* its lamps, ⁵and you shall set the Golden Altar for incense before the Testimony Chest and you shall put the Opening Screen for the Tabernacle, ⁶and you shall set the Ascending-offering Altar before the Meeting Tent Tabernacle Opening, ⁷and you shall set the Basin between Meeting Tent and between the Altar and set water there, ⁸and you shall put the Plaza around

and set the Plaza gate Screen, [9] and you shall take the Ointment Oil and anoint the Tabernacle and all that is in it, and you shall make it holy and all its implements, so that it will be a Holiness, [10] and you shall anoint the Ascending-offering Altar and all its implements, and you shall make the Altar holy, so that the Altar will be a Holiness of Holinesses, [11] and you shall anoint the Basin and its Stand and make it holy, [12] and you shall Bring Near Aaron and his sons to the Meeting Tent Opening and wash them with water, [13] and you shall make Aaron wear the Holiness Garments and anoint him and make him holy so that he may priest for me, [14] and his sons you shall Bring Near and make them wear shifts [15] and anoint them as you anointed their father so that they may priest for me. And their anointment shall be for being for them as an eternal priesthood *to their ages.*"

[16] And Moses did; as all that Yahweh commanded him, so he did.

[17] And it happened, in the first month, in the second year, on the first of the month, the Tabernacle was erected. [18] And Moses erected the Tabernacle, and he set its bases and put its frames and set its crossbars and erected its posts [19] and spread the Tent over the Tabernacle and put the Tent cover over it, above — as Yahweh commanded Moses — [20] and he took and set the Testimony into the Chest and put the poles on the Chest and set the *kappōret* on the Chest [21] and brought the Chest into the Tabernacle and put the Veil Screen and screened before the Testimony Chest — as Yahweh commanded Moses — [22] and he set the Table in Meeting Tent on the Tabernacle's northward flank, outside the Veil, [23] and arranged on it a bread arrangement before Yahweh — as Yahweh commanded Moses — [24] and he put the Lampstand in Meeting Tent opposite the Table, on the Tabernacle's southward flank [25] and *raised* the lamps before Yahweh — as Yahweh commanded Moses — [26] and he put the Golden Altar in Meeting Tent before the Veil [27] and censed Spice Incense on it — as Yahweh commanded Moses — [28] and he put the Opening Screen for the Tabernacle, [29] and the Ascending-offering Altar he put (at) the Meeting Tent Tabernacle Opening, and he *sent up* on it the Ascending-offering and the Tribute-offering — as Yahweh commanded Moses — [30] and he put the Basin between Meeting Tent and between the Altar and set there water for washing — [31] and Moses, Aaron and his sons would wash their hands and their feet from it, [32] in their coming into Meeting Tent or in their approaching to the Altar they would wash — as Yahweh commanded Moses — [33] and he erected the Plaza around the Tabernacle and the Altar and set the Plaza gate Screen.

And Moses completed the Task.

[34] And the cloud covered Meeting Tent, and Yahweh's Glory filled the Tabernacle. [35] But Moses could not enter into Meeting Tent, for the cloud tented upon it, and Yahweh's Glory filled the Tabernacle. [36] And at the cloud's lifting itself from over the Tabernacle, Israel's Sons would set forth upon all their settings forth; [37] but if the cloud would not lift itself, then they would not set forth until the day of its lifting itself. [38] For Yahweh's cloud (would be) over the Tabernacle by day, and a fire would be by night in it, to the eyes of all Israel's House, in all their settings forth.

INTRODUCTION

◆

INTRODUCTION

◆

CULT AND COVENANT

The pivot of Exodus's hinged narrative is the Song of the Sea. Exod 15:1–18 leads the reader up from the roiling Deep to Yahweh's unshakable mountain, "the firm seat for your sitting . . . the sanctum . . . your hands founded" (vol. I, pp. 37–38). From that exalted spot "Yahweh . . . will reign, for ever and eternity."

The Song essentially summarizes the whole Book of Exodus. In volume I, we saw how first the infant Moses and then all Israel were rescued from the threatening waters. And we left Israel camped at Yahweh's mountain, where Jethro and Moses instituted a rudimentary judicial administration (chap. 18). It still remained, however, for Yahweh formally to establish his sovereignty over Israel—by legal acclamation as covenanted overlord, by the promulgation of a law code and by the construction of a royal abode. This constitutes the matter of Exodus 19–40.

As we shall see under COMMENT to chaps. 35–40 (pp. 674–722), the second half of Exodus addresses a single question. How can Israel abide in relationship with the transcendent Deity, whose full essence the earth cannot bear? Yahweh proposes to make himself accessible in two ways that are related both conceptually and by anagrammatic wordplay: God and Israel will *yd^c* 'know' and *y^{c}d* 'meet' each other. The Book of Exodus is riddled with evocations of these roots (see further vol. I, p. 37; below, NOTE to 25:16).

Yahweh and Israel interact in two spheres that, at least for the Priestly Writer, are one and the same: Cult and Covenant. The people's regular offerings are nothing less than the periodic tribute owed to their contractual Overlord, whose benevolence is contingent on Israel's fidelity.

Central to both worship and political arrangements is the element of reciprocal manipulation. Ritual in general represents an effort to cajole if not control divine power. And in the biblical notion of Covenant, which is strictly *quid pro quo*, while Israel retains the option to break or keep the treaty, Yahweh has surrendered his own free will. He has bound himself robotically to reward or punish his people, depending upon their behavior. (One could compare the Greek notion that the gods themselves are subservient to Fate; see Vernant 1980: 92–109.)

What is the utility of such a theology? I regard Covenant and Cult as explanatory theories, alternatives to fate, luck, original sin, karma, mechanical energy, etc., to explain why things happen. In the Bible's dominant worldview, when bad things befall Israel, the cause *must* be ritual imperfection and/or Covenant dereliction.* At the cost of chronic guilt, Israelites could be assured that their personal and national vicissitudes made sense. (I suggest in Propp [2004c] that this theory was not shared by the masses, who probably attributed a far greater role in causing misfortune to sorcery and demons. [also below, pp. 772–73 n. 57])

THE FRACTURED COVENANT

The seminal insight of twentieth-century biblical scholarship, for which chief credit goes to Elias Bickermann (1976: 1.1–32), George E. Mendenhall (1954) and Klaus Baltzer (1971), is that the biblical Covenant is more than a general contract (see also Hillers 1969; McCarthy 1981). It is specifically a *political* treaty between a suzerain (Yahweh) and his vassal (Israel). Although each treaty document is unique, from the dozens of Hittite, Syrian and Assyrian exemplars we may abstract the following idealized covenant form:

- *a.* Identification of the document as a treaty.
- *b.* Identification of the two parties.
- *c.* Review of past relations between the parties, in particular the overlord's beneficence toward the vassal.
- *d.* Stipulations of what the suzerain requires of the vassal, especially exclusive fidelity and regularly submitted tribute.
- *e.* Provisions for the storage of the document and its public recitation.
- *f.* A list of divine witnesses.
- *g.* Blessings for obedience.
- *h.* Curses for disobedience.

The Torah does not contain the Covenant text per se. Instead, Scripture speaks *as if* quoting from or alluding to such a document, whose existence is only implicit. This is why, although we can locate all of the above covenantal elements, they do not stand in order together. Rather, they extend across the entire Torah, enhancing thematic coherence but obscuring the covenantal form.

Specifically: sections *a* and *b* are found in recurrent assertions that a Covenant

---

* One might advance the Book of Job as an exception to this theology. Indeed, Job's unmotivated sufferings are often viewed as an implicit critique of the simplistic Covenant theology. For me, however, Job is the exception that proves the rule. Its unhappy protagonist is a *non-Israelite*, probably a *pre-Israelite*. He is not necessarily Everyman; he may just be Every-Gentile. The Book of Job demonstrates how, absent Israelite Cult and Covenant, humans have no claim on God at all. Even the righteous Job, best of non-Israelites, notwithstanding his obsessive sacrifices and personal scrupulosity, can do nothing but succumb to Yahweh's arbitrary might. It is thus possible to view the Book of Job as outlining the problem to which the Torah provides the solution. Such, at least, was probably the rationale behind Job's inclusion in Scripture. At a deeper level, I share the common impression that the author of Job was questioning God's justice to all peoples, including Israel. The exotic setting is just a diversion.

exists between Yahweh and Israel. Section *c* is the entire pentateuchal narrative, chronicling Yahweh's benevolent acts toward Israel. Section *d* is the mass of pentateuchal legislation: ritual, civil and ethical. Section *e* is found in Exod 25:10–21; Deut 10:3–5, concerning the Chest for storing the Covenant tablets, and in Deut 31:10–13, which requires that the law be publicly recited every seven years. Section *f* is alluded to various statements that Heaven, Earth, Israel and Moses' own literary creation are to serve as Covenant witnesses — the most important witness, however, being Yahweh himself (Deut 4:26; 30:19; 31:21, 26, 28; 32:46; Josh 24:22). Sections *g–h*, the covenantal blessings and curses, are rehearsed briefly in Exod 15:25–26; 23:22–33 and extensively in Leviticus 26; Deuteronomy 27–28.

If it ever existed, the original Covenant document, describing Yahweh's and Israel's mutual obligations, is lost forever. But the Covenant *form* survived — as a vessel. Into it the pentateuchal authors poured all they had: tribal sagas, genealogical lists, chronological tables, topographical descriptions, ancient poems, royal edicts, civil laws, priestly regulations, farming techniques, parental wisdom, common sense, etc. Eventually the vessel burst, leaving its shards scattered throughout the Torah. Ever since, the Five Books of Moses themselves have served as Israel's functional Covenant document.

ABOUT THIS VOLUME

As with its predecessor, the contents of volume II are organized into an extremely literal TRANSLATION; numerous TEXTUAL NOTES that treat variant readings; a detailed SOURCE ANALYSIS on literary prehistory; a REDACTION ANALYSIS on the editing process; many NOTES on small matters of interpretation, and lengthy COMMENTS on larger issues. For the general reader, only the NOTES and COMMENTS will be of interest. The final COMMENT (pp. 674–722) is my attempt to synthesize the religion of ancient Israel, as refracted through the Priestly source and its image of the Tabernacle.

New in this volume is the frequent quotation of ancient Near Eastern laws that parallel, sometimes *verbatim*, statutes in Exodus; these are introduced by "COMPARE." The passages from cuneiform and hieroglyphic texts generally do not receive full discussion. Their presence will facilitate comparative study and alert the reader to the manifold ways in which biblical legislation is a regional variant of ancient Near Eastern common law.

At the end of this volume are five APPENDICES: A. The Documentary Hypothesis, B. The Historicity of the Exodus from Egypt, C. The Origins of Monotheism, D. The Theme of the Exodus in the Bible and E. Afterthoughts. Although they are briefer than originally envisioned (vol. I, pp. 53–54), these essays address broad issues beyond the scope of the commentary proper.

BIBLIOGRAPHY

◆

BIBLIOGRAPHY

◆

Whenever possible, I cite English editions of foreign-language works, some of which appeared decades after the original writing: e.g., Loewenstamm 1992 was published in 1965 (Hebrew), while Jacob 1992 was completed in 1945 in German, but not published in its original language until 1997. The inconvenience this method imposes upon the specialist is, I think, outweighed by its convenience for the nonscholarly English reader, for whom this work is also intended. For books (but not for reprinted articles), this bibliography gives all original publication dates, providing a clearer sense of the history of scholarship. Modern Hebrew titles will be transliterated according to my method for Biblical Hebrew; see pp. xxix–xxx above.

Abel, F. M.
  1933   *Géographie de la Palestine.* Paris: Gabalda.
Aberbach, M., and L. Smolar
  1967   Aaron, Jeroboam, and the Golden Calf. *JBL* 86: 129–40.
Abū Assāf, A.
  1990   *Der Tempel von ʿAin Dara.* Damaszener Forschungen 3. Mainz am
         Rhein: Philipp von Zabern.
Abū Assāf, A., P. Bordreuil and A. R. Millard
  1982   *La statue de Tell Fekherye.* Études Assyriologiques 7. Paris: Recherche
         sur les civilisations.
Abusch, T.
  1989   The Demonic Image of the Witch in Standard Babylonian Litera-
         ture. Pp. 27–58 in *Religion, Science, and Magic,* ed. J. Neusner,
         E. Frerichs and P. V. McC. Flesher. New York/Oxford: Oxford Uni-
         versity.
Ackerman, S.
  1992   *Under Every Green Tree.* HSM 46. Atlanta: Scholars Press.
Aejmelaeus, A.
  1987   What Can We Know about the Hebrew *Vorlage* of the Septuagint?
         ZAW 99: 58–89.
  1992   Septuagintal Translation Techniques—A Solution to the Problem of
         the Tabernacle Account. Pp. 381–402 in *Septuagint, Scrolls and Cog-*

nate Writings, ed. G. J. Brooke and B. Lindars. SBLSCS 33. Atlanta: Scholars Press.

Aharoni, Y.
1968 Arad: Its Inscriptions and Temple. *BA* 31: 2–32.
1973 The Solomonic Temple, the Tabernacle and the Arad Sanctuary. Pp. 1–8 in *Orient and Occident*, ed. H. A. Hoffman, Jr. Fs. C. H. Gordon. AOAT 22. Kevelaer: Butzon & Bercker; Neukirchen-Vluyn: Neukirchener Verlag.
1974 The Horned Altar of Beer-sheba. *BA* 37: 2–6.

Aḥituv, S.
1997 Pənê H'. Pp. 3*–11* in *Tehillah le-Moshe*, ed. M. Cogan, B. L. Eichler and J. H. Tigay. Fs. M. Greenberg. Winona Lake, Ind.: Eisenbrauns.

Aḥituv, Y., and H. Tadmor
1982 Tāḥaš. *EM* 8.520–21. Jerusalem: Bialik Institute.

Albright, W. F.
1935 The Names *Shaddai* and *Abram*. *JBL* 54: 173–204.
1950 The Psalm of Habakkuk. Pp. 1–18 in *Studies in Old Testament Prophecy Presented to Professor Theodore H. Robinson*, ed. H. H. Rowley. Edinburgh: Clark.
1957 *From the Stone Age to Christianity*. New York: Doubleday Anchor Books.

Almagro-Gorbea, M.
1982 Pozo Moro y el influjo fenicio en el periodo orientalizante de la península ibérica. *Revista di Studi Fenici* 10: 231–72.

Alquier, J., and P. Alquier
1931 Stèles votives à Saturne découvertes près de N'gaous (Algérie). *CRAIBL* 1931: 21–26.

Alt, A.
1968 *Essays on Old Testament History and Religion*. Garden City, N.Y.: Doubleday.

Amiran, R.
1969 *Ancient Pottery of the Holy Land*. Hebrew orig. 1963. Israel: Massada.

Andersen, F. I., and A. D. Forbes
1986 *Spelling in the Hebrew Bible*. BibOr 41. Rome: Pontifical Biblical Institute.

Andersen, F. I., and D. N. Freedman
2000 *Micah*. AB 24E. New York: Doubleday.

Anderson, G. A.
1987 *Sacrifices and Offerings in Ancient Israel*. HSM 41. Atlanta: Scholars Press.

Aptowitzer, V.
1930–31 Bêt hammiqdāš šel ma'ălâ 'al pî hā'aggādâ. *Tarbiz* 2: 137–53.

Arlotto, A.
1972 *Introduction to Historical Linguistics*. Washington, D. C.: University Press of America.

Armerding, C.
1958 The Atonement Money. *BS* 115: 334–40.
Arnold, W. R.
1917 *Ephod and Ark.* Cambridge, Mass.: Harvard University.
Artzy, M.
1990 Pomegranate Scepters and Incense Stand with Pomegranates Found in Priest's Grave. *BARev* 16.1: 48–51.
Assmann, J.
1997 *Moses the Egyptian.* Cambridge/London: Harvard University.
Aston, B. G., J. A. Harrell and I. Shaw
2000 Stone. Pp. 5–77 in *Ancient Egyptian Materials and Technologies,* ed. P. T. Nicholson and I. Shaw. Cambridge: Cambridge University.
Attridge, H. W., and R. A. Oden, Jr.
1976 *The Syrian Goddess.* SBLTT 9. Missoula, Mont.: Scholars Press.
1981 *Philo of Byblos: The Phoenician History.* CBQMS 9. Washington, D.C.: Catholic Biblical Association of America.
Ausloos, H.
1996 The Septuagint Version of Exod 23:20–33: A "Deuteronomist" at Work? *JNSL* 22: 89–106.
Avigad, N.
1990 The Inscribed Pomegranate from the "House of the Lord." *BA* 53: 157–66.
Avishur, Y.
1984 *Stylistic Studies of Word-Pairs in Biblical and Ancient Semitic Literatures.* AOAT 210. Kevelaer: Butzon & Bercker; Neukirchen-Vluyn: Neukirchener Verlag.
Avner, U.
1993 *Maṣṣeboth* Sites in the Negev and Sinai and Their Significance. Pp. 166–81 in *Biblical Archaeology Today, 1990,* ed. A. Brian and J. Aviram. Jerusalem: Israel Exploration Society.
2001 Sacred Stones in the Desert. *BARev* 27.3: 30–41.
Axelsson, L. E.
1987 *The Lord Rose up from Seir.* ConBOT 25. Lund: Almqvist & Wiksell.
Baentsch, B.
1903 *Exodus-Leviticus-Numeri.* HKAT. Göttingen: Vandenhoeck & Ruprecht.
Baethgen, F.
1888 *Beiträge zur semitischen Religionsgeschicte.* Berlin: Reuther.
Baker, D. W.
1992 Girgashite. *ABD* 2.1028. New York: Doubleday.
Baker, H. S.
1966 *Furniture in the Ancient World.* New York: Giniger.
Bakon, S.
1997 Creation, Tabernacle and Sabbath. *JBQ* 25: 79–85.
Balicki, A.
1970 *The Netsilik Eskimo.* Prospect Heights, Ill.: Waveland.

Ball, C. J.
    1899   *Light from the East*. London: Eyre and Spottiswoode.
Baltzer, K.
    1971   *The Covenant Formulary*. German orig. 1960. Oxford: Blackwell.
Barkay, G.
    1990   A Bowl with the Hebrew Inscription *qdš*. *IEJ* 40: 124–29, plate 14.
    1992   The Priestly Benediction on Silver Plaques from Ketef Hinnom in Jerusalem. *TA* 9: 139–92.
Barlett, J. R.
    1968   Zadok and His Successors at Jerusalem. *JTS* 19:1–18.
Barnett, R. D.
    1981   Bringing the God into the Temple. Pp. 10–17 in *Temples and High Places in Biblical Times*, ed. A. Biran. Jerusalem: Hebrew Union College–Jewish Institute of Religion.
Barth, J.
    1894   *Die Nominalbildung in den semitischen Sprachen*. Leipzig: Hinrichs.
Batto, B.
    1987   The Sleeping God: An Ancient Near Eastern Motif of Divine Sovereignty. *Bib* 68: 153–77.
    1992   *Slaying the Dragon*. Louisville: Westminster/John Knox.
Baudissin, W. W. von
    1929   *Kyrios als Gottesname in Judentum*. Giessen: Töpelmann.
Becking, B.
    1981–82   The Two Neo-Assyrian Documents from Gezer in their Historical Context. *Jaarbericht Ex Oriente Lux* 27: 76–89.
Beegle, D. M.
    1972   *Moses, the Servant of Yahweh*. Grand Rapids, Mich.: Eerdmans.
Beit-Arieh, I.
    1983   A First Temple Period Census Document. *PEQ* 115: 105–9.
Ben-Ḥayyim, Z.
    1977   *'Ibrît wa'ărāmît nōsaḥ šômərôn* IV. Jerusalem: Academy of the Hebrew Language.
Benichou-Safar, H.
    1988   Sur l'incinération des enfants aux tophets de Carthage et de Sousse. *RHR* 125: 57–67.
Ben-Tor, A.
    1992   Qiri, Tell. *ABD* 5.581–82. New York: Doubleday.
Ben-Tor, A., and M. T. Rubiato
    1999   Excavating Hazor Part Two. Did the Israelites Destroy the Canaanite City? *BARev* 25.3: 22–39.
Ben Zvi, E.
    1992   The Closing Words of the Pentateuchal Books: A Clue for the Historical Status of the Book of Genesis within the Pentateuch. *BN* 62: 7–10.

Benz, F. C.
   1972   *Personal Names in the Phoenician and Punic Inscriptions.* Studia Pohl
          8. Rome: Pontifical Biblical Institute.
Berlejung, A.
   1996   Der Handwerker als Theologe. *VT* 46: 145–68.
Berlin, A.
   1989   On the Meaning of *pll* in the Bible. *RB* 96: 345–51.
Bertram, G.
   1959   Zur Prägung der biblischen Gottesvorstellung in der griechischen
          Übersetzung des Alten Testaments. Die Wiedergabe von *schadad*
          und *schaddaj* im Griechischen. *WO* 2: 502–13.
Beyerlin, W.
   1965   *Origins and History of the Oldest Sinaitic Traditions.* German orig.
          1961. Oxford: Blackwell.
Bezold, C.
   1903   *Ninive und Babylon.* Bielefeld/Leipzig: Velhagen und Klasing.
Biale, D.
   1982   The God with Breasts: El Shaddai in the Bible. *History of Religions*
          20: 240–56.
Bickermann, E.
   1976   *Studies in Jewish and Christian History.* AGJU 9. Leiden: Brill.
Bienkowski, P., ed.
   1992   *Early Edom and Moab: The Beginning of the Iron Age in Southern Jor-
          dan.* Sheffield Archaeological Monographs 7. Sheffield: Collis.
Bietak, M.
   1981   *Avaris and Piramesse.* Proceedings of the British Academy, London
          65. Oxford: Oxford University.
   1992   An Iron Age Four-Room House in Ramesside Egypt. Pp. 10*–12* in
          Avraham Biran Volume. ErIsr 23. Jerusalem: Israel Exploration Society.
   2003   Israelites Found in Egypt. *BARev* 29.5: 40–49, 82–83.
Biran, A.
   1981   "To the God Who is in Dan." Pp. 142–51 in *Temples and High Places
          in Biblical Times,* ed. A. Biran. Jerusalem: Hebrew Union College–
          Jewish Institute of Religion.
   1994   *Biblical Dan.* Jerusalem: Israel Exploration Society, Hebrew Union
          College–Jewish Institute of Religion.
Blau, J.
   1987–88 Kəlûm ništtammərû ʿiqbôtā(y)w šel hazzûgî bithûm hakkin-
          nûyîm wəhappōʿal bəʿibrît hammiqrāʾ. *Leš* 52: 165–68.
Blenkinsopp, J.
   1976   The Structure of P. *CBQ* 38: 275–92.
   1992   *The Pentateuch.* ABRL. New York: Doubleday.
Blum, E.
   1990   *Studien zur Komposition des Pentateuch.* BZAW 189. Berlin/New
          York: de Gruyter.

Boer, P. A. H. de
    1948   Some Remarks on Exodus XXI 7–11. The Hebrew Female Slave. Pp. 162–66 in *Orientalia Neerlandica*. Leiden: Sijthoff.
    1972   An Aspect of Sacrifice. Pp. 27–47 in *Studies in the Religion of Ancient Israel*. VTSup 23. Leiden: Brill.

Bogaert, P. M.
    1981   L'Orientation du parvis du sanctuaire dans le version grecque de l'Exode (*Ex.* 27, 9–13 LXX). *L'Antiquité classique* 50: 79–85.

Bori, P. C.
    1990   *The Golden Calf and the Origins of the anti-Jewish Controversy.* South Florida Studies in the History of Judaism 16. Atlanta: Scholars Press.

Börker-Klähn, J., and W. Röllig
    1971   Granatapfel. *RlA* 3.616–32. Berlin: de Gruyter.

Borowski, O.
    1983   The Identity of the Biblical ṣirʿâ. Pp. 315–19 in *The Word of the Lord Shall Go Forth*, ed. C. L. Meyers and M. O'Connor. Fs. D. N. Freedman. American Schools of Oriental Research Special Volume Series 1. Winona Lake, Ind.: Eisenbrauns.
    1987   *Agriculture in Iron Age Israel.* Winona Lake, Ind.: Eisenbrauns.
    1998   *Every Living Thing.* Walnut Creek/London/New Delhi: Sage.

Bottéro, J.
    1954   *Le problème des Ḫabiru.* Cahiers de la Société Asiatique 12. Paris: Imprimerie Nationale.
    1981   L'ordalie en Mésopotamie ancienne. *Annali della Scuola Normale Superiore de Pisa.* Classe di lettere e filosofia, serie III,3. 11: 1005–67.
    1992   *Mesopotamia: Writing, Reasoning, and the Gods.* French orig. 1987. Chicago/London: University of Chicago.

Botterweck, G. J., D. N. Freedman and J. Lundbom
    1978   dôr. *TDOT* 3.169–81. Grand Rapids, Mich.: Eerdmans.

Boxall, B.
    2000   State's 150th No Different from 149th, *The Los Angeles Times* Sept. 8: A3, A20.

Braulik, G.
    1992   Haben in Israel auch Frauen geopfert? Pp. 19–28 in *Zur Aktualität des Alten Testaments*, ed. S. Kreuzer and K. Lüthi. Fs. G. Sauer. Frankfurt am Main/Bern/New York/Paris: Lang.

Braun, J.
    2002   *Music in Ancient Israel/Palestine.* German orig. 1999. Grand Rapids/ Cambridge: Eerdmans.

Breasted, J. H.
    1962   *Ancient Records of Egypt.* New York: Russell & Russell.

Brenner, A.
    1982   *Colour Terms in the Old Testament.* JSOTSup 21. Sheffield: JSOT Press.

Brenner, M. L.
    1991   *The Song of the Sea: Ex 15:1–21.* BZAW 195. Berlin/New York: de Gruyter.

Bretschneider, J.
    1991   *Architekturmodelle in Vorderasien und der östlichen Ägäis vom Neolithikum bis in das 1. Jahrtausend.* AOAT 229. Kevelaer: Butzon & Bercker; Neukirchen-Vluyn: Neukirchener Verlag.

Brichto, H. C.
    1963   *The Problem of "Curse" in the Hebrew Bible.* JBLMS 13. Philadelphia: Society of Biblical Literature and Exegesis.
    1974   Kin, Cult, Land and Afterlife—a Biblical Complex. *HUCA* 44: 1–54.

Bridgeman, J.
    1987   Purple Dye in Late Antiquity and Byzantium. Pp. 159–65 in *The Royal Purple and the Biblical Blue,* ed. E. Spanier. Jerusalem: Keter.

Brown, J. P.
    1980   The Sacrificial Cult and Its Critique in Greek and Hebrew (II). *JSS* 25: 1–21.

Brown, S.
    1991   *Late Carthaginian Child Sacrifice.* JSOT/ASOR Monograph Series. Sheffield: Sheffield Academic Press.

Bryan, B. M.
    1996   Art, Empire, and the End of the Late Bronze Age. Pp. 33–79 in *The Study of the Ancient Near East in the Twenty-first Century,* ed. J. S. Cooper and G. M. Schwartz. Winona Lake, Ind.: Eisenbrauns.

Buber, M.
    1949   *The Prophetic Faith.* New York: Macmillan.

Buber, M., and F. Rosenzweig
    1934   *Die Schrift.* Berlin: Schoken.
    1994   *Scripture and Translation.* German orig. 1936. Indiana Studies in Biblical Literature. Bloomington/Indianapolis: Indiana University.

Budde, K.
    1891   Bemerkungen zum Bundesbuch. ZAW 111: 99–114.
    1892   Aus einen Briefe von W. Robertson Smith vom 27.8. ZAW 12: 162–63.

Burkert, W.
    1972   *Lore and Science in Ancient Pythagoreanism.* German orig. 1962. Cambridge, Mass.: Harvard University.
    1983   *Homo Necans.* German orig. 1972. Berkeley/Los Angeles/London: University of California.
    1988   The Meaning and Function of the Temple in Classical Greece. Pp. 27–47 in *Temple in Society,* ed. M. V. Fox. Winona Lake, Ind.: Eisenbrauns.
    1992   *The Orientalizing Revolution.* Cambridge/London: Harvard University.
    1996   *Creation of the Sacred.* Cambridge/London: Harvard University.

Burrows, E.
  1940   The Meaning of El Šaddai. *JTS* 41: 152–61.
Burrows, M.
  1950–51   *The Dead Sea Scrolls of St. Mark's Monastery.* New Haven, Conn.: American Schools of Oriental Research.
Cahill, J. M.
  1997   Royal Rosettes Fit for a King. *BARev* 2.5: 48–57, 68–69.
Calmeyer, P.
  1969   Glocke. *RlA* 3.427–31. Berlin: de Gruyter.
Campbell, J.
  1976   *The Masks of God: Primitive Mythology.* New York: Penguin.
Cardellini, I.
  1981   Die biblischen "Sklaven"-Gesetze im Lichte des keilschriftlichen Sklavenrechts. BBB 55. Bonn: Hanstein.
Carr, D. M.
  1996   *Reading the Fractures of Genesis.* Louisville: Westminster John Knox.
Cartmill, M.
  1993   *A View to a Death in the Morning.* Cambridge/London: Harvard University.
Casanowicz, I. M.
  1894   *Paronomasia in the Old Testament.* Boston: Norwood.
Cassin, E.
  1968   *La splendeur divine.* École practique des hautes études, Sorbonne. Civilisations et sociétés 8. Paris: Mouton.
Cassuto, U.
  1967   *A Commentary of the Book of Exodus.* Hebrew orig. 1951. Jerusalem: Magnes.
Cassuto, M. D., and R. D. Barnett
  1962   Kərûb, kərûbîm. *EM* 4.238–44. Jerusalem: Bialik Institute.
Cazelles, H.
  1946   *Études sur le code de l'Alliance.* Paris: Letouzey et Ané.
Childs, B. S.
  1974   *The Book of Exodus.* OTL. Philadelphia: Westminster.
Chirichigno, G. C.
  1993   *Debt-Slavery in Israel and the Ancient Near East.* JSOTSup 141. Sheffield: Sheffield Academic Press.
Clements, R. E.
  1972   *Exodus.* The Cambridge Bible Commentary. Cambridge: Cambridge University.
Clifford, R. J.
  1971   The Tent of El and the Israelite Tent of Meeting. *CBQ* 33: 221–27.
  1972   *The Cosmic Mountain in Canaan and the Old Testament.* HSM 4. Cambridge, Mass.: Harvard University.
  1994   *Creation Accounts in the Ancient Near East and in the Bible.* CBQMS 26. Washington, D.C.: Catholic Biblical Association of America.

Cody, A.
  1969 A *History of the Old Testament Priesthood*. Rome: Pontifical Biblical Institute.

Cogan, M.
  1974 *Imperialism and Religion: Assyria, Judah and Israel in the Eighth and Seventh Centuries B.C.E.* SBLMS 19. Missoula, Mont.: Scholars Press.

Cogan, M., and H. Tadmor.
  1988 *II Kings*. AB 11. Garden City, N.Y.: Doubleday.

Cohen, S. J. D.
  1999 *The Beginnings of Jewishness*. Berkeley/Los Angeles/London: University of California.

Colby, B., and M. Cole
  1973 Culture, Memory and Narrative. Pp. 63–91 in *Modes of Thought*. London: Faber & Faber.

Cole, R. A.
  1973 *Exodus*. Downers Grove, Ill.: InterVarsity.

Collins, J. J.
  1995 *The Scepter and the Star*. ABRL. New York: Doubleday.

Cooke, S. A.
  1903 A Pre-Massoretic Biblical Papyrus. *Proceedings of the Society of Biblical Archaeology* 33: 34–56.

Cooper, A.
  1989 The Plain Sense of Exodus 23:5. *HUCA* 59: 1–22.

Coote, R. B., and D. R. Ord
  1991 *In the Beginning*. Minneapolis, Minn.: Fortress.

Cowley, A. E.
  1923 *Aramaic Papyri of the Fifth Century B.C.* Oxford: Clarendon.

Crawley, A. E.
  1961 Mirror. *Encyclopedia of Religion and Ethics* 8.695–97. New York: Scribner.

Cross, F. M.
  1961a The Development of the Jewish Scripts. Pp. 133–202 in *The Bible and the Ancient Near East*, ed. G. E. Wright. Fs. W. F. Albright. Garden City, N.Y.: Doubleday.
  1961b The Priestly Tabernacle. Pp. 201–21 in *The Biblical Archaeologist Reader Volume I*, ed. D. N. Freedman and G. E. Wright. Garden City, N.Y.: Doubleday.
  1973 *Canaanite Myth and Hebrew Epic*. Cambridge, Mass.: Harvard University.
  1976 The "Olden Gods" in Ancient Near Eastern Creation Myths. Pp. 329–38 in *Magnalia Dei*, ed. F. M. Cross, W. E. Lemke and P. D. Miller. Memorial G. E. Wright. Garden City, N.Y.: Doubleday.
  1981 The Priestly Tabernacle in the Light of Recent Research. Pp. 169–78 in *Temples and High Places in Biblical Times*, ed. A. Biran. Jerusalem:

Nelson Glueck School of Biblical Archaeology of Hebrew Union College–Jewish Institute of Religion.

1994   4QExod-Levᶠ. Pp. 133–44 in *Qumran Cave 4.VII*, ed. E. Ulrich et al. DJD 12. Oxford: Clarendon.

1998   *From Epic to Canon*. Baltimore/London: Johns Hopkins University.

1999   King Hezekiah's Seal Bears Phoenician Imagery. *BARev* 25.2: 42–45, 60.

Cross, F. M., et al.

1972   *Scrolls from Qumrân Cave I*. Jerusalem: Albright Institute of Archaeological Research and the Shrine of the Book.

Cross, F. M. , and D. N. Freedman

1997   *Studies in Ancient Yahwistic Poetry*. Orig. Ph.D. diss., Johns Hopkins University, 1950. The Biblical Resource Series. Grand Rapids, Mich./Cambridge: Eerdmans; Livonia, Mich.: Dove.

Crüsemann, F.

1987   "Auge um Auge . . ." (Ex 21,24f). *Evangelische Theologie* 47: 411–26.

1996   *The Torah*. German orig. 1992. Minneapolis, Minn.: Fortress.

Culican, W.

1980   Phoenician Incense Stands. Pp. 85–101 in *Oriental Studies Presented to Benedikt S. J. Isserlin*, ed. R. Y. Ebied and M. J. L. Young. Leeds University Oriental Studies, Near Eastern Researches 2. Leiden: Brill.

Dahlberg, B. T.

1962   Hur. *IDB* 2.664. Nashville, Tenn.: Abingdon.

Dalglish, E. R.

1992   Bethel (Deity). *ABD* 1.706–10. New York: Doubleday.

Dalley, S.

1989   *Myths from Mesopotamia*. Oxford/New York: Oxford University.

2000   Hebrew *taḥaš*, Akkadian *duḫšu*, Faience and Beadwork. *JSS* 45: 1–19.

Dalman, G.

1935   *Arbeit und Sitte in Palästina IV*. Gütersloh: Bertelsmann.

1937   *Arbeit und Sitte in Palästina V*. Gütersloh: Bertelsmann.

1939   *Arbeit und Sitte in Palästina VI*. Gütersloh: Bertelsmann.

Damrosch, D.

1987   *The Narrative Covenant*. San Francisco: Harper & Row.

Dandamaev, M. A., and V. G. Lukonin

1989   *The Culture and Social Institutions of Ancient Iran*. Cambridge/New York/New Rochelle/Melbourne/Sydney: Cambridge University.

Danker, F. W.

1992   Purple. *ABD* 5.557–60. New York: Doubleday.

Danthine, H.

1939   L'imagerie des trônes vides et des trônes porteurs de symboles dans le Proche Orient ancien. Pp. 857–66 in *Mélanges syriens offerts à M. René Dussaud*. Paris: Geuthner.

Daube, D.
1936   A Note on a Jewish Dietary Law. *JTS* 37: 289–91.
1947   *Studies in Biblical Law.* Cambridge: Cambridge University.
1963   *The Exodus Pattern in the Bible.* London: Faber & Faber.
D'Auria, S., P. Lacovara and C. H. Roehrig
1988   *Mummies and Magic.* Boston: Northeastern University.
Daviau, P. M. M., and M. Steiner
2000   A Moabite Sanctuary at Khirbat al-Mudayna. *BASOR* 320: 1–21.
Davies, G. H.
1967   *Exodus.* Torch Bible Commentaries. London: SCM.
Davies, G. I.
1990   The Wilderness Itineraries and Recent Archaeological Research. Pp.
       161–75 in *Studies in the Pentateuch,* ed. J. A. Emerton. VTSup 41.
       Leiden: Brill.
Davies, H.
1967   The Ark of the Covenant. *ASTI* 5: 30–47.
Davila, J. R.
2001   *Descenders to the Chariot.* Supplements to the Journal for the Study
       of Judaism 70. Leiden/Boston/Köln: Brill.
Davila, J. R., and B. Zuckerman
1993   The Throne of 'Ashtart Inscription. *BASOR* 289: 67–80.
Dawson, W. R.
1926   Some Observations on the Egyptian Calendars of Lucky and Un-
       lucky Days. *JEA* 12: 260–64.
Day, J.
1979   Echoes of Baal's Seven Thunders and Lightnings in Psalm XXIX and
       Habakkuk III 9 and the Identity of the Seraphim in Isaiah VI. *VT* 29:
       143–51.
1985   *God's Conflict with the Sea.* Cambridge: Cambridge University.
1989   *Molech: A God of Human Sacrifice in the Old Testament.* University
       of Cambridge Oriental Publications 41. Cambridge: Cambridge
       University Press.
De Groot van Houten, C.
1992   Remember That You Were Aliens: A Traditio-Historical Study. Pp.
       224–40 in *Priests, Prophets and Scribes,* ed. E. Ulrich et al. Fs. J. Blen-
       kinsopp. JSOTSup 149. Sheffield: Sheffield Academic Press.
Delcor, M.
1983   Les trônes d'Astarté. Pp. 777–87 in *Atti del I Congresso Internazionale
       di Studi Fenici e Punici, Roma 5–10 Novembre 1979.* Rome: Con-
       siglio Nazionale delle Ricerche.
1986   Réflexions sur l'investiture sacerdotale sans onction à la fête du nou-
       vel an d'après *le Rouleau du Temple* de Qumrân (XIV,15–17). Pp.
       155–64 in *Hellenica et Judaica,* ed. A. Caquot, M. Hadas-Lebel and
       J. Riaud. Fs. V. Nikiprowetzky. Leuven/Paris: Peeters.
1990   *Environnement et tradition de l'Ancien Testament.* AOAT 228. Keve-
       laer: Butzon & Bercker; Neukirchen-Vluyn: Neukirchener Verlag.

Del Olmo-Lete, G.
  1999   *Canaanite Religion According to the Liturgical Texts of Ugarit.* Be-
         thesda: CDL.
Deutsch, R., and M. Heltzer
  1994   *Forty New Ancient West Semitic Inscriptions.* Tel Aviv: Archaeologi-
         cal Center.
Dever, W. G.
  2001   *What Did the Biblical Writers Know and When Did they Know It?*
         Grand Rapids, Mich./Cambridge: Eerdmans.
  2003   *Who Were the Early Israelites and Where Did They Come From?*
         Grand Rapids, Mich./Cambridge: Eerdmans.
  2005   *Did God Have a Wife?* Grand Rapids, Mich./Cambridge: Eerdmans.
Dhorme, E. P.
  1920–23   L'emploi métaphorique des noms de parties du corps en hébreu
         et en akkadien. *RB* 29: 465–506; 30: 374–99, 517–40; 31: 215–33,
         489–517; 32: 185–212.
Di Cesnola, A. P.
  1884   *Salaminia.* London: Whiting.
Diamond, A. S.
  1957   An Eye for an Eye. *Iraq* 19: 151–55.
Dibelius, M.
  1906   *Die Lade Jahves.* FRLANT 7. Göttingen: Vandenhoeck & Ruprecht.
Dietrich, M., and O. Loretz
  1980   Das Porträt einer Königin in KTU 1.14 I 12–15. *UF* 12: 199–204.
Dick, M. B.
  2002   Worshiping Idols. *BRev* 18.2: 30–37.
Dickson, H. R. P.
  1983   *The Arab of the Desert:* London: George Allen & Unwin.
Dillmann, A.
  1880   *Exodus und Leviticus.* Kurzgefasstes exegetisches Handbuch. Leipzig:
         Hirzel.
Dion, P. E., and P. M. M. Daviau
  2000   An Inscribed Incense Altar of Iron Age II at Ḫirbet el-Mudēyine (Jor-
         dan). *ZDPV* 116: 1–13.
Dommershausen, W.
  1980   *chālal.* TDOT 4.417–21. Grand Rapids, Mich.: Eerdmans.
Dothan, T., and M. Dothan
  1992   *People of the Sea: The Search for the Philistines.* New York: Macmillan.
Doughty, C. M.
  1921   *Travels in Arabia Deserta.* New York: Boni & Liveright.
Douglas, M.
  1966   *Purity and Danger.* London/Henley: Routledge & Kegan Paul.
Dozeman, T. B.
  1989a *God on the Mountain.* SBLMS 37. Atlanta: Scholars Press.
  1989b Inner-biblical Interpretation of Yahweh's Gracious and Compassion-
         ate Character. *JBL* 108: 207–23.

Draffkorn, A. E.
1957   *Ilāni/Elohim. JBL* 76: 216–24.

Driver, G. R.
1954–59   Technical Terms in the Pentateuch. *WO* 2: 254–63.
1969   Ugaritic and Hebrew Words. *Ug* 6: 181–84.

Driver, S. R.
1891   *An Introduction to the Literature of the Old Testament.* New York: Scribner.
1911   *The Book of Exodus.* Cambridge Bible for Schools and Colleges. Cambridge: Cambridge University.

Drosnin, M.
1997   *The Bible Code.* New York: Simon & Schuster.

Dunand, F.
1979   Droit d'asile et refuge dans les temples en Égypte lagide. Pp. 77–97 in *Hommages à la mémoire de Serge Sauneron 1927–1976 II*, ed. J. Vercoutter. Bibliothèque d'Étude 82. Cairo: Institut Français d'Archéologie Orientale.

Duncan, J. A.
1992   Considerations of 4QDt^j in Light of the "All Souls Deuteronomy" and Cave 4 Phylactery Texts. Pp. 199–215 in *The Madrid Qumran Congress: Proceedings of the International Congress on the Dead Sea Scrolls, Madrid 18–21 March, 1991* STDJ. Leiden/New York/Cologne: Brill; Madrid: Editorial Complutense.

Durand, J. M., and M. Guichard
1997   Les rituels de Mari (textes no 2 à no 5). Pp. 19–78 in *Florilegium marianum III*, ed. D. Charpin and J. M. Durand. Mémoires de *N.A.B.U.* 4. Paris: Société pour l'Étude du Proche-Orient Ancien.

Durham, J. I.
1987   *Exodus.* WBC 3. Waco, Tex.: Word Books.

Durkheim, E.
1915   *The Elementary Forms of Religious Life.* French orig. 1912. London: George Allen & Unwin.

Ebeling, E.
1948   Mittelassyrische Rezepte zur Bereitung von wohlriechenden Salben. *Or* 17: 129–45, 299–313.

Eck, D.
1985   *Darśan. Seeing the Divine Image in India.* Chambersberg, Penn.: Anima Books.

Edelman, D.
1987   Biblical *Molek* Reassessed. *JAOS* 107: 727–31.

Edelman, R.
1966   To ʿannôt Exodus xxxii 18. *VT* 16: 355.

Eerdmans, B. D.
1939   *The Covenant at Mount Sinai Viewed in the Light of Antique Thought.* Leiden: Burgersdijk and Niermans.

Ehrlich, A. B.
    1908   *Randglossen zur hebräischen Bibel 1.* Leipzig: Hinrichs.
    1909   *Randglossen zur hebräischen Bibel 2.* Leipzig: Hinrichs.
    1969   *Mikrâ ki-Pheschutô 1.* Orig. pub. 1899. New York: KTAV.

Eichler, B.
    1977   Another Look at the Nuzi Sistership Contracts. Pp. 45–59 in *Essays on the Ancient Near East in Memory of Jacob Joel Finkelstein,* ed. M. de Jong Ellis. Memoirs of the Connecticut Academy of Arts and Sciences 19. Hamden, Conn.: Archon.

Eilberg-Schwartz, H.
    1990   *The Savage in Judaism.* Bloomington/Indianapolis: University of Indiana.
    1994   *God's Phallus.* Boston: Beacon Press.

Eising, H.
    1980   *zākar. TDOT* 4.64–82. Grand Rapids, Mich.: Eerdmans.

Eissfeldt, O.
    1935   *Molk als Opferbegriff im Punischen und Hebräischen und das Ende des Gottes Moloch.* Beiträge zur Religionsgeschichte des Altertums 3. Halle (Saale): Niemeyer.
    1937   Eine Einschmelzstelle am Tempel zu Jerusalem. *Forschungen und Fortschritte* 13: 163–64.

Elhorst, H. J.
    1910   Das Ephod. ZAW 30: 259–76.

Eliade, M.
    1954   *The Myth of the Eternal Return.* Bollingen Series 46. New York: Bollingen Foundation.
    1959   *The Sacred and the Profane.* German orig. 1957. New York: Harper.

Ellenbogen, M.
    1962   *Foreign Words in the Old Testament.* London: Luzac.

Emerton, J. A.
    1967   The Meaning of '*nšy qdš* in Lam 4 1. ZAW 79: 233–36.

Enns, P.
    2000   *Exodus.* NIV Application Commentary. Grand Rapids: Zondervan.

Evans-Pritchard, E. E.
    1956   *Nuer Religion.* Oxford: Clarendon.

Ewald, H.
    1876   *The Antiquities of Israel.* German orig. 1866. London: Longmans, Green.

Fabry, H. J.
    1995   *lēb. TDOT* 7.399–437. Grand Rapids, Mich.: Eerdmans.

Fales, F. M.
    1992   Census. *ABD* 1.882–83. New York: Doubleday.

Feliks, Y.
    1995   The Incense of the Tabernacle. Pp. 125–49 in *Pomegranates and Golden Bells,* ed. D. P. Wright, D. N. Freedman and A. Hurvitz. Fs. J. Milgrom. Winona Lake, Ind.: Eisenbrauns.

Fensham, F. C.
1959 New Light on Exod. 21 6 and 22 7 from the Laws of Eshnunna. *JBL* 78: 160–61.
1960 Exodus XXI:18–19 in the Light of Hittite Law §10. *VT* 10: 333–35.
1962 Widow, Orphan, and the Poor in Ancient Near Eastern Legal and Wisdom Literature. *JNES* 21: 129–39.
1963 Clauses of Protection in Hittite Vassal-Treaties and the Old Testament. *VT* 13: 133–43.
1966 The Burning of the Golden Calf and Ugarit. *IEJ* 16: 191–96.
1988 Liability of Animals in Biblical and Ancient Near Eastern Law. *JNWSL* 14: 85–90.

Fiddes, N.
1991 *Meat: A Natural Symbol.* London/New York: Routledge.

Finkelstein, I.
1988 *The Archaeology of the Israelite Settlement.* Jerusalem: Israel Exploration Society.

Finkelstein, J. J.
1961 Ammiṣaduqa's Edict and the Babylonian "Law Codes." *JCS* 15: 91–104.
1966 The Genealogy of the Hammurapi Dynasty. *JCS* 20: 95–118.
1981 *The Ox that Gored.* Transactions of the American Philosophical Society 72.2. Philadelphia: American Philosophical Society.

Fishbane, M.
1979 *Text and Texture.* New York: Schocken.
1985 *Biblical Interpretation in Ancient Israel.* Oxford: Clarendon.
1995 Census and Intercession in a Priestly Text (Exodus 30:11–16) and its Midrashic Transformation. Pp. 103–11 in *Pomegranates and Golden Bells*, ed. D. P. Wright, D. N. Freedman and A. Hurvitz. Fs. J. Milgrom. Winona Lake, Ind.: Eisenbrauns.

Fleming, D. E.
1992 *The Installation of Baal's High Priestess at Emar.* HSS 42. Atlanta: Scholars Press.
1999 If El is a Bull, Who is a Calf? Pp. 23*–27* in *Frank Moore Cross Volume.* ErIsr 26. Jerusalem: Israel Exploration Society.
2000 Mari's Large Public Tent and the Priestly Tent Sanctuary. *VT* 50: 484–98.

Forbes, R. J.
1957 *Studies in Ancient Technology* vol. 5. Leiden: Brill.
1964a *Studies in Ancient Technology* vol. 4. 2d ed. Leiden: Brill.
1964b *Studies in Ancient Technology* vols. 8–9. 2d ed. Leiden: Brill.
1966 *Studies in Ancient Technology* vol. 5. 2d ed. Leiden: Brill.

Forsyth, N.
1987 *The Old Enemy: Satan and the Combat Myth.* Princeton, N.J.: Princeton University.

Foster, B. R.
1993 *Before the Muses.* Bethesda: CDL.

Fowler, J. D.
    1988   *Theophoric Personal Names in Ancient Hebrew.* JSOTSup 49. Sheffield: Sheffield Academic Press.

Fowler, M. D.
    1992   Incense Altars. *ABD* 3.409–10. New York: Doubleday.

Fox, E.
    1986   *Now These are the Names.* New York: Schocken.

Fox, M. V.
    1973   ṬÔB as Covenant Terminology. *BASOR* 209: 41–42.
    1974   The Sign of the Covenant. *RB* 81: 557–96.

Frankel, D.
    1994   The Destruction of the Golden Calf: A New Solution. *VT* 44: 330–39.

Frankfort, H.
    1978   *Kingship and the Gods.* Chicago: University of Chicago.

Frazer, J.
    1919   *Folk-lore in the Old Testament.* London: Macmillian.

Freedman, D. N.
    1976   Divine Names and Titles in Early Hebrew Poetry. Pp. 55–107 in *Magnalia Dei,* ed. F. M. Cross, W. E. Lemke and P. D. Miller, Jr. Memorial G. E. Wright. Garden City, N.Y.: Doubleday.
    1981   Temple Without Hands. Pp. 21–30 in *Temples and High Places in Biblical Times,* ed. A. Biran. Jerusalem: Hebrew Union College–Jewish Institute of Religion.
    1997   *Divine Commitment and Human Obligation.* Grand Rapids/Cambridge: Eerdmans.
    2000   *The Nine Commandments.* New York: Doubleday.

Freedman, D. N., A. D. Forbes and F. I. Andersen
    1992   *Studies in Hebrew and Aramaic Orthography.* Biblical and Judaic Studies from the University of California, San Diego 2. Winona Lake, Ind.: Eisenbrauns.

Freedman, D. N., and M. O'Connor
    1986   *YHWH. TDOT* 5.500–21. Grand Rapids, Mich.: Eerdmans.
    1995   *kᵉrûḇ. TDOT* 7.307–19. Grand Rapids, Mich.: Eerdmans.

Fretheim, T. E.
    1968   The Priestly Document: Anti-Temple? *VT* 18: 313–29.
    1991   *Exodus* Interpretation. Louisville: John Knox.

Freud, S.
    1918   *Totem and Taboo.* German orig. 1913. New York: Moffat, Yard.

Freund, R. A.
    1989   Murder, Adultery and Theft? *SJOT* 2: 72-80.
    1990   *Understanding Jewish Ethics.* Lewiston, N.Y.: Mellen.

Fried, L. S.
    2004   *The Priest and the Great King.* Biblical and Judaic Studies from the University of California, San Diego 10. Winona Lake, Ind.: Eisenbrauns.

Friedman, R. E.
1981 *The Exile and Biblical Narrative*. HSM 22. Chico, Calif.: Scholars Press.
1987 *Who Wrote the Bible?* New York: Summit.
1992 Torah. *ABD* 6.605–22. New York: Doubleday.
1995 *The Disappearance of God*. Boston/New York/Toronto/London: Little, Brown.
1998 *The Hidden Book in the Bible*. San Francisco: HarperSanFrancisco.
2001 *Commentary on the Torah*. New York: HarperSanFrancisco.
2003 *The Bible with Sources Revealed*. New York: HarperSanFrancisco.
Friedrich, I.
1968 *Ephod und Choschen im Lichte des alten Orients*. Wiener Beiträge zur Theologie 20. Vienna: Herder.
Friedrich, J.
1975 *Hethitisches Wörterbuch*. Heidelberg: Winter.
Fritz, V.
1977 *Tempel und Zelt*. WMANT 47. Neukirchen-Vluyn: Neukirchener Verlag.
Frymer-Kensky, T.
1980 Tit for Tat: The Principle of Equal Retribution in Near Eastern and Biblical Law. *BA* 43: 230–34.
1983 Pollution, Purification, and Purgation in Biblical Israel. Pp. 399–414 in *The Word of the Lord Shall Go Forth*, ed. C. L. Meyers and M. O'Connor. Fs. D. N. Freedman. American Schools of Oriental Research Special Volume Series 1. Winona Lake, Ind.: Eisenbrauns.
1998 Virginity in the Bible. Pp. 79–96 in *Gender and Law in the Hebrew Bible and the Ancient Near East*, ed. V. Matthews, B. M. Levinson and T. Frymer-Kensky. JSOTSup 262. Sheffield: Sheffield Academic Press.
Fuhs, H. F.
1990 *yārēʾ; yirʾâ; môrāʾ*. *TDOT* 6.290–315. Grand Rapids, Mich.: Eerdmans.
Gadd, C. J.
1936 *The Stones of Assyria*. London: Chatto and Windus.
Gagarin, M.
1981 *Drakon and the Early Athenian Homicide Law*. Yale Classical Monographs 3. New Haven/London: Yale University.
1986 *Early Greek Law*. Berkeley/Los Angeles/London: University of California.
Gall, A. von
1918 *Der hebräische Pentateuch der Samaritaner*. Giessen: Töpelmann.
Galling, K.
1925 *Der Altar in den Kulturen des alten Orients*. Berlin: Karl Curtius.
Gandz, S.
1970 *Studies in Hebrew Astronomy and Mathematics*. New York: KTAV.

Gane, R.
    1992   "Bread of the Presence" and Creator-In-Residence. *VT* 42: 179–203.
Garber, P. L., and R. W. Funk
    1962   Jewels and Precious Stones. *IDB* 2.898–905. Nashville, Tenn.:
           Abingdon.
Garfinkel, Y.
    1987   The Meaning of the Word *MPQD* in the Tel Ira Inscription. *PEQ*
           119: 19–23.
Garr, W. R.
    1990   Interpreting Orthography. Pp. 53–80 in *The Hebrew Bible and Its In-*
           terpreters, ed. W. H. Propp, B. Halpern and D. N. Freedman. Biblical
           and Judaic Studies from the University of California, San Diego 1.
           Winona Lake, Ind.: Eisenbrauns.
Gaster, T. H.
    1962   Sacrifices and Offerings. *IDB* 4.147–59. Nashville, Tenn.: Abingdon.
Gazin-Schwartz, A., and C. Cornelius Holtrof, ed.
    1999   *Archaeology and Folklore*. Theoretical Archaeology Group. London/
           New York: Routledge.
Geoghegan, J. C.
    2004   The Abrahamic Passover. Pp. 47–62 in *Le-David Maskil*, ed. R. E.
           Friedman and W. H. C. Propp. Fs. D. N. Freedman. Biblical and Ju-
           daic Studies from the University of California, San Diego 9. Winona
           Lake, Ind.: Eisenbrauns.
Gevirtz, S.
    1984   *ḥereṭ* in the Manufacture of the Golden Calf. *Bib* 65: 377–81.
Ghirshman, R.
    1964   *The Arts of Ancient Iran*. New York: Golden.
Gianto, A.
    1987   Some Notes on the Mulk Inscription from Nebi Yunis (*RES* 367).
           Bib 68: 397–401.
Gibson, M., and R. D. Biggs, ed.
    1977   *Seals and Sealing in the Ancient Near East*. Bibliotheca Mesopotam-
           ica 6. Malibu: Undena.
Gilbert, M.
    1997   *Holocaust Journey*. New York: Columbia University.
Gillison, G.
    1993   *Between Culture and Fantasy*. Chicago/London: University of Chi-
           cago.
Ginsberg, H. L.
    1936   *The Ugarit Texts (Kitbê ʾÛgārît)*. Jerusalem: Bialik Foundation.
    1982   *The Israelian Heritage of Judaism*. New York: Jewish Theological
           Seminary.
Ginsburg, C. D.
    1926   *Tôrâ nəbîʾîm ûk(ə)tûbîm*. London: British and Foreign Bible Society.
    1966   *Introduction to the Massoretico-Critical Edition of the Hebrew Bible*.
           Orig. pub. 1897. New York: KTAV.

Ginsburger, M.
  1903   *Pseudo-Jonathan*. Berlin: Calvary.
Ginzberg, L.
  1928   *The Legends of the Jews*. Philadelphia: Jewish Publication Society.
Girard, R.
  1977   *Violence and the Sacred*. French orig. 1972. Baltimore/London: Johns Hopkins University.
Githuku, S.
  2001   Taboos on Counting. Pp. 113–17 in *Interpreting the Old Testament in Africa*, ed. M. Getui, K. Holter and V. Zinkuratire. Bible and Theology in Africa 2. New York/Washington, D.C./Baltimore/Boston/Bern/Frankfurt am Main/Berlin/Brussels/Vienna/Oxford: Lang.
Gitin, S.
  1989   Incense Altars from Ekron, Israel and Judah. Pp. 64*–65* in *Yigael Yadin Memorial Volume*. ErIsr 20. Jerusalem: Israel Exploration Society.
  1992   New Incense Altars from Ekron. Pp. 43*–49* in *Avraham Biran Volume*. ErIsr 23. Jerusalem: Israel Exploration Society; Hebrew Union College–Jewish Institute of Religion.
Gitin, S., and M. Cogan
  1999   A New Type of Dedicatory Inscription from Ekron. *IEJ* 49: 193–202.
Goetze, A.
  1956   *The Laws of Eshnunna*. Annual of the American Schools of Oriental Research 31. New Haven: American Schools of Oriental Research.
Goodblatt, D. M.
  1994   *The Monarchic Principle*. Texte und Studien zum Antiken Judentum 38. Tübingen: Mohr (Siebeck).
Gooding, D. W.
  1959   *The Account of the Tabernacle*. Texts and Studies 6. Cambridge: Cambridge University.
Gordon, C. H.
  1935   'Elōhîm in its Reputed Meaning of *Rulers, Judges*. *JBL* 54: 139–44.
  1962   *Before the Bible*. New York: Harper & Row.
Görg, M.
  1967   *Das Zelt der Begegnung*. BBB 27. Bonn: Hanstein.
  1976   Zur sogenannten priesterlichen Obergewand. *BZ* 20: 242–46.
  1977   Eine neue Deutung für *kăpporaet*. ZAW 89: 115–18
  1981a Zur Dekoration des Leuchters. *BN* 15: 21–29.
  1981b *Šaddaj*—Ehrenrettung einer Etymologie. *BN* 16: 13–15.
  1984   Der Spiegeldienst der Frauen (Ex 38,8). *BN* 23: 9–13.
  1991   *Aegyptiaca-Biblica*. Ägypten und Altes Testament 11. Wiesbaden: Harrassowitz.
  1992   Etham. *ABD* 2.644. New York: Doubleday.
Gorman, F. H. Jr.
  1990   *The Ideology of Ritual: Space, Time and Status in the Priestly Theology*. JSOTSup 91. Sheffield: Sheffield Academic Press.

Gosse, B.
1996 Transfert de l'onction et de marques royales au profit du Grand Prêtre en Ex 25 ss. *Henoch* 18: 3–8.

Gottwald, N. K.
1979 *The Tribes of Yahweh*. Maryknoll, N.Y.: Orbis.

Gradwohl, R.
1997 Drei Tage und der dritte Tag. *VT* 47: 373–78.

Gras, M., P. Rouillard and J. Teixidor
1991 The Phoenicians and Death. *Berytus* 39: 127–76.

Gray, J.
1983 Exodus. Pp. 89–184 in *The Pentateuch*. Interpreter's Concise Commentary I. Nashville, Tenn.: Abingdon.

Gray, G. B.
1971 *Sacrifice in the Old Testament*. Orig. pub. 1925. New York: KTAV.

Green, A. R. W.
2003 *The Storm-god in the Ancient Near East*. Biblical and Judaic Studies from the University of California, San Diego 8. Winona Lake, Ind.: Eisenbrauns.

Greenberg, M.
1951 Hebrew *segullā*: Akakdian *sikiltu*. *JAOS* 71: 172–74.
1955 *The Hab/piru*. AOS 39. New Haven: American Oriental Society.
1959 The Biblical Concept of Asylum. *JBL* 78: 125–32.
1962 Another Look at Rachel's Theft of the Teraphim. *JBL* 81: 239–48.
1983 *Ezekiel 1–20*. AB 22. Garden City, N.Y.: Doubleday.

Greenfield, J. C.
1959 Lexicographical Notes II. *HUCA* 30: 141–51.
1991 Asylum at Aleppo: a Note on Sfire III, 4–7. Pp. 272–78 in *Ah, Assyria . . .* , ed. M. Cogan and I. Eph'al. Fs. H. Tadmor. ScrHier 33. Jerusalem: Magnes.

Grintz, Y. M.
1975 Mûnāḥîm qədûmîm bətôrat kōhănîm. *Leš* 39: 5–20, 163–81.

Gröndahl, F.
1967 *Die Personennamen der Texte aus Ugarit*. Studia Pohl 1. Rome: Pontifical Biblical Institute.

Groom, N.
1981 *Frankincense and Myrrh*. London/New York: Longman; Beirut: Librarie du Liban.

Gruber, M. I.
1987 Women in the Cult according to the Priestly Code. Pp. 35–48 in *Judaic Perspectives on Ancient Israel*, ed. J. Neusner, B. A. Levine and E. S. Frerichs. Philadelphia: Fortress.

Gubel, E.
1987 *Phoenician Furniture*. Studia Phoenicia 7. Leuven: Peeters.

Guethner, M.
1999 *Tricksters and Trancers*. Bloomington/Indianapolis: Indiana University.

Haas, V.
1994 *Geschichte der hethitischen Religion.* Handbuch der Orientalistik 15. Leiden/New York/Köln: Brill.
Hachlili, R., and R. Merḥav.
1985 Mənôrat happulḥān bîmê bayit rī(')šôn ûbayit šēnî ʿal-pî hamməqôrôt wəhammimṣā' hā'arkê'ôlôgî. Pp. 256–67 in N. *Avigad Volume.* ErIsr 18. Jerusalem: Israel Exploration Society.
2001 *The Menorah, the Ancient Seven-armed Candelabrum.* Leiden/ Boston: Brill.
Hackett, J. A.
1980 *The Balaam Text from Deir ʿAllā.* HSM 31. Chico, Calif.: Scholars Press.
Hall, J. M.
2002 *Hellenicity.* Chicago/London: University of Chicago.
Hallo, W. W.
1995 Slave Release in the Biblical World in Light of a New Text. Pp. 79–93 in *Solving Riddles and Untying Knots,* ed. Z. Zevit, S. Gitin and M. Sokoloff. Fs. J. C. Greenfield. Winona Lake, Ind.: Eisenbrauns.
Halperin, D. J.
1988 *The Faces of the Chariot.* Texte und Studien zum Antiken Judentum 16. Tübingen: Mohr (Siebeck).
Halpern, B.
1978 The Ritual Background of Zechariah's Temple Song. *CBQ* 40: 167–90.
1983 *The Emergence of Israel in Canaan.* SBLMS 29. Chico, Calif.: Scholars Press.
1991 Jerusalem and the Lineages in the Seventh Century BCE: Kinship and the Rise of Individual Moral Liability. Pp. 11–107 in *Law and Ideology in Monarchic Israel,* ed. B. Halpern and D. W. Hobson. JSOTSup 124. Sheffield: JSOT.
1993a The Exodus and the Israelite Historians. Pp. 89*–96* in *Abraham Malamat Volume.* ErIsr 24. Jerusalem: Israel Exploration Society.
1993b The Baal (and the Asherah) in Seventh-Century Judah: Yhwh's Retainers Retired. Pp. 115–54 in *Konsequente Traditionsgeschichte,* ed. R. Bartelmus et al. Fs. K. Baltzer. OBO 126. Freiburg: Universitätsverlag; Göttingen: Vandenhoeck & Ruprecht.
2001 *David's Secret Demons.* Grand Rapids, Mich./Cambridge: Eerdmans.
Hansen, T.
1964 *Arabia Felix.* New York and Evanston: Harper & Row.
Hanson, P. D.
1975 *The Dawn of Apocalyptic.* Philadelphia: Fortress.
Haran, M.
1955 Ṣûrat hā'ēpōd bamməqôrôt hammiqrā'iyyîm. *Tarbiz* 24: 380–91.
1962a Leḥem happānîm. *EM* 4.493–95. Jerusalem: Bialik Institute.
1962b Shiloh and Jerusalem *JBL* 81: 14–24.
1968 Nəsākîm. *EM* 6.883–86. Jerusalem: Bialik Institute.

1978 *Temples and Temple-Service in Ancient Israel.* Oxford: Clarendon.

1979 Seething a Kid in Its Mother's Milk. *JJS* 30: 23–35.

1984 The Shining of Moses' Face: A Case Study in Biblical and Ancient Near Eastern Iconography. Pp. 159–73 in *In the Shelter of Elyon,* ed. W. B. Barrick and J. R. Spencer. Fs. G. W. Ählstrom. JSOTSup 31. Sheffield: JSOT.

Harris, J. S.

1966 The Stones of the High Priest's Breastplate. *ALUOS* 5: 40–62.

Hasel, G. F.

1992 Sabbath. *ABD* 5.849–56. New York: Doubleday.

1995 *kārat; kerutôt; keritut. TDOT* 7:339–52. Grand Rapids: Eerdmans.

Hassan, S.

1943 *Excavations at Gîza vol. iv.* Cairo: Government Press, Bulâq.

Hausmann, J.

1997 *mōr. TDOT* 8.557–60. Grand Rapids: Eerdmans.

Ḥayutin, M.

1993 Miškan 'ōhel mô'ēd — šiḥzûr 'aḥēr. *Beit Mikra* 38: 229–44.

Hayward, R.

1999 St Jerome and the Meaning of the High-Priestly Vestments. Pp. 20–105 in *Hebrew Study from Ezra to Ben-Yehuda,* ed. W. Horbury. Edinburgh: Clark.

Heger, P.

1997 *The Development of the Incense Cult in Israel.* BZAW 245. Berlin/ New York: de Gruyter.

1999 *The Three Biblical Altar Laws.* BZAW 279. New York: de Gruyter.

Heider, G. C.

1985 *The Cult of Molek.* JSOTSup 43. Sheffield: JSOT Press.

Helck, W.

1965 Ptaḥ. Pp. 387–89 in *Götter und Mythen im vorderen Orient,* ed. H. W. Häussig. *Wörterbuch der Mythologie* 1.1. Stuttgart: Klett.

1971 *Die Beziehungen Ägyptens zu Vorderasien im 3. und 2. Jahrtausend v. Chr.* 2nd ed. Ägyptologische Abhandlungen 5. Wiesbaden: Harrassowitz.

Held, M.

1954 Sətûmâ miqrā'ît ûmaqbîlātāh bə'ûgārîtît. Pp. 101–13 in *M. D. Cassuto Volume.* ErIsr 3. Jerusalem: Israel Exploration Society; Bialik Institute.

1961 A Faithful Lover in an Old Babylonian Dialogue. *JCS* 15: 1–26.

Helfmeyer, F. J.

1974 *'ôth. TDOT* 1.167–88. Grand Rapids: Eerdmans.

Heltzer, M.

1978 *Goods, Prices and the Organization of Trade in Ugarit.* Wiesbaden: Reichert.

Hendel, R. S.

1989 Sacrifice as a Cultural System: The Ritual Symbolism of Exodus 24, 3–8. *ZAW* 101: 366–90.

1997 Aniconism and Anthropomorphism in Ancient Israel. Pp. 212–18 in *The Image and the Book*, ed. K. van der Toorn. Leuven: Peeters.
1998 *The Text of Genesis 1–11*. New York/Oxford: Oxford University.
2005 *Remembering Abraham*. Oxford/New York: Oxford University.

Hendrix, R. E.
1992 The Use of *Miškān* and *'ōhel Mô'ēd* in Exodus 25–40. *AUSS* 30: 3–13.

Hennessey, J. B.
1985 Thirteenth Century B.C. Temple of Human Sacrifice at Amman. Pp. 85–104 in *Phoenicia and Its Neighbors*, ed. E. Gubel and E. Lipiński. Studia Phoenicia 3. Leuven: Peeters.

Henninger, J.
1975 *Les fêtes de printemps chez les Sémites et la Pâque israélite*. Ebib. Paris: LeCoffre.

Hepper, F. N.
1969 Arabian and African Frankincense Trees. *JEA* 55: 66–72.

Hertzberg, H. W.
1929 Mizpah. *ZAW* 47: 161–96.

Herzberg, W.
1979 Polysemy in the Hebrew Bible. Ph.D. diss., New York University.

Heschel, A. J.
1951 *The Sabbath*. New York: Farrar Straus and Giroux.

Hess R. S.
1992 Caphtor. *ABD* 1.869–70. New York: Doubleday.

Hestrin, R.
1987a The Lachish Ewer and the 'Asherah. *IEJ* 37: 212–23.
1987b The Cult Stand from Ta'anach and its Religious Background. Pp. 61–77 in *Phoenicia and the East Mediterranean in the First Millennium B.C.*, ed. E. Lipiński. Orientalia Lovaniensia Analecta 22. Studia Phoenicia 5. Leuven: Peeters.

Hestrin, R., and M. Dayagi-Mendels
1979 *Inscribed Seals: First Temple Period*. Jerusalem: Israel Museum.

Hiebert, P. S.
1989 "Whence Shall Help Come to Me?": the Biblical Widow. Pp. 125–41 in *Gender and Difference in Ancient Israel*, ed. P. L. Day. Minneapolis, Minn.: Fortress.

Higginbotham, C. R.
2000 *Egyptianization and Elite Emulation in Ramesside Palestine*. Culture and History of the Ancient Near East 2. Leiden/Boston/Köln: Brill.

Hill, A. E.
1998 *Malachi*. AB 25D. New York: Doubleday.

Hillers, D. R.
1967 Delocutive Verbs in Biblical Hebrew. *JBL* 86: 320–24.
1969 *Covenant: the History of a Biblical Idea*. Baltimore, Md.: Johns Hopkins University.
1972 MŠKN' "Temple" in Inscriptions from Hatra. *BASOR* 206: 54–56.

Hirzel, R.
  1967   *Die Strafe der Steinigung.* Darmstadt: Wissenschaftliche Buchge-
          sellschaft.
Hoch, J. E.
  1994   *Semitic Words in Egyptian Texts of the New Kingdom and Third Inter-
          mediate Period.* Princeton, N.J.: Princeton University.
Hoffmeier, J. K.
  1996   *Israel in Egypt.* New York: Oxford University.
Hoffner, H. A. Jr.
  1973a The Hittites and the Hurrians. Pp. 197–228 in *Peoples of Old Testa-
          ment Times,* ed. D. J. Wiseman. Oxford: Clarendon.
  1973b Incest, Sodomy and Bestiality in the Ancient Near East. Pp. 81–90 in
          Orient and Occident, ed. H. A. Hoffner. Fs. C. H. Gordon. Kevelaer:
          Butzon & Bercker; Neukirchen-Vluyn: Neukirchener Verlag.
  1980   *chābhal* II. *TDOT* 4.179–84. Grand Rapids: Eerdmans.
Hoftijzer, J.
  1957   Ex. xxi 8. *VT* 7: 390–91.
  1967   Das sogenannte Feueropfer. Pp. 114–34 in *Hebräische Wort-
          forschung,* ed. B. Hartmann et al. Fs. W. Baumgartner. VTSup 16.
          Leiden: Brill.
Hoftijzer, J., and K. Jongeling
  1995   *Dictionary of the North West Semitic Inscriptions.* Handbuch der
          Orientalistik. Leiden/New York/Köln: Brill.
Hoftijzer, J., and G. van der Kooij
  1976   *Aramaic Texts from Deir ʿAlla.* Documenta et Monumenta Orientis
          Antiqui 19. Leiden: Brill.
Holladay, J. S. Jr.
  1992   House, Israelite. *ABD* 3.308–18. New York: Doubleday.
Holzinger, H.
  1893   *Einleitung in den Hexateuch.* Leipzig: Mohr (Siebeck).
  1900   *Exodus.* Kurzer Hand-commentar zum Alten Testament 2. Tübin-
          gen: Mohr (Siebeck).
Homan, M. M.
  1998   A Tensile Etymology for Aaron: ʾahărōn > ʾahălōn. *BN* 95: 21–22.
  2002   *To Your Tents, O Israel!* Culture and History of the Ancient Near East
          12. Leiden/Boston/Köln: Brill.
Hopkins, D. C.
  1987   Life on the Land: The Subsistence Struggles of Early Israel. *BA* 50:
          178–91.
Horowitz, W., and V. Hurowitz
  1992   Urim and Thummim in Light of a Psephomancy Ritual from Assur
          (*LKA* 137). *JANES* 21: 95–115.
Houtman, C.
  1990a The Urim and Thummim: A New Suggestion. *VT* 40: 229–32.
  1990b On the Pomegranates and the Golden Bells of the High Priest's Man-
          tle. *VT* 40: 223–27.

1993a *Exodus Volume 1.* Dutch orig. 1986. Historical Commentary on the Old Testament. Kampen: Kok.

1993b *Der Himmel im Alten Testament.* OTS 30. Leiden/New York/Köln: Brill.

1994 Wie fiktiv ist das Zeltheiligtum von Exodus 25–40? *ZAW* 106: 107–13.

1996 *Exodus Volume 2.* Dutch orig. 1989. Historical Commentary on the Old Testament. Kampen: Kok.

2000 *Exodus Volume 3.* Dutch orig. 1996. Historical Commentary on the Old Testament. Leuven: Peeters.

Hrouda, B., and J. Krecher

1969 Göttersymbole. *RlA* 3: 483–98. Berlin: de Gruyter.

Hubert, H., and M. Mauss

1964 *Sacrifice: Its Nature and Function.* French orig. 1898. Chicago/London: University of Chicago.

Huddleston, J. R.

1992 Red Sea. *ABD* 5.633–42. New York: Doubleday.

Huffmon, H. B.

1965a *Amorite Personal Names in the Mari Texts.* Baltimore, Md.: Johns Hopkins University.

1965b The Exodus, Sinai and the Credo. *CBQ* 27: 101–13.

1966 The Treaty Background of Hebrew *yāda'*. *BASOR* 181: 31–37.

1974 Exodus 23:4–5: A Comparative Study. Pp. 271–78 in *A Light unto My Path*, ed. H. N. Bream, R. D. Heim and C. A. Moore. Fs. J. M. Myers. Philadelphia: Temple University.

Huffmon, H. B., and S. B. Parker

1966 A Further Note on the Treaty Background of Hebrew *yāda'*. *BASOR* 184: 36–38.

Huizinga, J.

1970 *Homo Ludens.* German orig. 1944. London: Temple Smith.

Humbert, P.

1939 Les adjectifs "zâr" et "nôkri" et la "femme étrangère" des proverbes bibliques. Pp. 1.259–66 in *Mélanges Syriens offerts à Monsieur René Dussaud.* Paris: Geuthner.

Humphrey, N.

1992 *A History of the Mind.* New York/London: Chatto & Windus.

Hurowitz, V.

1985 The Priestly Account of Building the Tabernacle. *JAOS* 105: 21–30.

1986 Another Fiscal Practice in the Ancient Near East: 2 Kings 12: 5–17 and a Letter to Esarhaddon (*LAS* 277). *JNES* 45: 289–94.

1987 Salted Incense—Exodus 30,35; *Maqlû* VI 111–113; IX 118–20. *Bib* 68: 178–94.

1992a *I Have Built You an Exalted House.* JSOTSup 115; JSOT/ASOR Monograph Series 5. Sheffield: Sheffield Academic Press.

1992b "His Master Shall Pierce His Ear with an Awl" (Exodus 21.6)—Marking Slaves in the Bible in Light of Akkadian Sources. *Proceedings of the American Academy for Jewish Research* 58: 47–77.

1995   The Form and Fate of the Tabernacle: Reflections on a Recent Proposal. *JQR* 86: 127–51.

2004   The Golden Calf—Made by Man . . . or God? *BRev* 20.2: 28–32, 47.

Hurvitz, A.
1982   A *Linguistic Study of the Relationship Between the Priestly Source and the Book of Ezekiel*. CahRB 20. Paris: Gabalda.

Hutton, R.
1994   *Charisma and Authority in Israelite Society*. Minneapolis, Minn.: Fortress.

Hyatt, J. P.
1980   *Commentary on Exodus*. New Century Bible. Grand Rapids: Eerdmans; London: Marshall, Morgan & Scott.

Iakovidies, S.
1981   A Peak Sanctuary in Bronze Age Thera. Pp. 54–62 in *Temples and High Places in Biblical Times*, ed. A. Biran. Jerusalem: Hebrew Union College–Jewish Institute of Religion.

Ishida, T.
1977   *The Royal Dynasties in Ancient Israel*. BZAW 142. Berlin/New York: de Gruyter.

1979   The Structure and Historical Implications of the Lists of the Pre-Israelite Nations. *Bib* 60: 461–90.

Isser, S.
1990   Two Traditions: The Law of Exodus 21:22–23 Revisited. *CBQ* 52: 30–45.

Isserlin, B. S. J.
1983   The Israelite Conquest of Canaan: A Comparative Review of the Arguments Applicable. *PEQ* 115: 85–94.

Jackson, B. S.
1975   *Essays in Jewish and Comparative Legal History*. Studies in Judaism in Late Antiquity 10. Leiden: Brill.

1976   A Note on Exodus 22:4 (MT). *JJS* 27: 139.

Jacob, B.
1992   *The Second Book of the Bible: Exodus*. Trans. W. Jacob. German orig. 1945, pub. 1997. Hoboken, N.J.: KTAV.

Jacobsen, T.
1970   *Toward the Image of Tammuz*, ed. W. L. Moran. HSS 21. Cambridge, Mass.: Harvard University.

1976   *The Treasures of Darkness*. New Haven/London: Yale University.

1987a The Graven Image. Pp. 15–32 in *Ancient Israelite Religion*, ed. P. D. Miller, Jr., P. D. Hanson and S. D. McBride. Fs. F. M. Cross. Philadelphia: Fortress.

1987b *The Harps that Once*. . . . New Haven/London: Yale University.

Janowski, B.
1980   Erwägungen zur Vorgeschichte des israelitischen Šelamîm-Opfers. *UF* 12: 232–59.

1982 *Sühne als Heilsgeschehen.* WMANT 55. Neukirchen-Vluyn: Neukirchener Verlag.

Janzen, J. G.

1997 *Exodus.* Westminster Bible Companion. Louisville, Kenn.: Westminster John Knox.

Jay, N.

1992 *Throughout Your Generations Forever.* Chicago/London: University of Chicago.

Jenson, P. P.

1992 *Graded Holiness: A Key to the Priestly Conception of the World.* JSOTSup 106. Sheffield: Sheffield Academic Press.

Joffe, A. H.

1993 *Settlement and Society in the Early Bronze Age I and II, Southern Levant.* Monographs in Mediterranean Archaeology 4. Sheffield: Sheffield Academic Press.

Johnson, A. R.

1947 Aspects of the Use of the Term *pānîm* in the Old Testament. Pp. 155–59 in *Festschrift Otto Eissfeldt zum 60. Geburtstage,* ed. J. Fück. Halle: Max Niemeyer.

1961 *The One and the Many in the Israelite Conception of God.* 2d ed. Cardiff: University of Wales.

Joüon, P.

1965 *Grammaire de l'hébreu biblique.* Rome: Pontifical Biblical Institute.

Kapelrud, A. S.

1963 Temple Building, a Task for Gods and Kings. *Or* 32: 56–62.

Karageorghis, V.

1981 The Sacred Area of Kition. Pp. 82–90 in *Temples and High Places in Biblical Times,* ed. A. Biran. Jerusalem: Hebrew Union College–Jewish Institute of Religion.

Kaufman, S. A.

1974 *The Akkadian Influences on Aramaic.* Assyriological Studies 19. Chicago/London: University of Chicago.

Kaufmann, Y.

1960 *The Religion of Israel.* Chicago: University of Chicago.

Kawashima, R. S.

2003 The Jubilee Year and the Return of Cosmic Purity. *CBQ* 65: 370–89.

2004 *Biblical Narrative and the Death of the Rhapsode.* Indiana Studies in Biblical Literature. Bloomington/Indianapolis: Indiana University.

Kearney, J. P.

1977 Creation and Liturgy: The P Redaction of Ex 25–40. *ZAW* 89: 375–87.

Keel, O.

1975 Kanaanäische Sühneriten auf ägyptischen Tempelreliefs. *VT* 25: 413–69.

1978 *The Symbolism of the Biblical World.* German orig. 1972. New York: Seabury.

1980 *Das Böcklein in der Milch seiner Mutter und Verwandtes.* OBO 33. Freiburg: Universitätsverlag; Göttingen: Vandenhoeck & Ruprecht.

Kellermann, D.
1975 *gûr.* TDOT 2.439–49. Grand Rapids: Eerdmans.

Kelso, J. L.
1948 *The Ceramic Vocabulary of the Old Testament.* BASORSup 5–6. New Haven: American Schools of Oriental Research.

Kempinski, A.
1990 He'omnām rimmôn mib"bêt yahwe(h)"? *Qad* 23: 126.

Kennedy, A. R. S.
1898 Tabernacle. *A Dictionary of the Bible,* ed. J. Hastings, 4.653–68. Edinburgh: Clark.
1903 Weaving. *Encyclopedia Biblica* 4.5276–90. London: Black.

Kennicott, B.
1776–80 *Vetus Testamentum Hebraicum.* Oxford: Clarendon.

Kerkeslager, A.
2000 Mt. Sinai—in Arabia? *BRev* 16.2: 31–39, 52.

Kerr, W. P., ed.
1900 *Essays of John Dryden.* Oxford: Clarendon.

Kessler, D.
2001 Bull Gods. *Oxford Encyclopedia of Ancient Egypt* 1.209–12. New York: Oxford University.

Kessler, R.
1972 Die Querverweise im Pentateuch. Ph.D. diss., University of Heidelberg.
1986 Silber und Gold, Gold und Silber: Zur Wertschätzung der Edelmetalle im Alten Israel. *BN* 31: 57–69.

King, L. W.
1912 *Babylonian Boundary Stones.* London: British Musem.

Kirschner, R.
1992 *Baraita de-Melekhet ha-Mishkan.* Monographs of the Hebrew Union College 15. Cincinnati, Oh.: Hebrew Union College.

Kitchen, K. A.
1979 Egypt, Ugarit, Qatna and Covenant. *UF* 11: 460.
1993 The Tabernacle—A Bronze Age Artefact. Pp. 119*–29* in *Avraham Malamat Volume.* ErIsr 24. Jerusalem: Israel Exploration Society.
1997 Sheba and Arabia. Pp. 126–53 in *The Age of Solomon,* ed. L. K. Handy. Studies in the History and Culture of the Ancient Near East 11. Leiden/New York/Köln: Brill.
2003 *On the Reliability of the Old Testament.* Grand Rapids: Eerdmans.

Kiuchi, N.
1987 *The Purification Offering in the Priestly Literature.* JSOTSup 56. Sheffield: Sheffield Academic Press.

Klawans, J.
  1997   The Impurity of Immorality in Ancient Judaism. *JJS* 48: 1–16.
Klein, E.
  1987   A *Comprehensive Etymological Dictionary of the Hebrew Language for Readers of English.* New York: Macmillan; London: Collier.
Klein, M. L.
  1980   *The Fragment-Targums of the Pentateuch.* AnBib 76. Rome: Pontifical Biblical Institute.
  1986   *Genizah Manuscripts of Palestinian Targum to the Pentateuch.* Cincinnati, Oh.: Hebrew Union College.
Klein, R. W.
  1996   Back to the Future: The Tabernacle in the Book of Exodus. *Int* 50: 264–76.
Kletter, R.
  1998   *Economic Keystones: The Weight System of the Kingdom of Judah.* JSOTSup 276. Sheffield: Sheffield Academic Press.
Klingbeil, G. A.
  1995   Ritual Space in the Ordination Ritual of Leviticus 8. *JNSL* 21: 59–82.
  1997   Ritual time in Leviticus 8 with special reference to the seven day period in the Old Testament. *ZAW* 109: 500–13.
Kloos, C.
  1986   *Yhwh's Combat with the Sea.* Amsterdam: van Oorschot; Leiden: Brill.
Knapp, A. B.
  1985   Alashiya, Caphtor/Keftiu, and Eastern Mediterranean Trade. *JFA* 12: 231–50.
Knauf, E. A.
  1982   Ḥaṭef Pataḥ in geschlossener Silbe im Codex Leningradensis. *BN* 19: 57–58.
  1984   Eine nabatäische Parallele zum hebräischen Gottesnamen. *BN* 23: 21–28.
  1988a   *Midian.* Abhandlungen des Deutschen Palästinavereins. Wiesbaden: Harrassowitz.
  1988b   Zur Herkunft und Sozialgeschichte Israels. "Das Böckchen in der Milch seiner Mutter." *Bib* 69: 153–69.
  1992   Horites. *ABD* 3.288. New York: Doubleday.
Knight, G. A. F.
  1976   *Theology as Narrative. A Commentary on the Book of Exodus.* Edinburgh: Handsel.
Knohl, I.
  1995   *The Sanctuary of Silence.* Hebrew orig. 1992. Minneapolis, Minn.: Fortress.
  1997   Two Aspects of the "Tent of Meeting." Pp. 73–79 in *Tehillah le-Moshe,* ed. M. Cogan, B. L. Eichler and J. H. Tigay. Fs. M. Greenberg. Winona Lake, Ind.: Eisenbrauns.

Knoppers, G. N.
1995 Aaron's Calf and Jeroboam's Calves. Pp. 92–104 in *Fortunate the Eyes That See*, ed. A. Beck et al. Fs. D. N. Freedman. Grand Rapids: Eerdmans.

Koch, K.
1959 *Die Priestserchrift von Exodus 25 bis Leviticus 16.* FRLANT 71. Göttingen: Vandenhoeck & Ruprecht.
1976 Šaddaj. *VT* 26: 299–332.
1993 Ḫazzi-Ṣafôn-Kasion. Die Geschichte eines Berges und seine Gottheiten. Pp. 171–223 in *Religionsgeschichtliche Beziehungen zwischen Kleinasien, Nordsyrien und dem Alten Testament*, ed. B. Janowski, K. Koch and G. Wilhelm. OBO 129. Freiburg: Universitätsverlag; Göttingen: Vandenhoeck & Ruprecht.
1995 Some Considerations on the Translation of *kappōret* in the Septuagint. Pp. 65–75 in *Pomegranates and Golden Bells*, ed. D. P. Wright, D. N. Freedman and A. Hurvitz. Fs. J. Milgrom. Winona Lake, Ind.: Eisenbrauns.
1999 *ʿāwōn. TDOT* 10.546–62. Grand Rapids: Eerdmans.

Koenen, K.
1994 Der Name ʿGLYW auf Samaria-Ostrakon Nr. 41. *VT* 44: 396–400.

Koester, C. R.
1989 *The Dwelling of God.* CBQMS 22. Washington, D.C.: Catholic Biblical Association of America.
2001 *Hebrews.* AB 36. New York: Doubleday.

Köhler, L.
1936 Hebräische Vokabeln I. *ZAW* 54: 287–93.

Kornfeld, W.
1978 *Onomastica Aramaica aus Ägypten.* Österreichische Akademie der Wissenschaften philosophisch-historische Klasse 333. Vienna: Österreichische Akademie der Wissenschaften.

Kraeling, E. G.
1953 *The Brooklyn Museum Aramaic Papyri.* New Haven, Conn.: Yale University.

Kraeling, C. H.
1956 *The Synagogue.* The Excavations of Dura-Europos Final Report 8.1. New Haven, Conn.: Yale University.

Kramer, S. N.
1988 The Temple in Sumerian Literature. Pp. 1–16 in *Temple in Society*, ed. M. V. Fox. Winona Lake, Ind.: Eisenbrauns.

Kronasser, H.
1963 *Die Umsiedlung der schwarzen Gottheit.* Vienna: Hermann Böhlaus.

Kugel, J. L.
1981 *The Idea of Biblical Poetry.* New Haven, Conn.: Yale University.

Kuhl, C.
1952 Die "Wiederaufnahme"—ein literarkritisches Prinzip? *ZAW* 64: 1–11.

Kupper, J. R.
　1950　Le recensement dans les textes de Mari. Pp. 99–110 in *Studia Mariana*, ed. A. Parrot. Leiden: Brill.
Kutsch, E.
　1963　*Salbung als Rechtsakt*. BZAW 87. Berlin: Töpelmann.
Kutsko, J. F.
　2000　*Between Heaven and Earth*. Biblical and Judaic Studies from the University of California, San Diego 7. Winona Lake, Ind.: Eisenbrauns.
Labuschagne, C. J.
　1966　*The Incomparability of Yahweh in the Old Testament*. Pretoria Oriental Series 5. Leiden: Brill.
　1992　"You Shall not Boil a Kid in Its Mother's Milk": A New Proposal for the Origin of the Prohibition. Pp. 6–17 in *The Scriptures and the Scrolls*, ed. F. García Martínez, A. Hilhorst and C. J. Labuschagne. Fs. A. S. van der Woude. VTSup 49. Leiden: Brill.
Lakoff, G., and M. Johnson
　1980　*Metaphors We Live By*. Chicago: University of Chicago.
Lambdin, T. O.
　1953　Egyptian Loan Words in the Old Testament. *JAOS* 73: 145–55.
Lambert, W. G., and A. R. Millard
　1969　*Atra-ḫasīs. The Babylonian Story of the Flood*. Oxford: Clarendon.
Lammens, H.
　1928　*L'Arabie occidentale avant l'Hégire*. Beyrouth: Imprimerie Catholique.
Landsberger, B.
　1929　Ḫabiru und Lulaḫḫu. *Kleinasiatische Forschungen* 3: 321–34.
Langdon, S.
　1935　*Babylonian Menologies and the Semitic Calendars*. London: Oxford University.
Langhe, R. de
　1959　L'autel d'or du temple de Jérusalem. *Bib* 40: 476–94.
Lauha, A.
　1945　*Die Geschichtsmotive in den alttestamentlichen Psalmen*. Annales Academiae Scientiarum Fennicae B 56. Helsinki: Finnische Literaturgesellschaft.
Le Déaut, R.
　1972　Critique textuelle et exégèse—*Exode* XXII 12 dans la Septante et le Targum. *VT* 22: 164–75.
Leibowitz, N.
　1976　*Studies in Shemot*. Jerusalem: World Zionist Organization.
Lemaire, A., and J. M. Durand
　1984　*Les Inscriptions araméennes de Sfiré et l'Assyrie de Shamshi-ilu*. Paris/Geneva: Droz.
Lemche, N. P.
　1975　The "Hebrew Slave." Comments on the Slave Law Ex. xxi 1–22. *VT* 25: 129–44.
　1992　Ḫabiru, Ḫapiru. *ABD* 3.6–10. New York: Doubleday.

Lesher, J. H.
     1992   *Xenophanes of Colophon.* Phoenix Supplementary Volume 30.
            Toronto/Buffalo/London: University of Toronto.
Lesko, B. S.
     1999   *The Great Goddesses of Egypt*: Norman: University of Oklahoma.
Levenson, J. D.
     1985   *Sinai and Zion.* Minneapolis/Chicago/New York: Winston.
     1988   *Creation and the Persistence of Evil.* San Francisco, Calif.: Harper
            & Row.
     1993   *The Death and Resurrection of the Beloved Son.* New Haven/London:
            Yale University.
Levi, D.
     1981   Features and Continuity of Cretan Peak Cults. Pp. 38–44 in *Temples
            and High Places in Biblical Times,* ed. A. Biran. Jerusalem: Hebrew
            Union College–Jewish Institute of Religion.
Levi, J.
     1987   *Die Inkongruenz im Hebräisch.* Wiesbaden: Harrassowitz.
Levi-Strauss, C.
     1978   *The Origin of Table Manners.* French orig. 1968. New York: Harper
            & Row.
Levin, S.
     1971   The Etymology of *nektar*: Exotic Scents in Early Greece. *Studi
            Micenei ed Egeo-Anatolici* 13: 31–50.
Levine, B. A.
     1963   Ugaritic Descriptive Rituals. *JCS* 17: 105–11.
     1965   The Descriptive Tabernacle Texts of the Pentateuch. *JAOS* 85:
            307–18.
     1968   On the Presence of God in Biblical Religion. Pp. 71–87 in *Religions
            in Antiquity,* ed. J. Neusner. Studies in the History of Religions 14.
            Leiden: Brill.
     1974   *In the Presence of the Lord.* Studies in Judaism in Late Antiquity 5.
            Leiden: Brill.
     1987   The Language of Holiness: Perceptions of the Sacred in the Hebrew
            Bible. Pp. 241–55 in *Backgrounds for the Bible,* ed. M. P. O'Connor
            and D. N. Freedman. Winona Lake, Ind.: Eisenbrauns.
     1993   *Numbers 1–20.* AB 4. New York: Doubleday.
Levine, E.
     1999   On Exodus 21,10 'Onah and Biblical Marriage. *ZABR* 5: 133–64.
Levinson, B. M.
     1997   *Deuteronomy and the Hermeneutics of Legal Innovation.* New York/
            Oxford: Oxford University.
     2003   *You Must Not Add Anything to What I Command You*: Paradoxes of
            Canon and Authorship in Ancient Israel. *Numen* 50: 1–51.
     2000   The Hermeneutics of Tradition in Deuteronomy. *JBL* 119: 269–86.
     2004   Is the Covenant Code an Exilic Composition? Pp. 272–325 in *In
            Search of Pre-exilic Israel,* ed. J. Day. London/New York: Clark.

Levinson, B. M., ed.

    1994   *Theory and Method in Biblical and Cuneiform Law.* JSOTSup 181. Sheffield: Sheffield Academic Press.

Levitt Kohn, R.

    2002   *A New Heart and a New Soul. Ezekiel, the Exile and the Torah.* JSOTSup 358. Sheffield: Sheffield Academic Press.

Levy, T. E., et al.

    2004   Reassessing the chronology of Biblical Edom. *Antiquity* 78: 865–79.

Levy-Feldblum, A.

    1986   Dîn ʿebed ʿibrî: hebdəlê signôn ûmašməʿûtām. *Beit Mikra* 107: 348–59.

Lewis, T. J.

    1998   Divine Images and Aniconism in Ancient Israel. *JAOS* 118: 36–53.

Licht, J. S.

    1968   Nəqāmâ. *EM* 5.917–21. Jerusalem: Bialik Institute.

Lichtheim, M.

    1976   *Ancient Egyptian Literature—Volume II: The New Kingdom.* Berkeley, Calif.: University of California.

Lidzbarski, M.

    1915   *Ephemeris für semitische Epigraphik* 3. Giessen: Töpelmann.

Lienhardt, G.

    1961   *Divinity and Experience.* Oxford: Clarendon.

Lipiński, E.

    1999   *nāqam; nāqām; nᵉqāmâ. TDOT* 10.1–9. Grand Rapids: Eerdmans.

Litvinski, B. A.

    1987   Mirrors. *Encyclopedia of Religion* 9.556–59. New York: Macmillan; London: Collier Macmillan.

Liverani, M.

    1973   The Amorites. Pp. 100–33 in *Peoples of Old Testament Times,* ed. D. J. Wiseman. Oxford: Clarendon.

Livingstone, A.

    1986   *Mystical and Mythological Explanatory Works of Assyrian and Babylonian Scholars.* Oxford: Clarendon.

Lockshin, M. I.

    1997   *Rashbam's Commentary on Exodus.* Brown Judaic Studies 310. Atlanta: Scholars Press.

Loewenstamm, S. E.

    1962a Mîddâ kəneged mîddâ. *EM* 4.840–46. Jerusalem: Bialik Institute.

    1962b The Ugaritic Fertility Myth—the Result of a Mistranslation. *IEJ* 12: 87–88.

    1967   The Making and Destruction of the Golden Calf. *Bib.* 48: 481–90.

    1968   Miškan H'. *EM* 5.532–48. Jerusalem: Bialik Institute.

    1969   *M/TRBYT* and *NŠK. JBL* 88: 78–80.

    1975   The Making and Destruction of the Golden Calf—a Rejoinder. *Bib* 56: 330–43.

1977 Exodus XXI 22–25. *VT* 27: 352–60.
1992 *The Evolution of the Exodus Tradition.* Hebrew orig. 1965. Jerusalem: Magnes.

Lohfink, N.
1986a *ḥopšî. TDOT* 5.114–18. Grand Rapids: Eerdmans.
1986b *ḥāram. TDOT* 5.180–99. Grand Rapids: Eerdmans.
1991 Poverty in the Laws of the Ancient Near East and of the Bible. *Theological Studies* 25: 34–50.
1994 *Theology of the Pentateuch.* German orig. 1988, 1990. Minneapolis, Minn.: Fortress.

Lorenz, K.
1966 *On Aggression.* German orig. 1963. New York: Harcourt, Brace & World.

Loretz, O.
1960 Ex 21,6; 22,8 und angebliche Nuzi-Parallelen. *Bib* 41: 167–75.
1977 Die hebräischen Termini *ḥpšj* "freigelassen, Freigelassener" und *ḥpšh* "Freilassung." *UF* 9: 163–67.
1980 Der kanaanäische Ursprung des biblischen Gottesnamens El Šaddaj. *UF* 12: 420–21.

Lorton, D.
1999 The Theology of Cult Statues in Ancient Egypt. Pp. 123–210 in *Born in Heaven, Made on Earth*, ed. M. B. Dick. Winona Lake, Ind.: Eisenbrauns.

Löw, I.
1967 *Die Flora der Juden.* Orig. pub. 1924–34. Hildesheim: Olms.

Lucas, A., and J. R. Harris
1962 *Ancient Egyptian Materials and Industries.* 4th ed. London: Arnold.

Luckenbill, D. D.
1926–27 *Ancient Records of Assyria and Babylonia.* New York: Greenwood.

Lundbom, J. R.
1978 God's Use of the *Idem per Idem* to Terminate Debate. *HTR* 71: 193–210.
1999 *Jeremiah 1–20.* AB 21A. New York: Doubleday.

Lutzky, H.
1998 Shadday as a Goddess Epithet. *VT* 48: 15–36.

Maccoby, H.
1999 *Ritual and Morality.* Cambridge: Cambridge University.

Machinist, P.
1991 The Question of Distinctiveness in Ancient Israel. Pp. 196–212 in *Ah, Assyria . . .* , ed. M. Cogan and Israel Eph'al. Fs. H. Tadmor. ScrHier 33. Jerusalem: Magnes Press.

Maier, J.
1965 *Das altisraelitische Ladeheiligtum.* BZAW 93. Berlin: Töpelmann.

Maier, W. A. III
1986 *'Ašerah: Extrabiblical Evidence.* HSM 37. Atlanta: Scholars Press.

Malamat, A.
1970 The Danite Migration and the Pan-Israelite Exodus: A Biblical Narrative Pattern. *Bib* 51: 1–16.

Malkin, I.
1994 *Myth and Territory in the Spartan Mediterranean.* Cambridge: Cambridge University.

Maloney, R. P.
1974 Usury and Restrictions on Interest-Taking in the Ancient Near East. *CBQ* 36: 1–20.

Malul, M.
1997 *Kappî* (Ex 33,22) and *bǝḥopnā(y)w* (Prov 30,4): Hand or Skirt? *ZAW* 109: 356–68.

Mandelkern, S.
1937 *Veteris Testamenti Concordantiae.* Leipzig: Schocken.

Mann, T. W.
1977 *Divine Presence and Guidance in Israelite Traditions: The Typology of Exaltation.* John Hopkins Near Eastern Studies. Baltimore, Md.: Johns Hopkins University.

Margalit, B.
1987 Ugaritic Contributions to Hebrew Lexicography. *ZAW* 99: 395–96.

Margalith, O.
1983 *bgdy śǝrād* = Fine Linen from Colchis? *ZAW* 95: 430–31.

Martinetz, D., K. Lohs and J. Janzen
1989 *Weihrauch und Myrrhe.* Stuttgart: Wissenschaftliche Verlagsgesellschaft.

Masetti-Rouault, M. G.
1999 Rôles et images de l'écriture en Mésopotamie ancienne. *Semitica* 49: 5–18.
2001 Les maquettes dans les textes mésopotamiens. Pp. 445–61 in *"Maquettes architecturales" de l'Antiquité,* ed. B. Muller. Université Strasbourg *Travaux du centre de recherche sur le Proche-Orient et la Gréce antiques* 17. Paris: de Boccard.

Matthews, V. H.
1994 The Anthropology of Slavery in the Covenant Code. Pp. 119–35 in *Theory and Method in Biblical and Cuneiform Law,* ed B. M. Levinson. JSOTSup 181. Sheffield: Sheffield Academic Press.

Mauss, M.
1967 *The Gift.* French orig. 1925. New York: Norton.

Maxwell-Hyslop, K. R.
1971 *Western Asiatic Jewellery c. 3000–612 B.C.* London: Methuen.

May, H. G.
1936 The Ark—a Miniature Temple. *AJSL* 52: 215–34.

Mayer, W. R.
1987 Ein Mythos von der Erschaffung des Menschen und des Königs. *Or* 56: 55–68.

Mazar, A.
1982 The "Bull Site"—an Iron Age I Open Cult Place. *BASOR* 247: 27–42.
Mazar, B., and I. Dunayevsky
1964 En-Gedi. Third Season of Excavations. *IEJ* 14: 121–30.
Mazar, B., M. Dothan and I. Dunayevsky
1961 'Ein Gev. Excavations in 1961. *IEJ* 14: 1–49.
McCarter, P. K. Jr.
1980 *I Samuel.* AB 8. Garden City, N.Y.: Doubleday.
1984 *II Samuel.* AB 9. Garden City, N.Y.: Doubleday.
McCarthy, C.
1981 *The Tiqqune Sopherim.* OBO 36. Freiburg: Universitäts Verlag; Göttingen: Vandenhoeck & Ruprecht.
McCarthy, D. J.
1981 *Treaty and Covenant.* 2nd ed. AnBib 21A. Rome: Pontifical Biblical Institute.
McEvenue, S. E.
1971 *The Narrative Style of the Priestly Writer.* AnBib 50. Rome: Pontifical Biblical Institute.
1974 The Style of a Building Instruction. *Semitics* 4: 1–9.
McNeile, A. H.
1908 *The Book of Exodus.* Westminster Commentaries. London: Methuen.
Melamed, E. Z.
1961 "Break-up" of Stereotype Phrases as an Artistic Device in Biblical Poetry. Pp. 115–53 in *Studies in the Bible,* ed. C. Rabin. ScrHier 8. Jerusalem: Magnes.
Mellinkoff, R.
1970 *The Horned Moses in Medieval Art and Thought.* Berkeley: University of California.
Mendelson, I.
1935 The Conditional Sale into Slavery of Free-born Daughters in Nuzi and the Law of Ex. 21:7–11. *JAOS* 55: 190–95.
1949 *Slavery in the Ancient Near East.* New York: Oxford University.
1955 On Slavery in Alalakh. *IEJ* 5: 65–72.
Mendenhall, G. E.
1954 Ancient Oriental and Biblical Law. *BA* 17: 26–76.
1962 The Hebrew Conquest of Palestine. *BA* 25: 66–87.
1973 *The Tenth Generation.* Baltimore/London: Johns Hopkins University.
Meshorer, Y.
1982 *Ancient Jewish Coinage.* Dix Hills, N.Y.: Amphora.
Mesnil du Buisson, R. du
1963 Origine et évolution du panthéon de Tyr. *RHR* 164: 133–63.
Mettinger, T. N. D.
1971 The Nominal Pattern "QeTULLA" in Biblical Hebrew. *JSS* 16: 2–14.

1974 Abbild oder Urbild? "Imago Dei" in traditionsgeschichtlicher Sicht. ZAW 86: 403–24.

1976 *King and Messiah.* ConBOT 8. Lund: Gleerup.

1982 *The Dethronement of Sabaoth.* ConBOT 18. Lund: Gleerup.

1995 *No Graven Images?* ConBOT 42. Stockholm: Almqvist & Wiksell.

Metzger, M.

1970 Himmlische und irdische Wohnstatt Jahwes. *UF* 2: 139–58.

1985 *Königsthron und Gottesthron.* AOAT 15. Kevelaer: Butzon & Bercker; Neukirchen-Vluyn: Neukirchener Verlag.

1994 Jahwe, der Kerubenthroner, die von Keruben flankierte Palmette und Sphingenthrone aus dem Libanon. Pp. 75–90 in *Wer ist wie du, HERR, unter den Göttern?*, ed. I. Kottsieper et al. Fs. O. Kaiser. Göttingen: Vandenhoeck & Ruprecht.

Meyers, C. L.

1976 *The Tabernacle Menorah.* ASORDS 2. Missoula, Mont.: Scholars Press.

1979 Was There a Seven Branched Lampstand in Solomon's Temple? *BARev* 5.5: 47–57.

1996 Realms of Sanctity: the Case of the "Misplaced" Incense Altar in the Tabernacle Texts of Exodus. Pp. 33–46 in *Texts, Temples, and Traditions,* ed. M. V. Fox et al. Fs. M. Haran. Winona Lake, Ind.: Eisenbrauns.

Meyers, C. L., and E. Meyers

1987 *Haggai, Zechariah 1–8.* AB 25B. Garden City, N.Y.: Doubleday.

Milgrom, J.

1971 Sin Offering or Purification Offering? *VT* 21: 237–39.

1972 Altar. *EncJud* 2.762–67. Jerusalem: Keter.

1981 Sancta Contagion and Altar/City Asylum. Pp. 278–310 in *Congress Volume Vienna 1980,* ed. J. A. Emerton. VTSup 32. Leiden: Brill.

1983a *Studies in Cultic Theology and Terminology.* Studies in Judaism in Late Antiquity 36. Leiden: Brill.

1983b Of Hems and Tassels. *BARev* 9.3: 61–65.

1990 *Numbers.* JPS Torah Commentary. Philadelphia/New York: Jewish Publication Society.

1991 *Leviticus 1–16.* AB 3. New York: Doubleday.

2000 *Leviticus 17–22.* AB 3A. New York: Doubleday.

2001 *Leviticus 23–27.* AB 3B. New York: Doubleday.

Milik, J. T.

1959 *Ten Years of Discovery in the Wilderness of Judaea.* French orig. 1957. SBT 26. Naperville, Ind.: Allenson.

Miller, P. D. Jr.

1970a Apotropaic Imagery in Proverbs 6:20–22. *JNES* 29: 129–30.

1970b Animal Names as Designations in Ugaritic and Hebrew. *UF* 2: 177–86.

1973 *The Divine Warrior in Early Israel.* HSM 5. Cambridge, Mass.: Harvard University.

1980 El, The Creator of Earth. *BASOR* 239: 43–46.

2000 *The Religion of Ancient Israel.* Library of Ancient Israel. London: SPCK; Louisville, Kenn.: Westminster John Knox.

Moberly, R. W. L.

1983 *At the Mountain of God.* JSOTSup 22. Sheffield: JSOT.

Moor, J. C. de

1997 *The Rise of Yahwism.* 2d ed. Leuven: University Press.

Moore, G. F.

1897 Biblical Notes: 3. The Image of Moloch. *JBL* 16: 161–65.

Moorey, P. R. S.

1994 *Ancient Mesopotamian Materials and Industries.* Oxord: Clarendon.

Moran, W. L.

1959 The Scandal of the "Great Sin" at Ugarit. *JNES* 18: 280–81.

1961 The Hebrew Language in its Northwest Semitic Background. Pp. 54–72 in *The Bible and the Ancient Near East,* ed. G. E. Wright. Garden City, N.Y.: Doubleday.

1992 *The Amarna Letters.* French orig. 1987. Baltimore/London: Johns Hopkins University.

Morenz, S.

1973 *Egyptian Religion.* German orig. 1960. Ithaca, N.Y.: Cornell University.

Morgenstern, J.

1966 *The Rites of Birth, Marriage, Death, and Kindred Occasions Among the Semites.* Cincinnati: Hebrew Union College Press.

Morrison, M. A.

1992 Hurrians. *ABD* 3.335–38. New York: Doubleday.

Mosca, P.

1975 Child Sacrifice in Canaanite and Israelite Religion. A Study in *Mulk* and *MLK.* Ph.D. diss., Harvard University.

Moscati, S.

1987 *Il sacrificio punico dei fanciulli: realtà o invenzione?* Problemi attuali di scienza e di cultura, quaderno 261. Rome: Accademia nazionale dei Lincei.

1988 *The Phoenicians.* Italian orig. 1988. New York: Abbeville.

Moscati, S., and S. Ribichini

1991 *Il sacrificio dei bambini: un aggiornamento.* Problemi attuali di scienza e di cultura, quaderno 266. Rome: Accademia nazionale dei Lincei.

Muchiki, Y.

1999 *Egyptian Proper Names and Loanwords in North-West Semitic.* SBLDS 173. Atlanta, Georg.: Society of Biblical Literature.

Muilenburg, J.

1961 The Linguistic and Rhetorical Usages of the Particle *ky* in the Old Testament. *HUCA* 32: 135–60.

Muller, B., ed.

2001 *"Maquettes architecturales" de l'Antiquité.* Université Strasbourg

Travaux du centre de recherche sur le Proche-Orient et la Gréce antiques 17. Paris: de Boccard.

Müller, D. H.
1903 *Die Gesetze Hammurabis und ihr Verhältnis zur mosäischen Gesetzgebung sowie zu den XII Tafeln.* Vienna: Fromme.

Müller, H. P.
1997 *mōlek. TDOT* 8.375–88. Grand Rapids: Eerdmans.

Müller, M.
1891 *Physical Religion.* London: Longmans.

Murray, G. W.
1935 *Sons of Ishmael.* London: Routledge.

Muscarella, O. W.
1981 *Ladders to Heaven.* Toronto: McClelland and Stewart.

Musil, A.
1928 *The Manners and Customs of the Rwala Bedouins.* American Geographical Society Oriental Explorations and Studies 6. New York: American Geographical Society.

Muthmann, F.
1982 *Der Granatapfel.* Bern: Abegg-Stiftung.

Na'aman, N.
1980 The Shihor of Egypt and Shur that is before Egypt. *TA* 7: 95–109.
1986 Ḫabiru and Hebrews: The Transfer of a Social Term to the Literary Sphere. *JNES* 45: 271–88.

Nam, D.
1989 The "Throne of God" Motif in the Hebrew Bible. Ph.D. diss., Andrews University.

Negev, A.
1967 Hakkərônôlôgyâ šel hammənôrâ ba'ălat šib'at haqqānîm. Pp. 193–210 in *E. L. Sukenik Volume.* ErIsr 8. Jerusalem: Israel Exploration Society.

Nestle, E.
1913 Das Böcklein in der Milch der Mutter. *ZAW* 33: 75–76.

Neufeld, E.
1955 The Prohibitions Against Loans at Interest in Ancient Hebrew Laws. *HUCA* 26: 355–412.
1980 Insects as Warfare Agents in the Ancient Near East (Ex. 23:28; Deut. 7:20; Josh. 24:12; Isa. 7:18–20). *Or* 49: 30–57.

Niditch, S.
1986 Ezekiel 40–48 in a Visionary Context. *CBQ* 48: 208–24.
1996 *Oral Word and Written Word.* Library of Ancient Israel. Louisville, Kenn.: Westminster John Knox.

Niehr, H.
1999 *nāśî'. TDOT* 10.44–53. Grand Rapids: Eerdmans.

Niehr, H., and G. Steins
2004 *šadday. TDOT* 14.418–46. Grand Rapids: Eerdmans.

Nielsen, K.
1986 *Incense in Ancient Israel.* VTSup 38. Leiden: Brill.

Nöldecke, T.
1886 Friedr. Delitzsch, Prolegomena eines neuen hebräisch-aramäischen Wörterbuchs zum Alten Testament. ZDMG 40: 718–43.

North, R.
1955 Flesh, Covering, and Response, Ex. xxi 10. *VT* 5: 204–6.
1970 Zechariah's Seven-Spout Lampstand. *Bib* 51: 183–206.

Noth, M.
1928 *Die israelitischen Personennamen.* Stuttgart: Kohlhammer.
1960 *The History of Israel.* 2d ed. New York/Evanston: Harper & Row.
1962 *Exodus.* German orig. 1959. OTL. Philadelphia: Westminster.
1981 *The Deuteronomistic History.* German orig. 1957. JSOTSup 15. Sheffield: JSOT Press.

Nötscher, F.
1969 *"Das Angesicht Gottes schauen" nach biblischer und babylonischer Auffassung.* 2d ed. Darmstadt: Wissenschaftliche Buchgesellschaft.

Nowack, H.
1992 Untersuchungen über die materialtechnischen Aspekte des Altars Ex 27. *BN* 63: 62–71.

Oates, D., and J. Oates
1976 *The Rise of Civilization. The Making of the Past.* Oxford: Elsevier Phaidon.

O'Connell, K. G.
1984 The List of Seven Peoples in Canaan: A Fresh Analysis. Pp. 221–42 in *The Answers Lie Below,* ed. H. O Thompson. Fs. L. E. Toombs. Lanham, Md.: University Press of America.

Oden, R. A. Jr.
1987 *The Bible Without Theology.* New Voices in Biblical Studies. San Francisco: Harper & Row.

Ogden, J.
1982 *Jewellery of the Ancient World.* London: Trefoil Books.
2000 Metals. Pp. 148–76 in *Ancient Egyptian Materials and Technologies,* ed. P. T. Nicholson and I. Shaw. Cambridge: Cambridge University.

Olyan, S. M.
1982 Zadok's Origins and the Tribal Politics of David. *JBL* 101: 177–93.
1988 *Asherah and the Cult of Yahweh in Israel.* HSM 34. Atlanta: Scholars Press.
1996 Why an Altar of Unfinished Stones? *ZAW* 108: 161–71.
1998 What Do Shaving Rites Accomplish and What Do They Signal in Biblical Narrative Contexts? *JBL* 117: 611–22.

Oppenheim, A. L.
1943 Akkadian *pul(u)ḫ(t)u* and *melammu.* *JAOS* 63: 31–34.
1947 A Fiscal Practice of the Ancient Near East. *JNES* 6: 116–20.
1949 The Golden Garments of the Gods. *JNES* 8: 172–93.

1964 *Ancient Mesopotamia*. Chicago/London: University of Chicago.
1967 *Letters From Mesopotamia*. Chicago/London: University of Chicago.
Oren, E. D.
1964 Lə'inyan "šə'ērāh kəsûtāh wə'ōnātāh" (šəmôt 21 10). *Tarbiz* 33: 317.
1987 The "Ways of Horus" in North Sinai. Pp. 69–119 in *Egypt, Israel, Sinai*, ed. A. R. Rainey. Tel Aviv: Tel Aviv University.
Oren, E. D., ed.
2000 *The Sea Peoples and Their World*. Philadelphia: The University Museum, University of Pennsylvania.
Otto, E.
1989 *Rechtsgeschichte der Redaktionen im Kodex Ešnunna und im "Bundesbuch."* OBO 85. Freiburg: Universitätsverlag; Göttingen: Vandenhoeck & Ruprecht.
1991 *Körperverletzungen in den Keilschriftrechten und im Alten Testament*. AOAT 226. Kevelaer: Butzon & Bercker; Neukirchen-Vluyn: Neukirchener Verlag.
Otto, R.
1936 *The Idea of the Holy*. German orig. 1917. Oxford: Oxford University/London: Milford.
Ottosson, M.
1980 *Temples and Cult Places in Palestine*. BOREAS. Uppsala Studies in Ancient Mediterranean and Near Eastern Civilizations 12. Uppsala: Almqvist & Wiksell.
Otzen, B.
1977 *bdl*. TDOT 2.1–3. Grand Rapids: Eerdmans.
Overton, S. D.
2002 Now You See It, Now You Don't: Biblical Perspectives on the Relationship Between Magic and Religion. Ph.D. diss., University of California, San Diego.
Owczarek, S.
1998 *Die Vorstellung vom Wohnen Gottes inmitten seines Volkes in der Priesterschrift*. Europäische Hochschulschriften Series 23, vol. 625. Frankfurt am Main/Berlin/Bern/New York/Paris/Vienna: Lang.
Paran, M.
1989 *Darkê hassignôn hakkōhănî battôrâ*. Jerusalem: Magnes.
Pardee, D.
1979 A New Ugaritic Letter. *Bibliotheca Orientalis* 34: 3–20.
Parnas, M.
1975 "'Ēdût," "'Ēdôt," "'Ēdəwôt" bəmiqrā' 'al reqa' tə'ûdôt ḥiṣôniyyôt. *Shnaton* 1: 235–46.
Parpola, S.
1980 The Murder of Sennacherib. Pp. 171–82 in *Death in Mesopotamia*. Proceedings of the 26th Rencontre assyriologique internationale, ed. B. Alster. Copenhagen: Akademisk Forlag.
1993 *Letters from Assyrian and Babylonian Scholars*. State Archives of Assyria 10. Helsinki: Helsinki University.

Parrot, A.
1961   *Arts of Assyria*. New York: Golden.
Patai, R.
1967   *The Hebrew Goddess*. New York: KTAV.
Paul, S. M.
1970   *Studies in the Book of the Covenant in the Light of Cuneiform and Biblical Law*. VTSup 18. Leiden: Brill.
Pentiuc, E. J.
2001   *West Semitic Vocabulary in the Akkadian Texts from Emar*. HSS 49. Winona Lake, Ind.: Eisenbrauns.
Perrot, G., and C. Chipiez
1884   *Histoire de l'art dans l'antiquité* II. Paris: Hachette.
Perrot, N.
1937   Les représentations de l'arbre sacré sur les monuments de Mésopotamie et d'Élam. *Babyloniaca* 17: 5–144.
Petrie, W. M. F.
1890   *Kahun, Gurob, and Hawara*. London: Kegan Paul, Trench, Trübner.
Pettazzoni, R.
1978   *The All-knowing God*. Italian orig. 1957. New York: Arno.
Pines, R.
1971   Şəbāʿîm. *EM* 6: 663–72. Jerusalem: Bialik Institute.
Plastaras, J.
1966   *The God of Exodus*. Milwaukee, Wisc.: Bruce.
Plautz, W.
1964   Die Form der Eheschliessung im Alten Testament. *ZAW* 76: 298–318.
Poebel, A.
1932   *Das appositionell bestimmte Pronomen der 1. Prs. sing. in den westsemitischen Inschriften und im Alten Testament*. Assyriological Studies 3. Chicago: Oriental Institute of the University of Chicago.
Pons, J.
1988   La référence au séjour en Égypte et à la sortie d'Égypte dans les codes de loi de l'Ancien Testament. *Études Théologiques et Religieuses* 63: 169–82.
Pope, M. H.
1955   *El in the Ugaritic Texts*. VTSup 2. Leiden: Brill.
1962a Seven, Seventh, Seventy. *IDB* 4.294–95. Nashville, Tenn.: Abingdon.
1962b Number. *IDB* 3.561–67. Nashville, Tenn.: Abingdon.
1965a *Job*. AB 15. Garden City, N.Y.: Doubleday.
1965b Kōtar. Pp. 295–97 in *Götter und Mythen im vorderen Orient*, ed. H. W. Häussig. *Wörterbuch der Mythologie* 1.1. Stuttgart: Klett.
Porten, B.
1968   *Archives from Elephantine*. Berkeley: University of California.
Powell, M. A.
1992   Weights and Measures. *ABD* 6.897–908. New York: Doubleday.

Powels, S.
  1992   Indische Lehnwörter in der Bibel. *ZAH* 5: 186–200.
Prawer, S. S.
  1983   *Heine's Jewish Comedy.* Oxford: Clarendon.
Preuss, H. D.
  1998   *nāgap. TDOT* 9.210–13. Grand Rapids: Eerdmans.
Price, M. J., and B. L. Trell
  1977   *Coins and Their Cities.* London: Vecchi; Detroit: Wayne State University.
Prijs, L.
  1948   *Jüdische Tradition in der Septuaginta.* Leiden: Brill.
Propp, W. H. C.
  1987a *Water in the Wilderness.* HSM 40. Atlanta: Scholars Press.
  1987b The Origins of Infant Circumcision in Israel. *HAR* 11: 355–70.
  1987c On Hebrew *śāde(h)*, "Highland." *VT* 37: 230–36.
  1987d The Skin of Moses' Face—Transfigured or Disfigured? *CBQ* 49: 375–86.
  1992   Ithamar. *ABD* 3.579–81. New York: Doubleday.
  1993   Kinship in 2 Samuel 13. *CBQ* 55: 39–53.
  1997   The Priestly Source Recovered Intact? *VT* 46: 458–78.
  1999   Milk and Honey: Biblical Comfort Food. *BRev* 15.3: 16, 54.
  2004a Symbolic Wounds. Pp. 17–24 in *Le-David Maskil*, ed. R. E. Friedman and W. H. C. Propp. Fs. D. N. Freedman. Biblical and Judaic Studies from the University of California, San Diego 9. Winona Lake, Ind.: Eisenbrauns.
  2004b Acting Like Apes. *BRev* 20.3: 35–40, 46.
  2004c Exorcising Demons. *BRev* 20.5: 14–21, 47.
Puech, E.
  1977   Documents épigraphiques de Buseirah. *Levant* 9: 11–20.
Purvis, J. D.
  1994   The Tabernacle in Samaritan Iconography and Thought. Pp. 223–36 in *Uncovering Ancient Stones: Essays in Memory of H. N. Richardson*, ed. L. M. Hopfe. Winona Lake, Ind.: Eisenbrauns.
Qafaḥ, Y.
  1963   *Pêrûšê Rabbênû Səʿadyâ Gāʾôn ʿal hattôrâ.* Jerusalem: Mossad Harav Kook.
Qimron, E.
  1972   Hahabḥānâ bên wāw ləyôd bitʿûdôt midbar yəhûdâ. *Beit Mikra* 18: 102–12.
  1986   *The Hebrew of the Dead Sea Scrolls.* HSS 29. Atlanta: Scholars Press.
Quaegebeur, J.
  1993   L'autel-à-jeu et l'abattoir en Égypte tardive. Pp. 329–53 in *Ritual and Sacrifice in the Ancient Near East*, ed. J. Quaegebeur. Leuven: Peeters.
Quirke, S.
  1992   *Ancient Egyptian Religion.* New York: Dover.

Rabin, C.
    1963   Hittite Words in Hebrew. *Or* 32: 113–39.
    1975   'Abnēṭ ûpiṭdâ. *Leš* 39: 182–86.
Rabinowitz, J. J.
    1959a Exodus xxii 4 and the Septuagint Version Thereof. *VT* 9: 40–46.
    1959b The "Great Sin" in Ancient Egyptian Marriage Contracts. *JNES* 18: 73.
Rad, G. von
    1965   *The Problem of the Hexateuch and Other Essays.* German orig. 1958.
           Edinburgh: Oliver and Boyd.
Rainey, A. F.
    1970   The Order of Sacrifices in Old Testament Ritual Texts. *Bib* 51:
           485–98.
    1994   Hezekiah's Reform and the Altars at Beer-sheba and Arad. Pp. 333–54
           in *Scripture and Other Artifacts,* ed. M. D. Coogan, J. C. Exum and
           L. E. Stager. Fs. P. J. King. Louisville, Kenn.: Westminster John
           Knox.
    1995   Unruly Elements in Late Bronze Canaanite Society. Pp. 481–96 in
           Pomegranates and Golden Bells, ed. D. P. Wright, D. N. Freedman
           and A. Hurvitz. Fs. J. Milgrom. Winona Lake, Ind.: Eisenbrauns.
    1996   Who Is a Canaanite? A Review of the Textual Evidence. *BASOR* 304:
           1–15.
Ratner, R., and B. Zuckerman
    1986   "A Kid in Milk?": New Photographs of *KTU* 1.23, Line 14. *HUCA* 57:
           15–60.
Rechenmacher, H.
    1996   *šabbāt[t]* — Nominalform und Etymologie. *ZAH* 9: 199–203.
Redford, D. B.
    1984   *Akhenaten the Heretic King.* Princeton, N.J.: Princeton University
           Press, 1984.
    1987   An Egyptological Perspective on the Exodus Narrative. Pp. 137–61
           in *Egypt, Israel, Sinai,* ed. A. R. Rainey. Tel Aviv: Tel Aviv Univer-
           sity.
    1992   *Egypt, Canaan, and Israel in Ancient Times.* Princeton, N.J.: Prince-
           ton University.
Reinhold, M.
    1970   *History of Purple as a Status Symbol in Antiquity.* Collection Latomus
           116. Brussels: Latomus.
Reisner, G. A., and W. S. Smith
    1955   *A History of the Giza Necropolis II.* Cambridge, Mass.: Harvard Uni-
           versity.
Renan, E.
    1859   Nouvelles considérations sur le caractère général des peuples sémi-
           tiques. *JA* 5 série. 13: 214–82.
Rendsburg, G. A.
    1990   The Internal Consistency and Historical Reliability of the Biblical
           Genealogies. *VT* 40: 185–206.

1992   The Date of the Exodus and the Conquest-Settlement: The Case for the 1100s. *VT* 42: 510–27.

Richter, G. M. A.
1915   *Greek, Etruscan and Roman Bronzes.* New York: Metropolitan Museum of Art.
1966   *The Furniture of the Greeks, Etruscans and Romans.* London: Phaidon.

Rieder, D.
1974   *Pseudo-Jonathan. Targum Jonathan Ben Uziel on the Pentateuch.* Jerusalem: American Academy for Jewish Studies.

Rigsby, K. J.
1996   *Asylia.* Berkeley/Los Angeles/London: University of California.

Ringgren, H.
1986   *Ḥāqaq. TDOT* 5: 139–47. Grand Rapids: Eerdmans.

Risto, N.
1998   *The Levites.* South Florida Studies in the History of Judaism 193. Atlanta: Scholars Press.

Roberts, J. J. M.
1971   The Hand of Yahweh. *VT* 21: 244–51.
1977   Nebuchadnezzar I's Elamite Crisis in Theological Perspective. Pp. 183–87 in *Essays on the Ancient Near East in Memory of J. J. Finkelstein,* ed. M. de Jong Ellis. Memoirs of the Connecticut Academy of Arts & Sciences. Hamden, Conn.: Archon.

Robertson, D. A.
1972   *Linguistic Evidence in Dating Early Hebrew Poetry.* SBLDS 3. Missoula, Mont.: Society of Biblical Literature.

Robinson, H. W.
1967   *Corporate Personality in Ancient Israel.* Philadelphia: Fortress.

Ross, J. F.
1962   The Prophet as Yahweh's Messenger. Pp. 98–107 in *Israel's Prophetic Heritage,* ed. B. W. Anderson and W. Harrelson. Fs. J. Muilenburg. London: SCM.

Rossi, J. B. de
1784–85   *Variae Lectiones Veteris Testamenti Librorum.* Parma: ex Regio Typographeo.

Roth, M. T., ed.
1995   *Law Collections from Mesopotamia and Asia Minor.* SBLWAW 6. Atlanta: Scholars Press.

Rothenberg, B.
1972   *Timna.* London: Thames and Hudson.

Russell, B. D.
2002   The Song of the Sea: the Date and Significance of Exodus 15:1–21. Ph.D. diss., Union Theological Seminary and Presbyterian School of Christian Education.

Ryckmans, G.
1934   *Les noms propres sud-sémitiques.* Bibliothèque du *Muséon* 2. Louvain: Bureaux du *Muséon.*

Rylaarsdam, J.
  1962 Weeks, Feast of. *IDB* 4.827–28. Nashville, Tenn.: Abingdon.

Sadaqa, A., and R. Sadaqa
  1964 *Jewish and Samaritan Version of the Pentateuch. Exodus.* Jerusalem: Rubin Mass.

Safrai, S.
  1965 *Hāʿăliyyâ ləregel bîmê habbayit haššēnî.* Tel Aviv: Am Hassefer.
  1976 The Temple. Pp. 865–907 in *The Jewish People in the First Century,* ed. S. Safrai and M. Stern. Compendia Rerum Iudaicarum ad Novum Testamentum 1. Assen/Amsterdam: Van Gorcum.

Sakenfeld, K. E.
  1978 *The Meaning of Ḥesed in the Hebrew Bible.* HSM 17. Missoula, Mont.: Scholars Press.

Sanderson, J. E.
  1986 *An Exodus Scroll From Qumran: 4QpaleoExod^m and the Samaritan Tradition.* HSS 30. Atlanta: Scholars Press.

Sarna, N.
  1986 *Exploring Exodus.* New York: Schocken.
  1991 *The JPS Torah Commentary: Exodus.* Philadelphia/New York/Jerusalem: Jewish Publication Society.

Sasson, J. M.
  1968 Bovine Symbolism and the Exodus Narrative. *VT* 18: 380–87.

Sauneron, S.
  2000 *The Priests of Ancient Egypt.* French orig. 1957. Ithaca/London: Cornell University.

Sayers, D. L.
  1941 *The Mind of the Maker.* New York: Harcourt, Brace.

Schacht, J.
  1964 *An Introduction to Islamic Law.* Oxford: Clarendon.

Schäfer, P.
  1974 Tempel und Schöpfung. *Kairos* 16: 122–33.

Scharbert, J.
  1975 *brk; bᵉrākhāh. TDOT* 2.279–308. Grand Rapids: Eerdmans.
  2004 *qll; qal; qᵉlālâ. TDOT* 13.37–44. Grand Rapids: Eerdmans.

Schenker, A.
  1988 Affranchissement d'une esclave selon Ex 21,7–11. *Bib* 69: 547–56.
  1994 Interprétations récentes et dimensions spécifiques du sacrifice ḥaṭṭāt. *Bib* 75: 59–70.
  2000 La différence des peines pour les vols de bétail selon le *Code de l'Alliance* (Ex XXI, 37 et XXII, 3). *RB* 107: 18–23.

Schmitt, R.
  1972 *Zelt und Lade als Thema alttestamentlicher Wissenschaft.* Gütersloh: Mohn.

Schoneveld, J.
  1973 Le sang du cambrioleur. Exode XXII 1,2. Pp. 335–40 in *Symbolae Bib-*

licae et Mesopotamicae, ed. M. A. Beek et al. Fs. F. M. Th. de
Liagre Böhl. Studia Francisci Scholten Memoriae Dicata 4. Leiden:
Brill.

Schottroff, W.
1967 *'Gendenken' im Alten Orient und im Alten Testament.* 2d ed.
WMANT 15. Neukirchen-Vluyn: Neukirchener Verlag.

Schroer, S.
1987 *In Israel gab es Bilder.* OBO 74. Freiburg: Universitätsverlag; Göttingen: Vandenhoeck & Ruprecht.

Schumacher, G.
1908 *Tell el Mutesellim I.* Leipzig: Haupt.

Schur, N.
1995 *The Karaite Encyclopedia.* Beiträge zur Erforschung des Alten Testaments und des antiken Judentums 38. Frankfurt am Main/Berlin/Bern/New York/Paris/Vienna: Lang.

Schürer, E.
1979 A *History of the Jewish People in the Age of Jesus Christ (175* B.C.–A.D. *135).* Edinburgh: Clark.

Schwally, F.
1891 Miscellen. *ZAW* 11: 169–83.

Schwartz, B. J.
1991 The Prohibitions Concerning the 'Eating' of Blood in Leviticus 17.
Pp. 34–66 in *Priesthood and Cult in Ancient Israel,* ed. G. A. Anderson and S. M. Olyan. JSOTSup 125. Sheffield: Sheffield Academic Press.
1995 The Bearing of Sin in the Priestly Literature. Pp. 3–21 in *Pomegranates and Golden Bells,* ed. D. P. Wright, D. N. Freedman and A. Hurvitz. Fs. J. Milgrom. Winona Lake, Ind.: Eisenbrauns.
1996 The Priestly Account of the Theophany and Lawgiving at Sinai.
Pp. 103–33 in *Texts, Temples, and Traditions,* ed. M. V. Fox et al. Fs. M. Haran. Winona Lake, Ind.: Eisenbrauns.

Schwienhorst, L.
1998 *mārâ. TDOT* 9.5–10. Grand Rapids: Eerdmans.

Schwienhorst-Schönberger, L.
1990 *Das Bundesbuch (Ex 20,22–23,33).* BZAW 188. Berlin/New York: de Gruyter.

Seebass, H.
1993 Noch einmal zum Depositenrecht Ex 22,6–14. Pp. 21–31 in *Gottes Recht als Lebensraum,* ed. P. Mommer et al. Fs. H. J. Boecker. Neukirchen-Vluyn: Neukirchener Verlag.

Seely, D. R.
1992 Shur, Wilderness of. *ABD* 5.1230. New York: Doubleday.

Seeman, D.
1998 "Where Is Sarah Your Wife?" Cultural Poetics of Gender and Nationhood in the Hebrew Bible. *HTR* 91: 103–25.

Segal, J. B.
  1963 *The Hebrew Passover.* London: Oxford University.
Seger, J. D., and O. Borowski
  1977 The First Two Seasons at Tell Halif. *BA* 40: 156–66.
Segert, S.
  1975 *Altaramäische Grammatik.* Leipzig: Verlag Enzyklopädie.
Sellin, E., et al.
  1926 *Die Ausgrabungen von Sichem.* Leipzig: Harrassowitz.
Seow, C. L.
  1984 The Designation of the Ark in Priestly Theology. *HAR* 8: 185–98.
  1989 *Myth, Drama, and the Politics of David's Dance.* HSM 44. Atlanta: Scholars Press.
  1992 Hosts, Lord of. *ABD* 3.304–7. New York: Doubleday.
  1997 *Ecclesiastes.* AB 18C. New York: Doubleday.
Serpel, J. A.
  1986 *In the Company of Animals.* Oxford: Blackwell.
Serpico, M., and R. White
  2000 Oil, fat and wax. Pp. 390–29 in *Ancient Egyptian Materials and Technologies,* ed. P. T. Nicholson and I. Shaw. Cambridge: Cambridge University.
Seybold, K.
  1986 *ḥāšab.* TDOT 5.228–45. Grand Rapids: Eerdmans.
Shafer, B. E.
  1997 Temples, Priests, and Rituals: an Overview. Pp. 1–30 in *Temples of Ancient Egypt,* ed. B. E. Shafer. Ithaca, N.Y.: Cornell University.
Sheffer, A.
  1978 The Textiles. In *Kuntillet Ajrud,* ed. Z. Meshel. Israel Museum Catalog 175. Jerusalem: Israel Museum.
Shelmerdine, C. W.
  1985 *The Perfume Industry of Mycenaean Pylos.* Göteborg: Paul Åströms Förlag.
Shiloh, Y.
  1971 Review of Marie-Louise Buhl & S. Holm-Nielsen: *Shiloh. IEJ* 21: 67–69.
Sigrist, M.
  1993 Gestes symboliques et rituels à Emar. Pp. 381–410 in *Ritual and Sacrifice in the Ancient Near East,* ed. J. Quaegebeur. AL 55. Leuven: Peeters.
Simian-Yofre, H.
  1999 *'wd.* TDOT 10.495–515. Grand Rapids: Eerdmans.
Singer, I.
  1999 A Political History of Ugarit. Pp. 603–33 in *Handbook of Ugaritic Studies,* ed. W. G. E. Watson and N. Wyatt. Handbuch der Orientalistik 1.39. Leiden/Boston/Köln: Brill.
Smith, M.
  1975 A Note on Burning Babies. *JAOS* 95: 477–79.

Smith, M. S.
1990 *The Early History of God.* San Francisco: Harper & Row.
1992 Rephaim. *ABD* 5.674–76. New York: Doubleday.
1997 *The Pilgrimage Pattern in Exodus.* JSOTSup 239. Sheffield: Sheffield Academic Press.
2001 *The Origins of Biblical Monotheism.* Oxford: Oxford University.
2002 *The Early History of God.* 2d ed. San Francisco: Harper & Row.

Smith, W. R.
1881 *The Old Testament in the Jewish Church.* Edinburgh: Black.
1927 *Lectures on the Religion of the Semites.* 3d ed. New York: Macmillan.

Snijders, L. A.
1980 *zûr/zār. TDOT* 4.52–58. Grand Rapids: Eerdmans.

Soden, W. von
1970 *Mirjām*-Maria "Gottesgeschenk." *UF* 2: 269–72.
1981 Zum hebräischen Wörterbuch. *UF* 13: 157–64.

Sommer, B. D.
2001 Conflicting Constructions of Divine Presence in the Priestly Tabernacle. *Biblical Interpretation* 9: 41–63.

Soukiassian, G.
1983 Les auels "à cornes" ou "à acrotères" en Égypt. *Bulletin de l'Institut Français d'Archéologie Orientale* 83: 317–33.

Spaey, J.
1994 Emblems in Rituals in the Old Babylonian Period. Pp. 411–20 in *Ritual and Sacrifice in the Ancient Near East*, ed. J. Quaegebeur. AL 55. Leuven: Peeters.

Spalinger, A.
1978 A Canaanite Ritual found in Egyptian Reliefs. *Journal of the Society for the Study of Egyptian Antiquities* 8: 47–60.

Spanier, E., ed.
1987 *The Royal Purple and the Biblical Blue.* Jerusalem: Keter.

Speiser, E. A.
1962 Man, ethnic divisions of. *IDB* 3: 235–42. Nashville/New York: Abingdon.
1963a The Stem *PLL* in Hebrew. *JBL* 82: 301–6.
1963b Background and Function of the Biblical Nāśîʾ. *CBQ* 25: 111–17.
1965 *Pālil* and Congeners: A Sampling of Apotropaic Symbols. Pp. 389–93 in *Studies in Honor of Benno Landsberger on his Seventy-fifth Birthday*, ed. H. G. Güterbock and T. Jacobsen. Assyriological Studies 16. Chicago: University of Chicago.
1967 Census and Ritual Expiation in Mari and Israel. Pp. 171–86 in *Oriental and Biblical Studies*, ed. J. J. Finkelstein and M. Greenberg. Philadelphia: University of Pennsylvania.

Sperber, A.
1959 *The Bible in Aramaic I.* Leiden: Brill.

Sperber, D.
1965 The History of the Menorah. *JJS* 16: 135–59.

Sperling, S. D.
    1998 *The Original Torah.* New York/London: New York University.
    1999 Pants, Persians, and the Priestly Source. Pp. 373–85 in *Ki Baruch Hu*,
          ed. R. Chazan, W. W. Hallo and L. H. Schiffman. Fs. B. A. Levine.
          Winona Lake, Ind.: Eisenbrauns.
Spinoza, B. de
    1951 A *Theologico-political Treatise and A Political Treatise.* Latin orig.
          1670. New York: Dover Publications.
Stager, L. E.
    1980 The Rite of Child Sacrifice at Carthage. Pp. 1–11 in *New Light
          on Ancient Carthage*, ed. J. G. Pedley. Ann Arbor: University of
          Michigan.
    1982 Carthage: A View from the Tophet. Pp. 155–66 in *Phönizier im
          Westen*, ed. H. G. Neimeyer. Madrider Beiträge 8. Mainz: Philipp
          von Zabern.
    1983 The Finest Olive Oil in Samaria. *JSS* 28: 241–45.
    1991 *Ashkelon Discovered.* Washington, D.C.: Biblical Archaeology
          Society.
Stager, L. E., and S. R. Wolff
    1981 Production and Commerce in Temple Courtyards. *BASOR* 243:
          95–102.
    1984 Child Sacrifice at Carthage—Religious Rite or Population Control?
          BARev 10: 30–51.
Stamm, J. J.
    1939 *Die akkadische Namengebung.* Mitteilungen der vorderasiatisch-
          aegyptischen Gesellschaft 44. Leipzig: Hinrichs.
Stark, J. K.
    1971 *Personal Names in Palmyrene Inscriptions.* Oxford: Oxford University.
Steiner, R. C.
    1977 *The Case for Fricative-Laterals in Proto-Semitic.* AOS 59. New Haven,
          Conn.: American Oriental Society.
Steiner, R. C., and C. F. Nims
    1984 You Can't Offer Your Sacrifice and Eat It Too: A Polemical Poem
          from the Aramaic Text in Demotic Script. *JNES* 43: 89–114.
Steins, G.
    1989 "Sie sollen mir ein Heligtum machen." Pp. 145–67 in *Vom Sinai
          zum Horeb*, ed. F. L. Hossfeld. Fs. E. Zenger. Würzburg: Echter.
Stern, E.
    2001 Pagan Yahwism: The Folk Religion of Ancient Israel. *BARev* 27.3:
          20–29.
Stewart, D. T.
    2000 Ancient Sexual Laws: Text and Intertext of the Biblical Holiness
          Code and Hittite Law. Ph.D. diss., University of California, Berkeley.
Stowers, S. K.
    1998 On the Comparison of Blood in Greek and Israelite Ritual. Pp.

179–94 in *Hesed Ve-emet,* ed. J. Magness and S. Gitin. Fs. E. S. Frerichs. Brown Judaic Studies 320. Atlanta: Scholars Press.

Strauss, H.

1960 Gôrālāh wəṣûrātāh šel mənôrat haḥašmônā'îm. Pp. 122–29 in *M. Narkiss Volume.* ErIsr 6. Jerusalem: Israel Exploration Society.

Strugnell, J.

1960 The Angelic Liturgy at Qumrân—4Q Serek Šîrôt ʿOlat Haššabbāt. Pp. 318–45 in *Congress Volume Oxford 1958.* VTSup 7. Leiden: Brill.

Süring, M. L.

1980 *The Horn-Motif in the Hebrew Bible and Related Ancient Near Eastern Literature and Iconography.* Andrews University Seminary Doctoral Dissertation Series 4. Berrien Springs, Mich: Andrews University.

Tadmor, H.

1994 *The Inscriptions of Tiglath-Pileser III King of Assyria.* Jerusalem: Israel Academy of Sciences and Humanities.

Tal, A.

2000 *A Dictionary of Samaritan Aramaic.* Handbuch der Orientalistik 1.50. Leiden/Boston/Köln: Brill.

Talmon, S.

1961 Synonymous Readings in the Textual Traditions of the Old Testament. Pp. 335–83 in *Studies in the Bible,* ed. C. Rabin. ScrHier 8. Jerusalem: Magnes.

1981 The Ancient Hebrew Alphabet and Biblical Text Criticism. Pp. 498–529 in *Mélanges D. Barthélemy,* ed. P. Casetti, O. Keel and A. Schenker. OBO 38. Fribourg: Éditions Universitaires; Göttingen: Vandenhoeck & Ruprecht.

1986 *King, Cult and Calendar in Ancient Israel.* Jerusalem: Magnes.

Tawil, H.

1980 Azazel the Prince of the Steppe: A Comparative Study. ZAW 92: 43–59.

Terrien, S.

1978 *The Elusive Presence.* San Francisco: Harper & Row.

Thomas, B.

1932 *Arabia Felix.* New York: Scribner.

Thomas, D. W.

1968 Some Further Remarks on Unusual Ways of Expressing the Superlative in Hebrew. *VT* 18: 120–24.

Thompson, H. O.

1992 Marah. *ABD* 4.513. New York: Doubleday.

Thompson, S. E.

1994 The Anointing of Officials in Ancient Egypt. *JNES* 53: 15–25.

Tigay, J. H.

1986 *You Shall Have No Other Gods.* HSS 31. Atlanta: Scholars Press.

1999 Some More Delocutives in Hebrew. Pp. 409–12 in *Ki Baruch Hu,*

> ed. R. Chazan, W. W. Hallo and L. H. Schiffman. Fs. B. A. Levine. Winona Lake, Ind.: Eisenbrauns.

Toeg, A.
>   1977   *Mattan tôrâ bəsînay*. Jerusalem: Magnes.

Torrey, C. C.
>   1943   The Evolution of a Financier in the Ancient Near East. *JNES* 2: 295–301.

Tov, E.
>   2001   *Textual Criticism of the Hebrew Bible*. 2d ed. Minneapolis, Minn.: Fortress; Aasen-Maastricht: Van Gorcum.

Tov, E., and S. White
>   1994   4QReworked Pentateuch[c]. Pp. 255–318 in *Qumran Cave 4.VIII*. DJD 13. Oxford: Clarendon.

Trible, P.
>   1978   *God and the Rhetoric of Sexuality*. Overtures to Biblical Theology 2. Philadelphia: Fortress.

Trumbull, H. C.
>   1885   *The Blood Covenant*. New York: Scribner.
>   1906   *The Threshold Covenant*. 2d ed. New York: Scribner.

Tur-Sinai, H.
>   1950   *Hallāšôn wəhassēper* 1. Jerusalem: Bialik Institute.
>   1950–51   The Origin of the Alphabet. *JQR* 41: 83–109, 159–79, 277–301.
>   1955   *Hallāšôn wəhassēper* 3. Jerusalem: Bialik Institute.
>   1957   *The Book of Job*. Jerusalem: Kiryath Sepher.

Turner, V. W.
>   1967   *The Forest of Symbols*. Ithaca, N.Y.: Cornell University.
>   1968   *Drums of Affliction*. Oxford: Clarendon.
>   1974   *Dramas, Fields, and Metaphors*. Ithaca/London: Cornell University.

Tuzin, D. F.
>   1978   Sex and Meat-Eating in Ilahita. *Canberra Anthropology* 1: 82–93.
>   1980   *The Voice of the Tambaran*. Berkeley/Los Angeles/London: University of California.
>   1984   Miraculous Voices: The Auditory Experience of Numinous Objects. *Current Anthropology* 25: 579–96.
>   1997   *The Cassowary's Revenge*. Chicago/London: University of Chicago.

Tvedtnes, J. A.
>   1982   Egyptian Etymologies for Biblical Cultic Paraphernalia. Pp. 215–21 in *Egyptological Studies*, ed. S. Israel-Groll. ScrHier 28. Jerusalem: Magnes.

Utzschneider, H.
>   1988   *Das Heiligtum und das Gesetz*. OBO 77. Freiburg (Schweiz): Universitätsverlag; Göttingen: Vandenhoeck & Ruprecht.

Van Beek, G.
>   1960   Frankincense and Myrrh. *BA* 23: 70–95.

Van Buren, E. D.
1945 *Symbols of the Gods in Mesopotamian Art.* AnOr 23. Rome: Pontifical Biblical Institute.
Van Dam, C.
1997 *The Urim and Thummim.* Winona Lake, Ind.: Eisenbrauns.
Van Den Eynde, S.
1996 Keeping God's Sabath: 'wt and bryt (Exod 31,12–17). Pp. 501–11 in *Studies in the Book of Exodus,* ed. M. Vervenne. Bibliotheca Ephemeridum Theologicarum Lovaniensium 126. Leuven: University Press/Peeters.
Van der Toorn, K.
1985 *Sin and Sanction in Israel and Mesopotamia.* SSN 22. Assen/Maastricht: van Gorcum.
1990 The Nature of the Biblical Teraphim in the Light of the Cuneiform Evidence. *CBQ* 52: 203–22.
1994 *From Her Cradle to Her Grave.* The Biblical Seminar 23. Sheffield: JSOT Press.
1995 The Significance of the Veil in the Ancient Near East. Pp. 327–39 in *Pomegranates and Golden Bells,* ed. D. P Wright, D. N. Freedman and A. Hurvitz. Fs. J. Milgrom. Winona Lake, Ind.: Eisenbrauns.
1997 The Iconic Book: Analogies between the Babylonian Cult of Images and the Veneration of the Torah. Pp. 229–48 in *The Image and the Book,* ed. K. van der Toorn. Leuven: Peeters.
Van Dijk, H. J.
1968 *Ezekiel's Prophecy on Tyre (Ez.26,1–28,19).* BibOr 20. Rome: Pontifical Biblical Institute.
Van Driel-Murray, C.
2000 Leatherwork and Skin Products. Pp. 299–319 in *Ancient Egyptian Materials and Technologies,* ed. P. T. Nicholson and I. Shaw. Cambridge: Cambridge University.
Van Gennep, A.
1960 *The Rites of Passage.* French orig. 1909. Chicago: University of Chicago.
Van Houten, C.
1991 *The Alien in Israelite Law.* JSOTSup 107. Sheffield: JSOT.
Van Seters, J.
1994 *The Life of Moses. The Yahwist as Historian in Exodus-Numbers.* Louisville, Kenn.: Westminster/John Knox.
1996 The Law of the Hebrew Slave. *ZAW* 108: 534–46.
2003 *A Law Book for the Diaspora.* Oxford/New York: Oxford University.
Vaux, R. de
1961 *Ancient Israel.* New York: McGraw-Hill.
1964 *Studies in Old Testament Sacrifice.* Cardiff: University of Wales.
1967 *Bible et Orient.* Paris: Les Éditions du Cerf.

1971 *The Bible and the Ancient Near East.* French orig. 1967. Garden City, N.Y.: Doubleday.

1983 The Revelation of the Divine Name YHWH. Pp. 48–75 in *Proclamation and Presence,* ed. J. I. Durham and J. R. Porter. 2nd ed. Macon, Georg.: Mercer University.

Vernant, J. P.
1980 *Myth and Society in Ancient Greece.* French orig. 1974. Sussex: Harvester Press; Atlantic Highlands, N.J.: Humanities Press.

Viberg, Å.
1992 *Symbols of Law.* ConBOT 34. Stockhold: Almqvist & Wiksell.

Vogelsang-Eastwood, G.
2000 Textiles. Pp. 268–98 in *Ancient Egyptian Materials and Technologies,* ed. P. T. Nicholson and I. Shaw. Cambridge: Cambridge University.

Volkwein, B.
1969 Masoretisches ʿēdūt, ʿēdwōt, ʿēdōt — "Zeugnis" oder "Bundesbestimmungen"? *BZ* 13: 18–40.

Vriezen, T. C.
1950 The Term *hizza*: Lustration and Consecration. *OTS* 7: 201–35.
1972 The exegesis of Exodus xxiv 9–11. *OTS* 17: 100–33.

Wacker, M. T.
1992 Kosmisches Sakrament oder Verpfändung des Körpers? "Kultprostitution" im biblischen und im hinduistischen Indien. *BN* 61: 51–75.

Wade, M. L.
2003 *Consistency of Translation Techniques in the Tabernacle Accounts of Exodus in the Old Greek.* SBLSCS 49. Leiden/Boston: Brill.

Walker, C., and M. B. Dick
1999 The Induction of the Cult Image in Ancient Mesopotamia: The Mesopotamian *mīs pî* Ritual. Pp. 55–121 in *Born in Heaven, Made on Earth,* ed. M. B. Dick. Winona Lake, Ind.: Eisenbrauns.

Waltke, B. K., and M. O'Connor
1990 *An Introduction to Biblical Hebrew Syntax.* Winona Lake, Ind.: Eisenbrauns.

Ward, W. A.
1992 Goshen. *ABD* 2.1076–77. New York: Doubleday.

Ward, W. H.
1910 *The Seal Cylinders of Western Asia.* Washington, D.C.: Carnegie Institution of Washington.

Warmington, E. H.
1979 *Remains of Old Latin III.* LCL. Cambridge, Mass: Harvard University; London: Heinemann.

Watson, A.
1991 *Roman & Comparative Law.* Athens, Georg./London: University of Georgia.

Watson, W. G. E.
1999 Non–Semitic Words in the Ugaritic Lexicon (4). *UF* 31: 785–99.

Watts, J. W.
1999 *Reading Law.* The Biblical Seminar 59. Sheffield: Sheffield Academic Press.

Wehr, H.
1976 A *Dictionary of Modern Written Arabic.* Ithaca, N.Y.: Spoken Languages Services.

Weimar, P.
1988 Sinai und Schöpfung. *RB* 95: 337–85.

Weiner, A. B., and J. Schneider, ed.
1989 *Cloth and Human Experience.* Smithsonian Series in Ethnographic Inquiry. Washington/London: Smithsonian Institution.

Weinfeld, M.
1970a The Covenant of Grant in the Old Testament and in the Ancient Near East. *JAOS* 90: 184–203.

1970b 'Rider of the Clouds' and 'Gatherer of the Clouds.' *JANES* 5: 421–26.

1972 The Worship of Molech and of the Queen of Heaven and Its Background. *UF* 4: 133–54.

1978 Pentecost as the Festival of the Giving of the Law. *Immanuel* 8: 7–18.

1981 Sabbath, Temple and the Enthronement of the Lord—the Problem of the Sitz im Leben of Genesis 1:1–2:3. Pp. 501–12 in *Mélanges bibliques et orientaux en l'honneur de M. Henri Cazelles.* AOAT 212. Kevelaer: Butzon & Bercker; Neukirchen-Vluyn: Neukirchener Verlag.

1987 The Tribal League at Sinai. Pp. 303–14 in *Ancient Israelite Religion,* ed. P. D. Miller, Jr., P. D. Hanson and S. D. McBride. Fs. F. M. Cross. Philadelphia: Fortress.

1990 Sabbatical Year and Jubilee in the Pentateuchal Laws and the Ancient Near Eastern Background. Pp. 39–62 in *The Law in the Bible and Its Environment,* ed. T. Veijola. Helsinki: Finnish Exegetical Society; Göttingen: Vandenhoeck & Ruprecht.

1991 The Census in Mari, in Ancient Israel and in Ancient Rome. Pp. 293–98 in *Storia e tradizioni di Israele,* ed. D. Garrone and F. Israel. Fs. J. A. Soggin. Brescia: Paideia.

1993 The Ban on the Canaanites in the Biblical Codes and Its Historical Development. Pp. 142–60 in *History and Traditions of Early Israel,* ed. A. Lemaire and B. Otzen. Fs. E. Nielsen. VTSup 50. Leiden/New York/Köln: Brill.

1995 *kābôd.* *TDOT* 7.22–38. Grand Rapids: Eerdmans.

Weippert, M.
1961 Erwägungen zur Etymologie des Gottesnamens 'Ēl Šadday. ZDMG 111: 42–62.

Weiss, D. H.
1962 A Note on 'šr l' 'rśh. *JBL* 81: 67–69.

Weissbach, F. H.
1911 *Die Keilinschriften der Achämeniden.* Vorderasiatische Bibliothek. Leipzig: Hinrichs.

Wellhausen, J.
 1885 *Prolegomena to the History of Ancient Israel.* German orig. 1883. Edinburgh: Black.
 1897 *Reste arabischen Heidentums.* 2d ed. Berlin: Reimer.
 1899 *Die Composition des Hexateuchs und der historischen Bücher des Alten Testaments.* 3d ed. Berlin: Reimer.
Wente, E. F.
 1992 Ramses. *ABD* 5.617–18. New York: Doubleday.
Westbrook, R.
 1988 *Studies in Biblical and Cuneiform Law.* CahRB 26. Paris: Gabalda.
 1994 The Deposit Law of Exodus 22,6–12. *ZAW* 106: 390–403.
Westphal, G.
 1906 Aaron und die Aaroniden. *ZAW* 26: 201–30.
Wevers, J. W.
 1990 *Notes on the Greek Text of Exodus.* SBLSCS 30. Atlanta: Scholars Press.
 1991 *Exodus.* Göttingen Septuagint II.1. Göttingen: Vandenhoeck & Ruprecht.
 1992 *Text History of the Greek Exodus.* Abhandlungen der Akademie der Wissenschaften in Göttingen, Philologisch-historische Klasse, 3d series, 192; MSU XXI. Göttingen: Vandenhoeck & Ruprecht.
Whibley, L.
 1963 *A Companion to Greek Studies.* New York/London: Hafner.
White, M.
 1990 The Elohistic Depiction of Aaron: A Study in the Levite-Zadokite Controversy. Pp. 149–59 in *Studies in the Pentateuch,* ed. J. A. Emerton. VTSup 41. Leiden/New York/Copenhagen/Köln: Brill.
White, S. A.
 1990 The All Souls Deuteronomy and the Decalogue. *JBL* 109: 193–206.
Whitelam, K. W.
 1992 King and Kingship. *ABD* 4: 40–48. New York: Doubleday.
Whybray, R. N.
 1967 *'annôt* in Exodus xxxii 18. *VT* 17: 122.
Wickens, G. E.
 1969 A study of *Acacia albida* Del. *(Mimosoïdeae). Kew Bulletin* 23: 181–200.
Williamson, H. G. M.
 1985 A Reconsideration of *'zb* II in Biblical Hebrew. *ZAW* 97: 74–85.
Wilson, E. J.
 1994 *"Holiness" and "Purity" in Mesopotamia.* AOAT 237. Kevelaer: Butzon & Bercker; Neukirchen-Vluyn: Neukirchener Verlag.
Wilson, J. A.
 1945 The Assembly of a Phoenician City. *JNES* 4: 245.
Winlock, H. E.
 1955 *Models of Daily Life in Ancient Egypt.* Publications of the Metropolitan Museum of Art Egyptian Expedition 18. Cambridge, Mass.: Harvard University.

Wiseman, D. J.
  1958 *The Vassal Treaties of Esarhaddon.* IRAQ 20.1. London: British School of Archaeology in Iraq.
Wolfson, E. R.
  1992 Images of God's Feet: Some Observations on the Divine Body in Judaism. Pp. 143–81 in *People of the Body*, ed. H. Eilberg-Schwartz. SUNY Series, the Body in Culture, History, and Religion. Albany: State University of New York.
Wood, B. G.
  1992 Kiln. *ABD* 4.38–39. New York: Doubleday.
Wright, C. J. H.
  1992 Sabbatical Year. *ABD* 5.857–61. New York: Doubleday.
Wright, D. P.
  1986 The Gesture of Hand Placement in the Hebrew Bible and in Hittite Literature. *JAOS* 106: 433–46.
  1987 *The Disposal of Impurity.* Atlanta: Scholars Press.
  2003 The Laws of Hammurabi as a Source for the Covenant Collection (Exodus 20:23–23:19). *MAARAV* 10: 11–87.
Wright, G. E.
  1954 The Levites in Deuteronomy. *VT* 4: 324–330.
  1961 The Temple in Palestine–Syria. Pp. 169–84 in *The Biblical Archaeologist Reader Volume I*, ed. D. N. Freedman and G. E. Wright. Garden City, N.Y.: Doubleday.
  1964 *God Who Acts.* London: SCM.
Wright, L. S.
  1989 *MKR* in 2 Kings xii 5–17 and Deuteronomy xviii 8. *VT* 39: 438–48.
Wright, R.
  1994 *The Moral Animal.* New York: Pantheon.
Yadin, Y.
  1963 *The Art of Warfare in Biblical Lands.* New York/Toronto/London: McGraw-Hill.
  1983 *The Temple Scroll.* Hebrew orig. 1977. Jerusalem: Israel Exploration Society.
Yarden, L.
  1971 *The Tree of Light.* Ithaca, N.Y.: Cornell University.
Yardeni, A.
  1991 Remarks on the Priestly Blessing on Two Ancient Amulets from Jerusalem. *VT* 41: 176–85.
Yaron, R.
  1971 The Goring Ox in Near Eastern Laws. Pp. 50–60 in *Jewish Law in Ancient and Modern Israel*. New York: KTAV.
Youssef, A. A. H., C. LeBlanc and M. Maher
  1977 *Le Ramesseum* IV. Cairo: Centre d'étude et de documentation sur l'ancienne Egypt.
Yurco, F. J.
  1990 3,200-Year-Old Picture of Israelites Found in Egypt. *BARev* 16.5: 20–38.

Zaccagnini, C.
1983 Patterns of Mobility Among Ancient Near Eastern Craftsmen. *JNES* 42: 245–64.

Zakovitch, Y.
1991 *"And You Shall Tell Your Son . . ." The Concept of the Exodus in the Bible.* Jerusalem: Magnes.
1994 Ancient Variants and Interpretations of Some Laws of the Book of the Covenant as Reflected in Early Prophets' Narratives. *The Jewish Law Annual* 11: 57–62.

Zeitlin, S.
1939 *The Book of Jubilees, Its Character and Its Significance.* Philadelphia: Dropsie College.

Zevit, Z.
1992 Timber for the Tabernacle: Text, Tradition, and *Realia.* Pp. 136*–43* in *Avraham Biran Volume.* ErIsr 23. Jerusalem: Israel Exploration Society; Hebrew Union College–Jewish Institute of Religion.
2001 *The Religions of Ancient Israel.* London/New York: Continuum.

Ziderman, I.
1987 First Identification of Authentic *Tĕkēlet. BASOR* 265: 25–33.

Zimmerli, W.
1983 *Ezekiel 2.* German orig. 1969. Hermeneia. Philadelphia: Fortress.

Zobel, H. J.
1977 *ʾărôn. TDOT* 1.363–74. Grand Rapids, Mich: Eerdmans.
1986 *ḥeseḏ. TDOT* 5.44–64. Grand Rapids, Mich: Eerdmans.
1993 Das Recht der Witwen und Waisen. Pp. 33–38 in *Gottes Recht als Lebensraum,* ed. P. Mommer et al. Fs. H. J. Boecker. Neukirchen-Vluyn: Neukirchener Verlag.

Zohar, N.
1988 Repentance and Purification: The Significance and Semantics of *ḥṭ't* in the Pentateuch. *JBL* 107: 609–18.

Zohary, M.
1958 ḥelbәnâ. *EM* 3.139–40. Jerusalem: Bialik Institute.
1962 lәbônâ. *EM* 4.418–19. Jerusalem: Bialik Institute.
1968 môr. *EM* 5.439–40. Jerusalem: Bialik Institute.
1976a Qiddâ. *EM* 7.25–26. Jerusalem: Bialik Institute.
1976b Qāne(h), qәnē(h)-bōśem, qāne(h) haṭṭôb. *EM* 7.199–201. Jerusalem: Bialik Institute.

Zohary, M., and C. Rabin
1976 Qinnāmôn, qinnәmon-beśem. *EM* 7.202–3. Jerusalem: Bialik Institute.

Zorell, F.
1927 Der Gottesname "Šaddai" in den alten Übersetzungen. *Bib* 8: 215–19.

Zucconi, L. M.
2005 Can No Physician be Found?: The Influence of Religion on Medical

Pluralism in Ancient Egypt, Mesopotamia and Israel. Ph.D. diss., University of California, San Diego.

Zwickel, W.
1990 *Räucherkult und Räuchergeräte.* OBO 97. Freiburg: Universitäts Verlag; Göttingen: Vandenhoeck & Ruprecht.

ANALYSIS, NOTES AND COMMENTS

◆

PART IV. THE FIRST COVENANT
(EXODUS 19–24)

◆

XVIII. *All that Yahweh spoke we will do and heed* (19:1–24:18)[*]

19 ¹⁽ᴾ⁾ In the third month of Israel's Sons going out from the land of Egypt, on this day, they came to the Sinai Wilderness. ²⁽ᴿ⁾ And they set forth from Rephidim and came to the Sinai Wilderness and camped in the wilderness. ⁽?⁾ And Israel camped there, opposite the mountain, ³⁽ᴱ⁾ but Moses, he ascended to the Deity.

⁽ᴱ/ᴰ⁻ˡⁱᵏᵉ⁾ And Yahweh called to him from the mountain, saying: "Thus you will say to Jacob's house, and tell to Israel's Sons: ⁴'You, you saw what I did to Egypt, and I carried you on vultures' wings and brought you to me. ⁵And now, if you will listen, listen to my voice and keep my Covenant, then you will become for me a treasure beyond all the peoples, for mine is all the earth. ⁶And you, you will become for me a priests' kingdom and a holy nation.' These are the words that you will speak to Israel's Sons."

⁷And Moses came and called to the people's elders and put before them all these words that Yahweh commanded him. ⁸And all the people answered as one and said, "All that Yahweh spoke we will do." And Moses brought the people's words back to Yahweh.

⁹⁽ᴱ⁾ And Yahweh said to Moses, "See: I am coming to you in the nimbus cloud, so that the people may hear during my speaking with you, and also in you they may trust to eternity." ⁽?⁾ And Moses told the people's words to Yahweh.

¹⁰⁽ᴶ⁾ And Yahweh said to Moses, "Go to the people, and you shall sanctify them today and tomorrow, and they shall wash their robes. ¹¹And they must be ready for the third day, for on the third day Yahweh will descend in all the people's *eyes* onto Mount Sinai. ¹²And you shall restrict the people all around, saying, "Guard yourselves (from) ascending on the mountain and infringing upon its edge. Any infringing upon the mountain must be put to death, death. ¹³A hand must not

---

[*] Printed editions of the Hebrew Bible vary in their verse enumeration for chap. 20 after v 13 (see NOTE to 20:1). This edition follows *BHS*, supplying in parentheses the alternative numbering.

touch him; but he must be stoned stoned or shot, shot: whether animal whether man, he shall not live. When the *ram pulls*, they, they shall ascend on the mountain."

¹⁴And Moses descended from the mountain to the people and sanctified the people, and they washed their robes. ¹⁵And he said to the people, "Be ready for three days; don't come near to a woman."

¹⁶And it happened on the third day at morning's happening, ⁽ᴱ⁾and there were *sounds* and lightnings and a heavy cloud on the mountain and a horn's sound, very strong. And all the people who were in the camp quaked. ¹⁷And Moses took the people out to meet the Deity from the camp, and they stationed themselves at the mountain's bottom. ¹⁸⁽ᴶ⁾And Mount Sinai, it smoked, all of it, forasmuch as Yahweh had descended upon it in fire, and its smoke ascended like furnace smoke, and all the mountain quaked greatly. ¹⁹⁽ᴱ⁾And the horn's sound was *going and strengthening* greatly; Moses, he would speak, and the Deity, he would answer him with sound. ²⁰⁽ᴶ⁾And Yahweh descended onto Mount Sinai, to the mountain's head, and Yahweh called Moses to the mountain's head. And Moses ascended.

²¹But Yahweh said to Moses, "Descend, warn the people, lest they break through to Yahweh to see, and many of it fall. ²²And also the priests approaching to Yahweh, they must sanctify themselves, lest Yahweh erupt against them."

²³But Moses said to Yahweh, "The people will not be able to ascend to Mount Sinai, for you, you warned us, saying, 'Restrict the mountain, and you shall sanctify it.' "

²⁴⁽ᴱ⁾And Yahweh said to him, "Go, descend, and you shall ascend, you and Aaron with you; but the priests and the people, they must not break through to ascend to Yahweh, lest he erupt against them."

²⁵So Moses descended to the people and said to them —

20   ¹⁽ᴿ⁾And Deity spoke all these words, saying: ²"I am Yahweh your deity who took you out from the land of Egypt, from a slaves' house.

³"There shall be for you no other gods before my face.

⁴"Don't make for yourself a statue or any image, what is in the heavens above or what is in the earth below or what is in the waters below the earth. ⁵Don't bow to them or serve them, for I am Yahweh your deity, a jealous deity, reckoning fathers' sin upon sons, upon a third and upon a fourth (generation) for my haters, ⁶but doing fidelity to a thousandth (generation) for my lovers and my command-keepers.

⁷"Don't raise Yahweh's name for nothing, for Yahweh will not clear whoever raises his name for nothing.

⁸"Remember the Sabbath day, to sanctify it. ⁹Six days you may work and do your every task, ¹⁰but the seventh day is Sabbath for Yahweh your deity. Don't do any task, you or your son or your daughter, your manservant or your maidservant or your animal or your sojourner who is in your gates. ¹¹For (in) six days Yahweh made the heavens and the earth, the sea and all that is in them, but he rested on the seventh day. Therefore Yahweh blessed the Sabbath day and sanctified it.

¹² "Honor your father and your mother, so that your days may lengthen upon the soil that Yahweh your deity is giving to you.

¹³ "Don't murder.

¹⁴⁽¹³⁾ "Don't commit adultery.

¹⁵⁽¹³⁾ "Don't steal.

¹⁶⁽¹³⁾ "Don't testify against your fellow as a false witness.

¹⁷⁽¹⁴⁾ "Don't covet your fellow's house; don't covet your fellow's wife or his manservant or his maidservant or his bull or his ass or anything of your fellow."

¹⁸⁽¹⁵⁾⁽ᴱ⁾ And all the people were seeing the *sounds* and the *torches* and the horn's sound and the mountain smoking, and the people feared and recoiled and stood from afar. ¹⁹⁽¹⁶⁾ And they said to Moses, "Speak you with us, that we may hear; but Deity must not speak with us, lest we die."

²⁰⁽¹⁷⁾ And Moses said to the people, "Don't fear; because for the sake of testing you has the Deity come, and for the sake of his fear will be *upon your face*, so that you won't sin."

²¹⁽¹⁸⁾ And the people stood from afar, but Moses, he approached to the dark-cloud where the Deity was there.

²²⁽¹⁹⁾⁽ᴱ/ᴰ⁻ˡⁱᵏᵉ⁾ And Yahweh said to Moses, "Thus you will say to Israel's Sons: 'You, you saw that from the sky I spoke with you. ²³⁽²⁰⁾ Don't make along with me silver gods, and gold gods don't make for yourselves. ²⁴⁽²¹⁾ An earthen altar you may make for me, and you will sacrifice on it your Ascending-offerings and your Concluding-offerings, your flock and your herd; in any place where I announce my name, I will come to you and bless you. ²⁵⁽²²⁾ But if an altar of stones you make for me, don't build them *cutstone*, for your blade you shall have lifted against it and profaned it. ²⁶⁽²³⁾ And don't ascend by steps up to my altar, at which your nudity must not be revealed.'

21 ⁽ᴱ?⁾¹ "These are the case-laws that you shall set before them:

² 'When you buy a Hebrew manservant, six years he shall serve, and in the seventh he shall depart as a freeman, gratis. ³ If with his *gap* he enters, with his *gap* he shall depart; if he is a woman's husband, then his woman shall depart with him. ⁴ If his master gives him a woman and she bears him sons or daughters, then the woman and her children, she shall belong to her master, and he, he shall depart with his *gap*.

⁵ 'If the manservant should say, say, "I love my master, my woman and my sons; I will not depart a freeman," ⁶ then his master shall bring him to the Deity and bring him to the door or to the doorpost. And his master shall drill his ear with a drill, and he must serve him forever.

⁷ 'And when a man sells his daughter as a maidservant, she shall not depart as the manservants' departing. ⁸ If she is bad in her master's eyes, who did not engage for her, then he must let her be ransomed; to alien kin he is not entitled to sell her, for his breach of contract with her. ⁹ And if for his son he engages for her, according to the daughters' case he shall do with her. ¹⁰ If another (woman) he takes for himself, her flesh, her covering and her *ʿōnâ* he may not stint. ¹¹ And if these three he does not do for her, then she may depart gratis; there is no silver.

¹² 'Whoever strikes a man and he dies must be put to death, death. ¹³ But the

one who did not lie in wait, but the Deity by happenstance brought it to his hand, then I will set for you a place whither he may flee. ¹⁴ But when a man presumes against his fellow to kill him by premeditation, from beside my altar you may take him to die.

¹⁵ 'Whoever strikes his father or his mother must be put to death, death. ¹⁶ And whoever steals a man — and he sells him and/or he/it is found *in his hand* — must be put to death, death.

¹⁷ 'And whoever curses his father or his mother must be put to death, death.

¹⁸ 'And when men contend, and a man strikes his fellow with a stone or with a fist, and he does not die, but falls to bed, ¹⁹ if he gets up and walks about outside upon his cane, then the striker is cleared; only (for?) his sitting idle he must give, and he must heal, heal.

²⁰ 'And when a man strikes his manservant or his maidservant with the rod, and he dies under his hand, he must be avenged, avenged. ²¹ However, if a day or two days he *stands*, he shall not be avenged, for he is his silver.

²² 'And when men fight, and they strike a pregnant woman, and her child comes out, and there is no injury, he must be fined, fined, as the woman's husband may stipulate against him, and he shall give what is fair. ²³ But if injury there is, then you must give — life for life, ²⁴ eye for eye, tooth for tooth, arm for arm, leg for leg, ²⁵ burn for burn, wound for wound, stripe for stripe.

²⁶ 'And when a man strikes his manservant's eye or his maidservant's eye and ruins it, as a freeman he must release him for his eye. ²⁷ And if his manservant's tooth or his maidservant's tooth he makes fall out, as a freeman he must release him for his tooth.

²⁸ 'And when a bull gores a man or woman and he dies, the bull must be stoned, stoned, and its meat may not be eaten; but the bull's owner is clear. ²⁹ But if it was a gorer bull *from yesterday-the day before*, and it was warned about to its owner, but he did not guard it, and it caused a man or a woman to die, the bull shall be stoned, and also its owner must be put to death. ³⁰ If a ransom is imposed upon him, then he must give his life's redemption, as whatever is imposed upon him. ³¹ Whether a son it gores or a daughter it gores, according to this case shall be done to it. ³² If a manservant the bull gores or a maidservant, silver, thirty shekels, he must give to his master, and the bull must be stoned.

³³ 'And when a man opens a pit or when a man digs a pit and does not cover it, and a bull or an ass falls therein, ³⁴ the pit's owner must reimburse; silver he must restore to its owner, and the dead shall be his.

³⁵ 'And when a man's bull injures his fellow's bull, and it dies, then they shall sell the living bull and divide its silver, and also the dead they shall divide. ³⁶ Or (if) it was known that it was a gorer bull *from yesterday-the day before*, and its owner did not guard it, he must reimburse, reimburse, bull for bull, and the dead shall be his.

³⁷ 'When a man steals a bull or a sheep and slaughters it or sells it, five large cattle for the bull he must reimburse, or four small cattle for the sheep. 22 ¹ If in breaking in the thief is found, and he strikes him and he dies, there is no *bloodiness* for him. ² If the sun shone upon him, there is *bloodiness* for him; he must pay,

pay. If he has nothing, then he shall be sold for his theft. ³ If the theft, from bull to ass to sheep, is found, found in his hand alive, twofold he must pay.

⁴ 'When a man clears a field or vineyard, and he releases his cattle, and it clears in another's field, he shall pay, pay from his field according to its yield; and if the entire field it clears, his field's best and his vineyard's best he shall pay. ⁵ If fire goes out and reaches briars, and stacked grain or the standing grain or the field is consumed, the fire-setter must pay, pay for the burning.

⁶ 'When a man gives to his fellow silver or objects to keep, and it is stolen from the man's house, if the thief is found, he shall pay twofold. ⁷ If the thief is not found, then the house owner shall approach to the Deity: if he did not send his hand against his fellow's property. . . . ⁸ In any crime case about a bull, about an ass, about a sheep, about a robe, about anything lost concerning which one says that, "That's it," unto the Deity the case of the two of them shall come. Whomever Deity finds guilty shall pay twofold to his fellow.

⁹ 'When a man gives to his fellow an ass or a bull or a sheep or any animal to keep, and it dies or suffers a break or is raided without one seeing, ¹⁰ an oath by Yahweh will be between the two of them: if he did not send his hand against his fellow's property. . . . And its owner shall accept, and he shall not pay. ¹¹ If it is stolen, stolen from with him, he must pay its owner. ¹² If it is torn, torn, let him bring it, evidence of the tearing; he shall not pay.

¹³ 'And when a man borrows from his fellow, and it suffers a break or dies, its owner not with it, he must pay, pay. ¹⁴ If its owner is with it, he shall not pay. If it is hired, it came in its payment.

¹⁵ 'And when a man seduces a virgin who was not betrothed and lies with her, he must pay, pay her bride-price as a wife to him. ¹⁶ If her father refuses, refuses to give her to him, silver he must weigh out, according to the virgins' bride-price.

¹⁷ 'A sorceress don't let live.

¹⁸ 'Everyone who lies with an animal must be put to death, death.

¹⁹ 'Whoever sacrifices to other gods must be destroyed.

²⁰ 'And a sojourner, don't afflict and don't oppress him, for sojourners you were in the land of Egypt. ²¹ Any widow or orphan don't oppress. ²² If you oppress, oppress him—for if he should cry out, cry out to me, I shall hear, hear his cry— ²³ then my *nose* will flare, and I shall kill you by the sword, and your wives will be widows and your sons orphans.

²⁴ 'If silver you lend my people, the poor man with you, don't be to him as a creditor; don't lay *bite* upon him. ²⁵ If you accept, accept as collateral your fellow's robe, by the sun's *entry* return it to him. ²⁶ For it alone is his covering, it is his robe for his skin: in what will he lie down? And it will happen, when he cries out to me, then I will hear, for I am gracious.

²⁷ 'Deity don't curse, and a leader among your people don't execrate.

²⁸ 'Your fullness and your *demaʿ* don't postpone. The firstborn of your sons you must give to me. ²⁹ You must do likewise for your bull, for your flock: seven days it will be with its mother; on the eighth day you must give it to me.

³⁰ And Holiness men you must become for me, and *torn meat* don't eat; to the dog you must throw it.

23   ¹'Don't carry a false rumor. Don't set your hand with a wicked man to be a criminal witness. ²Don't be consorting after a multitude, and don't testify about a dispute inclining after a multitude in order to influence. ³And a pauper don't exalt in his lawsuit.

⁴'When you encounter your enemy's bull or his ass astray, return, return it to him. ⁵When you see your adversary's ass recumbent under its burden and would refrain from leaving (it) to him, you must leave, leave (it) with him.

⁶'Don't influence your pauper's verdict in his lawsuit. ⁷From a false *word* keep distant, and an innocent or righteous one don't kill; for I shall not vindicate a guilty one. ⁸And a bribe don't take; for the bribe, it blinds the sighted and perverts the righteous's words.

⁹'And a sojourner don't oppress; for you, you have known the sojourner's soul, for sojourners you were in the land of Egypt.

¹⁰'And six years you may sow your land and gather its harvest. ¹¹But the seventh, abandon it and leave it alone, that your people's paupers may eat, and their leftovers the field animal may eat. So you will do for your vineyard, for your *olive*.

¹²'Six days you may do your doings, but on the seventh day you will cease, so that your bull and your ass may rest, and your maidservant's son and the sojourner may catch breath.

¹³'And through all that I have said to you, you will *keep* yourselves, and the name of other gods' don't mention. It shall not be heard upon your mouth.

¹⁴'Three *feet* you must celebrate to me in the year. ¹⁵The Unleavened Bread Festival you must keep: seven days you must eat unleavened bread as I commanded you, on the occasion of the New Grain Month, for on it you went out from Egypt. And my Face must not be seen emptily. ¹⁶And the Harvest Festival, the firstfruits of your produce that you sow in the field, and the Ingathering Festival at the year's *departure*, in your ingathering your produce from the field. ¹⁷Three times in the year all your malehood must appear to the Lord Yahweh's Face.

¹⁸'Don't offer with leavened food my Slaughter-offering blood, and my *festival* fat must not linger until morning.

¹⁹'Your soil's first firstfruits you shall bring to Yahweh your deity's House.

'Don't cook a kid in its mother's milk.

²⁰[D-like]'See: I am sending a Messenger before you to guard you on the way and to bring you to the place that I have prepared. ²¹ Guard yourself from his *face* and heed his voice; don't rebel against him, for he will not *lift* your offense, for my Name will be within him. ²²But if you heed, heed his voice and do all that I speak, then I will oppose your opponents and attack your attackers.

²³'For my Messenger will go before you and bring you to the Amorite and the Hittite and the Perizzite and the Canaanite and the Hivvite and the Jebusite, and I will eradicate him. ²⁴Don't bow to their gods and don't serve them and don't do like their deeds. Rather, you must destroy, destroy them and smash, smash their pillars.

²⁵'And you shall serve Yahweh your deity, and he will bless your bread and your water, and I will remove illness from your midst. ²⁶There will not be a bereft or barren (female) in your land; your days' number I will make full.

²⁷'My terror I will release before you and discomfit all the peoples that you come against them, and I will set all your enemies *with the back of the neck toward you*. ²⁸And I will send the ṣirʿâ before you, and it will expel the Hivvite, the Canaanite and the Hittite from before you. ²⁹I will not expel him before you in one year, lest the land become a waste and the field animals multiply against you. ³⁰Little by little I will expel him before you, until that you bear fruit and acquire the land. ³¹And I will set your border from the Suph Sea and to the Philistines' Sea, and from Desert to the River, for I will give into your hand the land's inhabitants, and you will expel them before you.

³²Don't *cut* with them or with their gods a covenant. ³³They may not dwell in your land, lest they cause you to sin against me; when you serve their gods, indeed it will become for you as a snare.' "

24 ¹⁽ᴱ⁾But to Moses he said, "Ascend to Yahweh, you and Aaron, Nadab and Abihu, and seventy from Israel's elders, and you shall bow down from afar. ²And Moses alone will approach to Yahweh, but they, they may not approach, and the people, they may not ascend with him."

³And Moses came and recounted to the people all Yahweh's words and all the case-laws. And the people answered in one voice and said, "All the words that Yahweh spoke we will do." ⁴And Moses wrote down all Yahweh's words.

And he got up early in the morning and built an altar *under* the mountain and twelve pillar for Israel's twelve tribes. ⁵And he sent the youths of Israel's Sons, and they *sent up* Ascending-offerings and *slaughtered* Slaughter-offerings, Concluding-offerings to Yahweh, bulls. ⁶And Moses took half the blood and put in the bowls, and half the blood he cast against the altar. ⁷And he took the Covenant Document and read in the people's ears. And they said, "All that Yahweh spoke we will do and heed."

⁸Then Moses took the blood and cast upon the people and said, "See: the Covenant blood that Yahweh has *cut* with you by all these words."

⁹Then Moses and Aaron, Nadab and Abihu and seventy from Israel's elders ascended ¹⁰and saw Israel's deity. And under his feet: like lapis lazuli brickwork, and like the heavens' *bone* for clarity. ¹¹And against the elite of Israel's Sons he did not send forth his arm, but they beheld the Deity and ate and drank.

¹²And Yahweh said to Moses, "Ascend to me to the mountain and be there, that I may give you the stone tablets, the Direction and the command that I have written to direct them."

¹³So Moses and Joshua his attendant got up, and Moses ascended to the Deity's mountain. ¹⁴But to the elders he had said, "Stay for us in this (place) until when we return to you. See: Aaron and Hur are with you; whoever has *words*, let him approach to them. ¹⁵And Moses ascended to the mountain, ⁽ᴾ⁾**and the cloud covered the mountain. ¹⁶And Yahweh's Glory settled upon Mount Sinai, and the cloud covered it six days.**

And he called to Moses on the seventh day from inside the cloud. ¹⁷Now, the appearance of Yahweh's Glory was like a consuming fire on the mountain's head to the eyes of Israel's Sons. ¹⁸And Moses came inside the cloud, ⁽ᴱ/ᴿ⁾and he ascended to the mountain. ⁽ᴱ⁾And Moses was on the mountain forty day and forty night.

ANALYSIS

TEXTUAL NOTES

19:1. *from the land of Egypt.* Against MT-Sam *mē'ereṣ miṣrāyim,* Syr lacks "land of," possibly lost by haplography *(m . . . m)* in its *Vorlage.*

Sinai. Syr has "Sin" as in MT 16:1; 17:1; Num 33:11–12. In Exod 19:2, however, Syr has "Sinai."

19:2. *and camped in the wilderness.* This clause is absent in LXX, probably due to homoioarkton with the following phrase *(wyḥnw . . . wyḥn),* or possibly in order to streamline a redundant original (cf. Wevers 1990: 292).

19:3. *to the Deity.* LXX has "to the God's *mountain,*" as if reading **'l hr h'lhym* for MT *'l h'lhym.* While haplography by homoioarkton *(h . . . h)* in MT-Sam is conceivable, more likely we have a deliberate effort to minimize the description of God as coming bodily to earth (Tov 2001: 128). Moreover, LXX solves a logical problem: if Moses is already before God, how can God summon him (Wevers 1990: 293)? In LXX, Moses presumably ascends from the valley to the foot of Mount Sinai. Cf. TEXTUAL NOTE on "from the mountain" below.

Yahweh. LXX, Kenn 199 and Syr have "the God." Throughout chap. 19 (see TEXTUAL NOTES to vv 7, 8, 18, 21, 22, 23, 24) and elsewhere, LXX often has "the God" for MT "Yahweh" (see Wevers 1992: 241). Since the other Versions generally support MT, Wevers (1990: 305) infers that LXX was chary of using God's proper name in describing his interaction with Moses. The less intimate appellation "God" was considered more reverent.

from the mountain. LXX[B] has "from the sky." One might initially adjudge this an inner-Greek confusion between *oros* 'mountain' and *ouranos* 'sky,' but the Hebrew MS Kenn 1 similarly has *min-haššāmayim* 'from the sky.' More likely "from the sky" is an intentional exegetical correction: assuming Moses has already ascended the mountain, it makes more sense for God to speak from the sky (cf. 20:22[19]). Yahweh promises to alight on Sinai in 19:9, 11, and will do so in 19:18, 20. The LXX admittedly reading fixes problems in chap. 19 (see SOURCE and REDACTION ANALYSES)—but for that very reason it should probably be rejected.

Israel's Sons. Kenn 13 (?), 109, one LXX MS (MS 799) and apparently the Severus scroll (Ginsburg 1966: 417) read *lbyt yśr'l* 'to Israel's *House.*'

† 19:4. *what I did.* Sam and Kenn 6, 84, 109, 129, 189, 248, 253 prepose the direct object marker *'t,* perhaps rightly; it could have dropped from MT due to homoioarkton *(' . . . ').* But MT is also attractive as the shorter text.

to Egypt. One might alternatively vocalize *lmṣrym* (MT *ləmiṣrāyim*) as **lammiṣrîm* 'to the *Egyptians.*' Superficially, the ancient Versions support this emendation, but in fact they consistently interpret *mṣrym* in this manner, whether appropriately or not. Better, then, to keep to standard MT. The common MT variant *bəmiṣrāyim* 'in Egypt' (Kennicott 1776–80: 146; de Rossi 1784–85: 62–63) refers unambiguously to the land of Egypt.

19:5. *a treasure.* LXX adds "people," assimilating to Deut 7:6; 14:2; 26:18.

all the peoples. Syr expands: "of the earth," reinforcing the connection with the following clause. *Tg. Ps.-Jonathan* features the same expansion, but then has lost the rest of the verse by haplography.

19:6. *Israel's Sons.* As often, Syr paraphrases: "Israel's *House.*"

19:7. *the people's elders.* LXX^A, *Fragmentary Targum* V, Kenn 84 and a Genizah MS *(BHS)* have "*Israel's* elders."

Yahweh. LXX has "the God." See TEXTUAL NOTE to 19:3, "Yahweh."

him. LXX^{AFM} have "them," i.e., the people.

19:8. *Yahweh spoke.* LXX has "the God said," not only using a different divine name (see TEXTUAL NOTE to 19:3, "Yahweh"), but possibly reflecting *^ʾ*mr* 'said' in the *Vorlage*, vs. MT-Sam *dibber* 'spoke' (Wevers 1990: 296); contrast LXX 24:3, 7. Syr, too, has "said" not "spoke."

† *we will do.* LXX adds "and heed," harmonizing with 24:7 (MT) and 24:3 (LXX). Alternatively, an original *wnšmʿ was dropped by haplography before *wyšb* 'and (he) brought back' (D. N. Freedman, privately).

the people's words. LXX^B has "these words," as in 19:7.

to Yahweh. LXX has "to *the God.*" See TEXTUAL NOTE to 19:3, "Yahweh."

† 19:9. *in the nimbus cloud.* For MT's unique *bʿb hʿnn*, Sam has *bʿby hʿnn* 'in the nimbus clouds,' 'in the cloud's *denseness*' or, conceivably, 'in *my* cloud, the nimbus' (S. Dolansky Overton, privately); *Samaritan Tg.*, however, appears to support MT. LXX has "in a cloud *pillar*," either paraphrasing or accurately rendering a third variant, *bʿmwd ʿnn, as in 13:21, etc.

to Yahweh. The fragment 2QExod^b uniquely continues with 34:10, before breaking off.

19:10. *Go to the people.* LXX has "*descend to warn* the people," probably harmonizing with 19:21.

† 19:12. *the people.* Sam has "the mountain" (cf. TEXTUAL NOTE to 19:18, "the mountain"), a variant possibly found also in Rabbinic texts (cf. ibn Ezra). Sam is probably a harmonization with 19:23, where Moses says that Yahweh told him to restrict *the mountain.* One might indeed expect the mountain rather than the people to be cordoned off, but it matters little: the point is that the people and the mountain are separated from one another (Cassuto 1967: 234; see, however, NOTE, "around"). Syr solves the minor problem by paraphrasing, "*warn* the people." For further evidence that Sam is secondary, see following TEXTUAL NOTE.

saying. Sam has "and to the people say." Assuming the originality of MT throughout the verse, this is a secondary alteration, made after "people" was changed to "mountain" (see TEXTUAL NOTE above).

Vg, which otherwise follows MT, instead of "saying" has "*and say to them.*" What stood in Jerome's *Vorlage* is unclear. He may have been reading a conflation of MT and Sam ("And you shall restrict the people all around [MT], and to the people say" [Sam]), which he compressed for stylistic reasons.

yourselves (from) ascending. Since a Niphʿal does not ordinarily take a direct object, we might make "from" explicit by restoring *lākem mēʿălôt for MT *lākem ʿălôt*, the mem having dropped either by haplography during copying or by mishearing during dictation (Ehrlich 1908: 338). But there are sufficient parallels to make MT an attractive *lectio difficilior* (see GKC §122*a–b*).

19:13. *shot, shot.* For MT *yrh yyrh,* Sam has an aural/graphic variant *yr' yr'h.* The first word is most naturally read as **yārō',* the infinite absolute of *yr'* 'fear'; the second appears to be **yir'e(h)* 'he must see.' *Samaritan Tg.,* however, regards both as active forms of the verb "to see." But neither "fear" nor "see" would make sense in context, and so MT is preferable.

When the ram pulls. For MT *bimšōk hayyōbēl,* LXX has "when the sounds and the trumpets and the cloud go away from the mountain." Again, LXX is attempting to make sense of its incoherent *Vorlage* (cf. TEXTUAL NOTES to 19:3). Moses has been warned that Yahweh's descent upon the mountain will endanger Israel (19:12). According to 19:16–19, thunder, lightning, cloud and horn blasts signal God's presence. Since we would expect Israel to ascend *after* God departs, LXX has freely rewritten the text (Wevers 1990: 300–1). Even the more literal versions of Symmachus ("when the clamor, the trumpeting, has been drawn off") and Theodotion ("when the *Iōbēl* departs") follow the general approach of LXX (see NOTE), as does Syr ("when the trumpet falls silent").

19:14. *sanctified the people.* LXX paraphrases: "sanctified *them.*"

19:15. *for three days.* Syr and Vg read or paraphrase "for the *third day,*" harmonizing with 19:11, 16. Sam and Kenn 109 have "*the* three days *(lšlšt hymym),*" tantamount to "for the *aforesaid* three days." True, three days have already been mentioned (19:11). But 19:11 is *Yahweh's* speech to Moses, while 19:15 is *Moses'* report to the people. Thus the article, though not impossible, is probably secondary.

19:16. *the mountain.* LXX specifies: "Mount *Sinai.*"

a horn's sound. Sam has "*the* horn's sound *(wqwl hšwpr),*" referring back to *hayyōbēl* 'ram, ram's horn' in 19:13 (cf. TEXTUAL NOTE to 19:15).

19:17. *the mountain's bottom.* LXX^B specifies: "under Mount *Sinai.*"

† 19:18. *Yahweh had descended upon it.* While MT has *yrd 'lyw yhwh,* Sam and Kenn 109, 152 have *yrd yhwh 'lyw;* LXX MSS also vary in word order. Either reading could be original, and the difference is probably random. LXX calls the Deity "the God"; see TEXTUAL NOTE to 19:3, "Yahweh."

† *the mountain.* Kenn 173, 191, 248, 426, 476 (?), 528, 551 (?), 642, Rossi 405, 585, the Paris MS of *Fragmentary Targum* P (Klein 1980: 1.83) and LXX have "the *people,*" i.e., **h'm,* for MT-Sam-Tgs.-Syr *hhr* 'the mountain.' Since the people quake in 19:16, in 19:18 MT is the more diverse and attractive reading. (*Fragmentary Targum* V fully assimilates 19:18 to 19:16, "And all the people quaked *that were in the camp.*") Dillmann (1880: 198) objects to MT on the grounds that only people can *ḥrd* 'fear, tremble.' But, even if this were so, the mountain might simply be personified, as in Ps 68:16–17; 114:4–6 (cf. Jacob 1992: 539); Hyatt (1971: 202) cites the quaking of inanimate objects in Isa 41:5 and Ezek 26:18. For a parallel case of confusion between "mountain" and "people," see TEXTUAL NOTE to 19:12, "the people."

quaked. Since in LXX the subject is the people (previous TEXTUAL NOTE), the verb *ḥrd* is paraphrased as *exestē* 'were astonished.'

19:19. *the horn's sound*. LXX "the trumpet's sounds" assimilates to the plural in 19:16—where the word *qōlōt/phōnai* 'sounds' refers to thunder—mediated by 19:13 (LXX), which mentions "sounds and trumpets."

† *with sound*. So MT (*bəqôl*) and LXX (*phōnēi*). On the possibility of reading *baqqôl 'with *the* (aforesaid) sound,' see NOTE.

19:20. *to the mountain's head* (second time). LXX has "*on* the mountaintop," as earlier in the verse. *Tg. Neofiti I* and *Fragmentary Targum* have "*from* the mountain's (head)," which we might have expected (cf. *Mek. baḥōdeš* 4).

19:21. *Yahweh said*. LXX has "*the God* said." See TEXTUAL NOTE to 19:3, "Yahweh."

Moses. LXX formulaically adds "saying."

to Yahweh. LXX has "to *the God*." See TEXTUAL NOTE to 19:3, "Yahweh."

19:22. *to Yahweh*. LXX MSS have either "to *the God*" or "to Lord (i.e., Yahweh), *the God*." See TEXTUAL NOTE to 19:3, "Yahweh."

19:23. *to Yahweh*. LXX has "to *the God*." See TEXTUAL NOTE to 19:3, "Yahweh."

19:24. *Aaron*. A few MSS of LXX and of Vetus Latina, Syr, a Genizah Targum (Klein 1986: 24) and Rossi 721 explicate: "Aaron *your brother*," as in 4:14; 7:1–2, etc.

to Yahweh. LXX has "to *the God*." See TEXTUAL NOTE to 19:3, "Yahweh."

he erupt. LXX specifies "*Yahweh* erupt," harmonizing with 19:22.

19:25. *descended*. Sam, Rossi 592 and *Tgs. Ps.-Jonathan* and *Neofiti I* add "from the mountain."

* 20:1. *Deity*. LXX, Vg and *Tgs*. have "(the) Lord," i.e., Yahweh.

spoke LXX^A specifies "to Moses."

20:4. *a statue*. Syr expands "*any* statue."

† *or any image*. The conjunction is absent in Kenn 4, 80, 129, 674 and in standard MT Deut 5:8, but present in many MSS and Versions of both Exodus and Deuteronomy (cf. also Deut 4:16, *pesel təmûnat kol sāmel* 'a statue [of?] the image of any icon). The shorter text may be correct. If so, then *təmûnâ* may denote not the idol itself but the form of the thing depicted (Dillmann 1880: 210).

†† 20:5. *jealous*. MT is vocalized *qannā'*, but Nash Papyrus has *qnw'*, a synonymous but rarer form found in Josh 24:19; Nah 1:2. Most likely Nash preserves the original pronunciation (*qannō'*), MT the original spelling (*qn'*).

† *upon a third*. Kenn 109, 181 and 369 have a variant *'l bnym (w)'l bny bnym (w)'l šlšym* 'upon sons *(and)* upon sons' sons *(and)* upon a third . . . ,' as in 34:7. This is probably the original text of Exod 20:5; Deut 5:9 as well, since it is both logical and liable to haplography (D. N. Freedman, privately). But the corruption probably occurred prior to canonization, and so is not remedied in my translation (see further under SOURCE ANALYSIS and NOTE). Many Sam MSS agree with Deut 5:9 (standard MT), inserting "and" before "upon sons' sons."

---

* The Decalog reappears in Deut 5:6–21(18) with numerous differences, major and minor. The following text critical analysis assumes that the two recensions differed maximally at the point of canonization, and were later harmonized to varying degrees in the Versions.

20:6. *but doing.* The conjunction is absent in some witnesses to Deuteronomy (e.g., 4QDeutⁿ, 4QPhylJ) but is probably original in Exodus.

my command. Against Exod 20:6 "my," MT Deut 5:10 Kethibh *mṣwtw* probably represents *miṣwōtāw* 'his commands,' less likely *miṣwātô* 'his command' (Deut 5:10 Qere = Exod 20:6). On waw-yodh confusion, see Cross (1961a); Qimron (1972).

20:7. *Yahweh will not.* LXXᴮ expands "Yahweh *your God* will not," as earlier in the verse.

whoever. 4QMezA has *k[l ']šr* 'anyone who,' supported by 4QPhylJ,O—all, strictly speaking, witnesses to Deuteronomy rather than Exodus.

20:8. *Remember.* For MT *zākôr,* Sam has *šmwr* 'keep,' as in Deut 5:12. MT is preferable as the more diverse text. Jacob (1992: 582) observes the same phenomenon apropos of the "New Grain Month": in Exod 13:3 one must "remember" it; in Deut 16:1 one must "keep it."

to sanctify it. Deut 5:12 expands: "as Yahweh your deity commanded you."

20:10. *but the seventh day.* Nash Papyrus, Kenn 5, 69, 129, 244, LXX, Vg and various Qumran witnesses to Deuteronomy (4QDeutⁿ, 4QPhylB,G,J, 8QPhyl) have "but *on* the Sabbath day" *(wbywm),* expanding and assimilating to Exod 16:26; 31:15; 35:2. The shortest reading is 4QMezA, "the seventh day," but this witness is too marginal to be followed here.

Yahweh. Absent in LXXᴬ.

† *any task.* Sam (Sadaqa 1964: 30; *Samaritan Tg.;* pace von Gall 1918: 157), LXX, Nash Papyrus, Syr MSS, Jub 50:7, Vg and many Syr MSS insert "in it" *(bh/bw),* as do various witnesses to Deut 5:14 (for parallels, cf. Exod 12:16; 35:2; Jer 17:24). While one tends to regard *bh* as an expansion, there is a possiblity of parablepsis with the preceding *t'śh* 'do' (homoioteleuton). One could also argue that the shorter text represents an assimilation to passages such as Lev 16:29; 23 *passim;* Numbers 28–29; Deut 16:8; Jer 17:22.

your manservant. Many MT MSS (Kennicott 1776–80: 148; a Genizah MS [*BHS*]) and early printed editions (Ginsburg 1926: 108), Syr and *Tg. Onqelos* insert "and," as in Deut 5:14 (standard MT). *Tg. Ps.-Jonathan* omits the manservant entirely.

† *or your animal.* Sam lacks "or," perhaps rightly—4QDeutⁿ, admittedly not a witness to Exodus, lacks most conjunctions in this series—while Kenn 155 and *Tg. Ps.-Jonathan* omit the animal entirely. 4QMezA, however, replaces "your animal" with "your bull or your ass," derived from Deut 5:14 (but without the initial conjunction), while LXX and Nash Papyrus offer a conflation: "*your bull or your ass* or *all* your animal(s)." While in theory the mention of bull and ass could be original, fallen from MT by haplography, the presence of "all" betrays Deuteronomy's influence upon LXX and Nash Papyrus.

20:11. *For.* Verse 11 is entirely different in Deut 5:15: "And you shall remember that a manservant you were in the land of Egypt, but Yahweh your deity took you out from there with a strong arm and with an extended limb; therefore Yahweh your deity commanded you to do the Sabbath day." Possibly the original Decalog underlying both Exodus and Deuteronomy contained a simple injunction to keep/remember the Sabbath, without any justification at all (see p. 146).

the sea. Some Sam MSS, many MT and *Tg. Onqelos* MSS (de Rossi 1784–85: 64), LXX, Vg, Syr, *Tg. Ps.-Jonathan* and *Fragmentary Targum* have *"and* the sea" (**w't hym*).

the Sabbath day. Nash Papyrus, LXX, *Bib. Ant.* 11:8 and Syr have instead "the *seventh* day," probably borrowed from Gen 2:3.

20:12. *mother.* Deut 5:16 expands: "as Yahweh your deity commanded you" (cf. TEXTUAL NOTE to 20:8).

so that. LXX and Nash Papyrus insert "so that it will be well for you, and," as in Deut 5:16. This seems to be original to Deuteronomy, since the phrase is characteristically Deuteronomic (Deut 5:29[26]; 6:18; 12:25, 28; 22:7; cf. also Deut 4:40; 6:3). Given the Versions' tendency to harmonize Exodus and Deuteronomy, one hesitates to follow this longer reading. Admittedly, however, there are other traces of Deuteronomic language in the Exodus Decalog (see pp. 145–46), and the sequence *ləmaʿan . . . ləmaʿan* would be ripe for haplography (cf. Aejmelaeus 1987: 85–86).

† *the soil.* LXX has instead "the good land," as if reading **h'rṣ ḥṭwbh,* a Deuteronomic expression (Deut 3:25; 4:22; 8:7, and esp. 8:10), albeit absent from Deut 5:16 in both MT and LXX. D. N. Freedman (privately) suggests that the LXX *Vorlage* and original text was **hā'ădāmâ haṭṭôbâ,* reduced in MT by parablepsis.

† 20:13–15. *murder . . . adultery . . . steal.* Deut 5:18–21(18) introduces the second and third negative commands with "and" (*wəlō [']*). For these three prohibitions, my translation follows the sequence of MT in both Exod 20:13–15 and Deut 5:17–19 (also Josephus *Ant.* 3.91; Matt 19:18). But there is considerable room for doubt. LXX[B] Exod 20:13–15 has: "adultery . . . steal . . . murder" (also Philo *Decal.* 36), while LXX Deut 5:17–19 and Nash Papyrus have: "adultery . . . murder . . . steal" (also Luke 18:20; Rom 13:9; Philo *Decalogue* 51, *Quis her.* 173, and assorted Church Fathers). Jas 2:11 and *Bib. Ant.* 11:10–11 forbid adultery and murder in that order, omitting theft entirely, thus supporting any of the above except MT. (Actually, the LXX situation is even more complicated, with MSS disagreeing among themselves; however, LXX[B] is probably original [cf. Wevers 1990: 314].) Hosea and Jeremiah both seemingly quote the Decalog: Hos 4:2 has "murder . . . steal . . . adultery" (preceded by oath-breaking), while Jer 7:9 has "steal, murder, adultery" (followed by a false oath; see also the sequence "thief . . . adulterers" in Ps 50:18).

The simplistic explanation for this variety is that the Decalogs of Exodus and Deuteronomy originally differed in order, as in LXX. But that should have left us with two versions, not three or more. Most likely, over the centuries all six possible permutations have appeared somewhere. Even a single writer such as Philo could be inconsistent; see further Freund (1989). For a comparable confusion in the order of apodictic laws, see TEXTUAL NOTE to 21:15–16.

20:16(13). *false.* Nash Papyrus replaces MT-Sam *šeqer* with its synonym *šāw('),* as in Deut 5:20 (standard MT).

20:17(14). *house . . . wife.* LXX, 4QBibPar, Nash Papyrus (reconstructed) and Kenn 1 (?) 82 (?), 622 reverse the direct objects vis-à-vis MT Exodus, in agreement with Deut 5:21(18). Also, the Vg *Vorlage* may have used a different verb for the second "covet," i.e., *tit'awwe(h)*, derived from Deuteronomy. (Nash Papyrus is unclear here; see Cooke 1903: 43.) In Sam and Kenn 5, 69, 84, 109, 193, 325, the second "don't covet" is preceded by *w-* 'and.'

† *or his manservant.* Kenn 4, 109, 181, 186, 204, 206, 674 have simply *'bdw* (without the conjunction), possibly original. Other witnesses offer longer readings: Sam has *śdhw 'bdw* '*his field,* his manservant' (also Sam Deut 5:21[18]; 4QPhylG), while MT Deut 5:21(18) and LXX (both Exodus and Deuteronomy) have *śdhw w'bdw* '*his field or* his manservant'). Kenn 136, 150 (?), 435, 593, 681 and Nash Papyrus also include "his field," but Nash is damaged; we cannot tell whether a conjunction followed. See also following TEXTUAL NOTE.

† *or his bull.* Sam Exod 20:17(14) and MT Deut 5:21(18) lack the conjunction, perhaps rightly. Since this passage contains a sequence of terms beginning and ending with waw, we would expect such variation, especially if the text originally lacked word divisions (see vol. I, INTRODUCTION, p. 46). We should also be open to the possibility that the longer readings are original, given abundant opportunities for parablepsis.

his ass. After this, LXX adds "or all his animals," derived from 20:10 (see TEXTUAL NOTE, "or your animal").

of your fellow. Sam features a substantial plus at the end of the verse, a pastiche of Deut 7:1; 11:29–30; 27:2–8 in the Samaritan version, in order to legitimate the Samaritans' claim that Shechem, not Jerusalem, was God's favored sanctuary (see Tov 2001: 94–95): "And it will happen, when Yahweh your deity brings you to the Canaanite's land, whither you are coming to acquire it, then you shall erect for yourself big stones and plaster them with plaster, and write on the stones all the words of this Direction. And it will happen, in your crossing the Jordan, then you shall erect these stones that I am commanding you today on Mount Gerizim, and you shall build there an altar to Yahweh your deity, an altar of stones. Don't lift iron against them; (of) whole stones you will build Yahweh your deity's altar, and you will send up upon it Ascending-offerings to Yahweh your deity, and you will sacrifice Concluding-offerings and eat there and rejoice before Yahweh your deity. That mountain is across the Jordan, *behind* (west of) the way of the sun's *entry* (setting) in the Canaanite's land, who dwells in the Arabah opposite the Gilgal, by the Moreh Terebinth, opposite Shechem."

20:18(15). *seeing the sounds and the torches.* Sam and probably 4QpaleoExod^m "fix" the jarring zeugma (see NOTE) by insertion and rearrangement: "*and all the people were hearing the* sounds *and the horn's sound,* and seeing the torches."

the people (second time). Sam, LXX, a Genizah MS *(BHS)*, Kenn 109 and *Tg. Pseudo-Jonathan* have "*all* the people," as earlier in the verse.

†† *feared.* The *BHS* apparatus is quite misleading here. Where MT and *Tg. Onqelos* have *wayyar(')* 'and . . . saw (sing.),' Sam reads *wyr'w* 'and saw (pl.),' supported by *Samaritan Tg.*, Syr, Kenn 129 (?) and *Tgs. Ps.-Jonathan* and *Neofiti I.* The plural participles of LXX *(phobēthentes)* and Vg *(perterriti)*, however, reflect a form of the verb *yr'* 'fear,' either **wayyīrā(')* (sing.) or more likely **wayyīrǝ'û* (pl.). Thus, there are two potential original consonantal readings, *wyr'* and *wyr'w*, each with two possible vocalizations.

My translation "feared" follows LXX-Vg. MT is redundant, since the verse begins "and all the people were *seeing*." Moreover, in v 20, Moses tells the people, "*Fear* not," suggesting their fear was already mentioned (note also *yir'ātô* 'his fear'). We cannot be certain, however, since MT makes sense and is to some extent *lectio difficilior*. (D. N. Freedman privately compares 1 Kgs 19:3, where standard MT reads "saw," but various MSS and Versions read "feared.")

and recoiled. The verb seems to be absent from LXX. Perhaps *wyn'w* was accidentally dropped from the *Vorlage* because of similarity to the following *wy'mdw*. Wevers (1990: 315), however, more plausibly suggests that LXX has deliberately compressed the quasi-synonymous "feared" and "recoiled."

20:19(16). *To Moses.* In Sam, 4QpaleoGen-Exod[1] and 4QpaleoExod[m], the verse continues, borrowing from Deut 5:24(21)–27(24), "See: Yahweh our deity let us see his honor and his greatness, and his voice we heard from the fire's midst. This day we saw that Deity may speak to Man and he can live. And now, why should we die, for this great fire will consume us; if we shall continue to hear Yahweh our deity's voice any longer, then we shall die. For who (is there) of all flesh that has heard the living Deity's voice speaking from the fire's midst and lived? Approach you and hear all that Yahweh our deity may say, and you, you speak to us all that Yahweh our deity speaks to you, that we may heed and do. But the Deity must not speak with us, lest we die."

† *that we may hear.* The phrase is absent from LXX, perhaps rightly, although haplography in the sequence *wnšm'h w'l* is possible (homoioarkton).

† *Deity.* Sam and possibly the LXX *Vorlage* read *h'lhym* 'the Deity,' against MT *'ĕlōhîm*.

† 20:20(17). *to the people.* LXX has simply "to *them*." This could be deliberate abbreviation during translation, although it is possible that the LXX *Vorlage* already had **lhm* or *'lyhm* (the latter more closely resembles in both shape and sound MT *'l h'm* 'to the people'). It is not certain which is the original reading, but the large amount of probable paraphrase in this section of LXX makes MT seem preferable.

has the Deity come. LXX adds "to you." Although an original reading **b' h'lhym 'l(y)km* is conceivable, being susceptible to haplography, more likely LXX is again paraphrasing.

20:21(18). *the people.* Many LXX MSS, Vetus Latina and *Bib. Ant.* 11:15 read "*all* the people."

where the Deity was there. In Sam, 4QpaleoGen-Exod[1] (Sanderson 1986: 208), 4QpaleoExod[m], 4QBibPar, 4QTestim (Tov 2001: 99) and SyrHex, the verse continues, adapting from Deut 5:28(25)–29(26); 18:18–22; 5:30(27)–31(28):

And Yahweh spoke to Moses, saying, 'I have heard the sound of this people's words that they spoke to you; they did well (in) all they said. Who will give that (if only), and this would be their *heart* (intention), to fear me and keep my commands all the days, so that it would be well for them and for their sons to eternity. A prophet I will raise up for them from their brothers' midst like you, and I will set my words in his mouth, and he will speak to them all that I will command him. And it will happen: the man who does not listen to his words that he will speak in my name, I, I will require it of him. However, the prophet that presumptuously speaks in my name what I did not command him to speak, or who speaks in the name of other gods, then that prophet shall die. And if you say in your heart, "How shall we know the word that Yahweh did not speak it, that the prophet speaks in Yahweh's name?"—the word will not happen and not come. That is the word that Yahweh did not speak it; in presumption the prophet spoke it. Don't dread before him.

"Go," say to them, "Return yourselves to your tents," and you stand here with me, and I will speak to you all the command, the statutes and the laws, that you will teach them; and they will do (them) in the land that I am giving to them to acquire it.'

The reason for the insertion is that, according to Deut 18:16–17, this exchange took place at Horeb, although it is unreported in MT Exodus. Sam, 4QpaleoGen-Exod[1] and 4QpaleoExod[m] characteristically harmonize by expanding contradictory reports of the same events in the Torah (Tov 2001: 88); cf. TEXTUAL NOTE to 6:9.

20:22(19). *to Moses, "Thus you will say.* Sam has instead "to Moses, *saying: 'Speak. . . .'*"

† Israel's Sons. LXX has a longer variant: "Thus you will say to Jacob's house, and you will tell to Israel's Sons." Perhaps this is borrowed from 19:3, but we cannot be certain. An original *kh t'mr lbyt (or 'l byt) y'qb wtg(y)d lbny ('l bny) yśr'l might have become kh t'mr 'l bny yśr'l (MT) by parablepsis.

20:23(20). *along with me.* LXX has instead "for yourselves," as if reading *lkm to match the following clause more closely. The more varied MT-Sam is presumably original. Syr conflates the variants, "along with me *for yourselves*," while Vg contains neither. And Luzzatto reads *'ōtî for 'ittî, producing the meaning, "Don't make *me* (into) a silver deity," i.e., an idol of Yahweh (cf. already Mek. baḥōdeš 10). This comports better with the trope, which puts a stop after 'ty, but would be unidiomatic Hebrew. MT makes perfect sense as it stands; see Jacob (1992: 750–51) for parallels.

silver . . . gold. Syr reverses the metals.

20:24(21). *you may make.* In MT, all the second person forms are singular, in contrast to the plurals of the preceding verse. In LXX, however, only the final clause "I will come to you and bless you" has "you" in the singular; the rest is plural.

† *your flock . . . herd.* Before "your flock," LXX[B], Syr and many MT MSS (de Rossi 1784–85: 64) insert "and." Sam and Tg. Onqelos have, perhaps correctly, "*from* your flock and *from* your herd" (mṣ'nk wmbqrk), vs. MT 't ṣ'nk w't bqrk; for a brief discussion, see Levinson (1997: 36–38). "Your" is singular in all Versions, but a superlinear correction to 4QBibPar makes it plural ('wlwtyk[m]h . . . šlmyk[m]h . . . ṣw'nyk[m]h).

in any place. Sam has simply "in *the* place," i.e., bmqwm for MT bəkol-hammāqôm. On the one hand, our preference for the shorter text favors Sam. On

the other hand, Sam makes the verse resemble more closely a ubiquitous Deuteronomic cliché for cultic centralization (Deut 12:14, 18; 15:20; 16:2, 7, 11, 15, etc.).
On Sam's characteristic assertion of Shechem's exclusive sanctity, cf. the following TEXTUAL NOTE and TEXTUAL NOTE to 20:17(14), "of your fellow."

I announce. Syr and *Tg. Neofiti I* have "*you* announce," shifting the act from
God to Israel ("you" is singular in Syr, plural in *Tg. Neofiti I*). For the MT imperfect *'azkîr*, Sam has the perfect *'zkrty = hizkartî* 'I *have* announced,' thus reinforcing the Samaritan claim that God's chosen city, all the way back to Genesis, was
Shechem (see Tov 2001: 94–95). The spelling *'zkrty* for *hzkrty* reflects (a) the
common exchange of gutturals in Samaritan Hebrew (Tov, pp. 95–96), (b) the influence of the Aramaic 'Aph'el conjugation and, in all likelihood, (c) knowledge
of the original reading, MT *'zk(y)r*.

† *my name.* Sam and LXX add "there," reading **šmy šmh*. Either MT has suffered corruption by haplography, or else LXX-Sam harmonizes with such passages
as 1 Kgs 8:16, 29; 9:3; 11:36; 2 Kgs 23:27; Jer 7:12, which contain the sequence
š(ə)mî šām 'my name there.'

† *I will come.* LXX preposes "and." On the one hand, this could be an inner-
Greek development arising from ambiguity as to clause division. Conceivably,
however, the LXX *Vorlage* really had a cohortative **wə'ābō(')* 'that I may come.'
In the latter case, the fact that the preceding letter is yodh, similar to waw in
Greco-Roman era script, might be a factor. That is, MT might be the result of hap-
lography, or LXX the result of dittography.

† *20:25(22). But.* The conjunction is absent in Kenn 132, 152, 600.

† *lifted against it and profaned it.* LXX paraphrases: "lifted against *them* and
they are profaned," thereby repairing a difficulty in MT: what is "it"? In MT, the
suffixes on *'āle(y)hā* 'against it' and *wattəhallehā* 'and profaned it' are feminine, so
the referent must be *gāzît* 'cutstone (fem.),' but this hardly makes sense. More logical, but therefore also suspect, is Sam *hnpt 'lyw wthllhw* 'lifted against it (masc.)
and profaned it (masc.)' (possibly also Syr), where the referent is *mizbēah* 'altar
(masc.).' Might there have been an intermediate variant, synonymous to Sam,
*hnpt 'lyhw wthllhw?

† *20:26(23). And.* The conjunction is absent in Kenn 69, 158, 181, 244.

at which. For MT *'lyw*, Sam has *'lyw* 'to which.'

† *your nudity must not be revealed.* While MT and all other witnesses read a
Niph'al *tiggāle(h)*, with the subject either the addressee or "your nudity," LXX
with equal plausibility reads a Pi'el *təgalle(h)*, so that the injunction is "Don't reveal your nudity."

†† 21:1. *These.* Although MT begins with a conjunction *w*, I have followed the
shorter text of Sam, Vg and 4QBibPar.

† 21:2. *serve.* Sam, LXX, Vg, *Tg. Neofiti I* and Syr expand: "serve *you*" (*y'bdk*).
Although this variant is widely distributed, our preference for the shorter reading
favors MT.

seventh. LXX and *Tg. Neofiti I* explicate: "seventh *year*."

†† *as a freeman.* This interpretation requires revocalizing MT *lahopšî* as
*ləhopšî. See NOTE.

21:3. *If* (first time). Many Syr MSS begin with the conjunction "and."

† *with his gap.* For the MT singular *bgpw (bəgappô)*, Sam and 4QBibPar have a plural *bgpyw*, possibly correct, since MT, too, could be read as an archaically spelled plural *(*bəgappāw)*. Notice that, each time in the verse, the word in question is followed by either yodh or waw, almost identical in Roman period script (Cross 1961a; Qimron 1972). See further NOTE.

he shall depart. LXX inserts a conjunction, as if its *Vorlage* read either **wyṣ' bgpw* or **wbgpw yṣ'* (vs. MT *bgpw yṣ'*). But more likely LXX is freely translating.

If (second time). Kenn 18, 84, 150, 686, LXX, Syr and *Tg. Ps.-Jonathan* insert "and."

21:4. *if.* Kenn 84, Rossi 419, LXX, Syr and Vg begin, "and."

sons. Where all other Versions have simply *bānîm* 'sons,' Kenn 109 has *bānîm ûb(ə)nê bānîm* 'sons *and sons' sons.'* Although the longer reading is easily liable to haplography and hence could be original, it is far easier to imagine that Kenn 109 has been expanded, given the isolation of its reading; cf. TEXTUAL NOTE to 20:5. D. N. Freedman (privately) observes that, assuming this is a six-year slave, he will not yet have grandchildren.

† *her master.* So MT *('ădōne[y]hā)*. Sam, most Syr MSS, the LXX *Vorlage* (Wevers 1990: 324) and apparently 4QBibPar have "*his* master" *('dwn[y]w)*. On the one hand, "his master" appears earlier in the verse, arguably making MT *lectio difficilior.* On the other hand, we find in even greater proximity *yəlāde(y)hā* 'her children' (see also *'ădōne[y]hā* in 21:8), making Sam-Syr-LXX equally *lectio difficilior.* The case is therefore difficult to judge. Ultimately, the master owns both man- and maidservant.

†† 21:5. *If.* I have followed the shorter reading of Sam and Kenn 4, 196, Rossi 440, 592. Standard MT begins, "*And* if."

21:6. *or to the doorpost.* LXX simply has "to the door, to the doorpost," as if its *Vorlage* read **'l hdlt 'l hmzwzh.* But MT *'l hdlt 'w 'l hmzwzh* 'to the door *or* to the doorpost' is likely correct. Either a scribe's eye skipped from *'w* 'or' to *'l* 'to,' or, more likely, LXX is paraphrasing, since MT is admittedly odd — how can there be a door without a doorpost? Other Versions also grapple with the peculiar phraseology: Vg has "to the door *and* to the doorpost," while *Tg. Ps.-Jonathan* has "before the door *which is* before the doorpost."

his master (second time). Vg lacks *'ădōna(y)w*, as if it had fallen out by homoioarkton before *'et.*

21:7. *the manservants'.* Upon first inspection, the LXX variant *hai doulai* 'the *maid*servants' seems to be an inner-Greek corruption. While Hebrew *hā'āmōt* 'the maidservants' and *hā'ăbādîm* 'the manservants' are quite distinct in appearance, Greek *hai doulai* 'the maidservants' closely resembles *hoi douloi* 'the manservants.' Thus, one might suppose that the original LXX read **hoi douloi*, matching MT.

However, LXX Exodus never uses *doulos* for Hebrew *'ebed*; the preferred term is *pais.* Moreover, despite Jerome's overall fidelity to the Hebrew, Vg *ancillae* 'the maidservants' follows LXX not MT. Conceivably there was a variant Hebrew *Vorlage *hā'āmōt* behind both LXX and Vg, which assume that the laws of slave manumission apply to females as well as to males, unless a woman had been sold into slavery by her own father. In any event, such a reading would not be original, but rather a harmonization with Deut 15:12, which explicitly sets a six-year term for both man- and maidservants.

21:8. *If.* Rossi 419, LXX[A] and some *Tg.* MSS (de Rossi 1784–85: 64) insert "And."

she. The pronoun is implicit in MT, explicit in Sam *(hy').*

† *did not engage for her.* The textual situation is far more complex than the *BHS* notes suggest. Some Versions read *lō(')* 'not'; others read *lô* 'for himself' (thus generating contradictory interpretations); some read *y'dh;* others read *h(w)'dh.* All four possible combinations may be attested. (Confusion of *lō[']* and *lô,* possibly due to aural error or memory lapse [see volume I, p. 46], is not confined to this verse; see also Lev 11:21; 25:30; 1 Sam 2:3; 2 Sam 16:18; 2 Kgs 8:10; Isa 9:2; 49:5; 63:9; Ps 100:3; 139:16; Prov 19:7; 26:2; Job 13:15; 41:4; Ezra 4:2; 1 Chr 11:20.)

My translation follows the MT Kethibh *'šr l' y'dh* 'who did *not* engage for her,' probably supported by LXX[AF] et al., Syr, Symmachus, Aquila, Theodotion, *Tg. Neofiti I* and MSS of *Tg. Onqelos* (see also de Rossi 1784–85: 65). On the meaning, see NOTE.

Standard MT Qere, Kenn 109, 247, 248, 249, 251 and Rossi 274, however, read *'šr lw y'dh* 'who engaged for her *for himself,*' probably supported by LXX[B] and MSS of *Tg. Onqelos* and *Tg. Ps.-Jonathan* (on the LXX variants, see Schenker 1988: 552–53). If this is the original text, then the MT Kethibh is corrupt, anticipating *'šr l'* in 21:13. Against the Qere, however, Budde (1891: 102) points out that the expected word order would be **'šr y'dh lw.*

Sam has *'šr l' h'dh,* which, according to *Samaritan Tg.,* is to be rendered "who did not warn/testify concerning her." I assume this means that the maidservant is entitled to a warning before she is let go. If this reading is correct, then MT has anticipated the Qal *yî'ādennâ* in v 9. If Sam is incorrect, it has brought forward the Hiph'il prefix of the following *wǝhepdâ.*

Finally, Vg "to whom she had been given" appears to read **'šr lw h(w)'dh (hû'ădâ),* literally, "for whom she had been appointed." This is essentially a conflation of the MT Qere and the Sam consonantal text.

SPECULATION: Positing metathesis in all the attested versions and following the MT Kethibh *lō(')* instead of the Qere *lô,* Holzinger (1900: 83) and Baentsch (1903: 190) adopt Budde's (1891: 101–4) conjectural emendation: **'šr l' yd'h* 'who did not (sexually) *know* her,' corrupted in MT by anticipation of the *yy'dnh* 'he has engaged for her' in the following verse. There is nothing to say against this theory—presumably the father has in fact not lain with the maidservant—but neither is there any evidence in its favor.

† *breach of contract.* At issue is the vocalization of *bgdw.* We would expect the infinitive construct **bogdô,* whereas MT *bigdô* suggests a noun *beged/bēged.* There is admittedly a rare noun *beged* 'treachery,' and nouns can replace true infinitives construct (cf. Waltke and O'Connor 1990: 6.1.1.d, p. 599). And yet, given

the pausal form *bāged* in Jer 12:1, we might have expected "his treachery" (< *beged*) to be vocalized *bagdô.

Perhaps the proper reading is after all *bogdô. The received vocalization *bigdô* may well reflect a midrashic reading "his *garment*," for *Mek. nəzîqîn* 3; *b. Qidd.* 18b cite the homiletical interpretation of R. Aqiba: one should read here *bəbigdô bāh* as "(after he spread) his garment upon her" as an act of betrothal (cf. Isa 4:1; Ezek 16:8; Ruth 3:9).

21:9. *And.* The conjunction is absent in Kenn 158.

engaged for her. Sam and several MT MSS (Kennicott 1776–80: 151) have *yᶜdnh* (vs. MT *yyᶜdnh*), which *Samaritan Tg.* parses as a Hiphᶜil imperfect: "warned her." Sam's defective spelling may be original, but the verb is certainly the Qal imperfect of *yᶜd*.

† *he shall do.* One might revocalize MT *yaᶜăśe(h)* as **yēᶜāśe(h)* 'it shall *be done*' without impairing the basic sense.

21:10. *If.* Many MT MSS (Kennicott 1776–80: 151; de Rossi 1784–85: 65), Sam, LXX, Vg and Syr have "*And* if."

her ᶜōnâ. On proposed emendations to MT *wəᶜōnātāh* and the word's possible meanings, see NOTE.

21:11. *And if.* Kenn 253 and *Tg. Ps.-Jonathan* lack the conjunction.

21:13. *to his hand.* LXX and *Tgs. Ps.-Jonathan* and *Neofiti I* have *lydyw* 'to his hands' (cf. TEXTUAL NOTES to 21:16, 20). On the inherent ambiguity of the pronominal suffix *-w* (plural in old orthography, singular in younger orthography), see Andersen and Forbes (1986: 62).

I will set. Syr, rather oddly, has "*he* [God] has set."

he may flee. LXX clarifies, "*the murderer* may flee."

21:14. *But when.* Kenn 152 omits the conjunction.

†† 21:15. *Whoever.* Standard MT begins with "And," but the conjunction is absent in Kenn 9, Rossi 766, some Sam MSS, LXX and possibly Vg.

† 21:15–16. *Whoever . . . whoever.* So the Hebrew Versions. The laws against manstealing and filial impiety are reversed in LXX vis-à-vis MT-Sam, so that LXX consecutively treats filial piety in vv 16–17 and more directly associates murder and kidnap. Vv 16 and 17 also seem to lack initial conjunctions in LXX, which may be a superior reading.

21:16. *a man.* The ancient translations variously harmonize 21:16 with the parallel but more restrictive law in Deut 24:7, "If a man is found stealing a *soul* (person) from his brothers, from Israel's Sons, and masters him and sells him. . . ." Syr simply substitutes *napšā* 'soul' (Hebrew *nepeš*) for the expected *gabrā* 'man' (Hebrew *ʾîš*), but otherwise renders Exod 21:16 faithfully. *Tgs. Onqelos* and *Ps.-Jonathan*, however, read "a *soul* from Israel's Sons"—thus the law does not forbid kidnapping Gentiles. LXX is the most slavishly harmonistic with Deuteronomy: "a *man* from Israel's Sons and having mastered him should sell" (for discussion, see Aejmelaeus 1987: 83–85). Elsewhere in this pericope, *Tgs.* (but not LXX) restrict various laws to crimes against Israelites (21:7, 9, 31, etc).

in his hand. Some Syr MSS read "in his hands"; cf. TEXTUAL NOTES to 21:13, 20.

21:17. *And whoever.* Syr lacks the conjunction.

21:18. *men.* Here and in 21:22, LXX and Syr probably expand *ad sensum:* "two men," possibly inspired by 2:13, "two Hebrew men fighting" (in LXX 2:13, however, the wording is different).

a man strikes. Sam unexpectedly and awkwardly puts the verb in the plural (*hkw*), necessitating a translation "if men fight and hit, a man his fellow. . . ."

† *with a stone . . . fist.* These words are absent from Sam. Initially, one might prefer this shorter text, supposing that standard MT represents early halakhah, explicating and limiting a cryptic statute. But, as we shall discover in 21:20, 28, 29, 32, 33, 35 (see TEXTUAL NOTES), Sam consistently attempts to make its laws as general as possible—equally a method for generating halakhah. Thus MT is likely original.

21:19. *If.* Kenn 69 and 129 have "*And if.*"

his cane. LXX has simply "*a cane,*" probably periphrastic but conceivably reflecting a *Vorlage* *'*l mš'nt* vs. MT '*l mš'ntw.* If so, since the next letter is waw, either haplography to produce LXX or dittography to produce MT would be equally possible, particularly in continuous writing.

† *his sitting idle.* Wevers (1990: 332) raises the possibility that we should read something like *šobtô* 'his inactivity' (< *šbt*) rather than MT *šibtô* 'his sitting' (< *yšb*). See further NOTE.

† *heal, heal.* Whereas MT has Pi'el verbs (*rappō' yərappē'*), Samaritan tradition reads a Qal (Ben-Ḥayyim 1977: 425), in Massoretic vocalization, *rāpō' yirpā(')*. The meaning is unaffected, and either could be correct.

† 21:20. *with the rod.* As in 21:18, Sam does not specify the weapon, thus making the statute more general (also Rossi 503). See also TEXTUAL NOTES to 21:18, 28, 29, 32, 33, 35.

his hand. LXX and Vg have "his hands" (cf. TEXTUAL NOTES to 21:13, 16).

avenged, avenged. Harmonizing with other laws in the chapter and glossing a rare and ambiguous lexeme, Sam has "he must be *put to death, death*" (*mwt ywmt*); see also NOTE and next TEXTUAL NOTE.

21:21. *avenged.* Sam again has *ywmt* 'he shall (not) be *put to death*,' vs. MT *yuqqam.* 4QReworked Pentateuch[b] *yqwm* 'he will get up' is a simple transposition (possibly motivated by the proximity of '*md* 'stand').

21:22. *And if.* Kenn 650 B lacks "And."

men. See TEXTUAL NOTE to 21:18.

†† *her child comes out.* Reading a singular verb and subject with Sam, LXX, Tg. *Neofiti I* and probably Vg: *wyṣ' wldh*, vs. MT *wyṣ'w yldyh* 'and her child*ren* come out.' The alternation between *wyṣ' w-* (Sam) and *wyṣ'w y-* (MT) may reflect the similarity of waw and yodh in Roman-period script (Cross 1961a; Qimron 1972). The plural subject of MT is hard to understand—unless it refers, not just to children, but to all that comes forth during parturition. More likely, however, *yldyh* has simply been copied from 21:4. The noun *wālād* used by Sam et al. is paralleled only in Gen 11:30 and 2 Sam 6:23 (Kethibh in many MSS), making it *lectio difficilior.* Syr appears to conflate the aforesaid variants: *wnpqwn 'wlh* 'and her fetus (sing.) come out (pl.).'

injury. Though correctly rendering *'āsôn* in Gen 42:4, 38; 44:29 as referring to injury or illness, in Exod 21:22–23 LXX has *exeikonismenon* 'fully formed,' or more literally, 'fashioned after the image,' referring both to a prototypical human and, by extension, to the Deity (so also Philo *Spec. Leg.* 3.108; *Congr.* 137). Since this cannot be a straight rendering of a Hebrew *Vorlage*, Freund (1990: 241–54) cleverly argues for a homiletical reinterpretation, barely sustained by a Greek etymology: Hebrew *'āsôn* = Greek *holhē* (sic!) *sōma* 'the body.' (An alternative would be to imagine *'āsôn* as fallaciously associated with the root *'śy* 'make.')

what is fair. To solve the mystery of MT-Sam *biplīlîm* (see NOTE), Budde (1891: 106–8) proposes a conjectural emendation **bannəpālîm* 'for miscarriage,' supposedly a plural of abstraction based upon *nēpel* 'stillborn.' This alteration does not recommend itself; there are satisfactory ways to interpret MT-Sam short of textual surgery (see NOTE).

21:25. *burn . . . burn.* For the unique MT *kəwiyyâ*, Sam has the synonym *mkwh*, paralleled in Lev 13:24, 25, 28.

21:26. *maidservant's eye.* Kenn 193 adds "with a rod."

21:28. *a bull* (first time). Sam makes the law more general, adding "or any animal." On the phenomenon, already visible in MT, see Fishbane (1985: 170–74).

gores. Sam replaces MT *yiggaḥ* with the more common and general term *ykh* 'strikes.'

bull (second and third time). Sam replaces MT *šôr* with the more vague *bhmh* 'animal.'

21:29. *gorer bull.* Sam generalizes: "striking animal."

it was warned about. Two parallel laws from Mesopotamia (see NOTE to 21:30) use the verb *šūdû* 'notify, inform.' Against MT-Sam *hwʿd* (*hûʿad*, root *yʿd*), this could conceivably indicate an original Hebrew reading **hwdʿ* (**hûdaʿ*, root *ydʿ*) 'it was made known' (cf. Goetze 1956: 136 n. 9). Note that the dangerous ox is similarly described as "known" (*nôdaʿ*, root *ydʿ*) in 21:36. But MT-Sam makes perfect sense and should not be emended.

† *guard it.* Here and in 21:36, LXX *aphanisēi auton* 'eliminate it' may reflect not MT-Sam *yšmrnw* but **yšm(y)dnw* 'destroy it' (BHS), for in all periods and scripts, resh and daleth have been similar in appearance. Either reading would make sense. I have followed MT, mainly because the reading **yšm(y)dnw* is reconstructed and not necessarily the LXX *Vorlage* (Wevers 1990: 336). Sarna (1991: 128), however, notes the possibility that the LXX reading informed the ruling of R. Eliezer, who recommended *slaughtering* a dangerous beast immediately (*Mek. nəzîqîn* 10).

bull (second time). Sam replaces with "animal."

† 21:30. *If.* Kenn 4, 84, 129, 181, Rossi 419, LXX, some *Tg.* MSS (de Rossi 1784–85: 65), Syr and Vg begin with "and." Whichever reading is original, that the previous word ends in waw may have been a factor — or the change could have been random.

as whatever. MT Sebhirin, Kenn 284, 683 and Rossi 264, 266, 669, 688 read *bkl* 'in all,' a simple graphic error for *kkl*.

21:31. *Whether.* For standard MT *'ô*, Rossi 223 reads *'im* 'If,' while LXX and Syr appear to read *wə'im* 'And if.'

gores. Sam replaces with "strikes."

21:32. *If.* Kenn 1, 4, Rossi 419, LXX and Syr insert "And."

the bull gores. Sam has "the animal strikes."

the bull (second time). Sam: "the animal."

21:33. *ass.* Sam adds "or any animal."

21:34. *silver.* Kenn 109 expands: "twofold to his fellow, silver."

21:35. *bull . . . bull.* Each time, Sam adds "or any animal (of him)."

bull (third time). Sam omits "bull," so that "dead" may modify any of the afore-mentioned animals.

21:36. *Or.* Instead of MT 'ô, LXX, Syr and 4QBibPar have '*m* 'If.'

gorer bull. Sam has "striking animal."

its owner did not guard it. LXX has a longer text, "and its master was warned about it, but he did not eliminate it," thus matching 21:29 (see TEXTUAL NOTE, "guard it"). Probably LXX has been expanded for specificity, since there is no obvious mechanical explanation for parablepsis in MT-Sam.

†† *bull for bull.* Reading *šôr taḥat šôr with LXX and *Tg. Neofiti I*, matching more closely 21:23–25, "life for life, eye for eye," etc. Sam supports LXX, with its usual substitution: "animal for animal." MT *šôr taḥat haššôr* 'a bull for *the* (afore-said) bull' probably anticipates *tḥt hšwr* in 21:37.

21:37. *When.* Kenn 84, 136, 150, Sam, LXX, Syr and *Tg. Neofiti I* insert "And." 4QBibPar has '*m* 'If,' vs. MT *kî*.

22:1. *If.* LXX, Syr, Vg and Kenn 9 have "And if."

†† *he strikes him.* So Sam (*whkhw* [*wəhikkāhû*]); MT and and 4QBibPar have *wəhukkâ* 'and *is struck*.' We cannot really say which is original. *Whkh wmt* (MT) could have become *whkhw wmt* (Sam) by dittography, or *whkhw wmt* (Sam) could have become *whkh wmt* (MT) by haplography, especially assuming continuous writing.

bloodiness. For the MT plural *dāmîm* 'bloodiness,' here and in the next verse, Sam has simply *dām* 'blood.' The sense is unaffected. (MT *dāmîm* = Sam *dām* also in Gen 4:10, 11; Lev 12:4; 20:9.)

22:2. *If* (first time). Kenn 4, 9, 101, 129, Rossi 419, 669, LXX, Syr, Vg and some *Tg.* MSS (de Rossi 1784–85: 65) have "And if."

† *shone.* MT puts the verb in the feminine (*zrḥh*), but some Sam MSS have the masculine (*zrḥ*). Since *šemeš* 'sun' is of ambivalent gender, either might be original. Perhaps a contributory factor is that the next word *hšmš* begins with he', creating an opportunity for either haplography or dittography.

bloodiness. See TEXTUAL NOTE to 22:1.

pay. On LXX "die in exchange," see NOTE.

If (second time). Kenn 4, 5, 9, 69, 75, 84, 129, Rossi 266, 419, 669, LXX, Syr and *Tg.* MSS (de Rossi 1784–85: 65) have "And if."

nothing. 2QExod[b] apparently adds "to pay," agreeing with Vg and *Tg. Ps.-Jonathan.*

22:3. *If.* LXX, Kenn 109, 686 (?) and Syr read "And if."

bull . . . ass . . . sheep. LXX has simply "from ass to sheep." (Did a variant **mḥmwr 'd šwr 'd śh* 'from ass to bull to sheep' become **mḥmwr 'd śh* 'from ass to sheep' by *wr . . . wr* haplography?) Sam, however, then expands MT by adding "to any animal"; cf. TEXTUAL NOTES to 20:17(14), "his ass"; 21:28, 29, 32, 33, 35, 36.

his hand. Syr has "his hands."

twofold. 4QpaleoExod^m, Sam, 4QBibPar, Syr and *Tgs. Onqelos* and *Ps.-Jonathan* explicate: "one, two" (*'ḥd šnym*), i.e., "two for one" (cf. Dan 3:19, *ḥad-šibʿâ* 'one, seven = sevenfold'). See also TEXTUAL NOTES to 22:6, 8, "twofold."

22:4. *When.* Kenn 69, 236, Sam, LXX, 4QBibPar and Syr have "*And* when."

†† *clears.* Where MT uses the verb *bʿr* twice (*yabʿer, biʿēr*), the longer Sam has *ybʿr . . . bʿr . . . ybʿh* (see below), and the fragmentary 4QBibPar has *wky ybʿh . . . [kt]bwʾtwʾm kl hśdh ybʿh.* I concur with Aejmelaeus (1987: 82–83) that the last deserves preference as *lectio difficilior* and would read the opening as *kî yabʿe(h) ʾîš.* The root *bʿy* appears also in Isa 64:1, probably describing a fire that burns up water (cf. 1 Kgs 18:38); in Obad 6, *bʿy* may mean "reveal" (parallel to *ḥpś* 'seek out' [or read *ḥśp* 'uncover'?]). By emendation, the word has also been found in Sir 6:2 (reading *tbʿh* for *tʿbh*; cf. the Greek Version). Even after the standardization of MT, the Rabbis call an animal that damages a field by grazing *mabʿe(h)*, from the root *bʿy* (*m. B. Qam.* 1:1; see also *Tg. Ps.-Jonathan* Num 22:4, translating MT *ləḥōk* 'lick up'). As for cognates, we may cite Ugaritic *bǵy* 'disclose, uncover' in *KTU* 1.3.iii.20; see further NOTE.

† *in another's field.* For MT *biśdēh ʾaḥēr,* Jackson (1976: 140) proposes to read *bəśāde(h) ʾaḥēr* 'in another field,' perhaps correctly; see NOTE.

†† *he must pay . . . clears.* The words *šlm yšlm mśdhw ktbwʾth wʾm kl hśdh ybʿh* are absent in MT, but present in Sam, LXX, 4QBibPar and probably 4Qpaleo-Exod^m and 4QReworkedPentateuch^d. I believe them to be original. While ordinarily we prefer the shorter text, here MT, in this case the plus is not a typical gloss, i.e., a clarifying phrase (*pace* Rabinowiz 1959a). Rather, it consists of two unconnected clauses respectively linked to preceding and following clauses.

To explain the loss of words in MT, I imagine the following scenario. The verse originally read, *ky ybʿh ʾyš śdh ʾw krm wšlḥ ʾt bʿyrh wbʿh bśdh ʾḥr šlm yšlm mśdhw ktbwʾth wʾm kl hśdh ybʿh mytb śdhw wmytb krmw yšlm* (cf. 4QBibPar). The references to *bəʿîr* 'cattle' in v 4 and to *bʿr* 'burn' in v 5 progressively caused corruption of *bʿy* to *bʿr* (note, too, the similarity of *ʾyš* 'man' and *ʾš* 'fire'). One variant was *ky ybʿr ʾyš śdh ʾw krm wšlḥ ʾt bʿyrh wbʿr bśdh ʾḥr šlm yšlm mśdhw ktbwʾth wʾm kl hśdh ybʿh mytb śdhw wmytb krmw yšlm* (cf. Sam). Another was *ky ybʿr ʾyš śdh ʾw krm wšlḥ ʾt bʿyrh wbʿr bśdh ʾḥr šlm yšlm mśdhw ktbwʾth wʾm kl hśdh ybʿr mytb śdhw wmytb krmw yšlm* (cf. LXX?). This last suffered major haplography, skipping from *ʾḥr* to *ybʿr* (Sanderson 1986: 76–77), producing *ky ybʿr ʾyš śdh ʾw krm wšlḥ ʾt bʿyrh wbʿr bśdh ʾḥr mytb śdhw wmytb krmw yšlm* (MT).

22:5. *If.* LXX has "*And* if."

goes out. For a conjectural emendation *tṣt (tîṣat)* 'is ignited' for MT-Sam *tṣʾ* 'goes out,' see Talmon (1981: 519); on the confusion of ʾaleph and taw in paleo-Hebrew script, see Tov (2001: 244–45).

† *the field.* So MT-Sam; LXX and *Tgs. Onqelos* and *Ps.-Jonathan* have "*a* field." Either might be original, but I follow MT-Sam, since this reading alone is attested in Hebrew MSS.

is consumed. LXX and Syr "and consumes" makes "fire" the subject, as if reading **wᵊklh* vs. MT-Sam *wn'kl*. Such a reading, however, is found in no Hebrew MS and may well be periphrastic.

22:6. *When.* Kenn 132, Rossi 196 (?), 262, Sam, LXX and Syr have "*And* when."

is stolen. In place of the MT ostensible Puʻal *wᵊgunnab* (really a Qal Passive **wᵊgunab*), 4QpaleoExod^m and Sam (here and in Gen 40:15) have the synonymous Niphʻal *ngnb*. MT, at least as vocalized, uses the Niphʻal of *gnb* in Exod 22:11, and so is preferable in 22:6 as the more diverse text.

twofold. Sam, Syr and *Tgs. Onqelos* and *Ps.-Jonathan* explicate: "*(for) one, two*" (*'ḥd šnym*). See also TEXTUAL NOTES to 22:3, 8.

22:7. *If* (first time). Kenn 9, 109, 132, 181, Rossi 16, 262, 479, 500, 503, 656, 669, 766, Sam, LXX and Syr have "*And* if."

he did not. For the remainder of this verse ("he has not done wrong concerning anything of his neighbor") and the next, LXX is periphrastic. It does not necessarily reflect a variant *Vorlage* (Wevers 1990: 344–45)

22:8. *about an ass . . . lost.* MSS of MT and of *Tg.* (Kennicott 1776–80: 153; de Rossi 1784–85: 65–66), LXX, Syr and Vg insert *wᵊ-* 'and' before *ʻal* 'about' in various places in the sequence.

robe. As usual, Sam replaces MT *ślmh* with the more common synonym *śmlh*; cf. TEXTUAL NOTE to 22:25, "robe," and Sanderson (1986: 60–61).

† *the Deity.* So MT. Sam and 4QBibPar have "Yahweh."

Whomever. LXX: "*And* whomever."

Deity finds guilty. In MT, the verb *yaršîʻūn* is plural. Even when denoting to God (see NOTE to 1:17), *'ĕlōhîm* 'Deity,' is occasionally treated as a plural (GKC §132h, 145i). Sam features a longer and easier reading, *yršyʻnw h'lhym* 'the Deity finds *him* guilty' (for similar differences between MT and Sam in number and pronominal suffix, compare TEXTUAL NOTE to 22:24 "lay" and contrast TEXTUAL NOTES to 22:12, "let him bring . . . pay," 20, "afflict . . . oppress him"). See further NOTE.

twofold. Sam, Syr and *Tgs. Onqelos* and *Ps.-Jonathan* explicate: "*one, two*" (*'ḥd šnym*). See also TEXTUAL NOTES to 22:3, 6.

22:9. *When.* Kenn 4, Rossi 196 (?), 265, Sam, LXX, Syr and *Tg. Neofiti I* have "*And* when."

or any. Although the meaning is unchanged, Rossi 503, Sam, Syr, 4QBibPar and possibly LXX have *'w kl* (vs. MT *wkl*) to match the previous items.

dies . . . suffers a break. LXX reverses the verbs vis-à-vis MT, to match 22:13.

22:10. *Yahweh.* LXX has "the God," perhaps both to conform to the divine appellation elsewhere in this section and to avoid confusion between *kyrios* 'master, owner' and *kyrios* '(the) Lord' (Wevers 1990: 346). Vg omits God's name *Dominus* entirely, presumably for the latter reason.

†† 22:11. *If.* So Sam, Kenn 84, 99, 168, 389 A, Rossi 419, 543, 766, Rossi *Tg.* 419. MT, LXX and Syr have "*But* if."

†† 22:12. *If.* Various MT and *Tg.* MSS (Kennicott 1776–80: 154; de Rossi 1784–85: 66), LXX and Syr have "*And* if."

†† *let him bring . . . pay.* The last part of v 12 presents two main problems (for general discussion, see Le Déaut 1972). First, where does one divide the clauses:

before or after *haṭṭərēpâ* 'the prey'? Second, should one read *'ēd* 'witness, evidence' or *'ad* 'up to'?

In MT (with cantillation) and *Tg. Neofiti I*, the final clause is *haṭṭərēpâ lō(')* *yəšallēm* '(for) the tearing he shall not pay.' But comparison with 22:10, 14 favors parsing "he shall not pay" as an independent clause and connecting "the tearing" to what precedes. In fact, Rossi 223, 543, Sam, LXX and Vg isolate "he shall not pay" by inserting the conjunction "and." For my translation, I have adopted not the conjunction, but the syntactic analysis of Sam, LXX, etc.

We have two Hebrew consonantal versions of the first clause: Sam *yby' 'd ḥtrph* and MT *yb'hw 'd ḥtrph* (on the presence or absence of the pronominal suffix *-hw*, compare TEXTUAL NOTES to 22:8, 20, 24). Sam, which seems here to be the *Vorlage* of *Tg. Onqelos*, is most naturally interpreted as "let him bring evidence/a witness of the tearing" (cf. *Samaritan Tg.*). Although this could be original, it is dubious as *lectio facilior*.

The MT consonants permit four translations. The first is "let him bring him up to (*'ad*) the tearing (i.e., the carcass)," the approach of LXX, Vg and R. Jonathan (*Mek. nəzîqîn* 16; cf. also *b. B. Qam.* 10b–11a). But why use *'ad* for the expected *'el* 'to'? (Cf., however, *'ad hā'ĕlōhîm* 'unto the Deity' in v 8.) The second possibility, "let him bring to him evidence/a witness (*'ēd*) of the tearing," is presupposed by *Fragmentary Targum* but requires an unusual use of the pronominal suffix for the dative (for parallels, see GKC §11x). The third option is "let him bring it, (as) evidence (*'ēd*) of the tearing," the understanding of Syr. Lastly, we could take the witness as the grammatical subject: "let him that witnessed the tearing bring it (the dead animal)." In a sense, the most honest version is *Tg. Ps.-Jonathan*, which presents us with alternatives: "He brings to him witnesses or he shall make him approach to the prey's carcass."

SPECULATION: Ehrlich (1908: 353) proffers a highly attractive albeit conjectural emendation, supposing daleth-resh confusion: **yəbî'ēhû* (Ehrlich prefers Sam *yābî'*) *'ōr haṭṭərēpâ* 'let him bring (him) the *skin* of the slain animal,' by which it may be identified. But this is not without practical difficulties. First, the skin may not be the part left over by the predator. Second, is the borrower really expected to flay the carcass? (Perhaps so, if the the skin is all of value that remains.)

22:13. *borrows . . . fellow.* Syr and 4QBibPar add an explicating *bhmh* 'animal.' Various LXX MSS similarly add an animal of some sort, and *Tg. Ps.-Jonathan* and Vg add a still vaguer "something."

suffers a break or dies. LXX[BF] puts at the end "or is stolen," probably a harmonizing addition to match 22:9.

SPECULATION: Conceivably the original was **wnšbr 'w nšbh 'w mt*, a variation of 22:9 (this is in fact the Byzantine LXX reading, but this tradition is generally expansionist [Wevers 1992: 59]). From this, **'w nšbh* might have dropped by haplography, producing MT. As for LXX[BF], either it enshrines an equally ancient variant, or *'*w nšbh* had fallen out in its tradition, too, only to be reinserted at the end of the sequence.

22:14. *If . . . If.* Kenn 9 and 225 put "And" before the first "if," while Kenn 5 puts "And" before the second. LXX and Syr both times have "*And* if."

† *it came.* Sam inserts a conjunction, absent in MT, creating a converted perfect: *wb' 'then* it *shall* come.' This may in fact be correct; MT *bā'*, whether construed as a perfect or as a participle, is somewhat unexpected. Although the insertion or deletion of a conjunction hardly requires special pleading, in this case the corruption might be aural, since the previous word (*hû'*) ends in the vowel *û*, phonetically similar to *w* 'and, then.'

22:16. *If.* Kenn 109, 136, 158, 181, 225, 244, Rossi 12, 223, 440, 716, 766, a few *Tg.* MSS (de Rossi 1784–85: 66), Sam, LXX and Syr have "*And* if."

her father refuses, refuses. LXX "And if her father refuses, refuses *and does not agree* to give . . ." is probably an expansion, since LXX is rather periphrastic in this section (see following).

SPECULATION: LXX is an unusual expansion, however, since MT-Sam "refuses . . . to give" is perfectly intelligible. Possibly, LXX preserves the original reading: **'m m'n ym'n 'byh wl' y'bh ltth*. If so, MT-Sam would be the result of haplography due to the similarity of *'byh* 'her father' and *y'bh* 'agree.'

give her. Harmonizing with 22:15, LXX expands: "as a wife."

weigh out. The LXX paraphrase "pay her father" makes it clear that the brideprice belongs to the father, not to the wife (Wevers 1990: 349).

† 22:17. *sorceress.* The Versions vary on the number and gender of the enchanter(s). Syr and *Tg. Onqelos* are inherently ambiguous, since *hārāšā'* might mean either "*a* sorceress" (absolute state) or "*the* sorcerer" (emphatic state). *Tg. Ps.-Jonathan kl* '*byd ḥršywt* 'any that works sorcery,' too, is ambiguous. LXX *pharmakous* and the synonymous Vg *maleficos* 'sorcerers' are grammatically masculine plural, but logically of common gender. Mek. *nəzîkîn* 17 and *Tg. Neofiti I* (*kl ḥrš wḥrš'* 'every sorcerer and sorceress') explicitly apply the law to both sexes (so *b. Sanh.* 67a). Our sole extant Hebrew reading, however, is MT-Sam, banning only the *məkaššēpâ* 'sorceress (fem. sing.),' the *lectio brevior et difficilior.* The other traditions appear deliberately to broaden a narrow statute.

† *let live.* Since the consonants *tḥyh* might be vocalized as Qal **tiḥye(h)* 'live' (vs. MT Pi'el *təḥayye[h]* 'let live'), an alternative reading of the consonantal text would be "A sorceress *must not live*," a less direct way of saying *môt tûmāt* 'must be put to death, death.' This is apparently the reading of Samaritan tradition (Ben-Hayyim 1977: 96, 426).

†† 22:19. *other gods . . . destroyed.* My translation follows Sam, *zbḥ l'lhym 'ḥrym yḥrm*, vs. the longer MT *zōbēaḥ lā'ĕlōhîm yoḥŏrām biltî ləyahwe(h) ləbaddô* 'whoever sacrifices to the gods must be destroyed, *apart from Yahweh alone*' (LXX[A] combines these variants). MT's awkwardness makes it somewhat attractive, but could be the result of secondary glossation. If Sam is original, *'ḥrym* fell

from MT by homoioteleuton after *l'lhym* and/or its general similarity to the following *yḥrm*. But the resulting **zbḥ l'lhym yḥrm* 'whoever sacrifices to gods/Deity must be destroyed' was dangerously ambiguous, necessitating the MT clarification "apart from Yahweh alone." Against Sam, however, is the ubiquity of *'ĕlōhîm 'ăḥērîm* 'other gods' in Deuteronom(ist)ic texts, with which 22:19 may have been harmonized.

Conceivably, the long LXX variant "The one sacrificing to gods except (the) Lord alone must be destroyed by death" is correct, for its *Vorlage* stands closest to 2 Kgs 5:17, "Your slave will never again make Ascending-offering or a Slaughter-offering *(zebaḥ)* to other gods *(lē['jlōhîm 'ăḥērîm)* apart from Yahweh *(kî 'im-ləyahwe[h])*" (cf. Zakovitch 1994: 59). Only the final *ləbaddô* of MT Exod 22:19 finds no reflection in 2 Kgs 5:17.

Finally, Alt (1968: 144 n. 73) opines that the law originally matched its neighbors, reading **zōbēaḥ lē(')lōhîm 'ăḥērîm môt yûmāt* 'whoever sacrifices to other gods must be put to death, death.' But there is no mechanical explanation for the loss of **mwt ywmt* in the surviving Versions.

22:20. afflict . . . oppress him. The Versions disagree on whether the verbs are singular or plural, and whether the second verb bears a pronominal suffix. MT *tône(h)* 'afflict' and *tilḥāṣennû* 'oppress' are singular, and the second verb has a 3 m.s. pronominal suffix. In LXX *(kakōsete . . . thlipsete auton)*, both verbs are plural, and the second has a 3 m.s. pronominal direct object. *Tg. Neofiti I* makes both verbs plural and has a 3 m.pl. pronominal suffix on the second ("oppress *them*"). But in Sam, Syr, *Tgs. Onqelos* and probably *Ps.-Jonathan*, both verbs are plural and neither bears a pronominal suffix *(twnw . . . tlḥṣw)* (on the presence/absence of the suffix, cf. TEXTUAL NOTES to 22:8, "Deity finds guilty," 12, "let him bring . . . pay," 24, "lay"). We might prefer Sam as the shorter reading, but since the following verse-and-a-half ("sojourners you were [*hĕyîtem*] in the land of Egypt . . . don't oppress [*taʿannûn*]") is definitely plural, MT is preferable as the diverse *lectio difficilior*. My impression is that MT singulars in legal texts are original; the Versions variously pluralize to make explicit the laws' universal applicability.

22:22. If (first time). As routinely, LXX and Syr have "And if" (also Rossi 223), while Sam reads *ky 'm* 'Indeed, if,' brought forward from later in the verse.

you . . . oppress him. While MT and *Tgs. Onqelos* and *Ps.-Jonathan* switch back to the collective singular, Sam *t'nw* puts the verb in the plural. And both subject and object are explicitly plural in LXX, Vg and Syr: "you (pl.) oppress *them . . . they* should cry . . . *their* cry." *Tg. Neofiti I* also begins, "if you (pl.) oppress, oppress them," but then changes to the singular, with MT. The inconsistent MT is presumably original (see TEXTUAL NOTE to 22:20)

hear, hear. Before the infinitive absolute *šāmōaʿ*, Kenn 223, many Sam MSS and possibly Vg insert an unexpected "and," either a random phenomenon or a dittograph of the preceding yodh (on waw-yodh confusion, see Cross 1961a; Qimron 1972).

22:24. If. LXX and Syr have "And if."

† **my people . . . poor man among you.** Despite misgivings—"my people" is somewhat unexpected—my translation follows MT *'et-ʿammî 'et-heʿānî ʿimmāk*.

4QpaleoExod^m-Sam *ʾt ʿmy ʾt ʿny ʿmk* is identical to MT, save for the ungrammatical absence of the definite article after *ʾet-* (for parallels, see GKC §117d and NOTE to 21:28, "gores a man . . . woman"). LXX, however, offers a *lectio facilior*, "if silver you lend to your poor *brother* with you," as if reading **ʾet-ʾāḥîkā heʿānî ʿimmāk*; cf. Lev 25:35; Deut 15:7, 9; 24:14 (LXX^F, however, equals MT). In this case, it is difficult to reconstruct an original and trace its later permutations, since the sequence *ʿmy . . . ʿny . . . ʿmk* might be either the cause or the result of ancient scribal error (mem and nun were similar in paleo-Hebrew script). LXX is especially hard to explain, since *ʿmy* and *ʾḥyk* look and sound nothing alike.

SPECULATION: Conceivably, the LXX *Vorlage* was **ʿmk hʿny* or **ʿmytk hʿny* 'your poor kinsman' (cf. Baentsch 1903: 202; McNeile 1908: 136). However, this would be the sole case of LXX rendering *ʿam* or *ʿāmît* by *adelphos*.

don't (second time). Preceded by "and" in *Tg. Neofiti I*, Syr, probably Vg, one MT MS (Ginsburg 1926: 113) and MT Sebhirin.

lay. The verb is plural in MT (*təśîmûn*) but singular in Sam, LXX and Syr. Sam, moreover, adds a pronominal suffix (*tśymnw*) (cf. TEXTUAL NOTES to 22:8, "Deity finds guilty," 12, "let him bring . . . pay," 20). Although I generally prefer singulars over plurals, in this case LXX and Syr may have harmonized the verb with the singular in the preceding clauses. I therefore follow MT. The suffixed Sam form makes little sense; it probably results either from metathesis (*tśymwn* > *tśymnw*) or more likely from confusion with *tśybnw* in 22:25 (sic; Sam now reads *tśybnh*; see TEXTUAL NOTE, "return it to him").

22:25. *If.* LXX and Syr have "*And* if."

robe. Here 4QpaleoExod^m agrees with MT *śalmat*, vs. Sam *śmlt*; cf. TEXTUAL NOTE to 22:8, "robe." In the next verse, all witnesses have *śmlt*.

return it to him. Since *śalmâ/śimlâ* is feminine, MT *təśîbennû lô* 'return it (masc.) to him' exemplifies gender incongruity, not a rare phenomenon (Levi 1987) and a potential sign of originality. Sam has the *lectio facilior tśybnh lw* 'return it (fem.) to him' but probably originally agreed with MT (see TEXTUAL NOTE to 22:24, "lay"). *Tg. Onqelos* skirts the problem entirely by paraphrasing Hebrew *taḥbōl* with Aramaic *tissab maškônāʾ* 'you take a deposit (masc.).' LXX lacks any pronominal object, but this is probably just good Greek, not evidence of a variant *Vorlage* (Wevers 1990: 354). To remove the gender incongruity in MT, ibn Ezra supposes that the object is not *śalmâ* but the infinitive absolute *ḥābōl*, which here functions as a noun meaning "collateral." I know no parallel for such a construction.

22:26. *it . . . it.* On the consonantal spelling of *hîʾ* (fem.) as *hwʾ* (masc.), see TEXTUAL NOTE to 1:16, "she."

alone. I follow MT, connecting *ləbaddāh* with the first clause. LXX, however, joins it to the second: "it alone is his robe for. . . ." This unbalances the clauses, both of which in MT begin "it is."

† *for his skin.* For MT-Sam *ləʿōrô* 'for his skin,' LXX has *aschēmosynēs autou* 'for his *shame*,' as if reading **ləʿerwātô* (otherwise, LXX renders *ʿōr* accurately with *derma* 'skin'). It is hard to say whether this is a paraphrase *ad sensum* (cf. TEX-

TUAL NOTE to 28:42) or evidence of a true Hebrew variant. In either case, MT is slightly preferable as the less common idiom. (That the previous word ends in -*tô* might also have been a factor behind LXX's rendering/interpretation *śimlātô lə'erwātô*.)

hear. LXX "hear *him*" is periphrastic.

22:27. *a leader*. LXX (not LXX^A) has "leaders.

† 22:29. *for your flock*. So the standard MT, which is perhaps too strange to be correct. Sam, Kenn 196, LXX, Syr, *Tg. Ps.-Jonathan* and Vg have the expected conjunction "*and* for your flock." LXX, moreover, adds "and your ass," to match 22:3, 8, 9 and especially the parallel law in 34:19–20. Since asses were not sacrificed, however, LXX presumably intends that one should *sell* the foal, then buy a sacrificial lamb or simply donate the proceeds to God (cf. 13:13; Lev 27:27; Num 18:1). In contrast, one sacrifices the bull and the sheep. (On what is done with the firstborn human in 22:28, see NOTE.)

† *on the eighth day*. MT Sebhirin, very many MT and *Tg.* MSS (Kennicott 1776–80: 154; de Rossi 1784–85: 66), Soncino Bible (1488), Sam, LXX, Syr and *Tgs. Ps.-Jonathan* and *Neofiti I* insert "*and* on the eighth day." Virtually all parallels "*x* days . . . on the *x* + 1 day" feature a conjunction (for "seven . . . eighth," see Lev 12:2–3; 15:13–14, 28–29; Neh 8:18; for exceptions, see Lev 23:8, 36). Thus one might argue that standard MT is too anomalous to be correct. But these parallels come mainly from the Priestly source, while 22:29 is from another author. Since standard MT is unique but comprehensible, it is slightly preferable as *lectio difficilior*. (Note that the previous word ends in waw, creating an opportunity for either haplography or dittography, especially in continuous writing.)

†† 22:30. *meat*. MT, Sam and *Tg. Neofiti I* continue, "in the field" (*baśśāde[h]*). However, in a rare agreement among distinct textual streams, LXX, Vg, Syr and *Tgs. Onqelos* and *Ps.-Jonathan* lack *bśdh*. It is probably a quasi-dittograph of the preceding *wbśr* (*d* and *r* are similar in appearance in all phases of Hebrew script). (One might argue the contrary, that an original sequence *wbśr bśdh* suffered haplography; this, however, should have resulted in the loss of *bśr*, not *bśdh*.) Accordingly, I would read either **bəśar ṭərēpâ* 'meat of a torn animal' or **bəśar haṭṭərēpâ* 'the meat of the torn animal' (Budde *apud* Holzinger 1900: 94).

> SPECULATION: Although all extant Versions read "*and* meat," it is tempting to conjecture that the original was simply *bśr* 'meat,' which more closely resembles *bśdh*. The conjunction of MT *et al.* would be a natural, minor expansion, and also a dittograph of the preceding yodh (cf. Cross 1961a; Qimron 1972).

† *to the dog*. Instead of MT *lakkeleb* 'to the dog,' Sam reads an emphatic infinitive absolute: *hšlk*. Assuming that MT is correct—*lklb tšlkwn* is a more varied reading than *hšlk tšlykw*—might there be for Sam hygienic or ideological reasons why one should not feed defiled meat to dogs (e.g., lest they spread disease or impurity)? Or was a scribe simply misled by the profusion of kaphs and lamedhs (*t'klw lklb tšlhwn*)? Quite possibly, both MT and Sam are haplographic, and the original was **lklb hšlk tšlkwn 'tw* 'to the dog you must throw, throw it.'

23:2. *and.* The conjunction is absent in LXX.

† *and don't testify about a dispute.* For MT-Sam *wəlō(')-ta'ăne(h)* '*al-rīb*, LXX has "and don't join yourself with a crowd (i.e., **rōb*)," deriving *rb* not from *ryb* 'quarrel' but from *rbb* 'be great, many,' a root that appears twice in the verse as *rab-bîm* 'multitude.' How LXX takes the verb *ta'ăne(h)* is less obvious. Wevers (1990: 359) cites Syriac '*ny*, connoting, among other things, intimacy and association. Perhaps a similar usage existed in the Egyptian Aramaic familiar to the LXX translator.

SPECULATION: Since both MT and the LXX *Vorlage* are rather awkward, I suspect an ancient, irremediable textual corruption involving conflated variants, possibly **lō(')-tihye(h)* '*ahărê-rabbîm* *lərā'ōt* 'don't be consorting after a multitude' and **lō(')-tihye(h)* '*ahărê-rabbîm* *ləhaṭṭōt* 'don't be after a multitude to influence' (cf. Baentsch 1903: 205) Within this was inserted a third precept, **wəlō(')-ta'ăne(h)* '*al-rīb* *linṭōt* 'and don't testify about a dispute in order to incline (toward injustice).'

Alternatively, we might read *rb* as *rab* 'magnate' (cf. *b. Sanh.* 36a; Rashi), hence: "and don't testify on behalf of a magnate in order to influence." The law would then balance the following ban on favoring the poor, just as the parallel in Lev 19:15 forbids leaning toward either rich or poor. (Admittedly, *rab* as an independent noun, though attested in Rabbinic Hebrew and Phoenician, is not otherwise found in Biblical Hebrew). See further NOTE.

influence. LXX adds an explanatory "a trial."
23:4. *When.* LXX and Syr have "*And* when."
his ass. Sam adds '*w kl bhmtw* 'or any animal of him'; cf. TEXTUAL NOTES to 21:28–36; 23:12.
23:5. *When.* LXX and Kenn 69 have "*And* if."

SPECULATION: It is tempting to replace the opening *kî* 'when' with *lō(')* 'not' as in the parallel Deut 22:4, assuming that the erroneous *kî* of v 5 was imported from v 4 (Ehrlich 1969: 184). This would produce a smooth reading for the first half-verse: "Don't see the ass of one who hates you recumbent under its burden and refrain from leaving (it) to him." But the rest remains problematic; see further NOTE.

† *would refrain . . . with him.* The second half of the verse is notoriously difficult and possibly corrupt; see NOTE.
23:6. *your pauper's.* LXX lacks the slightly awkward "your."

SPECULATION: Cassuto (1967: 298), too, feels that the pronominal suffix *-kā* 'your' in the term '*ebyōnəkā* is rather odd. He suggests that here '*ebyôn* has a unique meaning "enemy," citing as a cognate Arabic '*by* 'refuse, dislike.' Another way to accommodate Cassuto's observation would be simply to emend the text: read for MT '*bynk* 'your pauper'**'ybk* ('*ōyibkā*) 'your enemy.' Instinctually, I agree that 23:6 originally referred to one's enemy. But, since this is mere conjecture, I have refrained from imposing such an understanding onto the translation.

23:7. *From.* Syr has "*And* from."

false word. 1QS 5:15 and LXX expand: *mkwl dbr šqr* 'from *every* false word.'

† *and an innocent.* LXX lacks *w-* 'and,' possibly correctly. In addition to the random addition or deletion of conjunctions, a contributory factor may be the preceding yodh of *wnqy*, creating an opportunity for haplography/dittography in continuous writing (see Cross 1961a; Qimron 1972).

for I shall not vindicate. For MT *kî lō(')-'aṣdîq*, LXX has "and *you* shall not vindicate," as if reading either **ky l' tṣdyq* or **wl' tṣdyq*, apparently influenced by the surrounding 2 m.s. verbs in 23:1–12. (Noth [1962: 189], however, seems to favor the second person as original.) If the error is early, the graphic similarity of 'aleph and taw in paleo-Hebrew script may have been a factor (see Tov 2001: 244–45). Sam appears to have a third variant, *ky l' hṣdyq rš'*, but *hṣdyq* is the equivalent of MT *'aṣdîq* 'I shall . . . vindicate' (cf. *Samaritan Tg. J*), since Sam sometimes confuses the gutturals aleph and he' (see Tov, pp. 95–96).

SPECULATION: Alternatively, to account for MT and Sam, we might posit an original **ky l' hṣdyq* [sic] *'ṣdyq rš'* 'I will not vindicate, vindicate a guilty one,' variously reduced in the surviving witnesses. But guttural confusion is the simpler explanation.

a guilty one. LXX appends "for gifts," as if reading **bšḥd.* This is periphrastic expansion—specifically, a double reading of the following *wəšōḥad* 'and a bribe" (Prijs 1948: 13–14).

23:8. *And a bribe.* Syr lacks "And."

† *it blinds the sighted.* So MT and Vg (*y'wr pqḥym*), vs. 4QpaleoGen-Exod[1], Sam, several MT MSS and editions (Kennicott 1776–80: 155; de Rossi 1784–85: 66–67), LXX, *Tgs. Onqelos* and *Ps.-Jonathan* and Syr, which all read *y'wr 'yny pqḥym* 'it blinds the sighted's *eyes.*' Methodology favors MT's *lectio difficilior et brevior,* since the plus is unnecessary to the sense and agrees with the parallel in Deut 16:19 (cf. Sir 20:29); moreover, its loss cannot be explained mechanically. See further NOTE.

For "sighted," Kenn 109, 129, 153, Syr, *Tg. Onqelos* and probably Aquila (Wevers 1990: 362) have *ḥăkāmîm* 'wise,' both a suitable paraphrase of *piqḥîm* 'sighted, discerning' and a harmonization with Deut 16:19.

the righteous's words. So MT (*dibrê ṣaddîqîm*), Sam, Vg and Syr. The rendering in LXX, and *Tgs. Onqelos* and *Ps.-Jonathan,* "righteous words" (**dəbārîm ṣaddîqîm?*), seems periphrastic, perhaps taking *ṣaddîqîm* as an abstract plural (cf. *Tg. Neofiti I: mly dyn' zkyy* 'pure words of justice'). But it is hard to understand why paraphrase was necessary or desirable; in fact, LXX renders MT literally in the parallel, Deut 16:19. For further discussion, see Prijs 1948: 65–66.

† 23:9. *oppress.* Perhaps correctly, 4QpaleoGen-Exod[1], Sam, LXX, Syr and *Tgs.* have the second person plural *tlḥṣw* for the MT-Vg singular *tlḥṣ,* thus agreeing

with the following 2 m. pl. verbs. MT could have lost the final waw by haplography with the following letter (D. N. Freedman, privately). But if, conversely, the MT *lectio difficilior* is original, then the longer variant may be the result of dittography with the next word. There is also a tendency to pluralize singular commands to Israel throughout the ancient translations. Many LXX MSS expand: "don't *afflict or* oppress," harmonizing with 22:20.

† 23:10. *And (first time).* So standard MT. Kenn 69, 674, LXX, Syr and Vg lack the conjunction, which is indeed unexpected (see NOTE).

23:11. *So.* Syr has "*And so.*"

for your vineyard. Against MT *ləkarməkā*, many Sam MSS and Syr have "for your (s.) vineyards" (i.e., *lkrmyk*), while *Tg. Neofiti I* has "for your (pl.) vineyards." See also next TEXTUAL NOTE.

for your olive. Sam, Kenn 4, Rossi 14, 185, 262, 373, 592, LXX, Syr, some *Tg.* MSS (Rossi 1784–85: 67) and Vg insert the expected "and" (on its absence, see NOTE). Moreover, Syr, many Sam MSS and some MT MSS (Kennicott 1776–80: 155; Rossi 373, 405) read *(w)lzytyk* '(and) for your olives' (cf. previous TEXTUAL NOTE). Since "vineyards . . . olives" is a biblical cliché (Deut 6:11; Josh 24:13; 1 Sam 8:14, etc.), MT *lkrmk lzytk* 'for your vineyard, for your olive' is both the shorter and the more difficult reading.

23:12. *your bull . . . maidservant's son.* Sam has instead "your manservant and your maidservant like you and all your animals," influenced by Deut 5:14 (cf. TEXTUAL NOTES to 21:28–36; 23:4).

the sojourner. Syr adds "who is in your cities," adapted from 20:10.

† 23:13. *And through all that I have said . . . keep yourselves.* I follow the slightly difficult reading of MT and *Tgs.*: *ûb(ə)kōl ʾăšer-ʾāmartî ʾălêkem tiššāmērû.* Sam, Rossi 668 (first hand), LXX and Vg offer the *lectio facilior* "All that I have said to you, you will keep" (*kōl ʾăšer-ʾāmartî ʾălêkem tišmərû*). (Syr, Kenn 277, 683 and Sebhirin have a conflated [*wə*]*kōl ʾăšer-ʾāmartî ʾălêkem tiššāmērû*, difficult to translate.)

† *don't mention. It shall not be heard.* These words present three problems. The first is the presence or absence of the conjunction between the clauses. It is missing from 4QpaleoGen-Exod[1] and standard MT but present in many MT and *Tg.* MSS (Kennicott 1776–80: 155; de Rossi 1784–85: 67), Sam, LXX, *Tg. Neofiti I*, Syr and Vg.

The next problem is the number of the verb "mention." Against MT *lʾ tzkyrw* 'don't mention (pl.),' Sam has *lʾ tzkyr* 'don't mention (s.).' In MT, the verb matches the preceding second masculine plurals *ʾălêkem tiššāmērû* 'to you (pl.), you (pl.) will keep yourselves,' while in Sam the verb matches the following second masculine singular *pyk* 'your (s.) mouth.' Either might be original. (LXX and *Tgs.* level the plural throughout the verse.)

The two problems under consideration—the status of the conjunction and the number of the verb—may in fact be related. In essence we have three variants: *tzkyr wlʾ* (Sam), *tzkyrw lʾ* (standard MT) and *tzkyrw wlʾ* (nonstandard MT, LXX, *Tg. Neofiti I*, Syr and Vg). While omission or addition of a conjunction may be a random affair, here we have the likelihood of haplography or dittography.

The third problem: Sam has *wl' yšm'w* 'and *they* shall not be heard,' referring to the gods' names. I assume that collective singulars are generally more original than plurals, and hence follow MT *(wə)lō(')* *yiššāmaʿ*.

your mouth. The translations into Greek and Aramaic "fix" MT-Sam *pîkā* 'your (sing.) mouth' by pluralizing the pronoun (see previous TEXTUAL NOTE); *Tg. Neofiti I* also pluralizes the noun itself: "your (pl.) mouths." Syr presents the periphrastic variant "your (pl.) *heart.*"

23:14. *you must celebrate.* The verb is collective singular in MT-Sam but explicitly plural in LXX, Syr, Vg and *Tgs. Ps.-Jonathan* and *Neofiti I.*

23:15. *keep . . . eat.* The verbs are singular in MT-Sam but plural in LXX. LXX[B], moreover, expands "keep *to do,*" after Deut 5:32(29); 6:3, 25; 8:1, etc.

you went out. Although so far in this section, Syr has followed the second masculine singulars of MT, here it has *npqtwn* 'you (pl.) went out,' vs. MT *yāṣā(')tā* 'you (sing.) went out.' Either this is paraphrase, or the mem of *mmṣrym* 'from Egypt' was orally or graphically reduplicated and shifted to the end of *yṣ't*, producing *yṣ'tm* 'you (pl.) went out.' Syr keeps to the plural through the rest of vv 15–16 (vs. MT).

† *And.* The conjunction is absent from LXX, Kenn 181 and Vg, perhaps rightly.

my Face must not be seen. The LXX reading "he shall not appear before me," as if reading **lō'-yērā'e(h) 'el-pānay*, both harmonizes with 23:17 and avoids the implication that Yahweh is visible. See also TEXTUAL NOTE to 23:17.

23:16. *Harvest Festival.* LXX adds an explanatory "you shall make."

† 23:17. *must appear to the Lord Yahweh's Face.* So MT *(yr'h 'l pny h'd[w]n yhwh)* (cf. Kennicott 1776–80: 156). LXX, Vg and Syr basically support MT, but call God "Lord (i.e., Yahweh) your god," as in 23:19 (cf. also 34:23–24). This is not a true variant. Rather, since these Versions call Yahweh *kyrios/Dominus/ māryā'* 'the Lord,' they wish to avoid the redundant "the lord, the Lord" (Wevers 1990: 367).

Sam, however, has a real variant: *yr'h 't pny 'rwn yhwh* 'must appear before Yahweh's *Chest,*' i.e., the Ark of the Covenant. We find almost the same contradiction in the parallel 34:23 (see TEXTUAL NOTE). Which reading is correct, MT or Sam? Anachronism is not a valid objection to Sam, for, even though the Chest is not described until chap. 25, the next two verses presuppose Temple worship. Moreover, 16:33–34 has already alluded to the Chest (see NOTES). Whichever variant is original, the similarity of daleth and resh in all periods of Hebrew script is surely a factor in the confusion. But the omission or addition of *he'* before *'r/d(w)n* 'Chest/Lord' must have been intentional.

I consider MT the superior reading. Both here and in 34:23–24, Sam may easily be explained as censoring anthropomorphism, comparable to the problematic vocalization of *r'y* 'see' (see SPECULATION below). In fact, many Sam MSS have an ungrammatical *yr'h 't pny h'rwn yhwh* 'must appear before the Chest, Yahweh' (*sic*), with the definite article impossibly standing before a noun in construct. This variant is probably the intermediary between MT and standard Sam.

SPECULATION: In both MT and Samaritan tradition (Ben-Ḥayyim 1977: 427), the verb *yērā'e(h)* is Niphʿal in 23:17 and in parallel passages (34:20, 23–24;

Deut 16:16; 31:11; 1 Sam 1:22; Isa 1:12; Ps 42:3). Accordingly, even for Sam, *'t* is not the definite direct object marker *'ēt* I but *'ēt* II 'with, at, by' (cf. *Samaritan Tg.* *'m qdm* 'before the presence'). In other words, *'et-pǝnê* is synonymous to the more common *lipnê* 'before'; Aḥituv (1997: 5* n. 6) compares 1 Sam 2:11, "And the lad was ministering before (*'et-pǝnê*) Eli the priest." Many commentators, however, suspect that the clause's proper vocalization is **yir'e(h) kol-zǝkûrǝkā 'et-pǝnê hā'ādōn yahwe(h)* 'all your malehood must see the Lord Yahweh's Face' (e.g., Luzzatto on Isa 1:12; Dillmann 1880: 247; Noth 1962: 192; esp. C. McCarthy 1981: 197–204). Later copyists, finding the anthropomorphism too gross, supposedly exercised the license of *tiqqûn sōpǝrîm* 'scribes' correction' to create the Niph'al *yērā'e(h)*, implicitly converting *'ēt* I into *'ēt* II. Note that *Mek. kaspā'* 4 and *b. Ḥag.* 2a, 4b exempt the blind from this precept, understanding the requirement as both to be *seen* (Niph'al *yērā'e[h]*) and to *see* (Qal **yir'e[h]*).

Admittedly, many biblical passages refer to seeing God or his face (Exod 24:10–11; Isa 6:5; 38:11; Ps 17:15; 42:3 [Versions], etc.). Jacob (1992: 724–25), however, denies any relevance for Exod 23:17, citing other passages in which *'et-pǝnê* is adverbial, not accusative (Gen 19:13, 27; 1 Sam 2:17; 1 Kgs 12:6; Ps 16:11; 21:7; Prov 17:24) and providing further illustrations. 1 Sam 1:22 is a particularly strong argument for the Niph'al in Exod 23:17, etc., since in Samuel the Niph'al perfect form is almost certain: *wǝnir'â 'et-pǝnê yahwe(h)* 'and he will appear to Yahweh's face' (although C. McCarthy [1981: 199–200] less plausibly reads a cohortative "let us see"). Moreover, Sam Exod 34:24 features an unambiguous Niph'al *lhr'wt* (MT *lērā'ôt*). Still, some uncertainty remains. One wonders how, before the introduction of vowel points, a reader was expected to distinguish between *yir'e(h)* (Qal) and *yērā'e(h)* (Niph'al) in an unclear context. Probably the expression was quasi-proverbial.

Ultimately, it makes no difference whether we read the Qal or the Niph'al in 23:17. We were already told in 23:15 that Yahweh's face may be seen. Accepting the MT vocalization, the point of v 17 is that Deity and worshiper should behold one another.

23:18. *Don't offer.* LXX begins 23:18 with a secondary insertion borrowed from 34:24: "When I dispossess nations from before you and widen your borders."

Slaughter-offering . . . festival. Taking this as a general prescription, and also understanding *ḥag* as connoting a sacrifice (see NOTE), Dillmann (1880: 249) conjectures that the original vocalization was **zǝbāḥay . . . ḥaggay* 'my Slaughter-offerings . . . my festival *offerings*.' The MT singulars *zibḥî . . . ḥaggî* would be an effort to limit the rule to the Passover sacrifice (see NOTE).

23:19. *milk.* Sam ends with a plus vis-à-vis the other Versions: *ky 'śh z't kzbḥ škḥ w'brh hy' l'lhy y'qb* 'for anyone doing this is like a sacrificer of contempt, and it is a provocation to Jacob's deity' (cf. Tal 2000: 550). A host of LXX MSS feature a strikingly similar addition to Deut 14:21, "Don't boil a kid in its mother's milk, *for anyone doing this, it is as if he sacrifices rats (asplaka, perhaps translating Hebrew *tinšamōt* [cf. LXX Lev 11:30]), *for it is a sin/provocation (mēnima/miasma) to Jacob's God."* See further Nestle (1913).

23:20. See. LXX has "*And see.*"

a Messenger. Sam, LXX and Vg have "*my* Messenger," harmonizing with 23:23; 32:34. See also TEXTUAL NOTE to 33:2, "a Messenger."

the place. LXX and Syr have "the *land*," comparable to Gen 50:24; Exod 6:8; 12:25; 33:1.

prepared. LXX adds "for you."

23:21. don't. LXX (not LXX^AFM) and Kenn 181 insert "and."

†† *rebel.* While the meaning is in little doubt (but see Rashbam, ibn Ezra), the vocalization is uncertain. The MT Hiph'il *tammēr* appears to be influenced by Aramaic (GKC §67g, y) and assumes the root *mrr*, which ordinarily means "to be bitter" (so Symmachus). However, Sam *(tmry)*, LXX, Aquila, *Tgs.* and Syr read the Hiph'il of *mry* 'rebel,' as the context dictates. So we should probably vocalize **temer* (GKC §67y) or **tāmēr* (assuming a root *mrr* equivalent to *mry*; cf. GKC §77e).

lift. LXX "refrain" *(hypostellō)* implies that the angel will not stint in punishment. Why LXX does not translate the Hebrew literally is unclear. Wevers (1990: 370) supposes that the translators felt theological discomfort with the notion that any but God can remit sin. See also the following TEXTUAL NOTES.

within him. LXX has "*upon* him." The diminution of the Messenger's status (see also previous TEXTUAL NOTE) may indicate that for LXX he is not an angel but Moses himself (*pace* Wevers 1990: 370). See further NOTE to 23:20.

23:22. But if. Vs. MT-Sam *kî 'im*, Syr appears to read *wə'im* 'and if.'

heed. The verb is singular in MT but plural in Sam *(tšm'w)*, LXX (not LXX^A) and *Tg. Neofiti I* (which pluralizes all references to Israel).

† *his voice.* So standard MT *(bqwlw)*. Sam, some MT MSS (Kennicott 1776–80: 156), LXX and *Tg. Neofiti I* read *bqwly* 'my voice.' Whichever is original, the cause of confusion is threefold: the similarity of waw and yodh in the canon's formative period (Cross 1961a; Qimron 1972), the grammatical switch between first and third person in 23:20–23 and the overall interpenetrability of the personae of Deity and Messenger (see NOTE to 3:2).

On behalf of Sam et al., one might note that the next word begins with waw, so a corruption *yw*> *ww* in MT is quite conceivable. Moreover, the confusion between waw and yodh is possible only in the square script of MT, not in the Samaritan paleo-Hebrew. Finally, *bqwlw* has just appeared in 23:21, making Sam the more diverse text. On the other hand, LXX, at least, is strongly influenced by 19:5–6, and so is suspect as harmonistic (see below). In the end, I follow MT, which is *lectio difficilior* in terms of content. That is, we would expect a command to "do all that *I* speak" to be preceded by "hear *my* voice" (Sam), not "hear *his* voice" (MT).

do. The verb is plural in Sam *(w'śytm)* and LXX^B, singular in the other witnesses.

I speak. Uniquely, *Tg. Neofiti I* has "*he* speaks."

At this point LXX inserts a long plus derived from 19:5–6: "'. . . to you, and keep my Covenant, then you will become for me a most treasured nation among all peoples, for mine is all the earth. And you, you will become for me a priestly king-dom and a holy nation.' These words you shall say to Israel's Sons: 'If you hear, hear my voice and do all that I say to you. . . . ' "

† 23:23. *Canaanite . . . Hivvite.* Rossi 503 (first hand) and LXX interpolate "and the Girgashite." Sam does the same, also putting "the Canaanite" in the first spot. Ausloos (1996: 91–100) regards the longer list as a harmonization with Deut 7:1. The various witnesses include conjunctions in varying positions throughout the list; my translation follows L.

I will eradicate him. All the ancient translations periphrastically pluralize the pronominal object: "eradicate *them.*" Tg. *Neofiti I* also makes the verb imperative: "and (you) eradicate them," apparently reading **whkḥdtw/wəhikḥadtô* (vs. the MT first person *whkḥdtyw/wəhikḥadtîw*).

† 23:24. *And don't.* LXX and Kenn 129 omit the conjunction, possibly cor-rectly.

†† *destroy, destroy.* The vocalization of standard MT, *hārēs təhārəsēm*, with both verbs Piʿel, is questionable. Rashbam knew texts in France that read *hārēs taharsēm*, with the second verb in the Qal. In fact, all evidence favors the Qal over the Piʿel as the proper conjugation for this root (the only other Piʿel is Isa 49:17, but the Versions and 1QIsaᵃ do not support MT). In fact, the French MSS were probably only half-correct: the original should have been **hārōs taharsēm*. The Piʿel is due to attraction to the following *wəšabbēr təšabbēr*.

23:25. *you shall serve . . . your deity.* The second persons are plural in MT and Sam, but singular in LXX. Since all verbs in the immediate environment are 2 m.s., MT-Sam is preferable as the more diverse reading.

he will bless. LXX and Vg have "*I* will bless," anticipating the shift to the first person later in the verse.

† *your bread . . . your water.* LXX inserts in the middle: "and your wine." This could be either an expansion or the original reading, since a list **'t lḥmk w't yynk w't mymk* 'your food and your wine and your water' would be liable to parablepsis (D. N. Freedman, privately). Syr pluralizes the pronominal suffixes.

I will remove. Syr "*he* will remove" harmonizes with the preceding "he will bless."

your midst. "Your" is singular in MT, plural in LXX and Syr.

23:26. *There will not be.* Sam, Rossi 683 and Syr prefix "And."

23:27. *My terror.* LXX begins "And" and omits the pronoun "My," perhaps lest one think that God's "terror" is fear not *caused* but *experienced* by the Deity.

discomfit. For MT *wəhammōtî* 'and (I shall) discomfit,' Syr and Vg read the more common word **wəhēmattî* 'and (I shall) kill'—which, however, ill suits the context, since the enemies proceed to flee. A possible stimulus for this variant reading may have been the close homophony with *'êmātî* 'My terror.'

23:28. *it will expel.* LXXᴬ and Syr have "*I* will expel," presumably influenced by the surrounding first-person verbs, especially "I will expel" in 23:29–30. LXXᴮ has "*you* will expel"; cf. 23:31 MT (see TEXTUAL NOTE).

the Hivvite. Before the Hivvite, LXX has "and the Amorite." Sam lists seven na-tions, in the same order as in 23:23 (see TEXTUAL NOTE). Syr, however, has only the Canaanite and the Hittite. Various MSS of various witnesses put conjunctions at various points in the sequence. My translation follows L.

23:29. *expel him.* Here and in 23:30, while MT and Sam use the singular object pronoun "him," all the ancient translations paraphrase "expel *them*." (Less likely, there were Hebrew MSS actually reading **ʾgršm* for MT *ʾgršnw;* on the potential corruption *nw > m* in the square script, see Tov [2001: 249].)

† *before you. Mippāne(y)kā* was either absent from the LXX *Vorlage* or ignored by the translator. We might consider this the superior, shorter reading, MT having been supplemented from 23:30–31. But in the absence of Hebrew evidence, I follow MT-Sam.

23:30. *expel him.* See TEXTUAL NOTE to 23:29.

23:31. *and I will set.* Vs. MT-Sam *wəšattî,* 4QpaleoExod^m has the more common synonym *wśmty.*

the River. The ancient translations identify the River more precisely. *Tgs. Onqelos* and *Ps.-Jonathan* specify "the Euphrates," *Tg. Neofiti I* has "the great river" and LXX has "the great river Euphrates."

the land's inhabitants. A Genizah fragment *(apud BHS),* some MT MSS (Kennicott 1776–80: 157; de Rossi 1784–85: 68), the Soncino Bible (1488) and *Tgs. Ps.-Jonathan* and *Neofiti I* expand: *"all* the land's inhabitants."

† *and you will expel them.* So MT *(wəgēraštāmô).* LXX, Vg and *Tg. Neofiti I* have "and *I* will expel them," as if reading **wəgēraštîmô* or **wəgēraštîm* (= Sam, *Samaritan Tg.*). Although one cannot be certain, I favor MT, since in the most recent occurrences (23:29, 30), the subject of *grš* 'expel' was "I" (God) not Israel. Accordingly, MT presents the most varied text. Syr "you (pl.) will expel them" is probably paraphrase, less likely a third reading **wəgēraštūm(ô);* see also next TEXTUAL NOTE. On the differing forms of the pronominal suffix in MT and Sam, see NOTE.

before you. MT *mippāne(y)kā* is not reflected in Syr. It was probably deliberately ignored, permitting *wgrštm(w)* to be taken as a second masculine plural (see previous TEXTUAL NOTE). Conceivably, however, "before you" fell out by inner-Aramaic parablepsis, assuming pluralization of the suffix: **ʾnwn mn qdmykwn* 'them before you (pl.)' > *ʾnwn* 'them' (homoioteleuton).

23:33. *They may not dwell.* LXX and Syr prefix "And."

when you serve. Since MT is difficult to translate (see NOTE), Syr offers a *lectio facilior:* "*don't* serve."

it will become. So MT, in which *yhyh* refers to the act of apostasy (but see NOTE). In contrast, Sam, LXX, *Tgs.* and Syr use the plural *yhyw* 'they (the Canaanites) will be' (see Wevers 1990: 377–78). Throughout this section, we find a tendency to change singulars to plurals. MT is likely original.

24:1. *Nadab.* Here and in 24:9, LXX and Syr have *"and* Nadab."

Abihu. Here and in 24:9, 4QpaleoExod^m and Sam add "Eleazar and Ithamar," harmonizing with 28:1, etc.

you shall bow down. To solve a logical problem, LXX has "*they* shall bow down." Strictly speaking, Moses is not among those who worship "from afar" (Wevers 1990: 379). For further examples of LXX "fixing" MT-Sam's ambiguous stage directions, cf. TEXTUAL NOTES to 24:2, 13, 14, 15.

from afar. LXX adds an explanatory "to the Lord."

24:2. *Yahweh.* LXX has "the God."

†† *ascend.* The verb is plural in MT *(ya'ălû)*, singular in Sam *(y'lh)*. Since *'am* 'people' can be singular or plural, both versions are grammatical. Sam is slightly preferable as *lectio difficilior*, since the previous verb *yiggāšû* 'approach' is plural. Cf. TEXTUAL NOTE to 24:3, "answered."

with him. LXX has "with *them*" to clarify an ambiguity: MT-Sam could imply that the people ascend as high as the elders (Wevers 1990: 380). Cf. TEXTUAL NOTE to 24:1, "you shall bow down."

24:3. *Yahweh* (first time). LXX has "the God."

† *all the laws.* Attractively, LXX lacks "all."

† *answered.* The verb is plural in Sam *(wy'nw)*, Tg. *Neofiti I* and MT Sebhirin, singular in MT *(wayya'an)*. *'Am* 'people' can be singular or plural, but here MT is slightly preferable as *lectio difficilior*, since the next verb is plural *(wayyō[']mərû)*. Cf. TEXTUAL NOTE to 24:2, "ascend."

the words. The phrase is missing in Kenn 84, Rossi 503, Rossi Sam 64 and Syr, thus harmonizing with 24:7.

we will do. LXX continues "and we will hear," presumably derived from 24:7 (cf. TEXTUAL NOTE to 19:8, "we will do").

24:4. *he got up.* Since the Deity has just been mentioned, LXX and Kenn 686 clarify: "*Moses* got up."

pillar. For MT *maṣṣēbâ* 'pillar' (collective singular), Sam and LXX read *'bnym* 'stones,' both an assimilation to the analogous scene in Josh 4:20 (Joshua erects twelve stones) (Wevers 1990: 381) and an avoidance of the term "pillar," forbidden by 23:24; 34:13; Deut 16:22, etc. (Tov 2001: 273).

24:5. *sent.* Against MT *wayyišlaḥ*, the Sebhirin raises the possibility of *wayšallaḥ* 'released.'

Yahweh. LXX has "the God."

† *Slaughter-offerings, Concluding-offerings.* While in MT, the nouns *zəbāḥîm* and *šəlāmîm* are unexpectedly in apposition, Sam MSS offer the more typical construction *zbḥy šlmym* 'Slaughter-offerings of Concluding-offerings.' LXX appears to reflect a more attractive variant *zbḥ šlmym 'a* Slaughter-offering *of* Concluding-offerings'; this last would be my choice, if only it were confirmed in a Hebrew MS.

bulls. Sam expands: *bny bqr* 'sons of cattle.'

24:6. *the bowls.* Where MT has *'aggānōt* 'bowls,' we find in LXXᴬ, Syr and Tg. *Neofiti I* the singular, "*a* bowl." We might revocalize *'aggenet*, an otherwise unattested byform of *'aggān*; compare Arabic *'ijjānat* 'bowl.' But most likely the MT plural is correct; it is corroborated by 4QBibPar *b'gwnwt* (sic). The variant singular is a paraphrase to facilitate Moses' blood manipulation (see NOTE).

24:7. *do . . . heed.* 4QpaleoExodᵐ, Sam, LXXꟳ and Syr reverse the verbs vis-à-vis MT, thus undoing the hysteron proteron (see NOTE). Perhaps one of the verbs fell out and was wrongly reinserted.

24:8. *cast.* Sam expands: *wyzrqhw* 'and cast *it*.'

upon the people. Tgs. *Onqelos* and *Ps.-Jonathan* elaborate, based partly upon 24:6: "against the altar as *Clearing,* on (behalf of) the people" of (cf. Rashi).

these words. A Genizah fragment *(apud BHS)* has instead *hammišpāṭîm hā'ēlle(h)* 'these case-laws.'

24:9. *Nadab.* See TEXTUAL NOTE to 24:1.

Abihu. See TEXTUAL NOTE to 24:1.

24:10. *saw Israel's deity.* Alarmed by the plain sense (cf. esp. 33:20, "Man may not see me and live"), LXX bowdlerizes, "saw *the place where* Israel's God *stood there,*" with "stood" evidently inspired by the following mention of God's "feet." The Greek translator may have deliberately mistaken *'ēt* I, the direct object marker, for *'ēt* II 'with, by, at'; cf. TEXTUAL NOTE to 24:11, "beheld the Deity."

24:11. *he did not . . . his arm.* In order to minimize the anthropomorphism, LXX paraphrases, "not one was missing." *Tg. Onqelos* similarly reports, "there was no harm."

beheld the Deity. LXX drastically bowdlerizes: "they appeared in the God's place," apparently reading *wyḥzw* as if in the Niphʻal—unattested for this verb but inspired by *nirʾâ* 'appear'—and interpreting *'ēt* as "with, by, at" (cf. TEXTUAL NOTES to 23:17; 24:10). For MT *wayyeḥĕzû* 'beheld,' Sam MSS read *wy'ḥzw*, the interpretation of which is unclear: **wayyēʾāḥăzû* 'and they gathered (before)'? *wayyō(')ḥăzû* 'and they grasped'? orthographic variant of *wayyeḥĕzû* (= MT)? orthograpic variant of *wayyēḥāzû* (= LXX)?

24:12. *the stone tablets.* So MT: *lūḥōt hāʾeben,* paralleled only in 31:18 (MT). In both verses, Sam has *lwḥt h'bnym* 'the tablets of stones,' conforming to 34:1, 4; Deut 4:13; 5:19(22); 9:9–11; 10:1, 3; 1 Kgs 8:9. MT is preferable as *lectio difficilior.*

†† *the Direction.* Reading *hattôrâ* with 4QReworked Pentateuch[b], Sam and LXX as *lectio brevior.* Rashi similarly understands MT "*and* the Direction" to exemplify the explicative (i.e., superfluous) waw: "*namely,* the Direction and the command."

24:13. *Moses ascended.* So MT. 4QReworked Pentateuch[b] has "in order to ascend" *(lʻlwt),* while LXX has "and *they* ascended," i.e., Moses and Joshua (cf. Rossi 503, "and Moses *and Joshua* ascended"). See TEXTUAL NOTES to 24:14, "he had said," 15, "Moses ascended."

SPECULATION: These variants would be well explained by supposing a common source **wyʻl* 'and he ascended.' This *lectio brevior* was paraphrased in 4QReworked Pentateuch[b], and expanded in LXX and MT for the sake of clarity.

24:14. *he had said.* LXX has "*they* had said," i.e., Moses and Joshua. See TEXTUAL NOTES to 24:13, 15, "Moses ascended."

Stay for us. Tg. *Neofiti I* has "stay for *me.*" LXX "rest" *(hēsychazete)* and Vg "wait" *(expectate)* may reflect a *Vorlage* **šbw lkm* 'stay you,' vs. MT *šəbû-lānû;* cf. LXX Gen 22:5 (LXX *kathisate* 'sit' = MT *šəbû-lākem*). See NOTE.

†† *See.* So Sam and possibly Vg. MT and LXX have "*And* see."

† *approach.* Although MT is perfectly comprehensible, Ehrlich (1908: 364) plausibly revocalizes *yiggaš* as **yaggēš:* "whoever has *words,* let him *present* (them) to them." For *higgîš* in a legal context, compare Isa 41:21–22.

24:15. *Moses ascended.* So MT; many LXX MSS have "Moses *and Joshua* ascended." MT is *lectio brevior et difficilior*, with LXX "fixing" the slightly inconsistent and ambiguous MT. See also TEXTUAL NOTES to 24:1, 2, 13, 14.

24:16. *Yahweh's.* LXX has "the God's."

settled. LXX *katebē* 'descended' appears to read *wyrd as in 19:20, vs. MT-Sam *wayyiškōn* (E. W. Goldstein, privately), but could also be regarded as paraphrase.

he called. LXX, Kenn 84 and Syr clarify: "and *the Lord* called."

24:17. *Israel's Sons.* Kenn 69 has *kl yśr'l* 'all Israel,' while Syr paraphrases "*all* Israel's *House.*"

24:18. *Moses was.* LXX and Vg have instead "*he* was *there,*" harmonizing with 34:28; cf. 24:12.

SOURCE ANALYSIS

The Horeb-Sinai narrative (chaps. 19–24, 32–34) will always frustrate our attempts to understand its composition history. Depending on presuppositions and temperament, one scholar's source-break will be another's artistic effect. My goal here is to show how the text *could have* evolved, not how it *did* (influential past treatments include Beyerlin 1965; Toeg 1977; Moberly 1983 and Dozeman 1989a).

To begin with, 19:1–2 is somewhat awkward: "In the third month of Israel's Sons going out from the land of Egypt, on this day, they came to the Sinai Wilderness. And they set forth from Rephidim and came to the Sinai Wilderness and camped in the wilderness, and Israel camped there, opposite the mountain." Why are we told twice that Israel "came to the Sinai Wilderness" and twice that they "camped"?

On the one hand, this might be the composition of a single writer, who began his story with a kind of heading and then backtracked to explain whence the people had come (Houtman 1996: 439). In other words, "And they set forth from Rephidim" could be a digression framed by *Wiederaufnahme* (cf. Kuhl 1952).

On the other hand, given other evidence external to chap. 19 for an editorial itinerary stratum (Cross 1973: 308–17), I am more inclined to see a supplemented text. The Redactor deliberately placed the words "And they set forth from Rephidim and came to the Sinai Wilderness and camped in the wilderness" inside a preexisting "In the third month of Israel's Sons going out from the land of Egypt, on this day, they came to the Sinai Wilderness. And Israel camped there, opposite the mountain." Not that this explanation is entirely satisfactory, either. One might rather have expected, given the editor's procedure elsewhere, "And they set forth from Rephidim and came to the Sinai Wilderness. In the third month of Israel's Sons going out from the land of Egypt, on this day, they came to the Sinai Wilderness. And Israel camped there opposite the mountain." Apparently, the Redactor wished instead to emphasize the month of Israel's arrival.

SPECULATION: Many commentators suggest that the exact day of Israel's departure fell from 19:1 by accident (see NOTE for other explanations). If this happened, the most likely occasion was when the Redactor was weighing his options and departing from his usual practice. He lost his focus and did not catch his error later.

Into which source did the Redactor make his insertion? The date formula, the phrase *bayyôm hazze(h)* 'on this day,' the reference to "Sinai"—these are all hallmarks of P. The final clause, however, "and Israel camped there, opposite the mountain" could come from any source.

The Priestly source continues in 24:15b–18a, with the description of the fiery Glory descending upon Mount Sinai (not Horeb). P's Sinai narrative leads directly into chaps. 25–31, 35–40, the Tabernacle account (see below, pp. 365–70).

The Sinai narrative ends with Moses' descent in 34:29–35. Since the language is Priestly, this may be the original conclusion to P's Tabernacle instructions—or, more accurately, the fulcrum of P's double-jointed Tabernacle section. Admittedly, however, two of the best source indicators are slightly dubious: in 34:29, LXX lacks *sînay* and *ʿēdūt* (see TEXTUAL NOTES). Still, in addition to the overall redundant style, we have in v 31 *nəśîʾîm* 'leaders' and *ʿēdâ* 'congregation,' plus "entering before Yahweh" in v 34, all signs of P. (On the possibility that the story was not just interpolated but composed by the Redactor, see REDACTION ANALYSIS.)

By standard source critical procedures, the remainder of chaps. 19–24, 32–34, should go mainly to JE. In fact, both J and E are discernible in chap. 19. But not all the seams are obvious.

For example, we find a possible fissure in 19:3, "but Moses, he ascended to the Deity, and Yahweh called to him from the mountain." To one mind-set, this is self-contradictory, and manifest evidence of source conflation. I, however, would find little difficulty in attributing the words to a single author. Either the first clause is circumstantial, as indicated by the inverted syntax ("while Moses was ascending to the Deity"), or else it serves as a kind of summary of what follows: "The important thing is—Moses went up the mountain. When he was there, the following things were said." We might also just accept hysteron proteron as a feature of biblical narrative. Or there could be two sources after all. No doubt, ancient biblical editors strove to minimize the jarring among their sources, and reveled in virtuosic, scarcely noticeable juxtapositions. Our perplexity thus vindicates their craft. As for the source or sources of 19:3, the presence of "Deity" in the first clause suggests E for the first half if not the entire verse.

The rest of v 3, "saying, 'Thus you will say . . .'" opens a new section, with Yahweh's speech continuing through v 6. Commentators notice two salient characteristics of this passage: it falls into almost poetic parallelism, and it shares vocabulary with Deuteronomy and related literature: *ʾattem rəʾîtem* 'you, you saw' (cf. Deut 29:1; Josh 23:3); God "carrying" (*nśʾ*) Israel (cf. Deut 1:31; 32:11); "vultures' wings" (cf. Deut 32:11–12); *ʾim šāmôaʿ tišməʿû* 'if you will listen, listen' (cf. Deut 11:13; 15:5; 28:1; Jer 17:24; Zech 6:15; but also Exod 15:26; 23:22); *səgullâ* 'treasure' (Deut 7:6; 14:2; 26:18), and the notion that all Israel is holy (cf. Deut 7:6; 14:2, 21; 26:19; 28:9) (cf. D. J. McCarthy 1981: 270–71; Smith 1997: 235–39). As we have previously seen, the D-like language occurs mainly in E (cf. vol. I, pp. 376–77; but also below, p. 150; Appendix A).

Exod 19:7–8 presumes the preceding divine speech ("all these words") and refers to "elders," and so probably is also Elohistic (see vol. I, pp. 51–52). In 19:9, Yahweh announces that this time *he* will come to Moses, flying down in his cloud-chariot, so that the people can hear. The reference to "trust *(heʾĕmîn)*" may be a sign of E (vol. I, p. 481). In the composite text, one assumes that what Israel is about to hear is the Decalog. But this is not necessarily the original intent (see below).

The end of 19:9 is strange: "And Moses told the people's words to Yahweh." What words? Has something fallen out? Or, even though the verb is different (*wayyāšeb* 'brought back' vs. *wayyaggēd* 'told'), is this *Wiederaufnahme* with v 8 — perhaps written by whoever inserted the Decalog, most likely the Redactor (see below)? If so, Yahweh's speech in v 9 is pluperfective: "Yahweh *had* said."

SPECULATION: Many scholars observe that 20:18(15)–21(18), or part thereof, could belong elsewhere (see further below). What if the passage originally stood within 19:8–9, as follows?

19:9a(E) And Yahweh said to Moses, "See: I am coming to you in the nimbus cloud, so that the people may hear during my speaking with you, and also in you they may trust to eternity."

20:18(15) And all the people were seeing the *sounds* and the *torches* and the horn's sound and the mountain smoking, and the people feared and recoiled and stood from afar. 20:19(16) And they said to Moses, "Speak you with us, that we may listen; but Deity must not speak with us, lest we die."

20:20(17) And Moses said to the people, "Don't fear; because for the sake of test-ing you has the Deity come, and for the sake of his fear will be *upon your face*, so that you won't sin."

20:21(18) And the people stood from afar, but Moses, he approached to the darkcloud where the Deity was there. 19:9b And Moses told the people's words to Yahweh.

Against this move, however, note that the definite articles in 20:18(15) ("*the sounds . . . the* torches . . . *the* horn's sound") imply their previous mention, whereas in the rearranged version they first appear here (contrast 19:16, with-out the articles, and compare 19:19, with the article).

Furthermore: as long as we are shifting text, if 19:3–6 contains a Deuterono-mistic insertion (see above), perhaps Yahweh's original opening speech was that now contained in 20:22(19)–26(23). It is to these cultic requirements that the people assent in 19:8.

Such drastic theories, however, must always consider why an editor would have treated his sources so cavalierly. Childs (1974: 35), e.g., thinks it was to make room for the laws that follow in 21:1–23:19. But was textual rearrange-ment really necessary?

The narrative in 19:10–15 seems of a piece. It is not Priestly but like P calls the mountain "Sinai" not "Horeb." Therefore, it is probably J. Note that the expres-sion *hāyâ nākôn lə-* 'be ready for' (19:11, 15) is paralleled only in Exod 34:2 (J?)

and Josh 8:4 (J for Friedman 1998: 152). Yahweh likewise "descends *(yrd)"* from Heaven (19:11, 18, 20) in Gen 11:5, 7; 18:21 (J)—but also in non-Yahwistic passages (e.g., Exod 3:8 [E?]; Num 11:17 [E]; Isa 31:4, etc.). And the idiom *bimšōk hayyōbēl* 'when the *ram pulls'* is paralleled only in Josh 6:5, *bimšōk qeren hayyōbēl* 'when the ram's horn *pulls'* (possibly J [Friedman 1998: 147]).

As for 19:16, the opening reference to "the third day" is probably still Yahwistic. The rest could be J or E—I incline slightly toward the former, since in E Yahweh has already promised to come to the people in a cloud (19:9). Exod 19:17, 19 should also belong to E, both because the term "Deity" appears in narration (Friedman 2003: 10–11) and because God is coming to meet Israel. In contrast, I would assign to J vv 18 and 20, based on the mention of "Sinai" and *'ešen hakkibšān* 'furnace smoke,' the latter reminiscent of Gen 19:28 (J), *qîṭôr hakkibšān* 'furnace fumes.'

Here, then, are the putative J and E accounts of the mountain theophany:

J.[16]And it happened on the third day at morning's happening, [18]and Mount Sinai, it smoked, all of it, forasmuch as Yahweh had descended upon it in fire, and its smoke ascended like furnace smoke, and all the mountain quaked greatly. [20]And Yahweh descended onto Mount Sinai, to the mountain's head, and Yahweh called Moses to the mountain's head. And Moses ascended.

E.[16]And there were *sounds* and lightnings and a heavy cloud on the mountain and a horn's sound, very strong. And all the people who were in the camp quaked. [17]And Moses took the people out to meet the Deity from the camp, and they stationed themselves at the mountain's bottom. [19]And the horn's sound was *going and strengthening* greatly; Moses, he would speak, and the Deity, he would answer him with sound.

I would admit and even emphasize, however, that without evidence external to chap. 19 about the significance of the names for the Deity and for the mountain, I would not have partitioned vv 16–18 between sources at all. I would rather have imputed the redundancy to deliberate dramatic effect. For example, some critics object that we should not be told twice that Yahweh descended (vv 18, 20). But I have given both of these to J.

Similarly, many source critics find 19:21–23 difficult. Schooled to find in redundancy evidence of multiple hands, one might naturally suppose that 19:12–13 and 21–22 are doublets:

[12]And you shall restrict the people all around, saying, "Guard yourselves (from) ascending on the mountain and infringing upon its edge. Any infringing upon the mountain must be put to death, death. [13]A hand must not touch him; but he must be stoned, stoned, or shot, shot: whether animal whether man, he shall not live.

[21]But Yahweh said to Moses, "Descend, warn the people, lest they break through to Yahweh to see, and many of it fall. [22]And also the priests approaching to Yahweh, they must sanctify themselves, lest Yahweh erupt against them."

Pursuing this train, we might give the second passage to E, assuming the first to be Yahwistic. By this scenario, v 23 is R^JE's wry joke on his own activity, making Moses himself comment on the text's redundancy: "But Moses said to Yahweh, 'The people will not be able to ascend to Mount Sinai, for you, you warned us, saying, "Restrict the mountain, and you shall sanctify it."' "

Appealingly droll as I find this interpretation, I would note that the two passages are not truly redundant. Exod 19:21–22 omits the details of how the mountain should be guarded, on the one hand, and adds a codicil about the priests, on the other. It is not really difficult to read vv 12–13 and 21–22 as a piece. According to 19:13, "When the *ram pulls*, they, they shall ascend on the mountain." Is it too much to imagine, with the people trembling in anticipation of the signal horn, that Yahweh feels a need to reinforce his command? From the author's perspective, this largely superfluous exchange has the benefit of increasing the suspense. And by any reading, there is still humor in Moses' fatigued, querulous rejoinder.

I am most unsure how to treat 19:24. The command to "descend" is redundant with v 21, and we have a third expressed concern that the people may transgress their bounds. Since we have assigned the previous two episodes to J, and since Aaron has already appeared in E, it might seem logical to give v 24 to E. On the other hand, Friedman (1998: 328) finds that the root *prṣ* characterizes his more extensive J source, as in 19:22. Thus, 19:24 may be J after all, with Aaron making a sudden entrance. (Friedman [2003: 152–53], who gives the verse to J, attributes Aaron's inclusion to either R or R^JE.)

Exod 19:25 is strange: "So Moses descended to the people and *said* to them." What did he say? Should one suppose that here "said *(wayyō[']mer)*" is equivalent to "spoke *(*waydabbēr)*"? Friedman (2003: 152) similarly translates "said it," assuming, as often in biblical Hebrew, a tacit pronominal object. But almost always *wayyō(')mer* introduces a direct quotation (other possible exceptions are Gen 4:8 [MT]; Judg 17:2; 2 Chr 32:24.)

Seemingly just as implausible would be the notion that what Moses says is "And Deity spoke," followed by the Decalog as an embedded quote-within-a-quote. Admittedly, Deuteronomy 5 describes Moses as transmitting the Ten Words to Israel, who in their fear stand too distant to distinguish Yahweh's words, and hear only the sound of his voice. Still, if Moses were reciting the Decalog in Exod 20:1, he would surely begin "Thus said Yahweh," not "And Deity spoke." That sounds like a narrator. Either some text accidentally fell out of 19:25, or else the interpolator of the Decalog, at the price of considerable awkwardness, grafted an account of the Decalog, preceded by "And Deity spoke all these words, saying," onto an older narrative, in order to create the impression that Moses mediated the Ten Words as in Deuteronomy.

This brings us to the Decalog itself, Exod 20:1–17(14), and the difficult question of its original source. On the one hand, 20:11 clearly alludes to Gen 2:1–3 (P). On the other hand, we find D-like language in 20:10 ("your gates") and 12 ("your days may lengthen upon the soil that Yahweh your deity is giving to you"). To the former, compare Deut 5:14; 6:9; 11:20; 17:5; for the latter, compare Deut 4:26, 40; 5:16, 33; 6:2; 11:9, 21; 17:20; 22:7; 25:15; 30:18; 32:47. Also D-like is Exod 20:2, "took you out from the land of Egypt" (cf. Deut 6:12; 8:14; 13:6, 11;

Judg 2:12) (Holzinger 1900: 70) "from a slaves' house" (Deut 5:6; 6:12; 7:8; 8:14; 13:6, 10) and Exod 20:5, "jealous Deity" (cf. Deut 4:24; 6:15; Josh 24:19). Therefore, I suppose that the Redactor adapted a version of the Decalog like that found in Deut 5:6–21(18) and stuck it into Exodus (cf. Smith 1997:175). In other words, the Ten Words do not properly belong to J, E or P. (On "the Ten Words" in 34:28, see pp. 150, 617.)

> **SPECULATION:** A frequent and perhaps inevitable conjecture, given the common perception that the Decalog is ancient and foundational, is that Exod 20:1–17(14) and Deut 5:6–21(18) have each expanded upon a common original. If so, the original might have existed already in JE. It is not hard to strip away secondary-looking matter to achieve a hard core, e.g.:
>
> > I am Yahweh your deity; there shall be for you no other gods before
> > my face.
> > Don't make for yourself a statue or any image.
> > Don't raise Yahweh's name for nothing.
> > Remember the Sabbath day.
> > Honor your father and your mother.
> > Don't murder.
> > Don't commit adultery.
> > Don't steal.
> > Don't testify against your fellow as a false witness.
> > Don't covet anything of your fellow.

Whether such a text ever existed is another question. On the apparent citations of the Decalog in Hosea and Jeremiah, see TEXTUAL NOTE to 20:13–15.

Above, I suggested transposing some or all of 20:18(15)–21(18) to 19:9. The passage also could (and probably should) be left where it is. The references to *"the sounds," "the torches"* and *"the horn"* sound like allusions to things already mentioned (19:16). At any rate, Yahweh's commands to Moses in JE are now found in 20:22(19)ff. As for the original source of 20:18(15)–21(18), the references to "fear," "testing" and "Deity" suggest E (see vol. I, pp. 481, 575).

> **SPECULATION:** Here is another possibility for JE. Inserting 20:18(15)–21(18) between 19:17 and 19b would arguably enhance the narrative flow. (This arrangement makes *bā'* in 20:20(17), not a perfect, but a participle: "for the sake of testing you is the Deity *coming*.") The counterargument is that, were this the case, there would have been no reason to shift 20:18(15)–21(18) to its present location, whether during the combination of J with E or during the combination of JE with P. It is better to regard the initial participial clause in 20:18(15) as parenthetical, describing actions simultaneous with the preceding business. While Moses and God converse, the terrified people ask them to withdraw, precisely as in Deuteronomy 5.

We come next to 20:22(19)–26(23) and more D-like language—even though, ironically, the contents are *anti-Deuteronomic*, assuming and authorizing multiple local shrines and lay sacrifice. I take these verses to be the text of E's tablets, possibly continued in 22:17–23:19. The cultic focus sets up E's sacrificial Covenant rites in chap. 24, and opens what I call the First Code (20:22[19]–23:33); see pp. 304–8. Many of its heterogeneous cultic and civil laws appear in revised form in Deuteronomy, and some are found also in the Second Code, 34:11–26. Nowhere is the hand of P evident. Seekers after simplicity argue the following: We have two pre-Priestly narrative strands, J and E; *ergo*, the two codes of Exodus must each belong to one of these sources. The First Code in chaps. 20–23, contiguous with a basically Elohistic context in chaps. 19–20, 24 and calling God "(the) Deity" (21:5, 12; 22:7, 8, 27), goes to E. Exod 34:11–26 by default goes to J.

The core of the First Code is 21:1–22:16. The *mišpāṭîm* 'case-laws' are phrased in the "if . . . then" legal language of the ancient Near East and probably possessed their own prehistory as an independent source. Many of the statutes are paralleled, some virtually duplicated, in other ancient codes (see NOTES *passim*). Beginning in 22:17, however, the style changes. It may be significant that 34:17–26, J's parallel corpus, overlaps with or duplicates provisions in 20:23(20)–26(23) and 22:17–23:19, but does not reproduce any of the casuistic legislation of 21:1–22:16.

The First Code concludes in a harangue in which we again encounter D-like language and themes (23:20–33): xenophobia and cultic intolerance, no covenants with foreign nations, Canaanite religion as a "snare" (cf. Deut 7:16), God's *ṣirʿâ* 'hornets(?)' (cf. Deut 7:20; Josh 24:12) and an explanation/excuse for Israel's deferred conquest of Canaan (cf. Deut 7:22; also Judg 3:1–6). Since Exod 20:22(19)–26(23), too, evinces D-like traits, we might regard 20:22(19)–26(23) and 23:30–33 as blocks framing the intervening *mišpāṭîm* as prologue and epilogue (cf. Blenkinsopp 1992: 189).

Exodus 24 is composite; Friedman's (2003: 160–61) analysis, for example, contains mostly E but also P, R and J. We may readily attribute 24:16–17 to P, since it features *šākan* 'settle,' *kābôd* 'Glory' and *sînay* 'Sinai.' Vv 15b and 18a are probably also Priestly, referring to the "cloud" of v 16. In P, 24:15–18 leads into 25:1, the Tabernacle, as 40:34–38 leads into Lev 1:1, the laws of sacrifice (cf. Milgrom 1991: 136–37).

For 24:1–15a, many have found two sources and a complex compositional history (e.g., Holzinger 1900: 104; Blenkinsopp 1992: 190). Exod 24:15a, "and Moses ascended to the mountain," for example, is a potential doublet of 24:18b, "and he ascended to the mountain." There are also minor oddities in 24:1–2, 9–14 when the verses are read as a whole. We must suppose that the elders bow down "from afar" indeed (v 1)—so distant that they are virtually still in the camp (v 14, "in this [place]"). Both Moses and Yahweh write down the divine word (vv 4, 7, 12). Overriding these quibbles, however, is a chain of allusions or connections to Genesis 22, strongly suggesting that 24:1–15a is of single authorship. Friedman (2003: 160) succinctly summarizes the evidence:

The two stories have a chain of ten verbs in common: "and he said," "and he took . . . and he set," "and he got up early," "and he built an altar," "and he put out his hand," "and he/it was," "and he/they got up," "and he/they came," "and he/they saw." Here in Exodus Moses says to the elders, "Sit here . . . we'll come back to you." There Abraham says the same words to the servant boys. And here servant boys (nĕʿārîm) appear as well. Both accounts use the term "from a distance" (mērāḥōq). Both use the term "to bow" (hištaḥăwōt). Both Moses and Abraham come up a mountain. Both have a burnt offering (haʿălôt ʿōlāh). In Genesis Abraham is rewarded because "you did this thing"; and the people in Exodus here promise that "We'll do all the things." Abraham is rewarded because "you listened to my voice"; and here in Exodus the people "said with one voice," and they say, "we'll listen."

The complex story makes good sense as a depiction of diplomacy. The treaty is first negotiated orally, next recorded in a preliminary draft, then finally ratified.

All evidence favors assigning 24:1–15a to the Elohist. First, in 24:11, 13, God is called hāʾĕlōhîm 'the Deity' and his abode har hāʾĕlōhîm 'the Deity's mountain.' Second, there are echoes of 19:7–8 (E): the elders' presence and the people's unanimous "All that Yahweh spoke we will do" (recall, however, that 19:7–8 belong to a D-like section, possibly to be distinguished from E). Then there is the similarity between 24:1–2 and 20:21(18) (E): both contrast the people's position "from afar" (mērāḥōq) with Moses "approaching" (niggaš) Yahweh. Moreover, 24:13–14, 18b, where Moses and Joshua leave Aaron et al. in charge for forty days following Israel's acceptance of the Covenant, sets up chap. 32, the Gold Calf account, which is probably Elohistic (see below). Exodus 32 in turn connects to 33:1–6, which calls the mountain "Horeb," a sign of E. Moreover, Exod 17:8–13 features the same cast of characters as 24:1–14, 18b; 32 — Moses, Aaron, Hur and Joshua — and mentions maṭṭē(h) hāʾĕlōhîm 'the Deity's rod,' indicative of the Elohist. (Admittedly, one might object that Joshua's role in 24:13; 32:17; 33:7–11 as Moses' acolyte sorts oddly with Joshua the general of 17:8–13.) Finally, a set of shared motifs binds all these Elohistic sections of Exodus both to Genesis 22 (E) and to Numbers 11–12 (E).

After the Priestly Tabernacle account (25:1–31:17), we read in 31:18, "And he gave to Moses, as he concluded speaking with him at Mount Sinai, the two Testimony Tablets, stone tablets, written by Deity's finger." This appears to be an Elohistic verse, the continuation of 24:18b, with the words "at Mount Sinai, the two Testimony Tablets" interpolated by R in Priestly style.

Unlike most critics, I find that Exodus 32, the Gold Calf, story reads quite well. I am not bothered by the people's multiple punishments in 32:26–35. Many have noticed, however, that Yahweh's speech in 32:7–13 strongly manifests D-like language: šiḥēt 'ruin' (cf. Deut 9:12), mahēr 'quickly' (Deut 4:26; 7:4, 22; 9:3, 12, 16; 28:20; Josh 2:5; Judg 2:17, 23), sārû min hadderek 'departed from the way' (Deut 9:12, 16; 11:28; 31:29; Judg 2:17), 'ăšer ṣiwwîtî 'which I commanded' (Deut 9:12; 17:3; 18:20; 31:5, 29, etc.) (Holzinger 1900: 108); M. White (1990) argues that the identification of the idol as a calf (vv 4b–6) is also a Deuteronomistic interpolation. Moreover, many now hold that the theme of the promise to the Patriarchs is an interpolation wherever it appears; see below, pp. 725–29.

Still, vv 7–13 fit well enough with their context; absent the Deuteronomistic corpus, we would never suspect a second hand. For the rest, the positive role of Joshua and the Levites, the negative role of Aaron, the expression "Deity" (v 16) — all these indicate E. Moreover, the expression "bring a great sin upon" (32:21) is paralleled in Gen 20:9 (E). We are surprised, however, to find in 32:15 the term *ʿēdūt* 'Testimony,' otherwise characteristic of P and R and possibly interpolated here (Holzinger 1900: 109; Hyatt 1971: 307).

Exod 33:1–6 continues themes from chap. 32: Yahweh's oath to the Patriarchs, the people's remorse. The concluding reference to "Horeb" confirms what we would assume anyway, i.e., that we have more E. But matters may be more complex. As many have noted, Exod 33:1b–3a breaks the continuity between vv 1a and 3b and is probably intrusive. After all, read by itself, Yahweh's promise of a Messenger to lead Israel in conquest of the land of milk and honey is good news, as in 23:20, 23; 32:34. And yet the people "mourned" at "this bad word." Moreover, in 33:12, Moses explicitly cites 33:1a, but does not appear familiar with the reassurances of vv 2b–3a. Since vv 1–4 flow better without vv 1b–3a, I think that in v 12 Moses was originally complaining that Yahweh had proposed to abandon the people to Moses' own guidance, without supernatural assistance. If 33:1b–3a is an insertion, it mitigates the harshness of Yahweh's rejection in v 3 by renewing the promises of chap. 23.

As for 33:7–11, the role of Joshua and the connection to other non-Priestly Meeting Tent stories (Numbers 11–12) also signify E. Among the linchpins of the Documentary Hypothesis is the Torah's divergent images of the *miškān* 'Tabernacle' and *'ōhel mōʿēd* 'Meeting Tent.' For P, it stands in the *middle* of the armed camp, surrounded by a cordon sanitaire of Levites (Num 1:53; 2:17), just as the Carthaginian portable hut-shrine was kept within the camp (Diodorus Siculus 20.65) and just as a sumptuous tent housed the divine presence of Ramesses II amid the troops (Kitchen 1993: 121*; Homan 2002: 111–16). Access to the Tabernacle's interior is restricted to Moses and the House of Aaron. Yahweh's cloud is visible above the Tabernacle, showing the people when to make and when to break camp (40:34–38; Num 9:15–23). In one form or another, the cloud is a permanent feature. The Tent is really a portable temple, a place of sacrifice. It is called both "Tabernacle" and "Meeting Tent."

Other passages envision the Tent (never called *miškān* 'Tabernacle') standing *outside* the camp, maintained by Moses and his acolyte Joshua, who evidently is a non-Levite and certainly a non-Aaronite. (According to Num 13:8; Josh 24:29–30; 1 Chr 7:27, Joshua is an Ephraimite.) Yahweh's cloud descends now and then to meet with Moses by the doorway (Exod 33:9–11; Num 11:17, 25; 12:5, 10; Deut 31:14–15). All these passages except Numbers 12 feature the root *yṣb* (Loewenstamm 1968: 543). There is no mention of Aaron or worship; God's cloud is a temporary manifestation. Exod 33:7–11 may conclude the Elohistic Horeb account. The tablets are broken, but some sort of replacement relationship with Yahweh has been reestablished through Meeting Tent. (See, however, below.)

Recall that we found pieces of J in 19:10–16a, 18, 20–23. Where is the Yahwist's Covenant? A common view finds it in chap. 34, where the revelation of Yahweh's full name (34:6–7) corresponds to comparable scenes from E (3:13–15) and P (6:2–3). If so, the first tablets come from E, the second tablets from J; the idea of two Covenants comes from Redactor^JE. The Second Code in 34:11–26, much of it paralleled in 20:23(20), 23:12–19 (E), constitutes the contents of J's tablets. The reference to "the Ten Words" in 34:28, however, must come from R or whoever interpolated the Decalog in 20:1–17(14). The gloss reassures the reader that the second tablets bore the same text as the first. (I do not share the common view, first expressed by Goethe, that chap. 34 contains Ten Words, an alternate Yahwistic Decalog. Just try to count them!)

The beguilingly attractive view that each Covenant Code comes from a separate source entails significant difficulties, however. Elsewhere we have seen D-like language mainly associated with E, yet it appears again in 34:11–16 (Noth 1962: 262). Moreover, we have not yet assigned 33:12–23, which goes equally well with 32:1–33:6 (supposedly E) and 34:1–9 (supposedly J). The rare term *'ēpô* 'then' (33:16) is a specific sign of J; cf. Gen 27:33, 37; 43:11 (Dillmann 1880: 347). Also, there are similarities between 33:16, 18 and Gen 15:8, 17 (J) (see NOTE to 33:18, "your Glory"). Finally, is it really possible that E's account ended with broken tablets, i.e., no Covenant?

One is highly tempted to find Redactor^JE being even more active than is generally supposed throughout this section. Notwithstanding its links to the E stratum, the Gold Calf account would be more easily explicable as Redactor^JE's creation to justify two Covenant scenes and two Codes, the first E and the second J (cf. Holzinger 1900: 103). Ehrlich (1969: 198) observes that the Gold Calf story is known only to the late Psalm 106 but goes unmentioned by the early prophet Hosea, for whom Israel's greatest sin is Baal Peor not the Gold Calf (Hos 9:10) — and this despite Hosea's animus against calf-worship (Hos 8:5–6; 13:2). If the Gold Calf is an insertion, then, beside chap. 32, we must give to R^JE 24:12–15a, which introduces the Calf account, and 33:1–6, which concludes it.

Some difficulties with the "simple" analysis of the Sinai-Horeb materials laid out here will be discussed further in APPENDIX A.

REDACTION ANALYSIS

By the foregoing analysis, the Yahwist, the Elohist and the Priestly Writer each maintained a different conception of what occurred at the mountain J and P call Sinai and E (along with D) calls Horeb. In J, Yahweh physically descends onto Mount Sinai, causing its peak to smoke. Strict sanctity requirements are imposed. Moses requests and is granted a vision of Yahweh and a revelation of his name. He also fashions stone tablets, on which Yahweh writes somes laws.

In the E source, Moses is summoned to Mount Horeb in 17:1–7, while Israel follows after (see NOTE to 17:6). On the way, the people beat off an Amalekite attack, as Moses supervises from a nearby peak, probably Horeb (17:8–16) (vol. I, pp. 615–17, 620–21). At "the Deity's mountain," Jethro helps Moses to found a judiciary (18:5–12) (vol. I, p. 628). Then Yahweh arrives in a storm, and there are extensive conversations between God and Moses, including the transmission of a law-code. Israel hears God's word and ratifies the Covenant in a blood ceremony. Then Moses and certain magnates ascend to dine before Yahweh. Moses and Joshua climb further up the mountain to receive tablets containing some part of the Covenant. During Moses' unexpectedly protracted absence, the people commission Aaron to fashion a divine symbol to go before them, thus violating the ban on images in 20:23(20). Moses returns and breaks the tablets, then takes various steps to reconcile God to Israel. Finally, outside the camp he sets up Meeting Tent, permanently staffed by Joshua. There Israelites can still encounter Yahweh.

When Redactor^JE combined J with E, he apparently exercised considerable freedom, so that undoing his work is very difficult. I assume that he worked after the fall of the Northern Kingdom, when the Northern version of Yahwism, with its calf iconography, was decisively discredited in Judean eyes. I also assume that the JE document represented an effort to reach out to northern refugees, and to claim some of the northern religious heritage for the surviving state of Judah. It was natural for Redactor^JE to utilize the E and J covenant scenes as successive acts in a drama of concord, rebellion and reconciliation, involving the repudiation of calf worship. As we saw, it is even possible that chap. 32 is entirely R^JE's concoction. (For futher discussion of Exodus 32 as a reflection on events of the eighth century B.C.E., see below, pp. 579–80.) It is noteworthy that the previous time we found J and E so fused, it was at the Burning Bush (chaps. 3–4), Yahweh's first great revelation to Moses at Horeb (vol. I, pp. 190–97). Such scenes evidently inspired Redactor^JE to unusual feats of editorial legerdemain.

As is often noted, the composite JE narrative seems rather hard on Moses, making him repeatedly trudge up and down Sinai-Horeb. This was already a feature of J and E individually, which both depict Moses as an ambassador shuttling between two parties. (As an "anti-angel," so to speak, Moses' labored excursions between Heaven and Earth contrast with the effortless travel of divine Messengers [e.g., Jud 13:20].) The cumulative picture is of a delicate and complicated process whereby Israel becomes covenantally bound to Yahweh, a gradual bridging of the nigh-unbridgeable gulf between the divine and the earthly (see further below, pp. 675–95).

As always, the editor's collage technique created new effects. For example, in J the mountain "quakes" (19:18), paralleling the people's "quaking" in E (19:16). In JE the image is Man and Nature both atremble before Yahweh. There is also constructive interaction between E and J vis-à-vis Israel's sanctity. E calls Israel a "priests' kingdom and a holy nation" (19:6), while J describes a rigorous, quasi-priestly, three-day purification period for all Israel (19:10–15). In J (19:13), the people are told to ascend when the horn (*yōbēl*) sounds. Then a horn (*šôpār*) is blown in E (19:19). In JE, accordingly, Yahweh's repeated warning to Moses in 19:21–24 (J) seems a response to the second signal (E), which may have caused confusion (see NOTE to 19:21).

A possible contradiction within JE concerns the matter of seeing God. Yahweh states in 33:20 (J?), "Man may not see me and live." Yet in 24:10–11 (E), not just

Moses but other prominent Israelites "beheld the Deity" with impunity. One is obliged to understand that what Moses requests in chap. 33 is a more direct experience than he previously received. Chap. 24 may imply that the Israelites' gaze was more *beneath* than *at* Yahweh (NOTE to 24:10, "under his feet"). Now in chap. 33, Moses requests a full, frontal view.

Overall, J's Covenant scene is simpler than E's. This, too, works in the JE composite, where the second Covenant bears a somewhat somber aspect. Cassuto (1967: 437–38) captures the overall effect by an analogy: "The [second Covenant] ceremony was to be similar to the first one, but not so festive, just as the second wedding of one who remarries his divorced wife is not quite the same as the first. The breach has been healed, but it is not possible to undo the fact that at some time the breach had existed. . . . [T]o a second 'wedding', after a divorce, a large assembly is not invited."

If R[JE] created the idea of a renewed Covenant, we must briefly note its distant reverberation in the Christian idea of the New Covenant. For Christians, the Church succeeded the Synagogue as Judah superseded Israel in the eyes of Redactor[JE] and his contemporaries.

P's Sinai account contains scanty narrative (19:1; 24:15b–18a; perhaps 34:29–35). Israel camps in the Sinai wilderness. Moses ascends Mount Sinai, upon which Yahweh's fiery Glory descends. There God reveals to Moses the Tabernacle plans and the "Testimony," the nature and contents of which are unclear (NOTE to 25:16). Assuming that 34:29–35 are P not R (see below), Moses returns from this experience with his face altered by the divine radiance: it is either shining or charred (below, pp. 618, 620–23). If it is radiant, Moses' veiled visage is a "type" of the divine presence sheathed in the Tabernacle curtains. If he is burnt, Moses demonstrates on his body the danger incurred by ordinary Israelites should they approach too near to God. This passage is the center of the Priestly Tabernacle pericope (chaps. 25–31, 35–40). In chaps. 35–40, Moses and Israel proceed to build the Tabernacle. For P, Yahweh's fiery descent in 24:15b–17 creates a frame with the end of chap. 40, where God's Glory takes up residence in the Tabernacle.

Friedman (1981) powerfully argues that P is a polemical response to JE. The JE Sinai-Horeb account contains much that would have offended the Aaronic Priestly author: direct encounters between God and Israel, and between God and Moses; sacrifices by the Midianite priest Jethro in precedence over Aaron (18:12) (on P's hatred for Midian, see Numbers 25); a Meeting Tent outside the camp staffed by the nonpriests Moses and Joshua; Aaron portrayed as a weakling if not a traitor; the Levites as Yahweh's loyal avengers.

One could read 34:29–35 in particular as P's outraged revision of the proceedings of JE. Moses, as a special concession, enjoys continued access to Yahweh in the Tabernacle. But, instead of his vaunted face-to-face relationship in JE (33:11), Moses' face is disfigured. Instead of the people witnessing his intimacy with God, they witness his impairment, which in daily life he hides behind a veil. Aaron is abashed before Moses—not because he himself has sinned, but because his brother has become utterly hideous. In P, the Cloud precludes Moses from entering the Tent (40:35), his kindred Levites become hierodules (Num 8:6–22, etc.) and his successor Joshua is made subservient to Aaron's son Eleazar (Num 27:15a–23). The Priestly Tabernacle is inside the camp, in a sense more accessible than JE's (33:7–11), but it is absolutely off-limits to nonpriests.

The final Redactor had the difficult task of combining JE with P. His first move was to note Israel's arrival at the mountain in 19:2, thus seeming to detach chaps. 17–18 from the Sinai-Horeb narrative. This minimized the prominence of the tent minister and hero Joshua (17:8–16) and of the foreign priest Jethro.

It appears that the Redactor also rewrote the Decalog of Deut 5:6–21(18) and inserted it into a JE context. By retaining JE's statement "Moses descended to the people and said to them," he created ambiguity, perhaps deliberately. Did Yahweh speak directly to Israel, or did Moses mediate his words? The Redactor also carefully made it clear that the second pair of tablets contained the Ten Words of the Covenant, just like the first (34:28).

The Redactor could have put P's Sinai theophany (24:15b–18a) into chap. 19. But it fit equally well in chap. 24, closer to the Tabernacle account it originally preceded.

The two panels of the P Tabernacle account (chaps. 25–31 and 35–40), perhaps originally linked by 34:29–35 (Moses' face), are now separated also by the Gold Calf and reconciliation episodes from JE (chaps. 32–34). This move on the Redactor's part was particularly brilliant, and abundant in irony. While, unknown to Israel, Yahweh is making a disposition for his permanent presence in the camp, the Israelites are fabricating their own divine symbol. The ornaments that had been intended for the Tabernacle instead go to make the Calf. Aaron, not knowing he is destined for the supreme priesthood, instead commits the supreme crime. The orgy of chap. 32 contrasts with the calm majesty of the Tabernacle cult (Utzschneider 1988: 91–92). The Meeting Tent outside the camp, staffed by Joshua (33:7–11), becomes a poor substitute for the glorious Meeting Tent envisioned by P (*Exod. Rab.* 35:3)—a temporary expedient, while God is still so angry that he might destroy Israel (Rashi, Rashbam, Bekhor Shor). By great efforts, Moses effects reconciliation between Israel and Yahweh, and future offenses can be expiated by the Great Priest in P's Tabernacle. The sacral legislation in 34:13–26 is thus prefatory to the renewal of the Tabernacle (Luzzatto).

Particularly striking is the vignette of 34:29–35, the transformation of Moses' face. In JE, Yahweh promises to work dire wonders not just for Israel but also for Moses personally (33:13, 16–17; 34:10). In the composite JEP, this refers not just to Moses' vision of the divine, but to its consequences described in 34:29–35. In JE, there is some ambiguity as to the identity of the "Messenger" who will lead Israel to Canaan. Moses demands that Yahweh's Face lead the people, and God acquiesces (33:14–15). This Face appears to be the divine presence. That is, Yahweh agrees to accompany Israel himself (for some qualifications, however, see below, pp. 597, 604, 619). JE also recounts that Yahweh and Moses converse *pānîm ʾel-pānîm* 'face to face' or 'face for face' (33:11), while emphatically denying that a human can survive a complete vision of God's countenance (33:20). In the composite Torah, these threads converge in 34:29–35.

As we have noted, because the key verb *qāran* is unparalleled, just what happens to Moses' face is subject to dispute (below, pp. 618, 620–23). If in the original P, Moses is disfigured as a result of his close encounter with Yahweh's Glory (24:15b–18a), in the composite Torah this occurs as a result of beholding Yahweh's "backparts" (33:23). In other words, seeing the divine Face kills; seeing the divine back merely disfigures Moses' own face. If, however, Moses' face actually shines, then the implication is that he himself has become the divine Face — or perhaps its reverse side?

The scene in 34:29–35 works so well in its current location, I am tempted to suppose that it is Redactor's own creation. To be more precise, if *qāran* denotes a disfigurement, the scene makes the most sense as Priestly, given its anti-Moses stance. If, however, the verb denotes glorification or radiance, the scene best goes to R.

NOTES

19:1. *In the third month.* The lack of an initial *wayhî* 'And it happened' sets off the following episode as particularly noteworthy (Cassuto 1967: 223). In other words, it is an independent event, not logically consequent to what precedes.

on this day. Bayyôm hazze(h) highlights the arrival at Sinai as the culmination of all the preceding chapters of Exodus, ever since Yahweh's first promise that Israel would worship at the mountain (3:12). In other words, "this day" implies, "This was, at last, the day" (Ramban).

But which day is "this day"? The two possibilities are (a) exactly two months after the Exodus—i.e., on the fifteenth day (Houtman 1996: 440)—or (b) on the first day, assuming that *ḥōdeš* 'month' bears its alternative, original sense: "new moon" (*Mek. baḥōdeš* 1; *b. Šabb.* 86b). In either case, we might have expected a more specific date. Why the ambiguity?

Jewish tradition puts the giving of the Law on the sixth day of the third month (Babylonian Siwwan), coincident with the Rabbinic date for the Festival of Weeks (Shavuʿot/Pentecost). This reckoning presupposes the Rabbinic interpretation of Lev 23:15–16: the Festival of Weeks begins fifty days after the first ʿOmer, or measure of barley, is presented to Yahweh on the "day after the Sabbath," taken to mean the second day of Unleavened Bread. But this is probably not the original meaning of Lev 23:15–16 (see vol. I, pp. 429–32).

How old is the association of the third month festival with the lawgiving at Sinai? It is first stated explicitly in Jub 6:17 (second century B.C.E.). But might it have existed already in the biblical era? 2 Chr 15:10–15 reports that King Asa held a great assembly "in the third month"(Weinfeld 1978: 11)—no precise date is provided—whereat, admonished by a prophet, the people renewed their covenant with Yahweh, rebuilt the altar and swore fealty to God amid trumpet and horn blasts. Significantly, the covenant is termed a *šābūʿâ* 'oath' (2 Chr 15:14–15), evoking the festival's name *šābūʿôt*.

SPECULATION: The written word *šbʿt* can be understood as *šābūʿōt* 'weeks' or *šabūʿōt* 'oaths' (cf. Zeitlin 1939: 6; Weinfeld 1978: 11); the two words were probably pronounced the same in biblical times. Although in the Torah, only God's relationship with the Patriarchs is called an "oath" (Gen 26:3; cf. Gen 24:7; 50:24; Exod 13:5, etc.), two Persian-Hellenistic era texts describe the Sinai covenant as a *šəbûʿâ* (Dan 9:11; Neh 10:30). Perhaps the firstfruits festival, celebrated seven weeks *(šābūʿōt)* after the start of the barley harvest (Lev 23:15–16; Num 28:26; Deut 16:9–10), came to commemorate divine promises *(šəbūʿōt)* in general. Jub 6:17–22 and 22:1 explicitly ascribe to the Festival of Weeks a double nature, both as a harvest festival and as a covenant renewal—but the covenant in question seems to be that of Noah, not Sinai. Similarly, the Qumran community convened in the third month—as in Exod 19:1 and 2 Chr 15:10–15, no date is mentioned—to reenact a covenant with blessings and curses (Milik 1959: 117).

Unlike *Pesaḥ*-Unleavened Bread, the Torah nowhere links the Festival of Weeks to a specific historical moment. Rather, Pentecost celebrates the annual harvest of the firstfruits. The festival liturgy for Shavuʿot includes a summary of how Yahweh took Israel from Egypt to inhabit the fruitful land in order to fulfill his oath, but the Sinai/Horeb event is absent (Deut 26:1–11). For the Torah, then, we can say only that the covenant at Sinai and Shavuʿot fall within the same month. There is no explicit coincidence of the date.

This ambiguity is, I suspect, deliberate. I incline toward the theory that the date of the Weeks Festival "floated," depending upon the state of the barley harvest from year to year (vol. I, p. 432). The very lack of precision in the dating of the arrival at Sinai (19:1), plus the people's multiday sojourn there, permitted Shavuʿot always to be the "anniversary" of Sinai.

going out from . . . Egypt. The Exodus serves as a temporal reference point also in Num 1:1; 33:38; 1 Kgs 6:1 *(Mek. baḥōdeš* 1). It is the date on which Israel's national identity is established.

Sinai Wilderness. On the location of Sinai, see APPENDIX B, p. 752.

19:2. *Rephidim.* See NOTE to 17:1 and APPENDIX B, p. 751.

opposite the mountain. This sounds as if Israel were camped on one side only *(Mek. baḥōdeš* 1). Ibn Ezra, however, citing Num 2:2, "opposite, around Meeting Tent," envisions the people as encircling the mountain.

19:3. *but Moses, he.* The inverted syntax contrasts Moses with Israel, camped opposite the mountain (Cassuto 1967: 225). The sequence of events in the received text is somewhat obscure. We could regard the statement that Moses ascended the mountain as a summary of what is about to happen; i.e., when Yahweh speaks in v 5, Moses is still in the camp. Another possibility is that in v 3, Moses merely begins to ascend. On his way up, he receives the divine message (cf. Ehrlich 1908: 336).

ascended. Not all the way up the mountain, since Yahweh addresses him from the top (Luzzatto) (see, however, previous NOTE). Bekhor Shor infers that Moses must have been summoned by Yahweh; he surely would not presume to approach uninvited. (Cassuto [1967: 226], conversely, commends Moses' enthusiasm and initiative in anticipating Yahweh's command.)

say to Jacob's house . . . tell to Israel's Sons. Yahweh's syntax is formally parallelistic, almost poetic (Luzzatto). At least in the Torah, "Jacob" as a national appellation is confined to poetry (Numbers 23–24; Deuteronomy 33) (Holzinger 1900: 67).

Building upon Rashi, Ehrlich (1969: 169–70) discerns a distinction between the verbs *'āmar* 'say' and *higgîd* 'tell.' The former refers to any pronouncement, while the latter implies a recounting of past events. If so, what is "said" is the promise to elevate Israel; what is "told" is the story of the Exodus.

19:4. *You, you.* The superfluous pronouns in vv 4, 6 and the phrase *wihyîtem lî* 'and you will be for me' in v 5 evoke the Covenant formula "You, you will become for me as a people; and I, I will be for you as Deity" (cf. Jer 30:22; 32:28; Ezek 11:20; 14:11; 36:28; 37:23; Zech 8:8). In fact, we would expect a second clause with the first person *wa'ānî* 'and I.' But the focus remains instead on Israel.

saw. Their ancestors' eyewitness testimony is invoked to sway future readers. Unlike foreign nations (15:14–16; 18:1), this first generation of Israelites need not rely on hearsay.

what I did. I.e., the Plagues and the sea crossing.

vultures'. Both etymology (Arabic *na/isr*) and ornithology favor this rendering of *nešer* over the more comfortable "eagle." Although one might have expected a carrion-eater to be a negative symbol for purity-conscious Israelites, the biblical authors were more impressed with the vulture's prowess in flight and solicitude as a parent.

It is hard to tell just which characteristic of vultures 19:4 evokes. The parallel in Deut 32:11 (cf. also Ezek 17:3–8) makes one think that Yahweh is like a parental vulture bearing Israel upon its pinions from the lowlands of Egypt to Mount Sinai (Rashi) (on divine wings, see also below, pp. 386–87, 390–91, 677–81). Arguably, however, the plural *nəšārîm* means that the Israelites themselves sprout metaphorical wings (cf. Isa 40:31; Ps 103:5 and especially Deut 28:49, "Yahweh will [*nš*'] raise against you a nation from afar . . . as the vulture flies"). Either way, Israel's passage through sea and wilderness is described as effortless, for to arial flight there are no obstacles (cf. Rashbam).

to me. Was not Yahweh with them all along? But he has now brought Israel to his special abode and into a new relationship (Rashbam). Ehrlich (1969: 170) translates *'ēlāy* as "chez moi," inasmuch as the place was already known as "Deity's mountain" (3:1; 18:5) and is, in that sense, his proper home. Jacob (1992: 527) even finds matrimonial imagery in Yahweh taking Israel into his house.

There is another way to understand *'ēlāy.* The point may be that part of Yahweh, i.e., the cloud Messenger (vol. I, pp. 549–50), has conducted Israel to God's fuller presence, the Face (see below, pp. 604, 619).

19:5. *And now.* The function of *wə'attâ* is clarified by ancient epistolary usage: after polite opening greetings, *wə'attâ* means "and now to business." At the same time, in 19:5 it also implies, "Having discussed the past, let's turn to the present and the future."

then you will become. Possibly we should translate this conditionally "and *if* you will become," continuing the protasis. By this reading, the apodosis would come in the next verse, signaled by the redundant pronoun: "*then* you, you will become for me. . . ." The translations of LXX and Syr bar such an interpretation, however.

treasure. In ancient Near Eastern diplomatic parlance, an ordinary vassal was a "slave" (Hebrew *'ebed,* Ugaritic *'bd,* Akkadian *wardum*). The vassal with special prerogatives was the king's "treasure" (Hebrew *sǝgullâ,* Ugaritic *sglt* [*KTU* 2.39.7, 12]), Akkadian *sikiltum,* which originally connoted one's private wealth (see Greenberg 1951; Held 1961). Israel is called Yahweh's "treasure" also in Deut 7:6; 14:2; 26:18; for Mesopotamian parallels, see Held (p. 11).

for mine is all the earth. This clause explains why it is so great an honor to be Yahweh's "treasure." He owns everything, but Israel is his favorite possession. In this vein, ibn Janah (*apud* ibn Ezra) considers *kî* to be concessive: "*although* mine is all the earth." Deut 7:6; 14:1–21; 26:16–19; 32:8–9 progressively elaborate on the theme that, as Yahweh is supreme (*'elyôn*) among gods, so Israel is supreme among nations. On Israel's sense of distinctiveness, see further Machinist (1991).

19:6. *you, you.* The superfluous pronoun highlights a contrast between Israel and something else. It might be "all the peoples" or "all the earth" in v 5 (Dillmann 1880: 195). But more likely the contrast is with Yahweh, owner of Israel and all other peoples (Ehrlich 1908: 337; 1969: 170). Most likely of all, Israel is set apart from God, on the one hand, and the nations, on the other.

priests' kingdom . . . holy nation. The ceremonial, quasi-poetic language continues (cf. Cross 1998: 33). The phrase *mamleket kōhǎnîm* 'priests' kingdom' is unique and unparalleled. *Gôy qādôš* 'holy nation' is also unique, but paralleled by the more common *'am qādôš* 'holy people' (Deut 7:6; 14:2, 21; 26:18–19; Isa 62:12) (Dillmann 1880: 196). The two main nouns, here in parallel, can also appear in coordination: *gôy ûmamlākâ* 'nation and/or kingdom' (1 Kgs 18:10; 60:12) (Jacob 1992: 538).

The relationship between these coordinated expressions has stimulated much debate. To begin with, their sequence is slightly surprising. In typical parallelism, as in biblical poetry, the first element is often more specific and thus more intense than the second (cf. Kugel 1981). We would expect, therefore, "holy nation . . . priests' kingdom," with *kōhǎnîm* 'priests' exemplifying a particular kind of *qōdeš* 'holiness' and *mamlākâ* 'kingdom' a particular type of *gôy* 'nation' (*gôy* generally precedes *mamlākâ,* whether in conjunction [cited above] or parallel [Ps 46:7; 79:6; Ps 105:13 = 1 Chr 16:20; 2 Chr 32:15].)

Another minor item of note is that the expressions differ slightly in form: *mamleket kōhǎnîm* 'priests' kingdom' is a construct chain of two nouns, while *gôy qādôš* 'holy nation' is a noun plus adjective. But Hebrew plural nouns often function as abstractions; thus *kōhǎnîm* could be rendered "priestliness." And abstractions governing nouns in construct function essentially as adjectives, so that *mamleket kōhǎnîm* could be rendered "priestly kingdom," more closely balancing "holy nation" (so Vg: *regnum sacerdotale*).

Because *mamlākâ* means both "king*ship*" and "king*dom*," there are two basic approaches to 19:6, the one elitist and the other egalitarian. According to the first, *mamleket kōhǎnîm* 'priests' kingship' and *gôy qādôš* 'holy nation' are nonsynonymous. Rather, *mamleket kōhǎnîm* implies "monarchy of priests"; i.e., Israel is to be a holy nation ruled by (even holier) priests. Support from the immediate context might be the sudden mention of priests in 19:22—perhaps they have just been created pursuant to 19:6. Throughout much of the Persian and Hellenistic eras Judah was a theocracy (Goodblatt 1994: 6–56); the priestly Maccabees explicitly claimed the kingship, in defiance of tradition, which restricted the monarchy to the House of David. The phrase "royal priesthood" would describe the Hellenistic Jewish kingdom perfectly. (On priest-kings at Sidon and elsewhere, see briefly Goodblatt p. 56 nn. 71–73.)

Still, prior to Hasmonean times, the priest *(kōhēn)* was not a king *(melek)*. Therefore, most favor the alternative approach: *mamleket kōhănîm* and *gôy qādôš* cumulatively express the extreme sanctity of *all* Israel. That *mamlākâ* 'kingdom' and *gôy* 'nation' are functionally equivalent is suggested by their frequent parallelism cited above—after all, most all of Israel's neighbors were polities ruled by kings—while *kōhănîm* 'priests' operate under the most stringent requirements of holiness *(qōdeš)*.

The implication that all Israelites are priestly is borne out by both the immediate context and numerous biblical parallels. First, according to 19:10–15, all the people are to observe extra purity requirements of cleanliness and continence, so that they may approach Yahweh, whose holiness is absolute. Second, if read in conjunction with the preceding verse, 19:6 explains in what respect Israel is Yahweh's "treasure"—it is the holiest nation on Earth, the sole one whose proximity the Deity may tolerate. Third, 22:30 will stipulate of all individual Israelites, "men of holiness you must become for me." Fourth, in 24:5 the "youths of Israel's Sons," not a hereditary clergy, make sacrifices just like priests (see NOTE). Fifth, Deut 7:6; 26:19; 28:9, elaborating on Exod 19:5–6, describe the entire nation of Israel as "holy." Sixth, Korah objects to Moses and Aaron, "All the congregation are holy" (Num 16:3) (Ehrlich 1969: 170). Seventh, Ps 114:1–2 may also be related to Exod 19:4–6: "Upon Israel's departure from Egypt, Jacob's House from a foreign-tongued people, Judah became his holiness *(qodšô)*, Israel his regime *(mamšəlôtā[y]w)*" (for the association between *memšālâ* 'regime' and *mamlākâ/malkût* 'kingdom,' cf. Jer 34:1; Ps 145:13).

The notion that all Israel possesses a priestly quality, observing special restrictions in diet, marriage, sexuality, mourning, hygiene, etc., surfaces throughout the Bible (Levenson 1985: 24–32, 71–72; 1988: 115). Deut 14:1–21 in particular is a commentary on Exod 19:5–6: "You are sons to Yahweh your deity; do not gash yourselves (in mourning), and do not make a baldness *between your eyes* (on the forehead) for the dead, for you are a holy people to Yahweh your deity, and you Yahweh chose to become for him as a treasure people beyond all the peoples that are on the earth's *face*. . . . Don't eat any carcass . . . for you are a holy people to Yahweh your deity" (cf. also Deut 7:1–11, esp. v 6; 28:9).

Taking an extreme line, Ehrlich (1969: 170) regards Exod 19:6 as an assertion that Israel needs no priesthood at all. But the notions of national sanctity and priestly sanctity are hardly incompatible. Even the Priestly source, which above all others insists upon priestly prerogatives, requires that all Israelites be vigilant: "You must be holy; for I, Yahweh, your deity, am holy" (Lev 19:2). (On the so-called Holiness School and its attitude toward communal sanctity, see below, pp. 730–32).

The democratization of Israel's holiness is sometimes viewed as a postexilic development that reached fruition, after the Temple's demise, in Rabbinic Judaism and Christianity. Yet the roots of egalitarianism run deep. It appears that in earliest times any Israelite man could offer sacrifice, as throughout Genesis; possibly, however, firstborn sons were preferred (see vol. I, pp. 455–56). Gradually, the group known as Levites began to attract to themselves the sacred office. This is exactly the situation reflected in Judges 17 (note especially v 13), where Micaiehu/ Micah first consecrates his own son to officiate at his shrine (cf. also 1 Sam 7:1), but is pleased when he can replace him with an itinerant Levite. Later still, the House of Aaron asserted its special claims, with some accepting only the family of Zadok as priests. The Korah account (Numbers 16–17 *passim* [P]) addresses just this issue: the Levites following the rebel Korah chide Moses and Aaron for exalting themselves as Yahweh's servants, for "all the community is holy" (Num 16:3) — thus, ironically, the Levites lobby for the priesthood of all Israel. But Yahweh affirms that neither any Israelite nor any Levite may serve as priest, but only a descendant of Aaron. (For brief consideration of the Levite–Aaronid conflict, see vol. I, pp. 284–86; below, pp. 567–74).

Exod 19:6 is democratic insofar as it concerns Israel itself, elitist insofar as it concerns all humanity. Yahweh's "treasured" vassal Israel will serve as priest-king over all the nations of the Earth, just as Isa 61:6 envisions all Israel serving as priests vis-à-vis the nations. (Isa 66:21, however, extends the priesthood even to Gentiles.) An editorial stratum in Genesis (Carr 1996: 177–232; APPENDIX A, pp. 724–29) emphatically reiterates, "All the earth's families will optain blessing (*nibrəkû/hitbārəkû*) through you" (Gen 12:3; 18:18; 22:18; 26:4; 28:14). Like an effective priest and a pious king, Israel will channel God's blessing to humanity (cf. Carr, pp. 186–89). The same understanding is evident in 1 Pet 2:9: "You are a chosen people, a priestly kingdom, a holy people, a unique people, so that you may proclaim the virtues of him who called you out of darkness into his wondrous light."

How did Yahweh's "treasure" Israel acquire its special sanctity? As we learn in 4:22–23, Israel is both Yahweh's firstborn son and his personal slave (see NOTES). As we learn in 13:2, 11–16; 22:28–29, etc., every firstborn son is holy to Yahweh (vol. I, pp. 454–56). In 22:28–30, the assertion that all firstborn are holy leads directly to the admonition, "be Holiness men." Mal 3:17 combines these three metaphors of treasure, son and servant: "And they shall be . . . a *treasure*, and I will have compassion on them as a man has compassion for his *son* who *serves* him." As Yahweh's firstborn son, Israel naturally partakes of his father's royal and sacred attributes. And as Yahweh's property, Israel is classed as *qōdeš* 'Holiness' (cf. Jer 2:3, "Israel is Holiness of Yahweh, the first of his harvest; all who eat him incur guilt") (on Holiness, see further below, pp. 682–90).

Being God's son imposes both privileges and responsibilities. It is because Israel is Yahweh's child, for example, that they are forbidden excesses of mourning; their Father in Heaven can never die. And when sinful Israelites fall too far short of their Father's divine image, they commit public sacrilege.

The "royal" psalms arrogate many of these godlike attributes to the Davidic monarch (cf. Psalms 2, 72, 89). And in P, the Aaronic Great Priest likewise embodies the entire people, on the one hand, and is attired like a king, on the other (see below, pp. 523–27). Again, however: the notion that Israel is priest-king of all nations, God's image on Earth, does not preclude the existence of hierarchy within the nation. As the priest and the king are to Israel, so Israel is (or shall be) to all peoples (Houtman 1996: 444–47).

SPECULATION: If we read 19:5–6 together with 32:26–29, skipping the intervening Priestly matter, we encounter another possible reading in the JE context, one not necessarily incompatible with that proposed above. Originally, Yahweh intended all Israel to serve him as priests. But after Aaron led the people astray, and only the other Levites proved faithful, God restricted priesthood to the tribe of Levi.

19:7. *Elders.* Implicitly, the elders convey Yahweh's message to the people, and probably also report the people's assent back to Moses (v 8) (Cassuto 1967: 227). Alternatively, the elders simply speak for the people. On the elders' ambiguous role in legitimating Moses' office, see vol. I, pp. 232–33.

19:8. *All that Yahweh spoke.* Israel promises blind obedience to whatever is required of Yahweh's "priests' kingdom and . . . holy nation"—i.e., the total compliance already demanded in 15:26 and tested in 16:4.

19:9. *nimbus cloud.* On Yahweh's vehicle, see vol. I, pp. 549–50; below, p. 674. This nebulous carriage hides Yahweh from human eyes but permits his voice to be heard (Ehrlich 1908: 337; 1969: 170). Compare Deut 4:11–12: "the mountain was burning with fire . . . darkness, cloud and darkcloud; and Yahweh spoke to you from inside the fire; the sound of words you were hearing, but an image you were not seeing, except for a sound."

also in you. Yahweh refers obliquely to Moses' questionable authority among the people. In the event, even the theophany at Sinai-Horeb is insufficient to instill faith among the Israelites. The theme of Yahweh legitimating Moses continues in 33:13, 16–17; 34:10 and culminates in Moses' transfiguration in 34:29–35.

told. In the composite text, Moses has already informed Yahweh of Israel's answer (v 8). One could take the two comments as resumptive repetition (*Wiederaufnahme*) to convey simultaneous or prior action (cf. Kuhl 1952). That is, Moses went back to report to Yahweh; but, before he opened his mouth, Yahweh made the speech in v 9 (Rashbam).

19:10. *sanctify . . . wash.* Israel is to prepare itself for its quasi-royal, quasi-priestly investiture (Jacob 1992: 533). An integral part of ritual purification was bathing the body and washing or changing the clothes (e.g., 29:4–5; see further Blenkinsopp 1992: 188; Houtman 1996: 450). On the homology of ritual impurity and dirt, see below, pp. 682–90.

19:11. *third day.* On this narrative cliché for time's passage, see Gradwohl (1997).

will descend. Is not God already on the mountain (vv 3, 8)? Either he has been floating just above the summit, or more likely he has been moving back and forth between Heaven and Sinai, just as Moses shuttles back and forth between the camp and Sinai. God's previous descents were for private conversations; the next theophany will be a sound-and-light show for the whole people to witness (vv 18–19).

19:12. *restrict*. Presumably a physical barrier is established, if only a cord laid on the ground. The whole mountain becomes a sort of temple (Luzzatto; cf. the etymology of Greek *temenos* 'temple,' literally, 'what is cut off'). On the demarcation of Near Eastern shrines in various periods; see Smith (1927: 155–64). See also next NOTE.

around. *Sābîb* is unexpected here, and comports better with the Sam variant "restrict *the mountain*" (TEXTUAL NOTE). According to the literal meaning of v 12, the Israelites are penned in like a herd. Yet, according to v 23, the *mountain* is cordoned off, as we would anticipate. Due respect for MT's *lectio difficilior* notwithstanding, perhaps Sam is original after all. If not, then "around" must be elliptical for "around *the mountain*." Or Jacob (1992: 534–35) could be correct: Moses "restricts" Israel by word alone.

Any infringing. Since the original lacks punctuation, it is unclear whether these final words are still addressed to Israel by Moses, or to Moses by Yahweh.

19:13. *must not touch him*. So ibn Ezra and Rashbam, taking *bô* as referring to the errant human or animal. An alternative interpretation of *lō(*) tigga' bô* could be "must not infringe upon *it*," i.e., the mountain (*Mek. baḥōdeš* 3, implicitly).

stoned . . . shot. Fensham (1988: 89) suggests that stoning is the method for killing humans, shooting for killing beasts. In any case, even to apprehend an offender, one may not trespass on the sacred space. Rather, he or she must be shot down from a distance (ibn Ezra). (*Tgs. Ps.-Jonathan* and *Neofiti I*, however, assume that the stones and arrows are supernatural, while other authorities hold that *yry* 'shoot' refers to the casting down of the transgressor himself [*Mek. baḥōdeš* 3; *b. Sanh.* 45a; Rashi].) One might think that the corpse, lying on the mountain, would then be a source of further ritual contamination. But this consideration is outweighed by the greater offense of deliberate sacrilege, which is expiated by the transgressor's execution—and, perhaps, his "burial" beneath a pile of stones. If these precautions are neglected, the text implies, the entire community is jeopardized (Ehrlich 1908: 338).

ram. The term for "horn" is not the familiar *šōpār*, as in 20:18(15), but the less common *yōbēl*. Josh 6:4–13 associates the *yōbēl* with the battle horn (*qeren yōbēl, šôpǝrôt yôbǝlîm*), but it is not clear what *yōbēl* in isolation means. A connection with Latin *iubilare* 'shout' is intriguing, especially since the Semitic stem **qarn* 'horn' also appears in various Indo-European languages (Latin *cornus*, Greek *keras*, Germanic *horn*, etc.).

Etymologically, *yōbēl* appears to mean "that which or he who leads"—cf. Aquila *parapherōn* 'conductor, mover'—and so might refer to any kind of summoning agent or the summons itself. Ibn Ezra thinks it is the ram itself, perhaps a dominant bellwether, an interpretation going back to some early comparative Semitic analysis by Rabbi Aqiba (*b. Roš Haš.* 26a) and now apparently supported by the Marseilles Tariff (*KAI* 69.7) (Dillmann 1880: 197). Another possibility is that *yōbēl* 'ram' is a military classification; on the use of animal names as military titles, see Miller (1970b) and cf. 15:15. (P's use of *yōbēl* for the "Jubilee" year does not enter into this discussion, except to note that the Jubilee represents a return to primordial purity, such as existed at Mount Sinai-Horeb; cf. Kawashima [2003].)

pulls. Most commentators assume that here *mšk* means "blow," but the literal meaning is "draw." I would entertain the possibility that in 19:13 *mšk* rather means "summon"; in fact, the root meanings of *ybl* 'lead' and *mšk* 'pull' are semantically close. *Mšk* might also mean "stretch out" in the sense of "wield." Rashi, however, thinks the reference is simply to a prolonged tone (also Holzinger 1900: 68).

The Versions provide a different interpretation: LXX "when the sounds and the trumpets and the cloud *go away* from the mountain"; Symmachus "when the clamor has been *drawn off*"; Theodotion "when the *Iōbēl departs*"; Syr "when the horn *falls silent*." All of these take *mšk* as "withdraw" or "to pull away (from the lips)," presumably contrasting with *tqʿ* 'to insert, to blow.' Among Rabbinic commentators, Rashbam, Bekhor Shor and Ḥizquni favor this interpretation. While this might be possible for Exod 19:13, however, it is unlikely for Josh 6:5, where *bimšōk baqeren hayyôbēl* 'when the ram's horn *pulls*' parallels *bašomʿăkem ʾet-qôl haššôpār* 'upon your hearing the horn's sound.'

While one would assume that the horn of 19:13 is supernatural, as apparently in 20:18(15), Saadiah (*apud* ibn Ezra) thinks that this is an ordinary horn that Moses blows (cf. also Dillmann 1880: 197). Trumpet and horn blasts are traditional signals in both warfare and worship, often indicating the advent of either a divine figure (Ps 47:6; 1 Thess 4:16) or his symbol (2 Sam 6:15) (Dillmann 1880: 197–98). Perhaps, then, as Holzinger (1900: 68) suggests, Exodus mentions the horn to highlight Yahweh's role as war god. (Dillmann also registers some obsolete, rationalizing exegesis that explains the trumpet-like clangor by various loud natural phenomena.)

shall ascend on the mountain. Or "may ascend" (see SPECULATION below). Out of context, one would think that this means that the people climb to the top. But v 17 implies, at most, that they merely stand upon the mountain's lower flanks (see NOTE). Another possibility: ibn Ezra approvingly conveys an opinion of Samuel bar Hophni: "they" here are only Aaron, Nadab, Abihu and the seventy elders (24:1); no others are ever allowed to ascend, apart from Moses and Joshua (see also Luzzatto).

SPECULATION: Exod 20:20(17) speaks of a "test" that Israel must pass through God-fearing and avoiding sin. Yahweh's invitation to ascend the mountain in 19:13 may be this test. If so, Israel passes by refusing to ascend.

19:15. *Be ready.* Unlike v 11, "be ready for the third day," here *nakōnîm* must mean "be readying yourselves (for three days)." Since another meaning of *nākôn* is "be steadfast," it is also possible that the verb specifically connotes sexual continence.

three days. Although in Deuteronomic (Deut 22:12) and Priestly law (Lev 15:16–18), ordinary sexual impurity is dispelled at nightfall, 1 Sam 20:26 and 21:6, alongside our verse, may imply an older, three-day period for male purification.

come near to a woman. The verb *niggaš* 'approach' is probably related to *gāšaš* 'grope' and may originally have connoted touching (cf. Houtman 1996: 454). This command, addressed to the men, might be meant either euphemistically— do not have heterosexual intercourse—or literally—avoid women, lest they spread menstrual impurity. (Presumably, a menstruant would be excluded from the assembly *ipso facto*.) A male seminal emission elicited by proximity to a woman would also be ritually defiling.

Exod 19:15 raises unanswered questions. Does Yahweh's command to the Israelite men imply a symmetrical obligation for the women not to "come near" to men? Or does it imply that only the men are invited upon the mountain, while the women tend the children in the camp?

The requirement of at least temporary celibacy for worshipers is not limited to Israel. Herodotus 2.64 attributes the origins of the sex taboo to the Egyptians, and in 1.198 he imputes a similar view to the Babylonians and "Arabs" (i.e., Syro-Palestinians and desert nomads). In Egypt, priests and anyone else entering a temple had to abstain from sex during their period of service (Sauneron 2000: 40). This temporary continence does not imply that sex was sinful for Israelites and other ancient Near Easterners—any more than eating is sinful because people sometimes fast for religious reasons. Rather, one subjects oneself to a trial by forgoing a licit pleasurable activity.

One could frame various conjectures as to why sex should make one unfit for worship. While I accept Burkert's (1983: 58–72) basic premise that many religious rituals, particularly animal sacrifice, originated in a hunting context (see below, pp. 695–700), I would dispute his claim that "[p]recisely because the act of killing is sexually charged, sexual abstinence is frequently a part of preparing for sacrifice, for war, and for the hunt" (pp. 60–61). I would rather look to more practical considerations: specifically beliefs that sexual intercourse weakens men and that game animals can detect a woman's scent upon a man. For a culture close in time and space to Israel, consider the scene in the Mesopotamian *Epic of Gilgamesh* I.iv, where, advised by a hunter, the sacred prostitute deprives the wildman Enkidu of his ability to keep company with the animals. After a week of sex, he now runs too slowly; moreover, the woman "took away his scent" (*ilteqe napīssu* [I.173]) by which the animals recognized him, presumably replacing it with her own.

Another way to explain sexual abstinence is to consider patterns of male competition and subordination. That is, male competition for females may disrupt the cooperation necessary for a successful battle or hunt. Moreover, in the Bible, for a man or woman to act sexually is challenging to society's alpha male, Yahweh, who by his status theoretically owns all female sexuality. One could also say that Israelite men, who as submissive males constitute Yahweh's collective "wife," should not behave in a manly fashion in God's presence (cf. Eilberg-Schwartz 1994). (To be clear: I do not claim that Yahwism ever involved ritual sex; I do claim, however, that all male–male relationships, including those between humans and gods, potentially provoke unconscious sexual jealousies.) Read in this light, the command not to *niggaš* 'come near to, approach' a woman stands in antithesis with the priestly requirement to *niggaš* Yahweh (19:22). (For another approach to the question of sexual abstinence, see below, p. 453.)

19:16. *sounds.* The noun *qôl* may denote the human voice, the sound of an instrument or any noise at all. In present context, especially in the plural *qōlōt,* it is pealing thunder.

The storm theophany, a mythic *topos* with Canaanite antecedents, situates the divine in meteorological phenomena (see vol. I, pp. 554–59; Green 2003). The thunderstorm has both beneficent and frightening aspects. Even at a physiological level, intense, subsonic sound waves provoke terror in all animals, ourselves included (Tuzin 1984).

horn's sound. While the ram's horn is rather faint by modern, symphonic standards, it probably made a greater impression on the ancients, who inhabited a quieter world. Perhaps many were blown at once. Keel (1978: 341) notes that, according to Dio Cassius 66.23, a "trumpet blast" was heard at Vesuvius, even though, to our ears, a volcanic explosion sounds nothing like a shofar. Keel also observes that Gideon's guerillas use torches, horn calls and the noise of shattering crockery (!) to unnerve the foe (Judg 7:16–20). On one level, the purpose of the horn is to intimidate. But, on another level, the ram's horn is blown to introduce a festival (Lev 25:9; Isa 27:13; Ps 47:6; 81:4; 2 Chr 15:14) (Noth 1962: 158–59; Hyatt 1971: 201). In Zech 9:14, Yahweh himself is the trumpeter.

19:17. *mountain's bottom.* *Taḥtît hāhār* might be either the lower slopes or the surrounding plain. If it is the former, then perhaps this is the "ascent" authorized in v 13, when the horn is "pulled" (see NOTE).

19:18. *to meet.* This is the etymological meaning of *liqra(')t* (< *qry* 'meet'). "Toward" would be an acceptable alternative.

smoked . . . fire . . . quaked. While the modern reader is inevitably reminded of a volcanic eruption, it is not certain that the Israelites knew of the phenomenon (see, however, Job 28:5, 10, which speaks of subterranean fire and channels). I do not think in any case that an experience of smoking, flaming, shaking mountains was necessary for an author to imagine such a thing; in other words, "we need not send for seismologists" (Cross 1973: 169). What makes this theophany impressive is precisely its uniqueness. The text tells us why Sinai is acting in this manner: not because of plate-tectonic instability, but "foreasmuch as Yahweh had descended upon it in fire." Likewise, Ps 104:32 reports that when Yahweh so much as looks at the Earth, it shakes; when he touches the mountains, they smoke.

furnace smoke. From a conical oven (Noth 1962: 159); on the structure of ancient kilns, see Wood (1992).

The form *'ešen* 'smoke' is unique and unexpected. We would expect either **'ăšan* (construct noun) (Rashbam) or **'ăšōn* (infinitive construct). The simplest explanation of MT is to posit a *hapax legomenon* *'ešen* 'smoke' synonymous with the more common *'āšān.*

19:19. *going and strengthening.* I.e., getting louder and louder. This *crescendo poco a poco* is among the most graphic aspects of the description. Are more and more of the heavenly host arriving, advancing closer and closer? Does Yahweh gradually acclimate Israel's ears to the rising din (*Mek. baḥōdeš* 3, 4)?

he would speak. What does Moses say? Ramban thinks the reference is to Yahweh's instructions in v 21, which, according to v 9, were intended to be audible by the people (Bekhor Shor). For Rashi and ibn Ezra, however, what Yahweh speaks is the Decalog.

with sound. One might think that *bəqôl* means with Yahweh's own speaking voice, now loud enough for all to hear. He must shout, because the ram's horn is so loud (Rashbam) or because Moses is with the people down in the plain. Ehrlich (1908: 338–39), however, opines that the sense is "with pure sound," i.e., without any visible speaker. As Childs (1974: 343) observes, Deuteronomy 4–5 emphasizes that Israel heard a speaking voice, even if they required Moses to interpret its words. Some, however, revocalize *baqqôl* 'with *the* sound,' finding a reference either to the horn (Van Seters 1994: 277 n. 87) or to inarticulate thunder, interpreted by divination (Holzinger 1900: 68).

19:21. *Descend.* The testy exchange between Moses and Yahweh over restricting access to the mountain is somewhat peculiar. It seems that Yahweh wants to resume his tête-à-tête with Moses atop the mountain, instead of shouting down commands. So he summons Moses up (v 20)—but then gives him a renewed admonition not to transgress the mountain's sanctity (vv 21–22). Apparently, when the horn calls of v 16 summoned Israel to the mountain's lower area (v 17), there was a danger that the people would misunderstand their warrant to ascend as unlimited (v 13). Moses must descend once more to make it clear that they may not climb to the top.

His stamina seemingly overtaxed, Moses rejoins that this has already been taken care of. No one is likely to break through. Yahweh then makes an additional demand: Aaron must accompany Moses up the mountain. Apparently Moses must personally escort him across the barrier, making it clear that *hoi polloi* are still absolutely excluded.

Other explanations are possible. Perhaps Yahweh's main motive in dispatching Moses back down is so Moses can interpret the Decalog to the people. Also, by returning to the camp, Moses is spared the ear-shattering experience of Yahweh's descent. That is, God may be protecting Moses.

Finally, the Rabbinic commentators are wont to compare God's interactions with Moses to a king and his courtier. In this vein, one is tempted to see Yahweh testing Moses' obedience simply by giving him a redundant command. The perfect courtier silently complies. The imperfect courtier demeans his sovereign by crassly pointing out his error. Perhaps this vignette shows Yahweh putting Moses in his place (cf. Fretheim 1991: 219).

break through. The verb *ḥrs* literally means "break down," said of a stone fence in Prov 24:31. So the language is probably elliptical: "lest the people break down (the barrier)."

see. Ordinarily, to behold Yahweh is lethal (e.g., 33:20; Isa 6:5). God expects Israel to be naturally curious, with potentially disastrous results. Later, a select few will be granted a vision of the divine (24:9–11).

19:22. *priests.* It is not clear who these are. They may be the same as the "youths" of 24:5 (*b. Zebaḥ.* 115b; see NOTE). Or they may be Aaron, Nadab and Abihu (24:1), whom the Priestly source identifies as priests (*Mek. baḥōdeš* 4; Ehrlich 1969: 170).

approaching. That is, "about to approach." V 24 excludes the priests from literally approaching. But the verb approach *(niggaš),* like its synonym *qārab,* connotes sacred service (compare also *higgîš, hiqrîb* 'sacrifice').

erupt. The root *prṣ* describes a semi-spontaneous outburst of divine wrath and consequent damage; cf. 2 Sam 6:8; 1 Chr 15:13.

19:23. *Restrict the mountain.* In fact, Yahweh had said, "restrict *the people*" (v 12). The meaning is the same: the mountain and the people are cut off one from another (see, however, TEXTUAL NOTE to v 12). Holzinger (1900: 68) finds in the fenced-off mountain the inspiration for the famous Rabbinic maxim, "Make a fence around the Torah," justifying the more stringent aspects of Oral Torah (*m. 'Abot* 1:1).

sanctify. That is, declare it holy.

19:24. *Go, descend.* As in 32:7, it is possible that Yahweh's dismissal is somewhat peevish.

Aaron with you; but the priests and the people. It is slightly unclear who is and who is not to ascend the mountain. The MT cantillation puts a stop after Aaron: he may ascend, but the priests and people may not (so already LXX). This is the most natural reading.

The problem is that, according to v 22, the priests *are* to approach. Moreover, in 24:1, Aaron and the elders of Israel climb the mountain, together with Nadab and Abihu, who are Aaron's sons and co-priests, at least in P. In the context, it may make more sense to understand, "you shall ascend, you and Aaron with you and the priests; but the people, they must not break through to ascend. . . ." Admittedly, were this his intention, the writer would have done better to put "with you" after "the priests." In any case, it seems that the people must be reminded to stay put, precisely because a few will be allowed to pass the barrier (ibn Ezra).

lest he erupt. Yahweh briefly speaks of himself in the third person, as if he is not entirely in control of his own volatility.

19:25. *said to them.* We expect direct speech to follow. Thus, at least in the composite text, 20:1 could be taken as Moses' words, not the narrator's (see SOURCE ANALYSIS, p. 145). Alternatively, we may take "said" *(wayyō[ʾ]mer)* in the sense of "spoke" or "talked," or as bearing a tacit object (Friedman 2003: 152). Dillmann (1880: 199) thinks that Moses reports Yahweh's commands from vv 21–24.

20:1. *And Deity spoke.* As just observed, it is unclear whether we are to understand these as Moses' words or the narrator's. In 20:22(19); Deut 4:12–13, 33, 36; 5:4, 19(22)–20(23), the people hear the Decalog directly from Yahweh's own mouth, albeit mediated by Moses (Deut 5:5). See further SOURCE ANALYSIS.

Readers following the Hebrew text will note that the following verses contain two superimposed cantillations. Correspondingly, in different editions, the verse enumeration varies after 20:12. Some give each command its own verse; others run together murder, adultery, theft and false witness as a single verse. The Massoretes recorded two methods of chanting and clause division, leaving posterity to make sense of it. Later Jewish communities would use one for public and the other for private reading, or assign them different functions in the liturgical calendar (see further Houtman 2000: 4).

20:2. *I am Yahweh.* As in a royal proclamation, Yahweh first names himself (Holzinger 1900: 70). The statement "I am So-and-so" identifies an unseen speaker. In particular, God's "I am," like the oath "as Yahweh lives," serves as an assurance of reliability (see vol. I, pp. 271–71).

Instead of "I am Yahweh your deity," some translate, "I, Yahweh, am your deity. . . ." I doubt an Israelite would have perceived a difference. A more radical translation is "Don't have any gods before me, Yahweh, your deity who took you out from the land of Egypt, from a slaves' house" (Poebel 1932: 53–58), but the Akkadian parallels upon which Poebel draws in support are not fully apropos for Hebrew.

your deity. Inasmuch as Yahweh has reclaimed Israel from Pharaoh's grasp, he can rightfully claim to be their god (Ehrlich 1969: 171). (Although English cannot convey the distinction, "your" is singular; the Decalog addresses each Israelite individually.)

took you out. Since the root *yṣ'* refers to manumssion, *hôṣē(')tîkā* could also be paraphrased as "liberated you" (cf. Chirichigno 1993: 188).

slaves' house. Or "house of slavery" (ibn Ezra [shorter commentary]). Yahweh's liberation of Israel from bondage to Pharaoh, and claiming them as his own property, gives him the sovereign right to make rules for them (Dillmann 1880: 207).

20:3. *other gods.* One could also translate *'ĕlōhîm 'aḥērîm* as "another god" (*Tgs.*; Dillmann 1880: 207), tantamount to the expression, *'ēl 'aḥēr* 'another god' in 34:14 (Holzinger 1900: 70–71).

before my face. The Decalog neither concedes nor denies the existence and efficacy of other deities (Holzinger 1900: 71). *'Al-pānāy* literally means "against/opposite my face" (cf. Isa 65:3; Jer 6:7; 7:15; 15:1; 23:39), i.e., occupying the same time and/or space, as in Gen 11:28; Num 3:4 (cf. *Mek. baḥōdeš* 6; Rashi). If Yahweh inhabited an idol or stone, the command would simply be not to display other images in his cella (Houtman 2000: 19, 31), as was done around Allah, for example, in pre-Islamic Mecca. So one possible meaning is that no other deities may be worshiped in Yahweh-shrines. This understanding would provide a natural lead-in to vv 4–5. Ḥizquni and Luzzatto, however, argue for an interpretation "in despite of me" (cf. colloquial English "in one's face"). By the fullest rendering, the commandment bars acknowledgment of any gods beside or in precedence to Yahweh, forever.

20:4. *for yourself.* It is unclear how to take *lǝkā.* It could be akin to the ethical dative used with verbs of motion or change of stance (Saadiah). If so, one is simply forbidden to make an idol, whether for oneself or for another.

I rather think, however, that "for yourself" is meant literally. To account for Saadiah's scruple, "Don't make" would include commissioning another to make an idol.

statue . . . image. Strictly speaking, the "statue *(pesel)*" is the material object, the "image *(tǝmûnâ)*" is its shape. It is unclear whether 20:4 also prohibits flat sketches and bas-reliefs.

Why stifle what is probably a universal human impulse, starting in childhood, to depict Nature? Presumably, as the Rabbis would put it, to "make a fence around the Torah" (*m. 'Abot* 1:1). That is, lest one worship images, one may not even make an image. The Torah proscribes depictions of birds, mammals, reptiles, amphibians and fish, as well as humans and the astral bodies (Deut 4:15–19). All these were staples of ancient Near Eastern sacral iconography. (On classical sources indicating other aniconic forms of religion, see Dillmann [1880: 209]; for a broader, updated treatment and recent bibliography, see Mettinger [1995]; Lewis [1998].)

In fact, all peoples produce images; the Israelites were no exception (Schroer 1987). Around the word, people treat these images as divine personalities. Such icons reflect our human tendency to personalize the products of our own craft—a vehicle, a tool, a weapon—no less than we personalize the natural environment. As instinctively social creatures, we tend to form hierarchical relationships, even in the absence of appropriate beings with whom to interact. Children dress, feed and dominate their dolls; adults dress, feed and submit to their idols.

What is the Bible's objection to idolatry? Notably, history's first monotheist, the fourteenth-century B.C.E. Pharaoh Akhenaten, also banned images (see Redford 1984; below, pp. 762–94). But could not a monotheist focus his or her contemplation of the One on a material depiction without compromising the Godhead's unity (cf. Bekhor Shor)?

The Bible persistently and deliberately regards the sacred image as a numinous fetish, the god itself, despite all the evidence from the Near East and elsewhere that idols were understood only as pictures of the gods and receptacles for their divine presence (on the Egyptians, see Morenz [1973: 150–58]; on the Mesopotamians, see Jacobsen [1987a]; on the Greeks, Burkert [1988: 32–33]). Both Mesopotamians and Egyptians, for example, performed rituals to induct the divine spirit into the idol via the mouth (Walker and Dick 1999; Lorton 1999: 147–79). Many conclude that the Bible polemically misrepresents popular belief, but I doubt it. The Bible's image of the idolater, making no distinction between depiction and depicted, probably conveys a more accurate sense of the common person's experience than the learned speculations of Egyptian, Mesopotamian, Greek and Hindu savants. Many people today still do not want their photographs "taken" because a likeness is more than a likeness. It absorbs the essence of what it depicts.

It is easy to conceive reasons, therefore, why the Bible's theologians banned idols, even of Yahweh. Probably they felt that iconolatry infringed somehow on divine sovereignty. "Israel was forbidden to make images of Yahweh precisely because his presence was to be seen as the result of a free and personal decision on the part of God" (Plastaras 1966: 165). Moreover, given a popular tendency to equate god and idol, multiple depictions of Yahweh might lead to a fragmentation of his divinity. Creating too close an association between Yahweh and anything in the visible world—whether a living creature or its likeness—potentially conduces to treating that animal itself as a divinity—if not Yahweh himself, then a hypostasis, which in the course of time might receive independent divine status.

Like Hindus and like Baruch Spinoza, elite Egyptian theologians promulgated a pantheistic notion that one divine Essence had divided itself millions of times to produce all that we see around us, so that God is All and All is God (Assmann 1997). In contrast, biblical monotheism meticulously dissociates Creation from Creator (Kaufmann 1960: 7–121). Nothing on Earth is the least bit divine, with the single exception of humanity.

Theoretically, the Israelites could have venerated a single, authorized image of Yahweh and barred all others. But it is easy to imagine the inevitable result: the proliferation of unauthorized "knock-offs." For Akhenaten's less rigorous anicionism, multiple artistic depictions of the sun were perfectly licit, as was worship of the human incarnation of divine sunlight: the Pharaoh himself.

Not so for Israel. Israelite worship, i.e., prayer and sacrifice, is essentially a vertical affair, with Man on Earth and God in Heaven. Idolatry adds a new vector: worship may be conceived as horizontal, directed to God on Earth (see my discussion of the Tabernacle, below, pp. 495–96, 518–21, 675–95). Thus an idol binds the divine essence to the lower realm. The aniconic Deity possesses the option of withdrawing his presence whenever humanity, in particular Israel, falls short of his ethical and ritual standards.

All graphic representations are metaphors, not the thing itself. Metaphors can work in two directions. If my Love's like a red, red rose, then every red rose recalls my Love. A statue therefore creates a potential for sacrilege in two ways. First, what happens to the god when his image is captured, defiled or destroyed? Someone, possibly the Israelites, desecrated the statues of Canaanite Hazor (Ben Tor 1999), and the Bible repeatedly commands the destruction of all sacred imagery. Rather than have their god captured or killed in effigy, Israelite theologians may have reasoned, better to dispense with idols entirely. (On Assyrian attitudes toward the spoliation of idols, see Cogan 1974.)

Moreover, during the manufacture of an idol, the sacred and profane dangerously collide. While this is also a problem in the construction of the Tabernacle and Temple (see below, pp. 532, 686–90), how much more grave the plight of impure humans fashioning, not an earthly abode for God, but his earthly *body*. (Analogous concerns would lead the Church to postulate the sinless conceptions of both Jesus and Mary.) In Mesopotamia, elaborate rituals, including a mock severing of the craftsmen's hands, carefully disassociated the manufacture of idols from any earthly taint (Jacobsen 1987a). Israelites avoided the problem by eschewing idols altogether, thereby lending their national god a distinctive mystique.

While an idol provides an accessible form of the deity, it is also, ironically, quintessentially austere and impassive. Writes Fretheim (1991: 226), "Unlike plastic images, which are static and immobile, deaf and dumb, unfeeling and unthinking, and fix God at a point in time, Israel's God is one who can speak and feel and act in both nature and history (and in this sense is free)." An idol is both easy and challenging to relate to.

Another theological difficulty motivating the Bible's ban on images in general, not just sacred images, may be ambivalence toward human creativity. The ancient Near Eastern polytheists often associated the creation of humanity with divine craftsmen and/or mother goddesses, emblematic of human craftsmen and mothers. As the Israelite Heaven holds no creator apart from Yahweh, the fashioning of living creatures and their simulacra may have been regarded as a prerogative of the highest God. There is a point where *imitatio dei* ceases to be a virtue and becomes sacrilege.

Many of these same objections probably occurred to polytheists. For, just as one can conceive of idolatrous monotheism, one can imagine aniconic polytheism. A degree of aversion to depicting the divine has been found in many surrounding and contemporary cultures, especially the pre-Islamic Arab (Mettinger 1995: 69–79). According to Pseudo-Lucian *Syrian Goddess* 34, the powers of the sun and moon required no idols, since they were manifest to all (Attridge and Oden 1976: 45–57). This archaic aniconic tendency was elevated to a philosophical postulate by Xenophanes (c. 570–478 B.C.E.), who denied that the gods possessed human forms (frags. 14–16; Lesher 1992). And in the same era, the Persians would march to war with the empty divine chariot of "Zeus," i.e. Ahura-Mazda (Herodotus 7.40; cf. 1.131). Herodotus 1.181–82 also reports that the top of Bel's temple tower in Babylon held a couch but no idol, and further examples could be multiplied. Aniconism has always possessed certain appeals for polytheists and monotheists alike.

But the history of the Byzantine Church's Iconoclasic Controversy shows just how attached even monotheists can be to their images. For, the Decalog notwithstanding, the Israelites did make images. The Bible itself mentions Nehushtan (Num 21:8–9; 2 Kgs 18:4), several gold calves (see below, pp. 580–83), the Griffins of the Tabernacle and Temple (below, pp. 517–19), the bulls beneath the Temple's great basin (1 Kgs 7:25, 44) and figured bulls and lions (1 Kgs 7:29; 10:19–20). And archaeology has revealed numerous examples of Israelite pictorial art. But two impressions remain strong. First, there is a distinct paucity of excavated portrayals of humanoid males that one might potentially identify with Yahweh (see Lewis 1998: 42–43). Second, Israelite art in general is the crudest in the region. To judge from the Bible, Israelites were more eager to destroy than to create art. Were they Antiquity's true "philistines"?

As if to compensate for their poverty of graphic expression, the Israelites excelled in literature. While physical depictions are unconditionally banned, the Bible abounds in literary descriptions of Yahweh, who is almost always compared to a human male in his prime (for some exceptions, see Trible 1978). Conversely, for the Priestly Writer and Ezekiel, *human bodies* are material figurations of the divine (Kutsko 2000), and the crime of murder is compounded with desecration (Gen 9:6). (Naturally, a human must not be worshiped, but a likely, partial exception was the Davidic king [cf. Whitelam 1992: 45–46], belief in whose divinity would in time spawn Christianity.) For further discussion of iconism and aniconism, see pp. 703, 778–79.

or any image, what. The grammatical construction wəkol-təmûnâ 'ăšer baššāmayim bars the intuitive understanding "or any image *of* what is in the heavens. . . ." That would have been expressed by the construct form *təmûnat, as in Deut 4:16, 25 (cf. Holzinger 1900: 71). Instead, we have apposition.

heavens . . . earth . . . waters. Deut 4:16–19 elaborates: no male or female human figures, no domestic animals, no birds, no four-footed animals, no fish, no sun, moon or stars.

below the earth. In ancient cosmography, the Earth was a disk floating on water. The surrounding seas were believed to be the visible portions of this great Deep and continuous with it. Apparently, all marine life was assumed to exist also below the Earth.

20:5. *serve.* I.e., by sacrifice. In 20:5 and Deut 5:9, the peculiar vocalization of *t⁽bdm—tā⁽obdēm? to⁽obdēm?*—has occasioned discussion. (In 23:24, the first vowel bears a metheg, favoring the former vocalization.) What we would expect is **ta⁽abdēm* (cf. the 2nd masc. pl. *ta⁽abdû*). Only *ad hoc* explanations are possible. E.g., perhaps the expected *pataḥ* vowels were rounded to *qameṣ qaton* under the influence of the following bilabial consonants *b* and *m* (cf. Garr 1990: 58–65). A fuller discussion might also consider the use of *w* for an unexpected *u* in Qumran orthography (cf. Qimron 1986: 35–38). Some construe *to⁽obdēm* (*sic*) as a Hoph⁽al (e.g., Jacob 1992: 552), meaning something like "Don't let yourself be forced to serve them." But it is not clear that the Hoph⁽al can be used with a pronominal suffix in this manner, and I cannot conceive that this was the author's intent.

them. The referent of this masculine plural is somewhat ambiguous. It could be the denizens of Heaven, Earth and the seas, rather than their images (Dillmann 1880: 210). Alternatively, it could skip back over v 4 to the "other gods" of v 3 (Jacob 1992: 549, 551). Or it could be "statue or any image" (cf. Holzinger 1900: 72).

for. After a negative assertion, *kî* often has the force of "but rather." Here, it is unclear whether the better rendering would be "Don't bow to them, *because* I, Yahweh your deity, am a jealous deity . . ." or "Don't bow to them, *but rather* I, Yahweh, am your deity, a jealous deity. . . ." My translation above compromises between these possibilities, which would probably not be perceived as alternatives by speakers of ancient Hebrew.

jealous deity. Some argue that "zealous" or "impassioned" is a more accurate interpretation of *qannō⁾/qannā⁾* (e.g., Luzzatto; Sarna 1991: 110). Others regard jealous possessivity, as in romantic love or marriage, as the correct emotion (Ehrlich 1969: 172; Cassuto 1967: 242–43). In fact, both meanings apply in v 5: Yahweh is jealous when Israel serves another god; he is zealous in his vengeance. As Saadiah observes, *qannō⁾/qannā⁾* can also mean "punitive," as the text immediately explains.

The phrase *⁾ēl qannō⁾/qannā⁾* is paralleled in 34:14; Deut 4:24; 6:15; Josh 24:19 (see also Deut 29:19; 32:16, 21); on a possible precursor from Emar, see Pentiuc (2001: 149). Seekers after wordplays will find the phrase evocative of the root *qny*, as in the name *⁾elqānâ* 'God procreated' and the old Canaanite theology of *⁾ēl ⁽elyôn qōnē(h) šāmayim wā⁾āreṣ* 'Highest God, master/procreator of Sky and Land' (on Gen 14:22 and its antecedents, see Miller 1980). In the context of Exodus, Yahweh's jealousy (*qn⁾*) also resonates anagrammatically with his disinclination to "clear (*nqy*)" abusers of his name (v 7).

reckoning. The multivalent verb *pqd* (see NOTE to 3:15, "acknowledge") here combines nuances of record-keeping and punishment. According to Amos 3:2, it is precisely because Yahweh liberated Israel from Egypt and entered into the Covenant with them, that he punishes (*pqd*) them (Jacob 1992: 556).

sons. In context, *bānîm* are descendants in general—unless we read the longer text "upon sons and upon sons' sons" (TEXTUAL NOTE to "upon a third").

Third . . . fourth (generation). The plurals *šillēšîm* and *ribbē'îm* are probably adjectives describing *bānîm* 'sons'; compare Gen 50:23; 2 Kgs 10:30; 15:12 and *bny rb'* in the ninth-century B.C.E. Nerab inscription (*KAI* 226.5).

Morphologically, the forms *šillēšîm* and *ribbē'îm* are somewhat surprising. First, this pattern is generally used in Hebrew for bodily defects: *'iwwēr* 'blind,' *pissēaḥ* 'lame,' etc. Second, the normal rules for vowel reduction should have produced **šilləšîm, ribbə'îm* or possibly **šilšîm, rib'îm*. (For the latter word, a variant *rəbî'îm* is attested in 2 Kgs 10:30; 15:12.)

Moreover, the terms' meaning is unclear. Which generations are the "third" and "fourth"? From what point do we count? Exod 34:7, closely related to our verse, speaks first of "sons and . . . sons' sons," followed by the third and fourth generation (this may also have been the original reading of 20:5; see TEXTUAL NOTE). This suggests that the first generation are the sinner's children, and the fourth generation are his great-great-grandchildren. The proof is in 2 Kgs 10:30; 15:12, where Yahweh promises that four generations (*bənê rəbî'îm*) of Jehu's house will reign: Jehu, followed by Jehoahaz, Joash, Jeroboam II and Zechariah.

Gen 50:23, however, indicates that the first generation is the progenitor himself: "And Joseph saw, through Ephraim, *šillēšîm* sons; also the sons of Menasseh's son Machir were born on Joseph's knees." Thus the "third generation" are grandchildren. By this understanding, in Exod 20:5 the count starts with the sinner himself, his sons are the second generation, his grandsons are the third and the great-grandsons the fourth generation. The same understanding is likely present in Job 42:16, "And he saw his sons and his sons' sons, four generations." Here "four generations" may refer to the unmentioned generation of great-grandsons.

In adjudicating between these seemingly contradictory verses, I consider 2 Kgs 10:30; 15:12 decisively unambiguous. The fourth generation is that of the great-great-grandchildren. It follows that in Gen 50:23, the two clauses are not synonymous. Whereas Joseph survived to see grandchildren through Menasseh, he saw great-grandchildren through Ephraim. In Job 42:16, Job apparently lives to behold two more generations than those explicitly mentioned.

Just what Yahweh intends in Exodus is also uncertain. Does he clear the slate after the fourth generation? Or perhaps God waits for three generations for signs of repentance; then, finding none, he eradicates the whole lineage (ibn Ezra). This last view is, admittedly, a Rabbinic attempt to harmonize Exodus with Ezekiel 18, which denies the heritability of guilt. And yet it makes sense (see, however, Ramban's critique). For Cassuto (1967: 243), 20:5 is an incentive not to sin: one may live to see one's beloved progeny punished for one's own past misdeeds.

Yahweh does not apply this standard to Israel alone. Jacob (1992: 555) notes that Yahweh delays to punish the Amorites till the fourth generation, because their "sin is not yet full" (Gen 15:16). We have here a fatalistic notion that the sons of the wicked continue to "fill" their fathers' bag of sins. After four generations, the load is sufficient to justify their eradication.

The transgenerational transmission and accumulation of guilt may seem harsh, even smacking of blood feud. Luzzatto notes that Deut 24:16 bans precisely such an attitude for human judges (also 2 Kgs 14:3–6). Old Testament religion and Judaism would eventually reject the notion of hereditary guilt entirely (Jer 31:29–30; Ezekiel 18), concomitant with a rising sense of individual as opposed to clan identity and responsibility (Halpern 1991). Already in Exodus, however, the genetic inheritance of culpability is limited: God's vengeance lapses after the fourth generation. In contrast, the reward of virtue is near-infinite (see below). (Other passages treating congenital guilt include Lev 20:5; 26:39–40; Josh 7:24–25; 1 Sam 2:30–36; 2 Sam 3:29; 12;10; 1 Kgs 14:10; 2 Kgs 5:27; Isa 14:21; 65:7; Jer 14:20; 15:4; 16:11–13; Amos 7:17; Ps 109:14; Lam 5:7; Dan 9:16; Neh 9:2, 17–35; for other passages, see Houtman 2000:29; for parallel Classical discussion of the subject, see Dillmann 1880: 211.) In the course of time, Christianity would reinvent the notion of transgenerational guilt in its doctrine of Original Sin.

If our sources are not quite consistent on the matter, we should not be surprised. Even ordinary individuals, and certainly entire societies, will constantly readjust theodicy to mood and circumstance.

my haters. I.e., those who hate Yahweh by rejecting his commands and spurning the Covenant, in contrast to those who love God. This probably refers to the fathers not the sons (Luzzatto, after Gersonides). Those who find a reference to the sons (e.g., *Tg. Onqelos, Mek. baḥōdeš* 6, *b. Ber.* 7a) are trying to make it out that only *guilty* sons are punished for their fathers' faults, against the plain sense.

20:6. *doing fidelity.* This is a rather lame rendering of *'ōśe(h) ḥesed*. A more adequate paraphrase would be "faithfully requiting." On the nuances of *ḥesed* 'obligatory beneficence and benevolence,' see Sakenfeld (1978) and, for further bibliography, vol. I, p. 532.

thousandth (generation). There are three possible interpretations of *'ălāpîm*. The first is "thousands" (LXX, Vg), but this does not ideally suit the context, where the contrast is with "third . . . fourth *generation*." Moreover, in the parallel verse 34:7, Yahweh is not just "doing" but *"keeping (nōṣēr)* fidelity for *'ălāpîm*," which arguably implies the pasage of time. Most likely, therefore *'ălāpîm* refers to generations (Luzzatto). For the extact nuance, we have the options of following *Tgs.* "thousandth generation" or Syr "thousands of generations." The parallel in Deut 7:9; Ps 105:8 = 1 Chr 16:15 *'elep dôr* 'one thousand generations' supports the former interpretation for Exod 20:6. Ultimately, it does not matter. We should understand *'ălāpîm* as an expression of infinity (*Mek. baḥōdeš* 6).

lovers . . . command keepers. Although the text is poorly preserved, it is likely that the first Ketef Hinnom silver plaque employs similar phrases and concepts: [*'*]*hb hbr*[*yt wh*]*ḥsd l'h*[*byw w*]*bšmry* . . . 'the covenant-lover and fidelity to his lovers, and among those who keep . . . ' (*AHI* 4.301).

20:7. *raise.* I.e., "invoke" or "pronounce" (*nāśā*[*'*]). Implied is "on your mouth/lips" (Luzzatto); Jacob (1992: 557) cites other cases of *nśʾ* apropos of oral utterances such as weeping, song, prophecy, etc.—e.g., 23:1; 2 Kgs 9:25; Ps 15:3; 139:20.

Interpreters dispute precisely what is prohibited. Some think that the command specifically addresses false oaths (*Tgs.*; Syr; Josephus *Ant.* 3.91; Saadiah), comparing such passages as Ps 24:4, "did not *raise* (i.e., invoke") my (Yahweh's) *soul* (self) for nothing, and did not swear for deceit." Moreover, the partial Decalog synopsis in Jer 7:9 lists "stealing, murdering, committing adultery and swearing for falsehood" (cf. also Zech 5:3). Finally, the parallel in Deut 5:20 replaces "for nothing" with "for falsehood." To swear "as Yahweh lives" (e.g., Jer 4:2) and to then lie would be tantamount to saying "God is dead" (cf. ibn Ezra). The prophet Hosea (4:15) condemns all oaths "as Yahweh lives," probably for this reason (cf. also Jer 5:2). In contrast, when Israel swears only the truth, then "you are my witnesses" (Isa 43:10)—i.e., witnesses to my existence (cf. Leibowitz 1976: 327).

Others take the command more broadly, banning anything from execrating God directly to conjuring with his name, praying for the impossible or even idly mentioning him (cf. Dillmann 1880: 212; Houtman 2000: 37). Childs (1974: 409–11) translates, "You shall not abuse the name of Yahweh your God." One must not impugn Yahweh's reputation by invoking him in matters in which he is unlikely to respond.

A deity is acknowledged and reified by invocation and imprecation no less than by sacrifice. Compare Deut 6:13: "Yahweh your deity you must fear, and him you must serve, and by his name you must swear." Israel proves its exclusive fidelity to Yahweh not only by sacrifice to Yahweh alone, but also by swearing by Yahweh alone, and never falsely or for trivial purposes (cf. Bekhor Shor; Jacob 1992: 559). The false oath is injurious to society, ultimately undermining our ability to cope with reality, and is banned in all civilizations. E.g., Edward Gibbon (*Decline and Fall of the Roman Empire*, ch. 2) comments, "The [Roman] pontiffs . . . respected as the firmest bond of society, the useful persuasion that, either in this or in a future life, the crime of perjury is most assuredly punished by the avenging gods." Few cases so aptly illustrate Durkheim's (1915) insight that God is no more and no less than the principle binding society together.

name. The previous command prohibited idolatry. Like a picture, the name of a thing or person can be metaphorically equivalent to the thing or person it/him/herself. To know an entity's name is to possess power over it, as when the first Man names the animals and Woman (Gen 2:19, 23) and later renames Eve (Gen 3:20). Moses had early on asked to know Yahweh's name (Exod 3:13), a request that the Deity evidently finds threatening (vol. I, pp. 223–26). By continually revealing his true name to Israel, Yahweh makes himself vulnerable, no less than a god in plastic form. He can be "damaged" by the abuse of his appellation. Throughout Exodus, Yahweh is jealously concerned for his "name," i.e., his renown (see vol. I, pp. 36–37; Jacob 1992: 558–59).

clear. Niqqâ 'clean, clear' does not mean "forgive." Rather, it connotes acknowledging the discharge of a vow, as in Gen 24:41; Josh 2:20 (Bekhor Shor). If a man swears falsely by Yahweh, he incurs a debt to the Deity that can never be removed—save, presumably, by his death—whether or not human authorities take action (Sarna 1991: 111).

20:8. *Remember.* The command *zākôr* 'remember' is slightly odd. More expected would be *šāmôr* 'keep' (e.g., Deut 5:12) or even *ʿăśô(h)* 'do' (cf. Exod 31:16; Deut 5:15). Perhaps the focus is on remembering the two past events commemorated by this commandment: explicitly the Creation (Bekhor Shor) and implicitly the Lawgiving at Sinai. Compare the reference to the Sabbath as a "sign," i.e., mnemonic marker, in 31:17 (see NOTE).

It seems, moreover, that the root *zkr* implies not just recollection but action based upon memory. For example, in 13:3 the command to "remember" the Exodus from Egypt motivates the season's rituals. So too, remembering the Sabbath and the recollection of Yahweh's primordial rest prompt one to abstain from work.

At its simplest level, however, 20:8 simply means, "Don't forget the Sabbath." Before calendars and clocks, it would indeed have been easy to forget which day was the Sabbath—at least, after the cessation of the seven-day Manna cycle (ibn Ezra [shorter commentary], Bekhor Shor). Whereas the festivals are governed by the moon, the Sabbath relies solely on human record-keeping—which is to say, memory.

Sabbath. The derivation of the noun *šabbāt* is not certain. If it is an indigenous word correctly vocalized, there are three hypothetically possible roots: *šbb*, *šby* and *šbt*. Of these, the only one that suits semantically is *šbt* 'cease,' and probably the Israelites themselves made this connection. The plural *šabbātōt*, the extended noun *šabbātōn* and the pre-suffixal form *šabbatt-* (Lev 23:32; Num 28:10; Isa 66:23; Hos 2:13; cf. Lam 1:7 *mišbattehā*) all corroborate that the final taw is a root consonant.

The noun *šabbāt* is of ambiguous gender (see NOTE to "to sanctify it" below). It appears to merge two proto-Hebrew nominal stems, presumably synonymous: **šabbat* (m.) and **šabbatt* (f.). The noun's pattern is also somewhat unexpected. Words of the shape **qaṭṭāl(t)* generally denote professional activities such as *gannāb* 'thief,' *ḥā(r)rāš* 'smith,' etc., or else are verbal nouns of the Piʿel (Wright 1989). Thus, *šabbāt* would be expected to mean "terminator" (but see Rechenmacher 1996).

Many scholars argue, however, that the term is not native to Hebrew, but borrowed from Mesopotamia. Akkadian *šapattu* denotes the midpoint of the lunar month, the day of the full moon (Langdon 1935: 89–96). (Some even suppose that this is the meaning also of Hebrew *šabbāt* in 2 Kgs 4:23; Isa 1:3–14; Hos 2:13–15; Amos 8:4; see, however, Hasel [1992: 850].) This theory accounts for the occasional doubling of the final taw in *šabbāt*. For the shift $p > b$, the best explanation would be either a folk etymological association with *šbt* 'cease' or else with Akkadian *sibittum* 'seven' (Benzinger *apud* Holzinger 1900: 72). Note, too, that Akkadian *šapattu* has an alloform *šabattu*. The doubling of the second consonant in Hebrew still remains unexplained, however. And how did a foreign term for the full moon come to describe the last day of an Israelite seven-day week or, rarely, a week itself (Lev 23:15; 25:8; Isa 66:23)?

Here scholars invoke another Mesopotamian institution. In the late Assyrian calendar, certain occupations were proscribed on days 7, 14, 19, 21 and 28 of the month, due to bad luck (Langdon, pp. 83–89). Significantly, all these except the nineteenth day are multiples of seven, roughly corresponding to a quarter-lunation of c. 29.5 days. According to this theory, in some unattested intermediary form of tradition, the name *šapattu* came to denote these unlucky days—perhaps because the taboo day and the full moon would roughly coincide on the fourteenth–fifteenth. The Egyptians also observed various lucky and unlucky days on which various activities were forbidden because their success was unlikely (Dawson 1926). And in the modern Middle East, the Bedouin observe periods of good or bad luck days, at intervals of ten days (Musil 1928: 390).

If the biblical Sabbath is a borrowing from Mesopotamia, it is a creative borrowing several stages removed from its origin: applying the name of the mid-month point to the day of rest, broadening the concept of rest, suppressing the notion of bad luck, and detaching the system from the lunar cycle. If the Sabbath was deeply rooted in Israelite culture, however, then the seeming Mesopotamian connections may be mere coincidence, representing parallel developments in neighboring cultures. Given the late date of the Mesopotamian evidence, the seven-day taboo cycle might even reflect West Semitic influence upon Mesopotamia, not vice versa.

As Levenson (1988: 119–20) astutely notes, in biblical religion, the Sabbath replaces the absent New Year's Day. Whereas the New Year was marked in Mesopotamia, at least locally, by recitations of the Creation myth (see vol. I, pp. 442–43), Israel held no celebration on the first day of the first month (vol. I, pp. 386–87). Instead, the Sabbath leads the list of festivals in Leviticus 23. Time is ritually regenerated, not annually at a royal shrine but weekly in every home.

to sanctify it. The verb "remember" bears, as it were, a double object. The basic meaning is: "Remember to sanctify the Sabbath day." But *ləqaddəšô* could also be translated "by sanctifying it."

Instead of *ləqaddəšô*, one might have expected a feminine-suffixed form (*ləqaddəšāh*), since normally *šabbāt* is feminine. Perhaps the suffix refers to *yôm* 'day' (m.). But more likely *šabbāt* is here masculine after all, as in Num 28:10; Isa 56:2 (see previous NOTE). In the old orthography, the suffixed infinitive would have been written *lqdšh* whether the objectival suffix were masculine (-ô) or feminine (-āh). That is, the autograph was inherently ambiguous.

How can Israel sanctify what Yahweh has already sanctified (Gen 2:3; Exod 20:11)? *Pace* Levine (1987: 248), *ləqaddəšô* is probably not delocutive, meaning "*declare* the Sabbath holy." More likely it means: "*treat* the Sabbath as holy," like a sacrificial offering and as a thing proper to the divine realm, not to be mingled with the profane (Luzzatto). Just as one immolates valuable livestock to Yahweh, forgoing use for oneself, so one declines to make profitable use of a seventh of one's life, rendering the value of the time to God.

How does one keep the biblical Sabbath? Specific forbidden acts are Manna collecting and cooking (chap. 16), plowing and harvesting (34:21), kindling fire (35:3), wood chopping (Num 15:32–36) and trading (Jer 17:19–27; Amos 8:5; Neh 13:15–22). Rabbinic Judaism will considerably extend this list (*m. Šabbat*).

20:10. *seventh day.* The phrase *yôm haššбî'î* is odd, literally meaning "the day of the seventh" (cf. TEXTUAL NOTE). Presumably it is modeled after *yôm haššabbāt* 'the day of the Sabbath' in the preceding verse.

The number seven is a stereotypical patterning device in the Bible and the ancient Near East (Pope 1962a). At least as far as units of time are concerned, the cycle probably originated as an approximation of the four phases of the moon during a c. 29.5–day lunation (for parallels in other cultures, see Ewald 1876: 98, 350). In Hellenistic times (c. second century B.C.E.), each weekday was assigned to one of the seven "planets" then acknowledged: the Sun, Moon, Mercury, Venus, Mars, Jupiter and Saturn (see Gandz 1970: 171–210). The alternative calendar of Roman-era Judaism also exploits the fact that the 364 *(sic!)* days of the year are evenly divisible by 7 (on the Jewish solar calendar, see briefly vol. I, pp. 386, 431).

for Yahweh. The first Sabbath was observed by Yahweh himself (Gen 2:2–3), who continues once a week to abstain from creation (contrast John 5:17)— witness the cessation of Manna each Saturday (Exodus 16; see vol. I, p. 597).

Don't do any task. The rise of agriculture in Neolithic times created the first crisis of overwork, followed by the advent of capitalism in the Persian era (see Seow 1997) and, centuries later, the Industrial Revolution. The remediating Israelite Sabbath makes for good sanity and health, and has been widely imitated worldwide.

For the Torah, there is also a theological point, which Heschel (1951: 3) eloquently articulates in modern terms: "He who wants to enter the holiness of the day must first lay down the profanity of clattering commerce, of being yoked to toil. He must go away from the screech of dissonant days, from the nervousness and fury of acquisitiveness and the betrayal in embezzling his own life. He must say farewell to manual work and learn to understand that the world has already been created and will survive without the help of man."

son . . . daughter. The nonmention of "your wife" proves that, here at least, the command in the masculine singular applies also to the female (Luzzatto; contrast NOTE to 20:17[14], "write," below).

your animal. Not only must all human dependants keep the Sabbath, but so must domestic animals. On the personification of animals in biblical religion, see below, pp. 285, 695–701.

sojourner. It may not be coincidence that, on the *seventh* day, rest is enjoined upon *seven* entities: "you," "your son," "your daughter," "your slave," "your maidservant," "your animal" and "your sojourner" (Cassuto 1967: 245).

20:11. heavens . . . earth . . . sea. This partition echoes the trichotomy of v 4, which forbids graphically representing the denizens of these realms (Holzinger 1900: 74).

Comparison with other ancient Near Eastern mythology is instructive. In the Babylonian epics *Atra Ḥasīs* (Lambert and Millard 1969) and *Enūma Eliš* (*ANET*[3] 60–72, 501–3; Dalley 1989: 233–74), the gods' primordial labors lead ultimately to rest—but for them alone. Humanity is the robotic workforce created to assume their drudgery. In J, too, mankind's doom is to work (Gen 3:17–19, 23). In P, however, the Torah's dominant voice, Creation culminates in Yahweh's rest (Gen 2:1–4a), which he eventually imparts to Israel. Thus, by resting one day a week, later generations unite in imitation of God himself. Through the day of rest, they experience the original meaning of "recreation." Deut 5:15, in contrast, grounds the Sabbath command in the liberation from Egyptian bondage, when the Hebrews learned the meaning of rest.

20:12. *Honor your father and your mother.* There is probably no culture save for our own that does not place a supreme value upon respect for one's elders. Western Civilization is uniquely characterized by its belief in progress instead of decline, the superiority of the new over the old.

Filial piety is essentially an intergenerational bargain: I tend my children when they are young and weak, so that they will tend when I'm old and weak. In some archaic societies surviving till modern times, the elders, though feeble, are privy to the greatest secrets simply by virtue of having lived long enough to progress though the ranks of initiatory secret societies. Thereby, the very old wield a social power disproportionate to their physical power (Tuzin 1980). This background explains why the chief gods of Canaan and Mesopotamia, among other cultures, are often imagined as old men, past their physical prime, and why, in so many cultures, "old man" is a term of quintessential respect.

The Torah frequently endorses filial obedience (see also 21:15, 17; Lev 19:3; 20:9; Deut 5:16; 21:18–21; 27:16). The Book of Proverbs in particular reiterates the theme of the honor due one's parents, extolling them as the fonts of wisdom (Prov 1:8–9; 6:20–21; 10:1; 15:20, etc.). Like the Decalog, such texts frequently mention the mother as well as the father.

While presumably drummed into children from a young age, the obligation of filial piety continues throughout a parent's life. Some interpret this command as applying mainly to adults, warning them not to abuse or abandon the elderly (Noth 1962: 165; Houtman 2000: 50–56). For further discussion of honoring parents, see NOTES to 21:15, 17.

days may lengthen. The reward for honoring one's elders is, naturally enough, surviving to elderhood oneself (see also Prov 4:10). Bekhor Shor proffers a brief homily, "If you hold fast to the commands, your sons will honor you and support you through old age; you will not die in want before your time." Length of days is a common biblical reward (Deut 4:40; 5:30; 6:2; 11:9, 22; 22:7; 1 Kgs 3:14). In Deut 22:6–7, it is connected to respect for familial relations, even among the animals: one must not take eggs or chicks with the mother bird present, but must chase away the dam "so that it will be well for you, and you may lengthen days." In Eph 6:1–2, Paul appears to understand Exod 20:12 as promising both prosperity and longevity.

Ibn Ezra, however, also sees in v 12 an admonition to the people *en masse.* As long as they practice filial piety, the Israelites will not be exiled from Canaan. This is not just supernaturalism, for, as Ehrlich (1908: 344; 1969: 173–74) observes, it is precisely the honoring of ancestral customs that constitutes, unifies and stabilizes a society. Most likely, both interpretations of 20:12, the personal and the national, are correct (Dillmann 1880: 217).

One might think that the Hiph'il verb *he'ĕrîk* should be transitive (ibn Ezra). In that case, the subject might be the honored parents, who as empowered spirits will prolong their descendants' days from the grave (cf. Brichto 1974: 30–35). But it is hard to imagine a biblical author endorsing the ancestor cult as one of the ten foundations of Israelite society. Rather, we have an intransitive/impersonal Hiph'il, as in Deut 5:16; 6:2; 25:15; 1 Kgs 8:8. Perhaps it is a special, intensive form: "your days may lengthen *greatly*" (D. N. Freedman, privately).

upon the soil. Why is this necessary? Personal fulfillment is not just longevity; it is longevity on one's own ancestral soil, surrounded by numerous descendants, and culminating in interment in that very soil, among the bones of one's forebears.

20:13. *Don't murder.* The next three commands are curt statements. They require no justification or elaboration because they are the bases of all societies, not just the Israelite (Cassuto 1967: 237). When the Torah first articulates the murder ban, however, it provides a characteristically Israelite explanation, equating homicide with sacrilege: "for in Deity's image he made Man" (Gen 9:6; on Israelite attitudes toward life-taking, see further below, NOTES to 21:12–14; pp. 681–82, 695–701).

The verb *rāṣaḥ* means illegally to kill a human being (Rashbam; Bekhor Shor). (In Num 35:30 alone, the root refers to capital punishment, so that the offender gets his just deserts.) Misleading but seemingly ineradicable in the English-speaking world is the AV rendering "Thou shalt not kill," which is far too broad. By using the verb "kill," which appears only 128 times in the AV, rather than "slay" (473 occurrences), the translators may have been trying to convey the sense of "murder"; contrast AV Matt 19:18, "Thou shalt do no murder." ("Murder" as a verb appears only 3 times in the AV.)

20:14(13). *adultery.* Since the Bible accepts polygyny, adultery (*n'p*) is defined as sexual intercourse between a man, married or not, and a married woman who is not his wife. A married man is free to cohabit with whomever he likes, provided he does not infringe on another man's conjugal rights. But ibn Ezra, developing Saadiah's interpretation, regards *n'p* as connoting all forbidden sexual relations (see, however, Luzzatto). Israelite tribal affiliation was transmitted only through fathers; thus, the entire kinship system depended on female marital fidelity.

20:15(13). *steal.* With Saadiah, I take this command literally: "Don't take what is not yours." Some feel, however, that mere theft is too slight a crime to belong alongside murder and adultery, both capital offenses. Accordingly, Rashi suggests that the prohibition is on kidnapping (also *b. Sanh.* 86a; *Mek. baḥōdeš* 8). And Freedman (2000: 85–118) thinks that theft implies violation of *ḥerem,* or Yahweh's right to the spoils of war.

I, however, do not regard the Decalog as a catalogue of the most severe crimes—after all, what do we make of coveting (see below)? Rather, it is an implicit list of social rights, granted and enforced by Yahweh in exchange for Israel's exclusive obedience. These rights are weekly rest, respect from one's children, security from murder, secure possession of one's wife, secure possession of one's property and security from a rigged judicial process.

20:16(13). *testify.* The root *'ny* basically means "to answer," perhaps in this context "to respond to interrogation" (on the theory that the original meaning was "to open," see Levine 1999). This command naturally follows murder, theft and adultery, all offenses for which the accused and accuser are both entitled to a just trial

(Holzinger 1900: 75). Apropos of the expression 'ānâ bə-, Talmon (1986: 84) observes that when 'ny is follwed by the preposition bə- 'in, against,' the evidence is assumed to be damning (Deut 31:28; 1 Sam 8:9; 12:3; 2 Sam 1:16; Hos 5:5; Mic 6:3); when 'ny is followed by lə- 'for' as in the Yavneh Yam ostracon (AHI 7.10–11), it is expected to be exculpatory.

There is no explicit evidence that Israelite witnesses testified under oath. Still, Jer 7:9 and Hos 4:2 both associate oath-breaking with murder, theft and adultery. This may (or may not) be an ancient interpretation of Exod 20:16(13).

(as) a false witness. This translation follows ibn Ezra, taking 'ēd as in apposition to the implicit subject "you." It is also possible to regard 'ēd as equivalent to 'ēdût 'testimony' and as a direct object—hence, "Don't testify . . . false testimony." The latter has been the conventional understanding since LXX; Leibowitz (1976: 336) compares Gen 31:47, where 'ēd appears to bear this meaning. Luzzatto suggests a compromise, regarding the language as elliptical: "Don't testify . . . the testimony of a false witness." Concern for honest judicial testimony also motivates the requirement for two witnesses in capital cases (Num 35:30; Deut 17:6; 19:15). Deut 19:16–21 elaborates on the consequences of false testimony (see also Exod 23:1; Lev 19:16; Deut 5:20).

20:17(14). covet. Some exegetes feel that coveting (ḥmd) does not belong among the foregoing crimes, since it is hardly a prosecutable offense. Those who regard 20:15 as addressing some crime other than theft (NOTE to 20:15) find the ban on theft in 20:17(14), citing 34:24, where ḥmd may refer not just to coveting but to acting upon one's inclination by expropriating land (e.g., Noth 1962: 166; see, however, NOTE; for a general discussion against this view, see Cassuto 1967: 248).

This is reading far too much into the text, and also reducing the Decalog to a simple list of dos and don'ts. Rather, the Ten Words deliberately descend from the sublime font of Israelite society, Yahweh, to the base human motives of envy and acquisitiveness (cf. Houtman 2000: 68–69). The tenth command addresses desire as the emotional root of crime, most obviously of adultery and theft but sometimes also of murder (e.g., 2 Samuel 12) and false witness (e.g., 1 Kings 21). The appropriate illustration is Achan's confession, "I saw among the spoils one fine Shinar cloak and two hundred shekels of silver and one gold tongue (ingot), its weight fifty shekels, and I desired them (wā'ehmdēm) and took them" (Josh 7:21; cf. also Deut 7:25).

In the composite Torah, the Decalog adverts to Mankind's early history, when coveting (ḥmd) the forbidden fruit led to expulsion from the Garden (Gen 3:6). While it can never be eradicated, the legist implies that, for society's good, envy should be suppressed to the extent possible. The last of the Ten Words approaches the Buddha's insight that desire is the source of all unhappiness, and also Freud's insight that "libido" is a prime human motivator. Mere wishes, not just acts, can be displeasing to Yahweh (Cassuto 1967: 240, 249).

house. Here bayit connotes any elements of a household that possess economic value—not just the domicile per se, but also one's wife, servants and livestock. (Because they are not purchased, children do not belong in the list.) In Deut

5:21(18), in contrast, *bayit* seems to denote specifically a structure (Dillmann 1880: 218).

wife. The text addresses the male household head specifically. For a woman to desire another woman's husband is less problematic because he can take her as a second wife, assuming that she is unmarried.

anything of your fellow. I.e., his inanimate property.

20:18(15). *the people were seeing.* One could take the beginning of the verse as an extended circumstantial clause, as if to say, "Seeing the sounds and the *torches* and the horn's sound and the mountain smoking, the people feared and recoiled. . . ."

Since there is no initial consecutive verb, one might infer that the events of vv 18(15)–21(18) are temporally anterior to the Decalog, following upon the doings of chap. 19 (Ramban). In other words, the Decalog is inserted within a quasi-*Wiederaufnahme* (Kuhl 1952) framed by similar passages containing "Thus you will say . . . You, you saw" (19:3–6 to 20:22[19]). On the other hand, Deuteronomy 5 appears to follow the superficial order of Exodus 20, with the people's fear following the Decalog.

sounds. Here *qôlōt* means thunder. How could the people "see" thunder? This is the Bible's classic example of "zeugma," the incongruity created when a verb or adjective logically modifies only one of a pair of nouns. Obviously, the people saw only the lightning and smoke; they *heard* the sounds. Ibn Ezra (shorter commentary) perceptively notes that at issue may be the confusion of the human senses in Israelite parlance and experience. He compares, "See, my son's odor" (Gen 27:27); "you . . . have fouled our odor in Pharaoh's eyes" (Exod 5:21), and "the light is sweet" (Qoh 11:7). Other good examples are Exod 20:23(19), "you saw that from the sky I spoke with you," and Deut 4:12, "an image you were not seeing, except for a sound."

torches. *Lappîdîm* here connotes lightning (also in Ezek 1:13). Perhaps we are to imagine that minor deities bear torches or are themselves animate flambeaux (for Akkadian parallels, see *CAD* 3.156–57). The term *lappîd* may originally be Indo-European; Rabin (1963: 128–29) supports a derivation from Hittite *lappiya-* 'shining object, torch' (cf. also Greek *lampas* 'torch'). The description of Sinai-Horeb as swathed in furnace-smoke (19:18) and lit by torches (20:18[15]) recalls Gen 15:17, where the covenanting divine presence is represented by a smoking oven and a fiery torch.

recoiled. This translation of *nw'* mediates between "reeled, staggered, shook" (*Mek. bahōdeš* 9; Saadiah) and "moved, retired" (ibn Ezra; Ehrlich 1908: 345).

stood from afar. Or "stood still at a distance." Perhaps the people have refused to obey the summons of the horn (19:13, 19). If so, rather than take umbrage, Yahweh may actually approve of their diffidence (20:20[17]), as in Deut 5:28(25)–29(26).

20:19(16). *Speak you.* Despite Yahweh's previous concern that Israel would wish for a more immediate experience (19:12–13, 21–23), in the event, they are too intimidated to approach. They instead confirm Moses as intermediary. At last, he is elected not only by God but also by Israel (cf. vol. I, pp. 232–33).

20:20(17). *testing you.* It is not clear of what this trial consists. Since Moses is reassuring the people, perhaps they have just passed Yahweh's test by declining his invitation to ascend the mountain upon hearing the ram's horn. Or maybe they have not yet faced their trial, in which case it can only be Moses' prolonged, forty-day disappearance (24:18)—a test Israel fails by making the Gold Calf (chap. 32). I rather think, however, that the test is the Decalog itself: a rudimentary code that Israel may or may not be able to follow. It is also possible that the combination of sources has obscured what the test is.

Luzzatto, however, thinks that the sense of *nissâ* is not "test" but "train, inititate by ordeal"; similarly, Rashbam maintains that *nissâ* refers to instruction. If so, 20:20(17) explains that Israel will be instructed and ordained as Yahweh's priestly kingdom (19:6).

his fear. The fear of Yahweh is holy awe (Ezek 1:18; Ps 90:11); see Fuhs (1990).

upon your face. While this possibly refers to a frightened facial expression, more likely it means that fear of God should be in one's constant consciousness, as if before one's face. In other words, here *'al* means "opposite" not "on." In the composite text, moreover, it is noteworthy that Moses' face will either reflect or bear the consequences of Yahweh's own dread aspect (34:29–35) (COMMENT to 31:1–34:35). Yahweh's fear will literally be on his face.

20:21(18). *darkcloud.* This nimbus veils Yahweh's fiery presence from the people's sight.

20:22(19). *Thus you will say . . . . : You, you saw.* We return to the D-like diction and parallelistic style of 19:4–6 (note the quasi-poetic quality of v 23[20], suggesting we read 19:4–6 as the introduction to 20:22[19]–26[23]). The former unit appointed Israel as Yahweh's priests; the latter unit gives some basic principles for worship. Both paragraphs manifest a democratizing cast: all the nation are holy; sacrifice may be performed anywhere on any rude altar, presumably by anybody.

from the sky. This need not contradict the notion that Yahweh speaks from the mountain. On the assimilation of "mountain" and "heaven" in ancient religious language, see Metzger (1970).

I spoke. Ibn Ezra's (shorter commentary) observation is apropos: "Since I spoke myself with you, face to face, without intermediary, you need not make alongside me gods of silver and gold—for there are many idolaters who say to this day, that their image will intercede on my behalf and help me before God. . . . I have no need that you should make gods of gold, and neither have you any need." In other words, this verse is thematically linked to what follows. It essentially describes Israelite worship as vertical—aimed directly at the Deity in the sky—rather than horizontal—directed to the Deity on Earth. This contrasts with the ideology of Tabernacle and Temple; see below, pp. 495–96, 518–21, 675–95.

20:23(20). *Don't make.* I take the following laws as the likely contents of E's tablets, displaced in the redacted text by the Decalog.

silver . . . gold. While the syntax is pleasingly parallelistic—provided we ignore the MT cantillation, which sets a stop after *'ittî* 'with me'—it raises the question: what about simpler idols of stone or wood? These, too, are presumably banned. But this set of laws is aimed specifically against sumptuous temple complexes.

20:24(21). *earthen altar.* *'Ådāmâ* 'earth, dirt' contrasts with "silver" and "gold" in the preceding verse (and also, arguably, with the metal tool of v 25[22]). When the Syrian Naaman transports a supply of Israelite dirt to enable him to worship Yahweh in Damascus, he presumably fashions the earth into just such an altar (2 Kgs 5:17) (Sarna 1991: 116). On P's hollow Bronze Altar, apparently filled with earth or stones each time it is erected, see below, pp. 424, 499–501.

Whether a pile of soil or a structure of mud brick (Hyatt 1971: 225), it is important that the altar appear improvised and untidy. Preferably it should be of dirt, which the rains will swiftly wash away. If a more permanent stone installation is desired, it must still possess a rude appearance. "The law is a protest against the intrusion of culture into the cult, a reversion to the 'holy' simplicity of an older time" (Holzinger 1900: 81). Also, the very act of stone-shaping *(psl)* is suspect, since the same art can produce an idol *(pesel)*.

sacrifice. Because the verb *zābaḥ* means both "slaughter" and "sacrifice by fire," it is unclear whether the altar in 20:24(21) is just for burning the animal, or also for killing it. In 1 Sam 14:32–35, killing an animal on the ground is problematic, because the carcass soaks in its own blood. If the animal is slain on an elevated pile, however, then the blood drains down. (On the complex relationship between the altar and the slaughter block, see below, pp. 698–99.) *Mek. baḥōdeš* 11 solves the problem of 20:24(21) by translating, "you shall slaughter *near* it."

Ascending-offerings. The Ascending-offering *(ʿōlâ)* is a wholly burnt meat meal for Yahweh alone (Lev 1:3–17; 6:1–6); see pp. 702–3.

Concluding-offerings. The *šelem* is consumed mainly by worshipers, a token amount of fatty parts being burnt for Yahweh and some of the meat paid to the priest for his services (Lev 3:1–17; 7:11–34). This was the ordinary sacrifice whereby the Israelite obtained table meat (also called *zebaḥ* 'Slaughter-offering'). The *šelem* appears frequently outside the Priestly Source (e.g., 1 Sam 13:9; 2 Sam 6:18; 2 Kgs 16:13), and also in Ugaritic (e.g., *KTU* 1.14.v.40, vi.10, etc.) and Phoenician/Punic texts (*KAI* 37.B.4; 51.5; 120.2) (see further Janowski 1980).

The meaning of *šelem*, traditionally "peace offering," is uncertain. The semantic field of the root *šlm* includes "reconciliation" and "restitution," both ideas apropriate to sacrifice (cf. Levine 1974: 3–52). And yet, would they not better describe a gift given wholly to Yahweh (the *ʿōlâ*) or a purifying rite of reconciliation (the *ḥaṭṭā[ʾ]t*), rather than a meal intended mainly for the offerer? Another nuance of *šlm* is "perfection," and indeed the victim must meet stringent physical standards — but that is true for all sacrifices.

The verbal root *šlm* also means "to be concluded," and in fact the *šelem* always follows other offerings. Mere etiquette would dictate tending to the Deity's needs before one's own (below, p. 695). I slightly favor this last interpretation (*pace* Levine 1974: 20–21) and tentatively render *šelem* by "Concluding-offering" (for further discussion of the subject, see Milgrom 1991: 220–25).

your herd. My translation follows the MT trope, with the main pause (*ʾatnāḥ*) after *baqārekā* 'your herd.' LXX, however, divides the clauses differently (see Wevers 1990: 319), in essence deleting the semicolon after "herd" and inserting a conjunction to isolate the final clause: "you will sacrifice . . . your flock and your herd in any place where I proclaim my name, *and* I will come to you and bless you."

in any place. Like its Phoenician, Punic and Arabic cognates, Hebrew *māqôm* 'place' can specifically connote a temple. By erecting an altar, the worshiper creates an *ad hoc* shrine.

In 20:24(21), the interpetation of *bəkol-hammāqôm* as "any (or every) place" (LXX, Syr, *Tg. Onq.*) is not quite certain; for that, one might have expected **bəkol-māqôm*. *Bəkol-hammāqôm* would more naturally be translated as "throughout the entire land" or collectively "in all places." However, the translation "any place" is confirmed by Gen 20:13; Deut 11:24 (cf. Josh 1:3) (Levinson 1997: 32 n. 18). This verse articulates the popular and presumably original notion that one may sacrifice spontaneously to Yahweh wherever one chooses, rather than resorting to a temple and priesthood (Hyatt 1971: 226). The D and P sources combat this view, centralizing worship at one spot (Friedman 1987). While the usual inference is that Exod 20:24(21) is older than D or P, it could hypothetically represent a later challenge to D and P, when the people were in reduced circumstances (Ehrlich 1908: 346; Van Seters 2003; but see Levinson 2004). It could also be, as ibn Ezra infers, that the law simply acknowledges that worship would be conducted in various places—the wilderness, Nob, Shiloh, etc.—before permanently settling at Zion. But the adjoining reference to the simplest of altars would seem to indicate multiple, rude sanctuaries.

I announce. Why would Yahweh announce his own name? Holzinger (1900: 80) regards temples as places of theophany, where God announces, "I am Yahweh," as in his dealings with the Patriarchs and Moses (cf. already Saadiah).

An alternative interpretation of *'azkîr* is "I cause to be pronounced" (compare the exegetical variant "you pronounce" [TEXTUAL NOTE]). If so, wherever a person calls upon Yahweh's name, it is as if Yahweh has commanded him to do so. Forthwith, Yahweh draws near, and the site becomes a sanctuary and source of blessing. For Luzzatto, however, *hizkîr* simply connotes worship (cf. Isa 26:13; Ps 20:8).

20:25(22). *stones*. Fieldstone altars are mentioned in Gen 22:9; Deut 27:5–6; Josh 8:31; Judg 6:20; 13:19; 1 Sam 6:14–15; 14:33–34; Hos 12:12; 1 Macc 4:47, and probably Gen 22:9 and, in light of Joshua 22, Gen 30:44–54. In Exodus, the plural *'ăbānîm* implies a structure built of many stones, not hewn from a single stone. Olyan (1996) draws a parallel between the unhewn stone of an altar and the unblemished animal required for sacrifice, but I find the analogy inapt. Sacrificial animals are drastically "altered"—slaughtered and butchered—before presentation to God. I cannot see why stones should not be similarly prepared for divine service, unless there is some other objection (see further below).

blade. In some fashion, a cutting tool would profane the altar. Probably *ḥereb* 'blade' implies a *metal* blade (contrast, however, Josh 5:2–3 for flint blades). Merely chipping the stones to make them fit together is presumably allowed.

What is the problem with metal? Is the ban on a particular metal? Syr, *Tgs. Neofiti I* and *Ps.-Jonathan* understand that the prohibition is against *iron* blades, as stated explicitly in Deut 27:5, "an altar of stones, don't wield iron against them." Admittedly, biblical chronology places Moses in the Late Bronze Age, before the widespread use of iron (see p. 736). But this is no difficulty: the Torah mentions iron in several places, so its authors either were guilty of anachronism or put

Moses later than the chronological framework would suggest. Similarly, 1 Kgs 6:7 reports of the Temple, "picks and adzes (?), any iron implements, were not heard in the House while it was being built." (According to 1 Kgs 6:31, the stones were dressed off-site.)

Evidently, there was a taboo on iron in the holy places (ibn Ezra [shorter commentary]), doubtless because of its innovative status and, above all, its association with weaponry and violence (*Mek. baḥōdeš* 11; Ramban; cf. Cassuto 1967: 325). The Greeks similarly consider iron to be defiling (Rigsby 1996: 18), and, in European folklore, iron repels fairies and suchlike archaic creatures.

All this notwithstanding, the fact is that Exod 20:25(22) does not name the blade's substance. Perhaps this is another example of "making a fence around the Law." While the actual banned metal was iron, all tools were barred, Luzzatto suggests, to remove the temptation to engage in decorative art or idol-making (cf. ibn Ezra; Rashbam).

lifted. The verb *hēnîp* may be ironic, since the same root describes making offerings upon the altar (e.g., 29:24–27).

against it. The feminine singular suffixes on ʿ*āle(y)hā* and *wattəḥallehā* lack an obvious referent, unless it is *gāzît* 'cutstone' (Holzinger 1900: 81). Less likely, they may refer to the feminine singular *'eben* 'stone,' even though only the plural *'ăbānîm* appears.

profaned. Because of its function as a conduit to Yahweh, an altar should be supremely holy (29:37). A profaned altar will not function (on altars and sacrifice, see below, pp. 499–501, 695–703). The collocation of *ḥereb* 'blade' and *ḥillēl* 'profane' evokes the idiom *ḥălal ḥereb* 'pierced by the sword'—as if one had slain the altar (which in fact, by the proper, Priestly procedure, runs with blood [see pp. 698–99]).

20:26(23). *steps.* I.e., shaped stone slabs. The altar envisioned here must not be an expensive, monumental affair.

It is natural to elevate an altar to minimize its distance from Heaven. But still, a proper distance between Heaven and Earth must be maintained (Genesis 11). A sacrifice from a high place is no more pleasing than a sacrifice from a low place.

at which. The etymological locative sense of *'ăšer* 'that, which, where' may be in operation here. Saadiah, however, regards *'ăšer* as prefatory to a purpose clause "so that. . . ."

your nudity. It is unclear whether the officiant is a layman or priest. In either case, male nudity during worship is not approved; see NOTE to 28:42. Many scholars point out scenes of ritual nudity in ancient Near Eastern art (e.g., *ANEP* nos. 597, 600, 603, 605, 619) (e.g., Sarna 1991: 117). One suspects, however, that nudity per se was not too indecent for Israelites. Isaiah, for example, was commanded to forgo clothes to dramatize the plight of exile (Isaiah 20). It was more the peep show of skimpy garments alternately concealing and revealing that offended (e.g., 2 Sam 6:16–22).

21:1. *case-laws.* Derived from the root *špṭ* 'judge, administer,' *mišpāṭîm* are probably court decisions, i.e., legal precedents (Dillmann 1880: 225). If so, the designation *mišpāṭîm* technically applies only to passages in the First Code formulated in the dispassionate third-person "casuistic" form: "if a man . . . ," i.e.,

21:2–22:16 (Baentsch 1903: 188–89). Luzzatto, too, distinguishes the *mišpāṭîm* from more basic and absolute principles such as the commands of the Decalog, expressed through apodictic injunctions, which are not limited to or even necessarily relevant to jurisprudence (cf. the classic study of Alt 1968: 103–71). In historical reality, most if not all of the following "cases" probably arose out of the ordinary administration of justice, including legal training, and were only secondarily attributed to Yahweh (see further pp. COMMENT).

set. The verb *tāśîm* leaves it unclear whether Moses is to present the following laws in oral or in written form. Perhaps it is both; cf. 17:14; Deuteronomy 31–32.

21:2. *Hebrew.* As *Mek. nəzîqîn* 1 and Rashi observe, the phrase *'ebed 'ibrî* is grammatically ambiguous, It might mean either "a Hebrew manservant" or "a Hebrew's manservant," who might himself not be a Hebrew (cf. TEXTUAL NOTE to 1:15). The parallel law in Deut 15:12 is more explicit: "When *your brother* Hebrew is sold. . . ." And that is what makes sense here, too.

What is a "Hebrew"? For millennia, the term *'ibrî* has designated a Jew, and before that, tradition assumes, a biblical Israelite (for a good premodern, critical discussion, see ibn Ezra). Although there is room for doubt, I think that tradition is probably correct.

The genealogies of Genesis include an individual named Eber (*'ēber*, ancient pronunciation **'ibr*) (Gen 10:24–25; 11:14–17). Eber is the great-grandson of Noah's son Shem (for whom in modern times the "Semitic" peoples and languages were named). The name and character Eber were created, one would think, to provide an ancestor for all the *'ibrîm*. But, in that case, the term "Hebrew" includes not only the Israelites but the Arabs, Aramaeans, Moabites, Ammonites and Edomites, all "Eber's sons" (Gen 10:21) (cf. Halpern 1983: 53). Alternatively: the first man explicitly called a "Hebrew" is Abram (Gen 14:13). From this, one might reasonably infer that all nations to whom the Bible accords Abrahamic descent—i.e., Edom, Israel, the Arabian tribes—are the "Hebrews." (Ibn Ezra records [and rejects] a Qara'ite opinion to this effect.) The biblical usage of "Hebrew" is indeed perplexing. If the term denoted only Israelites, then we would expect to find "Eber" as a third name of Jacob-Israel, the ancestor of all Israelites and of no one else.

Discounting the eponymous Eber, what is the true derivation of the term *'ibrî*? With recourse only to Hebrew, we would most naturally assume it means "the one from across (*'ēber*)," presumably across the river, be it the Euphrates or the Jordan. In other words, from a Palestinian perspective, "Hebrew" connotes "Easterner." Biblical tradition in fact places Israel's immediate origin in northern Mesopotamia (Gen 11:31–32; 12:4–5) and ultimately in southern Mesopotamia (Gen 11:28, 31; 15:7). It is not quite clear, however, that the term assumes a Palestinian perspective. In Assyrian, Babylonian and Persian times, when the Torah was composed, Canaan was included in the region called "Across the River" (*eber nāri*)— i.e., across the Euphrates *from an Eastern perspective* (cf. Ezra 4:10; 8:36; Neh 2:79). In this case, *'ibrî* would connote a "Westerner," i.e., a denizen of Syria–Palestine, equivalent to the older Akkadian term *amurrû* 'westerner' (biblical Amorite).

Modern epigraphic discoveries have revolutionized our understanding of the term "Hebrew"—or else provided one or two mischievous red herrings. It turns out that, from Late Bronze Age Egypt to North Syria, a somewhat disreputable social class heavily represented among mercenaries, brigands and slaves was known by a term that was likely pronounced ʿ*abiru* or ʿ*apiru* (unfortunately, due to the inherent ambiguities of the cuneiform script, we cannot rule out entirely *ḫabiru, ḫapiru, ḫabiru, ḫapiru, habiru and hapiru*). Can these be the Hebrews (for general discussion, see Bottéro 1954; Greenberg. It is a curious fact that the term "Hebrew" appears in the Bible mainly in two contexts: in the mouths of foreigners (or when Israelites speak of themselves to foreigners) or describing slaves, as in 21:2. Might the term retain a self-deprecatory connotation lingering from the Late Bronze Age, and might it still be a social rather than an ethnic category, perhaps a type of slave (Alt 1968: 120–22; Cassuto 1967: 265–66)? Naturally, the contrary possibility also exists: ʿ*ab/piru* originally was an ethnic term for a Late Bronze people so widely disdained that any outsider or menial was labeled a "Hebrew" (cf. Halpern 1983: 52–55)

All references to ʿ*ab/piru* come from the Late Bronze Age; there are no ʿ*ab/piru*-outcasts in Iron Age texts contemporary with historical Israel. Lemche (1975) draws one possible conclusion: Exodus preserves pre-Israelite norms for ʿ*ab/piru* enslavement. Alternatively, we might divorce the biblical Hebrews entirely from the ʿ*ab/piru*-question.

The real question is whether the biblical term ʿ*ibrî* is better illuminated by pre-biblical Canaanite sources or by postbiblical Jewish sources. It should be obvious, however, that the best source would be the Israelites themselves. The Bible provides conclusive evidence that, notwithstanding that Jacob-Israel is never actually called a Hebrew, the term is restricted to his descendants, quite as tradition maintains (Durham 1987: 320). First, some passages appear to equate "Hebrew" and "Israelite," e.g., Deut 15:12, "your brother Hebrew" (Jacob 1992: 612–13). In Gen 39:17; 40:15, Joseph is called a "Hebrew slave" "from the Hebrews' land." More important, when Moses announces that the "Hebrews' deity" demands the release of his people (Exod 3:18; 5:3; 7:16; 9:1, 13), "Hebrews" is equivalent to "your fathers" (3:16) and "Israel" (5:1). And, while D and P are not always reliable guides as to the intent of older legislation, Deut 15:12–18 and even more explicitly Lev 25:25–55 make it clear that Israelite slaves have special rights, thus clarifying Exod 21:2–6. I admit that the ʿ*ab/piru* connection is tantalizing and probably valid on some level (see below, pp. 742–44). But, regardless of etymology, in the Bible ʿ*ibrî* 'Hebrew' functions as the ethnic term for an Israelite (for other scholars of this view and similar opinions, see Chirichigno 1993: 205 n. 1). I would compare the term "American," which logically and etymologically describes any denizen of South or North America, but which in almost all contexts is used worldwide to denote citizens of the United States of America.

After all, if not ʿ*ibrî*, what would be the generic Hebrew term for a descendant of Jacob? We read about the Edomite (ʾ*ădōmî*), the Ammonite (ʿ*ammōnî*), the Eygptian (*miṣrî*), etc. We also read about the Judahite (*yəhûdî*), the Zebulonite (*zəbûlōnî*), the Bethlehemite (*bêt-laḥmî*), etc. Yet, although we constantly use the term "Israelite," it corresponds to a Hebrew word appearing only in Lev 24:10–11: *yiśrə'ēlî(t)*. What was the normal ethnic adjective for an Israelite? The only plausible candidate is *'ibrî* (Landsberger 1929: 329).

In the literary context of the Book of Exodus, *'ebed 'ibrî* 'Hebrew manservant' in 21:2 echoes Moses' demand for liberation: "Thus has Yahweh the *Hebrews'* (*'ibrîm*) deity said: 'Release my people that they may *serve* (*'bd*) me' " (7:16; 9:1, 13) (Jacob 1992: 612). This implicit allusion is heightened and made explicit in the slave law of Deut 15:12–18: "And you must remember that you were a slave in the land of Egypt, and Yahweh your deity ransomed you; therefore I am commanding this matter today" (see also Jer 34:13–14). In other words, the humane treatment of slaves, at least Hebrew slaves, is predicated upon Israel's own experience of servitude. This is presumably why the First Code's case-law opens with this subject, instead of with crimes and their remedies (Sarna 1991: 118).

The Jewish sources devote considerable attention to the question of whether specific laws refer to Israelite or foreign slaves or both. On the one hand, one could argue that wherever the text mentions a slave without further qualification, the law is for all slaves. On the other hand, one could argue that the reference to the "Hebrew slave" in 21:2 covers all references to slaves in the following chapters. The Rabbis had a particular problem, in that they were obliged to reconcile the slightly variant laws of Exod 21:2–6 and Deut 15:12–18 with each other and with Lev 25:39–55, which abolishes slavery for all Israelites, limiting it to foreigners. Harmonizing E, D and P is not our concern, but the problem remains. The legislator must have thought that the answer was obvious, since he was probably codifying what was common or at least well-known practice.

Manservant. Persons mostly entered servitude due to economic distress (Lev 25:39; Deut 15:12; 28:68; Isa 50:1; Amos 2:6; 8:6). Throughout the Near East, debt was the main cause of slavery (Mendelson 1949; 1955: 66; Chirichigno 1993). Other ways to become a slave were sale by parents (Exod 21:7; 2 Kgs 4:1; Neh 5:2, 5), also due to poverty; judicial sentence (Exod 22:2); kidnapping (Gen 37:28; Exod 21:16; Deut 24:7), and capture in war (Gen 14:12–14; Num 31:9, 18; Deut 21:10–14; 1 Sam 30:3; 1 Kgs 20:39; 2 Kgs 5:2; 2 Chr 28:8–15). There was also the *yəlîd bayit* 'house-born,' the offspring of slaves (see Gen 14:14; 17:12, 23, 27; Exod 21:4–5; Lev 22:11; 25:45–46; Jer 2:14). After becoming a slave, during the term of servitude one was a chattel, much like domestic cattle (Gen 12:16; 20:14; 24:35; 30:43), i.e., owned but still possessed of some basic rights and the object of empathy (cf. Job 31:13–15). For a general discussion on the biblical institution of slavery, see Matthews (1994); on slavery in the ancient Near East, see Mendelsohn (1949), Cardellini (1981: 1–236) and Chirichigno (1993: 30–100).

Unlike many moderns who have deeply investigated the phenomenon of ancient Near Eastern slavery (e.g., Cardellini, Chirichigno), I do not think that it is valid to insert distinctions among various types of slaves that the biblical text itself does not make—i.e., to suppose that some laws refer only to debt-slaves and other to bought slaves. I read the laws as broadly as possible.

six years. Because it is older, this law does not reckon with P's Jubilee, by which all slaves are set free every fifty years, irrespective of their purchase date (Lev

25:8–55). Similar to Exod 21:2, Gen 29:18–30 seems to envision a renewable, seven-year term of service (Dillmann 1880: 226), and perhaps the original term was seven years. Subsequently, on the analogy of six work days + one rest day, the laborer was liberated one year early (cf. Dillmann 1880: 226; Jacob 1992: 614).

On the number seven in the Bible, see Pope (1962a); on the quasi-equivalence of the numbers six and seven, cf. Jer 34:14, according to which the term of service is both six and seven years (MT; contrast LXX).

seventh. The seventh year of his servitude (*Mek. nəzîqîn* 1). Bekhor Shor, however, opines that this is the sabbatical year, when agricultural labor is suspended (23:11; Lev 25:1–7, 20–22; Deut 15:1–11) (see also *Tg. Ps.-Jonathan* Exod 21:7). But Houtman (2000: 123–24) notes the obvious problem: if all slaves are liberated every seven years, most would not serve out their six-year terms. More likely, each slave has his own particular release year, independent of the sabbatical cycle. On the periodic liberation of slaves and remission of debt in the ancient Near East, see Weinfeld (1990).

as a freeman. By this law, the "Hebrew slave" is "less than a full citizen but . . . more than a full slave," who serves for life (Durham 1987: 321).

As ibn Ezra explains, MT *laḥopšî* presents us with a grammatical problem. The lamedh prefix implies that *ḥopšî* is an abstract noun ("freedom") (Rashi, Rashbam), but the yodh suffix implies an adjective or descriptive noun (cf. *Tgs. bar ḥôrîn* 'son of the free'). Luzzatto cleverly but without real evidence supposes that *ḥopšî* is a shortened form of an abstract noun **ḥopšît*, just as Aramaic abstract nouns end in *-û*, short for *-ût*. Perhaps the Massoretes followed some such theory to justify the definite article within the prefix *la-*.

I, however, have taken the liberty of emending the vocalization (see TEXTUAL NOTE). The final vowel I regard as the common adjectival-gentilic suffix, like that on *ʿibrî* 'Hebrew' (cf. Cazelles 1946: 45). The term thus means "a man characterized by *ḥōpeš* 'liberty, manumission.'"

As with the term "Hebrew," ancient Near Eastern texts have both clarified and clouded our picture of *ḥopšî*. The word is related to Akkadian *ḥupšu*, which describes a type of person in various Old Assyrian and Old Babylonian documents, the Nuzi tablets, the Amarna letters from Byblos and texts from Alalakh and Ugarit (for literature, see Lemche 1975: 140–41). At least in the Late Bronze Age, the *ḥupšu* served primarily as soldiers, although we also hear of *ḥupšu* artisans and shepherds. Lemche (p. 142) regards the *ḥupšu* as only semi-free, which could explain a slave's reluctance to be liberated in Exodus, quite apart from his emotional attachments to his master and family. Perhaps, like the Mesopotamian *muškēnu*, the *ḥopšî*/*ḥupšu* occupied an intermediate status between the ordinary free citizen (Hebrew *ʾîš*, Akkadian *awīlu*) and the slave (Hebrew *ʿebed*, Akkadian *wardu*) (cf. Lemche pp. 136–42). But, if this were so in Israel, it is hard to understand why Saul should offer, as a reward for battling Goliath, eternal *ḥopšî*-hood for the champion and his descendants, presumably meaning that neither he nor his heirs should ever be enslaved (1 Sam 17:25). In short, while the cuneiform sources may well assume a three-level social hierarchy, for the Bible all men fall into one of two categories, *ḥopšî* 'free' and *ʿebed* 'slave' (cf. Loretz 1977). For further discussion, see Lohfink (1986a). (I will not treat here the use of "Freedom House [*bêt ḥopšî/ût*]" to connote a leprosarium [2 Chr 26:21] and the parallel Ugaritic expression *bt ḥptt* to describe the land of Death [*KTU* 1.4.viii.7]. These are both presumably euphemisms for houses of detention [cf. also *ḥpš* in Ps 88:6; Job 3:19, apropos of the dead].)

gratis. This convenient Latin word ("by grace") precisely renders Hebrew *ḥinnām* (< *ḥēn* 'grace, favor'). The law may simply indicate that neither party owes the other money, a principle that Deut 15:13–14 will modify into a requirement that the master endow his released slave (Levy-Feldblum 1986: 357–58). Thus from the master's perspective, "buying" a Hebrew slave is more a lease than a purchase. The situation is not unique; on slave-release in Mesopotamian sources, see Hallo (1995).

The implicit motivation for this law is the ideology that all Israelites are Yahweh's slaves. They therefore do not have the power to sell their persons to another in perpetuity (Ḥizquni), just as Pharaoh had no right to enslave them. At the most, they may be leased to a master.

COMPARE: If an obligation is outstanding against a man and he sells or gives into debt service his wife, his son, or his daughter, they shall perform service in the house of their buyer or of the one who holds them in debt service for three years; their release shall be secured in the fourth year (Hammurapi §117). (LCMAM 103)

21:3. *with his gap.* I have left untranslated the Hebrew term *gap*, which appears only in these verses. Both tradition (*b. B. Qidd.* 20a) and almost all of modern critical literature agree as to the verse's intent: if a slave enters service as a bachelor, he must leave as a bachelor. That is, *bəgappô* means "alone" (LXX *monos*).

The principal dispute is as to the word's derivation. Rashi supposes the root to be **gnp* = *knp* 'garment' (cf. Vg *cum quali veste*), i.e., he came with only the clothes on his back (see also Luzzatto). For the idiom, Jacob (1992: 615) compares Gen 32:11 "with my staff," implying "and nothing else." Bekhor Shor, however, thinks that *gap* means "body," so that *bəgappô* literally means "with (only) his body" (cf. the opinion in *Mek. nəzîqîn* 1; *b. Qidd.* 20a that *bəgappô* means "with uninjured body," which works in v 3 but not v 4). While *gap* is not otherwise attested in this sense, three nearly homophonous terms are. Saadiah (see Qafaḥ 1963: 65 n. 3) compares *gab* 'back, body,' and Dillmann (1880: 226) adds *gēw/gəwiyyâ* with the same meaning; cf. esp. Gen 47:18; Neh 9:37. Ibn Ezra (shorter commentary), moreover, cites Prov 9:3, where *gap* is an architectural feature, presumably the "back" or top of a wall. As for the semantics, Paul (1970: 47 n. 4) notes that Akkadian *pagru* 'body' similarly means "self," while Ehrlich (1969: 176) compares Hebrew *ləbaddô* 'alone' from *bad* 'part (of body).' (A simple-minded solution along these lines would be to revocalize **bəgūpô*, postbiblical Hebrew for "with his body.")

SPECULATION: Ehrlich (1908: 347) makes a superficially attractive suggestion: *gap* is a synonym of *'ăgap* 'troop, attachment, dependent'—i.e., "entourage"—

and is presumably cognate to Arabic *jaffa* 'company, group.' (In Mishnaic Hebrew, however, *'ăgap* means "wing, arm.") Thus the second half of the verse is a clarifying gloss to the first half, and both deal with a slave who enters servitude with a family. By this interpretation, the better reading is Sam's plural *bgpyw* (see TEXTUAL NOTE). It is hard to make this work in vv 4–5, however, which seem to exclude wife and offspring from the man's *gap*. Ehrlich's approach could still be sustained, however, if the man's *gap* were taken as persons or possessions other than his immediate family, e.g., his own slaves or cattle.

enter . . . depart. In the context of slavery, the verbs *bā(')* and *yāṣā(')* connote respectively enslavement and manumission (Paul 1970: 47–48).

husband. To avoid confusion, in a marital context I have not literally translated *ba'al* as "owner," the term's true meaning. In Biblical Hebrew, the word for slave-owner is not *ba'al* but *'ādōn*. Thus a slave may be a *ba'al* but not an *'ādōn*. As far as we can tell, while a freeman may possess a slave-wife, a freewoman may not possess a slave-husband.

his woman. The Hebrew term for wife, *'iššâ*, simply means "woman."

This law does not explicitly address the status of children born prior to their father's enslavement. Common sense would suggest that, like his wife, any children the man brought into servitude would be released along with him. The status of children the couple produces during their service is less clear. Perhaps they must stay behind, as in the case where the master "gives" his slave a wife (v 4).

The question of a slave's family must have presented a frequent problem. Paul (1970: 48–49) notes that, at Nuzi, slaves sometimes entered servitude along with their families; in other cases, their masters gave them mates. In Exodus, this is the very subject of the dispute between Pharaoh and Moses: are the Israelite men entitled to leave with their families or not (10:8–10, 24–26) (Daube 1963: 48)? The same question also underlies the tense relationship between Laban and his indentured kinsman Jacob (Genesis 31) (Chirichigno 1993: 228–29).

21:4. *If his master gives.* The language suggests that a slave forfeits the right to contract a marriage on his own behalf during his term of service (Driver 1911: 210; *pace* Ehrlich 1969: 176). It is unclear whether the master is simply breeding slaves like cattle, or whether this is a real marriage with the owner acting *in loco parentis*. An Akkadian contract from eighth-century B.C.E. Gezer, where Israelite, Aramean and Assyrian influences mingled, includes in the sale of a property a slave, his two wives and his son (Becking 1981–82: 81).

a woman. Ehrlich (1908: 347–48) sees v 4 as continuing v 3, so that the sense would be: "If his master gives him a (second) woman." But for this we would rather have expected *wə'im-'aheret/šēnît yitten-lô 'adōnā(y)w* 'and if another/a second (woman) his master gives him'; for the syntax, cf. 21:10.

children. A child born into slavery is elsewhere called *ylîd bayit* 'house-born' (Gen 14:14: 17:12–13, 23, 27; Lev 22:11; Jer 2:14); cf. Akkadian *wilid bītim* (Finkelstein 1961: 99). Whereas the traditional Jewish view traces ethnic identity through the mother, all biblical evidence suggests that in Israelite times ethnic identity passed through the *father* (on the innovation of matrilineality, see Cohen 1999: 263–307). The law therefore seems to create its own contradiction: the son of an enslaved Hebrew ought himself to be a Hebrew and limited to six years of servitude, at least upon attaining his majority.

she shall belong. Although the subject is plural ("the woman and her children"), the verb *tihye(h)* is singular. Such incongruence is common when the verb precedes its subject, less common when, as here, it follows (GKC §145o). Since the text also says "her master" not "their master," Holzinger (1900: 82) feels that the children are an "appendix." The expected syntax would put the singular verb first: **wəhāyətâ la(ʾ)dōne(y)hā hāʾiššâ wîlāde(y)hā* 'then the woman, and her children, shall belong to her master.' The text's inverted word order emphasizes the detained wife and children, contrasting them with the liberated male slave.

her master. The term is actually plural: *ʾ(ă)dōne(y)hā* 'her masters.' Like *baʿal* 'owner, master, husband,' *ʾādôn* 'owner, lord' sometimes appears in the plural of abstraction or magnitude, as if to say "lord*ship*," in which case it may be treated as singular (GKC §124g; ibn Ezra; see also NOTE to 1:17, "The Deity"). *ʾĀdôn*, especially in the form *ʾădōnāy* 'my Lord' (or perhaps 'the Lordly'), is a common title of Yahweh, since Israel is his collective slave (cf. Jacob 1992: 616).

COMPARE: If a male slave marries a female slave, his beloved, and that male slave (later) is given his freedom, she/he will not leave (or: be evicted from?) the house (Ur-Namma §4). (*LCMAM 17*)

21:5. *should say.* It is unclear whether this is the slave's inner thought or the public declaration of a legal formula.

I love my master. What if, as is more likely, he loves only his wife and children but not his master? The manservant's ideal recourse, not spelled out here, would be to accept manumission and then try to buy his family's freedom.

If he has no prospect of amassing sufficient funds, then the slave faces a difficult choice. A slave to a kindly and prosperous owner might well prefer servitude over an impoverished and lonely liberty (Holzinger 1900: 82). Deut 15:13–14 redresses this very hindrance to liberation by requiring a manumission gift (Noth 1962: 178). This, one imagines, was often applied toward the purchase and freeing of the former manservant's family. Other slaves, however, presumably felt little loyalty to wives and children foisted upon them by a master.

21:6. *the Deity.* As a likely plural of abstraction (NOTE to 1:17), *hāʾĕlōhîm* almost always connotes Yahweh. The second most common usage is to indicate other gods. But a venerable tradition sees in 21:6 a reference not to God or lesser deities but to ordinary magistrates (LXX; *Tgs.*; Syr; Rashi). The underlying assumption is that *ʾĕlōhîm* properly connotes any authority, whether human or divine. In this case, it is supposed that the civic authorities must witness and certify the ceremony, to prevent the coerced retention of a slave entitled to his freedom (Luzzatto; McNeile 1908: 127). That would be tantamount to kidnapping, a capital offense (21:16).

I and most modern scholars, however, are not convinced that *ʾĕlōhîm* here or anywhere refers to human authorities (see Gordon 1935). While it is still possible that 21:6 refers to a judicial setting, we would have to suppose with Ramban that judges are called "Deity" because God inspires their judgments, inasmuch as they are his representatives and, so to speak, junior colleagues (cf. Deut 1:17; 19:17; 2 Chr 19:6).

Since the parallel statute in Deut 15:17 omits the term, many infer that *hā'ĕlōhîm* in Exodus refers to something distasteful to the Deuteronomist, i.e., polytheism and/or idolatry (e.g., Baentsch 1903: 190). If our law did not originate in an ultra-rigorous monotheistic context, perhaps *hā'ĕlōhîm* really are divinities, whether household gods (Schwally 1891: 181–82) like the Roman *penates* (Baentsch 1903: 190; Beer 1939: 108) or ancestral deities (van der Toorn 1990: 209–10). Paul (1970: 51) notes that, in Mesopotamia, symbols of gods were placed by the doorways of private homes and also by the portals of temples. Doorway divinities presumably served a protective role; hence, the ritual may render the slave neutral as a household member, so that the apotropaic genii will let him pass and extend to him their protection. For more discussion of household gods in the Bible, see Gordon (1935); Draffkorn (1957); Greenberg (1962), and Houtman (2000: 116–19).

Most likely, however, *hā'ĕlōhîm* in 21:6 bears its ordinary meaning. The master and slave resort to Yahweh, perhaps in order to swear that the commitment to lifelong servitude is voluntary (cf. 22:8).

bring him. The subject is still presumably the master, although Dillmann (1880: 226) supposes it to be the judge. As we shall see, it is unclear whether bringing the slave to the Deity and bringing him to the door are identical or sequential acts.

door . . . doorpost. Deut 15:17 makes it clear that the awl is thrust through the ear into the door. As Rashbam and Bekhor Shor observe, even in a stone house, an awl can be thrust into a wooden doorframe and door (vs. *Mek. nəzîqîn* 2).

Which door? Opinions are divided among three possibilities: the owner's house, the city gate and the temple.

1. The slave-bonding ritual in Deut 15:17 apparently takes place at home. Likewise, one might argue, in Exodus the rite is domestic—unless the Deuteronomist transformed a temple ritual into a domestic practice precisely to avoid resorting to local High Places (see below). In any case, the doorway of the home is fraught with symbolism in many cultures, and may have been particularly associated with covenantal rites of passage such as marriage and servitude (cf. Trumbull 1906; see also vol. I, pp. 434–41 and below pp. 456, 499). (Van der Toorn [1990: 208–11] imagines, however, that the door in question belongs to a sanctum at the *rear* of the house, where the ancestral "gods" were kept.)

Further, the role of the doorpost evokes the sign of the paschal blood (*b. Qidd.* 22b), a connection that might be interpreted in either of two ways. Assuming the *Pesaḥ* as the background for 21:6, the symbolism might imply, "Freed by Yahweh from Pharaoh, why would you voluntarily surrender your liberty?" (Saadiah *apud* ibn Ezra [shorter commentary]). In other words, the slave ritual is an anti-*Pesaḥ*. Conversely, the rite of 21:6 may inform the symbolism of the paschal night, when Israel passed from temporary servitude to Pharaoh into eternal servitude to Yahweh.

More mundanely, Ehrlich (1908: 348; 1969: 176–77) suggests that the significance of the doorway is simply that there is no avoiding it. Everyone leaving or entering the house must use it. The slave will continually see the hole in the wood and remember his obligation of service; compare the role of the inscribed doorpost as a mnemonic in Deut 6:9; 11:20. Essentially, the ritual defines the slave's sphere as ending at the threshold. He is henceforth to be a symbolic component of the house, "nailed in place" (cf. ibn Ezra [shorter commentary]). Hurowitz (1992a: 8, 76) compares the Mesopotamian custom of driving a spike into the ground or a wall to betoken ownership, as we say, "staking a claim." And equally important, the mark in the doorway reminds the *master* of his own lifelong obligation, even beyond his slave's productive years (Houtman 2000: 118–19).

2. Ibn Ezra plausibly argues that Exod 21:6 and Deut 15:17 refer to the *city* gate, where the elders would gather to ratify legal transactions (Deut 21:19; 22:24; Ruth 4:1). Although his interpretation is inspired by the dubious identification of *'ĕlōhîm* as "judges" (see above), it still makes considerable sense. The gateway is such a significant feature of a city that, via metonymy, *ša'ar* 'gate' is frequently tantamount to "city" (e.g., Deut 5:14; 15:7). Like the domestic doorpost, the city gate is envisioned as reminding the Israelite of his obligations to God (Deut 6:9; 11:20).

3. Assuming that the doorway is also where Yahweh is to be found, one would naturally think of a shrine, e.g., Shiloh, whose doorposts are mentioned in 1 Sam 1:9 (Dillmann 1880: 226), or the Temple, whose doorposts are envisioned in Ezek 41:21; 43:8; 45:19. In the context of the Torah, however, the only shrine is the Tabernacle, where Yahweh is wont to manifest himself by the opening (33:9–10; Num 12:5; 16:19; 20:6; Deut 31:15) but which does not possess a wooden door or doorframe. For the oath at the sacred portal, Fensham (1959) and Loretz (1960) note that Laws of Eshnunna §37 mentions an oath sworn at the entry of the temple of the god Tishpak *(ina bāb Tišpak)*.

We have reached an impasse, with sound arguments for each opinion. The meaning of the ritual will be discussed further in the NOTES that follow.

drill. What is the purpose of piercing the ear? First, it is a mildly disagreeable act, as one would anticipate in a rite of passage (see below). In fact, if the drilling is an ordeal pure and simple, the hole may have been allowed to close after the procedure (Chirichigno 1993: 243). But we expect an initiatory mutilation to leave its mark. Was a pierced ear a sign of servitude in Israel? Probably not, since many Israelites likely wore earrings (32:2–3, but cf. Gen 35:4), as did Assyrians and in later times Mesopotamians (Juvenal *Satires* 1.104), Arabs (Judg 8:24; Petronius *Satyricon* 102) and Carthaginians (Plautus *Poenulus* 5.2.21). If boring the ear was meant to leave a permanent slave mark, the operation had to be either something out of the ordinary—a very large hole—or else an opportunity to insert a token of servitude into the hole instead of a ring (Mendelsohn 1949: 49; Hurowitz 1992b: 49 n. 2). Another possiblity is that the pierced ear, like circumcision (Gen 17:9–14) and the tassel on the garment (Num 15:38–40), is a sign for him who bears it, not a mark distinguishing him from others. In other words, all might have pierced ears, but the slave's pierced ear reminds him of the day he entered lifelong bondage.

As Viberg (1992: 86) notes, the very act of piercing can betoken subjugation. In Job 40:24, 26, for example, God claims to have pierced and harnessed Leviathan, making him his *'ebed 'ôlām* 'eternal slave' (cf. *wa'ăbādô lə'ōlām* 'he must serve him forever,' Exod 21:6). Leviathan was admittedly pierced through the *nose*, just as, in Mesopotamia, a judicial penalty was to have one's nose bored in the manner of an animal (Finkelstein 1981: 40 n. 1). In Israel, the lifelong slave may have worn in his ear not a label but a cattle-ring, representing the invisible rope binding him to his owner and his household. He must always "incline his ear" to his master's commands.

In the classic rite of passage, the initiate leaves his original location, spends time in a special place, the so-called liminal zone, where he is subjected to an ordeal and/or marked, and is finally reincorporated into his community (Van Gennep 1960; Turner 1967). In the present case, the beginning and end of the slave's journey is the home. For his liminal rites, he must go somewhere else. The slave resorts to "the Deity," presumably at the most convenient shrine, to undergo transformation from temporary Hebrew slave to eternal slave, perhaps no longer classed as a Hebrew. What happens there we do not know. Quite possibly, as we have seen, it is there his ear is permanently marked. Alternatively, some unknown rite takes place in the temple, while the ear piercing is the final stage of initiation performed at the master's doorway, effecting the servant's final surrender of autonomy.

ear. Why this body part? Mainly because it can be marked with minimal trauma. But this does not preclude homiletical interpretations, of which the most obvious is that the slave is forever at his master's beck and call. It may not be coincidental that in Babylon, a rebellious slave is punished by the excision of his ear (Cassuto 1967: 267; quoted below). Similarly, the Aaronid priest is consecrated as Yahweh's chattel by the application of blood to his *ear*, hand and foot (see below pp. 529–31 and Propp 2004a). Blood must be drawn to seal and sanctify the rite, just as blood is shed when Israel undertakes eternal vassalhood to Yahweh (below, pp. 308–9).

Some commentators ask, "Which ear?" They answer the right, since that is involved in rites of passage described in 29:20; Lev 8:23–24; 14:14, 17. More likely, if the text does not say which, it does not matter.

forever. The word *lə'ōlām* has two usages. Absolutely, it refers to eternity or the end of time; subjectively, it connotes one's lifetime or the end thereof. Here we have the latter usage: the Hebrew is enslaved till death (Rashbam). This is always the nuance when social relations are called "forever"; Driver (1911: 212) compares 1 Sam 1:22, where Samuel is given to Yahweh "forever," and 1 Sam 27:12, where Achish thinks David will be his "eternal slave" (cf. also Job 40:28). Cazelles (1946: 47) and Paul (1970: 49) also cite the formula whereby, in Ugaritic myth, the storm god enters the sea god's service, *'bdk 'an wd'lmk* 'I am your servant, yea, the one of your eternity' (*KTU* 1.5.ii.12, 19–20), and the gods' gift to Kirta of *'bd 'lm* 'slave(s) of eternity' (*KTU* 1.14.iii.24 etc.). We find the same nonliteral meaning of "forever" in the biblical matrimonial formula "I betroth you to me forever" (Hos 2:21) and in marriage contracts at Elephantine (Cowley 1923: 15.4; Kraeling 1953: 2.7); compare also Ugaritic *'att.'il.w'lmh* 'Ilu's wives, yea, unto his eternity' (*KTU* 1.23.42, 48–49). (The pronominal suffixes applied to Ugaritic *'lm* also indicate that "eternity" can be tantamount to "lifetime"; compare the evolution of Canaanite *dārdār* 'eternity' into Hebrew *lədōrōte[y]kā* 'for *your* ages.')

For traditionalists who do not reckon with separate sources, this law is disturbingly contradicted by the Jubilee legislation in Lev 25:10 (P), which enacts a universal manumission in the fiftieth year (cf. Josephus *Ant.* 4.273; *Mek. nəzîqîn* 2; *m. Qidd.* 1:2; Rashi; ibn Ezra). This dilemma necessitated the Rabbinic view that in Exod 21:6 *lə'ōlām* just means "for a long time."

COMPARE: 205. If *awīlu's* slave should strike the cheek of a member of the *awīlu*-class, they shall cut off his ear. . . . 282. If a slave should declare to his master, "You are not my master," he (the master) shall bring charge and proof against him that he is indeed his slave, and his master shall cut off his ear (Hammurapi §§205, 282). (*LCMAM* 122, 132)

21:7. *a man.* Presumably a Hebrew man, as in 21:2.

sells. In the preceding case of the manservant, 21:2 makes the buyer not the slave the grammatical subject. In 21:7, the subject is the girl's father not her purchaser. In contrast, the paraphrase in Deut 15:12, "When your Hebrew brother or sister sells him/herself," empathizes more with the slave, and in fact contains more liberal provisions. Exodus stresses rather the woman's passivity, subject to the authority first of her father and then of her purchaser.

his daughter. Although Exodus does not explicitly impose this limitation, by Rabbinic law only a minor may be sold into slavery (*Mek. nəzîqîn* 3; *b. Ketub.* 46b; *Arak.* 29b). To judge from Deut 15:12, a woman may also sell herself, presumably if she is a widow or an orphan, i.e., a female without a guardian.

May not a man also sell his son? One would assume so (*pace Mek. nəzîqîn* 3). But, if we are speaking of Hebrews, then the son is covered by the previous statute. He is entitled to liberation after six years.

Daughters are sold as slaves in situations of extreme need, as when a parent cannot provide for his family, or else simply to create an advantageous social bond (Driver 1911: 212). As we shall see, the line between slavery and marriage, concubinage and wifehood, is rather fine. Laban's daughters disparagingly use the term *mkr* 'sell' of their own marriage (Gen 31:15)

maidservant. An *'āmâ* is a nonfree, working female, as likely as not owned by another woman (e.g., Gen 30:3; Exod 2:5; Nah 2:8). An ordinary maidservant may sometimes advance to the status of secondary wife, like Hagar, Bilhah and Zilpah (Gen 16:3; 30:3–4, 9). Elsewhere, it was the practice for a maidservant's bill of sale to stipulate that the purchaser must marry the girl himself or give her in marriage to one of his sons or slaves. At Nuzi, for instance, through a contract called *ṭuppi mārtūti u kallūti* 'tablet of daughtership and daughter-in-lawship,' a daughter is sold into servitude with the proviso that she will eventually (after a trial period? after puberty?) be married either to the purchaser or to his son. In this case, under no condition may she be married to a slave (Mendelsohn 1935). Our law in Exodus seems similarly to afford protection to a maidservant by arranging for her marriage.

as in the manservants' departing. That is, a Hebrew maidservant is not released after six years (Rashbam, Luzzatto), even if she is married to a Hebrew slave (21:4). The provisions of 21:7 are directly contradicted by Deut 15:12, according to which Hebrew man- and maidservants alike are liberated in the seventh year (also Jer 34:9). (The harmonizing Rabbinic solution supposes that v 7 refers not to seventh-year manumission but to liberation for mutilation as per 21:26–27 [Rashi; cf. also *Mek. nəzîqîn* 3] — which makes the law far more brutal, because now a maidservant is not freed even for physical abuse!)

While at first glance the nonliberation of the maidservant may seem oppressive, the statute is designed to *protect* her. Instead of liberating a menial to shift for herself, the law encourages the owner to elevate her to the status of wife or at least concubine (*m. Bek.*1:7; Rashi; Rashbam; Bekhor Shor). (Deuteronomy's solution is to require a manumission gift to all liberated slaves, male and female alike.)

21:8. *bad.* Since the maidservant is not yet a wife or concubine, *rā'â* indicates not sexual disatisfaction but general incompatiblity, as in Gen 28:8 (Isaac's displeasure with Esau's wives) (Schenker 1988: 551). But here, the woman is in fact a *prospective* wife, and so "bad" might include unattractiveness. Note that, whereas the male slave has the discretion to choose liberty or servitude, for the female slave, the choice lies with her master.

who. Cazelles (1946: 48) takes '*ăšer* not as a relative pronoun but as a conjunction (cf. Waltke and O'Connor 1990: 331 n. 1): "if she is bad in her master's eyes, so *that* he does not contract for her." I do not think this is likely, for then the verb should be the imperfect **yîʿādennâ*, not the perfect *yəʿādāh*.

engaged for her. With LXX-Aquila-Symmachus-Theodotion, I take the verb *yāʿad* as meaning "to make a commitment," in this case to elevate the maidservant into a concubine or wife (cf., e.g., *Mek. nəzîqîn* 3; *b. Qidd.* 18b; ibn Ezra). Moreover, the root *yʿd* probably includes the notion of setting a specific time limit to her menial status (*Tgs. Neofiti I, Ps.-Jonathan*), as in the idiom *yāʿad môʿēd* in 2 Sam 20:5 (Ramban). Compare Arabic *waʿada* 'promise, set a time' and Syriac *waʿdāʾ* 'set time or place, agreement' (Cazelles 1946: 48).

The owner does not necessarily promise to marry the maidservant himself; that would be expressed by the verb '*ēraś* 'betroth' (Schenker 1988: 549). As appears more clearly in v 9, the verb *yāʿad* implies making an engagement *concerning* a woman. That is, the verb refers to the action of her guardian, who has the right to bestow her on whom he pleases (W. R. Smith *apud* Budde 1892; compare, e.g., Middle Assyrian Law §39). This includes the option of marrying her himself.

Our efforts to understand the text are hindered by the existence of two contradictory variants, even within the MT tradition (see TEXTUAL NOTE). According to the Kethibh '*ăšer-lō(ʾ) yəʿādāh* 'who did *not* engage for her,' the master did not, at the time of sale or subsequently, undertake to promote the maidservant into a wife or concubine or to marry her to another. According to the Qere '*ăšer-lô yəʿādāh* 'who engaged for her *for himself*,' at some point he promised to marry her himself, most likely when he bought her from her father. (It is even possible that the subject of *yəʿādāh* is the *father*, who assigned the girl to the purchaser.)

In a careful study, Schenker (1988) favors the MT Kethibh. He describes the laws of slavery in 21:2–11 as a "diptych," with the rules for the man- and the maidservant opposed to one another: "Exod 21:2–6 concerns the end of service for menservants in general. Symmetrically, Exod 21:7–11 treats the term of service of maidservants in general. Vv 4–6 introduce the case of non-liberation of a manservant, just as vv 8–11 present the case of the liberation of a maidservant. In both cases, there is an identical but opposing structure: a general rule followed by an exception. In the case of the male, the general rule is liberation after six years, the exception being non-liberation . . . due to the slave's fidelity to his marriage with a woman whom his master has given him, and who continues to belong to his master. Conversely, in the woman's case, the general rule is non-liberation after six years . . . the exception being emancipation because her liberation [i.e., redemption] or marriage overrides the condition of servitude" (p. 550).

Schenker understands v 7, "she shall not depart as the menservants' departing," to indicate that a woman is ordinarily enslaved for life. I find the Rabbinic view, however, that generally a slave girl was promoted to a wife or concubine, more in keeping with the spirit of the text, which seems designed to protect all slaves, male and female. This brings us back to the Qere, with its parallel "if" clauses implying a pair of alternatives (cf. Jacob 1992: 614). If a man buys a maidservant, there is an assumption that, at the time of purchase or subsequently, he will take her on as a concubine or else give her to his son in that capacity.

While we may feel stymied by these opposite readings, we must also remember that they occupy a subordinate clause. The law's main effect is clear: "If she is bad in her master's eyes . . . then he must let her be ransomed."

he must let her be ransomed. Ideally, the father refunds her purchase price to the displeased owner. But, assuming the girl was sold into slavery due to her family's poverty, they may still lack the means to purchase her freedom. In that case, it appears that the master would naturally seek a buyer elsewhere—unless *hipdâ* simply means "liberate." Ehrlich (1908: 349), in a quasi-talmudic fashion, argues that the owner must lessen her price to facilitate her redemption.

alien kin. In any other context, the phrase '*am nokrî* would be immediately explicable as "foreign nation." In other words, *nokrî* is the opposite of '*ibrî.* The implicit point would be that foreigners do not follow the rules of Exodus and so would not be appropriate slave-owners (Luzzatto). This approach entails two difficulties, however. The first problem is why not simply say *nokrî* 'foreigner'; i.e, why mention a "people"? The second problem is that, by this understanding, the law neglects to say whether the owner is entitled to sell his maidservant to another Israelite; Driver (1911: 213) simply infers that he may. By this interpretation, the law forbids not only deporting a maidservant but also selling her to an ethnic non-Israelite within the confines of Canaan. Bekhor Shor, for example, integrates the statute with 21:4: you may not marry a spurned maidservant to a non-Israelite slave (he interprets *mkr* 'sell' as "transfer," as in Judg 4:9).

Overall, I find an alternative approach preferable. The connotation of *nokrî* 'alien' really depends on what it is contrasted with. Ordinarily it is Israel, and so *nokrî* describes a non-Israelite. But Luzzatto notes that *nokrî* sometimes is simply a nonrelation (cf. Gen 31:15; Ps 69:9; Prov 5:10; Job 19:15; Eccl 6:2) or a person other than one's self (Prov 27:2); similarly in Ugaritic, *nkr* connotes a nonhusband (*KTU* 1.14.ii.49; iv.28). Thus '*am nokrî* in Exod 21:8 may describe *persons unre-*

lated to the maidservant. The displeased owner is to offer her to her family for redemption, ideally by marriage to a kinsman (Houtman 2000: 128) or else by simple monetary compensation (Schenker 1988: 547). Likewise, the Priestly Source requires the family to ransom debt slaves (Lev 25:48–54). As for *ʿam* meaning "clan, kin," Luzzatto compares Gen 28:3; 48:4, *qəhal ʿammîm* 'assembly of tribes.' (Since *ʿam* sometimes also denotes an individual "kinsman" [Sarna 1991: 121], the phrase *ʿam nokrî* could be viewed as an ironic oxymoron.)

Finally, it is possible that "alien" takes the perspective not of the woman but of her owner. As the price of not taking her as concubine and thus breaking his contract with the father (reading with the Qere *ʾăšer-lô yəʿādāh* 'who engaged for her for himself*)*, the master forfeits his right to sell her *to anyone* beside himself (cf. Humbert 1939: 262; Ehrlich 1969: 177).

he is not entitled to sell her. The root *mšl* 'possess authority, be entitled' connotes the authority of the family head also in Gen 3:16; 24:2; 37:8 (Jacob 1992: 624). Presumably "he" is the disatisfied purchaser (Houtman 2000: 128). But for *b. Qidd.* 18a and ibn Ezra, "he" is the woman's father after her ransom, and Rashi thinks "he" could be either the owner or the father (see also next NOTE).

his breach of contract. The referent of "his" is the master not the father, for the father dealt in good faith (Jacob 1992: 624).

Most view the noun *beged* as connoting treachery or marital infidelity (cf. Jer 3:20; Mal 2:14). De Boer (1948: 165), however, shows that more likely *bgd* means simply "to abrogate a relationship or contract" without necessarily negative moral connotations (compare Akkadian *nabalkutu* 'break an agreement, rebel'). In essence, *bgd* is the antonym of *yʿd* 'engage.' Baentsch (1903: 191) comments that a master owes his maidservant a kindly disposition. Even to dislike her is tantamount to breaking faith. See also TEXTUAL NOTE.

COMPARE: If a man <wants to give in marriage> his debtor's daughter who is residing in his house as a pledge, he shall ask permission of her father and then he shall give her to a husband. If her father does not agree, he shall not give her. If her father is dead, he shall ask permission of one of her brothers and the latter shall consult with her (other) brothers. If one brother so desires he shall declare, "I will redeem my sister within one month"; if he should not redeem her within one month, the creditor, if he so pleases, shall clear her of encumbrances and shall give her to a husband (Middle Assyrian Laws A §48). (*LCMAM* 173)

21:9. *for his son.* Why for his son? In order to give him a sexual education and the comforts of a concubine at a suitable age, lest he become entangled in inappropriate liaisons, and in order to produce a grandchild.

The law probably assumes that the maidservant had not already lain with the father, for sexual intercourse with both father and son would count as an offense both to the father (Gen 35:22; 49:4; see Propp 2004b) and to God (Lev 18:8; 20:11; Amos 2:7). See also below.

he engages for her. The relationship of v 9 to v 8 is unclear. It is possible to understand that, although the maidservant may be "bad" in her master's eyes, he is still willing to affiance her to his son. But this is counterintuitive, and I think the case is independent. A man might buy a slave girl with the intent of taking her as a concubine or of giving her to his son as a concubine. But should she prove unsuitable, then the deal is off, as per v 8b.

according to the daughters' case. This is another obscurity. Most understand *mišpāṭ* 'case' here as connoting custom (see below). But since the term appears within a code of *mišpāṭîm*, we must consider whether it bears its proper legal meaning of "legal precedent, statute." If so, there are two possibilities: (a) the reference is to a law not included in Exodus 21; (b) the reference is to 21:7, a father's right to sell his daughter into slavery (cf. Houtman 2000: 129). I do not think that this can be the case, however, since the woman is already affianced to the master's son. The grammar is decisive. Had the text read a perfect **yaʿ ādāh* instead of the imperfect *yîʿādennâ*, then one could understand that the master had engaged to marry the woman to his son, but later broke it off because "she was bad in his eyes." Either 21:9 refers to another law not preserved in the Torah, or else *mišpāṭ* bears a nonjudicial sense.

Kamišpaṭ habbānôt may most simply be interpreted "as is the legal standard for young women," which the following verse clarifies (cf. Rashi; Dillmann 1880: 229): i.e., her entitlement to "flesh," "covering" and *ʿōnâ*. That is, *bat* 'daughter' here connotes a young woman; for a similar use of *mišpāṭ*, see Deut 21:17; 1 Sam 8:9; Ezek 16:38; 23:45, etc.

Paul (1970: 55) argues, however, that "according to the daughter's case" means "like a free, Hebrew woman" (also Ehrlich 1908: 349; Childs 1974: 442, 448). He cites as parallels the Akkadian phrases "he must treat her like a daughter of [the city] Arrapḫa" and "he must treat her like his own daughter, an Assyrian." The problem, however, is that Exodus does not say **kamišpaṭ habbānôt hāʿibriyyōt* 'according to the case of *the Hebrew daughters*,' which would indeed parallel the Mesopotamian texts.

More likely, to my mind, 21:9 refers to the rights and responsibilities of fatherhood. The master has assumed the right to marry off his maidservant *in loco parentis* (Cazelles 1946: 49; cf. Ramban). Both as surrogate daughter and daughter-in-law, the woman is now as forbidden to him as his own daughter, according to the laws of incest (cf. Sarna 1991: 121).

he shall do. The subject is the father-master.

21:10. *another (woman).* Biblical narratives and laws attempt respectively to describe and control the inevitable tensions engendered by polygamy: ambiguous inheritance rights, jealousy among co-wives and half siblings, and the attendant headaches for the family patriarch (cf. Propp 1993). Comments Levine (1999: 156), "[A]lthough the Bible does acknowledge the existence of polygamy, it does not make peace with it." The implication of the prototypical marriage of Adam and Eve (Genesis 3–4) and also of the Covenant-as-marriage metaphor (Isa 50:1; 54:6–7; 62:4–5; Jer 2:2; Hosea 1–2) is that monogamy is the ideal (but contrast Jer 3:6–11; Ezekiel 23, for Yahweh's *two* wives, Israel and Judah).

It is not clear, however, that the subject of v 10 is technically polygamy, since the law does not consider the maidservant as more than promised *(yʿd)* to become a wife or concubine. *'Aḥeret* is just another female in the household, whether slave, concubine or wife.

flesh . . . covering . . . 'ōnâ. This law refers to the case of a relatively prosperous man who can afford to add a member to his household without stinting on the present occupants' prerogatives (Beer 1939: 109). The verse has become an exegetical Rohrschach test of what interpreters think a woman should be entitled to, whether as necessities or luxuries. The text, which sounds rather like a proverb, uses peculiar terms, perhaps elevated diction (Levine 1999: 143). Of the three items, one is slightly unclear, one is unclear and one is very unclear.

The least ambiguous term is the second. Almost all find in *kəsût* (< *ksy* 'cover') a reference to clothing, as in 22:26, etc., although shelter is not inconceivable. (I find implausible North's [1955] view that *kəsût* is "protection [in the harem].") If *kəsût* is clothing, then a further question is whether it connotes the bare minimum or an extensive wardrobe. A final possibility is that the referent is not clothing in general but a particular item: perhaps the veil, worn by legitimately married women throughout the ancient and modern Middle East (but not clearly so in biblical Israel).

Less certain is the import of the first item, *šə'ēr*. The majority view is that it means "meat." But some raise two objections: (a) *šə'ēr* rarely if ever in Hebrew connotes dead, edible meat; rather, it is the living flesh (North 1955); (b) meat was not a staple of the Israelite diet, which was largely vegetarian. These objections may easily be met, however: (a) in Ps 78:20, 27, *šə'ēr* clearly means "meat" or "food, like the Semitic cognates *š'r* (Punic) and *šīru* (Akkadian); (b) perhaps the text mandates not necessities but luxuries (Dillmann 1880: 229). Holzinger (1900: 83) sees a requirement that the woman be allowed to participate fully in family meals of sacrificial meat (cf. 1 Sam 1:4–5). Less plausibly, ibn Ezra (see both shorter and longer commentaries) suggests that "her flesh" refers not to the meat the woman consumes, but her own flesh, nourished by various comestibles. That is, she must be kept contentedly plump. Finally, for North (1955), "her flesh" is the pleasure of sexual intercourse; compare *bāśār* 'flesh, penis.' But by far the simplest understanding, assuming that *šə'ēr* is "flesh," is that the woman must not eat less well than the rest of the household.

SPECULATION: *Šə'ēr* has another meaning: "kinsman." One might think that this is was an extension of the meaning "flesh" to connote blood kin. But the testimony of Ugaritic and Arabic proves that two roots merged into Hebrew *šə'ēr*: **š'r* and **ṯ'r* (Dietrich and Loretz 1980: 202). Maimonides (*apud* Jacob 1992: 626) interprets that the woman must not be denied access to her relatives (cf. *šə'ēr* in Lev 18:6; 21:2; Num 27:11). In a similar vein, A. P. Covici (privately) suggests that the right is access to her children, or even the right to procreate. And Jerome translates *šə'ēr* as *nuptiae* 'marriage,' i.e., acquisition of new kin. That is, the woman must not be kept celibate. Ramban, who also sees the meaning of kinship as primary, thinks that here *šə'ēr* simply connotes sexual intercourse (so already R. Judah the Prince [*Mek. nəzîqîn* 3]). He notes that *šə'ēr* often appears in a sexual context (e.g., Lev 18:6; 20:19; 21:2; 25:49).

All the foregoing explanations of *šǝ'ēr* amount to basically three: the woman is entitled to either food, her family or sexual intercourse. Lacking more evidence, it is hard to choose among these options. (Already *b. Ketub.* 47a–48a weighs the various options, including an opinion that the verse mandates naked as opposed to clothed sexual intercourse!)

This brings us to the most obscure term of all: *'ōnātāh*, or her *'ōnâ*, which appears derived from a root *'ny* or conceivably *'wn* (see below). There are four basic approaches:

1. *'Ōnâ* means "sexual relations" or "sexual pleasure." This is the oldest attested interpretation, found in LXX, *Tgs.* and Syr; among its subsequent defenders are Saadiah, ibn Ezra and, latterly, Levine (1999). The etymology is uncertain, however. A. Schultens *apud* de Boer (1948: 163) compares Arabic *'wn* 'help' (cf. *'ezer* 'help, mate' in Gen 2:18, 20). But, as vocalized, the more likely root is *'ny*, which ordinarily means "answer" and here might mean "respond sexually" (cf. Mandelkern 1937: 834). Levine (pp. 144–45), however, argues that the basic meaning of *'ny* is "open," whence the usual meaning "answer" in the sense of "open the mouth" or "open a discourse." In 21:10, for Levine, *'ny* means opening for sexual intercourse, a nuance he detects also in 32:18 (see NOTE); Hos 2:17 (cf. also Hos 2:23–24) and in the frequent use of *'innâ* apropos of rape (see already *Mek. nǝzîqîn* 3; *b. Ketub.* 47b). To prove that a woman is entitled to procreate, Levine (pp. 151–52) also cites the tale of Tamar in Genesis 38 as a defense of conjugal rights (but the real issue here is the levirate obligation, not sex per se). Levine makes a better case from 2 Sam 20:3, where David supports but has no conjugal relations with his harem, so that they live in "widowhood during (the husband's) life" (?) (MT *'almǝnût ḥayyût*). Why mention this, he asks, even using a special term, unless it is contrary to the norm? Levine (p. 138) observes that while ancient Near Eastern law codes do not mandate a woman's right to sexual satisfaction, the Talmud emphatically does (*m. Ketub.* 5:6–7; *Ned.* 2:1; *b. Ketub.* 61b–63a). By his reading, Exod 21:10 anticipates later Jewish law. If *'ōnâ* does refer to sexual intercourse, we might compare to the triad of 21:10 the archetypical marriage described in Genesis 2:21–4:1, where the first man and woman share food (= *šǝ'ēr?*), clothing (= *kǝsût*) and their bodies (= *'ōnâ?*).

There are others who understand *'ōnâ* sexually, but somewhat differently. Since *'ōnâ* is well attested in the sense of "time" or "season," Ehrlich (1908: 349) says it can be "time" in the sense of "turn," for in polygamy, the wives must take turns (cf. Gen 30:14–16). Similarly, *m. Ketub.* 5:6 understands 21:10 as mandating set times for intercourse. It is also conceivable that "season" could mean privacy during menstruation (cf. English "period").

Note that Exodus 21 describes a maidservant, probably a virgin engaged to be married at some future time. So, if it refers to conjugal rights, the clause in v 10 jumps ahead to her status as wife or concubine.

2. Others argue that *'ōnâ* means "shelter," as in our cliché "food (= *šǝ'ēr*), clothing (= *kǝsût*) and shelter (= *'ōnâ*)." The root *'wn* 'to shelter' is well attested in Hebrew (cf. *'ān* 'reside,' *mā'ōn* 'dwelling'), although von Soden (1981: 159–60) observes that we might have expected a vocalization **'ūnātāh* instead of MT *'ōnātāh*.

That 21:10 requires a man to house his maidservant is the view of Rashbam, Bekhor Shor (tentatively) and, in modern times, Cassuto (1967: 269). One may compare Lipit-Ishtar §28, "If a man's first-ranking wife loses her attractiveness or becomes a paralytic, she will not be evicted from the house; however, her husband may marry a healthy wife, and the second wife shall support the first-ranking wife," and Hammurapi §148, "If a man marries a woman, and later *la'bum*-disease seizes her and he decides to marry another woman, he will not divorce his wife whom *la'bum*-disease seized; she shall reside in quarters he constructs and he shall continue to support her as long as she lives."

3. Another common view is that '*ōnâ* means "cosmetics, scented oils" or the like (Oren 1964; Paul 1970: 57–61; cf. Jacob 1992: 627). In an impressive range of ancient Near Eastern texts, a dependent, often a woman, is entitled to food, clothing, and ointment; e.g., Hammurapi §178, "the brothers shall take her field and her orchard and they shall give to her food, oil, and clothing *(ipram piššatam u lubūšam)* allowances . . . and they shall thereby satisfy her"; Lipit-Ishtar §27, "he shall provide grain, oil, and clothing rations for the prostitute" (see also the "Instruction of Ptaḥ-hotep" [*ANET* 413]). A somewhat similar collocation may be observed in Hos 2:7: "my lovers who give me my bread/food *(laḥmî)* and my water (= *šə'ēr*), my wool and my flax (= *kəsût*), my oil and my fluids (= '*ōnâ*)," and Eccl 9:7–9, "Eat your bread in joy, and drink your wine with a merry heart . . . let your garments be white, and may oil not be absent upon your head."

The main objection to this approach is a lack of etymological justification. Basically, it assumes rather than proves that a dependent Israelite maidservant had the same entitlements as elsewhere in the Near East. To address the linguistic problem, Oren (1964) proffers an emendation: for MT '*nth* read **'ngh* (also conceivable would be '*ngth*) 'her delicacies.' (Along these lines, one might propose **'dnh* 'her finery'; cf. 2 Sam 1:24.) Or we could maintain MT-Sam '*nth*, comparing Arabic *ġaniya* 'to be rich, content' or Syriac *y'n* 'to be greedy.' (Either of these potential cognates would also be compatible with the sexual interpretation of '*ōnâ*.)

4. Lastly, '*ōnâ* might mean "responsibility," as in the English idiom "to be answerable." Support might be found in Isa 4:1, where destitute women are willing to forgo a man's feeding (= *šə'ēr?*) and clothing them (= *kəsût*), begging only that "his name be called" over them, i.e., that he take responsibility (= '*ōnâ*) for them.

In light of these complications, we must leave the three entitlements of the maidservant an unresolved mystery.

21:11.*these three*. Although "these three" most obviously refers to "flesh . . . covering . . . '*ōnâ*" (Cassuto 1967: 269), normative Rabbinic tradition identifies the three actions as (a) marrying the woman, (b) marrying her to a son, (c) allowing her to be redeemed (e.g., *Mek. nəzîqîn* 3; Rashi; cf. also Chirichigno 1993: 253). And it is true that, if v 10 were missing, that would be the only possible reading. But since v 10 is there and mentions three obligations, there is no reason to deny its precedence as the closer referent.

does not do for her. In this conditional language, we may detect the wording of actual contracts of marriage and indenture, as in documents from Elephantine (Kraeling 1953: 7.38–39) and Wadi Murabba'at (DJD 9 text 7) (cf. Levine 1999: 137 n. 8).

gratis; no silver. I.e., she need not buy her freedom. But neither is she explicitly entitled to any parting gift (contrast Deut 15:12–14).

SPECULATION: In the spirit of the Rabbis, who believed no word of Scripture to be superfluous, one might scrutinize the redundancy of *ḥinnām 'ên kāsep* 'gratis; there is no silver.' After all, above in v 2, *ḥinnām* alone sufficed. There is another root *ksp*, 'to feel shame,' with a possible abstract noun *kesep*, homophonous with the common term for "silver" (Hos 9:6; see *HALOT*). So perhaps the end of v 11 should be interpreted with *double entente*: "gratis, without *shame*."

21:12. *Whoever strikes*. With v 12, there is a marked break in literary style. No longer do we find the lengthy "if . . . then" casuistic style with its subclauses and qualifications. That will resume in v 18. Instead we have curt, apodictic phrasing using an injunctive verbal mood: the jussive *yûmāt* 'let him be put to death' (Alt 1968: 133–71). The participle (here, *makkē[h]*, literally "the striker of") replaces the "if" clause only for ten capital offenses: adultery (Gen 26:11), sacrilege (Exod 19:12), murder (21:12; cf. also Gen 9:6; Lev 24:17–21), kidnapping (21:16), filial impiety (21:15, 17), sorcery (22:17), bestiality (22:18), apostasy (22:19), Sabbath violation (31:14–15) and blasphemy (Lev 24:16) (cf. Jacob 1992: 631). The language creates a most shocking effect after the preceding legalese; Jacob speaks of "the pathos of outrage." Exod 21:12 emphatically states a basic principle about the protection of persons (Cazelles 1946: 50), one that the rest of the chapter will variously qualify.

SPECULATION: The apodictic style appears only in 21:15–17 and in 22:17–19, raising the suspicion that the laws against murder, parental abuse, kidnapping, filial impiety, sorcery, bestiality and apostasy—seven altogether—are excerpted from a list of capital offenses (Baentsch 1903: 192).

Both the striker *(makke([h])* and his victim (*'îš* 'man') are grammatically masculine. This reflects both the conventions of Hebrew—the masculine is the default gender—and also the simple fact that men are more likely than women to be involved in lethal altercations. But there is no reason to think that the following laws would not apply to perpetrators and victims of both sexes. As we learn in 21:28–29, the principle covers even a manslaying animal (cf. Gen 9:5–6). It also does not appear to matter whether a weapon is involved (Luzzatto); cf. v 18.

and he dies. This is necessary to specify, because *hikkâ* 'strike' can but need not imply a fatal outcome (cf. Rashi and NOTE to 2:12).

put to death, death. Môt *yûmāt* exemplifies the emphatic use of the infinite absolute (GKC §113n–r). The law is most unlikely to mean "*may* be put to death" (*pace* Westbrook 1988: 78). Because the verb is passive, the statute does not explain *how* the murderer is to be executed. That is apparently assumed knowledge and in any case less important than the basic principle. The method of execution most commonly mentioned in the Bible is stoning (Lev 24:23; Num 15:35–36; Deut 13:11; 17:5; 21:21; 22:21, 24; Josh 7:25; 1 Kgs 21:10), although we occasionally read of burning (Gen 38:24; Lev 20:14; 21:9); the Rabbis will add strangulation and beheading with the sword (on capital punishment, see *Mek. nəzîqîn passim*; *m. Sanh.* 6–7; *b. Sanh.* 45a–53a). Perhaps, where the Torah does not specify a method, it is up to the executioner. If so, the most convenient method may have indeed been the sword (Jackson 1975: 111).

The passive voice also conceals *who* executes the murderer. According to Num 35:19, 21, 27; Deut 19:6, 12; 2 Sam 14:11, after a proper judicial inquiry, this task preferably falls to one or several of the victim's kin, called *gōʾēl/gōʾălê haddām* 'the Blood Redeemer(s).' The term "Redeemer" implies that, by shedding the killer's blood, the executioner symbolically brings back his kinsman's lost blood (Daube 1947: 124–25). In the absence of close relatives, the community itself presumably acts as executioner; compare the punishment of the apostate in Deut 13:10: "Your hand, it shall be first against him to kill him, and all the people's hand afterward."

That, ideally, is the end of the affair. Although both may occur, lynching and vendetta are discouraged (e.g., 2 Samuel 2–3; 14:4–11). Exodus 21 is notably silent, however, on the Blood Redeemer's role, focusing rather on the judicial process (Houtman 2000: 136). We find at most indirect reference to vengeance in v 14: when the killer takes refuge at the altar, we may assume that he is pursued by Blood Redeemers (Luzzatto). Consequently, the addressee of "you may take him" in v 14 could well be the avenger (see NOTE).

The law codes and narratives agree on one thing: murder cannot be compounded by monetary restitution (Num 35:31–33). *Pace* Westbrook (1988: 39–83), this inflexibility sets the Bible apart from most societal norms, ancient (e.g., Hittite Laws §§1–6; but see below for Ur-Namma) and modern (e.g., the Bedouin [Musil 1928: 489–503]). Even though the victim's family gains nothing by the murderer's death, Yahweh requires that they and society extirpate all homicides. In our terms, homicide is a criminal not a civil offense. The potentially divisive aspects of blood vengeance are mitigated by the consideration that the true avenger is God, not one's fellow citizen. An impartial and thorough judicial inquiry should convince the community, and maybe even the murderer's kin, that his execution was deserved. And the aggrieved are allowed to vent their rage in a controlled manner by functioning as authorized Blood Redeemers.

One important matter that the First Code does not treat explicitly is killing in self-defense. From the case of the thief in the night (22:1), we may infer *a fortiori* a right to protect one's own life. But presumably, as in our society, self-defense must be established before a court.

At the level of form, the five-word verse *(makkē[h] ʾîš wāmēt môt yûmāt)* is notable for its *m*-alliteration and for a threefold repetition of the root *mwt* 'die' (Blenkinsopp 1992: 198).

COMPARE: If a man commits a homicide, they shall kill that man (Ur-Namma §1). (*LCMAM* 17)

If a man, who has not yet received his inheritance share, takes a life, they shall hand him over to the next-of-kin. Should the next-of-kin so choose, he shall kill him, or, if he chooses to come to an accommodation, then he shall take his inheritance share (Middle Assyrian Laws B §2). (*LCMAM* 176)

They do not kill anybody in the land of the Hittites. . . . If the king hears about such a thing, they seize the killer of such a person and hand him over to the brothers of the murdered man. His brothers take the monetary compensation for the murdered man and they perform the expiatory ritual on the murderer. . . . But if the brothers do not want to accept a monetary compensation, they execute the man who has taken a life (letter of Hattusilis III of Hatti to the king of Babylon [thirteenth century B.C.E]; trans. Oppenheim 1967: 144).

21:13. *the one who.* On this use of *'ăšer,* see Waltke and O'Connor (1990: §3.2.1 p. 529).

lie in wait. Although v 12 seems simple enough—all killers must be killed—vv 13–14, 18–23 introduce necessary subtleties. E.g., what if it was just an accident?

The rare verb *ṣādâ* 'lie in wait' is paralleled in 1 Sam 24:12 and possibly Lam 4:18; we also have a noun *ṣədîyâ* used of premeditated murder in Num 35:20, 22. Jacob (1992: 634) notes that in Num 35:23, *ṣədîyâ* appears to be glossed as *rə'ôt* 'seeing,' but that does not exclude the connotion of lying in wait. After all, in Exod 21:14, *zw/yd* 'to act with presumption, to plot' could equally be taken as equivalent to *ṣādâ* in v 13.

the Deity. The designation of God as *'ĕlōhîm* is noteworthy. On the one hand, this is the First Code's routine title for Yahweh (21:6, 13; 22:7–8), whose proper name appears only in 22:10. On the other hand, *'ĕlōhîm* 'Deity' has a somewhat less specific connotation as a plural of abstraction. Indeed, at times the most appropriate rendering is "the supernatural" (vol. I, pp. 216, 328). Cazelles (1946: 51) compares Akkadian *ilum* 'god,' which can connote unfortunate supernatural causation, as in Hammurapi §249, *ilum imḫassu* 'a god strikes it [an ox] down.' Exod 21:13 leaves it unclear whether the author attributes all fortune specifically to Yahweh or more vaguely to supernatural influences. In any case, what the law describes is an accidental homicide. The killer did not intend to kill, but divinity decreed otherwise and properly bears responsibility (cf. Luzzatto).

What specifically does 21:13 envision as an act of God? The parallel legislation in Num 35:22–23; Deut 19:4–5 indicates primarily workplace accidents, such as a flying axehead or a shove in the wrong direction; see also the Roman Twelve Tables 8.24 (Warmington 1979: 494). *Mek. nəzîqîn* 4 and *b. Mak.* 7a–8b provide further elaboration on accidental homicide.

Nowhere does the Torah clearly address the spontaneous crime of passion, in which the assailant does not "lie in wait" but nonetheless kills deliberately, e.g., Moses' murder of the Egyptian taskmaster (2:11–12; see vol. I, pp. 166–68) or the brawl described in 21:18 (see below). Also undiscussed is an act of violence due to loss of self-control, e.g., from drunkenness or mental illness (e.g., Saul's "bad spirit" in 1 Sam 16:14–16, 23; 18:10; 19:9). These Houtman (2000: 145) assumes would also be exempted from the category of murder.

by happenstance brought. The verb *'innâ* properly means "to create an opportunity," always for harm; cf. 2 Kgs 5:7; Ps 91:10; Prov 12:21.

I will set. Since God caused the accident, he undertakes to protect the guiltless manslayer (Jacob 1992: 634).

a place. Sometimes *māqôm* has a special connotation of "holy place," like the Arabic cognate *maqām* (Sarna 1991: 122). Here, the "place" in question possesses an altar. But the people are not yet in the land. Is the law only for the next generation?

In the JE context, the wilderness asylum may be Meeting Tent, assuming that it is associated with an otherwise unmentioned altar. For the composite Torah, however, this would be impossible, because the Tabernacle Altar is off-limits to laymen (see below). *Mek. nəzîqîn* 4 and *b. Mak.* 12b logically deduce that the whole camp of Levi is the temporary place of refuge, pending the establishment of the six Levitical Asylum Cities (Numbers 35; Deuteronomy 4:41–43; 19:1–13; Joshua 20). The prevalent view among criticial scholars, however, is that, in its original context (see pp. 306–8), the law visualized a local High Place. When these were abolished in order to foster cult centralization, a provision had to be made for manslayers; hence the regional Asylum Cities. These are not temples, yet they partake of the Temple's protective aura (e.g., Baentsch 1903: 192).

he may flee. One would think that the accidental manslayer is completely guiltless. Yet it would not be socially practicable merely to declare him so. The victim's kin would feel an unsatisfied thirst for revenge, and more mischief would ensue. The principle of asylum is a logical albeit imperfect solution. The unfortunate killer is consigned to a circumscribed existence, with the avengers' sword hanging above his head. But at least he is not executed.

This may seem unfair to all parties—but that is the point: it is a compromise. Both P and D explicitly clear the Blood Redeemer of guilt, should he manage to catch and kill the manslayer outside of his refuge (Num 35:27; Deut 19:6).

In fact, one might argue that the killer is not guiltless after all. Even a witless beast who kills a man must be punished (21:28–32). Yahweh is offended by improperly shed blood, whatever the circumstances (see, e.g., Frymer-Kensky 1983; below, pp. 695–703). Jacob (1992: 634–35) supposes that, by normative biblical belief, the innocent simply do not incur mishaps. Bad things happen only to bad people (on misfortune and the Covenant, see above, pp. 33–34). Jacob infers that both the accidental manslayer and his victim must bear guilt for some previous crimes; the lethal mishap is their joint punishment from God. By this quasi-karmic logic, the slain must have been a greater sinner than his slayer! While this goes well beyond the Torah's plain sense, Jacob correctly notes that at the very least the manslayer has been guilty of negligence.

How is intentionality determined? Presumably by weighing both the manner of death and the motivation. The judges are community leaders, men of experience and influence whom consensus or human authority has appointed as wise and impartial arbiters (see de Vaux 1961: 143–63). In the meantime, the killer may stay at the altar in temporary detention. Or perhaps he is taken elsewhere and protected from avengers pending a verdict (cf. Num 35:12; Josh 20:6 [P] *re* the Asylum City).

If the manslayer is convicted of murder, then he is executed. If he is declared innocent, however, Exodus leaves it unclear what happens to him. Does he live out his days at the shrine, protected from extralegal vengeance? Or does he return to society after a "cooling-off" period? How many killers are there at any time, and how many can a sanctuary support? Should the killer pay for his own upkeep, or are some of the temple's funds allocated for that purpose? Does the manslayer make any monetary restitution to his victim's kin?

The more detailed provisions of Numbers 35 and Deuteronomy 19, probably composed later, answer most of these questions. Manslayers are relegated to internal, protective "exile" in six Asylum Cities, which are also Levitical cities. Within the town's confines, they are protected from vengeance; outside, they have no immunity. They may return safely to their communities only upon the Great Priest's death (Num 35:25, 28; Josh 20:6). Presumably, this means that any further act of vengeance against them is accounted murder. In some mysterious fashion, the Great Priest's passing purges the land of bloodguilt (Greenberg 1959; see vol. I, p. 235; below, pp. 501, 531).

This limitation of private vengeance by institutionalized asylum is part of a larger social process: the weakening of clan and tribal loyalties, and the increasing power of the center (Halpern 1991). According to the newer ethos, Yahweh does not reckon guilt by the family but by the individual (Jer 31:29–30; Ezekiel 18). By implication, so should the courts and people generally (Deut 24:16).

21:14. *presumes.* In this context, the root *zw/yd* 'to act with arrogance' may connote premeditation. Its opposite would be *šgg* 'err' (Num 35:11) (Jacob 1992: 636). The root *zw/yd* was possibly chosen to pun with *ṣdy* 'lie in wait' (v 13).

premeditation. An alternative rendering of *'ormâ* might be "malice." The Hebrew root *'rm* refers to cleverness or forethought, whether for good or ill. But the Arabic cognate *'aruma* denotes exclusively enmity (Cassuto 1967: 270).

my altar. Rather than be explicit, the statute simply assumes the principle of sacred asylum. Throughout the Mediterranean world, an altar or its surrounding temple protected an accused criminal from his would-be prosecutors (see, e.g., *Thucydides* 4.98; Smith 1927: 148–49 n. 2; Greenfield 1991; Rigsby 1996). The notion is well reflected in the semantics of the English word "sanctuary," meaning both "holy place" and "refuge." Privileged temples functioned as jails, removing undesirables from society for the protection of all. Their immunity sometimes created tension with the secular judicial authorities (for examples from Hellenistic Egypt, see Dunand 1979).

The Bible often invokes asylum imagery apropos of the Temple. E.g., the Psalms celebrate the security of dwelling in Yahweh's House: "My soul longs and even perishes for Yahweh's courtyards. . . . Even the bird found a house, and the swallow a nest for herself where she laid her chicks beside your altars. . . . How fortunate are they who dwell in your House!" (Ps 84:3–5; cf. Smith 1997: 81–109). Conversely, Jeremiah 7 attacks the people's confidence that, however great their crimes, the Temple will protect them, even calling the sanctuary a "robbers' cave" (v 11). While this is mainly invective, it might also reflect the presence of criminals within the sacred precincts (cf. Sforno).

How asylum worked is easy to visualize. Once one man killed another, a foot race began. The killer had two choices: to flee to an altar or to flee abroad. The latter alternative surely was as common in Israel as in Greece (see Gagarin 1981). But it is ignored by biblical law because it is outside of Israelite jurisdiction (cf. Exod 2:15; 2 Sam 13:38). If the killer was confident of proving his innocence and his ability to reach sanctuary, he would seek an altar. Meanwhile, the kin of the slain would try to guess his direction and overtake him, since he was fair game until he reached the asylum. The law protected avengers from the accusation of murder, provided they won the race (Westbrook 1988: 79).

The principle of asylum is illustrated in 1 Kgs 1:50–53 and 2:28–34. In the first vignette, David's son Adonijah, who has committed no crime apart from claiming the royal succession, preventively seeks refuge once it is apparent that his younger half-brother Solomon will be king:

> And Adonijah feared from before Solomon. So he arose and went and seized the Altar's horns. And it was told to Solomon, saying, "See, Adonijah fears King Solomon, and see, he has grasped the Altar's horns, saying, 'Let King Solomon swear to me this day: if he will put to death his servant with the sword . . .' " (i.e, Solomon must swear not to kill Adonijah).
>
> And Solomon said, "If he becomes a *son of worth* (i.e., a "good boy"), not (one) of his hairs shall fall to the ground. But if wrong should be found in him, then he must die."
>
> So King Solomon sent, and they took him down from by the Altar, and he entered and bowed to King Solomon.

In this case, a man leaves his asylum because he has made at least a probationary peace with his pursuer, as might also happen in cases of accidental homicide. Later, however, Solomon has Adonijah executed, apparently on trumped-up charges (1 Kgs 2:13–25; see Cross 1973: 237; Halpern 2001: 398–99). Forthwith, he purges his brother's supporters, including David's general Joab, an inveterate but now retired murderer.

> And the news reached Joab . . . and Joab fled to Yahweh's Tent and seized the Altar's horns. . . . So Solomon sent Benaiah Jehoiada's son, saying, "Strike him down."
>
> Then Benaiah entered Yahweh's Tent and said to him, "Thus says the King: 'Leave!' "
>
> But he said, "No, but I will die here."
>
> Then Benaiah brought back word to the king, saying, "Thus spoke Joab, and thus he answered me."
>
> And the King said to him, "Do as he spoke, and strike him down and bury him. So you will remove the gratuitous bloodiness that Joab has shed, from upon me and from upon my father's house. And may Yahweh bring back his blood upon his (own) head, who struck down two men more righteous and good than he. . . ."
>
> So Benaiah Jehoiada's son went up and struck him down and put him to death. And he was buried in his home in the wilderness.

1 Kgs 2:28–34 shows the application of Exod 21:14. Solomon, later famous as a judge (1 Kings 3), rules that Joab has no right to asylum because he bears blood-

guilt. But 1 Kgs 2:28–34 implies that Benaiah kills Joab right by the Altar, whereas Exod 21:14 requires removing the criminal first.

As observed above, in its original context, 21:14 likely referred to any altar, whether of the regional High Place or Meeting Tent. The notion that anyone, even an alleged murderer, might touch the Tabernacle Altar creates a problem in the composite Torah, however, for the notion is anathema to P. First, unjustly shed human blood is the ultimate pollutant (Num 35:31–34; Deut 19:10; 21:1–9; cf. Gen 4:10–11). Second, while P retains the old principle underlying asylum, "And the Altar shall be Holiness of Holinesses; any touching the Altar becomes holy" (Exod 29:37), this sanctity now excludes rather than protects the profane, even if one is free of ritual impurity. Instead, P like D provides six Asylum Cities for the manslayer (Numbers 35).

The Rabbis, who undertook to harmonize the different sources, provide a much more limited and rather far-fetched reading of 21:14. "From beside my altar you may take him" means that the murderer must be immediately arrested and executed, *even should he be a priest and in the very act of sacrifice* (cf. *Mek. nəzîqîn* 3; *Mak.* 12a; Rashi; ibn Ezra [shorter commentary]). The law, in other words, makes its point *a fortiori*: if you may take even a murderous priest from Yahweh's very Altar, how much more a common Israelite from an Asylum City (Bekhor Shor)! As for the bloody Joab seeking asylum at the Altar (1 Kgs 2:28–34), this the Rabbis regard as sacrilege, further evidence that he deserved his fate (*b. Mak.* 12a).

The biblical notion of asylum derives its symbolism from two contexts. The first is Middle Eastern mores of hospitality, most celebrated among the Bedouin, for whom a guest is absolutely inviolable (Musil 1928: 455–70). How much more when the host is Yahweh, and the refugee takes shelter at God's table, the Altar. To harm him is no less than to injure the Deity's honor. The second context is sacrificial: consigned to sacred asylum, the fugitive symbolically immolates himself, becoming Yahweh's property, elsewhere called *qōdeš* 'Holiness' or *ḥērem* 'taboo.' To injure the fugitive is to steal from Yahweh and thus to violate his Holiness.

SPECULATION: In Priestly theology, Yahweh's Holiness reaches out to destroy whenever the impure intrudes into his presence (see below, pp. 689–90). If the same notion obtained among those who practiced altar asylum (which, as we have seen, P does not endorse), then perhaps the quest for sacred refuge was also a judicial ordeal. Anyone who could touch an altar with impunity must *ipso facto* be clear of bloodguilt.

you may take him. It is unclear how much urgency is expressed by the verb *tiqqāḥennû*. An equally valid translation would be "you *must* take him," both because the murderer must be executed, and because the Altar must be kept apart from bloodguilt, the aforementioned case of Joab notwithstanding (cf. Philo *Spec. Leg.* 3.88–91). When Josiah sets out deliberately to defile forbidden altars, he makes human sacrifices upon them (2 Kgs 23:20).

The addressee of the injunction "you may take" is uncertain. Jacob (1992: 637) thinks it is the judge or elder, as in Deut 19:12, and as generally in the First Code. But, to judge from 21:14 alone, it could equally be the avenger or a member of an impromptu lynch mob. Num 35:12, 24–25 simply places authority in the hands of "the community" *(hāʿēdâ)*. It probably does not matter. The overriding considerations are (a) that the murderer be executed and (b) that this not take place at the altar. For further discussion of asylum, see Houtman (2000: 132–44).

21:15. *Whoever strikes.* Due to the ambiguity of the verb *hikkâ*, 21:15 can be read in two different ways. To incur the death penalty, must one kill a parent, or does a mere blow suffice? In other words, does the qualification "and he dies" in v 12 apply also here? That would be more believable if the intervening qualifications of vv 13–14 were secondary, so that the similarly phrased injunctions against murder and striking a parent originally stood one after another, as follows: "Whoever strikes a man and he dies must be put to death, death. Whoever strikes his father or his mother must be put to death, death."

I think, however, that the very lack of a qualification, in contrast to v 12, should be decisive. If we assume that the legislator wrote exactly what he meant, then merely striking a parent is a capital offense (Dillmann 1880: 230; Driver 1911: 216). Otherwise, the law would be unnecessary, since murder was already treated in vv 12–14. In other words, so great is the reverence due one's parents, to hit them is equivalent to killing anyone else. According to 21:17, even verbally abusing them is tantamount to homicide.

These punishments go far beyond the talionic principle of "eye for eye, tooth for tooth" *(Mek. nəzîqîn* 5), because parent and child are not social equals. After all, a naughty child might argue, if parents spank children, then talion requires that children repay blow for blow! (The equivalent Babylonian law [quoted below], while also not talionic, is milder and more appropriate: the son's offending hand is severed, as was apparently also the practice among Hellenistic Jews [Philo *Spec. Leg.* 2.244–48].) Deut 21:18–21 is even more severe than Exodus: a disobedient, worthless son, even if he has not lifted a finger against his parents, is publicly condemned by his father and mother and then stoned to death by the whole community.

Striking a parent is a reversal of the natural order, whereby parents cuff or beat children for their misdeeds, not vice versa (Durham 1987: 23); e.g., Prov 13:24: 23:13–14; 29:15. To be sure, most children at one time or another strike a parent. But this law, like all laws, applies mainly to adults. (Rabbinic sources will also add the requirement that the blow cause an injury [*Mek. nəzîqîn* 5; *b. Sanh.* 84b].) Thus, although 21:15 may well have been cited to admonish difficult children, the subject is really abuse of the *elderly* by their *adult* children. (Houtman [2000: 147–48] compares a Ugaritic myth wherein a young goddess threatens to batter an elderly god bloody if he refuses her requests [*KTU* 1.3.v.23–25].)

or his mother. Although the conjunction *wə-* 'and, or' is ambiguous, obviously one need not strike *both* parents to incur the death penalty. Either one will do (Ehrlich 1969: 177). Despite the Bible's overall patriarchal cast, it consistently mandates reverence toward both parents; see further NOTES to 20:12.

The parricide taboo is universal, and all cultures espouse filial piety. Yet parricide is equally the subject of myths and legends worldwide. The theories of Sigmund Freud (1918) and Sir James Frazer (1911), that these tales are memories of actual homicides, is neither provable nor likely. But that they arise from the kind of intergenerational competition manifest throughout the animal kingdom, including our closest primate relations, seems an inescapable conclusion (cf. Propp 2004b). The way to exorcise these guilt-provoking tendencies is, on the one hand, to depict them in stories, and, on the other hand, to make them the subject of the most stringent taboos. A society's elders, past their physical prime but responsible for shaping and promulgating the traditional culture, understandably make their own persons legally sacred.

COMPARE: If a child should strike his father, they shall cut off his hand (Hammurapi §195). (*LCMAM* 120)

21:16. *sells him.* Comparing v 8 "alien kin," Driver (1911: 216) thinks that 21:16 probably bans selling the victim into a foreign country. But surely sale to another Israelite, or to a non-Israelite resident of Canaan, would be equally criminal. Moreover, even v 8 probably does not refer to transportation abroad (see NOTE, "alien kin").

and/or he/it is found in his hand. The words ûm(ə)kārô wənimṣā(ʾ) bəyādô have evoked much commentary. Literally they mean, "and he sold him and he/it is found in his hand." (Since Hebrew has no neuter gender, any "he" or "she" might be an "it.") Most agree that "hand" here implies "power, possession" (Durham 1987: 312; on Akkadian parallels, see Paul 1970: 66). But concerning the rest, there is much disagreement.

Since wə-/û can also mean "or," Saadiah takes the two clauses as parenthetically expressing alternatives: "Whoever steals a man—whether he sells him or retains him. . . ." But that could have been said more clearly by *ʾim-nimṣā(ʾ) bəyādô ʾim-məkārô or *ʾô-nimṣā(ʾ) bəyādô ʾô-məkārô. Perhaps, then, "or he is found in his hand" is a kind of afterthought, tantamount to "*even if he is only* found in his hand," i.e., not yet sold (cf. Houtman 2000: 151). Still, 21:16 appears to put matters backward (Rashi, ibn Ezra). We would rather have expected *wənimṣā(ʾ) bəyādô ûm(ə)kārô 'whether he is found in his hand or he sold him.' Compare the laws for stolen animals in 21:37; 22:3, which distinguish the cases of the cattle thief who has disposed of the animal from the one caught with the goods—although, in that case, the punishments are different, whereas it makes no difference when one steals a person (Jacob 1992: 638–39). For these and other reasons, Daube (1947: 95) concludes that the clause wənimṣā(ʾ) bəyādô is a later interpolation into a short, apodictic law, "Whoever steals a man must be put to death, death."

And there are at least five other plausible ways of reading 21:16. First, "and he is found in his hand" might imply that the slave has been paid for but not delivered (cf. *b. Sanh.* 85b). Second, "and he is found in his hand" might refer to the purchaser's having taken possession (Ramban). Third, "and he is found in his hand" might refer to the seller: "he is caught (with the victim) in his hand" (Houtman [2000: 150] compares Deut 24:7, where the kidnapper is the subject of nimṣā[ʾ]).

Fourth, "and it is found in his hand" might refer to the payment, constituting proof of sale (Noth 1962: 180). And fifth, "and it is found in his hand" might idiomatically mean "and it is proved" (Vg; Bekhor Shor).

If Saadiah is correct that "he is found in his hand" and "he sold him" are alternatives, which I find the most natural reading, then the question is raised: suppose one abducts a child not in order to sell it but to raise it. When King Solomon confronts this issue, he does not in fact decree death for the kidnapping harlot—but 1 Kgs 3:16–28 is just a fable, not necessarily a model of case law.

Another question is why, in MT, the law against kidnapping appears sandwiched between two statutes concerning filial piety (see, however, TEXTUAL NOTE to 21:15–16). Can we find a rationale, or is the sequence haphazard?

These three cases deal with abrogation of the normal parent–child relationship, wherein the parents first raise the child and the child later reveres the parents. As a kidnapper deprives his victim of the chance to observe filial piety, he is himself a causer of filial impiety. (In Saadiah's imaginative scenario, perhaps inspired by the myth of Oedipus or similar tales, an abducted child unknowingly commits a capital offense against his parent, in which case the kidnapper would be mortally culpable.)

put to death. As in the surrounding cases of physical or verbal abuse against a parent, here the punishment is more than "eye for eye." According to the principle of talion, the kidnapper should himself be sold into slavery (see below, pp. 224–31). Kidnapping plus involuntary enslavement (of a man? of anybody?) is instead classified as an act of violence, tantamount to murder.

In the Laws of Hammurapi, too, kidnapping is a capital offense (see also Dillmann [1880: 230] for Classical references). In the Hittite Laws (§§19–24), however, abduction may be compounded with a payment. We should note that, in the most prominent biblical story about kidnapping, the tale of Joseph (Genesis 37, 39–50), Joseph's brothers are tormented for their crime, but they are not killed.

COMPARE: If a man should kidnap the young child of another man, he shall be killed (Hammurapi §14). (*LCMAM* 84)

21:17. *curses.* Just what is forbidden here is unclear. The verb *qillēl*, literally 'to treat as insignificant' or 'to make insignificant,' combines "to call down misfortune," "to insult" and "to maltreat," thus corresponding to the various nuances of English "curse" and "abuse." Its principal antonyms are *bērak* 'bless,' i.e., confer or wish for well-being, and *kibbēd* 'honor,' i.e., make or treat as important (Ehrlich 1908: 349; Cassuto 1967: 271). (For general discussions of *qillēl*, see Brichto 1963; Scharbert 2004.) Houtman (2000: 149) notes the absence of a law requiring parents not to abuse children (contrast Eph 6:4; Col 3:21).

Usually, context permits us easily to differentiate among the usages of *qillēl*. E.g., when Yahweh (Gen 8:21) or a prophet (2 Kgs 2:24; Neh 13:2) is the grammatical *subject*, he is removing blessing and sending misfortune, and likewise when the curser calls upon a deity (1 Sam 17:43). But when God is the direct *object* (Lev 24:15, 23; cf. 1 Kgs 21:10, 13; Job 1:5; 2:9), he must be the recipient of mere verbal abuse, since imprecations cannot harm him or diminish his well-being. And when one is forbidden to "curse" the deaf, most likely one is not to mock or insult him or her (Lev 19:14).

What if, as here, the object is a parent (also Lev 20:9; Deut 27:16; Prov 20:20; 30:11)? Is one forbidden to speak slightingly to or about a father or mother? Or is one commanded not to recite a spell or prayer aimed to bring about a parent's death, e.g., in order to speed one's inheritance (Jacob 1992: 640)? *Mek. nəzîqîn* 5; *b. Šebu.* 35b–36a; *Sanh.* 66a leniently reserve capital punishment for him who specifically dishonors a parent in the name of God. But, given the ambiguity, more likely the Bible intends the broadest possible meaning: one may not do anything that diminishes parental honor (*qillēl*). Similarly, in an Akkadian legal document from Ugarit, the cognate *qullulu* connotes filial impiety and is contrasted with *kubbutu* 'to honor' (Paul 1970: 67); cf. also the Canaanite glosses *qll* and *kbd* in EA 245:39. For further discussion of reverence toward parents, see pp. 178, 211–12.

Like the law against striking a parent, this statute seems rather harsh by modern standards. Luzzatto sees the filial piety provisions as rooted in an older time when, in Roman fashion, the paterfamilias exercised total authority over his household and demanded unconditional respect. As an extreme case, Luzzatto cites Judah's apparent authority to summarily sentence his betrothed daughter-in-law Tamar to death (Gen 38:24).

put to death. Who enforces this? Since the overall cast of the First Code is judicial, most likely the law envisions a proper inquiry, with witnesses and judges. As for the executioners, these might be the parents themselves. Deut 21:18–21 describes parents prosecuting their child before the entire community. But that need not be the intention of Exodus. While it is indeed hard to imagine parents prosecuting their own children, one could imagine, say, a brother accusing another brother of filial impiety, either during or after their parents' lifetime.

> COMPARE: 192. If the child of (i.e., reared by) a courtier or the child of (i.e., reared by) a *sekretu* should say to the father who raised him or to the mother who raised him, "You are not my father" or "You are not my mother," they shall cut out his tongue. 193. If the child of (i.e., reared by) a courtier or the child of (i.e., reared by) a *sekretu* identifies with his father's house and repudiates the father who raised him or the mother who raised him and departs for his father's house, they shall pluck out his eye (Hammurapi §§192–93). (*LCMAM* 120)

21:18. *men contend.* Ordinarily, the root *ryb* refers to a verbal quarrel. It is to be distinguished from *nṣy*, the actual fight (Paul 1970: 74 n. 1). But what is the implication here? Either *ryb* euphemistically connotes a physical fight, or else we are to imagine a verbal quarrel that breaks into violence (Sarna 1991: 123). By the latter reading, the text is elliptical, merely implying a brawl. In any case, the law is about a homicide that is the result neither of malice aforethought nor of mischance, but of ordinary enmity that gets out of hand.

stone. The rock might be swung, hurled or held in the fist to weight the blow.

fist. This translation of *'egrōp* is not quite secure. Although in postbiblical Hebrew it denotes the fist, some translators and interpreters going back to the *Tgs.* think that here *'egrōp* is an implement (also Saadiah; ibn Ezra; Rashbam; ibn Janaḥ [*Root Book*, under *g-r-p*], ibn Ezra, NEB). The Semitic root *grp* means "to sweep away" (ibn Ezra), which can be done with either the hand or a tool. A *megrāp* (Joel 1:17) is apparently a shovel, with cognates in Syriac and Arabic *(mijrafa)*. Is an *'egrōp* similarly a farming tool?

Probably not. The term *'egrōp* 'fist' is adequately attested in Rabbinic Hebrew, and it is inherently unlikely that a name for a body part was excavated out of the Torah and given a new meaning. More likely it was handed down orally since Israelite times. If "fist" is the correct sense for Exodus, then the law must be paradigmatic: "stone" represents any implement and "fist" the use of a limb (thus, covering, say, a lethal kick) (Cazelles 1946: 53).

Still, we cannot be certain. When P undertakes to list the types of objects that can be used as instruments of murder, it omits the fist: "whether with a iron implement/weapon *(kəlî barzel)* he struck him . . . or whether with a hand stone *('eben yād)* . . . or whether with a hand stick *('ēṣ-yād)*" (Num 35:16–18). That is, only metal, stone and wood are considered sufficiently heavy and hard to cause a fatality. It is much harder to kill with the fist. But Exod 21:18 is not completely comparable to Num 35:16–18 since the latter deals with premeditated murder.

To adjudicate, I would cite Isa 58:4, which describes the people's lack of decorum on fast days: "If with quarreling *(ryb)* and fighting *(nṣy)* you fast, and with hitting with the guilty *'egrōp*. . . . " As in Exod 21:18, a quarrel leads to brawling, involving hitting with something. The only natural interpretations of *'egrōp* here would be either "fist" or "weapon." But since there is no evidence, textual or etymological, that an *'egrōp* denotes weapons in general, and since the interpretation "shovel" would be comically inappropriate in Isaiah, I prefer the interpretation "fist" for Biblical Hebrew, quite as in postbiblical Hebrew.

Curiously, Exod 21:18 does not mention the staff, which men ordinarily carried (cf. Num 35:18 [P]). Maybe it was customary for freemen to fight without weapons, in contrast to caning a slave (21:20) or a child (Prov 13:24). Or maybe it is assumed that clubbing with a staff *ipso facto* constitutes intentional homicide. It is to avoid such difficulties that Sam omits the implements entirely (TEXTUAL NOTE).

21:19. *outside.* Publicly, before witnesses. This law is designed to protect the assailant, and to provide a motivation for him to support his incapacitated victim (Schwienhorst-Schönberger 1990: 56). Only once the injured man is sufficiently recovered to leave his house is his adversary safe from capital punishment. Presumably, the law remedies an earlier situation, in which persons were executed on mere suspicion of having caused a death, even if the victim appeared temporarily to recover.

upon his cane. The "cane" *(miš'enet)* has been understood in two ways. On the one hand, since in modern Western society only the infirm use walking sticks, we naturally assume that the attacker is cleared once his victim is minimally ambulatory, i.e., does not need to be carried by others but hobbles on his own (cf. Philo *Spec. Leg.* 3.106; *Mek. nəzîqîn* 6; ibn Ezra; Dillmann 1880: 230). But the cane might alternatively be viewed not as a crutch but as a staff borne by men of dignity. If so, to "walk about outside on his cane" would imply a full return to health (cf. Rashi; Jacob 1992: 645).

I incline toward the former interpretation. It is true that Gidon's angel, who is presumably hale and hearty, carries a cane (Judg 6:21). But Zech 8:4 associates a cane with infirmity: "old men and old women . . . each with a cane in his hand because of abundance of days." I infer that the cane was properly carried by the elderly, who truly needed a "third leg." But because of the prestige attached to old age, any man of honor might sport a cane as a token of symbolic elderhood, like the Victorian walking stick or the earlier powdered wig. In the context of an injured man, it is most natural to suppose that the cane is a necessity, not an affectation.

cleared. The root *nqy*, which properly means "to be clean," almost always connotes freedom from guilt and exemption from punishment (Baentsch 1903: 193). Even if the victim subsequently dies, the attacker is cleared, for, having gone abroad, the former invalid may have encountered other accidents (Driver 1911: 216).

This law, were it ever applied literally, might produce unfortunate side effects. Imagine a fistfight in which one party falls down, not really injured, takes to his bed *and refuses to get up* since he is still receiving compensation from his adversary. That is, there is an incentive to malinger.

What the law implies but does not state is that, should the victim fall to bed and then die without having left his house, then the attacker is not "cleared." He is guilty of murder and, after a proper investigation, will be executed (Philo *Spec. Leg.* 3.10). It would no longer matter who started the fight or why. For this law to be practicable, we must assume that the striker is detained, at the altar or elsewhere, pending his victim's death or recovery (*Mek. nəzîqîn* 6; *b. Ketub.* 33b; *Sanh.* 78b).

only. Jacob (1992: 646–47) shows that *raq* here is tantamount to "however" (cf. Gen 19:8; 24:8; Deut 20:6). He further argues that the wording does not necessarily exclude other compensation, beyond medical bills.

sitting idle. The consonants *šbtw* have been variously parsed. The MT vocalization *šibtô* implies the root *yšb* 'sit, dwell,' the state that officially expires when the invalid leaves his house. Schwienhorst-Schönberger (1990: 57) supports this interpretation, arguing that as *qwm* 'get up' is paired against its antonym *npl* 'fall,' so *hlk* 'walk' should be paired against *yšb* 'sit.'

Saadiah, however, favors the root *šbt* 'cease, be idle,' which makes equally good sense (cf. LXX *argia* 'idleness, unemployment'). Luzzatto compares Roman law, according to which the injured are entitled to the costs of healing, damages and *idleness.* The root *šbt* may connote a temporary rest from paid labor also in the seventh-century B.C.E. letter from Meṣad Ḥashavyahu (*AHI* 7.001.5–7), but there, a more likely interpretation is "Sabbath" (ultimately from the same root; see pp. 175–76). The only objection to this approach to 21:19 is that we would expect from *šbt* a vocalization **šobtô* (cf. Wevers 1990: 332).

Finally, it is not certain that remuneration is the topic at all. *Šibtô yittēn* could also be translated "he must give him a place to live" or even "he must give him his home" (cf. Cazelles 1946: 53, but also Fensham 1960). Thus the law may require the striker to take the stricken into his home and nurse him back to health (see next NOTE).

heal, heal. Like the previous phrase, the words *rappō' yərappē'/rəpō' yirpā(')* (see TEXTUAL NOTE) are somewhat ambiguous. Superficially, they would appear to mean that the aggressor must himself heal his victim—despite the social awkwardness this would entail. But such is not the tradition. After all, most Israelites presumably lacked medical expertise (see *AHI* 100.804 for epigraphic evidence of healers). The majority view is that the guilty party is obliged to *pay a doctor* (Tgs.; Syr; *b. B. Qam.* 85a–b), an interpretation with parallels in cuneiform law (see below). Alternatively, one might suppose that the offender must support the invalid *until he is healed (rp' yrp')*; Luzzatto embraces both interpretations. The Rabbis (*Mek. nəzîqîn* 6) homiletically understand the emphatic repetition of the infinitive absolute as covering relapses and subsequent related disabilities. (See also *b. B. Qam.* 85a on the limits of liability.)

Whatever the exact meaning, 21:18–19 offers another case in which talion does not operate (see above, pp. 211, 213; below, pp. 225–26, 229, 231, 235). If it did, the aggressor would be beaten until he, too, is an invalid. Instead, practicality prevails, and the culpable party repays his debt to the man he injured, who may even come to feel gratitude for the support.

The words *rappō' yərappē'* are often cited as the Bible's sole positive reference to the practice of medicine. Otherwise, the healing of injuries and the postponement of death are regarded as infringements upon Yahweh's sovereignty (cf. 15:26; Deut 28:27; 32:39; Hos 6:1; Job 5:18; 2 Chr 16:12). See further ibn Ezra (shorter commentary) and vol. I, pp. 579–82. On Israelite medicine in a cross-cultural context, see Zucconi (2005).

COMPARE: 47. If a man should inflict(?) any other injuries(?) on another man in the course of a fray, he shall weigh and deliver 10 shekels of silver. 47A. If a man, in the course of a brawl, should cause the death of another member of the *awīlu*-class, he shall weigh and deliver 40 shekels of silver (Eshnunna §§47–47A). (*LCMAM* 66)

206. If an *awīlu* should strike another *awīlu* during a brawl and inflict upon him a wound, that *awīlu* shall swear, "I did not strike intentionally," and he shall satisfy the physician (i.e., pay his fees). 207. If he should die from his beating, he shall also swear ("I did not strike him intentionally"); if he (the victim) is a member of the *awīlu*-class, he shall weigh and deliver 30 shekels of silver. 208. If he (the victim) is a member of the common-class, he shall weigh and deliver 20 shekels of silver (Hammurapi §§206–8). (*LCMAM* 122)

10. If anyone injures a person and temporarily incapacitates him, he shall provide medical care for him. In his place he shall provide a person to work on his estate until he recovers. When he recovers, his assailant shall pay him 6 shekels of silver and shall pay the physician's fee as well. . . . 174. If men are hitting each other, and one of them dies, the other shall give one slave (Hittite Laws §§10, 174). (*LCMAM* 218–19, 234)

21:20. *strikes his manservant . . . dies.* Should not this case fall under the general laws of murder already laid out in vv 12–14 (Rashi)? Like the following discussion of the fetus, 21:20–21 treats a special case: the slave is neither a full person nor simple property but something in between.

As we have already noted, the First Code does not clearly distinguish among various types of slaves: Hebrew slaves, foreign slaves, purchased slaves, debt slaves, bred slaves, war captives and impressed thieves. The ancient Near Eastern codes regard harming another's menial slave as a crime against the slave owner, not the slave himself (Hammurapi §§199, 213, 217, 223, 231; Hittite Laws §§8, 12, 14, 16, 18). But, at least at Nuzi, a slave apparently could prosecute an abusive master (Paul 1970: 70). Similarly, the Code of Hammurapi §§115–16 (quoted below) explicitly protects from violence the debt slave *(nipûtum)*, as opposed to the completely unfree *wardum*-slave (Schwienhorst-Schönberger 1990: 68–69).

with the rod. The implication may be that to use any weapon on a slave is cruel and reckless. A kind master and a prudent owner would limit himself to, say, slapping a recalcitrant servant—but not in the face (21:26–27). A rod too is liable to maim or kill (e.g., Num 35:18).

More likely, however, as with guiding a sheep or chastising a child, the rod was ordinarily used to direct and admonish slaves, notwithstanding the potential for abuse (Rashbam). The staff appears as a legitimate instrument of guidance also in Isa 9:3; Prov 10:13; 13:23; 19:25; 22:15; 23:13–14; 26:3. Moreover, Prov 29:19, "a slave is not chastised with words," seems implicitly to advocate beating one's servants (Jacob 1992: 648). As with the following provisions dealing with maiming slaves, the law's point is probably that, if you must cudgel your slave, do so gently—and you might be wiser to refrain from violence entirely.

By focusing on a rod, this law leaves undiscussed the cases of a lethal beating administered by bare hands or with a true weapon. I would assume that this law applies whenever a slave dies from a beating (Rashbam); cf. Sam (TEXTUAL NOTE).

under his hand. Presumably this means during the beating and not later (Ramban).

he must be avenged, avenged. The exact nuance of *nāqōm yinnāqēm* is uncertain. The phrase might alternatively mean "it (the crime) must be avenged" (Holzinger 1900: 85; Schwienhorst-Schönberger 1990: 72). And Cazelles (1946: 54) raises another possibility. Noting that the form **yuqqam* would be expected for the passive, as in the following verse, and observing that the Sam variant *mwt ywmt* 'he must be put to death, death' has the master as the subject (TEXTUAL NOTE), he makes the master the subject of both clauses: "he must undergo vengeance."

More important and also uncertain is the practical import of "vengeance," since the root *nqm* does not otherwise appear in biblical law (ibn Ezra; for a general discussion, see Lipiński 1999). Perhaps the word was chosen for reasons of assonance, as it chimes with *nqy* 'to be innocent' (v 19) and *nky* 'to be struck' (vv 12, 15, 18, 20) (cf. Jacob 1992: 649). But we would expect a legislator to be more interested in clarity than in wordplay.

There is no doubt that "vengeance" implies punishment. The only question is:

of what sort? For some exegetes, the use of *nāqōm yinnāqēm* instead of *môt yûmāt* 'must be put to death, death' (v 12) shows that the text distinguishes between the death of a freeman and a slave. For Baentsch (1903: 195), *nqm* implies simply paying a fine to the shrine (also McNeile 1908: 129). Arguably, the law regards it as self-evident that a man would not deliberately kill his own slave, who is, after all, "his silver" (v 21). Such deaths are by definition classed as manslaughter not murder (Beer 1939: 111).

For most interpreters, however, the phrase *nāqōm yinnāqēm* is synonymous to *môt yûmāt* 'must be put to death, death' (= Sam [see TEXTUAL NOTE]); e.g., Philo *Spec. Leg.* 3.141. In other words, after a trial, either the slave's kin or their proxies execute the abusive owner. Elsewhere, the root *nqm* always refers to lethal vengeance (Licht 1968). In particular, Ehrlich (1969: 178) compares Gen 4:15, "I would *kill (hrg)* a man for my wound. . . . If Cain is avenged *(nqm)* sevenfold, then Lamech seventy-sevenfold." (The Rabbis [*Mek. nəzîqîn* 7; *b. Sanh.* 52b] opine that *nqm* refers specifically to death by the sword, comparing Lev 26:25, *ḥereb nōqemet nəqam-bərît* 'a sword exacting Covenant-vengeance' [cf. also *ḥereb . . . nəqāmâ* in Ps 149:6–7].) As for the atypical use of *nqm* in a legal context, the ambiguity may be deliberate, since a slave would probably not possess kin to act as Blood Redeemers—or else they would have ransomed him—and more likely the court and/or community must act in their stead (Sarna 1991: 124). Should they fail in this duty, Yahweh himself will take vengeance, at the least upon the murderer and probably upon the entire community that shelters him (Chirichigno 1993: 155–69).

There are still other possibilities. Westbrook (1988: 91), whose axiom is that biblical and Mesopotamian law are maximally similar (see Hammurapi §116 below), supposes that the root *nqm* specifically connotes talion, i.e., exact retribution (below, pp. 225–31): "'He shall be avenged' means that the appropriate member of the creditor's family is liable to be killed by way of revenge: if the victim were a son—his son; if a daughter—his daughter." This would be the system abolished by Deut 24:16, "Fathers shall not be put to death on account of sons, and sons shall not be put to death on account of fathers; each man for his own sin, they shall be put to death."

Lastly, seeking a middle ground, Houtman (2000: 157–59) thinks that *nqm* most likely implies a criminal prosecution, as in LXX 'he shall be judged with a judgment' (cf. Vg). But, unlike a simple case of murder (v 12), the law does not limit the judges' discretion. They might impose the death penalty, but they might not—particularly in the absence of kindred avengers, e.g., if the slave were a non-Israelite (cf. Cazelles 1946: 54).

If "avenged" here connotes capital punishment, whether of the owner or a family member, the Torah accords the slave ultimate human dignity. In Yahweh's sight, his life is as valuable as another's. This accords with later Muslim law (Schacht 1964: 127, 178) and the practice of first-century B.C.E. Egyptians and Athenians (Diodorus Siculus 1.77). If, however, deliberately killing a slave can be compounded by a fine, then the biblical law resembles more the Mesopotamian custom, which places a variable value on the lives of different social classes.

21:21. *day . . . two days.* As in 21:18–19, the benefit of doubt protects the assailant in a case when death is not immediate. If the victim is a slave, his mere survival for a day or two suffices to clear his owner of culpability. If, however, the victim is a free man, his recovery must be publicly certified. In other words, the law protects the enslaved slightly less than the free.

stands. I.e., survives (Ehrlich 1969: 178). Although the verb here (*'md* 'be standing') is different from that in 21:19 (*qwm* 'stand up'), both verses presume that an erect posture and the ability to walk constitute evidence of good health (Jacob 1992: 649).

Chirichigno (1993: 174), however, proposes a novel interpretation of *'im-yôm 'ô yômayim ya'ămōd:* "If . . . within a day or two he gets up [out of bed]." This is most unlikely, on two counts. First, I do not know where else *yôm* means "within a day" as opposed to "for a day." Second, Chirichigno's claim, that the meaning "survive, persist" for *'āmad* is unparalleled, is inexplicable; the root *'md* very frequently connotes endurance (Exod 9:16; Lev 13:5, 37; 1 Kgs 15:4; Jer 32:14; 48:11; Ps 19:10; 33:11, etc.). Far more rarely is *'md* used as a synonymn for *qwm* 'rise (from a seated or supine position)' as in Chirichigno's translation; the best examples come from Daniel (e.g., 8:22–23; 11:2–3). (For the other verses Chirichigno cites [p. 175 n. 2], the accepted meanings "stand still" and "stand firm" are more likely than "stand up.") I also regard as unlikely Schwienhorst-Schönberger's (1990: 65) understanding of *'md* as "perform service." That would have been **ya'ămōd ləpānā[y]w* 'stand *before him.*' Rather, in 21:20–21, *'md* is the opposite of *mwt* 'die,' just as "a day or two days" is the opposite of "under his hand," i.e., immediately.

not be avenged. Modern scholars do not regard the form *yuqqam* as a Hoph'al, as it appears, but rather as the Qal passive (Beer 1939: 110; cf. Waltke and O'-Connor 1990: §22.6 pp. 373–76). The two patterns coalesced, as proto-Northwest Semitic **yahunqam* and **yunqam* merged into Hebrew *yuqqam.*

he is his silver. I.e., the slave is only property, either purchased from a previous owner or detained for his own failure to repay a loan. The master who abuses his slave so that he dies slowly is sufficiently punished by loss of the slave's worth, whether it is market value or the money the slave owes him (cf. Schwienhorst-Schönberger 1990: 66–67). He is not a criminal but a fool (Philo *Spec. Leg.* 3.142)—the archetype of such brutish stewardship being Pharaoh himself, who chose to oppress his own Hebrew slaves. Only in the most extreme case, when the slave dies "under his hand," does the law intervene.

COMPARE: *115.* If a man has a claim of grain or silver against another man, distrains a member of his household, and the distrainee dies a natural death while in the house of her or his distrainer, that case has no basis for a claim. *116.* If the distrainee should die from the effects of a beating or other physical abuse while in the house of her or his distrainer, the owner of the distrainee shall charge and convict his merchant, and if (the distrainee is) the man's son, they shall kill his (the distrainer's) son; if the man's slave, he shall weigh and deliver 20 shekels of silver; moreover, he shall forfeit whatever he originally gave as the loan (Hammurapi §§115–16). (*LCMAM* 103)

2. [If] anyone kills [a male] or female slave in a quarrel, he shall bring him for burial [and] shall give [2] persons (lit., heads), male or female respectively. He shall look to his house for it. . . . *4.* If anyone strikes a male or female slave so that he dies, but it is an accident, he shall bring him for burial and shall give one person. He shall look to his house for it (Hittite Laws §§2, 4). (*LCMAM* 217)

21:22. *men fight.* In a somewhat confusing but still comprehensible manner, 21:22–25 treats at least three ambiguities raised by the preceding laws (cf. Loewenstamm 1977: 346–57): What happens when a third party is injured in the course of a fight? If the third party is a pregnant woman who miscarries, is the abortion manslaughter? How does one redress nondeadly injuries? Rather than resort to textual dissection, as in most critical treatments, I regard this complexity as an original characteristic of the First Code. Unlike the cuneiform law collections, which delight in listing numerous eventualities, Israelite legal scholars proved their virtuosity by posing a small number of cases possessing broad implications.

Thus the basic question, that of the innocent bystander, is not answered directly. We are not told what happens should a male onlooker suffer such-and-such an injury. Rather, a pregnant woman is posited. From her case, we are presumably meant to extrapolate for all unintended harm (so *Mek. nəzîqîn* 8). Combatants who hurt a bystander are subject to punishment, depending upon the nature of the injury.

The second issue this law treats is more philosophical: is a fetus a person? Is a pregnant woman comparable to, say, a woman carrying her infant in her arms? Is the death of the fetus manslaughter, so that he who jostled the mother is subject to blood vengeance? Is he entitled to asylum?

The answer to the third question, what is the punishment for nonlethal injuries, is simple: "eye for eye, tooth for tooth," etc. I will discuss the Torah's famous *lex talionis* below.

Although many ancient Near Eastern law codes treat injury to a pregnant woman and her fetus (or even gravid livestock; see Hittite Laws §77, 84), this surely cannot have been a common occurrence. Paul (1970: 71 n. 1) infers that we have a case of literary interdependence among the codes, and Finkelstein (1981: 19 n. 11) rather simplistically posits an origin in a single, real case of premature labor and miscarriage. But these suppositions do not answer the question: why among all crimes and accidents likely and unlikely should the codes have borrowed and shared legislation concerning miscarriage? The answer is that, like legal scholars everywhere, ancient legislators were attracted to the unusual and ambiguous (e.g., on Roman law, see Watson 1991: 12).

they strike. Either of the men, not both together (Luzzatto).

a pregnant woman. I assume that the woman is an innocent bystander, not a participant as in Deut 25:11–12. (I find unwarranted Daube's [1947: 108] inference that she is wife to one of the parties, and that the blow is therefore deliberate.)

her child. My translation follows Sam, LXX, etc. *wəlādāh* 'her child' (see TEX-TUAL NOTE). MT, however, reads *yəlāde(y)hā* 'her children.' This must be taken as referring either to the potential for multiple pregnancies—"(all) her babies, (however many)"—or else to all the stuff of childbirth: water, blood, child(ren), afterbirth.

comes out. The minority view is that the verb *yāṣā(ʾ)* here connotes a success-ful albeit premature birth (Jackson 1975: 95, 99; Durham 1987: 323). The major-ity view is that *yāṣā(ʾ)* indicates a miscarriage (most recently, Houtman 2000: 161). It is true that the ancient Near Eastern parallels (quoted below) envision an aborted pregnancy, and it is true that the expression "come out" (*yṣʾ*) is used apropos of abortion or the immediate death of a newborn in Num 12:12; Job 3:11 (Schwienhorst-Schönberger 1990: 94). But, as we shall observe, the cuneiform law codes have a different aim than the First Code. In fact, the Hebrew verb *yāṣā(ʾ)* more often refers to live births (e.g., Gen 25:25–26; 38:28–30).

The text seems deliberately ambiguous. Something comes out of the pregnant woman. There are four possible outcomes: healthy mother and child, dead-or-injured mother and healthy child, healthy mother and dead-or-injured child, and dead-or-injured mother and child. The following clauses attempt to address these eventualities.

injury. The disputed noun *ʾāsôn* otherwise appears only in Gen 42:4, 38; 44:29; Sir 31/34:22; 38:18; 41:9. Both the biblical context and the Arabic cognate *ʾasiya* 'be distressed' suggest the meaning "harm" (e.g., Baentsch 1903: 193). Some claim, however, that the meaning is more specifically "fatality" (e.g., Josephus *Ant.* 4.8.278). The Rabbis, for example, think that *ʾāsôn* here refers to the woman's death (*Mek. nəzîqîn* 8). (For more discussion of the history of interpreta-tion, see Isser [1990] and TEXTUAL NOTE.)

Even though the argument that *ʾāsôn* implies a fatality draws support from the ancient Near Eastern codes, which consider only the *death* of mother or child, I think this approach is incorrect. As observed above, the First Code is in one im-portant way not comparable to the cuneiform documents. The Hittite Laws con-tain 200 clauses and the Code of Hammurapi 282, treating all manner of torts. In contrast, the technique in Exodus 21 is to compress multiple legal issues into a small number of complex, paradigmatic cases. In my holistic reading, 21:22–25 is about all injuries caused to third parties, and indeed about all injuries. If the bib-lical writer wished clearly to describe the death of the woman or her offspring, he would have used the verb *mwt* 'die.' On the contrary, he makes it explicit what constitutes *ʾāsôn*: death; damage to an eye, a tooth, an arm, a leg; a burn, a wound or a stripe (Schwienhorst-Schönberger 1990: 93). Not all of these can occur dur-ing childbirth to either mother or offspring, but, again, the case is intended to have broad application.

It remains unclear whether "injury" applies only to the mother, or to mother and child. By the theory that v 22 describes a miscarriage, *ʾāsôn* can only connote the mother's death or injury; the baby is already dead. But if, as I think, v 22 de-scribes premature labor, then the "injury" would be to either the mother or the in-fant. If the child is viable and the mother is unharmed, then the man who accidentally jostled her owes the woman's husband a modest fine for endangerment and inconvenience (Durham 1987: 323).

fined. Arguably, the root 'nš refers to punishment in general rather than compensation in goods or silver (see SPECULATION below). Rashi, who assumes a miscarriage, suggests that the fine is determined by the price differential between a pregnant and a nonpregnant slave.

stipulate against him. Since I cannot imagine that the husband has the unrestricted right arbitrarily to impose a fine, I take *yāšît ʿālā(y)w* as referring to a legal claim, to be settled by a judge. See also following NOTES.

he shall give. Both the subject and exact nuance of the verb *nātan* 'give' are unclear. The sentence could mean either that the *striker* must *pay* the fine (*Mek. nəzîqîn* 8) or that the *husband* may *impose* the fine (Ramban).

what is fair. My translation of *biplīlîm* is an inadequate compromise. The traditional Jewish view is that *pəlīlîm* are "judges" (Josephus *Ant.* 4.8.278; *b. Sanh.* 111b; Bekhor Shor), an interpretation shared by Syr. Daube (1947: 108) regards the reference to the judiciary as supplementary to the original law, which gave the husband unrestricted authority.

Another opinion is that *pəlīlîm* means "estimation, reckoning" (Saadiah). (Arabic *falla* 'break, notch' may provide an etymology, if we envision a notched tally stick.) "Estimation," then, might mean one of two things. First, it may refer to money: the law does not set a specific fine, but leaves it to the discretion of either the husband or the authorities. Second: some moderns suggest that what is calculated or estimated is not the payment but the age of the dead baby (recall that, by the majority view, 21:22 describes a miscarriage). Speiser (1963a: 303) compares Hittite Laws §§17–18 (quoted below), awarding different damages according to the age of an aborted fetus. This same principle is implicit in LXX (TEXTUAL NOTE to "injury") and remains part of Bedouin culture (Musil 1928: 494). This second approach, moreover, is still sustainable if 21:22 describes a live birth: the fine corresponds to the estimated age of the premature infant. In fact, these two approaches amount to the same thing. The fine is adjusted *(pll)* based upon an evaluation *(pll)* of the birth: live or dead, how many offspring, perhaps the sex. In a somewhat similar fashion, Leviticus 27 assigns to citizens monetary values for payment of vows that vary according to gender and age (Isser 1990: 43).

The view that *pll* refers to estimation and calculation finds additional support in two other passages. In Gen 48:11, Jacob exclaims to Joseph, "To see your face I did not expect *(pillāltî,* cf. colloquial English "figure, reckon"); but, see, Deity has let me behold your seed!" The second text is Ezek 16:52, "And you, bear your shame that you reckoned *(pillalt)* to your sister."

Other evidence, however, suggests that *pll* refers to intercession and arbitration. By far the most frequent attestation of the root *pll* is the Hithpaʿel *hitpallēl* 'to intercede, pray'—i.e., to call on a higher power to remedy a wrong or misfortune. Though much less common, the Piʿel also means "to intercede" or perhaps "to request intercession": e.g., "And Phinehas stood and interceded *(waypallēl),* and the plague was stopped" (Ps 106:30). Most illuminating is 1 Sam 2:25: "If a man sins against a man, then Deity arbitrates for him *(ûpillô);* but if against Yahweh a man sins, who will seek intercession for him *(yitpallel-lô)*?" Accordingly, one might understand *biplīlîm* in Exod 21:22 as "by arbitration," i.e., submitting the claim to a neutral party for adjustment. Is it possible, after all, that the law grants a husband unlimited discretion to punish a man who has not necessarily injured his wife and child (cf. *Mek. nəzîqîn* 8)?

Exod 21:22 does not use the verb *pll*, however, but rather the derived noun *pəlīlîm*, apparently a plural of abstraction (GKC §124g). *Pəlīlîm* is attested in two other passages. The first, Deut 32:31, may not be relevant. "Our enemies are *pəlīlîm*" strikes me as meaningless and probably corrupt (the context suggests rather **'ĕlīlîm* or **gillûlîm*, both disparaging terms for false gods). But certainly pertinent is Job 31:9–11, where Job swears with delicate euphemism,

If ever my heart was seduced by a woman,
And I lay in wait by my fellow's "doorway" —
May my wife "grind" for another,
May others "bend" over her.
For that would be evil,
And that would be the penalty *('āwōn)* of *pəlīlîm*.

Here, *pəlīlîm* initially appears to mean exact retribution: if Job lay with his fellow's wife, may other men lie with his own (Loewenstamm 1962a: 844). This is the punishment of David: as he lay with Bathsheba, so his own harem is violated (similiarly by Middle Assyrian Laws §55, a rapist is punished with the rape of his own wife). Later in the same chapter, a similar term *pəlīlî* appears. Job admits that, if his heart had been seduced to pride by his great wealth, then his sufferings "would be the penalty *('āwōn)* of *pəlīlî*, because I would have offended God above" (Job 31:28). Again, the nuance of exact retaliation fits: had Job been grasping, he would have deserved to loose all his wealth.

This raises a problem. In Exod 21:22–23, giving *biplīlîm* appears to be the *opposite* of the talionic principle "life for life, eye for eye, tooth for tooth. . . ." Apparently in both Job and Exodus, *pəlīlîm* means something like "justice" or "settlement," potentially but not necessarily talionic.

SPECULATION: If, however, Job is decisive, and *pəlīlîm* literally denotes talion, then my understanding of Exodus must be revised. We must suppose that the law in fact describes an abortion, not premature labor; that *'āsôn*, which I argued means "injury," really indicates the mother's death; that *'nš* implies, not paying a fine, but suffering punishment. We might then parse Exod 21:22–23 as follows: If two men fight and cause a pregnant woman to miscarry, but she herself does not die *('āsôn)*, the offender is punished *('nš)* by his wife being made to miscarry in retaliation *(biplīlîm)*. But if the pregnant woman dies or suffers permanent injury, then talion demands that the same be inflicted on the assailant (or on his wife).

Overall, I do not find the foregoing SPECULATION compelling. While in Job *pəlīlî(m)* appears to connote "retaliation," two other Hebrew nouns derived from *pll* do not. Although the overall sense is unclear, in Isa 16:3 *pəlîlâ* parallels *ʿēṣâ* 'counsel, deliberation.' (In Deut 32:28–31, however, *pəlîlîm* appears to be the opposite of *ʿēṣâ* 'counsel,' *təbûnâ* 'discernment' and the verbs *ḥkm, śkl* and *byn*, all connoting wisdom.) More revealing, but not decisive, is Isa 28:7: "Even these were careless through wine, erred through beer: priest and prophet were careless through beer, were babbling/confused/drunken *(blʿ)* through wine, erred through beer, were careless in seeing, stumbled in *pəlîliyyâ*." As the prophet's job is to see *(rʾy*; cf. *rōʾe[h]* 'seer'), the priest's is apparently to *pll*. But this does not resolve our dilemma, since a priest's office includes both fair judgment (Deut 17:8–13; 19:17; 33:10; Jer 18:18; Ezek 7:26; Micah 3:11) and interceding between Israel and Yahweh. Lastly, we have the names *pəlalyâ* (Neh 11:12) and its short form *pālāl* (Neh 3:25), indicating that *pll* is something Yahweh does (cf. 1 Sam 2:25).

In short, our evidence points in three directions: *pll* = "calculate," *pll* = "judge" and *pll* = "arbitrate." One possibility would be to posit the existence of multiple roots. More realistic, however, would be to modify our understanding of what constituted judgment for Israel. A judge is not a ruler handing down decisions. He is an arbiter between conflicting parties, be they two humans or God and Israel. His delicate task is to present solutions both in accordance with tradition and acceptable to all concerned: the plaintiff, the defendant, society at large, the government and Yahweh. In other words, keeping the peace requires judgment and calculation. In the case at hand, that includes estimating the suffering caused by premature delivery and, potentially, the loss of an infant. All this may be implied in *biplīlîm*.

21:23. *injury there is.* As discussed above, I think this means any damage to mother or child.

you must give. Who is "you"? Is it the offender (Beer 1939: 111)? Or is it the judge who imposes the sentence, as elsewhere in the code (Jacob 1992: 659; Schwienhorst-Schönberger 1990: 126)? More important, who is the recipient? The offended party, in which case compensation is intended? Or God (i.e., society), in which case the law speaks of retaliation, up to the death penalty? The use of the verb *nātan* 'give' instead of *šillēm* 'repay' suggests the latter (cf. Daube 1947: 134–47). See also following NOTES.

life for life. This NOTE and the following treat the Old Testament's notorious *lex talionis* or "law of retribution" (Exod 21:23–25; Lev 24:17–22; cf. Deut 19:19). In this context, "life for life" almost certainly prescribes capital punishment (Luzzatto). (Hypothetically, *nepeš taḥat nepeš* could also indicate *giving* the aggrieved party a child or a wife to replace the deceased — cf. Gen 4:25 — but such recompense would be impossible with eyes, teeth etc., and so probably is not intended here, especially since no recipient is specified.)

The principle "life for life" appears also in nonjudicial contexts. Jehu admonishes his guard, 2 Kgs 10:24, "The man who escapes from among the men I am about to bring upon your hands — his life for his life *(napšô taḥat napšô)*," apparently meaning that anyone who lets a Baal-worshiper escape will forfeit his own life. And in 1 Kgs 20:39, a prisoner is entrusted to a soldier with the words, "Your life for his life *(napšəkā taḥat napšô)*; or you must weigh out a talent of silver."

For Exod 21:23, a question immediately arises. Is this not an accidental injury?

It is, but evidently not one exempted by 21:13. In other words, we are to interpret 21:13 in the manner of Num 35:22–23; Deut 19:5: "acts of God" are true accidents like workplace injuries, not the unintended consequences of animosity. The same might be inferred from Exod 21:18: two men fight and one kills the other without previous intent. If the stricken party recovers, his assailant is cleared. The tacit assumption is that, if he does not recover, his adversary is a murderer, even in the absence of premeditation. In other words, what we reckon as manslaughter, the Bible considers murder. If people wish to brawl, they may, but they risk incurring capital charges if either a participant or a bystander dies.

Exod 21:23 mandates execution should the pregnant woman die. But execution of whom, the male combatant or his wife? Strict talion in a patriarchal society would require the latter (Houtman 2000: 165). Hammurapi §§116, 210, 230 and Middle Assyrian Laws §55 offer examples of a man's wife or children being harmed for his offenses against another's wife or children. Still, we cannot be certain.

What if the pregnant woman merely miscarries? If fetal death counts under "injury," then someone must die. But who? It must be either the assailant (cf. Middle Assyrian Laws A §50 [quoted below]) or perhaps his youngest child, in the true spirit of talion. (One might argue that Deut 24:16, "Fathers shall not be put to death on account of sons; and sons, they shall not be put to death on account of fathers," attacks this very practice, but, more likely, the subject is vicarious punishment; e.g., if a murderer fled abroad, his son was executed in his stead.)

"Life for life" raises one other question: the term *nepeš* technically refers to both human and animal life. Obviously, one cannot compound a murder or manslaughter just by killing a sheep. But if I kill your sheep, is my punishment to kill one of my own? Or do I owe you a sheep? Lev 24:17–18, 21 explicitly addresses these issues:

> And a man, should he strike (dead) any human's life *(nepeš)*, must be put to death, death. And should one strike (dead) an animal's life, he must repay it, life for life *(nepeš taḥat nepeš)*. . . . And whoever strikes (dead) a beast must repay it, but whoever strikes a human must be put to death.

COMPARE: *d.* If [a . . .] strikes the daughter of a man and causes her to lose her fetus, he shall weigh and deliver 30 shekels of silver. *e.* If she dies, that male shall be killed. *f.* If a . . . strikes the slave woman of a man and causes her to lose her fetus, he shall weigh and deliver 5 shekels of silver (Lipit-Ishtar §§d–f). (*LCMAM* 26–27)

1. If he jostles the daughter of a man and causes her to miscarry her fetus, he shall weigh and deliver 10 shekels of silver. 2. If he strikes the daughter of a man and causes her to miscarry her fetus, he shall weigh and deliver 20 shekels of silver (Sumerian Laws Exercise Tablet §§1–2). (*LCMAM* 43)

209. If an *awīlu* strikes a woman of the *awīlu*-class and thereby causes her to miscarry her fetus, he shall weigh and deliver 10 shekels of silver for her fetus.

210. If that woman should die, they shall kill his daughter. *211.* If he should cause a woman of the commoner-class to miscarry her fetus by the beating, he shall weigh and deliver 5 shekels of silver. *212.* If that woman should die, he shall weigh and deliver 30 shekels of silver. *213.* If he strikes an *awīlu's* slave woman and thereby causes her to miscarry her fetus, he shall weigh and deliver 2 shekels of silver. *214.* If that slave woman should die, he shall weigh and deliver 20 shekels of silver (Hammurapi §§209–14). (*LCMAM* 122–23)

21. If a man strikes a woman of the *a'īlu*-class thereby causing her to abort her fetus, and they prove the charges against him and find him guilty—he shall pay 9,000 shekels of lead; they shall strike him 50 blows with rods; he shall perform the king's service for one full month. . . . *50.* [If a man] strikes [another man's wife thereby causing her to abort her fetus, . . .] a man's wife [. . .] and they shall treat him as he treated her; he shall make full payment of a life for her fetus. And if that woman dies, they shall kill that man; he shall make full payment of a life for her fetus. And if there is no son of that woman's husband, and his wife whom he struck aborted her fetus, they shall kill the assailant for her fetus. If the fetus was a female, he shall make full payment of a life only. *51.* If a man strikes another man's wife who does not raise her child, causing her to abort her fetus, it is a punishable offense; he shall give 7,200 shekels of lead. *52.* If a man strikes a prostitute causing her to abort her fetus, they shall assess him blow for blow, he shall make full payment of a life. *53.* If a woman aborts her fetus by her own action and they then prove the charges against her and find her guilty, they shall impale her, they shall not bury her. If she dies as a result of aborting her fetus, they shall impale her, they shall not bury her. If any persons should hide that woman because she aborted her fetus [. . .] (Middle Assyrian Laws A §§21, 50–53). (*LCMAM* 160, 173–74)

17. If anyone causes a free woman to miscarry, [if] it is her tenth month, he shall pay 10 shekels of silver, if it is her fifth month, he shall pay 5 shekels of silver. He shall look to his house for it. *18.* If anyone causes a female slave to miscarry, if it is her tenth month, he shall pay 5 shekels of silver (Hittite Laws §§17–18). (*LCMAM* 219)

21:24. *eye . . . tooth . . . arm . . . leg.* This is the universal instinct of retaliation, self-evident to all four year olds, that every society in its own way seeks to curb. The legal theory of talion (< Latin *talio* 'similar retribution for injury') is particularly characteristic of biblical and second millennium B.C.E. Mesopotamian law, perhaps as a common heritage from the Amorite past (Frymer-Kensky 1980). The older commentaries (e.g., Dillmann 1880: 232) learnedly cite various ancient and modern societies practicing or at least advocating talionic punishment alongside or instead of compensation. Compare, for example, the Roman *Twelve Tables* 8:2: *Si membrum rupsit, ni cum eo pacit, talio esto* 'If he broke [another's] limb, unless he appeases him, let it be talion' (Warmington 1979: 476). The most striking Greek parallel, of roughly the same antiquity as the Torah (c. seventh century B.C.E.) is from the Greek colony Locri: "If someone puts out an eye, he must submit to having his own put out, and there shall be no material restitution" (Crüsemann 1987: 419; but see also Gagarin [1986: 66 n. 63] on the tradition's dubious authenticity and questionable association with the lawgiver Zaleucus).

Although talion is often cited as exemplary of "savagery" in both senses—primitivism and cruelty—wherever we can track the evolution of law, whether in Mesopotamia or Europe, we discover that monetary restitution *precedes* corporal retaliation (Diamond 1957). There is nothing inevitable or unidirectional about this historical progression; rather, the implementation of talion is a corollary of centralized administrative authority, which happens to increase over time in the societies with the oldest records (Crüsemann pp. 416–17). One can well imagine the reverse process, as authority is fragmented and restitution replaces talion.

In the ancient Near Eastern context, at least, one might in fact argue that talion represents an *advance* in equity, by making previously private grievances the business of society as a whole (Finkelstein 1961: 98). In Mesopotamia's more "progressive" version of talion, however, some eyes are more equal than others, and talionic retribution is a privilege of the upper class (Paul 1970: 76). Biblical law, the product of a simpler, less stratified society, acknowledges no upper class. Talion applies to all freemen.

Two related questions pertain to *lex talionis:* (a) is it literal or metaphorical? (b) why is it invoked here?

Some critical scholars follow the Rabbinic opinion that "eye for eye" must refer to monetary compensation: "the value of an eye for an eye" or "no more than the value of an eye for an eye" (*b. B. Qam.* 83b–84a; Jacob 1992: 659–62; Cassuto 1967: 278–79; Schwienhorst-Schönberger 1990: 100–105; cf. Westbrook 1988: 39–83). Arguably, the fact that Num 35:31 forbids a ransom payment for murder implies that any other crime may be compounded, including manslaughter (21:18–19) and the case of the pregnant woman (21:22–23) (*b. B. Qam.* 83b; Luzzatto). Josephus *Ant.* 8.280, for example, believes that at the parties' discretion, the retaliatory maiming may be commuted into a fine (also Mendenhall 1954: 40). But what is the monetary value of a life, or an eye? Perhaps the determining factor is the current price of a slave, and how much the price decreases as (s)he is maimed (cf. *m. B. Qam.* 8:1; *b. Sanh.* 79a; *Mek. nəzîqîn* 8). Although a statute stipulating that an eye is worth an eye might seem unnecessary, Exod 21:23–25 and Lev 24:17–22 may be read as an implicit critique of Babylonian law, in which an aristocrat's and a commoner's eyes were of different value. Still, Daube (1947: 108) raises a valid objection: a fine was already stipulated for a lesser offense—i.e., no "injury." Logically, vv 23–25 must decree a more severe penalty, i.e., mutilation.

A related view is that *lex talionis* is no law at all, but a kind of philosophy of justice (Frymer-Kensky 1980: 232), just as the requirement to surrender one's firstborn to God can be realized in many ways, not necessarily literal (cf. Levenson 1993: 8–9; below, pp. 264–71). One might understand that, by rehearsing the mantra "life for life, eye for eye, tooth for tooth," which he perhaps learned as a pupil (Schwienhorst-Schönberger 1990: 125), the legislator is *freed* from his obligation to follow the precept literally. (On this strategy of legal reformers, more often associated with Jesus and the Rabbis, see Levinson 2003). Although from

21:23b–25 one might conclude that all biblical justice is talionic, in fact none of the laws of chaps. 21–23 exhibit exact retribution, with the sole exception of capital punishment for murder. As Jacob (1992: 650–51) notes, we rarely find true talio even in Hammurapi's Code, which frequently prescribes mutilations. Rather, the punishment is a permanent marking, generally of the offending body part: a nursemaid's breasts, a thief's hands, a rebellious son's ears, etc.

I, however, like the Qara'ites (*apud* ibn Ezra), take the Bible's *lex talionis* at face value (also Dillmann 1880: 232). After all, it is hard to disassociate "life for life" in v 23 from the principle that all murderers must die in v 12. And Lev 24:19–20 (P) is unambiguous: "A man who makes an injury in his fellow—as he did, so it shall be done to him: break for break, eye for eye, tooth for tooth, as he makes an injury in a (fellow) human, so it shall be done to him." B. M. Levinson (1997: 15 n. 15) convincingly draws a dichotomy between two classes of crime and their remedies: "Within biblical law, *talion* ('measure for measure') is invoked for crimes against the person, whether bodily injury (Exod 21:23–25; Lev 24:17, 19–21) or perjury (Deut 19:19–21). In contrast, *financial compensation* is levied in the case of property damage or theft (Exod 21:36, 37; 22:3, 4, 5, 6, 11, 13). The two systems of punishment are mutually exclusive and explicitly contrasted (Lev 24:17–21)." Islamic law, too, theoretically prescribes exact, retaliatory mutilation for cases of criminal bodily injury (Schacht 1964: 185).

The source of confusion is simply this: the text demands retribution *in the language of compensation.* That is, one can literally replace animals "for" *(taḥat)* stolen livestock (21:36–37). One can even replace a life by handing over another human to become a household member (cf. Hittite Laws §§1–4; Gen 4:25). Were organ and limb transplantation practicable, it would be equally just to literally give "eye for eye, tooth for tooth." But that is scarcely possible today—and not at all in Antiquity. To whom, then, does one "give" the offender's body part? To God? To society? It is simply excised. In short, *lex talionis* is a policy of retribution dressed up in the phraseology of repayment, thereby satisfying the respective demands of what we call criminal and civil law (cf. Daube 1947: 102–53). If the originally injured party derives no tangible benefit from mutilating his offender, at least the parity between them is restored (Daube, p. 128).

Which system is the more just, literal talion or monetary composition, is not necessarily relevant or even clear. Each system has its advantages. On the one hand, it does not help a blind man to remove the eye of the one who blinded him. He might prefer to receive payment (Bekhor Shor). On the other hand, talion removes distinctions between rich and poor. The rich man may need his shekel less than the pauper, but they value their eyes equally (Luzzatto). Differently put: talion is the greater deterrent for the would-be criminal; monetary restitution is of greater benfit to the victim.

And there is a final factor, not to be underrated for ancient or modern societies. Talion satisfies our esthetic appreciation for and expectation of a villain's receiving his just deserts (Loewenstamm 1962a: 845). This is why talionic comeuppance frequently appears in biblical narratives of crime-and-punishment and in proverbs for proper behavior. The parade example of retributive mutilation is the ruler of Bezek, whose thumbs and big toes the Judahites cut off, whereupon he confesses ruefully, "Seventy kings, with the thumbs of their hands and feet severed, used to crumb-pick under my table. As I did, so Deity has repaid me" (Judg 1:7) (Jackson 1975: 83).

Yahweh, who boasts "Vengeance is mine!" and threatens "So I shall do to you (just) as you did" (Ezek 16:59), is the great dispenser of talion. Sometimes he punishes individuals, as when David, who took his neighbor's wife, lives to see his own harem violated (2 Sam 12:11; 16:21–22) (Daube 1947: 168), or as when Yahweh threatens Ahab, "In place of (?) the dogs lapping Naboth's blood, the dogs will lap your blood, even yours too" (1 Kgs 21:19), or as when Samuel chastizes Agag, "As your sword bereaved women, so your mother shall be the most bereft of women" (1 Sam 15:33). The criminal can even be an entire nation, as when God says to Edom, "As you did shall be done to you; your payback will return upon your head. For as you drank upon my Holiness Mountain, all nations will drink always; and they will drink and swallow, and they (the Edomites) will be as if they had never been" (Obad 16), or as when God threatens Israel, "For you plundered many nations; all the rest of the peoples shall plunder you" (Hab 2:8). The fates of Haman, hanged on the very gallows he had prepared for Mordechai (Esth 7:10), and of Daniel's accusers, cast into the lion's den (Daniel 6), fully satisfy the reader's expectations.

The motif of fair, ironic recompense also informs such apothegms as "The pit-digger, he falls into it; the stone-roller, it returns upon him" (Prov 26:27; cf. Ps 7:15; Prov 21:13; Eccl 10:8). And the First Code itself includes a threat, should Israelite men mistreat widows and orphans, that their own wives and children will become widows and orphans (22:21–23). For further examples, see Loewenstamm (1962a: 844–45); for Greek parallels, see Crüsemann (1987: 417).

In theory, *lex talionis* has the salutary effect of banning escalating vengeance among Israelites. The biblical paradigms for pre-talionic justice would be Lamech and Samson. The former boasts that he "would kill a man for my wound, or a boy for my stripe. If Cain is avenged sevenfold, then Lamech seventy-sevenfold" (Gen 4:23–24) (Houtman 2000: 167). And in Judg 15:11, Samson slaughters many Philistines who have burned to death his father-in-law and wife, commenting somewhat inaccurately, "As they did to me, so I did to them" (Jacob 1992: 658). We may compare also Judg 16:28, where Samson brings down the roof on a banqueting hall full of Philistines in order to "wreak vengeance for one of my two eyes." Between Israelites, vengeance must be pursued in a court of law and is limited to exact talion.

What about the immediate context? Childbirth is always dangerous, but not because of potential mutilation or laceration. For the case at hand, the assailant of the pregnant woman (or the assailant's wife [Houtman 2000: 166, 168]) is sentenced to suffer the same injuries that occurred during the altercation, from death to—one supposes—simply being kicked in the stomach or scratched in the face. But, in my view, this one complicated case is intended also to address the question of all injuries, however incurred. Presumably to make his point clear—but to the confusion of modern, hypercritical scholarship—the writer lists injuries that are not necessarily relevant to childbirth.

SPECULATION: The old Northwest Semitic *lex talionis* may have a surprising afterlife. Algerian Punic inscriptions in Latin from c. 200 C.E. use the following formula, apropos of the sacrificial substitution of a lamb for a child: *anima pro anima sanguine pro sanguine vita pro vita* 'spirit for spirit, blood for blood, life for life' (Alquier and Alquier 1931). The Punic original must have resembled the Bible's *lex talionis* (Eissfeldt 1935: 1–4), which was conceivably preserved among the Phoenicians and their colonists. But here the subject is not paying the gods what they are owed, but, so to speak, tricking them with a substitute: expecting a human life, they receive a beast's.

In Christianity's double Bible, *lex talionis* implicitly foreshadow's Jesus' famous sayings "Do to others as you would have them do to you" (Matt 7:12; Luke 6:31) and "If anyone strikes you on the right cheek, turn the other also" (Matt 5:39). What originated as retroactive judicial vengence is converted into proactive altruism for day-to-day life.

21:25. *wound . . . stripe*. The exact meanings of *peṣaʿ* and *ḥabbûrâ* are uncertain, but commentators agree that the former is the more serious. Saadiah says a *peṣaʿ* is a broken bone, while *ḥabbûrâ* denotes a surface injury, as when blood is drawn. Ibn Ezra, however, cites an opinion that a *peṣaʿ* is a bloody wound, while a *ḥabbûrâ* is bloodless. Luzzatto thinks that *ḥabbûrâ* means "bruise," since it also describes a leopard's spots (Jer 13:23) and is comparable to Arabic *ḥabīr* 'striped.' And the meaning "scar" is suggested by another cognate: Arabic *ḥabr* 'scar.'

The entire list "life . . . eye . . . tooth . . . arm . . . leg . . . burn . . . wound . . . stripe" contains eight items: the entire person plus seven potential injuries. Presumably the body part and injuries named are paradigmatic. That is, they would cover other types of injury to other parts of the body.

21:26. *strikes*. By implication, with the rod, as in v 20; cf. Prov 10:13; 13:24; 29:19.

In 21:12–14, 18–19, after describing the consequences for murder and battery, the writer then discusses to what extent the law is the same for slaves (vv 20–21). Similarly, in 21:26–27, having just enunciated the principle of talion, he raises the question: are slaves entitled to talionic retribution? The answer is No; instead, they are generously compensated for their injuries. As in Babylon, talion applies only between social equals (Driver 1911: 220).

release him for his eye. This law is intended to curb slave abuse, particularly beating around the head, which may result not just in loss of an eye or a tooth but in death. The Rabbis will extend this law to twenty-two other body parts; they also deal with the loss of baby teeth, which presumably would not count (*Mek. nəzîqîn* 9; *b. Qidd.* 24a–b). Against the Rabbis, however, it is unclear whether the mention of eyes and teeth really is paradigmatic as in v 24 (see above). One could argue that the Torah restricts its focus to body parts whose loss would not necessarily impair a slave's productivity and so might be treated carelessly. The law makes destroying a slave's eye or tooth equivalent to, say, breaking his leg and thereby losing his labor (Schwienhorst-Schönberger 1990: 76–77).

Although it treats the murder or mutilation of a slave, the First Code never prescribes a remedy for ordinary injuries. To release a severely crippled slave would be no favor. Common sense suggests that injured servants would be entitled to lifelong support.

COMPARE: *196.* If an *awīlu* should blind the eye of another *awīlu*, they shall blind his eye. *197.* If he should break the bone of another *awīlu*, they shall break his bone. *198.* If he should blind the eye of a commoner or break the bone of a commoner, he shall weigh and deliver 60 shekels of silver. *199.* If he should blind the eye of an *awīlu's* slave or break the bone of an *awīlu's* slave, he shall weigh and deliver one-half of his value (in silver). *200.* If an *awīlu* should knock out the tooth of another *awīlu* of his own rank, they shall knock out his tooth. *201.* If he should knock out the tooth of a commoner, he shall weigh and deliver 20 shekels of silver (Hammurapi §§196–201). (*LCMAM* 121)

21:27. *tooth.* The equivalence of eye and tooth may seem surprising. Who would not rather lose a tooth than an eye? Indeed, given the ancients' poor diet and lack of oral hygiene, people of all classes must have been losing teeth all the time. In the interests of curbing abuse, however, a slave's eye and even his tooth are made economically equivalent to his entire value (cf. Philo *Spec. Leg.* 3.201–2).

COMPARE: If an *awīlu's* slave should strike the cheek of a member of the *awīlu* class, they shall cut off his ear (Hammurapi §205). (*LCMAM* 122)

7. If anyone blinds a free person or knocks out his tooth, they used to pay 40 shekels of silver. But now he shall pay 20 shekels of silver. He shall look to his house for it. 8. If anyone blinds a male or female slave or knocks out his tooth, he shall pay 10 shekels of silver. He shall look to his house for it (Hittite Laws §§7–8). (*LCMAM* 218) (§§12, 14, 16, 18 similarly assess fines for injuring a slave's arm, leg, nose or ear, or unborn child.)

21:28. *bull.* The goring ox is a preoccupation of both biblical and Mesopotamian law (see below). And yet, such incidents were extremely rare. Finkelstein (1981: 21) notes that, in thousands of cuneiform documents, there is not a single case of an ox killing a human, and only one allegation that a bull killed another bull. As with the case of the pregnant woman, however, ancient legal scholars may simply have been fascinated by the situation's ambiguity. Given that livestock are chattels possessed of volition but not full intelligence, who is responsible for their actions? (The same problem applies to the misdemeanors of minors, not treated by the Near Eastern codes.)

On a deeper level, the theme's popularity expresses an ambivalence toward the domestication of very large mammals, especially those potentially aggressive. The productive exploitation of strong, meat-bearing draft animals more than compensated for the occasional injury. It is notable that, while the docile flock is a frequent metaphor for society in the Bible (Eilberg-Schwartz 1990: 120–21), the herd almost never is. The bull is too dangerous and unpredictable; although he condescends to serve us, he demands our respect. Rather, he and his cousin the wild ox symbolize royalty and divinity throughout the ancient Near East (Green 2003; see below, pp 580–83). (For further information on the uses of the domesticated bovine, see Borowski 1998: 71–85.)

Jacob (1992: 668) observes that *šôr*, the theme word of 21:28–32, appears seven times.

gores a man . . . woman. In the phrase *'et-'îš 'ô 'et-'iššâ,* indefinite direct objects are anomalously preceded by *'et-* (see GKC §117*d*). Perhaps the author wished to avoid the sequence *šôr 'îš 'ô 'iššâ,* liable to misinterpretation as "a man's or woman's bull" (Cassuto 1967: 278–79).

and he dies. The law does not treat, save indirectly (see below), what surely was more common: *non*fatal injuries caused by cattle.

stoned. Unmentioned but understood is that the stoning be preceded by a legal inquiry, during which the animal and possibly its owner should be detained. Oxen are too valuable to be destroyed casually. And, as the law later states, one must determine whether this is the animal's first offense.

How does one stone a bull to death? If thrown from a safe distance, surely stones would just enrage the animal. Perhaps the bull is roped as if for ordinary slaughter and then stoned (on stoning in the Classical world, see Hirzel 1967). And why stone the bull at all? Why not just slit the throat? The messy process of stoning deliberately renders the carcass what 22:30 calls *ṭarēpâ* 'torn'; it may not be sacrificed or eaten (Rashi; Houtman 2000: 179). Stoning, moreover, is a highly symbolic manner of killing, otherwise reserved for *human* malefeasants. It is a way for the whole community to serve as corporate executioner by engaging, so to speak, in controlled mob violence (Finkelstein 1981: 27). Perhaps 21:28 prescribes the formal execution of a "murderous" animal, as in the folkways of many peoples from Antiquity until today (see Finkelstein pp. 48–85). (*M. Sanh.* 1:4 even envisions the goring ox being condemned by a judicial panel.) If so, the point may be merely to make an impression *a fortiori*: if a beast is slain for homicide, how much more guilty is a man?

But is the animal really culpable? Gen 9:4–5 (P) states clearly that animals can bear bloodguilt: "However, flesh with its soul *(nepeš)*, its blood, you may not eat. And, however, blood for your souls I shall demand. From every animal's hand I shall demand it" (cf. Luzzatto; Sarna 1991: 128). This is why carnivores are not kosher. Eating a homicidal bull would similarly be tantamount to eating a forbidden predator (Leviticus 11; Deut 14:3–21; cf. Philo *Spec. Leg.* 3.144). And if the beast is considered a murderer, there is a risk of his polluting not just the individual Israelite (Driver 1911: 221) but the entire land with bloodshed (Num 35:33–34; Deut 21:1–9) (Holzinger 1900: 86). The bull's execution may be regarded as talionic, only, in this case, the "life for life" principle equates a human and an animal life (Beer 1939: 112) (cf. my discussion of the vicarious nature of animal sacrifice, below pp. 695–702).

In addition, since stoning generally punishes *religious* offenses (e.g., 19:12–13), the ox arguably is stoned for sacrilege, i.e., "insurrection against the divinely ordained hierarchy of terrestrial authority," in which men are authorized to kill cattle but not vice versa (cf. Finkelstein 1981: 28, 47). For the same reason, the animal party to an incident of sexual bestiality must be killed for violating Yahweh's primordial distinctions among the species (Lev 20:15–16 [P]) (Fensham 1988: 88). For eliminating sources of pollution, the technique of stoning possesses a special advantage: there is no actual contact between executed and executioner (cf. Exod 19:13) (Jackson 1975: 113–14).

According to 21:28, the guiltless owner, too, is punished: not with a judicial penalty but with the loss of his bull. He is not indemnified by the community. Thus, besides disease, theft and predation, the assumed risks of cattle raising include owning a dangerous ox.

eaten. Meat-eating is intimately connected with sacrifice, for one must share the first taste with Yahweh upon an altar (see pp. 695–96). Neither human nor Deity should consume the flesh of a homicidal beast, which would pollute the altar with bloodguilt (cf. Westbrook 1988: 87–88). Such an offering could even be construed as an indirect human sacrifice! To judge from the passive "may not be eaten," the meat cannot be sold as food to non-Israelites either (also Lev 17:15; contrast Deut 14:21). The Rabbis dispute whether it may be put to other purposes; see *b. B. Qam.* 41a; *Qidd.* 56b; Rashbam.

clear. The owner of the bull cannot be prosecuted for negligent homicide.

COMPARE: If an ox gores to death a man while it is passing through the streets, that case has no basis for a claim (Hammurapi §250). (*LCMAM* 128)

21:29. *gorer bull.* An ox can kill only once, before it is destroyed. The inveterate gorer *(naggāḥ)* treated by 21:29 has not previously taken human life, but it has demonstrated its potential to do so by persistent, aggressive behavior toward other oxen. In such cases, the law implies, the owner must take responsibility for protecting the public from future occurrences. If he fails to do so, he incurs capital punishment, even for a first offense.

yesterday-the day before. The expression *təmōl šilšōm* refers to the past in general, not literally the previous two days.

it was warned about. The subject of the verb *hûʿad* might be either the bull or the fact of its being dangerous. The former alternative is suggested by Talmudic *mûʿād,* describing a dangerous beast about which its owner was warned.

The verb's passive voice conceals who is responsible for warning the owner—it would seem that everybody is. The parallel Mesopotamian law entrusts this task to the municipal authorities, and similarly in Exodus, *hûʿad* may imply a formal procedure with the calling of witnesses *(ʿēdîm)* or a public remonstrance before witnesses (cf. *b. B. Qam.* 112b; Cazelles 1946: 58; Jacob 1992: 666).

guard it. This might refer literally to confining the animal, but possibly *šmr* indicates precautions in general; e.g., Hammurapi §251 envisions blunting or buffering the horns (see below). For further discussion, see Paul (1970: 80–81 n. 6).

put to death. The text reads simply *yûmāt,* without the emphatic infinitive *môt.* Is the distinction meaningful? Is this a milder sentence (McNeile 1908: 130; Beer 1939: 112)? Despite liberalizing Rabbinic tradition, it is unlikely that v 29 simply *predicts* that God will avenge the fault (*Mek. nəzîqîn* 10 [cf. *b. B. Qam.* 84a]; Rashi; Ramban; Jacob 1992: 667) or that the owner "deserves to die" (ibn Ezra). The Rabbis are attempting to reconcile 21:29 with Num 35:31, which forbids commuting a death sentence with a fine, by denying that 21:29 describes a capital offense at all. But even some Jewish sources admit the obvious sense of v 29: the negligent owner will be executed (*Tg. Onqelos*; Bekhor Shor; Luzzatto), unless the kinfolk of the slain accept a ransom (v 30). I would understand the lack of the infinitive absolute as leaving options open, "he *may* be put to death" (Holzinger 1900: 87).

The basic principle seems simple: all murderers must die (21:12). But the First Code revels in the ambiguous. What if the death is a simple accident, if it is a by-product of a fight, if a fetus dies, if a slave dies, if the death is caused indirectly by an animal? Only in the last case is blood money an option.

21:30. *ransom.* As we have observed, 21:30 appears to contradict Num 35:31 (P), which bans all monetary compensation for murder. But the case of the dangerous ox is the proverbial "exception that proves the rule." It is really one of negligence as opposed to homicide, and so damages may be awarded (ibn Ezra). As Luzzatto observes, whether the ransom is set by the court or by the victim's kin is unstated. Perhaps it is negotiated by the court on behalf of the family, as apparently in the case of the pregnant woman (see NOTES to 21:22). On the noun *kōper* 'ransom' and the root *kpr*, see below, pp. 385–86, 466–68.

his life's redemption. It is unclear whether "his" refers to the slain person or to the owner, whose own life is forfeit (*Mek. nəzîqîn* 10).

COMPARE: If an ox is a gorer and the ward authorities so notify its owner, but he fails to keep his ox in check and it gores a man and thus causes his death, the owner of the ox shall weigh and deliver 40 shekels of silver (Eshnunna §54). (*LCMAM* 67)

If a man's ox is a known gorer, and the authorities of his city quarter notify him that it is a known gorer, but he does not blunt (?) its horns or control his ox, and that ox gores to death a member of the *awīlu*-class, he (the owner) shall give 30 shekels of silver (Hammurapi §251). (*LCMAM* 128)

21:31. *son . . . daughter.* These must be minors—otherwise why distinguish them from the "man" and "woman" of v 28 (Rashi)? Apparently there was some question as to whether the life of a free minor was worth that of an adult. The answer is yes; contrast the law for slaves that follows.

A second consideration may be that this arguably superfluous clause implicitly rejects the Mesopotamian version of talion, whereby the owner's son or daughter might be executed (Müller 1903: 166–69; Sarna 1991: 128). The following laws will illustrate:

COMPARE: *116.* If the distrainee should die from the effects of a beating or other physical abuse while in the house of her or his distrainer, the owner of the distrainee shall charge and convict his merchant, and if (the distrainee is) the man's son, they shall kill his (the distrainer's) son; if the man's slave, he shall weigh and deliver 20 shekels of silver; moreover, he shall forfeit whatever he originally gave as the loan.

209. If an *awīlu* strikes a woman of the *awīlu*-class and thereby causes her to miscarry her fetus, he shall weigh and deliver 10 shekels of silver for her fetus. 210. If that woman should die, they shall kill his daughter.

229. If a builder constructs a house for a man but does not make his work sound, and the house that he constructs collapses and causes the death of the householder, that builder shall be killed. 230. If it should cause the death of a son of the householder, they shall kill a son of that builder (Hammurapi §§116, 209–10, 229–30). (*LCMAM* 103, 122, 125)

gores. One must supply "and he dies."

this case. I.e., the rules for injuries to adults.

21:32. *manservant.* A bondsman is here regarded as a chattel, not as a full human. The case is intermediate between one bull killing another and a bull killing a freeman. Notably, when a slave is murdered by a master, the slain is probably accounted a full human (cf. NOTE to 21:20, "he must be avenged, avenged"); when a slave is killed by an animal, the slain is property (Paul 1970: 83). The only reason for the distinction I can conceive is that the law in 21:20–21 can potentially deter masters from slave abuse, whereas bulls will always be bulls.

gores. One must again supply "and he dies."

thirty shekels. Since the price of a slave varied, ibn Ezra (shorter commentary) plausibly opines that thirty shekels is the *average* price of a slave. In late Late Bronze Age Syria, this would have been a reasonable evaluation (Mendelsohn 1955: 68). The older laws of Eshnunna and Hammurapi value the slave's life more cheaply (see below), so presumably there was inflation over the centuries (but the Mesopotamian and Israelite shekels were not of the same weight).

The law for gored slaves does not trouble to distinguish between a bull's first offense and the inveterate gorer. There may have been more severe consequences for the owner if his bull presented a known hazard.

COMPARE: If it gores a slave and thus causes his death, he shall weigh and deliver 15 shekels of silver (Eshnunna §55). (*LCMAM* 67)

If it is a man's slave (who is fatally gored), he shall give 20 shekels of silver (Hammurapi §252). (*LCMAM* 128)

21:33. *opens.* To "open" a pit presumably is to uncover one that was dug previously and covered over or filled in (Saadiah; Rashi); cf. Gen 26:15. Having opened a hole, one is obliged to keep it covered with planks or surrounded by a fence, so that it may conveniently be used without the risk of persons or animals falling in (Josephus *Ant.* 4.8.283; Philo *Spec. Leg.* 3.147). As Jacob (1992: 672) observes, the previous law of the bull referred to a roving hazard. The present law is about a stationary hazard. (For Rabbinic discussion, see *b. B. Qam.* 51a–55a.)

pit. The most common uses of pits were to store water as a cistern or grain as a granary. It seems that the original digger is implicitly cleared in this case, since he took the proper precaution of covering the well.

bull . . . ass. The cliché refers to any domestic beast (Rashi), as Sam makes explicit (TEXTUAL NOTE).

21:34. *owner.* According to *m. B. Qam.* 4:5, a cistern may be owned by someone other than the owner of the land where it is situated (cf. the disputes over water rights in Gen 26:15–22). In Middle Assyrian Laws B §§10, 13, however, it is a crime to open a well in another's field.

reimburse. It may be no coincidence that the verb *šillēm* appears in 21:34–22:14 fourteen times, i.e., 2 × 7. The root *šlm* 'be whole, complete' implies making whole a deficit or debt, and also perhaps restoring peace (*šālôm*) between men (cf. Jacob 1992: 673).

silver. Not a replacement animal, but the slain beast's market value (Strack *apud* Holzinger 1900: 87).

restore. The verb is not *nātan* 'give' but *hēšîb* 'cause to return.' The silver replaces the lost animal.

his. This is ambiguous. I assume that the *owner of the pit*, having paid for the bull, is allowed to keep and use the carcass—e.g., to make leather, to sell to a foreigner (cf. Deut 14:21) or to feed to dogs (Exod 22:30) (Rashbam; ibn Ezra [shorter commentary]; Ramban; Luzzatto; Dillmann 1880: 234). Admittedly, Talmudic authority holds that the *owner of the animal* is rewarded for his inconvenience with both a payment and the carcass (*Mek. nəzîqîn* 11; *b. B. Qam.* 10b; Rashi). But then we would have expected either "he must restore silver *and the dead* to its owner," or "silver he must restore to its owner, and *also* the dead shall be his."

21:35. *injures.* The verb *ngp* describes any blow or injury, not necessarily goring with the horns *(ngḥ)* (Luzzatto).

dead . . . divide. Tgs. make the meaning explicit: "divide the *proceeds* of the dead." This is treated as a no-fault accident, even if inequities arise in the case of animals of unequal value (*m. B. Qam.* 3:9; *Mek. nəzîqîn* 12; Houtman 2000: 184). (Or perhaps the money is divided not *exactly* in half but in proportion to the animals' worth [Jacob 1992: 675].) The same legal principle underlies Solomon's judgment that a baby claimed by two women should be divided (2 Kgs 3:16–28) (cf. Yaron 1971: 52).

COMPARE: If an ox gores another ox and thus causes its death, the two ox-owners shall divide the value of the living ox and the carcass of the dead ox (Eshnunna §53). (*LCMAM* 67)

21:36. *known.* The conditions of v 29—that the owner was warned but had not taken precautions—tacitly apply here, too (cf. Jacob 1992: 676).

his. Again, the Rabbis implausibly understand that the owner of the slain bull receives both payment and the carcass (Rashi); see NOTE above to 21:34, "his." More likely, the two parties exchange bulls, a dead animal for a live (Dillmann 1880: 234).

In the case of a first offense, where there was no fault, the two ox-owners shared the damage equally (v 35). In this case, where one party is guilty of negligence because his animal presents a known danger, they still share the damage, but in proportions disadvantageous to the careless owner. The goal is to minimize resentment between the parties and restore social equilibrium (Finkelstein 1981: 36).

21:37. *slaughters . . . sells.* The case differs from mere theft, where the restitution is twofold (22:3, 6, 8). Why is the fine greater when the animal is disposed of? For Schenker (2000: 19), the distinction is premeditation: to have already sold or slaughtered the beast implies an "operation," not an opportunistic crime; whereas the man caught with the goods has not yet profited from his act. The obvious objection is that the thief's whole intent may have been to enlarge his own flock, not to sell the animal. Ibn Ezra (shorter commentary) suggests that the penalty is less when the animal is still alive and in the thief's possession, so that he may repent and return it. The crime is certainly easier to resolve when the animal is still on hand. Indeed, the ideal solution would be just to return the creature without involving the law at all.

five . . . four. In 21:37–22:3, reparations range from 200 to 500 percent, whereas Lev 5:24 (P) sets restitution at 120 percent. According to Driver (1911: 223), fourfold repayment for cattle theft is the rule in later Roman law and among the Bedouin. Multiple reparations are a natural crime deterrent (cf. double compensation for ordinary theft in 22:3, 6, 8; fourfold compensation for a lamb in MT 2 Sam 12:6 [Dillmann 1880: 234]; sevenfold compensation in OG 2 Sam 12:6 and MT Prov 6:31).

Bulls cost more than sheep, because oxen yield more meat, can pull loads and reproduce more slowly (cf. Philo *Spec. Leg.* 4.11–12; *Mek. nəzîqîn* 12; *m. Bab. Qam.* 7:1; Schenker 2000). But why compute the animals' relative value exponentially? (Hittite law shows a comparable phenomenon; see below.) Apparently cattle rustling requires a greater disincentive than sheep stealing. Although Exodus does not directly treat the theft of inanimate objects, 21:37 appears to establish a general principle: the more valuable a stolen object, the higher the rate of multiple recompense. The Torah addresses the ratio only for stolen livestock, leaving other cases to the judges' discretion.

This law must be understood alongside those against kidnapping and homicide, where we find a kind of exponentially ascending scale reaching infinity. For stealing any animal or object, the compensation rate is twofold (22:3, 6, 8). For theft plus sale or slaughter of a sheep, it is fourfold. For theft plus sale or slaughter of a bull, it is fivefold. For stealing and disposing of items of even greater value, it is *x*-fold. For stealing and selling or murdering a human—the fine is the maximum: death. (Even beyond this penalty is P's transgenerational punishment of *kārēt* 'excision' for the worst offenses to Yahweh; see vol. I, pp. 403–4.)

COMPARE: If a man steals an ox, a sheep, a donkey, a pig, or a boat—if it belongs either to the god or to the palace, he shall give thirtyfold; if it belongs to a commoner, he shall replace it tenfold; if the thief does not have anything to give, he shall be killed (Hammurapi §8). (*LCMAM* 82)

[If a man should steal] either [. . .], or an animal, or anything else, and they prove the charges against him and find him guilty, he shall repay [the stolen goods]; they shall strike him 50 blows with rods; he shall perform [the king's service for x days]; the judges . . . shall render this judgment. [But if . . .] he/it should "reach" [. . . (in volume?)], he shall return the stolen goods, as much as he stole, to the full value, as much as it may be; they shall impose upon him the punishment determined by the king (Middle Assyrian Laws C §8). (*LCMAM* 184)

57. If anyone steals a bull — if it is a weanling calf, it is not a "bull"; if it is a yearling calf, it is not a "bull"; if it is a 2-year-old bovine, that is a "bull." Formerly they gave 30 cattle. But now he shall give 15 cattle: 5 two-year-olds, 5 yearlings, and 5 weanlings. He shall look to his house for it.

58. If anyone steals a stallion — if it is weanling, it is not a "stallion"; if it is a yearling, it is not a "stallion"; if it is a two-year-old, that is a "stallion." They used to give 30 horses. But now he shall give 15 horses: 5 two-year-olds, 5 yearlings, and 5 weanlings. He shall look to his house for it.

59. If anyone steals a ram, they used to give 30 sheep. Now he shall give [15] sheep: he shall give 5 ewes, 5 wethers, and 5 lambs. And he shall look to his house for it.

63. If anyone steals a plow ox, formerly they gave 15 cattle, but now he shall give 10 cattle: 3 two-year-olds, 3 yearlings, and 4 weanlings. He shall look to his house for it.

67. If anyone steals a cow, they used to give 12 oxen. Now he shall give 6 oxen: he shall give 2 two-year-old oxen, 2 yearling oxen, and 2 weanlings. He shall look to his house for it.

68. If anyone steals a mare, its disposition is the same (i.e., 2 two-year-olds, 2 yearlings, and 2 weanlings).

69. If anyone steals either a ewe or a wether, they used to give 12 sheep, but now he shall give 6 sheep; he shall give 2 ewes, 2 wethers, and 2 (sexually) immature sheep. He shall look to his house for it.

70. If anyone steals an ox, a horse, a mule, or an ass, when its owner claims it, [he shall take] it in full. In addition the thief shall give to him double. He shall look to his house for it (Hittite Laws §§57–59, 63, 67–70).

22:1. *in breaking in. Bammaḥteret* implies "*while* breaking in" not "*after* breaking in" (Rashi). To be subject to summary justice, the burglar must be caught in the act.

Just what the thief breaks into is uncertain. One at first thinks of a house. But the context (21:37; 22:3) refers to the theft of livestock. Perhaps, then, he breaks into a sheep or cattle enclosure (Houtman [2000: 189] compares John 10:1–2). More likely, however, the text's ambiguity is deliberate. As it happens, the Israelites kept some of their animals inside their house enclosures (Holladay 1992); others were kept outside. The law covers the theft of any animals that involves breaking into an enclosed area (as opposed to, say, stealing a stray beast).

no bloodiness for him. Commentators vigorously debate whether *lô* 'for him' refers to the burglar (*m. Sanh.* 8:6; Rashi; Luzzatto; Schoneveld 1973) or the homeowner (ibn Ezra; Rashbam). Since the homeowner is not specifically mentioned, my slight preference is for the first option, and similarly for the parallel in Num 35:28. The real issue is whether *dāmîm* here refers to bloodguilt proper, which the homeowner might acquire for killing the burglar, or the sanctity of life itself. Differently put, one could translate *'ên lô dāmîm* as either "he [the thief] has no protection" or "no bloodguilt is created (for killing) him." There is no sense disputing the exact nuance, however, because it all amounts to the same thing. The homeowner does not incur bloodguilt for killing the nocturnal burglar because the thief was fair game.

It is noteworthy that an ostensible law on theft does not confine itself to theft per se, but also establishes a principle in the matter of homicide. The author continues to focus on his initial proccupation in chap. 21: the value of persons and their lives (Finkelstein 1981: 39). Having banned all homicide and then made exceptions for unusual circumstances—accident, a brawl, a miscarriage, an animal attack—he then asks whether an ordinary criminal, not a murderer, may be killed without bloodguilt. Making such decisions is the office of the judge, who, according to Deut 17:8, must differentiate "between blood and blood" (Levinson 1997: 128).

COMPARE: *21.* If a man breaks into a house, they shall kill him and hang (?) him in front of that very breach. . . . *22.* If a man commits a robbery and is then seized, that man shall be killed (Hammurapi §§21–22). (*LCMAM* 85)

22:2. If the sun shone. What does this mean? The distinction might be either spatial or temporal. That is, the text might be differentiating between robbing an open-air enclosure as opposed to a roofed domicile. Or it could be a simple day vs. night distinction.

Bekhor Shor's view is similar to the first position. The burglar may not be killed "if he has emerged from the break-in into the fresh air, where the sun shines." This makes some sense: a man breaking *into* a house may be presumed to be a murderer; a man breaking *out* has already shown his milder intentions by stealing (cf. Ramban). In fact, Hittite Laws §93 treats separately the case of a man apprehended before breaking into a house.

As we shall see, however, it is far more likely that "the sun shone" has a temporal meaning. Again, there are two possible interpretations. One is that it refers to sunrise; i.e., if a day has passed, then to kill the burglar would be a crime of cold blood not self-defense. Schoneveld (1973: 337) and Schwienhorst-Schönberger (1990: 177) similarly argue that the man is technically not a thief until he has escaped with the goods, and that therefore "the sun shone" must refer to the time of the arrest, not of the crime. I do not feel that this is necessary. To me, vv 1–2 speak of strangers apprehended while rummaging inside a house with presumed guilty intentions (see also Daube 1947: 91–92).

The preponderance of evidence supports Saadiah, ibn Ezra and Rashbam: "if the sun shone" simply means "by day." Job 24:13–17 associates the nighttime with nefarious deeds in general, including housebreaking (vv 14, 16) (ibn Ezra [shorter commentary]). Houtman (2000: 190) also cites Matt 24:43; Luke 12:38–39, apropos of Jesus' stealthy, nocturnal return. It makes sense to be more cautious at night. By day, a thief might assume that a house is empty; at night, his assumption would be that it is occupied. Moreover, by night there can be no testimony as to the thief's identity, nor can he be easily tracked. Extreme measures to detain him are justified. Doubtless the ideal would be to knock him out and bind him, but restraint may not be practicable in the dark.

Decisive are the parallels from other cultures that permit a man to defend his property to the utmost—but only at night (Dillmann 1880: 234). Such was the ordinance of Solon of Athens (Demosthenes *Against Timocrates* 113; Plato *Laws* 9.874) and also Rome's Twelve Tables 8.12: "If by night the theft is committed, if he kills him, let him be held legally killed" (Warmington 1979: 482). Nocturnal homicide is also judged more leniently among the Bedouin (Musil 1928: 495). As for the ancient Near East, the Laws of Eshnunna §§13–14 (quoted below) likewise distinguish between nocturnal and diurnal theft and their remedies.

bloodiness for him. The law contains a double warning: against houseowners not to kill by day, and against burglars not to burgle at night (cf. Luzzatto). But the sanction on the homeowner is merely implied. Should he kill the thief by day, he himself will presumably be detained, tried and executed as a murderer (Driver 1911: 224; see also next NOTE on LXX). Some may have held, however, that killing a housebreaker by day or night was licit or at most a peccadillo. Compare Jer 2:34, "Also on your skirts they have been found, the lifeblood of the innocent poor; you did not find them while breaking in *(bammaḥteret)*" (Leibowitz 1976: 376–78).

pay, pay. Apparently concerned that the consequences for the houseowner are too vague, LXX makes him the subject of *šallēm yəšallēm* and translates "he shall die in exchange." But the more obvious interpretation, in keeping with the usage for *šillēm*, is that the thief, instead of dying, must repay what he stole, plus damages.

sold. So that he may repay his victim from the proceeds. Bekhor Shor contrasts the Egyptian justice of Joseph, who feigned readiness to enslave the alleged thief Benjamin even after Pharaoh's stolen property was recovered (Gen 44:10). It is unclear whether the owner is still owed twice the value of the theft. According to b. *Qidd.* 18a, he is not entitled, but this may reflect the Rabbis' continuing efforts to make biblical criminal law less Draconian. After all, six years of labor (assuming seventh-year liberation as per 21:2) would seem to be worth far more than a single animal or two animals (Ehrlich 1969: 176). But perhaps not. At least in the Late Bronze Age, an ox and a slave possessed the same approximate value (Heltzer 1978: 86–87, 92–93).

for his theft. Bignēbātô means "in exchange for what he stole" and may also imply "as a consequence of his theft."

COMPARE: A man who is seized in the field of a commoner among the sheaves at midday shall weigh and deliver 10 shekels of silver; he who is seized at night among the sheaves shall die, he will not live. A man who is seized in the house of a commoner, within the house, at midday, shall weigh and deliver 10 shekels of silver; he who is seized at night within the house shall die, he will not live (Eshnunna §§13–14). (*LCMAM* 61)

22:3. *in his hand.* This verse alludes back to 21:37, making the intervening material in a sense parenthetical (Cassuto 1967: 282; for the view that 22:1–2 is secondary, see Schwienhorst-Schönberger 1990: 162–87). Luzzatto observes that "found in his hand" in 22:3 is the opposite of "sells it" in 21:37 (cf. 21:16), while "alive" in 22:3 is the opposite of "slaughters" in 21:37. Thus the basic law is: ordinarily a cattle thief must repay twofold. If, however, he has sold or slaughtered the animal, the rate increases to four- or fivefold restitution, depending on the species. Theoretically, such a law would deter a thief from disposing of a stolen animal, which in turn would increase the likelihood of its recovery (Luzzatto).

twofold. The thief repays the stolen animal plus one of his own. Luzzatto regards twofold restitution as measure-for-measure retaliation: as the thief tried to make his one sheep into two by theft, so the owner is entitled to "double" his stolen animal.

Although the law in 21:37–22:3 is framed to apply to lifestock alone, we can infer, and vv 6 and 8 confirm, that twofold restitution is the rule for all recovered stolen objects (Jacob 1992: 689). The law does not address, however, what happens when a precious object is stolen and then broken or sold. From 21:37, we may understand that the rate of repayment rises exponentially with the object's value. Presumably the judges determine the size of the multiplier.

22:3. *ass.* This animal was not mentioned in 21:37, perhaps because that verse referred to slaughter, and Israelites did not eat donkey meat (Jacob 1992: 681).

The subject of larceny is treated extensively in the ancient law codes: Lipit-Ishtar §§9, 11; Sumerian Laws Handbook of Forms §§iii 10–15; Eshnunna §§6, 12–13, 36–37, 40, 49–50; Hammurapi §§6–13, 21–25, gap e, 125, 253–56, 259–60, 265; Middle Assyrian Laws A §§1, 3–6; B §§8–9; C §§5, 8–10; F §1; M §§3; N §§1–2; O §6; Hittite Laws §§57–71, 81–83, 91–97, 101–103, 108, 110, 119–43. Of these, I quote just two examples.

COMPARE: If he steals a boat, he shall double (its value) as compensation. If he steals a pig, he shall double (its value) as compensation (Sumerian Laws Handbook of Forms §§iii 10–15). (*LCMAM* 49)

If a man steals an ox, a sheep, a donkey, a pig, or a boat—if it belongs either to the god or to the palace, he shall give thirtyfold; if it belongs to a commoner, he shall replace it tenfold; if the thief does not have anything to give, he shall be killed (Hammurapi §8) (*LCMAM* 82)

22:4. *clears.* Exod 22:4 is an ancient crux. The law's basic premise, at least, is fairly clear. A farmer deliberately denudes his own land. (Jackson [1976], however, supposes that he has been hired to de-vegetate another's plot.) The operation gets out of hand, and a neighbor's plot is stripped bare as well, against the neighbor's desires. Naturally, the first farmer owes damages for his negligence. The debate is over by what method he cleared his land.

To complicate the discussion, the MSS are in disagreement: there are two candidates for the verb in question: *b'r* and *b'y* (on my preference for the latter, see TEXTUAL NOTE). *B'r* can mean either "burn" or "remove" and possibly "graze"; *b'y* probably means "expose, clear away," whether by fire (cf. Isa 64:1) or grazing (cf. *m. B. Qam.* 1:1; possibly Sir 6:2). Thus by either reading, it is still not obvious by what method the farmer clears his soil.

Some translators understand that the farmer *burns* his land, since this is the meaning of *b'r* in v 5. If so, then v 4 describes a fire deliberately set to clear brush, while in v 5 the combustion is spontaneous (*Tg. Neofiti I*; Baentsch 1903: 197–98; McNeile 1908: 132; Ehrlich 1908: 251–52; cf. Zakovitch 1994: 60–62). One might ask, why destroy a vineyard? Either in order to clear a plot to be used *henceforth* as a vineyard, or to clear a *former* vineyard for another use (cf. Vergil *Georgics* 1.84–85).

But this interpretation encounters a serious objection. While there is no bar to translating *kî yab'er-'îš śāde(h) 'ô kerem* (MT-Sam) as "when a man burns a field or a vineyard," it is not so easy to interpret the following *wəšillaḥ 'et-bə'îrō(h)* as "he releases the burning." For that, we would have expected **wəšillaḥ 'et-habbə'ērâ*, similar to v 5. In other words, one must emend *b'yrh* into *hb'rh* to make combustion the topic of v 4 (cf. Baentsch 1903: 197–98).

The alternative view starts from the fact that, in all other contexts, the noun *bā'îr* denotes cattle (on the vocalization, see below). Thus, irrespective of context, *wəšillaḥ 'et-bə'îrō(h)* should mean "and he releases his cattle." It follows that, in 22:4, the root *b'r/b'y* describes destruction by cattle, whether through grazing (LXX; Syr; *Tg. Onqelos*; Vg; *Samaritan Tg.*; *b. B. Qam.* 2b–3a; Ehrlich 1969: 179–80) or trampling (Jacob [1992: 682] compares Dan 7:7; cf. *Tg. Ps.-Jonathan* "trespass"). By this reading, v 4 follows naturally after 21:28–22:3, which treats harm caused by or to livestock (cf. ibn Ezra).

A potential objection to this translation, at least for MT, is that it supposes two unparalleled and implausible denominative verbs derived from *bā'îr*: *bi'ēr* 'to act like cattle' and *hib'îr* 'to cause to act like cattle.' The better analysis would be that underlying *bā'îr* is a verbal root *b'r* meaning something like "range," "graze" or even "eat"; *bā'îr* originally meant "that which ranges" or "that which grazes." This theory potentially explains why, in Arabic, *ba'îr* denotes a camel, while in other languages it is a bovine or any domestic herd animal. (Jacob [1992: 682] opines that *b'r* referred originally not only to eating but to digestion and defecation [cf. Arabic *ba'r* 'dung']; on the importance of manure in cereal farming, see Theophrastus *Plants* 8.8.4.)

If the above seems too speculative, an acceptable alternative explanation of MT-Sam would be to cite the common Hebrew verb *b'r* II 'to remove,' paralleled in Aramaic and Ugaritic. In fact, in Aramaic the root can connote gleaning or harvesting, similar to the procedure in Exodus.

Why would one use a field as a pasture? Presumably to clear and/or fertilize it.

In the modern Middle East, cattle trample newly plowed and planted soil to push down the seeds (Borowski 1987: 54; cf. Isa 32:20). Moreover, Pliny *Natural History* 18.161 reports that in Babylonia maximal grain yields were achieved by letting cattle graze down excess growth.

In support of the notion that cattle, not fire, remove the vegetation in 22:4, even if we read *b'r* with MT, compare Isa 5:5. Yahweh punishes a vineyard representing Israel: "I will remove its hedge, and it will be for *b'r*; break down its fence, and it will be for trampling" (see also Sir 36:30, "without a fence, a vineyard will be eaten up [*ybw'r*]). The verb *b'r* describes destroying a vineyard also in Isa 3:14, but the context is ambiguous: Yahweh accuses Israel's leaders: *wə'attem biʿartem hakkerem gəzēlat heʿānî bəbāttêkem* 'and you, you *b'r*-ed the vineyard; the poor's stolen property is in your houses' (ibn Ezra). (In a third passage featuring the verb *b'r* and the noun *kerem* 'vineyard, orchard,' the verb clearly means "to burn" [Judg 15:5].)

Lastly, the fact that Hittite Laws §§105–7 link damage to a field caused by fire or sheep, albeit in the reverse order from Exodus, favors the notion that 22:4 refers to damage by cattle (Cassuto 1967: 284). Somewhat similarly, Hammurapi §§57–58 treat first damage from irrigation that gets out of control, followed by damage from grazing. And, although the tablet is broken, it appears that Neo-Babylonian Laws §§2–3 cover in sequence damage to a neighbor's field caused by grazing and damage caused by irrigation.

cattle. The term *bāʿîr* was chosen to include all domestic herd animals: sheep, goats and bovines. Based on the Arabic cognate *baʿir* 'camel,' I consider the vocalization *bāʿîr* more likely than the accepted *bəʿîr*.

in another's field. Jackson (1976: 140) argues that this cannot be the meaning. For that, the author would have written "in his *neighbor's* field" (**biśdē[h] rēʿēhû*). He therefore emends MT *biśdē(h) 'aḥēr* into **bəśāde(h) 'aḥēr* 'in another field,' i.e., not the field he had been hired to de-vegetate with his animals. This may be correct.

according to its yield. Kitbû'ātō(h) might mean that the offender pays exactly what he destroyed: barley for barley, grape for grape, etc. More likely, however, the reference is to the overall value of the lost crop, taking into account both the amount and the quality. For payments of estimated agricultural damages, compare Sumerian Laws Handbook of Forms §§iv.45–41 and Hammurapi §§42, 53, 55, 65.

his field's best . . . his vineyard's best. The referent of "his" is slightly unclear (cf. Rashbam, Luzzatto). It could mean that the rate of compensation is as if the damaged crop itself were of the highest quality, so that monetary compensation is an option. But more likely the negligent farmer gives his neighbor a suitable quantity of the finest produce, irrespective of the quality of the damaged crop (*Mek. nəzîqîn* 14; *m. Giṭ.* 5:1; *b. B. Qam.* 6b). This is supported by the previous clause (absent in MT), where "his field" must be the offending farmer's.

Assuming that damages are paid in kind, it is unclear whether the injured neighbor is compensated with harvested produce or with the right to tend and harvest his neighbor's plot, until he is repaid (cf. Ehrlich 1969: 178–79).

COMPARE: 57. If a shepherd does not make an agreement with the owner of the field to graze sheep and goats, and without the permission of the owner of the field grazes sheep and goats on the field, the owner of the field shall harvest his field and the shepherd who grazed sheep and goats on the field without the permission of the owner of the field shall give in addition 6,000 silas of grain per 18 ikus (of the field) to the owner of the field. 58. If, after the sheep and goats come up from the common irrigated area when the pennants announcing the termination of pasturing are wound around the main city-gate, the shepherd releases the sheep and goats into a field and allows the sheep and goats to graze in the field — the shepherd shall guard the field in which he allowed them to graze and at the harvest he shall measure and deliver to the owner of the field 18,000 silas of grain per 18 ikus (of field). (Hammurapi §§57–58) (*LCMAM* 92–93)

22:5. *fire goes out.* This law is connected to the preceding by the subject — damage to a field — and the punning, double use of *bʿr/bʿy* 'clear' (ibn Ezra; see above). The Bible in general appears to associate cattle and fire as ravenous (compare Num 22:4 with 1 Kgs 18:38; Isa 5:24 [Jacob 1992: 686]; see also Sir 6:2–3 comparing oxen and fire). The two laws in 22:4–5 treat damage caused by entities lacking volition (fire) or possessing limited volition but no malice (cattle). The law never deals with intentional, direct harm. This characteristic of dealing with the unusual or nonobvious is shared with early Roman law (Watson 1991: 12).

It is suprising that the author did not say, "When a man lights a fire. . . ." Making the fire itself the subject changes the nuance slightly: a man has lit a fire, presumably to clear his land (Bekhor Shor), but it gets out of hand. It is natural to personify fire as capricious and hungry; compare, e.g., "Let fire go out from the bramble and eat Lebanon's cedars" (Judg 9:15). Although Bekhor Shor thinks that this is a case of negligence not arson, presumably v 5 covers both.

reaches. The Hebrew verb *māṣā(ʾ)* fuses two proto-Semitic roots: *mṣʾ* 'find' and *mẓy* 'arrive at.'

briars. These were left standing to serve as hedges (Wevers 1990: 343); Dillmann (1880: 236) compares Isa 5:5; Sir 28:24.

stacked grain . . . standing grain . . . field. The law passes from the most severe damage to the least (Rashbam): from stacked grain (*gādîš*) in which the labor of reaping has been invested, to grain still growing (*qāmâ*), to the field itself (*śāde[h]*) (i.e., the rocks, soil and the seeds or sprouts therein; compare, e.g., Isa 5:24 [cf. *b. B. Qam.* 60a]). *Qāmâ* is somewhat uncertain; perhaps it denotes any standing crop, including fruit trees (Houtman 2000: 195).

COMPARE: 105. [If] anyone sets [fire] to a field, and the fire catches a vineyard with fruit on its vines, if a vine, an apple tree, a pear (?) tree or plum tree burns, he shall pay 6 shekels of silver for each tree. He shall replant [the planting]. And he shall look to his house for it. If it is a slave, he shall pay 3 shekels of silver for each tree. 106. If anyone carries embers into his field, catches (??) it while in fruit, and ignites the field, he who sets the fire shall himself take the burnt-over field. He shall give a good field to the owner of the burnt-over field, and he will reap it. *107*. If a person lets his sheep into a productive vineyard, and ruins it, if it has fruit on the vines, he shall pay 10 shekels of silver for each 3,600 square meters. But if it is bare, he shall pay 3 shekels of silver (Hittite Laws §§105–7). (*LCMAM* 230)

22:6. *gives*. By its lack of specifity, the law seems to cover items entrusted to a guardian who might or might not be paid (Luzzatto; cf. *m. Šebu.* 8:1; *b. B. Meṣ.* 94b). A man might guard an item for a neighbor who needed to leave his home, whether to follow the flocks, to engage in warfare, to pursue trade or to make a pilgrimage (on deposits among the Bedouin, see Doughty 1921: 1.176, 267, 280; 2.301).

objects. *Kēlîm* can be anything from vessels to musical instruments to weapons to food.

it is stolen. Since the item has disappeared, it must either have been hidden by the guardian or stolen by a third party. The form *gunnab* (originally **gunab*) exemplifies the Qal passive (Beer 1939: 110; cf. Waltke and O'Connor 1990: §22.6 pp. 373–76).

twofold. Twofold restitution is the ordinary penalty for theft (cf. 22:3, 8). The text does not address the question of whether the bailor and the bailee had a monetary arrangement, so that one might owe the other money in addition. Perhaps that was settled by prior contract.

22:7. *approach*. Presumably the suspected guardian is accompanied by the owner of the stolen property (Dillmann 1880: 236). See further below.

the Deity. Ordinarily, *hā'ĕlōhîm* refers to Yahweh, Israel's god. Modern scholarship does not accept that the term ever connotes human judges (*pace* Tgs.; Syr; *Mek. nəzîqîn* 15). Since it is technically plural (see vol. I, p. 140), however, *hā'ĕlōhîm* can also be rendered "the gods." The Bible's overall monotheism might appear to exclude that possibility, and yet in v 8, *hā'ĕlōhîm* is accompanied by a plural verb *yaršî'ûn* (MT). Gordon (1935) and Paul (1970: 90–91 n. 6) conclude that the correct translation here is "the gods," in Paul's words a "reflex of pre-Israelite times." This is unlikely to be the understanding of whoever incorporated the law into Exodus, however. More likely, either the plural is incorrect (it is not supported by Sam [TEXTUAL NOTE]), or else here, as in Gen 20:13; 31:53; 35:7; Josh 24:19, *'ĕlōhîm* is treated as a true plural even apropos of Yahweh. (See also below, pp. 551–52.)

Why mention God or gods at all? The text may be distinguishing between judgment by priests at a shrine and judgment by the elders in the gate (Deut 21:19; 22:15; 25:7; Amos 5:12, 15) (Baentsch 1903: 198). According to Deut 17:8–12; 19:15–21, the high court is sponsored by Yahweh himself (see further Levinson 1997: 110–16, 127; on Yahweh and his Temple as the source of judgment, cf. also 1 Kgs 8:31–32). The idea is not unique to Israel; Childs (1974: 449) compares from Mesopotamia the formal deposition *maḥar ilim* 'before a god' in cases in which material evidence is lacking or inadequate (e.g., Hammurapi §§9, 23, 106, 240, 266, 281; on Mesopotamian judicial oaths, see van der Toorn [1985: 46]).

if he did not send his hand. This clause and its twin in v 10 have occasioned much confusion. The context implies an oath-curse *(šəbûʿâ, ʾālâ)* conveyed in indirect discourse, as explicitly in v 10 (Rashi). That is, we expect the guardian, now a defendant, to acquit himself by swearing to his innocence, as in the laws of Eshnunna §37 and in Bedouin custom (Doughty 1921: 1.267); see also *b. B. Qam.* 63b. There is a problem, however. If the defendant were asserting his innocence, we would expect the text to read **ʾim-šālaḥ yādô bimle(ʾ)ket rēʿēhû* 'if he *did send* his hand against his fellow's property . . . , ' the silent conclusion being a curse "may such-and-such befall him" (on the syntax of cursing, see Waltke and O'Connor 1990 §40.4.4 pp. 687–80). Why in 22:7, 10 do we find *ʾim-lō(ʾ)* 'if . . . not,' which would seem to be an oath that he *was* the thief?

One possibility is that the writer, like modern neophytes in Biblical Hebrew, just was confused, and forgot that a negative oath is expressed in the positive (so, implicitly, LXX: "he shall swear that he surely did not act wickedly"). But this seems most unlikely. Another possibility is that, contrary to our expectations, the syntax for oaths in indirect speech differs from direct speech.

Not all find an oath in 22:7, however. Holzinger (1900: 89) understands: he shall swear to "*whether* he did not take the property of his neighbor," i.e., we have an indirect question. Others understand, "the house owner shall approach to the Deity *if he did not send his hand against his fellow's property.*" But whether or not he stole the goods is precisely what is unknown! And for what purpose does he approach God, unless for judgment? Luzzatto thinks that the wording is elliptical; the intent is "the homeowner (i.e., the guardian) shall approach the Deity *so that it may be ascertained whether* he did not send his hand against his neighbor's property . . . by judicial inquiry." One might compare 2 Kgs 1:2: "Go, inquire of Baal Zebub, Ekron's deity, *whether (ʾim)* I shall recover from this illness."

If only based upon the Mesopotamian parallels, we expect difficult cases to be settled by an oath-curse. That is, the party invites God to harm him if he lies. But, as we see, there are problems if the speaker is the defendant. *What if the swearer is the plaintiff,* quoted in indirect speech? "If he (the defendant) did not send his hand against his (the plaintiff's) property," may such-and-such a fate befall the plaintiff—that might be the bailor's accusation. If so, then in cases when entrusted property disappears, both parties, owner and guardian, must approach the shrine; compare 22:10, "an oath by Yahweh shall be between the two of them." The plaintiff lodges his complaint in the form of an oath. Presumably, although this is unstated, the defendant responds with a counter-oath, and finally Yahweh renders judgment. For plaintiffs as well as defendants deposing before the deity, compare Hammurapi §120 (quoted below). (See further NOTES to 22:10.)

In other words, the defendant does not approach God alone. The plaintiff also comes forward and assumes a risk in pressing his suit, for, at least in some cases, both parties may be under suspicion (Durham 1987: 326). Each potentially incurs divine punishment—"an oath by Yahweh will be between the two of them"—a strong incentive to settle matters out of court. Reciprocal oath-curses appear also in Gen 26:28–31; 1 Sam 20:42; 2 Sam 21:7; indeed, all covenants come under this category, which is why *ʾālâ* means both "curse" and "covenant."

One would think that justice by the parties' oaths is a poor procedure. It would work, however, if there were a deeply ingrained fear of lying under oath, tantamount to a violation of the Decalog (see NOTE to 20:7, "raise"). 1 Kgs 8:31–32 illustrates the principle: "In the case that a man sins against his fellow, and he raises against him/himself a oath-curse (*'ālâ*) by swearing-cursing upon himself *(ləha'ălōtô)*, and he comes making an oath-curse (read: **'ālō[h]?*) before your Altar in this House, then you, you will hear in the Heavens and act and judge your servants, convicting a guilty one to return his own behavior upon his head, and acquitting an innocent, giving to him according to his innocence."

COMPARE: 36. If a man gives his goods to a *naptaru* for safekeeping, and he (the *naptaru*) then allows the goods which he gave to him for safekeeping to become lost — without evidence that the house has been broken into, the doorjamb scraped, the window forced — he shall replace his goods for him. 37. If the man's house has been burglarized, and the owner of the house incurs a loss along with the goods which the depositor gave to him, the owner of the house shall swear an oath to satisfy him at the gate of (the temple of) Tishpak: "My goods have been lost along with your goods; I have not committed a fraud or misdeed"; thus shall he swear an oath to satisfy him and he will have no claim against him (Eshnunna §§36–37). (*LCMAM* 64–65)

120. If a man stores his grain in another man's house, and a loss occurs in the storage bin or the householder opens the granary and takes the grain or he completely denies receiving the grain that was stored in his house — the owner of the grain shall establish his grain before the god, and the householder shall give to the owner of the grain, twofold the grain that he took (in storage). 121. If a man stores grain in another man's house, he shall give 5 silas of grain per kur (i.e., per 300 silas) of grain as annual rent of the granary. 122. If a man intends to give silver, gold, or anything else to another man for safekeeping, he shall exhibit before witnesses anything which he intends to give, he shall draw up a written contract, and (in this manner) he shall give goods for safekeeping. 123. If he gives goods for safekeeping without witnesses or a written contract, and they deny that he gave anything, that case has no basis for a claim. 124. If a man gives silver, gold, or anything else before witnesses to another man for safekeeping and he denies it, they shall charge and convict that man, and he shall give twofold that which he denied. 125. If a man gives his property for safekeeping and his property together with the householder's property is lost either by (theft achieved through) a breach or by scaling over a wall, the householder who was careless shall make restitution and shall restore to the owner of the property that which was given to him for safekeeping and which he allowed to be lost; the householder shall continue to search for his own lost property, and he shall take it from the one who stole it from him. 126. If a man whose property is not lost should declare, "My property is lost," and accuse his city quarter, his city quarter shall establish against him before the god that no property of his is lost, and he shall give to his city quarter twofold whatever he claimed (Hammurapi §§120–26). (*LCMAM* 104–5)

If a man's wife should place goods for safekeeping outside of the family, the receiver of the goods shall bear liability for stolen property (Middle Assyrian Laws A §6). (*LCMAM* 156)

22:8. *crime case. Peša*ʿ, connoting disobedience or lawlessness, ordinarily refers to offenses graver than theft. Accordingly, ibn Ezra adopts a Qaraʾite opinion (attributed to R. Yeshuah) that *pš*ʿ actually means to depart from a person's power and possession, as in 2 Kgs 8:22, "Edom *pš*ʿ-d from under Judah's hand." If so, instead of "crime case," *dəbar peša*ʿ means "lost item" or "case about a lost item," whether lost by negligence or theft.

"That's it." The simple words *hûʾ ze(h)* 'This is it/he' receive varying interpretations. Most likely the law refers to any item that is distinctive and easily identifiable, so that when it is found in another's possession, one can say, "That's it" (Luzzatto; Baentsch 1903: 199; Cassuto 1967: 286; compare Daube's [1947: 5–10] analysis of the legal implications of *hikkîr* 'recognize' in Gen 31:32; 37:32–33; 38:25–26). Alternatively, *hûʾ ze(h)* might mean that one can point to a person and say, "He's the one (who stole my property)" (Westbrook 1994: 397). For Dillmann (1880: 236), "That's it" means "That's a criminal case (*dəbar peša*ʿ)." Decisive for me is Hammurapi §§9–11, which stress the importance of witnesses who can identify allegedly stolen property, e.g., unique vessels or branded animals, as opposed to, say, heaps of grain.

the Deity. See NOTE to 22:7, "the Deity."

finds guilty. In MT, the verb *yaršîʿūn* is plural, even though its subject is *hāʾĕlōhîm*, a formal plural that is almost always construed as a singular when the subject is Yahweh. As it is unlikely that the verse assumes polytheism (NOTE to 21:6, "the Deity"), we should rather just register an exception, comparable to Gen 20:13; 31:53; 35:7; Josh 24:19. In all these cases except Gen 35:7, the subject is Yahweh.

In fact, however, the consonants *yršyʿn* are ambiguous. Although MT vocalizes a plural with paragogic nun, we might also read an archaic energic singular suffix (*-an[na]*) or a defectively written pronominal suffix (*-nū*). To judge from Sam (TEXTUAL NOTE), the latter seems the most likely (Loretz 1960: 170–1 n. 3).

We are not told how God convicts the guilty. Is his wisdom delegated to the judges? Do they consult some oracle such as the Urim and Thummim (cf. *Mek. nəzîqîn* 15) (below, pp. 442–43, 523)?

twofold. If the defendant is convicted, he owes the plaintiff 200 percent restitution as a thief. If the defendant is acquitted, however, then the plaintiff is counted as having made a false accusation. He owes the same amount to his neighbor (Luzzatto), thus losing triple the value of what he originally possessed. Compare Deut 19:16–21, according to which a false witness must suffer the very fate that would have befallen the one against whom he testified.

The Priestly Source, which contains somewhat different legislation about stolen deposits, mandates returning the deposit plus only 20 percent damages (Lev 5:21–24). Apparently contrition, sacrifice and voluntary restitution mitigate the fine (Milgrom 1991: 328–30)

22:9. *to keep.* As in the previous law concerning deposits, the Jewish commentators assume that this is a paid arrangement, since cattle-keeping involves considerable labor (Jacob 1992: 694–95). Cassuto (1967: 285) thinks that the law includes a hired shepherd, who bears some liability for the protection of the flock, just as Jacob recompenses Laban for losses to his employer's flock (Gen 31:39).

suffers a break. It is unclear whether *nišbar* refers to any injury at all (Lev 22:22; Ezek 34:4; Zech 11:16) or only to harm from a wild beast (1 Kgs 13:26, 28) (Rashbam).

raided. Nišbâ must mean something other than *nignab* 'stolen' in v 11. Apparently, it refers to an organized cattle raid, as opposed to an isolated theft (cf. 1 Sam 30:1–20; Jer 13:17; Job 1:17; 1 Chr 5:21). The terms *nišbar* 'suffers a break' and *nišbâ* 'is raided' were presumably chosen for their alliteration (Cassuto 1967: 287).

22:10. *oath by Yahweh.* I.e., an oath "As Yahweh lives. . . ." Despite the fact that the loss occurred "without one [human] seeing," God witnessed what happened. He will not acquit the one who swears falsely in his name (Jacob 1992: 694; see further NOTES to 20:7; 22:7). This is the only place where the name "Yahweh" appears in the First Code; elsewhere we find "the Deity" (21:6; 22:7–8).

between the two of them. The expression, paralleled in Gen 26:28; 2 Sam 21:7, may imply that each party swears an oath (Ehrlich 1969: 181; see NOTE to 22:7, "if he did not send his hand," and next NOTE). Similarly in 1 Kgs 2:42–44, Shimei swears not to leave Jerusalem, and Solomon apparently swears to kill him if he does.

Whether one or two oaths are sworn, Yahweh, the divine guarantor of oaths, stands between two contending parties like a boxing referee, keeping the peace by separating the two (cf. ibn Ezra [shorter commentary]). Instead of directly confronting each other, they communicate through oaths in Yahweh's name.

if he did not send his hand. As argued above, it is likely that each party has the opportunity to swear an oath. Confusingly, however, the text quotes in direct speech only the owner's accusation, not the guardian's exculpation. The law assumes that one party will shy away from taking a false oath; otherwise magistrates will adjudicate between them.

property. For this connotation of *malā(ʾ)kâ* 'work, object' indicating livestock, see Gen 33:14 (ibn Ezra).

And its owner shall accept. The root *lqḥ* means "accept" or "take." What shall the owner accept or take? Syr and *Tgs. Onqelos* and *Ps.-Jonathan* render "its owner shall accept from him *the oath*" (also *b. Šebu.* 45a; *B. Qam.* 106a). Ehrlich (1969: 181) compares Ps 6:10, where acceptance implies hearing and belief, noting as well parallels in other languages (see also Prov 2:1; 4:10; Job 22:22). English "take it from me" likewise means "hear me and trust me."

But *lāqaḥ* may also indicate that the owner takes *the carcass* (Abarbanel, Luzzatto; cf. *Mek. nazîqîn* 16 and ibn Ezra [shorter commentary]). Admittedly, for a stolen animal, there would be nothing to take. But if there are remains of any value, surely they should belong to the owner (Hyatt 1971: 239). Luzzatto sensibly observes that it all amounts to the same thing: the owner accepts either the animal's remains or, if was stolen, an oath.

22:11. *stolen.* While an organized cattle raid is not held against the keeper, he should to be able to prevent smaller-scale theft and therefore is still liable (Houtman 2000: 204). The bailee is supposed to be in a better position to protect the item than its owner. That is why he was entrusted with the goods in the first place.

22:12. *torn.* Killed by a predator, rather than slaughtered.

bring it, evidence. Although ʿēd is normally translated "witness," here it refers to impersonal "evidence" or "testimony" as in Deut 31:21; Isa 19:20 (Dillmann 1880: 237); see also NOTE to 20:16, "(as) a false witness."

If an animal simply disappears without witnesses or evidence, then the owner must be pacified by an oath (v 10). Ideally, however, the bailee will produce evidence that he did not himself dispose of the animal. If it was killed by a predator, there may be a carcass; compare Amos 3:12: "The shepherd may rescue from the lion's mouth two shanks or an ear tip" (*Mek. nəziqîn* 16). The custom of producing evidence also underlies the action of Joseph's brothers, who do not simply assert that their brother was mangled but bring spurious evidence in the form of a blood-spattered robe (Gen 37:31–33) (Daube 1947: 3–15; Jacob 1992: 685). A more scrupulous shepherd, in lieu of bringing the carcass, might even take responsibility and simply replace the destroyed animal, as in Hammurapi §263 or Jacob in Gen 31:39 (Luzzatto), or, if he were especially heroic, he would attempt to rescue the animal (David in 1 Sam 17:34–36).

SPECULATION: In addition to the various readings of this verse explored under TEXTUAL NOTE, it is also conceivable that we should read **ʿad haṭṭərēpâ* as "the spoils of the tearing" (Cassuto 1967: 287). The noun ʿad connotes both plunder and predation; compare the phrase ḥullaq ʿad-šālāl 'plunder-spoil is apportioned' in Isa 33:23, and Gen 49:27, "Benjamin is a wolf; he tears *(yiṭrāp)*: in the morning he eats prey *(ʿad)*, and in the evening he apportions spoil."

COMPARE: 262. If a man [gives] an ox or a sheep to a [herdsman . . .] 263. If he should cause the loss of the ox or sheep which were given to him, he shall replace the ox with an ox of comparable value or the sheep with a sheep of comparable value for its owner. 264. If a shepherd, to whom cattle or sheep and goats were given for shepherding, is in receipt of his complete hire to his satisfaction, then allows the number of cattle to decrease, or the number of sheep and goats to decrease, or the number of offspring to diminish, he shall give for the (loss of) offspring and by-products in accordance with the terms of his contract. 265. If a shepherd, to whom cattle or sheep and goats were given for shepherding, acts criminally and alters the brand and sells them, they shall charge and convict him and he shall replace for their owner cattle or sheep and goats tenfold that which he stole. 266. If, in the enclosure, an epidemic should break out or a lion make a kill, the shepherd shall clear himself before the god, and the owner of the enclosure shall accept responsibility for him for the loss sustained in the enclosure. 267. If the shepherd is negligent and allows mange (?) to spread in the enclosure, the shepherd shall make restitution — in cattle or in sheep and goats — for the damage caused by the mange (?) which he allowed to spread in the enclosure, and give it to their owner (Hammurapi §§262–67). (*LCMAM* 129–30)

If any shepherd throws a sheep to a wolf, its owner shall take the meat, but the shepherd shall take the sheepskin (Hittite Laws §80). (*LCMAM* 228)

22:13. *borrows.* The borrower assumes greater liability than a guardian. The guardian has been commissioned by the owner, whereas the borrower initiates the loan and perhaps pays the owner for the use of his animal (Childs 1974: 476).

The creature in question is most likely a draft animal. To judge from the topic's popularity in ancient Near Eastern legal texts, borrowing oxen was as common as borrowing farm equipment in modern times.

suffers and break . . . dies. Unlike v 9, 22:13 does not mention the possibility that the animal was carried off in a raid (but see TEXTUAL NOTE).

22:14. *its owner . . . with it.* Presumably working alongside the animal (Rashbam), e.g., plowing a field, possibly for hire (*m. Šebu.* 8:1; *b. B. Meṣ.* 94a–96b). If he is there, the owner retains responsibility for his beast's welfare (Bekhor Shor). One who borrows an animal but does not solicit or receive its owner's assistance assumes an extra responsibility (Luzzatto).

it is hired. Since almost everywhere else a *śākîr* is a hired laborer of quasi-indentured status, some render *śākîr hû'* as "he is a hireling" (Rashbam; Bekhor Shor; Ḥizquni; Daube 1947: 16–17; Noth 1962: 185). This, then, provokes the questions: who is the hireling: the lender or the borrower? And why introduce this special case (Childs 1974: 476)?

Almost certainly *śākîr* here describes *the animal* (Dillmann 1880: 238). Much ancient Near Eastern legislation regulates the hiring of draft animals. As for the exceptional use of *śākîr*, in Isa 7:20 the term appears to describe a borrowed razor, so why not an ox (Luzzatto; Holzinger 1900: 90)?

it came in its payment. The phrase *bā' biśkārô* is opaque. We cannot tell whether MT *bā'* is a perfect verb or a participle; moreover, if we read *wb'* with Sam, the tense is future (TEXTUAL NOTE). And what is the subject: the owner, the renter (Rashbam), the ox (Rashi) or the ox's lost value (ibn Ezra [shorter commentary])? The sense of the beth preposition in *biśkārô* is equally unclear. And what is the purpose of the phrase? Is it a judicial ruling? Or is it a philosophical shrug: "That's what he gets for hiring out his animal" (ibn Ezra [shorter commentary])? Durham (1987: 309) paraphrases "the loss is the owner's risk," commenting, "the owner had rented it for a fee and so had already calculated the risk he was taking and provided for compensation in the fees he charged" (p. 327). Alternatively, in addition to the rental fee, there was a security deposit, to be refunded upon the ox's safe return but in this case forfeited, so that it is included in the hire.

COMPARE: 34. If a man rents an ox and cuts the hoof tendon, he shall weigh and deliver one-third of its value (in silver). 35. If a man rents an ox and destroys its eye, he shall weigh and deliver one-half of its value (in silver). 36. If a man rents an ox and breaks its horn, he shall weigh and deliver one-quarter of its value (in silver). 37. If a man rents an ox and breaks its tail, he shall weigh and deliver one-quarter of its value (in silver) (Lipit-Ishtar §§34–37). (*LCMAM* 33)

1. If he (the renter) destroys the eye of the ox, he shall weigh and deliver one-half of its value (in silver). 2. If he (the renter) cuts off the horn of the ox, he shall weigh and deliver one-third of its value (in silver). 3. If he (the renter) severs (?) the hoof tendon of the ox, he shall weigh and deliver one-quarter of its value (in silver). 4. If he (the renter) cuts off the tail of the ox, [he shall weigh and deliver one-. . . of its value (in silver)]. 5. If he (the renter) [. . .]-s . . . of the ox, he shall weigh and deliver one-quarter of its value (in silver). 6. If an ox dies while crossing a river, he (the renter) shall weigh and deliver (silver) according to its full value. 7. If a lion kills a yoked ox engaged in pulling (a plow or wagon), he (the renter) will not replace (the ox). 8. If a lion kills an ox or an ass (?) [. . .] in that place, he (the renter) will not replace (the ox). 9. If [. . .] crossing (?) [. . .] he shall [weigh and deliver] one- [. . . of its value (in silver)] (Sumerian Laws about Rented Oxen from Nippur §§1–9). (*LCMAM* 40–41)

244. If a man rents an ox or a donkey and a lion kills it in the open country, it is the owner's loss. 245. If a man rents an ox and causes its death either by negligence or by physical abuse, he shall replace the ox with an ox of comparable value for the owner of the ox. 246. If a man rents an ox and breaks its leg or cuts its neck tendon, he shall replace the ox with an ox of comparable value for the owner of the ox. 247. If a man rents an ox and blinds its eye, he shall give silver equal to half of its value to the owner of the ox. 248. If a man rents an ox and breaks its horn, cuts off its tail, or injures its hoof tendon, he shall give silver equal to one quarter of its value. 249. If a man rents an ox, and a god strikes it down dead, the man who rented the ox shall swear an oath by the god and he shall be released (Hammurapi §244–49). (*LCMAM* 127–28)

22:15. *seduces.* Like other ancient peoples, the Israelites probably lacked our clear distinctions between elopement, abduction and rape. Even English "rape" originally referred to "stealing" a woman from her male relatives. Seduction, whether violent or consensual, was legally an affair between men, both in Israel and in the ancient world generally (Propp 1993; Houtman 2000: 206–7); see especially Middle Assyrian Laws A §55 (quoted below). In Exodus 22, abduction/rape is classified as an example of theft—specifically, of borrowing property and not returning it intact (Holzinger 1900: 91; cf. ibn Ezra). Violence need not be involved. Since the root *pty* refers to taking advantage of another's simplicity, our law can refer to a consensual situation, presumably including a false promise of marriage (Ramban, Luzzatto).

virgin. The case of a marriageable nonvirgin, e.g., a widow or divorcée, is not addressed, as she sustains no loss in monetary value (Ehrlich 1969: 181).

A bride's virginity was an important economic asset to her male guardians. If a man is misled into marrying a nonvirgin under false pretenses, this simple case of fraud may become a capital crime for the woman (Deut 22:13–21). (On virginity in the Hebrew Bible, see further Frymer-Kensky [1998].)

was not betrothed. If she was betrothed to another man, both the woman and her lover are mortally culpable as adulterers (cf. Deut 22:23–24) and violators of the Decalog (20:14). Monetary resolution is not an option. Weiss (1962), however, supports a Tannaitic interpretation (cf. *Mek. nəzîqîn* 17): the perfect verb *'ōrāśâ* implies that "she *never had* been betrothed" to anyone, and hence that her father had never received a bride-price for his daughter.

pay her bride-price. The seducer must marry the woman, whether or not he wishes to (Bekhor Shor).

22:16. *refuses.* Legally, the woman has no say in her fate. She might be prevented from marrying a man with whom she had willingly lain (as perhaps in Genesis 34) or might be forced to wed the man who had violently raped her. In real life, one assumes that the woman's wishes were often consulted, like Rebecca in Gen 24:57–58. Public opinion may also have influenced a father's decision-making.

In addition to the remedies prescribed in 22:16, in real life some rapists were probably killed (Genesis 34; cf. 2 Sam 13:28–29). On the comparably flexible mores of the Bedouin, which include both composition and lynching for rape, see Murray (1935: 220).

virgins' bride-price. To judge from Deut 22:29, this may have been fifty shekels (*Mek. nəzîqîn* 17). The father is recompensed for the lost value of his daughter as a bride (Luzzatto) and as a domestic worker (Houtman 2000: 209), and for the resources he invested in raising her. Should he succeed in marrying her off to another man, he will actually make more money. On the marriage transaction, see Plautz (1964).

This statute concludes the *mišpāṭîm* 'case-laws' proper.

COMPARE: 7. If he deflowers in the street the daughter of a man, her father and mother do not identify (?) him, (but) he declares, "I will marry you"—her father and her mother shall give her to him in marriage. 8. If he deflowers in the street the daughter of a man, her father and her mother identify (?) him, (but) the deflowerer disputes the identification (?)—he shall swear an oath . . . at the temple gate (Sumerian Laws Exercise Tablet §§7–8). (*LCMAM* 44)

27. If a man marries the daughter of another man without the consent of her father and mother, and moreover does not conclude the nuptial feast and the contract for (?) her father and mother, should she reside in his house for even one full year, she is not a wife. 28. If he concludes the contract and the nuptial feast for (?) her father and mother and he marries her, she is indeed a wife; the day she is seized in the lap of another man, she shall die, she will not live (Eshnunna §§27–28). (*LCMAM* 63)

55. If a man forcibly seizes and rapes a maiden who is residing in her father's house, [. . .] who is not betrothed (?), whose [womb (?)] is not opened, who is not married, and against her father's house there is no outstanding claim—whether within the city or in the countryside, or at night whether in the main thoroughfare, or in a granary, or during the city festival—the father of the

maiden shall take the wife of the fornicator of the maiden and hand her over to be raped; he shall not return her to her husband, but he shall take (and keep?) her; the father shall give his daughter who is the victim of fornication into the protection of the household of her fornicator. If he (the fornicator) has no wife, the fornicator shall give "triple" the silver as the value of the maiden to her father; her fornicator shall marry her; he shall not reject (?) her. If the father does not desire it so, he shall receive "triple" silver for the maiden, and he shall give his daughter in marriage to whomever he chooses. 56. If a maiden should willingly give herself to a man, the man shall so swear; they shall have no claim to his wife; the fornicator shall pay "triple" the silver as the value of the maiden; the father shall treat his daughter in whatever manner he chooses (Middle Assyrian Laws A §§55–56). (*LCMAM* 174–75)

22:17. *sorceress.* In my understanding, witchcraft (*kšp*) means causing action at a distance, without commonsense cause-and-effect. This would also include obtaining information without direct experience. Both of these are abilities of Yahweh's servants and various unauthorized practitioners (Overton 2002).

Why mention only the female sorcerer (*məkaššēpâ*)? The Jewish commentators answer that women are (or are assumed to be) more given to sorcery than are men (*b. Sanh.* 67a; Rashi; ibn Ezra, etc.); see 2 Kgs 9:22; Isa 47:12; Nahum 3:4 (Luzzatto); 1 Sam 28:7 (Holzinger 1900: 91); Ezek 13:18–23 (Noth 1962: 185). It remains a question whether Exod 22:17 also bans a male sorcerer (so *Mek. nəzîqîn* 17, presumably harmonizing with Lev 19:26b, 31; 20:6, 27; Deut 18:9–14; Overton 2002: 67). In Mesopotamia, too, most witches were female (Abusch 1989; Van der Toorn 1994: 113–16). But unlike Exodus, the cuneiform law codes refer to sorcerers of both sexes (see below)

Not all commentators agree, however, that Exod 22:17 is aimed at magic. Ehrlich (1908: 354–55) observes that in 2 Kgs 9:22; Nah 3:4; Mal 3:5, the root *kšp* appears alongside verbs connoting sexual activity (*zny, n'p*). Continuing along this line, Houtman (2000: 211–12) infers that the command in Exodus is really directed against all particularly "charming" women, i.e, those of extreme sexual attraction. In a sense, this suits the context, since the preceding law concerns the male seducer, and the following concerns bestiality. But could the Torah really command that all pretty or flirtatious girls be executed?

don't let live. Just what *lō(')* *təhayye(h)* requires is debated. We might have expected instead "Every sorceress must be put to death, death," implying a judicial proceeding (Holzinger 1900: 91). For some, that is the point. Bekhor Shor spells out the implicit brutality: "It means that one does not make her stand trial. Rather, because she is a known witch, anyone who promptly killed her would be meritorious. For if one brought her before a court, she would perform sorceries in order to save herself or work some harm." Bekhor Shor supports this interpretation by drawing the parallel with the command concerning the Canaanites, "Let not a soul live" (Deut 20:16), which also refers to prompt execution without a trial (cf. *Mek. nəzîqîn* 17; also Philo *Spec. Leg.* 3.92–103). One must take great pains to root out witches, lest even one survive through negligence (Rashbam). Her very existence is an affront to the Deity. By this interpretation, the law contrasts unfavorably with the Hammurapi Code (see below), which is well aware that people may be falsely accused of witchcraft.

Ibn Ezra (shorter commentary), however, has a different approach, with far milder implications. Lō(') təḥayye(h) means that one may not do business with a witch, thereby supporting her (another meaning of ḥiyyâ 'let live'; cf. Dillmann 1880: 238).

But more in keeping with both ancient Near Eastern law and ordinary decency would be the following scenario: Exod 22:17 is addressed to the judges. A woman is accused of witchcraft and put on trial. Once she is convicted as a witch, she must be executed. One might naturally be tempted to spare her, whether out of fear, compassion or a desire to use her services. Nevertheless, the law enjoins severity. The paradigmatic violator of this precept is King Saul, who does not arrest but rather consults the witch of Endor and afterward leaves her in peace (1 Sam 28:7–25).

Why persecute witches? One reason is that they infringe on the prophets' control over wonders and divination. Saul, for example, turns to the witch of Endor because Yahweh has cut him off, sending no prophetic messengers, no revelatory dreams and no response by Urim and Thummim (1 Sam 27:6, 15). A more basic reason, however, is that witches are assumed to be given mostly to harmful magic and therefore are social pests. Lastly, in Israel's patriarchal society, 22:17 might be a veiled attack on empowered women and female cultic practices in general. Most male thaumaturges are called "prophets," with a few exceptions; most female thaumaturges are called "witches," again with a few counterexamples.

COMPARE: If a man charges another man with practicing witchcraft but cannot bring proof against him, he who is charged with witchcraft shall go the divine River Ordeal, he shall indeed submit to the divine River Ordeal; if the divine River Ordeal should overwhelm him, his accuser shall take full legal possession of his estate; if the divine River Ordeal should clear that man and should he survive, he who made the charge of witchcraft against him shall be killed; he who submitted to the divine River Ordeal shall take full legal possession of his accuser's estate (Hammurapi §2). (LCMAM 81)

If either a man or a woman should be discovered practicing witchcraft, and should they prove the charges against them and find them guilty, they shall kill the practitioner of witchcraft. A man who heard from an eyewitness to the witchcraft that he witnessed the practice of the witchcraft, who said to him, "I myself saw it," that hearsay-witness shall go and inform the king. If the eyewitness should deny what he (i.e., the hearsay-witness) reports to the king, he (i.e., the hearsay witness) shall declare before the divine Bull-the-Son-of-the-Sun-God, "He surely told me"—and thus he is clear. As for the eyewitness who spoke (of witnessing the deed to his comrade) and then denied (it to the king), the king shall interrogate him as he sees fit, in order to determine his intentions; an exorcist shall have the man make a declaration when they make a purification, and then he himself (i.e., the exorcist) shall say as follows, "No one shall release any of you from the oath you swore by the king and by his son; you are bound by oath to the stipulations of the agreement to which you swore by the king and by his son (Middle Assyrian Laws A §47). (*LCMAM* 172–73)

22:18. *lies with an animal.* The Bible's ban on bestiality (see also Lev 18:23; Deut 27:21) is presumably aimed mainly at barnyard experimentation. To judge from Genesis 1 (P), bestiality constitutes an unacceptable breach of Yahweh's division of the species "each according to its type" and undermines the ordained relationship between men and women.

Some, however, find in 22:18 a religious polemic against supposed ritual bestiality, which crops up mainly in legends. It is true that Ugaritic myth (*KTU* 1.5.v.18–21) describes a god coupling with a heifer; and the similar adventures of the Greek gods are well known (Cassuto 1967: 290). It is also true that Lev 18:23–30 accuses the Canaanites of bestiality, among other sexual offenses. And Herodotus 2.46 mentions an incident of Egyptian bestiality, perhaps to provide an explanation for Egypt's hybrid sacred iconography. But I hestitate to extract rituals from mythology that is equally likely to reflect suppressed emotional drives. As Plato acknowledges (*Republic* 571C), an inclination toward bestiality may be more widespread than its actual practice.

Even if 22:18 is motivated by religious polemic—which I doubt—it is hard to imagine that, for the First Code, *profane* bestiality would be unobjectionable. The ban is absolute. On the topic of bestiality in ancient Near Eastern literature, see Hoffner (1973b) and Stewart (2000: 96–130, 288–311).

COMPARE: *187.* If a man has sexual relations with a cow, it is an unpermitted sexual pairing: he will be put to death. They shall conduct him to the king's court. Whether the king orders him killed or spares his life, he shall not appear before the king (lest he defile the royal person). *188.* If a man has sexual relations with a sheep, it is an unpermitted sexual pairing: he will be put to death. They shall conduct him [to the] king's [court]. The king may have him executed or may spare his life. But he shall not appear before the king. . . . *199.* If anyone has sexual relations with a pig or a dog, he shall die. He shall bring him to the palace gate (i.e., the royal court). The king may have them (i.e., the human and the animal) killed or he may spare them, but the human shall not approach the king. If an ox leaps on a man (in sexual excitement), the ox shall die; the man shall not die. They shall substitute one sheep for the man and put it to death. If a pig leaps on a man (in sexual excitement), it is not an offense. *200a.* If a man has sexual relations with either a horse or a mule, it is not an offense, but he shall not approach the king, nor shall he become a priest (Hittite Laws §§187–88, 199–200a). (*LCMAM* 236–37)

22:19. *to . . . gods.* The unique vocalization *lā'ĕlōhîm* probably shows that these are "gods" with a lower-case "g." If the referent were Yahweh, the Masoretes would have written **lē(')lōhîm* (Rashi; Ramban).

destroyed. The root *ḥrm* entails, at the minimum, execution. It may also imply the eradication of the culprit's family and forfeiture of all his property to the Deity, as in Lev 27:28–29; Deut 13:18; Josh 7:16–26 (Luzzatto; Beer 1939: 116); for further literature on *ḥrm,* see Lohfink (1986b) and Houtman (2000: 216 n. 183).

Meyer (*apud* Beer 1939: 116) oberves a climaxing effect in vv 17–19: "do not let live," "must be put to death, death," "must be destroyed." This may imply that the crimes of witchcraft, bestiality and apostasy appear in order of mounting severity.

22:20. sojourner. The following exhortations address social stratification. How should the average citizen treat the prince, the sojourner, the widow, the orphan, the pauper (cf. Beer 1939: 116)?

As a nonnative resident distant from any kinsmen to assist or avenge him, the *gēr* is a likely target for exploitation (cf. Rashbam). He is called a "sojourner," because, no matter how many generations his family may have lived in the land, as a nontribesman he is not entitled to a hereditary patrimony. The classic example of sojourning, as the text immediately notes, is Israel's centuries-long residence in Egypt (also 23:9; Lev 19:33–34; Deut 10:19; 24:17–22).

Biblical texts often do not specify whether the sojourner is or is not an Israelite. It appears that, for most purposes, an individual's primary identity was tribal not national. In other words, in day-to-day life, the differences between Israelite and non-Israelite might have been less important than, say, between Ephraimite and non-Ephraimite.

It might seem surprising that non-Israelites possessed any rights at all. After all, as nations and city-states, the Canaanites were to be exterminated (e.g., 23:20–33). As individuals, however, they were afforded considerable rights and protections. In P, at least, sojourners are expected to follow some Israelite religious norms such as Unleavened Bread (12:19), Clearing Day (Lev 16:29), blood avoidance (Lev 17:10–13) and sexual taboos (Lev 18:26)—hence the postbiblical usage of *gēr* to denote a convert. Jacob (1992: 703) thinks that much the same is implied in Exodus 22, in which a ban on apostasy is followed by a law protecting "sojourners." In their tone, the following merciful statutes mollify to some extent the harsh absolutism of 22:17–19. According to *b. B. Meṣ.* 59b and Leibowitz (1976: 380), the most frequently reiterated command in the Torah is to treat the sojourner fairly (thirty-six times). For further discussion of *gērîm,* see Kellermann (1975), van Houten (1991) and De Groot van Houten (1992).

oppress. For Rashbam, the root *lḥṣ* refers specifically to forced labor, as in 3:9 (also Ehrlich 1969: 182). But Luzzatto argues that *lḥṣ* refers more broadly to economic oppression, less plausibly adding that it metaphorically also connotes defamation, as in Rabbinic literature.

for sojourners you were. Although one naturally takes this as an appeal to empathy (Rashbam; Bekhor Shor; cf. 23:9), *Mek. nəzîqîn* 18 provides a more cynical explanation. If you rebuke a sojourner for being an alien, he may throw the rebuke back in your face: "Your ancestors, too, were sojourners" (cf. *b. B. Meṣ.* 59b). While this seems unlikely, the evocation of the Exodus in 22:20–23 does convey an explicit threat: just as you cried out to me and I heard your voice, so I will hear the sojourner's plea (Ramban). In other words, Pharaoh's fate can be yours, too (see vol. I, p. 354). The text appeals to both compassion and self-interest (Luzzatto). On Israel's Egyptian experience as the basis of law, see Pons (1988).

22:21. *widow*. Then as now, the widow and orphan were proverbially destitute (Fensham 1962). At least in some privileged cases, however, widowhood *empowered* a woman, since she no longer was under the authority of a father, brother or husband (Hiebert 1989).

Exod 22:20 opens a new section, with exhortation replacing legalistic style. And in fact, the subject—protection of the poor—is not part of ancient Near Eastern statutory law. Rather, it is law's *goal*, as expressed in the prologues and epilogues of the cuneiform codes (Lohfink 1991). This is another example of how biblical law fuses the older genres of law, proverb, royal apology and political treaty (cf. pp. 34–35).

orphan. Houtman (2000: 221–22) observes that a *yātôm* is specifically a *fatherless* child; see Ps 109:9; Lam 5:3. Throughout the ancient Near East, the gods entrusted society and its ruling classes with protecting those without a living male guardian (Fensham 1962). The Bible generalizes the requirement, addressing each Israelite citizen (Zobel 1993).

oppress. Rashbam takes ʿinnâ here as connoting forced labor, as in 1:11; cf. NOTE to 22:20, "oppress."

22:22. *If . . . if*. How to parse these clauses is unclear. We could assume a compound conditional (Ramban): "If you oppress, oppress him, indeed, if he should cry out, cry out to me, then I shall hear, hear his cry, and my *nose* will rage. . . ." Rashi, however, sees after the first clause an unstated consequence (may such-and-such happen to you), as is often found in oaths (GKC §149*b*), followed by a second conditional (cf. Bekhor Shor). If that is correct, then we could paraphrase v 22 with two positive injunctions: "You must not oppress him" and "He must not cry out." My translation follows Luzzatto, however, who sees nested conditional sentences.

oppress, oppress. In conditional clauses, the infinitive absolute intensifies uncertainty (Joüon 1965: 349–50 §123*f–g*; Waltke and O'Connor 1990: §35.5.1*g*, pp. 586–87).

him . . . he. The widow is included in the third-person masculine singular; cf. the Versions (TEXTUAL NOTE, "you . . . oppress him").

cry out. The implication of this common biblical theme is that Yahweh has his ear particularly cocked for the plea of those without resources and recourses. Prov 22:22–23 and 23:10–11 graphically articulate the notion that Yahweh is the legal guardian and avenger of those who lack human protection (Sarna 1991: 138).

22:23. *nose*. On this idiom for anger, see vol. I, p. 213.

widows . . . orphans. As often, divine vengeance is tit-for-tat (ibn Ezra [shorter commentary]; Houtman 2000: 226; above pp. 229–30). Again, we have the element of empathy: in the past, your fathers and mothers were sojourners; in the future, your wives and children may become widows and orphans (Luzzatto).

22:24. *silver*. The inverted syntax emphasizes *kesep* 'silver.' The text ignores loans of grain, very common in ancient Near Eastern sources (Maloney 1974; see below). Paying interest on seed grain is probably permitted, since there is a reasonable expectation of a good return (cf. Lev 25:37; Deut 23:20). Silver is far less likely to multiply through business ventures (see below).

my people. If MT is correct (see TEXTUAL NOTE), the awkward *'ammî* must mean "*one of* my people" (Baentsch 1903: 202). It emphasizes that the following prohibition on usury applies only to Israelites (ibn Ezra [shorter commentary]), as stated explicitly in Deut 23:21 (cf. also Lev 25:36). The lender is reminded that the debtor, no less than himself, is Yahweh's dependent. Ehrlich (1969: 183) frames a homily: "The one you think poor, to whom popular opinion considers you superior, since you are rich—him I nevertheless call 'my people.' "

SPECULATION: In the phrases "gathered to his kin *('ammā[y]w)*" and "cut off from its kin *('amme[y]hā)*," *'am* is tantamount to "kinsman," perhaps on the father's side (cf. Arabic *'amm* 'paternal uncle'). Thus a literal rendering of v 24 might be, "If silver you lend to my *kinsman*, to the poor man among you." Yahweh claims the pauper as his own close family member, under his personal protection (cf. *Exod. Rab.* 31:5). Many Israelite personal names similarly proclaim that Yahweh is the bearer's *'am—'ĕlî'ām*, *'ammî'ēl*, etc.

with you. This presumably means living in the same village (cf. *b. B. Meṣ.* 71a; Rashi).

do not be . . . a creditor. How can a creditor not be a creditor? Rashi, following *Mek. kaspā'* 1, supposes that the law really refers to behavior: don't *act like* a creditor, i.e., don't shame the borrower. Rashbam notes that the root *nš'/y* often appears when a creditor is about to confiscate property (Deut 15:2; 24:10–11; 2 Kgs 4:1; Isa 50:1; Ps 109:11; Neh 5:10–11). Conceivably, the text means that the creditor has no right to seize the debtor's goods but must resort to the court (*m. B. Meṣ* 13:1). Or perhaps a *nōše(h)* is specifically an exploitative creditor who charges interest.

bite. *Nešek* is the colorful biblical term for interest, possibly inspired by the similar-sounding *nš'/y* 'lend.' The law might refer specifically to a creditor who extends the term of an existent loan on the condition of interest (Rashbam), or perhaps *nešek* refers specifically to exorbitant interest (cf. Baentsch 1903: 202–3). It is also quite possible, as is generally assumed, that 22:24 bars all interest. As for the metaphor of the "bite," Rashi explains, "It is like a snake bite that makes a slight, imperceptible wound in one's foot, which suddenly erupts and swells (the entire body) up to the head. So is interest imperceptible, not noticed until the interest mounts and eliminates much of one's wealth."

Loewenstamm (1969) argues that *nešek* refers specifically to interest paid on a monetary loan, in contrast to *t/marbît* 'multiplication,' interest paid on a loan of grain (cf. Lev 25:36, but also Deut 23:20 and compare the discussion in *b. B. Meṣ.* 60b–61a). In the ancient Near East, interest rates ranged from 20 percent to 50 percent, with the norm being 20 percent for silver and 33 1/3 percent for grain (Maloney 1974).

It is important not to impose our capitalist assumptions on ancient Israel. McNeile (1908: 136) contrasts the modern loan, often a business investment, with the biblical loan to alleviate poverty. Houtman (2000: 218) gives the example of someone who has exhausted his/her food supplies and needs charity to tide them over until the next harvest. The needy one would be entitled to borrow from a more fortunate neighbor without paying interest, for "such aid is thought of as a charitable deed; the giving is done *gratis et amore*" (Neufeld 1955: 407). A creditor must treat his debtor gently, lest debt should lead to slavery, as in 2 Kgs 4:1 (Sarna 1991: 138), or exile, as in 1 Sam 22:2 (Houtman 2000: 219). On borrowing and debt in the ancient Near East generally, see Maloney (1974); on the interrelation among the biblical codes in regard to borrowing, see Fishbane (1985: 174–77).

22:25. *collateral.* This statute follows logically upon and qualifies the law concerning interest. In the case of potential default, you may demand and keep collateral. In other words, 22:24 protects borrowers, while 22:25 protects creditors. Although debtors' rights are a more frequent biblical topic, compare Ps 37:21, "A wicked borrower, then he does not repay; but whoever is charitable and gives is righteous." On Hebrew terminology for pledges, see Hoffner (1980).

robe. Almost the only collateral the Bible mentions, also appearing epigraphically (*KAI* 200; *AHI* 700.1), is the garment (Deut 24:10–13, 17; Ezek 18:7; Amos 2:8; Prov 20:16; 27:13; Job 22:6). Is the point that the indigent were so poor, they owned only the clothes on their back? Or that borrowed amounts were generally trivial? Or that the deposits were of only symbolic value? The last is most likely, since in fact the creditor is not even allowed to hold the deposit for more than a day (next NOTE). Household implements (Deut 24:6) and livestock (Job 24:3) would seem more appropriate as serious collateral.

by the sun's entry. I.e., by sunset. In an effort to eliminate the ostensible redundancy with Deut 24:13, the Rabbis (*Mek. kaspā'* 1; *b. B. Meṣ.* 114b) reverse the plain sense of Exod 22:25: the debtor may keep his robe all day, giving it to the creditor to hold for the night (see Rashi)!

Noting that it is unclear whether the creditor may repossess the garment upon the following sunrise, Luzzatto supposes that he can keep the robe for only a half-day. After that, the poor man repossesses his clothes. Thus, as Noth (1962: 187) observes, the collateral is a legal fiction—arguably, to save the pauper's honor, assuming that the robe is deposited in public and returned in secret.

22:26. *For it alone.* Ibn Ezra takes *kî* as "for," explaining why one should be compassionate. Since, however, not every pauper has only one robe, Saadiah and Bekhor Shor understand *kî* as conditional: "*If* that should be his sole covering . . . in what will he lie down?"

Ehrlich (1969: 183) cites (and rejects) an interpretation I have not otherwise seen that reads *lbdh* as *ləbaddō(h)* and understands this etymologically as "for his body part" (in Job 18:13, *bad* parallels '*ôr* 'skin'). While this produces elegant parallelism—"covering for his body//robe for his skin"—Ehrlich observes that it also effaces the entire point, that *all* the pauper owns for covering is his one robe.

SPECULATION: Another difficulty Ehrlich notes with the foregoing is that *bad* does not exactly mean "body." One could retain the parallelism by reading *lbdh* as **lbśrh* 'for his flesh' (*d* and *r* are similar in appearance). But this sort of radical emendation has been passé for over a century (see, e.g., Budde 1891), with good reason.

lie down. As Bedouin of South Arabia sleep on sand, using their garments as bedding (Thomas 1932: 154–55), Israelites slept on their garments (Deut 24:12–13; Amos 2:8).

gracious. Strict justice may entitle one to keep a poor man's robe. But like any good ruler, Yahweh is motivated not by equity alone but also by mercy (Rashbam; Bekhor Shor). After the threats of vv 22–23, God needs merely to allude to the sanction for being uncharitable — as if to say, "I am gracious, and it would be dangerously presumptuous for you to be less gracious than I."

22:27. *Deity . . . leader.* The meanings of the two terms, *'ĕlōhîm* and *nāśî'*, are disputed, at least in this context. The latter is a royal designation, although some argue that originally it means "tribal leader," as we find throughout the Priestly source (Speiser 1963b; for general discussion, see Niehr 1999). In the Bible, *'ĕlōhîm* most often refers to Yahweh, less often to other deities; and sometimes, at least by traditional Jewish interpretation, it can also denote *human* dignitaries. The exegetical literature explores all three possibilities. Given the parallelism with "leader," *Tgs.*, Syr, Rashbam, Bekhor Shor and Luzzatto think that the *'ĕlōhîm* are "judges" (cf. also Mek. *kaspā'* 1; *b. Sanh.* 66a–b; Rashi). Modern scholarship, however, does not acknowledge that *'ĕlōhîm* anywhere refers to humans (NOTE to 21:6).

Rather surprisingly, in 22:27 LXX renders *'ĕlōhîm* as "gods," perhaps reflecting the translator's religious milieu in Egypt (Wevers 1990: 355). We find the same in Josephus *Ant.* 4.8.207; *Ap.* 2.336; Philo *Spec. leg.* 1.53, and Jerome's Vulgate. These authors, too, were struggling for accommodation with a polytheistic environment. The emperor Julian even officially promulgated LXX Exod 22:27 in his futile effort to re-paganize the Roman empire (*Against the Galilaeans* 238C). By this understanding, Exodus requires one to speak respectfully of others' religions. But such delicacy is hardly a prominent theme in the Old Testament.

By the most natural reading of 22:27, *'ĕlōhîm* simply refers to Yahweh, while the *nāśî'* is the king. Thus, in a manner adumbrating Christian-European theories of kingship, Exodus associates blasphemy with *lèse majesté*, insofar as Deity and Ruler are symbols of one another, and both represent society (cf. Durkheim 1915). Already in the pre-monarchic era, we find the war cry, "For [the god] Yahweh and for [the judge] Gideon!" (Judg 7:18). The association is not limited to Israel; for example, a seventh-century B.C.E. Philistine jar is dedicated "to [the god] Baal and to [the king] Padi" (Gitin and Cogan 1999). Sargon II of Assyria boasts of teaching nations "to fear god and the king" (Luckenbill 1926–27: 2.66), which in turn evokes Prov 24:21, "Fear Yahweh, my son, and a king." In fact, a host of biblical passages associate Yahweh and the king; a maximalist list would include Exod 22:27; 1 Sam 12:3, 5; 29:9; 2 Sam 7:14; 14:17, 20; 15:21; 19:28; 1 Kgs 21:10, 13; Isa 8:21; 9:5; Jer 30:9; Micah 2:13; Zeph 1:5; Zech 12:8; Ps 2:7; 45:7; 89:26–30, 37–38; Prov 24:21; 25:2; Eccl 8:2; 2 Chr 19:11. Some of these passages strongly imply that the king was accorded divine status (see Smith 2001: 157–63, below, p. 770). (On the relationship between the Deity, society's theoretical alpha male, and the king, the flesh-and-blood alpha male, see also Burkert [1996: 93–97].)

curse . . . execrate. One may not denigrate Yahweh (also Lev 24:10–16, 23), and one may not call down supernatural harm upon a ruler (on the verbs *qillēl* and *ʾārar,* see NOTE to 21:17). That cursing God is wrong and stupid is self-evident. Who would deliberately malign a virtually all-knowing, supremely powerful, jealous being, unless seeking death (Job 1:5; 2:9; cf. Isa 8:21)? But often, secretly (or publicly) cursing a human ruler is the poor man's sole recourse and revenge (cf. Rashbam and Bekhor Shor); compare, e.g., Judg 9:26–29; 2 Sam 16:5–13; 1 Kgs 2:8–9; Qoh 10:20. Exodus bars even this meager consolation, in the interests of civil stability. The Bible's illustration of Exod 22:27 is Jezebel's trumped-up charge against Naboth, "He *blessed* [i.e., cursed—*bērak*] Deity and king" (1 Kgs 21:10, 13), whereupon Naboth is duly stoned to death.

SPECULATION: In this context, cursing may include more than direct imprecation. Both Yahweh and king were the objects of oaths (2 Sam 15:21; Zeph 1:5). Most likely, to swear "As Yahweh lives . . ." or "As the king lives . . ." to a falsehood would be reckoned forms of cursing, implicitly denying the life of Deity or king.

22:28. *fullness and . . . demaʿ.* Both the terms *məlēʾātəkâ* and *dimʿăkā* are obscure. The first is derived from the root *mlʾ* 'to be full'; the latter recalls *dimʿâ* 'teardrop.' Most translators see a reference to agricultural and horticultural produce, but they disagree on which is which. LXX *aparchas halōnos kai lēnou* 'firstfruits of threshing floor and vat' understands *məlēʾâ* to be cereal and *demaʿ* to be oil or wine. In support, we may note that grain is called "fullness" in Deut 22:9 (Rashbam). Like LXX, Saadiah (*apud* ibn Ezra) explains *demaʿ* as olive oil, while for Rashbam, Bekhor Shor and Driver (1911: 234) it is both wine and oil, related to *dimʿâ* 'teardrop.' Sarna (1991: 141) further compares Arabic *dammāʿ* denoting juice oozing from a vine; ibn Janaḥ (*Root Book*) similarly notes the Arabic idiom "vine tear" for wine. (For a different etymology, Sarna also observes that *Sam Tg.* renders "fat, fatness, best" [*ḥēleb*] in Gen 45:18; Deut 32:14 by a word *dmʿ*, presumably related to Arabic *dimāġ* 'brain.')

Arguing the contrary, however, ibn Ezra observes that "fullness" can be the overflow of the winepress (cf. Num 18:27), and Ramban claims (not quite accurately) that Joel 2:24 applies "full" to wine and oil. Childs (1974: 450) thinks that *məlēʾâ* and *demaʿ* both refer to grape juice, while Schwienhorst-Schönberger (1990: 363) considers *məlēʾâ* to be wine and *demaʿ* oil. Lastly, Fishbane (1985: 60–61) argues from Deut 22:9 that *məlēʾâ* is both cereal and wine. The possibilities are all exhausted.

It is not even certain, moreover, that the terms refer to agriculture. Vg, for instance, translates "tithe" and "firstling." And it is quite possible that the language is poetic. Durham (1987: 329) renders "your fullness and your dripping," evoking the image of an overflowing vat or cup (cf. Ps 23:5). That is, Israel is promised a perennial surplus. Equally plausibly, Ehrlich (1969: 355) thinks that the verse features merism: hold nothing back, from your overflowing to your merest drop.

SPECULATION: Conceivably, the whole verse is in antithetical poetic parallelism, addressing a single subject. In that case, v 28a might have something to do with human reproduction or firstborn consecration. Ibn Ezra conveys (and rejects) a Qara'ite exegesis that "fullness" is pregnancy (cf. Eccl 11:5) and *dema'* is ejaculation, thus linked to the following clause about children. The injunction is against deferring marriage, although one could also take it as a command not to abstain from intercourse. Along these lines, we could also identify *mǝlē'â* and *dem'a* as respectively "tumescence" and "ejaculation," so that the text would ban *coitus interruptus* (cf. Gen 38:9).

don't postpone. Assuming that the subject is agriculture (previous NOTE), this means either: do not submit the firstfruits offering late (Bekhor Shor) or do not treat firstfruits, reserved for Yahweh, like later fruits, fit for human consumption. One must set aside Yahweh's due in proper order, be it Firstfruits, Donation, Tithe, etc. (*Mek. kaspā'* 1; cf. Rashi).

Whether the subject is specifically agriculture or fertility in general, *lō(')* *tǝ'aḥēr* 'don't postpone' sets up by contrast *tittēn* 'you must give' in the next verse.

firstborn. *Bǝkôr* ordinarily connotes a *man's* firstborn. The parallel pentateuchal passages, however, make it clear that Yahweh's claim is on a *woman's* firstborn (13:2, 11–16; 34:19–20; Lev 27:26–27; Num 3:12–13, 40–51; 8:17–18; 18:15–18). Up until modern DNA testing, maternity has always been reckoned a fact, paternity a plausible inference. In the case of small cattle, at least, it is unlikely that shepherds kept track of sires.

sons. It is a biblical principle that the firstfruits of reproduction—vegetable, animal, human—belong to Yahweh. When you have only one fruitful tree, only one lamb, only one calf—instead of putting it to use, you must set it aside and at the first opportunity give it to Yahweh by sacrifice. Destroying the firstfruits and firstlings is basically an investment or a wager. One gives all to God in hopes that he will repay the offering many times over. The sacrifice also represents deference to a Master, who naturally eats before his servants partake (below, pp. 695–96).

What about firstborn children? Here the Torah makes an exception. A firstborn son must be redeemed from Yahweh by sacrificing an animal in its stead or by making an equivalent payment. In addition, the entire tribe of Levi serves God in place of the firstborn males (13:2, 11–16; 34:19–20; Lev 27:26–27; Num 3:12–13, 40–59; 8:16–18; 18:15–18). And yet 22:28 mandates no substitution. On the contrary, the adverb *kēn* 'likewise' in v 29 suggests that the child is treated no differently from a sheep or calf. Tradition, which ascribes all the Torah to a single author, has no difficulty with 22:28, since it does not explicitly contradict the law of redemption. Even modern critical scholarship might come to a similar conclusion, assuming that 22:28 is part of the E source (see p. 147), which already mandated redemption in 13:11–16. But what if the law of 22:28 is older than E? Modern scholarship raises a shocking question: is it possible that 22:28 originally mandated the *sacrifice* of firstborn sons?

First, we must ask whether firstborn human sacrifice to Yahweh was ever an Israelite practice. Micah 6:6–8 is often read as indirectly proving its acceptability, at least in some circles (see the discussion in Heider 1985: 316–19):

With what shall I come before Yahweh,
Bow down to the deity of the *Height* (heaven)?
Should I come before him with Ascending-offerings,
With calves *sons of* a year?
Does Yahweh delight in thousands of rams,
In tens of thousands of oil streams?
Should I give my firstborn (for/as) my fault,
My belly's fruit (for/as) my soul's Sin-offering?
It has been told to you, Man: what is good,
And what does Yahweh require of you,
But doing justice and loving fidelity
And walking humbly with your deity?

Micah rejects human sacrifice. But his language suggests that it is no more reprehensible than ordinary vegetable and animal sacrifice, all of which please Yahweh far less than simple righteousness. Such, at any rate, is a common reading of Micah. But I think it is inaccurate. The prophet's rhetoric begins with Ascending-offerings and yearling calves, which any person of means might offer. Then it begins an ascent to hyperbole with "thousands of rams . . . tens of thousands of oil streams," supposed to please God more than ordinary sacrifice. It follows that the concluding reference to infant sacrifice to expiate sin is meant ironically. The prophet follows the logic "if a little sacrifice is good, more is better" to its horrifying conclusion: the most valuable sacrifice, a child can best atone for sin *(ḥaṭṭa[ʾ]t)* — as if such a sacrifice were not the most heinous sin *(peša‘)* itself. Having exposed the limitations of sacrifice, Micah proposes a simpler alternative: "doing justice and loving fidelity and walking humbly with your deity." Thus Micah 6:6–8 does not afford credible evidence of Israelite firstborn human sacrifice (cf. de Vaux 1964: 69; *pace* Andersen and Freedman 2000: 532–39).

The story of the Aqedah (Genesis 22) revolves on a similar point. Need one go so far as to kill one's wife's firstborn, in hopes that more sons and daughters will follow? The story's moral: while God is theoretically entitled to the literal sacrifice of the child, an animal sacrifice obtains the same reward (Levenson 1993: 111–12). Like Micah 6:6–8, Genesis 22 proves that firstborn sacrifice existed as a concept in the writers' minds, not necessarily as an institution.

Another passage often cited to support the notion that Exod 22:28 authorizes ritual infanticide of the firstborn to Yahweh is Ezek 20:18–31a:

By your fathers' statutes do not walk, and their laws do not keep, and with their turd-gods do not be defiled. I am Yahweh your deity; by my statutes walk and my laws keep, and do them. . . . But the sons disobeyed me: by my statutes they did not walk, and my laws they did not keep by doing them, which men may do and stay alive through them. . . . Because my laws they did not do and my statutes they spurned . . . I in turn gave them statutes that were not good and laws by which one cannot stay alive, and I defiled them with their offerings, *transferring* every *loosening* of the womb *(bəha‘ăbîr kol-peṭer rāḥam)*, so that I might horrify them. . . . You have polluted yourselves in your fathers' way . . .

and in raising your offerings, in transferring your sons in fire (*bəha'ăbîr bənêkem bā'ēš*), you are polluting yourselves with all your turd-gods until this day.

Ezekiel explicitly claims that Yahweh had commanded firstborn sacrifice—in order to make the people sin! (Cf. my discussion of theodicy in vol. I, pp. 353–54.) The relevance for Exod 22:28 is ambiguous. On the one hand, it is hard to imagine what Ezekiel is referring to, if not to Exod 22:28 alongside 34:19 (cf. Heider 1985: 372 n. 737). On the other hand, in the Exodus narrative the people have not yet sinned, and Yahweh has no reason to punish them. This is not a reasonable reading of Exodus. Given the overall polemical cast of Ezekiel's prophecy and the manner in which he ironically bends older traditions for rhetorical ends (Levitt Kohn 2002), I do not consider him a reliable exegete.

Ezekiel's reference to "*transferring* your sons in the fire" brings firstborn sacrifice into the orbit of an originally distinct practice: the mass burning of young children, irrespective of sex and birth order. Characteristic vocabulary associated with this rite includes *he'ĕbîr* 'transfer, make pass,' *bā'ēš* 'into/through the fire,' *śārap* 'burn' and, above all, *mōlek*, a term whose meaning is disputed (see below). At least in Jerusalem, these practices were carried out in a place called *tōpet*, possibly an Aramaic term for "oven" (cf. Smith 1927: 377 n. 2). Passages referring to the Topheth-cult include Lev 18:21; 20:2–5; Deut 12:31; 18:10; 2 Kgs 16:3; 17:17; 21:6; 23:10; Isa 30:33; 57:5, 9; Jer 7:30–32; 19:5; 32:35; Ezek 16:21; 20:25–31; 23:36–39; Ps 106:37–38; cf. also Isa 30:27–33; 57:9; Jer 2:23; 3:24.

What went on at the Topheth is the subject of considerable debate. Some note correctly that *he'ĕbîr* need not refer to actual sacrifice (e.g., Weinfeld 1972). But the accompanying references to fire and burning (esp. Jer 7:31; 32:35) make it hard to imagine anything other than a burnt offering (Smith 1975: 478).

The Bible's tarring the Topheth-cult as Canaanite (Lev 18:21, 24–30; Deut 12:31; 18:10–12; 2 Kgs 16:3) is amply borne out by evidence from the Punic colonies established around the Mediterranean, the heirs of Canaanite culture. Greek and Latin texts from the fifth century B.C.E. to the fifth century C.E. consistently describe the Phoenicians and their Punic descendants as responding to emergencies by sacrificing children to the local high god, generally called *Kronos* in Greek and *Saturnus* in Latin; authors include Sophocles, Cicero, Diodorus Siculus, Pliny the Elder, Plutarch, Justin Martyr, Tertullian, Porphyry and lesser luminaries (Mosca 1975: 2–35; Brown 1991: 21–35). For example, Porphyry *On Abstinence* 2.56 cites war, drought and plague as occasions for ritual infanticide, while Diodorus Siculus (20.14.5) records the sacrifice of five hundred Carthaginian children during a military crisis. He also describes the infamous bronze statue of Kronos, down whose arms the tiny victims rolled into a fire pit. In the second century C.E., a Carthaginian-turned-Christian describes the practice, though outlawed, as still carried out secretly in his own day (Tertullian *Apology* IX:2–4). Jewish midrashim describe the cult in the same lurid terms as the Greco-Roman, with babies tumbling down an idol's brazen arms into an inferno (Moore 1897). To slightly mitigate the horror, most Greco-Roman sources imply that the babies were first slaughtered then burnt (but see Mosca [1975: 22–23] on Kleitarchos's reports to the contrary).

In addition to this hearsay evidence, archaeologists have uncovered at Carthage some 20,000 burnt babies, both full-term and aborted, together with the bones of many sacrificial lambs or kids (Stager 1980). Similar discoveries have been made at Punic sites in Sousse (Tunisia), Motya (Sicily) and Tharros, Sulcis, Monte Sirae, Bythia and Nova (Sardinia) (for a general discussion, see Brown 1991). From Pozo Moro, Spain, we even have a large crematorium with a relief showing a two-headed monster and a horse-headed monster probably dining on children and a pig (Heider 1985: 188–91; Almagro-Gorbea 1982: 254, pl. LIV). We should note that neither the Israelite nor the Phoenician mainlands have yielded comparable finds, probably because continuous occupation has either destroyed the evidence or made it inaccessible. In Late Bronze Age Jordan, however, a temple was used for ritual human cremations, possibly in a sacrificial context (Hennessey 1985).

What did the Punic colonists call ritual infanticide? Although their interpretation is disputed, inscriptions in Punic and Latin indicate that one type of offering was called *molk*, the exact cognate of Hebrew *mōlek* (Israelite pronunciation *mulk* or *molk*). But the Punic *molk* was not necessarily a human sacrifice; it could also be a lamb as a substitute. In fact, several Punic stelae from Algeria describe the *molk* sacrifice in Latin as *anima pro anima sanguine pro sanguine vita pro vita* 'soul for soul, blood for blood, life for life' . . . *agnum pro vikario* 'a lamb as a substitute,' i.e., for a child (Alquier and Alquier 1931: 24). The term *molk* may also appear on a mainland Phoenician stele (Gianto 1987; Smith 2002: 172). The term's etymology, however, remains a mystery. In a Canaanite dialect, one would expect *molk* to mean something like "kingship" (see below).

Prior to the Punic evidence, Hebrew *mōlek* had always been considered a god's name, "Molech," to whom an infant was "transferred," just as one may "transfer (*he'ĕbîr*)" a child to Yahweh (13:12) or an inheritance to an heir (Num 27:7–8). Some still argue for this interpretation, citing evidence for a god *mālik* and chthonian deities called *mlkm* (Weinfeld 1972; Heider 1985; Day 1989). But, since we would reconstruct the Israelite pronunciation of *mōlek* as *mulk/molk* on independent grounds, the similarity to Punic *molk* cannot be dismissed as coincidence. Despite some ambiguities, Hebrew *mōlek*, too, is best understood as a type of offering (Eissfeldt 1935; Olyan 1988: 11–13, 53, 59 n. 93, 65–69; Ackerman 1992: 117–43; Müller 1997). Although *mōleks* might be offered to Baal (Jer 19:5), most were probably directed to Yahweh, evoking Jeremiah's vehement denials that God had ever required such a thing (Jer 7:31; 19:5; 32:35). The *mōlek* apparently differed from an ordinary altar sacrifice, although a human may also be sacrificed as an *'ōlâ* 'Ascending-offering' (Genesis 22; 2 Kgs 3:27). *Molk* was evidently a special procedure, performed not on an ordinary altar but on a pyre at the Topheth.

SPECULATION: As a compromise, I would propose that *molk/mōlek* was *both* a deity and a type of offering (also Edelman 1987). Similarly, Hebrew *qōdeš*

'Holiness' connotes an offering, while in related languages the cognate *qudš* is a goddess, and the plural *qdšm* denotes gods in general (see vol. I, p. 527). More remote parallels are *'aštārôt* 'Astarte-goddesses' or 'young animals' (Deut 7:13; 28:4, 18, 51) and *'ăšērâ* '(the goddess) Asherah' or a 'sacred pole' (NOTE to 34:13).

At a remove of over two millennia, it is hard to know, let alone to understand, what used to happen at the Israelite Topheth and analogous shrines along the Mediterranean. Here is a summary of my impressions, along with an important *caveat:*

I take it as axiomatic that a kind of natural selection weeds out customs inimical to the survival of the family and the society. Infanticide per se is not maladaptive in this sense. Many communities employ exposure or abortion to control the population and eliminate the deformed. But it is hard to construe such "hygienic" infanticide as an act of worship (*pace* Stager and Wolff 1984). And killing every male firstborn, supposedly mandated by 22:28, would be no less than Darwinian suicide. Below (pp. 309, 529–31, 695–701), I shall argue that animal sacrifice *symbolizes* human sacrifice (see also vol. I, pp. 454–56). But this need not imply an actual superseded practice of ritual infanticide, at least in ordinary times.

What about extraordinary times, in crises brought on by plague or invasion? Then people would turn to asceticism: fasting, sackcloth-and-ashes, self-flagellation, etc. With death all around, it would be natural to assume that the gods are no longer satisfied with *ersatz* sacrifices. While Death cannot be repelled completely, perhaps he can be controlled if society selects his victims for him. One can imagine different experiments to discover what human offering would appease the gods. One expedient would be to sacrifice a royal child on behalf of the entire kingdom. Of the Carthaginians, Diodorus Siculus *Bibliotheca Historica* 20.14 reports that only the "noblest" *(tous kratistous)* were offered as infant sacrifices. Famously, Sir James Frazer's *Golden Bough* posited that kings were originally killed once they had lost the physical vigor that brought blessing upon their people. This could provide the etymology of *molk* 'royalty, royal sacrifice' (and also provide a symbolic background for the redeeming death of King Jesus).

We probably have a biblical record of this practice in 2 Kgs 3:26–27, describing a siege: "When the king of Moab saw that the war was too strong for him, he took with him seven hundred men drawing the sword, to break through to the king of Edom, but they could not. Then he took his firstborn son who would rule *under him* (i.e., in his place) and sent him up as an Ascending-offering upon the wall," whereupon *qeṣep-gādôl* 'great wrath' (i.e., disgust? divine anger?) assailed Israel, and they quit the field. In light of the Phoenician and Punic parallels, it appears that the king of Moab sacrifices his own infant firstborn son to avert a crisis. (For alleged iconographic evidence of the practice, see Keel 1975; 1978: 102, fig. 132a; Spalinger 1978; for the idea that the offering consists simply of gently *lowering* a child as a symbolic sacrifice, see Pseudo-Lucian *Syrian Goddess* 58.) Similarly,

the first Israelite credited with sacrificing his son is King Ahaz (2 Kgs 16:3); perhaps this was in response to the siege laid against Jerusalem by the Northern Kingdom and Aram. The cautionary tale of Jephthah could also be read in this light:
Tricked by fate, the war-leader in effect sacrificed his own daughter in order to obtain victory (Judg 11:29–40), thus reversing the customary substitution of an animal for a human.

A more democratic albeit more sanguinary solution than royal infanticide,
however, would have been to require that all families surrender a child, so that
others might live. We still do this in times of war, through military conscription.
When food is scarce and suffering great, infanticide would be a perennial temptation. As we have seen, this appears to have been the practice at Carthage and other
Punic colonies. The Israelite equivalent is the cult of the Topheth, the mass sacrifice of infants.

Since the prophets considered infant sacrifice a Canaanite abomination, and
since the only culture of the Iron Age explicitly to continue the traditions of the
Bronze Age Canaanites was the Phoenician, and since the Punic colonies
founded by the Phoenicians practiced ritual infanticide, it is only natural to seek
the practice's font and origin in Phoenicia and Canaan. Because the same cities
have been inhabited in Lebanon since time immemorial, however, no Topheth
precincts have been uncovered (but see Heider [1985: 24–25] on the debate over
Middle-Late Bronze Age Gezer). But there is literary evidence. Quintus Curtius
4.3.23 reports that during Alexander's siege of Tyre in 322 B.C.E., the Tyrians debated reviving the old custom of infant sacrifice, which they had bequeathed to
the Carthaginians. And the following (admittedly late) paraphrase of Byblian
mythology is as close as we are likely to get to the foundation legend of Canaanite
child sacrifice:

> At the occurrence of a fatal plague [the god] Kronos immolated his only son to
> his [deceased] father Ouranos [Heaven]. . . . Among ancient peoples in criti-
> cally dangerous situations it was customary for the rulers of a city or nation,
> rather than lose everyone, to provide the dearest of their children as a propitia-
> tory sacrifice to the avenging deities. The children thus given up were slaugh-
> tered according to a secret ritual. Now Kronos, whom the Phoenicians call El,
> who was in their land and who was later divinized after his death as the star of
> Kronos, had an only son by a local bride named Anobret, and therefore they
> called him Ieoud [*sic?*].—Even now among the Phoenicians the only son is
> given this name.—When war's gravest dangers gripped the land, Kronos
> dressed his son in royal attire, prepared an altar and sacrificed him. (Eusebius,
> *Praeparatio Evangelica* 1.10.33, 44; trans. Attridge and Oden 1981: 61, 63)

Philo of Byblos, supposedly quoting a Phoenician priest Sanchuniathon,
touches on the following themes: (a) the ritual is a response to plague; (b) the
death of a few ransoms the many; (c) the child in the myth is an only child; (d) he
is royally attired. The myth points, on the one hand, to the Punic offering of *molk*
'royalty,' on the other, to the alleged Israelite practice of offering the firstborn (see

below). (The reference to secrecy, moreover, recalls the evidence that the infant sacrifice was a nocturnal ritual, *sacrum magnum nocturnum* in the N'gaous stelae; see also Isa 30:29 [Mosca 1975: 215]. (Another tradition associated with Byblos may also distantly reflect *molk* ritual infanticide: according to Plutarch *De Iside et Osiride* 15–16, the Egyptian goddess Isis, while in Byblos, first nurtured and then burned the son of King Malkathros.)

A hypothetical compromise between the extremes of killing a single prince and killing many children of each sex would be to offer only the firstborn, recalling the gods' claim on the first of everything. As we have seen, some have read Exod 22:28 in this light, and the notion is paralleled in Micah 6:6–8 and Ezek 20:18–31.

While I concede that the Israelites sometimes engaged in infant sacrifice, and while it would have been natural for them to sacrifice their firstborn, I find no explicit evidence that they did so — say, in the fulminations of the Deuteronomistic Historian. The sacrifice of the firstborn appears as a *literary* theme, both explicitly in Genesis 22 and implicitly in the stories of firstborn sons who are lost and found again, undergoing their own narrative *rites de passage*, starting with Abel, the animal sacrificer who is himself killed (Gen 4:1–16), and continuing through Isaac, firstborn of Abraham's wife Sarah, who is nearly made a burnt offering (Genesis 22), and through Joseph, firstborn to Rachel, who is symbolically slain and replaced by a goat (Gen 37:18–35). No doubt, the tradition of the Tenth Plague, in which Yahweh killed the Egyptian firstborn, builds upon an older idea that, when the firstborn die for God during a crisis, their death ransoms others. In the Christian Bible, as already noted, the theme of the sacrificed firstborn culminates with Jesus (Levenson 1993). As for Micah and Ezekiel, I find it easy to believe that each prophet in his own way, was attacking popular religion by carrying it to extremes, just as the prophets consistently portrayed idolatry as the idiotic veneration of sticks and stones (see p. 778). In sum: while I feel little doubt that some Israelites sacrificed their children, I am unconvinced that *firstborn* sacrifice was widespread or even practiced at all. I am equally unconvinced that Exod 22:28 was ever invoked to justify it (so also Mosca 1975: 235–38).

Where does that leave us in interpreting Exod 22:28? I would start with v 29, which mandates giving *(nātan)* Yahweh firstling animals on the eighth day "likewise." I do not imagine that this necessarily means sacrifice; it could simply indicate setting apart. Certainly with cultic centralization in Jerusalem, it became impossible to sacrifice every firstling on its eighth day of life (see below). Segal (1963: 181) reasonably supposes that animals were merely *dedicated* to God on the eighth day, i.e., reserved for future sacrifice and precluded from any other use, as in Rabbinic law (see below, NOTE to 22:29, "you must give"). Similarly, the firstborn son, once he has survived a week, is set apart in some fashion.

Perhaps in some cases, he is destined to become a sacrifice. Perhaps in other situations, he will be donated to a shrine like the young Samuel (for other examples, see vol. I, p. 455–56; see also NOTE to 33:11, "youth"). Most often, however, his life would be redeemed with an animal sacrifice. (For P, as an extra measure, the entire tribe of Levi replaces the Israelite firstborn [Numbers 3; 8:16–18; compare Judges 17].) Levenson (1993: 9) puts the matter well: "Exod 22:28b articulates a theological ideal about the special place of the firstborn son, an ideal whose realization could range from literal to non-literal implementation, that is, from sacrifice to redemption, or even to mere intellectual assent without any cultic act whatsoever."

The basic rationale for donating a firstborn child to God is to produce more off-spring. Thus in Gen 22:15–18, God promises Abraham numerous descendants in reward for his willingness to sacrifice Isaac. Note, too, that after receiving Hannah's firstborn Samuel as a Nazirite hierodule, Yahweh gives her five more children (1 Sam 2:21). To obtain the maximum benefit, one must first be at least theoretically willing to surrender all that one has, i.e., even an only child.

The *caveat*: In justice to the Israelites, Phoenicians and Carthaginians, I must acknowledge that the evidence for ritual infanticide, though voluminous and damning, is entirely circumstantial. If they were arraigned in an American court and represented by a good lawyer, these peoples would surely be acquitted of criminal charges. For there still exists "reasonable doubt." Like cannibalism, ritual sex, incest, etc., human sacrifice is a canard societies have cast at one another since time immemorial (cf. Oden 1987: 131–53). Romans accused the early Christians of practicing ritual cannibalism in their secret masses, eating flesh and drinking blood (Justin Martyr *Apology* 2.12.5). Centuries later, the Christians turned the same accusation against the Jews and their Passover celebration. Both ideas have roots in the biblical notion that animal sacrifice is symbolically equivalent to human sacrifice (vol. I, pp. 454–56; below, pp. 309, 529–31, 695–703). And yet both are false. We may not blindly accept Greek and Roman accusations against the Phoenicians, often clearly biased, without the closest scrutiny. Thousands of burnt babies might seem proof enough, but some defenders of the Carthaginians insist that these are the cremations of children who died naturally (Moscati 1987; Benichou-Safar 1988; Moscati and Ribichini 1991; Gras, Rouillard and Teixidor 1991: 171–73; but see also Stager 1982: 165). Even these authors, however, accept that, in extreme situations, the Carthaginians probably did sacrifice living children to the gods.

22:29. *do likewise.* The phrase *kēn-taʿăśe(h)* implies that the firstling animal is treated in a manner identical or analogous to the firstborn child of v 28b. One possible inference is that both verses mandate the slaughter and sacrifice of animal and human alike on the eighth day (previous NOTE). A second possibility is that, on the eighth day, both the firstling animal and the firstborn son are designated for eventual sacrifice at a convenient time. The third possibility is that both man and beast are singled out on the eighth day for their respective fates: sacrifice for cattle and something else for the human, presumably donation to the shrine or redemption.

seven days. Sarna (1991: 141) sees this law as humanitarian. Just as one may not take chicks or eggs from under a brooding mother (Deut 22:6–7) or kill parent and child on the same day (Lev 22:28), so one must not prematurely separate suckling and dam. More important, however, is that one must not present Yahweh with a newborn calf or lamb that may be defective. The animal must first have demonstrated its viability (Bekhor Shor; Sforno).

on the eighth day. Haran (1979: 28 n. 15) supports the interpretation of *Mek. kaspā'* 1 that *bayyôm haššəmînî* means *"from* the eighth day *onward."* He argues that it was impractical to sacrifice each firstling on the eighth day, even assuming the existence of numerous local shrines. If this is indeed a problem, however, I think it less forced to reinterpret "give *(nātan)"* as connoting dedication; see also next NOTE.

give. As already noted, in vv 28b–29 the verb *nātan* is ambiguous; it may but need not connote actual sacrifice. Lev 22:27 (P) seemingly provides the answer: "A bull or a sheep or a goat, when it is born, then it shall be seven days under its mother; and from the eighth day and onward, it will be acceptable as an offering. . . ." But we cannot simply assume that the Priestly Writer has provided a straightforward interpretation of Exod 22:29. Unlike the First Code (20:24[21]–26[23]), P explicitly envisions one Altar for the entire people. Sacrifice of every firstling exactly on its eighth day would be practicable in the wilderness, in the Tabernacle's proximity (cf. D. Ashkenazi *apud* Luzzatto). But in the Promised Land, a shepherd from Dan or Gilead could not reasonably trek to Jerusalem whenever a young ewe lambed and a heifer calved for the first time. The same observations apply to Deut 15:19–20: "All the firstborn that will be born among your herd and among your flock, the male, you must consecrate to Yahweh your deity. Do not work with your bull's firstborn and do not shear your flock's firstborn. Before Yahweh your deity you must eat it, year by year, in the place that Yahweh will choose, you and your house." That is, the firstlings are raised at home, then led to Jerusalem for sacrifice during a pilgrimage festival. Later Jewish practice, which could not accept contradictions within the Law, necessarily understood that animals were merely designated as *set aside* for Yahweh on the eighth day; one has a year to make the actual sacrifice (*m. Bekor.* 4:1). The First Code, however, appears to envision a more convenient recourse to God (20:24[21]–26[23]; 21:6, 14; 22:7–8, 10) and probably assumes the local High Place, in which case eighth-day sacrifice would be possible (Driver 1911: 235; *pace* Haran 1979: 28 n. 15). If so, there would be a glut in the springtime, when most lambs are born.

22:30. *Holiness men . . . for me.* One could also render *'anšê qōdeš . . . lî* as "my men of Holiness." Sforno links this injunction to the preceding: one becomes holy by donating sons to Yahweh's service. In fact, the connection is even deeper. The implication of 22:28b–30 is that Israel is Yahweh's flock, with firstborn consecration shedding its protective aura over the whole people. Israel may not eat torn meat, because that would make them scavengers, tainted by bloodshed and unworthy of the divine presence. The overall theme of 22:28–30 is that a portion of the crops, firstborn sons, firstling animals and ultimately the entire people must be treated as *qōdeš* 'Holiness,' i.e., Yahweh's sanctified portion.

torn meat. It is not entirely clear whether *ṭərēpâ* here implies the act of tearing in general or a torn animal in particular. The parallels in Lev 7:24; 11:39–40; 17:15; 22:8; Ezek 44:31 appear to support the latter. In later Jewish parlance, *ṭārēp* 'torn' (Yiddish *treyf*) denotes nonkosher meat and eventually all nonkosher food.

While the perennial game of finding health justifications for Jewish and other dietary systems can be played with only limited success—ecological considerations and arbitrary ethnic marking are far more significant factors—we must acknowledge the obvious: the human stomach cannot easily digest rotten meat. We make poor scavengers. But, as the reference to *qōdeš* 'Holiness' suggests, the ritual-symbolic aspect still applies: one may consume meat only after draining the spurting blood into a bowl and offering a portion to Yahweh, which is not possible unless the kill is fresh (Childs 1974: 480).

the dog. One may interpret *lakkeleb* as collective, i.e., "to the dogs," or as implicitly bound to a suffix, i.e., "to *your* dog" (ibn Ezra). In Israel, some dogs were domesticated for herding, watching and hunting (Isa 56:10–11; Ps 22:17), while others ran wild (Borowski 1998: 133–40). All were contemptible as scavengers (1 Kgs 14:11; 16:4; 21:19, 23–24; 22:38; 2 Kgs 9:10, 36); on dog veneration in other cultures, see Stager (1991: 20–36). Deut 14:21 will revise Exod 22:30 to eliminate the wastage: "Don't eat any carrion. To the sojourner who is in your gates you may give it, and he may eat it; or sell it to a foreigner. For you are a holy people to Yahweh your deity." Lev 11:43–44; 19:2; 20:7, 26 ground Israel's particular sanctity on Yahweh's own Holiness: "You shall be holy, for I, Yahweh your deity am holy."

23:1. *carry.* For Luzzatto (on 20:7), the idiom is elliptical. Implied is "carry *on your mouth/lips*." But because the verb *nāśā(ʾ)* corresponds to both English "carry" and "take up," the law is slightly ambiguous. On the surface, it seems a straightforward prohibition against *spreading* slander (Bekhor Shor). But LXX, Tgs., *Mek. kaspāʾ* 2 and *b. Pesaḥ.* 118a see a prohibition on *listening* to slander, particularly if one is a judge. Either way, there is a degree of redundancy, whether with the immediately following law against false testimony (cf. Luzzatto) or with v 7, which warns against accepting false testimony in court. Sarna (1991: 142) regards 23:1a as addressing everyone in the court—litigants, witnesses and judge.

It is not completely clear, however, that the context is judicial at all. Bekhor Shor and Cassuto (1967: 296) detect an implicit *a fortiori* argument: do not speak slander even in private (cf. Lev 19:16), let alone in court.

set your hand. I.e., conspire or collaborate.

wicked man. It is unclear whether here *rāšāʿ* connotes a guilty litigant (Rashi) or a false witness (Rashbam). Ibn Ezra (shorter commentary) observes that there must be two or more witnesses, at least in capital cases (Deut 17:6; 19:15). A single, malicious witness might well attempt to suborn corroboration (see also *Mek. kaspāʾ* 2; *b. Šebu.* 31a). It is best to take the admonition as broadly as possible: one may not conspire with either a guilty party or a false witness.

criminal witness. An *ʿēd ḥāmās* commits a crime through false testimony (Deut 19:16; Ps 35:11). He becomes tantamount to a robber or even a murderer by bringing about false judgments against the innocent.

23:2. *consorting.* Most often the word *lārāʿōt* is taken as referring to evil or evil-doing, as a plural of abstraction (see GKC §124)—literally, "for bad things" (cf. Jer 3:5; Ezek 6:9; Hos 7:1). This is an admonition not to follow a wicked majority, whether in the courtroom or in life generally.

It is also possible to understand *lārāʿōt* as an infinitive verb. Rabbinic opinion (e.g., *m. Sanh.* 1:6), for instance, takes it simply to mean "to convict." This makes some sense, given the parallelism with the infinitives *linṭōt* 'inclining' and *ləhaṭṭōt* 'to influence.' One problem is that the root of *lərā'ōt* must be *r'y*, whereas the root meaning "to be bad" is *r''*. Still, the phenomenon of alloform geminate and final-weak roots interchanging is well known (GKC §77e); a root *r'y* 'to be evil' is quite conceivable. In that case, however, more likely than a Pi'el *lərā'ōt* might be be a syncopated Hiph'il **lar'ōt* (cf. GKC §53q).

My translation "consort," however, assumes that the root is *r'y* II 'to associate with,' almost always used in the context of ill-advised company (e.g., Prov 13:12; 22:24; 28:7; 29:3; Job 24:21)—perhaps due to the homophony with *r''* 'to be evil.' For Exod 23:2, "consort" fits both the context and the form *lərā'ōt* slightly better than the conventional translation "to work evil."

multitude. Either a wrongheaded judicial majority or perhaps public opinion in general.

testify. Despite the common use of *'ny* apropos of testimony, Ehrlich (1969: 184) thinks that this injunction addresses the judge, not witnesses, and connotes judicial deliberation or judgment.

dispute. In this context, *rīb* connotes both a lawsuit and the quarrel that motivated it.

inclining . . . influence. The root *nṭy* means "to stretch" and also "to turn aside." The first verb is the intransitive Qal *linṭōt*, while the second is the causative Hiph'il *ləhaṭṭōt*. In both cases, that from which one deviates or causes others to deviate is implicitly "justice" (cf. v 6) or "the truth" (Vg); cf. *hiṭṭâ mišpāṭ* in Deut 16:19; 24:17; 27:19; 1 Sam 8:3; Lam 3:35. Sometimes, however, the object is the person one wrongs in judgment; cf. Isa 10:2; Amos 5:12; Mal 3:5; Prov 18:5 (Baentsch 1903: 205).

multitude (second time). This verse apparently enunciates an important legal principle that would provoke considerable Rabbinic discussion (see, e.g., Rashi). But just what is the principle is unclear; the passage may even be corrupt (see TEXTUAL NOTE). Some suggest that here *rabbîm* does not mean "a multitude" but rather "great men." If so, then the clause is to be connected with v 3 and may be paraphrased, "Don't testify in a lawsuit (or 'concerning a magnate' [TEXTUAL NOTE]) showing favoritism in order to incline (others) toward the great, neither should you exalt a pauper in his lawsuit." This principle would match the substance of Lev 19:15. It is also possible that earlier in the verse, *rabbîm* likewise means "the great." If so, the prohibition is not against following the herd but against following the influential. But the most likely and traditional view is that the verse warns against being swayed by an unjust consensus.

As already noted, commentators dispute as to whom the admonition is addressed. The possibilities are a judicial panel, who should not be affected by popular opinion (Jacob 1992: 712); individual judges, who should not be swayed by other judges (Bekhor Shor), or witnesses, who should not report common prejudice as attested fact (Luzzatto). These are not mutually exclusive interpretations. Indeed, the main point could be whole-life wisdom: never follow a malicious majority against your conscience.

23:3. *don't exalt.* This prohibition obliquely fosters consideration for the poor by *assuming* that one would be more sympathetic to their plight. Comments Luzzatto, "See how the Torah tries to strengthen the feeling of compassion and favor for individuals but forbids this to judges, the reason being that the individual bestows what belongs to him, whereas the judge bestows what belongs to others." More even-handed, Lev 19:15 forbids favoring either rich or poor.

23:4. *When.* Although the text returns to the conditional syntax characteristic of 21:2–22:16, the *mišpāṭîm* 'case-laws' proper, there is an important difference. Exod 23:4 is not a third-person legal instruction to a judge ("When a man encounters his enemy's bull . . .") but a second-person moral exhortation to the individual Israelite. This is preaching couched in quasi-legalistic language.

you encounter. Since *pāgaʿ* also means "strike," a closer translation might be "when you hit upon." Notice that the text does not say, "When you *see*"; apparently, one need not go too far out of one's way to help (*Mek. kaspāʾ* 2; *b. B. Meṣ.* 33a). In the following law, however, which involves also the suffering of the animal, one must intervene more assertively, cooperating even with an enemy (cf. Luzzatto).

your enemy's. As is often noted, the contents of vv 4–5 do not jibe with their overall context, which concerns the administration of justice (see below, pp. 278–79, 307–8). Conceivably, however, the "enemy" and "one who hates you" are adversaries at law, not just people whom you find distasteful (Hyatt 1971: 245–46). Bekhor Shor spells out the obvious implication of vv 4–5: if you must help your enemy, then you also must help your friend (and presumably the stranger, too). The interpretation that 23:4–5 has an *a fortiori* application to all Israelites, friend or foe, goes back to Deut 22:1–4, which paraphrases Exod 23:4–5 but speaks of "your brother" rather than "your enemy."

return. One may not exploit the chance encounter for self-enrichment. To keep the animal would be tantamount to theft, as other Near Eastern law codes make explicit (Eshnunna §50; Hittite Laws §§45, 71, 79). Stealing an enemy's property is easy for the conscience to rationalize but invites retaliation.

Cattle-rustling is endemic to pastoral peoples, providing opportunities for the display of male prowess. But just as biblical law attempts to regulate blood vengeance (see pp. 207–11, 501), so it takes precautions to avoid raids. A person in possession of another's cattle, friend or foe, must take *immediate* steps to restore it, before misunderstandings and violence arise. The parallel in Deut 22:1–3, however, which speaks of the lost property of one's "brother" not one's "enemy," instructs one to take in the animal or item for safekeeping, until it can be returned.

COMPARE: *71.* If anyone finds an ox, a horse, or a mule, he shall drive it to the king's gate. If he finds it in the country, they shall present it to the elders. The finder shall harness it (i.e., use it while it is in his custody). When its owner finds it, he shall take it in fully, but he shall not have the finder arrested as a thief. But if the finder does not present it to the elders, he shall be considered a thief. . . . *79.* If oxen enter another man's field, and the field's owner finds them, he may hitch them up for one day until the stars come out. Then he shall drive them back to their owner (Hittite Laws §§71, 79). (*LCMAM* 227)

23:5. *your adversary*. Is there a difference between 'ōyēb 'enemy' in v 4 and śōnē' 'hater' in v 5? Luzzatto infers that the former is more dangerous than the latter, since you are not obliged to confront the "enemy" personally, whereas you must cooperate with the mere "hater."

recumbent. The pack animal is not necessarily in trouble (contrast Deut 22:4). It could also be plain uncooperative, like Balaam's ass in Num 22:27 (Huffmon 1974: 274; Houtman 2000: 244).

and would refrain. Because of the law's overall ambiguity, it is unclear whether wəhādaltā should be taken as part of the protasis ("if/when" clause) or the apodosis ("then" clause). My translation follows the first option. Saadiah, ibn Ezra and Cassuto (1967: 297), however, understand wəhādaltā as a positive injunction: "Then stop yourself (from abandoning him with his problem)" (cf. hǎdal-ləkā in 2 Chr 25:16).

leaving . . . leave, leave. The meaning of 23:5 is an ancient crux (see Cooper 1989). What both helps and hinders our understanding is the existence of a parallel in Deut 22:4, which instructs one to help raise one's "brother's" (not "adversary's") ass or ox (not just ass) that has "fallen" (not "lain") down (not necessarily under a burden). Is Exod 23:5 talking about the same situation or a different one? LXX (*synegereis*), Syr (*šql*) and Vg (*sublevabis*) assume the former, i.e., that Exod 23:5 requires one to *raise* an enemy's ass. Given the fact that several of the conditions are explicitly different, however, I prefer to interpret each passage independently. Deuteronomy may be modifying or subverting the older law's intent (Cooper 1989).

It helps to visualize the scenario. A man is on a journey with his ass, transporting some valuables. Suddenly, the beast lies or falls down. Because of the weight it bears, it cannot or will not rise, nor can its owner lift it single-handed. While in this vulnerable position, the traveler sees a neighbor with whom he has been at odds. He needs his help, and yet he cannot trust him. The passerby, for his part, is greatly tempted to leave his adversary to his problem—or perhaps somehow to exploit his misfortune (e.g., gather comrades and make off with the property). Therefore, even if his intentions are good, the passer-by must approach the situation cautiously, lest his actions be misinterpreted. Both parties are extremely tense, the owner more so as he is frustrated with his beast. The potential for violence is great.

What is unclear is how 23:5 advises the passerby to respond to his enemy's plight. The chief obstacle to our comprehension is the strange use of the verb 'āzab (3x) and its accompanying prepositions lə- 'to, for' and 'im 'with.' The common Hebrew root 'zb means "abandon, forsake, leave." In the first instance, this makes fairly good sense: when one encounters an enemy's animal in trouble, one might naturally be inclined to leave him and it alone, thereby doing some mischief but remaining within the law. It is difficult, however, to translate 'ăzōb lô as "leaving *it*"; that should have been *'ăzōb 'ōtô or *'ozbô. More likely the object (the animal) is merely implied. Lô 'to him' then would refer to the owner.

The concluding instruction 'āzōb ta'ăzōb 'immô presents greater difficulties. The surface interpretation would be "you must leave, leave with him," i.e., you and your enemy must together walk away and abandon the animal. But that would make little sense (unless they are seeking more help).

A preferable translation, as in the preceding clause, would regard the animal or its load as the implicit object: "you must leave, leave (it) with him." This in turn might mean one of two things: either (a) you must just leave the scene and not get involved, or (b) you must leave the load with the animal or with the owner (rather than steal it). *Mek. kaspā'* 2 and *b. Meṣ.* 32a–33a reflect this ambiguity by offering examples of when one is and is not obliged to help. Interpretation (a) implies that, when an enemy's property is involved, it is wisest just to pass by (Cooper 1989). It is true that Deut 22:4 instructs one to help, but there the distressed party is "your brother" not "your adversary." Equally plausible, however, is possibility (b): just as one has no right to confiscate an enemy's lost animal (Exod 23:4), no more has one the right to steal his ass's burden on the specious grounds of offering assistance. One may and must loosen the load to spare the animal, but then one should quit the scene.

Some commentators have attempted to circumvent the ordinary meaning of *'āzab* either by altering the text or by attributing to the familiar root an unusual meaning. Most simple is to emend *'zb* 'abandon' to *'zr* 'assist' for the second and third verbs (Bochart *apud* Dillmann 1880: 243; Baentsch 1903: 206), since in paleo-Hebrew script beth and resh were similar in appearance. Thus the verse may be read: "When you see the ass of one who hates you recumbent under its burden and would refrain from leaving (it) to him, you must help, help (it) with him." As conjectural emendations go, this is fairly attractive.

An alternative approach is to locate a meaning for *'zb* other than "leave, abandon." With *Tg. Onqelos*, both Rashi and Dillmann (1880: 243) take *'āzab* as "release," comparing the obscure cliché *'āṣûr wə'āzûb* 'detained or released (?)' (Deut 32:36; 1 Kgs 14:10; 21:21; 2 Kgs 9:8; 14:26). The case would be strengthened, however by clearer examples and cognates from related languages. I would discount an appeal to Akkadian *šūzubu* 'rescue' (< *ezēbu* 'abandon' = *'zb*) (e.g., Casanowicz 1894: 68 n. 99, 296). If a loanword, *šūzubu* should have entered Biblical Hebrew as **šēzîb*, the postbiblical form (< Aramaic *šēzēb* 'rescue'). And if *šūzubu* is just a cognate, then it would correspond to a Hebrew Hiph'il **he'ĕzîb* not the Qal *'āzab*.

A more attractive theory sees a merger of two distinct proto-Semitic roots: **'zb* 'abandon' and **ḏb* 'lay down, prepare, restore,' the latter attested in Ugaritic, Old South Arabic and possibly in Mishnaic Hebrew *ma'ăzîbâ* 'cement, paving.' (Another potential biblical attestation might be *'zb* 'pave, repair' in Neh 3:8 [Cassuto 1967: 297–98], but see Williamson [1985: 78–82] for counterarguments.) If so, Exod 23:5 instructs one to help the owner *reload* the beast. (Also from this root might be *'izzābôn* 'merchandise.') Margalit (1987: 395–97), however, by comparing Exod 23:5 and Deut 22:4, infers that *'zb* can mean "raise up" (cf. LXX Exod 23:5), a meaning he also plausibly detects in Neh 3:8, 34.

One last approach returns us to the familiar *'āzab* 'leave, abandon.' The *Tgs.* render 23:5b as follows: "abandon, abandon *what is in your heart* concerning him, and unpack (it) with him, *Tgs. Ps.-Jonathan* and *Neofiti I* inserting "and reload (it)." Thus *'āzab* may simply connote relinquishing a grudge, in one or in all three cases: "When you see your adversary's ass recumbent under its burden and would refrain from letting go (of your anger) at him, you must let go, let go (of your anger) with him." But this is not satisfactory, either, because now the verse does not actually instruct one to do anything.

with him. The last word of the verse encourages a homiletical reading. By working together (if that is what is meant), the two enemies might begin to reduce their mutual hostility (Leibowitz 1976: 432–33; Jacob 1990: 714–15). Helping one's enemies is also recommended in Prov 25:21–22; Job 31:29. If Exod 23:4 tells one how to avoid a false accusation of theft by an enemy, 23:5 may take an additional step, describing an opportunity for reconciliation.

23:6. *influence*. Since v 3 already forbade favoring the poor, *hiṭṭâ* here may imply doing the opposite (Bekhor Shor). *Mek. kaspā* 3, however, thinks that vv 3 and 6 both forbid favoring the pauper. Perhaps 23:6 bans bias in either direction, whether to the poor man's advantage or his detriment. On judicial impartiality, see also Deut 16:19; 27:19; 1 Sam 8:3; Lam 3:35.

your pauper's. *'Ebyōnəkā*, if the correct reading (see TEXTUAL NOTE), may be a shorthand equivalent to *'ebyōn(ê) 'ammekā* 'your *people's* pauper(s)' (cf. 23:11). Or perhaps it refers to a single dependent, as when a slave sues his master for justice (cf. Job 31:13) (Jacob 1992: 715; Houtman 2000: 247). Nowadays, a judge with personal involvement would recuse himself owing to a conflict of interest. But all that the Bible demands is that he be as fair as possible. Houtman shows how Deut 16:19 converts Exod 23:6 into a general prohibition on injustice.

23:7. *false word*. Since *dābār* 'word' can be used figuratively, perhaps the law is referring not just to slander (cf. Prov 29:12) but to all shady business (Baentsch 1903: 206).

keep distant. If still speaking of court proceedings, the meaning is: whether as plaintiff, witness or judge, do not get involved with a trumped-up lawsuit. Always render justice in fear (cf. Luzzatto). Alternatively, if the context is not solely judicial, v 7 may be an admonition against gossip. (*Mek. kaspā* 3 gives both possibilities; for other interpretations, see *b. Šebu.* 30b–31a.)

righteous one. In this context, *ṣaddîq* specifically connotes a person who is legally innocent. The law envisions a case where a suspect has been cleared by the court but might nonetheless be subject to a private vendetta (Bekhor Shor) or may be persecuted by the judge himself, who knows him to be guilty of other offenses (ibn Ezra). After the court has acted, further punishment must be left to God (see also *Mek. kaspā* 3; *b. Sanh.* 33b).

kill. *Hārag* is not the term for judicial execution (*hēmît*). The law probably addresses extrajudicial lynching, or perhaps indirect murder through false testimony and baseless prosecution (Baentsch 1903: 206).

I shall not vindicate a guilty one. In the context, there are at least three ways to take this clause. First, Yahweh may be threatening that whoever kills an innocent person, whether spontaneously or by judicial injustice, will him/herself incur divine punishment as a "guilty one" (cf. Cassuto 1967: 299), for Yahweh abominates equally *maṣdîq rāšā' ûmaršîa' ṣaddîq* 'whoever vindicates the guilty one or convicts the righteous one' (Prov 17:15). Second and perhaps more likely, the verse may warn that, in cases when criminals are acquitted for want of evidence or by miscarriage of justice, God himself will exact vengeance. The third possibility is that Yahweh directs and inspires all human judges. (Compare the Rabbinic view that magistrates are called *'ĕlōhîm* 'Deity' [NOTE to 21:6].) If so, the text asserts that a court's decisions are infallible. Anyone whom the court acquits is acquited by God himself, who will not "vindicate a guilty one."

23:8. *bribe.* To judge from the frequency with which the Bible discusses this topic, judicial corruption must have been a constant concern if not a widespread problem (Deut 10:17; 16:19; 27:25; Isa 1:23; 5:23; 33:15; Ezek 22:12; Micah 3:11; 7:3; Ps 15:5; 26:10; Prov 17:8, 23; 18:16). It is certain that Exod 23:8 forbids bribing a judge. It likely also prohibits suborning a witness.

blinds. Whether we read with Sam-LXX or with MT (see TEXTUAL NOTE), v 8b contains poetic parallelism, probaby indicative of a proverbial origin (Cassuto 1967: 299). But the original reading is uncertain. Superficially, Sam-LXX feels more poetic: *haššōḥad yəʿawwēr ʿênê piqḥîm wîsallēp dibrê ṣaddîqîm* 'The bribe blinds the sighted's eyes / And perverts the righteous's words.' There is exact parallelism between "blinds/perverts," "eyes/words" and "sighted/righteous." But the result is to orphan the subject of the sentence, "the bribe," which finds no place within the bicolon. The MT reading, in contrast, is more consonant with the techniques of Hebrew poetry: *haššōḥad yəʿawwēr piqḥîm wîsallēp dibrê ṣaddîqîm* 'The bribe blinds the sighted / And perverts the righteous's words.' The subject "bribe" in the first colon is balanced in the second colon by the extra element "words."

righteous's. One might think that the *ṣaddîqîm* 'righteous' are impartial judges. But in a judicial context, the *ṣaddîq* is usually the acquitted party. Accordingly, for ibn Ezra the "righteous" are the *innocent*, who might be falsely condemned through bribery (for others in agreement, see Leibowitz 1976: 454).

words. The proverb refers to the power of greed to affect both perception ("blinds the sighted") and judgment ("words"). The maxim may admonish equally the witnesses, who see, and the judges, who speak. Both groups must shun all remuneration from interested parties. Or perhaps judges alone are addressed, as in the parallel in Deut 16:18–19.

COMPARE:
Do not confound a man in the law court,
In order to brush aside one who is right.
Do not incline to the well-dressed man,
And rebuff the one in rags.
Don't accept the gift of a powerful man,
And deprive the weak for his sake.
Maat [justice] is a great gift of god,
He gives it to whom he wishes . . .
Do not make for yourself false documents,
They are a deadly provocation (Instruction of Amenemope 20
    [XX.21–XXI.10]). (Lichtheim 1976: 158)

23:9. *oppress.* Seeking to account for the apparent change of subject, ibn Ezra and Bekhor Shor infer that the specific "oppression" envisioned is the perversion of justice.

Following N. Lohfink, Houtman (2000: 224) regards 22:20–23:9 as a unit framed by inclusio. Exod 23:9 is not really a conclusion, however, but a transition to vv 10–12, which protect the indigent in a different way.

known . . . soul. To "know (*yādaʿ*)" the "soul (*nepeš*)" implies empathy. Jacob (1992: 715) compares Prov 12:10: "The righteous one *knows* his (domestic) animal's *soul.*"

23:10. *And six.* As in v 9, the opening conjunction mitigates slightly the change of subject. The Sabbatical law appears also in Lev 25:2–7, 20–22; Deut 15:1–11; 31:10–13, which do not envision the poor as eating from the wild growth (see also Neh 10:32). For discussion, see Wright (1992).

your land. The use of *ʾereṣ* 'land' rather than *śāde(h)* 'field' (cf. Lev 25:3) indicates that the entire land of Canaan must enjoy the Sabbatical year (cf. Jacob 1992: 716).

gather. The verb *ʾāsap* probably connotes storage not reaping (Rashi).

field animal. Ḥayyat haśśāde(h) presumably includes anything from deer to rodents. Domestic cattle (*bəhēmâ*) are not mentioned, because they are grazed in their usual pasturage during the seventh year.

23:11. *But the seventh.* The syntax is a little peculiar. Since the object of the following verbs is "the land," one might have expected *ûbaššəbîʿît 'But *on* the seventh' instead of *wəhaššəbîʿît* (ibn Ezra [shorter commentary]). In his longer commentary, ibn Ezra supposes that the grammatical object of "abandon it and leave it alone" is "the seventh (year)," citing Neh 10:32. Jacob (1992: 716) accordingly translates, "But you shall omit the seventh [year]." An alternative could be to recognize the "accusative of time" (Waltke and O'Connor 1990: 171 §10.2.2c).

abandon . . . leave alone. Rabbinic commentators devote considerable discussion to the difference between *šmṭ* and *nṭš.* The most careful analyst is Ramban, who concludes that they are the respective opposites of "plant" and "gather" in the preceding verse. Since one may not even plant, the only growth will come from seeds dropped in the last harvest.

Dillmann (1880: 244) raises the practical question of whether there was a standard seventh year throughout the land, or whether it varied for every farmer and even every field. We may compare the case of the Hebrew slave, who had, it seems, an individual "time clock" (above, pp. 188–89); also analogous is the fruit tree, taboo until its own fifth year (Lev 19:23–25). As Baentsch (1903: 206) observes, a flexible Sabbatical year would have caused less economic upheaval. And one does the poor no favor by granting extra assistance only once every seven years (Houtman 2000: 252).

For Dillmann, however the explicit parallel with the Sabbath in v 12 favors a standard Sabbatical year, as does the reference in v 10 to "your land" (as opposed to "your field"). Lev 25:2–7, 18–22; Deut 15:1–11 explicitly mandate a single Sabbatical year for the whole land, and this is the practice of later Judaism (Neh 10:31; 1 Macc 6:49, 53; Josephus *Ant.* 13.8.1; 14.10.6; *m. Šeb.*).

their leftovers. I.e., what the poor leave behind (Sforno).

vineyard . . . olive. These plus "land" (23:10) describe cultivated soil in general (Houtman 2000: 256).

The implied purpose of the Sabbatical year is rest and refreshment. In this, it is comparable to the Sabbath day, ordained in the next verse. Cassuto (1967: 301), moreover, compares the law of servitude: "Every Israelite resembles the Hebrew slave in . . . that he, too, shall work for only six consecutive years, and after this period he also shall be freed, in the seventh year, from the yoke of hard toil." According to Lev 26:34, 43 (P), the land itself is capable of enjoying a Sabbath, since, in general, the biblical authors were averse to a continuous time-flow and inclined toward periodic returns to stasis in both ritual and history (vol. I, p. 434; cf. Kawashima 2003). Every seventh year, the land returns to the seventh day of Creation, when all was perfection. Symbolism apart, experience had probably taught the advisability of a periodic fallow year to minimize soil depletion (Sarna [1991: 143–44]; on agricultural nutrient replenishment, see Hopkins [1987: 185] and Borowski [1987: 148–51]).

The general principle is the same as for consecrating firstfruits and firstlings (see above pp. 264, 271). One forgoes a short-term gain for a long-term benefit.

23:12. *cease.* Tišbōt, from the root *šbt*, could also be understood denominatively: "keep the Sabbath *(šabbāt)*" (Holzinger 1900: 96).

bull . . . ass. On empathy with animals in the Bible, see pp. 177, 285, 695–701.

maidservant's son. Luzzatto opines that the *ben-'āmâ* is a born slave of the lowest rank. This is too narrow. He could also be the master's child with certain privileges (e.g., Ishmael in Gen 21:10).

sojourner. Who might be a migrant farm worker or the like (ibn Ezra [shorter commentary]).

catch breath. The form *yinnāpēš/ yinnāpaš* will recur in 31:17 apropos of God resting on the first Sabbath after Creation. Comments Buber (1949: 54), "The crass anthropomorphism binds the deity and the tired, exhausted slave, and with words arousing the soul calls the attention of the free man's indolent heart to the slave. . . . Everyone . . . shall be able to imitate YHVH without hindrance."

Although the clauses are too long for true poetry, Cassuto (1967: 301) catches quasi-poetic parallelism in v 12: " your bull and your ass may rest, / And your maidservant's son and the sojourner may catch breath."

On the Sabbath, see pp. 175–78.

23:13. *all that I have said.* This refers to the ordinances of chaps. 21–23 and possibly also the Decalog of chap. 20 (Jacob 1992: 720).

keep yourselves. Tiššāmērû combines the notions of "observe carefully" and "keep yourselves alive." Again, we have a jump of subject from both what precedes and what follows. And again, traditional Jewish exegetes try to smooth the transition, commenting that solicitude for sojourners (for the Rabbis, *gērîm* are religious converts), while laudable, incurs the risk of religious deviation, e.g., mentioning other gods (Bekhor Shor; Cassuto 1967: 302). Here *tiššāmērû* is understood as "protect yourselves."

mention. In the ancient Near East, to name a god is both to invoke and to praise him/her, as is most graphically illustrated by the recitation of Marduk's fifty names culminating the Babylonian *Enūma Eliš* (*ANET*³ 60–72, 501–3; Dalley 1989: 233–74). The Hebrew verb *hizkîr* 'mention, name, commemorate' is associated with praise in Isa 26:13; Ps 45:18; 71:16; cf. Isa 62:6. Like the later Rabbis, the legist of Exodus appears to be erecting a "fence" around the basic principle of monotheism: don't worship other gods, don't praise them, *don't even mention them* (cf. Sforno). (See also Josh 23:7; Hos 2:19; Zech 13:2; Ps 16:4.) Presumably, the author would have objected to the Deuteronomistic historian's frequent mentions of Baal, Milcom, Chemosh et al., and would have favored the later dysphemistic replacement of *baʿal* with *bōšet* 'shame' in the names Ishbaal/ Ishbosheth and Meribbaal/Mephibosheth (McNeile 1908: 140). The principle of Exod 23:13 may also underlie the insertion of *šiqqûṣ* 'abomination' after naming a foreign god (1 Kgs 11:5, 7; 2 Kgs 23:13) (*Mek. kaspā*ʾ 4; Ramban).

In addition to pure worship, ancient texts name gods as witnesses to oaths; compare Gen 31:54, where Jacob and Laban swear by "Abraham's Deity" and "Nahor's Deity." By implication, 23:13 bans such covenants that Israel might make with non-Yahwistic nations (ibn Ezra [shorter commentary]). The Israelites may have habitually sworn by other gods, whether in earnest or reflexively (compare Jer 5:7; 12:16; Amos 8:14; Zeph 1:5). But the Bible authorizes oaths by Yahweh alone (Deut 6:13; 10:20) (Houtman 2000: 263; *Mek. kaspā*ʾ 4).

23:14. *Three feet.* I.e., "three times." Hebrew knows two words for "foot": the more common is *regel* (used here) and the less common is *paʿam* (used in v 17). The same two words also mean "time, instance," but for this usage the frequency is reversed, with *paʿam* being more common. *Regel* in the sense of "time" occurs only in 23:14; Num 22:28, 32, 33, always with the number "three." The mention of the "foot" may deliberately invoke the image of a walking pilgrimage; compare the postbiblical expression *ʿaliyyâ ləregel* 'ascent (to the Temple) on foot' (cf. *Mek. kaspā*ʾ 4).

Exod 23:14 presents another abrupt break in subject. Some find a connection with v 13 via contrast: instead of celebrating for other gods, you must observe three pilgrimage festivals *to me* (ibn Ezra [shorter commentary]).

Biblical festival calendars appear in 23:14–19; 34:18–23; Leviticus 23; Numbers 28–29; Deut 16:1–17; Ezek 45:18–25. Some calendars give precise dates; others, such as Exod 23:14–19, do not. McNeile (1908: 141–42) sees the lack of dates as original and pragmatic: as crops ripened differently in different regions in different years, farmers would present their produce at the local High Place only when it was ready. The cultic centralization required by D and P, in contrast, would impose a certain artificiality in the interests of uniformity.

celebrate. The root *ḥgg* implies a pilgrimage, like the Arabic *ḥajj*. The *ḥag* 'pilgrimage festival' is to be distinguished from the broader category of *mōʿēd* '(holy) occasion' (Driver 1911: 242).

23:15. *Unleavened Bread Festival.* For detailed discussion of the springtime *Maṣṣôt* festival complex (modern Passover), see vol. I, pp. 427–61.

as I commanded you. In 13:6 (Levinson 1997: 67). This cross-reference could be the work of the Elohist, assuming that chaps. 13 and 23 are both Elohistic. Or it could be a later hand (cf. below, pp. 725–27).

New Grain. On *ʾābîb*, see NOTE to 13:4.

Month. On the meaning of *ḥōdeš* 'month, new moon,' see NOTE to 13:4 and Levinson (1997: 68 n. 51).

my Face. On Yahweh's *pānîm*, i.e., his presence, see below, pp. 604, 619–20, 622–23.

must not be seen. In ancient Near Eastern parlance, "seeing the face" implies either attendance at the royal court (if the face is a king's) or temple worship (if it is a god's) (vol. I, p. 342; Nötscher 1969).

emptily. Empty-handed. That is, one must not present oneself before Yahweh without gifts of sacrifices.

23:16. *Harvest Festival.* The unique term *ḥag haqqāṣîr* denotes a festival probably observed also by Canaanites (Judg 9:27) (Cassuto 1967: 303). It marked the culmination of the wheat harvest, what the Gezer Calendar (*AHI* 10.001.5) calls *yrḥ qṣr wkl* 'month of reaping and measuring (?)' (Borowski 1987: 36). As with all the agricultural festivals, scholars question whether these were always celebrated on the same date, or varied by locale and annual climate (cf. Dillmann 1880: 248). This Harvest Festival would become Jewish Shavuʿot/Pentecost.

the firstfruits of your produce. Rashi suggests that the language is elliptical, tantamount to "*at the time of* the firstfruits of your produce." I would rather regard *bikkûrê maʿăśe(y)kā* as in apposition to *qāṣîr*, which means both "the act of harvesting" and "that which is harvested."

Ingathering Festival. The fruit harvest in the autumn, which would become Jewish Sukkot. The most important fruit picked at this time is the olive. On *yrḥw 'sp* 'two months of ingathering' in the Gezer Calendar (*AHI* 10.001.1), see Borowski (1987: 32–34).

year's departure. It is unclear whether *ṣē(')t haššānâ* connotes the year's midpoint, when it begins to go out, or its final day, when it ends and a new year begins. On the vexed matter of the biblical calendars, see vol. I, pp. 383–87.

23:17. *malehood.* *Zəkûr* denotes males no longer dependent upon their mothers, to judge from Deut 20:13 (*ṭap* 'dependents' are distinguished from *zəkûr* 'malehood') and 1 Sam 1:22 (Samuel appears to Yahweh's Face after he is weaned) (Ehrlich 1908: 359; Jacob 1992: 722–23). Deut 31:10–13, however, requires that even the smallest children "appear to Yahweh's Face."

Our meager biblical sources about pilgrimage (Smith 1997: 52–141) can be considerably supplemented by a judicious reading of Second Temple materials (Safrai 1965). Josephus *Ant.* 4.8.7 emphasizes the sense of national cohesion created by pilgrimage. It is hard to imagine, however, that three times annually each adult male from Dan to Beersheba dropped whatever he was doing and took his family to Jerusalem. In later Jewish practice, pilgrimage was not considered obligatory (Safrai 1976: 899–900). As for Exodus 23, since it appears not to reckon with a single cult center, a trip to the local High Place probably suffices.

appear. On "seeing Yahweh" or being "seen" by Yahweh as the essence of pilgrimage, see Smith (1997: 100–9).

the Lord Yahweh's. The peculiar idiom *hā'ādōn yahwe(h)* means "Boss Yahweh," as if Israel were indentured servants farming his land (ibn Ezra, Ramban). Sforno compares Lev 25:22, "Mine is the land, for you are sojourners and settlers beside me." *'Ādōn* also evokes Yahweh's title *'ădōn kol-hā'āreṣ* 'Lord of all the land/world' (Josh 3:11,13; Micah 4:13; Zech 4:14; 6:5; Ps 97:5), inasmuch as God receives Israel's agricultural products in tribute (Jacob 1992: 725).

Face. On the one hand, *pānay* 'my face' is simply equivalent to *ləpānay* 'in my face, in my presence' (ibn Ezra). On the other hand, Yahweh's *pānîm* "Face, Front" bears a special significance as his manifestation on Earth. See below, pp. 604, 619–20, 622–23.

23:18. *my Slaughter-offering.* *Zibḥî* ostensibly describes any eaten sacrifice (Dillmann 1880: 249). According to Lev 2:5–6 explicitly and numerous other Priestly passages implicitly, cereal offerings burnt on the Altar must be unleavened. For possible reasons, see vol. I, pp. 433–34.

A very ancient and possibly correct interpretation, however, sees in 23:18 a specific reference to *Pesaḥ-Maṣṣôt*, i.e., Passover, which can be celebrated only in the absence of leavened bread (34:25; *Mek. kaspā'* 4; *b. Pesaḥ.* 64a; Holzinger 1900: 97; Baentsch 1903: 209; Sarna 1991: 146). For further discussion, see NOTE to 34:25, "*Pesaḥ* festival Slaughter-offering," and Haran (1978: 327–29).

blood. Cassuto (1967: 304) interprets *dam zibḥî* as "my blood-sacrifice." But this translation obscures the essential point: purifying blood must not contact impure leaven (see vol. I, pp. 433–34; below, pp. 683–90).

festival fat. Here as in Mal 2:3; Ps 118:27, *ḥag* 'festival' probably connotes a festival *sacrifice.* "Fat" is specificically kidney and liver fat (Driver 1911: 245).

morning. The fat of pilgrimage feasts must be consumed before morning, implicitly burnt upon the Altar. We find similar laws in 12:10; 34:25; Deut 16:4 apropos of the paschal offering, and many other sacrifices must be finished within a set time (see NOTE to 12:10). On the transformation of Exod 23:14–19 in Deuteronomy 16, see Levinson (1997: 81–93).

23:19. *first firstfruits.* The phrase *rē'šît bikkûrê* is equivalent to "your finest firstfruits" (Luzzatto).

Yahweh your deity's House. Since for the immediate future, Yahweh will be worshiped in a Tent, *bayit* 'house' might be regarded as anachronistic or at least anticipatory. But Holzinger (1900: 97) and Baentsch (1903: 209) correctly understand the phrase as tantamount to "any Yahweh shrine," comparing Gen 28:22; see also Josh 6:24; 9:23; 2 Sam 12:20 and, for a general discussion, Homan (2002: 23–27).

cook. Meat was usually boiled in water (Exod 12:9; Ezek 24:3–5). Milk-boiled meat was presumably a luxury, as it was more nutritious. Bekhor Shor, however, understands *bšl*, which also connotes the ripening of fruit (Gen 40:10 [see vol. I, p. 395), as "raise": "Don't raise a (firstling) kid on its mother's milk," i.e., past its eighth day of life. This interpretation, refuted already by ibn Ezra (longer commentary), appears to have originated among the Qara'ites (Haran 1979: 28 n. 15).

Ibn Ezra (shorter commentary) spells out the obvious. If *you* may not boil a kid in its mother's milk, neither may you eat a kid that *another* has seethed in its mother's millk.

kid. LXX translates *arnos* 'lamb.' Possibly *gədî* denotes both a kid and a lamb (*b. Ḥul.* 113a–b; ibn Ezra; *HALOT*; cf. Rashi, who also thinks it can even be a calf). Already Philo *Virt.* 144 takes the law to apply to all domestic mammal flesh. But ibn Ezra notes that the Arabic cognate *jady* refers only to a kid (for further cognates, see Haran 1979: 32 n. 25). Rashi's view is doubtless swayed by Rabbinic exegesis banning the intermingling of all milk and all meat (including that of fowl, but excluding fish and locusts); see *Mek. kaspā'* 5; *m. Ḥul.* 8:4; *b. Ḥul.* 113a–16a; *b. Qidd.* 57b; ibn Ezra.

mother's milk. This law appears three times in the Torah: in 23:19 (E?); 34:26 (J?) and Deut 14:21 (D). Four questions require consideration: (a) what exactly is "milk"? (b) why boil a kid in its own mother's milk? (c) why ban the practice? (d) how is this law related to its context(s)? (As for why the principle is absent from P, the law may presuppose domestic meat consumption, forbidden in Leviticus 17 [P].)

a. *What is milk?* Fresh, raw milk boils over and crusts. In the modern Middle East, milk is always slightly soured, and this fluid yogurt is frequently used for seething a meat stew (Haran 1979: 30–31; Knauf 1988b: 164–66).

b. *Why use mother's milk?* Rashbam thinks that boiling a kid in its mother's milk is a mere convenience. Suppose a goat bears two kids and has an ample milk supply. It would be natural to slaughter one and use the milk at hand for cooking. Ibn Ezra observes that Arabs esteem kid (and meat in general) boiled in milk as a delicacy (see also Doughty 1936: 1.75), and Labuschagne (1992: 10) notes an ancient reference already in the "Tale of Sinuhe" (*ANET* 20). But there is no evidence of kid boiled in its own mother's milk as a common Near Eastern repast.

Maimonides *Guide* iii.48 takes a different approach, identifying boiling a kid in its mother's milk as a polytheistic custom. For a while, twentieth-century scholars believed that a Ugaritic ritual text (*KTU* 1.23.14) described boiling a kid in milk—not its mother's, however. But more recent study has dispelled this misinterpretation (Ratner and Zuckerman 1986).

Lastly, Luzzatto conjectures that it was customary to offer to the Temple priests the first milk, like the first wool (Deut 18:4). The desanctification of the first milk is indeed a widespread Arab custom (Henninger 1975), and its absence from biblical law is surprising (Smith 1927: 220–21; cf. Daube 1936). If so, the kid in question would presumably be a firstling that one has shared with the Deity.

c. *Why the ban?* Even if boiling a kid in its mother's milk were a Canaanite practice—for which, I repeat, there is no evidence—that would not explain why the Torah forbids it. Almost all aspects of Israelite sacrifice are paralleled among their neighbors. Why single out this? Many exegetes regard the statute as humanitarian, citing prohibitions on taking chicks in their mother's sight (Deut 22:6–7) or killing an animal and its parent on the same day (Lev 22:28) (ibn Ezra; Rashbam). Overall, the Bible displays a tendency to identify empathetically with domestic animals (see pp. 177, 695–98, and Keel 1980: 142–44). Other biblical laws ban certain *mixtures* as contrary to God's design (e.g., Deut 22:9–11, etc), and, in at least one instance, this overlaps with a humanitarian concern (Deut 22:10 *re* yoking together an ox and an ass). Eilberg-Schwartz (1990: 128–34) reads Exod 23:19 in the specific context of the incest taboo: mother and son should never mingle substances (on cooking and sex as homologous, see also Tuzin 1978; Fiddes 1991: 144–62).

While there may or may not be a subliminal sexual message, there surely is an incongruity in putting a dead kid inside nourishing milk, not the milk inside a live kid (cf. Philo *Virt.* 143). For Douglas (1966), such dislocations are the essence of ritual defilement. (I do not find attractive Labuschagne's [1992: 14–15] thesis that the taboo addresses the presence of blood elements in new goat's milk. The law permits one to boil a kid in another she-goat's milk, which too might contain the reddish tinge.)

d. *What is the relation to the context?* I have already remarked upon the seeming disjointedness of 23:1–19. Nonetheless, interpreters have taken pains to read connections into every juncture, and this is no exception. For some, as already noted, boiling a kid in milk is a ritual practice. If so, the law bears some association with its context—if only because much meat was consumed during the pilgrimage festival (Rashbam). More specifically, Sarna (1991: 147) suspects that, just as v 18 arguably refers to the Unleavened Bread Festival and v 19a more clearly alludes to the Firstfruits Festival, so by elimination v 19b, boiling a kid, should be a practice associated with the Booths Festival (see also Haran 1979: 34–35). Goldstein and Cooper (1990: 29), however, associate the ban on cooking a kid in its mother's milk with the paschal ritual—in which case, if vv 18–19 follow a calendrical sequence, v 18 should refer to Sukkot. Or perhaps the connection lies within v 19, and the kid in 19b is a firstling, comparable to the firstfruits of v 19a. (Labuschagne [1992: 13–15] attempts to embrace all of the above.)

It is also possible to view 23:19b as pointing forward to the ban on intermingling with the Canaanites, hence Maimonides' conjecture that boiling a kid in its mother's milk was a Canaanite practice. More loosely and more plausibly, one could regard the rule, like many dietary regulations, as an ethnic marker. Canaanites (allegedly) boil kids in their mothers' milk; Israelites do not—and the two groups should not be confused. One should note that Exod 34:26 likewise links the kid in milk prohibition to the festal calendar, while Deut 14:21 makes it the sequel to the dietary laws.

SPECULATION: My intuition is that v 19b is really a proverb. After all, we never read of anybody in the Bible cooking a kid or lamb in any milk at all, and certainly not in its own mother's. But, if so, what does the saying mean?

One possibility is that it inculcates empathy. What is the most disgusting thing someone can do? Causing a mother to be instrumental in the eating of her son, which is but a step away from cannibalism. Thus, I would relate 23:19 to the Assyrian cursing ritual of putting fetal lambs into ewes' mouths (Vassal Treaty of Esarhaddon 547 [*ANET*³ 539), and also to the situation described in 2 Kgs 6:26–30, when two women conspire to boil and eat their own offspring. By this reading, 23:19b concludes the legal section with an oblique reference to the emotion on which all civil society is based: empathy, i.e., the ability to imagine another person as possessing feelings and rights as valid as one's own.

And we must not overlook the obvious. The previous verse contained a rule about ḥēleb 'fat.' The "catchword" principle may have led the arranger to introduce a precept about ḥālāb 'milk' (on catchwords, see Lundbom 1999: 87–91). The principle would not apply, however, in 34:26 or Deut 14:21, where "fat" does not appear.

23:20. *sending.* The participle *(šōlēaḥ)* often indicates the imminent future. This Messenger will lead the people from Sinai and on to Canaan, until they subdue the land. (See also next NOTE.)

Like the Book of Deuteronomy, which it resembles in style and content, 23:20–33 addresses the coming settlement in the land. It discloses the Covenant's reward, an incentive to the ratification ceremony in chap. 24.

Messenger. To what does *mal'āk* refer here: an angelic or a human emissary? Normally, the term connotes the former. Ibn Ezra cites the common biblical theme of God's guiding, battling angel (Gen 24:7; 48:16; Num 20:16; 2 Sam 24:16; Isa 37:36; 63:9; see further Mann 1977), and, following midrashic sources, Rashbam and Ramban identify this Messenger specifically with "Yahweh's Army Captain," who joins Israel after their entry into the land (Josh 5:13–15).

Bekhor Shor, however, thinks that here *mal'āk* connotes a prophet, who like an angel serves as envoy from the divine council (compare 1 Kgs 22:19–23 and Isaiah 6; for further discussion, see Ross 1962). If so, the obvious candidate is Moses, who might be described as an "anti-angel," i.e., a human envoy from Earth to Heaven. One might object that Moses does not personally lead the people to conquer Canaan—but perhaps that is still Yahweh's plan at this point (Gersonides; Luzzatto). Alternatively, one might see a reference not to Moses but to a "prophet like Moses" (cf. Deut 18:18–19) (Maimonides *Guide* 2.34).

At least in the composite text, it is a little surprising that Yahweh promises a Messenger at this late point. An angelic cloud has already led the Israelites to Sinai and will accompany them to Canaan (see vol. I, pp. 549–50). Is this the same entity (Knobel *apud* Dillmann 1880: 251)? It sounds like something new. Are we in a different literary source? Might the Messenger in question be Yahweh's "terror" (v 27) or the *ṣir'â* 'hornet (?)' (v 28)? Moreover, in 33:2–3, Yahweh seems to send his Messenger as a *punishment* for the Gold Calf affair, in lieu of his "Face," i.e., his fuller presence (see below, pp. 597–98). How does that Messenger relate to this Messenger? Is the envoy of 23:20 Yahweh's hypostatic Name (see the following NOTES)?

The simplest answer—admittedly a dodge—is that Yahweh is deliberately delphic. While reassuring the people that, come what may, he will not abandon them, the Deity keeps his options open. He does not specify the form of his guiding Messenger, whether human or divine. He promises only that the divine Name will be in him. (In the composite text, Moses eventually realizes this and objects to Yahweh's equivocations; see NOTE to 33:2.)

the place. I.e., the land of Canaan (Baentsch 1903: 210).

23:21. *from his face.* The word *mippānā(y)w* basically means "from him" and also evokes Yahweh's hypostatic *pānîm* 'Face' (following NOTES and pp. 604, 619–20, 622–23).

rebel. The root *mry/mrr* (see TEXTUAL NOTE) denotes disobedience, particularly to God (Schwienhorst 1998). Bekhor Shor paraphrases the clause as follows: "If you rebel against him, he has no authority to forgive your sin, for who rebels against him sins against me."

lift your offense. To "lift" or "bear" *(nāśā[')])* sin, said of a deity, means to "pardon." That is, the god relieves the sinner of his fault. When a human "bears" sin, however, he is mortally culpable (Koch 1999: 551, 559–60; NOTE to 28:38). The noun *pešaʿ* 'offense' may specifically connote covenant infidelity (1 Kgs 12:19; 2 Kgs 1:1; 3:5, 7; 8:20, 22) (Sarna 1991: 148).

for (second time). Saadiah understands *kî* differently: "Don't rebel against him . . . *although* my Name (i.e., the "merciful and benevolent," etc. [34:6]) is within him" (so also Houtman 2000: 274). But for such a concessive clause, I would rather have expected *gam/ʾap kî* 'even though.'

my Name. In the biblical conception, Yahweh cannot be fully manifested on Earth. But he makes parts of himself accessible to humans as hypostases. These go by many names: "Face," "Name," "Messenger," etc. To explain the relationship, ibn Ezra resorts to an astronomical analogy. As the moon shines in the reflected light of the sun, so that one could claim that moonlight is actually sunlight, so an angel is and is not God himself.

This paradoxical relationship is paralleled in surrounding cultures. In Ugaritic, the independent goddess ʿAṭtartu is called *šm bʿl* 'Baʿlu's name' (*KTU* 1.16.vi.56). An Israelite inscription from Kuntillet ʿAjrūd refers to a deity as "God's name" (*šm ʾl*) (*AHI* 8.023.3). And in Egyptian art, the Pharaonic cartouche may stand in for the king's portrait.

Like our passage, Deuteronomy and Deuteronomistic literature prefer the hypostasis of Yahweh's *šēm* 'Name.' Yahweh is not physically manifest on Earth, nor is his presence represented by a statue. Rather, he is symbolized by the word *yahwe(h)*. Here the Hebrew concept of *šēm* 'name' approaches our notion of "idea" (or Greek *logos*). Moreover, at least for a poet, the "Name" may have the physical characteristics of a person. Compare the ambiguous anthropomorphism of Isa 30:27, "See, Yahweh's Name coming from a distance, its/his *nose* (anger) flaring . . . its/his lips full of wrath, its/his tongue like a consuming fire" (Luzzatto). For further discussion, see below, pp. 619–20.

within him. This Messenger is most likely the familiar hypostasis of Yahweh's "Name" (*šēm*) (previous NOTE). But the reference to the name being inside the Messenger (*bəqirbô*) is unique, and has engendered other readings. Ibn Ezra, for instance, cites (and rejects) a view that the Messenger that must be obeyed is the Torah scroll, which contains the sacred Name. Along the same lines, one might think of the Covenant Chest. But the traditional angelic interpretation is more compelling.

23:22. *oppose your opponents.* The redundancy of *wəʾāyabtî ʾet-ʾōyəbe(y)kā wəṣartî ʾet-ṣōrəre(y)kā* 'then I will oppose your opponents and attack your attackers' is typical of biblical poetry (see vol. I, pp. 502–8). In fact, the language of vv 20–33 as a whole is quasi-poetic, with vv 24–26 approaching true poetry (see below). On possible antecedents in Hittite international treaties, see Fensham (1963).

the Amorite . . . him. The language is collective, equivalent to "the Amorites . . . them."

23:24. *bow . . . serve.* We find the same phrasing in the Decalog (20:5).

don't do like their deeds. This might be a general condemnation of Canaanite customs (compare Lev 18:3) or a specific disparagement of their sacrifices. Dillmann (1880: 252) interprets *walō(')* *ta'ăśe(h)* *kəma'ăśêhem* as "don't make like their makings," i.e., do not build idols, taking "their" to refer to the gods, as later in the verse (so also Ehrlich 1908: 360; 1969: 185). But, while *ma'ăśe(h)* sometimes refers to a solid structure (Num 8:4; 1 Kgs 7:28), and while the verbs *hrs* 'destroy' and *šbr* 'smash' function as antonyms to *'śy* 'make, do' in 23:24, nowhere else does *ma'ăśe(h)* connote an idol.

This passage explains why the indigenous peoples of Canaan must be eliminated (Houtman 2000: 271). We are no longer in the idyllic past of Genesis—though even then there were tensions, specifically about intermarriage (e.g., Genesis 24, 28, 34). The only solution is eliminating the non-Israelites as nations. Only a few will survive as *gērîm* 'sojourners,' largely sharing Israelite culture.

Rather. This is Saadiah's interpretation of *kî* following a negative clause.

them . . . their. In the first case, the likely referents are the Canaanites' gods, i.e., their idols, not the Canaanites themselves (Baentsch 1903: 210). In the case of "their pillars," however, it is less clear to whom the pronominal suffix refers. In any event, the Canaanite nations and their gods are equally doomed.

pillars. On the Canaanites' sacred pillars *(maṣṣēbōt)*, see NOTE to 34:13.

23:25. *bread . . . water.* Tgs. *Onqelos* and *Ps.-Jonathan* capture the sense with "food and drink" (cf. 1 Sam 25:11; Isa 3:1; 33:16; Hos 2:7).

23:26. *bereft or barren.* Ibn Ezra plausibly understands this to include both women and cattle; cf. Deut 7:14. Similar themes—fertility/sterility, health/disease—appear in a covenantal context in Exod 15:26; Leviticus 26; Deut 7:13–15; 30:9. For further discussion, see Lohfink (1994: 60–61 n. 79); vol I, pp. 579–82.

your days' number. This promise may be read on two levels (McNeile 1908: 145). On the individual level, the biblical ideal is to die at an old age surrounded by numerous descendants, e.g., Gen 25:8–9; 35:29; Job 42:16–17 (Houtman 2000: 278–79). On the national level, the ideal is eternal residence in the land.

While falling short of true poetry in terms of rhythm, concision and stringent parallelism (see vol. I, pp. 502–8), 23:24–26 possesses a quasi-poetic eloquence proper to hortatory rhetoric:

> Don't bow to their gods and don't serve them
> And don't do according to their deeds;
> Rather, you must destroy, destroy them
> And smash, smash their pillars.
> And you shall serve Yahweh your deity,
> And he will bless your food and your water,
> And I will remove illness from your midst.
> There will not be a bereft or barren (female) in your land;
> Your days' number I shall make full.

23:27. *My terror.* In context, *'ēmātî* means "fear of me (Yahweh)." Cassuto (1967: 308) notes the wordplay with the verb *hammōtî* 'I will discomfit.'

back of the neck. As we say, "turn tail." For the idiom, see Josh 7:8, 12; Ps 18:41.

Unlike the Suph Sea, where Israel had but to stand and watch Yahweh fight, they will have to participate in the battle for Canaan. Yahweh will demoralize the foe, but Israel must conquer them.

23:28. *the ṣirʿâ*. The meaning of this term is disputed, here and in the parallels Deut 7:20; Josh 24:12. The least likely approach, but nonetheless possible, correlates it with ṣāraʿat 'leprosy' (ibn Ezra; cf. Saadiah). If so, the disease is personified. The conquest traditions make no mention of an epidemic among the Canaanites, however. Slightly more plausible is Köhler's (1936: 291) equation with Arabic *ḍaraʿa* 'to be dejected'; better still is Klein's (1987: 557) invocation of Arabic *ṣaraʿa* 'throw down.' By these interpretations, Yahweh promises to dishearten or prostrate the Canaanites.

The most likely understanding, however, is that the *ṣirʿâ* is a stinging insect, as in Rabbinic Hebrew and Aramaic (*ʿarʿîtāʾ*) (Klein, p. 557; on a possible parallel in a New Kingdom Egyptian text, see ANET 477 n. 36). One possibility is that the language is metaphorical: the *ṣirʿâ* symbolizes terror (*ʾêmâ*), to which it is parallel (vv 27–28) (cf. Cassuto 1967: 308). It is also possible that this *ṣirʿâ* is a minor deity, like the Messenger in vv 20–23. Likewise in Ugaritic, among the gods' monstrous adversaries is *ʾil dbb* 'Fly God' (*KTU* 1.3.iii.46). (The similar epithet Beelzebub [*baʿal zəbûb*] 'Lord Fly,' god of Ekron, however, is a dysphemistic pun on *baʿal zəbûl* 'Lord Prince,' a Canaanite divine title.) Overly subtle and yet too naive is the argument that the "hornet" is Pharaoh Merneptah, whose invasion of Canaan otherwise goes unmentioned in the Bible (see Borowski 1983).

More likely, however, the language is collective (LXX, Vg). Exodus envisions an actual swarm of biting or stinging insects (compare Ps 118:12, which likens enemies to bees). Why send such a tiny army? The context provides the answer: to extirpate the Canaanites only gradually, lest the land be neglected. Thus Wis 12:8–10 cites Exod 23:28–30 to palliate the violence of the Conquest: Yahweh deployed stinging insects as a humane gesture, so that the Canaanites might *voluntarily* vacate the land. (Admittedly, Josh 24:12 appears to envision the expulsion by *ṣirʿâ* as rather sudden.)

Overall, I am inclined to understand the *ṣirʿâ* on the analogy of the Plagues of Egypt, which include insect swarms in both E (8:16–27; 10:3–19) and P (8:12–15) (compare also Isa 7:18, where Yahweh threatens Ahaz with flies and bees). Exod 23:28–30 similarly envisions a period when Israel is trying to oust the Canaanites, who are simultaneously beset by a plague of biting or stinging insects. These may serve the function of disheartening them, or the author may have had an intuition of insect-borne disease (on the real and metaphorical use of insects as weapons, see Neufeld 1980). By this reading, it is ironic that in their first encounter, the Canaanites "chase after [Israel] as bees would do" (Deut 1:44). I admit, however, that the narrative of Joshua does not explicitly describe any such pests.

expel. The image of a deity expelling (*grš*) his human foes is paralleled in the Moabite Mesha stele (*KAI* 181.19): "And Chemosh expelled him from before hi[m]"; see Mann (1977: 101 n. 4).

Hivvite . . . Hittite. The catalogue of Canaanite nations, which can contain as many as eleven or twelve elements (Gen 10:15–18; 1 Chr 1:13–16) and most often has six, is curtailed here to avoid too many words between *wəgērəšâ* 'expel' and *milləpāne(y)kā* 'from before you' (Cassuto 1967: 308). Had the sentence begun *wəgērəšâ milləpāne(y)kā*, however, it would have been feasible to cite the entire list. On the enumeration of the Canaanite peoples, see Ishida (1979), O'Connell (1984) and Ausloos (1996: 91–100).

23:29. *field animals.* The term *ḥayyat haśśāde(h)* is collective. It includes both dangerous predators and garden pests, the very creatures left unmolested in the Sabbatical year (23:11).

multiply against you. The phrase *rabbâ ʿāle(y)kā* combines three notions: (a) multiply and attack you, (b) multiply in your presence and (c) become too numerous for you. This implies an Israel that has yet to reach its starlike, sandlike overabundance (e.g., Gen 22:17; 32:13; 1 Kgs 4:20).

23:31. *border.* Gəbūl can also be translated "territory" (Baentsch 1903: 212).

Suph Sea . . . Philistines' Sea. Perpetuating a trope from Canaanite myth, Israel's mythical limits are from "sea to sea" (Amos 8:12; Ps 72:8; cf. Micah 7:12) or "on sea and on rivers" (Ps 89: 26) (Keel 1978: 21). The grandiose imagery hints at universal domain over the (flat) Earth. Yet, the distance from the Red Sea to the Mediterranean is only c. 130 miles/210 km. Moreover, as McNeile (1908: 146) observes, the Israelites never controlled any coastal cities until Jonathan the Hasmonean captured Joppa in 148 B.C.E. (1 Macc 10:76). V 31a gives the land's theoretical dimensions approximately from the southeast to the northwest.

Desert. The text treats *midbār* 'Desert' as a proper name, without a definite article (this is supplied in the ancient translations, however). The name of the desert is unstated, but it is the vast expanse stretching from the Sinai across the Negeb and the Arabah and into Arabia.

the River. Which river? According to most exegetes (e.g., Rashi), it is the Euphrates; cf. Deut 11:24, "from the River, the Euphrates River. . . ." But possibly the author is equivocating, referring vaguely to the *Jordan* as if it were the mighty Eurphrates (cf. Halpern's [2001: 164–74, 187–98, 248–59] discussion of David's conquests).

Whatever the Desert and whatever the River, together they function as opposites (dry and barren vs. wet and teeming) that express a totality (merism).

you will expel them. The meaning of MT *wəgēraštāmô* is not in doubt (on whether the verb was originally second masculine singular or first person singular, see TEXTUAL NOTE). But the suffix *-mô* 'them' is unexpected. Of its twenty-three occurrences, all are in poetry save this one instance (GKC §58g). In prose, we expect the ordinary form *-m* (= Sam). Phonologically, *-mô* is more archaic than *-m* (both go back to *-humu*), but its presence in poetry is no proof of antiquity, since it is favored also by late poets as a pseudo-archaism (GKC §91l; Robertson 1972: 65–69). Since 23:31 is prose, however (*pace* Jacob 1992: 736), *-mô* could be taken as truly archaic. Overall, Cassuto (1967: 309) detects the use of elevated language and quasi-poetic style to mark the epilogue in vv 20–33. On the expulsion of the Canaanites, see also 34:11; Deut 33:27; Josh 24:18; Judg 2:21; 6:9; Ps 78:55; 80:9.

23:32. *with them.* For the expected **ʾittām*, we find *lāhem* 'to them, for them.' To Cassuto (1967: 308), this suggests a covenant of vassalage rather than a treaty between equals. I doubt that we can be so precise.

covenant. The Israelites' covenantal relationship with Yahweh is exclusive. They may not enter into treaties with other parties, whether human (the Canaanites) or divine (their gods). Moreover, as ibn Ezra (shorter commentary) observes, to make an alliance whereby Israel owes the Canaanites aid would undermine God's plan to eliminate them and their gods from the land. The counterexample are the Gibeonites, who trick Israel into a covenant relationship (Joshua 9). Such arrangements are forbidden also by Exod 34:12, 15–16; Deut 7:2–3; Josh 23:12–13; Judg 2:2–3.

23:33. *lest they cause you to sin.* Due to the ambivalence of *kî,* the end of the verse is syntactically very difficult. LXX and Vg take the first *kî* as "if," the second as "indeed." According to Rashi, both *kîs* are quasi-relatives equivalent to *'ăšer:* "lest they cause you to sin against me *in the fact that* you serve their gods, *which* would become for you as a snare." Ramban compares 34:12, "lest *(pen)* it become a snare."

it will become. The subject of *yihye(h)* is unclear. Luzzatto thinks it is the foreign nation under discussion, whereas for Sforno "it" is simply the condition of living among the Canaanites.

snare. The comparison of foreigners to an animal trap is paralleled in Deut 7:16; Josh 23:13; Judg 2:3; 8:27; Ps 106:36. As Exod 34:15–16; Deut 7:2–4; Josh 23:12 spell out, the implicit reference is probably to marriage. On the biblical theme of the destruction/expulsion/subjugation of the Canaanites, see further Weinfeld (1993).

However we parse the clauses, Yahweh's speech concludes in quasi-poetic language:

> They may not dwell in your land,
> Lest they cause you to sin against me;
> When you serve their gods,
> Indeed it will become for you as a snare.

24:1. *But to Moses he said.* The inverted syntax of 24:1, *wǝ'el-mōše(h) 'āmar,* implies one of two things. Either the tense is pluperfect—i.e., prior to speaking chaps. 21–23, Yahweh *had* instructed Moses to bring up Aaron et al. (Rashi)—or else Yahweh has been speaking to someone else, but now turns to Moses personally.

The latter interpretation seems more natural. The diverse legal and hortatory materials in chaps. 20–23 are really for the people. Now Yahweh addresses Moses himself (Ehrlich 1908: 362; 1969: 186). The syntactic disjunction jolts the reader back into the narrative time line and launches a new series of waw-consecutive clauses.

Ascend. Since Moses is already on the mountain, the contextual meaning is "go down and come back up."

to Yahweh. God frequently speaks of himself in the third person.

Aaron. Moses' brother in P, his kinsman in JE (see NOTE to 4:14).

Nadab and Abihu. The names *nādāb* and *'ăbîhû'* respectively mean "Noble" and "He (i.e., God) is my father." In the Priestly source, Nadab and Abihu are Aaron's two elder sons, killed by Yahweh for desecrating the Tabernacle (Leviticus 10). Here in E, while their identity is not stated, a reasonable surmise is that they are likewise Aaron's sons. (The unnamed priests of 19:22 might be Aaron, Nadab and Abihu.)

If Aaron, Nadab and Abihu are priests already in JE, then P's story in Leviticus 10 would be the literary equivalent of a coup. It displaces the authentic Aaronic lines of Nadab and Abihu with Eleazar and Ithamar, whose own Aaronic pedigree, one might further speculate, was disputed or even spurious (on priestly rivalries, see vol. I, pp. 284–86; below, pp. 567–74).

seventy from Israel's elders. The wording implies that there are more than seventy to choose from. Seventy may constitute a theoretical national quorum; compare the seventy elders who appear in Ezek 8:11. Probably the number also represents the seventy Israelite clans of Gen 46:8–27 (see also TEXTUAL NOTE to 1:5). In addition, seventy may have been the ideal number of guests for a sumptuous banquet; Vriezen (1972: 107) notes the invitation of seventy guests to meals in Egyptian and Ugaritic myths.

bow down. All, including Moses, are to prostrate themselves from a distance. Moses alone will approach closer to the Deity.

from afar. As in 20:21(18), this is meant literally—even the magnates may not approach too closely the divine presence—and also idiomatically. At Ugarit (*PRU* 4: 221, 226), to "bow down from afar" means to express homage (Sarna 1991: 151). Sarna compares Jacob's elaborate prostrations, starting at a distance, before his reunion with his estranged brother Esau (Gen 33:3).

24:2. *And Moses.* We might have expected "and you . . . will approach" (ibn Ezra). The reason for the third person is that Moses will relay Yahweh's words to Israel.

the people. As in 19:12–13, 21–24; 34:3, Yahweh is very concerned that the people not come near him.

24:3. *words . . . case-laws.* The latter term, *mišpāṭîm* 'judgments, cases, laws,' refers to the casuistic legal material in 21:1–22:16. The *dəbārîm* 'words' indicate everything else in chaps. 21–23. Also possibly included is the ritual legislation of 20:23(20)–26(23). The Decalog, Yahweh's "words" *par excellence*, may also be meant, assuming that, although the people heard Yahweh's voice, they required Moses to "translate" (see above, pp. 145, 166).

24:4. *wrote down.* The people assent while the laws are still oral. The divine words are then immediately transcribed for posterity.

under the mountain. As in 19:17; 32:19, this refers to either the lower slopes or the plain surrounding the mountain. In any case, it is the region permitted to the common people.

twelve pillar. Stone pillars are common symbols of the divine in Canaanite shrines and as such are frequently condemned in the Bible (NOTE to 34:13). Hence the text is quick to explain, "for Israel's twelve tribes"—not for the gods. Elijah is said to have built a somewhat similar structure at Mount Carmel: an altar made of twelve stones representing the tribes of Israel (1 Kgs 18:31–32) (ibn Ezra [shorter commentary]). A monumental heap of twelve stones appears also in Joshua 4.

for Israel's twelve tribes. Does this means that the stones somehow stand for the tribes (Saadiah paraphrases "equivalent to")? Or was each pillar used by a single tribe? Exactly what are the stones for? Perhaps they stand as monumental witnesses to the Covenant (Dillmann 1880: 256), like the mound erected by Jacob and Laban (Gen 31:45–52), the altar by the Jordan (Joshua 22) and the stela at Shechem (Josh 24:26–27). Or, given the enigmatic sequence of events in the Sinai pericope, it is possible that these pillars are boundary stones separating Israel from the mountain (cf. 19:12, 21–24; Bekhor Shor). Another possibility: the pillars are assembled into an altar, as in 1 Kgs 18:31–32.

Herodotus 3.8 may shed interesting if ambiguous light on Exodus. He reports that when two "Arabs," i.e., Semites, take an oath, they find a third to stand between them, cut their hands with a flint and apply their blood to *seven stones*. This sounds rather like the Covenant between Yahweh and Israel at Sinai-Horeb, with Moses as the arbitrating third party. So perhaps the stones stand as a vestige of an ancient cult practice without any surviving ritual function at all. Sarna (1991: 151) suggests, however, that when Moses "cast [blood] upon the people" (24:8), he really bloodied the pillars that stood for them (cf. Ginsberg 1982: 45–46).

However that may be, as described in the JE document (17:1–7; 19:3–25; 24:1–14; 33), Sinai-Horeb is the classic Semitic shrine (biblical *bāmâ* 'High Place'). It features a mountain, a grotto, a spring, an altar and pillars (cf. Smith 1927: 165–212). All that is missing is a sacred tree—but that role was already played by the burning bush (chaps. 3–4) (see vol. I, p. 199; below, NOTE to 34:13).

SPECULATION: Ehrlich (1908: 362) makes an intriguing suggestion. *Mṣbh* is not the familiar *maṣṣēbâ* 'pillar' but a unique word **maṣṣābâ* 'station.' That is, Moses designates separate places for the tribes to stand. Although Ehrlich takes pains to explain how one "builds" a station, I would uncouple this clause from the preceding and take the end of v 4 as nonverbal and parenthetical: "there being twelve station(s) for Israel's twelve tribes."

24:5. *youths.* Why are youngsters deputized as sacrificers? Some argue that *na'ar* can connote a cultic functionary of any age. The assumed semantic progression would be "youth" > "servant" > "minister" (i.e., one who serves the community by serving the Deity). But it appears that young men sometimes were deputized as priests (cf. 33:11; Judg 17:7–13; 1 Samuel 1:24; 2–3) (Holzinger 1900: 105). *Tgs.* Onqelos and Ps.-Jonathan paraphrase *na'ărê* in 24:5 as "firstborn," the latter explaining they were Israel's original clergy—in agreement with some modern scholarship (e.g., vol. I, pp. 455–56).

I, however, think that here "youths" simply means "non-elders," since the elders accompany Moses partway up the mountain (Mendelssohn *Biur* [*apud* Jacob 1992: 741]). For further discussion of the role of *na'ar*, see NOTE to 33:11, "youth."

sent up. I.e., burned (*he'ĕlâ*).

Ascending-offerings. On the wholly burnt *'ōlâ*, see pp. 702–3.

slaughtered. The verb *zābaḥ* 'slaughter' usually connotes making a meat sacrifice (*zebaḥ*) shared by Yahweh and worshipers (Milgrom 1991: 218). On the relationship between slaughter and sacrifice, see below, pp. 695–701.

Exod 24:5 marks the fulfillment of Moses' request of Pharaoh, "Release my people, that they may celebrate to me in the wilderness" (5:1, etc.) (Jacob 1992: 742–43).

Slaughter-offerings, Concluding-offerings. It is not clear whether there is a difference between *zəbāḥîm* and *šəlāmîm*. Both terms indicate a sacrifice wherein the worshiper consumes most of the meat.

bulls. While the plain sense is that the bulls are for both types of offerings, the MT cantillation could be taken to indicate that they are only for the Concluding-offerings (cf. *b. Yoma* 52b; *Ḥag.* 6b; Bekhor Shor). But this would make no sense. Surely Yahweh is entitled to a holocaust of the most valuable animal, i.e., a bull.

The text does not state the total number of animals. Ibn Ezra (shorter commentary) opines that there are twenty-four victims, two per tribe for the two varieties of sacrifice.

24:6. *half the blood.* Was the blood from the two types of offerings kept separate (so Rashi)? Or were the collections mixed and poured? The blood is not necessarily divided literally in half; rather, it may simply be divided. Obviously, more fluid is required to spatter the people than to spatter the altar (Ehrlich 1908: 363; 1969: 187).

The scene in 24:6 reminds Bekhor Shor of Abram halving the animals in Genesis 15, when he enters into a covenant with Yahweh. Cutting things in two parts symbolizes the reciprocity of a compact, and the fate of mutilation that will befall whichever party proves faithless. Similarly, in Exodus, the sacrificial blood probably represents the blood of each party, theoretically forfeit in case of treachery (cf. Dillmann 1880: 257); compare the Herodotean report cited above (NOTE to 24:4, "for Israel's twelve tribes") and see below, pp. 308–9.

in the bowls. The definite article (not "in [some] bowls") implies that the reader is familiar with sacrificial ritual. Several bowls are needed to speed the process of spattering the people.

he cast. Presumably this blood, too, was collected in a vessel *(mizrāq)* or vessels and conveyed to the altar; cf. NOTE to 27:3, "bowls." Or perhaps a hyssop bunch was dipped directly into the animal's blood (cf. 12:22).

24:7. *Covenant Document.* The term *sēper habbərît* has entered into scholarly parlance as a technical term, the "Book of the Covenant" or "Covenant Code," defining a portion of Exodus. Unfortunately, scholars disagree on what is included: all of 20:22(19)–23:33 (already Spinoza 1951: 125) or only 21:1–23:33? It is also possible that the Covenant Document is 23:20–23, Yahweh's promise to Israel. (For Rashi, however, the Covenant Document is Genesis 1 through Exodus 15!) In fact, it is unclear whether the expression denotes a specific corpus at all or simply means "the text of the Covenant."

Most likely, at least for the composite text, the "Covenant Document" is none other than the stone tablets. Deuteronomy, a commentary on an early form of Exodus, explicitly calls the Ten Words the Covenant, in distinction from the various specific statutes (Deut 4:13; 9:9). D's expression "Covenant Chest *('ărôn habbərît)*" also implicitly equates the tablets with the Covenant.

do and heed. At one level, this is hysteron proteron, since audition should precede performance (see also TEXTUAL NOTE). But *šāmaʿ* 'hear, heed' also connotes obedience (cf. Vg). Accordingly, the meaning is: "We will perform it with a will."

Already in 19:8, the people promised to "do." Ibn Ezra (shorter commentary) and Rashbam proffer an attractive interpretation of 24:7: "we will do" refers to all that has been commanded so far. "We will heed" refers to all that may be commanded in the future. And for Ehrlich (1908: 363), "do" refers to commands, "heed" to admonitions and promises.

24:8. *cast.* Presumably, Moses has assistants carry the bowls among the people for the sparging.

the people. Ibn Ezra supposes that, for practicality's sake, the elders stand in for the entire people. But we would rather expect the pillars to serve this function (cf. Cassuto 1967: 313); see NOTE to 24:4, "for Israel's twelve tribes."

Covenant blood. On the relationship between blood and covenant, see below, pp. 308–9.

cut. For unclear reasons, the verb *kārat* 'cut, cut down, sever, hew' connotes covenant-making in Hebrew and Phoenician (*KAI* 27.9–11 [Arslan Tash]). For discussion, see Hasel (1995).

all these words. These are the laws and principles of chaps. 21–23 (Saadiah).

24:10. *saw.* Exod 33:12–23 states emphatically that humans cannot survive a direct vision of Yahweh's Face. In 24:9–11, however, select members of the people are granted a vision of Yahweh enthroned in glory. The text comments that, contrary to expectation, they were not harmed: Yahweh "did not send forth his arm."

under his feet. Better, "at his feet," i.e., surrounding his feet (Ehrlich 1908: 363); cf. the expression "under the mountain" (19:17; 24:4; 32:19). The text describes a stone pavement, not a stone footstool. On the theology of divine feet, see below, pp. 519–20.

Although the elders see Yahweh, the author conceals the divine appearance from the reader. We may see in our minds only the pavement beneath his feet. Possibly the text's reticence implies that the elders themselves, glimpsing God from the corners of their eyes, did not actually dare to lift their gaze (Noth 1962: 195). Childs (1974: 506) imagines that the elders gaze upward through a translucent, blue barrier that partially obscures their view.

lapis lazuli. The blue color is that of the sky, just as, in Canaanite myth, the storm god's sky-palace is constructed of gold, silver and lapis lazuli (*KTU* 1.4.v.15–19, 31–35, 38–40; vi.34–38). The Babylonian god Bel-Marduk, too, sits on a lapis lazuli throne in Heaven (Livingstone 1986: 82–83). And Ezek 1:26 similarly implies that the transparent sky receives its hue from Yahweh's lapis lazuli throne placed directly above.

brickwork. The sky—our ceiling, so to speak—is simultaneously God's palace floor (cf. Ezek 1:26). Akkadian texts, too, mention a heaven of stone (Livingstone 1986: 86).

heaven's bone. "Bone" is an overliteral rendering. *ʿEṣem haššāmayim* means "the sky's substance" or "the sky itself."

The text never says clearly what is under Yahweh's feet, only that it is solid and blue. It is presumably the firmament that sustains the waters above—P's "plating *(rāqîaʿ)*" (Gen 1:6–8), Ezekiel's "plating appearing like dreadful ice" (Ezek 1:22, 25), Job's "polished mirror" (Job 37:18) and the "Glass Sea" of Rev 4:6; 15:2. Similarly, Ps 29:10 probably describes Yahweh as enthroned on or next to the celestial waters *(mabbûl)* (see Kloos 1986: 62–66). In Exodus, as Israel's leaders climb above the cloud level, they see Yahweh standing or more likely sitting enthroned above the firmament (LXX; cf. Ezek 1:22–26).

clarity. *Ṭōhar* here refers both to a gemstone's pure color and to a cloudless sky (cf. Job 37:21). But its most frequent meaning is also apposite: the ritual *purity* of Heaven.

24:11. *elite.* There is little doubt that Hebrew *ʾāṣîl* is cognate to Arabic *ʾaṣīl* 'noble.' But the Israelites may have created a folk association with the architectural and anatomical term *ʾaṣṣîl* (< Proto-Semitic **wṣl*), perhaps meaning "joint" or "edge" (cf. Holzinger 1900: 106). Dillmann (1880: 258) notes Ewald's comparison of the expression *pinnôt hāʿām* 'the people's corners (i.e., elite) in Judg 20:2; 1 Sam 14:38; cf. Isa 19:13. A similar association underlies *qəṣôt hāʿām* 'the people's edges' in 1 Kgs 12:31; 13:33 (note Isa 41:9, where both *ʾăṣîlîm* and *qāṣôt* appear).

The term *ʾăṣîlîm* for chieftains foreshadows Num 11:17, 25, where Yahweh proposes to *ʾṣl* 'remove the excess' of Moses' prophetic power to share it among seventy elders (Rashi).

did not send forth his arm. The divine "arm" symbolizes injury or mischance (Roberts 1971). Yahweh does not harm the elders at Sinai-Horeb, even though in other circumstances it is death to see God.

beheld. It is important for the parties making an agreement physically to see one another. The verb is *ḥāzâ*, not the more familiar *rāʾâ*, perhaps because the text denies that Man can *rāʾâ* 'see' Yahweh and live (33:20) (Ehrlich 1908: 363–64). For Jacob 1992: 746), *ḥāzâ* specifically connotes prophetic vision *(ḥāzôn)*, but I cannot find a real distinction from *rāʾâ*. Cross-culturally, the archetypical worship experience is when worshiper and deity behold one another (for India, see Eck 1985).

ate and drank. To eat before someone is to acknowledge his authority and beneficence, and conversely one's own dependence and vulnerability (cf. the aristocracy eating and drinking before Adonijah [1 Kgs 1:25] and the prince eating bread before Yahweh [Ezek 44:3]). Covenants in particular, whether or not between equals, are celebrated by a feast, to terminate the sometimes tense negotiations and to restore good cheer or its semblance (cf. Gen 26:28–31; 31:44–54; Josh 9:11–15; 2 Sam 3:20–21; Isa 55:1–3).

Subservient to God's law and dependent on his protective power, at Sinai-Horeb Israel's leaders are fêted as loyal vassals. Ps 81:9–11, 14–17 likewise associates the Decalog with victory and dining:

Hear, my people, and I will testify to you;
Israel, if you would listen to me:
You shall have no strange god,

Nor bow to a foreign god.
I am Yahweh your deity who brought you up from the land of Egypt.
Open your mouth and I will fill it. . . .
If only my people would heed me,
(If) Israel would walk in my ways,
I would . . . subdue their enemies. . . .
He (*sic!*) would feed you from wheat-fat,
And from a mountain I'd sate you with grape-honey.

A literary theme with deep roots in Near Eastern myth is a god's victory over his foes at a mountain, followed by the proclamation of his kingship, the fashioning of his dwelling and a celebratory party (see *KTU* 1.4.vii.49–52). These motifs appear in the redacted Sinai-Horeb pericope as the battle with Amalek (17:8–16), the Covenant (19:3–24:8), the visit to Yahweh's celestial palace for a feast (24:9–11) and the construction of the Tabernacle (chaps. 25–31, 35–40). Such a victory banquet is described also in Ps 23:5, "You lay a table before me, in my adversaries' presence, you smeared my head with oil, my cup overflows."

What dish does Yahweh serve the elders? Possibly they partake of the etherealized stuff of Israel's sacrifices, Yahweh's own food. Alternatively, they are consuming their sacrificial portions of the Slaughter-offerings (cf. ibn Ezra). "The eating and drinking of the elders is an admittedly one-sided covenant-meal" (Holzinger 1900: 106)—perhaps because the parties are not social equals. As suzerain, God does not eat in his subjects' presence. The elders' feasting contrasts with Moses' own ascetic fast before Yahweh (34:28; Deut 9:9) (ibn Ezra), and also with their next feast—while celebrating before the Gold Calf (32:6).

24:12. *Ascend.* Either Moses and the elders are tacitly supposed to have descended (ibn Ezra [shorter commentary]), or else Moses ascends even closer to Yahweh.

tablets. Engraved tablets might be of wood, clay or metal, but stone is preferable for its imperishability; what is engraved cannot easily be erased or altered (Bekhor Shor). Roman treaties, similarly, were inscribed on bronze tablets (Sarna 1991: 108). But unlike metal, stone is a natural substance not requiring human manufacture. Carved stone thus is symbolically suitable for the recording and monumental display of immutable laws, be they Rome's Twelve Tables or Yahweh's Decalog.

We are not told here how many tablets Moses receives. In 31:18; 32:15, they are said to be two. According to 34:28; Deut 4:13; 10:4, they contain the Decalog. It is unclear whether each tablet bears half of the Decalog, or the two tablets are duplicates. In comparable ancient Near Eastern treaties, each party keeps his own copy. Hence, one might think that the Covenant Tablets are duplicates. But why would Yahweh give Israel his own copy? P's notion of the Tabernacle as the intersection of Heaven and Earth potentially makes sense of this notion (below, pp. 675–95). But I remain uncertain of what the Elohist originally had in mind.

Direction . . . command. LXX plausibly takes *haṭṭôrâ* and *hammiṣwâ* as collectives, tantamount to plurals; for Vg only the second is collective.

Did not Moses already transcribe "all Yahweh's words" as the "Covenant Document" (24:4, 7)? It is unclear whether what Yahweh proposes to write in 24:12 is the same or a different text.

I have written. Yahweh had not only proclaimed the Decalog; he had inscribed it. In Israel's semiliterate culture, a message was official only once it had been both written and read aloud; see NOTE to 17:14.

24:13. *Moses ascended.* Tacitly accompanied by Joshua, who reappears in 32:17.

24:14. *he had said.* The pluperfect is expressed by inverted syntax (Rashi).

Stay for us. The expected words would be **šabû-lākem* 'stay you,' as in Gen 22:5 (see above, pp. 147–48). "For us" is ambivalent; it means "wait for us" and also "be here in our place while we're on the mountain." The elders are to stand between the camp and the mountaintop, from which position they can govern the people.

Aaron and Hur. In E, Aaron is Moses' kinsman not brother (vol. I, p. 214). On Hur, see NOTE to 17:10. Moses' delegation of authority to Aaron sets up the debacle of chap. 32, the Gold Calf.

has words. Ba'al *dabārîm* literally means "owner of words." *Dabārîm* 'words' implies a dispute (Rashi; Dillmann [1880: 260], comparing 18:16–19, 26; 22:8). Either this passage does not know of the judicial innovations of chap. 18 (Ehrlich 1908: 364), or else Aaron and Hur simply take Moses' place as the court of last resort.

24:15. *Moses ascended.* I take this as *Wiederaufnahme* (Kuhl 1952). That is, this is the same ascent mentioned in v 13, reiterated after the pluperfect digression in v 14.

the cloud. He'ānān could also be translated collectively: "clouds."

24:16. *Glory . . . cloud.* P inclines occasionally toward quasi-poetic parallelism: "And Yahweh's Glory settled upon Mount Sinai, / And the cloud covered it six days" (cf. Cross 1973: 166–67 n. 87). It appears that the Glory abides only on the mountaintop, while the smoke sheathes the entire mountain downward (ibn Ezra).

covered it. Ibn Ezra understands *waykassēhû* as "covered *him*," i.e., Moses.

24:16. *Glory.* On Yahweh's effulgence, see Weinfeld (1995) and p. 674.

settled. The verb *šākan* evokes the derived noun *miškān* 'Tabernacle,' where Yahweh's presence will reside (40:34–35) (Cassuto 1967: 316).

six days. The reason for this time lapse is unspecified. Ehrlich (1908: 365) and Batto (1992: 120) attractively suggest that Yahweh spends six days making the model for the Tabernacle (25:9, 40), just as he spent six days making the world (see further below, pp. 675–76). One might also suppose that Moses is purifying himself (cf. 29:30, 35, 37) (Cassuto 1967: 316), or that Yahweh's Glory is cauterizing Sinai of its impurities.

24:17. *appearance.* The text says what the Glory looked like to the Israelites, not what it actually was. This coyness in describing the Glory is still more pronounced in Ezekiel 1 (cf. Terrien 1978: 137).

consuming fire. Although Moses approaches the blazing fire, he is not consumed, rather like the Bush that initiated his mission (3:2–3 [JE]). On whether he suffers an injury from this proximity, see below, pp. 620–23. On fire as a theme in Exodus, see briefly vol. I, p. 36.

24:18. *forty.* On this stereotypical number in the Bible, see Pope (1962b: 565). Exod 34:28 and Deut 9:9 will add the detail that Moses fasts during this period. At least in the composite text, a reasonable inference is that it takes forty days for Yahweh to explain the Tabernacle (chaps. 25–31) to Moses (Ehrlich 1908: 365).

COMMENT

STAND AT SINAI

Rooted on Earth, piercing the clouds—a mountain literally connects Heaven and Earth (see Metzger 1970). At Sinai, *Mek. baḥōdeš* 4 (cf. 9) explains with a homely analogy, God "bent the lower Heavens and upper Supreme Heavens onto the mountaintop, and Glory descended, and he laid them on top of Mount Sinai as a man would lay a mattress upon a bed." When Moses climbs the mountain, he approaches Heaven itself, in order to mediate a pact between Yahweh and Israel.

Like all matters religious, the Covenant operates along horizontal and vertical axes. Horizontally, its practical function is to unite the people into a common society and nation. For materialists, this is the beginning and end of religion (Durkheim 1915). In the Bible's terms, however, lateral social cohesion is merely the precondition for the more important relationship between all Israel beneath and Yahweh above. The conical mountain, wide at its terrestrial base but narrowing to a single point in Heaven, perfectly symbolizes Israelite religion and culture.

Just as the Tabernacle has been described as a "portable Sinai" (see pp. 687–88), so one could call the mountain a "stationary Tabernacle." Writes Sarna (1991: 105),

> A close similarity to the wilderness Tabernacle is suggested by several shared characteristics. Both Sinai and the Tabernacle evidence a tripartite division. The summit corresponds to the inner sanctum, or Holy of Holies. The second zone, partway up the mountain, is the equivalent of the Tabernacle's outer sanctum, or Holy Place. The third zone, at the foot of the mountian, is analogous to the outer court. As with the Tabernacle, the three distinct zones of Sinai feature three gradations of holiness in descending order. Just as Moses alone may ascend to the peak of the mountain, so all but one are barred from the Holy of Holies in the Tabernacle. Just as the Holy Place is the exclusive preserve of the priesthood, so only the priests and elders are allowed to ascend to a specific point on the mountain. The confinement of the laity to the outer court of the Tabernacle, where the altar of burnt offering was located, evokes the parallel with Sinai in the restriction of the laity to the foot of the mountain, where the altar was built. The graduated restrictions on access, touch, and sight are the counterparts of the repeated regulations about the unlawful invasion of sacred domain in the same three ways. God is said to "descend" upon the mountain as

upon the Tabernacle, and He communicates with Moses on the summit as He does in the Holy of Holies. Finally, the vivid descriptions of smoke, dense cloud, and fire that issued from and enveloped Sinai are paralleled by the cloud and fire that become associated with the Tabernacle.

Why must Israel and Yahweh enter into a new covenant? Had not Yahweh already covenantally promised Israel's ancestors numerous progeny and the possession of Canaan? The intervening centuries have witnessed the seeming realization of God's first obligation: the Hebrews are now a teeming multitude (chap. 1; 12:37). But at Sinai, Israel learns that the promise of land has strings attached, and great amounts of fine print. Like any solid compact, the Covenant entails specific obligations, as well as specific consequences for compliance and noncompliance.

At Sinai, Yahweh begins to disclose to Moses and Israel what he apparently concealed from the Patriarchs: Israel's continued residence in Canaan will be contingent upon their adherence to a legal and cultic standard that will set them apart from the indigenous peoples. But God is not yet fully candid. On the positive side, he promises that Israel will become Yahweh's "treasure beyond all the peoples . . . a priests' kingdom and a holy nation." On the negative side, he merely warns, "Be careful for yourself" (34:12). As if not wishing to spoil the joyous occasion with notes of doom, Yahweh does not spell out the drastic consequences for disobedience. Later, Leviticus 26 and Deuteronomy 27–30 will explicitly announce that the gift of land is conditional. Apostasy's ultimate price will be loss of the land, i.e., exile.

KING YAHWEH AND VASSAL ISRAEL

As stated above (pp. 34–35), modern scholars recognize that the biblical Covenant between Israel and Yahweh was modeled primarily on international political treaties, rather than, say, articles of servitude, land sales or marriage contracts (Bickermann 1976: 1.1–32; Mendenhall 1954; Baltzer 1971). Unfortunately, critics have gotten somewhat sidetracked debating the matter of form, i.e., whether there is such a thing as a uniform ancient Near Eastern vassal treaty, and whether specific biblical texts manifest all its features, etc. I am content to observe that an ancient political treaty *may* exhibit many of the following elements:

 a. Identification of the document as a treaty.
 b. Identification of the two parties.
 c. Review of past relations between the parties, in particular the overlord's beneficence toward the vassal.
 d. Stipulations of what the suzerain requires of the vassal, including exclusive fidelity and regular submission of tribute.
 e. Provisions for the storage of the document and its future public recitation.
 f. A list of divine witnesses.
 g. Blessings for obedience.
 h. Curses for disobedience.

The compact was then ratified before the gods with sacrifices. Various disagreeable acts might be performed to dramatize the fate of a perfidious vassal.

Nowhere does the Bible actually represent the text of the Covenant between Yahweh and Israel. The important thing is that a Covenant exists. (Compare the "Constitution" of Great Britain.) Its contents may be imagined, and even discovered by experience, as specific actions on Israel's part seem to provoke divine responses. The prophets' special role was to interpret the Covenant to the people, the light of the people's behavior and the nation's historical vicissitudes.

Among other things, the Covenant may be viewed as an exercise in practical theodicy. Under the assumptions that Yahweh is just and that Yahweh is in charge, when Israelites suffer individually or corporately, the only possible inference is that they have violated the Covenant. Covenant ideology, in other words, is a device to explain fortune and misfortune. (For a comparison with ancient beliefs concerning demons, see Propp 2004c.)

NINE–TEN–ELEVEN–TWELVE WORDS

The ordinances that Israel must follow to receive the benefit of Yahweh's promises open with the Decalog. In English, these are known as the "Ten Commandments." Their original Hebrew name, however, is "the Ten Words (*'ăśeret haddəbārîm*)" (34:28; Deut 4:13; 10:4), which is also the etymology of "deca-log." This is an important point, because, as we shall see, many exegetes find in 20:2–17(14) not ten *commands* but ten *statements*.

Chapter 20 nowhere says that vv 2–17(14) contain ten laws. That is first stated in 34:28; Deut 4:13; 10:4. Still, the number ten bears tradition's authorizing stamp and is probably the author's intention. Yet counting the commands proves surprisingly difficult. Even leaving out the Samaritan version, which appends a final commandment concerning worship at Mount Gerizim (TEXTUAL NOTE to 20:17[14], "of your fellow"), mainstream Jewish and Christian interpretations proffer three contradictory divisions of the laws, with the differences clustered at the beginning (20:2–6) and end (20:17[14]). (For a convenient chart, see Freedman 2000: 15–16.)

The least likely partition, in my view, is that espoused by Clement of Alexandria and Augustine and perpetuated in the Catholic Church. It takes 20:2 as prefatory and vv 3–6 as the first commandment. The ninth and tenth commandments are found within 20:17(14): first not to covet another's house, second not to covet his wife, slaves, livestock and property. The problem is that here *bayit* does not connote a stone structure, a domicile, but a household, which includes humans and animals. Thus this verse contains a basic directive, "Don't covet your fellow's house," the meaning of which is then explained. To my mind, breaking v 17(14) into two commands is as illogical as, say, breaking vv 8–10 into three commands: to remember the Sabbath, to work for six days, and to desist on the seventh. No one would read the text that way.

Probably the most popular view is that proposed by Philo *Quis Her.* 169 and Josephus *Ant.* 3.91 and revived by Zwingli and Calvin. It regards 20:2 as introductory and takes v 17(14) as containing only one commandment. Vv 3–6 are then divided between the first and second commands, against worshiping other gods and fashioning images of them. This seems the most obvious division, as it contains ten distinct injunctions.

And yet normative Jewish tradition (there are Rabbinic dissenters) takes God's self-identification in 20:2 as the first Word (see already Philo *Mut.* 23). The second Word is then contained in vv 3–6, and so on, with 20:17(14) a single injunction against coveting. The chief immediate drawback of this classification is that v 2, "I am Yahweh . . . ," contains no imperative and thus stands apart formally from the following nine Words, which are true commands. Even if we are counting ten "words" not ten "commands," this seems a little strange. A second potential drawback of the Rabbinic division is that 20:3–6, which forbids both the worship of other gods and idolatry, is classed as one long provision, whereas one might be inclined to see two separate commands with Philo and Josephus. But this last problem is no problem at all. The Bible makes little distinction between polytheism per se and idolatry per se (see pp. 778–79). I now find it most natural to read the basic command as v 3, with vv 4–6 providing some elaboration.

Barring unforeseen epigraphic discoveries, the matter cannot be decided. I share the Christian impression that 20:2 is a preface, not part of a list. I share the Jewish view that vv 3–6 are a single Word. And I share the Jewish-Protestant view that v 17(14) is a single command. And yet that leaves me with only nine Words.

> SPECULATION: It is curious that, if we combine the three prevalent divisions of 20:2–17(14), we arrive at a "dodecalog." Is it possible that, Deuteronomy notwithstanding, we are meant to find *twelve* commands, one per tribe? I have trouble imagining, however, that this was the author's intention, especially against the ancient witness of 34:28; Deut 4:13; 10:4 that Yahweh's Words number ten.

However we enumerate its provisions, the Decalog represents someone's notion of what it meant to belong to Israel, Yahweh's "priests' kingdom and holy nation." But what is distinctive in the Ten Words? What culture does not espouse respect for the elderly; regard for life, property and marital ties; adherence to the truth, and the cultivation of a good attitude toward one's neighbor? In the Decalog, only the demand for worshiping Yahweh alone, the ban on images and Sabbath observance are distinctively Israelite.

Thus the Torah, one might say, elevates common decency into a divine statute. The genius of the biblical author was to take what everybody acknowledged was right, and attribute its origin to Yahweh as a special gift to Israel. In part, the intention was rhetorical, even polemical. It is a time-approved strategy to buttress one's ideological platform with platitudes. By attaching the noncontroversial to the controversial, the latter goes down more smoothly. Anyone who worships idols and other gods, the Decalog implies, is likely a killer, adulterer, elder-abuser, liar and thief. Anyone opposed to murder, adultery, falsehood, elder-abuse and theft will worship Yahweh alone and keep his Sabbath. Because they lack the Ten Words, foreigners are basically immoral. In short, the Decalog's gist is to be found in its opening provisions. The rest is just good advice.

This move was entirely characteristic of biblical and later Jewish religion. Anyone can wear a fringed garment; the Israelite does so in obedience to Yahweh and so earns special merit (Num 15:38–39; Deut 22:12). Any man can be circumcised; the Israelite removes his foreskin in obedience to Yahweh and so earns special merit (Genesis 17; Propp 1987b). The Decalog's moral: people all over the world may tell the truth and honor the elderly. But when an Israelite does this, he is strengthening his people's bond with God.

Against appearances, the Decalog is probably no ancient foundational document. More likely, it is a pithy attempt to render the essence of society and law, comparable to the celebrated, "golden" formulations of Hillel and Jesus (cf. Houtman 2000: 7–8). A society regulated solely by the Decalog would not last very long. The Ten Words provide merely the basic principles of behavior, a theoretical standard of limited practical value.

The Decalog is not the Covenant (*pace* Mendenhall 1954). The Decalog is the *symbol* of the Covenant, a text short enough to be engraved on one or two tablets and deposited in a chest. The true Covenant lies in the details, elaborated with each level of redaction, as P, D and E were successively added to J. At the far end, the process would yield the beliefs that the Covenant was subject to near-infinite interpretation and elaboration (Judaism) or had been replaced by God (Christianity).

The elusive number ten is probably symbolic. Just as the numbering of the twelve tribes of Israel is somewhat fluid—does one count Levi; are Ephraim and Manesseh one tribe or two?—so we cannot easily enumerate the Ten Words. Perhaps part of their mystique lies in the fact, like the trees of Christopher Robin's enchanted place, they will never by definitively counted. (With varying success, scholars have attempted to extract other decalogs from 21:2–11; 34:11–26; Lev 18:6–18; 19:2–18; 20:2–21; Deut 27:15–26; Ezek 18:5–9; Ps 15:2–5; for bibliography, see Houtman 2000: 9 n. 12.)

THE FIRST CODE

In the current state of the text, Exodus 19–20 sets the stage for what I call the "First Code" (20:22[19]–23:19). It is not the oldest law-code in history; it merely stands first in the Torah. (Others use the names "Book of the Covenant" and "Covenant Code," disagreeing as to its precise delimitation [see further NOTE to 24:7].) As we have seen, many of its provisions are paralleled in the legal literature of other peoples.

The First Code opens with cultic ordinances for proper worship (20:23[20]–26[23]). These I would connect to the epilogue in 23:14–33, concerning worship and the dire risk of apostasy.

The heart of the First Code is a set of *mišpāṭîm* 'case-laws' couched in the casuistic "if . . . then" syntax characteristic of ancient Near East legal corpora (21:1–22:16). Finkelstein (1981) proposes a sensible partition of these "cases" based upon their content. The first section, 21:1–32, one may call the "Law of Persons," regulating cases in which individuals are deprived of liberty or life, whether legally (servitude, execution) or illegally (kidnapping, murder). In 21:33–22:16, we have the "Law of Things," i.e., theft and damage. Here the penalties are generally monetary.

To an extent, however, Finkelstein's partition is undermined by numerical patterns that overleap his sectional divisions. It is noteworthy that 21:2–36 contains ten main laws, each introduced by *kî* 'when': (21:2, 7, 14, 18, 20, 22, 26, 28, 33, 35) (e.g., Dillmann 1880: 225). (In fact, however, 21:14 is a subordinate law concerning the limits of asylum; the main law is enunciated participially in v 12, "Whoever strikes a man and he dies must be put to death, death.") The laws on personal injuries alone comprise seven *kî* clauses (21:18, 20, 22, 26, 28, 33, 35) as do the laws of property (21:37; 22:4, 5, 6, 9, 13, 15) (Jacob 1992: 607, 678). These number patterns may have served as memorization aids—or may just have symbolized order and perfection.

The remaining contents of 22:17–23:19 are hard to classify. They treat mainly two topics: (a) maintaining internal social harmony by proper dealings with the poor and even one's enemies; and (b) maintaining harmony with Yahweh by negative acts (minimizing ritual impurity) and positive acts (festival worship). The First Code ends with exhortations to avoid contamination from Canaanite religion, as the people take possession of the land (23:20–33).

THE DECALOG AND THE FIRST CODE

In the composite text, one can read much of the First Code as a commentary on the Decalog—even if, in reality, the Decalog could have originated as a synopsis of the older First Code. The Ten Words begin, "I am Yahweh . . . who took you out . . . from a slaves' house" (20:2); the First Code's case-laws begin with the treatment and liberation of slaves. Exod 21:2–11 is itself a sort of decalog, with symmetrical five-clause provisions governing respectively male and female servants.

The Decalog's first explicit injunction concerns the exclusive worship of Yahweh (20:3); closely linked is the following prohibition on images (20:4–6). These two requirements, monolatry and aniconism, frame the First Code. Exod 20:22(19)–26(23) restates that Israel witnessed Yahweh's role in the Covenant ("You, you saw that from the sky I spoke with you"), forbids idolatry and describes the proper mode of altar-worship. These subjects return in 22:19 (not sacrificing to other gods), 23:13 (not mentioning other gods) and especially 23:23–33 (not making covenants with the Canaanites or their gods, but destroying them and their idols).

The Decalog's next command concerns sullying Yahweh's "name," i.e., his honor and reputation (20:7). This recurs in 22:27, "Deity don't curse."

The next command is Sabbath-keeping (20:8–11). This subject returns in 23:10–12, the seven-year agricultural cycle and the seven-day work cycle.

The next command concerns filial piety (20:12). This is covered in 21:15, 17, "Whoever strikes his father or his mother must be put to death, death. . . . And whoever curses his father or his mother must be put to death, death."

The next command concerns murder (20:13). What constitutes murder? What if the homicide is unpremeditated? What if the cause of death is unclear? What about nondeadly assaults? What if the victim is a fetus? What if the killer is an animal? What if the victim is a slave or a minor or an animal? What if the killing is a judicial execution? Are there acts so heinous they are legally equivalent to murder? All these topics are treated in 21:12–36.

The next command concerns sexual crimes (20:14). Although the First Code does not address adultery per se, it does discuss seduction in the context of damage to property (22:15–16).

The next command concerns theft (20:15), more broadly definable as illegitimate transfer of ownership. This constitutes the matter of 21:37–22:16.

The next command returns to the matter of false testimony (20:16). Without reliable court procedure, no one can be prosecuted for the violation of any laws. Exod 23:1–3, 6–8 concerns the fair administration of justice.

The final command (20:17[14]) is not really a law at all, but an acknowledgment that desire is the root of unhappiness. Murder, theft, adultery, perjury—all are usually motivated by greed. Perhaps this clause may be linked specifically to the First Code's exhortations not to oppress one's indigent neighbors (22:20–26; 23:9).

Overall, the laws of the First Code appear to be grouped but not really organized. They are heterogenous in style and content. This is partly a result of the hazards of redaction and accretion. But it also reflects a mind-set less concerned than ours with classificatory hierarchies. There is some evidence that non-Western peoples organize material differently for purposes of memorization, with far less use of sorting or classifying (Colby and Cole 1973). It is undeniable, for example, that 21:26–27 (injuries to slaves) would make more sense preceding v 20 (killing a slave) (Ehrlich 1908: 349), and yet the principle of verbal association ("eye, tooth") takes precedence. To me, the First Code and other biblical codes create the impression of being recounted by an elderly legist with a rather fragmented memory. But the ancient Israelites doubtless perceived things differently.

Though under the NOTES I have quoted numerous examples, I shall not enter deeply into the question of the apparent dependency of Israelite upon Mesopotamian law. For that, see Paul (1970), Finkelstein (1981), Westbrook (1988), Otto (1989, 1991), Van Seters (2003) and Wright (2003). The influence might have occurred in many ways: e.g., imported by a crucial element in Israel from Mesopotamia (the Abrahamic tradition), or mediated by the dominance of cuneiform culture in the Late Bronze Age, or during later Israel's interactions with the great powers of Mesopotamia. We might also posit common sources, since the two Mesopotamian corpora most similar to the Bible, the Laws of Eshnunna and of Hammurapi, arose in a milieu of strong Northwest Semitic (Amorite) influence. One must also distinguish between two questions: the dependence of discrete Israelite laws upon Mesopotamian prototypes, and the dependence of the biblical redactional process upon Mesopotamian legal scholarship (Otto 1991).

It remains an open question what the ancient Near Eastern law codes, including the Bible's First Code, were used for. Like the Decalog, the First Code would have been insufficient to regulate a society, as it leaves many important matters unaddressed. What if one kills or injures another's slave? What if a slave injures a free man? What if one makes a false accusation? What if one receives stolen goods? In contrast with Mesopotamian legislation, biblical law seems largely indifferent to economic matters (e.g., trade) and family life (marriage, inheritance). Finkelstein (1981: 38) writes, "The biblical attitude towards wrongful taking . . . may be described as almost complacent. This stands out especially in comparison with the severity with which biblical law treats wrongs against persons, and even more when we consider the stern treatment of wrongful taking in Hammurapi's laws, which often invoke the capital penalty (e.g., §§7–13)." This distinctive trait is strikingly illustrated by 22:1–2, which focuses on the value of a burglar's life, not the punishment he must suffer for his theft. Unlike the more encyclopedic Mesopotamian and Hittite compendia, the First Code focuses on complex, ambiguous cases, as is especially visible in the laws on personal injuries (21:18–36). Basic principles are left to inference—or rather they are assumed.

So far as we can tell, judges did not consult or follow ancient Near Eastern law codes. These texts functioned more as *symbols* of justice, generally issued by monarchs to celebrate their godly rule (Bottéro 1992: 156–84). Thus law codes were inscribed on monuments and publicly proclaimed (Watts 1999: 15–31). Quite apart from justice, among the law's purposes was simply to cause people to assemble and assent to authority. A secondary function was to serve as a canonical master-text for future generations of scribal students, whose rote copying would perpetuate the legislator's glory.

The First Code probably originated in such a compilation, as we can see in its rhetorical strategy. Writes Watts (1999: 64), "Hearers and readers are likely to feel directly addressed and therefore obliged to respond. Second-person address . . . highlights the rhetorical function of law, a function closely related . . . to passages of proverbial wisdom." As for who would create such a document, the natural candidates are the kings of Israel, who would have claimed the credit for Israelite common law by turning it into royal edict (Crüsemann 1996: 109–200).

When the Elohist made the First Code part of the story of Israel's origins, the common law was attributed not to a monarch in Jerusalem or Samaria but to King Yahweh at Sinai. Upon him devolved the credit for what in reality was the local manifestation of the ancient Near Eastern jurisprudential tradition. If the goal of Near Eastern legislation was "the characterization of the law-giver as just according to internationally recognized standards of law" (Watts 1999: 98), how better to honor God—and gain credit for one's own literary work and religio-social agenda? Further: the law code was set into a new context, whereby it served as the list of stipulations in the Covenant between Yahweh and Israel (see above, pp. 34–35, 301–2).

This literary recontextualization created a degree of unclarity in the laws. Who is their addressee? Originally, it would have been judges—and so it still may be, for, in an earlier Elohistic narrative (chap. 18), Moses had founded the national judiciary. But the First Code can also be read as addressing ordinary citizens. Perhaps it does not matter. If "all the world's a stage," it is no less a court of law, with the individual continually required to speak truthfully, eschew malice and judge fairly. The court is merely a backup to common decency; disputes that reach formal arbitration represent a failure of the more basic system.

Lastly, we should note that the First Code is framed by religio-cultic legislation (20:23[20]–26[23]; 23:14–33). This genre, too, has ancient Near Eastern roots: in royal sanctions for rebuilding or repairing shrines, supplying their ritual needs through grants or taxes, specifying offerings, and issuing regulations concerning the priesthood. If civil legislation originally served the purpose of proving its author to be just, these regulations proved him also to be pious (for a brief discussion, see Watts 1999: 99).

COVENANT BLOOD

Dillmann (1880: 257) lists various ways in which compacts are sealed in the Bible: through gift exchange (Gen 21:27–32), through a shared meal (Gen 26:30; 2 Sam 3:20)—in particular bread and salt (Lev 2:13; Num 18:19; 2 Chr 13:5)—through cutting animals in half (Genesis 15) and through a sacrifice *cum* meal (Gen 31:54; Exod 24:8–11; 1 Sam 11:15; Ps 50:5). The acts are not all equivalent. The exchange of gifts and sharing of food creates fellowship between the parties, as does worshiping together. The act of severing animals, however, appears to be a pre-enactment of the covenant violator's fate (compare Jer 34:12–22).

In Exodus 24, we find sacred stones (on their possible meaning, see NOTES to v 4), sacrifices and sacred meals—both the Slaughter-offerings of v 5, eaten by the people and shared with God (see below, pp. 695–96), and the elders' banquet before the visible Deity (v 11), which many have described as a Covenant meal (e.g., Noth 1962: 196). The most impressive aspect of the ritual, however, involves applying sacrificial blood to both the people and the altar (24:6, 8). This act is heavily freighted with symbolism. Exodus 24 describes a rite of passage whereby Israel enters into vassalage under Yahweh. Initiation rituals generally feature an inflicted trauma, real or symbolic, that symbolizes the candidate's death. Having survived his ordeal, he is symbolically reborn to a new status (Propp 2004a). In Exodus 24, the people are literally bloodied, thus symbolically injured.

Because the blood comes from a common source, it symbolizes the horizontal, literal kinship of all Israelites and also their vertical, fictive kinship with their Heavenly Father (on blood brotherhood and its role in Exodus 24, see Trumbull 1885, esp. 238–40, 298.). Herodotus 3.8 describes a similar Semitic ritual whereby parties to an oath mingle their blood on sacred pillars, presumably symbolizing their fictive kinship. In a Greek parallel, Aeschylus *Seven Against Thebes* 43–47 describes heroes taking an oath by touching bull's blood collected in a shield (cf. also Xenophon *Anabasis* 2.2.9).

Covenantal bloodletting has another function: it represents the sanguinary fate that awaits the traitor to the pact. In 24:8, sprinkling the people is as much as to say, "If you do not keep the Covenant, your blood is forfeit like this blood" (Saadiah *apud* ibn Ezra). It follows that the blood sprinkled against the altar in v 6 constitutes Yahweh's own bleeding wound. He, too, must keep his promises (cf. Ehrlich 1969: 187); compare the divine fire that passes amid the severed animals in Gen 15:17 to seal Yahweh's vows to Abram. (For further discussion of symbolic injuries, see vol. I, pp. 33, 233–40; vol. II, pp. 529–31; Propp 2004a.)

Moreover, the blood of Exodus 24 comes from *sacrificed animals.* The people hence are implicitly equated with the slain victims. They are like human sacrifices, transferred into Yahweh's domain as *qōdeš* 'Holiness, sacred offering.' (On animal sacrifice and priestly consecration as vicarious human sacrifices, see further below, pp. 531, 695–705.)

Apropos of circumcision and the paschal rite, I have had occasion to describe the Arab rite of *fidya/fedu* 'redemption,' wherein, during rites of passage, blood is applied to persons or things—originally to repel demons (vol. I, pp. 233–41, 434–38, 441). In Exodus 24, "Covenant blood" has a similar purifying, protective function. According to Zech 9:11, for example, "covenant blood" liberates captives from "the pit" (i.e., exile).

Exodus 24 may in fact be read as the mirror image of the *Pesaḥ.* The blood ritual in Exodus 12 initiates Israel's freedom; the blood ritual of Exodus 24 terminates it. Released from involuntary servitude to Pharaoh, Israel voluntarily enters Yahweh's servitude. (Compare 21:6, where a man becomes a permanent slave by standing "before the Deity" [see NOTE] and having blood drawn from his ear.) Later Judaism would apply the phrase of 24:8, *dam bərît* 'Covenant blood,' to the surgical operation whereby each Jewish boy separately enters into the Covenant, symbolically dramatizing the conceit that all later generations stood with their ancestors at Sinai (see already Deut 5:2–4; 29:13–14). The people will finally leave Sinai after making the second *Pesaḥ* (Num [P]).

In 19:6, Yahweh promised to make Israel "a priests' kingdom and a holy nation." The prerogative of holy priesthood is to approach God without suffering harm. The blood of Exodus 24 functions like the blood applied to the priest in 29:20, 21: it is a symbolic wound that confers protection from the divine presence. From Sinai onward, all Israel is Yahweh's "priests' kingdom and holy nation." In confirmation that the rite of passage has been efficacious, Exodus 24 describes Israel's representative elders beholding God unscathed.

Heb 9:19–22 makes explicit the analogy to purification rites by attaching the cleansing agents of wool, water and hyssop (cf. Leviticus 14) to the doings at Sinai:

> For when every command of the law had been declared by Moses to all the people, taking the blood of calves and goats, with water and scarlet wool and hyssop, he sprinkled both the [Covenant] document itself and all the people, saying, "This is the blood of the covenant which God commanded you." And in the same way he sprinkled with the blood both the Tent and all the vessels for worship. Indeed, under the law almost everything is purified with blood, and without blood-shedding there is no forgiveness.

In the Christian Bible, the sacrifices at Sinai that inaugurate the First Covenant are the explicit type of the final Covenant, inaugurated by the joint slaughter of God and Man in the person of Jesus, who enjoins his followers to drink "my Covenant blood" (Mark 14:24).

PART V. THE TABERNACLE DIRECTIONS (EXODUS 25–31)

◆

XIX. *Take for me a Donation-offering* (25:1–31:18)

25 [1(P)]And Yahweh spoke to Moses, saying: [2]"Speak to Israel's Sons, and they shall take for me a Donation-offering. From every man whose heart ennobles him you shall take my Donation-offering. [3]And this is the Donation-offering that you shall take from them: gold, silver and bronze, [4]blue and purple and worm-crimson and linen and *goats* [5]and reddened ram skins and beaded skins and acacia wood, [6]oil for illumination, fragrances for the Ointment Oil and for the Spice Incense, [7]carnelian stones and *filling* stones for the Ephod and for the *ḥošen*. [8]And they shall make for me a Sanctum, and I will tent in your midst. [9]According to all that I am making you see, the Tabernacle's model and the model of all its implements, so you shall make.

[10]"And you shall make a chest, acacia wood: two cubits and a half its length and a cubit and a half its breadth and a cubit and a half its height. [11]And you shall plate it pure gold, from inside and from outside you shall plate it. And you shall make atop it a gold *zēr* around. [12]And you shall cast four gold rings for it, and you shall set on its four *feet*, and two rings on its one flank and two rings on its second flank. [13]And you shall make acacia wood poles and plate them gold. [14]And you shall insert the poles into the rings on the Chest's flanks for carrying the Chest by them. [15]In the Chest's rings the poles shall be; they shall not be removed from it. [16]And you shall set into the Chest the Testimony that I will give you.

[17]"And you shall make a pure gold *kappōret*: two cubits and a half its length and a cubit and a half its breadth. [18]And you shall make two Griffins, gold: *miqšâ* you shall make them; on the *kappōret*'s two ends [19]they shall be made; one Griffin on this end here and one Griffin on this end here; on the *kappōret* you shall make the Griffins on its two ends, [20]so that the Griffins will be spreading wings above, screening over the *kappōret* with their wings, and their faces (each) *man toward his brother*, toward the *kappōret* the Griffins' faces shall be. [21]And you shall set the *kappōret* on the Chest, above, and into the

Chest you shall set the Testimony. ²² And I will be meetable for you there, and I shall speak with you from atop the *kappōret*—from between the two Griffins that are on the Testimony Chest—everything that I shall command you for Israel's Sons.

²³ "And you shall make a table, acacia wood: two cubits its length and a cubit its breadth and a cubit and a half its height. ²⁴ And you shall plate it pure gold. And you shall make for it a gold *zēr* around. ²⁵ And you shall make for it a hand-breadth's frame around. And you shall make a gold *zēr* for its frame around. ²⁶ And you shall make four gold rings for it and set the rings on the four corners which are of its four legs. ²⁷ Aligned with the frame the rings shall be, housings for poles for carrying the Table. ²⁸ And you shall make the poles, acacia wood, and plate them gold; and the Table shall be carried by them. ²⁹ And you shall make its bowls and its spoons and its dippers and its rinsers from which may be poured; pure gold you shall make them. ³⁰ And you shall set on the Table *Face Bread* before my face continually.

³¹ "And you shall make a pure gold lampstand: *miqšâ* the Lampstand shall be made, its *thigh* and its *reeds*, its cups, its *kaptōrîm* and its *flowers*, they shall be from it. ³² And six *reeds* going out from its sides—three Lampstand *reeds* from its one side and three Lampstand *reeds* from its second side—³³ three 'almondized' cups on the one *reed—kaptōr* and *flower*—and three 'almondized' cups on the one *reed—kaptōr* and *flower*—thus for the six *reeds* going out from the Lampstand. ³⁴ And on the Lampstand four 'almondized' cups—its *kaptōrîm* and its *flowers*—³⁵ and a *kaptōr* under the two *reeds* from it, and a *kaptōr* under the two *reeds* from it, and a *kaptōr* under the two *reeds* from it, for the six *reeds* going out from the Lampstand. ³⁶ Their *kaptōrîm* and their *reeds*, they shall be from it, all of it one *miqšâ*, pure gold. ³⁷ And you shall make its lamps seven, and one shall *raise* its lamps and illumine opposite its front; ³⁸ and its tweezers and its fire-pans, pure gold. ³⁹ A talent, pure gold one shall make it, along with all these implements. ⁴⁰ And see and make by their model that you are being made to see on the mountain.

26 ¹ "And the Tabernacle you shall make, ten curtains: twisted linen, blue and purple and worm-crimson, Griffins, webster's work you shall make them. ² The one curtain's length eight-and-twenty by the cubit, and breadth four by the cubit, the one curtain. One measure for all the curtains. ³ Five of the curtains, they shall be fastening (each) *woman to her sister*, and five curtains fastening (each) *woman to her sister*. ⁴ And you shall make blue loops on the one curtain's *lip*, on the edge on the *fastening*, and so you shall make on the outer curtain's *lip*, on the second *fastening*. ⁵ Fifty loops you shall make on the one curtain, and fifty loops you shall make on the edge of the curtain that is on the second *fastening*, the loops aligning (each) *woman to her sister*. ⁶ And you shall make fifty gold clasps and fasten the curtains (each) *woman to her sister* with the clasps, so that the Tabernacle shall be one.

⁷ "And you shall make *goat* curtains to tent over the Tabernacle: eleven curtains you shall make them. ⁸ The one curtain's length thirty by the cubit, and breadth four by the cubit the one curtain. One measure for the eleven curtains.

⁹And you shall fasten the five curtains separate and the six curtains separate. And you shall double the sixth curtain against the Tent's front. ¹⁰And you shall make loops fifty on the one curtain's *lip*, the outermost on the *fastening*, and fifty loops on the *lip* of the curtain, the second *fastening*. ¹¹And you shall make bronze clasps, fifty, and bring the clasps into the loops and fasten the Tent, so that it shall be one. ¹²And the superfluous overhang of the Tent's curtains: half of the superfluous curtain shall hang over the Tent's back; ¹³and the cubit on this (side) and the cubit on this (side) as the superfluity along the Tent curtains' length shall be overhung on the Tabernacle's sides, on this (side) and on this (side) to cover it. ¹⁴And you shall make a cover for the Tent: reddened ram skins, and a beaded skins cover above.

¹⁵"And you shall make the *qərāšîm* for the Tabernacle: standing acacia wood, ¹⁶ten cubits the *qereš*'s length, a cubit and a half-cubit the one *qereš*'s breadth, ¹⁷two *arms* for the one *qereš*, pegged (each) *woman to her sister*; so you shall make for all the Tabernacle's *qərāšîm*. ¹⁸And you shall make the *qərāšîm* for the Tabernacle: twenty *qereš* for the austral, southward side. ¹⁹And forty silver bases you shall make under the twenty *qereš*, two bases under the one *qereš* for its two *arms*, and two bases under the one *qereš* for its two *arms*. ²⁰And for the Tabernacle's second flank, for the north side, twenty *qereš* ²¹and their forty bases, silver, two bases under the one *qereš* and two bases under the one *qereš*. ²²And for the Tabernacle's *seaward* backparts you shall make six *qərāšîm*. ²³And two *qərāšîm* you shall make for the Tabernacle's corners at the backparts. ²⁴And they shall be twinning from below; together they shall be whole up to its *head*, to the one ring. So shall it be for the two of them, for the two corners they shall be. ²⁵And there shall be eight *qərāšîm* and their bases, silver; sixteen bases, two bases under the one *qereš*, and two bases under the one *qereš*. ²⁶And you shall make crossbars, acacia wood: five for the *qərāšîm* of the Tabernacle's one flank ²⁷and five crossbars for the *qərāšîm* of the Tabernacle's second flank and five crossbars for the Tabernacle's *qərāšîm* at the *seaward* backparts, ²⁸and the inner crossbar amid the *qərāšîm* barring from end to end. ²⁹And the *qərāšîm* you shall plate gold; and their rings you shall make gold, housings for the crossbars; and you shall plate the crossbars gold. ³⁰And you shall erect the Tabernacle according to its rule that you were made to see on the mountain.

³¹"And you shall make a veil: blue and purple and worm-crimson and twisted linen; webster's work one shall make it, Griffins. ³²And you shall set it on four gold-plated acacia posts, their Y-brackets gold, on four silver bases. ³³And you shall set the Veil under the clasps, and you shall insert there, inside the Veil, the Testimony Chest, so that the Veil will separate for you between the Holiness and between the Holiness of Holinesses. ³⁴And you shall set the *kappōret* on the Testimony Chest in the Holiness of Holinesses. ³⁵And you shall put the Table outside the Veil, and the Lampstand opposite the Table by the Tabernacle's flank southward, and the Table you shall set by the north flank.

³⁶"And you shall make a screen for the Tent Opening, blue and purple and

worm-crimson and twisted linen, embroiderer's work. ³⁷And you shall make for the Screen five acacia posts and plate them gold, their Y-brackets gold, and you shall cast for them five bronze bases.

27   ¹"And you shall make the Altar, acacia wood: five cubits length and five cubits breadth—foursquare the Altar shall be—and three cubits its height. ²And you shall make its *horns* on its four corners—from it its *horns* shall be—and you shall plate it bronze. ³And you shall make its pots for de-ashing it and its shovels and its bowls and its forks and its fire-pans—in short, all its implements you shall make bronze. ⁴And you shall make for it a mesh, lattice work, bronze; and you shall make on the lattice four bronze rings on its four corners. ⁵And you shall set it under the Altar's rim beneath, and the lattice shall as be far as half the Altar. ⁶And you shall make poles for the Altar, acacia-wood poles, and plate them bronze. ⁷And its poles shall be inserted into the rings, so that the poles will be on the Altar's two flanks in carrying it. ⁸Hollow-planked you shall make it. As he made you see on the mountain, so they shall make.

⁹"And you shall make the Tabernacle's Plaza: on the austral, southward side, sheets for the Plaza, twisted linen, length one hundred by the cubit on the one side, ¹⁰and its posts twenty and their bases twenty, bronze; their Y-brackets and their *ḥăšūqîm*, silver. ¹¹And likewise on the north side in length: sheets, one hundred by the cubit, and its posts twenty and their bases twenty, bronze; their Y-brackets and their *ḥăšūqîm*, silver. ¹²And the Plaza's breadth on the sea side: sheets, fifty cubit, their posts ten and their bases ten. ¹³And the Plaza's breadth on the *forward, sunrise* side: fifty cubit. ¹⁴Fifteen cubit, sheets for the *shoulder,* their posts three and their bases three. ¹⁵And for the second *shoulder,* fifteen sheets, their posts three and their bases three. ¹⁶And for the Plaza gate a screen, twenty cubit, blue and purple and worm-crimson and twisted linen, embroiderer's work, its posts four and their bases four. ¹⁷All the Plaza's posts around, *məḥuššāqîm* silver, their Y-brackets, silver, and their bases, bronze—¹⁸the Plaza's length one hundred upon one hundred, and breadth fifty upon fifty, and height five cubits, twisted linen—and their bases, bronze—¹⁹in short, all the Tabernacle's implements in all its Work and all its tent-pegs and all the Plaza's tent-pegs, bronze.

²⁰"And you, you shall command Israel's Sons: and they shall take to you pure, crushed olive oil for illumination, to *raise* a continual lamp ²¹in Meeting Tent, outside the Veil that is before the Testimony. Let Aaron and his sons arrange it from evening till morning before Yahweh. An eternal rule *for their ages* from Israel's Sons.

28   ¹"And you, Bring Near to yourself Aaron your brother and his sons with him from the midst of Israel's Sons to priest for me: Aaron, Nadab and Abihu, Eleazar and Ithamar, Aaron's sons. ²And you shall make Holiness Garments for Aaron your brother for glory and for splendor. ³And you, you shall speak to all wise-hearted whom I have filled (with) wisdom's spirit, and they shall make Aaron's garments, to make him holy to priest for me. ⁴And these are the garments that they shall make: a *ḥōšen* and an ephod and a robe and a woven shift, a turban and a sash; and they shall make Holiness garments for Aaron and for

his sons to priest for me. ⁵And they, they shall take the gold and the blue and the purple and the worm-crimson and the linen.

⁶"And they shall make the Ephod: gold, blue and purple, worm-crimson and twisted linen, webster's work. ⁷Two fastening shoulder-pieces, it shall be for it; at its two sides it shall be fastened. ⁸And the woven-band for its ephod-binding that is on it, like its work, from it shall it be: gold, blue and purple and worm-crimson and twisted linen. ⁹And you shall take two carnelian stones and engrave on them the names of Israel's sons: ¹⁰six of their names on the one stone and the names of the remaining six on the second stone, according to their genealogy. ¹¹Stone-cutter's work, seal engravings, one shall engrave the two stones by the names of Israel's sons; set in gold plait-rings you shall make them. ¹²And you shall put the two stones on the Ephod's shoulder-pieces, Memorial stones for Israel's Sons, so that Aaron may bear their names before Yahweh on his two shoulder-pieces as a Memorial.

¹³"And you shall make gold plait-rings. ¹⁴And two pure gold chains: *migbālōt* you shall make them, rope work. And you shall set the rope chains on the plait-rings.

¹⁵"And you shall make the Judgment *ḥōšen*, webster's work, like an ephod's work you shall make it, gold; blue and purple and worm-crimson and twisted linen you shall make it. ¹⁶Foursquare it shall be, doubled; a span its length and a span its breadth. ¹⁷And you shall *fill* in it stone *filling*, four rows, stone. A row: *'ōdem*, *piṭdâ* and emerald, the one row; ¹⁸and the second row: turquoise, lapis lazuli and *yāhǎlōm*; ¹⁹and the third row: *lešem*, *šǝbô* and jasper; ²⁰and the fourth row: *taršîš*, carnelian and jade. Plait-ringed in gold they shall be in their *fillings*. ²¹And the stones, they shall be by the names of Israel's sons, twelve by their names, seal engravings, (each) *man* by his name they shall be, for twelve tribe. ²²And you shall make upon the *ḥōšen gablūt* chains, rope work, pure gold. ²³And you shall make upon the *ḥōšen* two gold rings, and you shall set the rings on the *ḥōšen*'s edges. ²⁴And you shall set the two gold ropes on the two rings on the *ḥōšen*'s edges. ²⁵And the two ropes' two ends you shall set on the two plait-rings; and you shall set on the Ephod's shoulder-pieces, against its front. ²⁶And you shall make two gold rings and put them on the *ḥōšen*'s two edges, at its *lip* that is against the Ephod inside. ²⁷And you shall make two gold rings and set them on the Ephod's two shoulder-pieces below, against its front, opposite its fastening, above the Ephod's woven-band. ²⁸And they must tie the *ḥōšen* by its rings to the Ephod's rings with blue cord for being over the Ephod's woven-band, so the *ḥōšen* will not slip from upon the Ephod. ²⁹And Aaron shall bear the names of Israel's sons in the Judgment *ḥōšen* over his heart in his coming into the Holiness as a Memorial before Yahweh continually. ³⁰And you shall set into the Judgment *ḥōšen* the Urim and the Thummim, so that they will be over Aaron's heart in his coming before Yahweh. And Aaron shall bear the Judgment of Israel's Sons over his heart before Yahweh continually.

³¹"And you shall make the Ephod's Robe: completely blue. ³²And its *head mouth* shall be in its midst; a *lip* will be for its *mouth* around, weaver's work,

like an anus *mouth* will be for it; it will not be torn. ³³ And you shall make on its skirts pomegranates of blue and purple and worm-crimson on its skirts around, and gold bells in their midst around—³⁴ a gold bell and a pomegranate, a gold bell and a pomegranate—on the Robe's skirts around. ³⁵ And it shall be upon Aaron for attending, so that his sound will be heard in his coming into the Holiness before Yahweh and in his leaving, and he shall not die.

³⁶ "And you shall make a pure gold blossom and engrave on it seal engravings: 'a Holiness of Yahweh.' ³⁷ And you shall put it on blue cord, and it shall be on the Turban; against the Turban's front it shall be. ³⁸ And it shall be upon Aaron's forehead, and Aaron shall Bear the Transgression of the Holinesses that Israel's Sons shall make holy, for all their holy gifts; and it shall be upon his forehead continually, for favor for them before Yahweh.

³⁹ "And you shall plait the Shift, linen, and make a linen Turban, and a Sash you shall make, embroiderer's work.

⁴⁰ "And for Aaron's sons you shall make shifts, and you shall make sashes for them, and hats you shall make for them, for glory and for splendor. ⁴¹ And you shall make Aaron your brother and his sons with him wear them, and you shall anoint them and *fill their hand* and make them holy, so that they may priest for me.

⁴² "And make for them linen underpants to cover naked *flesh*; from hips and to thighs they shall be. ⁴³ And they shall be on Aaron and on his sons in their coming into Meeting Tent or in their approaching to the Altar to attend in the Holiness, lest they Bear Transgression and die. An eternal rule for him and for his *seed* after him.

29   ¹ "And this is the thing that you shall do to them to make them holy to priest for me: take one bull, cattle's son, and rams, two, perfect, ² and bread, unleavened bread, and unleavened *ḥallōt* saturated with oil and unleavened bread wafers anointed with oil, wheat bran you shall make them. ³ And you shall set them on one basket and Bring them Near in the basket, and the bull and the two rams, ⁴ and Aaron and his sons you shall Bring Near to Meeting Tent Opening and wash them with water. ⁵ And you shall take the garments and make Aaron wear the Shift and the Ephod's Robe and the Ephod and the *ḥōšen*, and you shall "ephod" to him with the Ephod's *woven-band*. ⁶ And you shall set the Turban on his head and put the Holiness Crown on the Turban. ⁷ And you shall take the Ointment Oil and pour on his head and anoint him. ⁸ And his sons you shall Bring Near and make them wear shifts ⁹ and gird them with a sash, Aaron and his sons, and bind hats for them. And priesthood shall be for them as an eternal rule.

"And you shall *fill* Aaron's *hand* and his sons' *hand*. ¹⁰ And you shall Bring Near the bull before Meeting Tent, and Aaron and his sons shall press their hands on the bull's head. ¹¹ And you shall slaughter the bull before Yahweh (at) Meeting Tent Opening. ¹² And you shall take from the bull's blood and apply on the Altar's *horns* with your finger, and all the blood you shall pour toward the Altar's fundament. ¹³ And you shall take all the fat covering the entrails and all the excrescence on the liver and the two kidneys and the fat that is on them and *smoke* them on the Altar. [14] And the bull's meat and his skin and his dung you shall burn with fire outside the camp. He is a Sin-offering.

[15] "And the one ram you shall take, and Aaron and his sons shall press their hands on the ram's head. [16] And you shall slaughter the ram and take his blood and dash it against the Altar around. [17] And the ram you shall dismember into his members, and wash his entrails and his shanks and set with his members and with his head. [18] And you shall *smoke* the entire ram on the Altar. He is an Ascending-offering for Yahweh; a Soothing Scent, a Gift for Yahweh is he.

[19] "And you shall take the second ram, and Aaron and his sons shall press their hands on the ram's head. [20] And you shall slaughter the ram and take from his blood and apply on Aaron's earlobe and on his sons' right earlobe and on their right hand-thumb and on their right *foot-thumb*, and you shall dash the blood against the Altar around. [21] And you shall take from the blood that is against the Altar and from the Ointment Oil and sprinkle upon Aaron and upon his garments and upon his sons and upon his sons' garments with him. And he and his garments and his sons and his sons' garments with him shall become holy. [22] And you shall take from the ram the fat: the fat-tail and the fat covering the entrails and the liver's excrescence and the two kidneys and the fat that is on them and the right thigh—for he is a *Filling* Ram—[23] and one bread loaf and one oil bread *ḥallâ* and one wafer from the unleavened bread basket that is before Yahweh. [24] And you shall put the whole on Aaron's palms and his sons' palms, and you shall elevate them (as) an Elevation-offering before Yahweh. [25] And you shall take them from their hand and *smoke* on the Altar in addition to the Ascending-offering as a Soothing Scent before Yahweh. It is a Gift to Yahweh.

[26] "And you shall take the breast from the *Filling* Ram that is Aaron's and elevate it (as) an Elevation-offering before Yahweh, and it will be as a portion for you. [27] And you shall make holy the Elevation breast and the Donation thigh, that is elevated and that is donated from the *Filling* Ram, from what is Aaron's and from what is his sons', [28] and he shall be for Aaron and for his sons as an eternal rule from Israel's Sons. For it is a Donation-offering, and a Donation-offering he will be from Israel's Sons from their Concluding Slaughter-offerings, their Donation-offering for Yahweh.

[29] "And the Holiness Garments that are Aaron's will be for his sons after him, for being anointed in them and for *filling their hand* in them. [30] Seven days the priest replacing him, from his sons, who will come into Meeting Tent to attend in the Holiness, must wear them.

[31] "And the *Filling* ram you shall take and boil his meat in a holy place. [32] And Aaron and his sons shall eat the ram's meat and the bread that is in the basket (at) Meeting Tent Opening. [33] They must eat them by which Clearing was effected, for *filling their hand* for making them holy. But an outsider may not eat, for they are Holiness. [34] And if (any) of the *Filling* meat or of the bread is left over until the morning, then you shall burn the leftover in fire. It may not be eaten, for it is Holiness. [35] And you shall do for Aaron and for his sons likewise, as all that I have commanded you; seven days you shall *fill their hand*.

³⁶ "And a Sin bull you shall do (each) day concerning the Clearing. And you shall Un-sin upon the Altar in your effecting Clearing upon it. And you shall anoint it to make it holy. ³⁷ Seven days you shall effect Clearing upon the Altar and make it holy. And the Altar shall be Holiness of Holinesses; any touching the Altar becomes holy.

³⁸ "And this is what you must do upon the Altar: lambs, *sons of* a year, two per day (as a) Continual-offering. ³⁹ The one lamb you shall do in the morning, and the second lamb you shall do *between the two evenings,* ⁴⁰ and a tenth of bran saturated with a quarter-hin crushed oil, and a quarter-hin wine libation, for the one lamb. ⁴¹ And the second lamb you shall do *between the two evenings*; like the morning Tribute-offering and like its libation you shall do for it, a Soothing Scent, a Gift for Yahweh, ⁴² a Continual Ascending-offering *for your ages* (at) Meeting Tent Opening before Yahweh, where I will be meetable for you to speak to you there.

⁴³ "And I will be inquirable there for Israel's Sons, and it/one will be made holy by my Glory. ⁴⁴ And I will make holy Meeting Tent and the Altar, and Aaron and his sons I will make holy to priest for me. ⁴⁵ And I will tent in Israel's Sons' midst, and I will be for them as a deity, ⁴⁶ and they will know that I am Yahweh their deity who took them out from the land of Egypt by my tenting among them—I am Yahweh their deity.

30 ¹ "And you shall make an altar, an incense censer: acacia wood you shall make it, ² a cubit its length and a cubit its breadth—foursquare it shall be— and two cubits its height; from it its *horns.* ³ And you shall plate it pure gold: its *roof* and its *walls* around and its *horns.* And you shall make for it a gold *zēr* around. ⁴ And two gold rings you shall make for it beneath its *zēr* on its two flanks, you shall make on its two sides, and they shall be as housings for poles for carrying it with them. ⁵ And you shall make the poles, acacia wood, and plate them gold. ⁶ And you shall set it before the Veil that is before the Testimony Chest, where I will be meetable for you there. ⁷ And Aaron shall cense on it Spice Incense by morning by morning, in his adjusting the lamps let him cense it; ⁸ and in Aaron's *raising* the lamps *between the two evenings* let him cense it, continual incense before Yahweh *for your ages.* ⁹ Do not *send up* on it alien incense or an Ascending-offering or a Tribute-offering, and a libation do not libate on it. ¹⁰ And Aaron shall effect Clearing on its *horns* once in the year from the blood of the Clearing Sin-offering; once in the year he shall effect Clearing on it *for your ages.* It is a Holiness of Holinesses for Yahweh."

¹¹ And Yahweh spoke to Moses, saying: ¹² "When you *lift the head* of Israel's Sons in their accountings, then (each) man shall give to Yahweh his *soul's* ransom in their being accounted, lest there be harm against them in accounting them. ¹³ This they must give, each passing over the accountings: the half-shekel by the Holiness Shekel—twenty gerah the shekel—the half-shekel (as) a Donation-offering for Yahweh. ¹⁴ Each *passing over* the accountings, from the *son of* twenty year and upward, must give Yahweh's Donation-offering. ¹⁵ The rich may not (give) more and the poor may not (give) less than than the half-shekel, to give Yahweh's Donation-offering to effect Clearing for your *souls.*

¹⁶And you shall take the Clearing Silver from Israel's Sons and give it toward the Meeting Tent Work, so that it will be for Israel's Sons as a Memorial before Yahweh, to effect Clearing for your *souls*."

¹⁷And Yahweh spoke to Moses, saying: ¹⁸"And you shall make a basin, bronze, and its stand, bronze, for washing, and you shall set it between Meeting Tent and between the Altar, and set there water. ¹⁹And Aaron and his sons shall wash their hands and their feet from it; ²⁰in their coming into Meeting Tent they must wash with water, lest they die; or in their approaching to the Altar to attend, to *smoke* a Gift to Yahweh, ²¹they must wash their hands and their feet, lest they die. And it will be for them an eternal rule, for him and for his *seed for their ages*."

²²And Yahweh spoke to Moses, saying: ²³"And you, take for yourself fragrances: *head* of *dərôr* myrrh, five hundred; and fragrant cinnamon half as much, fifty and two hundred; and fragrant cane, fifty and two hundred; ²⁴and *qiddâ*, five hundred by the Holiness Shekel; and olive oil, a hin. ²⁵And you shall make it (into) Holiness Ointment Oil, a compounding compound, compounder's work; Holiness Ointment it shall be. ²⁶And you shall anoint with it Meeting Tent and the Testimony Chest, ²⁷the Table and all its implements, the Lamp and all its implements, the Incense Altar ²⁸and the Ascending-offering Altar and all its implements, the Basin and its Stand. ²⁹And you shall make them holy, and they shall be a Holiness of Holinesses. Any touching them becomes holy. ³⁰And Aaron and his sons you shall anoint, and you shall make them holy to priest for me. ³¹And to Israel's Sons you shall speak, saying: 'Holiness Ointment Oil this shall be for me *for your ages*. ³²On a human's flesh it must not be poured, and in its composition you shall not make its like. It is a Holiness; a Holiness shall it be for you. ³³A man who compounds its like or who puts (any) of it on an outsider, then he shall be Cut Off from his kin.' "

³⁴And Yahweh said to Moses, "Take for yourself spices—gumdrop and *šəhēlet* and galbanum—spices and pure frankincense, part for part it shall be. ³⁵And you shall make it (into) incense, a compound, compounder's work, salted, pure, Holiness. ³⁶And you shall pulverize (some) of it fine and set (some) of it before the Testimony in Meeting Tent, where I will be meetable for you there. A Holiness of Holinesses it shall be for you. ³⁷And the incense that you make, in its composition you shall not make for yourselves. A Holiness for Yahweh it shall be for you. ³⁸A man who makes its like to smell it, then he shall be Cut Off from his kin."

31 ¹And Yahweh spoke to Moses, saying: ²"See, I have called by name Bezalel son of Uri son of Hur from the tribe of Judah ³and filled him with a divine spirit in wisdom and in understanding and in knowledge and in every task, ⁴for planning plans, to make in gold and in silver and in bronze ⁵and in stone carving for *filling* and in wood carving, to do every task. ⁶And I, see: I have given with him Oholiab son of Ahisamach from the tribe of Dan, and into the heart of every wise-hearted I have set wisdom.

"And they shall make all that I commanded you: ⁷Meeting Tent and the Chest for the Testimony and the *kappōret* that is over it and all the Tent's implements, [8] the Table and its implements, the pure Lampstand and all its implements, the Incense Altar [9] and the Ascending-offering Altar and all its implements, the Basin and its stand, [10] the Textile Garments and the Holiness Garments for Aaron the priest and his sons' garments for priesting, [11] the Ointment Oil and the Spice Incense for the Holiness. As all that I commanded you they shall make."

[12][R?] And Yahweh said to Moses, saying: [13] "And you, speak to Israel's Sons, saying: 'Nevertheless, my Sabbaths you must keep. For it is a sign between me and between you *for your ages*, to know that I, Yahweh, am your sanctifier. [14] And you shall observe the Sabbath, for it is a Holiness for you. Its desecrater must be put to death, death; for any doing a task on it—then that *soul* shall be Cut Off from its kinfolks' midst. [15] Six days a task may be done. But on the seventh day: a Sabbatical Sabbath, a Holiness of Yahweh. Anyone doing a task on the Sabbath day must be put to death, death. [16] And Israel's Sons shall observe the Sabbath, doing the Sabbath *for their ages*, an eternal covenant. [17] Between me and between Israel's Sons it is a sign for eternity; for six days Yahweh made the heavens and the earth, but on the seventh day he ceased and caught his breath.'"

[18][E] And he gave to Moses, as he concluded speaking with him [R] at Mount Sinai, the two Testimony Tablets, [E] stone tablets, written by Deity's finger.

ANALYSIS

TEXTUAL NOTES

25:2. *Speak*. The LXX-Syr *Vorlage* may have read *'ĕmōr 'say,' vs. MT-Sam *dabbēr*. But the latter is preferable as the reading actually attested in Hebrew.

and they shall take. LXX "and *you* (pl.) shall take" anticipates the verb at the end of the verse. The error could have been committed in either Hebrew or Greek.

for me. Absent in LXX[B].

you shall take. LXX[B] and presumably the original LXX insert "and," as if reading *wtqḥw, vs. MT-Sam *tiqqəḥû*. This would produce a different clause division for the verse: "and they shall take for me a Donation-offering from every man whose heart ennobles him; *and* you shall take my Donation-offering." If this is not just freedom in LXX, we should note that the waw ending the preceding word could have been reduplicated across the word boundary to create the LXX *Vorlage*: *lbw wtqḥw.

† *my Donation-offering*. Tg. Neofiti I uniquely reads 'pršwtyh 'his (i.e., each man's) Donation-offering.' But the parallel in 35:5 has "Yahweh's Donation-offering," supporting MT-Sam-LXX 25:2.

†† 25:3. *silver*. So Sam; MT has "and silver." See also TEXTUAL NOTE to 35:5.

and bronze. LXX[A] omits "and."

†† 25:4. *blue.* So Sam, LXX MSS and possibly Vg; MT has "*and* blue."

† *and purple.* Some LXX MSS omit "and."

linen. LXX has "*twisted* linen," as if reading the cliché **šēš mošzār* (26:1, 31, 36, etc.). I follow the shorter text of MT-Sam. See also TEXTUAL NOTE to 35:6.

25:6. *oil . . . fragrances.* Sam and Syr insert "and" before each substance, as in 35:8.

This whole verse is missing from LXX, both here and in the parallel 35:8 (see TEXTUAL NOTE). If this is a deliberate deletion, perhaps the copyist was motivated by the consideration that oil and spices are not really construction materials (Dillmann 1880: 277; Wevers 1990: 392; cf. NOTE), or because oil will be discussed below in 27:20 (Cassuto 1967: 327). Alternatively, LXX may well be the result of haplography by homoioteleuton from *štym* in v 5 to *smym* in v 6 in one passage, followed by the harmonization of the other (Cassuto). Finally, it is possible that LXX is original and that MT-Sam has been supplemented. See further pp. 369, 514–15.

† 25:7. *carnelian stones.* Sam and LXX prefix "and," as in 35:9.

ḥōšen. Although this Hebrew term refers to the priest's oracle-pouch, LXX here has *podērē* '(full-length) robe' rather than its usual *logion*; see Wevers (1990: 395).

† 25:8. *And they shall make.* LXX has "And *you* (sing.) shall make," as if reading **w'śyt* like LXX-Sam 25:10 (see TEXTUAL NOTE). Vis-à-vis MT, LXX replaces the third person in this section with the second person—plural in 25:2, singular in vv 8, 10. LXX emphasizes that, whereas the people are directly commanded to contribute, Moses must supervise the actual construction.

I may tent. LXX paraphrases "I will *appear.*" Presumably, the Diasporic translators were uncomfortable with God permanently residing in a single place (Wevers 1990: 395). We find the same trend in *Tgs. Onqelos* and *Ps.-Jonathan*, which paraphrase, "I will make my Presence settle among them."

†† *in your midst.* Reading *btwkkm* 'in *your* (pl.) midst' with Sam, LXX and *Bib. Ant.* 11:15, against MT *btwkm* 'in *their* midst.' It is hard to judge which reading is more probable. My preference for the slightly difficult Sam assumes that MT has leveled the third person plural from earlier in the verse *(wə'āśû)* and/or committed a simple haplography *(kk > k)*.

25:9. *According to all.* LXX inserts an additional "And you (sing.) shall make for me," presumably to clarify that the verbs of the preceding and succeeding clauses govern this clause, too.

making you see. Sam and LXX add "in the mountain," evidently borrowed from the parallels in 25:40; 26:30; 27:8.

†† *so.* Here I read with LXX, Syr and probably Vg **kn*, vs. MT-Sam *wəkēn* '*and* so.' Admittedly, the variant is attested in but a single Hebrew MS (Kenn 80), perhaps by coincidence; admittedly, MT-Sam is the more difficult text, with slightly garbled syntax: "According to all that I am making you see . . . *and* so you shall make." But MT-Sam may be too eccentric to be correct. The LXX-Syr variant, with *kə-/ka'ăšer* 'according to/as' coordinate with *kēn* 'thus/so,' conforms to standard diction in P (e.g., Gen 6:22; Exod 7:6, 10; 12:28, 50) and elsewhere (Gen 41:13; 44:10; 50:12; Exod 1:12, etc.). The scribe responsible for the MT-Sam

reading may have been influenced by the sequence *-yw* ending the preceding word (Holzinger 1900: 120) and/or by the phrase "*and* so *(wəkēn)* . . . make/ made" elsewhere in the Torah (e.g., Gen 34:7; Exod 26:4; Lev 16:16; Deut 22:3). In defense of MT, however, Cassuto (1967: 328) cites Num 1:19, which features a comparable anomaly. And Rashi neatly solves the difficulty by joining the first part of v 9 to the beginning of v 8: "And they shall make for me a Sanctum . . . according to all that I am making you see, the Tabernacle's model and the model of all its implements. *And* so you shall make."

† *you shall make.* "You" is plural in MT *(ta'ăśû)*, singular in LXX and Sam *(t'śh).* Some Syr MSS support MT, while others duplicate "*they* shall make" from the following verse. Within the context of v 9, MT is the more varied and hence more attractive reading, since it uses the second person in both the singular (for Moses) and the plural (for Israel). The second person singular in LXX-Sam may reflect assimilation both to the preceding *'ôtəkā* 'you (sing.)' and to the immediately following *wə'āśîtā* 'and you (sing.) shall make' (v 10; see next TEXTUAL NOTE).

†† 25:10. *and you shall make.* Reading *w'śyt* with Sam and LXX, to match the following commands, all addressed to Moses (Holzinger 1900: 121). MT *wə'āśû* 'and *they* shall make' is admittedly *lectio difficilior*, but it may be influenced by the preceding *ta'ăśû* 'you (pl.) shall make.' Vg supports the MT consonants *w'św* but interprets them as a plural imperative: **wa'ăśû* 'and make!' In MT and Vg, all Israelites are responsible for making the holiest object, the Chest, presumably through their donations (*Exod. Rab.* 34:3; Ramban; Leibowitz 1976: 487–89).

In 25:8–11, as we have seen, the Versions differ concerning the person and number of pronominal references to Moses/Israel, switching from Israel to Moses at different points. The tradition's fluidity indicates that, just as Moses' persona and God's sometimes interpenetrate (see NOTES to 7:17; 11:8), so do the personae of Moses and Israel mingle when he is their representative. My translation somewhat arbitrarily follows MT, except for v 11.

a chest. LXX expands: "a chest *of the Testimony.*"

† 25:11. *atop it.* For standard MT *'ālā(y)w*, Sam, Kenn 69, 84, 196, Rossi 10, 503 and probably the *Vorlagen* of LXX, Tg. *Neofiti* I and Syr read *lô* 'for it,' as in 37:2 (also 30:3). Either might be correct, but my translation assumes that the Sam-LXX-Syr variant has harmonized the two accounts.

around. Uniquely, 4QpaleoGen-Exod[1] lacks *sbyb.* While we often prefer the shorter reading, it is more likely here that a scribe skipped *sbyb* due to homoioteleuton with the preceding *zhb* 'gold.'

† 25:12. *and two rings* (first time). The conjunction, which is somewhat unexpected (see NOTE, "and two rings . . . and two rings"), is not reflected in LXX, Syr, Vg and Kenn 69, a MS containing many old variants. Possibly the waw in MT-Sam is a dittograph of the preceding *-yw* (Ehrlich 1908: 366) and anticipatory of *ûštê* later in the verse.

25:15. *be removed.* Literally, "depart" — unless we revocalize a passive Hoph'al **yūsərû* (cf. Ehrlich 1908: 366).

from it. Syr has "from *them*" (i.e., the rings)."

25:17. *its length . . . its breadth.* In MT, the suffixes are properly feminine (*'orkāh . . . roḥbāh*) to agree with the feminine *kappōret.* In Sam, however, the suffixes are masculine (*'rkw . . . rḥbw*), under the influence of 25:10 and because this is the more common expression in the Bible (23 masc. examples vs. 7 fem. examples). The autograph presumably had an ambiguous *'*rkh . . . rḥbh* in old-style orthography, in which the suffix -*h* could correspond to either Massoretic -*ô* or -*āh.* See further TEXTUAL NOTE to 37:6.

25:18. *Griffins, gold; miqšâ.* On the LXX paraphrase, see NOTE.

†† 25:19. *they shall be made.* This verb has no parallel in 37:7–8. Since waw-yodh confusion is more likely in the square script than in Samaritan paleo-Hebrew, I read with Sam-LXX a passive Niphʿal *yēʿāśû* (cf. *Samaritan Tg.*), rather than MT *waʿăśē(h)*, a Qal imperative breaking the pattern of converted perfects *waʿāśîtā* 'and you shall make.' (Another possible reading is an infinitive absolute **waʿāśō[h]* [Ehrlich 1908: 367].)

I also follow Sam, against MT-LXX, in attaching the verb to the preceding verse. This yields a clause division more graceful and in keeping with Priestly style. The parallelistic "*miqšâ* you shall make them; on the two corners of the *kappōret* they shall be made" recalls many other Priestly verses featuring "short-circuit inclusio" (below, pp. 380, 641, 713; McEvenue 1971: 43–44; Paran 1989: 49–97).

> SPECULATION: The autograph could well have had a Niphʿal singular **yēʿāśe(h)*, grammatically permissible though unusual (on such incongruence between verb and subject, see GKC §145). This hypothetical reading could have generated MT *wʿśh*, both by waw-yodh confusion (cf. Cross 1961a; Qimron 1972) and as an attempt to "fix" the grammar. The Sam plural *yʿśw* would be an analogous correction.

this end here; on the kappōret. LXX runs this together, paraphrasing "this side of the Propitiation."

†† *you shall make.* The verb is plural in standard MT (*taʿăśû*), which uses both the second-person singular (*taʿăśē[h]*) and the plural (*taʿăśû*) in v 19. But "you shall make" is singular (*taʿăśe[h]*) in a Genizah MS (*apud BHS*), the lost Codex Hilleli, Kenn 5, 94, 160, 466, 601 and Rossi 14, 16, 248, 262, 266, 503, as well as LXX, Sam, Syr and some *Tg.* MSS (de Rossi 1784–85: 69; Sperber 1959: 131; Rieder 1974: 121 n. 10), including *Neofiti I.* Moreover, the execution report in 37:8 uses the third person singular verb *ʿāśâ* 'he made.' In fact, except for the first word in MT 25:10, all verbs pertaining to making the Chest in this section are second-person singular. Standard MT 25:19 is clearly *lectio difficilior*, but in my judgment too difficult. I read *taʿăśe(h)* (with Dillmann 1880: 281).

Before the verb, LXX and some Syr MSS prepose "and," perhaps because they have read together *miqqāṣâ mizze(h) min-hakkappōret* 'on this end here on the *kappōret*' (see above).

the Griffins. LXX, Syr and Rossi 12 have "the *two* Griffins," as in 25:22.

25:20. *so that . . . will be.* LXX lacks a conjunction, perhaps reflecting a *Vorlage* *yhyw as later in the verse (Wevers 1990: 400), vs. MT-Sam *wǝhāyû* (on waw-yodh confusion, see Cross 1961a; Qimron 1972).

(each) man toward his brother. Here and in 26:3, for MT and 4QpaleoGen-Exod[1] *'îš 'el-'āḥîw*, we find in 4QpaleoExod[m] and Sam *'ḥd 'l-'ḥd* 'one to one,' an expression paralleled in 36:10, 12–13, 22 but not otherwise in chaps. 25–31.

toward the kappōret. Syr repeats *"above the kappōret"* from earlier in the verse—but there it described the Griffins' wings, not their faces.

†† 25:21. *the Testimony.* So Sam; other Versions continue: "that I will give you." Since there is no obvious reason for the phrase to have been dropped accidentally or deliberately, and since Sam of all the witnesses tends the most toward expansion, I take its short reading as original. The longer text is borrowed from 25:16.

25:22. *I will be meetable.* For MT-Sam *wnw'dty*, LXX has *gnōsthēsomai* 'I will make myself known.' Most commentators (e.g., BHS) infer an LXX *Vorlage* **wnwd'ty* 'I will be *known*,' a case of accidental metathesis. But Wevers (1990: 401), noting the same "error" in LXX 29:42; 30:6, 36, sensibly argues that we have not recurring corruption but deliberate paraphrase, a punning midrash (Rabbinic *'al tiqrê*) to avoid the anthropomorphism implicit in a face-to-face meeting between Man and God. Out of the same motives, the *Tgs.* paraphrase, "I will make *my Word* present" in all three instances.

atop the kappōret . . . Testimony Chest. Tg. Neofiti I uniquely rearranges the contents: "atop the *kappōret* that is on the Testimony Chest, from between the two Griffins."

everything. My translation follows standard MT-Sam. LXX has *"and according to (kai kata)* everything, which I shall command you for Israel's Sons," as if reading **wkkl 'šr*, vs. MT *'ēt kol-'ăšer*. LXX is difficult, because it would seem to require a concluding "so you shall make." Possibly, however, the LXX *Vorlage* was rather *w't kl 'šr* (= Kenn 4, 5, 111, 129, 132, 150, 153, 157, 158, 168, 191, 199, 228, 615, Rossi 2, 10, 11, 16, 262, 440, 443, 476, 479, 656, 716, 766; Rashi; ibn Ezra), with *'ēt* understood not as *'ēt* I the direct object marker but as *'ēt* II, ordinarily "with" but here "as." It is also possible the LXX *Vorlage* equaled standard MT-Sam, and that *kai* is simply an emphatic "indeed" (cf. Wevers 1990: 401).

for Israel's Sons. Against MT-Sam *'el-bənê yiśrā'ēl*, Syr and Tg. Neofiti I appear to read *"concerning ('al)* Israel's Sons"—although sometimes *'el* can mean "about, concerning."

25:23. *a table, acacia wood.* LXX has "a table, *gold* (LXX[B])/*of pure gold*." See next TEXTUAL NOTE.

25:24. *And you shall plate . . . gold.* The first half of v 24 is missing in LXX, a minus related to the LXX variant in 25:23 (previous TEXTUAL NOTE). Both MT-Sam-4QpaleoExod[m] and LXX indicate that the Table has a gold component, but LXX creates the impression it is solid gold, like, it seems, the Tables of the First (1 Kgs 7:48) and Second (Josephus *War* 7.148) Temples.

† 25:26. *for it.* "For it" is not reflected in LXX and Vg, which present the more attractively varied text (cf. vv 24–25). Still, as this variant is not reflected in any extant Hebrew MS, I have followed MT-Sam (see, however, TEXTUAL NOTE to 37:13, "cast").

set. Syr replaces this verb with a slightly varied repetition of the first clause, rendering the entire verse as follows: "And make four gold rings for it, *and you shall make rings, four, of gold* on its four corners above its four legs" (see below).

the rings. LXX[B] and Syr (see previous TEXTUAL NOTE) insert "four," matching the first half of the verse.

are of. Syr (*l'l mn*) appears to read *'l* 'are *on*,' vs. MT-Sam *lə-* 'are of, belonging to'; cf. TEXTUAL NOTE to 37:13, "of."

25:27. Aligned with the frame. LXX connects these words to v 26 by inserting a conjunction absent in MT-Sam: "and set the rings on the four parts of its four legs under the frame; *and* the rings shall be. . . ." In the MT-Sam *lectio difficilior*, the verb *tihye(y)nā* does double duty, referring both backward to the rings' location ("against the frame") and forward to their purpose ("housings for poles for carrying the Table"). LXX simplifies by attaching the first words of v 27 to v 26.

†† *housings.* Reading *btym* with Sam, vs. MT-LXX-Tgs. *ləbāttîm* 'as housings'; the parallel in MT 37:14 also has simply *bāttîm*. It is easier to imagine *btym lbdym* 'housings for poles' becoming *lbtym lbdym* 'as housings for poles' than vice versa. Compare, too, *bāttîm labbərîḥīm* 'housings for the crossbars' in 26:29.

for carrying the Table. LXX (not, originally, LXX[AF]) adds "by them," as in all Versions of 25:14, 28 but not 37:15 (except in Syr; see TEXTUAL NOTE).

25:28. gold. LXX and Kenn 69, 237 (marg.), 248 expand: "*pure* gold," as in 25:11, 24 (standard MT-Sam). In contrast, MT and Sam, which I take to be original, consistently describe the poles as plated with simple "gold," presumably a somewhat harder alloy than the "pure gold" of the holy objects themselves.

the Table shall be carried by them. Reading with MT *wəniśśā(')-bām 'ethaššulḥān*. Sam alleviates the slight anomaly of the direct object marker in a passive construction (GKC §121) by adding a waw to make the verb transitive: *wnś'w bhm 't-hšlḥn* 'and *they shall carry* the table by them.'

According to BHS, Tgs. Onqelos and Ps.-Jonathan and Syr share Sam's reading, but in fact this is far from clear. *Wîhôn nāṭəlîn* (Tgs.)/*wnehwôn šāqlîn* (Syr) 'and they shall be carrying' might well be a paraphrase of an awkward *Vorlage* such as MT. In contrast, the Sam variant *wənāśə'û* would most naturally come out in Aramaic as the imperfect **wəyiṭṭəlûn/wnešqlûn* 'and they shall carry' (cf. *Samaritan Tg. wysblwn*). Tg. *Neofiti I* has "for carrying the Table by them"—a paraphrase of MT inspired by v 27.

† *25:29. its dippers and its rinsers.* So MT, 4QpaleoExod[m] and LXX. The items are reversed in Sam, thus matching 37:16 (cf. Num 4:7 *qəśôt hannāsek*). Still, in a sequence of three nouns all beginning with *w-* and ending in *-tyw*, we cannot exclude the possibility that 25:29 and 37:16 originally matched each other as in Sam, and that in MT-4QpaleoExod[m]-LXX, *mənaqqiyyōt* fell out accidentally, to be reinserted at the end (see further NOTE).

† *from which.* MT has the grammatically correct and rarer form *bāhen* (fem.), whereas Sam, 4QpaleoExod[m] and Kenn 5, 69, 104, 107 (?), 109, 110, 152, 196, 251, 260, 359B and the Soncino Bible (1488) have the more common but here incongruous masculine *bhm*. The original reading is hard to judge, since gender (in)congruence is not ordinarily a factor in textual criticism (Levi 1987).

may be poured. So MT (*yussak*). LXX "*you* will pour" is probably periphrastic.

Sam *yskw* 'they will pour' carries forward the active voice from the previous verse in Sam (see TEXTUAL NOTE to 25:25, "the Table shall be carried by them").

† 25:31. *shall be made.* So standard MT (i.e., L) and standard *Tgs.* Onqelos and *Ps.-Jonathan.* But Sam, LXX, Syr and very many MSS of MT and *Tgs.* (Kennicott 1776–80: 160; de Rossi 1784–85: 70–71; Ginsburg 1926: 146; Sperber 1959: 132) have "*you* shall make," with Sam and some MT MSS even adding '*t* to indicate a transitive verb. Vg, which drops the word entirely, probably also read "you shall make" in its *Vorlage.*

Since the consonants *t'śh* are ambiguous, this was originally a matter of oral tradition. MT vocalizes a Niph'al *tēʿāśe(h)* (note the MT consonantal variant *tyʿśh* [Codices Mugah, Yerushalmi; Second Rabbinic Bible]), while LXX-Sam reads a Qal **taʿāśe(h).* Either could be correct. Since MT features the more unusual Niph'al conjugation, I have followed its reading (minus the inserted yodh of some MSS).

†† *its thigh and its reeds.* Reading **yrkh wqnyh* with the presumed LXX-Vg-Syr *Vorlage* (probably also *Tgs.* Ps.-Jonathan and Neofiti I), since the following makes it clear that the Lampstand possesses several "reeds," i.e., branches (on the "thigh," see NOTE). MT *yarēkāh wəqānāh* 'its *thigh* and its *reed,*' supported by 4QpaleoExod^m (extant only for the second word) and *Tg.* Onqelos, has apparently leveled the singular, while Sam *yrkyh wqnyh* 'its *thighs* and its *reeds*' seems to borrow the plural suffixes from the following words *gbyʿyh kptyrh wprḥyh* 'its *cups,* its *kaptōrîm* and its *flowers.*' But we cannot be certain; for MT, the singular "its reed" might refer to the central shaft above the "thigh" (Rashi), to all the branches collectively (Cassuto 1967: 342) or to a crossbar. We find a comparable distribution of readings in Num 8:4, MT *ʿad-yarēkāh ʿad-pirḥāh.* See further NOTE.

cups . . . kaptōrîm . . . flowers. Before each feature, LXX and Syr insert "and."

25:32. *and six reeds.* According to Hachlili and Merḥav (1985), since the seven-branched Lampstand does not otherwise appear in the textual or artifactual record till Roman times, these "reeds" must have been interpolated into Exodus. The original Lampstand, they say, was a simple pedestal. I would not head down this methodological path, however, especially since the branches are mentioned already in LXX, and since Num 8:2 mentions seven lamps.

† 25:33. *Three . . . flower.* The entire first clause is missing from LXX. Most likely, whether accidentally or purposely, LXX skipped from one "three" to the next. *Tg.* Neofiti I analogously omits the second clause (also in 37:19). The original, longer text of MT-Sam uses repetition to convey symmetry (cf. 25:32, 35).

thus. Sam and LXX MSS add "you shall make," as in 22:29; 23:11; 26:17.

25:34. *'almondized' cups.* Many LXX MSS add "for the one *reed*" (cf. 25:33), presumably for clarification (but see Wevers 1990: 407).

Syr lacks "almondized" or rather its Syriac equivalent *qbîʿîn* 'affixed, permanent.' While the longer text of other Versions could be a harmonization to v 33, in this case it is more likely that Syr has suffered corruption due to homoioteleuton, whether in Hebrew (*gbʿym mšqdym* > **gbʿym*) or Syriac (*ʾspqyn qbyʿyn* > *ʾspqyn*).

† 25:35. *and a kaptōr* (first time). LXX and Syr lack the conjunction, perhaps correctly. MT-Sam could have borrowed it from the following, parallel phrases.

and a kaptōr under the two reeds from it (second and third times). *Tg. Neofiti I* omits one repetition; cf. TEXTUAL NOTE to 33:21, "and a *kaptōr*."

After the first phrase, LXX differs considerably from MT-Sam and is apparently streamlining. Retroverted into Hebrew, LXX would read **wkptr tht 'rb't hqnym mmnh kn lššt hqnym hyṣ'ym mn hmnrh* 'and a *kaptōr* under the *four reeds* from it, *thus* for the six *reeds* going out from the Lampstand.' The addition of *ken* 'thus' (also in Syr) may be explained as a borrowing from 25:33. In any case, it is necessary once the repetition is eliminated (cf. Rashbam). On the possible parallel in 11QTemple IX:8, see Yadin (1983: 2.36).

25:36. *Their . . . their.* Syr has "its . . . its," to match 25:31, 34. Syr also begins the verse with "and."

† *reeds.* Although I would not emend the text without manuscript evidence, I consider it highly likely that, here and in 37:22, *wqntm* is an ancient error. I suspect that the original read **wprhyhm* 'and their *flowers*,' which is what we would expect (see NOTE).

† *one.* The numeral is feminine in MT (*'ht*) but masculine (*'ḥd*) in Sam. The noun modified, *miqšâ*, appears feminine (but one could read a masculine **miqše[h]*). On gender incongruence, see Levi (1987).

† 25:37. *and one shall raise.* So MT (*wəheʿĕlâ*), reading the third-person converted perfect as an impersonal construction. Sam, LXX, Tgs. and Vg, however, have a second person *wh'lyt* 'and *you* shall *raise*.' Syr combines these approaches by understanding an imperative, **wəhaʿălē(h)* 'and raise!' See also following.

† *illumine.* The Hiph'il of the root *'wr* can mean "shine," "illumine" or "cause to shine, kindle." In MT, the masculine singular verb *wəhēʾîr* must refer to the one who kindles the fire, not to the flames themselves. This is indeed odd. Sam, LXX, Vg, Syr and Tgs. *Onqelos* and *Ps.-Jonathan* present the *lectio facilior wh'yrw* 'and *they* (the flames) shall illumine,' as in 8:2. This might be the original reading here, too.

> **SPECULATION:** We could dispose of the troublesome third-person singulars in 25:37 by reading second-person singular imperatives: *wəhaʿălē(h)* . . . *wəhāʾêr* 'and *raise* and illumine,' anticipating the imperatives in 25:40 (cf. Rashi). Better still, we could interpret the same forms as infinitives absolute, which can replace any finite verbal form including the imperative. This may be the approach of the *Tgs.*, since their *Vorlagen* are usually identical to MT. *Tg. Neofiti I*, "in order to illumine," also sounds like a rendering of the infinitive absolute.

25:38. *fire-pans.* On the different spellings in MT and Sam, see NOTE.

pure gold. Between vv 38 and 39, LXX has "you shall make," which can be read with either verse (see also following TEXTUAL NOTE). Originally, however, it went with v 38 (Wevers 1990: 410). *Tg. Neofiti I*, too, feels the need to supply a verb in v 38: "one shall make it," duplicated from v 39. And Syr adds an imperative "make!"

† 25:39. *A talent, pure gold . . . all these implements.* MT has an unusual im-

personal third-person singular *yaʿăśe(h)*. But MT Sebhirin, Sam, Syr, some *Tg.*
MSS (de Rossi 1784–85: 71; Sperber 1959: 132) and Kenn 9, Rossi 174, 562 have
the *lectio facilior taʿăśe(h)* 'you shall make,' probably also behind the LXX of
vv 38–39. By one reading, LXX has no verb at all: "all these implements a talent of
pure gold" (previous TEXTUAL NOTE).

SPECULATION: One expedient to account for this diversity of readings is to
posit an original Niphʿal **yēʿāśe(h)* 'it shall be made,' misunderstood by all the
Versions. On the passive "illogically" used with the direct object marker, see
GKC §121.

Although MT *kikkār zāhāb ṭāhôr* 'a talent, pure gold' must be taken as apposition, one might revocalize **kikkar zāhāb ṭāhôr* and translate "a talent *of* pure
gold." See also TEXTUAL NOTE to 37:24.

  † *along with.* Standard MT can be understood only by taking *ʾēt* as *ʾēt* II 'with'
(so Vg). The alternative is to follow the *lectio facilior* of Sam, Syr and Kenn 236,
Rossi 2, 6, 414, which insert a conjunction *(wəʾēt)*, making *ʾēt* the expected direct
object marker. Then the whole verse reads, "A talent, pure gold one/you [see previous TEXTUAL NOTE] shall make it *and* all these implements," corresponding
to the parallel in 37:24. Either might be original.

  † *25:40. And see and make.* LXX omits the conjunctions before these commands.

  † *by their model.* For standard MT-Sam-Syr *bətabnîtām*, many MSS and editions of MT and of *Tgs.* (Kennicott 1776–80: 161; de Rossi 1784–85: 71; Sperber
1959: 132) and perhaps LXX and Vg read *kətabnîtām*. The variants are synonymous; cf. Gen 1:26, *naʿăśe(h) ʾādām bəṣalmēnû kidmûtēnû* 'Let us make Man in
(bə-) our image, as *(ki-)* our likeness.' Moreover, beth and kaph are easily confused
in the square script (Tov 2001: 248).

  that you are being made to see. Syr has "that I am going to show you," as in 25:9;
cf. TEXTUAL NOTES to 26:30, "that you were made to see"; 27:8, "as he made
you see."

  †† *26:1. blue.* So Sam and Syr; MT and LXX have "*and* blue."

  Griffins. Two Versions evidently feel discomfort with the depiction of supernatural beings portrayed anywhere other than upon the Chest cover. *Tg. Neofiti I*
paraphrases *kərûbîm* as *ṣywryn* 'figured, embroidered' (also Saadiah), while Vg
even more loosely has "variegated in feathery work" for MT *kərûbîm maʿăśēh
ḥōšēb*; see also TEXTUAL NOTES to 26:31, "webster's work . . . Griffins"; 36:35,
"Griffins." Houtman (2000: 420–21) notes that Josephus *Ant.* 3.113, 126 and
Philo *Moses* 2.84; *Quaest. in Exod.* 2.85, 91 similarly do not mention Griffins, instead stressing the absence of any animal figures. See NOTE for the possibilty that
in fact *kərûbîm* does not mean "Griffins" in 26:1, 31; 36:35.

  26:2. eight-and-twenty by the cubit. Uniquely, *Tg. Neofiti I* adds "the one curtain," to match the next clause.

  † *26:3. Five.* Sam, Kenn 95 and LXX begin "and," as in 36:10.

  of the curtains. LXX and Syr possibly read **(w)ḥmš yryʿt* '(and) five curtains' as later in the verse, vs. MT *ḥămēš hayrî'ōt* 'the five of the curtains.' Cf. further below; also TEXTUAL NOTES to 26:8, "for the eleven curtains"; 36:10, 15.

woman to her sister (both times). Whenever this phrase (*'iššâ 'el-'ăḥōtāh*) occurs in chap. 26, Sam has *'ḥt 'l 'ḥt* 'one to one' (also Syr and *Tgs.*, which, however, probably reflect MT). Since "one to one" is found in MT-Sam 36:10, 12, 13, 22, Sam is probably harmonizing and/or replacing an obsolete idiom.

and five curtains fastened. I follow MT *wǝhāmēš yǝrî'ōt ḥōbǝrōt*, the shortest and most varied text. Sam has *wḥmš hyry'wt thyynh ḥbrwt* 'and five *of the* curtains *shall be* fastened' as earlier in the verse (also Syr and *Tgs.*). Cf. TEXTUAL NOTES to 26:8, "for the eleven curtains"; 36:10, 15.

† 26:4. *And you shall make.* LXX adds "for them," as if reading *lhn*, which could indeed have dropped before *ll't* in MT-Sam due to homoioarkton. But this would also be a natural expansion.

† *at the edge.* Here and in 36:11, against MT *mqṣh* (*miqqāṣâ*), Sam has a synonymous *bqṣh*. Either could be original. On the one hand, the word *qāṣe(h)* is more often preceded by *min/mi-* than by *bǝ-*, making Sam *lectio difficilior*. On the other hand, the Sam prefix *b-* could be borrowed from the following word *b(m)ḥbrt* (see following TEXTUAL NOTE).

†† *on the fastening.* I read with Sam *bmḥbrt* as in 36:11, 17, against MT *baḥōbāret* (see also TEXTUAL NOTE to 26:10, "of the fastening"). *Ḥōberet* is properly a participle as in v 10, while *maḥbāret* should denote an assemblage.

26:5. *Fifty.* Kenn 95 and LXX (but not LXX[B]) appear to begin with a conjunction before "fifty," as we find later in the verse.

on the one curtain. Syr explicates: "on the one curtain's *lip*," as in the prior verse.

on the edge of the curtain. Syr expands: "on the edge of the *second* curtain."

the loops aligning. LXX omits "the loops." This could be either deliberate compression or accident, *ll't* having dropped from the *Vorlage* due to homoioteleuton after *mqbylt* 'aligning.'

woman to her sister. See TEXTUAL NOTE to 26:3.

26:6. *woman to her sister.* See TEXTUAL NOTE to 26:3.

26:7. *to tent.* On this interpretation of *l'hl*, based upon Syr and *Tg. Neofiti I*, see NOTE.

† 26:8. *and breadth four by the cubit the one curtain.* Vs. MT *wrḥb 'rb' b'mh hyry'h h'ḥt*, Sam and LXX have "and four cubits the one curtain's breadth" (*w'rb' 'mwt rḥb hyry'h h'ḥt*) as in MT 36:15. I favor MT as the more diverse text.

†† *for the eleven curtains.* Reading with Sam and LXX *l'šty 'šrh hyry'wt*, vs. MT-4QpaleoExod[m] *l'šty 'šrh yry'wt* 'for eleven curtains.' Since the curtains have already been mentioned, the article *ha-* is expected. It probably fell from MT by haplography (*hh > h*) (Ehrlich 1908: 369). But we cannot exclude the possibility that Sam and LXX are "fixing" MT to the norm. See also TEXTUAL NOTES to 25:3, "and five curtains fastened," and 36:10, 15.

†† 26:10. *loops fifty.* Reading with 4QpaleoExod[m]-Sam-LXX *ll'wt ḥmšym* (also 36:17), vs. MT *ḥămiššîm lūlā'ōt* 'fifty loops.' MT, it appears, has simply borrowed "fifty loops" from later in the verse. (Alternatively, 4QpaleoExod[m]-Sam-LXX may be conforming to 36:17.)

the outermost. LXX has *ana meson* 'innermost, central,' as if reading **htyknh (hattîkōnâ)*, a word found in 26:28; 36:33, vs. MT *haqqîṣōnâ* 'the outermost.' A Cairo Genizah MS *(apud BHS)* reads *haḥîṣônâ*, a more common synonym to *haqqîṣōnâ* (25 occurrences for *ḥîṣôn*, vs. 4 for *qîṣōn*).

†† *of the fastening.* As in 26:4 (see TEXTUAL NOTE), MT reads *baḥōbāret*, while Sam has *bmḥbrt*. I incline toward Sam, supposing that MT has leveled *ḥōberet* throughout the verse. In both MT and Sam, the parallel in 36:17 reads *bammaḥbāret* (also 36:11).

† *and fifty loops.* Sam, LXX and Tg. *Neofiti I* add *tʿśh* 'you shall make.' The result is a symmetrical *wʿśyt llʾwt ḥmšym . . . wḥmšym llʾwt tʿśh* 'and you shall make loops, fifty . . . and fifty loops you shall make,' analogous to 36:17, "and he made loops fifty . . . and fifty loops he made." My preference for the shorter and more diverse text favors MT, but we cannot be certain.

† *the second fastening.* Although all Versions have *hḥbrt hšnyt* here and in 36:17, and although I have retained this reading as *lectio difficilior*, the language is so awkward (see NOTE) that we might posit an original **b(m)ḥbrt hšnyt* 'of the second fastening' as earlier in the verse and in vv 4, 5.

26:12. *and the superfluous . . . back.* LXX is considerably longer than MT: "And *you shall let down* the superfluity in the Tent's curtains; the excess half-curtain you shall fold over, *the excess of the Tent's skins you shall fold over* behind the Tent." LXX appears to understand *srḥ* 'overhang' as a transitive verb, perhaps reading a Hiphʿil (which, however, would be unattested for this root). It also seems to take the initial word of v 12 as a verb, either an imperative **ûs[ə]raḥ* or another imperfect **wətisraḥ*, vs. the MT noun *wəseraḥ*.

† 26:13. *the superfluity.* LXX has "the *curtains'* excess." This sounds like a clarifying expansion, and yet the verse is reasonably intelligible without it. I would consider, then, the possibility of a variant *Vorlage*: **bʿdp hyryʿt*, vs. MT *bāʿōdep*. Even if so, we could regard the longer text as expanded on the rough analogy of 26:12 *hʿdp byryʿt*.

† *cover it.* LXX uncharacteristically omits the direct object. Possibly the *Vorlage* read simply **lkst* 'to cover,' vs. MT *lkstw*. Since the next word begins in waw, dittography and haplography are equally likely to have occurred, assuming continuous writing. Alternatively, if the LXX *Vorlage* used a fuller orthography than MT, we could have a case of metathesis (**lkswt* vs. *lkstw*).

26:14. *beaded skins.* Syr adds, "of rams."

† 26:15. *the qərāšîm.* So MT-Sam-Syr-Tgs. *(haqqərāšîm).* One is tempted to read with the presumed LXX *Vorlage* **qršym* since, throughout this section, commands to make (*ʿśy*) a thing are usually followed by the noun in the indefinite form, as befits their first mention (GKC §126d). Moreover, it is easy to imagine MT-Sam importing the definite article from the parallel in 26:18 (see TEXTUAL NOTE, "the *qərāšîm*) or from the execution in 36:20. We encounter an analogous situation in 27:1, 9; see TEXTUAL NOTES.

standing. LXX does not translate MT-Sam *ʿmdym*, which probably fell from its *Vorlage* either by homoioteleuton with the preceding *šṭym* 'acacia' or by homoioarkton with the following *ʿśr* 'ten.' It is also possible that "standing" is simply implicit in LXX's rendering of Hebrew *qərāšîm* as *styloi* 'pillars' (Wevers 1990: 420).

† 26:16. *ten cubits the* qereš's *length.* The Versions differ in their rendition of this simple phrase, both here and in 36:21. My translation follows MT. Sam and Syr have "ten cubits the *one* qereš's length," while LXX has "ten cubits *you shall make* the *one* qereš," omitting "length" but adding a verb. "You shall make" in LXX is probably a simple expansion; it is absent in LXX^AFM. But explaining the loss of "length" in LXX is difficult, whether in Hebrew or in Greek (see below).

One might favor Sam-Syr over MT, since we would expect "the *one* qereš's length" (cf. 26:2, 8, 10, 19, etc.). Indeed, MT might be considered too difficult to be correct. And yet, there is no mechanical explanation for the loss of **hā'eḥād* 'the one,' while one could easily imagine Sam-LXX-Syr adapting MT to the expected phraseology. See also TEXTUAL NOTES to 27:14, "the shoulder"; 36:17, "the curtain outermost," 21, "the qereš's length."

SPECULATION: If we insist upon the shortest possible reading, we might conjecture that underlying all attested variants is a laconic **śr 'mwt hqrš* 'ten cubits the qereš,' diversely elaborated in MT, Sam and LXX.

†† *a cubit.* So Sam and Kenn 95, 181. MT and LXX insert "and"; see also TEXTUAL NOTE to 36:21.

26:17. *Two.* Syr and Kenn 95 insert "and."

woman to her sister. See TEXTUAL NOTE to 26:3.

26:18. *the* qərāšîm. LXX again has simply "*qərāšîm*" as in LXX 26:15 (see TEXTUAL NOTE). I follow MT-Sam-Syr, since the definite article is now expected, tantamount to "the *aforesaid* qərāšîm." Were we to follow LXX in 26:15, we would have to assume that the MT-Sam-Syr tradition modified 26:15 to match 26:18, while the opposite process occurred in LXX.

twenty qereš. In 26:18–20, Sam, Kenn 132, 136, 253 and Rossi 592, 656 have the expected plural *qršym* (as in 36:23–25) vs. the more unusual MT collective singular *qereš* (see GKC §134e). The plurals in LXX-Syr-Tgs. could reflect either Sam or MT. See also TEXTUAL NOTES to 26:19, 20.

austral, southward. LXX has instead "northward." See TEXTUAL NOTE to 26:20, "north."

26:19. *the twenty* qereš. Sam, Kenn 18 and Rossi 476 have the expected definite plural *hqršym*, as in 36:24, vs. the more unusual and text-critically preferable MT singular *haqqāreš* (see TEXTUAL NOTE to 26:18).

its arms. Instead of *ydtyw*, many Sam MSS read *ytdtyw* 'its pegs,' as in 27:19. See also TEXTUAL NOTES to 36:22, 24. LXX interprets "arms" here as "sides"; cf. NOTE to 26:17.

† 26:20. *Tabernacle's.* LXX lacks "Tabernacle." Presumably, **hmškn* dropped from the *Vorlage* by homoioarkton before *hšnyt* 'second.' But we cannot exclude the possibility that LXX preserves the original text, and that other Versions contain an explicating plus.

north. LXX has "south," reversing the treatment of the two sides vis-à-vis

MT-Sam (see TEXTUAL NOTE to 26:18, "austral, southward"). The reason for the interchange is unfathomable, but it might be related to the reorientation of the Plaza in LXX (see TEXTUAL NOTE to 27:9, "austral, southward").

twenty qereš. Sam expands: "*you shall make* twenty *qərāšîm*," corresponding more closely to 36:25 (plural also in Rossi 265 and the ancient translations) (see TEXTUAL NOTE to 26:18).

26:21. *the one qereš . . . the one qereš.* Each time, LXX adds "for its two sides," derived from v 19 (see also TEXTUAL NOTE to 26:25, "the one *qereš*").

26:23. *And two qərāšîm.* Uniquely, a Cairo Genizah MS (*apud BHS*) has instead "and two *bases*," borrowed from 26:19, 21, 25.

†† 26:24. *And let them be.* Reading a converted perfect *wəhāyû* with Sam, Kenn 84, 102, 107, 199, 244, Rossi 16, 274, 825. Standard MT features instead a jussive *wəyihyû.* LXXᴮ *kai estai* appears to read **whyh*, which makes little sense (but LXXᴬ has the expected plural *kai esontai*). My preference for *wəhāyû* is based upon 36:29, 30 (see TEXTUAL NOTES).

†† *together.* So Sam. MT and 4QpaleoExodᵐ insert a conjunction *wə-* ʿand.' An original **yḥdw* 'together' could have become *wyḥdw* 'and together' by dittography plus waw-yodh confusion in the square script (see Cross 1961a; Qimron 1972). (LXX MSS exhibit comparable variants, an original *kai kata* [= MT] probably having become *kata* [= Sam] by homoioarkton during Greek transmission [Wevers 1990: 424].)

† *whole.* Reading with MT *tammîm* (cf. Syr, Tg. *Neofiti* I). Sam has *tʾmym* 'twinning' as previously in the verse. LXX and Tgs. *Onqelos* and *Ps.-Jonathan* may follow Sam, since they translate the two words identically (see also Tg. *Neofiti* I in the parallel 36:29). In any case, MT is preferable as the more diverse reading.

† *up to.* For MT *ʿal,* Sam and Kenn 101, 136 read the preposition *ʾel* 'to' as in MT 36:29. The meaning is unaffected.

its head. The reading in LXX and Tgs. *Onqelos* and *Ps.-Jonathan* "the(ir) heads" is not a variant but the pluralization of a Hebrew collective in translation. Tg. *Neofiti* I "the head" is closer to the Hebrew; some early editions of Tg. *Onqelos* accurately reflect MT *rō(ʾ)šô* 'its head' (Sperber 1959: 134).

to the one ring. LXX has *eis symblēsin mian* 'to one *fastening*,' as if reading **ʾel-maḥberet ʾeḥāt* or **ʾel-hammaḥberet hāʾeḥāt* for MT *ʾel-haṭṭābaʿat hāʾeḥāt.* This could be a clarifying paraphrase but alternatively might reflect a variant *Vorlage,* as LXX otherwise renders Hebrew *ṭābaʿat* with *daktylios.* Syr appears to read the preposition *ʿal,* as in the previous phrase.

† *shall it be.* LXX "you shall make" seems to reflect a *Vorlage *tʿśh*, vs. MT-Sam *yhyh.* On the one hand, LXX tends frequently to insert the verb *poiein* 'do, make' in this section. And the LXX *Vorlage* may have been adapted specifically to 36:29, "so he *made* for the two of them." On the other hand, MT-Sam may have been influenced by the presence of *yihyû* earlier in the verse. Since the LXX variant is merely reconstructed, I follow MT-Sam.

SPECULATION: Though Syr is not our oldest or best witness, here it contains an attractively short text: "thus for the two," with no verb at all. This could be the laconic original variously expanded by LXX and MT-Sam.

the two of them. Syr adds in explication "bases," a far-fetched effort to cope with the ambiguities of v 24 (below, pp. 414–15, 503).

† *they shall be.* Though reflected in all witnesses, I wonder whether the awkward *yhyw*, not paralleled in 36:29, is a corruption inspired by the presence of this verb twice previously in the verse and the similarity to the verb *whyw* immediately following.

For the possibility that v 24 has suffered major corruption, see NOTE (SPECULATION, p. 415).

† 26:25. *sixteen bases.* LXX and Syr omit "bases," presumably for fluidity but possibly reflecting a shorter and superior *Vorlage* subsequently expanded in MT-Sam.

the one qereš (first time). LXX adds "for its two sides," derived from v 19; cf. TEXTUAL NOTE to 26:21.

† *two bases under the one qereš . . . the one qereš.* So MT *(šnê 'ădānîm taḥat haqqereš hā'eḥād ûš[ə]nê 'ădānîm taḥat haqqereš hā'eḥād).* Sam has a less repetitive *šny 'dnym šny 'dnym lqrš h'ḥd* 'two bases, two bases *for* the one qereš.' This implies that each frame has *four* bases, two on each side — or so I would read Sam. In 36:30, both MT and Sam seem defective; my assumption is that Sam has adapted 26:25 to an already corrupt 36:30 (see TEXTUAL NOTE).

† 26:26. *crossbars, acacia wood.* So MT *(bərîḥîm 'ăṣê šiṭṭîm).* Sam and 4Qpaleo-Exod[m] have *bryḥy 'ṣy šṭym* 'acacia-wood crossbars' as in 36:31. Both are good Hebrew, the former using apposition (GKC §131d) and the latter the construct (GKC §128o) to describe the relationship between artifact and material.

†† *one flank.* Ṣēla' 'flank' is generally feminine, yet the number *'eḥād* 'one' (MT-Sam) is masculine (the only other case of masculine *ṣēla'* is 1 Kgs 6:34). In the parallel 36:31, however, we find the expected feminine *'eḥāt.* Even though gender incongruity is common enough (Levi 1987), in this case the masculine number may be a corruption imported from v 25; alternatively, the proximity of the masculine noun *miškān* may have influenced the choice of *'eḥād* (D. N. Freedman, privately). (That LXX applies the number "one" to the *qərāšîm,* which it translates as if singular, may be an expedient to solve this problem [contrast Wevers 1990: 425].)

26:27. *crossbars* (second time). According to tradition, the Roman-era Severus Scroll omitted *bərîḥîm* and simply read "and five for the *qərāšîm*" as in the preceding verse (Ginsburg 1966: 417).

†† *for the Tabernacle's qərāšîm at the seaward backparts.* Here I venture a quasi-conjectural emendation *ləqaršê hammiškān layyarkātayim yāmmâ,* the reading of the parallel 36:32 (see, however, TEXTUAL NOTE). Most witnesses to 26:27 read *ləqaršê ṣela' hammiškān layyarkātayim yāmmâ* 'for the *qərāšîm* of the Tabernacle's *flank* at the seaward backparts' (Syr further expands "*the Tabernacle's seaward* backparts" as in 26:22.). But the term *ṣēla'* otherwise indicates the Tabernacle's north and south sides (see, however, TEXTUAL NOTE to 26:35). Moreover, the reference to the "second" flank earlier in the verse implies that there is no third. I suppose, therefore, that *ṣela'* was carelessly duplicated from earlier in the verse in our surviving witnesses.

†† 26:28. *barring.* Following Ehrlich (1908: 370), I read the Qal participle **brḥ (bōrēaḥ)* for the MT-Sam Hiphʿil participle *mbrḥ (mabrīaḥ)*, since the Qal is used in this sense in the parallel passage, 36:33 (but see TEXTUAL NOTE). MT-Sam *mbrḥ* arose from reduplication of the preceding *m.*

† 26:30. *according to its rule.* So MT-Sam *(kəmišpāṭô).* Quite possibly, however, the superior reading is 4QpaleoGen-Exod^l-LXX-Vg *kmšpṭ* 'according to *the* rule.' The case is difficult to judge. *Kmšpṭ* is the shorter reading but also the more common form (*kmšpṭw* appears otherwise only in Num 9:14 [MT]; 1 Kgs 5:8).

that you were made to see. Syr paraphrases: "that I showed you"; cf. TEXTUAL NOTES to 25:40, "that you are being made to see"; 27:8, "as he made you see."

† 26:31. *one shall make.* Against the MT *lectio difficilior yaʿăśe(h)*, LXX, Syr, a Cairo Genizah MS *(BHS)*, Kenn 132, 152, 244, 248, Rossi 419, 656, *Tg. Onqelos* in the Ixar Bible (1490), a marginal correction to *Tg. Neofiti I* and MT Sebhirin all read *taʿăśe(h)* 'you shall make,' a harmonization both with the initial verb and with the parallel in 26:1. Sam, however, has *yʿśw* 'they shall make,' while Kenn 260, 384 and the Soncino Bible (1488) read an impossible perfect *ʿāśâ* 'he made,' derived from 36:35 (conceivable, however, would be an imperative **[wa]ʿăśē[h]* or an infinitive absolute *[wə]ʿāśō[h]* [note Kenn 5 *wʿśh*, first hand]).

webster's work . . . Griffins. On the paraphrase in *Tg. Neofiti I* and Vg *(opere plumario et pulchra varietate contextum* 'of a feathery work and interwoven with lovely variety'), see TEXTUAL NOTES to 26:1, "Griffins"; 36:35, "Griffins."

26:32. *their Y-brackets.* Here and wherever the sequence *wwyhm* occurs, LXX, Syr, *Samaritan Tg.* and *Tg. Neofiti I* ostensibly insert a conjunction "and." This reflects not a variant Hebrew text but a different (and incorrect) parsing of the consonants *wwyhm.* That the plural of *wāw* is *wāwîm*, not **wîm*, is clear from 36:38; 38:28. Ibn Ezra (shorter commentary) notes that we would in fact expect a conjunction in 26:32, etc., but thinks **ûwāwêhem* would have been too hard to say.

on four silver bases. LXX either employs unusually free translation or else reflects a variant *Vorlage:* "and their bases, four, silver," somewhat similar to 26:19, 25.

26:33. *under the clasps.* Overall, it is astonishing how infrequently the MSS and Versions confuse the Hebrew words *qereš* 'frame' and *qeres* 'clasp.' The copyists must have been extra-vigilant. But here there has been a mistake of some sort. Against MT-Sam-Syr *tḥt hqrsym* 'under the clasps,' LXX has *epi tous stylous* 'over the pillars.' Commentators (e.g., *BHS*) often infer that LXX read **hqršym* in its *Vorlage*, a variant also found in Kenn 5, 9, 17, 18, 132, 152, 158, 160, 171, 196, 601 and a Cario Genizah MS *(apud BHS).* If so, it would appear that, to make the best of a dubious text, a scribe changed the preposition from "under" to "over" to make the picture more comprehensible. Wevers (1990: 428) notes that, according to 26:32, the Veil is hung upon *pillars* (Hebrew *ʿammûdîm*), and perhaps this is what LXX had in mind, since it uses *stylos* to render both *qereš* and *ʿammûd.*

On Friedman's (1981: 50–51) proposal to combine the readings of MT-Sam and LXX into **taḥat haqqərāšîm*, see below, pp. 503–4.

† 26:34. *set the kappōret.* Two other words that are easily confused are *kprt*

(kappōret), the Chest's cover, and *prkt (pārōket)*, the Veil shielding the Chest (cf. TEXTUAL NOTE to 40:3, "Veil"). Here, against MT-Sam-Syr *hakkappōret*, LXX and *Tg. Neofiti I* (first hand) reflect **hprkt*, thus exactly reproducing the beginning of v 33. MT-Sam is preferable as *lectio difficilior*, since the *pārōket* 'Veil' is the subject of the surrounding discussion. Indeed, v 33 already specified that the Chest was placed within the Veil.

26:35. *the Tabernacle's flank.* For MT *ṣelaʿ hammiškān*, Sam and a Cairo Genizah MS *(apud BHS)* have *yrk hmškn* 'the Tabernacle's *backpart*.' MT, however, reserves *yārēk* for the Tabernacle's rear, to the west (26:22, 23, 27); see also TEXTUAL NOTE to 26:27, "for the Tabernacle's *qərāšîm* at the seaward backparts."

† *the north flank.* LXX has "the *Tabernacle's* flank, north*ward*," as if reading **l ṣlʿ hmškn ṣpwnh*, vs. MT-Sam-4QpaleoGen-Exod[1] *ʿl ṣlʿ ṣpwn(h)*. The wording of LXX matches better the previous clause; therefore, MT-Sam is the more diverse and preferable text.

After v 35, Sam and 4QpaleoExod[m] insert their version of 30:1–10, thereby associating the Golden Altar with the other Tabernacle furniture. There is a chance that this is correct, and that in MT 30:1–10 was lost by homoioarkton *wʿśyt . . . wʿśyt* 'and you shall make . . . and you shall make.' If so, the omitted matter was subsequently reinserted into MT in its present location.

I do not favor this theory, however, because Sam is throughout prone to rearranging, harmonizing and supplementing (see, e.g., TEXTUAL NOTES to 6:9; 7:8–11:10 *passim*; 20:1–17[14]). The MT-LXX reading, which has the Golden Altar in chap. 30, is preferable as the more difficult text, especially since we can find a somewhat plausible rationale for the Incense Altar's postponement (below, pp. 716–17). For futher discussion on the problem of the Incense Altar, see pp. 369, 514–15.

† 26:36. *for the Tent Opening.* These words are missing in LXX (contrast LXX 37:5; see TEXTUAL NOTE to 36:37). Although this is *lectio brevior et difficilior*, it should not be adopted without corroboration from a Hebrew MS.

† 26:37. *acacia posts.* LXX has simply "posts," as if reading *ʿmwdym* for MT-Sam *ʿmwdy šṭym*. This is probably an inner-Greek haplography: *stylous aseptous* > *stylous* (D. N. Freedman, privately).

gold. Sam expands "pure gold"; cf. LXX 25:28 (TEXTUAL NOTE, "gold").

† 27:1. *the Altar.* So MT *(ʾet-hammizbēaḥ)*, as if the Altar were already known to the reader (see also TEXTUAL NOTES to 26:15, 18; 27:9, "and you shall make the Tabernacle's Plaza"; 28:9, 39, "the Shift, linen"; 36:15; 38:20, 27). Sam and LXX have simply *mzbḥ* 'an altar,' which we would have expected for the Altar's first appearance. In a parallel instance, we found reason to doubt MT (TEXTUAL NOTE to 26:15, "the *qərāšîm*). Here, mechanical error is less likely, although conceivably MT imported *hammizbēaḥ* from later in the verse. I have retained MT as *lectio difficilior*, supposing that LXX-Sam corrected the reading to the norm.

For Sam, moreover, there is a second consideration. In both Sam and 4QpaleoExod[m], 27:1 is immediately preceded by 30:1–10, describing the Incense Altar (TEXTUAL NOTE to 26:35, "the north flank"). With this textual arrangement, referring to "*the* Altar" would have been confusing (cf. Childs 1974: 525)—

although Sam would have done better to specify "the *Ascending-offering* Altar" as in 38:1.

27:2. *plate it.* Against MT-Sam '*tw,* LXX has "plate *them,*" referring to the horns, or to the horns plus the Altar.

27:3. *its pots . . . shovels.* Corresponding to MT-Sam *sîrōtā(y)w ləd̲aššənô wəyā'ā(y)w,* LXX has "a crown/rim *(stephanē)* for the Altar and its cover *(kalyptēra).*" Presumably, "crown" refers to either the four horns or an otherwise unmentioned decorative rim. But *sîr* 'pot' is not a rare word, and the Greek Bible generally understands it correctly (e.g., in 16:3). One might infer that LXX read a different word in 27:3, perhaps a form of *sgr (misgeret = stephanē* in 25:25, 27) or *zēr* 'rim' (for which, however, LXX uses *kymatia strepta* in 25:11, 24, etc.); the translator may even have made an association with Aramaic *zîrā'* 'crown.'

But, more likely, LXX is based upon MT-Sam *sîrōtā(y)w* after all, even if we cannot explain why. In Jer 52:18, also a catalog of sacred implements, Hebrew *sîrôt* 'pots' again corresponds to the Greek singular *stephanē* 'crown,' completely against the plain sense (in the parallel 2 Kgs 25:14, the Greek correctly has *lebētai* 'bowls').

That leaves MT-Sam *ləd̲aššənô wəyā'ā(y)w* as ostensibly corresponding to LXX "for the Altar and its cover." But nowhere else does LXX render *yā'(e[h])* (see NOTE) as "cover," while the Old Greek generally understands *diššēn* as "fatten" (Ps 20:4; 23:5; Prov 15:30). What is going on? It appears that the translator of LXX Exod 27:3 looked to Num 4:13, where MT *wəd̲iššənû 'et-hammizbēaḥ* 'and they shall de-ash the Altar' occurs in the context of *covering* the Altar and is accordingly mistranslated: *kai ton kalyptēra epithēsei(s) epi to thysiastērion* 'and he/you (LXX MSS disagree with one another and with MT) shall put the cover upon the Altar.' Thus, in two places, LXX erroneously takes *diššēn* to mean "to cover an altar." As for *wy'yw,* it is not reflected in LXX. It could have been dropped either by homoioteleuton with *ldšnw* or by homoioarkton with *wmzrqtyw,* or it could be a casualty of very loose translation.

for de-ashing it. Ehrlich (1908: 371) repoints the MT infinitive *ləd̲aššənô* as a noun *ləd̲išnô* 'for its *ash*' (see also Saadiah). Since, however, the verb is paralleled in Num 4:13, revocalization is unwarranted.

SPECULATION: The mention of pots for removing ash is surprising and not paralleled in 38:3. Without it, we would have assumed that the pots are for *boiling* the meat (Heger 1999: 179–81; compare 16:3; 2 Kgs 4:38–41; Jer 1:13; Ezek 11:3–11; 24:3–6; Micah 3:3; Zech 14:21; Job 41:23; Eccl 7:6). Perhaps, then, MT-Sam has suffered metathesis of an original **sîrōtā(y)w wəyā'ā(y)w ləd̲aššənô* 'its pots and its shovels for de-ashing it,' which would be more logical (see, however, NOTES).

shovels . . . bowls . . . forks. Vg lacks one implement, mentioning only "tongs" and "forks." Jerome is generally lax in his enumeration of sacred utensils, and so we cannot be certain what he read in his *Vorlage.* Possibly he or his text omitted either *wmzrqtyw* 'and its bowls' or *wmzlgtyw* 'and its forks' due to their graphic similarity.

and its fire-pans. LXX translates in the singular (*kai to pyreion autou* 'and its fire-pan'), as if reading **wmḥtw* vs. MT *wmḥttyw*/Sam *wmḥty(w)tyw.* Perhaps the LXX proto-V*orlage* read **wmḥtwtw,* which became **wmḥtw* by haplography.

in short, all. So MT and Sam (on this usage of *l-,* see NOTE to 14:28). LXX (not LXX^A) and Syr, however, appear to read the more expected *wkl* 'and all' (also MT Sebhirin)—but this is probably paraphrase, since we find the same correspondence in 27:19 (see TEXTUAL NOTE). A Cairo Genizah MS *(apud* BHS) and Tgs. *Ps.-Jonathan* and *Neofiti I,* as well as Tg. *Onqelos* in the 1490 Ixar edition, read simply *kl* as in 38:3.

27:4. *for it.* Not reflected in Syr.

on the lattice. Here and in v 5, Syr "on the mesh" and LXX "on the *hearth*" are unlikely to represent a variant V*orlage *ʿal hammikbār* but are rather elucidating paraphrases (Wevers 1990: 433, *pace* BHS).

on its four corners. LXX^B "*under* its four sides" is related to LXX's understanding of v 5; see TEXTUAL NOTES below.

† 27:5. *it.* Where MT has the feminine singular *'ōtāh,* referring to the lattice (*rešet,* fem.), Sam has the masculine singular *'tw,* referring to the mesh (*mikbār,* masc.). The difference is negligible, especially since in the ancient autograph, *'th* probably stood for both *'ōtāh* and *'ōtô.* LXX-Vg may preserve a third variant, "them," as if reading **'(w)tn,* referring to the *rings* not the mesh.

rim. For MT-Sam *krkb,* LXX has *eschara* 'hearth,' which corresponds to MT-Sam *mkbr* 'mesh' in 27:4.

the lattice. See TEXTUAL NOTE to 27:4, "on the lattice."

as far as. MSS of Tgs. vary between *ʿad* (= MT) and *ʿal* 'upon.'

27:6. *acacia-wood poles.* LXX has simply "acacia wood," which is admittedly the shorter reading *(lectio brevior)* but also what one might expect *(lectio facilior).* In the absence of grounds for mechanical error, I assume that LXX is streamlining. Its reading is attested in no extant Hebrew MS.

† 27:7. *And its poles shall be inserted.* So MT and 4QpaleoGen-Exod^l: *wəhûbā(') 'et-baddā(y)w.* Tg. *Onqelos* has "and you shall insert *its* poles," while LXX, Syr, Vg and Tg. *Neofiti I* have "and you shall insert *the* poles." One would ordinarily dismiss these translations as periphrastic, but Sam preserves the LXX-Syr-Vg-Tg. *Neofiti I* V*orlage: whb't 't hbdym.* (Tg. *Onqelos* compromises, so to speak, between MT and Sam, reflecting **whb't 't bdyw.*) If these variations result from mechanical error, either dittography (*'t > ' 't*) produced Sam, or haplography (*' 't > 't*) produced MT.

I have followed MT *wəhûbā('),* because it employs a somewhat unusual passive construction with a direct object (GKC §121) and because it breaks the expected sequence: "and you shall . . . and you shall." As for "*its* poles *(bdyw)*" vs. "*the* poles *(hbdym),*" I again favor MT, since *(h)bdym* occurs twice in proximity, while *bdyw* is unique in this section.

SPECULATION: Assuming that behind MT lay a defectively-spelled form without waw, the consonants **whb'* would be susceptible to other interpretations as well. Tg. *Ps.-Jonathan wyhnʿl* 'and one shall insert' appears to read a converted perfect *wəhēbî* or possibly an infinitive absolute *wəhābē*. Likewise, the second-person renderings cited above conceivably reflect not Sam *wəhēbē(')tā* but an imperative or infinitive absolute command *wəhābē* 'and insert!'

two flanks. LXX originally omitted "two" — it is restored in some MSS — probably not by textual error but because the number of poles was obvious (Wevers 1990: 434). But two MT MSS, Kenn 193 and 244, also lack "two."
27:8. *as he made you see.* LXX-Vg "as you were shown" and Syr-Tg. *Ps.-Jonathan* "as I showed you" are probably not variants but paraphrases based upon 25:9, 40; 26:30; Num 8:4. (Admittedly, however, the Hebrew equivalent of the latter reading, *hr'ʾt(y)k*, would resemble both visually and aurally MT-Sam *hr'ʾh 'tk* [Holzinger 1900: 131].)
so they shall make. Sam inserts a conjunction: "*and so* . . . ," probably influenced by the cliché "and so they/you shall make/do" (25:9; 26:4; Lev 16:16; Deut 22:3; Josh 11:15, etc.). LXX "so *you* shall make *it*" duplicates the phrase from earlier in the verse.
27:9. *And you shall make the Tabernacle's Plaza.* We might have expected, against MT-Sam *wə'āśîtā 'ēt ḥăṣar hammiškān*, **wə'āśîtā ḥāṣēr lammiškān* 'and you shall make *a* Plaza *for* the Tabernacle," since this is the Plaza's first mention (see TEXTUAL NOTE to 27:1; GKC §126d). LXX does translate in this manner, but it is presumably paraphrasing.
austral, southward. LXX "westward" reflects its peculiar rotation of the Plaza by 90 degrees (Bogaert 1981). In Egypt, "forward" is south not east, "seaward" is north (cf. NOTES to 10:13; 14:21; TEXTUAL NOTES to 26:20, "north"; 27:11, "north," 13, "forward, eastward"). Wevers (1990: 435) conjectures that for LXX the inner sanctum symbolized Jerusalem, while the outer courtyard connoted the Alexandrian Diaspora. Despite his own reservations, I find Wevers's thesis compelling, especially given the apparently deliberate reworking of 27:11, 19 in LXX to deemphasize the Tabernacle and emphasize the Plaza (see TEXTUAL NOTES).
the Plaza. A Cairo Genizah MS *(BHS)* expands "the *Tabernacle's* Plaza," to match the Plaza's first mention.
twisted linen. The absence of this phrase in LXX^B raises two possibilities: either *ek byssou keklōsmenēs* was lost after *aulēs* 'Plaza' during Greek transmission (homoioteleuton), or LXX^B preserves the original LXX reading, which other MSS expand to match MT-Sam. If it was originally not reflected in LXX, *šš mšzr* could have dropped from the Hebrew *Vorlage* by homoioteleuton after *ḥṣr* 'Plaza.' (Although LXX^B is *lectio brevior et difficilior*, it is too short and difficult — and uncorroborated in a Hebrew MS — to be adopted.) Note that the LXX fulfillment narrative (LXX 37:7) does mention twisted linen.
27:10. *and its posts.* Against MT-Sam-4QpaleoExod^m-Tgs.-Syr *wə'ammûdā(y)w*, LXX has "and *their* posts," as if reading **w'mdyhm*, referring to the curtains (cf. 38:11). See also TEXTUAL NOTES to 27:11, 16.
†† *their Y-brackets.* Reading **wāwêhem* with Sam-LXX, against MT *wāwê hā'ammûdîm* 'the *posts'* Y-brackets.' My assumption (not necessarily correct) is

that originally 27:10–11 consistently had "their Y-brackets," while 38:10–11 had "the posts' Y-brackets." If so, MT has harmonized commission and fulfillment.

27:11. *And likewise*. LXX lacks the conjunction.

north. LXX "east" reflects its 90 degree rotation of the Tabernacle; see TEXTUAL NOTE to 27:9, "austral, southward."

†† *in length: sheets, one hundred by the cubit*. After much vacillation, I have concluded that Sam *b'rk ql'ym m'h b'mh* is the best extant reading (also Syr and Vg; cf. 38:11). LXX reads a synonymous **ql'ym m'h b'mh 'rk* 'sheets, one hundred by the cubit, length,' probably in imitation of 27:9. MT, 4QpaleoGen-Exod[1] and Tgs., however, offer the most difficult text: *bā'ōrek qəlā'îm mē'â 'ōrek* 'in length: sheets, one hundred length,' with "length" repeated and "cubits" understood. Possibly proto-MT conflated Sam and LXX, yielding **b'rk ql'ym m'h b'mh 'rk* 'in length, sheets, one hundred by the cubit, length,' from which *b'mh* 'by the cubit' fell by haplography *(*m'h b'mh > m'h)*, yielding MT.

> SPECULATION: We might conjecture that no MS preserves the original reading. One could easily imagine that the autograph had a shorthand *ql'ym m'h* 'sheets, one hundred,' which later scribes clarified, variously adding "cubits" and "(in) length" lest one think there are 100 curtains. Cf. TEXTUAL NOTES to 27:15, "fifteen, sheets," 18.

† *and its posts*. So MT-Syr (*wə'ammûdāw* [Qere]). Sam and Kenn 107 have *'mwdyhm* 'their posts,' as in 38:11, while LXX and Tg. *Ps.-Jonathan* read *w'mwdyhm* "and their posts," as in LXX 27:10 (see TEXTUAL NOTE). I assume, perhaps wrongly, that 27:10–11 originally had "its posts" and 38:10–11 "their posts," as in MT. In any case, it hardly matters: "its" refers to the Plaza, "their" to the curtains comprising the Plaza. See also TEXTUAL NOTE to 27:16.

†† *their Y-brackets*. Reading *wwyhm* with Sam, against MT *wāwê hā'ammûdîm* 'the *posts*' Y-brackets.' See TEXTUAL NOTE to 27:10.

† *silver*. LXX has "and the(ir) bases plated in silver," so that the Plaza's bases superficially resemble the Tabernacle's silver bases. If for LXX, the Plaza symbolizes the Diaspora, the extra ornamentation makes sense (see TEXTUAL NOTES to 27:9, "astral, southward," 19).

† 27:12. *ten*. Here and in 27:14, 15, 16, Sam and 4QpaleoGen-Exod[1] (extant only in v 12) add "bronze" to match vv 10, 11, 17, 18. Cf. TEXTUAL NOTES to 27:15, "three," 16, "four"; 38:10.

> SPECULATION: We would expect the verse to continue: **wwyhm/wwy h'mdym wḥšqyhm ksp* 'the pillars'/their Y-brackets and their *ḥăšūqîm* silver' as in vv 10–11. Indeed, the parallel in 38:12 continues in this wise. Perhaps, then, a scribe's eye jumped to the waw that begins v 13 and dropped the reconstructed text.

27:13. *forward, eastward*. As elsewhere, LXX understands *qedem* in the Alexandrian mode to denote the south (see NOTES to 10:13; 14:21; TEXTUAL NOTE to 27:9, "austral, southward").

† *fifty cubit.* LXX adds "their posts ten and their bases ten," so that v 13 matches v 12 exactly. The expansion, if such it is, could be accidental or deliberate. But it is also possible that MT is the result of parablepsis from he' (*'mh* 'cubit') to he' (**'śrh* 'ten'). The parallel in 38:13 also lacks the LXX plus.

†† 27:14. *fifteen.* So Sam (*lectio brevior*); MT and LXX begin "and."

cubit. LXX adds "the height," either an explicating plus or the original text **ḥmš 'śrh 'mh qmh [sic] hql'ym,* reduced by homoioteleuton (*mh . . . mh*) and haplography to MT-Sam *(w)ḥmš 'śrh 'mh ql'ym.* Overall, LXX appears to be expansionistic in this section, however. Moreover, its sense is not clear; one must infer that here, uniquely, *hypsos* 'height' really means "length" (see Wevers 1990: 439); cf. the Rabbinic discussion of whether fifteen cubits refers to height or width (*b. 'Erub.* 2b; *Zebaḥ.* 59b–60a).

the shoulder. LXX is longer, presumably expansionistic: "the *one* shoulder," to correlate with "the second shoulder" in v 15.

bases three. Sam adds a final "bronze"; see TEXTUAL NOTE to 27:12.

27:15. *shoulder.* Against MT *kātēp,* Sam uses *pē'â* 'side,' which has appeared five times in 27:9–13. Sam accordingly lacks a distinction that is meaningful in MT: *pē'â* is a complete side, while the fabrics flanking the portal are each a *kātēp.*

†† *fifteen, sheets.* I have tentatively followed MT-Syr-Tgs. *ḥmš 'śrh ql'ym* 'fifteen, sheets,' with "cubit" understood. Sam *ḥmš 'śrh 'mh ql'ym* (also Vg) matches 27:14 and is presumably a clarifying expansion (cf. TEXTUAL NOTE to 27:11, "in length: sheets, one hundred by the cubit"). LXX "fifteen *cubits the* sheets' height (i.e., length)" (see Wevers 1990: 439) is probably a paraphrase of Sam. (But against MT, one could argue that Sam *ḥmš 'śrh 'mh ql'ym* became MT *ḥmš 'śrh ql'ym* by a copyist skipping from one he' to the next.)

three. Sam adds "bronze"; see TEXTUAL NOTE to 27:12.

27:16. *screen, twenty cubit.* LXX adds "the height," as if reading **msk 'śrym 'mh qmh,* from which *qmh* was lost by homoioteleuton with *'mh.* But it is clear that LXX is expansionistic in this section, and, in any case, the use of *hypsos* 'height' for length is peculiar to the Greek (see Wevers 1990: 439).

†† *its posts.* All extant Versions agree with MT: *'ammûdêhem . . . wǝ'adnêhem* 'their posts . . . and their bases.' But this makes no sense, since there is no masculine plural noun to which the pronominal suffixes might refer. Rather, it is the *screen* (*māsāk,* m.s.) that has four posts. It follows that we must emend the first word to **'ammûdā(y)w* as in MT-Sam 27:10 (see TEXTUAL NOTE; also TEXTUAL NOTE to 27:11). The corruption is due to the presence of *'ammûdêhem* in 27:12, 14, 15.

four. Sam adds "bronze"; see TEXTUAL NOTE to 27:12.

†† 27:18. *one hundred upon one hundred.* Reading *m'h bm'h* with LXX and some Sam MSS. MT-standard Sam-Syr-Vg-Tgs. all have *m'h b'mh* 'one hundred by the cubit.' Whichever reading is original, the other arose either by the graphic similarity of *bm'h* and *b'mh* (metathesis) or by an effort to clarify that the number refers to cubits (one might also confect a hypothetical **m'h bm'h b'mh* 'one hundred upon one hundred by the cubit,' variously reduced by haplography in the extant witnesses). Ordinarily we prefer mechanical explanations, but in this case an

overriding consideration is that the same phenomenon—mention or nonmention of cubits—occurs also in 27:11, and later in v 18 (see TEXTUAL NOTE to 27:11, "in length: sheets, one hundred by the cubit"; next TEXTUAL NOTE).

fifty upon fifty. So MT-LXX-Syr-*Tgs.* (*hămiššîm bahămiššîm*). Sam reads *hmšym b'mh*, and Vg has simply "fifty," which could be a paraphrase of either MT or Sam—Jerome is quite free—or a corruption of MT: *hmšym bhmšym > *hmšym*. My assumption in v 18 and my suspicion in v 11 is that all references to "cubits" are secondary (see TEXTUAL NOTES).

27:19. *in short, all.* So MT (*ləkōl*), Tg. *Neofiti I* and presumably Syr and Vg (on this usage of *l-*, see NOTE to 14:28). LXX ostensibly reads **wkl 'and all,'* as in the following phrases, but this may be a paraphrase of MT; cf. TEXTUAL NOTE to 27:3. Sam has the longest reading: *w'śyt 't kl 'and you shall make all . . . ,'* supplying the implicit verb and making the verse match other instructions in the pericope.

† *all the Tabernacle's implements in all its Work.* Here, MT-Sam differs considerably from LXX, which has "all the implements *and* all its *tools.*" LXX and MT-Sam are speaking of different things: LXX of the Plaza and MT-Sam of the Tabernacle. LXX is probably a deliberate alteration to exalt the outer Plaza, symbolic of the Diaspora (see TEXTUAL NOTES to 27:9, "austral, southward," 11, "silver"; also next TEXTUAL NOTE).

Other variants are less significant. Syr appears to read **(l)kl kly hmškn wkl 'bdtw* '(in short), all the Tabernacle's implements *and* all its Work,' so that like LXX, Syr borrows *wəkol* 'and all' from the following phrases. Conversely, Tg. *Neofiti I* reproduces *lkl 'for all'* (vs. MT-Sam *bkl*) from earlier in the verse. Finally, a Cairo Genizah MS (*apud BHS*) reads "in all *their* Work (*bkl 'bdtm*)."

† *and all its tent-pegs . . . bronze.* Sam equals MT, except that it has carelessly duplicated *wbkl 'and in* all' from the previous phrase (also Kenn 600). LXX, however, has a shorter text: "and the Plaza's tent-pegs, bronze." At first glance, it would seem that LXX has accidentally reduced the sequence *wkl ytdtyw wkl ytdt* (MT) to **wkl ytdt.* But the overall evidence shows rather that LXX reflects a deliberate rewriting to deemphasize the Tabernacle in v 19 (see previous TEXTUAL NOTE; TEXTUAL NOTES to 27:9, "austral, southward," 11, "silver").

At the end of v 19, Sam, 4QpaleoExod[m] and the *f* family of LXX MSS add "and you shall make garments of blue and purple and worm-crimson for serving in them in the Holiness," easing the introduction of the priesthood in the following verses. It is not impossible that this is original, having dropped from MT by waw . . . waw ("and . . . and") parablepsis. But it would also be a typical expansion.

27:20. *you shall command.* For MT *təṣawwe(h)*, LXX has the imperative *syntaxon*, as if reading **ṣaw,* as in Lev 24:2.

27:21. *Let . . . arrange.* Syr and Vg begin "And." While the conjunction is text-critically insignificant, it points to a different clause division from MT; see NOTE.

† *till.* Kenn 4, 5, 17, 18, 69, 84, 107, 129, 150, 153, 158, 168, 181, 193, 237, 615, 686, Syr and a Tg. *Onqelos* MS (Sperber 1959: 136) have "*and* till."

† *and his sons.* For Haran (1978: 209, 227), the reference to Aaron's sons is an

interpolation. Admittedly, "and his sons" is absent in the parallel in Lev 24:3, and otherwise only Aaron may enter the Tabernacle to perform the "inner rites." For the opposite view, that "and his sons" is to be supplied in Lev 24:3 following Sam, LXX and MT MSS, see Milgrom (2001: 2088). See further NOTE.

† *for their ages.* Reading *lədōrōtām* with MT-*Tgs.*-Vg. We find in Sam, Kenn 173, LXX and Syr the variant *ldrtykm* 'to *your* ages,' a more common idiom in conjunction with *ḥuqqat ʿôlām* 'eternal rule' (12:14, 17; Lev 3:17; 10:9; 23:14, 21, 31, 41; 24:3; Num 10:8; 15:15; 18:23; cf. Num 35:29). The reading of Sam-LXX-Syr implies that the commandment is primarily for all Israel—but then "*from* (*mēʾēt*) Israel's Sons" would not make sense. "To *their* ages," however, referring to Aaron and his sons, is logical: the priests kindle the lamps as an eternal charge from both Yahweh and Israel (see NOTE). The third-person plural phrasing is paralleled in Gen 17:7,9; Exod 12:42; 27:21; 30:21; 31:16; 40:15; Lev 7:36; 17:7; 21:17; Num 15:38; compare also Exod 28:43, "an eternal rule for him [Aaron] and for his *seed* after him."

28:1. *with him.* LXX does not reflect Hebrew *ʾtw*. It was omitted either deliberately for ease of translation or accidentally due to homoioteleuton, whether in Hebrew *(bnyw ʾtw)* or in Greek *(*autou met' autou)*.

† *to priest.* Here and in 28:3, 4, MT adds a suffixed waw *(lkhnw)* absent in Sam *(lkhn)* and unreflected in LXX, Syr, Vg and *Tgs. Onqelos* and *Ps.-Jonathan* (contrast the *Neofiti I* paraphrase "for serving in the priesthood before *him,*" i.e., God). In the parallel 29:1, MT itself lacks the suffix, reading *lkhn.* If this *-w* is pronominal, then we have a meaningful if minor variant: Sam "to priest" vs. MT "for *his* priesting" (the last is the interpretation of the Three). But *-w* may be an archaic case ending (cf. GKC §90o) that LXX duly ignored and Sam deleted as unnecessary. See further NOTE.

Nadab. LXX and Syr prefix "and."

Abihu. The LXX transcription *Abioud* evidently reflects not MT-Sam *ʾbyhwʾ* but *ʾbyhwd,* a name attested in 1 Chr 8:3.

Eleazar. By their deployment of the conjunction, MT, Sam, Vg and *Tgs.* divide between Aaron's doomed elder sons and the two younger survivors to whom the priesthood will pass (Leviticus 10). LXX and Syr lack this distinction, inserting "and" before "Eleazar."

28:2. *Garments.* LXX has the singular; see TEXTUAL NOTE to 28:3, "Aaron's garments, to make him holy."

28:3. *speak.* Syr "say" (properly, Hebrew *tō[ʾ]mar*) is probably a loose translation of MT-Sam *tədabbēr.*

all. Vg is admittedly quite free in the Tabernacle pericope, but its omission of "all" here could indicate that *kl* had fallen from its *Vorlage* due to homoioteleuton with the preceding *ʾl* 'to.'

† *wise-hearted.* This is plural in MT-LXX-Vg-Syr-*Tgs.* (*kl ḥkmy lb* 'all wise-hearted') but singular in Sam and Kenn 170 (*kl ḥkm lb* 'each wise-hearted [man]'). Textual variation has arisen from the fact that, in both MT and Sam, 28:3 refers to the craftsmen in both singular and plural. If MT is original, Sam has "fixed" the text to match the singular suffix on *millē(ʾ)tîw,* literally "I filled *him.*"

If, however, Sam is original, MT has pluralized *ḥăkam* 'wise [man]' to match *wəʿāśû* 'and *they* shall make.' See further NOTE.

Aaron's garments, to make him holy. LXX "Aaron's *holy* garment *for the Holiness*" differs in several respects from MT-Sam-4QpaleoExod^m *bigdê ʾahărōn ləqaddəšô*. Some of the variation is simple paraphrase. For example, here and in v 2, the Greek singular *stolēn* for the Hebrew plural *bigdê* exemplifies the Greek collective, tantamount to English "clothing" (Wevers 1990: 444; cf. Vg). The insertion of "holy" before "garment" in LXX (also Syr), thus matching v 2, likewise probably does not represent a variant *Vorlage*, which would be quite different from MT-Sam: **bigdê haqqōdeš ʾăšer ləʾahărōn*.

> SPECULATION: For the final word, however, LXX may have followed a variant Hebrew text uniquely reading **lqdš* (**laqqōdeš*), vs. MT-Sam *lqdšw* (*ləqaddəšô*). Wevers (1990: 445) sees the change as deliberate, arguing that anointing not robing sanctifies a priest. But to judge from 28:41, investiture and anointment *together* constitute consecration. It is at least as possible that, just as the following infinitive "to priest" is attested as both *lkhn* and *lkhnw* (TEXTUAL NOTE to 28:1, "to priest"; next TEXTUAL NOTE), so there was variation between **lqdš* and *lqdšw*. Specifically, if an original *lkhnw* was modernized into *lkhn*, a scribe might have absentmindedly dropped the waw from the preceding infinitive, creating a consonantal text *lqdš* that LXX read not as **ləqaddēš* 'to priest,' but as **laqqōdeš* 'for the Holiness.'

† *to priest.* See TEXTUAL NOTES to 28:1, 4. Note that, if Sam's shorter reading is original, the MT corruption probably originated in v 3: *lqdšw lkhn* (Sam) > *lqdšw lkhnw* (MT).

28:4. *they shall make.* Syr adds "for them."

a . . . an . . . an. LXX inserts the definite article before the first three vestments, I suppose since they were well known to readers.

ephod. LXX calls this vest-like garment a "shoulder strap," apparently making a forced connection between Greek *epōmis* and Hebrew *ʾēpôd* (on the latter's true derivation, see NOTE). The choice is doubly unfortunate, since *epōmis* also renders *kātēp* 'shoulder' in the following verses.

and a robe. Vg omits the conjunction, thus grouping the vestments in pairs: "a *ḥōšen* and an ephod, a robe and a woven shift, a turban and a sash."

† *and a . . . shift.* Sam and LXX^B omit the conjunction, perhaps correctly. Tgs. Onqelos and Ps.-Jonathan pluralize "shifts . . . turbans . . . sashes," since, according to 28:40, the minor clergy also wear these garments (*Tg. Neofiti I* pluralizes only "turbans"). Evidently, the Tgs. take the MT singulars as collectives. Cf. TEXTUAL NOTE to 39:29, "the Sash."

a turban. Kenn 5, 17, 75, 95, 136, 196 and Syr insert "and."

†† *for Aaron.* So LXX and Kenn 84, 199; MT and Sam add "your brother" as in 28:1, 2, 4, 41. (Admittedly, LXX could be an adaptation to 29:28, 35; 39:27, etc.) In the absence of grounds for parablepsis, I follow the shorter reading. Cf. TEXTUAL NOTE to 29:5, "Aaron."

† *to priest.* See TEXTUAL NOTES to 28:1, 3.

† 28:5. *and the blue.* Many MT MSS, including a Genizah fragment *(BHS)*, omit the conjunction, perhaps rightly (Kennicott 1776–80: 166; de Rossi 1784–85: 72).

linen. Many Syr MSS expand: "*twisted* linen."

† 28:6. *gold, blue and purple, worm-crimson and.* As often in lists, the Versions vary in their deployment of conjunctions. My translation follows standard MT. Vg inserts a conjunction before "blue," while Sam, many MT MSS (Kennicott 1776–80: 166; de Rossi 1784–85: 72), Aquila, Symmachus, Vg, *Tgs.* and Syr put a conjunction before "worm-crimson." Overall, there appears to be an attempt to adapt v 6 to v 5.

LXX omits all these materials, simply commanding, "and they shall make the Ephod from twisted linen." In LXX 36:9 (= MT 39:2), however, the list is full: "gold and blue and purple and worm-crimson and twisted linen." LXX 28:6 seems to be the result of random textual loss.

28:7. *fastening . . . for it.* LXX adds "the other [i.e., the one] to the other." While this is probably paraphrase, LXX conceivably preserves an original **z't 'l z't* 'this to this,' lost by homoioteleuton after *ḥbrt* 'fastening.'

† *at.* Here and in 28:24, for MT-*Tgs.* *'el*, Sam, Kenn 17, 69, 81, 129, 181, 190, 602 (cf. Kenn 3), a Genizah MS *(apud BHS)* and probably Syr read *'al*, as in 39:4 (see TEXTUAL NOTE). The meaning is unaffected.

†† *it shall be fastened.* I read with Sam-LXX *yḥbr* (**yəḥubbār*). This creates a "short-circuit inclusio" typical of P (McEvenue 1971: 43–44, 108; Paran 1989: 49–97) and matches more closely the fulfillment account, 39:4: "at its two sides it was fastened *(ḥubbār)*." MT, Syr, Vg and *Tgs.* offer a slightly more awkward *wəḥubbār* 'and it shall be fastened,' probably a corruption inspired by the form but not the syntax of 39:4. The corruption also reflects the similarity of waw and yodh in Roman era square script (Cross 1961a and Qimron 1972) and the fact that the previous word ends *-yw*.

28:8. *blue.* Kenn 155 (first hand), Syr and Vg insert "and."

† 28:9. *two carnelian stones.* The Versions offer three readings, one slightly un-grammatical (MT) and two fully grammatical (Sam, LXX). MT has *'et-štê 'abnê šōham*, in which the definite direct object marker *'et* irregularly precedes an in-definite *'abnê šōham*. Sam and Kenn 18, 75, 80 have the more grammatical *'t-šty 'bny hšhm*, with an explicitly definite direct object. LXX ostensibly reads **'t-šty h'bnym 'bny šhm* 'the two stones, carnelian stones,' perhaps trying to "fix" MT, although Wevers (1990: 448) opines that LXX *lithous lithous* 'stones, stones' is simply a Greek dittography. Nonetheless, if the LXX *Vorlage* was as I have recon-structed it, then one could explain MT, at least, as resulting from haplography: **'t šty h'bnym 'bny > 't šty 'bny.*

SPECULATION: No Version contains what we would really expect: simply **štê 'abnê šōham* 'two carnelian stones,' indefinite because this is the stones' first mention (GKC §126d). If this was in fact the original, all our extant witnesses anticipate "*the* two stones" in vv 11–12.

† *on them.* MT contains a grammatical "error": *'ălêhem* 'on them (masc.)' referring to *'ăbānîm* 'stones' (fem.). Sam, however, correctly has *'lyhn* (fem.). We cannot say which is original, but incongruence alone is not evidence of corruption. We similarly find the "incorrect" masculine *'ōtām* 'them' for the feminine **'ōtān* in 28:11, 14, 26, 27; 39:7 (on the phenomenon, see Levi 1987). (Although D. N. Freedman privately suggests that we have a *dual* suffix, referring to *two* stones, Blau [1987–88] casts serious doubt on the existence of dual pronouns in Hebrew.)

28:10. *on . . . on.* Both times, Syr supplies "engrave."

names of the remaining six. LXX simplifies: "the six remaining names."

†† 28:11. *one shall engrave.* I follow the unique *lectio difficilior* of 4QpaleoExod^m: *ypth.* All other Versions read *tpth* 'you shall engrave.'

† *set in gold . . . them.* Between *mūsabbōt* 'set' and *mišbəṣōt* 'plait-rings,' Theodotion, SyrHex, Vg and Syr insert a conjunction, perhaps reading a participle **məšubbāṣōt* (cf. *məšubbāṣîm* in v 20). See further NOTE, "plait-rings."

The end of v 11, after "Israel's Sons," is lacking in LXX. Absent a mechanical explanation for haplography in either Hebrew or Greek, LXX might conceivably preserve the original *lectio brevior.* But it is also possible that LXX has suffered either random corruption or deliberate simplification (Wevers 1990: 449).

28:12. *Memorial stones.* Sam and LXX add *hnh* 'they are,' breaking up MT's slightly awkward use of apposition ("two stones . . . Memorial stones").

their names. LXX explicates: "the names *of Israel's Sons,*" matching v 11. See also next TEXTUAL NOTE.

a Memorial. LXX adds "for them," in effect transferring the pronominal suffix from "names" (MT *šəmōtām*) to the end of the verse (see previous TEXTUAL NOTE).

28:13. *gold.* LXX has "*pure* gold," as in the next verse.

28:14. *And two.* LXX begins "And you shall make," to match the prior verse. In effect, LXX transfers the command to "make" from the middle of the verse to the beginning; see next TEXTUAL NOTE.

† *you shall make them, rope work.* The phrase *t'śh 'tm* 'you shall make them' is absent from a Genizah MS *(BHS),* LXX and Vg (which tends in any case to compression). Its loss is possibly due to similarity with the following *m'śh 'bt* 'rope work.' At least in LXX, however, the command to make is supplied at the beginning of the verse; see previous TEXTUAL NOTE.

SPECULATION: Note that in the Genizah MS and Vg, 28:14 is governed by "and you shall make" in 28:13. It is remotely possible that this is the original state of affairs, and that both MT and LXX have inserted commands to "make" into v 14.

the rope chains. Syr ostensibly reads **šty šršrt (h)mgblt* 'the *two* chains, migbālōt.' Although this is likely just paraphrase harmonizing the two halves of v 14, we must acknowledge the slight possiblity that **šty šršrt* was reduced to *šršrt* in all other Versions due to homoioarkton.

on the mišbāṣôt. LXX continues: "on their shoulder-pieces in front," derived from 28:25.

† 28:15. *like an ephod's work.* So MT *(kmʿšh ʾpd)*, against Sam-LXX *kmʿšh h'pwd* 'like *the* Ephod's work.' Whichever is the original, the other may be the result of haplography/dittography of he', especially assuming continuous writing. But if the change is deliberate, then Sam-LXX is probably "correcting" the more difficult MT (for parallels with *maʿăśē[h]*, see Jacob 1992: 812). Some deliberation must be present in any case, since 39:8 features the same distribution of variants (see TEXTUAL NOTE).

blue. LXX and Syr insert "and"; see also TEXTUAL NOTE to 39:8.

† 28:17. *four rows, stone. A row.* This is the only reasonable interpretation of MT's slightly awkward *ʾarbāʿâ ṭûrîm ʾāben ṭûr.* Syr, Vg and Tgs. paraphrase "four rows *of* stones. A row," as if *ṭûrîm* were in construct with *ʾāben* (cf. MT-Sam *ṭûrê ʾāben* in 39:10). These same Versions also expand the following "a row" into "*the first* row."

Sam and Kenn 95, however, offer a *lectio brevior et facilior ʾrbʿh ṭwrym ṭwr* 'four rows. A row. . . .' Sam may have lost *ʾbn* 'stone' due to its similarity with the following *ʾdm* (in paleo-Hebrew script, mem and nun are similar). But it is also possible that the superfluous *ʾāben* 'stone' in MT-LXX-Syr is a gloss or an accidental addition.

and emerald. The conjunction is absent in LXX^AFM. See further below.

†† 28:20. *carnelian.* Standard MT has "*and* carnelian." I arbitrarily follow Sam, Kenn 2, 4, 8, 18, 75, 84, 101, 107, 108, 129, 132, 136, 150, 152, 158, 168, 181, 200, 244, 248, 260 and most Tg. Onqelos MSS, which employ a consistent "*a, b* and *c*" pattern for each row in 28:17–20 (also MT-Sam 39:10–13). Equally consistent are Syr and Tg. *Neofiti I:* "*a* and *b* and *c*." Other Versions are inconsistent. In standard MT, for example, the first three rows are "*a, b* and *c*," but the fourth is "*a* and *b* and *c*." LXX MSS vary considerably, as one might expect.

† *Plait-ringed in gold.* I follow the short and difficult MT-Vg *məšubbāṣîm zāhāb.* Sam and Syr have *mwsbt mšbṣwt (mišbaṣôt) zhb* 'Set in gold *plait-rings*,' matching MT-Sam 28:11 and especially the parallel 39:13. Sam must also underlie LXX *perikekalymmena chrysiōi (kai) syndedemena en chrysiōi* 'Set in gold *(and)* bound together with gold' (on the conjunction, cf. TEXTUAL NOTE to 28:11, "set in gold . . . them"). LXX probably repeats "gold" because it takes the phrase not as a construct chain but as two nouns, *mûsabbōt* and *mišbaṣôt,* each in construct to *zāhāb* 'gold' (cf. GKC §128a). While it is tempting to adopt the longer reading of Sam *(mwsbt mšbṣwt zhb),* haplography should have produced an unattested **mšbṣwt zhb,* not MT *mšbṣym zhb.* It is easier instead to believe that Sam-LXX-Syr is adapted to 28:11.

fillings. LXX has "row," which I take as a paraphrase of MT *bəmillûʾōtām.* BHS, however, suggests that LXX actually reads **kṭwrm.*

28:22. *gablūt.* LXX *sympeplegmenous* 'twined' appears to read a passive participle **gəbūlōt* (Baentsch 1903: 242).

†† *chains.* Standard MT *šršt* is meaningless. I follow Sam *šršrt,* as in the parallel 39:15 (also several MT MSS [Kennicott 1776–80: 167]).

pure gold. At this point, LXX jumps to v 29. One might attribute this to parablepsis: either from *wʿśyt* 'and you shall make' (v 23) to *wnśʾ* 'and (Aaron) shall bear' (v 29) (waw-waw homoioarkton) or from *ṭhwr* 'pure' (v 22) to *hʾpwd* 'the

Ephod' (v 28) (resh-daleth homoioteleuton; cf. Tov 2001: 245–46). Also possible would be a skip in Greek from *kai* 'and' to *kai*. Since, however, in v 29 LXX partially summarizes the missing matter, more likely the omission was deliberate (see further TEXTUAL NOTE to 28:29, "continually").

† 28:23. *two gold rings*. So MT-*Tgs.*-Vg. Syr and *Tg. Ps.-Jonathan* expand: "two *pure* gold rings." Sam, too, has a longer reading: *šty mšbṣwt zhb wšty ṭbʿt zhb* 'two gold *mišbaṣôt and* two gold rings,' matching 39:16 (see, however, TEXTUAL NOTE). If Sam is original, MT must be considered haplographic (*šty . . . šty*).

†† *the rings . . . edges*. So Sam, Kenn 181 and a *Tg. Onqelos* MS (Sperber 1959: 138), assuming that MT et al. inserted "two" before "rings" and "edges" for clarification and to match 39:16. But one might argue with equal plausibility that Sam deleted "two" to match 28:24.

† 28:24. *at*. See TEXTUAL NOTE to 28:7, "at." Here, Kenn 69 and 107 (firsthand?) also read *ʿal*, as earlier in the verse.

edges. Rossi 592 and Syr expand: "*two* edges."

† 28:25. *the two ropes' two ends*. So MT, both here and in the parallel 39:18: *štê qaṣôt štê hāʿăbōtōt*. In both places, however, Sam uses apposition in place of a construct chain: *šty hqṣwt šty hʿbtwt* 'the two ends, the two ropes' (cf. also TEXTUAL NOTE to 39:32, "all the Work of the Meeting Tent Tabernacle"). This *lectio difficilior* is conceivably correct, but more likely it arose from the frequency of *šty h-* 'the two' throughout this section.

Syr appears entirely to have lost *šty (h)qṣwt* '(the) two ends' by parablepsis—but perhaps the words were dropped deliberately. *Tgs. Onqelos* and *Ps.-Jonathan*, too, seem disturbed by this innocuous clause and resort to paraphrase: "and the two ropes that are on its two edges you shall put." It appears that *Tg. Onqelos*, at least, does not recognize that *qāṣôt* might connote either the corners of a foursquare object or the ends of a cord.

28:26. *two*. A Cairo Genizah MS *(apud BHS)* incorrectly "corrects" MT-Sam, reading *šty* (fem.) for *šny* (masc.). *Qaṣôt* appears feminine but is often masculine (see BDB).

† *against*. While standard MT has *ʾel-ʿēber*, Sam and Kenn 18, 69, 129 have *ʿl ʿbr*. Cf. TEXTUAL NOTE to 28:7, "at."

28:29. *before Yahweh*. Here LXX has "before *the God*," although in v 30 it has "before *the Lord* (= MT 'Yahweh')."

continually. The last word is absent from LXX, which instead continues: "and you shall put the chains on the Judgment *ḥōšen*; the ropes on both sides of the *ḥōšen* you shall put, and the two plait-rings you shall put on both the Ephod's shoulder-pieces in front." This plus vis-à-vis MT-Sam is related to the missing matter in vv 23–28 (see TEXTUAL NOTE to 28:22, "pure gold"). Thus, more briefly than MT-Sam, LXX explains how the *ḥōšen* is fastened to the Ephod. This summarizing style of translation anticipates LXX chaps. 35–40; see EXCURSUS, pp. 631–37.

† 28:30. *And you shall set into*. At the start of v 30, Sam has *wʿśyt ʾt hʾrym wʾt htmym* 'and you shall make the Urim and the Thummim.' If this is original, it fell from MT-LXX by parablepsis from *wʿśyt* 'and you shall make' to *wntt* 'and you

shall set.' I rather imagine, however, that Sam is expansionistic, alleviating the abrupt introduction of the Urim and Thummim in MT. Were the Sam plus original, we might have expected a clarification of what these items were made. Again in chap. 39, MT does not report the making of the Urim and Thummim, but Sam 39:21 does (see TEXTUAL NOTE, "Moses").

Against MT *wntt 'l* 'and you shall set *into*' (also *Tgs.*), Sam and LXX (and probably Syr) read *wntt 'l* 'and you shall set *upon.*' Ostensibly in this latter variant, the Urim and Thummim are outside not inside the *ḥōšen*, and are presumably equated with the engraved stones (cf. Josephus *Ant.* 3.217–28). But sometimes there is no real difference between the prepositions *'el* and *'al*; cf. TEXTUAL NOTE to 28:7, "at."

they shall be. LXX has "*it* shall be," referring to the *ḥōšen*, which, for LXX, may be equivalent to the Urim and Thummim that rest in or upon it (previous TEXTUAL NOTE).

on Aaron's heart. Syr has "on *his* heart," apparently imported from the latter half of the verse.

before Yahweh. LXX explicates: "*into the Holy*, before the Lord."

† 28:31. *the Ephod's Robe.* LXX has "*an undergarment* robe." The indefinite is what one expects for the first reference (GKC §126d). The use of *hypodytēs* 'undergarment' describes more specifically the relationship between the Robe and the Ephod; it is unlikely to be based upon a distinct Hebrew term. The LXX *Vorlage* probably had simply **m'yl* with Sam 39:22, against MT-Sam *'t m'yl h'pd*; cf. TEXTUAL NOTES to 29:5; 39:22. If so, this would be the preferred reading.

completely blue. Uniquely, Tg. *Ps.-Jonathan* substitutes "blue *cord*," as if reading *ptyl tklt* (cf. 28:37) for MT-Sam *klyl tklt*.

† 28:32. *it will not be torn.* The asyndetic MT-Sam *lō(') yiqqārēa'* feels unnecessarily dramatic for what is, essentially, a tailoring tip (cf. Rashi). I suspect that behind LXX-Syr-*Tgs.*-Vg "lest it be torn" is an unattested variant **wl' yqr'* (compare *wəlō[']* in 28:28, 35). Since the previous letter is waw, either dittography to produce LXX-Syr-*Tgs.*-Vg or haplography to produce MT-Sam might have occurred.

28:33. *its skirts.* In both cases, LXX explicates, "the *Robe's* skirts," the first time also adding "beneath."

worm-crimson. Sam and LXX add "and twisted linen," a variant favored by Haran (1978: 169 n. 44). See further TEXTUAL NOTE to 39:24.

and gold bells. LXX has a fuller text, "(and) the same shape of gold pomegranates and bells," as if paraphrasing a *Vorlage* **wrm(w)ny zhb wp'm(w)nym* or **wrm(w)ny zhb wp'm(w)ny zhb* or conceivably **wrm(w)ny wp'm(w)ny zhb*, vs. MT-Sam-Syr *wp'mwny zhb*. Regarded in isolation, the LXX reading might be preferred as original, with MT-Sam-Syr the product of haplography. See next TEXTUAL NOTE, however.

28:34. *a gold bell and . . . pomegranate.* LXX has a considerably different text: "beside a gold pomegranate, a bell and a flower-like object *(anthinon)*," the last being LXX's term for the textile pomegranates. Thus LXX describes *three* interspersed hanging items: bells (composition unspecified), fabric pomegranates and golden pomegranates. In contrast, MT and Sam do not mention golden pomegranates and instead envision golden bells.

While I cannot account for LXX in detail, I assume that MT-Sam is original and that LXX in effect harmonizes two variants, one with golden pomegranates and one with golden bells. If a scribe wrote from memory, these variants might have arisen from the acoustic similarity of Israelite Hebrew *rammōn 'pomegranate' (MT rimmōn) and *pa'mōn 'bell' (MT pa'ămōn). See further NOTE to 28:33, "and gold bells."

Syr presents a shorter reading than either MT-Sam or LXX: "and a bell, a bell of gold and pomegranates." Apart from adding a conjunction, Syr has lost zhb wrm(w)n 'gold and a pomegranate' by homoioteleuton after the first p'm(w)n 'a bell.'

28:37. against the Turban's front. Absent in Vg. Although Jerome is given to deliberate compression, in this case the omission might be due to parablepsis from one hammiṣnepet 'the Turban' to the next.

† it shall be. Although the verb is attested in all Versions, one wonders whether the superfluous yhyh is a quasi-dittograph of the following whyh 'and it shall be' (on waw-yodh confusion, see Cross 1961a and Qimron 1972).

28:38. his forehead. LXX clarifies: "on Aaron's forehead."

28:39. And you shall plait. Against the MT-Sam wšbṣt, LXX kosymboi 'tassels' reflects a slightly different Vorlage, probably *wtšbṣt (cf. kosymbōton = tašbēṣ in 28:4). Syr "and make" may indicate uncertainty as to the meaning of šbṣ.

† the Shift, linen. Against the standard MT-Sam singular hakkətōnet, referring to Aaron's garment, LXX, Kenn 1, 69, 80, 129, 152 and Symmachus read a plural *hakkuttŏnōt as in v 40, referring to the shifts of all the priests. But it is fairly clear that v 39 refers to the garments of Aaron alone. Even in LXX, the other vestments in v 40 are singular.

More worthy of consideration is Syr-Tgs. "and you shall make a linen shift," which we might have expected, since this is the Shift's first mention (cf. TEXTUAL NOTE 27:1; GKC §126d).

SPECULATION: Conceivably, the Aramaic Versions have actually reinvented or preserved the lost original, *wšbṣth ktnt šš, with the second-person singular suffix on wəšibbaṣtâ spelled plene with final he' (GKC §44g). If so, that h migrated across the word boundary in MT-Sam.

a turban. Doubtless thinking of the minor clergy, Tg. Neofiti I pluralizes, as if reading *miṣnəpōt.

28:40. and you shall make for them. Omitted by LXX, presumably for fluidity's sake (also Vg).

28:41. and you shall make . . . wear. So MT-Sam (wəhilbaštā [2 m.s.] 'ōtām). 4QpaleoExodᵐ has [w]hlbštm 'wtm, which might be read either as "[and] you (pl.) shall make them wear [*wəhilbaštem] them" or "[and] you (sing.) shall clothe them [*wəhilbaštām] with them."

their hand. LXX modifies the Hebrew idiom: "their hands."

28:42. naked flesh. LXX "shame of their skin" appears to associate 'erwâ 'nudity' with 'ôr 'skin'; cf. TEXTUAL NOTE to 22:26, "for his skin." (A twelfth-century C.E.

German codex [Kenn 84] merits commemoration in the annals of hilarious typographical/scribal errors committed during the Bible's transmission: *bəśar 'orlātô* 'the flesh *of his foreskin.*')

28:43. *him . . . his . . . him. Tg.* Neofiti I pluralizes "them . . . their . . . them," referring to Aaron and his sons (who, for Neofiti, are not Aaron's four sons but the future Great Priestly succession through Eleazar).

29:1. *And this is the thing that.* Apparently bothered by the use of the singular "this" to describe a series of actions, LXX and Syr respectively paraphrase "And *these* are what" and "And do thus."

for me. Tgs. Neofiti I and Ps.-Jonathan (Rieder 1974: 126 n. 1) read "for *him.*" But these Versions are generally periphrastic; it is scarcely conceivable that they alone preserve an ancient variant.

take. Syr inserts "and."

one bull. Kenn 111, Rossi 2, 10 and ostensibly Vg omit "one." This is either an assimilation to the common expression "*a* bull, cattle's son" (e.g., Lev 4:3; Num 8:8; 15:24, etc.) or conceivably a skip in Hebrew, from the resh in *par* 'bull' to the similar-appearing daleth in *'eḥād* 'one.'

29:2. *bread, unleavened bread, and unleavened cakes.* Where MT-Sam has two synonymous expressions connected by "and" *(leḥem maṣṣôt wəḥallōt maṣṣōt),* Syr drops the conjunction, putting "bread, unleavened bread" in apposition with "unleavened cakes." LXX, however, has simply "unleavened cakes." There are several possible explanations for the discrepancy. One is that LXX has deliberately shortened a redundant *Vorlage.* Another is that LXX lost **wḥl(w)t mṣ(w)t* 'and bread, unleavened bread' after *wlḥm mṣ(w)t* due to homoioteleuton. A final possibility is that MT-Sam incorporates synonymous variants, one of which underlies LXX. Comparison with 29:23 suggests, however, that the first explanation is correct: LXX is deliberately streamlining a verbose *Vorlage* (see TEXTUAL NOTE).

† *anointed with oil.* The words *məšuḥîm baššāmen* do not appear in 4Qpaleo-Exod^m, Sam and Kenn 18, 94, 128. Absent an obvious cause for scribal error, one might prefer this shorter reading. Exod 29:23, however, which refers back to the bread, also does not mention that the wafers are oiled. Since I have chosen in general to reconstruct maximally different command and fulfillment narratives (cf. pp. 807–8), and since precisely these two witnesses, 4QpaleoExod^m and Sam, are most prone to harmonization—admittedly, generally by addition not subtraction—I have followed MT.

† 29:5. *Aaron.* LXX adds "your brother." While this would be a typical expansion, it is also possible that MT lost **'ḥyk* before *'t* due to homoioarkton.

† *with the Shift and the Ephod's Robe and the Ephod.* So MT: *'et-hakkuttōnet wə'ēt mə'îl hā'ēpōd wə'et-hā'ēpōd.* Sam has a far longer text: *'t hkytnt [sic] wḥgrt 'tw 'bnyṭ whlbšt 'tw 't hm'yl wntth 'lyw 't h'pwd* '(and make Aaron wear) the Shift *and gird him (with) a sash and make him wear the Robe and put on him the Ephod.'* Characteristically, Sam has expanded the text to match the fulfillment narrative in Lev 8:7—although the omission of the Sash from 29:5 MT is surprising and might be the result of haplography (cf. Driver 1911: 315).

LXX, in contrast, offers a shorter text than MT: "*both* with the Shift-Robe *(kai ton chitōna ton podērē*) and with the Ephod." Possibly the unexpected initial *kai* reflects **w't* in the *Vorlage*, rather than simply *'t*. For the rest, one might at first think that LXX simply skipped from one "Ephod" to the next. But the residuum should have been **(w)'t-hktnt w't m'yl h'pd* '(and) the Shift and the Ephod's Robe,' whereas the LXX *Vorlage* appears to have been something like **'t-hktnt w't hm'yl w't-h'pd*—compared to MT, a shorter, more ambiguous and arguably superior reading (see also TEXTUAL NOTES to 28:31, "the Ephod's Robe"; 39:22, "the Robe"). Note that the parallel in Lev 8:7 also calls the Robe *ham'îl*.

Somewhat similar to LXX is Syr "the Shift and the Robe *and the Turban* and the Ephod," an expansion presumably inspired by the Turban's appearance in the next verse and by the queston that, if the lesser priests' hats are included in 29:8–9, why not Aaron's here?

Vg has the shortest text of all: "both the linen Shift and the Ephod." Although Jerome is prone to paraphrase and compression, this might reflect a haplographic *Vorlage*, skipping from *w't hm'yl/m'yl h'pd* to *w't-h'pd*.

and you shall "ephod" for him with the Ephod's woven-band. LXX "and you shall fasten for him the Oracle (i.e., the *ḥōšen*) on the Ephod" may well be a paraphrase of the difficult MT, but additionally seems to confuse the similar-looking *ḥšn* (*ḥōšen*) and *ḥšb* 'weave.' On the interpretations of Syr, Vg and *Tgs.*, see NOTE.

29:9. *a sash.* Sam, Kenn 193, LXX, Syr and *Tgs.* all read the plural *'abnēṭîm*, vs. the MT-Vg collective singular *'abnēṭ*. This is presumably a secondary correction, harmonizing with the plurals *kuttŏnōt* 'shifts' and *migbā'ōt* 'hump-hats' in vv 8–9. The parallel in Lev 8:13 is also singular in MT and plural in other Versions (including Vg).

> **Speculation:** The MT singular *'abnēṭ* raises the possibility that, in fact, the "shifts" and "hats" were also originally collective singulars, to be vocalized **kuttōnet* and **migba'at*.

† *Aaron and his sons.* These words are absent from LXX. The mention of Aaron seems slightly odd, since the text is primarily discussing his sons (cf. b. *Yoma* 5b–6a; Ramban; Noth 1962: 230). If original, the phrase refers only to the preceding sash, which all the priests wore (28:39–40), not the following *migbā'ōt* 'hats,' worn only by the lesser clergy. Ehrlich (1908: 377) supposes that Aaron was added here precisely because his Sash was omitted in v 5 (see TEXTUAL NOTE, "with the Shift and the Ephod's Robe and the Ephod").

† *priesthood.* LXX adds "for me," presumably to resemble the similar expression "to priest for me" in 28:3, 4, 41; 29:1. But we cannot exclude the possibility that the original was **lkhnh ly* (old spelling), with *lî* 'for me' lost in the other Versions due to homoioarkton before *ləḥuqqat*.

an eternal rule. LXX paraphrases "eternally."

hand . . . hand. LXX and Tg. *Neofiti I* pluralize both hands; Syr pluralizes only the sons' hands. This is a matter of idiomatic translation, not of Hebrew variants.

29:10. *before Meeting Tent.* Against MT-Syr-Vg *lpny 'hl mw'd* (= Lev 3:8, 13; 4:14; Num 3:7, 38; 8:9), LXX reflects the more common **'l-ptḥ 'hl mw'd* 'to Meeting Tent *Opening*,' as in 29:4; 40:12; Lev 1:3, etc. [24 examples total]). Combining elements from MT and LXX, Sam has *lpny yhwh ptḥ ʾhl mwʿd* 'before Yahweh *(at)* Meeting Tent *Opening*,' as in 29:11 (also Lev 14:11; 15:14; 16:7; Josh 19:51). See further next TEXTUAL NOTE.

bull's head. LXX continues the verse: "before the Lord at the doors of the Tent of Witness," Sam's plus in the first half of the verse (previous TEXTUAL NOTE). Both LXX and Sam have in different ways brought forward text from 29:11, where we find in all Versions "the bull before Yahweh (at) Meeting Tent Opening."

29:12. *all the blood.* LXX makes explicit what the Hebrew must mean: "all the *remaining* blood." Vg similarly has "the remaining blood," without "all."

you shall pour. Ibn Ezra seems to read *yšpk* 'he shall pour,' a reading not to my knowledge attested in any MS. It may be a careless error on the part of ibn Ezra or his copyist.

toward. For MT-Sam-*Tgs. Onqelos* and *Ps.-Jonathan ʾel*, Syr and *Tg. Neofiti I* appear to read ʿ*al* 'upon.' This is not a true variant, just a matter of translation; cf. Syr and *Tg. Neofiti I* at Lev 4:7, 18, 25, 30, 34; 5:9; 8:15; 9:9.

29:13. *all the excrescence on the liver.* Against MT *hayyōteret ʿal-hakkābēd*, Sam and Kenn 107 have *ywtrt hkbd* as in Lev 8:16 (also Exod 29:22). Both expressions are paralleled, but in this case, MT is preferable as the more varied reading.

the fat that is on them. Syr "their fat" is a periphrastic adaptation to Lev 8:16.

† 29:14. *he is.* In MT, "he" *(hwʾ)* refers to the bull; in Sam and *Tg. Ps.-Jonathan,* "she/it" *(hyʾ)* refers to the *ḥaṭṭā(ʾ)t* 'Sin-offering.' The ambiguity arises from the fact that, throughout the Torah, both the masculine and the feminine third-person singular pronouns are generally spelled *hwʾ* (TEXTUAL NOTE to 1:16).

† 29:15. *shall press.* MT puts the verb in the plural *wəsāməkû*, while Sam has the singular *wsmk* as in 29:10, 19. Either would be grammatically acceptable. In Lev 8:18, which parallels Exod 29:15, MT again uses the plural and Sam the singular. We might call upon LXX to adjudicate, since it agrees with MT in Exodus *(kai epithēsousin)* and with Sam in Leviticus *(kai epethēken)*.

† 29:16. *the ram.* LXX offers a *lectio brevior* "him," as if reading *ʾ(w)tw* (cf. also Vg). Most likely the *Vorlage* read simply *wšḥṭṭ* 'and you shall slaughter' without any object at all, to parallel Lev 8:19 *wayyišḥāṭ* (where, however, LXX supplies a subject—"Moses"—rather than an object as in Exod 29:16). Absent corroboration from a Hebrew MS, I would not embrace LXX as the superior reading in 29:16. But it remains possible that MT-Sam added "the ram" for clarification. See also TEXTUAL NOTE to 29:20.

take its blood. Kenn 190, Syr and Vg have "take *from* its blood," to match 29:12, 20, 21, etc.

29:17. *wash . . . shanks.* LXX adds an explicating "with water," derived from 29:4. There is no mechanical reason for the loss of a putative *ʾbmym* in MT-Sam.

upon his members and upon his head. So MT-Sam. *Pace* Wevers (1990: 473), LXX "upon his members *with* (*syn*) his head" probably translates a variant *Vorlage* *ʾl nthyw ʾl rʾšw*, the reading of Kenn 150—although it is admittedly not certain that LXX knew this use of ʿ*al*. The LXX *Vorlage* presumably arose out of MT-Sam ʿ*l nthyw wʿl rʾšw* either by haplography *(ww > w)* or by the random insertion of a conjunction.

29:18. *he is* (first time). LXX does not translate the first *hûʾ* but only the second, presumably for fluidity's sake. Kenn 80, Syr and Vg also omit the second *hû'*. Finally, against MT *ləyahwe(h) hû'*, Sam and Kenn 4 have the synonymous *hû' ləyahwe(h)*, matching 29:18b, 25 and the parallel in Lev 8:21.

a Soothing Scent. LXX, Syr and Tgs. have *"as* a Soothing Scent," i.e., *ləreaḥ nîḥôaḥ*, the reading of Kenn 109, 128 (?), 152, 186 and Rossi 10, 262, 440, 543. This is presumably a secondary harmonization with 29:25, 41 and Lev 8:21. See also TEXTUAL NOTE to 29:41.

29:20. *the ram.* LXX has "him" (cf. also Vg)—i.e., the *Vorlage* simply had the verb *wšḥṭṭ* with no object at all, as in Lev 8:23 *wayyišḥāṭ* (where LXX likewise supplies *auton*). See also TEXTUAL NOTE to 29:16.

† *on Aaron's earlobe.* So MT-Sam: *'al-tənûk 'ōzen 'ahărōn*. The LXX *Vorlage* apparently read **'l tnwk 'zn 'hr(w)n hymnyt w'l bhn ydw hymnyt w'l bhn rglw hymnyt* 'on Aaron's *right* earlobe *and on his right hand-thumb and on his right foot-thumb'* as in Lev 8:23, before proceeding to the sons. One might initially favor this longer reading, attributing the shorter MT-Sam text to parablepsis within a list of similar terms. But, were that the case, we might rather have expected **'al-tənûk 'ōzen 'ahărôn haymānît wə'al-tənûk 'ōzen bānā(y)w haymānît* 'on Aaron's *right* earlobe and on his sons' right earlobe,' skipping from one *w'l* 'and on' to the next. (This is in fact the reading of Syr and Tg. Ps.-Jonathan.) Admittedly, the impression that LXX preserves the original reading is hard to resist. Given, however, the pervasive efforts of both Sam and LXX to harmonize Exodus 29 with Leviticus 8, it is at least as likely that LXX 29:20 is expanded to resemble Lev 8:23–24.

and you shall dash . . . around. So MT. In 4QReworked Pentateuch[c] and LXX, these words conclude 29:21. As we shall see, Sam shifts the position of v 21 vis-à-vis MT (TEXTUAL NOTES to 29:21, "And you shall take," 28, "for Yahweh"), and something similar probably happened in 4QReworked Pentateuch[c] and LXX: v 21 was actually put *inside* v 20. The motive, I suppose, was to make the command to sprinkle blood around the Altar (end of 29:20) connect directly into the disposition of the fat parts (29:22), as in Lev 8:24–25.

29:21. *And you shall take.* In Sam and almost certainly 4QpaleoExod[m], all of 29:21 is located after 29:28; see TEXTUAL NOTE to 29:28, "for Yahweh."

from the blood . . . from the Ointment Oil. These are reversed in Sam, conforming to Lev 8:30.

shall become holy. Sam has *wqdštw* 'and *you* shall *make him holy*,' borrowing the Pi'el verb from Lev 8:30 *wayqaddēš*.

with him. LXX continues, "and the ram's blood you shall pour against the Altar around," more or less the final words of 29:20 in MT-Sam (see TEXTUAL NOTE).

†† 29:22. *the fat—the fat-tail.* Against MT-Syr *haḥēleb wəhā'alyâ*, I tentatively follow the more syntactically varied Sam, *ḥḥlb 't h'lyh*. MT is in fact redundant, since "the fat" should include the following fatty items. "The fat-tail" is entirely absent from LXX, perhaps due to haplography by homoioarkton in a Hebrew variant combining aspects of MT and Sam: *w't h'lyh w't ḥḥlb* (so one Sam MS [von Gall 1918: 179] and probably 4QpaleoExod[m] and 4QReworked Pentateuch[c]) > **w't ḥḥlb* (LXX *Vorlage*). For the parallel Lev 8:25, MT, supported by LXX, has

both conjunction and direct object marker, *wə'et-hā'alyâ*, while Sam MSS are divided regarding the presence of the conjunction.

† *the liver's excrescence*. One would initially dismiss 4QpaleoExod^m *hyw[trt 'l hkbd]* 'the excr[escence on the liver]' as a harmonization with 29:13 (see TEXTUAL NOTE). It is conceivable, however, that as Lev 8:16, 25 consistently use *yôteret hakkābēd*, so the original text of Exodus 29 had *hayyôteret 'al hakkābēd* in both vv 13 and 22, with 4QpaleoExod^m the sole witness for the latter.

† *a Filling ram*. Unexpectedly, LXX lacks "ram"; compare 29:34; Lev 7:37; 8:28; contrast *'êl hammillū'îm* in 29:26, 27, 31; Lev 8:22, 29. This *lectio brevior et difficilior* might be correct.

† 29:23. *one bread loaf and one oil bread cake*. So MT-Sam-Syr: *wkkr lḥm 'ḥt wḥlt lḥm šmn 'ḥt*. LXX has a shorter reading, "one bread from oil," as if reading **wkkr lḥm šmn 'ḥt*. Upon first glance, LXX seems clearly haplographic; the scribe has skipped from one *lḥm* to the next. But we find precisely the same phenomenon in 29:2, also apropos of bread (see TEXTUAL NOTE). The odds of accidental corruption in two parallel passages are less than the likelihood that LXX methodically streamlined a redundant *Vorlage* (Wevers 1990: 476). Note that, in the parallel Lev 8:26, LXX renders MT literally.

† 29:25. *smoke*. Sam makes explicit the implicit object "them" (*'tm*). Syr is more explicit still, borrowing from the next verse: "the breast from the ram." While I have followed the MT-LXX *lectio brevior*, note that the parallel, Lev 8:28, also lacks an object for "smoke." It is therefore possible that MT-LXX is harmonistic.

on the Altar in addition to the Ascending-offering. Against MT *hmzbḥh 'l h'lh* (= Lev 8:28), LXX has "on the Altar *of* the Holocaust," as if reading **'l mzbḥ h'lh*, either a memory lapse or more likely a paraphrase; cf. the LXX treatment of *layyôm 'al-hakkippūrîm* in 29:36 (see TEXTUAL NOTE, "for [each] day concerning the Clearing"). (It is also possible, assuming no word divisions, that *hmzbḥh'lh'lh* [MT] became a difficult **hmzbḥh'lh*, of which LXX made the best sense it could.) Syr and Vg also differ slightly from MT-Sam: "on the Altar *as an* Ascending-offering," as if reading **hmzbḥh l'lh*.

† *before Yahweh*. These words are absent in Sam, which is *lectio brevior* but also *lectio facilior*, since the parallels in 29:18, 41 and especially Lev 8:28 lack "before Yahweh."

29:26. *that is*. So MT (*'ăšer*). Sam *m'šr* 'from what is' anticipates 29:27 and also reduplicates the mem ending the preceding word.

29:28. *their šəlāmîm Slaughter-offerings*. Many witnesses to LXX replace "their" with "Israel's Sons'" for clarity, but this is probably neither the original LXX (Wevers 1992: 248) nor the superior reading. It may be a harmonization with Lev 10:14.

for Yahweh. Sam follows with 29:21. If the change was accidental, v 21 probably was dropped because both it and v 22 begin *wlqḥt* 'and you shall take'; v 21 was then reinserted lower in the text. But more likely the change was deliberate, to match Lev 8:24–25, 30.

29:29. *for being anointed*. LXX "for *their* being anointed" is either an intentional clarification or an accidental corruption: *ləmošḥâ bām > *ləmošḥām bām*.

in them (second time). Presumably in the interests of economy, LXX omits the second "in them" *(bām)*; also Kenn 95, 200.

†† 29:33. *must eat.* LXX lacks a conjunction, thus reading the jussive/imperfect *y'klw* with Sam, vs. the MT converted perfect *w'klw.* I follow Sam, since waw-yodh confusion is more likely in the square script of MT (Cross 1961a; Qimron 1972).

for filling. Sam adds *bm* 'with them' to match v 29.

for making them holy. Kenn 129, 153, 186 and Syr insert "and."

eat (second time). LXX and Vg expand: "from them."

29:34. *you shall burn.* The command is plural in some Syr MSS but singular in more reliable witnesses.

It may not be eaten. Syr inserts a conjunction.

† 29:36. *a Sin bull.* LXX makes this definite, as if reading **wpr hḥṭ't* (= Kenn 5, 84, 129, 223), vs. MT-Sam *wpr ḥṭ't.* This could be loose translation, but we cannot dismiss the possibility that LXX enshrines a variant *Vorlage* to be weighed against MT-Sam; note that ḥet and he' were somewhat similar in paleo-Hebrew and almost identical in the later square script. We do not expect the definite article, since this is the bull's first mention (GKC §126d)—but that is a potential sign of authenticity; cf. TEXTUAL NOTES to 26:15, 18; 27:1; 28:9; 36:15; 38:20, 27.

for (each) day concerning the Clearing. For MT-Sam *layyôm 'al-hakkippūrîm,* LXX has "for the day of Clearing," as if reading **ləyôm hakkippūrîm*—here, apropos not of Yom Kippur but of the priestly ordination. This is probably a paraphrase; cf. TEXTUAL NOTE to 29:25, "on the Altar in addition to the Ascending-offering." Notice that, whereas MT and Sam prescribe one bull per diem for seven in total, LXX ostensibly requires only one, perhaps on the first day (Wevers 1990: 482).

29:37. *any touching.* Syr and Kenn 186 insert "and."

† 29:38. *lambs, sons of a year, two per day (as a) Continual-offering.* Against MT *kəbāśîm bənê-šānâ šnayim layyôm tāmîd,* LXX has a much longer text: "lambs, one-year-olds, *flawless,* two per day, *on the Altar continually,* a Continual-offering," as if reading **kbśym bny šnh tmymym šnym lywm 'l hmzbḥ tmyd 'lt tmyd,* for which the closest parallel is Num 28:3: *kəbāśîm bənê-šānâ təmîmîm šnayim layyôm 'ôlâ/'ôlat tāmîd* 'lambs, sons of a year, perfect, two per day, a Continual-offering.'

Sam matches MT, except that, like LXX, it ends with *'lt tmyd* 'a Continual Ascending-offering.' This may very well be the original reading, with MT the result of haplography: *tmyd 'lt tmyd* (Sam) > *tmyd* (MT). Our text-critical criteria are exquisitely balanced: Sam is thoroughly expansionistic and harmonistic in this section, yet its reading is very susceptible to corruption.

29:40. *quarter . . . quarter.* In MT (also Tg. Onqelos), the forms are different: *reba'* and *rəbî'ît.* Sam and Kenn 109, however, have *rəbî'ît* both times. Although the reason for the difference is unclear, one naturally favors the more diverse reading.

† 29:41. *its libation.* "Its" is feminine in MT and Tgs. *(niskāh),* masculine in LXX-Sam-Kenn 69 (first hand) *(nskw).* In MT, the referent is the "Tribute-

offering"; in LXX-Sam, it is either the lamb or the morning (cf. ibn Ezra). Since the masculine and feminine suffixes were not distinguished in early Israelite orthography, the autograph must have read an ambiguous *nskh. Note that, in the almost *verbatim* doublet in Num 28:8, MT has *niskô*. See also next TEXTUAL NOTE.

† *you shall do for it.* In MT and Tgs. *Onqelos* and *Ps.-Jonathan*, "for it" *(lāh)* is feminine, referring to the evening ʿōlâ 'Ascending-offering' (ibn Ezra [shorter commentary]). Sam, however, has *lw* (masc.), referring to the lamb (also Tg. *Neo-fiti I*). And LXX lacks "for it" entirely, perhaps lost due to homoioarkton with the following *lərêaḥ* 'as a . . . scent' (but see next TEXTUAL NOTE) or else omitted as unnecessary.

Both readings are correct in a sense. That is, the autograph probably read an ambiguous *lh, the original spelling of both *lāh* and *lô* (cf. previous TEXTUAL NOTE). MT may have preserved the original orthography, Sam the intended pronunciation.

†† *a Soothing Scent.* Reading *ryḥ nyḥḥ* with Sam, Kenn 103, 181, 686 and LXX, as *lectio brevior*. MT has "*as* a Soothing Scent" *(lərēaḥ nîḥōaḥ)*. Cf. TEXTUAL NOTE to 29:18.

29:42. *I will be meetable.* Pace BHS, LXX "I will be *known*" probably does not represent a *Vorlage* *ʾwdʿ, against MT-Sam ʾwʿd (see TEXTUAL NOTE to 25:22; Wevers 1990: 486). Whether out of purely theological scruples or the particular concerns of Diaspora Judaism, LXX continually manifests discomfort at the no-tion that God is "meetable" by humans on Earth. The translators solved the prob-lem with a graphic pun analogous to a Rabbinic 'al tiqrê 'do not read' midrash, rendering the root yʿd 'meet' as if ydʿ 'know.' But this is unlikely to be a true vari-ant. See also TEXTUAL NOTE to 29:45.

† *for you.* This is plural *(lākem)* in MT (cf. Num 17:19 [MT]), singular *(ləkā)* in Sam, LXX and Kenn 69, 153 (cf. 25:22; 30:6, 36). The plural refers to all Israel or to Moses and Aaron (ibn Ezra), while the singular indicates Moses alone.

This disagreement among our witnesses arises from the fact that, in all Ver-sions, the verse begins in the plural and ends in the singular. Where did the shift originally fall? Defending MT, Ehrlich (1969: 195) observes that, since Moses and Yahweh meet at the *kappōret* over the Testimony Chest (25:22), it must be Is-rael who meets Yahweh in the Plaza (see NOTE, "where . . . there"). But Sam-LXX also makes sense: Moses meets Yahweh in the Tent (29:42), where all Israel may inquire through Moses (v 43; see TEXTUAL NOTE to "I will be inquirable" below).

† *there.* The final *šām* is unreflected in LXX and Syr. Either the translators felt that three times in two verses was too much, or else their *Vorlagen* were shorter than MT-Sam—which would make an attractive variant.

†† 29:43. *I will be inquirable.* I follow the Sam *lectio difficilior wndršty*, against MT-Syr *wənôʿadtî* 'and I will be *meetable*' and against LXX *kai taxomai* 'and I will *command*' (cf. Vg *praecipiam* 'I will *instruct*'). MT is probably influenced by the diction of 29:42, repeating the root yʿd. Sam, in contrast, makes a fine distinction: Israel may "inquire" *(drš)* of God, but Moses is the one who "meets" *(yʿd)* the

Deity. Indeed, the only other occurrence of *drš* in Exodus is 18:15, where the people inquire of God through Moses. Thus, if MT is perchance correct, Sam is harmonizing 28:43 with 18:15 and perhaps also misreading the following *wnqdš[ty]* (*d* and *r* are easily confused in all periods). But Sam is the more probable reading in v 43.

What LXX and Vg read is unclear. In 2 Sam 20:5, the Qal of *yʿd* is rendered with *tassō*; thus LXX may be reading as if **wyʿdty* (**wəyāʿadtî*). Another possibility would be a variant **whʿdty* (**wahăʿîdōtî*) 'and I will admonish.' Or both Versions might be reading **whdʿty* (**wəhōdaʿtî*) 'and I will make known'; cf. TEXTUAL NOTE to 6:3. Lastly, LXX and Vg may even follow Sam, since the root *drš* can have additional connotations of demanding and studying.

and it/one will be made holy. Against the difficult MT-Sam *wəniqdaš*, LXX, Syr and Tgs. *Onqelos* and *Ps.-Jonathan* have "and I will be made holy," as if reading **wəniqdaštî* (cf. the preceding first-person verb, and also *wəniqdaštî* in Lev 22:32). See further NOTE.

29:45. *And I will tent in.* Against MT-Sam *wəšākantî*, LXX has *kai epiklēthēsomai* 'and I will be *invoked* by.' There is no possibility of innocent graphic confusion; rather, LXX felt embarrassment at the notion of God residing on Earth (Wevers 1990: 487). The LXX paraphrase may be inspired specifically by the Deuteronomic idiom whereby Yahweh causes his Name (*šēm*) to "tent" (*škn*) in Israel. It is unclear whether this is a matter of abstract theology or of Diaspora politics; see also TEXTUAL NOTES to 29:42, "I will be meetable," and to 29:46, "for my tenting. . . ."

29:46. *their deity . . . their deity.* The first time, Kenn 4, 69, 103 read "*your* (pl.) deity," confusing *ʾĕlōhêhem* (third person) with *ʾĕlōhêkem* (second person). The second time, Kenn 69, 80, 84, 128, Rossi 265, 440, 503 read "*your* (pl.) deity."

who took them out. LXX "taking them out" harmonizes with 6:7; Lev 22:33; Deut 8:14; 13:6, 11; Judg 2:12, reading a participle (**hammôṣîʾ*) rather than a relative clause (*ʾăšer hôṣēʾ[ʾ]tî*). Compare MT and LXX on Deut 5:6 and contrast Exod 20:2.

for my tenting among them—I am Yahweh their deity. LXX radically paraphrases: "for being *invoked* by them *and to be their God.*" See TEXTUAL NOTE to 29:45, "And I will tent in."

† 30:1. *And you shall make.* In Sam and 4QpaleoExod^m, 30:1–10 follows 26:35; see TEXTUAL NOTE to 26:35.

† *an altar, an incense censer.* LXX has simply "an altar of incense," possibly reading a quasi-haplographic **mzbḥ qṭrt* against MT-Sam *mizbēaḥ miqṭar qəṭōret*; that is, the sequence *mqṭr qṭrt* lost its first element due to the words' overall similarity. But harmonization with 37:25 is an equally likely explanation.

you shall make it. LXX has "*and* you shall make it," attached to 30:2. While a *Vorlage* reading either **wtʿśh* or **wʿśyt* is not inconceivable (against MT-Sam *taʿăse[h]*), this could also be an inner Greek corruption, a reduplication of *kai poiēseis* from the beginning of the verse. Wevers (1990: 489) thinks, however, that the translator simply wished to supply a main verb for v 2.

30:4. *gold.* LXX has "pure gold," as in the preceding verse.

for it. Some LXX MSS do not reflect *lô*, but see Wevers (1992: 189) for the originality of *autōi*.

†† *and they shall be.* Against standard MT, *wəhāyâ* 'and *it* shall be' (= Tg. Ps.-Jonathan and most Tg. Onqelos MSS), Sam, Kenn 80, 181, LXX, Syr and some Tg. MSS have *whyw* 'and *they* shall be.' MT is not just *lectio difficilior* but so difficult as to be impossible. I follow Sam et al.

†† 30:6. *before the Veil that is before the Testimony Chest.* So Sam, LXX and Kenn 69, 83, 84, 110, 132, 205, 325A, 348, 395, 474, 480, 486, 507, 519, 545, 563, 593, 620, Rossi 12, 17, 264, 265, 450, 592, 674, 688, 825. Standard MT, Syr, Vg and Tgs. continue: "before the *kappōret* that is over the Testimony" *(Tg. Neofiti I* begins "and," as do many MSS and editions of MT and Tg. [*BHS*; Rossi 1784–85: 73]; some MSS also have "before the Testimony *Chest*," matching the preceding phrase). While the shorter reading might be haplographic (Wevers 1990: 491), the rare convergence of so many MT MSS with Sam and LXX deserves consideration. Moreover, the reference to the *pārōket* 'Veil' before the Chest makes more sense in context than the ultra-holy *kappōret*. Indeed, if MT is correct, the Incense Altar should be inside the Veil, in the innermost and holiest recess of the Tabernacle, where Aaron is supposed to enter but once a year (Leviticus 16); cf. Heb 9:4. How, then, can he burn daily incense there (30:8)? It seems that this is a rare case of standard MT incorporating parallel versions of a single phrase (cf. Talmon 1961: 373–74; for the confusion of *pārōket* and *kappōret*, see TEXTUAL NOTES to 26:34; 40:3). See further NOTE.

I will be meetable. On LXX "I will be *known*," see TEXTUAL NOTES to 29:42, 45.

†† 30:7. *let him cense it.* LXX "he shall cense *on* it" seems to repeat the phrasing of the beginning of v 7, but may alternatively read with Sam *yqṭyrnw* (also Syr and Tg. Neofiti I), with the masculine suffix referring to the Incense Altar. In MT *yaqṭîrennâ*, the feminine suffix refers to *qəṭōret* 'incense' (also Tgs. Onqelos and Ps.-Jonathan). See also TEXTUAL NOTE to the same phrase in 30:8.

† 30:8. *the two evenings.* The L vocalization *hă'arbayim* [sic] looks like a careless error (we expect *hā'arbayim*), but Knauf (1982) has assembled other examples of the phenomenon, which remains unexplained.

† *let him cense it.* LXX again has "he shall cense *on* it," as if reading **yqṭyrnw* (also probably Syr and Tg. Neofiti I). But this time, both MT and Sam have *yqṭrnh* (also Tgs. Onqelos and Ps.-Jonathan). Thus in vv 7–8, MT both times has *yqṭrnh*; the LXX *Vorlage* both times has **yqṭyrnw*; Sam has first *yqṭyrnw*, then *yqṭrnh*. The principle *lectio difficilior praeferenda est* favors Sam as the most diverse text.

30:9. *Do not.* LXX begins "And."

† *send up . . . pour.* The verbs are plural in MT-Sam *(ta'ălû . . . tissəkû)*, singular in the original LXX *(anoiseis . . . speiseis)* (Wevers 1990: 493). MT-Sam anticipates *lədōrōtêkem* 'for your (pl.) ages' in 30:10. Should the presumed LXX *Vorlage* **t'lh . . . tsk* ever surface in a Hebrew MS, it might be considered the superior reading.

† *or an Ascending-offering or a Tribute-offering.* LXX is unexpectedly asyndetic:

karpōma thysian 'offering, sacrifice.' A corresponding *Vorlage* *ᶜlh mnḥh would be *lectio difficilior* but perhaps too difficult to be correct.

30:10. *Aaron shall effect Clearing.* Probably independently, LXX, Kenn 69, 95 and *Tg. Neofiti I* insert "on it," as if reading **wkpr ᶜlyw 'hrn*, adapting to the second half of the verse.

its horns. Most Syr MSS specify "*the altar's* horns."

over it. Tg. Neofiti I adds "over its horns" to match the first half of the verse.

† *for your ages.* LXX uniquely has "for *their* ages," as if reading *ldrtm, vs. MT-Sam *ldrtykm*. LXX is slightly preferable as *lectio difficilior*—we find *ldrtykm* in 30:8—but may be too odd to be correct. Since the variant is in any case reconstructed, I have followed MT-Sam.

† 30:12. *in their mustering them* (first time). This is missing in LXX and Vg, probably dropped in the interests of concision (Wevers 1990: 494).

lest there be harm against them in accounting them. This clause is missing from *Tg. Ps.-Jonathan* in Rieder's (1974) edition, dropped by homoioteleuton with the preceding. Contrast the edition of Ginsburger (1903: 153).

30:13. *This they shall give.* LXX expands: "*and* this *is what* they shall give." Vg also begins with a conjunction.

† *the half shekel by the Holiness Shekel—twenty gerah the shekel—the half-shekel.* So MT-Syr-Tgs.: *mḥṣyt hšql bšql hqdš ᶜśrym grh hšql mḥṣyt hšql trwmh lyhwh.* LXX is similar, but inserts "but" before the second "half shekel," as if reading *wmḥṣyt (= Kenn 84). Sam differs considerably: Israel must give *mḥṣyt hšql bšql hqdš wšql hqdš ᶜśrym grh hw' hšql trwmh lyhwh* 'the half-shekel by the Holiness Shekel—and the Holiness Shekel, it is twenty gerah the shekel—a Donation-offering for Yahweh.' On the one hand, MT might be haplographic, reducing *bšql hqdš wšql hqdš* into *bšql hqdš* and dropping *hw'* before *hšql* due to homoioarkton. On the other hand, Sam itself might be defective at the end of the verse, losing *mḥṣyt hšql* after *hšql* by homoioteleuton.

> **SPECULATION:** One is greatly tempted to posit a hybrid original: **mḥṣyt hšql bšql hqdš wšql hqdš ᶜśrym grh hw' hšql mḥṣyt hšql trwmh lyhwh* 'the half-shekel by the Holiness Shekel—and the Holiness Shekel, it is twenty gerah the shekel—the half-shekel a Donation-offering for Yahweh.'

† 30:14. *must give Yahweh's Donation-offering.* Against MT *ytn trwmt yhwh*, with the verb in the singular, Sam has *ytnw 't trwmt yhwh*, putting the verb in the plural and adding the optional direct object marker. Either is grammatically acceptable, but MT is slightly preferable as the more diverse reading (the plural *yittənû* appears in 30:13).

† 30:16. *the Clearing Silver.* LXX *to argyrion tēs eisphoras* should correspond to Hebrew *kesep hattərûmâ 'the Donation Silver,' a reading found in no Hebrew MS. Perhaps it is simply an interpretation of MT-Sam *kesep hakkippūrîm*, for LXX sometimes has difficulty, as do I (NOTE to 29:33), rendering Hebrew *kpr* (cf. Wevers 1990: 480–81).

† *your souls.* Most Syr MSS have "*their* souls," ostensibly assimilating to the previous third-person reference to Israel. Since the two variants are more similar in

Syriac *(npšthwn/npštkwn)* than in Hebrew *(npštm/npštykm)*, this is probably an inner-Syriac development. Yet it remains possible that, since "your souls" appears also in 30:15, Syr alone preserves the original Hebrew **npštm*.

† 30:18. *And you shall make.* LXX has an imperative "Make," as if reading **ʿśh*, vs. MT *wʿśyt.* Although this is probably paraphrase, we cannot be certain, since LXX generally follows its *Vorlage* closely in this matter. Moreover, we do not expect the converted perfect at the start of discourse. Conceivably, LXX is correct, and MT-Sam has assimilated to other commands begining *wəʿāśîtā.*

†† 30:19. *wash.* The verb is plural in MT *(wərāḥăṣû)*, singular in Sam *(wrḥṣ).* Either would be grammatically correct, although the latter is slightly preferable, as the verb occurs in the plural in vv 20–21 (see also TEXTUAL NOTE to 40:31).

† *their feet.* LXX adds "with water," anticipating 30:20; cf. TEXTUAL NOTES to 30:21. D. N. Freedman privately observes, however, that LXX might be original, other Versions having reduced **rglyhm bmym* to *rglyhm* due to homoioteleuton.

† *from it.* In Sam, *mmnw* follows the initial verb "wash," thus matching 40:31.

30:20. *to attend, to smoke.* LXX and Syr insert a conjunction between the verbs.

†† 30:21. *they shall wash.* Reading with Sam, LXX and most Syr MSS *yrḥṣw*, vs. MT *wrḥṣw* '*and* they shall wash' (on waw-yodh confusion in the square script, see Cross 1961a; Qimron 1972). I slightly favor Sam as *lectio difficilior*, since the large majority of clauses in this section begin with waw consecutive (although the imperfect/jussive *yirḥăṣû* appears in 30:20).

and their feet. LXX^ABM continues: "with water, when they enter into the Tent of Witness, they shall wash with water," then concurring with MT-Sam "lest they die." This is most likely a dittograph of v 20, whether in Hebrew or in Greek (but D. N. Freedman privately observes that, as in 30:19, the shorter Versions might be haplographic, skipping from *rglyhm* 'their feet' to **bmym* 'with water').

† *eternal rule.* Against MT *ḥoq-ʿôlām*, Sam and Kenn 84 have *ḥqt ʿlm.* Both are common expressions.

for his seed for their ages. LXX paraphrases, "for his generations after him."

30:23. *And.* The conjunction is absent in Syr and Vg.

for yourself. This is unreflected in LXX, probably because it was considered redundant with "you."

† *fragrances: head.* My phrase division follows LXX and Vg. On the possibility that the words *bəśāmîm* and *rō(ʾ)š* have been transposed, see NOTE.

30:25. *Holiness Ointment Oil it shall be.* Most Syr MSS insert an implausible conjunction: "Ointment Oil, *and* it shall be a Holiness"; other MSS, however, support MT.

†† 30:27. *the Table.* Following Sam and Kenn 5, 150, 227, Rossi 716 as *lectio brevior*; standard MT begins "and." Throughout the list, MT features more conjunctions than Sam, which groups the objects in pairs. LXX includes the Table in 30:28, just before the Basin.

and all its implements. Kenn 80, 200, Rossi 174 and Vg omit *kl* 'all,' either by haplography before *klyw* 'its implements' or to match 31:8 (TEXTUAL NOTE); see further below.

†† *the Lamp.* So Sam; MT inserts "and."

†† *and all its implements.* Reading with Sam, LXX and Kenn 69, 109, 152, 160,

199, 600, Rossi 405 *w't kl klyh; kl* 'all' is absent from standard MT, *Tg. Onqelos,* Vg and Syr. Either the shorter reading is the result of haplography or the longer reading is expansionistic/dittographic. The problem is epidemic; cf. TEXTUAL NOTES to "and all its implements" above and to 31:8; 35:13, 14, 16.

†† *the Incense Altar.* So Sam; MT inserts "and."

†† 30:28. *the Basin and its Stand.* So Sam; MT inserts "and." Before the Basin, LXX treats the Table. Vg omits the Basin altogether, whether by homoioarkton *(w't . . . wqdšt)* or by homoioteleuton *(klyw . . . knw).*

† 30:29. *and they shall be.* LXX has *kai estai* 'and *it* shall be,' an unexpected reading that could reflect a *Vorlage whyh,* vs. MT-Sam *whyw;* cf. TEXTUAL NOTE to 30:4 "and they shall be." The singular verb is probably too difficult to be correct, however; its ostensible subject would be "a Holiness of Holinesses."

any touching. Syr inserts "and."

30:31. *for me.* Kenn 69–LXX "for *you* (pl.)" is probably a secondary assimilation to "for your (pl.) *ages*" (Wevers 1990: 501) and also a harmonization with 30:37 (see TEXTUAL NOTE, "for you").

†† 30:32. *be poured.* Reading either *ysk* with several MT MSS (Kennicott 1776–80: 175) or *ywsk* with Sam, confirmed by LXX, *Tgs.* and Syr. The form is either Hophʻal or Qal Passive (Houtman 2000: 578). I attribute the MT Qal *yîsak* 'one shall (not) pour'—from an otherwise unexampled root **ysk*—to waw-yodh confusion in the square script (see Cross 1961a; Qimron 1972). Ibn Ezra compares Gen 50:26, where MT has *wyyśm (wayyîśem),* vs. the expected **wayyûśam* (= Sam).

† *and in its composition.* Against MT *ûb(ə)matkuntô,* Sam has *wbtkntw,* which would correspond to Massoretic **ûbitkūnātô* 'and in its preparation.' Sam has diversity in its favor, since it has *bəmatkuntāh* in 30:37 with MT. But *təkûnâ* does not elsewhere refer to chemical preparations.

† *you shall not make.* So MT-Sam. LXX MSS are divided between *ou poiēthēsetai* 'it shall not be made' and *ou poiēsete* 'you (pl.) shall not make' (= MT-Sam). Wevers (1992: 231) considers the former the original LXX. If so, its *Vorlage* possibly read with Kenn 109 (first hand) **tʻśh (tēʻāśe[h]),* a more difficult and hence more probable reading than MT-Sam *taʻăśû.*

its like. LXX and *Tg. Neofiti I* add "for yourselves," borrowed from 30:37.

† *it is a Holiness; a Holiness it shall be.* Sam, LXX, Syr and Vg insert "and" between the clauses. Ordinarily, I prefer the shorter text, in this case MT-*Tgs.* After the second "Holiness," 4QBibParaph adds *qdšym* 'of Holinesses'; cf. 30:10.

SPECULATION: In light of the variants possibly reflected in 4QReworked Pentateuch[c] 30:37 (TEXTUAL NOTE), it is conceivable that 30:32 conflates two ancient variants: **qdš hwʾ lkm* 'it is a Holiness for you' (unattested) and *qdš yhyh lkm* 'a Holiness it shall be for you' (Kenn 69).

30:33. *A man.* Syr inserts "And."

† 30:34. *said to Moses.* So standard MT. Sam, Kenn 18 and Vg have a longer reading, "*spoke* to Moses, *saying,*" as in 30:11, 17, 22, etc.

spices. Tg. Neofiti I considerably expands the list: "the *head* of incenses, sweet perfumes, balsam, spikenard, myrrh and galbanum and pure frankincense."

† *and šəḥēlet and galbanum.* LXX omits the conjunctions, perhaps rightly.

† 30:35. *And you shall make it.* LXX unexpectedly has "And *they* shall make," as if reading a converted perfect **wʿśw/wəʿāśû* (which, however, could also be read as an imperative **waʿăśû* 'And make!'). If it were attested in Hebrew, this reading might be considered superior to MT-Sam *wəʿāśîtā.*

† *it.* The pronoun is feminine in MT (*ʾōtāh*), matching *qəṭōret* 'incense' (fem.), but masculine in Sam (*ʾtw*), to match *yihye(h)* 'it (masc.) shall be' in v 34 (probably also LXX and Syr). MSS and editions of *Tgs.* have "it" in both masculine *(ytyh)* and feminine *(yth).* The biblical autograph presumably read **ʾth*, which in old spelling could have been construed as either masculine (**ʾōtō[h]*) or feminine (**ʾōtâ*). See also next TEXTUAL NOTE and TEXTUAL NOTE to 30:36, "some of it."

† *salted.* This time, MT has the masculine participle *məmullāḥ*, modifying *rōqaḥ* 'compound' (masc.), while Sam has the feminine *mmlḥt*, modifying *qəṭōret* 'incense' (fem.) (cf. preceding TEXTUAL NOTE). In this case, aural error might be a contributory factor, since the following consonant is ṭeth, similar in sound to taw. (See also TEXTUAL NOTE to 30:36, "some of it.")

† 30:36. *(some) of it* (first time). LXX has "some of *them*," referring to all the ingredients. Both times, in MT "it" is feminine *(mimmennâ)* (also Syr); in Sam and Kenn 5 (first hand), "it" is masculine *(mmnw).* And Kenn 84 offers a mixed reading: *mmnw . . . mmnh.* Cf. TEXTUAL NOTES to 30:35.

(some) of it (second time). This is unreflected in LXX; perhaps the *Vorlage* had lost *mmnh* due to homoioteleuton after *wnṭth* 'and you shall put.' But LXX is given to eliminating redundancies of this sort; cf. TEXTUAL NOTE to 30:12, "in their mustering them."

I will be meetable. On LXX "I will be known," see TEXTUAL NOTE to 29:42.

30:37. *And the incense that you make, in its composition.* LXX simplifies considerably: "Incense according to this composition," as if reading simply **qṭrt kmtknh.* This resembles more closely the parallel injunction in 30:32, and also obviates a grammatical anomaly in MT-Sam: the shift between the second-person singular and plural within the verse (see NOTE). Syr "fixes" the problem by reading the first verb as if **taʿăśû* 'you (pl.) make' (vs. MT-Sam *taʿăśe[h]* 'you [sing.] make').

† *you shall not make.* Some LXX MSS have a passive "shall not be made," as if reading a Niphʿal **tēʿāśe(h)*, against MT-Sam *taʿăśû*; cf. TEXTUAL NOTE to 30:32, "you shall not make," and Wevers (1992: 231).

A Holiness it shall be. 4QReworked Pentateuch[c] originally read *[qd]š h[y]ʾ* 'it *is* a Holiness'; cf. 30:32 *qōdeš hûʾ*. A later scribe inserted a raised *t* before *h[y]ʾ*, as if to write a variant of *thyh*, the reading of all other witnesses. Possibly there were two ancient variants, **qdš hy* and *qdš thyh*—although, admittedly, 4QReworked Pentateuch[c] is sometimes periphrastic.

† *for you.* This is singular *(lk)* in standard MT, 2 Syr MSS and *Tg. Onqelos*, plural *(lkm)* in Sam, 4QReworked Pentateuch[c], LXX, *Tgs. Ps.-Jonathan* and *Neofiti I*

and two early editions of *Tg. Onqelos* (Sperber 1959: 144). Syr, which pluralized the first verb in v 37 (see above), here supports MT in most witnesses. The reading *ləkā* (sing.) is *lectio difficilior*, since we find *lākem* (pl.) both earlier in the verse and in the parallel phrase in 30:32 (cf. also TEXTUAL NOTE to 31:14, "it is a Holiness for you"). On the verse's strange grammar, see NOTE.

In 4QReworked Pentateuch^c, an illegible word follows *lkmh* [*sic*], not found in any other witness.

30:38. *A man*. Syr inserts a conjunction.

† 31:3. *and in understanding*. Perhaps rightly, many MSS of MT and of Tgs. omit the conjunction (Kennicott 1776–80: 175; de Rossi 1784–85: 74). Cf. TEXTUAL NOTE to 35:31.

† *and in knowledge and in every task*. So MT-Sam-Syr-Tgs.: *ûb(ə)daʿat ûb(ə)kol-məlā(ʾ)kâ*. LXX-Vg "and with knowledge *in* every task," if not an ameliorating paraphrase, should reflect a *Vorlage* *wbdʿt bkl mlʾkh, without the second conjunction.

SPECULATION: The most expected reading would be simply *wbdʿt kl mlʾkh 'and with knowledge *of* every task,' found in no MS or tradition. Conceivably, both LXX and MT-Sam represent progressive corruptions of this conjectural *lectio facilior*, influenced by the double *ûbə-* previously in the verse. See also TEXTUAL NOTE to 35:31.

† 31:4. *for planning plans, to make*. Sam, Kenn 5, 9, 181, 198, Rossi 699 (?), Tg. *Neofiti I* and a *Tg. Onqelos* MS (Sperber 1959: 144) begin "and." *Tg. Neofiti I* also has "and" before "to make." LXX *dianoeisthai kai architektonēsai ergazesthai* 'to conceive *and to design* to work' might be a paraphrase of MT *laḥšōb maḥăšābōt laʿăśôt*, but may alternatively represent a variant *Vorlage*, perhaps *lḥšb wlḥrš lʿśwt or *lḥrš wlḥšb lʿśwt* (for the roots *ḥrš* and *ḥšb* in association; cf. 35:33, 35; 38:23; Prov 6:18).

† *bronze*. LXX continues: "and in blue and in purple and in worm-crimson and in twisted linen." On the one hand, the commissioning of Bezalel would seem the proper occasion for a full inventory of materials (cf. 35:5–9), and a list of items each beginning *wb-* 'and in' would be liable to haplography. On the other hand, the longer text could be a typical expansion.

† 31:5. *for filling*. *Ləmallō(ʾ)t* is not reflected in LXX and is also surprisingly absent from a Genizah MS (*BHS*). As Wevers (1990: 508) observes, LXX implies that Bezalel is a stonemason not a gem cutter. It is conceivable, then, that "for *filling*" was added in MT-Sam as a clarifying gloss.

31:6. *I have given with him Oholiab*. LXX uniquely has "I have given *him and* Eliab," as if reading **ntty ʾtw (ʾōtô) wʾt ʾhlyb*, against MT-Sam *ntty ʾtw (ʾittô) ʾt ʾhlyb* (cf. 38:23, *wəʾittô ʾohŏlîʾāb*). I.e., there occurred dittography of waw across a word boundary.

The LXX rendition of the name *(Eliab)* seems to reflect a *Vorlage* with the more familiar *ʾlyʾb 'My god is the Father,' against MT-Sam *ʾhlyʾb*. Syr *ʾlyhb* is presumably another oral garbling that yields an Aramaic folk etymology: *ʾēlîyhab* 'My god gave.' On the true meaning of *ʾohŏlîʾāb*, see NOTE.

and into the heart of every wise-hearted. LXX "to every wise of heart" is either a simplifying paraphrase of MT-Sam (Wevers 1990: 509) or a literal rendering of an unattested variant **wlkl ḥkm lb* (favored as original by Ehrlich 1908: 387). It is remotely possible that MT-Sam *ûb(ə)lēb kol-ḥăkam-lēb* conflates older readings: **ûb(ə)lēb kol-ḥākām* 'and into the heart of every wise' (Kenn 1, Rossi 33, possibly Vg) and **ûb(ə)kol-ḥăkam-lēb* 'and into every wise-hearted' (or: **ûl[ə]kol-ḥăkam-lēb* = LXX). But the redundancy of MT-Sam is really inoffensive in Priestly style; cf. 36:2: "every wise-*hearted* man, in whose *heart* Yahweh gave wisdom, everyone whose *heart* lifted him."

31:7. *the Chest for the Testimony.* Kenn 2, 84 and LXX have the more common expression "the Chest *of* the Testimony."

† *and all the . . . implements.* As elsewhere, our witnesses are divided between *wkl kly* 'and *all* the implements' (MT-Sam-LXX [see Wevers 1990: 510]) and *wkly* 'and the implements' (Vg) (cf. TEXTUAL NOTES to 30:27; 31:8; 35:13, 14, 16).

†† 31:8. *the Table.* So Sam, Kenn 198, 225, Rossi 197, 248, 500, 668, Vg and *Tg. Onqelos* MSS (Sperber 1959: 144); other Versions begin "and." In vv 8–11, I follow Sam and Vg, which group the holy furniture into pairs.

Before the Table, LXX uniquely has "and the Altars," i.e., the Bronze Altar for burnt offerings and the Golden Altar for incense. See further TEXTUAL NOTE to 31:9.

† *and its implements.* Here, against standard MT-Vg *w't klyw*, Sam, very many MT MSS (Kennicott 1776–80: 176; de Rossi 1784–85: 74–75) including a Genizah MS *(BHS)*, LXX, Syr, *Tg. Ps.-Jonathan*, a marginal note to *Tg. Neofiti I* and *Tg. Onqelos* in the Ixar Bible (1490) read **w't kl klyw* 'and *all* its implements.' Whichever is original, the variation is the result either of expansion/dittography *(kly > kl kly)* to produce Sam-LXX etc. or haplography *(kl kly > kl)* to produce standard MT. See also TEXTUAL NOTES below and to 30:27; 31:7; 35:13, 14, 16.

†† *the pure Lampstand.* Omitting the conjunction with Sam, Kenn 5, 129, 198, 225, 355, Rossi 197, 668, Vg and a *Tg. Onqelos* MS (Sperber 1959: 144); see TEXTUAL NOTE to "the Table" above.

and all its implements. Vg does not reflect *kl* 'all,' which is absent from Kenn 81, Rossi 296, 649, 766, 789. The shorter reading might be attributed to parablepsis by homoioarkton *(kl kly > kl)*, but, at least for the MT MSS, there may be an effort to harmonize with 30:27 (see, however, TEXTUAL NOTE). See also TEXTUAL NOTES above and to 30:27, 28; 31:7; 35:13, 14, 16.

†† *the Incense Altar.* Omitting the conjunction with Sam, Vg and a *Tg. Onqelos* MS (Sperber 1959: 144); see TEXTUAL NOTE to "the Table" above.

The Incense Altar is missing from LXX, which some take as evidence that it was a late addition to the text (see pp. 369, 514–15, 716–17). But the Incense Altar is at least alluded to in LXX 31:8 (see TEXTUAL NOTE, "the Table"), and one can explain LXX as haplographic; see also next TEXTUAL NOTE.

31:9. *and the Ascending-offering Altar and all its implements.* This, too is missing from LXX. Therefore, I would not read too much into the nonmention of the Incense Altar (previous TEXTUAL NOTE). Rather, it appears that the LXX *Vorlage* suffered a major loss of text by homoioarkton *w't . . . w't*, a corruption hastily remedied by the insertion of "and the Altars" into 31:8 (TEXTUAL NOTE).

†† *the Basin.* Omitting the conjunction with Sam, Vg and a *Tg. Onqelos* MS (Sperber 1959: 144); see TEXTUAL NOTE to 31:8, "the Table."

†† 31:10. *the Textile Garments.* Omitting the conjunction with Sam and Vg (TEXTUAL NOTE to 31:8, "the Table").

In v 10 as a whole, LXX differs considerably from other Versions: "and the ministerial robes for Aaron and his sons' robes for priesting for me," as if reading **w't bgdy hšrt l'hrn w't bgdy bnyw lkhn ly,* against MT-Sam *w't bgdy hšrd w't bgdy hqdš l'hrn hkhn w't bgdy bnyw lkhn.* Each variant and phrase must be considered separately.

For the first, LXX "and the ministerial *(leitourgikos)* robes" ostensibly reads **wə'et-bigdê haśśārēt* with two Sam MSS (von Gall 1918: 183). But I think it most unlikely that this was the actual *Vorlage.* Syr and *Tgs.* also translate "ministerial garments," and at least the latter almost certainly have MT before them. Rather, there was an exegetical tradition, first attested in LXX, that *śrd* is a synonym of *šrt* 'attend.' Aside from graphic similarity, this understanding draws inspiration from 35:19; 39:1, 41, *('et-)bigdê haśśərād ləśārēt baqqōdeš* 'the Textile Garments to attend in the Holiness'—in fact, Kenn 69, 82, 136, Rossi 10, 265, 543, 549, 592 read *wə'et-bigdê haśśərād ləśārēt baqqōdeš* in 31:10 as well (see de Rossi 1784–85: 75). (For the possibility that *śrd* actually *is* a synonym of *šrt*, see NOTE.)

LXX's tendency to compress redundancies is also evident in its omission of "and the Holiness Garments." It appears that "ministry . . . Holiness" was construed as hendiadys for ritual service (Wevers 1990: 511) (cf. Vg).

The nonmention of "the priest" in LXX might be attributed to two factors. First, it may have been included in the general notion of *leitourgia* 'ministry.' But a mechanical explanation lies near to hand: *hkhn* dropped after *l'hrn* by homoioteleuton. The least likely possibility is that *hkhn* is a secondary gloss in MT-Sam.

Finally, the addition of "for me" at the end of the verse in LXX (also Syr) is an assimilation to 28:1, 3, 4, 41; 29:1, 44; 30:30.

†† 31:11. *the Ointment Oil.* Omitting the conjunction with Sam and Vg; see TEXTUAL NOTE to 31:8, "the Table."

As all. Kenn 109, Syr, Vg and *Tg. Neofiti I* have simply "all," as if reading **kl*, vs. MT-Sam *kkl.* This initially appears to be simple haplography. But we cannot be sure; the same phenomenon recurs in Syr-*Tg. Neofiti I* 39:32; 40:16, and in *Tg. Neofiti I* 25:9. It is more likely deliberate interpretation, not careless error.

† 31:12. *said.* So MT-Sam *(wayyō[']mer).* Kenn 136, LXX, Vg and a *Tg. Onqelos* MS (Sperber 1959: 144) have "spoke," as if reading **wydbr*—which is what we would expect; cf. 30:11, 17, 22; 31:1, etc. This variant, which alleviates the redundancy of MT-Sam *wayyō(')mer . . . lē(')mōr* 'said . . . saying,' I would reject as *lectio facilior.*

31:13. *And you.* Syr omits the conjunction.

my Sabbaths you must keep. Syr's surprising translation "you *have been keeping* Sabbaths" evidently has in mind chap. 16, where Israel refrains from collecting Manna on the Sabbath.

for it is a sign. LXX[B] does not reflect "for." In LXX[A], "for" *(gar)* may be a correction toward MT, but see Wevers (1992: 172).

After *'wt hy[']*, 4QpaleoExod^m jumps to *[l]km mḥll[yh]* '[for] you; [its] desecrater' in v 14, which is likewise preceded by *hy'* 'it is.' That is, we have parablepsis.

† 31:14. *it is a Holiness for you.* LXX^BM etc. "it is holy *for the Lord* for you (pl.)"
resembles LXX 30:37 (see TEXTUAL NOTE to 30:37, "for you"); on the Sabbath
as Yahweh's property, cf. 16:23, 25; 20:10; 35:2, etc. While we ordinarily prefer
the shorter reading, in this case the putative LXX *Vorlage* *qdš hy/w' lyhwh lkm*
conceivably was reduced to MT-Sam *qdš hy/w' lkm* by homoioarkton. LXX^A
agrees with MT-Sam. Cf. TEXTUAL NOTE to 31:16, "the Sabbath, doing."

for any doing a task. Again, LXX unexpectedly omits "for" (cf. TEXTUAL
NOTE to 31:13).

its kinfolks' midst. Kenn 69, Rossi 18, 419, 543, 766, Syr, *Tg. Ps.-Jonathan* and a
Tg. Onqelos MS (Sperber 1959: 145) have simply "from its people," as in Gen
17:14; Lev 7:20, etc.

† 31:15. *a task may be done.* So MT-Sam-*Tgs.* (*yēʿāśe[h]*), even though the verb
is masculine and the subject *məlā(')kâ* feminine (on incongruence, see Levi
1987).

But there are other possibilities. First, we might "fix" MT-Sam by revocalizing a
third person impersonal **yaʿăśe(h)* 'one may do.' Second, LXX reads "you (sing.)
will do works" as if reading a Qal **taʿăśe(h)* (cf. 20:9–10; Deut 5:13–14). Vg and
Syr similarly have "you (pl.) will do work," harmonizing with the second masculine plural in v 14. In fact, LXX may have misunderstood its *Vorlage*, for **tʿśh*, to
judge from MT 35:2; Lev 23:3, should be read as a passive **tēʿāśe(h)* 'may be done'
(*tʿśh* is also the reading of Kenn 9, 84). See also TEXTUAL NOTE to 35:2.

on the Sabbath day. LXX^B "on the *seventh* day" is probably an assimilation to
bayyôm haššəbîʿî in 31:15, 17 (LXX^AM = MT-Sam). Vg temporizes with "on *this*
day."

a Holiness of Yahweh. Syr has "*it is* a Holiness for Yahweh," to resemble more
closely 31:14.

† 31:16. *the Sabbath, doing.* Syr expands "the Sabbath *for the Lord*, doing," as if
reading **ḥšbt lyhwh lʿśwt*. Ordinarily, we would consider this a typical Syr expansion, but in fact its *Vorlage* is found in 2QExod^b. Thus, there is a chance that is the
original text, all other Versions reading *ḥšbt lʿśwt* due to parablepsis (homoioarkton). For the expression "Sabbath for Yahweh," cf. 16:25; 20:10; Lev 23:3; 25:2, 4;
Deut 5:14. See also the first TEXTUAL NOTE to 31:14.

doing the Sabbath. LXX "doing *them* (i.e., Sabbaths)" and Vg "celebrating *it*"
are probably paraphrases to avoid repeating "the Sabbath."

31:17. *and the earth.* Syr and one LXX MS expand after 20:11, adding "and the
sea(s) and all that is in them" (cf. Kenn 109, 129).

31:18. *stone tablets.* Sam reads *lwḥwt 'bnym* 'tablets of stones,' vs. MT *lūḥōt
'eben*. See TEXTUAL NOTE to 24:12.

SOURCE ANALYSIS

Although scholars have attempted to isolate various subdivisions and strata (see
below), the Tabernacle pericope (chaps. 25–31, 35–40) is widely regarded as the

parade example of the Priestly Source—for its vocabulary, its style, its tone and its ideology.

For style, I would note the following expressions, either unique to P or particularly characteristic of it (see Holzinger 1893: 338–49): *mibbayit ûmîḥûṣ* 'from inside and from outside' (25:11; 37:2); *wə'et-bānā(y)w 'ittô* 'and his sons with him' (28:1, 41; 29:21); *bānā(y)w/zar'ô 'aḥărā(y)w* 'his sons/seed after him' (28:43; 29:29); *laggulgōlet* 'for the skull' (38:26); *day* 'enough' (36:5, 7); *lədōrōt* 'for ages' (27:21; 29:42; 30:8, 10, 21, 31; 31:13, 16; 40:15); *zkr* 'remember' (apropos of God) (28:12, 29; 30:16; 39:7); *zrq* 'dash' (29:16, 20); *kābôd/kəbôd yahwe(h)* '(Yahweh's) Glory' (29:43; 40:34, 35); *kihhēn* 'to priest' (28:1, 3–4, 41; 29:1, 44; 30:30; 31:10; 35:19; 39:41; 40:13, 15); *kəhunnâ* 'priesthood' (29:9; 40:15); *ləkōl* 'for all/in short, all' (27:3, 19; 28:38; 36:1); *kpr* 'Clear' (29:33, 36; 30:10, 15–16); *wənikrətâ* 'shall be cut off' (31:14); *mə'at* 'hundred' (38:25, 27); *bəkōl mōšəbōtêkem* 'in all your dwellings' (35:3); *maḥăṣît* 'half' (30:13, 15, 23; 38:26); *maṭṭe(h)* 'tribe' (31:2, 6; 35:30, 34; 38:22, 23); *məlā(')kâ* 'task' (31:3, 5, 14–15; 35 *passim*; 36:1–8; 38:24; 39:43; 40:33); *wāma'lâ* 'and upward' (30:14; 38:26); *hammiškān* 'the Tabernacle' (25:9; 26 *passim*; 27:9, 19; 35:11, 15, 18, etc.); *negep* 'harm' (30:12); *hēnîp* 'elevate' (29:24, 26–27; 35:22); *nōkaḥ* 'opposite' (26:35; 40:24); *nāśî'* 'chieftain' (35:27); *sammîm* 'spices' (30:7; 31:11; 35:8, 15, 28; 37:29; 39:38; 40:27); *sāmak yād* 'press the hand' (29:10, 15, 19); *kol-'ădat bənê yiśrā'ēl* 'all the congregation of Israel's Sons' (35:4, 20); *hā'ēdût* 'the Testimony' (25:16, 21–22; 26:33–34; 27:21, etc.); *'dp* 'be superfluous' (26:12–13); *lə'ummat* 'aligned' (25:27; 28:27; 37:14; 38:18; 39:20); *ḥoq/ḥuqqat 'ôlām* 'eternal rule' (27:21; 28:43; 29:9, 28; 30:21); *bərît 'ôlām* 'eternal covenant' (31:16); *bên hā'arbayim* 'between the two evenings' (29:39, 41; 30:8); *'ērek* 'arrangement' (40:4, 23); *qōdeš qŏdāšîm* 'Holiness of Holinesses' (26:33, 34; 29:37; 30:10, 29; 40:10); *rêaḥ nîḥôaḥ* 'Soothing Scent' (29:18, 25, 41); *šabbātôn* 'sabbatical' (31:15); *tōlədōt* 'genealogy' (28:10); *tənûpâ* 'Elevation' (29:24, 26–27; 35:22; 38:24, 29); *tərûmâ* 'Donation' (25:2–3; 29:27–28; 30:13–15; 35:5, 21, 24; 36:3, 6); the designation of months by number (40:2, 17). P abundantly features formulaic language: *waydabbēr yahwe(h) 'el-mōše(h) lē(')mōr* "And Yahweh spoke to Moses, saying"; *kəkōl 'ăšer . . . kēn* 'as/according to all . . . so.' And there is a fondness for redundancy, particularly the "short-circuit inclusio," e.g., "And you shall plate it pure gold, from inside and from outside you shall plate it" (25:11; see further below, p. 713).

As for tone, i.e., aspects of the writer's personality reflected in his work, most noteworthy in the Tabernacle pericope is a penchant for precise linear measurements related to P's frequent citation of chronological and genealogical information elsewhere. P's ideology—centralized worship, purification through sacrifice, Yahweh's presence among the people, the exclusive prerogative of the Aaronic priesthood—will be analyzed extensively below (esp. pp. 674–703).

A few verses within this section, however, may not belong to P. The clearest case is 31:18, "And he gave to Moses, as he concluded speaking with him at Mount Sinai, the two Testimony Tablets, stone tablets, written by Deity's finger." The beginning of the verse sounds Priestly, with the expressions *killâ lədabbēr* (Dillmann 1880: 335, comparing Gen 17:22; 49:33), *har sînay* 'Mount Sinai' and *hāʿēdūt* 'the Testimony.' As for the remaining "stone tablets, written by Deity's finger," the near *verbatim* parallel is a non-Priestly text, Deut 9:10 (for God's finger, cf. also Exod 8:15 [E]; for Yahweh's fabrication of the tablets, see also 32:16 [E?]). "Stone tablets" alone appeared already in 24:12 (E). Accordingly, Holzinger (1900: 148) gives 31:18b to E. If so, the ostensibly Priestly language in v 18 was inserted by the final Redactor (cf. Johnstone 1990: 77). Alternatively, we could suppose that 31:18 as a whole is an editorial seam composed by the Redactor, who knew and could quote all the Torah's sources, in order to smooth the transition to the non-Priestly Gold Calf account. Schwartz (1996: 126–27) could well be right that originally P spoke simply of "the Testimony," the phrase "two Testimony Tablets" in 31:18; 32:15; 34:29 being R's concoction. Otherwise, the Tabernacle texts proper speak simply of *hāʿēdūt*, as does the rest of the Priestly narrative (16:34; 27:21; 30:6, 36; Lev 16:13; 24:3; Num 17:19, 25). This in turn raises the question of what *ʿēdūt* meant for the Priestly Writer. Was it necessarily the two stone tablets containing the Decalog? For discussion, see NOTE to 25:16.

Moreover, some of 31:12–17 may also be Redactorial. Although P uses the roots *ʿśy* and *šmr* 'keep' in parallel (Lev 18:5; 19:37; 20:8, 22; 22:31; 25:18; 26:3), the expression *šmr . . . laʿăśôt* 'observe . . . doing' in 31:16 is paralleled not in P but frequently elsewhere, especially in Deuteronomy (5:1, 32; 6:3, 25; 7:11; 8:1; 11:22, 32; 12:1; 13:1, 19; 15:5; 17:10, 19; 24:8; 28:1, 13, 15, 58; 31:12; 32:46).

A widely accepted case of Redactorial composition is in 40:38 and probably 40:36–37 as well. Koch (1959: 45–46) argues that 40:35 originally flowed directly into Lev 1:1 as follows: "But Moses could not enter into Meeting Tent, for the cloud dwelt upon it, and Yahweh's Glory filled the Tabernacle. And Yahweh called to Moses, and Yahweh spoke to him from Meeting Tent." The present conclusion of Exodus, moreover, referring to the people's witnessing the cloud (v 38), resembles Deut 34:12, "all the great dread that Moses worked *to the eyes of all Israel*," suggesting an overarching editorial framework produced by the final redaction (Ben Zvi 1992). The jarring chronological displacement (see pp. 691–94), the redundancy with Num 9:15–23 and the references to way stations may all point to the final Redactor's hand. Thus P's original Tabernacle pericope probably concluded, "and Moses could not enter into Meeting Tent, for the cloud dwelt upon it, and Yahweh's Glory filled the Tabernacle." (Friedman [1987: 252], however, opts for the alternative solution: giving Exodus 40 entirely to P and Num 9:15–23 to R.)

A more pervasive difficulty for source analysis is the redundancy between the commands in chaps. 25–31 and their execution in chaps. 35–39. To the well-ordered modern mind, Exodus 35–39 is "utterly meaningless in terms of content . . . [it] would not be missed, if it were absent" (Wellhausen 1899: 142).

Taken alone, this argument does not sway me in the least. Economy may have been Wellhausen's ideal, but it plainly was not the Priestly Writer's (e.g. Num 7:12–83, the catalogue of the chieftains' donations). Would we really expect P merely to *imply* that Moses and Israel carried out Yahweh's decrees? We have many other examples, admittedly far briefer, where P presents parallel command and execution reports (Genesis 1; Gen 17:11–12, 23; Exod 14:16, 21, 26–27;

Num 13:1–3, 17; 20:23, 28; 27:18–23). In fact, the problem of redundancy extends beyond the Book of Exodus: Leviticus 8 carries out the instructions of Exodus 29, again with a degree of variation but with considerable repetition (see McNeile 1908: lxxii; Milgrom 1991: 545–48). Similarly, the census authorized in 30:1–16 is executed in Numbers 1 (see below, pp. 536–37). As for ancient Near Eastern parallels, these too predict a degree of redundancy, as well as variation in order (Rainey 1970; Hurowitz 1985; Milgrom 1991: 495–97). It is even possible to find a positive value in the prolixity of description, late nineteenth-century German sensibilities notwithstanding (below, pp. 710–20).

But Wellhausen's case rests on more than redundancy. We also note certain minor but systematic linguistic and orthographic differences between chaps. 25–31 and 35–40: e.g., the replacement of *'îš 'el-'ăḥîw/'iššâ 'el-'ăḥōtāh* '(each) man/woman toward his/her brother/sister' (25:20; 26:3) with *'eḥād 'el-'eḥād/'aḥat 'el-'aḥat* 'one to one' (36:10, 12–13, 22) (cf. TEXTUAL NOTE to 25:20); also the plene spelling *qṣwwt* (Kethibh) in 37:8; 39:4 against the defective *qṣwt* in 25:19; 27:4; 28:7. Further: while both panels of the Tabernacle pericope use the expressions *mizbaḥ haqqəṭōret* 'the Incense Altar' (30:27; 31:8; 35:15; 37:25) and *mizbaḥ hā'ōlâ* 'the Ascending-offering Altar' (30:28; 31:9; 35:16; 38:1; 40:6, 10, 29; also Leviticus 4 *passim*), only chaps. 35–40 refer to these items also as *mizbaḥ hazzāhāb* 'the Golden Altar' (39:38; 40:5, 26; also Num 4:11) and *mizbaḥ hannəḥōšet* (38:30; 39:39) 'the Bronze Altar.' Moreover, in my reconstructed text, 27:10–11 consistently uses *'ammūdā(y)w* 'its posts' and *wāwêhem* 'their Y-brackets,' while 38:10–11 has *'ammūdêhem* 'their posts' and *wāwê hā'ammūdîm* 'the posts' Y-brackets' (TEXTUAL NOTES to 27:10, 11, "and its posts"). Are these differences evidence of separate authorial hands or of one author introducing deliberate variation?

The entire affair has been muddied further by the consideration that chaps. 35–40 are very different in LXX vis-à-vis MT-Sam, and, within LXX, very different from chaps. 25–31. It is as if in LXX chaps. 35–40, we have a different Greek translator rendering a different Hebrew *Vorlage* (see further pp. 631–37).

How this relates to the foregoing problem is unclear. The most radical conjecture would be that, prior to the Greco-Roman era, Exodus lacked any explicit fulfillment narrative at all. The Hebrew and Greek texts were independently supplemented to fill out chaps. 35–40. If this is what happened, however, one must admit that the MT-Sam interpolator was a skilled mimic of Priestly style, avoiding linguistic giveaways (e.g., borrowings from Aramaic, Persian or Greek; contacts with Mishnaic Hebrew). While this is not unthinkable—a modern scholar might bring it off—we must concede that the Books of Chronicles, Daniel and Song of Songs frequently betray their late origins. Even if chaps. 35–40 are a late supplement, it is hard to imagine they were composed after the third century B.C.E., when LXX was translated.

SPECULATION: If we consider only the minor divergences between chaps. 25–31 and 35–40 within MT, without reference to LXX, a better scenario is tentatively proposed by R. E. Friedman (privately). Against Wellhausen, maybe chaps. 35–40 are the original, chaps. 25–31 the supplement. That is, originally

P (or P's source) simply narrated the Tabernacle's construction and erection. Yahweh's instructions may come from a later hand, just as the Temple Scroll (11QTemple) imaginatively reconstitutes the divine speech underlying Moses' summation in Deuteronomy.

A related matter is the problematic placement of the Golden Incense Altar, whose introduction in 30:1 seems like an afterthought. We do not expect any further building details after the majestic rhetoric of 29:42–46, which features many of P's theme words (cf. Janowski 1982: 317–20): ". . . *for your ages (lədōrōtêkem)* (at) Meeting Tent Opening *(petaḥ 'ōhel-mô'ēd)* before Yahweh *(lipnê yahwe[h])*, where I will be meetable *(y'd)* for you to speak *(dbr)* to you there. And I will be inquirable there for Israel's Sons *(bənê yiśrā'ēl)*. . . . And I will make holy *(qdš)* Meeting Tent and the Altar *(hammizbēaḥ)*. . . . And I will tent *(škn)* in Israel's Sons' midst *(tôk)*, and I will be for them as a deity *('ĕlōhîm)*, and they will know *(yd')* that I am Yahweh their deity who took them out *(hôṣî')* from the land of Egypt by my tenting *(škn)* among them—I am Yahweh their deity" (Hyatt 1980: 291). After this summation, what needs to be said?

For Wellhausen (1885: 65–67) and most of his followers, the Golden Altar's inclusion in chap. 30 (MT-LXX), rather than in chap. 25 alongside the other Tabernacle furniture (i.e., the Chest, Table and Lampstand), indicates that it was added secondarily (see also Noth 1962: 234–35; below, pp. 514–15, 716–17). The connection with the problem just discussed is that, in the fulfillment narrative of chaps. 35–40, the Incense Altar is regularly mentioned with the Chest, Table and Lamp as expected (35:15; 37:25; 39:38; 40:5, 26). Thus one might deduce that the same hand that inserted the Golden Altar in chap. 30 composed chaps. 35–40 as a supplement to the original P commandment narrative. We should note, too, that in Sam and 4QpaleoExod^m, the Incense Altar instructions (MT 30:1–10) follow 26:35 (see TEXTUAL NOTE).

To create yet more confusion, LXX sometimes omits the Incense Altar vis-à-vis MT (TEXTUAL NOTE to 35:15; see also TEXTUAL NOTES to 31:8, "the Incense Altar," 9), although it is present in LXX 40:5, 26. Manifestly, something is going on with the Incense Altar in all textual traditions, that is, throughout the Judaisms of the Graeco-Roman period, when the manuscript streams diverged. Although I do not share his belief in the intrusiveness of 30:1–10, I agree with Heger's (1997) basic thesis that some controversy over cultic practices—specifically, the legitimacy of censing without sacrifice—led to the deletion and reinsertion of the Incense Altar in our various witnesses.

As some have sought various late stages of redaction, others have attempted to isolate older materials utilized by the Priestly Writer. Hendrix (1992), for example, shows that in 25:1–27:19, the shrine is consistently called *hammiškān* 'the Tabernacle'; in 27:20–33:11 (which includes both P and non-P material), we find *'ōhel mō'ēd* 'Meeting Tent,' and chaps. 35–40 use mixed terminology. Hendrix suggests that "Tabernacle" describes a place and "Meeting Tent" a function. But, from the same evidence, Cross (1981: 169 n. 3) infers a proto-Priestly document using *hammiškān* alone.

Finally, we may briefly consider the relationship between P and JE (see also

REDACTION ANALYSIS below). In the narrative position where JE describes the scene of Israel's and Aaron's deepest disgrace, the Gold Calf (chap. 32), P narrates their greatest glory: the Tabernacle, where sins can be erased and impurity cleansed. While in chap. 32 Moses intercedes and obtains Clearing (*kpr*) (32:30) by his prophetic stature, in P's Tabernacle pericope Moses never speaks to Yahweh (Utzschneider 1988: 95). In fact, P makes no room for prophets, using the term *nābî'* only apropos of Aaron (7:1) It is the priest not the prophet who performs *kippūr*.

In 24:9–11 (JE), Moses, Aaron, Nadab, Abihu and seventy elders ascend the mountain, behold Yahweh, eat and drink before him and return unscathed. The Priestly Writer makes no mention of this scene, which by his standards would be scandalous. Instead, the tribes and their elders merely fund the Tabernacle, where eating and communion with the Divine are mediated by the Aaronid priests.

Similarly, in 33:12–34:9 (JE), Moses experiences his closest encounter with Yahweh and obtains God's pardon for the people. P substitutes for this a description of Moses' injury as a result of proximity to God (34:29–35; see, however, pp. 620–32). Instead, the closest Man and Yahweh may come is through Tabernacle worship, especially on Yom Kippur, when the Great Priest enters the inner sanctum and suffers no harm (30:10; Leviticus 16).

Moreover, where JE dwells in detail on the Covenant *ritual* between Yahweh and Israel (chap. 24), P emphasizes instead the Covenant *document*, i.e., the Testimony. P's Covenant is not ratified by a one-time ritual; instead it serves as the focus of ongoing ritual. JE's Meeting Tent, staffed by the nonpriests Moses and Joshua, is a place for personal prayer and prophetic communication. It stands outside the camp (33:7–11), which, for P, is a zone of impurity (Knohl 1997: 72). P's "Meeting Tent Tabernacle," in contrast, is erected in the camp's very heart (25:8; Num 1:50–2:32) and constitutes the focus of sacrificial worship; it is accessible only to the House of Aaron but sheds its sanctity upon all. In JE, now and then Yahweh parks his cloud-vehicle by the door; in P, he leaves it for long durations on the roof. P's God does not sporadically descend from some higher realm; rather, he remains immanent in the Tent and in the camp (see Sommer 2001: 45).

REDACTION ANALYSIS

The combination of JE with P produced many new meanings and implications, ranging from the trivial to the profound. For example, P never divulges the source of the people's treasures (25:3–7, etc.). In JEP, the answer is obvious: it is the recycled plunder of Egypt (3:22; 11:2; 12:35) (Baentsch 1903: 221), which in JE implicitly goes to make the Gold Calf (NOTE to 32:2). The composite text thus provides the prototype for the later belief that the wealth of nations should enrich the Temple (e.g., Isa 45:14; 60:5–6; 61:6; 66:11; Zech 14:14).

Another minor matter: in the received text, one naturally equates JE's Hur, Aaron's colleague of unspecified lineage (17:10, 12; 24:14), with Bezalel's grandfather, Hur of Judah (31:2; 35:20; 38:22). As Hur and Aaron once helped Moses to channel Yahweh's saving might (17:8–16), they now are associated respectively with the building and the service of Yahweh's Tent, the locus of God's power on Earth.

The JE narrative shows non-Aaronids offering sacrifices both creditable (24:5–8) and discreditable (32:6 [MT, see TEXTUAL NOTE]). In the edited whole, the Tabernacle pericope stands as a definitive rejection of uncontrolled, uncentralized worship. After Sinai, all sacrifice belongs to the House of Aaron.

It is indeed ironic that P's Tabernacle pericope now frames the JE text that it was intended to supplant (cf. Friedman 1987: 217–41). In the edited text, before he learns of his election to the priesthood (chap. 29) and Bezalel's designation as chief artificer (31:2–5), Aaron has already fabricated an idol and led the people in forbidden worship (chap. 32). Since Aaron is nonetheless sanctified (Leviticus 8), we infer that Moses has somehow obtained pardon for him (cf. Deut 9:20), against the clear implication of 32:33, "Whoever has sinned against me, I will erase him from my Document." Aaron's ritual purification in Leviticus 8, in fact, may serve as his implicit atonement for the Gold Calf affair. The composite story of Aaron's fall and redemption enriches the portrayals both of Aaron and of Yahweh.

Similarly, even though the life-saving, expiatory census is mandated before the Gold Calf (30:11–16), it is taken afterward. In effect, the half-shekel of silver atones for Israel's apostasy (for Midrashic sources to this effect, see Ginzberg 1928: 3.146–48). The making of the Calf, in JE wholly negative and in P too horrible to mention, becomes in the composite Torah a sort of *felix culpa* for Aaron and Israel, necessitating the Tabernacle's atoning cultus.

The addition of Exodus 32 considerably lessens the impression of P's great sin episodes: the transgression of Nadab and Abihu (Leviticus 10), the Levites' revolt led by Korah (Numbers 16, *passim*) and the apostasy at Baal Peor (Num 25:6–15). The crime most readers remember instead is JE's Gold Calf. In the redacted text, Exodus 32 mitigates P's unflattering portrayal of the Levites and super-flattering portrayal of Aaron (see further vol. I, pp. 284–86, and below, pp. 567–74).

Finally, redaction brought together JE, which records a Covenant ratification ceremony (24:1–11) but no institutionalized sacrifice, with P, which knows the Covenant but lacks a ratification ceremony per se (see below, pp. 694–95). In other words, JE and P each complete gaps in the other's account.

In their compositional diversity, chaps. 19–40 ponder E's question, "Is there Yahweh in our midst or not?" (17:7) (Fox 1986: 137; cf. Utzschneider 1988: 88–91). Is the mountain God's permanent home or a temporary residence? Is his presence contingent on Moses' presence? Can he be brought to Israel in the form of an idol? Will God go before or among the people? What is the essence of Israel's relationship to Yahweh: Covenant or Cult? These highly edited chapters possess a thematic coherence and theological richness that far transcend their original components.

NOTES

25:1. *And Yahweh spoke.* The Deity begins his address while Moses is still on Mount Sinai, within the cloud and fire (24:16–18). Exod 25:1 opens one very long speech by Yahweh, comprising 25:2–30:10. It contrasts with the following six short utterances in 30:11–31:17, perhaps to be understood as spoken on separate occasions (cf. Abarbanel).

25:2. *take.* Both the people and the leaders are to "take" *(lqḥ)* the Donation. In the first instance, the people are the subject; "take" means to select and bring an offering to Yahweh. In the second instance (and also in v 3), *tiqqəḥû* 'you shall take' refers to Moses and the priests receiving the Israelites' contributions (Cassuto 1967: 324).

for me. That is, for Yahweh, the Tabernacle's owner.

Donation-offering. The root of *tərûmâ* is ostensibly *rwm* 'to be high' (NOTE to 29:27), as if the contribution were lifted up from the mass (BDB) or displayed aloft; hence KJV "heave offering." Von Soden (1970), however, has assembled evidence suggestive of a Northwest Semitic root **rym* 'give' (also Ehrlich 1969: 194 [on 29:27]); see also NOTE to 15:20, "Miriam" (for reservations, cf. Anderson 1987: 137–44). Hence my translation "Donation-offering." Since otherwise *tərûmâ* generally connotes a sacrifice (e.g., 29:27–28), Israel's contribution is itself an act of worship (Durham 1987: 354). Their voluntary endowment will contrast with Solomon's exacted service and taxation to build his Temple (1 Kgs 5:27–30; 10:14) (Gray 1983: 162).

Unlike the half-shekel poll tax (30:11–16), no amount is specified for this gift to the Sanctuary. Exod 35:21–36:7 stresses that the people's participation is enthusiastic and voluntary.

heart. The seat of intellect and rational emotion (Fabry 1995).

ennobles him. I am uncertain how best to render *yiddəbennû.* On the one hand, one might translate "moves him," based upon Arabic *nadaba* 'incite, summon'; compare also the Phoenician inscription from Zinjirli (*KAI* 214.33), where *ndb* probably means "instigation." On the other hand, Hebrew *ndb* appears only in the specific context of generosity. It is thus more semantically akin to the Arabic eighth form *'intadaba* 'be amenable' and Aramaic *nədab* 'be willing'; cf. also Arabic *naduba* 'be clever, capable, noble.'

My translation "ennobles him" is inspired by the comparable expression *nədîb lēb* 'noble-hearted' in 35:5, 22 and by the noun *nādîb* 'aristocrat.' The people's gift is "princely" (cf. Utzschneider 1988: 292); 36:3–7 provides the telling detail that they were so enthusiastic they had to be restrained. Israel's generosity of heart contrasts with Pharaoh's chronic "strength" *(ḥzq),* "firmness" *(kbd)* and "hardness" *(qšy)* of heart in chaps. 7–14 (see vol. I, pp. 353–54). The Israelites, rich and poor alike, dispense their riches as freely as lords; whereas Pharaoh, a true king, would not grant his human chattel a reprieve. See further NOTE to 35:10.

you shall take my Donation-offering. The orotundity of this superfluous phrase is typical of the Priestly Source (Paran 1989: 49–97).

25:3. *gold, silver and bronze*. The metals are listed in order of descending value. The basic principle is that objects closest to Yahweh's holy presence are made of gold, whose luster never tarnishes (ibn Ezra [shorter commentary]). Although silver does blacken, this may have been considered desirable (Ogden 2000: 171). On the use and manufacture of these metals in antiquity, see Forbes (1964b), Lucas (1962: 195–53), Moorey (1994) and Ogden (2000); on the order in which the Bible mentions metals (silver usually precedes gold), see Kessler (1986).

The silver Donation in particular has occasioned some comment. Exod 30:11–16 and 38:25–28 imply that the silver is not really a voluntary contribution but is gathered by taxation. Saadiah (*apud* ibn Ezra) opines, however, that the silver of 25:3 is a separate donation of silver for making the trumpets (Num 10:1–10) and other vessels. Or perhaps this silver goes directly into the Tabernacle treasury, to purchase animals and supplies. Most likely, however, the text is speaking loosely about all the materials, however gathered (cf. *y. Sheqal.* 1:1; Rashi; ibn Ezra).

The nonmention of iron has also elicited comment (already Philo *Quaest. in Exod.* 102 compares the absence of iron in Homeric epic). Might this be evidence that the historical Tabernacle was a Bronze Age artifact (Cole 1973: 189)? Not necessarily, for P assumes the use of iron in Lev 26:19; Num 31:22; 35:16. The real reason for iron's absence is twofold: (a) it is not a decorative metal, and (b) it is associated with defiling bloodshed (Beer 1939: 130; cf. NOTES to 20:25[22]).

25:4. *blue . . . purple . . . worm-crimson*. Technically, these are dyes not fabrics. Although the material is unspecified, the Rabbinic tradition that these are woolen textiles (*b. Yebam.* 4b) is confirmed by extrabiblical sources (e.g., the annals of Tiglath-Pileser III [*ANET* 282–83; Tadmor 1994: 170–71]). Like gold, silver and bronze, so blue, purple and worm-crimson are probably listed in order of descending value (Milgrom 2000: 1661).

Təkēlet 'blue' (Akkadian *takiltu*) is derived from crushed snails (Pliny *Natural History* 9.125–42; *b. Šabb.* 75a; *b. Menaḥ.* 44a), especially *T. trunculus*. How it differs from *'argāmān* 'purple' is not clear; it is generally assumed that *təkēlet* is somewhat greener and *'argāmān* somewhat redder. These dyes were the celebrated Tyrian "purple," an expensive status symbol in Antiquity (Reinhold 1970; on the linguistic history of the word *'argāmān*, see Ellenbogen 1962: 38–39; Rabin 1963: 116–18). Ezek 27:7 associates blue and purple with Cyprus, but in fact they were the products of the Phoenician littoral generally. Purple was expensive because laborious to extract; it may have taken as many as 12,000 snails to produce 1.4 grams of dye (Danker 1992: 558). In Roman times, a pound of purple silk cost the equivalent of $100,000 in the 1980s (Milgrom 1983b: 63).

Tôlaʿat šānî, literally "crimson worm," or *šənî tôlaʿat* 'worm's crimson' is kermes (Saadiah), the red dye obtained principally from *Kermococcus vermilis*, a scale insect that lives on oak trees (Borowski 1998: 160). The color is also called simply *tôlāʿ* 'worm' (Lam 4:5; cf. Isa 1:18). The exact meaning and etymology of *šānî* are unknown. The LXX-Vg understanding of *tôlaʿat šānî* as "double crimson" implausibly associates it with the root *šny* 'to be two' (Wevers 1990: 393)— but Jacob (1992: 776–77) notes that purple wool was often double-dipped (Pliny

Natural History 9.134–35, 137). For more information on dyed wool, see Forbes (1964a: 1–26, 99–150), Ziderman (1987), Danker (1992), Borowski (1998: 177–80), Houtman (1993a: 143) and the definitive essays in Spanier (1987).

linen. Like several other Hebrew terms for luxury items, *šēš* is a borrowing; compare Egyptian *šś* 'linen' (Lambdin 1953: 155; Ellenbogen 1962: 164; Muchiki 1999: 257–58; for Rabbinic etymological discussion, see *b. Yoma* 71b). Pharaoh dresses Joseph in *šēš* (Gen 41:42), and, according to Ezek 27:7, *šēš* was imported from Egypt. Since no color is mentioned, this must be plain white linen (cf. ibn Ezra), hence perhaps the homophony with terms for "alabaster" (Hebrew *šayiš*, Egyptian *šś*).

Generally, chaps. 25–31, 35–40 call the linen *šēš mošzār* 'twisted linen,' a phrase possibly favored for its assonance. It is not clear whether *šēš mošzār* denotes a special type of linen or merely expresses the obvious: to make flax into threads, the strands must be finely twined. (According to *b. Yoma* 71b, "twisted linen" is eightfold thread.) It is also possible that *mošzār* is a technique not of spinning but of weaving (Hayutin 1993: 240–41). For more information on ancient flax and linen, see Lucas and Harris (1962: 142–46), Forbes (1964a: 27–43, 151–74) and Vogelsang-Eastwood (2000: 269–78). On Palestinian textile production in modern times, see Dalman (1937: 1–144).

goats. This is shorthand for goats' *hair*, spun into threads and woven into textiles (also Num 31:20; 1 Sam 19:13). To this day, goats' hair is the most common covering for Middle Eastern tents.

25:5. *reddened ramskins.* Either painted or dyed (cf. Forbes 1957: 9, 27). The Pu'al participle *mə'oddām* 'reddened,' rather than *'ădōm* 'red,' implies an artificial process, not natural coloration (Rashi). Although the Hebrew root *'dm* 'to be red' seems etymologically sufficient, Ehrlich (1908: 365) and Pines (1971: 665) point to Arabic *'addam/'adamiyy* 'tanner' and *'adīm* 'hide.' Has Arabic borrowed *'dm* from a Northwest Semitic language, or does Arabic preserve the original meaning, found vestigially in Hebrew *mə'oddām* (Brenner 1982: 111)? The former scenario is more likely, since loanwords are most often nouns for professions and products (Arlotto 1972: 184–88). On techniques for leatherworking in Antiquity, see Forbes (1957: 1–77) and Van Driel-Murray (2000). On the color red, evocative of blood and danger in many cultures, see briefly Fiddes (1991: 68–69).

beaded skins. Təḥāšîm (singular *taḥaš*) is an ancient riddle solved only recently. Apart from the Exodus Tabernacle texts and Numbers 4, where *taḥaš* skins wrap the sacred objects in transit, it appears only in Ezek 16:10 as sandal leather.

To judge from the parallel with "reddened ram skins," *təḥāšîm* should denote either an animal or a color. Many proposals for the former have an improbable air—a unique, extinct creature such as a unicorn (*b. Šabb.* 28b; Rashi); a badger (Martin Luther and AV, based on German *Dachs*); a crocodile (Borowski 1998: 206); a giraffe (cf. Mandelkern 1937: 1242). More likely candidates are the dugong or dolphin (Arabic *d/tuḫas*; see Dillmann 1880: 276–77).

The most common suggestion since antiquity, however, is that *taḥaš* is a bluish, blackish, reddish color (the sources are rather vague) corresponding to Greek *hyacinthos* (LXX; Josephus *Ant.* 3.102; Vg; *y. Šabb.* 2:3; *Qoh. Rab.* 1:9) and to Aramaic *sasgônā'* (*Tgs.*-Syr). A great step forward was taken by Aḥituv and Tadmor (1982), anticipated by Jacob (1992: 768), who correlate *taḥaš* with Akkadian *dušû/duḫšû*, Hurrian *tuḫšiwe*, Sumerian DUḪ.ŠI.A, a reddish-yellow stone or leather of that color used for sandals and other purposes. (This cognate may indicate that the Hebrew singular should be vocalized *tōḥaš*, not *taḥaš*.) But Dalley (2000), in a *tour de force* marshaling of philological and archaeological evidence, proves that *dušû/duḫšû/taḥaš* is neither a substance nor a color, but a technique of sewing blue faience beads onto leather to attain various chromatic effects.

acacia. *Šiṭṭîm* is a loanword from Egyptian *šnḏt* (Lambdin 1953: 154; Ellenbogen 1962: 160; Muchiki 1999: 256; cf. Arabic s/*ṣanṭ*, Akkadian š/*samṭu*). LXX "imperishable wood" accurately describes acacia's resistance to rot (midrashically noted also in *b. Yoma* 72a; *Sukk.* 45b). Of the over 700 varieties of acacia large and small, Zevit (1992) favors *Acacia albida* as meeting the Tabernacle's requirements of size. It does not, however, grow in the desert, from which Zevit infers that, at least in this detail, the account is unhistorical (see further pp. 411, 709–10). For a detailed description of the distribution, characteristics and uses of *Acacia albida*, see Wickens (1969).

25:6. *oil for illumination.* I.e., pure olive oil (27:20). *Mā'ôr* 'illumination' may also be understood as referring to the lamps themselves, just as it describes the sun and moon in Gen 1:16 (Ehrlich 1908: 365–66).

fragrances. One could also translate *bəśāmîm* more specifically as "(resin of) balsam trees," the incense-yielding shrubs of South Arabia and Somaliland (Van Beek 1960). See further NOTES to 30:23.

Ointment Oil. For anointing and consecrating the sacred vessels and personnel (40:9–15).

Spice Incense. *Sammîm* finds apparent cognates in Aramaic *sammā'*, Arabic *samm*, Akkadian *šammu* and Egyptian *smw* (Grintz 1975: 173), all describing herbs, especially of magical, toxic or medicinal virtue. These are not the expected phonetic correspondences, however (cf. Kaufman 1974: 100). One possibility is that in some of these languages, the term is borrowed, borne by the active trade in South Arabian aromatics (cf. Arlotto 1972: 184–88). It is also possible that the resemblance is fortuitous, that we have two different roots: **šmm* 'sprout' and **śmm* 'be fragrant (for the latter, cf. Arabic *šamma* 'to smell').

Bekhor Shor rhetorically questions the relevance of this verse to chap. 25. Do not oil and incense pertain to worship rather than to construction (cf. TEXTUAL NOTE on LXX)? He responds that both oil and perfumes are used to prepare the Tabernacle for Yahweh's presence. Only with lighting, anointing and censing will the construction be complete.

25:7. *carnelian.* *Šōham* is probably carnelian (LXX *sardion*); likely cognates are Akkadian *sāmtu* 'carnelian' (< *siāmu* 'to be red'), Ugaritic *šmt*, a precious mineral, and Ge'ez *sōm/sāwm*, a gem. Again, the phonetic correspondences are not as expected, perhaps because this was a trade item. According to Gen 2:12, *šōham* comes from South Arabia; Akkadian texts link *sāmtu* to India and the East (*CAD* 15.121–22). These exotic gems are donated by the tribal leaders (35:27).

Since the carnelians each will bear *six* names (28:9–12), unlike the gemstones on the priest's oracular pouch (28:21), either they are larger than the pectoral jewels (Abarbanel) or else the writing is simply finer.

filling. To judge from 28:17 (see NOTE), *millū'îm* (< *ml'* 'be full') refers to textile settings for gemstones.

Ephod. This is the vest or tunic described in 28:6–8; see NOTE to 28:4 and COMMENT p. 523.

ḥōšen. The oracular pouch worn on the priest's breast; see NOTES to 28:15–30 and COMMENT p. 523.

25:8. *Sanctum. Miqdāš,* literally "holy place" (< *qdš* 'to be holy'), denotes any place Yahweh is wont to appear, most often the Temple (Durham 1987: 354–55). See also NOTE to 15:17 (vol. I, p. 543–44).

tent. Not the ordinary verb for habitation, *yāšab,* but the more specialized *šākan,* associated with tent-dwelling (Cassuto 1967: 345–46; Cross 1961b: 225–27; Sarna 1986: 197). See also NOTE to 25:9, "the Tabernacle's."

in your midst. We would have expected "in *its* midst" i.e., within the Tabernacle (Sarna 1991: 158). For P, it is crucial that Yahweh, despite his unapproachable holiness, should dwell in the middle of the camp, imparting some of his sanctity to Israel (Lev 15:31; 16:16; 22:32; 26:11–12; Num 16:3; 18:20; 35:34); see below, pp. 686–91.

SPECULATION: If P was written when neither Tabernacle nor Temple still stood (see p. 732), then 25:8 takes on an additional meaning. Yahweh is present on Earth only in and through Israel, his living Tabernacle. Yahweh "tents" in their midst both individually and communally, especially when they keep the Sabbath (cf. Bakon 1997: 83; on the parallel between the Tabernacle and the Sabbath, see pp. 675–76, 691–94). On the use of these themes in the Gospel of John, see pp. 720–21.

25:9. *making you see . . . model.* As Yahweh speaks, Moses is shown a *tabnît* (< *bny* 'build') for the Tabernacle (cf. 25:40; 26:30; 27:8; Num 8:4). The same word appears in Akkadian *(tabnītu)* meaning "(beatiful) arrangement, creation," and "Tabnit" is also a Phoenician personal name (*KAI* 13), although its meaning is disputed (Benz 1972: 428). Here *tabnît* could connote one of three things: (a) a large-scale prototype, i.e., Yahweh's celestial Tent; (b) a small architect's model, or (c) a set of plans.

A. Many have thought that Moses sees Yahweh's heavenly Tabernacle (e.g., Cassuto 1967: 322; Clifford 1971: 226; cf. Letter to the Hebrews *passim*); according to Rabbinic sources, it is made of colored fire (*Pesiq. Rab Kah.* 1:3; *Cant. Rab.* 3:11). At least in the composite text, such a structure might be alluded to in 15:17, "The sanctum . . . your hands founded" (Freedman 1981: 26). The Canaanite analogue would be the tent of 'Ilu 'God,' head of the Ugaritic pantheon, which also may be located on a mountain (Clifford 1972: 34–57). It is certain that, throughout the ancient Near East, temples were thought to be modeled on celestial prototypes (Weinfeld 1981: 505). But this interpretation is somewhat far-fetched for Exodus. The Tabernacle itself should be the *tabnît* of Yahweh's heavenly dwelling, not vice versa (see following).

B. The *tabnît* of Exodus might rather be a small model, somewhat like the miniature homes and shops from Egyptian tombs or the clay model houses found throughout the ancient Near East (Bretschneider 1991; Muller 2001). That a *tabnît* can be three dimensional is suggested by Josh 22:28, where the Transjordanian tribes claim to have built no functioning altar, only a replica *tabnît*. Similarly, *tabnît* can connote an idol, i.e., a god's solid image in the form of a human (Deut 4:16–18; Isa 44:13). Hurowitz (1992a: 168–70) makes the strongest case for this interpretation, citing parallels from Mesopotamia of supernaturally revealed scale models (see also Masetti-Rouault 2001).

C. The *tabnît* could be a drawing. In Ezek 8:10, the term describes wall etchings or reliefs, and Loewenstamm (1968: 534) compares the god Ea sketching in the dirt to instruct the Babylonian Flood hero Atra-ḫasīs how to build a ship (Lambert and Millard 1969: 129). Again, when King Ahaz, impressed by a foreign, monumental altar, sends back to the Great Priest its "likeness *(dəmût)* and its construction *(tabnît)*, pertaining to all its fabrication," one might envision a plan with verbal indications rather than a scale model (2 Kgs 16:10). According to 1 Chr 28:11–12, 18–19, Yahweh inspired David to produce the Temple's *tabnît* "in writing" *(biktāb)*, probably referring to verbal instructions but conceivably a drawing. The Samaritan Tabernacle illustrations analysed by Purvis (1994) may be considered attempts to reconstruct Moses' *tabnît*.

Whatever the *tabnît* of Exodus may be, the text never indicates that Moses brings it down the mountain and shows it to anyone. One rather gets the impression that he describes it to the craftsmen by memory.

Unlike the Temple of Solomon (but cf. 1 Chr 28:19; Aptowitzer 1930–31), the Tabernacle is designed not by humans but by God. This corresponds to a pervasive ancient mind-set minimizing human involvement in the planning and construction of sacred objects (e.g., *Enūma Eliš* IV–VI [*ANET* 66–69; Dalley 1989: 255–63]; cf. Jacobsen 1987a, apropos of idols). On the term *tabnît* as faintly evocative of Creation, see NOTE to 25:40.

the Tabernacle's. While *miškān* at times metaphorically connotes any habitation, even a tomb (Isa 22:16; Ps 49:12) or an animal's lair (Job 39:6), there is a clear association with tent-dwelling, hence the traditional rendering "Tabernacle" (< Latin *tabernaculum* 'tent'). In general, the root *škn* connotes transitory encampment, as opposed to the more permanent *yšb* 'sit, inhabit, reside (in one place)' (Gen 9:27; Judg 8:11; Isa 13:20; Ps 78:55; Job 11:14; 18:15) (Görg 1967: 97–124). *Miškān* often parallels *'ōhel* 'tent' or *maḥăne(h)* 'camp' both in Hebrew (Num 16:24–27; 24:5; 2 Sam 7:6; Isa 54:2; Jer 30:18; Ps 15:1; 78:28; Job 21:28) and in Ugaritic (*KTU* 1.15.iii.18–19; 17.v.32–33). Both *'ōhel* and *miškān* interchangeably denote the wilderness Tabernacle, and they may even stand together, as in 40:2, 6: *miškan 'ōhel-mô'ēd* 'the Meeting Tent Tabernacle.' In 26:1–14; 36:8–19; 40:19; Num 3:25, however, the Priestly Writer makes a distinction: the "Tabernacle" is the inner curtain of wool and linen, the "Tent" is the outer curtain of goat hair. Nomads and shepherds live in encampments called *miškānōt* (Num 16:26–27; 24:5; Ezek 25:4; Cant 1:8). For cognates, Akkadian *maškanu* and Aramaic *maškənā'* can similarly denote a tent or canopy; compare also Arabic *maskan* 'abode' (< *sakana* 'rest, be still'). Even Greek *skēnē* 'tent' may be a borrowing of this Semitic term (Homan 2002: 11–12 n. 23).

In the Ugaritic references, the tabernacles in question are divine dwellings, like

FIGURE 1a. Chest and *kappōret*

Yahweh's abode in Exodus and like the *mšk[n']* probably mentioned in a Hatra inscription (*KAI* 247.5; Hillers 1972). David's sacred Tent in Zion, too, is designated by the plural *miškānōt* 'encampment' (2 Sam 7:6; Ps 132:5, 7), and even the Temple is called *miškān(ōt)* (Ezek 37:27; Ps 43:3; 84:2). (On the interchange between terms for "tent" and "house," see below, pp. 703–5)

its implements. Num 1:50; 4:15; 18:3 imply that *kēlā(y)w* refers to all the Tabernacle's contents, not just the minor utensils such as pans and forks (*pace* Jacob 1992: 769) or construction tools such as hammers and chisels (*pace* Rashi, Sforno on 27:19).

25:10. *you shall make.* That is, Moses is to commission the artificers. Compare 28:2–3, when Moses is first commanded to make the priestly garments, but then is immediately told to entrust the work to skilled tailors. The initial fabrication of the holy objects will be performed under the supervision of Bezalel and Oholiab (31:1–11). But Moses will assemble the whole (40:1–8).

a chest. Hebrew *'ărōn* denotes any type of box, e.g., a coffin (Gen 50:26) or a coffer (2 Kgs 2:10–11). Synonymous cognates include *'rn* in Phoenician (*KAI* 1.1–2; 9.A.2, B.4; 11; 13.2, 3, 5; 29.1) and inscriptional Aramaic (see Hoftijzer and Jongeling 1995: 109–10), Akkadian *arānu* and Arabic *'irān*. The underlying ver-

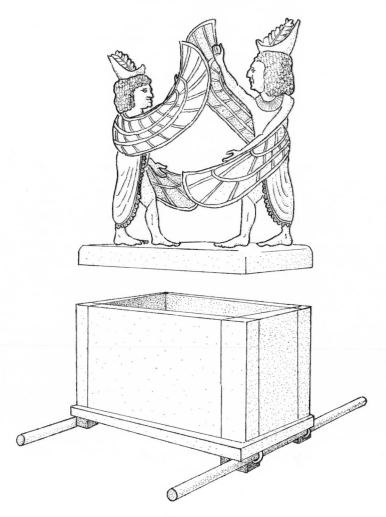

Figure 1b. Chest and *kappōret* (alternative structure)

bal root is most likely *'ry* 'gather.' On the signficance of the Chest, see below, pp. 512–21; for illustrations, see figs. 1a–b.

acacia wood. Bekhor Shor notes that, given its extreme sanctity, one might have expected the Chest to be solid gold. The use of wood may be a concession to portability, like the hollow Bronze Altar (27:1–8).

Because the Massoretic vocalization *'ărôn* is both the absolute (2 Kgs 12:10 = 2 Chr 24:8) and the construct form, it is unclear whether the relationship between *'ărôn* and *'ăṣê šiṭṭîm* is apposition (my translation; cf. 37:1 *hā'ārōn 'ăṣê šiṭṭîm* and GKC §131*d*), double accusative of fabricated object and material (GKC §117*hh*)—which may be the same as apposition—or simply construct state (i.e., "a chest *of* acacia wood"). That the author himself did not distinguish clearly is evident from comparing the following expressions: on the one hand, *šnayim kərūbîm zāhāb* (25:18); *habbaddîm 'ăṣê šiṭṭîm* (25:28); *bərîḥîm 'ăṣê šiṭṭîm* (26:26); *hammizbēaḥ 'ăṣê šiṭṭîm* (27:1); *hammənōrâ zāhāb ṭāhôr* (37:17) (all with apposition/double accusative); and, on the other hand, *baddê 'ăṣê šiṭṭîm* (25:13); *mənōrat zāhāb ṭāhôr* (25:31); *bərîḥê 'ăṣê šiṭṭîm* (36:31) (construct).

cubits. The *'ammâ* is probably the distance from an average man's elbow to his fingertips (cf. Deut 3:11, "by a man's *'ammâ*): c. 1.5 feet/0.5 m. The Chest was thus roughly 3.75 feet/1.25 m. in length and 2.25 feet/.75 m. in height and depth. As with the Tabernacle itself, the text does not distinguish between the outer and interior measurements, presumably because the walls are of negligible thickness (cf. ibn Ezra).

25:11. *plate.* Gold both preserves and beautifies. In Egypt, wooden furniture was covered with gold either by nailing on hammered plates or by gluing on foil (Ogden 2000: 164). Cassuto (1967: 329) suggests that the former method is more appropriate here, since the tablets, rolling around during transport, would abrade thin gold foil.

The inverted, chiastic word order is high Priestly style, the "short-circuit inclusio": "you shall plate it pure gold, from inside and from outside you shall plate it" (McEvenue 1971: 43–44; Paran 1989: 47–97).

pure gold. "Pure *(ṭāhôr)*" is meant both literally—the Chest is plated with unalloyed gold—and figuratively—only the most valuable and perdurable metal befits God's absolute Holiness. There is also a practical consideration: the purest gold is the most malleable.

What exactly the Priestly Writer intended by *zāhāb ṭāhôr* depends on when P was written (see p. 732). The mass refinment of gold was unknown before the sixth century B.C.E. If he lived during or after the sixth century, as most believe, the Priestly Writer may have attributed an innovative metallurgic technique to Mosaic antiquity. But if P antedates the sixth century, the reference is doubtless to *relatively* pure gold in its natural state. On the use and manufacture of gold in Israel and the ancient Near East, see Meyers (1976: 28–31, 41–43), Moorey (1994: 217–32) and Ogden (2000: 161–66).

from inside . . . from outside. We would say, "On the inside, on the outside."

zēr. This enigmatic feature of the Chest, Table (25:24–25) and Incense Altar (30:3–4) is of disputed etymology, form and purpose. For the etymology, Luzzatto implausibly compares Hebrew *nēzer* 'headband.' Cassuto (1967: 329) more aptly invokes Aramaic *zîrā'* 'wreath, crown,' envisioning a band with a floral motif. Some derivatives of Arabic *zwr*, moreover, imply a meaning "to be bent," which might suit a rim or molding. And Grintz (1975: 17) proffers a derivation from Egyptian *dr* 'limit, wall, side.'

Where is the *zēr* located? If it runs around the top, it could simply be a molding to cover the bare wood of the Chest's upper edge (Bekhor Shor; cf. *Mel. Mišk.* 7). Or perhaps the *zēr* is a protruding rim within which the *kappōret* nests (Rashi; Kennedy 1898: 665). But it might also be a band running around the side or bottom.

Jacob (1992: 772–73) finds significance in the fact that, besides possessing a *zēr*, the Chest, Table and Incense Altar are also borne by poles. According to 30:4, the Incense Altar's poles are inserted into gold rings "beneath its *zēr*." Likewise for the Chest and for the Table, the matter of the *zēr* is followed directly by a description of the rings and poles. The Chest, Incense Altar and Table, Jacob further notes, are covered in *pure* gold (25:11, 24; 30:3), while the *zēr* and poles apparently use ordinary gold. He infers that the *zēr*'s function is both to affix the rings to the sacred objects and (if I understand him properly) to insulate those who carry them from Holiness contagion (cf. below, pp. 683–90).

Jacob glides over a problem, however. In 30:4, we would expect the rings to be not "under" (*mittaḥat*) the *zēr*, but "aligned with" (*ləʿummat*) it, as in 25:27. Rather than hold the rings and poles away from the Chest, the *zēr* may be a molding running midway around its sides, with the rings directly below (fig. 1a). Perhaps the function is to distribute weight, so that when the priests lift the Chest, the stress is more vertical than horizontal (although the *zēr* itself would be a potential structural weakness). See also NOTES to 25:24, 25.

around. Fox (1986: 143) notes the assonance in *zēr zāhāb sābîb*.

25:12. *rings.* Hebrew *ṭābaʿat* originally denoted a finger-ring or signet. By the time of P, however, if not earlier, it described any small metal hoop, such as the Tabernacle's fasteners. The term is paralleled in Arabic *ṭābaʿ*, Syriac *ṭabʿāʾ* and Amarna (i.e., Canaanite) *timbuʾu* (EA 11.rev.25; 25.1.69 [?]). These words are all apparently borrowed from Egyptian *ḏbʿt* 'seal' (Lambdin 1953: 151; Muchiki 1999: 247), in turn derived from Egyptian *ḏbʿ* 'finger.'

its four feet. The intepretation is uncertain. Since *paʿam* normally means "foot," the simple interpretation of *ʾarbaʿ paʿămōtā(y)w* is that the Chest stands upon squat feet, insulating it from the potentially impure ground (ibn Ezra). But why would feet be introduced so casually, rather than explicitly ordained (Jacob 1992: 774)? Are they understood to be a normal feature of such chests (Dillmann 1880: 279; Houtman 2000: 377), just as the Table's legs are assumed in 25:26? By this approach, the rings are attached to the feet themselves, perhaps with the *zēr* just above to support the Chest (see NOTE to 24:11, "elite"). The Table's rings, similarly, are attached to its legs.

Another approach holds that *pəʿāmōt* here are "corners" (Tg. Onqelos, Rashi), in which case we may compare *pēʾâ* 'corner' in 25:26. Luzzatto observes that in 1 Kgs 7:30, 34, *paʿam* seems to interchange with *pinnâ* 'corner' (*ʾarbaʿ paʿămōtā[y]w . . . ʾarbaʿ pinnōt*). If this is correct, to which of the Chest's eight corners are the rings attached? Rashi says the upper corners, which would make the Chest easier to hoist—but the use of *paʿam* 'foot' suggests rather a bottom corner (Ramban, Sforno), so that the Chest would be borne higher.

SPECULATION: We are not told how the Chest's sides are held together. Assuming vertical corner braces to which the sides are mortised, "corners" and "feet" would be one and the same (figs. 1a–b).

Jacob (1992: 802) offers an ingenious argument for placing the rings at the bottom for both Chest and Table. Each of these objects stands 1.5 cubits tall. Similarly, according to 27:4–5, the Altar's rings are placed halfway up, or 1.5 cubits from the top. Thus, when the priests carry the Chest, Table and Altar, their tops would be level, assuming that the poles are at the bottom of the first two items (figs. 1b, 3a). I am not sure, however, that Jacob's reconstruction of the Table is correct; it depends upon the placement of the "frame" (see NOTES to 25:25–26).

and two rings . . . and two rings. Ibn Ezra (longer commentary) and Bekhor Shor think that these are different from the previously mentioned rings and merely decorative. For them, the Chest really has eight rings, not four. But this is surely an overreaction to the first conjunction, which is simply explicative (GKC §154; ibn Ezra [shorter commentary]; Rashbam) and need not be translated (Rashi).

flank. Ṣēlāʿ, literally "rib" (Gen 2:21–22; *m. Ḥul.* 3:1; *b. Ḥul.* 42b, 52a), often connotes the sides of structures (Exod 26:20, 26–27, 35; 27:7; 30:4; 1 Kgs 6:5, 15–16), as opposed to front *(pānîm)* and back *(yarkātayim, ʾāhōr[ayim])* (cf. Jacob 1992: 774; NOTE to 30:4, "its . . . flanks . . . its . . . sides").

Commentators debate whether the Chest's poles are affixed to its long sides (Josephus *Ant.* 3.136; ibn Ezra; Sforno; Dillmann 1880: 279) or its short sides (*b. Menaḥ.* 98a–b; Rashi; Rashbam; Kennedy 1898: 665; Cassuto 1967: 329–30; Jacob 1992: 774). The answer depends on which angle the Chest is meant to be viewed from. One would think the front is the long side, so that both Griffins would be visible on the ends (see figs. 1a–b). Accordingly, the poles are attached to the short sides. In Solomon's Temple, too, the Chest's poles will run east-to-west, protruding beyond the inner cella (1 Kgs 8:8).

25:13. *poles.* Boxes with carrying poles are common back to the Egyptian Old Kingdom, including a good example from Tutankhamun's tomb (Kitchen 1993: 125*).

25:14. *for carrying.* The Chest is too holy to be lifted in any other fashion. If the poles are affixed to the short sides, the Chest is presumably carried by four men (cf. *b. Menaḥ.* 98a–b). These must be consecrated priests (e.g., Num 4:5–6; Joshua 3–4, 6). 1 Sam 6:19 and 2 Sam 6:6–7 describe the dire consequences if a layman handles the Chest.

The Bible describes the Chest as being carried before the people on the march and borne into battle as a palladium (Num 10:33–36; 14:44; Joshua 6; 1 Samuel 4; 2 Sam 11:11). Seow (1989: 79–144) contends that the Chest was also paraded about in occasional religious processions, just as in Egypt the naos housing the divine image was taken on frequent outings (Sauneron 2000: 92–98) and just as the symbols of Assyrian gods went on periodic parade (e.g., *ANEP* 181 no. 538; see Van Buren 1945; Hrouda and Krecher 1969; Spaey 1994). Ugaritic myth similarly refers to the golden carrying poles of ʾIlu's litter (*KTU* 1.4.i.36–37). And closer to Israel in space but considerably later in time, a third-century C.E. Tyrian coin depicts a shrine with four carrying poles on the bottom (Price and Trell 1977: fig. 40).

25:15. *they shall not be removed from it.* The same is not said for the carrying poles of the Table and the two Altars. On the one hand, that the same rule applies for all four objects might simply be inferred. But, assuming that the staves for the

Table and Altars were stowed when the Tabernacle was assembled, one asks: What is different about the Chest? Cassuto (1967: 330) suggests that since the Chest travels before the people, it must be portable from the instant the cloud lifts from over the Tent (40:36–37; Numbers 9:15–23). In other words, the poles' perpetual emplacement signifies the impermanence of Yahweh's and Israel's desert habitations.

The Priestly Source appears inconsistent, however. For one thing, as Houtman (2000: 378) notes, the poles' installation is recorded in both Exod 37:5 and 40:20 (see NOTES). More important, according to Num 4:6, when Israel breaks camp, the priests wrap the Chest in fabrics and "set (i.e., insert) its poles," just as is said for the Table and Altar (Num 4:8, 11, 14). Ibn Ezra's solution, that *waśāmû badda(y)w* means "they put its poles (on their shoulders)," is forced, as is Bekhor Shor's inference that Numbers 4 describes only the Tabernacle's *first* disassembly; ever after, the Chest's poles will be left in place.

To resolve this contradiction, I would rather reinterpret Exodus 25:15 to mean *"lest* they [the poles] depart from it" (compare NOTE to 28:32, "it will not be torn"). In other words, *lō(') yāsūrû mimmennû* is not a command for all time but a precaution during transit. Once the Chest is safely deposited, its poles may be removed (cf. Ehrlich 1908: 366–67). But this understanding, too, is difficult. According to 1 Kgs 8:8, the Chest retained its poles in Solomon's Temple, as if Exod 24:15 were understood as an eternal proscription. Perhaps the Priestly Writer just made a mistake in Num 4:6, or there was a contradiction in his sources.

25:16. *Testimony.* In *'ēdūt* (generally spelled *'ēdût*), several semantic and etymological streams converge, making it difficult to distinguish denotation from connotation, basic meaning from evocative allusion (see below, and Simian-Yofre [1999] for full data and bibliographical references).

In Exod 25:16, *'ēdūt* primarily connotes the Chest's contents, i.e., the tablets (ibn Ezra, Rashbam; cf. Seow 1984: 193–94). The Chest can therefore be called *'ărôn hā'ēdût* 'the Testimony Chest' (25:22, 26:33–34, etc.; also *hā'ēdût* alone in Exod 16:34; 27:21; 30:36; Num 17:19, 25). Similarly, the Tabernacle is *miškan hā'ēdût* 'the Testimony Tabernacle' (38:21; Num 1:50, 53; 10:11) or *'ōhel hā'ēdût* 'the Testimony Tent' (Num 9:15; 17:22–23; 18:2; cf. 2 Chr 24:6). The fabric screening the Chest is *pārōket hā'ēdût* 'the Testimony Veil' (Lev 24:3).

As vocalized in MT, *'ēdūt* is composed of *'ēd* 'witness' plus the suffix *-ūt* connoting abstraction (GKC §86k)—hence "Testimony" (LXX *martyria/on*). In Rabbinic Hebrew (but not Biblical), *'ēdūt* connotes an ordinary judicial deposition. *'Ēd* 'witness' is related to the verb *hē'îd* (root *'wd*) meaning both "depose, call as witness" and "admonish, warn" (Schwartz 1996: 126 n. 52). In poetry, *'ēdût* is associated with *tôrâ* 'direction, law' (Ps 19:8; 78:5), *ḥōq* 'rule' and *mišpāṭ* 'judgment, law' (Ps 81:5–6).

What is a "Testimony"? The Bible calls various objects "witnesses" (*'ēd*): lambs, a cairn, a carcass (?), an altar (Gen 21:30; 31:44, 48, 52; Exod 22:12 [?]; Josh 22:27–28, 34; Isa 19:20). Recall that the Priestly Source conceives of its laws as the terms of a covenant. The typical ancient Near Eastern political covenant treaty features blessings and curses, along with the invocation of divine *witnesses* to enforce them (see pp. 34–35, 301–2). Deuteronomy frequently refers to covenant witnesses—Heaven and Earth (Deut 4:26; 30:19), Moses' song (Deut 31:19–21, 28), the Law (Deut 31:26)—and in Josh 24:22, the people themselves are covenant witnesses. Blessings and curses we find in Leviticus 26 (P), but where are the witnesses to P's covenant? Presumably inside the Testimony Chest.

Modern epigraphic discoveries from the Semitic realm have further enriched and complicated the semantic profile of *ʿēdût*. We find in the eighth-century B.C.E. Aramaic inscriptions from Sefire (*KAI* 222–24) a plural noun *ʿdy* (absolute *ʿdn*; construct *ʿdy*) describing a suzerainty treaty (for discussion, see Lemaire and Durand 1984: 91–106). Although the term is found nowhere else in Aramaic, it must have been quite common, since in the eighth century it was borrowed by Akkadian as *adê*. We even find the expression *ṭuppī adê* 'treaty tablets' (*CAD* 1.1.133), recalling Hebrew *lūḥōt hāʿēdût* 'the Testimony Tablets' (31:18; 32:15; 34:29).

Why Aramaic *ʿdy* (pronounced **ʿadayyā*) should be plural is unclear. It may connote the abstraction of a political relationship (cf. Segert 1975: 333–34); it may refer to the specific treaty stipulations (Volkwein 1969: 33; Seow 1984: 193; cf. Hebrew *ʿēd[əw]ōt* in 2 Kgs 17:15; 23:3; Ps 25:10; 132:12); it may refer to divine witnesses to the treaty (Hebrew *ʿēdîm*) (see Parnas 1975). In any case, given the striking similarity to *ʿadayyā*, many today simply render Hebrew *ʿēdût* as "Covenant" (as did I in Exod 16:34). In premodern times, exegetes had already suggested this meaning, especially since the Chest is called both *ʾărôn hāʿēdût* and *ʾărôn habbərît*, the latter clearly meaning "Covenant Chest" (cf. already Calvin). Presumably, Hebrew appropriated Aramaic *ʿadayyā* as *ʿēdût* when Israel came into painful contact with the Assyrian Empire, which often conducted its foreign affairs in Aramaic (2 Kgs 18:26).

I am slightly uneasy, however, at the casual assumptions that *ʿēdût* and *bərît* are synonyms, and that the former is borrowed from Aramaic. If they meant the same thing, why did the Priestly Writer not stick with the traditional *bərît* (cf. Seow 1984: 191–92)? The equation *ʿadayyā* = *ʿēdût* is also too facile; we should rather have expected a Hebrew form **ʿādîm*. And yet the vocalization *ʿēdût* goes back at least to the third century B.C.E., as shown by LXX *martyria/on* 'testimony.' Indeed, it is possible that *ʿēdût* existed as a loanword already in twelfth-century B.C.E. Egyptian *ʿdwti*, connoting a relationship among partners (Grintz 1975: 171; Kitchen 1979: 460). If so, the Hebrew form is actually older than the Aramaic and cannot be derived from it (see, however, Lemaire and Durand [1984: 98] for reservations on the Egyptian evidence).

Given these difficulties, I think a better parallel to Hebrew *ʿēdût* is Ugaritic *tʿdt*, which means something like "legally valid sign" or "evidence" (cf. Smith 1997: 246 n. 85; note that Hebrew *təʿûdâ* parallels *tôrâ* in Isa 8:16, 20). The Aramaic term closest in meaning to *ʿēdût* is not *ʿadayyā* but rather *ś/sāhădû(tā)* 'testimony,' which translates *ʿēdût* in Syr and Tgs. and is the equivalent of Hebrew *ʿēd* 'witness' in Gen 31:47.

SPECULATION: Our difficulty ascertaining the precise meaning of *ʿēdût* suggests that two or three distinct Semitic roots may have coalesced in Hebrew.

Most directly underlying *'ēdût* is *'wd*, which probably originally meant "repeat," as in Arabic *'āda* 'return' and Ethiopic *'ōda* 'go around' (cf. Hebrew *'ôd* 'iteration, continuance, again'). On the other hand, *'hd* in Arabic and Old South Arabic means "entrust, promise, contract," whence Aramaic *'dy'* 'treaty' (Lemaire and Durand 1984: 100-1; on the linguistic development, cf. GKC §77.5). Arabic also has *wa'ada* 'promise,' while South Arabic has *'wd* 'establish peaceful relations,' also apropos of covenants. Perhaps the fullest interpretation of *'ēdût* would be "token of a pact."

However he understood the term, the Priestly Writer probably favored *'ēdût* for its resonance with other theme words. For example, *'ēdût* chimes with P's common designation for Israel: *(hā)'ēdâ* '(the) congregation.' Moreover, the phrase *'ōhel hā'ēdût* "the Testimony Tent" evokes the Tabernacle's frequent designation *'ōhel mô'ēd* 'Meeting Tent' (cf. LXX *hē skēnē tou martyriou* 'the Tent of the Testimony'). While *'ēdâ* and *mô'ēd* both derive from the root *y'd* 'to meet,' another important Priestly theme word is an anagram: *yd'* 'to know (experientially, covenantally)' (Huffmon 1966; Huffmon and Parker 1966). Thus the Testimony (*'ēdût*) Tablets bear witness (*'ēd*), admonishing (*hē'îd*) the community (*'ēdâ*) to fulfill its covenant obligations (*'ēd[əw]ōt*), since God has made himself "known" (*yd'*) to them and continues to encounter (*y'd*) them at Meeting (*mô'ēd*) Tent. (See also pp. 691-94.)

Lastly, what exactly is the *'ēdūt* stored inside the Chest? In the received text, it is the stone tablets containing the Decalog (31:18; 32:15; 34:28-29). But I am not sure that the pristine Priestly source knows either tablets or Decalog (cf. Dillmann 1880: 262-63; above, pp. 366-67). One might instead suppose that in P, the Chest contains the Tabernacle instructions (cf. Beegle 1972: 262) or perhaps the model or plans revealed to Moses. But why should the heart of the Tabernacle be a verbal or material image of itself? Overall, it is more reasonable to suppose that for P, the *'ēdūt* is a covenant document of some sort, perhaps the Decalog after all. But it functions more as talisman than text, an artifact whose mere existence validates the unchanging Covenant between Yahweh and Israel (similarly Schwartz 1996: 126).

25:17. *pure gold.* Since Yahweh's presence will appear over the *kappōret*, it must be *pure* gold, unlike the gold-plated Chest beneath (Bekhor Shor).

kappōret. This is another richly ambivalent term, unique to P (*kprt* in an alphabetic cuneiform tablet from Taanak has nothing to do with Exodus and is in any case a disputed reading [Janowski 1982: 62-63]). To express the main alternatives, LXX uses a double rendering: *hilastērion epithema* 'Propitiatory Lid' (Koch 1995: 67-68). Still today, some consider *kappōret* a ritual term describing purification and atonement; for others, it simply means "cover."

On the one hand, the Hebrew root *kpr* most often connotes ritual purification, expiation and reconciliation—in my translation, "Clearing" (NOTE to 29:33). Presumably, then, *kappōret* means "place of Clearing (*kippūrîm*)." As the centerpiece of Yahweh's holy Tabernacle, each year on Yom Kippur the *kappōret* receives the blood of the Sin-offering whereby both the people and the Tabernacle are "cleared" and Yahweh's continued presence is assured (Lev 16:14–15) (*Exod. Rab.* 50:4; cf. ibn Ezra). Yahweh's spirit can abide only in a place of utmost ritual cleanliness, atop the *kappōret.*

The alternative approach is mundanely literal: *kappōret* simply means "cover, lid" (Saadiah, Rashi, *Root Books* of ibn Janaḥ and Qimḥi). After the equivocating LXX, our oldest exponent of this interpretation is 4QtgLev 1:6, which renders *kappōret* as *ksy'* 'covering.' Linguists marshal philological support from Arabic *kafara* 'cover' and from select biblical passages (NOTE to 29:33). Admittedly, the Bible calls no other lid *kappōret*, the ordinary term being *delet* (2 Kgs 12:10) (Baentsch 1903: 224). Still, the syntax of 25:17—"make *a kappōret*," not "*the kappōret*"—implies that we have a common noun, albeit rare. In any case, P treats the *kappōret* as a distinctive item, associated with but not simply part of the Chest (Haran 1978: 250).

However he understood the word, the Priestly Writer probably chose *kappōret* (original pronunciation **kappurt*) to evoke *kippūrîm* and possibly also the Tabernacle Veil (*pārōket*, originally pronounced **parrukt*). There is also a certain similarity to **kurūb (kərûb)* 'Griffin.'

SPECULATION: I should mention two additional, Egyptological approaches to *kappōret*, though they currently seem far-fetched. First, Grintz (1975: 163–67) supposes a metathesis of Egyptian *k3p* 'cover.' Second, since some Israelites conceived the Chest to be Yahweh's footstool (below, pp. 519–21), Görg (1977) detects a borrowing from Egyptian *kp (n) rdwy* 'soles of the two feet.' But *kp (n) rdwy* does not mean "footstool" in Egyptian.

length . . . breadth. Like the Chest on which it rests, the *kappōret* measures c. 3.75 feet/1.25 m. by 2.25 feet/0.75 m. As no width is indicated, it must be fairly thin (*pace b. Sukk.* 4b–5b, which claims that the *kappōret* was a span in thickness).

25:18. *Griffins.* Although Hebrew *kərūb* has entered English as "cherub," I have chosen instead "Griffin," lest one envision a humanoid angel or, worse, a pudgy toddler (cf. already *b. Sukk.* 5b; *Ḥag.* 13b). English "Griffin" comes from Greek *gryps, gryphos*, probably in turn derived from Semitic *kərūb* (Wellhausen 1885: 304; Cassuto and Barnett 1962: 240). The link to Greece may have been the Phoenicians; a damaged Punic text from Saint-Monique contains the sequence *krbm* in an unclear context (*KAI* 96.2).

The etymology of *kərūb* is uncertain. Since the Griffin is Yahweh's mount, a perennial guess with little foundation sees an anagram of *rkb* 'ride' (e.g., I. Reggio *apud* Luzzatto), but we do find wordplay between *kərūb* and *rəkûb* 'mount, chariot' in 2 Sam 22 = Ps 18:11; Ps 104:3. More likely, *kərūb* is related to Akkadian *karābu* 'bless' and means "the Blessed" (compare also Old South Arabic *krb* 'vow, consecrate, sacrifice').

While the proper definition of a "Griffin" in English is a winged lion with a falcon's head, the precise composition of the biblical *kərūb* is unclear, and perhaps the term connotes any chimerical being. Griffins appear in three biblical contexts: as a decorative motif in sacred architecture (25:18–22; 26:1, 31; 1 Kgs

6:23–35; 7:36; Ezek 41:18–25), as guardians or denizens of Paradise (Gen 3:24; Ezek 28:14–16) and as the supports of Yahweh's throne or chariot (below, pp. 516–21). Their most consistently mentioned feature is wings (e.g., Exod 25:20; 2 Sam 22:11; 1 Kgs 6:24, 27; Ezek 10:1–19). Ezekiel 1 and 10 portray the Griffins in greatest detail, but these four-winged, four-faced, wheeled creatures correspond to nothing in ancient art, and the prophet himself does not recognize them at first (Ezek 10:20, but cf. 9:3). Most likely Ezekiel synthesizes several types of monsters—the winged, bird-headed human; the winged, human-headed ox, and the winged, human-headed lion (cf. Metzger 1985: 312–25; Freedman and O'Connor 1995: 316–18). All these are well attested in ancient art, particularly from Mesopotamia, and may have been regarded by Ezekiel as partial representations or manifestations of a single creature. It is even possible that Hebrew *kərūb* (original pronunciation **kurūb*) is a borrowing from Akkadian *kāribu/kāribtu/ kurību*, describing cultic images (Hyatt 1980: 267; see, however, the cautions of Freedman and O'Connor 1995: 308–9). For exemplary illustrations of composite monsters from seventh-century B.C.E. Urartu, see Muscarella (1981: 183).

Scholars most often imagine Yahweh's Griffins in the Tabernacle and Temple as constituting his throne (see COMMENT, pp. 515–21). But on what exactly does God sit? While Haran (1978: 252) and Mettinger (1982: 22–23) envision the Griffins' inner wings meeting to form a seat, I know of no pictorial evidence supporting such a view and have difficulty interpreting 1 Kgs 6:23–27; 8:7; 1 Chr 28:18; 2 Chr 3:10–13; 5:7–8 in this manner. In Ezekiel 1 and in all ancient depictions (e.g., Megiddo ivory, fig. 2 [*ANEP* fig. 332, p. 111]; Ahiram sarcophagus [*ANEP* fig. 458, p. 158]), the Griffins do not support the god or king directly but rather uphold his chair.

What does the biblical Griffin symbolize? Perpetuating ancient imagery, Hebrew poetry often depicts Yahweh as a sky-riding storm god (among many discussions, see Cross 1973: 91–194; Weinfeld 1970b; Day 1985; Batto 1992; Green 2003). Accordingly, Yahweh's celestial servitors are sometimes called *rûḥōt* 'spirits, winds.' For example, 1 Kgs 22:19–24 describes Yahweh as enthroned among beings called both *rûḥōt* 'winds/spirits' and *ṣəbā' haššāmayim* 'Heavens' Army.' One of these spirits descends to inspire the prophets. Ps 104:3 describes Heaven's *rûḥōt* as *winged* storms, while 2 Sam 22:11 = Ps 18:11 further identifies the *rûḥōt* with Yahweh's Griffin(s) (on *kərūb* as possibly collective [cf. Ezek 10:2, 4], see Cassuto and Barnett 1962: 239). In 2 Sam 22:11 = Ps 18:11, Yahweh "mounts" *(rkb)* the Griffin(s); similarly, Ps 104:3 anagrammatically calls the winged wind Yahweh's "mount" or "chariot" *(rəkûb)*. Ezekiel 1 describes the Griffins as gusting, flaring and roaring like a storm. In short the biblical Griffins personify the tempest, recalling Sumerian *IM.DUGUD*, the lion-headed storm bird of the gods (Jacobsen 1976: 128–29).

SPECULATION: In light of the Akkadian and South Arabic cognates referring to blessing and worship, one might also understand the Griffins as conveying Israel's hymns and prayers up to Heaven, and Yahweh's blessings down to Earth. Playing with the cliché *yōšēb hakkərūbîm* 'seated (upon) the Griffins,' Ps 22:4 calls Yahweh *yōšēb təhillôt yiśrā'ēl* 'seated (upon) Israel's psalms' (Houtman 2000: 385).

FIGURE 2. Megiddo ivory (detail restored)

For more about the Griffins, see NOTES to 25:20 and COMMENT, pp. 517–19.

gold; miqšâ. The MT trope requires this syntactic division. A pause between *zāhāb* and *miqšâ* is also suggested by the parallel in 25:31, "And you shall make a Lampstand of pure gold; *miqšâ* the Lampstand shall be made." LXX, however, considers *zhb mqšh* a compound, paraphrasing the verse: "And you shall make two cherubim *of* carved gold *and* you shall *put* them on both the sides of the Propitiation (i.e., *kappōret*)."

The meaning of *miqšâ* is uncertain. It is used here and in 37:7 of the Griffins, and also of the golden Lampstand (25:31, 36; 37:17, 22; Num 8:4) and the silver trumpets (Num 10:2). Since the root *qšy* means "to be hard," one might imagine a particularly durable alloy, but that seems incompatible with "pure gold" (25:31). Meyers (1976: 32–33) suggests that *miqšâ* refers to a wooden substructure, but, while this might work for the Griffins and the Lampstand, it is less likely for the trumpets.

The consensus is rather that *miqšâ* refers to hammered metalwork, since that is how one shapes a brass instrument (LXX, Vg, *b. Menaḥ.* 28a). Perhaps the beating not only shapes but also makes designs *(repoussé)*. Accordingly, the Griffins are fashioned hollow from hammered sheets of gold. As for etymology, Rashi aptly cites Aramaic *nəqaš* 'knock, beat' (we might repoint MT as **miqqəšâ* or *maqqāšâ*

< *nqš*), while Meyers (1976: 34) adds the Aramaic quadriliteral roots *qšqš/kškš/ gšgš*, which onomatopoetically mean "strike, knock." But to my knowledge, these terms are not used of metalworking.

The text declines to give the Griffins' dimensions, which would presumably depend on Israel's generosity. And the Griffins' physical relation to the *kappōret* is also moot. By the conventional understanding of *min-hakkappōret* (v 19), the Griffins are of one piece with the pure gold lid (see NOTE, "on the *kappōret*"), and so must be pure gold themselves, even if v 18 refers simply to "gold" (Holzinger 1900: 121). But more likely they are made of a lesser grade of gold and subsequently soldered on (see further below).

on the kappōret's . . . ends. Perhaps *miššənê qəṣôt hakkappōret* should be understood as "*slightly in from* the *kappōret's* two ends"; see NOTE to 25:19, "on this end here." In any case, the Griffins are placed at the *kappōret's* two short sides (figs. 1a–b).

two. The masculine number *šnê* is correct. Although the plural *qāṣôt* 'ends' looks feminine, it is generally construed as masculine (25:18, 19; 28:7, 23, 26; 37:7–8; 39:4, 16, 19; Isa 41:5). There are only four examples of the feminine (Exod 27:4; 28:25; 39:18; Jer 49:36).

25:19. *on this end here. Miqqāṣâ mizze(h)*, literally "*from* an end, from here," may mean that the Griffins are not quite at the *kappōret's* extremities but slightly to the center (Jacob 1992: 776).

on the kappōret. Most commentators take *min-hakkappōret* in a quasi-partitive sense: "as a part of, of one piece with the *kappōret*" (Rashi). Similar expressions appear in 25:26, 31, 35; 27:2; 28:8; 30:2; 37:8, 17; 38:2; 39:5 (see NOTES). If so, we must read v 17 in the light of v 18 and vice versa. That is, both the *kappōret* and the Griffins are made of beaten, pure gold.

The Syriac Version, however, exhibits some instructive vacillation. In 37:8, Syr paraphrases "*above* the *kappōret*"; in 25:19, it joins the phrase to what precedes, perhaps correctly: "the other side of the *kappōret*." Why does Syr decline the more obvious rendering "from, out of the *kappōret*"?

It is clear in the preceding matter that *miššənê qəṣôt hakkappōret* (v 18) and *miqqāṣâ mizze(h)* (v 19) describe the Griffins' location: they are not *from*, but *on* or *in from* the ends (see NOTES above). *Min-hakkappōret*, therefore, may clarify *miqqāṣâ mizze(h)* 'from this end here'—i.e., this end of the *kappōret*, thus reiterating v 19. This rather orotund description is further rounded out and clarified at the end of v 19, where *ʿal-šnê qəṣôtā(y)w* can only mean "*on* its ends." As further evidence that *min* 'from' is here synonymous to *ʿal* 'on,' in 25:19 *ʿal-šnê qəṣôtā(y)w* corresponds to *miššənê qəṣôtā(y)w* in 37:8. In short, I think that v 19 tells us not *how* the Griffins are connected to the *kappōret* but *where* they are located.

Even by the usual interpretation, *min-hakkappōret* need not mean that the Griffins and *kappōret* are formed from a single ingot. They might simply protude from the *kappōret*, permanently soldered on (Kennedy 1898: 665), just as the Ephod's girdle is attached to the Ephod (28:8) (see further NOTES to 25:31, "from it"; 28:8, "from it"). If so, the Griffins are presumably made from a harder grade of gold (Jacob 1992: 776), since they are delicate in structure. (Admittedly, this concession to practicality would violate the general principle that objects closest to the divine presence are of the purest gold.)

its two ends. This seems the most likely interpretation, despite the fact that *kappōret* is feminine, while the pronominal suffix on *qaṣôtā(y)w* 'its ends' is masculine (*pace* Jacob [1992: 776], who thinks the suffix refers to each Griffin).

The chances are excellent that here and throughout Exodus 25–28, 37, 39, MT misvocalizes the consonants *qṣwt*. We should read the plural not as MT *qāṣôt* (suffixed *qaṣôtā[y]w* in 25:19) but as **qaṣāwōt* (i.e., we should vocalize **qiṣwōtā[y]w* in 25:19). The evidence is twofold. First, against the tendency in this section of Exodus to spell the feminine plural defectively (e.g., *-t* vs. *-wt*), this word is always written *qṣwt* (in fact, in the entire MT we never find **qṣt/qāṣōt*). Second and more significant, in 37:8; 39:4, the Kethibh is the *lectio difficilior qṣwwt*, as one might expect at Qumran. In other words, while *qṣwt* is ambiguous, *qṣwwt* is not and points to the vocalization **qaṣāwōt*, a form MT preserves in 38:5; Ps 65:9; note, too, *qaṣwê* 'ends (of),' with the construct masculine plural suffix, in Isa 26:15; Ps 48:11; 65:6.

25:20. *spreading.* The root *prś* here refers to wings (also Deut 32:11; 1 Kgs 6:27). Elsewhere, however, it describes extending fabric, e.g., of a garment (Num 4:7–13; Deut 22:17; Judg 8:25; Ezek 16:8; Ruth 3:9) or a tent (Exod 40:19). *Pōraśê* is the first of three words in v 20 that, while ostensibly describing the winged Griffins, evoke textile and protective imagery. See following NOTES.

wings. Literally, "two wings" (*kənāpayim*). The word *kānāp* can also describe the ends of a garment (e.g., Deut 22:12; 23:1; 1 Sam 15:27; 24:5–12; Ezek 16:8; Ruth 3:9). See NOTES above and below.

screening. Although Griffins can be associated with enthronement (pp. 517–18), Exodus 25 does not describe a throne (*pace* Haran 1978: 251, 254). There is no seat, no armrests, no footstool; the creatures do not stand side-by-side but face each other. To judge from the iconographic parallels, they either kneel or stand with wings swept forward (figs. 1a–b, pp. 378–79) (Metzger 1985: 1.312, 331). There is no way this can be envisioned as a throne (see further COMMENT, pp. 518–19).

The root *skk* 'screen, shelter, canopy' culminates the textile allusions in v 20 (see previous NOTES). The derived nouns *sukkâ/sōk/sāk* refer to tents and other shelters, including the Tabernacle's successor, the Temple (Ps 27:5; 31:21; 42:5; 76:3; Lam 2:6) (see Homan 2002: 9–11). Ezek 28:14–16, too, in an obscure context, refers to *kərûb hassōkēk* 'the screening Griffin.' The golden Griffins of the *kappōret* "screen" (*skk*) over Yahweh's presence by spreading (*prś*) their wings (*kənāpayim*) (cf. 1 Kgs 6:27; 8:7; 1 Chr 28:18; 2 Chr 5:8). This creates a sort of miniature Tabernacle within the Tabernacle.

What does this canopy of wings represent? According to P, Yahweh's presence is hidden/revealed in a cloud ('*ānān*) of incense above the *kappōret*, thus beneath the Griffins' sheltering wings (Lev 16:2, 13). Heavenly clouds (also '*ānān*) are themselves sometimes compared to a tent or canopy and described as "spread" (Exod 40:35 [note *škn*]; Ps 105:39; Job 36:29) or winged (see below). In particular, the theophany in 2 Sam 22:11–12 features several linguistic contacts with Exod 25:20: "And he mounted on Griffin (*kərûb*) and took flight (MT 'appeared') and soared on wind's wings *(kanpê)*; and he set the dark around him (as) his shelter *(sukkôt)*" (compare Ps 18:11–12). Ps 104:2–4 also describes Yahweh as a storm god both wearing and inhabiting the luminous tissue *(śalmâ, yərî'â)* of the heavens and mounted on the storm cloud, soaring with "wind's wings" (see below, pp. 677–80). Also evocative of Exod 25:20 is Job 36:29: *miprəśê-'āb . . . sukkātô* 'spreading cloud . . . his canopy.' And cloud and canopy are again associated in Isa 4:5–6: "cloud *('ānān)* by day and smoke and radiance of flame-fire by night, indeed a pavilion over all Glory; and a shelter *(sukkâ)* will be for a shade by day." So in one sense, the cloud of incense between the Griffins may symbolize Yahweh's heavenly presence amid the storm clouds.

There is another network of passages, primarily psalmic, that apply the terms "spread," "wing" and "canopy" to God's tent. The imagery is not frightening or even majestic but rather comforting, with associated vocabulary such as *ḥsy* 'take refuge,' *sēter* 'hiding place' and *ṣel* 'shadow, shelter.' For example, Yahweh is said to protect his elect in "his *wings'* shelter" (Ps 17:8; 31:21 [emended]; 36:8; 57:2; 63:8) (cf. NOTE to 31:2, "Bezalel"). In Ps 91:4, 11, for instance, we read, "With his pinion he screens *(skk)* for you, and under his wings you take refuge. . . . For he commands his (angelic) Messengers concerning you, to guard you in all your ways." The imagery simultaneously evokes a mother bird shielding her chicks and Yahweh's winged Griffins. God's protecting *kənāpayim* may also be his skirts, which a man spreads over a woman to offer his protection, generally in marriage (Ezek 16:8). For example, Boaz lauds Ruth for figuratively "taking refuge under his [Yahweh's] *kənāpayim* 'wings' " (2:12)—but she literally takes refuge under Boaz's outspread *(prś)* skirt *(kānāp)* (3:9). The homology of garments, tents and winged creatures is explicit in Ps 104:1–4 and implicit in Exodus, where the Tabernacle curtains and the priestly vestments are made of the same fabric, and the former are patterned with Griffins (but see NOTE to 26:1, "Griffins").

These passages illuminate Exodus primarily through contrast. In the Psalter, the image of God's winged, overspreading presence is reassuring. Yahweh is like a mother bird sheltering her young, or like a man extending his possessive protection over a woman, or like a nomad patriarch offering asylum to the fugitive. In P's world, however, the protection afforded by Yahweh's wings is entirely different. The psalmists sing as if anyone could take shelter within the Tabernacle, even in the Holy of Holies, even beneath the Griffins' very wings. Such a notion would be anathema for P, which insists that Israelites keep their proper distance. Only the Great Priest, the maximally pure human, and he but once a year, may approach the *kappōret* to obtain Clearing *(kippūr)* for the nation—and under no circumstance would he actually mount the *kappōret*. In P, Yahweh does not shelter *(skk)* over the oppressed. Instead his sculpted servants shelter over the divine Presence itself.

their faces (each) man toward his brother, toward the kappōret. On first reading, the description seems confusing. How can the Griffins face both one another and the lid? One possibility is that, like the Griffins of Ezek 41:18–19, each has two faces (for iconographic parallels, see de Vaux 1967: 242 n. 1). But surely P would have made this clear. The majority view is that the Griffins face each other with heads reverently bowed toward the Chest and *kappōret*, so as not to behold Yahweh (ibn Ezra [shorter commentary]; Bekhor Shor; Cassuto 1967: 335; Haran 1978: 153; Sarna 1986: 195–96). Yet, out of hundreds of representations of such beasts from around the ancient Near East, not one is depicted in so neck-straining a position. Cutting the Gordian Knot, some commentators even cite the supposed impossibility of the posture as evidence of textual conflation or expansion (e.g., Koch 1959: 12).

More likely, 25:20 simply says the same thing twice chiastically: facing each other, the Griffins gaze across the *kappōret*, rather than turning outward away from it (Japheth ben Ali *apud* ibn Ezra; Rashbam; Holzinger 1900: 122; Jacob 1992: 777). Similarly in 2 Chr 3:13, a text combining aspects of Solomon's Temple with the Tabernacle, the Griffins of the Temple are said to face inward (*ûp[ə]nêhem labbayit*). In emphasizing that the Griffins face one another rather than stand side-by-side, the Priestly Writer minimizes the *kappōret*'s similarity to a throne. See further pp. 390, 518–19.

25:21. *you shall set the Testimony.* The redundancy, even greater in MT than in my translation (see TEXTUAL NOTE), creates a chiastic frame with 25:16, surrounding the *kappōret* instructions: "And you shall set into the Chest the Testimony . . . and into the Chest you shall set the Testimony" (cf. Rashi). The purpose is to remind the reader of the first reason that the *kappōret* is important: it covers the Testimony within the Chest. The second reason is made plain in the next verse.

25:22. *I will be meetable.* Or "I will make myself available"; cf. 29:42–43; 30:6, 36; Num 17:19 (compare also Lev 16:2; Num 7:89). The space over the *kappōret* is the locus for Yahweh's presence on Earth.

The choice of the verb *wanô'adtî* creates numerous paronomastic overtones. First, the root *y'd* provides P's explanation for the Tabernacle's other name, *'ōhel mô'ēd* 'Meeting Tent.' Second, P's contribution to the Book of Exodus is framed by wordplay between *y'd* 'meet' and *yd'* 'know, experience, have a covenantal relationship' (6:3; 29:43; see Smith 1997: 268–69). (On "knowledge" as a theme in all sources of Exodus, see INTRODUCTION, vol. I, p. 37; but correct my careless misreading of 25:22.) Third, we must recognize the allusion to *'ēdūt* 'Testimony' (cf. Cassuto 1967: 336; NOTE to 25:16). Again, the punning is not gratuitous or decorative: it discloses P's understanding of Yahweh's relationship with the profane world, otherwise too impure to coexist with his Holiness. By the terms of his Covenant, Yahweh's presence is drawn to the Testimony in Meeting Tent, where an annual rite of purification over the *kappōret* permits him and Israel to remain in physical and legal contact (Leviticus 16).

there. The text precisely delineates the small space from which the cosmic God's voice will emerge: "there," "atop the *kappōret*," "from between the two Griffins," "on the Testimony Chest." The Tabernacle's two foci, together corresponding to the polytheist's idol, are Yahweh's intangible, transitory presence above the Chest and his eternal pact with Israel inside it (see further pp. 518–19, 694–95).

According to 25:22; 30:6; Num 7:89, Yahweh continues to speak to Moses from the *kappōret* throughout his life — even though, as a nonpriest, Moses should be barred from entry. Evidently, the Lawgiver stands above these rules.

There is no indication that the Great Priest will ever hear Yahweh's voice from between the Griffins. I infer that, for P, God falls silent after Moses' death, his Word enshrined in the written Testimony. Since P foresees no future role for prophecy, messages from God will be conveyed through the Urim and Thummim (NOTE to 28:29).

I shall command you for Israel's Sons. In other words, Moses is the intermediary between Yahweh and the people. See TEXTUAL NOTE for the Syr and *Tg. Neofiti I* interpretation "*concerning ('al)* Israel's Sons."

Other ancient Near Easterners also heard voices emerging from within their divine images, functionally equivalent to the Bible's Chest-*kappōret* ensemble (see pp. 518–19, 694–95). But this was no miracle. By secret hiding places and hidden tubes, the priests (cynically? piously?) caused the gods to speak (e.g., Sauneron 2000: 99). Whether Israelite priests also engaged in holy ventriloquism is unknown. If they did, we would expect to hear about it from their critics the prophets.

25:23. *table.* It is also called "the Pure Table" (Lev 24:4, 6) and "the *Face* Table," because it held the "*Face* Bread" (Num 4:7; see NOTE to 25:30). On the function and symbolism of sacred tables, see COMMENT, pp. 507–9; on Phoenician tables, see Gubel (1987: 241–61).

cubits. The Table is roughly 3 feet long (1 m.), 1.5 feet (0.5 m.) wide and c. 2.25 feet (0.75 m.) tall.

25:24. *plate.* See NOTE to 25:11.

zēr. On this problematic term, see NOTE to 25:11. In this case, the *zēr* is either a raised band around the table top to prevent the bread from sliding off, or else a molding around the side to cover the bare wood (Rashbam), perhaps with a wreath-like motif (cf. Aramaic *zîrā'* 'wreath, crown'). It may or may not be the same as the *zēr* on the frame mentioned in v 25 (see NOTE below).

25:25. *frame.* The *misgeret*, literally "enclosure," apparently provides structural support. The Table's carrying poles are thrust through rings attached to its legs. The ensuing stress is distributed by affixing the frame at the same height (see figs. 3a–b).

It is unclear at what height the poles and frame are attached. On the weathered Arch of Titus, the Roman conquerors hoist the Second Temple's Table shoulder-high, with the sacred trumpets fastened to its side (fig. 4). But these poles could have been supplied by the Romans themselves, since the Lampstand is carried in the same manner, even though no biblical text indicates that it had poles (fig. 6, p. 400). For the Table of Exodus, if the poles are at the feet, so that the Table is borne as high as possible (cf. Jacob 1992: 802), the frame actually constitutes a base (see fig. 3a). Or the frame and poles might be halfway down the legs, for maximal strength (Cassuto 1976: 338), as with the Bronze Altar (27:4–5). If, however, the poles are just under the table top and bear some of its weight, then the frame also attaches the legs to the top (fig. 3b; cf. *b. Menaḥ.* 96b; *Sukk.* 5a; Jacob 1992: 778). (Another approach, which I find less plausible, sees the frame as resting *upon* the table top, holding the bread in place [cf. *b. Menaḥ.* 96b; Rashbam; Luzzatto]. I

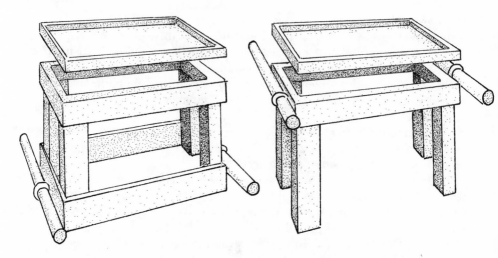

FIGURES 3a–b. Table (alternative, exploded views)

FIGURE 4. Arch of Titus (detail)

suppose that, by this theory, the rings for the poles are located upon the legs directly under the table top, hence "aligned with the frame" [see, however, Luzzatto].)

handbreadth's. C. 3 inches/8 cm.

zēr. It is not clear whether this rim is identical to that of the preceding verse (see NOTE). Jacob (1992: 779) agrees with Rashi and ibn Ezra: there is only one *zēr.* It is mentioned first in v 24; then v 25 digresses to explain that it is attached to the frame. In other words, we have a type of *Wiederaufnahme,* or resumptive repetition (cf. Kuhl 1952). Dillmann (1880: 283), however, finds two "rims," one associated with the table top, the other with the legs and frame. On the possible relationship between the *zēr* and the poles, see NOTE to 25:11, "*zēr.*"

25:26. *make.* Previously in 25:12, Moses was told to "cast" (*ysq*) gold rings (cf. 37:13; 38:5). After specifying their technique of manufacture, the text uses the less precise *'śy* 'make' (Jacob 1992: 779).

and set the rings. The clause division in 25:26–27 is not entirely clear; my punctuation follows the MT cantillation. An alternative rendering would be "and set the rings on the four corners which are of its four legs, aligned with the frame. The rings shall be housings for poles. . . ." But in that case, we might have expected the verb to be the converted perfect *wəhāyû, not the jussive *tihye(y)nā.*

four corners . . . four legs. Why not simply say "on the four legs"? One possibility is that here *pē'â* is a synonym for *pa'am* 'foot,' used in a comparable context in 25:12. If so, the text is clarifying the location of the poles, and probably the frame as well, at the bottom of the Table (fig. 3a).

The text never states whether the poles run parallel to the two-cubit sides or to the one-cubit sides; cf. my discussion of the Chest above (NOTE to 25:12, "flank"). If we follow the analogy of the Chest, they should be affixed to the short sides.

25:27. *Aligned with the frame.* On the interpretation of *lə'ummat hammisgeret,* see NOTE to 25:25, "frame."

housings. Here and in 26:29; 30:4; 36:34; 37:14, 27; 38:5, the unusual term *bāttîm,* literally "houses," may have been chosen for its assonance with *baddîm* 'poles' (Cassuto 1967: 338–39).

poles. Like the Chest, the Table was too sacred to be touched directly.

25:28. *and the Table shall be carried by them.* On the superfluous direct object marker *'et-* before the subject of a passive verb, see GKC §121*a–b.*

25:29. *bowls . . . spoons . . . dippers . . . rinsers.* We are not told the number or size of these golden vessels, nor is their relation to the Table and its bread arrangement entirely clear. According to 37:16, they are set directly on the Table.

The first item, *qə'ārōt,* are dishes or bowls; compare Arabic *q'r* 'be deep' (sometimes describing a bowl) (Luzzatto; Dillmann 1880: 283). Num 7:13, etc., mention large, silver *qə'ārōt* weighing 130 shekels (c. 4.3 lbs./1.5 kg.), filled with oil and bran. In Exod 25:29, since the following items are probably for censing and libating, most commentators infer that the bowls are for the bread itself. Bekhor Shor thinks of mixing bowls for dough, while Rashbam envisions molds in which the bread is baked. One might think, however, that these preparations were performed in a bakery, not in the Tabernacle itself. The more common view is that the dishes are for *displaying* the baked bread (cf. Rashi), although we might have expected a flat vessel, more a tray than a bowl. So the bowls' function remains moot.

Kappōt are spoons, presumably for incense as in Numbers 7. Lev 24:7 states more clearly that the Face Bread is accompanied by incense, most likely burned upon the adjacent Golden Altar (Milgrom 2001: 2095–96). Incense is generally associated with grain offerings (e.g., Lev 2:1–9; Isa 1:13; 43:23; Jer 17:26; 41:5; Ps 141:2; Neh 13:5, 9; on the practice at Elephantine, see Cowley 1923: 30.21, 25; 31.21; 32.9; 33.11).

The tradition regarding the *kappōt* is somewhat diverse. Josephus *Ant.* 3.143, 256 speaks not of spoons but of golden *cups*. And according to 11QTemple VIII:9, 12, incense was set directly upon the bread. But *kappōt* literally are "hands, palms." Archaeologists have uncovered hand-shaped spoons, presumably used for censing, at En-Gev, Megiddo and other sites in Syria-Palestine (Mazar, Dothan and Dunayevsky 1961: 26, pl. 11).

The remaining two items, *qəśāwōt* 'dippers (?)' and *mənaqqiyyōt* 'rinsers (?),' are explicitly associated with liquids (also 37:16; Num 4:7; see next NOTE). The first also appears in Ugaritic, where *qś* parallels *ks* 'cup' (*KTU* 1.3.v.33–34, 4.iv.45–46). (More remote, but also possibly related, is Arabic *qašwiyya*, denoting a container made of straw.) As for the *mənaqqiyyōt* 'rinsers,' the root *nqy* has two basic connotations in Semitic: "to be clean, innocent" (Hebrew, Aramaic, Arabic) and "to pour, libate" (Akkadian, Syriac). Probably these go back to a common proto-Semitic meaning, either "to rinse" or "to empty." Here, Hebrew *mənaqqiyyâ* uniquely bears the Akkadian-Syriac meaning of *nqy* (but note also Ps 26:6; 73:13, "I *wash* my hands in innocence [*niqqāyyôn*]").

from which may be poured. Since P uses the root *nsk* in both the Hiph'il (Num 28:7) and the Qal (Exod 30:9 [MT vocalization]), the verb *yussak* might be construed as either Hoph'al or Qal Passive (cf. Waltke and O'Connor 1990: 373–76 §22.6). For Saadiah and Rashi, however, the root in question is not *nsk* 'pour' but *skk* 'cover.' This follows an implausible Rabbinic tradition that 25:29 describes not vessels but a complicated system of dispay racks (*m. Menaḥ.* 11:6; *b. Menaḥ.* 97a; see the illustration in Lockshin 1997: 316).

The clarification "from which may be poured" may be stimulated by the vessels' unusual names, possibly unfamiliar to readers (see previous NOTE). One might think that the phrase refers only to the "rinsers," named last. But the parallel in 37:16 reads "*its rinsers and the dippers* from which may be poured," reversing the order of 25:29 (see also Num 4:7, "the rinsers and the libation dippers"). If 25:29 is not corrupt (see TEXTUAL NOTE, "its dippers and its rinsers"), the natural inference is that *qəśāwōt* and *mənaqqiyyōt* are *both* used in pouring (Cassuto 1967: 339). And if so, one was probably a large jar in which liquid was transported, the other a dipper.

The greater question is what these vessels are doing on the Table at all. Bekhor Shor suggests they are for pouring water into the bowls for mixing dough—but would one do this in the Tabernacle? Haran (1968: 885) conjectures that they are not used at all but contain symbolic wine changed weekly along with the Face Bread (see next NOTE). But why does the text mention pouring, if one is not supposed to use the vessels? Elsewhere, the root *nsk* connotes a ritual libation of wine vaporized upon the Altar (Num 15:7, 10, 13; 2 Kgs 16:13, 15; see NOTE to 29:40, "libation"), and libations accompany bread offerings in other ancient Near Eastern cultic texts (Gane 1992: 190–91). Perhaps the "dippers" and "rinsers" are for libations upon the Bronze Altar in the Plaza (Luzzatto; Cassuto 1967: 339; but see Milgrom 2001: 2093); according to 30:9, no libations may be made upon the inner Golden Altar standing near the Table. For a fuller discussion, including the possibility of libations within the Tabernacle itself (cf. Num 28:7), presumably on the floor, see Gane (1992: 183–89).

SPECULATION: There are other approaches to the problem. Since the root *nsk* has an alloform *swk* 'wash, cleanse,' the *qəśāwōt* and *mənaqqiyyōt* might be for *rinsing*, as the name of the latter particularly suggests. Just as the Deity symbolically eats bread (see below), so he should be able symbolically to wash his hands when at table. Or perhaps these vessels are for cleaning the Tabernacle furniture, especially the Incense Altar.

Another possibility: *m. Sukk.* 4:9–10; 5:1 describes a yearly water libation on the festival of *Sukkôt* to encourage God to provide rain in the coming year. The Torah mentions no such rite, but its practice could account for the presence of libation vessels in the Tabernacle.

A final explanation for the fluid containers, which to me seems the most reasonable, is that they hold *oil*. Although the Table is generally associated with the twelve loaves of "Face Bread," it also holds incense, presumably to be burnt on the Golden Altar. The third piece of cultic furniture in the room is the Lampstand. Although we read about snuff pans and wick tweezers, we never learn where the lamp oil is kept. Why not upon the Table? Most often the root *swk* refers to pouring oil (admittedly upon the body): e.g., 30:32; Deut 28:40; 2 Sam 14:2; Ezek 16:9; Micah 6:15.

25:30. *Face Bread.* Rabbinic authorities proffer many explanations for the term *leḥem pānîm*, some quite fantastical (Haran 1962a: 493). But the simplest understanding is that Face Bread are cakes deposited *lipnê yahwe(h)* 'to Yahweh's *face*,' as 25:30 (*ləpānay* 'before me, to my face') makes explicit (ibn Ezra; Cassuto 1967: 340). In Hebrew, *pānîm* 'face' also has the connotations of "presence" and "self" (e.g., 2 Sam 17:11; Prov 7:15; Hyatt 1980: 269) and bears particular theological significance when said of God (see below, pp. 619–20). The bread is also called *leḥem hattāmîd* 'the Continual Bread' (Num 4:7), *leḥem hammaʿăreket* 'the Arrangement Bread' (Neh 10:34; 1 Chr 9:32; 23:29), *leḥem qōdeš* 'Holiness Bread' (1 Sam 21:5), *maʿăreket tāmîd* 'Continual Arrangement' (2 Chr 2:3) and simply *hammaʿăreket* 'the Arrangement' (1 Chr 28:16; 2 Chr 13:11; 29:18). See further COMMENT, pp. 507–9.

Lev 24:5–9 describes the Face Bread in detail: twelve cakes (one for each tribe?) are made from semolina. According to Josephus *Ant.* 3.142 and Philo *Laws* 2.161 (also *m. Menaḥ.* 5:1; *b. Menaḥ.* 57a), the loaves are unleavened, as befits an offering to Yahweh; see NOTE to 23:18, "my Slaughter-offering." The practice of offering Face Bread may be illustrated by four clay model bread offerings found at Beth Shan (c. 1100 B.C.E.), stamped "daily offering" in Egyptian (Ottosson 1980: 49–50).

The bread is set out in two "arrangements" (*maʿărākōt*). Are these rows or piles? On the one hand, when said of the lamps on the Lampstand, *maʿărākâ* describes a horizontal row (39:37). On the other hand, Lev 24:7 requires that incense be put *ʿal-hammaʿăreket* 'upon (each) arrangement.' Given the limited surface of the table top and the size of each cake, it is most likely that the loaves are piled vertically (Gane 1992: 186–97 n. 53), rather than spread out horizontally as in an Old Kingdom Egyptian depiction of a table with twelve loaves (D'Auria et al. 1988: 95 fig. 27).

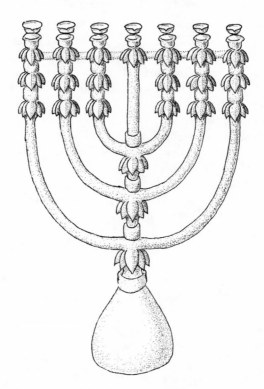

FIGURE 5a. Lampstand

25:31. *pure gold.* See NOTE to 25:11. Perhaps because of its substance as well as its sacred function, the Lampstand is also called the "pure Lampstand" (31:8; 39:37; Lev 24:4). I find it surprising that the Lampstand should be made of unalloyed, soft gold, without any supporting armature. Would not the branches bend, even break? Perhaps what the text calls "pure gold" is not 24–carat but a harder alloy (accurate tests to assay purity were developed only in the sixth century B.C.E.). Whatever its exact composition, the Lampstand would be structurally weak, unless there were a crossbar connecting the branches at the top as in Late Antique depictions (c. 350–450 C.E.) (see SPECULATION below). The text provides no basis for the wooden substructure posited by Meyers (1976: 32–33; see NOTE to 25:18, "gold; *miqšâ*").

lampstand. Mənōrâ (from the root *nwr* 'burn, shine') appears to mean "lampstand," in distinction to the *nēr* 'lamp' placed upon it, the mem prefix connoting both location and utensil. *Gen. Rab.* 20:7 is explicit: "a mənōrâ of gold and a *nēr* of pottery on top of it" (Sperber 1965: 146 n. 42). The seven-lamp Tabernacle mənōrâ is the prototype for the later nine-lamp mənōrâ or *ḥǎnukkiyyâ* that Jews light during the postbiblical festival of Hanukkah. On the Lampstand's form and symbolism, see following NOTES and COMMENT, pp. 509–12, and figs. 5a–b.

miqšâ. The term probably refers to hammered gold (NOTE to 25:18, "gold;

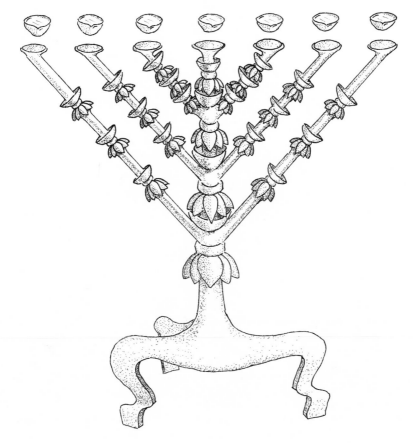

FIGURE 5b. Lampstand (alternative structure)

miqšâ"). The Lampstand was not gold-plated (*ṣpy*) (*pace* Meyers 1976: 32–33) but made in a manner analogous to the Griffins, by beating out solid gold.

thigh. The context suggests that *yārēk* 'thigh, loin' (plural in Sam) connotes the Lampstand's base (Meyers 1976: 20–22; Hachlili and Merḥav 1985). On the metaphorical use of body parts in architecture and other contexts, see Dhorme (1920–23).

There are two current reconstructions of the Lampstand's base, each with support from Roman-era and later iconography (no known depiction of the Lampstand antedates the first century B.C.E). Some envision the Lampstand standing on a tripod, as in many early depictions (Noth 1962: 208; Cassuto 1967: 342; Strauss 1960; for illustrations see Yarden 1971; Hachlili 2001 and my fig. 5b). But Exodus, so lavish with detail, makes no mention of this. Was the reader expected simply to understand that a *yārēk* has three legs? In contrast, we find explicit reference to feet in the cases of the Table and possibly the Chest (25:12, 26).

More likely, the shaft simply swells at its base, forming a "pelvis" on which the

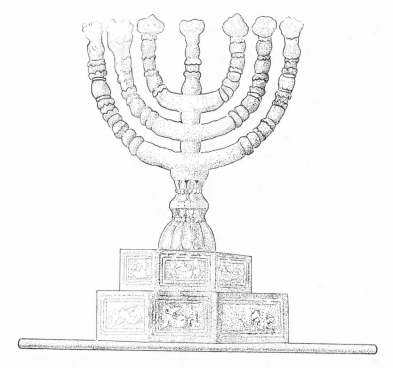

FIGURE 6. Arch of Titus (detail, restored)

Lampstand "sits" (cf. Meyers 1976: 21; my fig. 5a). This is how the Menorah is shown in the oldest depictions, prior to the third century c.e. (Hachlili and Merhav 1985: 267 n. 53): a wall carving from Jerusalem (Yarden 1971: fig. 19) and the coinage of Mattathias Antigonus, last of the Maccabees (Yarden figs. 20–22). If the Lampstand is really pure gold, a solid pedestal would be far stronger than spindly legs. (The elaborate base depicted in the Arch of Titus [fig. 6], adorned with classical mythological motifs that must have infuriated pious Jews, was probably an innovation of Herod's devising.)

It is somewhat surprising that, unlike the Chest, Table and two Altars, no carrying poles are assigned to the Lampstand. There are poles on the Arch of Titus, although these may have been supplied by the Romans. According to Num 4:9–10, the Menorah was wrapped in wool and leather and apparently hung from a yoke (môṭ).

reeds. The term is qāne(h), related to English "cane." Whether or not the Lampstand is a symbolic tree, we might expect its ramifications to be called *'ănāpîm or *maṭṭōt 'branches' (see COMMENT, p. 511). Yet qāne(h), though a botanical term, is not known to describe a tree branch, either in Hebrew or in cognate languages. Why is it used here?

We expect a "reed" to be something cylindrical and straight (Noth 1962: 208). Ibn Ezra adds that a "reed" ought to be hollow (also Merhav and Hachlili 1985:

262), but the examples do not bear this out. As in English, in Hebrew "cane" connotes a walking stick (2 Kgs 18:21; Isa 36:6; 42:3; Ezek 29:6), and also a balance beam (Isa 46:6) and a unit of linear measure (Ezek 40:3–8; 42:16–19; cf. Akkadian *qanû*, Greek *kanōn* and *kalamos*). In Job 31:22, the "reed" is a body part, perhaps the collarbone from which the arms seemingly hang; see further below.

Against the conventional iconography, the Lampstand in Exodus may have straight branches (fig. 5b). While the image of a curved-branch Lampstand is familiar from many Roman-era depictions, most famously the Arch of Titus (fig. 6), we find the Lampstand with straight or nearly straight arms at Dura Europos (Yarden 1971 fig. 91; contrast fig. 89) and elsewhere (Yarden, figs. 43, 46–47, 129–30, 158, 170). My fig. 5a attempts to compromise between the bent and the straight.

SPECULATION: Like my translation, the foregoing discussion follows LXX-Vg-Syr (see TEXTUAL NOTE, "its *thigh* and its *reeds*"). If, however, we retain the singular *qānâ* of MT, other possible interpretations emerge. One is that the "reed" in question is the vertical shaft above the base, from which the side branches emerge. Another is that, like the balance beam called *qāne(h)* in Isa 46:6, this "reed" is *horizontal*, i.e., a bar connecting the structurally weak branches at the top, as in numerous ancient depictions (Yarden 1971: 19, figs. 61, 62, 66, 71–74, 76, 84–88, 93–95, 98, 110, 128–30, 136, 173–74, 188–92, 198–99, 206, 209–12; my fig. 5a). Though the interpretation is uncertain, we may also find "reed" connoting a horizontal suspension system or brace (the collarbone?) in Job 31:22: "may my shoulder (blade?) fall from its shoulder (reading **šikmā[h]*); may my arm be broken from its *reed* (reading **qānāh*)."

cups. All we can say for certain is that *gābîaʿ* and its cognates ordinarily connote drinking vessels but that it must be something else here (Meyers 1976: 22–23). If each arm is surmounted by a "cup" holding a lamp—which the text never specifies—then we may compare a stand from Gezer with this setup (Meyers 1976: 75, fig. 32). The lower "cups" of the Lampstand, however, simply encircle the shaft of each branch and are presumably decorative (fig. 5b). (Hachilil and Merḥav [1985: 261–63] suggest that the composite flower ornaments are also functional, concealing and reinforcing joints.) In Akkadian, similarly, *gullatu* 'bowl' can describe a base, a capital or a circular molding on a pillar (Meyers, p. 23).

Then there is the problematic relationship between the "cups," the *kaptōrîm* 'rings (?)' and the "flowers." From 25:31 alone, one naturally infers these are three associated but distinct motifs. But v 33 may imply that each *gābîaʿ* consists of a *kaptōr* and a flower (Noth 1962: 208; Cassuto 1967: 343; Hachlili and Merḥav 1985: 261; my fig. 5a). (In light of the association with "flowers," one wonders whether *gābîaʿ* might have a meaning here closer to *gibʿōl* '[flax] bud' [cf. Dillmann 1880: 284].) I incline to see the cups as independent, however, because v 34 ascribes to the Lampstand's central shaft "four . . . cups—*its kaptōrîm* and *its flowers (kaptōre[y]hā ûp[ə]rāḥe[y]hā*)," not **kaptōrêhem ûpirḥêhem* 'their *kaptōrîm* and *their flowers*.' That is, "cups," "*kaptōrîm*" and "*flowers*" are in equivalent relationship to the Lampstand; the last two are not subsumed by the first.

A stand from Megiddo is crowned with stacked flowers, surmounted by a bowl decorated with petals (Meyers 1976: 74; Schumacher 1908: frontispiece and p. 128). Although the Megiddo piece is broken, Meyers notes that parallels from the Mediterranean suggest there was originally a triple flower. This could indicate that, at least for the six side branches, the Menorah's floral decorations were grouped at the ends of the arms (fig. 5a), not evenly spaced as is generally supposed (fig. 5b).

kaptōrîm. We do not know the meaning of this word, which describes a feature of a pillar (Amos 9:1; Zeph 2:14) and of the Tabernacle Lampstand. It does not look Semitic at all, unless we engage in philological legerdemain, e.g., positing a portmanteau of *ktr* 'surround' and *kpp* 'curve.'

Many scholars, noting the association with flowers in 25:31–34, suppose a *kaptōr* to be the calyx beneath the petals (e.g., Hyatt 1980: 270). According to LXX and Vg, the *kaptōrîm* are "spheres" *(sphairōtēres, sphaerulae)* — note the globule motif on ancient Menorah depictions (Yarden 1971) — while *b. Menah.* 28b compares them to *tp̱hy hkrtyym* 'Cretan apples' (or possibly *tp̱hy hbyrwtyym* 'cypress cones'; see Kirschner [1992: 248–49 n. 66]). Similarly, the Aramaic Versions render *kaptōr* with *h̠zwr* 'apple, round fruit.' Meyers (1976: 24) tentatively identifies the *kaptōr* as connoting a capital, originally pear-shaped but later of any botanical form. She proffers, however, no examples of fruit-shaped capitals.

Generally, however, *kaptōr* is a place name, probably Crete (Knapp 1985) but conceivably a vague term for the Mediterranean islands in general. The Ugaritic craftsman god Koṯaru dwells in *kptr*, presumably a center of skilled artisans (*KTU* [1.1.iii.1, 18; 2.iii.2]; 3.vi.14; 100.46). One would therefore expect a *kaptōr* to be a decoration characteristic of Mediterranean art (cf. Cole 1973: 193; Rendsburg 1990: 205). Although she does not make the Caphtor connection, Meyers (1976) observes the frequency of stacked blossoms separated by rings on metal, stone and ceramic stands from the Mediterranean, counting 57 examples in total, 32 from Cyprus alone (pp. 77–78, figs. 34–36; see also Richter 1915: 366–68). Similar artifacts are found in the Phoenician-Punic world (Meyers, figs. 27, 37–41), to which they may be native (Culican 1980; on Phoenician influence in both Cyprus and Crete, see briefly Burkert 1992: 27). In fact, the image closest in form to the Tabernacle Lampstand is an object, presumably a tree, depicted on a Late Bronze Age seal from Cyprus (Meyers, fig. 65; de Cesnola 1884: p. xiii, 2). In Exodus, *kaptōr* cannot connote the entire blossom motif, as it is clearly distinguished from the "flower." Perhaps, with Hachlili and Merḥav (1985: 261), we should equate the *kaptōr* with the ring component of the flower stack.

flowers. A *peraḥ* is simply a flower, here used as a decorative motif. It might be either right-side-up or inverted, the latter having more extensive iconographic support (Meyers 1976: figs. 20, 25–27, 36–37, 39). Note especially the stands plundered from Judah by Sennacherib (for a clear photo and drawing, see Stern 2001: 26). Meyers (1976: 25) suggests that the specific flower type is the lily *(šôšān)*, a motif in Solomon's Temple (1 Kgs 7:19, 22, 26).

from it. Mimennû probably does not imply that the branches and their adornments are beaten out of the same ingot as the main shaft (*pace* Rashi et al.). This would present considerable challenges to the goldsmith. Rather, the point is that the "reeds" *protrude* "from it," i.e, from the Lampstand shaft, but are secondarily affixed (cf. Hachlili and Merḥav 1985: 262). See also NOTES to 25:19, "on the *kappōret*"; 28:8, "from it."

25:32. *from its sides.* Or "from its *two* sides." I.e., *miṣṣidde(y)hā* could be construed as either plural or dual.

Lampstand reeds. I.e., each arm is itself a lampstand.

25:33. *'almondized'.* I almost wrote "amygdaline," probably as unfamiliar in English as *məšuqqād* would be in ancient Hebrew. All commentators associate *məšuqqād* with the noun *šāqēd* 'almond,' denoting both the nut and the tree. Assuming this is correct, how can the "cups" be like almonds? One possibility is that, if each cup consists of "*kaptōr* and *flower*" (see NOTE on "cups" above), the petals are inspired by the almond blossom, or the *kaptōr* by the almond calyx (Dillmann 1880: 285). Alternatively, the cups may have almond-shaped lozenges as a decorative motif (Meyers 1976: 23).

The presence of an almond-like, branched object in the Tabernacle brings to mind Num 17:16–26, where Aaron's rod, transmogrified into a budding almond branch, is deposited before the Chest (Cole 1973: 192; see p. 511). (There is also a verbal root *šqd* 'observe,' not entirely inappropriate for a Lampstand; Jer 1:11–12 puns upon the two meanings of the root.)

SPECULATION: While evidence of the Ugaritic/Aramaic Shaphʿel conjugation in Hebrew is extremely sparse, we might also consider the root *nqd* 'to make little points.' If so, *məšuqqād* would mean "dotted" and have nothing to do with almonds.

on the one reed . . . on the one reed. I.e., on each "reed."

kaptōr and flower. The trope implies that each "cup" is "'almondized' *in respect of kaptōr* and flower" (on the ambiguous syntax, cf. *b. Yoma* 52a–b; Rashi). See NOTE to 25:31 for the view that the cups are not separate from the floral elements, but are composed of these elements.

25:34. *Lampstand.* Here *mənōrâ* must connote the central shaft. It has four, not three, floral elements, among which emerge the arms.

25:35. *a kaptōr under the two reeds from it.* The threefold repetition conveys that all three sets of branches protrude in the same manner. Here the theory of Hachlili and Merḥav (1985: 261–63), that the *kaptōrîm* strengthen the joints, seems particularly attractive. Assyrian depictions of a sacred tree sometimes similarly feature ring-moldings along the main stem, between which branches emerge (Ward 1910: figs. 679, 688, 689; Perrot 1937: pls. 18–21, 23, 25–27, 29, 31–32).

25:36. *their kaptōrîm and their reeds.* Noth (1962: 208) notes that "their" lacks an antecedent. In TEXTUAL NOTE, I propose that we read instead "their *kaptōrîm* and their *flowers*," referring to the six arms described in v 35. If this emendation is too drastic, we might follow Cassuto (1967: 343–44): *qənōtām* does not mean "their *reeds*"—that should be **qənêhem*—but "their *joints*," based on the MT of Job 31:22. (See, however, GKC §87 *m–o* for nouns with both *-îm* and

-ōt plurals; note, too, that the Aramaic and Arabic cognates to qāne[h] exhibit both plural types.)

they shall be from it. I.e., protruding; see NOTE to 25:31, "from it."

one miqšâ. This is generally taken to mean that a single ingot is hammered out to make the Lampstand, branches and all (e.g., Sarna 1986: 195). Meyers (1976: 32), however, thinks a single sheet of gold foil is attached to a wooden form. But more likely, "one" here simply connotes an assembled whole (also Hachlili and Merhav 1985: 263), just as the composite Tabernacle is said to be "one" when erected (26:6, 11; 36:13, 18).

25:37. *lamps.* The first time, *nērōt* denotes small, spouted oil lamps perched atop the Lampstand's arms (Meyers 1976: 57–58). Although 25:37 does not specify what they are made of, 37:23–24 implies that the lamps are golden (*b. Menah.* 88b–89a; Ramban), like those of Solomon's Temple (1 Kgs 7:49). But we cannot exclude the possibility that the Tabernacle's lamps are of the ceramic, disposable variety.

one. No subject is specified. We learn from 27:21; Num 8:1–3 that caring for the lamps is the priests' office.

raise. LXX and Vg understand *he'ĕlâ* as referring to installation *(epithēseis/ pones)*, hence NEB "mount" (also Driver 1911: 277). But for that we might have expected either *nātan* 'set' or *śām* 'put.' More likely, we have the common connotation of *he'ĕlâ* to connote lighting a fire (ibn Ezra [shorter commentary] on 27:20). For the semantic development "send up" > "kindle," Luzzatto compares Aramaic *'assêq* with both meanings.

its lamps. Here *nērōt* may mean "flames" rather than "lamps."

and illumine opposite its front. The sense is that one installs the lamps *so that* the Menorah illuminates forward (cf. *Tg. Neofiti I* [TEXTUAL NOTE]) (figs. 5a–b). The spouted lamps should all point in the same direction (cf. LXX "*from* its one face"), across the Tabernacle toward the Table (Rashbam, Bekhor Shor); cf. Num 8:2–3.

25:38. *tweezers.* In Isa 6:6, *malqāhayim* are tongs used to remove a coal from the fire (< *lqh* 'take'). Here, they are probably tweezers for manipulating or trimming lamp wicks (Rashi, Rashbam). That they are golden indicates the flames' sanctity.

fire-pans. Against MT *mahtōte(y)hā* (presumed singular **mahtâ*), Sam has *mhtytyh* (cf. Sam Exod 27:3, 37:23; Num 4:9), i.e., **mahtiyyōte(y)hā* (presumed singular *mahtît*; cf. *Tgs. mahtiyyātahā*). Elsewhere, however, Sam agrees with MT.

Many suggest that the *mahtōt* are ashtrays for removing spent wicks (e.g., Rashi). But it is clear from Lev 10:1; 16:12; Num 16:18; 17:11 that their purpose is instead to convey fire, the proper meaning of the root verb *hty* (Isa 30:14; Prov 6:27; 25:22). It follows that the *mahtōt* of the Lampstand and likewise the bronze *mahtōt* of the Altar (27:3) carry coals with which to kindle the fires. (On the possibility that the pans are also used for incense, see p. 514.) For Israelite-period iron fire-pans from Tel Dan, see Biran (1994: 192–95, color plate 33, ill. 152).

25:39. *talent.* A talent (Greek *talantos*, Hebrew *kikkār*) is 3,000 shekels, c. 75.5 lbs./34 kgs. The Lampstand itself must weigh slightly less, since some of this gold goes to its utensils (cf. *b. Menah.* 88b).

We are told only the Lampstand's weight, not its dimensions; according to *Mel. Mišk.* 10; *b. Menaḥ.* 28b, it was 18 palms high (3 cubits; c. 4.5 feet/1.5 m.). Why is weight the Torah's main consideration?

Hachlili and Merḥav (p. 256) observe that, for the gold-plated Chest, Table and Tabernacle frames, a relatively small amount of gold is required, determined by the scale of the wooden substructure. For a solid gold piece such as the Lampstand, however, the weight is more significant. (By this argument, however, we would expect to be told the weight of the *kappōret* and Griffins, likewise of solid gold and of irregular shape.)

along with. I have taken *'ēt* as *'ēt* II, synonymous to *'im* 'with.' Alternatively, we might read the redundant definite direct object marker (*'ēt* I), tantamount to "including" or "in short" (cf. Ehrlich 1908: 368–69).

25:40. *And see.* *Ûr(ə)'ē(h)* has both a general sense "see (to it)" and a particular sense "see (what I am showing you)," since the construction of the Lampstand is hard to understand from words alone (cf. Rashi).

model. While *tabnît* may apply to all the paraphernalia of chap. 25, it is most apt after the Lampstand (see also Num 8:4), since the directions are so confusing (cf. *b. Menaḥ.* 29a). The author assures us that Moses possesses more information than what we read in Exodus.

26:1. *And the Tabernacle.* The paragraph begins with emphatic inversion (not: "And you shall make the Tabernacle"), as if to say, "We've finished with the holiest objects; now, for the Tabernacle itself . . ." (Cassuto 1967: 348).

Throughout this section, *miškān* 'Tabernacle' connotes the inner covering of linen and wool, distinguished from the outer *'ōhel* 'Tent' of goat hair (Rashbam; Ramban on 39:33). This is a curiously rationalistic breakup of the stereotypical synonymous pair "tent/tabernacle" (cf. Utzschneider 1988: 131).

ten curtains. It is unclear whether the relationship between the "Tabernacle" and "curtains" is apposition, double accusative or construct; see NOTE to 25:10, "acacia wood."

twisted linen . . . blue . . . purple . . . worm-crimson. On these fabrics, see NOTES to 25:4. The list is stereotyped, but only here and in 39:29 does the linen come first. Dillmann (1880: 286) infers that, for the Tabernacle curtains at least, the basic fabric is white linen, with colored threads interwoven to create Griffin designs. Haran (1978: 162) concurs, adding that the mainly linen composition indicates a lesser degree of sanctity than the mostly woolen Veil. Excavations at Timna have uncovered a Midianite sacred tent of woven flax and wool, dyed red and yellow (Rothenberg 1972: 151). And, at the Israelite cult site of Kuntillet 'Ajrūd, archaeologists have found nearly a hundred textile fragments, mostly linen but also some dyed wool and linen mixed (Sheffer 1978).

Griffins. On these hybrid servants of Yahweh — part lion, part bird and probably part human — see NOTE to 25:18 and COMMENT, pp. 516–19. For curtains resembling those of the Tabernacle, see a fifth-century B.C.E. Greek vase depicting Penelope weaving a griffin tapestry (Forbes 1964a: 203 fig. 29) and also various Persian-era tapestries found frozen in Siberia that depict winged quadrupeds and other beasts (Ghirshman 1964: 361, pl. 467).

Here and in 36:8, 35, the grammatical status of *kərûbîm* is somewhat obscure. It apparently describes the *manner* in which the threads are to be woven: so as to produce the images of Griffins, which also adorned the walls of Solomon's Temple (1 Kgs 6:29, 32, 35) and of the Syrian temple at 'Ein Dara (Abū Assāf 1990). Apropos of the Veil (26:31), 2 Chr 3:14 paraphrases Exodus: *wayya'al 'ālā(y)w kərûbîm* 'and he raised (*sic*?) upon it Griffins.'

SPECULATION: 2 Chr 3:14 notwithstanding, there is a possibility that *kərûbîm* does not mean "Griffins" in 26:1; 36:8, 35. As we have seen, Tg. Neofiti I, Philo, Josephus, Jerome and Saadiah make no mention of Griffins (TEXTUAL NOTE). The Arabic verb *karaba* means "afflict" and also "tighten," referring to threads (as in *makrūb* 'tied tightly') and tent cords (Musil 1928: 62, 73). In 25:1; 36:8, a translation 'pulled tight' apropos of woven curtains would work better than "Griffins" (in 36:35, however, "pulled tight" is slightly awkward).

webster's work. The skilled weaver of complex patterns is called *ḥōšēb* 'calculator.' Ordinary weaving of a single color is denominated by the root *'rg* (39:22, 27) (Haran 1978: 160); see also NOTE to 26:36, "embroiderer's work." On ancient weaving techniques, see Forbes (1964a: 175–258) and Vogelsang-Eastwood (2000: 274–78).

them. As often, the masculine (*'ōtām*) displaces the grammatically required feminine (*'ōtān*); cf. Levi (1987).

26:2. *The one curtain's length.* I.e., each curtain's length.

four cubits. According to Homan (2002: 152), this is the greatest width a hand loom can accommodate.

one measure. I.e., the same dimensions.

26:3. *Five of the curtains.* Ordinarily, *ḥămēš hayrî'ōt* would mean "the five curtains." For semantically indefinite nouns standing in construct to definite nouns, see Joüon (1965: 431 §139b–c).

fastening. The cloths are presumably sewn together (Rashi). Assuming that MT is correctly vocalized, the panels are not "fastened" (**ḥăbûrōt*, passive) but "fastening" (*ḥōbərōt*, active), as if grasping one another (cf. Cassuto 1967: 348). Together, they constitute a *maḥberet* 'fastening, assembly.' (Haran [1978: 166] and Houtman [2000: 421], however, understand *ḥōbərōt* and *maḥberet* as denoting the *place* of juncture, i.e., the seam.)

(each) woman to her sister. I.e., each to each. The ten panels are assembled into two equal curtains, each measuring 20 × 28 cubits (c. 30 × 42 feet or 10 × 14 m.). A single long curtain of 40 × 28 cubits would perhaps be too cumbersome to transport (Bekhor Shor; Cassuto 1967: 348). On Friedman's (1981: 50–51) theory that the two curtains are folded back at the seam, creating a double layer, see COMMENT, pp. 503–4.

and five curtains. The repetition "Five of the curtains . . . and five curtains" means "five on this side and five on that."

26:4. *loops.* The term *lūlā'ōt* is unique to the Tabernacle pericope. The meaning is inferred primarily from context, since the etymology is somewhat uncertain.

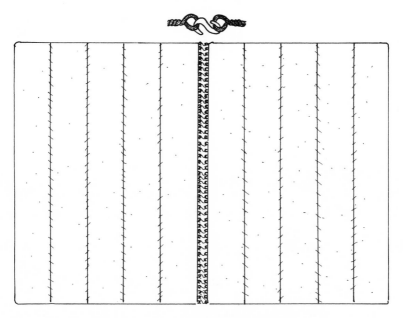

FIGURE 7. Inner curtain of linen and wool

BDB and KB see a reduplicated derivative of the root *lwy* 'twist, surround,' i.e., **lwlw*, which became *lwl'* by dissimilation, probably via **lwly* (see GKC §93*x*); compare Arabic *lawlaba* 'twist, screw.' It is not clear whether these blue "loops" are sewn-on woolen threads or tied-off loose ends from the weaving.

on the outer curtain's lip. In the phrase *biśpat hayrî'â haqqiṣônâ*, the adjective *qîṣônâ* 'outer' could modify equally *yərî'â* 'curtain' and *śəpat* 'lip,' since both are feminine.

26:5. *fifty . . . fifty.* On each curtain's edge, the loops would be spaced at intervals of c. 0.57 cubits (cf. Bekhor Shor). The large number minimizes the strain on each individual loop.

aligning. Maqbîlōt means that the loops should be placed exactly, so that they meet (*qbl*) when laid together (Rashi). This usage is characteristic of later Hebrew and Aramaic (cf. ibn Ezra [shorter commentary]).

26:6. *clasps.* These would temporarily bind the matching loops of the two large, composite curtains, until camp was struck and the Tent disassembled (fig. 7).

The etymology of *qeres* is uncertain. (The LXX rendering *krikos* 'ring' exploits fortuitous phonetic similarity.) The verbal root *qrs* 'bow down' does not seen apposite, unless the basic meaning is "curve." More likely would be a slightly irregular derivative of the root *qrṣ* 'pinch.'

so that the Tabernacle shall be one. As we say, a "unit."

26:7. *goat.* To this day, Bedouin tents are typically made of spun black goat hair (cf. Cant 1:5, "black as the tents of Salmah [in Arabia]," reading **śalmâ* for MT *šəlōmō[h]* 'Solomon').

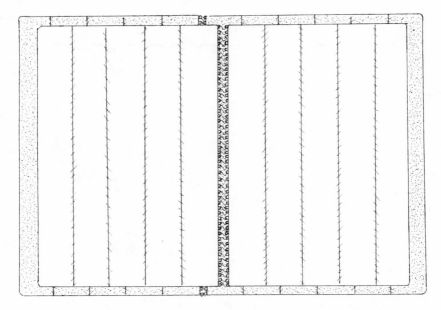

FIGURE 8. Inner curtain of linen and wool against outer curtain of goat hair

to tent. Or "as a tent." My rendering highlights the ambiguity of the form *l'hl.* Assuming MT *lə'ōhel* is correctly vocalized, the noun *'ōhel* 'tent' replaces the expected infinitive construct **'ĕhōl* (compare *lə'ahăbâ* 'to love,' *lîrā'* 'to fear,' etc.). While *Tg. Ps.-Jonathan* translates *lə'ōhel* as an infinitive, most other Versions make it a noun, and Vg has a double rendering *(ad operiendum tectum.)* See further NOTE to 36:14.

It is clear from vv 11, 13 that this outer goat-hair curtain is called the "Tent," in distinction to the inner fabric of the "Tabernacle" *(miškān)* proper; see COMMENT, to pp. 505–6.

eleven. Thus the outer goat-hair curtain contains one panel more than the inner curtain of linsey-woolsey. Since in both cases, each panel is 4 cubits wide, the outer curtain's length will exceed the inner curtain's by 4 cubits (fig. 8). The outer curtain measures 44 cubits × 30 cubits (c. 66 × 45 feet or 22 × 15 m.). See further pp. 505–6

them. See NOTE to 26:2, "them."

26:8. *thirty.* The goat-hair curtain is two cubits wider than the inner curtain, which is only 28 cubits broad (26:2). Thus there is a superfluity of one cubit on each side (26:13). See pp. 505–6.

26:9. *five . . . six.* Since there are eleven panels, they cannot be evenly divided into two "fastenings," unlike the inner curtains. See further NOTE to 26:3, "(each) woman to her sister."

double. In theory, this might mean either that the eleventh curtain is folded in half, or that it is folded over the tenth. The former is more likely; see pp. 505–6.

against the Tent's front. This probably means that the folded half-curtain bends

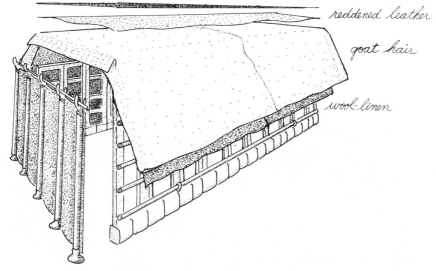

beaded leather

reddened leather

goat hair

wool-linen

Figure 9. Tabernacle coverings (exploded view)

at 90 degrees to shroud the Tabernacle's open front, covering the top two cubits to keep out rain and light (Kennedy 1898: 662); see fig. 9.

26:10. *loops.* Unlike the the blue woolen loops of the inner curtain (26:4), we are not told the substance of these loops. Probably they are of less valuable goat hair, just as the outer Tent's bronze clasps are of less value than the inner Tabernacle's golden clasps (Cassuto 1967: 350).

the second fastening. Accepting MT or Sam, I would take *h(m)ḥbrt hšnyt* in 26:10; 36:17 as "*thus* the second fastening." But we would really expect **b(m)ḥbrt hšnyt 'of* the second *fastening'* (see TEXTUAL NOTE).

26:11. *clasps.* In contrast to the golden clasps of the inner curtain, the outer curtain is fastened by less expensive bronze clasps, since it is farther from the inner Holiness (ibn Ezra).

one. See NOTE to 26:6, "so that the Tabernacle shall be one."

26:12. *superfluous overhang.* The "overhang *(seraḥ)*" is half a panel, or two cubits. It is "superfluous *('ōdēp)*" either because it is longer than the inner curtain (Rashi), or because it actually rests upon the ground (*b. Šabb.* 98b; Rashbam; Cassuto 1967: 353). On the curtains' alignment, see pp. 505–6.

shall hang. My translation assumes that *tisraḥ* is a 3 f.s. intransitive verb. The passive participle *sārûaḥ* 'overhung' in 26:13 (also Ezek 23:15; Amos 6:4, 7) implies, however, that *sāraḥ* is properly transitive. In that case, we could read *tisraḥ* as 2 m.s. transitive: "*you shall hang* half of the superfluous curtain." Or we could vocalize a passive **tissāraḥ* (Niphʿal).

26:14. *cover.* A tough, leather cover shelters the more delicate goat-hair and linen-wool textiles. The Romans frequently did just this to protect their military tents in winter (references in Dillmann 1880: 288), as did Libyans in the Early Iron Age (Breasted 1962: 3.251) and Bedouin today (Cassuto 1967: 353). This shields the Tabernacle from the elements, but also makes the interior even darker.

The cover's dimensions are unspecified. According to *Mel. Mišk.* 3, it measures 30 by 10 cubits and thus covers only the Tabernacle's roof (also Rashi; Luzzatto). It is also possibile that the cover stretches down obliquely on the sides, held taut with pegs. (I doubt that it hangs straight down the sides—that would make the interior unbearably stuffy.)

reddened. Mesopotamians and Egyptians dyed leather with madder (Van Driel-Murray 2000: 306). The color red, evocative of blood and danger, is sacred or taboo in many cultures (see Fiddes 1991: 68–69). The Arabian holy pavilion *qubba* was of red leather (Lammens 1928: 127–28), and a red-painted tent shrine is portrayed on a Palmyra relief (third–first century B.C.E.).

skins . . . skins. Why does the text mention two types of decorated leather (on *taḥaš* as beadwork, see NOTE to 25:5)? Are these two layers, with the bottom one unseen, or a single cover both composed of dyed skins and adorned with beadwork? Rabbinic literature contains both interpretations: either there are two covers with the *taḥaš* above or else there is a single cover with the two leathers in a checkerboard pattern (*paspîsîn*, literally "mosaic tiles") (*Mel. Mišk.* 3). The latter would resemble the leather tent of Queen Isi-em-Kheb from Egypt (Forbes 1966: fig. 11; Homan 2002: 106–7). Exod 35:11 and 40:19 mention only one cover, while Num 4:25 refers explicitly only to the beaded cover. Nevertheless, the repetition of "cover" in 26:14; 39:34 decisively indicates two covers, the red below and the beaded above (Jacob 1992: 790), as does the Massoretic trope, which puts a major pause after "reddened ram skins" (Luzzatto). Consequently, in 35:11; 40:19, the singular "cover" must refer collectively to both layers. As for Num 4:25, "its cover," over which the beaded leather is laid, must be the red leather cover.

26:15. *qərāšîm.* Although the noun *qereš* is known from both biblical and prebiblical contexts, its meaning remains uncertain. In the Tabernacle pericope, the *qərāšîm* are a wooden structure supporting the curtains. An eighteenth-century B.C.E. tablet from Mari (M.6873) similarly refers to a large tent with ten wooden *qersū* (also ARM XXVII.124:5'), transported by twenty men (Durand and Guichard 1997: 65–66; Fleming 2000). And Ugaritic mythology of the fourteenth century B.C.E. calls the high god Ilu's tent a *qrš*, apparently by synecdoche (*KTU* [1.1.iii.23; 2.iii.5; 3.v.8]; 4.iv.24; [17.vi.9]). None of this tells us exactly what a *qereš* looks like.

The traditional understanding of *qereš*, perpetuated in Modern Hebrew, sees a solid board or pillar. E.g., according to Philo *Moses* 2.78; Josephus *Ant.* 3.118, the Tabernacle's gold-plated *qərāšîm* constitute a solid, glittering wall (cf. figs. 12a–b, pp. 416, 417). The source of this interpretation may be Ezek 27:6, where the prophet envisions a fantastic ship with an ivory *qereš*, often understood as its deck. But this *qereš* is more likely either an onboard pavilion (van Dijk 1968: 63) or a wooden frame, inlaid with ivory like the "ivory houses" and "ivory couches" of 1 Kgs 22:39; Amos 3:15; 6:4. (For a tent-cabin on an Egyptian model ship, see Winlock [1955: pl. 51]; for textual references, see Herodotus 7.100 [on the Persians] and Skylax *Periplus* 20.65.1 [the Phoenicians].) Below we shall see that the *qereš* of Exodus is more likely a ladder-like trellis.

standing. That is, the *qərāšîm* are upright (*'ōmədîm*), not stacked horizontally. Cassuto (1967: 354–55) detects an allusion to the *'ammūdîm* 'posts' that support an ordinary tent, and perhaps the same association underlies the LXX rendering *styloi* 'pillars.'

26:16. *length . . . breadth.* We are not told the depth of each *qereš*. Although Rabbinic sources envision cubit-thick, solid *qərāšîm* (e.g., *b. Šabb.* 98b; Rashi), the weight of each would enormous, c. 1,772 lbs./804 kg. (Homan 2002: 139). In fact, most species of acacia are too small to produce beams of this size (Zevit 1992). Kennedy's (1898: 661) influential treatment makes the *qərāšîm* ½ cubit thick in order to achieve a pretermined width for the entire structure—which he miscalculates (see p. 496)—but such *qərāšîm* would still be very heavy (cf. Homan 2002: 143). More likely, the *qərāšîm* are of negligible depth (see below, p. 497); Josephus estimates four fingers (*Ant.* 3.116, 119; cf. also Cassuto 1967: 354–57), while Ehrlich (1908: 370) argues that the *qərāšîm* must be thinner still, perhaps two fingers, since four fingers would have been called a *ṭōpaḥ* 'handbreadth.' Indeed, a *qereš* would quickly topple if it vastly outweighed its two bases, which according to 38:27, together weigh c. 151.2 lbs./68.6 kg. (Cassuto 1967: 357).

There is an indirect way to estimate the weight of each *qereš* (cf. Bekhor Shor; Homan 2002: 143–44). Of the six oxcarts allocated for transporting the Tabernacle (Num 7:6–7), four are reserved for the Merarites, whose charge is the Tabernacle and the Plaza (Num 4:31–32). Since a two-ox team can draw c. 4,400 lbs./ 2,000 kg. (Homan p. 144), the Merarites' carts can carry at most 17,600 lbs. We know the weight of the metal bases of the Tabernacle and Plaza: 7,560 lbs. silver (100 talents, 38:27) and 5,292 lbs. bronze (c. 70 talents, 38:29), for a total weight of 12,852 lbs. That leaves 4,748 lbs. for the wooden components, i.e., the 60 Plaza posts and the 48 *qərāšîm* of the Tabernacle.

Here our calculations are seemingly at an impasse. We do know, however, that a *qereš* is twice the height (10 cubits) of a post (5 cubits), and that each *qereš* contains two vertical components (next NOTE). If we arbitrarily assume that a *qereš* is four times as heavy as a post, then each post weighs c. 19 lbs./41.8 kg. and each *qereš* 76 lbs./167.2 kg. (60 × 19 lbs. + 48 × 76 lbs. = 4788 lbs.). This estimation can then be confirmed by the aforesaid Mari text, where one *qersu* is a two-man load (NOTE to 26:15).

26:17. *two arms.* Even though the "arms" are two, the text uses the plural (*štê yādôt*), not the dual (**yādayim*), because these are not literal "arms" (GKC §87*o*).

From the English translation, one might mistakenly think that the "arms" connect one *qereš* to another. But it is the "arms" (fem.) not the *qərāšîm* (masc.) that are "pegged (*məšullābōt*)" each to each (*'iššâ 'el-'ăḥōtāh*) (see below). Moreover, according to 26:19, the *qereš*'s "two arms" are each inserted into a silver base. Are these additional "arms"? Indeed, if a *qereš* is solid, as in the traditional view (NOTE to 26:15), why would it require two bases at all?

All these objections are answered, along with the weight problem noted above, by Kennedy's (1898: 660) exegesis, which has gained wide acceptance (but not by Homan 2002: 137–48). The two connected "arms," which Kennedy takes in the sense of "sides," in fact constitute the *qereš*. That is, v 17 describes not a feature of the *qereš* but the entire *qereš* itself. The basic structure is two vertical shafts (*yādôt*), each inserted into a silver socket for stability and preservation. These "arms" are *məšullābōt*, i.e., connected with horizontal rungs (see next NOTE), so that each *qereš* is essentially a trellis (see fig. 10). Kennedy may err in computing the *qereš*'s thickness (see above), but otherwise his model answers all objections. Somewhat similar is the gold-plated tent frame of Hetepheres, Cheops' mother, consisting of vertical posts connected horizontally at top and bottom (Kitchen 1993: 119*–120*; for an illustration, see Reisner and Smith 1955: pl. 5). (On Hayutin's [1993: 231] theory that *štê yādôt* is the fraction ⅔, see the following NOTE and p. 504.)

pegged. The Puʿal participle *məšullābōt* is unique to this context. It must be related to the *šəlabbîm* of 1 Kgs 7:28–29, but these, too, are of unclear nature. More helpful are Rabbinic Hebrew *šəlîbâ* 'ladder rung' and Talmudic Aramaic *šəlā(ʾ)bāʾ* 'bottle stopper' (*b. Šabb.* 112b, but the reading is not quite certain). Similarly, Akkadian *šulbû* is a door lock, perhaps a bar (KB), while Punic *šlb* (*KAI* 69.4) is a body part, probably a rib (Levine 1974: 118–19).

According to Kennedy (1898), *məšullābōt* means "joined with cross bars," so that each *qereš* resembles a ladder. Hayutin (1993), however, thinks the *qərāšîm* are pegged together *overlapping*, each covering two-thirds of its neighbor; see further below, pp. 504–5.

(each) woman to her sister. I.e., "each to each," referring not to the *qərāšîm* (masc.) but to the "arms" (*yādôt*, fem.).

26:18. *austral . . . southward.* Here and in 27:9; 36:23; 38:9, P employs rhetorical redundancy (for *negbâ têmānâ*, see also Ezek 47:19; 48:28). Since the first term means literally "to the Negev wilderness," while Teiman is in Edom, further south and east, the perspective is Palestinian (Ramban). See also NOTES to 27:12–13.

26:19. *silver.* How the bases are to be made is not specified here. According to 38:27, they are mass produced by casting, like the bronze bases for the Screen (26:37) and the silver bases for the Veil (36:36). Even for the inner sanctum, the bases are made of silver not gold. Perhaps the ground was considered liable to pollution and hence not suitable to touch the holy metal.

bases. Although the meaning is fairly certain, *ʾeden* is of unknown etymology.

Since the bases' shape and dimesions are unstated, I assume they do not contribute to the Tabernacle's height (below, pp. 497, 503). More likely, they *encase* the vertical components of the *qərāšîm* (Rashi), rather like the stone post-bases recovered at Gizeh (Reisner and Smith 1955: 14 and pl. 3).

two bases . . . two bases. The sense is distributive: for each frame, two bases.

26:20. *flank.* On *ṣēlāʿ* in the sense of "side," see NOTE to 25:12, "flank."

26:22. *backparts.* Yarkātayim is a dual derivative of *yārēk* 'thigh, loin.' "Backparts" connotes remoteness in any direction; cf. *yarkətê ʾāreṣ* 'Earth's extremities' (Jer 6:22, etc.), *yarkətê ṣāpôn* '(Mount) Zaphon's peak' (Isa 14:13) and *yarkətê bôr*

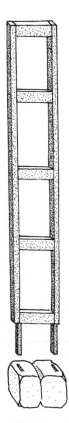

FIGURE 10. *Qereš* and bases

'the Pit's bottom' (Isa 14:15). In Exodus, *yarkātayim* connotes the back of the Tabernacle, in contrast to the *ṣəlā'ōt* 'flanks' and *pānîm* 'face, front.' It is the protected recess where Yahweh's spirit will rest.

seaward. The perspective is again Palestinian; *yāmmâ* means "westward," i.e., toward the Mediterranean (cf. NOTE to 26:18).

26:23. *And two qərāšîm.* As becomes clear in v 25 ("eight *qərāšîm*"), these are in addition to the six back frames of v 22.

Exod 26:23–24 is the crux of the riddle of the Tabernacle's dimensions. Since we do not understand how the corners are assembled, we cannot know how (and whether) they contribute to the structure's overall length and width (see further the following NOTES and p. 503).

corners. For the consonants *mqṣ't*, we find two vocalizations in MT: *məquṣ'ōt* (26:23; 36:28) and *miqṣō'ōt* (26:24; 36:29). In Exodus, at least, it might appear that the former is construct, the latter absolute. There are two difficulties, however. First, we find *miqṣō'ōt* in construct in Ezek 41:22; 46:22. Second, *məquṣ'ōt* should be the construct not of *miqṣō'ōt* but of the (unattested) Pu'al participle **məquṣṣā'ōt* 'cornered off.' Apparently, the Massoretes distinguished between the two words, but on what basis we do not know. (Jacob [1992: 793] implausibly guesses that *məquṣ'ōt* are *exterior* corner angles, while *miqṣō'ôt* are *interior* corner angles.)

26:24. *twinning . . . whole.* Our efforts to comprehend the text are thwarted both by our ignorance of Hebrew architectural terminology and by the author's punning diction (Cassuto 1967: 356): *tō'ămîm . . . tammîm.* (On the possibility that the ambiguity is deliberate, see p. 497.) The root *tmm* 'to be whole, complete' is common enough. The verb *t'm* 'to be a twin,' however, is unique in Biblical Hebrew. Rabbinic Hebrew has the Hiph'il *hit'îm* 'match, correspond, be double, be in the middle,' and so Houtman (2000: 434) suggests that the two corners are mirror images of one another. But this should be too obvious to mention.

In Kennedy's (1898) model, the corner frames are doubled or "twinning," reinforced by leaning buttresses or frames adjoining them at the top (see fig. 11a). Why the rear corners should require such support is unclear to me. Also unclear from his drawing is how the extra frames relate to the bases.

The real problem that 26:24 may be addressing is what holds the sides together, which otherwise the text never makes clear (on ancient Near Eastern joinery techniques, see Baker 1966: 21–26, 39–45, 127–224, 292–307). The most obvious understanding of 26:24 is that the corner frames are L-shaped (Homan 2002: 147–48), but this theory, too, requires modification (below, p. 503).

I provisionally suppose that each rear corner piece is attached by a ring to its perpendicular side piece (fig. 11b; see below). As for "twinning below . . . whole up to its *head*," if I am correct that the side pieces contribute only to the Tabernacle's width, then "twinning" *(tō'ămîm)* might mean "separate" or "corresponding," while "whole" *(tammîm)* implies "permanently joined" (cf. Syr *gāpîn* 'catching, being fastened'). In this way, we can have L-shaped corners that do not create extra length or necessitate additional bases (below, p. 503).

to its head. Comentators have speculated what "it" is. One possibility is "the Tabernacle" in v 23 (Cassuto 1967: 356), but this seems too remote an antecedent. More likely it is each individual corner *qereš*, hence the clarifying "for the two of them" in the following phrase.

to the one ring. The text uses the definite article *(haṭṭabba'at hā'eḥāt)*, as if we already knew about the ring (cf. Ramban), yet no ring has been mentioned. This is only slightly surprising, however; the rings for the crossbars will be introduced just as casually in 26:29. And what is the point of "one"? Houtman (2000: 435) thinks *haṭṭabba'at hā'eḥāt* means "the number-one ring," counting from the top; compare Gen 1:5 "day one" = "first day."

I see two main possibilities. First, at the corners, the adjacent vertical "arms" of the neighboring *qərāšîm* may be bound together with a fillet; Cassuto (1967: 356) cites an Egyptian parallel I have been unable to confirm. Second, the ring or rings may constitute a hinge, so that the two pairs of corner frames can be permanently assembled and yet stored flat. Dibelius (1906: 88) shows a framework housed in the Berlin Museum (Egyptian collection item 8708) whose parts are connected in an L-shape by rings.

Figure 11a [left]. Corner *qereš*
Figure 11b [right]. Corner *qereš* (alternative structure)

Speculation: Ordinarily, *hā'eḥāt* 'the one' is followed by *haššēnît* 'the second' (cf. 1:15; 25:32; 29:39; 37:18, etc.). Moreover, preceding *milləmaṭṭâ* 'from below,' we would expect *milmaʿlâ* 'from above' (cf. Deut 28:13; Jer 31:37; Ezek 1:27; Eccl 3:21). I wonder, then, whether 26:24 and in consequence 36:29 suffered an early, major loss of text. But I would not venture to restore the lacuna.

26:25. *two bases . . . two bases.* On the repetition, see NOTE to 26:19.

26:26. *crossbars.* Staves running along each side unite the *qərāšîm* into a fence that is easy to assemble and disassemble. The number, length and placement of the crossbars are disputed (see below).

five. One would initially think that the side bars are thirty cubits, running the walls' entire length (Rashbam), while the rear bars are twelve cubits (see p. 503). See next NOTE, however.

26:28. *the inner crossbar.* In what sense is this bar "inner" *(tîkôn)*? And is it one of the aforementioned five (Rashi) or an additional sixth bar (*Num. Rab.* 6:4; Rashbam)?

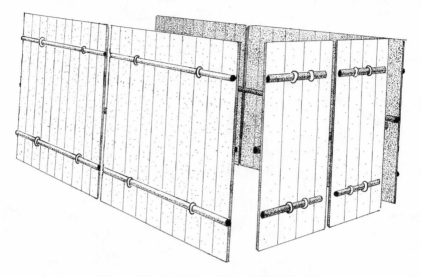

Figure 12a. *Qərāšîm* and bars (exploded view)

A popular model supposes that each of the walls is divided into two halves, just as the curtains are composed of two fastened sections (26:3–6, 9–11). To make the side walls, first two 15–cubit panels of twenty *qərāšîm* are assembled with poles at top and bottom (four bars). Then a longer, 30–cubit bar is inserted from end to end, holding the two half-walls in place (Rashi; Kennedy 1898: 660) (30–cubit acacia poles, admittedly, would require unsually large trees; see Zevit 1992.) Analogously, the rear wall is composed of two half-walls of six cubits. Thus the "inner crossbar" is the central among the three rows; there really are three "inner crossbars" for the entire Tabernacle.

But this explanation does not account for *bətôk haqqərāšîm* 'amid the *qərāšîm*,' for which Rashi and Dillmann proffer conflicting interpretations (see following). Another difficulty is the construction of the back wall. Why, if it is feasible to make 15–cubit units for the sides, should the 12–cubit back not be assembled whole, instead of in two panels?

amid the qərāšîm. What is the sense of *bətôk* 'amid, inside'? For Rashi, who envisions cubit-thick *qərāšîm*, the central pole passes *through* the frames themselves. The rings mentioned in v 29 are only for the upper and lower bars. Dillmann (1880: 291), however, suggests that the middle pole is simply *halfway up* the *qərāšîm*, although this would be a peculiar use of *bətôk*. The best interpretation is that, while the other bars are on the outside, this one runs along the interior (fig. 12a; cf. Homan 2002: 149).

barring from end to end. It is usually understood that each wall has one pole running its entire length—which in turn suggests that the other four or five bars do not (previous NOTE). Although his model is hard to square with Exodus, Josephus *Ant.* 3.120 adds the novel notion that the side bars plug into the rear bars for added stability at the corners.

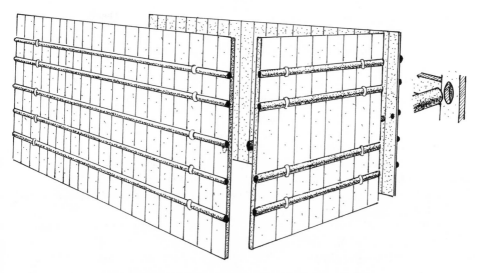

FIGURE 12b. *Qərāšîm* and bars (alternative, exploded view)

SPECULATION: As observed above (NOTES to 26:24), the text does not specify clearly what holds the corners together. Inspired by Josephus and by *Mel. Mišk.*, I tentatively propose the following. Each of three sides has five bars running the entire length, as one would initially assume from vv 26–27. Since v 28 follows directly out of v 27b, it applies to the rear wall alone. Of the rear wall's five cross-bars, the middle one *(tîkôn)* passes not only through the rings but also through *(bətôk)* the side *qərāšîm* themselves, thus holding the corners together. It alone is inside the Tabernacle framework; the other bars are outside (fig. 12b).

26:29. *rings.* We are not told how many rings are made, nor how they are arranged. Their number depends upon whether all the bars run the entire length and width (previous NOTES).

26:30. *its rule.* Hebrew *mišpāṭ* properly denotes legal judgment but sometimes connotes exact measurement (e.g., 1 Kgs 5:8; 6:38; Jer 30:18) or description (e.g., *mišpaṭ hammelek* 'the king's attributes' [1 Sam 8:9, 11]).

you were made to see. The text reiterates that Moses was shown something on the mountain, presumably to supplement the Torah's confusing and incomplete verbal instructions (cf. Cassuto 1967: 351; NOTES to 25:9; 27:8, "he made you see"). Here the verb *hor'êtā* is past tense not present. Thus, as in 27:8, the author drops the pretense that Moses is simultaneously observing a model or plan (contrast 25:9, 40). To preserve chronological integrity, we might take the verb as future perfect—"you shall have been made to see" (Rashi)—but then why "on *the* mountain" and not "on *this* mountain"? Rather, the author is writing from his own temporal perspective.

26:31. *veil.* Parōket, unique to the Tabernacle texts, is of debated derivation and meaning. Its ancient pronunciation was probably **parrukt*. For the etymology, most scholars look either to Akkadian *parāku* 'lie across, obstruct' or to Akkadian *parakku* 'shrine' (Driver 1911: 289; Cassuto 1967: 359), the latter derived from Sumerian BARAG and borrowed into Syriac and Hatra Aramaic as *prakkā'/praktā'* 'pagan shrine' (Kaufman 1974: 80). Perhaps, then, two etymological streams have coalesced in Hebrew *pārōket*. But the closest linguistic parallel, to my knowledge not previously noticed, is Akkadian *paruktu* (**parruktu?*), denoting a woolen sail. Since *par(r)uktu* appears only rarely and only in Late Babylonian, we cannot be certain whether it is a West Semitic (Phoenician?) term borrowed into Akkadian or vice versa. (This is not the only case of nautical terminology in the Tabernacle pericope; see also NOTES to 26:15; 27:9, "sheets." And Ezekiel's description of the Tyrian ship of state [chap. 27] manifests striking similarities to P's Tabernacle.)

With most commentators, I understand the *pārōket* as a curtain analogous to that of the Second Temple (Matt 27:51; Mark 15:38; Luke 23:45; cf. Heb 6:19; 10:19–32). Friedman (1981: 52), however, suggests it is rather a canopy, a miniature tent-within-a-tent (cf. below, pp. 503–4).

webster's work . . . Griffins. See NOTES to 26:1. If actual Griffins are intended, note that they protect access to Yahweh, just as the Griffins of Eden guard the portal to Paradise (Gen 3:24).

26:32. *acacia posts*. 'Ammûdê šiṭṭîm is shorthand for "acacia-wood posts" (*'ammûdê 'ăṣê šiṭṭîm), just as goat-hair curtains are called simply "goat(s)" (e.g., 25:4). Their height is not mentioned. Haran (1978: 154 n. 10) supposes them to be only five cubits tall, like the Plaza's posts—but, as he acknowledges, in that case they would not reach the ceiling. The maximum is ten cubits, the height of the Tabernacle.

Y-brackets. I have chosen "Y-bracket" to translate *wāw*, ordinarily the name of the sixth letter of the Hebrew alphabet. As an architectural feature, a *wāw* must be something shaped like the letter. But in what form? And which came first, the letter name or the object?

A priori, we might assume the object came first, since all or almost all the Hebrew letters were originally pictures of common objects: 'aleph was an ox head, beth a house, gimel a boomerang, etc. If so, we must look to the *original* shape of waw in earliest, pre-Hebrew inscriptions of the Middle and Late Bronze Age: a circle atop a vertical line (a "lollipop"). Since LXX and Syr interpret *wāw* in Exodus as "capital," we might suppose that the letter waw originally depicted a finial atop a pole.

It is more likely, however, that the object *wāw* was named after the letter, which in the Iron Age resembled English "Y." (If there had been an ancient Semitic term *waw, it ought to have become *yāw in Hebrew [Tur-Sinai 1950: 170–74].) Assyrian depictions of both Arabian tents (Yadin 1963: 451; Homan 2002: pl. 18) and their own military tents (Bezold 1903: 16; Homan, pl. 17), as well as Egyptian representations of tents (Hassan 1943: 80; Youssef, LeBlanc and Maher 1977: pl. xxii; Hayutin 1993: 235; Homan 2002: pl. 32b), all show vertical posts forking at the top. The bracket always supports a crossing pole, which may or may not be the Hebrew *ḥāšûq* (see further NOTE to 27:10, "*ḥăšūqîm*").

From 26:32, 37; 27:10–11, etc., one would think that the *wāw* is solid metal.

But we can infer from 38:28 that the metallic portion of each Y-bracket weighs under 11.9 oz./338 g., far too little for a separate fixture (see NOTE). Since 36:38 and 38:28 refer to plating the "head" of a post apropos of the Y-bracket, I conclude that each pole bifurcates at the top. This fork is plated in gold or silver, constituting the *wāw*.

gold. I.e., gold-plated; see preceding NOTE.

bases. These weigh a talent each, c. 75.5 lbs./34 kg. (38:27). The bases must be sufficiently heavy to prevent the posts and Veil from toppling, yet light enough to be shifted when the priest enters the inner chamber (Leviticus 16).

26:33. *under the clasps.* That is, the Veil hangs directly under the golden clasps of the inner curtains, twenty cubits from the entrance (see p. 503).

separate. On the theme of "separation" *(hibdîl)* in P, see briefly Otzen (1977) and below, pp. 688–89.

for you. Houtman (2000: 441) asks who is the addressee: Aaron's sons or all Israel? Only for the former would the distinction matter. Ordinary Israelites are barred from the Tent in any case.

Holiness . . . Holiness of Holinesses. The former *(haqqōdeš)* is the Tabernacle's outer chamber; the latter *(qōdeš haqqŏdāšîm)*, which might be paraphrased "the utmost Holiness," is the inner room where God's presence sojourns. The same superlative also describes the Bronze Altar (29:37; 40:10), the Golden Altar (30:10) and even the whole Tabernacle (30:29). On P's notion of Holiness, see pp. 683–90.

26:34. *on the Testimony Chest in the Holiness of Holinesses.* The verse combines two commands. Moses must first set the *kappōret* on the Testimony Chest, and then put them both in the Holiness of Holinesses.

26:35. *southward . . . north.* In other words, as one enters the Tabernacle from the east, the Lampstand is on the left and the Table on the right (fig. 13). The order of description is implicitly chiastic: "Table . . . Lampstand . . . south (for the Lampstand) . . . north (for the Table)."

26:36. *screen.* The noun *māsāk* derives from the root *skk* (also *ś/swk*) 'to cover, obstruct, protect.' Josephus *Ant.* 3.127 imagines the priests creeping under the Screen in a forced obeisance. More likely, it was simply pushed aside.

Opening. As with Solomon's Temple (Ezek 8:16), the Tabernacle opens to the east side.

embroiderer's work. The root *rqm* denotes some sort of textile decoration. "Embroider" comes from the Arabic cognate, but we are not told what the pattern is. Haran (1978: 160–62) thinks that *rqm* is a grade of weaving less demanding and hence less valuable than *ḥšb*, which has figures, but more challenging than ordinary *'rg*.

26:37. *posts.* Again, the height is unmentioned (cf. NOTE to 26:32, "acacia posts").

Y-brackets gold. On the nature of the gold-plated *wāwîm*, see NOTE to 26:32, "Y-brackets." On the nonmention of *ḥăšūqîm*, see NOTE to 27:10, "*ḥăšūqîm*."

bases. We do not know their weight, which must be sufficient to support the posts and the Screen. The total amount of bronze for the entire Tabernacle is

FIGURE 13. Tabernacle interior

seventy talents plus 2,400 shekels; most likely, the 70 talents go to make the sixty bases for the Plaza and its Screen (38:29–31) (NOTE to 38:30). If so, each base weighs c. 193.6 lbs./88 kg.

27:1. *the Altar.* On the unexpected definite article, see TEXTUAL NOTE. Ehrlich (1908: 371) suggests that it is called "*the* Altar" from the start, because a sacrificial installation is the *sine qua non* of any cult site.

Mizbēaḥ 'altar' is composed of the prefix *m-*, indicating the place where an activity is performed (GKC §85*e*), plus the root *zbḥ*, which ordinarily means "to sacrifice" but originally meant "to slaughter" (Arabic *ḏbḥ*; see Milgrom 1972). This etymology has led to speculation that *mizbēaḥ* originally meant "slaughter block" (Smith 1927: 341; see further pp. 695–705).

acacia wood. On the syntax, see NOTE to 25:10, "acacia wood."

five . . . five . . . three. I.e., c. 7.5 × 7.5 × 4.5 feet or 2.5 × 2.5 × 1.5 m. These are the exact dimensions of an altar unearthed at Arad—made, however, of plastered stone and earth, not bronze-plated wood (Aharoni 1968: 21, 25). Against the plain sense, a widespread Rabbinic tradition makes the Altar ten cubits high; see Jacob (1992: 802–5); Heger (1999: 172–73 n. 3).

foursquare. Viewed from above, the Altar would appear square *(rābûaʻ).*

27:2. *horns.* Ordinary stone altars display protuberances at the corners, called *qərānōt* 'horns' after their curved contour; for the most famous specimen, the altar of Beer-Sheba, see Aharoni (1974) or any handbook of biblical archaeology. The horns lend the structure an impressive air, like a crown, and may define a vertical zone of sanctity (below, pp. 499–51). But they were likely functional as well. At least in one case, it seems that the horns supported a metal barbecue (Rainey 1994: 338). And, though somewhat obscure, Ps 118:27, "bind the *ḥag* [festival sacrifice?] with ropes up to [ʻ*ad*] the Altar's horns," suggests that the meat might be literally tied down (cf. Calvin). But neither of these reflects the horns' primary purpose, I think.

The altar top is essentially a bowl with the sides cut away. The horn's function is to contain the fuel and meat while not unduly restricting the airflow (cf. Clements 1972: 175). This is also the function of the Assyrian "bench altar," which, seen from the side, resembles the Syro-Palestinian horned altar (Galling 1925: 46–48; additional illustration in Parrot 1961: 5). Horned altars are common in Hellenistic Egypt (Soukiassian 1983), with some depictions clearly showing the butchered animal parts supported between the horns (e.g., Quaegebeur 1993: 353 pl. V a). Other specimens are known from Cyprus and the Greek world (Karageorghis 1981). (As for an allegedly relevant prehistoric custom of mounting bulls' skulls on the altar, we may suppose it was long forgotten by biblical times [on the Neolithic bull cult at Çatalhöyük, see Oates and Oates 1976: 87–94].)

While the Bible is silent on the horns' practical purpose, it is explicit about their two religious functions. First, for Sin-offerings, they are anointed with purifying blood (29:12; see further pp. 698–703). Second, a fugitive may grasp an altar's horns to obtain temporary asylum (NOTE to 21:14 and below, p. 501).

from it. I.e., the horns are permanently attached; see NOTES to 25:19, "on the *kappōret*," 36, "they shall be from it."

bronze. The Altar stands in the Plaza, a place of lesser sanctity than the Tabernacle proper. Accordingly, it is made of bronze and is sometimes called the "Bronze Altar" (38:30; 39:39; 1 Kgs 8:64; 2 Kgs 16:14–15; Ezek 9:2; 2 Chr 1:5–6; 7:7), in contrast to the "Golden Altar" of incense situated within the Tabernacle (39:38; 40:5, 26; Num 4:11; 1 Kgs 7:48; 2 Chr 4:19). The metallic plating is decorative (though liable to oxidation) and also prevents both rot and scorching. In addition to the Bible's Bronze Altar, we are told that the altar of Hierapolis in Syria was of bronze (pseudo-Lucian *Dea Syria* 39 [Attridge and Oden 1976: 48–49]). Phoenician (*KAI* 10.4) and Punic (*KAI* 66.1) texts likewise mention bronze altars. On the anachronism with Num 17:3, see NOTE to 38:2.

27:3. *pots.* The *sîrōt* are generally assumed to be for conveying ashes outside the camp (cf. Lev 1:16; 4:12; 6:3–4; Num 4:13; Jer 31:40) (e.g., Cassuto 1967: 363). I should think, however, that shovels would suffice for this purpose (see TEXTUAL NOTE). If the received text is correct, perhaps the pots are for rinsing the Altar.

de-ashing. Diššēn means "to remove *dešen*," i.e., fat or fat ashes, a procedure described in Lev 6:3–4. Accumulating on the Altar (cf. 1 Kgs 13:3, 5), burnt fat would require frequent cleaning. For the semantic development, Rashi compares *šēreš* 'uproot' (< *šōreš* 'root'), *sēʿēp* 'lop off' (< *sāʿîp* 'branch') and *ʿiṣṣēm* 'break bones' (< *ʿeṣem* 'bone'). The most prominent example of this "privative" Piʿel is *ḥiṭṭēʾ* 'purify' (< *ḥēṭ[ʾ]* 'sin') (GKC §52h).

shovels. The singular of *yāʿîm* is unattested, and the exact meaning is uncertain. Although BDB gives *yāʿ*, to judge from the verbal root *yʿy* 'sweep away' (?) (Isa 28:17), we would expect rather a singular **yāʿe(h)*. (Compare also Arabic *wʿy* 'gather' and possibly Egyptian *iʿi* 'wash, rinse away' [Grintz 1975: 19].) From the nearby mention of removing ashes, most infer that the *yāʿîm* are shovels or sweepers for transfering burnt fat from the Altar to the "de-ashing" pots (e.g., Cassuto 1967: 363); see, however, NOTE to "pots" above. For images of such shovels, see Zwickel (1990: 161–65).

bowls. *Mizrāq* derives from the root *zrq* 'cast, sprinkle,' often used apropos of sacrificial blood (24:6; 29:16, 20, etc.). These vessels are probably used to collect blood for splashing against the Altar (Rashbam).

forks. *Mizlāgōt* is presumably related to *mazlēg*, a tridentate fork used to manipulate sacrificial meat (1 Sam 2:13–14) (Rashi; Rashbam); compare also Cappadocian Akkadian *mazlagu*. On such forks recovered in excavations, see Zwickel (1990: 157–65). The "forks" are probably listed between "bowls" and "fire pans" for assonance: *ûmizrəqōtā(y)w ûmizləgōtā(y)w ûmaḥtōtā(y)w* (cf. Cassuto 1967: 363).

in short. On this usage of *lə-*, see NOTE to 1:14.

27:4. *mesh, lattice work.* *Mikbār* is of the same root as *kəbārâ* 'sieve' (Rashi) and is some kind of metal reticulation (*rešet*). According to v 5, it is installed halfway up the Altar's height.

Exegetes differ on whether the *mikbār* is inside or outside the Altar. Many envision a grill set inside the hollow Altar, allowing ash to fall and air to enter (LXX; Josephus *Ant.* 3.149; Calvin; Cole 1973: 196–97; Durham 1987: 372). The altar at Beersheba, to judge from stain marks, once had a metal grill on top (Rainey 1994: 338). But why emphasize that the grate is under the collar that presumably runs around the outside (NOTE to 27:5)? It is also hard to understand how and why the carrying poles are attached to an interior grate, rather than to the Altar itself. (A possibility: the rings pass through the Altar's sides, so that the poles lock the grate into the Altar [see fig. 14b].)

The alternative opinion, to which I incline, regards the *mikbār* as a netting around the Altar's sides, keeping them in alignment and attaching them to the poles (see fig. 14a). A third-century C.E. coin from Byblos depicts a horned altar with meshwork sides (Keel 1978: 183 fig. 246). See further NOTES to 27:5; 29:16, and, for further discussion, Houtman (2000: 444–46).

its four corners. The suffix on *qəṣôtā(y)w* is masculine, so the antecedent is probably not *rešet* 'lattice' (fem.) but either *mikbār* 'mesh' or, less likely, *mizbēaḥ* 'Altar' (Jacob 1992: 802), both masculine.

27:5. *rim.* Morphologically, *karkōb* is peculiar; for the pattern $C_1C_2C_1C_3$, cf. *qarqaʿ* 'floor, ground.' *Karkōb* is presumably related to various words containing *k*

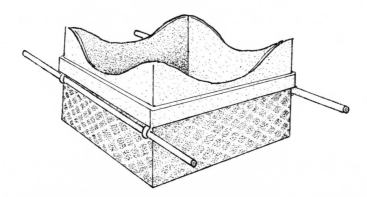

FIGURE 14a. Bronze altar

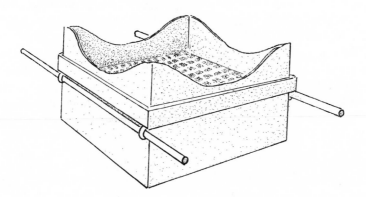

FIGURE 14b. Bronze altar (alternative structure)

and *r* or *k* and *b* referring to circularity: *kikkār* 'flat, round object or area' and *kirkēr* 'whirl' (Biblical Hebrew); *krk* 'encircle' (Rabbinic Hebrew and Aramaic); Arabic *kabbaba* 'roll (thread)'; Ethiopic *kababa* 'orbit'; cf. also Hebrew *kôkāb* (< **kawkab* < **kabkab*) 'star'; Aramaic *kubbā'* 'barrel'; Arabic *kūb* 'cup.' On an Edomite ostracon, the letters *krkb* are legible, but without a clarifying context (Puech 1977: 17).

Many think the Altar's *karkōb* is a broad ledge on which the priests stand (*b. Zebaḥ.* 62a; Childs 1974: 526). But it is surprising that Exodus should not mention more clearly so prominent a feature. To me, the natural interpretation is that the *karkōb* is a collar halfway up the Altar, such as we find on horned incense altars, e.g., from Megiddo (Cassuto 1967: 364; Milgrom 1972: 762; NOTE to 30:2, "from it its horns"). *Pace* Cassuto, however, the *karkōb* is not just ornamental, at least in the case of the Tabernacle Altar. The rim would let the Altar nest snugly within the mesh-and-pole assembly without falling through when lifted (fig. 14a). This reading also works for LXX, where it is the *rings* not the poles that are under the rim (TEXTUAL NOTE, "it"). See also next NOTE.

as far as half the Altar. The external meshwork evidently surrounds the lower half of the Altar (but Milgrom [1972: 762] thinks the upper), holding the sides in place and allowing the entire assembly to be carried securely by poles. Since the Altar's lower parts receive sacrificial blood, the *mikbār* may also serve to retain the blood against the Altar's sides and shield the Altar from human touch (NOTES to 29:12, 16). On Cassuto's theory of the mesh's function, see NOTE to 27:8, "Hollow-planked."

27:7. *And its poles shall be inserted.* On MT's slightly unusual grammar, with the passive verb *wəhûbā'* plus a direct object *'et-baddā(y)w*, see GKC §121 *a,b*; Waltke and O'Connor 1990: 177–78.

in carrying it. The Altar's carrying poles are stored when not in use. Cf. NOTE to 25:15.

27:8. *Hollow-planked. Nəbûb lūḥōt* is a slightly strange expression. By the consensus (but see below), it means that the Altar is constructed of wooden planks with a hollow center (e.g., *Tg. Ps.-Jonathan; Mek. baḥōdeš* 11; *b. Zebaḥ.* 61b; Rashi). Why a hollow Altar? Presumably to lighten the load during transit; a large stone altar would be impossible to carry.

Unlike the Incense Altar (30:3), the Bronze Altar does not explicitly have an upper surface to hold the fire and offering itself. Some assume that there is a bronze-plated top (e.g., Kennedy 1898: 657–58), which, against intuition (e.g., Ginzberg 1928: 3.162), has been shown capable of withstanding high temperatures (Nowack 1992). Another possibility is that the *mikbār* of v 4 is a cooking grate inside the Altar's cavity, but there are difficulties with this view (see NOTE to 27:4).

If the *mikbār* is instead an external structure and there is no top, then how might the Altar be used? Dillmann (1880: 295) and Cassuto (1967: 362) suggest that the hollow space is filled with dirt or stones, upon which the sacrifice is burnt. This is admittedly an attempt to harmonize P with JE, which ordains an altar of earth or rough stones (20:24–25)—but that does not make the interpretation incorrect. I find its simplicity compelling.

SPECULATION: Let us further consider Cassuto's reconstruction of the Altar, as it suggests an alternative understanding of *nəbûb lūḥōt*. To facilitate air flow, he argues, the planks must be perforated, allowing air to rise through the presumably loose filling. The surrounding bronze lattice is intended, then, to keep dirt and stones from falling out the air holes. Although Cassuto upholds the traditional interpretation of *nəbûb lūḥōt*, by his model the phrase could be rendered "with pierced planks" (to *nbb* compare the roots *ḥll* and *nqb*, which connote both hollowness and perforation). Somewhat similarly, Saadiah envisions the Altar as consisting of four posts surmounted by the horns, with the empty space between covered by mesh below and left open above (see Qafaḥ 1963: 72 n. 3).

he made you see. "He" is presumably Yahweh, but the lack of a specified subject may imply that the verb is impersonal: "one showed you." If so, *her'â 'ōtəkā* is tantamount to *hor'êtā* 'you were made to see' (26:30). As in 25:9, 40; 26:30; Num 8:4, the author seems to sense the inadequacy of his descriptions. He reassures the reader that Moses knew exactly what he was doing, even if we do not.

on the mountain. See NOTE to 26:30, "you were made to see."

27:9. *Plaza.* Ḥāṣēr designates an enclosed area where people congregate.

austral, southward. On the redundancy, see NOTE to 26:18.

sheets. These qəlāʿîm are of fine linen, unlike the heavier linen and wool curtains (yərîʿōt) that define the inner Tabernacle. The same word, like Arabic qilʿ, denotes a ship's sail (Rashi; Noth 1962: 216; cf. Philo *Moses* 2.90; *Mel. Mišk.* 5). The Plaza sheets are probably suspended from spars mounted on a central "mast" (see p. 498).

Since the posts are set at intervals of five cubits, most infer that to be the width of each sheet (e.g., *Mel. Mišk.* 5). Their height is explicitly five cubits (27:18). Unlike the curtains of the Tabernacle, the Plaza's sheets are not said to be combined into long panels, as one might expect (Cassuto 1967: 365). Is each anchored individually to flap in the wind? Overall, the text devotes less detail to the Plaza than to the holier Tabernacle.

twisted linen. As no dye is mentioned, the sheets are presumably their natural, off-white color (Cassuto 1967: 365).

27:10. *its posts.* Their material is not specified; presumably it is acacia wood, the only lumber donated (25:5; 35:24) (Haran 1978: 164; Jacob 1992: 807). On the number of the posts, see p. 498.

their (second time). "Their" (*-hem*) probably refers to the posts, less likely to the Y-brackets. This is Hebrew's necessary circumlocution for "the posts' Y-brackets and ḥăšūqîm" (GKC §128a).

Y-brackets. On the nature of the wāw, see NOTE to 26:32, "Y-brackets."

ḥăšūqîm. The meaning is uncertain. As the root ḥšq means "attach, bind," most envision bindings of silver around each post (e.g., Rashi), whether to secure the Y-bracket (fig. 15) or merely for decoration. (The tent poles of the prince of Megiddo, despoiled by Thutmose III, were similarly adorned with silver [Lichtheim 1976: 34].) An alternative sees the ḥāšūq as a curtain rod or spar supported by the Y-bracket (Cassuto 1967: 365) (fig. 15). For illustrations of tents with Y-brackets and curtain rods, see Bezold (1903: 16); Hassan (1943: 80); Yadin (1963: 451); Youssef, LeBlanc and Maher (1977: pl. xxii), and Ḥayutin (1993: 235).

A complication is that the metal component of the ḥāšūq must be very light (NOTE to 38:28). If it is a decorative binding, there is no problem. If it is a rod, however, it must be silver-plated, not solid silver.

Significantly, the Veil and the Tabernacle Screen are supported by posts and Y-brackets but lack ḥăšūqîm (26:32, 37; 27:16). Whatever they are, perhaps ḥăšūqîm would have impeded ingress and egress by holding the posts and/or the curtains in place. Perhaps they were also omitted from the Plaza Screen.

silver. This probably means silver-plated; see NOTES to 26:32, "Y-brackets"; 38:38.

27:12. *sea side.* Hebrew yām connotes the direction of the Mediterranean from the perspective of Canaan, i.e., the west.

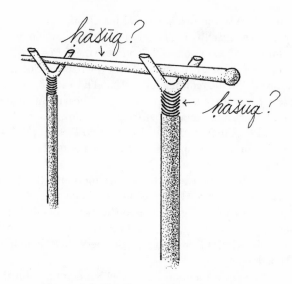

Figure 15. Y-brackets and alternative *ḥăšūqîm*

posts . . . bases. While 27:12 does not refer to Y-brackets or *ḥăšūqîm* for the west side, 27:17 makes their presence clear (Jacob 1992: 807).

27:13. *forward.* Because Israelites "oriented" themselves by facing toward the sunrise, *qēdmâ* implies "eastward."

sunrise. The root of *mizrāḥ* is *zrḥ* 'shine out.' On the rhetorical redundancy of *qēdmâ mizrāḥâ* here and in 38:13 (also Num 2:3; 34:15; Josh 19:13), see NOTE to 26:18.

27:14. *shoulder.* *Kātēp* is another anatomical-architectural term (see COMMENT, pp. 717–18), connoting the short sides flanking the doorway.

27:16. *screen.* Unlike the Veil and the Tabernacle Screen, we are not told how the Plaza Screen is attached to its posts. See NOTE to 27:10, "*ḥăšūqîm.*"

blue . . . purple . . . worm-crimson . . . linen. Unlike the white sheets, the Plaza Screen wears the Tabernacle's colors, as if to permit a glimpse of the splendor within. But the work is *rqm*, not the more prestigious *ḥšb*, presumably because there are no figures (contrast 26:1, 31). Its description matches that of the inner Screen in 26:36, equally a border between different degrees of sanctity. On these fabrics and dyes, see NOTES to 26:1.

embroiderer's work. See NOTE to 26:36.

27:17. *All the Plaza's posts.* This is not redundant, because, in fact, only the posts of the north and south sides have been described fully (Rashi). I am uncertain whether it includes the posts of the Plaza Screen, which may have lacked *ḥăšūqîm* (NOTE to 27:10, "*ḥăšūqîm*").

məḥuššāqîm. This is another of P's characteristic Puʿal technical terms (COMMENT, pp. 717–18); it means "featuring *ḥăšūqîm*," which are most likely either fillets or curtain rods (see NOTE to 27:10).

27:18. *one hundred upon one hundred . . . fifty upon fifty.* I.e., each of the two long sides measures 100 cubits, and each of the short sides measures 50 (cf. ibn Ezra).

My text follows LXX and Sam (TEXTUAL NOTE). MT, however, has "one hundred *by the cubit* and fifty upon fifty.' The last phrase *(ḥămiššîm baḥămiššîm)* is traditionally understood as giving the forecourt's dimensions—50 × 50 (Philo *Moses* 2.91–92; *Mel. Mišk.* 5; Rashi; *b. ʿErub.* 23b; Jacob 1992: 806)—and hence the Tabernacle's location within the Plaza. In fact, we do not know where in the Plaza the Tent stands (below, p. 498).

and their bases, bronze. V 18 ends with the same words as v 17, showing that the enclosed material is a digression (cf. Kuhl 1952).

27:19. *in short.* See NOTE to 1:14.

all the Tabernacle's implements. It is not clear whether *kəlê hammiškān* refers to the bronze tools used in constructing the Tabernacle—chisels, saws, etc. (Rashi; Cassuto 1967: 368)—or rather the sacred implements of the Altar. If building tools are intended, the nonmention of iron is striking. It could reflect either the narrative's Late Bronze Age setting or else taboos against using iron to fashion sacred objects (NOTE to 20:25[22]).

its Work. Cassuto (1967: 368) understands *ʿăbōdātô* to mean "its construction." But *ʿăbōdâ* also means "worship," admittedly mostly outside of P (Milgrom 1983a: 18–46). See further NOTE to 30:16, "Meeting Tent Work."

tent-pegs . . . tent-pegs. The fabric is tied down to keep it from blowing in the wind (Rashbam). From the first *yətēdōtā(y)w* we learn that the fabrics draped about the Tabernacle's wooden frames *(qərāšîm)* are also anchored with pegs and cords (cf. 35:18; 38:20, 31). The tent-pegs receive far more attention in the actual construction of the Tabernacle than in its blueprint (39:40; Num 3:37; 4:32), presumably because they are ordinary objects requiring no special design.

27:20. *And you.* In the preceding paragraphs, the command "(and) you shall make" does not mean that Moses is to fashion the Tabernacle himself. Rather, he is to oversee its construction. Now, however, Yahweh addresses Moses specifically (Ramban) with an emphatic, threefold *wə'attâ* 'And you' (27:20; 28:1, 3), telling him to order the oil, to summon Aaron's family and to commission the priestly garments (Sforno). Because the switch in tone is so striking, scribal tradition begins a new weekly reading *(pārāšâ)* here. The Christian arranger of chapters and verses, in contrast, finds a more pronounced break after v 21.

pure, crushed olive oil. Exod 27:20 repeats the demand in 25:6 for an oil donation, adding the qualification that, since the need is perpetual, the offering is continual and mandatory (cf. Cassuto 1967: 269). The Hebrew diction is loose, for in terms of manufacture, it is the olive itself, not the oil, that is *kātît* 'crushed' (cf. ibn Ezra, both commentaries). This is the finest grade, probably hand-ground in a mortar *(m. Menaḥ.* 8:4–5), not crushed in a large press (Cassuto 1967: 369–70; Durham 1987: 379). The goal is to eliminate impurities that would create smoke (Stager and Wolff 1981: 97) and smudge the curtains. Oil of such purity is used only for the Lampstand (Lev 24:2) and the daily grain offering (Exod 29:40; Num 28:5). For other purposes, a lesser grade suffices. On ancient techniques of oil manufacture, see Stager (1983); Serpico and White (2000: 405–7), and for modern Palestine, Dalman (1935: 153–290).

for illumination. Since the Lampstand is called *mənōrat hammā'ôr* 'the Illumination Lampstand' (35:14; Num 4:9), Hyatt (1980: 279) suggests that here and in 25:6; 35:28; Num 4:16, "illumination" is shorthand for "the Illumination Lampstand."

raise. On this idiom for kindling a fire or installing a lamp, see NOTE to 25:37, "raise."

continual. In Exod 27:20–21, *tāmîd* need not describe something that never ceases, but possibly an act performed at regular, daily intervals (Rashi; cf. 30:7–8; Lev 24:3). I think, however, that the flames are truly perpetual (with Ramban, but for different reasons); see further below.

lamp. Nēr can also be translated "flame." Cole (1973: 198) raises the possibility that this is not the great Lampstand but a simple night light.

27:21. in Meeting Tent. Though it scarcely matters, it is not clear whether "in Meeting Tent" goes with what precedes or what follows. My translation reflects Syr-Vg (TEXTUAL NOTE, "Let . . . arrange").

'Ōhel mō'ēd is grammatically definite; i.e., it functions as a proper name. The lack of a definite article (i.e., **'ōhel hammō'ēd*) bespeaks the term's archaic provenance (Ehrlich 1908: 377). In prebiblical literature, *m'd* denotes the gods' meeting tent (Clifford 1971) or a municipal council, as in the Egyptian "Voyage of Wen-Amon" (ANET 29; Wilson 1945). For the Priestly Writer, however, "Meeting Tent" is not where the gods assemble on a distant mountain or in Heaven, but where God meets Israel in their very midst, traveling among them (on the priests as representing the lesser members of the pantheon, see below, pp. 525–26).

SPECULATION: We do not know how, prior to P, Israelites understood the term *mō'ēd*. Perhaps they shared P's interpretation. Or they may have used "Meeting Tent" to describe where the tribes would gather, especially on festival days (another meaning of *mō'ēd*—e.g., Lev 23:4, "These are Yahweh's *mō'ădîm*"). On *mō'ēd*, see further pp. 691–94.

before the Testimony. '*Ēdūt* 'Testimony' often implies "Testimony Chest" (ibn Ezra); see p. 383. In this context, '*al-hā'ēdūt* must mean "*before* the Testimony (Chest)," not "*over* the Testimony (Chest)"; cf., however, Friedman's (1981: 52) theory that the *pārōket* is a canopy (NOTE to 26:31, "veil").

and his sons. In Lev 24:3, Aaron alone is commanded to kindle the lamps. Haran (1978: 209, 227) infers that *ûbānā(y)w* 'and his sons' in Exod 27:21 is a misguided gloss (cf. the slightly different conclusion of Levine 1965: 311–12). If necessary, however, we can eliminate the minor contradiction by identifying these offspring not as the minor clergy but as the future Great Priestly succession (cf. NOTE to 29:29, "his sons after him").

arrange. Since the root '*rk* can mean "estimate, evaluate," Yepheth ben 'Ali (*apud* ibn Ezra) interprets *ya'ărōk* as "measure," the point being that the oil must suffice for the entire night. But the parallel with the Table's "arrangement" (*'erek/ma'ăreket*) of bread (40:4; Lev 24:6–7) suggests rather lamps arranged in a row (ibn Ezra); cf. *nērôt hamma'ărākâ* 'the arrangement lamps' (39:37).

from evening till morning. By the plain sense, the lamps burn only at night. According to 30:7–8, Aaron "adjusts" *(hêṭîb)* them in the morning and "raises" *(he'ĕlâ)* their fire again in the evening (see NOTES). Milgrom [2001: 2089] cites a comparable Hittite practice at Nerik.

SPECULATION: There is a tradition, however, first attested in Josephus *Ant.* 3.199, that at least some lamps burn by both day and night, whence the custom of a perpetual light above the synagogue ark (cf. *m. Tamid* 3:9; *Sifra 'ĕmōr* 13:7). After all, the Tabernacle's interior, shrouded in wool and leather, would presumably be pitch dark even by day. How can the priests see what they are doing?

If the lamps never go out, what is the point of 27:21? Perhaps during the night, when one ordinarily sleeps, Aaron or his designee must keep a vigil to tend the flames. Or perhaps the priest must remember to use a longer wick and more oil before retiring (ibn Ezra). Or the Priestly Writer may be emphatically repudiating an older practice of letting the fire go out during the night (1 Sam 3:3).

before Yahweh. *Lipnê yahwe(h)*, literally "to Yahweh's face," is a technical expression describing the Tabernacle's inner sanctum, where part of Yahweh's essence is supposed to be concentrated (see pp. 619–20, 686–88).

an eternal rule for their ages. I.e., tending the lamps is the priests' constant duty forever. See also following NOTE.

from Israel's Sons. In context, the phrase cannot mean that the decree originates from Israel (contrast Gen 47:22, "a rule for the priests *from Pharaoh*"). Rather, *mē'ēt bənê yiśrā'ēl* implies two things. First, that lighting the lamps is the priests' task performed on Israel's behalf (Luzzatto, comparing Deut 18:3; Cassuto 1967: 370). Second, Israel, too, has its duty: supplying the priests with oil (Lev 24:2). Compare Exod 29:28, "for Aaron and for his sons as an eternal rule from Israel's Sons, for it is a Donation-offering."

Exod 27:20–21 reappears in a nearly identical form in Lev 24:2–3. For an explanation, see Milgrom (2001: 2084).

28:1. *And you.* See NOTE to 27:20.

Bring Near to yourself. In this context, *haqrēb* 'bring near' might mean "select out" from the mass of Israelites (Dillmann 1880: 298). "To yourself" may additionally imply that Aaron's family will be elevated like Moses himself (Ehrlich 1969: 191). The priests will not actually be robed and consecrated until after the Tabernacle is built (Leviticus 8). The command is therefore prospective, not intended for immediate fulfillment.

Since, however, *hiqrîb* (< *qrb* "approach") is usually a technical term for consecrating something *to* God (NOTE to 29:3) — hence my capitalization — we might have expected "Bring Near to *me* (cf. Ehrlich 1908: 372). For their ordination, the priests will be "Brought Near" to Meeting Tent and to Yahweh (29:4, 8; Lev 8:6,

13), and thereafter they will help Israel "Bring Near" their sacred offerings called *qorbānōt* (< *qrb*). Similarly, Yahweh will later command Aaron to "Bring Near" his fellow Levites for consecration (Num 18:2) (Luzzatto). Those sanctified to Yahweh are henceforth called his *qərôbîm* 'Near Ones' (Lev 10:3; Ezek 42:13; 43:19) (Ehrlich 1908: 373).

from the midst of Israel's Sons. We might have expected "from the midst of *Levi's* Sons." But that tribe has not yet received its sacred status (cf. 32:28–29 [E?]; Numbers 3, 8, 18 [P]). Aaron is elected, not as Moses' relation or as the chief Levite, but as the representative of all Israel (see pp. 522–32).

Aaron and his sons. Implicit is the equation of Aaron with all future Great Priests, and his sons with the ordinary priesthood.

Why Aaron deserves the honor of priesthood is unstated. Yahweh will reconfirm the appointment in perpetuity after Aaron's grandson Phinehas has proved his zeal for God (Num 25:10–13 [P]), but initially Aaron's election seems arbitrary. Like an oriental potentate, Yahweh bestows the priesthood where he wishes (for Egypt, see Sauneron 2000: 45–47).

to priest. I have exhumed this obsolete but useful English verb to correspond to Hebrew *kihhēn*, derived from *kōhēn* 'priest.' Outside the Torah, *kihhēn* clearly means "*serve* as priest" (Ezek 44:13; Hos 4:6; 1 Chr 5:36; 24:2; 2 Chr 11:14). In the Torah, however, the context is always priestly *ordination*, and arguably the verb is better rendered "to *become* a priest." (In many instances, including 28:1, 3, 4, one might be tempted to understand a transitive "to *install* as priest," but in 28:43; 40:13, 15; Num 3:4; Deut 10:6, the subject is definitely the initiate not God [cf. ibn Ezra, shorter commentary; Luzzatto].)

SPECULATION: Isa 61:10 uses *kihhēn* of a metaphorical bridegroom donning a glorious turban. Arguably, the verb in the Torah likewise connotes a priest donning his regalia upon initiation and continuing to display and wield it during his ministrations (cf. Luzzatto).

If the suffix on the infinitive *ləkahănô* is pronominal, the correct rendering would be "for *his* priesting," and likewise in v 4. With some hesitation, however, I understand the suffix as nonpronominal, which would explain its absence in the Versions (see TEXTUAL NOTE). Even in MT, the infinitive *kahēn* otherwise stands without a suffix. The *-ô* might be either a fossilized case ending in a compound expression (cf. ibn Ezra; admittedly, the parallels are all in construct [GKC §90*k–o*]) or else something akin to the Amarna suffix *-ī* used on infinitives (absolute, not construct; cf. Moran 1961: 60). Luzzatto also compares the suffix *-û(t)* in Aramaic infinitives.

glory and splendor. Kābôd 'glory' connotes both luxury and dignity, as an attribute of either God or an important human such as a king (see Weinfeld 1995: 25–31; for specific comparisons between the Great Priestly vestments and royal attire, see Ramban and COMMENT pp. 524–25). *Tip'eret* 'splendor' connotes fame, beauty and in particular a splendid headdress (Isa 62:3; Jer 13:18; Ezek 16:12; 23:42; Prov 4:9; 16:31); cf. *pə'ēr* 'splendor-hat' (Exod 39:28). The Great

Priest's finery honors not only himself but also Yahweh (cf. Sforno), whose very servants dress like kings.

28:2. *Holiness Garments*. The vestments are called *bigdê qōdeš* because they are worn in the *qōdeš* 'Holiness,' i.e., the Tabernacle, and nowhere else; and because they themselves bear the contagious quality of Holiness (see pp. 682–90). Ibn Ezra compares Ezek 44:19: "[the priests] must strip off their clothes . . . and not *sanctify (qdš)* the people through their clothes."

28:3. *wise-hearted*. The heart is the seat of cognition and skill (see Fabry 1995: 412–34); on the root *ḥkm* connoting artistic craft, see 1 Kgs 7:14; Isa 3:3; 40:20; Jer 10:9. P implicitly confers on the craftsman the honorary status of sage *(ḥākām)*.

Just as the ordinary Israelites are to be "*generous*-hearted" (25:2; 35:21, 29), so Yahweh makes the artisans "*wise*-hearted." Presumably, they practice their craft *gratis*, just as the people contribute their valuables voluntarily. In other words, that which Yahweh gave them—their skill—the craftsmen will give back to God (Ehrlich 1969: 191). See also NOTE to 31:3.

whom. There is a minor grammatical problem: the ostensible subject in MT is the plural *kol-ḥakəmê-lēb* 'all wise-hearted,' yet the objectival verbal suffix on *millē(ʾ)tîw* is singular (see TEXTUAL NOTE, "wise-hearted"). Ibn Ezra (longer commentary), Ehrlich (1969: 191) and Wevers (1990: 445) think that the antecedent is the singular "heart." But, grammatical incongruence notwithstanding, the more natural referent is each individual, wise-hearted man (ibn Ezra [shorter commentary]). Or, as Dillmann (1880: 299) notes, the true antecedent might be *kōl* 'all,' technically a singular noun meaning "totality" (cf. Isa 64:10; Nah 3:7; Prov 16:2; GKC §146c).

I have filled. This might refer either to the bestowal of aptitude at birth or to a recent spiritual gift. Probably both are intended: under renewed inspiration, the already talented artisans will surpass themselves. Cf. 31:6; 35:10, 25; 36:1, 2, 4, 8.

to make him holy. A more precise rendering of *ləqaddəšô* would be "for his being made holy." The garments themselves do not sanctify Aaron, but he cannot be consecrated without them, since both Aaron and his clothes will receive the mingled blood and oil of Holiness (29:21, 29).

to priest. See NOTE to 28:1, "to priest."

28:4. *ḥōšen*. The exact meaning and etymology of this term are unknown. As described in vv 15–30, the *ḥōšen* is a bejeweled pouch of fabric holding sacred lots (see NOTES to 28:16, 30). As for derivation, the root *ḥšn* is otherwise unknown in Northwest Semitic, though Cassuto (1967: 375) cites a textually dubious Ugaritic *ḥšn* (*KTU* 1.5.iii.3–4). Probably we should look to Arabic *ḥasuna* 'be beautiful,' *ḥusn* 'beauty' (BDB, KB); the latter noun would correspond exactly to Hebrew *ḥōšen*, which should then be rendered "Beauty." (Ehrlich [1969: 188] proffers instead Arabic *ḥawš* 'chest,' *ḥawšan* 'chest, coat of mail,' but neither the vowels nor the MT sibilant sustain this etymology [Arabic *š* = Hebrew *ś*].)

On the *ḥōšen*'s symbolism, see below, pp. 443, 523–24.

ephod. As we are uncertain what an *ʾēpôd* actually was, I have retained this familiar transliteration. The term is paralleled in assorted ancient Near Eastern texts, but none, unfortunately, reveal an ephod's exact shape. Old Assyrian texts from Cappadocia (twentieth century B.C.E.) mention a garment called *epattu* (plural *epadātu*) (*CAD* 4.183); at Ugarit, an *'ipd* costs twenty-five shekels (*KTU* 707.13–14), and Middle Kingdom Egypt knows a sacred garment called *ifd nṯr* 'divine ephod' (for further discussion, see Friedrich 1968: 29–33). In addition, Watson (1999: 786) compares the Hittite garment *ipantu*.

The Bible mentions ephods in three contexts (see de Vaux 1971: 349–53). The ordinary ephod is a priestly garment, typically made of linen (1 Sam 2:18; 22:18; 2 Sam 6:14; 1 Chr 15:27). It is rather revealing, whether because it is brief or because it is translucent (2 Sam 6:20–23; cf. NOTES to 20:26[23]; 28:42). It is girt (*ḥgr*) around the waist (Lev 8:7; 1 Sam 2:18; 2 Sam 6:14). Perhaps this simple ephod is a loincloth, akin to the *'izār* worn by pilgrims to Mecca. The Great Priestly ephod of Exodus, however, is an extra-fancy ceremonial model, made not just of linen but of dyed wool and gold thread. Moreover, it is not worn against the skin, but outside other garments. It also is suspended from the shoulders, like various garments depicted in New Kingdom Egyptian art (Van Dam 1997: 77–80). The ephods mentioned in other ancient Near Eastern texts must also be more luxurious than mere loincloths.

Confusingly, a second set of biblical verses describes an ephod as an oracular device, probably containing the Urim and Thummim (see below, NOTE to 28:30). It seemingly is not worn but carried (1 Sam 14:3, 18–19 [OG; MT different], 36–42; 22:18; 23:9–11; 30:7–8; cf. Judg 18:5). As many have observed, the contradiction is not irreconcilable, since the ephod of Exodus is attached to an oracular pouch containing the Urim and Thummim (cf. Friedrich [1968], who regards P's Ephod-and-*ḥōšen* ensemble as combining the originally distinct connotations of the ephod). Moreover, references to carrying (*nś'*) the ephod might reflect its being suspended from the shoulders, as in Exodus.

Other passages, however, associate an ephod with idolatry. In fact, taken alone, Judg 8:24–27; 17:5; 18:14–20; Hos 3:4 would indicate that an ephod is a golden idol, proscribed along with pillars and Teraphim (sacred images).

To reconcile these conflicting data, three explanations might suggest themselves. First, an ephod may have been a special garment put upon an idol and hence the object of independent worship (in Ugaritic myth, a god wears an *'ipd* [*KTU* 1.5.i.5]) (see Haran 1955: 384–91). Second, some biblical authors may have considered divining by an ephod tantamount to idolatry (for forbidden forms of divination, cf. Lev 19:26, 31; 20:27; Deut 18:10–11, etc.). Lastly, the ephod, the priestly vestment *par excellence*, may for some authors have represented an illegitimate priesthood. At least for the Priestly Writer, a non-Aaronid's donning an ephod would probably be a transgression (compare David's experiments in ephod-wearing and sacrifice [2 Sam 6:14–23].)

In sum: because of its association with idolatry, divination and priestly legitimacy, the ephod was controversial in ancient Israel. The Priestly Writer coopted this symbolic vestment by limiting its use to the Aaronid priesthood and to Yahweh's cult. For a more extensive discussion of the ephod, see Houtman (2000: 477–85).

woven. The form *tašbēṣ* 'woven' (?) is *hapax legomenon*, but other derivatives of the root *šbṣ* 'plait' appear apropos of the priestly vestments (see NOTE to 28:11, "plait-rings"). The interpretation "weave" is not secure. In Syriac, the nuance is more "mix," and many think that Hebrew *tašbēṣ* refers to a checkered pattern, while Houtman (2000: 473–75) inclines more toward the idea of "tailored." Another possibility is "adorned with braidwork" (cf. Vogelsang-Eastwood 2000: 280–81).

shift. The *kətōnet* is described only briefly in v 39, for it was well known to Israelite readers. Worn against the body, it is the first garment put on (Lev 8:7, 13; 16:4) and the last removed (Cant 5:3). It might even be one's only garment (Gen 3:21; 37 *passim*; 2 Sam 13:18; 15:32). It is tied on with a sash (Exod 28:40; Isa 22:21).

The word *kətōnet* is paralleled in many ancient languages (Ugaritic *ktn*, Phoenician *ktn* [*KAI* 24.12], Aramaic *kt(w)n*, Akkadian *kutinnu/kitû* [see Kaufman 1974: 28]), Greek *chitōn*, Latin *tunica* (metathesis). Also possibly related are various words for linen and perhaps even Arabic *quṭ(u)n*, the source of English "cotton" (Brown 1980: 7–8). And underlying all these words may be Sumerian GAD 'linen' (Ellenbogen 1962: 96).

robe. Commentators debate the dimensions of the Great Priest's blue woolen Robe (28:31–35). Since leggings must be worn for modesty's sake (NOTE to 28:42, "underpants"), the *məʿîl* may be more like a coat (Rashi) or a short skirt. More likely, however, it is a full-length robe (Josephus *Ant.* 3.159), with "skirts" (*šûlayim*, 28:33) reaching the ground (cf. Isa 6:1; Jer 13:22) (Ramban). The Black Obelisk of Shalmaneser III depicts King Jehu of Israel wearing a full-length robe, probably with short sleeves (*ANEP* fig. 355; see similar garments in *ANEP* fig. 371 [siege of Lachish]).

As it has a single hole for the head (28:32) with no special provision for the arms, Aaron's Robe is probably like a long poncho, perhaps with the sides tied loosely together (see fig. 16). As Hyatt (1980: 284) observes, the *məʿîl* is associated with persons of high status (1 Sam 2:19; 15:27 [Samuel]; 18:4 [Jonathan]; 24:5, 12 [Saul]; Ezek 26:16 [Tyrian rulers]; Job 1:20; 2:12 [Job]; Ezra 9:3–4 [Ezra]; 1 Chr 15:27 [David]). It has no intrinsic sanctity: e.g., as a priest, young Samuel ministers in an ephod, whereas every year his mother brings him a new robe (1 Sam 2:19). Although Noth (1962: 224–25) thinks that the Robe goes over the Ephod, the reverse is suggested by 29:5–6; Lev 8:7–9. As for etymology, while no clear cognates are known (see, however, Görg 1976; Redford 1992: 384 n. 77), there may be a connection with the verbal root *mʿl* 'act treacherously'; compare the semantic fields of *bgd* (*beged* 'garment,' *bāgad* 'betray') (Klein 1987).

turban. This conventional interpretation of *miṣnepet* is not quite certain; outside of Exodus, the term reappears only in Ezek 21:31. The verbal root *ṣnp* occurs only in Lev 16:4, where it means "to don a *miṣnepet*, and in Isa 22:18, where it is enigmatic (wind up into a ball? wind up to throw?). The closest potential cognate proposed is Akkadian *sanāp/bu* 'tie on,' and even though the initial consonants do not correspond, the meaning suits. (Phonologically impeccable but somewhat remote semantically is Arabic *ṣinfa*, the corner of a cloth [< *ṣannafa* 'sort, classify'], suggesting that the *miṣnepet* is a triangular fabric somewhat like the modern Arabian headdress [P. Bikai, privately].)

FIGURE 16. Great Priest and lesser priest

Since it is a royal symbol (Ezek 21:31), like the ṣānîp (Isa 62:3; Zech 3:5; Job 29:14) the miṣnepet is probably a tall headdress. Our sole depicted Israelite monarch, Jehu of Israel, wears a conical hat on Shalmaneser III's Black Obelisk (*ANEP* fig. 355).

sash. Although the two are separated in 28:39 by the Turban, the Sash is generally connected with the Shift (28:40; Lev 8:7, 13; Isa 22:21). The noun ʾabnēṭ is possibly of Egyptian derivation (< *bnd*; see Lambdin 1953: 146; Ellenbogen 1962: 2; Muchiki 1999: 237; but also Rabin 1975; Hoch 1994: 98–99). The Assyrian Black Obelisk depicts Jehu of Israel wearing a fringed sash around his long robe (*ANEP* fig. 355).

to priest. See NOTE to 28:1.

28:5. *they, they*. The repetition emphasizes the change of subject: not the priests but the craftsmen.

the gold . . . blue . . . purple . . . worm-crimson . . . linen. On these precious substances, see NOTES to 25:3–4, where their donation is mandated. The priest is clad in the same fabrics that constitute the Tabernacle (below, p. 528).

Properly attired, he is no alien intruder when he enters the Dwelling. Rather, as the inscription on his headgear proclaims (28:36), he fully belongs to Yahweh (Houtman 2000: 467). The woolen priestly garments of Exodus contrast strikingly with those worn by Egyptian priests, to whom wool was forbidden (Sauneron 2000: 40); compare Gen 46:34 on the Egyptians' supposed aversion to shepherds.

28:6. *Ephod.* See NOTE to 28:4.

gold. This was hammered flat, cut into wire and then twisted together with the strands of wool and flax (NOTES to 39:3; cf. *b. Yoma* 72a). Although there is no proof, Haran (1955: 383–84) thinks that gold receives the first mention, not just because it is the most precious but because it is the predominant element of the Ephod, which he conceives as heavy, shiny and rigid.

blue . . . purple . . . worm-crimson . . . linen. Interweaving blue, purple and crimson wool with linen violates the law against mingling wool and flax (*ša'aṭnēz*) in Lev 19:19; Deut 22:11. Presumably such a mixture is forbidden precisely because it is reserved for the Tabernacle and its personnel (Josephus *Ant.* 4.8.208; Milgrom 2000: 1660–64), like the special formula incense and the anointing oil (30:22–38) (Maccoby 1999: 133). In contrast, Ezek 44:17–18 requires the ministering priests to wear only linen, never wool (see further COMMENT pp. 523–24). Presumably because an ephod was a familiar garment, the text describes only its components, not its actual construction.

webster's work. See NOTE to 26:1, "webster's work."

28:7. *Two fastening shoulder-pieces.* The nature of these shoulder-pieces and their relationship to the Ephod is unclear. The use of the plural *kətēpōt*, not the dual **kətēpayim*, confirms the obvious: these are not literal "shoulders" but something pertaining to the shoulders. Actually, shoulder-pieces is not quite accurate; if *kātēp* here connotes the shoulder blade, then the "shoulder-pieces" may actually cover the upper back, and a better translation might be "scapular."

What does "fastening (*ḥōbərōt*)" mean? On the analogy of the phrase *ḥōbərōt 'iššâ 'el-'ăḥōtāh* 'fastening (each) *woman* to her *sister*,' i.e., joined together (26:3; Ezek 1:9), one might argue that the shoulder-pieces themselves are sewn together to cover the upper back (Rashbam; Jacob 1992: 812). Our verse, however, lacks the crucial phrase *'iššâ 'el-'ăḥōtāh* and so may mean something different: e.g., that the shoulder-pieces are attached as suspenders to the Ephod and/or the woven-band, but not to each other (Rashi). Noth (1962: 221) points to an Egyptian Old Kingdom depiction of men wearing loincloths with braces (*ANEP* 66 fig. 210). Haran (1955), for whom the Ephod is half gold, observes that galluses would be necessary to support the weight. And Houtman (2000: 486) adds that suspenders would make the Ephod easily adjustable, so that Aaron's heirs may wear it irrespective of stature.

at its two sides it shall be fastened. The clause division is uncertain. It is also possible to read "Two fastening shoulder-pieces, they shall be for it at its two sides; it shall be fastened." My translation brings out the parallelistic syntax we expect in P; the first clause says in general what the second says in particular (see Paran 1989: 98–136).

The exact meaning of qəṣôtā(y)w here is unclear; it might be rendered either "edges" or "sides." Are these the edges of the two side-pieces covering the shoulder blades (Rashbam; Jacob 1992: 812) or the left and right sides of the Ephod itself (Rashi)? Also, how are the edges/sides fastened—with metal rings, woolen loops, metal clasps or some other system (cf. 26:1–11)? Haran (1955: 381) supposes that the fastenings are undone whenever the priest dons or doffs the Ephod.

28:8. *woven-band for its ephod-binding.* Although we cannot be certain, the ḥēšeb 'woven-band' (< ḥšb 'reckon, calculate, weave') is traditionally understood as a woven corset fastened around the Ephod's upper part. Driver (1954–59: 258), however, compares the rare Egyptian ḥsb 'cross band,' while Grintz (1975: 18) proffers Egyptian ḥbs 'garment' (supposedly > Hebrew ḥšb via metathesis). It is also possible, even likely, that the two shoulder-pieces plus the "woven-band" simply constitute the Ephod, just as in 26:17 two vertical "arms" connected with rungs probably constitute a qereš.

SPECULATION: Ḥēšeb (ancient pronunciation *ḥišb) is rather a strange term for a cummerbund. Dillmann (1880: 300) suspects metathesis from an original *ḥēbeš (ancient *ḥibš) 'binding,' comparing kebeś/keśeb (< *kibś/kiśb) 'lamb' (see TEXTUAL NOTE to 12:5). If so, the conditioning factor for the metathesis could be the prominence of the root ḥšb throughout the Tabernacle pericope (26:1, 31; 28:6, 15, etc.).

The entire phrase ḥēšeb 'ăpuddātô 'ăšer 'ālā(y)w is somewhat enigmatic. First, what is the distinction between 'ēpôd and the derived noun 'ăpuddâ (on nouns of this class, see Mettinger 1971)? Second, how does ḥēšeb 'ăpuddātô 'ăšer 'ālā(y)w differ from ḥēšeb hā'ēpôd 'the Ephod's woven-band' (28:27, 28; 29:5, etc.)? The connection seems to be the verbal use of 'pd in 29:5; Lev 8:7, describing the affixing not of the Ephod per se but of its corset (ḥēšeb). In other words, 'pd means not "to wear an ephod" but "to bind on an ephod by means of a woven-band." 'Ăpuddâ, then, would mean "system for binding on an ephod" (cf. Rashi). (Ugaritic possesses an apparent cognate 'updt (KTU 4.264.1), but it is not a garment; Mettinger [p. 11] instead suggests a translation "corporation of ephod-priests.") These fine distinctions would be eliminated by the supposition that the Ephod consists of the "woven-band" suspended by the "shoulder-pieces," as suggested above.

like its work. That is, made in the same manner and from the same stuff.

from it. Permanently affixed and of the same material as the Ephod; on mimmennû, see NOTES to 25:19, "on the kappōret," 31, "from it."

28:9. *two carnelian stones.* On MT 'et-štê 'abnê šōham, see TEXTUAL NOTE.

engrave. The rare root ptḥ II 'engrave' (< PS *ptḥ [Akkadian patāḥu 'pierce']) is to be distinguished from the more familiar ptḥ I 'open' (< *ptḥ; cf. Akkadian petû, Arabic fataḥa).

on them. On the grammatical incongruence, see TEXTUAL NOTE.

Israel's sons. In 28:9, 11, 21, 29, bənê yiśrā'ēl are the original twelve sons of Jacob-Israel, not their myriad descendants.

28:10. *six . . . six . . . according to their genealogy*. I.e., by birth order according to Gen 29:31–30:24; 35:16–18 (Josephus *Ant*. 3.169, Vg, Tg. *Ps.-Jonathan*). Possibly each carnelian bears twenty-five letters: (a) *r'wbn, šm'wn, lwy, yhwdh, dn, nptly;* (b) *gd, 'šr, yśśkr, zbwln, ywsp, bnymyn* (admittedly, there is some flexibility in spelling; see *b. Soṭa* 36a–b). It seems that these gems are considerably larger than those on the *ḥōšen*, none of which bears more than six letters (Haran 1978: 168).

28:11. *seal engravings*. The names are incised in the fine letters used on gem signets, such as are frequently uncovered in excavations (e.g., Hestrin and Dayagi-Mendels 1979). Due to the hardness of the medium and the tiny scale, gem cutting is the most demanding of the scribal arts; the result is the most exquisite and durable of writing surfaces. On the production and use of ancient seals, see Gibson and Biggs (1977); Moorey (1994: 103–6); on gems and gem-cutting, see Ogden (1982: 89–150).

SPECULATION: The phrase "seal engravings" could also imply that the letters should be written backward, since mirror-writing is the most characteristic feature of signets. On the Great Priest's inscribed gems as personal seals, see further NOTES to 28:30, "heart" and COMMENT pp. 523–25.

one shall engrave. The impersonal construction (see TEXTUAL NOTE) is tantamount to a passive: "the two stones *shall be engraved*."

set. Fox (1986: 213) notes the assonance in *musabbōt mišbəṣôt* 'set in . . . plait-rings.'

plait-rings. The meaning of *mišbəṣôt* is uncertain (it appears again in Ps 45:14, apropos of a princess's attire). Driver (1954–59: 262) compares the noun *šābāṣ* 'cramp,' as if the stones were secured by a crimped setting. If, however, the root *šbṣ* means "braid," we may imagine a circlet of twined gold wire. The oldest example known to me comes from seventh-century B.C.E. Assyria (Maxwell-Hyslop 1971: pl. 216; see also a sixth/fifth-century gold-set Phoenician scarab [Moscati 1988: 372]). It is also conceivable that we should read **məšubbāṣôt* (see TEXTUAL NOTE), in which case we could translate "set in gold, gold-woven you shall make them"—i.e., the carnelian buttons are pierced and tied to the shoulder-pieces with gold threads. On beads and sequins sewn onto or woven into Egyptian textiles, see Vogelsang-Eastwood (2000: 280); for Mesopotamia, see Dalley (2000).

them. On the gender incongruence, see TEXTUAL NOTE to 28:9, "on them."

28:12. *put . . . on the Ephod's shoulder-pieces*. According to v 25 "against its front," the plait-rings and carnelians are not atop the shoulder or on the back, but lie against the Ephod's anterior side.

bear . . . on his two shoulder-pieces. On the shoulders—admittedly called *šekem* not *kātēp*—is where one carries a weighty office (Isa 9:5; 22:22) (Dillmann 1880: 305). To Aaron's bearing the names of Jacob's sons, Ehrlich (1969: 192) compares a father literally carrying his son(s) upon his shoulders (e.g., Isa 49:22). Is this why some passages refer not to "wearing" *(lbš, ḥgr)* but "carrying" an ephod (above, p. 432)?

Memorial. *Zikkārôn* denotes both something taken to heart and something written down, a "memorandum" (e.g., 17:14; Mal 3:16). In what sense are the inscribed stones a *zikkārôn*? Are the people supposed to remember their tribal ancestors? Is the priest to be eternally mindful of those he represents? Must Yahweh remember his obligations to Israel, particularly on Clearing Day (Yom Kippur) (*Exod. Rab.* 38:8)? Does the "Memorial" obtain atonement, like the census silver (30:12, 16) and the Midianite spoils (Num 31:50, 54)? Does it establish Israel's right to worship in the Tabernacle, just as Nehemiah repudiates Sanballat's "share . . . entitlement and . . . memorial" in Jerusalem (Neh 2:20)? Especially in the Priestly Source, the root *zkr* 'remember' is thematic: God "remembers" his Covenant with Israel (Gen 9:15–16; Exod 2:24; 6:5; Lev 26:42, 45; also Jer 14:21; Ezek 16:60; Amos 1:9; Ps 106:45). The very names of Israel's sons thus may be a kind of covenant witness—legal signatures, so to speak—reminding Yahweh and Israel of their mutual obligations (see COMMENT pp. 523–25; also Schottroff 1967 and Eising 1980).

28:13. *plait-rings.* Their function will be explained in v 25. Are these the gem-settings mentioned in v 11 or additional "plait-rings"? They sound like something new, an impression confirmed by 39:6, 16.

28:14. *chains.* These, too, will be explained in vv 22–25.

migbālōt. The meaning of this term is unknown, and likewise the related *gablūt* in 28:22; 39:15. LXX "variegated with flowers" appears to be a guess, conceivably on the basis of the slight similarity to *gibʿōl* 'bud.' In all three passages, the text immediately glosses *maʿăśē(h) ʿăbōt* 'rope work,' as if clarifying an unusual term (see below).

The root *gbl* is not otherwise connected with ropes; instead, *gəbûl* means "territory, border" (cf. Arabic *jabal* 'mountain'). One potential association is through the practice of measuring and demarcating territory by means of cords (cf. *ḥebel* 'rope, territory'; also Greek *zōnē* 'girdle, territory'). It is possible, too, that *gbl* is simply a byform of *ḥbl* and/or *kbl*, both of which connote binding (Dillmann 1880: 301). Or *migbālōt* might mean "*terminated* in a special manner," perhaps in a button or hook connecting to the shoulder-pieces (Rashbam). More promising is a connection with Aramaic *gbl* 'pound, knead, shape,' conceivably here referring to soldering (Driver 1954–59: 254–55). Lastly, if the basic form is *gablūt*, we might infer a particular style or technique associated with *gəbal* 'Byblos.'

them. On the gender incongruence, see TEXTUAL NOTE to 28:9, "in them."

rope work. I.e., the chains are twisted wire strands, not concatenated links (Rashi; Baentsch 1903: 240). Perhaps this is also the meaning of *migbālōt* and *gablūt* (see above).

28:15. *ḥōšen.* I.e., the bejeweled pouch resting on Aaron's breast (see NOTE to v 4). It is here called "the Judgment *ḥōšen*" (*ḥōšen hammišpāṭ* [also vv 29, 30]), because the Urim and Thummim inside it help to solve intractable legal disputes (ibn Ezra [shorter commentary]; Rashbam). After Moses' death, Yahweh will not speak directly to Joshua, but rather Joshua will seek *mišpaṭ hāʾûrîm* 'the Urim's decision' through the intermediacy of Eleazar the Great Priest (Num 27:21). On the Urim and Thummim, see further NOTE to 28:30 and pp. 523–25.

like the Ephod's work. I.e., made of the same stuff and in the same manner.

28:16. *Foursquare . . . doubled.* The *ḥōšen* is square when doubled, but un-folded it measures one by two spans (cf. Rashi). Most assume that it is sewn up the sides, forming a pouch with the top open (Noth 1962: 222), but I have my doubts (NOTE to 28:26, "on the *ḥōšen*'s two edges, at its lip"). For a portrayal of Ramesses II wearing a rectangular pectoral ornament, see Ball (1899: 103).

span. The *zeret* or half-cubit measures approximately nine inches/23 cm. Like the units of measure ephah and hin (NOTES to 16:36; 29:40), the word's origin is Egyptian: < *ḏrt* 'hand' (Lambdin 1958: 145; Muchiki 1999: 243).

28:17. *fill . . . filling.* To judge from the context, the verb *millēʾ* 'fill' connotes the setting of gems, presumably because one fills a cavity with the stone (Rashi; for an Akkadian parallel, see Maxwell-Hyslop 1971: lxiii).

I do not understand, however, how one sets gems in fabric, unless they are se-quins or buttons woven into or sewed onto the cloth. Ordinarily, gemstones are set in metal, as the verb "fill" might suggest. For example, the closest known parallel to the *ḥōšen* is a Middle Bronze Age Byblian rectangular gold pectoral, set with eleven gems and hanging from a gold chain (Noth 1962: 222–23; for pictures, see Moscati 1988: 522; Van Dam 1997: 73). So the gems in Exodus may be set into unmentioned metal casings that are sewn into the *ḥōšen*.

four rows. Perhaps corresponding to the tribes camping in four groups around the Tabernacle (Jenson 1992: 127).

stone. When it comes to identifying the gemstones, "we all grope at the wall, as if blind" (ibn Ezra [shorter commentary, quoting Isa 59:10]). When completely at a loss, I simply transliterate the Hebrew. For the rest, we have educated guesses. (In general, I cite information from KB; an interesting mineralogical discussion, brimming with classical erudition, is Dillmann [1880: 302–4]; see more recently Harris [1966] and Houtman [2000: 497–501]; on gemstones used by Mesopo-tamian craftsmen, see Moorey [1994: 74–103]; for Egypt, see Aston, Harrell and Shaw [2000: 21–63]; on sequins sewn onto or woven into fabrics, see Vogelsang-Eastwood [2000: 280].)

Precious, lustrous minerals betoken authority and beauty. They are associated in particular with Heaven and God's presence (24:10; Isa 54:12; Ezek 1:16, 26; 10:1, 9; 28:13–14, 16; Dan 10:6; Rev 4:3; 21:18–21). Their purpose here is to dig-nify the priest in the people's eyes, to make him like a heavenly being worthy to serve Yahweh. The inscription of Israel's tribal names on the stones permits them vicariously to enter the Holiness along with the Great Priest (see further below, pp. 526–27).

ʾŌdem. From the root *ʾdm* 'to be red.' Not the ruby, which was unknown at this time, but perhaps chalcedony (cf. Garber and Funk 1962: 900–1).

piṭdâ. Grintz (1975: 9) postulates an Egyptian origin, **pddt*, although no such word is attested. Others cite Sanskrit *pīta* 'yellow,' even though it is not the name of a gemstone (for more extended discussion, see Ellenbogen 1962: 133; Rabin 1975). Since Job 28:19 associates *piṭdâ* with Ethiopia, Powels (1992: 197–98) sug-gests that the biblical stone is green-yellow chrysolith, found on St. John's Island (Jazīrat Zabarjad) in the Red Sea.

emerald. Despite a superficially promising association of *bāreqet* with *brq* 'flash' (ibn Ezra; Jacob 1992: 815), probably made by the Israelites themselves, the true derivation is more likely non-Semitic (KB; contrast Dillman 1880: 303). Cognates are Akkadian *baraktu*, Greek *smaragdos*, Sanskrit *marakatam* and ultimately English "emerald" (Burkert 1992: 37; for fuller discussion, see *HALOT*).

28:18. *turquoise.* *Nōpek* probably derives from Egyptian *mfk(3)t* (Muchiki 1999: 251), vocalized in Assyrian as *npiki* (Lambdin 1953: 152). It is either turquoise or malachite.

lapis lazuli. As Powels (1992: 198) shows, the noun *sappîr* is probably not derived from Sanskrit *śanipriya* 'emerald or sapphire' (cf. Ellenbogen 1962: 125). More likely it is a loanword from an unknown Semitic dialect in which *spr* means "to be beautiful" (Aramaic *špr*) (Grintz 1975: 9).

yāhălōm. Identity unknown. The name recalls the verb *hālam* 'hammer.'

28:19. *lešem.* Unknown. The Egyptian cognate or source word is *nšmt* (Lambdin 1953: 152; Ellenbogen 1962: 97; Muchiki 1999: 248).

šəbô. Cf. the yellow Akkadian gem *šubû/šabû*, whose name derives from Sumerian ŠUBA (Ellenbogen 1962: 155).

jasper. 'Ahlāmâ derives from Egyptian *hnmt*, probably red-brown jasper (Lambdin 1953: 147; Ellenbogen 1962: 22; Muchiki 1999: 238–39).

28:20. *taršîš.* An unknown stone, perhaps imported from Tarshish in the Mediterranean.

carnelian. See NOTE to 25:7.

jade. *Yāšəpē(h)* is cognate to Akkadian *yašpû* and presumably Arabic *yaṣf/b* 'jasper' and *yašm* 'jade' (cf. also Ellenbogen 1962: 81).

28:21. *by the names of Israel's sons.* That is, of the same number (twelve) and each inscribed with a tribal name. We do not know whether there is any particular correlation between the tribal name and its respective gem—or, for that matter, in what order the tribes are listed. Perhaps it is birth order as in the two shoulder gems (v 10).

seal engravings. See NOTES to 28:11, 30, "heart."

(each) man. 'Îš means "each one," referring to the tribes.

28:22. *upon the hōšen.* The chains are not literally "upon the hōšen," as the following clauses make clear. Perhaps the preposition *'al* is better rendered "for" or "in addition to" (Rashi).

gablūt chains, rope work. Presumably these are the same cords referred to in v 14 (see NOTES), which together with v 22 frames the description of the hōšen. Chap. 39, the execution narrative, mentions only one pair of chains.

28:23. *edges.* In vv 23–24, *qəṣôt* presumably connotes the hōšen's top corners (Rashi). Elsewhere, *qāṣe(h)* refers to an end of a chain (e.g, 28:25) and an end of the Tabernacle (e.g., 26:28). The basic meaning is "extremity" (< *qṣy* 'cut').

28:24. *set the two gold ropes.* The two chains are somehow attached to rings at the hōšen's upper corners.

28:25. *two plait-rings.* The chains' other ends are attached to the mišbəṣōt mentioned in v 13 as part of the shoulder-pieces (fig. 16, p. 434). Literarily, v 25 returns us to the matter of v 13, thus creating a frame around the chains (vv 14, 22), which in turn frame the hōšen.

28:26. *two gold rings.* In addition to those previously mentioned (but see below).

them. On the gender incongruence, see TEXTUAL NOTE to 28:9, "on them."

on the ḥōšen's two edges, at its lip. As we have seen, the consensus is that the ḥōšen is a pouch open at the top (NOTE to 28:16). Scholars also agree that śāpâ 'lip' here describes the ḥōšen's bottom fold and that the "edges" in question are the lower corners. This explains in what sense the rings are tied "on the Ephod's two shoulder-pieces, *below*"; i.e., the ḥōšen has rings at its four corners, so that it is held flat against the priest's chest. I am unconvinced, however.

The difficulty is that, ordinarily, śāpâ conotes a strip bordering a cavity: the shore of the sea or the rim of a cup or the collar of a robe. Here it should describe the pouch's *opening.* If so, the rings may be at the top corners underneath the rings of v 23, since both pairs are said to be "on the ḥōšen's two edges." Indeed, it is not impossible that vv 23 and 26 are speaking of a single pair of rings. But it would be odd that the the gold chains suspending the ḥōšen from above and the blue cord(s) binding it down should be affixed alike at the upper corners, leaving the pectoral free to flap.

There is a third possibility reconciling these two approaches. What if the ḥōšen's opening were *downward,* with the fold at the top, and the Urim and Thummim somehow attached so as not to fall out (see NOTE to 28:30)? Then v 26 would make perfect sense. The "lip" is the nether opening, and rings at top and bottom bind the pectoral upward and downward (fig. 16, p. 434).

against the Ephod inside. In other words, the ḥōšen's "lip" lies directly on the Ephod.

28:27. *them.* On the gender incongruence, see TEXTUAL NOTE to 28:9, "on them."

the Ephod's two shoulder-pieces below, against its front. That is, these two rings are placed not directly over Aaron's shoulders but lower down *(millamaṭṭâ)* upon the front surface *(mimmûl pānā[y]w)* of the shoulder-pieces. See also next NOTE.

opposite its fastening, above the Ephod's woven-band. "Fastening" *(maḥberet)* implies something composite, fastened together (cf. 26:4–5). That is, these rings are set where the shoulder-pieces meet the woven band (Rashi; see fig. 16).

28:28. *with blue cord.* One could also render biptîl tǝkēlet as "with *a* blue cord," i.e., there was only one strand. Quite possibly, however, there was one for each, like the gold chains for the upper rings; see also NOTE to 28:37. My translation leaves the matter open.

Why only wool thread below, but gold ropes above? Because the nether cord bears no weight, and so may be less substantial (Cassuto 1967: 377–78).

slip. Or bounce around as the priest walks (Rashi). Perhaps there is a fear that the Urim and Thummim might pop out. The root of yizzaḥ appears to be zwḥ, based upon Arabic and Syriac cognates (cf. KB, which lists it under zḥḥ). Ramban also compares the quasi-synonymous root nsḥ 'be displaced, uprooted.'

It is questionable whether the verse mandates that, once assembled, the ḥōšen may never be detached from the Ephod (Ibn Ezra [shorter commentary]); on the intrinsic association of the Ephod with the Urim and Thummim, see NOTE to

28:4, "ephod"). I should think it more likely, however, that the assemblage is to be rigged anew each day, to facilitate dressing and undressing, not to mention laundering (compare my discussion of 25:15, "they shall not be removed from it").

28:30. *Urim and Thummim.* The Priestly Writer does not explain what these are or how they are to be made. Was the information widely known or deliberately suppressed? In either case, it is irretrievably lost. Ramban (on Lev 8:8) reasonably considers the Urim and Thummim a mysterious gift from Heaven. Otherwise, they appear only in Lev 8:8; Num 27:21; Deut 33:8; 1 Sam 14:41 (cf. LXX); 28:6; Ezra 2:63 = Neh 7:65.

Etymologically, *'ûrîm* and *tummîm* should respectively mean "lights" (< *'wr* 'shine') and "perfections" (< *tmm* 'to be whole, complete'), perhaps as abstract plurals, implying that they perfectly illuminate Yahweh's will. Given their judicial use, however, some associate Urim with *'rr* 'curse' (but for that we would expect **'ōrîm*) and Thummim with *tmm* in the sense of innocence (e.g., Gen 20:5–6; 1 Kgs 9:4; Ps 7:9; 25:21; 26:1, 11). 1 Sam 14:24–29 points in both directions; note especially the exchange, punning with *'ûrîm*: "Cursed *('ārûr)* be the man who eats food today". . . . "See, then, that my eyes shine *('ōrû)*, since I have tasted a little of this honey" (vv 28–29). (The root *'rr* may also refer to a legal conviction in Num 5:18, *mê hammārîm ham'ārārîm* 'bitter, cursing waters.') As for Thummim, 1 Sam 14:41 (MT) similarly appears to make a pun with *tāmîm* 'innocent.'

The nature and function of the Urim and Thummim remain unsettled; Van Dam (1997) surveys past proposals and comparable techniques of ancient Near Eastern sortition (also Horowitz and Hurowitz 1992). The closest parallel is Prov 16:33, which might be rendered: "The lot is cast from the fold/bosom, and (but?) all judgment is from Yahweh." P itself describes the Urim and Thummim in operation only in Num 17:21: "He [Joshua] shall inquire of him [Eleazar] by the judgment of the Urim."

It is generally held that the Urim and Thummim are used to distinguish between alternative propositions (generally "yes" and "no," as in "Shall we attack?"). (Most likely, even where Urim and Thummim are not mentioned, a yes/no question addressed to Yahweh may be understood as answered by the Urim and Thummim, e.g., in Judg 18:5–6; 20:23; 1 Sam 10:22; 23:2; 2 Sam 2:1; 5:19; cf. 1 Sam 14:36b–41.) The Urim and Thummim may have been used in thorny legal disputes, which, according to Exod 22:8; Num 27:1–11; Deut 17:8–12; 19:17, were adjudicated at the shrine. For futher discusion, see Milgrom (1991: 507–11), who argues strongly for a more flexible system than a binary yes/no choice.

SPECULATION: It is not quite certain, however, that the Urim and Thummim are lots. Josephus *Ant.* 3.217–28 appears to think they are rather the twelve engraved gems themselves, which communicate by shining in patterns (admittedly, however, Josephus does not explicitly mention "Urim and Thummim"). (The *Apocryphon of Moses* [1Q375–76] appears similarly to describe the Urim and Thummim as stones lighting up with "fire tongues.") And Philo *Spec. Leg.*

1.88 envisions the Urim and Thummim as two cloths sewn onto the ḥōšen. It may even be—admittedly, against the plain sense of Num 27:21—that P's Urim and Thummim are never drawn from their pocket, but just worn. Their mere presence over Aaron's heart makes his judgment tantamount to a divine oracle (cf. Houtman 1990a; 2000: 496). By this theory, the Priestly Writer coopted an ancient divinatory symbol about which he felt considerable ambivalence.

The Urim and Thummim are last mentioned in David's day. After the Exile and Return, Ezra 2:63 = Neh 7:65 laments their loss in a time when prophecy, too, had failed, although Josephus reports that the pectoral oracle functioned through Hasmonean times (*Ant.* 3.218). By the days of the Talmud, at any rate, divination by Urim and Thummim is a distant memory (*m. Soṭa* 9:12; *b. Yoma* 21b).

Judgment. Is mišpāṭ ellipsis for ḥōšen hammišpāṭ 'the Judgment ḥōšen,' just as ʿēdūt 'Testimony' stands for ʾărōn hāʿēdūt 'Testimony Chest' (16:34; 30:36; Num 17:19, 25)? Or does Aaron in some sense bear upon his breast Israel's "government" or even "Fate," other nuances of mišpāṭ (see further pp. 525–26)? The priest is similarly said to bear (nśʾ) the people's ʿāwōn 'transgression' (v 38). In fact, both mišpāṭ and ʿāwōn can connote "punishment." In some sense, then, the priest bears culpability for the entire people (cf. vol. I, p. 235; Greenberg 1959; below, pp. 448–50, 523–27).

heart. For the ancients, this organ houses the intellect (Fabry 1995: 412–34). Perhaps Yahweh is supposed to give Aaron's heart wisdom to interpret the Urim and Thummim (Houtman 2000: 497), or possibly the Urim and Thummim themselves impart wisdom by osmosis (cf. Houtman 1990a; 2000: 496). Similarly, according to late sources, Egyptian viziers wore the gemstone emblem of Truth (m3ʿt) as a pendant (Aelian *Varia Historia* 14.34; Diodorus Siculus *Bibliotheca Historica* 1.75.5).

Other nuances may be present, too: e.g., Aaron is constantly to be mindful of his people. We find the image of an engraved pectoral again in Jer 17:1, "Judah's sin is written with an iron stylus . . . engraved on their heart's tablet," and in Prov 7:1–3, "My son, observe my sayings. . . . Write them on your heart's tablet." And inasmuch as the ḥōšen is adorned with the personal seals of Israel's tribes, we could also compare Cant 8:6, "Put me as a signet on your heart" (cf. Ehrlich 1969: 192). As a woman desires physical and symbolic nearness to her beloved's breast/consciousness/heart (lēb), so should Israel yearn for Aaron, who bears their love to Yahweh. God, in turn, should constantly contemplate his cherished people. In all these senses, the pectoral serves as a zikkārōn 'Memorial.' For general discussions of amulets and amulet imagery, see Speiser (1965) and Miller (1970a). On Aaron as intermediary between Israel and Yahweh, see pp. 525–26, 688–91.

28:31. *the Ephod's Robe.* Just as the woven-band and the ḥōšen are physically inseparable from the Ephod (NOTE to 28:4, "ephod"), so the Robe is described as pertaining to the Ephod.

completely blue. I.e., of blue wool, without admixture of other colors or of linen.

Driver (1954–59: 259), however, prefers to translate *kəlîl təkēlet* as "of one piece, blue" (i.e., **kālîl təkēlet*).

28:32. *its head mouth.* More loosely, *pî rō(ʾ)šô* may be rendered "its top opening." But Ehrlich (1969: 192) thinks the meaning is "the *mouth* [opening] for his [Aaron's] head."

in its midst. The Robe is a simple expanse of fabric with a neck hole in the middle (NOTE to 28:4, "robe").

a lip . . . for its mouth. That is, the edges of the hole are finished with a collar, not left ragged.

weaver's work. To judge from 39:22, this phrase describes the entire Robe, not just the collar.

anus mouth. The meaning of *taḥrāʾ* is an old mystery. The word does not seem to be Egyptian (Lambdin 1953: 155), although Tvedtnes (1982) and Muchiki (1999: 258) compare Egyptian *tḥr* 'leather part of a carriage.' The *Tgs.* understand a type of armor, which seems inappropriate to the context and claims no philological support.

The only remotely plausible explanation of *taḥrāʾ* is Tur-Sinai's (1950: 219–23) avowedly outrageous proposal: *taḥrāʾ* is the anatomical term for the anus. His etymology, at least, is unexceptionable: if *taḥrāʾ* is a Semitic word, its root must be *ḥrʾ* 'defecate,' attested in Hebrew, Ugaritic, Aramaic, Arabic and Akkadian (for a possible Egyptian borrowing, see Hoch 1994: 232–33). Tur-Sinai further argues that Syr preserves this interpretation, and that the other Aramaic Versions originally read not *širyān* 'armor' but something like **šerîn* 'rings,' supposedly connoting the anal sphincter (cf. Latin *anus* 'ring,' Talmudic *pî tabbaʿat*, etc.).

Is this conceivable? Not at first blush; for the Israelites' negative attitude to elimination, see Deut 23:13–15; 1 Kgs 14:10; 2 Kgs 18:27; Isa 4:4; 28:8; 36:12; Ezek 4:12–14; Prov 30:12. The very word *ḥārāʾ* 'shit' was later censored by scribal tradition (see the Qere in 2 Kgs 6:25; 18:27; Isa 36:12). And yet, unlike blood and semen, feces and urine are so far as we know neutral in P's canons of Holiness. At any rate, pending a better explanation, I favor "anus" as the most likely interpretation of *taḥrāʾ*.

it will not be torn. This abrupt command (see TEXTUAL NOTE) has been taken in a number of ways (*b. Yoma* 72a). First, it might mean that the collar should be reinforced "*lest* it be torn" (Saadiah). Alternatively, it might be a command not to cut open a slit afterward but to make the hole during the weaving process (Rashbam; Bekhor Shor). Finally, *kəpî taḥrāʾ . . . lō(ʾ) yiqqārēaʿ* might be taken as a broken phrase tantamount to "an un-tearable anus mouth" (cf. Cassuto 1967: 383).

28:33. *skirts.* The dual *šûlayim* probably denotes the bottom edge of a hanging garment (compare Arabic *sawila* 'hang down'). Here, however, it may connote the two large flaps of a poncho-like robe (Houtman 2000: 509; see NOTE to 28:4, "robe"). The priest's Robe is adorned with an elaborate variation upon the fringe, ubiquitous in ancient Near Eastern haute couture. (On the social and religious symbolism of hem and tassels in the ancient Near East, see Milgrom 1983b.)

pomegranates. Not the actual fruit, but most likely clumps of dangling yarn

(Dillmann 1880: 309), less likely an embroidered pattern (Noth 1962: 224). For photographs of comparable metal pomegranate pendants from thirteenth–twelfth-century B.C.E. Canaan, see Artzy (1990: 48); for seventh-century B.C.E. Rhodian examples, see Muthman (1982: 36–37); for repeated pomegranates as a decorative motive, often alternating with other forms, see Muthmann (pp. 16–17, 19, 27–31). Hanging pomegranates were especially popular as earrings; for examples, see Maxwell-Hyslop (1971: figs. 115, 135–36; pl. 153).

Although the seedy pomegranate was a pregnant symbol associated with goddesses such as Cybele and Aphrodite (Börker-Klähn and Röllig 1971; Muthman 1982), it could have had no such meaning for P. Perhaps the Priestly Writer wished to retain the symbol but strip away its mythological baggage. Pomegranates similarly adorned Solomon's Temple (1 Kgs 7:18, 20, 42; Jer 52:22–23; 2 Chr 3:16; 4:13), and an eighth-century B.C.E. Israelite ivory pomegranate (of now-questioned authenticity) bears the inscription *lbyt . . . h qdš khnm* 'belonging to [divine name]'s House, the priests' Holiness' (Avigad 1990; on the missing deity, most likely Yahweh or Asherah, see Kempinski 1990). Another eighth-century Israelite pomegranate in relief is found inside a bowl from Lahav (Seger and Borowski 1977: 166).

and gold bells. According to 39:25, these are of pure gold. We have small chimes (minus clappers) from ninth-century B.C.E. Megiddo and from eighth–seventh century B.C.E. Achzib and Ziklag (see Braun 2002: 195–202 for discussion and pictures). True bells with clappers first appear in the Near East in the eighth century B.C.E. as ornaments for animals (cf. Zech 14:20). Actual golden bells survive from the Persian era, roughly contemporary with the Priestly source (Calmeyer 1969); see below, p. 732.

Again, some details are lacking. While Rashi supposes that the priest's bells have clappers, Rashbam envisions clapper-less chimes that collide, despite the intervening cloth "pomegranates." (As if combining Aaron's two fringe ornaments, metallic balls and wool pomegranates, a tripod from Ugarit boasts dangling, tinkling pomegranates [*ANEP* 588].) We are not told the number of Aaron's bells and pomegranates; according to *b. Zebaḥ.* 88b, there were seventy-two of each (on other guesses in early Christian sources, see Hayward 1999: 97–98).

The term *paʿămōn*, literally, "beater," may mentally resonate with *paʿam* 'foot,' since these bells encircled Aaron's feet and tinkled as he walked.

28:35. *his sound.* It is unclear whether the suffix on *qôlô* refers to Aaron or to his Robe. If the latter, we should render "*its* sound" (ibn Ezra [shorter commentary]). But more likely the reference is Aaron; the prooftext is Gen 3:8, 10, where the sound of Yahweh walking is called his *qôl* (Ehrlich 1908: 376).

in their midst. Most assume that the bells and pomegranates alternate (e.g., Rashi). Ramban, however, imagines that the bells are literally inside (*bǝtôk*) the pomegranates—which would completely dampen their resonance!

and he shall not die. What is the purpose of the bells? Our verse implies that (a) if the priest entered without the proper attire, Yahweh would kill him (*b. Sanh.* 83b; Rashi); but (b) Aaron is spared by virtue of the bells. One's initial impression might be that the bells apprise God of the priest's approach. Reassured that the encroacher is no layman but a sanctified minister, Yahweh restrains his overwhelming aura. As Bekhor Shor edifyingly comments: the priest must make a sound "lest he come before him [God] in stealth, like a thief. From this we learn common courtesy."

But the text does not actually say who hears the bells. Rather, it uses the ambiguous passive wǝnišmaʿ: the sound "will be heard." And if warning God is the entire point, why add "and in his leaving" (Ramban)? Aaron is no less in jeopardy when he departs the sanctuary than when he enters. Apparently, both God and Man need warning at the approach of the quintessentially "liminal" priest, who stands between the Holy and the Impure, conditions inherently inimical to one another (see pp. 683–91). Similarly, according to Lev 16:4, 23, on Yom Kippur the Great Priest must wash both before entering and before exiting the inner sanctum. What belongs to the profane realm must remain there; what belongs to Holiness must stay in the Tabernacle.

In practice, the tinkling bells on the Great Priest's Robe as he goes about his business would also reassure those *outside* that he still lives and has not brought impurity into contact with the sancta (G. H. Davies 1967: 216; Cole 1973: 202). (Note, however, that when Aaron approaches closest to Yahweh on Yom Kippur, his linen vestments make no sound [Lev 16:4].) Conversely, if the sound ceased, his death would be known, and his defiling corpse could be removed immediately (cf. Lev 10:4–5). The sound also allows hearers to participate vicariously in the service. If they can never see them, at least they can smell and hear Aaron's ministrations (cf. Dillmann 1880: 309). Thus, just as it has a characteristic scent and appearance, Tabernacle worship has a characteristic sound.

> **SPECULATION:** Noth (1962: 224) perceives in 28:35 a vestige of demonism (see also Frazer 1919: 3.446–80). The bells are intended to frighten off malicious spirits, attracted whenever and wherever boundaries are crossed (cf. Milgrom 1991: 504). This view is anticipated by Ramban, who identifies the potentially hostile beings as angels. Although this was presumably not the Priestly Writer's belief, he retained an ancient intuition that thresholds are dangerous (see further vol. I, pp. 440–41).
>
> I wonder, too, whether naive Israelites believed—or were told?—that the sound they heard in the Shrine was actually Yahweh moving about his business. On the popular belief that one could hear deities from without the temple, cf. Pseudo-Lucian *Syrian Goddess* 10; and, on Yahweh's sound, compare Gen 3:8–10; 2 Sam 5:24. On the priest as representing Yahweh, see below, p. 525–26.

28:36. *Blossom.* Whatever its precise definition, ṣîṣ connotes a head ornament, equivalent to a crown (*nēzer*) (29:6; 39:30; Lev 8:9 and cf. Sir 45:12; Wis 18:24; Josephus *Ant.* 3.172–78; Philo *Moses* 2.114; Milgrom 1991: 512–13). Comparable is the golden diadem worn by the high priest of Hierapolis (pseudo-Lucian *Syrian Goddess* 42). There are three principal proposals for rendering ṣîṣ:

A. The most common definition of ṣîṣ is "blossom" (Num 17:23; Isa 28:1, 4; 40:7–8; Ps 103:15; Job 14:2), from the root ṣwṣ 'sprout, flower.' Compare Qatna

Akkadian *ṣiṣṣatu* and Egyptian <u>*ḏiḏi*</u>, both West Semitic loanwords (?) connoting floral decorations (Görg 1991: 125; Redford 1992: 384 n. 77). Many believe that Aaron wears a golden rosette on his forehead, like the Temple's decorative floral motif called *pǝṭûrê ṣiṣṣîm* (1 Kgs 6:18, 29, 32, 35). Ancient Near Eastern gods and kings wear such golden rosettes on their headbands and indeed all over their persons (Oppenheim 1949; Maxwell-Hyslop 1971: 151–57, 218, 254–60; pls. 16, 72; Cahill 1997). The difficulty is that an inscribed surface should be flat, not in raised relief.

B. The root *ṣwṣ* has another meaning: "glint, glimpse." While the notions are distinct for us, Semitic languages often associate vegetal growth with radiance (Greenfield 1959; compare in particularly Hebrew *nṣṣ* 'sparkle/blossom'). Many scholars interpret *ṣîṣ* in Exodus as "shining object," presumably a plaque (e.g., Dillmann 1880: 309). And yet, of many examples of flat frontlet plaques, none bears a text (Maxwell-Hyslop 1971: 251–53; figs. 13, 46, 84–86; pls. 46–47, 123). Moreover, calling a plaque "shining object" is rather bland; we expect from P greater specificity.

C. Ibn Ezra (shorter commentary) cites Ezek 8:3, where Yahweh hoists the prophet by his *ṣîṣīt rō(')š*, generally understood to be a lock of hair (see Greenberg 1983: 167–68). Otherwise *ṣîṣīt* denotes a tassel on the corner of a garment (Num 15:38, 39). We might infer that the *ṣîṣ* of Exod 28:36 is something hanging upon the forehead, either a forelock or a gold pendant like a phylactery (cf. *Tg. Ps.-Jonathan*; Cassuto 1967: 384).

Our challenge is not to choose among these understandings but somehow to synthesize them. Josephus *Ant.* 3.172–78, for example, describes the *ṣîṣ* as no mere rosette or plaque, but as a complex floral crown with an inscribed plate in front. For my part, I envision the priestly *ṣîṣ* as a pendant plaque upon the forehead, incised with a rosette and an inscription above and/or below (fig. 16); for a golden plaque engraved with a rosette, see Maxwell-Hyslop (1971: pl. 16); for letters surrounding a figure, see the seals in Hestrin and Dayagi-Mendels (1979). Ibn Ezra (longer commentary) compares Ps 132:18, which exemplifies well the triple associations of the priestly head ornament: "There I will cause a *horn* to *sprout* for David, / I have trimmed a *lamp* for my Anointed. / His enemies I shall clothe in shame; / But upon him his *crown* will *shine/blossom* (*yāṣîṣ nizrô*)."

pure gold. The finest metal, since it is to receive God's name.

engrave on it. If my foregoing reconstruction of the Blossom is correct, *ûpittaḥtā ʿālā(y)w* is better rendered "engrave *around* it." See also next NOTE.

seal engravings. On the expression *pittûḥê ḥōtām*, see NOTE to 28:11. Maimonides (*Sēper ʿĂbôdâ* 9.1) suggests that, while the entire text might be written on one line, the preferred arrangement is *lyhwh* above and *qdš* below (fig. 16, p. 434). The reverse is also possible; compare the two-line inscription on a clay bulla from the first Temple period *yhwdh / lḥzkyhw ʾḥz mlk* 'Judah / of Hezekiah [son of] Ahaz king of' (Cross 1999). For letters engraved on precious metal, compare the silver plaques bearing versions of Num 6:24–26 discovered in Jerusalem (Yardeni 1991; Barkay 1992).

a Holiness of Yahweh. *Qōdeš* 'Holiness' qualifies any holy place, thing or being, very often a sacrifice. The phrase *qōdeš ləyahwe(h)* 'a Holiness of Yahweh' usually describes goods donated to God and also any sacred space, thing or person. Israelite pottery inscribed with *qdš* or an abbreviation thereof indicates that the contents were intended for God (*AHI* 2.102.1, 103.1, 104.1; 5.005.1; 24.014.2–3; Barkay 1990).

Thus the Blossom marks Aaron as Yahweh's chattel. But he is no mere slave; he is Yahweh's major domo, free to come and go. In another sense, he is a living human sacrifice—an idea less outlandish than it seems because the entire tribe of Levi will be consecrated to Yahweh to replace Israel's firstborn sons, theoretically forfeit to God (see vol. I, pp. 454–56; vol. II, pp. 264–71, 524–25); indeed, Num 8:13, 21 explicitly calls the Levites a *tənûpâ* 'Elevation-offering' (see NOTES to 29:24, 27). Just like a sacrificial victim (Lev 22:21–25; Deut 15:21; 17:1; Mal 1:8–14, etc.), the officiating priest must be sound of body (Lev 21:17–23) and free from impurity (Lev 22:1–16). Aaron's sanctity cannot compare with that of the Tabernacle itself, which is *qōdeš qŏdāšîm* 'Holiness of Holinesses.' But it is the greatest sanctity to which a mere human can attain.

Further: because Aaron bears in duplicate the names of the twelve tribes, all Israel is by extension "a Holiness of Yahweh" (cf. Durham 1987: 388); compare Jer 2:3, "Israel is a Holiness of Yahweh, his first harvest; all eating it shall be held guilty." (On the association of the priest and the whole people, see also NOTE to 19:6.)

SPECULATION: I must register a suprising tradition, in violation of the plain sense of 28:36, that only the Tetragrammaton was inscribed on Aaron's Blossom (Aristeas 98; Josephus *Ant.* 3.178, 187; *War* 5.235; Philo *Moses* 2.114, 132 [contrast *Quaest. in Exod.* 122]). Perhaps the divine name was featured more prominently than the word "Holiness." One could imagine, for instance, an upper line reading *lyhwh* and a lower line with *qdš*, separated by a rosette (see above, NOTE to "seal engravings; fig. 16, p. 434").

28:37. *on blue cord.* Presumably, the *ṣîṣ* was pierced. It is unclear how many strings are intended; see NOTES to 28:28; 39:31.

28:38. *Bear the Transgression of the Holinesses.* The clause *wənāśā'* ... *'et-'ăwōn haqqŏdāšîm* bears many interpretations. *Pace* Rashi and Milgrom (1991: 149), I doubt it refers only to atonement for improper sacrifice (*qŏdāšîm*), although that probably is included (see also *t. Pesaḥ.* 6:5; cf. *m. Pesaḥ.* 7:7). Nor do I think it is a bland "Aaron must bear responsibility and punishment for the Holinesses" (Ehrlich 1969: 192).

The term *'āwōn* is really untranslatable into English. It connotes a ritual or moral violation as well as the responsibility and punishment for that violation. It is often likened to a heavy burden (e.g., Isa 1:4, "a transgression-heavy people"). And the cliché *nāśā' 'āwōn* 'Bear Transgression' implies one of two situations. Said of the sinner himself, it means to be culpable, to bear both responsibility and punishment (my capitalization indicates that this is part of P's technical phraseology). If someone other than the sinner "Bears Transgression," however, then the innocent party assumes the burden, while the transgressor gets off scot free (cf. Schwartz 1995: 8–15). When it is Yahweh who assumes the guilt, the phrase simply connotes something like forgiveness: the guilt is removed or absorbed by God (34:7; Num 14:18; Isa 33:24; Hos 14:3; Micah 7:18; Ps 32:5; 85:3). When the party assuming the transgression is human, however, matters are more complicated. The anonymous man of Isaiah 53 pays a heavy price for bearing (*sābal*) his people's transgressions (v 11). And when Abigail in 1 Sam 25:24 and the Tekoite woman in 2 Sam 14:9 voluntarily assume ʿ*āwōn*, they are staking their lives.

In what sense does Aaron "Bear Transgression" (also Lev 22:16; Num 18:1)? First, the priests consume and digest the people's Sin-offerings (Kiuchi 1987: 135, 162). The connection is explicit in Lev 10:17, "Why did you not eat the Sin-offering . . . for it is Holiness of Holinesses for you [priests] for Bearing the Community's Transgression to make Clearing for them before Yahweh." Likewise, according to Hos 4:1–10, the people violate the laws of society (perjury, murder, theft, adultery) and of God's purity (corpse contamination), whereupon the priests "eat my people's Sin-offering and lift (*nś'*) their soul to transgression (ʿ*āwōn*), so that the priest becomes like the people" (vv 8–9a). In other words, the priest absorbs Israel's sins and becomes tainted with them. Lev 4:3, too, implies an equivalency between the sins of priest and people, so that where the crime actually originates becomes ambiguous and irrelevant: "If the anointed priest should sin for the people's fault. . . ."

Like any transference of objects or persons from the human to the divine realm, sacrifice creates the potential, even the likelihood, of the impure contaminating the pure. According to Lev 17:4, the very act of slaughter generates blood guilt that must be dispelled or absorbed by Tabernacle ritual (below, pp. 698–703). I assume that this is the "Transgression of the Holiness" that Aaron "Bears": all venial violations of Yahweh's Holiness caused by Israel's interactions with Yahweh. These include the sundry transgressions listed in Leviticus 22: consuming sacrificial meat in a state of impurity, an unauthorized person eating sacrificial meat, the offering of a defective animal.

SPECULATION: If Schwartz (1995: 6–7) is right that sins do not so much defile the Tabernacle as literally accrue in it, to be removed on Yom Kippur along with actual impurities (Lev 16:16) (see also Zohar 1988 and below p. 700), then "Bearing Transgression" into the Sanctuary may actually be desirable. Why? Because the land of Canaan is more susceptible to defilement than the Tabernacle is (cf. Frymer-Kensky 1983: 406–412). Without the ritual removal of impurities such as blood guilt, Canaan would spew forth Israel like tainted food (Lev 18:24–29; 20:22–25). The Tabernacle and its personnel function for the land like an antacid, absorbing the people's unsettling transgressions. The priest bears Israel's sins on his head, and once a year he lays them on the scapegoat's head, who "Bears all their Transgression" away from the camp (Lev 16:21) (see also NOTE to 29:14, "Sin-offering").

Aaron's temporary assumption of Israel's "transgression" also potentially explains why all manslayers except the most guilty are pardoned whenever a

Great Priest dies (Num 35:25; Josh 20:6). His death discharges the vicarious guilt he has accrued throughout his final year of service (cf. *b. Mak.* 11b; Greenberg 1959). Again, the Great Priest resembles a human sacrifice, dying to release others from sin (cf. NOTE to 28:36, "a Holiness of Yahweh").

Exod 28:38 conveys an implicit threat. We have just been told that Aaron's golden bells protect him from death whenever he crosses the Sanctuary's threshold (v 35). V 43 will similarly admonish that the priests' underpants must be worn, "lest they Bear Transgression and die." The implication of v 38 is that, without the Blossom to obtain Yahweh's favor, the Great Priest would pay with his life for the full weight of Israel's misdeeds. On the risks the priests bear on Israel's behalf, see for example Num 18:1–7: "You [Aaron] and your sons . . . shall Bear (*nśʾ*) the Holiness's Transgression (*ʿăwōn hammiqdāš*) and . . . the Transgression of your priesthood. . . . [The Levites] may not approach the Holiness equipment and the Altar, lest they die, both they and you. . . . And the alien approaching shall be put to death."

P's repeatedly sanguinary tales all make one point. It is death for any but the Aaronid priests to serve Yahweh, and even they must be very careful. This claim plainly served the interests of the clergy who penned the Priestly Source (see below, p. 732).

continually. I.e., whenever Aaron officiates.

for favor for them. Here and in Lev 26:41–43; Isa 40:2; Jer 14:10; Hos 8:13, "favor" (*rṣy*) serves as the opposite of *ʿāwōn* 'transgression.'

Like the individual priest, ordinary sacrificial offerings are called "Holiness"; they procure Yahweh's *rāṣôn* "favor" (see Milgrom 1991: 149). Although lack of favor is not necessarily lethal (e.g., Lev 7:18; 19:7; 22:23), Exodus implies the threat of violent rejection (see NOTE to "Bear the Transgression of the sancta" above).

before Yahweh. P's cliché *lipnê yahwe(h)*, literally "to Yahweh's face/presence," is tantamount to "within the Tabernacle."

28:39. *plait.* On *šbṣ*, see NOTE 28:4, "woven."

linen. It seems that the lower clergy dress entirely in white linen, like the Great Priest on Clearing Day (Lev 16:4, 23, 32), perhap as a sign of humility (fig. 16, p. 434). For parallels to white-robed priests, see Dillmann (1880: 311–12; NOTE to 28:42, "linen").

Sash. According to Josephus *Ant.* 3.154–56, its ends hang to the feet but are sometimes thrown over the left shoulder. How the *ʾabnēṭ* differs from the ordinary girdle, the *ʾēzôr*, is unclear. Presumably it is more splendid (cf. Noth 1962: 226), or P may just be using a recondite term. It is also unclear whether the Great Priest's Sash differs from those of the lower clergy (*b. Yoma* 12a).

embroiderer's work. See NOTE to 26:36. According to 39:29, the Sash is made of twisted linen and wool dyed blue, purple and crimson.

28:40. *hats.* The etymology and exact meaning of *migbāʿôt* are uncertain. A *migbaʿat* might be a tall, mounded hat. Ibn Ezra (shorter commentary) compares *gibʿâ* 'mountain'; also possibly related is *gābîaʿ* 'goblet' (Dillmann 1880: 310; cf.

Holzinger 1900: 138). But the best suggestion is Ramban's correlation with *k/qôbaʿ* 'helmet' (cf. Aramaic *kôbaʿ* 'turban'). Although I can cite no exact parallels from Hebrew, an assimilation *mikb-/miqb-* to *migb-* would not be surprising.

glory . . . splendor. Because the MT cantillation puts a stop after "sashes," Rashbam supposes that the headgear alone is "for glory and for splendor." I prefer to ignore the trope and conclude that, like Aaron's vestments (28:2), the lesser clergy's entire wardrobe is "for glory and for splendor" (Lockshin 1997: 374 n. 89).

28:41. *make wear.* Moses is not necessarily to dress the priests himself, although that cannot be excluded. I doubt the Great Priest can dress himself, particularly when it comes to rigging the *ḥōšen.*

anoint them. "Them" is the priests not the garments, to judge from the following clauses (Rashi). As is apparent from comparison with Leviticus 8, all the commands in v 41 are prospective, referring to the time when the Tabernacle will be completed. Only then can the priests be robed and sanctified (Rashbam).

We do not know exactly how anointment was carried out. According to a much later tradition, in addition to oil poured upon the head, a Greek chi (i.e., an X) was traced on the priest's forehead (through an association with Greek *chriō* anoint?) (*b. Ker.* 5b). For kings, a crown was supposedly traced.

Why anoint at all? On the most basic level, oil restores the skin in a harsh, dry climate (Houtman 1993a: 166). Houtman (2000: 523) summarizes the further associations of anointment in nonritual contexts: "application of anointing oil refreshes a person, restores vitality, and produces a feeling of well-being and self-confidence. . . . In case of sickness, it can reinvigorate him or her and numb pain. . . . Therefore one forgoes anointing oneself with oil in time of mourning. . . . 'Applying ointment' has an energizing and cleansing effect . . . , and it can revive and renew a person, remake him or her as it were into another, a new human being." Anointment is the natural complement of bathing: first one rinses off dirt and all that it symbolizes, and then smears oneself with fresh oil.

Such is the secular basis of anointing. In the Hebrew Bible, however, anointment is a ritual specifically associated with the inauguration of kings (Judg 9:15; 1 Sam 9:16; 10:1; 16:3; 1 Kgs 1:39; 2 Kgs 9:6; 11:12; 23:30), who were sometimes called *māšîaḥ* 'Anointed.' (In the Ugaritic texts, a queen is anointed, although the context is not clear [Pardee 1979: 14–20].) Occasionally, prophets, too, are anointed (1 Kgs 19:16; Isa 61:1). In both cases, the absorbed oil conveys Yahweh's spirit (1 Sam 16:13–14; Isa 61:1) and strength (Ps 89:21–26).

In the priest's case, however, oil confers Holiness. The Priestly Source calls the Great Priest "the anointed priest" (Lev 4:3, 5, 16; 6:15; cf. 16:32; 21:10; Num 35:25), and priests were similarly anointed in Hatti (Hoffner 1973a: 218) and Emar (Fleming 1992: 63–69). An Akkadian title for a priest was *pašīšu* 'anointed.' Whether of a king, a prophet or a priest, anointment is a rite of passage, a ritual elevation of status (Milgrom 1991: 553). In the case of the king, moreover, anointment betokens vassalhood to Yahweh (for a Canaanite parallel, see EA 51:4–9).

Why oil is poured on the initiate's *head* we do not know. Perhaps his gleaming face is considered reflective of the divine aura. To be sure, more mundane proposals have been advanced. Jacobsen (1970: 325–26), for example, learnedly derives the rite from a de-lousing technique. But all explanations are complicated by the fact that objects, too, may be anointed (e.g., Gen 28:18; 35:14), including the Altar and Tabernacle (Exod 29:36; 30:26; 40:10; Lev 8:10).

The effect of anointment is not necessarily benign. Most illuminating is the curse ceremony for an Assyrian vassal, which includes among other acts of sympathetic magic an application of oil: "[As oil en]ters your flesh, [just so may] they make this curse to enter into your flesh, [the flesh of your brothers], your sons and your daughters" (Wiseman 1958: 78, ll. 622–24; ANET³ 540). Compare also Ps 109:18, "And he wore curse (qəlālâ) as his vestment, and it entered like water into his midst and like oil into his bones." Like the vassal–suzerain relationship itself, anointment probably conveys potential blessing and curse. And anointment, like vassalhood, is heritable (cf. Exod 40:15, "their anointment shall be . . . for them as an eternal priesthood").

In the course of time, the fact that both kings and priests were anointed would contribute to the temporary fusion of the monarchy and sacerdocy under the Hasmoneans, as well as the expectation of two messiahs among the Qumran community and other Jews, and ultimately the image of Jesus as both King and Great Priest (see Collins 1995: 74–101). (For further discussion of anointing, see Kutsch 1963; Mettinger 1976: 185–232; Milgrom 1991: 516–17; Viberg 1992: 89–119; Thompson 1994.)

fill their hand. The Hebrew idiom *millēʾ ʾet-hayyād* 'fill the hand' is used only in the context of priestly ordination (e.g., 28:41; 29:9, 29, 33, 35; cf. 32:29). The corresponding noun for ordination is the abstract plural *millūʾîm* 'Fillings' (29:22–27, 34). The Hebrew expression is paralled by Mari *mullû qātam/qatē* 'fill the hand(s), hand over, entrust' (CAD 10.1.187), connoting a divine commissioning, a transfer of authority from a god to a sacred human: e.g., "(the gods) Shamash and Adad filled my hands for diviner-ship." Sarna (1991: 185) also compares English "mandate" (< Latin *mandatus* 'given into the hand').

make . . . holy. Ibn Ezra takes the verb as delocutive: "declare holy" (on such verbs, cf. Hillers 1967; on *qiddēš* in post-Biblical Hebrew, see Tigay 1999). But I rather think this is a reference to the sanctification procedure: washing, vesting, anointment.

28:42. *linen.* Not the *šēš* 'linen' of the Great Priest's robes and the Tabernacle curtains but *bad*, perhaps an inferior grade (Haran 1978: 174). If so, the Great Priest's wearing only *bad* on Clearing Day (Lev 16:4, 23) must be a form of abasement. The priest also dresses entirely in linen for the menial task of cleaning the Altar (Lev 6:3; on holy officiants clad in *bad*, see also 1 Sam 2:18; 22:18; 2 Sam 6:14). But, if *bad* is lesser stuff, it is slightly surprising that angels should wear it (Ezek 9:2–3, 11; 10:2, 6, 7; Dan 10:5; 12:6, 7).

Not all agree that *bad* is a textile. No one, after all, has proffered a convincing linguistic derivation (for forced Rabbinic etymology, see *b. Zebaḥ.* 18b; for an Egyptian derivation involving part of a ship and Osiris' severed phallus, see Grintz 1975: 14–15). Since the noun *bad* otherwise connotes distinction (< *bdd* 'be isolated, unique'), some regard the term as connoting holiness, equivalent to *qōdeš* (Elhorst 1910: 266–68; Houtman 1993a: 160–61).

underpants. This translation of *miknāsayim* (28:42; 39:28; Lev 6:3; 16:4; Ezek 44:18) is based on context; ordinarily the root *kns* means "to gather." We learn little about undergarments from ancient texts and art, but see Vogelsang-Eastwood (2000: 286–88) for surviving Egyptian specimens. The understanding of *miknāsayim* as trousers can be traced as far back as Greek *periskelē* 'drawers' (LXX) and *anaxyrides* (Josephus *Ant.* 3.152; *War* 5.231); Herodotus applies the latter term to the pants worn by the Persians, Scythians and other easterners (*Histories* 1.7; 5.49; 7.61, etc.) with or without kilts (for illustrations, see Ghirshman 1964: pls. 209, 229, 232, 236, 244, 245, 259). But *miknāsayim* might alternatively be a loincloth covering only the genitals (cf. Houtman 2000: 482–83; Josephus *Ant.* 3.152 [although, in context, Greek *diazōma* 'girdle' seems to connote drawers]). Houtman regards the *miknāsayim* as identical to the ephod of ordinary priests (see NOTE to 28:4, "ephod").

The need for some kind of coverage for modesty's sake is demonstrated by 1 Sam 6:20, where Michal berates her husband David for the skimpiness of his ephod (1 Chr 15:27 adds a proper robe to David's attire). And Exod 20:26(23) addresses the same concern not by prescribing priestly underwear but by forbidding that altars be elevated, "at which your nudity may not be revealed."

Admittedly, the concern is a little puzzling, for the Great Priest wears a great Robe with *šûlayim* 'skirts' (28:33, 34) that, according to Jer 13:22, 26; Nah 3:5, generally suffice for modesty. The underpants make more sense for the ordinary priests, who are clad only in shifts. This may explain why they are appended as a kind of afterthought to the major priestly vestments.

What is wrong with exposing one's genitals? Cassuto (1967: 387) sees the law as a rejection of ritual nudity, supposedly an old pagan practice (compare nude prophecy in 1 Sam 19:24; Isa 20:2–4; also the unclad Sumerian priests in *ANEP* 171 fig. 502). I think rather the offense lies in implicit sexuality: a man should approach Yahweh as submissive (i.e., feminized), not displaying his sex before his master (cf. Eilberg-Schwartz 1994: 137–62). According to Aulus Gellius 10:15, the Roman priest *flamen dialis* similarly wore a special garment "lest he appear nude under the heavens or under Jove's eye."

The relevant biblical passages suggest, however, that the main offense lies in priest's nudity being seen not by God but by the people. Again, a genital display before Israelite women could be construed as a challenge to Yahweh's status as Israel's "alpha male." And another danger could be homosexual arousal, since an ejaculation of semen would cause ritual impurity (19:5; Lev 15:16–18; cf. Deut 23:10–15; 1 Sam 21:4–7). Or perhaps the priest is regarded in some sense as Yahweh's image; uncovering his nudity would be tantamount to uncovering God's (on the concealment of Yahweh's genitals, see Eilberg-Schwartz 1994). In any event, it is striking that the biblical idiom for adultery is "uncovering nudity" (e.g., Leviticus 18, 20). Adultery is a capital offense; and the priest who exposes his genitals will likewise be killed by Yahweh.

SPECULATION: The *miknāsayim* may also create a zone of insulation between the priest's body and his sacred vestments. If the priest has a seminal emission while wearing consecrated robes, the result might be the garments' pollution and the priest's death. Perhaps the undergarments absorb but do not transmit Holiness, on the one hand, and impurity, on the other. This might explain, too, why the text is inconsistent as to their Holiness status.

Assuming that *miknāsayim* are after all pants, the question arises when trousers were first introduced into the Near East. That the Persians and Scythians wore pants is sometimes cited as objective evidence for P's postexilic date (most recently Sperling 1999). See further below, pp. 524, 732.

28:43. *coming into Meeting Tent.* To change the lamps or the bread, or to burn incense.

Bear Transgression and die. On this idiom, see NOTE to 28:38.

his seed after him. To judge from the nonmention of footwear, it seems that the Israelite priests officiated barefoot (so explicitly *y. Šeqal.* 5:1; *Exod. Rab.* 2:6; cf. *b. Roš Haš.* 31b; *Soṭa* 40a for the priestly benediction in later Judaism). In this, they resemble Moses at Horeb (3:5), Joshua before the angel (Josh 5:15) and the priests of Melcarth at Cades (Silius Italicus *Punica* 3.28). On the symbolism of the custom, see vol. I, p. 200. At the Temple of 'Ein Dara, the god him/herself enters the shrine unshod (Abū Assāf 1990).

29:1. *to make them holy to priest.* Having described their garments in detail, Yahweh now discloses the process by which Aaron and his sons will be separated from their fellow Israelites and made into priests. According to Lev 8:3, their ordination will be witnessed by the entire community.

Throughout this section, there is thoroughgoing ambiguity as to who does the consecrating: Yahweh (29:44; 31:13), Moses (29:27, 37; 30:29–30; 40:9–11, 13) or unspecified (28:3; 29:1, 33, 36). Sanctification is apparently a cooperative procedure: Moses conducts the rituals whereby God imparts Holiness to the Tabernacle, its personnel and ultimately all Israel. On the verb *ləkahēn* 'to priest,' see NOTE to 28:1, "to priest."

bull. This will be for the Sin-offering of the first day; see 29:14. In all, seven bulls and fourteen rams are probably used (NOTES to 29:35).

cattle's son. After *pār* 'bull,' one would think *ben bāqār* 'cattle's son' (or "son of the herd") would be superfluous. Is the language simply orotund, or is some distinction intended? Ibn Ezra supposes that *ben bāqār* implies a young animal; cf. Gen 18:7, "a bull, cattle's son, *tender and sweet.*" (Analogously, *banê 'ēlīm* 'gods' sons' and *banê nabî'îm* 'prophets' sons' connote subordinate gods and junior prophets.) Alternatively, Milgrom (1991: 232) conveys S. Rattray's attractive suggestion: the command excludes *wild* bovines.

rams, two. One animal will be the wholly burnt Ascending-offering (*'ōlâ*) (29:16–18); the other will be the Filling-offering (*millū'îm*) of ordination, partly consumed by the celebrants and partly burnt upon the Altar (vv 19–28).

perfect. One sacrifices to Yahweh only an animal whose vitality and physical qualities are unimpaired, who is neither sick nor deformed.

29:2. *bread, unleavened bread.* Moses will offer one loaf each of three types of unleavened bread, all made of wheat bran. Rabbinic authorities dispute whether *leḥem* 'bread' is necessarily baked (Rashbam) or whether in this case it is boiled in water (Rashi on Lev 6:14). On the etymology of *maṣṣâ* 'unleavened bread,' see NOTE to 12:8 (vol. I, pp. 393–94). On bread-making in modern Palestine, see Dalman (1935: 1–152).

ḥallōt. While we are not sure what *ḥallōt* are, they are clearly not the leavened "challah" of modern Judaism. The root *ḥll* 'pierce' may provide a clue; thus KB (p. 300) translates "ring-shaped bread." Ibn Ezra, however, infers from the context that it means "thick," the opposite of "wafers" (also Milgrom 1991: 184). An alternative etymology would derive the term from Hittite *ḥali-* '(sacred) cake.'

Although oil is not mentioned apropos of the first type of bread, Rashi and Rashbam deduce its presence from alleged parallels in 29:23; Lev 2:4–5; 8:26. But none of these really bear on the issue. Bekhor Shor, in contrast, concludes that the first cakes are oil-less. The solution may lie in Lev 7:12, where, reminiscent of Exod 29:2, the Gratitude-offering *(tôdâ)* is accompanied by three types of bread. The first is *murbeket,* which according to Lev 6:14 may mean "fried" *(Tg. Ps.-Jon.* Lev 6:14; Maimonides on *m. Menaḥ.* 9:3). If so, the oil is not a true ingredient, though some is absorbed. Admittedly, however, Lev 6:14 is not perfectly clear. For further discussion, see Milgrom (1991: 179, 399–40, 530), who thinks *murbeket* means "well soaked in oil" (also *t. Menaḥ.* 7:13; 8:17), and thus that all three types of bread in Exod 29:2 are oiled. For an Egyptian borrowing of the root *rbk* apropos of bread, see Hoch (1994: 204).

saturated with oil. The second type of unleavened bread may have oil baked into it *(b. Menaḥ.* 75a), presumably because it is too thick to be permeated by surface oil (Houtman 2000: 530). *Bālûl* literally means "mixed." A third-century B.C.E. Phoenician text known as the "Marseilles Tariff" also calls an offering *bll* in association with *mnḥ[t]* '(grain?) offering' (*KAI* 69.14; *ANET*[3] 656–57).

wafers. *Rāqîq* derives from the root *rqq* 'to be thin' (compare Arabic *raqqa* 'to be thin,' Nejd dialect *raqîq* 'thin bread' [Wehr 1976: 352]).

anointed with oil. The third type of bread is spread with oil after baking (cf. *b. Menaḥ.* 75a), still a common Middle-Eastern and Mediterranean repast (e.g., Hansen 1964: 209). Micah 6:7 ridicules the lavish use of oil in worship: "Does Yahweh delight . . . in tens of thousands of oil streams?"

SPECULATION: Since the priestly initiates assume symbolic identity with sacrificial animals (see pp. 448, 531), it may be no coincidence that the grain offerings are "anointed" *(məšūḥîm),* as if also representing the anointed priests *(hakkōhănîm hamməšūḥîm;* Num 3:3) given to God.

wheat bran. *Sōlet* is semolina or wheat bran, twice as expensive as ordinary barley (2 Kgs 7:1, 16, 18). Cognates are Akkadian *siltu* and Arabic *sult* with the same meaning (for Rabbinic citations, see Milgrom 1991: 179). The word may also appear as a loan in New Kingdom Egyptian (Hoch 1994: 369–70).

29:3. Bring them Near. Literally bring them to the Tabernacle, with the additional connotations of consecration and sacrifice (cf. *qorbān* 'offering,' lit. "what is brought near"; also Akkadian *qurrubu,* Arabic *qarraba* and Ugaritic *šqrb,* all referring to sacrifice). The verb *hiqrîb* 'Bring Near' is a *Leitmotif* of this section, which describes the transfer of sanctified offerings and humans from the mundane to the sacred sphere (28:1; 29:3–4, 8, 10). See also NOTE to 28:1, "Bring Near to yourself."

29:4. *Meeting Tent Opening*. *Petaḥ ʾōhel mōʿēd*, barred by a fabric screen, is as close to Yahweh as a layman may approach. On initiation at the doorway, cf. also NOTES to 21:6. Here as elsewhere, however, the phrase by extension connotes the entire Plaza (Milgrom 1991: 147); see p. 499.

wash. It is moot whether Moses personally washes Aaron's family or just makes them wash themselves. Lev 8:6 seems to indicate the former, but see Milgrom (1991: 500–1).

The water presumably comes from the Basin described in Exod 30:17–21; it is poured over Aaron and his sons. On pain of death, the priests must wash their hands and feet whenever they enter the Tabernacle or make sacrifice (30:20–21).

In 29:4, it is unclear how much of the body is washed. Most likely it is the entire surface (Driver 1911: 315), like the Great Priest on Yom Kippur (Lev 16:4, 24). But since the donning of underpants is not mentioned, they at least are perhaps worn during the bath (Holzinger 1900: 141).

In general, one washes before and sometimes also after contact with the holy (de Vaux 1971: 460–61; on ablutions at Ugarit, see Levine 1963: 105–7). Does the bath physically remove impurity or merely symbolize its removal? In the present case, I suppose that washing with water is a necessary-but-not-sufficient stage in the priests' purification. It eliminates gross particles, but full Clearing *(kpr)* requires blood (pp. 700–701).

29:5. *the garments*. Those described in 28:2–41 (all but the underpants).

Ephod . . . ḥōšen. See NOTES to 28:4.

and you shall "ephod" for him with the Ephod's woven-band. There are two plausible interpretations of *wəʾāpadtā lô bəḥēšeb hāʾēpōd*. The verb *ʾāpad* seems to be a denominative derived from *ʾēpōd*; it ostensibly means "to bind on an ephod" by means of a *ḥēšeb* 'woven-band' (NOTE to 28:8). Thus the clause might mean: "you shall fasten on his Ephod with the corset." Vg, Syr and *Tgs.*, however, understand the implicit object as not the Ephod but the *ḥōšen* attached to its front, in which case we would paraphrase: "fasten [the *ḥōšen*] to it [the Ephod] on the Ephod's corset" by the blue cord (28:28).

29:6. *Holiness Crown*. *Nēzer haqqōdeš* is the golden *ṣîṣ* inscribed "Holiness for Yahweh" (28:36). The etymology of *nēzer* is unclear; Grintz (1975: 169) derives it from Egyptian *nzrt* 'uraeus,' the symbolic serpent worn on Pharaoh's brow. There may also, as with *ṣîṣ*, be an association with hair (Num 6:9, 18, 19; Jer 7:29) and vegetal growth (Lev 25:5, 11). On the roots *nzr* and *ṣyṣ* in association, cf. Ps 132:18 (see further NOTE to 28:36, "Blossom").

29:7. *Ointment Oil*. Its formula is revealed in 30:23–25.

pour. In considerable quantity, and before the Turban is donned, to judge from Ps 133:2, which compares fraternal harmony to "the sweet oil upon the head, descending onto the beard, Aaron's beard that descends to the *mouth* (collar) of his garments" (Milgrom 1991: 518) (see, however, NOTE to 30:26). But Ramban notes that in Lev 8:9, 12, Aaron is anointed *after* putting on the Turban—so either some of the head is left bare, or perhaps Aaron doffs his hat to receive the oil. All the priests are anointed (28:41; 29:29; 30:30; 40:15; Lev 10:7), but apparently only Aaron is anointed on the head (note Lev 21:10, 12).

anoint. Aaron receives the sacred oil twice: once poured upon his head (29:7) and once sprinkled, together with blood, on his body and clothes (29:21). According to Lev 8:12, the first anointment sanctifies. But according to 29:31, the second application also sanctifies. Is the point that Aaron is twice as holy as other priests? For further discussion of anointment, see NOTE to 28:41.

29:8. *shifts.* The underpants (*miknāsayim*) are unmentioned, probably because they are worn during the washing (NOTE to 29:4, "wash").

29:9. *Aaron and his sons.* This has the air of an afterthought, as though the Priestly Writer realized he had neglected to mention Aaron's Sash in vv 5–6. See further TEXTUAL NOTE.

bind hats. From the verb *ḥbš* 'bind,' Milgrom (1991: 520) infers that the priests' special hats, the *mibgā'ōt*, have chin straps. But they might alternatively be wound around the head—or, as in Modern Hebrew, *ḥbš* might refer to the donning of any headgear.

priesthood . . . an eternal rule. One might initially take the phrase as retrospective, as if clothes alone make the priest. But instead this clause sets up the following ordination ritual.

fill Aaron's hand. I.e., ordain him; see NOTE to 28:41, "fill their hand."

29:10. *press. Sāmak* implies a light pressure (Milgrom 1991: 150).

their hands. In 29:10, 15, 19; Lev 8:14, 18, 22, it is somewhat unclear whether each man lays one or two hands upon the victim (the same ambiguity obtains in Lev 4:15; 24:14; Num 8:10, 12; 2 Chr 29:23). If it were one hand, we might have expected in Exod 29:10 **yādām* 'their hand' not *yədêhem* 'their hands.' Moreover, Aaron is expressly said to lay "his two hands (*štê yādāw*)" on the goat for Azazel (Lev 16:21). In other cases, however, an offerer presses with "his hand (*yādô*)" (Lev 1:4; 3:2, 8, 13; 4:4, 24, 29, 33). But even here there is room for doubt, because *ydw* 'his hand' could also be read as an archaic **yādāw* 'his hands.' Perfectly illustrating the problem are Num 27:18, 23; Deut 34:9, where the Versions disagree within and among themselves as to how many hands Moses lays upon Joshua.

Explanations of sacrificial hand-laying vary (see Milgrom 1991: 151). The most obvious interpretation, to which I subscribe (NOTE to 29:14, "burn"), is that the act transfers to the victim sin and impurity from which the offerer disassociates him/herself (Hubert and Mauss 1964: 32; Zohar 1988: 612–15). Thus there is symbolic identification between the sacrificer and what is sacrificed, in effect self-immolation (see further pp. 695–703). In this connection, Ehrlich (1969: 193) cites Lev 8:10–12, where the Israelites lay their hands upon their proxies, the Levites, who in turn lay their hands upon sacrificial animals; and likewise Num 27:18, 23; Deut 34:9, where Moses lays his hand(s) on his successor and surrogate Joshua.

Others take different approaches. For Baentsch (1903: 239), hand-laying is tantamount to manumission: the property leaves the owner's possession and enters God's. And Milgrom (1991: 151–53) claims that the laying of hands symbolizes ownership: the offerer is certified as the donor of the sacrifice, even if he can not literally carry in the victim because it is too large. While this may be P's rationale—there are corroborating parallels from Hatti (Wright 1986)—I would remain open-minded as to popular understandings of the ceremony. None of the interpretations proffered above excludes the others.

29:11. *slaughter.* By slitting the throat (Milgrom 1991: 154). Against the surface interpretation, Moses himself probably does not kill the animal, for the officiant does not ordinarily slaughter the sacrifice. The syntax of Lev 8:15, 19, 23 also suggests that someone else kills the bull (Milgrom, pp. 520–21)—most likely Aaron, on whose behalf the sacrifice is made.

before Yahweh (at) Meeting Tent opening. Lipnê yahwe(h) 'before Yahweh' is a common technical term for the Tabernacle or its inner sanctum. In chap. 29 and elsewhere, however, it can also refer to the Plaza before the Tabernacle's entrance, especially the vicinity of the Altar.

29:12. *apply on the Altar's horns . . . fundament.* We are not sure exactly what yəsôd 'fundament' connotes. It might be the Altar's lower half covered by the bronze mesh (NOTES to 27:4–5; cf. *m. Mid.* 3:1), or it might be where the Altar meets the ground. 1 Kgs 18:32 and perhaps Ezek 43:13–17 describe trenches surrounding an altar, but on this the Torah is silent (cf. Wright 1987: 149–59). Bloodying the Altar's horns (see NOTE to 27:2, "horns") and pouring blood around its base characterize the *ḥaṭṭā(')t* 'Sin-offering.' On the symbolism, see below pp. 698–701.

your finger. The manual manipulation of blood is a priestly prerogative associated with rituals of purification; cf. Lev 4:6, 17, 25, 34; 9:9 (Sin-offering); 16:14–19 (Clearing Day); Num 19:4 (Red Heifer).

all the blood. I.e., all the remaining blood not applied to the horns (LXX; Saadiah; Rashi).

29:13. *all the fat covering the entrails.* Milgrom (1991: 205) provides the anatomical details: *ḥēleb* is "layers of fat beneath the surface of the animal's skin and around its organs, which can be peeled off, in contrast to the fat that is inextricably entwined in the musculature." The fat covering the entrails is the "caul or greater omentum, referring to the fatty membrane, at times more than an inch thick, that surrounds the intestines and therefore secures for them a proper degree of warmth."

The Bible never explains why fat is reserved for God (Lev 3:17). On the one hand, "fat" sometimes connotes "the best" (e.g., Num 18:12), and fatty meat is the tastiest. On the other hand, the suet described in 29:13 and parallel passages is inedible, at least on its own (Milgrom, p. 427). It appears something of a legal trick: one takes the worst part, calls it the best, and gives it to God (on sacrifice as a deception of the gods, cf. Hesiod *Theogony* 535–40). Too, the oils in the fat facilitate burning and yield a pleasing odor.

excrescence. The yōteret is the caudate lobe on the liver (Milgrom 1991: 208).

and the two kidneys and the fat. Mentioned last, because they are removed last.

Buried deep in the adipose, the kidneys are treated like fat and burned on the Altar (Milgrom 1991: 207–8).

smoke. Hiqṭîr literally means "burn, turn to smoke." The savor is inhaled by Yahweh in Heaven, who, as a being of *rûaḥ* 'wind, breath, spirit,' naturally eats in this manner (below, pp. 702–3). Similarly, when Gideon proposes to feed Yahweh's Messenger, i.e., a divine emanation, the being declines to dine in human fashion but instead with the touch of his rod burns up bread, meat and broth on an improvised altar.

29:14. *meat and . . . skin and . . . dung.* These parts are simply discarded: the meat may not be eaten; the skin may not be tanned; the dung may not be used for fuel. See following NOTE.

burn. Why is a valuable animal wasted — neither burnt upon the Altar nor eaten by worshipers? In a routine Sin-offering to purge the impurity brought about by individual laymen, the priests eat the meat (Lev 6:18–23; cf. 10:18–19) (see pp. 449, 699–700). In the higher-level Sin-offerings for priestly or national violations, however, the meat is not eaten but destroyed (Lev 6:23).

The reason for the distinction is unclear. Perhaps it is simply that no man should benefit from the worst violation of purity strictures; in particular, a priest should not eat his own Sin-offering. Gorman (1990: 81) supposes, however, that the victim's body maintains a postmortem link with its drained blood: once the latter has absorbed the Tabernacle's impurity, the carcass must be eliminated safely outside the camp (also Wright 1987: 130; Milgrom 1991: 239, 261–62). (The more logical alternative, rejected by Wright and Milgrom, is that the laying of hands transfers the offerer's impurities to the animal *before* it is slain; see NOTE to 29:10.)

In Exodus 29, the Sin-offering of priestly consecration constitutes an intermediate, transitional case (on the equally exceptional Sin-offering of Lev 9:7–11, see Milgrom 1991: 580–81). On the one hand, since Aaron and his sons are initially laymen, their offering takes place in the Plaza, with Moses presiding. One might expect Moses, as *pontifex maximus pro tempore*, to eat their offering. But no: because Aaron and his sons are becoming priests and Moses is surrendering his sacerdocy, no one eats their offering (cf. Milgrom 1991: 525, 555–58). On Moses' ambiguous status, see further p. 532.

outside the camp. The nonsacrificial parts of the Sin-offering are always conveyed outside the camp, to a place that, while not sacred, is at least devoid of impurity (Lev 4:12, 21) — i.e., does not contain carcasses or fresh blood, is not under medical quarantine and is not a latrine (Deut 23:13–15; Ezek 4:12–14; see, however, Milgrom [1991: 536] for the view that feces are not defiling for P).

The reason for this removal is not stated. The parallel cases of the Red Heifer (Num 19:9), which cleanses the taint of death, and the "scapegoat," which bears the community's sins into the wilderness (Lev 16:21–22), strongly suggest a symbolic transferral of impurity to without the camp (cf. Milgrom 1991: 261–64).

he. The bull.

Sin-offering. The text names this complex procedure: *ḥaṭṭā(ʾ)t.* I maintain the traditional interpretation "Sin-offering" despite its unequivocal rejection by Milgrom (1971; 1991: 253–92), who proposes instead "Purification Offering." I concede that the ḥaṭṭā(ʾ)t effects purification and is associated with the roots ṭhr 'be pure' (e.g., Num 19:12; Ps 51:9) and kpr 'Clear, purge' (e.g., Lev 8:15; Ezek 43:20; 2 Chr 29:24) (for all three roots, see Num 8:21). In particular, the double middle radical of ḥaṭṭā(ʾ)t evokes the verb ḥiṭṭēʾ, conventionally rendered "purify" and associated with the ḥaṭṭā(ʾ)t in Exod 29:36; Lev 9:15; Ezek 43:22. (On ḥiṭṭēʾ, see further NOTE to 29:36, "Un-sin.")

Despite the strength of Milgrom's arguments, decisive for me is that, in the vast majority of contexts, ḥaṭṭā(ʾ)t means simply "sin" (but see Levine [1974: 102] on the possible Massoretic confusion of ḥāṭāʾt 'sin' and ḥaṭṭāʾt 'impurity'). For Priestly usage in particular, compare Lev 4:3, "He shall Bring Near for his sin that he sinned (ḥaṭṭāʾtô ʾăšer ḥāṭāʾ) a bull . . . to Yahweh as a Sin-offering (ḥaṭṭāʾt)." Even in 29:36; Lev 6:19; 9:15; Ezek 43:22; 2 Chr 29:24, ḥiṭṭēʾ does not so much mean "purify" as "perform the ḥaṭṭā(ʾ)t blood rite" (Milgrom 1991: 583). Moreover, I consider deriving the sense of ḥaṭṭā(ʾ)t from ḥiṭṭēʾ methodologically backward. The real question should be: since the root ḥṭʾ undeniably means "sin, offend, err," how came the Piʿel to connote ritual purification? Why, for instance, is a "Sin-offering" made for innocent happenstances such as childbirth (Leviticus 12) and genital flux (Lev 15:15)? Why does Hebrew, which shares so much cultic terminology with its cognate tongues, alone among the Semitic langauges call a purification sacrifice "Sin-offering"?

The most reasonable explanation is that Priestly theology subsumes moral and purity violations under one category: ḥaṭṭā(ʾ)t. This is the implication of Lev 16:16, "He [the Great Priest] shall effect Clearing (wǝkipper) for the Holiness from the impurities (ṭumʾōt) of Israel's Sons and from their crimes (pišʿêhem), for all their sins (ḥaṭṭōʾtām); and so he shall do for Meeting Tent that tents amid their impurities (ṭumʾōtām)." Since humanity cannot avoid ritual impurity, we cannot but offend Yahweh. If nonetheless we crave his proximity, we must avoid high crimes—murder, theft, adultery, etc.—and for accidental or unavoidable purity offenses make the Sin-offering as needed. This is why the Sin-offering generally precedes other types of burnt offerings (Sifra Maṣōrāʿ 3:13; cf. t. Para 1:1; Milgrom 1991: 488–89). To commune with God, humans must first be in a state of maximal purity (e.g., 19:10, 14–15) (see further pp. 682–701). The Sin-offering, I should reemphasize, does not effect Clearing for deliberate crimes, only for the accidental.

The Sin-offering will be performed seven times during the week of ordination, as Aaron and his sons are gradually made into priests and the Altar is gradually purified (29:36). Then, on the eighth day, the fully consecrated Aaron will make two more Sin-offerings, one for himself and one for the entire community (Lev 9:7–15). That the Altar has now been made as holy as possible by the ninefold Sin-offering is shown by the aftermath. When the requisite animal parts are laid upon the Altar, this time the priests need not kindle a fire. Yahweh's own Glory extends a fiery pseudopod from inside the Tabernacle to consume the offering (Lev 9:24); see below, pp. 532, 689–90.

29:15. *hands.* See NOTE to 29:10.

29:16. dash. The blood is tossed or perhaps sprinkled *(zāraq)* from a vessel called *mizrāq* (27:3; Num 4:14).

against the Altar around. Just what is bloodied is slightly unclear. Most understand that the Altar's sides are meant (e.g., b. *Zebaḥ.* 10b). But possibly one is to pour blood on the ground *around, nearby* the Altar (Philo *Spec. Leg.* 1.205); for this use of *ʿal,* cf. 32:1; 2 Sam 12:17, etc.

Blood-casting is a frequent aspect of animal sacrifice (29:16, 20; Lev 1:5, 11; 3:2, 8, 13; 7:2; 8:19, 24; 9:12, 18, etc.). The exception is the Sin-offering, whose blood is instead dabbed on the Altar's horns—or, in some cases, sprinkled inside the Tabernacle (Leviticus 4; 16:14–15)—and also poured out at the Altar's base (NOTE to 29:12).

As the embodiment of the life force, blood is taboo for humans (Gen 9:4; Lev 17:10–14; Deut 12:23). Like suet, it is reserved for God (Lev 3:17). But, unlike fat, blood does not burn. Accordingly, it is not sent Heavenward as smoke but deposited on various parts of the Tabernacle or poured at the Altar's base. Addressing the same problem, Deut 12:16, 23–24; 15:23 prescribe pouring out blood on the ground. (On the symbolism inherent in these quasi-libations, see pp. 698–701.)

Applying it to the Altar places blood within the divine domain. Possibly the mesh surrounding the Altar's lower sides retains the fluid, which would not adhere to its sides of sheer bronze (NOTES to 27:4–5). In any case, the gore-bespattered *mizbēaḥ,* literally "place of slaughter," jars the viewer into consciousness of the enormity of taking life—for, at heart, the Priestly Writer was a vegetarian (see pp. 681–82, 696–98).

29:17. dismember into his members. I.e., cut the ram's joints.

wash his entrails. To remove dung (Lev 4:11).

shanks. On *keraʿ* as denoting the lower leg, see Milgrom (1991: 159–60).

with his members . . . head. Nɘtāḥā(y)w here means its other parts, not counting the legs and entrails (Rashi). The butchered carcass is reassembled and set between the Altar's horns.

29:18. smoke. See NOTE to 29:13, "smoke."

all the ram. That is, the head and the members and the suet, plus the washed entrails and legs. Cf. Lev 8:20–21.

Ascending-offering. The literal meaning of *ʿōlâ,* traditionally rendered "burnt offering" or "holocaust," is "that which ascends (by fire)," i.e., to God. The victim is always a male (Lev 1:3). On the Ascending-offering as a gift to Yahweh, see Milgrom (1991: 172–77).

Soothing Scent. My alliteration imitates the assonance of *rêaḥ nîḥôaḥ.* Traditionally, *nîḥôaḥ* has been associated with the root *nwḥ* 'rest,' especially in the sense of *naḥat* 'ease' (BDB). But this is not certain. The form suggests rather a Niphʿal participle of an otherwise unknown Hebrew root **nḥḥ* (for parallels, see GKC §67u). And **nḥḥ* cannot be an alternate form of *nwḥ* (cf. GKC §77), because as an intransitive verb, *nwḥ/nḥḥ* would not used be in the Niphʿal. (Arabic *naḥḥa* 'propel' does not help either because the verb is probably onomatopoeic, from the sound one makes to start a beast.) Possibly related is the Ugaritic name *nḥḥy* (*KTU* 4.687.2), but we do not know its meaning. Farther afield, we might note Egyptian *nḥḥ* 'eternity.'

Whatever its literal sense, *rêaḥ nîḥôaḥ* describes the wholly burnt Ascending-offering (e.g., 29:18, 41; Lev 1:9, 13, 17), the Filling-offering (29:25), the Concluding-offering (Lev 3:5, 16; 17:6, etc.), the Tribute-offering of perfumed cereal (Lev 2:2, 9, 12) and the wine libation (Num 15:7). Yahweh is believed to snuff up the vitality of these sacrifices through his nostrils (Gen 8:21; Lev 26:31–32; Num 28:3–24). Contrary to what one might expect, however, "Soothing Scent" does not describe incense, because incense is not a food. It may be pleasing to God, but it is nonnutritious and does not qualify as *nîḥôaḥ*. (Perhaps *rêaḥ nîḥôaḥ* means "edible vapor"?)

Whether or not God in Heaven really smelled Israel's offerings, the people themselves assuredly did. The odor of roast meat is extremely complex and, like all scents, affects the human mind deeply, triggering buried emotions and memories. Compare pp. 513–14 below.

Gift. Closely associated with the cliché "Soothing Scent" is the technical term *'išše(h)* (29:18; 25; Lev 1:9, 13, 17, etc.). *Pace* Rashi and some moderns (BDB), most now disassociate *'išše(h)* from *'ēš* 'fire': on the one hand, it describes the non-burnt, spiced Face Bread (Lev 24:7, 9); and, on the other, *'išše(h)* does not describe the burnt "Sin-offering."

There are three more plausible etymologies. First, *'išše(h)* might be related to Arabic *'anisa* 'associate,' also cognate to Hebrew *'ănāšîm* 'men, people' (Gray 1971: 10–12). Second, *'išše(h)* could be related to Arabic *'aws* 'gift,' although *'išše(h)* is not quite what one would expect in Hebrew. The common opinion today, however, is that *'išše(h)* corresponds to Ugaritic *'iṯṯ* 'gift' (*KTU* 2.13.15, 30.14) and Arabic *'aṯāṯ* 'possessions' (< *'ṯṯ* 'to be fat, luxuriant') (e.g., Ehrlich 1909: 5; Hoftijzer 1967; Driver 1969: 181–84; Milgrom 1991: 161–62). From a related hollow root may be the biblical names *yəhô'āš* and *yō(')šiyyāhû* and the common epigraphic *'šyh(w)* (for attestations, see *AHI* p. 292).

29:19. *the second ram.* This is the "*Filling* ram" with which the priests are ordained.

press. See NOTES to 29:10.

29:20. *right.* The favored side in the ancient Near East; see Milgrom (1991: 528).

earlobe. A guess. We do not know what part of the ear is the *tənûk.*

hand-thumb . . . foot-thumb. As the same term *'eṣba'* denotes fingers and toes, so both the thumb and big toe are called *bōhen* 'thumb.' On the meaning of bloodying the ears, hands and feet, see pp. 530–31.

29:21. *blood . . . Oil.* Having symbolically shed their own blood by the vicarious Sin-offering, the priests receive it back from the Altar, which is simultaneously undergoing consecration (29:36). In other words, Yahweh symbolically gives them their lives back (see further below, p. 531).

It is not quite clear that the blood is to be mixed into the Ointment Oil, which is inherently holy (30:32). Possibly the fluids are sprinkled separately, as in 29:36; Lev 14:14–18: first the blood to purge, then the oil to consecrate (Houtman 2000: 541).

sprinkle. On the consecrating and purifying virtues of aspersion, see Vriezen

(1950); Milgrom (1991: 233–34). In several parallel cases, the blood is sprinkled seven times (Lev 4:6, 17; 8:11; 14:7, 16, 27, 51; 16:14, 15, 19). In Exod 29:35 Aaron and his sons are sparged once a day for seven days.

upon Aaron and upon his garments. For ibn Ezra, "upon Aaron" means upon his naked body, beneath his clothing—why else mention the garments separately? One would have thought it more convenient, however, to anoint the body between washing and robing (29:4–5) (see below, p. 529). On Aaron's redundant anointment, see NOTE to 29:7, "anoint."

Just as this procedure renders the priests' bodies holy, so does it consecrate their special garments. One would think that repeated applications of rams' blood and oil would create laundry problems, especially for the ordinary priests' linen vestments. Presumably, the stains are permanent signs of holiness, heritable by Aaron's descendants.

holy. Ordinarily, blood does not sanctify but purges. One might infer that in this case, the blood acquires contagious sanctity from the Altar (cf. 29:37) (Milgrom 1991: 534). But more likely it is the *oil* that consecrates.

29:22. the fat. See NOTES to 29:13.

the fat-tail. The *'alyâ* is a sheep's posterior adipose excrescence weighing from fifteen to fifty pounds. From ancient days until our own, shepherds have fashioned wheeled carts to help the animals bear the weight of their own tails (Milgrom 1991: 212)! According to Classical sources, the fat-tail was sacrificed in both Egypt (Herodotus *Histories*, 2.47) and Greece (references in Milgrom, p. 212).

the right thigh. There is some dispute as to whether *šôq* denotes the fore- or hindleg. Milgrom (1991: 431–32) interprets it as part of the hindleg, like Arabic *sāq* and Syriac *šāqā'*. On the other hand, a collection of ovine right *fore*legs has been uncovered in an eleventh-century B.C.E. cultic context at Tell Qiri (Ben-Tor 1992: 582).

for. To explain its peculiarities, the text specifies that this is a unique type of sacrifice: the *millū'îm* 'Filling' (see following).

Filling ram. Pace Rashi, who associates "Filling" with perfection, *millū'îm* is more likely derived from the idiom *millē' 'et-hayyād* 'fill the hand, consecrate as priest' (ibn Ezra); see NOTE to 28:41, "fill their hand." The "Filling ram" is the sacrifice by which priests are made. Linguistically, *millū'îm* belongs to the class of D-stem (i.e., with doubled middle radical) technical terms favored by the Priestly Writer; see p. 717.

29:23. one . . . one . . . one. These loaves will be consumed by Aaron's family (29:32).

loaf. For variety's sake, the text uses *kikkār*, probably a synonym of *ḥallâ* (29:2). On the bread offerings, see NOTES to 29:2.

wafer. Smeared with oil (29:2).

29:24. elevate them (as) an Elevation-offering. On this translation of *tənûpâ*, conventionally "Wave Offering," see Milgrom (1991: 461–73)—but also Anderson (1987: 133–35) for evidence that the basic meaning is "extra payment." All agree that *tənûpâ* is a rite symbolically transferring ownership to Yahweh (cf. Luzzatto). See further NOTES to 29:27.

29:25. *Ascending-offering . . . Soothing Scent . . . Gift.* On these terms, see NOTES to 29:18. The sacrifice consists of the fatty parts and the breads.

29:26. *breast.* Our text presupposes a butchering procedure that does not split the breastbone; see the comments of S. Rattray *apud* Milgrom (1991: 430–31).

Aaron. Aaron's sons are forgotten, as they are the lesser characters (ibn Ezra; contrast Ramban).

elevate it (as) an Elevation-offering. Rashi asks: if Aaron and his sons are holding the offerings, how can Moses be commanded to elevate them (*wəhēnaptā*, sing.)? He infers that when an offering is elevated, the officiating priest (here, Moses) and the donor (Aaron) put their hands together. But Lev 8:28–29 says clearly that Moses took the offering from the candidates' hands.

before Yahweh. See NOTES to 23:17; 27:21, "before Yahweh."

a portion for you. Rashi (on v 22) compares Moses' portion to the priests' share of the *šəlāmîm* 'Concluding-offerings.' As ibn Ezra observes, Moses is now "the priests' priest." But this is not the entire story.

As in the ordinary Concluding-offering, the breast here goes to the officiant (Lev 7:30–31). However, for Concluding-offerings, the priest also takes the right thigh as a Donation-offering (*tərûmâ*) (Lev 7:32–33). This Moses does not receive; instead, it is burnt on the Altar. Thus the Priestly Writer portrays Moses as only a temporary half-priest (cf. Milgrom 1991: 525, 531, 555–58). (On Levite-Aaronid competition and its influence on the portrayal of Moses and Aaron, see vol. I, pp. 284–85; vol. II, pp. 567–74.)

29:27. *consecrate.* Here the root *qdš* connotes not only receiving the supernatural quality of Holiness but also separation, which some take to be the root's original meaning. (Levine [1987: 248] perceives here an additional nuance of public declaration of sanctity, but I do not find this necessary.)

Although we do not at first realize it, 29:27–28 is a precept for the Concluding-offering of future times. And yet the text mentions the Filling-offering, from which, in fact, Aaron receives neither breast nor thigh. Why the furtive change of subject?

On principle, I dislike arbitrary assumptions of secondary interpolations, the first recourse of too many critics for too long (e.g., Noth 1962: 233). Rather, as if alarmed at having granted the Levite Moses the "Elevation breast," the Priestly Writer quickly points out that henceforth both the breast and thigh will go only to the priests (cf. Lev 7:30–33). The primal Filling ceremony of priestly ordination, where Moses receives the breast and the thigh is burnt on the Altar, is a one-time dispensation. (The parallel in Lev 8:29 will omit this rule because the matter will already have been treated in Leviticus 7.)

Donation thigh. Milgrom (1991: 415–16, 473–81) shows that *tərûmâ* connotes a gift to Yahweh (cf. Akkadian *tarīmtu* 'gift'), often preceded by an Elevation-offering representing the transfer of ownership (*tənûpâ*). To an extent, the terms are interchangeable; e.g., the Tabernacle bronze is called both a "Donation-offering" (35:24) and an "Elevation-offering" (38:29). On the etymology of *tərûmâ*, see NOTE to 25:2.

With Luzzatto, I put the main syntactic break after *hattərûmâ* 'the Donation,' not after *hûrām* 'is donated' (MT).

elevated . . . donated. In the context, this describes both the breast and the thigh, each a priestly portion (Lev 7:30–33).

29:28. *it shall be for Aaron . . . a Donation-offering.* I.e., both the breast of the Elevation-offering and the thigh of the Donation-offering will be Israel's Donation-offering to the priests, their share forever. Although the previous verse mentioned the Filling-offering, the subject here is really the *šəlāmîm* Concluding-offerings, the ordinary sacrifice.

eternal rule. Ḥōq sometimes combines the nuances of "decree" and "allot-ment" (cf. Gen 47:22, 26; Exod 5:14; Ezek 16:27; Prov 30:8; 31:5). For further dis-cussion, see Ringgren (1986).

from Israel's Sons. Who donate the shoulder and thigh to the priests.

Concluding. On *šəlāmîm*, see NOTE to 20:24(21), "Concluding-offerings."

29:29. *his sons after him.* Since the expression *bigdê haqqōdeš* 'the Holiness gar-ments' refers exclusively to the Great Priest's costume (NOTE to 31:10), "his sons after him" here connotes not all of Aaron's descendants but only the line of first-born heirs (Rashi). The author declines to state how to deal with vestments that are worn out or ill-fitting (cf. Ehrlich 1969: 194).

in them . . . them. I.e., dressed in them. Theoretically, one could also under-stand *bām* as "by them," as if donning the vestments were tantamount to conse-cration (cf. Num 20:25–28).

filling their hand. On this idiom for priestly ordination, see NOTE to 28:41.

29:30. *Seven days.* This prescription for future generations anticipates v 35, which makes it clear that Aaron and his sons also undergo a week of ordination (cf. Ezek 44:26–27).

the priest. Here one might take *kōhēn* in its original participial sense: "the one functioning as priest" (Ehrlich 1908: 381).

replacing him. Literally, "under him" *(taḥtā[y]w)*.

from his sons. Among his sons.

must wear them. Ibn Ezra (shorter commentary) assumes the sense is by day and night. But I should think that they were put off at night, for fear of defiling seminal emissions (see NOTES to 19:15).

29:31. *the Filling ram.* At first, one might think we are still discussing the ordi-nation of future priests—and perhaps we are—but v 32 shows that the command is really addressed to Moses and his contemporaries. The author subtly eases away from the digression in 29:27–30 to resume his narrative.

boil. This is the normal manner in which meat is prepared for human con-sumption (e.g., 12:9; 23:19; 34:26; Deut 16:7; 1 Sam 2:13–15; 1 Kgs 19:21; Ezek 24:5; Zech 14:21); see also NOTE to 12:9 (vol. I, p. 395). Lev 8:31 makes it clear that Moses does not himself boil the meat, but has the priests do it.

in a holy place. I.e., in the Plaza (Lev 6:9, 19) by the Tabernacle entrance (Lev 8:31), where the priests will also consume the meat (Exod 29:32).

29:32. *eat.* They eat the ram as donors, not officiants, whose portion would be the breast and thigh (29:27–28). Until the week of ordination is completed, Aaron and his sons are not full priests.

the bread that is in the basket. I.e., what remains after the cereal offering ac-companying the holocaust (29:23–25) (ibn Ezra).

(at) Meeting Tent Opening. I.e., in the Plaza, not in the Tabernacle proper (Rashi).

29:33. *Clearing.* P at last names its great mystery: the process whereby the Tabernacle accumulates and discharges the sins and impurities that otherwise would repel the divine (cf. above, NOTE to 29:14, "Sin-offering"; below pp. 698–700).

The root *kpr* (Pi'el *kipper*) presents a major difficulty for translators, exegetes and any who try to comprehend empathetically the biblical worldview (see Levine 1974: 56–77, 123–27; Wright 1987: 291–98; Kiuchi 1987: 87–109; Schwartz 1991: 52–60). The traditional "atone," i.e., "put at one, reconcile," places *kpr* primarily into the realm of social relationships. Milgrom (1991: 1079–84) insists, however, that the basic meaning is "purge," putting *kpr* into the realm of ritual purity (compare his treatment of *ḥaṭṭā['*]t, briefly discussed above [NOTE to 29:14, "Sin-offering"]).

The philological approach offers limited, ambiguous assistance. On the one hand, within Hebrew, *kpr* is often associated with *ṭhr* 'to be pure' (Lev 12:7–8; 14:20, 53; 16:18, 20; Num 8:21; Ezek 43:26), suggesting a meaning akin to "cleanse." Note, too, the parallelism between *kpr* and *mḥy* 'wipe away, erase' in Jer 18:23. On the other hand, the specific technique of *kpr* involves dirtying, i.e., smearing blood. (Milgrom [1991: 1081] explains that the Sin-offering blood wipes *off* impurity, but then why is it left on the Altar, not rinsed off as, e.g., in Greek and Mesopotamian purifications [e.g., Burkert 1992: 57–58, 61]?)

Perhaps *kpr* means not to wipe sins away but to cover them with blood. Although covering over *(kissâ)* sin is a wrong when done by a human (Deut 13:9; Ps 32:5; Prov 17:9; 28:13; Job 31:33), God may cover over the sin of the otherwise righteous (Ps 85:3; Neh 3:37), who is then *kəsûy ḥăṭā'â* 'covered of sin' (Ps 32:1) (compare the meanings of "bear transgression," NOTE to 28:38). Most noteworthy is Neh 3:37, which paraphrases Jer 18:23, replacing *kpr* with *ksy*:

Do not Clear *(kpr)* for their transgression, and their sin from before you do not wipe *(mḥy)*. (Jer 18:23)

And do not cover *(ksy)* for their transgression, and may their transgression from before you not be wiped *(mḥy)*. (Neh 3:37)

Moreover, we normally look to the Qal conjugation for a root's basic meaning. The sole instance of *kāpar* is Gen 6:14, "smear" (with *kōper* 'pitch'). The notion of "smearing, covering over" potentially accounts for the three meanings of the noun *kōper*: "henna," "pitch" and "ransom/bribe" (see below). Arabic *kafara* 'cover,' too, may indicate that the essence of *kpr* is covering or smearing over (see also NOTE to 25:17, "*kappōret*").

This ambivalence is not unique to Hebrew. Akkadian *kapāru/kuppuru* similarly means both "to clean" and "to smear," including an association with ritual purification (*CAD* 8.178–80). Accordingly, we might see the original meaning of *kpr* as not "smear" but "wipe," which would explain how a single root can mean both "cleanse" and "smear" (cf. Milgrom 1991: 1080). Both "wiping away" and "covering over" would be natural metaphors for the process by which sin and impurity are nullified. To us they seem mutually exclusive, but compare again Neh 3:37, where God is described as both *ksy ʿal* 'covering over' and *mḥy* 'wiping away' sin.

We have yet to treat the social sense of *kpr* 'to reconcile, appease,' exemplified in Gen 32:21: Jacob through gifts hopes to *kpr* Esau's face *(ʾăkappərâ pānā[y]w)*. The same meaning is found in Prov 16:14: "A king's anger is (like) Death Messengers, but a wise man will *kpr* it." Similarly, to lift the covenant curse of famine, David must appease *(ʾăkappēr)* the Gibeonites for a past injustice (2 Sam 21:3). These passages return us to the traditional rendering of *kipper:* "atone." But certainly in Gen 32:21 and possibly in Prov 16:14, *kipper* might have a more concrete sense: "bribe." An assocation between *kipper* and *kōper* 'ransom' is implicit in Exod 30:12, 16; Num 35:31–33; compare, too, the idom *kipper ʿal hannepeš* 'to make *kpr* for one's life' (30:15; Lev 17:11; Num 31:50). Also belonging in this category may be Isa 47:11: "Calamity shall befall you; you cannot buy it off *(kappərā[h])*."

Finally, there is another implication of *kpr* found commonly in Aramaic and Arabic: "annul, deny." In Isa 28:18, *kpr* refers to annulling a covenant, and in cultic contexts, *kipper* describes the annulment of violations: e.g., Isa 6:7, *wəsār ʿăwōnekā wəḥaṭṭā(ʾ)təkā təkuppār* 'and your transgression will go away and your sin will be canceled.' But one would ordinarily take this meaning as secondary and metaphorical, derived from a more concrete "wipe away" or "cover over" (cf. Levine 1974: 124–27).

Our philological foray is, admittedly, somewhat beside the point. Cognates and hypothetical proto-Semitic definitions are not necessarily germane to the semantics of Biblical Hebrew, let alone P's characteristic terminology. And yet the evidence is illuminating. Every one of the meanings suggested for *kpr*—purge, cover over, smear, appease, ransom, annul—suits Hebrew usage. With the Sin-offering and its blood rite, the offerant *ransoms* his life from Yahweh; *smearing* the Altar *cleanses* him and effects *reconciliation* with Yahweh, who *covers over* and *annuls* his sin/impurity.

We must forgo the quest for a single, original meaning of *kpr*. Even in proto-Semitic, some roots must have been polysemous. And polysemy can be a virtue. In all its overtones, *kpr* perfectly captures the paradox of purification and expiation, whereby sins and impurity are reconciled with Holiness (see further pp. 681–95).

How best to render *kpr* in English? After considering both "atone" and "purge," I have opted for "Clear"—capitalized to indicate a technical term—as a feeble attempt to express cleansing, nullification, reconciliation and the removal of an obstruction. See also next NOTE.

was effected. Notably, P always uses *kipper* as a factitive, i.e., intransitive verb (Levine 1974: 63–67). This is why I translate it as "effected Clearing," or, in the passive, "Clearing was effected." The priest does not himself Clear; only Yahweh can. Similarly, P employs the circumlocution *wənislaḥ lô* 'and it will be forgiven him,' because it is not actually the priest who confers the pardon, and yet pardon follows automatically (Lev 4:26, 31, 35; 5:10, etc.). (This was still an issue centuries later when Jesus scandalized other Jews by declaring a remission of sins [Matt 9:2–8; Mark 2:1–12; Luke 5:17–26; 7:47–50].)

Against one's initial impression, it is not eating the Filling ram that effects Clearing. Rather, the *blood* applied to both the priests' bodies and the Altar Clears for them, purging their impurities (Milgrom 1991: 528–29). This, along with the case of the skin-diseased person (Lev 14:1–32), is the only instance of a person rather than a thing being cleansed with blood (see further pp. 528–32). The bread, too, some of which is incinerated (Exod 29:25), may also have a purifying and expiatory function (cf. Lev 14:20; 1 Sam 3:14; Milgrom 1991: 196–97).

outsider. In this context, *zār* connotes a nonpriest (ibn Ezra). The antonym is *qārôb*, describing a person "near" to Yahweh (Ehrlich 1908: 382). The prohibition seems aimed also at future generations.

they are Holiness. As Milgrom (1991: 527, 534–35) observes, the Filling-offering by which the semi-priest Moses converts his brethren into full priests possesses an appropriately transitional status. In the sacrificial catalogue of Lev 7:37, Filling *(millū'îm)* follows the Ascending *('ōlâ)*, Tribute *(minḥâ)*, Sin *(ḥaṭṭā[']t)* and Guilt *('āšām)* offerings, all of which are super-sacred *(qōdeš qŏdāšîm)* and forbidden to laymen. And Filling precedes the least sacred Concluding-offerings *(šəlāmîm)*, permitted to nonpriests. Thus, on the one hand, like the holiest offerings, the Filling ram is eaten in the Tabernacle Plaza. On the other hand, as with the Concluding-offerings, the breast and thigh are separated out (NOTES to vv 26–28). And as with the Concluding Offerings known as Gratitude *(tôdâ)*, the Filling ram is accompanied by oiled bread and consumed within a day (Lev 7:11–15).

29:34. *until the morning . . . burn.* We find the same one-day limit for the paschal offering (12:10), the Gratitude-offering (Lev 7:15; 22:30) and perhaps the Nazirite's ram *(m. Zebaḥ. 5:6)*; see also NOTE to 23:18, "morning." Ordinary Concluding-offerings *(šəlāmîm)*, in contrast, are eaten within *two* days (Lev 7:16–17; 19:6–7). Sacrifices must be eaten as near as possible, in both time and space, their presentation upon the Altar; their inherent sanctity does not survive long in our corrupt world. See further vol. I, pp. 396–97, and Milgrom (1991: 219–20).

29:35. *likewise.* It is unclear whether the entire ritual of chap. 29 is performed each day: i.e., the Sin bull and the two rams for the Ascending- and Filling-offerings, together with the blood and oil rites. V 36 mentions only the bull, but perhaps the rest is assumed (see NOTE, "Sin bull"). Milgrom argues that the entire rite is repeated (1991: 537–40; *Lev. Rab.* 10:8), comparing other seven-day rites of passage: e.g., for birth-circumcision (Gen 17:12), marriage (Gen 29:27) and mourning (Gen 50:10) (see also Klingbeil 1997). As the Altar undergoes seven days of sanctification (v 37), the priests are simultaneously being purified and consecrated (Lev 8:33–35).

you. Here the pausal form of *'ōtəkâ* is *'ōtākâ*, not the expected **'ōtāk* (Sam *'tk*). Evidently the Massoretes were constrained by the consonantal text *'tkh*, which perhaps was influenced by the preceding (and rhyming) *kākâ* 'likewise.' On such full spellings, see Freedman, Forbes and Andersen (1992).

seven days. During the final week of the first year of the Exodus (*Tg. Neofiti I*, Rashi), Moses temporarily performs the priestly duties, surrendering them forever to the house of Aaron on the eighth day (Lev 9:1) (cf. *Lev. Rab.* 11:6). On the number seven, ubiquitous in biblical and ancient Near Eastern literature, see Pope (1962a).

To the details of Exodus 29, Lev 8:33, 35 adds that the priests may not leave the Tent Opening during their consecratory week, on pain of death (see Milgrom 1991: 535–36). Presumably, they sleep on the ground (compare Samuel and Eli in the shrine of Shiloh [1 Samuel 3]) and eliminate into pots. Lev 21:12, although dealing with the special case of mourning, implies *a fortiori* that the Great Priest never leaves the sacred compound at all (Milgrom 1991: 564)—which would imply that Great Priests were expected to remain celibate after their elevation. According to Lev 14:36–44, however, some priests do leave the Tabernacle to perform home inspections.

The Priestly Source may be characterized as Aaronid-triumphalist. Part of P's propagandistic rhetoric is a kind of pathos, as it depicts the priests' dangerous proximity to the divine, undertaken on the people's behalf by no choice of their own (see pp. 688–90). In Exodus 29, the Aaronids' seclusion during their ordination constitues a kind of initiatory ordeal, as they bid farewell to ordinary life (see further pp. 528–32).

29:36. Sin bull. Is this the identical offering mandated in 29:10–14 or an additional sacrifice (so Driver 1911: 324)? One initially assumes it is the same, so that a Sin bull is offered upon the Altar every day of the joint purification and consecration of the priests and the Altar. With each day, they and it become purer and more holy. In 11QTemple XV:16–18, 14–18, however, *two* Sin bulls are offered: one for any impurities generated by the priests and one for the people (cf. Lev 4:3–21); see further Milgrom (1991: 562).

concerning the Clearing. The phrase *ʿal-hakkippūrîm* is unique and somewhat obscure. Upon first reading, one naturally understands *"in addition to* the Clearing," a common usage of *ʿal* (e.g., in v 25). Thus ibn Ezra and Ramban identify the Clearing with the two rams, the second of which explicitly effects Clearing (29:33) and the first of which, as an Ascending-offering, may implicitly effect Clearing too (cf. Lev 1:4; 16:24; Ezek 45:15).

More plausibly, however, Rashi and Ehrlich (1969: 194) interpret *ʿal-hakkippūrîm* as *"for* the Clearing." That is, the phrase explains the *purpose* of the Sin bull. But since I cannot find another example of *ʿal* to express purpose, I have chosen instead "concerning," another frequent meaning.

Un-sin. Ḥiṭṭēʾ is the Piʿel of *ḥāṭāʾ(ʾ)* 'sin, violate, err.' It appears to be a special example of the privative Piʿel and means "to remove sin *(ḥēṭ[ʾ]/ḥāṭāʾâ/ḥaṭṭā[ʾ]t/ ḥāṭā[ʾ]t)*" (GKC §52h). In Priestly terminology, "sin" includes unavoidable ritual defilement, e.g., from an infected house (Lev 14:52) (see further NOTE to 29:14, "Sin-offering").

effecting Clearing upon it. In this context, *kapperkā ʿālā(y)w* might even be translated "your smearing (blood) on it" (likewise in 30:10; Lev 6:23; 8:15; 16:18, 27); see NOTE to 29:33, "Clearing."

anoint. Not just the Altar but all of the Tabernacle apparatus is anointed (30:26–28). The Altar is singled out here, because, unlike the other sancta, it is sanctified for seven days along with the priests (Milgrom 1991: 233); see next NOTE.

make it holy. As the priestly candidates day-by-day transfer their sins/impurities to the Altar through the Sin-offering, both they and it simultaneously receive Holiness by virtue of the anointing oil. Their purification and sanctification are gradual, lest defilement and the sacred collide, killing Aaron and his sons. The "impure" *(ṭāmēʾ)* and the "holy" *(qādôš)*, both construed as active forces or substances, must never come into contact (Milgrom 1991: 524); below, pp. 689–90.

What, then, of the Altar? How does receiving the candidates' sins and impurities comport with its sanctification? This is the mystery of *kippūrîm* 'Clearing.' By bloodying its extremities with the Sin-offering, Moses prepares the Altar to receive full Holiness. Unlike a human, the Altar will take no harm thereby—provided that it is cleansed and resanctified once a year in the annual Clearing Day (Yom Kippur) in the Fall (Leviticus 16). For more discussion, see pp. 700–701.

29:37. *seven.* According to 1 Kgs 8:65–66; 2 Chr 7:8–9, Solomon dedicated the Temple, which took seven years to build, in a seven-day festival in the seventh month (in all, the festivities lasted *two* weeks, since the inauguration was followed immediately by the seven-day Festival of Sukkot). Ezekiel's Temple, too, undergoes a seven-day consecration (Ezek 43:25–26). From elsewhere in the ancient Near East, Gudea of Lagash performs a seven-day temple dedication (Kramer 1988: 6; Jacobsen 1987b: 440), and, in Ugaritic myth, Baal's palace is created in seven days (Levenson 1988: 78–79). On the correlation with the biblical seven days of Creation, see pp. 675–76.

effect Clearing upon the Altar. Again (NOTE to v 36), this might mean "*smearing blood on* the Altar."

Holiness of Holinesses. Even though it stands outside the Tabernacle, the Altar possesses the highest degree of sanctity. It is a link between the contaminated world of ordinary people and Yahweh in purest Heaven (see pp. 499–501). This is why a physically defective priest "may not enter to the Veil, nor approach to the Altar" (Lev 21:22). By their quality of ultimate Holiness, the Tabernacle and Altar are able to sustain the weight of Israel's sins and impurities laid upon them during the Sin-offering (see pp. 699–701).

any. *Kōl* might in theory mean "any*body*" or "any*thing.*" Milgrom (1991: 446–56) shows that the latter is more likely: anything touching the Altar absorbs sanctity, even a pot or a garment (cf. Lev 6:20–21; Hag 2:12). Any unauthorized human touching Holiness must be killed (e.g., Num 1:51; 3:10, 38; 18:7). But the proscription does not affect the priests, who are already holy themselves (Ehrlich 1908: 382).

SPECULATION: Ehrlich (1908: 382) raises the intriguing and attractive notion that this principle is aimed against the custom of obtaining asylum by grasping the Altar by the horns (see NOTES to 21:13–14). Instead, P will designate cities of refuge for accidental killers who do not deserve execution (Num 35:9–34).

But it is also possible that the Holiness principle *explains* the asylum law. That is, by touching the Altar horns, charged with Israel's sins and impurities, and still surviving, the manslayer proves his innocence by ordeal. Instead of killing him, the horns accept his bloodguilt as a Sin-offering. As a theoretical principle, the killer is cleared in the eyes of God, but, given human nature, he still is not safe from the hand of Man. He becomes Yahweh's protected chattel, part of the sacred realm and confined to a Levitical city until released by the Great Priest's death. See also NOTE to 27:2, "horns."

will become holy. Rashi implausibly finds here a promise that even improper offerings will "become holy," i.e., acceptable, at the consecrated Altar. Others, however, think that v 37 articulates a requirement: everyone *must* be purified before touching holy things (Rashbam; Levine 1987: 246). But we would expect not the Qal conjugation for this meaning but rather the Hithpaʿel (Milgrom 1991: 445). More likely, the point is that, just as anything touching oil becomes oily, so the sacred anointing oil conveys contagious Holiness (see Milgrom, pp. 443–56). For the principle, see also 30:29; Lev 6:11, 20.

29:38. *sons of a year.* On this term for yearlings, see NOTE to 12:5 (vol. I, pp. 389–90).

(as a) Continual-offering. Upon first reading, one takes *tāmîd* as an adverb: "continually." But *tāmîd* denotes the daily offering of two yearling lambs along with grain and wine, prescribed in Num 28:3–8. Thus, as v 42 makes explicit, the Filling-offering is prototypical for the Continual-offering *(tāmîd)*, just as it anticipates the Concluding-offering *(šelem)*; see NOTES to 29:26.

29:39. *morning.* On P's day as beginning with sunrise, see vol. I, pp. 391–92.

between the two evenings. I.e., at evening (NOTE to 12:6 [vol. I, pp. 390–91]).

29:40. *tenth.* We learn from Num 28:5 that this is one-tenth of an ephah, which would be a little more than one quart (c. 1.2 liters). When measuring grain, the same volume is also called an *ʿōmer* (Rattray *apud* Milgrom 1991: 895).

crushed oil. See NOTE to 27:20, "pure, crushed olive oil."

quarter. A quarter-hin was presumably standard for libations (cf. also Lev 23:13). An Israelite inscription reads, "wine for libation, one fourth"—presumably, of the hin (Deutsch and Heltzer 1994: 23–26).

hin. This is a liquid measure of c. three quarts (3.6 liters). The hin is also mentioned in Egyptian Aramaic (Lidzbarski 1915: 128). The name is borrowed from Egyptian *hnw,* both a type of vessel and a liquid measure (Ellenbogen 1962: 68). (The hin may also appear in EA 14.iii.62, spelled syllabically *ḫi-na* [Lambdin 1953: 149], but Moran [1992: 33] considers *ḫina* a type of stone.) Muchiki (1999: 243), however, emphasizes that, although the words seem related, the biblical hin is considerably larger than its Egyptian counterpart (c. 0.5 liter).

Stager and Wolff (1981: 100 v. 3) have attempted to recreate experimentally the cereal offering. Their compound "formed a paste with the consistency of peanut butter. When placed over a gas flame, the small cakes . . . ignited readily and burned with a bright flame for nearly ten minutes. Combustion reduced the cake to a charred mass of solid, but brittle residue."

libation. Nēsek connotes a liquid offering of wine, which, mocking popular belief, Deut 32:38 describes as the gods' drink. Wine frequently accompanies festival offerings (Leviticus 23; Numbers 28–29). According to 2 Kgs 16:13, 15, the fluid is vaporized on the Altar, rising to Yahweh as a Soothing Scent (Num 15:7, 10). The sacrificial use of wine is somewhat surprising, because fermented substances (leavened bread, date-honey) are otherwise associated with impurity (vol. I, pp. 429–34). In Second Temple times, libations were apparently poured into trenches around the Altar's base (Sir 50:15; cf. Josephus *Ant.* 3.234).

29:41. *between the two evenings.* I.e., at evening (NOTE to 12:6).

Tribute-offering. In nonsacral contexts, *minḥâ* denotes a politically motivated gift, often symbolizing submission (Gen 32:14, 19, 21; Judg 3:15, 17; 1 Sam 10:27; 2 Kgs 20:12); cf. Arabic *manaḥa* 'endow,' *minḥa* 'gift, loan'; Ugaritic *mnḥ* (*KTU* 4.91.1) and the Late Egyptian loanword *mnḥt* (Hoch 1994: 128). Only Hebrew, however, uses *minḥâ* to describe a sacrifice. In non-Priestly contexts, it can be any burnt offering (e.g., Gen 4:3–4; Judg 6:18; 1 Sam 2:17, 29; Mal 8:14), perhaps even incense (Num 16:15); in P, however, the Tribute-offering is always a cereal sacrifice (e.g., Leviticus 2; 6:12–16; 7:9–10).

Why does the Bible call burnt sacrifices "Tribute-offerings," and why does P restrict the term to the cereal offering, as if it were the "Tribute" *par excellence*? Because Yahweh is Israel's covenanted suzerain, to whom sacrifice combines aspects of taxation and gift (cf. pp. 301–2). It seems, moreover, that Priestly tradition has deliberately made Yahweh's "Tribute" into something every Israelite can afford (on P's consciousness of economic inequities, see Lev 5:7–13, esp. vv 11–12, conceding the adequacy of a grain offering for the poorest Israelite).

its libation. On the referent of "its," see TEXTUAL NOTE.

29:42. *for your ages.* I.e., to eternity; see vol. I, pp. 205–6.

where . . . there. It is unclear whether the referent is the Tabernacle or the Plaza. For Yahweh appearing to Israel at the Tabernacle's doorway, see 33:9–10; Num 11:24–25; 12:5; Deut 31:15 (all E); Num 16:19; 20:6 (P).

I will be meetable. On the root *yʿd*, see NOTE to 25:22.

for you. On whether "you" is Moses or the Israelites, see TEXTUAL NOTE.

29:43. *I will be inquirable.* That is, Israel may meet Yahweh indirectly, ascertaining Yahweh's will through the mediation of either Moses or Aaron (see, however, TEXTUAL NOTE).

it/one will be made holy. Wəniqdaš is ambiguous, perhaps deliberately. The ancient translations supply various subjects: LXX, Syr, *Tgs. Onqelos* and *Ps.-Jonathan* have "I will be made holy," while Vg has "the Altar will be made holy." Most elaborate is *Tg. Neofiti I*, which, reading the consonants *šm* as both *šēm* 'name' and *šām* 'there,' paraphrases the entire verse: "I will be present *in my Name there* for Israel's Sons, and it [the Name] will be made holy in the midst of my Glory."

Since none of these efforts inspires confidence, we must try to make sense of

MT-Sam *wəniqdaš*. First, the point might be that *anything* is sanctified by Yahweh's presence: Israel as a nation, each individual Israelite or indeed any object (cf. NOTES to 29:37, "any," "will become holy"). Or the referent could be the Tabernacle (Rashbam) or its doorway (G. H. Davies 1967: 221–22). I incline, however, toward Jerome's interpretation: vv 38–42a are essentially a digression; vv 42b–43 return us to the Altar, whose Holiness is the subject of v 37. See also following NOTE.

by my Glory. Yahweh's presence, which descends upon the Tabernacle in 40:34, culminates the sanctification process. If we suppose that 29:43 is speaking of the Altar (previous NOTE), then the reference may be specifically to Lev 9:23–24, where Yahweh's Glory appears to the people and sends forth fire to kindle the Altar (cf. Rashbam).

29:46. *by my tenting*. This is Ehrlich's (1969: 195) interpretation of *ləšoknî*, more idiomatic than Rashi's "*for the sake of* my tenting." Ehrlich paraphrases the entire verse as follows: "When I, Yahweh their Deity, tent among them, and no other god tents among them as I tent, thus they shall know that I am Yahweh their Deity, who took them out from the land of Egypt." In other words, the formula "I am Yahweh . . . Egypt" is the kerygma that they shall know (also Durham 1987: 392). Its visible proof is the Tabernacle in their midst, glowing with the divine presence. And in the Priestly Writer's day, when the Tabernacle no longer stood, the Priestly document is implicitly Yahweh's testament to Israel. Reading the Tabernacle specifications, we are meant to experience vicariously God's salvific, purifying presence (see p. 722).

I am Yahweh. One would expect this redundant flourish to conclude Yahweh's speech (Cassuto 1967: 389). But he adds a few details in chap. 30.

As a whole, v 46 echoes previous episodes: Moses's first encounter with Yahweh in P (6:7), the Manna incident (16:6) and the preamble of the Decalog (20:2); on "knowing" (*yd'*) as a theme in Exodus, see vol. I, pp. 37, 272, 630; vol. II, p. 385. On the rhetorical function of *'ănî yahwe(h)* 'I am Yahweh,' see NOTE to 6:2 (vol. I, pp. 270–71).

30:1. *an altar*. Etymologically, *mizbēaḥ* (< *zbḥ* 'slaughter') should denote an altar for animal sacrifice (see pp. 420, 695–703). In fact, no cognate language calls an incense burner an "altar" (Heger 1997: 6). Cassuto (1967: 390) supposes that the Hebrew term had come to connote any platform for burnt offerings. But incense is not technically a sacrifice (pp. 513–14).

Maybe *mizbēaḥ* describes the four-horned *shape* rather than its function. Many excavated Israelite incense altars are horned (see below), and in Hellenistic Egypt, too, horned altars were used for both meat and incense (Soukiassian 1983). According to 30:9, actual burnt sacrifice upon the Golden Altar, though prohibited, would not be unthinkable. And, more important, the Golden Altar receives the blood of the most potent Sin-offerings (Lev 4:7, 18) so that, like the Bronze Altar outside, it may be a *symbolic* slaughter block (see pp. 695–703).

incense censer. *Miqṭar qəṭōret* lends clarification: *mizbēaḥ* does not bear its etymological meaning (previous NOTE).

One might be tempted to revocalize the preceding word as a construct, i.e., *mizbaḥ miqṭar qəṭōret, and to read the second as an Aramaic infinitive. The translation would be "an altar *for the act of* censing incense" (Rashi, ibn Ezra). As pointed, however, MT mizbēaḥ miqṭar qəṭōret must mean "an altar, *a place of* censing incense" (cf. BDB, p. 883). This interpretation is confirmed by *mqṭr* 'incense altar' in Moabite (Dion and Daviau 2000) and South Arabic (de Langhe 1959: 490); compare also Hebrew *miqṭeret* '(handheld) censer.'

30:2. *cubit . . . cubit . . . two cubits.* The Golden Altar measures c. 1.5 feet (0.5 m.) wide by c. 1.5 feet (0.5 m.) deep by 3 feet (1 m.) tall. Its pillar-like form thus resembles that of excavated Near Eastern incense altars (Elliger 1943: 135).

from it its horns. This probably means that the horns protrude upward from the altar's sides. See NOTES to 25:19, "on the *kappōret*"; 25:31, "from it."

Qərānōt 'horns' are vertical protrusions on the upper corners (see figs. 13, p. 420; 14a and b, p. 423). Of six small stone altars found at Megiddo, five have horns. Other examples come from Tell en-Naṣbeh, Arad, Gezer and Tell Beit Mirsim (Nielsen 1986: 46; Gitin 1989, 1992; Zwickel 1990: 110–44; Fowler 1992). Sacrificial altars, too, are surmounted by crowns, on whose function and symbolism see NOTE to 27:2, "horns."

30:3. *pure gold.* See NOTE to 25:11.

roof . . . walls. In this context, *gag* and *qîrōt* simply mean "top" and "sides"; for the latter, cf. Lev 1:15; 5:9; Ezek 41:22. It is unclear whether the smoldering incense is put directly on the golden "roof," set in a bowl resting between the horns or placed there in a hand-held censer (see Lev 10:1; 16:12; Num 16:6–7, 17–18; 17:3–4; Ezek 8:11; 2 Chr 26:19).

zēr. This is probably a protruding rim transferring the Altar's weight to the poles. See NOTES to 25:11, 24, 25.

30:4. *two rings.* Does this mean two rings per side (Vg) or two in total? The Chest, Table and Altar explicitly have four rings, two per side (25:12, 26; 27:4). One ring on each side is probably intended here (Jacob 1992: 828); because the Golden Altar is so light, two rings suffice to bear its weight (Bekhor Shor).

its . . . flanks . . . its . . . sides. Is there any difference between ṣal'ōtā(y)w 'its flanks' and ṣiddā(y)w 'its sides'? Against ordinary usage, Rashi understands the first word as denoting corners. Rather, I take the second term as clarifying the first (ibn Ezra). That is, because the Incense Altar is foursquare, there is some ambiguity as to which are its "flanks." Ṣiddā(y)w clarifies that the rings go on the Altar's sides *vis-à-vis* the west-facing onlooker (Cassuto 1967: 391; see also NOTE to 25:12, "flank").

30:6. *before the Veil.* The Incense Altar presumably stands in the middle of the chamber (see fig. 13, p. 420). A tradition that it stood within the innermost chamber, before the Chest (Heb 9:4), probably reflects the corrupt MT, which confusingly puts the Altar both "before the Veil *(pārōket)*" and "before the *kappōret*" (see TEXTUAL NOTE).

I will be meetable. On the wordplay between 'iwwā'ēd (root y'd), mō'ēd 'Meeting' and 'ēdūt 'Testimony,' see p. 385. On Yahweh's presence between the two Griffins, see pp. 516–21.

30:7. *Spice Incense.* The aromatics will be specified in 30:34; see NOTES.

adjusting. Hệțîb literally means "make good." Here it might connote adding oil, replacing the wick and/or cleaning out deposits.

30:8. *raising the lamps.* There are two slightly different interpretations of *heʿĕlâ nēr. Heʿĕlâ* can mean either "raise up" or "set on fire" (NOTE to 25:37, "raise"), and *nēr* can mean either "lamp" or "flame." Accordingly, it is uncertain whether the exact meaning is "lifting up and replacing the lamps"—somewhat unlikely, I think—or "lighting the lamps/flames."

On when the lamps burn—by night alone or by day and night—see NOTE to 27:21, "from evening till morning."

between the two evenings. I.e., at evening (cf. 27:21); see NOTE to 12:6.

continual. I.e., in the morning and evening.

for your ages. Lᵊdōrōtêkem combines the nuances of "in all your generations" and "forever." Even though only Aaron is named, his descendants must also perform the rite (ibn Ezra [shorter commentary]).

30:9. *send up.* Here *heʿĕlâ* clearly means "send up to Heaven by burning"; contrast NOTE to 30:8 above, "raising the lamps."

alien incense. Qᵊțōret zārâ is probably incense with any procedural irregularity—of the wrong composition, offered at the wrong time or in the wrong place (Vg; Rashi). An equivalent term is *'ēš zārâ* 'alien fire,' applied to improper incense in Lev 10:1; Num 3:4; 26:61. Somewhat similarly, Num 17:5 forbids the *zār* 'outsider,' i.e., the nonpriest, from offering incense (cf. also Exod 29:33; on *zār* 'alien,' see Snijders 1980).

In 30:9, the Priestly Writer polemicizes against the popular use of incense for religious and other purposes (Nielsen 1986: 51). He later tells two stories about the hazards of censing. In Leviticus 10, the right people (the priests Nadab and Abihu) use the wrong materials ("alien fire"; see Milgrom 1991: 598) and die; in Numbers 16, the wrong people (Korah the Levite and his followers) use the right materials and die. Similarly, in 2 Chr 26:16–21, when King Uzziah presumes to burn incense himself, Yahweh strikes him with skin disease.

Ascending-offering. A holocaust of meat (*ʿōlâ*).

Tribute-offering. A grain offering (*minḥâ*).

libation. In other words, the three substances burnt to Yahweh as true sacrifices—meat, cereal and wine—are all illicit upon the Incense Altar. There is bread and possibly wine on the golden Table standing nearby (NOTES to 25:29), but they may not be sacrificed on the Incense Altar (Haran 1968). Cole (1973: 206) adds a practical consideration: unlike the Bronze Altar, the Golden Altar is indoors. One would not want to smoke out the priests or ignite the curtains.

30:10. *effect Clearing . . . Clearing Sin-offering.* Leviticus 16 describes the purifying and atoning rite of *kippūr*, whereby blood is applied to the Golden Altar's horns on *yôm hakkippûrîm* 'Clearing Day.' On the terms "Clear" and "Sin-offering" (*ḥaṭṭā[']t*), see NOTES to 29:14, 33.

30:12. *When.* Commentators have noted that Yahweh does not actually *command* Moses to take a census (e.g., Abarbanel). Rather, he *assumes* that he will. Are we to take this as an implicit command? If so, is it a one-time head-count or a periodic requirement for future generations (Ramban)?

The Torah also does not state clearly when Moses carries out this census. It would seem to be immediate, as its purpose is to amass silver for the Tabernacle's components (38:25–28) (Rashi; Houtman 2000: 565). Rashbam reasonably supposes that the tax is collected and the people counted when Moses assembles them in 35:1. If so, the head-count represents the population just before the first anniversary of Israel's Exodus (40:2, 17). But it is more likely that the command implied in Exodus 30:12 is reiterated and executed in Numbers 1 (see below, pp. 536–38).

lift the head. The expression *nāśā(ʾ) ʾet-hārō(ʾ)š* bears several meanings, depending upon context (cf. Speiser 1967: 177–78). In Gen 40:19; 1 Chr 10:9, it means "to decapitate." In Gen 40:13, 20, it means "to honor"; in Judg 8:28; Isa 9:14; Zech 2:4; Ps 83:3; Job 10:15, it means "to behave with self-respect." In Exod 30:12; Num 1:2; 4:2, 22; 26:2; 31:26, 49, however, it refers to census-taking. Like us, the Israelites took a *per capita* "head-count." (Cf. also *gulgōlet* 'skull' in Exod 16:16; 38:26; also Old Akkadian *qaqqadu* 'head, person, tax.') This "poll tax" has two purposes: (a) collecting revenue and (b) obtaining an accurate census without actually counting anyone (see further NOTE to "harm" below and pp. 534–38).

accountings. This interpretation of *pəqūdîm* as an abstract noun is not universally accepted. Others understand *pəqūdîm* as "those who are counted," i.e., as a Qal Passive participle (e.g., Jacob 1992: 830). And in Num 31:14, 48; 2 Kgs 11:15, *pəqūdîm* is most easily understood as denoting military officers.

At least for Exod 29:12, I would take *pəqūdîm* as an abstract plural comparable to *bətūlîm* 'virginity,' *zəqūnîm* 'old age,' *ḥănūṭîm* 'embalming,' *məgūrîm* 'sojourn,' *nəʿūrîm* 'youth,' etc. Moreover, a reference to *pəqūdîm* is generally followed by a number, and in Numbers 14:29, *pəqūdîm* is parallel to *mispār* 'counting, number.' The final proof is Exod 38:21, 25, where *pəqūdîm* is an inventory not of people but of valuables. (Speiser's [1967: 178–79] contention that *pqd* connotes not counting per se but registration by name seems to be supported by an ostracon from Tel ʿIra containing *mpqd* followed by several names [Beit-Arieh 1983]; but see Garfinkel [1987], who argues for the meaning "guard unit" here and in a Cypriote Phoenician inscription [see also Hoftijzer and Jongeling 1995: 673–74].)

soul's ransom. The half-shekel payment literally saves each life, since, as we shall directly see, the processes of taxation and census-taking are considered perilous. A cynic would call this payment extortion, a far cry from the voluntary contribution celebrated in 25:2; 35:5, 21–29; 36:3–7. The Priestly Writer would presumably rejoin that, if Yahweh is to dwell in Israel's midst, the people must incur the dangers as well as the blessings of his proximity (see pp. 682–703).

The key concept in this paragraph is the root *kpr*, which in the simple form denotes ransom *(kōper)* and with reduplicated middle radical *(kipper)* refers to purification and reconciliation with God, what I call "Clearing" (NOTE to 29:33). Exod 30:15–16 implies that this *kōper* payment effects *kippūrîm* 'Clearing,' as if supplying the latter's etymology (ibn Ezra [shorter commentary]). (For a speculative parallel from Emar, see Pentiuc 2001: 97.)

For what sin or impurity does the ransom silver effect Clearing? Perhaps it is the very act of making the Tabernacle, transforming earthly ingredients into Yahweh's ultrapure abode and thus dangerously mingling the corrupt and the holy. But more likely the impurity is generated by the the the specific act of counting the people, which infringes on divine prerogatives (see pp. 535–36). (By concluding with *napšōtêkem* 'your [masculine plural] *souls*,' Yahweh addresses future Israelite readers, who, by sacrifice, may still obtain continual Clearing for their day-to-day defilements.)

SPECULATION: As they complete the Tabernacle, the Israelites may already bear two specific and potent forms of ritual impurity—at least in the composite Torah. First, many of the people have recently worshiped the Gold Calf, a major transgression calling for Clearing (32:30 [E?]). Second, Israelite warriors, admittedly acting at Moses' behest, have lately slaughtered the Amalekites (17:8–16 [E]) and also some 3,000 Israelite Calf-worshipers (32:27–28 [E?]).

In this last connection, Jacob (1992: 835) notes the extensive parallels between Exod 30:11–16 and Numbers 31, Israel's Holy War against Midian: *nāśā(')* *'et-hārō(')š* 'lift the head' (Exod 30:12; Num 31:26, 49), *pəqûdîm* 'accountings' (Exod 30:12; Num 31:14, 48), *tərûmâ ləyahwe(h)/tərûmat yahwe(h)* 'a Donation-offering for/of Yahweh' (Exod 30:13–15; Num 31:29, 41, 52), *libnê yiśrā'ēl ləzikkārôn lipnê yahwe(h)/zikkārôn lipnê yahwe(h) libnê yiśrā'ēl* 'for Israel's Sons as a Memorial Before Yahweh' (Exod 30:16; Num 31:54) and *ləkappēr 'al-hannəpāšōt* 'to effect Clearing for the souls' (Exod 30:15–16; Num 31:50). We know from other biblical passages that building Yahweh's earthly abode with bloodstained hands is taboo; see 1 Chr 22:8; 28:3; NOTE to 20:25(22), "blade." In the immediate context of Num 31:50, however, it is more likely that the deed requiring *kippûr* is again census-taking (Rashbam; Milgrom 1990: 264; see further pp. 534–38).

As Cassuto (1967: 393) observes, the root *kpr* plays a structural role in 30:1–16 as a whole, binding together vv 1–10 (esp. v 10), on the one hand, and 11–16, on the other, despite their disparate subject matters (the Golden Altar and the census).

harm. Negep (< *nāgap* 'strike') probably bears the special connotation of disease, as in Num 17:11, 12; Josh 22:17 (see Preuss 1998). Peeping through is an ancient, widespread belief that to count persons attracts misfortune, often personified as demonic—in medieval parlance the "Evil Eye" (Rashi). For further discussion, see pp. 534–36.

30:13. *passing over the accountings.* The expression *'ōbēr 'al-happəqûdîm* is somewhat cryptic. The image might be that of a flock passing by *('al)* the shepherd (Jer 33:13; cf. Lev 27:32; Ezek 20:37). To pass *over*, however, might imply crossing a boundary. But what boundary is crossed here? Ibn Ezra thinks that what is passed is twenty years. Or, as Israel pays the "ransom silver," one could imagine them crossing from Death to Life, or passing into Yahweh's possession (cf. Deut 29:11). A more mundane explanation would be that the men pass from the category of the uncounted into the category of the counted (Durham 1987:

403)—perhaps literally, if they stand in line (Driver 1911: 333). Finally, if *pəqūdîm* are military officers, we could translate "passing *before* the registrars" (compare NOTE to 30:12, "accountings"). Echoing Exod 30:11–16, 2 Kgs 12:5 (MT) calls the Temple tax *kesep ʿōbēr kesep napšôt ʿerkô* 'crossing silver, silver of souls of its value,' which Cogan and Tadmor (1988: 135; cf. p. 137) paraphrase: "silver of the census tax, silver from the valuation of persons."

half-shekel. A *šeqel* is not a coin but a measure of weight (< *šql* 'to weigh'), roughly 11.4 grams. When no other substance is specified, it is always silver.

Holiness Shekel. There are two possible interpretations for P's frequent expression *šeqel haqqōdeš*. Some infer that there were two shekels, an ordinary shekel and a lighter "Holiness Shekel" (see next NOTE). On the other hand, since *šeqel* literally means "weight," while *qōdeš* can refer to the Tabernacle, one could paraphrase *šeqel haqqōdeš* as "by the Tabernacle's weighing" (Vg). That is, the Tabernacle may have maintained a standard set of weights to ensure equity (on the injustice caused by inconsistent measures, see Lev 19:35–36; Deut 25:13–16; Ezek 45:10–12; Hos 12:8; Amos 8:5; Micah 6:11; Prov 11:1; 20:23; Job 31:6). In the case at hand, exact weight would be crucial, since even slight deviations would skew the census. The Mishnah analogously requires that all Temple offerings be weighed against the "Tyrian Shekel" (*m. Bek.* 8:7).

In any case, the Priestly Writer is asserting the Tabernacle's prerogative to set weights, normally a royal function in the ancient Near East (cf. Kletter 1998: 128–29). For Israel, compare 2 Kgs 12:5–17; 22:3–7, where the kings and not the priests count the people's silver donations. For further evidence of P's antimonarchic animus, see pp. 483, 533, 708.

twenty gerah. From Judean inscribed stone weights, we know that the average *gērâ* weighed 0.55 gram (Kletter 1998: 81), about one-twentieth of the c. 11.4 gram shekel.

Why define the shekel in this redundant fashion (also Lev 27:25; Num 3:47; 18:16; Ezek 45:12)? Perhaps the intent is to facilitate weighing the half-shekel, or ten gerah. We have other examples of the text gratuitously defining its units of measure (e.g,. Exod 16:36, "the *ʿōmer* . . . is the tenth of the *ʾêpâ*"). But it is also possible that the 20–gerah "Holiness Shekel" is deliberately distinguished from a 24–gerah standard shekel of Mesopotamia (the matter is too complicated to pursue here; see Kletter 1998: 80–82, 101–2, 116).

Jacob (1992: 835) notes that wherever the Torah mentions "twenty gerah," it is associated with paying ransom to Yahweh. Apparently, one must be extra-punctilious when doing business with God.

son of twenty year. Twenty years of age is when an Israelite man becomes eligible for military service (Num 1:3; 26:2). Therefore, the census is related to P's notion of Israel as Yahweh's army (see vol. I, p. 281).

Twenty is slightly older than one might expect. In ancient Greece, although twenty was the age for participation in public affairs, army service began at eighteen (Whibley 1963: 448). Perhaps the Bible delays so that one has an opportunity to marry, settle down and reproduce (compare the military exemption for newlyweds in Deut 20:5–7).

Exod 30:14 supports the argument that this census excludes the Levites, who will be counted from the age of twenty-five (Num 8:4) or thirty (Num 4:3), when they begin their service (Levine 1993: 133–34). See further pp. 536–37.

30:15. *rich . . . poor*. One is reminded of the gift of Manna, equally allotted to all (16:18). As Holzinger (1900: 145) notes, even in Israel's austere, formative period, there are already distinctions in wealth (also Cassuto 1967: 394). The Bible never advocates total wealth redistribution ("the poor shall never cease from the land," Deut 15:11). Rather, it attempts to alleviate the plight of the poor, e.g., through the Sabbatical year and the Jubilee (Leviticus 25, etc.).

The requirement for all men to give the same amount has elicited edifying homily: the tax is low so that all men are equal; no man's life is worth more than another's (ibn Ezra); all men are equally qualified to worship Yahweh and obtain his blessing (Clements 1972: 195). All that may be true, but it is beside the point. Since the census is taken by weighing the amassed silver, it is a practical imperative that all give the same amount (Ehrlich 1969: 197; for a Roman parallel, see Dionysus of Halicarnassus *Roman Antiquities* 4.15). For other purposes such as sacrifices and tithes, the rich are expected to give according to their means (Houtman 2000: 566).

to effect Clearing. Unlike later Judaism, the Bible never addresses at what age one incurs religious obligations. One might infer from 30:15 that the necessity for *kippūr* and other religious rites begins at twenty, along with military service (contrast Ramban, who sets the age at thirteen—the "Bar Mitzvah").

30:16. *for*. Although the diction is peculiar, it is hard to find another meaning for *'al* 'upon, in addition to' that fits this context (see next NOTE, however).

Meeting Tent Work. As in 35:24; 36:1, 3, 5; 39:32, 42, *'ăbōdâ* 'work' must connote not worship (*pace* Noth 1962: 236) but construction (cf. Milgrom 1983a: 18–46). The silver does not purchase offerings; it is built directly into the Tabernacle (38:27–28).

SPECULATION: In 36:5, 7, the terms *'ăbōdâ* and *məlā(')kâ*, both ordinarily denoting labor, may refer to *materials* (cf. NOTE to 36:7, "the Task"). If the same is true in 30:16, then I would render the first half-verse as follows: "And you shall take the Clearing Silver from Israel's Sons and give it *in addition to* the *(other)* Meeting Tent materials," solving the problem raised in the previous NOTE).

Memorial. Although appearing widely outside of P, *zikkārôn* is characteristic of the Priestly Source. The day of *Pesaḥ* (12:14 [P/R]), the engraved stones on the Great Priest's shoulders (28:12) and breast (28:29), Blasting Day (*yôm tərû'â*) on the first day of the seventh month (Jewish Rosh Hashanah) (Lev 23:24), the silver trumpets (Num 10:10), the Altar's bronze plating (Num 17:5) and the dedicated Midianite war booty (Num 31:54) are each called a "Memorial" (Fishbane 1995: 106–7). What is the term's significance here?

Often a *zikkārôn* is something written down, a memorandum (e.g., Exod 17:14; 28:12, 29). Or it may be audible but inarticulate, such as a horn call attracting

Yahweh's attention (Lev 23:24; Num 10:10). Or it may be a silent witness to a historical event (e.g., the stones of Josh 4:7). Exod 30:16 falls in the last category. Since the silver is incorporated into and defines the Tabernacle courtyard's perimeter (38:27–28), the Plaza itself is a memorial (Luzzatto). And more than just commemorate the Tabernacle's foundation, the silver continually Clears and atones. In other words, the Plaza's silver pedestals and capitals remind both Man and God that the Israelites of yore ransomed *(kpr)* their lives from the Deity. Now, thanks to the Tabernacle cultus, their descendants may periodically effect Clearing *(kipper)* for their impurities, and so keep the divine presence in their midst (see pp. 682–703). (On the root *zkr* and the theme of memory in general, see Eising 1980 and the literature cited therein.)

Before Yahweh. Lipnê yahwe(h) 'Before Yahweh, to Yahweh's face' is P's special designation for the Tabernacle or its interior.

30:18. *basin.* Although the meaning is not in doubt, the derivation of *kiyyôr* is uncertain (see Ellenbogen 1962: 84). If Semitic, *kiyyôr* likely comes from a root *kwr* 'go round' as in Arabic *kwr* 'wind around' (BDB); also likely related is Hebrew *kûr* 'furnace, smelting pot.' In the late period, Akkadian knows a word *kiūru* 'metal bowl' (CAD 8.476), for which a Canaanite origin cannot be excluded (but *AHw* p. 496 suggests a derivation from Urartean *kiri*).

Stand. Kēn 'that which holds firm' is equivalent to *məkônâ,* denoting a basin stand in 1 Kgs 7:38; 2 Chr 4:14. Both terms are related to *mākôn* 'foundation' (ibn Ezra; see NOTE to 15:17, "firm seat for your sitting/throne/dwelling"). Probably intended is a pedestal stand of the sort frequently uncovered in excavations (Meyers 1976) or perhaps a stand with legs (cf. *ANEP* figs. 370, 624, 625; Amiran 1969: 304–6). We are not told the measurements of either the Basin or its Stand, presumably because this will depend upon how many mirrors are donated by the women (ibn Ezra on 38:8) and because these items are considered relatively uninteresting.

between Meeting Tent and between the Altar. According to 40:6, the Bronze Altar stands "before the Opening of the Meeting Tent Tabernacle." Thus a passing priest cannot but remember to wash (ibn Ezra [shorter commentary]).

30:19. *Aaron and his sons.* In contrast to 40:31, Moses is not mentioned here, because the topic is the regular Tabernacle service for future generations (ibn Ezra).

hands and . . . feet. Because these parts are liable to tread upon or handle impurity (ibn Ezra).

from it. The priests presumably do not dip their hands and feet into the basin, but draw water from it (ibn Ezra [shorter commentary]).

30:20. *in their coming.* A priest enters the inner chamber to light the lamps, to renew the incense or to effect Clearing with the blood of the Sin-offering (Leviticus 4, 16) (Rashi). Although this command is addressed to the priests alone, the parallel in 40:31 includes Moses, too.

to attend. That is, the priests must wash before sacrificing. For other activities such as cleaning the Altar, they need not wash (Cassuto 1967: 396).

lest they die. Although the tone is positive, we cannot miss the implied threat: if they neglect to wash, they will die (Rashi). See further COMMENT, pp. 501–2.

the Altar. Unless the context requires otherwise, *mizbēaḥ* refers to the Bronze

Altar of the Plaza. According to 29:37, it shares with the Tabernacle's inner chamber the quality of *qōdeš qŏdāšîm* 'Holiness of Holinesses,' i.e., ultimate sanctity; see further pp. 499–501.

to attend, to smoke. I.e., to worship by burnt offering.

Gift. See NOTE to 29:18.

30:21. *wash*. The repetition from v 19 emphasizes the death threat (ibn Ezra).

for their ages. See NOTE to 30:8, "for your ages."

30:23. *you, take for yourself*. The emphatic language implies not that the oil will be for Moses' benefit but that he personally must compound it and anoint the Tabernacle, without delegating these tasks.

fragrances: head of. This is not the usual interpretation. Rashi, following the MT cantillation, takes *bəśāmîm rō(ʾ)š* as a phrase: "head (i.e., best) of fragrances." The problem is that we would have expected not apposition but construct: **bośmê rō(ʾ)š*, or, better still, **rō(ʾ)š bəśāmîm* (cf. Ezek 27:22 *rō[ʾ]š kol-bōśem*; Cant 4:14 *kol-rā[ʾ]šê bəśāmîm*). One possibility is that a scribe inadvertently transposed the two words. I have elected, however, to follow LXX and Vg, connecting *rō(ʾ)š* 'head, chief' to the following *mor-dərôr*.

SPECULATION: Some of these ingredients are rather pungent. In fact, *mōr* 'myrrh' derives its name from the root *mrr* 'to be bitter, strong.' Therefore, it is worth considering whether in these verses we do not have *rō(ʾ)š* II 'bitter flavor' not *rō(ʾ)š* II 'head chief.'

I translate *bəśāmîm* as "fragrances." The term generally refers to incense and may have originally denoted the balsam tree (Greek *balsamon*), whose resins were prized for their fragrance (on the linguistic borrowing from Semitic — probably Phoenician — into Greek, see Steiner 1977: 123–29). I do not understand the Massoretes' distinction between *bešem* and *bōśem*, both of which I translate "fragrance." Perhaps originally the former denoted the balsam tree, the second fragrance in general. In 30:23, in any case, they appear to be synonymous.

dərôr myrrh. We are not always sure what is the difference among the Israelites' many terms for odoriferous resins or indeed how precise their terminology was. Although most earlier medieval Jewish commentators regarded myrrh *(mōr)* as an animal product, since Ramban's definitive treatment it has been known to be the resin of various trees loosely called "balsam," native to South Arabia, Ethiopia and Somalia (Pliny *Natural History* 12.51–72); on the etymology and cognates, see Hausmann (1997: 557–58). Myrrh was valued for both its aromatic and medicinal properties (e.g., EA 269.16–17; Mark 15:23). In addition to censing, it was also used to embalm the dead (e.g., John 19:39–40). (For general discussions of incense production and trade, see van Beek 1960; Groom 1981; Nielsen 1986.)

In 30:23, *mōr* is qualified by *dərôr*; Punic *mrdr* (sic) seems to denote the same substance (*KAI* 161.8). *Dərôr* elsewhere means "liberty" (Lev 25:10; Isa 61:1; Jer 34:8, 15, 17; Ezek 46:17) or else is a type of bird (Ps 84:4). As neither will do here, scholars have resorted to one of two etymologies. (1) Since Arabic *darra* means "flow," Hebrew *mōr dərôr* may be the finest myrrh that flows spontaneously from the tree (cf. Pliny *Natural History* 12.35; Theophrastus *Plants* 9.4) or, alternatively, a liquid imbued with essence of myrrh (Ramban; cf. Cant 5:5, 13 "dripping myrrh" and Esther's bath in "myrrh oil" [Esth 2:12]) (Dillmann 1880: 320; BDB). (2) Others look to Arabic *durr* 'pearl,' understanding *mōr dərôr* as hardened myrrh droplets (Löw 1967: 1.307; cf. Pliny 12.61–62). Houtman (1993a: 167) makes a good argument in favor of the latter theory: since *dərôr* myrrh is measured by weight not volume, it should be solid not liquid.

half as much . . . fifty and two hundred. Against the plain sense, *b. Kerit.* 5a interprets this to mean that half of the cinnamon would weigh 250 shekels, and hence that the quantities of myrrh and cinnamon are both 500 shekels (also Rashi). Presumably the Rabbis are trying to account for the text's redundancy: 250 is obviously half of 500.

fragrant cinnamon. "Cinnamon" bark, really cassia (Powels 1992: 190–91), was imported from Southeast Asia and South Arabia (Strabo *Geography* 15.1.22; 16.4.19, 25). According to classical sources, it was very rare and costly (Theophrastus *Plants* 9.5; Pliny *Natural History* 12.85–98; 13.15; also Zohary and Rabin 1976).

fragrant cane. Qənē(h) bōśem is also called *qāne(h) haṭṭôb* 'the sweet cane' (Jer 6:20; cf. Akkadian *qanû ṭābu*) and simply *qāne(h)* 'cane' (Isa 43:24; Ezek 27:19). Although reeds are found in Israel itself, it is clear from the prophets that this special cane, like frankincense, was imported "from a distant land." Of various grasses valued in Antiquity for their aromatic essences, most prominent is that which classical writers call "calamus odoratus," imported from India (Dioscorides *De materia medica* 1.17), Arabia (Strabo *Geography* 16.4.19) and Syria (Theophrastus *Plants* 9.7; Pliny *Natural History* 12.104–6; 13.9–14). The variety most familiar to my readers will be East Asian "lemongrass." For further discussion, see Zohary (1976b).

30:24. *qiddâ.* We do not know the identity of this plant, mentioned only here and in Ezek 27:19. Most equate it with cassia (e.g., *b. Kerit.* 6a; *Tg. Onqelos*), with possible confirmation from Dioscorides (*Materia medica* 1.13), who identifies *kittō* as a type of cassia (Dillmann 1880: 321; on this and other older proposals, see Zohary 1976a). Powels (1992: 191), however, has more plausibly equated *qiddâ* with Sanskrit *kunda-* and various Indian derivatives denoting aromatics, especially balsam and incense.

The four dry spices are used in the following proportion: two parts myrrh, two parts *qiddâ*, one part each cinnamon and "cane." The total weight is 1,000 shekels, c. 25 lbs./11.4 kg. Although the recipe's main consideration is presumably olfactory, we note the alliterative quality of the last three ingredients: *qinnāmôn . . . qāne(h) . . . qiddâ* (cf. Ezek 27:19, *qiddâ wəqāne[h]*; Cant 4:14, *qāne[h] wəqinnāmôn*). (Is this a mnemonic aid for the compounder?)

olive oil. Because it is absorbed into the skin, oil is a perfect medium for perfume; the Bible mentions scented oil again in Cant 1:3; 4:10; Esth 2:12. *Šmn mr/šaman murri* 'myrrh oil' also appears repeatedly in Northwest Semitic texts (*KTU* 4.14.2, 8, 15; 4.91.16; 4.786.14; 5.23.1; EA 25.iv.51). Ancient Egypt was particularly renowned for its myrrh perfume (Van Beek 1960: 84–85).

hin. See NOTE to 29:40.

30:25. *compounding compound, compounder's work.* Because the manner of combination would be known to any perfumer, it is left unstated. To the uninformed reader, however, it is not clear how one imparts the essence of some twenty-five pounds of herbs to three quarts of oil (Sforno). They cannot simply be mixed like salad dressing.

Job 41:23 implies that "compounder's work" involves boiling (Houtman 1993a: 165). The Talmud preserves one method for imparting scent to oil, corroborated by Egyptian, Mesopotamian and classical sources (Shelmerdine 1985: 11–16; Ebeling 1948; Theophrastus *Odors*). Moreover, archaeological evidence of a Judean perfume industry has been found at Ein Gedi (Mazar and Dunayevsky 1964: 123; cf. *b. Šabb.* 26a). The herbs were soaked in water and oil, and then either the water was boiled away or the oil skimmed off (*b. Hor.* 11b; *Kerit.* 5a). Thus savor was transferred from the spices to the water to the oil (see further Lucas 1962: 85–90; Serpico 2000: 261–64). For a few drops of scented oil, one expended a large quantity of extremely valuable stuff—which is why perfume was and is so costly. Josephus *Ant.* 14.72 reports that the Second Temple possessed among its treasures large quantities of spices.

30:26. *anoint . . . Meeting Tent.* If the intent is that the very curtains are anointed as well as the Tabernacle's contents (cf. 40:9–11; Lev 8:10–11; Num 7:1), then this cannot be a wholesale smearing, which would require much more than a hin of oil (and would ruin the dyed fabric). More likely a sprinkling is envisioned, as in Lev 8:11 (Dillmann 1880: 322; Cassuto 1967: 398). The function of the oil is made clear in Exod 30:29: it imparts the quality of Holiness. Similarly, oil transfers Yahweh's spirit to individuals (NOTE to 28:41, "anoint them"), a notion increasingly potent in the religion of *ho Christos* 'the Anointed' (Luke 4:18; Acts 10:38; cf. Calvin).

30:29. *any touching . . . holy.* See NOTES to 29:37.

30:30. *Aaron and his sons.* This is redundant with 28:41 and seems to be an afterthought—which is not to say it must be a secondary insertion (vs. Noth 1962: 238).

30:32. *a human's flesh.* The context makes it fairly certain that '*ādām* here means "any person other than a priest," what v 33 calls a *zār* 'outsider.'

Exodus clearly forbids the cosmetic or recreational use of the sacred oil. In the greater biblical context, however, 30:32 raises an obvious question: what about various nonpriests who receive divinely sanctioned anointment, especially kings? Several answers are possible. First, these may simply have been anointed with a different compound. Second—a remote possibility—30:32 may specifically forbid pouring anointing oil on "flesh," i.e., on parts of the body not covered by hair. The prohibition would then include the priests themselves (ibn Ezra, Ramban). I, however, would rather detect a polemic against royal anointment, especially as the Priestly Source seems scarcely to envision the institution of kingship (the sole references are Gen 17:6; 35:11 and possibly Lev 4:22–35; see pp. 478, 533, 708). According to 1 Kgs 1:39, the oil with which Solomon was anointed had been kept in Yahweh's sacred tent. If so, this would have outraged the Priestly Writer.

poured. The root *swk* is reserved for nonceremonial oil applications; ritual anointment is *mšḥ*.

in its composition. It is unclear whether this refers to the ingredients alone or to the ingredients in their exact proportions (cf. Rashi, ibn Ezra).

30:33. *or who.* Two acts are proscribed: (a) making anointing oil, and (b) putting it on a nonpriest. Either one makes one liable to "Cutting Off" (see below). It cannot be that one must do *both* to incur the curse, for then the wording would be **'îš 'ăšer yirqaḥ kāmōhû wənātan mimmennû 'al-zār*. That is, the repetition of the relative pronoun *'ăšer* implies two separate acts. The text does not actually curse the "outsider" who receives the oil; presumably he, too, would be culpable.

Taken literally, the text implies that this oil was made but once in history, by Moses himself (Rashi). But in fact priestly anointment is to be renewed in every generation (see p. 532).

outsider. In context, *zār* must connote a nonpriest *(Tg. Ps.-Jonathan)*, a usage paralleled in Num 3:10; 17:5 (ibn Ezra). See also above, NOTE to 30:9, "alien incense."

Cut Off. I.e., will die prematurely and suffer post mortem the eradication of his lineage; on the *kārēt* penalty, see vol. I, pp. 403–4, and next NOTE. This curse presumably applies both to the one who makes the compound and the one who uses it for private purposes *(pace b. Kerit. 5a; Rashi).*

kin. The term *'am* here does not bear its usual meaning "people" but rather denotes a kinsman. This usage is restricted to the *kārēt* formula, the euphemism for death *ne'ĕsap 'el-'ammā(y)w* 'gathered to his kin,' names such as *'ammî'ēl* 'God is my kinsman' and Lev 19:16 (MT, but cf. the Versions and MSS). It is confirmed in Amorite usage (Huffmon 1965a: 196–98) and Arabic, where *'amm* means "paternal uncle." It is the totality of *'ammîm* in this original sense—the living, the dead and the unborn—that constitute the entire *'am* 'people.' In other words, *'am* 'people' appears to have originated as a collective noun for people related patrilineally. Inasmuch as the *kārēt* curse entails alienation in the afterlife (Propp 1987b), to be "cut off from one's kin" is the opposite of being "gathered to one's kin."

30:34. *Take for yourself.* See NOTE to 30:23.

spices . . . spices. This seems to be a miniature *Wiederaufnahme* (cf. Kuhl 1952): Yahweh commands Moses to gather spices, digresses to name them, then resumes with a repetition (ibn Ezra and esp. Rashbam). For a contrary view, see *b. Kerit.* 6a; Ramban.

gumdrop . . . šəḥēlet . . . galbanum. On these substances, see Nielsen (1986: 65–66) and Serpico (2000: 430–43, 456–59). The first item, *nāṭāp* (< *ntp* 'drip'), is probably a kind of Arabian balsam resin or stacte (Ramban) but possibly a Palestinian product (Löw 1967: 3.389; see further Houtman 1993a: 169; Feliks 1995).

Šəḥēlet is thought by most, including the Versions, to be a kind of shellfish native to the Red Sea and Indian Ocean (e.g., Ramban). Here the referent would be a snail-derived musk, whose manufacture is described in *b. Ker.* 6b. Cassuto (1967: 399), however, identifies *šəḥēlet* with the Akkadian *hapax legomenon suḥullatu*, an exotic plant; KB similarly cites Rabbinic Hebrew *šəḥālîm/šiḥlayim* and Aramaic *taḥlê* 'garden cress' (Löw 1967: 1.506–9). The ordinary Akkadian term for "cress" is *saḥlû/saḥlānu*, used as a spice and a medicine (*CAD* 15.61–65;

AHw p. 1009 compares Hittite *zaḫḫeli-*). Cassuto in addition cites Ugaritic *šḥlt*, apparently a comestible (*KTU* 4.14.4, 16). But there are problems. First, Hebrew *ḥ* can correspond to either Akkadian *ḫ* or Ugaritic *ḥ*, but not both (Ginsberg 1936: 102–3). Second, Hebrew and Akkadian *š* can correspond to Ugaritic *š*, but then not also to Aramaic *t*. Third, Hebrew *š* does not ordinarily correspond to Akkadian *s*. Given these phonological anomalies, we may be dealing with loanwords rather than genetic cognates. As for ultimate etymology, one might look to Arabic *saḥala* 'peel' (note also *'isḥil*, a tamarisk-like tree).

Ḥelbǝnâ, Greek *chalbanē*, Latin *galbanum*, is resin from *Ferula galbaniflua Boisser et Buhse* and related species originally indigenous to Persia and Afghanistan. In Antiquity, galbanum was generally accorded medicinal properties (e.g., Pliny *Natural History* 12.126–27; 24.1–22; see Zohary 1958). On its use to perfume water in Egypt and Mesopotamia, see Hoch (1994: 249–50).

Various other ingredients may also have been added to increase the output of smoke (cf. *b. Ker.* 6a; *y. Yoma* 4:5). For a more detailed discussion of incense compounding, see Milgrom (1991: 1026–31).

pure frankincense. Lǝbōnâ is the fragrant resin of *Boswellia* trees from southern Arabia, Ethiopia, Somalia and India. It comes in various colors and grades and in Antiquity (but not the Bible) was accorded medicinal value (Zohary 1962; Hepper 1969).

part for part. Bad bǝbad is slightly unclear. It could mean "separately" (ibn, Ezra), but more likely the intent is "in equal measure" (Saadiah; Rashi, and Dillmann [1880: 327], comparing *ḥēleq kǝḥēleq* 'share by share' in Deut 18:8). Otherwise, there would be no indication of proportions. Even so, it remains ambiguous whether the formula calls for all four spices in equal parts (Dillmann) or equal parts frankinense and gumdrop-*šǝḥēlet*-galbanum (in which case, the recipe is still incomplete).

it shall be. Because the ostensible subject, *qǝṭōret* 'incense,' is feminine, whereas the verb *yihye(h)* 'shall be' is masculine, an alternative translation would be "part shall be for part," i.e., the subject is *bad* 'part' (masculine) (cf. Cassuto 1967: 400).

30:35. *salted*. The Versions unanimously understand *mǝmullāḥ* as "mixed." But it is hard to ignore the connection with *melaḥ* 'salt' (*b. Kerit.* 6a; ibn Ezra). Cassuto (1967: 400) objects that we would not expect a Puʿal "salted," as there is no Piʿel **millaḥ* 'to salt' in Biblical Hebrew. This is but a slight difficulty. First, cognate languages such as Syriac and Arabic use the D-stem of *mlḥ* in just this sense. Second, since the root is attested in the Hophʿal (Ezek 16:4), we could always vocalize **momlaḥ* in Exod 30:35. Decisive are Mesopotamian magical texts, according to which salt was added to incense to enhance combustion (cf. also *b. Šabb.* 67b). Salt was also used to season food (Job 6:6) and appears to have connoted purity (2 Kgs 2:19–22) (ibn Ezra [shorter commentary]; Driver 1911: 340; vol. I, p. 433; on Mesopotamia, see Wilson 1994: 79). Cereal offerings were always salted (Lev 2:13; cf. Ezek 43:24). Still, the lack of a convincing explanation for the rendering "mixed" means that we should not entirely eliminate it from consideration (see Rashi for a far-fetched connection with *mallāḥ* 'sailor' and scrambled eggs!). For further discussion of mixed/salted incense, see Hurowitz (1987).

A grammatical note: the masculine adjectives *məmullāḥ* 'salted' and *ṭāhôr* 'pure' technically modify *rōqaḥ* 'compound' (masc.) not *qəṭōret* 'incense' (fem.).

pure. Does *ṭāhôr* here literally mean free from dross (Sforno), or is it directed specifically against ritual defilement (e.g., from insect carcasses)?

30:36. *set.* Burning on the Golden Altar is presumably intended.

(some) of it. As one would expect, incense is manufactured in large quantities, from which a suitable amount is extracted as needed for the regular incense offering (Noth 1962: 239).

fine. The fineness of the incense is noted again in Lev 16:12 (Rashbam; cf. Rashi on Lev 16:12).

before the Testimony. This phrase, paralleled in 16:34 (Manna) and Num 17:19, 25 (Aaron's rod), could be interpreted in either of two ways here. Superficially, *lipnê hā'ēdūt* would appear to mean "directly before the Testimony Chest" inside the Veil (so Heb 9:4). In that case, 30:36 could be speaking only of Clearing Day (*yôm hakkippūrm*), when the Priest brings incense into the inner sanctum (Lev 16:12–13). More likely, however, "before the Testimony" simply means "inside the Tabernacle," and the reference is to the Golden Altar of Incense standing outside the Veil. (This is probably also where the Manna pot and Aaron's rod are stored, not in the inner sanctum or within the Chest.)

30:37. *for Yahweh . . . for you.* In other words, the sacred incense belongs exclusively to the intimate Yahweh-Israel connection created by Tabernacle worship. Outside that context, it is forbidden. There is an implicit polemic here against unauthorized cultic censing (cf. pp. 369, 515).

30:38. *smell.* Although there are no parallels, I wonder whether *ləhārîaḥ* could mean "to make a smell" (cf. Arabic *'arwaḥa* 'stink').

Cut Off. It is a high sin for a human to appropriate Yahweh's own perfume in order simply to luxuriate.

31:2. *See.* The imperative *rə'ē(h)* recalls Moses to attention, signaling a change of subject after the preceding welter of technical details. On "See" as indicating a formal commission, compare Gen 41:41; Exod 7:1; Deut 1:8, 21; 2:24, 31 (Jacob 1992: 841).

called by name. *Qārā(')* *bəšēm* means to "summon" or "designate"; Luzzatto cites Isa 43:1, "I have called you by your name; you are mine." Bezalel's name, like that of his assistant Oholiab, providentially foreshadows his appointed task of building God's abode—ordained, according to *Exod. Rab.* 40:2, since Creation (see below).

Bezalel. *Bəṣal'ēl* means "In God's shelter/shade," befitting the builder of the Tabernacle (Jacob 1992: 842; cf. NOTE to 31:6 on the name Oholiab). For this use of *ṣēl,* compare the Ugaritic myth in which King Kirta worships *bẓl ḥmt* 'in the tent's shelter' (*KTU* 1.14.iii.55) (Coote and Ord 1991: 98). The element *ṣill-* 'shelter, shade' was popular also in Babylonian names, followed by the name of a god, city or temple (Stamm 1939: 84, 85, 91, 276, 314). One Ṣil(li)-ba'l was king of Gaza in Hezekiah's day (*ANET* 288, 291). (More remotely, Bezalel's name recalls the Akkadian proverb *ṣilli ili amēlu* 'god's shadow is Man' [Parpola 1993: 166].)

Uri. *'Ûrî* means "My Fire" or "My Light," probably short for *'ûrî'ēl* 'God is my Light' (cf. 1 Chr 6:9; 15:5, 11) and comparable to later *'ûrîyāh(û)* 'Yah(w) is my light' (2 Samuel 11, etc.). See further Fowler (1988: 156, 335).

Hur. LXX *Ōr* might reflect a vocalization *ḥôr*, vs. MT *ḥûr* (contrast LXX *Ourios* = MT *'ûrî*). The name probably comes from Egyptian *ḥr* 'Horus,' a popular element in Ugaritic (Gröndahl 1967: 136), Phoenician (Benz 1972: 317), epigraphic Israelite (Tigay 1986: 66, 76–66) and Egypto-Aramaic personal names (Kornfeld 1978: 80–82). Possible biblical parallels are *pašḥûr* and *'ašḥûr*.

We cannot be certain of Egyptian derivation, however. Alternative explanations for *ḥr* would be "Pale-face," "Hurrian" (Durham 1987: 233) or "Freeman" (Arabic *ḥurr*, Aramaic *ḥōr[în]*), and there might be a connection with the Old South Arabic name *ḥwr* (Ryckmans 1934: 3.58).

Meaning aside, commentators are divided on whether this Hur is (Jacob 1992: 842) or is not (Hyatt 1980: 297) the same as the Hur in 17:10; 24:14. If so, he is probably fairly young. The question is moot, especially since 17:10 and 24:14 are JE, while 30:1 is P, and we cannot know what the Redactor had in mind. Also moot, and beyond the scope of this commentary, is the relationship with the two Hurs of 1 Chr 2:19–20; 4:1, 4, and the relationship of the clan of Hur to the Calebites/Edomites (Dahlberg 1962; Axelsson 1987: 71–72).

Judah. The two artisans may be taken to represent the totality of tribes: from the descendants of Jacob's chief wife Leah (Judah) to those of Rachel's slave (Dan) (cf. Rashi on 35:34). Also, Oholiab and Bezalel come from what would be the northernmost and southernmost tribes, as if representing the entire land of Israel "from Dan to Beersheba" (Houtman 2000: 356). The Midrash notes that the Temple, too, was built by a Judahite (Solomon) and a Danite (Hiram) (Ginzberg 1928: 156). Clements (1972: 199) speculates that Bezalel and Oholiab were celebrated as ancestors of guilds.

31:3. I have filled. When did Bezalel receive his inspiration? Was he always talented? Ramban thinks that he was destined for his great task from birth, when he received his name (see NOTE to 31:2, "Bezalel"). But it is also possible that Yahweh has suddenly transformed him into a genius. On the inspiration of craftsmen, see also next NOTE and NOTES to 28:3.

a divine spirit. My rendering follows LXX *pneuma theion.* Hebrew *rûaḥ 'ĕlōhîm*, which might also be translated "Deity's spirit" (see NOTE to 8:15), is a pregnant phrase. In Gen 41:38, it refers to Joseph's uncanny ability to interpret dreams. In Num 24:2 and many other passages, it describes prophetic inspiration. But in Exod 31:3, *rûaḥ 'ĕlōhîm* connotes wondrous manual skill, the ability to actualize the divine intent.

The image of the inspired artist is not original to the Bible. By general ancient belief, the fine arts were founded in primordial, mythic time (cf. Gen 4:21–22), and the very first makers were gods (on divine craftsmen, see Pope 1965b; Helck 1965b). Latterday cultic craftsmen, by the gods' grace, are qualified to transform inert, profane matter into a semblance of the celestial. To design and build even ordinary structures requires divine assistance, for "if Yahweh, he does not build a house, in vain its builders toil" (Ps 127:1). In this sense, the artist is a "theologian" (Berlejung 1996), exampling divine activity and rendering it active and comprehensible. Like the prophet, he can also misuse his gift (Berlejung pp. 155–56, 161).

The expression *rûaḥ ʾělōhîm* connotes more than Bezalel's "inspiration" in our vague sense. Apart from describing Bezalel's skill in 31:3; 35:31, *rûaḥ ʾělōhîm* appears just one other time in P: "and Deity's 'spirit/wind/breath' fluttered over the waters' face" (Gen 1:2) (Kearney 1977: 378; Janzen 1997: 194). The moral: by building the Tabernacle, the workers renew and complete Creation, the firstfruits of Yahweh's *rûaḥ* (see also following NOTE and below, pp. 675–76).

By emphasizing Bezalel's role, P stands apart from ancient Near Eastern mythology, which ascribes temple-building historically to monarchs and mythically to the gods themselves (see vol. I, p. 554). Because P presents itself as history, its main actors are humans. But the Book of Exodus includes an overtly mythopoetic strain as well. Contrast 15:17: "The sanctum, my Lordship, *your* hands founded."

wisdom . . . understanding . . . knowledge. Commentators medieval and modern attempt to distinguish among *ḥokmâ, təbûnâ* and *daʿat;* the rationalist ibn Ezra even locates them in different sectors of the brain. But we really cannot differentiate among the Hebrew terms for learning, experience, skill, intuition, ingenuity, inspiration, genius, etc. The point is that Bezalel possesses all the requisite qualities in supernatural measure (cf. Ehrlich 1908: 387) and will handily solve any structural problems not explicitly treated in his instructions (ibn Ezra [shorter commentary]; Cassuto 1967: 402).

The Bible regards the artificer as a kind of sage; on the special "wisdom" of craftsmen, compare Isa 3:3; 40:20; Jer 10:9, and especially Prov 24:3–4: "By *wisdom* a house is built, and by *understanding* it is made firm, and by *knowledge* the rooms are filled." Bezalel seems to be the archetype of Hi/uram of Tyre, chief designer of Solomon's Temple, who likewise "was filled with the *wisdom* and the *understanding* and the *knowledge* to do all work in bronze" (1 Kgs 7:14; cf. 2 Chr 2:12–13).

The Bible's supreme artisan is naturally God himself. For Yahweh's Creation by his wisdom, cf. Isa 40:12–14, 28; Prov 8:22–31. In fact, Prov 3:19–20 attributes Bezalel's exact mental attributes to the Creator: "Yahweh by *wisdom* founded earth, / Established heavens by *understanding* / By his *knowledge* Deeps were cleft" (*b. Ber.* 55a; *Pirqei R. El.* 3; Leibowitz 1976: 675). As Israel's divine craftsman, Yahweh fills the role allotted in ancient religions to Ptaḥ, Hephaistos, Kotaru-wa-Ḥasīsu et al. (cf. pp. 762, 787).

and in every task. The wording is somewhat surprising; we might have expected simply **bəkol-məlā(ʾ)kâ* 'in every task,' without the conjunction *û-* (LXX–Vg; cf. TEXTUAL NOTE). Ibn Ezra thinks the waw in MT is emphatic: Bezalel is inspired "in wisdom and in understanding and in knowledge, *even* in every task" (also Ehrlich 1908: 387). We could also treat the conjunction as explicative: "*namely* in every task" (cf. GKC §154 n. 1). Or we might understand *məlā(ʾ)kâ* to connote not just the work but also its planning. Most likely, however, the author preferred alliterative parallelism (*ûbə- . . . ûbə- . . . ûbə-* 'and in . . . and in . . . and in') to strict grammatical logic. The following verse specifies what "every task" entails.

31:4. *planning plans.* The interpretation of *laḥšōb maḥăšābōt* is disputed. At issue is whether the root *ḥšb* here connotes an intellectual faculty (ibn Ezra [shorter commentary]) or more specifically weaving (Rashi). In the Tabernacle pericope, *ḥšb* frequently describes the most demanding textile work, generally in the expression *maʿăśē(h) ḥōšēb* (see NOTE to 26:1, "webster's work"). But the phrases *laḥšōb maḥăšābōt* and *ḥōšəbê maḥăšābōt* seem to be used more inclusively, preceding or following an inventory of skills (35:32–35). In 31:3, it is almost certain that *ḥšb* connotes invention in general, and likewise in Amos 6:5; 2 Chr 26:15. In Prov 6:18, *ḥšb* is associated with *ḥrš* 'fabricate': *lēb ḥōrēš maḥšəbōt ʾāwen* 'a heart fabricating evil plans.' (For further discussion of *ḥšb*, see Seybold 1986.)

31:5. *stone carving . . . wood carving.* *Ḥărōšet ʾeben* and *ḥărōšet ʿēṣ* could also be translated "stone work" and "wood work," but, at least etymologically, *ḥrš* refers to cutting. The specific tasks relevant to the Tabernacle are cutting and engraving gemstones and shaping planks and poles.

for filling. *Ləmallō(ʾ)t* is a Piʿel infinitive construct influenced by the III-y paradigm (i.e., as if the root were *mly, not *mlʾ*; see GKC §74h, 75qq). The term apparently refers to setting gemstones; see NOTES to 25:7, "filling"; 28:17, "fill . . . filling."

to do every task. This refers to other tasks here unspecified, e.g., textile work, as is made clear in 35:35 (ibn Ezra). See also TEXTUAL NOTE to 31:4, "bronze."

31:6. *I have given with him.* I.e., I have appointed as a colleague. This is a short way of saying that Oholiab, too, knows all crafts, as 35:35 explains.

Oholiab. *ʾOhŏlîʾāb* probably means "The Father is my Tent." As is often noted (e.g., Jacob 1992: 842), Oholiab's name matches his occupation. Given their pastoral nomadic antecedents, such names are expected among the Northwest Semites (see pp. 703–7; APPENDIX B). For example, an Israelite seal bears the woman's name *ḥmyʾhl* 'The Father-in-law is a Tent' (Fowler 1988: 334). Hyatt (1980: 297–98) compares Phoenician *ʾhlbʿl* 'Baal is my Tent,' *ʾhlmlk* 'The King is my tent' and *grʾhl* 'Client of the Tent' (Benz 1972: 262). South Arabic *ʾhlʾl* and *tʾlʾhl* may be relevant as well (although here *ʾhl* possibly means "family" not "tent") (Ryckmans 1934: 1.218, 271). Lastly, from the Bible we have the Edomite Oholibamah (Gen 36:2, 41) and the symbolic names for Israel and Judah Oholah and Oholibah (Ezekiel 23). For an argument that the name "Aaron" also derives from this root, see Homan (2002: 120–23).

Ahisamach. *ʾĂḥîsāmāk* means "My Brother has supported." On such kinship names as Oholiab and Ahisamach, see Noth (1928: 66–82), Huffmon (1965a) and Cross (1973: 3–12; 1998: 6–7). For other names with the element *smk*, see Fowler (1988: 104, 353).

Dan. On the symbolism of craftsmen from Judah and Dan, see NOTE to 31:2, "Judah." The later Danites may have derived special artistic know-how from the neighboring Phoenicians; in 2 Chr 2:13, the designer of Solomon's Temple is half-Tyrian, half-Danite (according to 1 Kgs 7:13–14, however, he is of Naphtali).

into the heart of every wise-hearted I have set wisdom. When did this happen? Providentially at birth? Or has Yahweh lately augmented the existing aptitude of certain individuals (e.g., Durham 1987: 410)? There is a parallel with the ordinary folk, whose generosity of heart is also evoked by the project (NOTE to 28:3, "wise-hearted"). Each donates something valuable, be it gold, gems, cloth or skill. On the heart as seat of wisdom and other qualities, see Fabry (1995: 412–34).

31:7. *Chest for the Testimony.* "Testimony" is ellipsis for "Testimony *Tablets*" (Rashi).

the Tent's implements. What are these *kēlîm?* Not really "implements" but apparently all the components unmentioned in vv 7–11: the Veil, the Screen, the *qərāšîm-*frames, the crossbars, the cords and the pegs (cf. ibn Ezra).

31:8. *pure Lampstand.* The language is elliptical; the sense is probably "pure *gold* Lampstand" (Saadiah on 39:37; Rashi; contrast Jacob 1992: 843); cf. 25:31. Similarly, Lev 24:6 speaks of the "pure Table."

31:10. *the Textile Garments.* The meaning of the phrase *bigdê haśśərād* and its relation to the priest's "Holiness Garments" are vexed questions. First, what does *śərād* mean? The root *śrd* is well known, but its ordinary meaning, "escape, survive," does not suit the context easily (see below, however). The favored theory, which my translation follows, makes a connection with Aramaic *sərādā'* 'netting' and Syriac *sardā'* 'sieve' (cf. Rashi). And there are other possibilities. Although the initial sibilants do not correspond, another promising cognate is Arabic *srd,* which refers to the repeated actions necessary to making garments (armor, leather) and also telling stories (compare English "yarn, spin, embroider, text," etc.) (cf. Dillmann 1880: 329). Lastly, Margalith (1983) identifies *śərād* as a type of linen from Colchis, which Greek calls *sardōnikon.*

The ancient translations, however, understand *śərād* to mean "worship." One would lightly dismiss this as a guess based upon 35:19; 39:1, 41, where *śərād* appears alongside *šrt* 'attend, minister,' except that Ugaritic knows a verb *šrd* 'attend, worship,' theoretically corresponding to Hebrew *śərād* (Held 1954). This approach assumes that the *śərād* garments and the "Holiness Garments" are one and the same. But this violates the plain sense of 31:10; 39:1, where they are distinguished. Even if in 31:10 we take the waw as explicative, we cannot so easily account for 39:1, "they made Textile Garments for attending in the Holiness; and they made the Holiness Garments. . . ."

Accordingly, commentators have sought other fabrics that might be meant, aside from clerical vestments. Rashi and ibn Ezra identify the *śərād* garments as the woolen wrappings for the sacred objects (Num 4:5–14). In support, Rashi notes that, according to 39:1, the *śərād* garments are pure wool, without the admixture of linen always mentioned apropos of the priestly robes. Ibn Ezra even finds the etymology of *śərād* in *śrd* 'to be a fugitive,' understanding *bigdê śərād* as tantamount to "temporary transport wrappings." (For Ehrlich [1969: 198], the definite article in *haśśərād* also implies that *śərād* is not a fabric but the purpose of the garment.)

The best analysis is Haran's (1978: 172–73): whatever its precise etymology, *bigdê haśśərād* serves as a general term for priestly garb. *Bigdê haqqōdeš* 'the Holiness Garments,' in contrast, are specifically Aaron's vestments (cf. 40:13; Lev 16:32). Assuming that Aaron's opulent robes and his sons' simpler outfits together constitute *bigdê haśśərād* makes sense of all occurrences. It follows that the conjunction in 31:10 is explicative: "the *śərād* garments: *namely* the Holiness Garments for Aaron the priest and his sons' garments" (cf. GKC §154 n. 1). As for the nonmention of linen in 39:1, I would note that, by Rashi's theory, no materials at all are mentioned for Aaron's garments in 39:1, which does not seem likely either. I cannot understand linen's absence, except as the result of carelessness (see TEXTUAL NOTE); cf. Ramban.

31:11. *for the Holiness.* *Laqqōdeš* most likely here refers to the outer sanctum, where the Incense Altar stands (cf. 26:33; 28:29, 35, etc.) (Rashi). Luzzatto less plausibly takes it in the sense of **ləqaddēš* 'to sanctify' as referring to the oil, which imparts Holiness to people and things (see NOTE to 28:41, "make . . . holy").

31:13. *you, you.* The redundancy emphasizes Moses' responsibility for teaching Israel about the Sabbath.

Israel's Sons. This is a precept not just for the workmen, although they are included, but for all Israel.

Nevertheless. 'Ak introduces a qualification: even though you are about to engage in the manufacture *(məlā[']kâ)* of the Tabernacle, you must still observe the Sabbath, when Yahweh rested from his own work *(məlā[']kâ)* (Gen 2:2). On references to Creation in the Tabernacle account, see pp. 675–76.

my Sabbaths. The plural emphasizes the Sabbath as a recurring institution. On the term *šabbāt*, see NOTE to 20:8, "Sabbath." (Although Cassuto [1967: 405] is correct that *šbt* is the theme root of 31:12–17, he miscounts: it occurs eight times, not seven.)

keep. The root *šmr* 'protect, watch' refers to Sabbath observance also in Lev 19:3, 30; 26:2; Isa 56:4. It implies both that the Sabbath must be defended from encroachments, and also that one must not lose track of time (ibn Ezra).

it is. Even though appearing in the plural *šabbətōtay* 'my Sabbaths,' the singular *šabbāt* is the implicit antecedent of *hī(w)*' 'it' (Jacob 1992: 847). (One could also "fix" the grammar, though it is hardly necessary, by rendering *'ōt hī[w]'* as "a sign exists.")

sign between you and between me. The sign *('ōt)* has been an important theme in the Priestly Source since Creation (Gen 1:14), when the astral bodies were designed "as signs *('ōtōt)* and as festivals and as days and as years." Some signs are aimed at humans alone, such as the wonders Moses works for Israel (chap. 4) and against Egypt (7:3; 8:19; 10:1–2, etc.). Others are primarily for Yahweh, like the paschal blood that protects Israel's houses (12:13). As a Covenant sign, however, the Sabbath bears significance for both God and Israel (31:13, 17; also Ezek 20:12, 20). We may compare two other Priestly Covenant signs: the rainbow (Gen 9:8–17) and circumcision (Gen 17:11).

Paradoxically, the Sabbath day is an invisible sign. It is also inevitable, built into time itself (Fox 1974: 577). That is, as day follows night, so the Sabbath comes, whether humanity marks it or not. Yet if a Sabbath may pass unnoted, how can it be a sign?

As far as Israel is concerned, the Sabbath like circumcision is a sign that Israel bears responsibility for actuating, or, according to 31:16, "making/doing" *(laʿăśôt).* Their desisting from work makes visible and valid Yahweh's legal relationship with Israel. If they did not keep the Sabbath, perhaps Israel and even Yahweh might forget the Covenant, with disastrous results for humanity.

Both the Sabbath and circumcision stand apart from the Torah's ordinary stipulations. Since they remind the parties of the Covenant's existence, they are comparable both to the treaty document itself and to the provision that it be periodically republished (see further pp. 301–2). (For futher consideration of signs in the Bible, see Helfmeyer [1974] and Fox [1974]; on the Sabbath and Covenant, see NOTE to 31:16, "eternal covenant.")

for your ages. I.e., eternally, in each generation; on *dōr,* see Botterweck, Freedman and Lundbom (1978) and NOTE to 3:15.

By the Priestly Writer's day the Tabernacle was no more, if it ever existed (see pp. 709–10). By the Redactor's day, much of Israel lived in exile, unable to worship in the biblically mandated manner. But the Sabbath, woven into Time's fabric, still served as an eternal and universal token of Yahweh's Covenants with the world and with Israel (cf. Jacob 1992: 854)

to know. Who is to know? According to LXX, it is Israel; according to Rashi, it is the nations. I think that the verse supplies the true answer: the Sabbath reminds both Israel and God of their covenant (cf. my discussion of *zkr* 'remember' in vol. I, pp. 179–80).

that. *Kî* is polyvalent, meaning "that," "because," "indeed," etc. (Muilenburg 1961). In the immediate context, after the verb *yd'* 'know,' "that" is the preferred translation (also Ezek 20:12; 37:28). In many parallel statements, however, "because" is called for (Lev 20:8; 21:8, 15, 23; 22:16). And in Lev 22:9, 32, the formula "I, Yahweh, am your/their sanctifier" simply provides an emphatic close to an injunction. In our verse, the ambiguity seems intentional. "I, Yahweh, am your sanctifier" is both *what* Israel knows, and the *reason* it knows; moreover, it emphatically punctuates the preceding statement.

I, Yahweh, am your sanctifier. One could also translate "I am Yahweh, your sanctifier"; on such first-person statements of self-identification, see vol. I, pp. 270–71, 578. In addition to its other functions (see previous NOTE), this pronouncement explains how the Sabbath works for Israel. It is not a sterile memorial, but it confers the recurrent benefit of sanctification. At the same time, in the larger context of Exodus, "I . . . am your sanctifier" refers to the task at hand: building Yahweh's holy abode that sheds sanctity upon all. (On the parallels between the Sabbath and the Tabernacle, see further pp. 675–76, 691–94.) Finally, the statement identifies by name the Deity who consecrates Israel, thereby reemphasizing the Torah's requirement to serve no god but Yahweh.

For the Priestly Source, the whole goal of religion, in all its facets, is to maximize and prolong contact between Yahweh and Israel (see pp. 675–703). When they keep the Sabbath, Israelites imitate God and partake of his Holiness; Yahweh draws near. Conversely, Sabbath violation threatens the entire community. No less than murderers and adulterers, Sabbath-breakers must be extirpated lest they spread pollution and bring about alienation from God.

31:14. *a Holiness for you.* The following verse will call the seventh day "a Holiness of Yahweh." (The preposition *lə-* may be translated as both "for" and "of.") The Sabbath belongs to both God and Israel.

its desecrater. That is, one who treats the Sabbath as an ordinary day (Rashi) and thereby causes ritual pollution. *Məhalle(y)hā* 'its desecrater' stands in antithetical parallelism to the preceding suffixed Pi'el participle *məqaddiškem* 'your sanctifier.' The verb *hillēl* refers to Sabbath violation also in Isa 56:2, 6; Ezek 20:13, 16, 21, 24; 22:8; 23:38; Neh 13:17–18; for a general study, see Dommershausen (1980).

put to death. According to Num 15:32–36, by stoning. For the number incongruence *məhalle(y)hā* (plural participle) . . . *yûmāt* (singular finite verb), Dillmann (1880: 330) compares Gen 27:29; Lev 17:14; 19:8.

a task. Məlā(')kâ refers both to an individual task and collectively to labors of all sorts. Here, the context naturally makes one think first of building the Tabernacle (cf. *məlā[']kâ* in 31:3, 5; chaps. 35–36 *passim*, etc.). The Rabbis, who presumably inherited a popular tradition of what constituted prohibited work, attempted theoretically to ground their Sabbath laws in the acts required for making the wilderness sanctuary (*b. Šabb.* 49b; *y. Šabb.* 7:2).

Cut Off. On the penalty of *kārēt*—loss of posterity and alienation from the land, often in addition to judicial execution—see vol. I, pp. 403–4. Note that Ezekiel blames the destruction and exile of Judah specifically on Sabbath desecration (Ezekiel 20; 22:8, 26; 23:38).

31:15. *Sabbatical Sabbath.* The expressions *šabbātôn* 'Sabbatical' and *šabbat šabbātôn* 'Sabbatical Sabbath' describe Blasting Day (Jewish Rosh Hashanah) (Lev 23:24), Clearing Day (Yom Kippur) (Lev 16:31; 23:32), the first and eighth days of Shelters (Sukkoth) (Lev 23:39), the year of Release *(šəmittâ)* (Lev 25:4–5) and the Sabbath itself (Exod 16:23; 31:15; 35:2; Lev 23:3). Like other nouns of the pattern *qittālôn* (< **qattalōn*), *šabbātôn* denotes a concrete example or the condition of its root meaning, in this case *šbt* 'cease, rest' (cf. Barth 1894: 324). In other words, *šabbātôn* means something like "quintessential cessation." (The reason we do not find the expected evolution **šabbatōn > *šibbātôn* was doubtless the influence of *šabbāt* 'Sabbath.')

To call the Sabbath a "Sabbatical" provides emphasis through tautology; indeed, much of the language in 31:12–17 is redundant (see p. 715). *Šabbat šabbātôn* is also coordinated with *qōdeš* 'Holiness' (16:23; 31:15; 35:2; Lev 23:3), evoking the phrase *qōdeš qŏdāšîm* 'Holiness of Holinesses.'

a Holiness of Yahweh. Applied to the Sabbath in 16:23; 31:15; Lev 23:3, the same formula is engraved on the Great Priest's "blossom" (28:36; 39:30). Elsewhere, it describes property transferred to God and therefore taboo for ordinary human use (Leviticus 27); see further NOTE to 28:36. The seventh day might similarly be described as time that an Israelite donates to Yahweh, rather than using it for private purposes.

It should occasion little surprise that God speaks of himself briefly in the third person. First, "a Holiness for Yahweh" is a cliché. Second, this is a common phenomenon; cf. 19:11, 22, 24 and numerous other examples.

31:16. *doing the Sabbath.* The paradoxical phrase *la'ăśôt 'et-haššabbāt*, paralleled in Deut 5:15, has occasioned some comment. Surely, one keeps the Sabbath by *not* doing; in Gen 2:4, for instance, *šbt* 'cease' and *'śy* 'do, make' are quasi-antonyms. Ibn Ezra infers that 31:16 really mandates making preparations *before* the Sabbath.

But the diction is not so strange. One similarly "makes" a festival by performing its prescribed actions (Num 9:4, 6, 13; Deut 16:10; cf. Ps 118:24). In Exod 31:16, refraining from work is simply viewed as a positive act. In a sense, '*śy* is tantamount to *šmr* 'keep, observe, guard,' with which it is associated here and elsewhere (e.g., Lev 18:4–5; 19:37; 20:8, 22; 22:31, etc.).

The main point is that the Sabbath does not just happen. Even merely noticing it is insufficient. The Sabbath must be "made," just as the Tabernacle and the world itself were both made (31:17) (Van Den Eynde 1996: 508). Noting that '*śy* 'make' has appeared and will appear again over 100 times in the Tabernacle pericope, Jacob (1992: 853–54) aptly characterizes the Sabbath as a Tabernacle in time (see also Heschel 1951; below, pp. 675–76, 691–94).

eternal covenant. It is not clear in what sense a special day can be a *bərît* 'covenant, treaty, pact' (for discussion, see Van Den Eynde 1996: 509–11). Perhaps here *bərît* connotes a covenant *stipulation*, as in Rabbinic Hebrew (generally apropos of circumcision, however). We may also compare the allotment of the "Face Bread," called an "eternal covenant" in Lev 24:8. Another possibility is that "covenant" is shorthand for "covenant *sign*," like circumcision (Gen 17:11) and the rainbow (Gen 9:8–17) (see NOTE to 31:13, "sign between you and between me"). Or the Sabbath might conceivably be understood as a covenant *blessing.* The best interpretation is that the Sabbath, as the Covenant's symbol, is metaphorically equivalent to the Covenant itself, i.e., is an icon in time rather than space. The term "covenant" may also imply conditionality: there is not just a penalty for ignoring the Sabbath but also a reward for its observance (Van Den Eynde, pp. 508–9). For further discussion of covenants, see pp. 301–2, 694–95.

31:17. *Between me and between Israel's Sons.* It is unclear how to divide the clauses across vv 16–17. One might equally render with Vg, ". . . an eternal covenant between me and between Israel's Sons. It is a sign . . ."; cf. Gen 9:16, "an eternal covenant between Deity and between each living *soul.*"

sign, for seven days. The word *kî* is ambiguous (Muilenburg 1961). By my translation, the Sabbath is a sign for Israel *because* Yahweh created the world in six days and then rested. Ibn Ezra interprets differently, however: "it is a sign for eternity *that* six days . . ."; i.e., the Sabbath bears witness to Yahweh's creation of the world. To deny one is to deny the other.

caught his breath. Or perhaps "revitalized himself." *Wayyinnāpaš* derives from *nepeš* 'soul, life, breath' and may properly refer to respiration (Rashi; compare Gen 2:7). The verb otherwise applies to weary humans refreshing themselves (Exod 23:12; 2 Sam 16:14); recall, too, Israel's "shortness of breath" when in bondage (Janzen 1997: 222). But here it is God himself who catches his breath, after the labor of speaking all Being into existence (cf. Driver 1911: 345). (In Exodus, the verb fittingly concludes seven chapters of uninterrupted divine discourse.) Although Holzinger (1900: 147) finds the image of a weary Deity surprising in P, Priestly theology is in fact quintessentially anthropomorphic. Man is formed in God's image, and vice versa (Gen 1:26–27; 5:1–2). It would be more accurate to describe P's God as transhuman in substance and social status but humanoid in form (Johnson 1961: 14; see further pp. 680–82, 685, 769). The other gods of the ancient Near East, too, labor and rest; see Batto (1987).

In the composite text, with the expression "ceased and caught his breath" the story itself pauses. Bezalel and company do not immediately set to work. When the tale is resumed, we read not of the Tabernacle's construction but of the Gold Calf.

31:18. *two Testimony Tablets.* After the lengthy Tabernacle instructions, we are returned to the matter of 24:12–18, where Moses was summoned to receive the Law.

written by Deity's finger. Just what is implied by the phrase *kətûbîm bə'eṣba' 'ĕlōhîm*, paralleled in Deut 9:10 (cf. Exod 32:16)? Why not say "written by Yahweh's finger?" In Exod 8:15, I tentatively rendered *'eṣba' 'ĕlōhîm* as "a divine finger," with a NOTE explaining it could also be translated "Deity's finger" (vol. I, p. 328; see also NOTE to 31:3, "a divine spirit," above). Here, although one may presume that Yahweh himself has inscribed the tablets (see further NOTE to 32:16, "Deity's . . . Deity's"), I would not eliminate "written by a divine finger," since the diction seems deliberately vague. The phrase could even be understood as "supremely skillful writing" (cf. Thomas 1968: 120–21).

Why the reference to a "finger" in particular? I would draw one of two inferences: either "finger" here is tantamount to *yād* 'hand, arm' in the sense of "agency"; or, more likely, Yahweh has literally engraved the stone with his adamantine digit as easily as a man might write in the dust with his finger.

COMMENT

THE PROBLEM OF MEANING

To the religious sensibility, the manufacture of numinous objects is inherently mysterious. How can the man-made be or become divine? The biblical prophets deride polytheists for the folly of worshiping images made by man from lifeless stone and wood (below, p. 778 n. 84). Yet the Israelites confront an analogous dilemma. Can a human-built structure of metal, wood and cloth really be God's home?

In fact, idolaters were and are considerably more sophisticated than an Isaiah or an Ezekiel would allow. Mesopotamian artisans performed complex rituals for converting raw and shaped materials into receptacles for the gods' spirits (Jacobsen 1987a; Walker and Dick 1999). Sacred icons were acknowledged to be artificial yet simultaneously acclaimed as divine. Temples similarly were known to be sponsored by kings and built by craftsmen and yet were venerated as manifestations of a divine prototype and as portals to Heaven (see Berlejung 1996).

This is not a quirk of some extinct "proto-logical" or "mythopoetic" mentality that the West has long transcended. For centuries, theologians have been exercised over whether and how flour and water might become Christ's literal body. And even secular moderns unconcernedly call a flat, painted canvas *Mona Lisa*, whereas its subject has been dead for centuries. René Magritte's famous painting *Ceci n'est pas une pipe*, among many other works of modern art, sets out deliberately to expose our ingrained tendency to confound signifier and signified.

In Exodus 25–31, 35–40, we see the Priestly Writer wrestling with the Tabernacle's dual nature as human artifact and divine abode. Concentrating on materials and measurements, he carefully skirts questions of meaning. What do the various elements represent? In what sense is Yahweh present?

Despite the matter-of-fact tone, we get a general sense of the structure's significance. The men and women who build the Tabernacle are inspired by Yahweh and follow a divinely revealed pattern. A ritual sequence in which blood figures prominently translates the finished product from the impure, mundane realm to the domain of Holiness. Although literally built by humans, the resulting structure is nonetheless "The sanctum . . . [Yahweh's] hands founded" (15:17). (For further discussion of the Tabernacle's significance as holy space, see below, pp. 686–95.)

METHODOLOGY

The modern reader of the Tabernacle pericope confronts a predicament that is, alas, too familiar. How may we comprehend this technical manual, written in inscrutable jargon, at times unnecessarily full and at times maddeningly vague, referring to illustrations that somehow have gotten lost (25:9, 40; 26:30; 27:8; Num 8:4)?

All analyses, including my own, necessarily negotiate between two interrelated questions: How is the Tabernacle constructed? And is it real or fictitious? By synthesizing two disparate bodies of evidence, the biblical text and archaeological realia, we risk entrapment in circular logic. The supposed verisimilitude of an archaeologically informed Tabernacle reconstruction cannot legitimately be cited as evidence of its historicity. But neither can a model contrived without recourse to archaeology be proffered as evidence of ahistoricity. We must consult the archaeological record judiciously, without straining to make the Tabernacle real or unreal, and postpone the question of reality. Provisionally, I shall accept at face value the text's claim to describe an actual object. But if some details appear to contradict the archaeological record and/or sound engineering principles—so be it.

A more easily avoided and hence less excusable error is the importation of alien esthetics and even numerology. One may pardon Philo (*Moses* 2.71–108), an avowed allegorist who lived long ago, but I feel less charitable toward Kennedy (1898), whose classic study invokes such specious evidence as the equilateral shape of New Jerusalem (Rev 21:16) to justify the Tabernacle's supposedly cubic inner chamber (p. 667). That Kennedy's (pp. 660–61) reckoning is in fact wrong or at least inconsistent further betrays his bias (on the problematic thickness of Kennedy's frames, cf. Homan 2002: 142). McNeile (1908: lxxxviii–lxxxix), for his part, takes the numbers three, four, seven and ten to represent God (3), Humanity (4), Unity (7 and 12) and Completeness (10). On what evidence? Scholars also err to worry whether certain richly decorated parts of the Tabernacle might be hidden from view—as though unseen they would no longer serve to glorify God and impress the reader. If my reconstruction seems asymmetrical, devoid of numerological significance, wasteful or downright ugly—so be it.

Another misguided presupposition is that the Tabernacle's dimensions must be proportional to the Jerusalem Temple's, whether First or Second, whether the Tabernacle is based on the Temple or vice versa (e.g., *Mel. Mišk.* 1; ibn Ezra on 26:31; Wellhausen [1885: 17–51]; see Utzschneider [1988: 270–79] for an overview). These matters had best be kept separate. And I have the same objection to comparisons between the Tabernacle and the Arad Temple (Aharoni 1973; Friedman 1987: 183). In the following discussion, parallels will be noted but not insisted on. If in some dimensions the structures are congruent, in others not—so be it.

The challenges before us are formidable. No one has yet definitively calculated the Tabernacle's dimensions, and a conclusive solution seems most unlikely. (On the history of scholarship, too voluminous to survey here, see Homan [2002: 89–185 *passim*]; for an unusually clear presentation of rabbinic interpretations, see Lockshin [1997] *ad loc.*) Of its very nature, the equation eludes a definitive solution because there are simply too many variables. All approaches must make certain assumptions, so here is mine: *An omitted measurement is treated as negligible*, unless the result is nonsense (e.g., the height of the pillars for the three screens). Without this modest axiom, I would not venture to reconstruct the Tabernacle at all.

SPECULATION: Although the artisans are told clearly how to make the Tabernacle's components, Moses alone beholds the plans or model *(tabnît)* and alone knows how to assemble the whole (cf. *Exod. Rab.* 52:4; Utzschneider 1988: 153–54; NOTE to 40:18). It is striking that the text's chief ambiguities pertain precisely to the points of juncture (see below). Rather than fault the Priestly Writer for imprecision, we might conclude that *we are not meant to understand*, lest we make a Tabernacle ourselves.

If the Priestly Writer does not permit us exactly to comprehend the Tabernacle's structure, still less does he tell us what it all means. This "muteness" (Levenson 1988: 95) should temper but not ban scholarly interpretation. Whether or not P admits it, the Tabernacle necessarily possessed symbolic resonances for ancient readers and the author himself, not to mention those who worshiped there, if it ever stood. The Priestly Writer's reticence is ultimately related to P's oft-noted lack of liturgy or incantations (cf. Kaufman 1960: 108–10). To speak aloud is to qualify, to explain, to engage in myth.

SPECULATION: P's muteness is indeed impressive. But it also incurs the risk of independent interpretations—such as mine—and a degree of theological pluralism that was probably the farthest thing from the author's mind. I cannot imagine that the Priestly Writer simply held no convictions in these matters. I can easily believe, however, that he forbore to publicize his opinion. Perhaps, as in countless mystery religions and secret societies, the authorized interpretations of ritual acts and equipment were revealed only to priestly candidates in the course of their training and indoctrination.

I shall now take the reader on a leisurely guided tour of the Tabernacle, beginning as an actual worshiper would, with the outer court. We will cross its zones of increasing sanctity, until finally we penetrate the "Holiness of Holinesses" beyond the Veil, a privilege accorded only to a Great Priest and only on Yom Kippur.

THE PEOPLE'S COURT: THE PLAZA
(ordained in 27:9–19, built in 38:9–20)

I would define a minimal shrine as an altar standing in a sacred enclosure (for archaeological examples of the *bāmâ* 'High Place,' see Mazar 1992: 169–70). Worship, i.e., sacrifice, is sent straight up to Heaven. There is no attempt to bring the god down to Earth into a statue or sacred cella, as in a true temple and the Tabernacle (see further below, pp. 519, 681–703).

According to the Torah, located in the middle of the Israelite camp is an enclosure. It smells of butchery and cooking. The *ḥāṣēr* 'Plaza' measures fifty cubits (c. 75 feet/25 m.) wide and one hundred cubits (c. 150 feet/50 m.) long. Its space is defined by five-cubit high poles (c. 7.5 feet/2.5 m.), twenty on the long sides and ten in the back, spaced at five-cubit intervals. Between are suspended white linen sheets, each panel five cubits wide, as may be inferred from 38:18 (see NOTE). The sheets are tied down with cords and pegs and may depend from horizontal spars, if that is the meaning of *ḥăšūqîm* (NOTE to 27:10). Whether the curtains hang inside, outside or between the posts is not clearly stated, but the numbers work only if we assume that each upright stands at the midpoint of its hanging, like a ship's mast (*Mel. Mišk.* 5; Loewenstamm 1968: 537; Haran 1978: 154–55 n. 11; NOTE to 27:9, "sheets"; fig. 17). The panels are perhaps stitched together to bar side entry, but this is only an inference. The posts are anchored with bronze stakes, presumably to prevent the walls from being blown down (27:19). Still, it all appears rather rickety. Perhaps the *ḥăšūqîm* have the additional function of joining the uprights one to another for greater stability. The Plaza's fluttering, translucent sheets stand only slightly higher than a man's head. They both reveal and conceal, lending an attractive mystery to the space they enclose (Cole 1973: 197).

The text does not say where in the Plaza the Tabernacle and Altar stand. Virtually all scholars divide the Plaza into two 50 × 50 cubit squares. At the center of one, they place the Testimony Chest, the Tabernacle's focal point. At the center of the other, they place the Bronze Altar (e.g., *b.* '*Erub.* 23b; *Mel. Mišk.* 5; Kennedy 1898: 657; Cassuto 1967: 368; cf. Philo *Moses* 2.91–94). The portal of the Tabernacle thus falls at the Plaza's exact midpoint. None of this comes from Exodus. I think it more likely that the Tabernacle is jammed against the Plaza's western wall, permitting a maximal number to congregate before its opening and around the Altar. But we cannot be sure; perhaps the space behind the Tabernacle was put to good use (see below). In general, the author's reticence on the Plaza contrasts with his volubility on the Tabernacle, reflecting the two spaces' relative grades of sanctity.

What is the Plaza's purpose? Unlike the Tabernacle, it is accessible to lay wor-

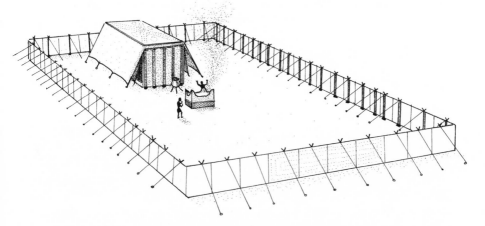

FIGURE 17. Tabernacle compound

shipers for slaughtering their sacrifices and for assemblies, provided participants are ritually clean (e.g., Lev 1:11; 8:3). The Plaza also affords a level of insulation, shielding the divine presence from contact with corruption in the camp (see further pp. 527–28, 682–703). Haran (1978: 184–85) argues that there are realms of graduated Holiness even within the Plaza, but P does not make this explicit.

Paradoxically, the Plaza is often called "Meeting Tent's Opening." Its expanse is, as it were, a three-dimensional threshold, a liminal space that is not just crossed but can be inhabited, at least temporarily. Worshiping in the Plaza, the people are neither in nor out of the world, neither inside nor outside the Tabernacle.

Exodus makes no provision for storerooms or living quarters, such as would be found in a permanent temple. Presumably these are in the camp, which may be considered part of the extended Tabernacle complex. (Alternatively, the portion of the Plaza behind the Tabernacle may be designated for utilitarian purposes.)

We enter the Plaza through the gap in its east side, a portal measuring twenty cubits. The opening is normally blocked by a curtain suspended on four posts. How one passes the Screen is unexplained — is it pushed aside, pulled up or simply removed? At any rate, gazing through, we see first the Bronze Altar and beyond it the Basin and finally the Tabernacle.

PIPELINE TO HEAVEN: THE BRONZE ALTAR
(ordained in 27:1–8, built in 38:1–7)

There are three basic ways to feed a god: by libations, by symbolic food presentations and by burnt offerings. When one burns cereal, meat or liquid on the Altar, the food ascends directly to Heaven as smoke. As the corrupt is to the pure, as matter is to spirit, so food is to smoke. What else would ethereal beings of human form but inhuman substance eat, if not translucent, intangible, gravity-defying vapors (see Judg 13:9–23; *Iliad* 8.550–52)? Fire sacrifice was universal in the ancient

Near East, and the Israelites shared with their neighbors common techniques and terminology (see Gaster 1962). (The Bible stands apart, however, in the disposition of liquids: while other cultures libated on the ground, the Bible, which acknowledges no chthonian powers, has wine poured directly onto the Altar [Num 15:5–10; Cassuto 1967: 337].)

As we learn indirectly from the prophets' condemnations of empty worship (e.g., Isa 1:11–14; Amos 5:21–23; Micah 6:6–7), sacrifice was supremely important to the common Israelite. Few could minister directly to Yahweh as priests; few could commune directly with him as prophets. But any man or woman could "nourish" God with the prescribed offerings in hopes of a good return. (On the rationale of sacrifice, see further below, pp. 702–3.)

Altars take many forms. On the one hand, the preferred, archaic shape is a simple mound of earth or a heap of uncut stones (20:24[21]–26[23]; cf. Gen 31:46–54; Judg 13:19–20; 1 Sam 6:14; 14:33–35; 1 Kgs 1:9; 18:31–32). But this apparently did not suit the Priestly Writer, perhaps because anyone can build such an altar and sacrifice upon it. The other extreme is the monumental altar favored in the great temples of the ancient Near East. (On the forms of ancient altars, Galling's [1925] classic treatment is still useful.)

Because the Tabernacle complex is continually on the move, and a large pile of dirt or stone would be impractical to transport, its Altar is something of a compromise. Instead of building a new installation at each campsite (cf. 17:15; 18:12), Bezalel constructs a hollow box that is probably to be filled with new earth and/or stones whenever the Tabernacle is erected (NOTES to 27:4–8). The Altar stands three cubits tall (c. 4.5 feet/1.5 m.); its cooking surface measures twenty-five square cubits (c. 7.5 × 7.5 feet/2.5 × 2.5 m.), dimensions replicated in a stone altar excavated at Arad (NOTE to 27:1, "five . . . five . . . three"). But some commentators raise a problem: how could an ancient priest standing, say, five feet tall, reach over to manipulate the offerings in the center of the Altar or tend the fire and clean the ashes? Many have inferred that the Altar is surrounded by a ledge for priests to stand on, while *Mel. Mišk.* 11 envisions a ramp. I have trouble finding any of this in Exodus, however (NOTE to 27:5)—indeed, 20:26(23) forbids it—and think that an average-sized officiant would probably do fine with proper implements. (For the priests' greater convenience, however, we might lower the sacrificial surface by supposing that the 4.5 cubit height includes the horns.)

We are not told the structure of the Altar in Solomon's Temple, but 1 Kgs 8:64 and 2 Kgs 16:14–15 imply that the Tabernacle's Bronze Altar continued in use for centuries (cf. Ezek 9:2; 2 Chr 4:1). Eventually, however, King Ahaz would build a more sumptuous installation (2 Kgs 16:10–16), while Ezekiel envisioned a grand, stepped affair for a restored and reformed Temple (Ezek 43:13–17).

As with the Tabernacle, just where the Bronze Altar stands in the Plaza is unspecified. By the accepted reconstruction (e.g., *Mel. Mišk.* 11), it occupies the center, as in the Arad temple Stratum XI (tenth century B.C.E.; in Stratum X, however, the courtyard was reconfigured so that the altar stood against a wall [Aharoni 1968: 18–23; for an updated discussion, see Zevit 2001: 156–71]). And yet the

Tabernacle Altar is said to be by "Meeting Tent's Opening" (29:42; Lev 4:7, 18 etc.). This may imply that it stands near the Tabernacle entrance, with the Basin closer still (Exod 30:18).

The Altar embodies the paradox at the Tabernacle's heart: how can impure humans interact with a pure God? On the one hand, as a direct channel to Heaven, the Altar is "Holiness of Holinesses," no less than the Tabernacle proper (29:37). A nonpriest may not officiate at the Altar, any more than he may enter the Tabernacle. Sacrificial animals must be "clean," i.e., legally edible and without defect (Leviticus 1; 22:19–24; Deut 15:21; 17:1; cf. Mal 1:7, 13). Any grain presented must be unleavened (Exod 23:18; Lev 2:11; cf. Judg 6:19–21; Amos 4:5; vol. I, pp. 433–34). The officiant himself must be of sound body in order to approach the Tabernacle and the Altar (Lev 21:17–23). And the fire by which the offering ascends to Yahweh's nostrils removes any remaining taint. In fact, it was originally kindled by Yahweh himself (Lev 9:24).

And yet the Altar's metal—bronze not gold—associates it with a realm of lesser purity, as perhaps does the fact that it is wrapped for transport in purple, not blue (Num 4:13) (Milgrom 1972: 763; below, pp. 527–28). Whereas the layman cannot even see the contents of the inner chamber (Num 4:20), he may at least see (but not touch) the Altar (Exod 29:37) (Milgrom, p. 763). The cumulative import of these observations is that the Altar, like the Plaza surrounding it, is liminal, a boundary between Heaven and Earth.

By this understanding, the Altar's horns, whatever their practical function (see NOTE to 27:2), may been seen as arrows pointing up, as forming the lower terminus of a conduit to Heaven. After the Altar's horns are purified with blood and consecrated with oil (29:36–37; Lev 8:15), the space they define belongs to God's realm, not Man's. (On the horns as creating a zone of asylum, see NOTE to 21:14, "my altar.") To desecrate an altar, one either de-horns it (Amos 3:14) or burns on it unclean, dead matter (2 Kgs 23:16, 20).

SPECULATION: Girard (1977: 36–38) regards blood sacrifices as replacing society's ultimate sanction, capital punishment. I similarly imagine the imbrued Altar horns, tokens of divine pardon for inadvertent violations (see NOTE to 21:14), as a *symbolic threat* against anyone violating the narrow bounds of acceptable bloodshed (compare the Roman *fasces* and the various divine weapons paraded about by the Assyrians [Van Buren 1945; Hrouda and Krecher 1969; Spaey 1994]). While proof in such matters is not attainable, that the involuntary manslayer, guilty before Man but innocent before God, receives asylum at the horns is most suggestive. See further pp. 206–11, 531.

NEXT TO GODLINESS: THE BASIN
(ordained in 30:17–21, built in 38:8)

Moving inward, we next pass by the Basin. The association of water with ritual purity is natural. Except in the most arid climes, water is the most common detergent. And everywhere pure water is the prime requisite for life, thus the symbolic opposite of disease, death and corruption. Ancient sanctuaries were often located near springs, which provided water for drinking, lustration and libation, as well as constituting a channel to the underworld spirits. For example, Dagan's temple at Ugarit had a spring, real or artificial (Del Olmo-Lete 1999: 30); compare also Pseudo-Lucian *Syrian Goddess* 45–48 on the pools of Hierapolis. Egyptian temples, too, featured bathing facilities for the priests (Sauneron 2000: 36). Solomon's Temple on Mount Zion was located near the Gihon spring and contained a huge basin called "the Sea" (1 Kgs 7:23–26) in addition to ten smaller lavers on wheeled carts (1 Kgs 7:27–39; 2 Chr 4:6).

The Tabernacle Basin enables priests to wash their hands and feet before entering the Tabernacle proper. Because these body parts most frequently contact the world, they must not, on pain of death, bring impurity upon the Tabernacle's sacred vessels or even its earthen floor; cf. Ps 24:4, where the one who enters Yahweh's abode must be not only pure-hearted but also *nəqî kappayim* 'pure of hands/feet.' Because the Basin stands by the door (30:18), the priests cannot miss it. Perhaps for the same reason, it is made of highly reflective bronze (see further NOTE to 38:8, "mirrors").

The Basin may have had further uses. First, we often read of sacrifices being washed (29:17; Lev 1:9, 13, etc.); perhaps this was done with the Basin's water. And the ordeal of the suspected adulteress, the "Bitter Cursing Waters" (Numbers 5), may also use water drawn from the Basin (Bekhor Shor).

Why is the Basin described apart from the other features of the Tabernacle and Plaza? Why are we not told its dimensions? Why is it not explicitly included in the transportation instructions of Numbers 4? Perhaps because the main commandment is to wash, and the vessel itself bears little inherent sanctity (Ramban) and is unnoteworthy compared to the other sacred furniture. After all, laving per se is not an act of worship but a preparation for worship (Cassuto 1967: 395). Still, according to 30:28–29; Lev 8:10–11, the Basin is endowed with ultimate Holiness through anointment. The scarcity of its mention is surprising, rather analogous to the ambiguous Holiness status of the priestly undergarments (below pp. 522–23).

THE SECRET OF HIS TABERNACLE:
THE SACRED TENT
(ordained in chap. 26; built in 36:8–38)

Finally, we approach the Tabernacle itself, standing resplendent at the enclosure's far end and emitting a heavy musk. In addition to the mystery that always attends the Holy, the Tabernacle possesses an extra measure of fascination because of the riddle of its construction. As already indicated, I do not believe in a definitive solution. But some readers may wish to appreciate fully the difficulties, and more will want to know what I consider the most likely reconstruction. To the rest, I apologize for the length and detail of the following discussion.

The Tabernacle consists of a framework of gilded wood, the *qərāšîm*, over which are draped an inner curtain of variegated wool and linen, a second curtain of goat hair and a two-ply cover of skins. The leather roof glistens with beadwork.

Although some have supposed that the two fabric curtains hang *inside* the frame (recently, Houtman 2000: 420), we know of no such inside-out tents. The closest parallel would be the tent within Tutankhamun's golden catafalque, but it, too, is draped over a frame (see Homan 2002: 107–9). As the curtains are said to *cover* (*ləkassôtô*) the Tabernacle (26:13), one would naturally assume that they are outside.

The solid substructure is composed of twenty units on each long side, plus six at the west end. The east end is left open as an entryway, comparable to the east-facing doorways of the First Temple (1 Kgs 7:39), Ezekiel's temple (Ezek 43:1–4) and the Arad shrine (Ottosson 1980: 109). Since each *qereš* is 1.5 cubits wide, one might initially think that the structure is thirty cubits long and nine cubits wide.

But here we encounter the crux of the matter, at the corners: "And two *qərāšîm* you shall make for the Tabernacle's corners at the backparts. And they shall be twinning from below; together they shall be whole up to its *head*, to the one ring. So shall it be for the two of them, for the two corners they shall be. And there shall be eight *qərāšîm* and their bases, silver; sixteen bases, two bases under the one *qereš*, and two bases under the one *qereš*" (26:23–25). What does this mean?

It turns out that the rear of the Tabernacle is composed of not six but eight *qərāšîm*. The structure of the corner pieces is unfortunately obscure. The reference to "twinning" suggests to Homan (2002: 148, 178–80) a special corner piece, a double, L-shaped unit connected by mortise and tenon — but then the text should say that each side has *twenty-one qərāšîm*. Moreover, the total of 100 silver bases (38:27) — 96 for the *qərāšîm* and 4 for the Veil — allows only two for each corner piece, not three or four as one might expect for an L-shape.

The matter is not trivial, because the Tabernacle's overall width depends upon the width of these corner pieces, which the text does not reveal. We face two options: (a) the author has forgotten to tell us, so we are entitled to guess (the majority view); (b) the text is silent because the width is the same as all the other *qərāšîm*, i.e., 1.5 cubits, and because the corners do not contribute to the length at all (my axiom). Modifying Homan, I take 26:24 to mean that each corner frame is attached permanently to one of the twenty side frames (see NOTES to 26:24 and fig. 11b). This yields a Tabernacle twelve cubits (c. 18 feet/6 m.) wide and thirty cubits (c. 45 feet/15 m.) long.

As for the structure's height, each *qereš* is said to be ten cubits tall, resting upon a "base" (*'eden*) of unspecified size. With other commentators, I assume that these bases are "shoes" enclosing the *qərāšîm*'s side pieces. They contribute weight and stability, but no additional height. Thus I envision a Tabernacle thirty cubits long, twelve cubits wide and ten cubits high.

A radically different model is adumbrated by Aharoni (1968: 25) and independently propounded in detail by Friedman (1981: 50–51). By making the *qərāšîm* overlap, the Aharoni–Friedman model shrinks the Tabernacle's length to twenty cubits and its breadth to between six and eight cubits (depending on the corner construction [see Friedman 1987: 179]). I find this theory unconvincing, however, for several reasons (see also Hurowitz 1995). First, *pace* Friedman, it is not at all "unusual" that the *qərāšîm* are 1 1/2 cubits wide, rather than one or two cubits—the half-cubit figures also in the dimensions of the Chest-*kappōret* (25:10, 17) and the Table (25:23) (cf. also 1 Kgs 7:31–32; Ezek 40:42; 43:17). Second, it is arbitrary to suppose that the frames overlap by a half-cubit; one might as well imagine half-cubit gaps in between. Third, it is equally arbitrary to suppose that the fabrics are folded in half, as they must be to cover this smaller structure. Fourth, Friedman understands '*el-mûl pǝnê hā'ōhel* 'against the Tent's front,' where the excess of the goat-hair curtain is folded, to mean "*opposite* the Tent's front"—i.e., in back—against all parallels to the phrase *mûl pǝnê* (28:25, 27, 37; 39:18, 20; Lev 8:9; Num 8:2; 2 Sam 11:15). In fact, the text has a special term for the Tabernacle's rear wall, *yarkātayim* 'backparts' (26:22, 23, 27). Fifth, Friedman's drawing (p. 140, fig. 5) does not show the large amount of excess drapery that must be bunched at the Tabernacle's rear, making it less tidy than he indicates. Sixth, in Friedman's model, the gold and bronze clasps align at the Tabernacle's opening, whereas MT states that the Veil shielding the Chest is *taḥat haqqǝrāsîm* 'under the clasps' (26:33). Since the Chest is clearly not in the doorway, Friedman halfway follows LXX *epi tōn stylōn* 'upon/against the pillars (i.e., *qǝrāsîm*),' reconstructing an unattested original **taḥat haqqǝrāsîm* 'under the frames,' which he then understands, against the normal meaning of *taḥat* 'under,' as "under *the level of* the frames." Seventh, *pace* Aharoni, that the Arad Temple measures twenty by six cubits is irrelevant. In short, the Aharoni-Friedman hypothesis creates more problems than it solves (for a defense of Friedman, however, see Homan 2002: 167–74; on Friedman's theory that the Tabernacle was lodged in the Temple's inner chamber, see below, p. 708.)

SPECULATION: Overlooked by Aharoni and Friedman, or perhaps considered too dubious for their purposes, is Ezek 41:1, "six cubits, the tent's width." If MT is correct, it is hard to imagine what *hā'ōhel* "the tent" could be if not the Tabernacle. This would constitute near-proof of the reduced Tabernacle theory. But OG (*ailam*) seems to reflect a *Vorlage* **h'ylm* (**hā'êlîm*) (BHS), in turn a miswriting of **h'wlm* (*hā'ûlām*) 'the entryway,' which makes considerably more sense (cf. Ezek 40:9; contrast Zimmerli 1983: 342).

Similar to Aharoni-Friedman but open to fewer objections is the relatively unknown analysis of Ḥayutin (1993). For Ḥayutin, that the *qǝrāsîm* overlap is not an arbitrary assumption but is stated specifically in 26:17, which he interprets: "Each *qereš* shall have *two thirds joined and overlapping*, one to the other." This translation is not impossible, although Ḥayutin's claim that '*iššâ 'el-'ǎḥōtāh* 'woman to her sister' connotes a specific mortising technique is implausible (the idiom appears in other contexts). Thus the *qǝrāsîm* define a space twenty by eight cubits, in agreement with Aharoni and Friedman. As for the curtains, Ḥayutin imagines them as extending thirty cubits, as in the standard model. Further, Ḥayutin identifies the inner structure of *qǝrāsîm* as the Tabernacle (*miškān*) proper, while the outer tent is '*ōhel mō'ēd* 'Meeting Tent.' Whereas all other models divide the Tabernacle into two chambers, Ḥayutin's Meeting Tent contains three zones of increasing sanctity: a pavilion extending in front, the outer sanctum and the inner sanctum. That P makes some such distinction seems plausible in such passages as 40:34–35; Num 3:38, but the author's penchant for quasi-poetic repetition may be a better explanation. Ultimately, I am unpersuaded by Ḥayutin as well.

If thirty by twelve by ten cubits are the Tabernacle's most likely outer dimensions, what of the interior? Again, since the text does not tell us the *qərāšîm*'s width, I take it to be negligible. The inner and outer dimensions are not appreciably different.

Securing the *qərāšîm* side by side is a set of crossbars, whose disposition is uncertain. A Rabbinic interpretation elicited by the definite article in "*the* inner crossbar" (26:28) visualizes a single pole with two right angles (⊓) running through the south, east and north walls (*b. Šabb.* 98b; illustration in Lockshin 1997: 339). While this is fantastical, it raises the real question of stability. In addition to the "one ring" in each corner, what holds the walls together (see NOTES to 26:24)? Maximal stability would require crossed diagonal beams (i.e., an X) to keep the corners just. Instead, it seems that the curtains' weight and the tension of the ropes suffice to anchor the sides.

The Tabernacle's inner curtain of linen and wool (the "Tabernacle") is composed of ten panels, each measuring 4×28 cubits. Assembled, they form a grand fabric of 40×28 cubits (c. 2,520 square feet/280 square meters) (fig. 7, p. 407). The goat-hair curtain (the "Tent") is slightly larger. It contains eleven panels each measuring 4×30 cubits, yielding a total of 44×30 cubits (c. 2,970 square feet/330 square meters) (fig. 8). If it hangs vertically, the inner curtain ends two cubits from the ground, while the outer ends one cubit from the ground. Presumably this space is at least partly if not entirely filled by the silver bases enveloping the *qərāšîm* at the bottom.

According to 26:9, one panel of the goat-hair curtain is "doubled." This might mean one of two things: either it is folded in half, so that the outer curtain really covers 42×30 cubits; or it is entirely folded over its neighbor, so that the total is 40×30. The answer is provided in 26:12–13, which addresses the discrepancy between the two curtains. According to 26:13, the outer curtain overhangs the inner curtain by a cubit on each side, for a total excess of two cubits. This is as we would expect, since the inner curtain is 28 cubits wide, while the outer is 30. Exod 26:12, however, makes the excess in the rear a half-panel, or two cubits. This resolves the meaning of 26:9, assuming the two curtains align in the Tabernacle's front. The outer curtain's eleventh panel must be folded in half, so that the whole covers 42 cubits, two more than the inner curtain. This excess half-curtain is said to lie "against the Tent's front." Most likely, the two extra cubits are draped over the opening as a valance to keep out light and rain (fig. 9, p. 409; Kennedy 1898: 662).

Inside the Tabernacle, the Veil hangs on four posts. Its dimensions are unspecified, but if it reaches from floor to ceiling, it should be twelve cubits wide by ten cubits high. It is placed exactly "under the clasps" (26:33), i.e., the golden fasteners of the inner curtain, partitioning the Tabernacle into a twenty-cubit-long outer chamber, the "Holiness," and a ten-cubit long inner chamber, the "Holiness of Holinesses." The Veil has been compared, on the one hand, to the partition-hangings of Bedouin tents; on the other hand, to cultic screens such as apparently existed at Late Bronze Age Hazor (Mazar 1992: 172) and Beth Shan (Ottosson 1980: 66) (cf. also Clement of Alexandria's [*Pedagogue* 3.4.2] description of the hangings shrouding the interior of an Egyptian temple.) The bipartite Tabernacle is far simpler than its mythological prototype: the tent of Canaanite 'Ilu (below pp. 376, 410, 703–5), with its seven or eight chambers (*KTU* 1.3.v.11, 26).

At the Tabernacle's eastward opening stands the *māsāk* 'Screen' suspended on five posts. Presumably it is twelve cubits wide and either eight or ten cubits tall, depending on whether it meets or is tucked under the goat-hair valance (figs. 9, 17).

My reconstruction may raise some objections. As already noted, if the Tabernacle's wooden framework measures 30 cubits long by 12 cubits wide by 10 cubits high, then the inner curtain covers only the top eight cubits of each side, leaving the lower two cubits bare (8 + 8 + 12 = 28). In the rear, however, the curtain covers the structure's entire height (10 + 30 = 40). As for the goat-hair curtain, it would cover the top nine cubits on each side (9 + 9 + 12 = 30) and would have an excess of two cubits in the rear (2 + 10 + 30 = 42). Moreover, the clasps holding the two curtains together are not aligned, as one might have expected, especially from 26:33 "under the clasps" (ibn Ezra; fig. 8). (This nonalignment could be intentional, however, to minimize leakage.)

The whole thing seems esthetically strange, like a poorly fitting garment. But all reconstructions involve overhangs, shortfalls and bunches of fabric. The Tabernacle also resembles no tent known from antiquity or modernity (on Bedouin tents, see Musil 1928: 61–76; Dalman 1939: 1–44; Dickson 1983: 54–60). To cover the substructure tidily would require not a rectangular curtain but a cruciform, like the Egyptian tent of Queen Isi-em-Kheb (Forbes 1957: 43 fig. 11). I infer that the curtains do not hang straight down but extend to the sides, secured by guylines and pegs (27:19; 35:18; 38:20, 31; 39:40) to allow glimpses of the golden *qərāšîm* and their silver bases (Bekhor Shor), to let light and air into the Tabernacle, and to make the structure less boxlike and more tentlike (fig. 17). (The alternatives are that the outer curtain's rear excess is draped on the ground [Cassuto 1967: 352–53] or folded over like the extra two cubits in the front, perhaps sheathing the inner curtain.)

Finally, to shelter the Tabernacle from the elements, there is a doubled covering of leather (see NOTE to 26:14, "skins . . . skins"). Because its dimensions are not given, we do not know whether the cover protects more than just the roof.

Compared to ancient temples, the Tabernacle of Exodus is of modest size (c. 45 feet long × 18 feet wide × 15 feet tall/15 m. × 6 m. × 5 m.). Whereas Solomon's Temple takes seven years to build (1 Kgs 6:37–38), the Tabernacle is finished in nine months or less (19:1; 40:2, 17) (Kennedy 1898: 666). Yet, in one sense, the Tabernacle is more complex than a solid temple. It is modular, designed for quick disassembly, easy transport and rapid reassembly. Durham (1987: 373) notes the frequent reference to carrying poles, frames set in separate bases, crossbars, hooks, clasps, etc. The roving, flimsy Tabernacle contrasts with stereotype of the ancient temple as the immovable, eternal *omphalus mundi*.

THOU PREPAREST A TABLE:
THE GOLDEN TABLE OF FACE BREAD
(ordained in 25:23–30, built in 37:10–16)

Exercising in our minds the priests' privilege of entering the Tabernacle, we are surrounded by Griffins, heavenly denizens woven into the tapestries (see, however, NOTE to 26:1, "Griffins"). These two-dimensional figures offer a foretaste of the solid Griffins of gold, still concealed behind the Veil. The room is musty from the Spice Incense. In it are three items of furniture, all golden (fig. 13, p. 420). First, on our right, we see the Golden Table, with twelve unleavened loaves, incense and libation vessels.

We humans express love by care and feeding—generally, of our families. The cosmic powers, one would think, should require nothing of humanity (cf. Plato *Laws* 899E). On the other hand, since a god can be childishly truculent, one might do well to treat him like a child—or, according to one sardonic Mesopotamian text, "like a dog" (*ANET* 438), coddling him in order to cultivate a degree of dependency (for parallels, see Burkert 1996: 144). For their part, the gods may condescend to be fed by us, just as we might eat a simple meal prepared and proudly presented by a child (Janzen 1997: 198).

Ancient literature, including the Bible, is equivocal on whether the gods actually need such nourishment. While Mesopotamian hymns and prayers praise deities as essentially omnipotent, mythology depicts the same gods as starving when temporarily deprived of sacrifices, then gathering about an offering "like flies" (*Gilgamesh* XI:161 [*ANET* 95]). Similarly in the Bible, the Torah mandates daily offerings called God's "food/bread *(leḥem)*" (Lev 3:11, 16; 21:6, 8, 17, 21, 22; 22:25; Num 28:2, 24 [all P]; cf. Ezek 44:7). And yet Micah 6:7 scoffs, "Does Yahweh delight in thousands of rams, in tens of thousands of oil streams?" and Ps 50:12–13 protests, "If I [Yahweh] were hungry, I would not tell you; for mine is the earth and its fullness. Should I eat bulls' flesh, drink goats' blood?" (see also 1 Sam 15:22; Isa 1:10–17; 29:13; Jer 6:20; 7:4, 8, 21–26; Hos 6:6; Amos 5:21–27; Ps 40:7–8; 51:18–19; Prov 15:8; 21:3, 27). Evidently, there was some disagreement on the matter even among the Bible's authors.

In the ancient Near East, as already noted, gods received food in three basic ways. First, liquid nourishment was poured onto the earth as a libation. Second, solid food was sent skyward by being burnt on an altar. With both methods, the food went directly to the deities, whose labile essences were most like the liquids or vapors they absorbed. In a third practice, however, edibles were placed before the god's statue upon a table, the earthly equivalent of a heavenly table (cf. *KTU* 1.4.i.38; 22.i.16; 109.31; 161.15; Isa 65:11). After a decorous time, the food was removed and consumed by priests performing the happy duty of *imitatio dei.*

It is possible to characterize this practice with empathy. "The food was evidently not consumed by the god. Only a part of his incorporeal soul was present in his statue, and the god's meal thus transpired beyond the limits of human perception, the immaterial spirit of the food passing into the divine soul without any apparent change in the arrangement of the offerings heaped on the altars"

(Sauneron 2000: 82–83). But one might take a jaundiced view even in antiquity—witness the satire in the apocryphon Bel and the Dragon, or in an Aramaic text from Egypt (Steiner and Nims 1984). Aristophanes *Plutus* 676–81 is an even more instructive example because it comes from a polytheistic society:

> I beheld the priest
> Whipping the cheese-cakes and the figs from off
> The holy table; thence he coasted round
> To every altar, spying what was left,
> And everything he found he consecrated
> Into a sort of sack. (trans. B. B. Roger, LCL)

What is placed on the table varies from culture to culture. While ancient Near Eastern art and texts depict offering tables heaped daily with bread (references in Gane 1992: 190–91) and also fruit and meat (e.g., ANEP figs. 392, 400, 624–28, 630–35, 637; ANET 343), the Torah mandates only a weekly presentation of twelve unleavened loaves. The Table is not placed directly before Yahweh's presence, i.e., the Chest and *kappōret*. Instead, it stands to one side. After a week, the priests eat the cakes (Lev 24:5–9), since, unlike fruit and meat, unleavened bread retains its edibility. Perhaps the absence of leaven and the ultra-pure environment were even believed to retard decay (cf. vol. I, pp. 433–34, 439–40, 600).

In addition to bread, the Tabernacle Table carries incense and libation vessels (see NOTES to 25:29). The ensemble is reminiscent of the great golden table of Babylon described by Diodorus Siculus *Bibliotheca Historica* 2.9.7–8, which supposedly weighed 500 talents and was set with two drinking cups and two censers (cf. Herodotus 1.181, 183).

Num 4:7 calls the Tabernacle Table *šulḥan happānîm* 'the Face Table'; the bread upon it is *leḥem happānîm* 'the Face Bread.' What is the connotation of "Face"? In NOTE to 25:30, we saw that *pānîm* frequently implies "front" and "presence," especially of a monarch. Compare Hushai's advice to the would-be king Absalom: "Your *face* should go in their midst" (2 Sam 17:11; cf. also Gen 43:3, 5; 44:23, 26; Exod 10:28–29; 2 Sam 14:24, 28, 32; 2 Kgs 25:19; Esth 1:14). Yahweh's "Face" is his partial manifestation on Earth and can be equivalent to God himself (see further NOTE to 33:14). For more discussion—and a far-fetched theory that Yahweh's actual portrait was stamped upon the cakes—see de Boer (1972: 27–36).

P makes no pretense that Yahweh eats the bread on the Table. Rather, Yahweh's portion of the Table offering is the incense, which he inhales as an *'azkārâ* when he relaxes on the Sabbath (Gane 1992: 182, 194–97, 201). In any case, the food set before Yahweh is by no means a full diet, even for a man (cf. Milgrom 2001: 2096). For P, God's true "food" is a burnt offering of meat or grain. The "Face Bread" is more for display, symbolic morsels that Yahweh deigns to grant the priests. Thereby, God dignifies both his ministers and himself (cf. Rashbam), since to eat bread at the king's table is to be his faithful servant (2 Sam 9:7–13; 19:29; 1 Kgs 2:7; 5:7; 10:5; 18:19; Dan 1:5; on God's laying a table, see Ps 23:5; 78:19).

The offering table will remain a feature of the shrines of Nob (1 Sam 21:1–7) and Jerusalem, although it is unclear whether Solomon made one table (1 Kgs 7:48; 10:5; 2 Chr 13:11; 29:18) or ten (1 Chr 28:16; 2 Chr 4:8, 19). The Second Temple also had at least one table (1 Macc 1:22; 4:49), depicted on the Arch of Titus (fig. 4, p. 394). It seems to be simpler than the table Ptolemy II had supposedly once donated to the Temple (Letter of Aristaeus 51–82).

THE LIGHT SHINETH IN THE DARKNESS: THE LAMPSTAND
(ordained in 25:31–40, built in 37:17–24)

On our left, opposite the Table, stands a complicated item that seems to have thwarted the Priestly Writer's descriptive powers. The Midrash records Moses' own perplexity upon first receiving God's verbal instructions, until being shown an actual model of the Lampstand (e.g., Ginzberg 1928: 3.160, 219; 6.65 n. 338, 79 n. 421).

In contrast to the simpler Chest and Table, the Lampstand's dimensions are not recorded (according to Mel. Mišk. 10; b. Menaḥ. 28b, it stood three cubits tall [c. 4.5 feet/1.5 m.] and had a maximum spread of two cubits [c. 3 feet/1 m.]). In fact, we cannot really know its size because, while the Lampstand's weight is stated—somewhat less than a talent (c. 75.5 lbs./34 kg.) (25:39)—we are not sure whether it is conceived as solid or hollow (the references to miqšâ and "reeds" suggest the latter; see NOTES to 25:18, "gold; miqšâ," and 25:31, "reeds"). Josephus Ant. 3.144, perhaps really describing the corresponding object of his own day, reports that the Tabernacle Lampstand was hollow and weighed 100 minae, or 1⅔ talents (c. 126 lbs./57 kg.). Whether it is hollow or not, I assume, pace Meyers (1976: 32–33), that the Lampstand is wholly metallic; otherwise, we would expect the text to mention a wooden substructure (contrast 25:10–11, 23–24; 26:32; 30:1–3). Yet the graceful, thin-branched candelabrum generally reconstructed (cf. Josephus War 7.149) would have been fragile indeed, especially if literally of "pure gold" (see NOTE to 25:11). This is probably why most ancient depictions (but not the Arch of Titus) supply a brace across the top (see further SPECULA-TION in NOTE to 25:31).

Additional structural details are potentially available in Zechariah's vision of the Lampstand (Zechariah 4). But the text is difficult, the prophet need not be describing something actually before him, and we cannot even assume that Zechariah and Exodus have the same object in mind (Meyers and Meyers 1987: 235–38). Most now regard Zechariah's Lampstand as a separate problem with little or no bearing on Exodus (e.g., North 1970; see below, however).

Another promising source of information is archaeology, but to date no rami-form, metallic lampstands have emerged. Scholars routinely cite the many seven-spouted saucer lamps from various periods found throughout Syria–Palestine (for illustrations, see North 1970), but these ashtray-like ceramic vessels are quite different from the resplendent Tabernacle Menorah. The closest parallel in fact comes from the tomb of Tutankamun: an alabaster lamp with three lotus blossom cups, which probably employed floating wicks (Görg 1981a). But the similarities are still meager.

According to 40:24, the Lampstand is installed against the Tabernacle's southern wall (fig. 13, p. 420). Its orientation, however, is unclear. *Tanḥ. wayyaqhēl* 10.10 and Rashbam claim that it illuminates the Table northward, while Josephus (*Ant.* 3.146) has the Lampstand on an angle, facing south and east. We cannot tell. Perhaps its stance is to be adjusted as needed.

What do the Lampstand and its seven lamps represent? For P, which eschews explicit mythic symbolism, they are just a source of light in the otherwise dark tent. But the author's reticence has not deterred speculation about what the Lampstand may have meant for Israelites. There are two basic approaches: the astronomical and the botanical.

First, the lamps may have symbolized the stellar angels. Many Israelites believed that God sat in state in Heaven, surrounded by servants called *malʾākîm* 'Messengers' or *banê ʾĕlōhîm/ʾēlîm* 'Deity's Sons.' Some passages equate these latter with the stars (Job 38:7; cf. Josh 5:14; Judg 5:20; Ps 148:2–3; see also NOTE to 15:11, "gods"). From biblical polemics, moreover, we can infer that many Israelites worshiped "Heaven's Army" (Halpern 1993b). In fact, Zech 3:9 and 4:10 seem to identify the seven Temple lamps, whose image was engraved on a stone (Halpern 1978: 170, 174–76), as "Yahweh's eyes roaming (*maśôṭaṭîm*) in all the earth," recalling the Greek *planētes* 'wanderering (stars)' as well as the Persian secret service, the King's "Eyes and Ears" (Dandamaev and Lukonin 1989: 111). But the closest parallel is Yahweh's "roaming" (*šûṭ*) spy Satan, attending God among "Deity's Sons," i.e., the star gods (Job 1:7). Quite logically, later tradition identifies Satan himself with the astral god "Shining son of Dawn" or Lucifer (Isaiah 14; see Forsyth 1987: 134–39, 237–38, 254, 269). Other texts refer to a comparable class of astral angels as *ʿîr(în)* 'watcher(s)' (Dan 4:10, 14, 20; 1 Enoch 1:4; 10:9; 12:2–4, etc.). The equation of stars or angels with Yahweh's eyes is suggested also in the expression *ʿapʿappê-šāḥar* 'Dawn's eyeballs' (Job 3:9; 41:10) and in Ezekiel's visions of God's eye-studded Chariot wheels (Ezek 1:16; 10:12) (see Halpern 1993b: 145).

The association of stellar bodies with eyes and watching is natural and not limited to the Bible. The Phoenicians, too, knew astral deities transliterated in Greek as *Zophasemin*, probably Phoenician **ṣōpê-šamêm* 'Heaven's Watchers' (Attridge and Oden 1981: 36–37, 77 n. 33). The Egyptians considered the Sun and Moon to be the Eyes of Horus. (On the association between stars and eyes in general, see Pettazzoni 1978: 6–7, 110–11.)

Viewed in this context, the Tabernacle's seven lamps specifically recall the seven major heavenly bodies known to ancient, geocentric astronomy: the Sun, the Moon, Mercury, Venus, Mars, Jupiter and Saturn (Philo *Moses* 2.102–3; *Quaest. in Exod.* 78–79 [cf. 75–77, 104]; Josephus *Ant.* 3.146; *War* 5.217; *Tg. Ps.-Jonathan* 39:37) (on the relation to the seven-day week, see p. 177). This understanding presumably also underlies Rev 1:12–20, where seven lampstands represent the seven churches, and seven stars their respective guardian angels. By this theory, the Lampstand was in effect a stationary orrery. But the Menorah need not have been a planetarium per se. It could have symbolized the seven-day week. Or its lamps might have represented the seven visible stars of the Pleiades, "God's stars" in the far north (Isa 14:13) (Beer and Galling 1939: 133; on seven stars in Mesopotamian iconography, see van Buren 1945: 74–82). Also possible is an association with Yahweh's "seven thunder arrows (?)," i.e., the lightning (Hab 3:9; for discussion see Day 1979). Lastly, the lamps could symbolize the astral gods that make up Yahweh's court, as in the Book of Job.

Having given the astronomical approach its due and more, let us consider the alternative: that the Lampstand represents a sacred tree (especially Meyers [1976: 95–164], though she also finds possible celestial associations [pp. 106–7, 121, 176, 207, fig. 7]). It is undeniable that, as generally reconstructed, the Lampstand recalls to our minds a tree; and Meyers (1979: 55–56) stresses the special prominence of the six-branched tree motif in Late Bronze II art. Indeed, since her book was written, archaeology has recovered an important Israelite example from the biblical period: the tree flanked by ibexes at Kuntillet ʿAjrūd. It is also undeniable that the tree is a pregnant symbol of life and divinity throughout ancient Near Eastern literature and iconography, including the Bible (Meyers 1976: 133–64; see pp. 613–14 below). And it is frequently associated with Griffins (see below, p. 519). By this approach, the Lampstand is the "Life Tree," even potentially the tree symbol of the Great Goddess (see below).

The astral and botanical interpretations are not necessarily incompatible. Jacob (1992: 785) observes that Semitic terms for shining and vegetal growth often overlap (see also Greenfield 1959). The example *par excellence* of what Yarden calls "The Tree of Light" is the Burning Bush of Exodus 3–4 (cf. Meyers 1976: 144–46; Van Seters 1994: 40–41). Like vegetal growth, light symbolizes Life (e.g., Ps 36:10; 49:20; 56:14; Job 3:16, 20; 33:28) (Sarna 1991: 165). But there is a difficulty with taking the Menorah as a symbolic tree: except for "flower" (*peraḥ*), the text eschews arboreal terminology. The fundament and main stem are not called "trunk" (*gezaʿ*) but "thigh" (*yārēk*). The arms are not called "branches" (*ʿānāp, ḥōṭer, maṭṭe[h]*, etc.), but "reeds" (*qāne[h]*). The Lampstand, as P describes it, is emphatically not a tree.

SPECULATION: An adherent of the botanical approach might find this suspicious. In P, things are seldom what they seem. We have already caught the Priestly Writer ordaining a paschal rite that it is not a sacrifice (vol. I, pp. 445–51) and a Table from which God does not eat; below we shall find Griffins that are not a throne and a Covenant Chest that is not a footstool. Now we have a tree that is not a tree. Why? Maybe in order to quash veneration of the tree symbol called Asherah (cf. the hints of Meyers [1976: 186, 200 n. 87]; on Asherah, see pp. 613–14 below). Later, the Priestly Writer will admit that a flowering branch was kept in the Tabernacle's inner sanctum, but again he provides an innocuous explanation: it is Aaron's almond-budding rod (Num 17:16–26) (see Yarden 1971: 40–42; Durham 1987: 365 for the Menorah as a stylized almond tree; cf. also Dillmann 1880: 284).

Lamps were common in Israelite shrines. The Shiloh sanctuary featured a special lamp (1 Sam 3:3), and the First Temple had not one but ten lampstands (on the single Lampstand in 2 Chr 13:11, see Meyers and Meyers 1987: 230). While Ezekiel 40–48 provides no lamp for his imagined Temple—further evidence that it was controversial in Priestly circles?—the Second Temple contained a prominent Lampstand (1 Macc 1:21; 4:49–50; 2 Macc 10:3; Sir 26:17; Josephus *Ant.* 12.250, 318), depicted on Titus' Arch (fig. 6, p . 400). (The Menorah's afterlife in Jewish thought and art cannot detain us; see the studies of Strauss 1960; Sperber 1965; Negev 1967; Yarden 1971, and Hachlili 2001.)

Light betokens Yahweh's presence and his favor (e.g., Num 6:25; Isa 10:17; 60:1; Micah 7:8; Ps 4:7; 27:1, etc.; see Keel 1978: 186–90; Meyers 1976: 144–46, 176–78). The idea of a light shining within the otherwise obscure outer chamber is a perfect symbol for "Yahweh, my lamp . . . who illumines my dark" (2 Sam 22:29; cf. Ps 18:29), who by his word created light amid the primordial gloom (Gen 1:3).

Finally, lest we neglect the obvious: the curtained Tabernacle needs illumination so that the priests can see what they are doing (Enns 2000: 515). Whatever its precise structure and symbolism, P's image of a broad-spreading Lampstand may be primarily motivated by a desire to cast light as widely as possible. Seven may simply have been a stereotyped but arbitrary number (cf. Pope 1962a).

As for the Lampstand's historical reality, Meyers (1976: 182) concludes, "On every level, the details of its fabricature and form point to it as a manifestation of a material culture than can be located in time at the end of the Late Bronze Age." But her data leave me, at least, with quite the opposite impression. First, Meyers must provide a wooden armature to make the Lampstand viable at all. Second, her only parallels for its branches are in depictions not of cultic stands but of trees. Third, she does not sufficiently discuss the strange fusion of pillar and arboreal motifs on the branches, whose shape she never actually reconstructs. Especially after attempting to draw it (figs. 5a–b, 13), I strongly suspect that the Tabernacle Lampstand is a baroque fantasy comparable to Ezekiel's Chariot. Nowadays a familiar icon, the seven-branched Lampstand is archaeologically so bizarre, given our current knowledge, one wonders whether it could have existed prior to Greco-Roman times. Like the rest of the Tabernacle, it may be a conceit of the Priestly Writer (below, pp. 709–10).

PILLARS OF SMOKE, PERFUMED WITH MYRRH AND FRANKINCENSE: THE GOLDEN ALTAR
(ordained in 30:1–10, built in 37:25–28)

Looking inward from the center of the Tabernacle, we see a third gold object standing directly before the Veil (fig. 13, p. 420). The Golden Incense Altar fills the entire space with scented clouds.

Incense played an important role in ancient life, especially religious life (Dillmann 1880: 324–25; Nielsen 1986; Martinez, Lohs and Janzen 1989; Zwickel 1990). In Mesopotamia, an incense burner was placed directly before the divine presence (Nielsen 1986: 30–33). Canaanite temples similarly featured incense installations before the sacred cellae or niches housing the divine image (e.g., LB I

Hazor [Ottosson 1980: 29, 32]; see also Gubel [1987: pls. IV, VI–VIII, X–XI] for incense stands before divine thrones in Phoenician art). The Egyptians called incense *snṯr,* meaning either "divine fragrance" or "what makes one a god" (Nielsen 1986: 109 n. 22).

Costly frankincense and myrrh were imported by caravan from Arabia, where they were extracted from trees (cf. 1 Kgs 10:1–10; Isa 60:6; Jer 6:20; Cant 3:6; van Beek 1960). In Israel, kings employed incense extravagantly (1 Sam 8:13; 2 Kgs 20:13; Ps 45:8–9; Cant 3:6–7), and censing ranked as a priestly task alongside sacrifice, teaching and divination (e.g., Lev 10:1; Num 16:6, 17–18; Deut 33:10; 1 Sam 2:28). The Temple maintained abundant stores of aromatics (Neh 13:5, 9; 1 Chr 9:29). Nonofficial worship also employed incense, much to the chagrin of the biblical authors (e.g., 1 Kgs 11:8; 22:44; 2 Kgs 23:5; Isa 65:3; Jer 7:9; 11:13; 19:13; 32:29; 44:17–23; Hos 2:15; on incense at Elephantine, see Porten 1968: 111–13, 291–93). The small Israelite altars recovered from excavations are usually understood as unofficial incense altars (Gitin 1989, 1992; Zwickel 1990: 110–44; Fowler 1992).

In the biblical Tabernacle, incense is presented in four ways: on the Table of Face Bread (Lev 24:7), in pans (Lev 10:1; 16:12; Num 16:6, 17–18), with the Tribute-offering of grain *(minḥâ)* (e.g., Lev 2:1–2; Isa 1:13; 43:23; 66:3; Jer 41:5; Ps 141:2; Neh 13:5, 9) and on the Golden Altar. It is donated to the Tabernacle by the chieftains in golden "hands" (Numbers 7; for illustrations, see Nielsen 1986: 4 nos. 24–34).

What was the purpose of incense in Israelite worship? Some suppose that it covered the stench of sacrifice. But I doubt Israelites were as sensitive as Americans to the fetor of butchery, which in any case was mitigated by the appealing odor of sizzling flesh. Still, the incense may have repelled insects attracted by the slaughter in the Plaza (Fowler 1992: 409; on galbanum as an insect repellent, see Pliny *Natural History* 19.58; on flies attracted to sacrifice, cf. Gilgamesh XI.161 [*ANET* 95]).

Perhaps, too, incense was believed to purify the air in a more metaphysical sense. The Egyptians considered incense the holy sweat of the gods. The Mesopotamians believed that aromatics could dispel impurity and attract the divine (Nielsen 1986: 8–9, 30–33). It is even possible that Greek *nektar,* the gods' vitalizing beverage, derives from a Semitic form **niqṭar* or **muqṭar,* denoting incense or scented fluid (cf. Levin 1971).

Most important, incense is simply to be enjoyed (cf. Prov 27:9; Cant 1:13; 5:5; Esth 2:12; Sir 24:15; see Nielsen 1986: 89–100). One creates a pleasant environment to attract Yahweh's presence, just as one perfumes a bedroom to attract a lover (cf. Ps 45:9; Prov 7:17; Cant 3:6–7; Esth 2:12; 3 Macc 4:6). By sweetening God's mood in the morning and evening (Exod 30:7–8), the priests increase the efficacy of Israel's worship (Houtman 2000: 583–84). As in Assyria (Luckenbill 1926–27: 2.385–86), incense is closely associated with prayer—see, e.g., Ps 141:1–2: "May my prayer stand before you (as) incense" (cf. also Luke 1:10–11; Rev 5:8; 8:3–5 [Calvin]). By placating the angry Deity, incense can also protect, as when it averts a plague in Num 17:11–13. The mechanism is almost physical: the odor enters God's *'appayim* 'nostrils' (cf. Deut 33:10), appeasing his *'ap* 'nose, anger' (Ramban on 30:1; Keel 1978: 147–48).

From the worshiper's standpoint, incense acts like a drug, elevating the senses and altering one's mood. In the Tabernacle's proximity, one undergoes a change of consciousness, for nothing so stirs the emotions and memories as a scent (is this why the perfumed grain offering is called *'azkārâ* 'Remembrancer'?). With its patented formula (30:34–38), the Tabernacle incense "marks" Yahweh's house and its personnel (cf. de Boer 1972: 37–47; Houtman 2000: 575). As a Holiness, i.e., Yahweh's prerogative, the Spice Incense may be appropriated for no other purpose, religious or recreational. Its fragrance is unique. Compare Pseudo-Lucian *Syrian Goddess* 30, apropos of the shrine of Mabbug, Syria: "An ambrosial fragrance comes from it, such as they say comes from the land of Arabia. And as you approach even from a distance it sends forth a scent that is very pleasant. And as you depart, it does not leave you. Your clothes retain the scent for a long time, and you remember it forever" (trans. Attridge and Oden 1976: 43).

The Tabernacle incense is more than a perfume to delight Yahweh and his worshipers. Its odoriferous clouds are a medium for God's manifestation, housing and shielding his presence over the Chest (Lev 16:2, 13). The billowing, scented fumes remind those who behold or smell them of Yahweh's various sacred clouds: the guiding pillar of cloud and fire; the cloudy presence on Sinai; the fiery, nebulous Glory in which God appears to humanity—and, ultimately, the very clouds of Heaven among which Yahweh resides (Nielsen 1986: 83–84; vol. I, pp. 549–50). Like fire and light, vapors are an eloquent symbol for the ungraspable divine.

As for its form, the Golden Altar is basically a box of gold-plated wood. Unlike the Bronze Altar for burnt offerings, it has a solid roof. Like the Bronze Altar, it is supported by a rim and poles and is presumably hollow, although the text never says so. Because of its light weight, the carrying poles are each anchored by a single ring (NOTES to 30:4). Like the Bronze Altar, the Incense Altar is crowned by horns. These are not necessarily high; see the examples from Shechem (Sellin 1926: 232–33, pl. 31B–C) and Transjordan (Daviau and Steiner 2000).

Surprisingly, exactly what is done with the incense is not explained, and no utensils are mentioned. Since incense burns at a low temperature (Sforno), it may be set directly on the Golden Altar or else perhaps in the fire pans mentioned in 25:38 (ostensibly pertaining to the lamps). Or the incense might be placed in a bowl (Cassuto 1967: 392) resting upon the horns.

I must revert at least briefly to the vexed matter of the originality of the Golden Altar (see also above, pp. 369, 716–17). Because of its unexpected mention in MT chap. 30; because Sam and 4QpaleoExod^m instead treat the Incense Altar after 26:35; because P most often calls the Bronze Altar *hammizbēaḥ* 'the Altar,' as if there were no other; because incense offerings are not mentioned unambiguously by First Isaiah, Hosea, Amos and Micah (the oldest literary prophets); because Ezekiel 43–46 does not mention incense or an incense altar (but note the condemnation of incense in Ezek 8:11); because in LXX the Incense Altar is absent from Exodus 38 but present in the corresponding MT chap. 37; because in LXX the Incense Altar is absent from 39:13–23 but present in MT 39:33–43 (v 38) (on these last two points, see Gooding 1959: 66–69); because LXX treats the incense and anointing oil differently from MT-Sam (TEXTUAL NOTES to 25:6; 35:8); because Ezra, Nehemiah, and the Temple Scroll (11QTemple) do not provide for a daily incense offering; because Chronicles inserts explicit references to incense absent in older sources—many consider the Incense Altar a late Second Temple period intrusion made unevenly in the various traditions (e.g., Wellhausen 1885: 64–67; Kennedy 1898: 664). Even the reference to the Temple's Golden Altar in 1 Kgs 7:48 can be dismissed either as an insertion (Wellhausen, p. 67) or as irrelevant, since incense is not explicitly mentioned (Heger 1997: 174). Although Wellhausen's arguments have had their detractors (e.g., Haran 1978: 230–45), the case is forcefully reasserted by Heger (1997).

There *is* something fishy about the affair. But for present purposes, the fact remains: every extant Version of Exodus includes the Incense Altar somewhere. All efforts to explain how it got there are conjectural. One does not get the impression of a simple evolution (*pace* Wellhausen), but it does seem that incense was controversial. Like artwork in the Church, it may well have been periodically expunged and reinstituted throughout the Second Temple period and afterward.

BOX AND THRONE: THE CHEST AND *KAPPŌRET* (ordained in 25:10–22, built in 37:1–9)

Thrusting aside the Veil, we finally enter the Tabernacle's *sanctum sanctorum*, a zone permitted only to the Great Priest and only on Clearing Day (*yôm hakkippūrîm*) (Leviticus 16). What we find inside is a surprise.

A typical ancient Near Eastern temple's inner chamber contains a statue toward which service is directed. The idol (< Greek *eidolon* 'image') is a concrete, man-made divine manifestation, a projection onto our earthly plane of a transmundane form. Like any visual icon or verbal metaphor, this artificial theophany is and yet is not the thing depicted (cf. Jacobsen 1987a; above pp. 167–70, 519).

Accordingly, within the Tabernacle one might expect to find a statue of Yahweh, either standing or seated. But, as we know, the Bible bans all idolatry (see p. 778). Instead, the symbol of the divine presence and the focus of Tabernacle worship is a two-part affair: a gold-plated wooden box (the '*ărōn* 'Chest') with a solid gold lid surmounted by two golden Griffins (the *kappōret*, see NOTE to 25:17).

The epithet "Testimony Chest" ('*ărōn hā'ēdūt*) implies that within are stored the "Testimony Tablets," symbol of the treaty between Yahweh and Israel. For the received, composite Torah, their contents are the Decalog (Deut 10:1–5; see p. 385), incised by God himself in stone hewn from Mount Sinai (34:1 [R^JE]).

SPECULATION: 1 Kgs 8:9 states most emphatically, "Nothing was in the Chest except the two stone tablets"—as if refuting claims to the contrary (Schmitt 1972: 102). Later tradition will furnish the Chest with additional objects: shards of the first tablets, a Torah scroll, the Manna pot, Aaron's rod (Heb 9:4; *Mel.*

Mišk. 6; *b. B. Bat.* 14b). There is also scant evidence of an archaic belief that within the Chest were once stored the Urim and Thummim (e.g., Arnold 1917; May 1936: 220 n. 11; cf. Judg 20:27–28; 1 Sam 14:17–19, 41; NOTE to 28:30). And on the basis of parallels from the ancient and modern Middle East, some scholars even conjecture that in earliest times, the Chest was a shrine containing sacred stones or idols (e.g., Baentsch 1903: 223; Dibelius 1906: 86–93; May 1936; for further references, see Maier 1965: 56; Houtman 2000: 373). As far as P is concerned, however, the sole contents are the Testimony.

All cultures foster diverse interpretations of religious symbols. Predictably, P's image of the Chest-*kappōret* assemblage reflects a complex ideological evolution and ongoing debate within Israel. Two originally distinct images converged in some circles, to be disentangled only partially by the Priestly Writer. These are the utilitarian tablet box, on the one hand, and God's sublime throne, on the other. The first may be treated briefly; the latter will require a lengthy discussion. (For extensive albeit outdated bibliography on the Chest, see Schmitt [1972] and Zobel [1977]).

In Mesopotamia, important documents written on clay or stone tablets might be sealed for safekeeping in a box called *tupšinnu/tupninnu.* The most famous is that mentioned in the prologue to the *Epic of Gilgamesh* (I:22–24, partly reconstructed): "[Seek out] the copper tablet box, [re]lease its bronze lock, [open] the door of the secret, [take] up the lapis lazuli tablet; read it!"—"it" being the tale of Gilgamesh. In Hebrew, the multipurpose word *'ărōn* denotes any solid container: a coffin (Gen 50:26), a coffer (2 Kgs 12:10–11) or, in Exodus, a tablet box. Of all documents, it is not surprising that the Covenant, a unique heritage from the past, should be preserved in a special container in a sacred place (on the deposition and safekeeping of legal documents, see Tur-Sinai 1955: 54–61).

Seemingly unrelated would be the notion that King Yahweh sits in state upon a celestial throne. The ancient Near Eastern religious imagination characteristically translated the trappings of human political power to the divine realm, envisioning Heaven as a vast palace-temple bureaucracy. Just as the fleshly king sat in a lofty seat surrounded by his courtiers, so literature and art portrayed the god(s) enthroned amid monarchic pomp. This iconography exalted not only the divine ruler but also the human ruler; god and king were symbols of each other. Naturally, a monarch would richly endow a cult that glorified not only the gods but himself.

CHAIR AND CHARIOT

One potent symbol of monarchy then and now, so familiar we take it for granted, is an ultra-luxurious, enormous *chair.* In Egypt, the throne was even personified as the chief goddess Isis (Lesko 1999: 156). Why a chair? Because a fancy seat represents property and leisure—the prerogatives of the rich and powerful.

Many commoners, to be sure, might own at least a simple chair (e.g., 2 Kgs 4:10). But in order to move, ordinary people must still get up and travel on their

own feet. Not so the high and mighty of old, who to avoid such indignity devised lit-
ters, sedan chairs and chariot-thrones (Perrot and Chipiez 1884: 100, fig. 23; Gad
1936: pl. 23). Since Egyptian times, whimsy has also endowed the legs of expensive chairs with animal paws, as if they might walk on their own. The oldest examples of quadrupeds built into the sides of a throne come from Old Kingdom Egypt;
from the Near East the motif would ultimately spread west to the Greco-Roman
world (e.g., Richter 1966: figs. 142, 145, 150–51, 156–64) and thence to us.

One might expect a god to have an even better solution than a walking chair.
Imagine a seat borne by creatures that not only walk but fly, traversing vast dis-
tances in an eyeblink. Ancient Near Eastern art offers dozens of deities or kings
whose thrones are flanked or supported by winged monsters, which I generically
call "Griffins" (NOTE to 25:18) and others call "Cherubim" (the basic iconographic study is Metzger 1985: esp. 1.259–82; see also Gubel 1987: 37–84, 87 fig.
7, 184 fig. 25, pls. I–XIV; for textual references to divine thrones, see Nam 1989:
59–118). The static depiction of a moving being challenges both artist and viewer.
Mettinger (1982: 35–36) comments: "The outstretched wings of the cherubim
help to create an iconographic impression of 'frozen motion,' and thus through a
brilliant paradox unify the idea of static presence implicit in the throne motif with
the dynamic *parousia* implicit in the theophany."

That gods should sit on mythological beasts is not surprising. What does it
mean when a human monarch is so depicted? Is he a god-king? Yes and no. Even
in cultures like the Mesopotamian where the individual king is usually considered mortal, the monarchic institution per se is divine and eternal (Frankfort
1978: 215–312; Mayer 1987). It makes sense that the throne, an emblem of kingship, should be flanked by sculpted supernatural beings, even if its temporary occupant is fully human. To be sure, Griffins and other chimerae are more than
royal beasts of transport. In ancient art, they also flank portals, shelter the divine
presence with their wings and stand independently (for pictures and discussion,
see Keel 1978: 142–43, 160, 169–71, 315; Metzger 1985; 1994; also NOTES to
25:18, 20). Still, the association of Griffins with thrones would become so ingrained that, for example, Ezek 28:2, 14–16 can compare the Prince of Tyre both
to God enthroned and to a Griffin with minimal incongruity.

The iconographic tradition of the Griffin-borne throne provides the background for Yahweh's epithet *yōšēb hakkərūbîm* (2 Kgs 19:15; Ps 80:2; 99:1; 1 Chr
13:6), sometimes preceded by *yahwe(h) ṣəbā'ōt* (1 Sam 4:4; 2 Sam 6:2; Isa 37:16).
Yahwe(h) ṣəbā'ōt means "Yahweh of Brigades," the soldiers in question being
Israel's hosts and/or God's celestial retinue (see Schmitt 1972: 145–59; vol. I, pp.
281, 515; Seow 1992). *Yōšēb hakkərūbîm*, literally "the Griffins-sitter," is usually
interpreted as "seated *upon* the Griffins." Yet the absence of a preposition between *yōšēb* and *hakkərūbîm* permits alternative readings. After all, one does not
sit so much *on* as *between* Griffins (Houtman 2000: 384–85). Moreover, since the
verb *yšb* can mean not only "sit" but also "dwell," some interpret *yōšēb*
hakkərūbîm as "dwelling *among* the Griffins" (e.g., Arnold 1917: 37–39). This,
too, makes sense, since Griffins are featured prominently throughout the Tabernacle (Exodus 25–26, 36–37) and the Temple (1 Kings 6–7; Ezek 41:18–25), both

facsimiles of God's Heavenly abode (below, pp. 686–88). In a similar vein, Griffins are also associated with Yahweh's primordial, earthly Paradise of Eden, guarding its miraculous trees (Gen 3:24; cf. Ezek 28:14–15). Finally, *yošēb* can also be translated "ruler" (Isa 10:13; Amos 1:5, 8); the full epithet would then simply mean "Ruler of the Griffins."

Our most detailed descriptions of Griffins are found in Ezekiel 1; 9:3; 10. But the prophet's human-bovine-aquiline-leonine winged monstrosities are difficult to visualize and quite unlike any known graphic representations. Evidently, the prophet is describing not statues but the living spirits of Heaven (see also pp. 677–80). They stand not beside but beneath Yahweh's throne. When aloft, they flap their wings; when on the Earth, they roll on wheels (cf. Dan 7:9). Jewish tradition calls this apparition *hammerkābâ* 'the Chariot' (see already 1 Chr 28:18). (Yahweh's chariot, *sans* Griffins, also appears in Isa 66:15; Hab 3:8; cf. 2 Kgs 2:11–12; 6:17; 7:6; Zech 6:1–8; Ps 68:18; 77:19. A coin of the Second Temple period even shows a male figure, perhaps God, seated on a wheeled Griffin-seat [Meshorer 1982: 1.21–26].)

We can now appreciate what is innovative and what is conservative in the Bible's descriptions of the Griffins of the Tabernacle and Temple. Let us start with the latter. In the inner chamber of Solomon's Temple stand side by side two immense Griffins of gold-plated olive wood. Between them rests the Testimony Chest (1 Kgs 6:23–28; 8:6–9). There is little doubt that for some Israelites (see further below), this ensemble represented Yahweh's royal presence on Earth, with the Griffins flanking God's invisible throne.

Functionally, the Temple's Griffins differ little from idols. Where they are, God is. In 2 Kgs 19:14–15, for example, King Hezekiah enters "before Yahweh," i.e., before the Griffins, and invokes God's attention by proclaiming him "Israel's deity, the Griffins-sitter." But the Griffins' very tangibility emphasizes the void between them, the lack of a throne and a kingly figure, and thus the mind's inability to comprehend Yahweh's royal essence. For abstraction, this arrangement surpasses the empty divine thrones widely attested in other cultures (see Danthine 1939; de Vaux 1967: 250–52; Delcor 1983; Metzger 1985: 1.295–96; Davila and Zuckerman 1993; Mettinger 1995; Hendel 1997). In Zion, not only the Deity but also his seat are undepicted.

The emptiness at the Temple's heart further implies that Yahweh's presence is not limited to the building, as the Deuteronomistic editor (cf. Noth 1981: 60) emphasizes in Solomon's peroration (1 Kings 8): "I have built, built a princely house for you, the firm seat for your sitting/throne/dwelling forever." (On the phrase *mākôn ləšibtəkā*, which in this context probably connotes the Griffins, see NOTE to 15:17 [vol. I, pp. 542–43].) The speech goes on to explain that the Temple is not the true abode of God, whom the Heavens cannot contain. Rather, the Temple increases the efficacy of Israel's prayers by directing Yahweh's attention to the Earth (vv 27–53). The Deuteronomistic Historian does not simply deny Yahweh's presence on Earth, but offers a more abstract theory: in the Temple resides Yahweh's "name" (*šēm*), connoting the sound "Yah-weh," the grapheme *yhwh* and the very concept of his divinity (1 Kgs 8:16–20, 29, 44, 48; cf. Mettinger 1982: 46–50, 52–66). None of these is God's full essence. All are aspects of the divine with which humanity can interact.

The Temple's Griffins are best regarded as a compromise between iconism and aniconism. While not a portrait, they are a plastic symbol of the divine presence. One could say that the whole Temple is a simulacrum, only metaphorically identical to Heaven, where God sits enthroned in his true Temple-palace *(hêkāl)*; compare Ps 11:4, "Yahweh, from his Holiness' Temple-palace; Yahweh, from the Heavens, his throne—his eyes behold, his orbs examine the sons of Man" (cf. Deut 26:15; Isa 63:15; Ps 33:13–14; see further Metzger 1970). Because of the Temple's stringent ritual purity and because of its celestial imagery, it was hoped that Yahweh would "hear from his (heavenly) Temple-palace, thrust the Heavens aside and descend . . . mount upon the Griffin(s) and fly, glide upon the wind's wings" to answer his people's petition (Ps 18:7, 10–11; cf. 2 Sam 22:7, 10–11). This is nothing but "sympathetic magic," whereby a static image exerts an influence over the living soul it represents. In Egypt, similarly, Osiris' bird-like *ba* spirit is said to fly down from Heaven to fill his idol, making it receptive to prayer (cf. Morenz 1973: 150–53; see also Lorton 1999: 189–200). In Mesopotamia, too, the gods' spirits fly from and presumably to their images "like birds" (Dick 2002: 36).

Above I said that *for some Israelites*, the Temple Griffins symbolized Yahweh's enthronement in Jerusalem. One assumes *a priori* that the kings fostered this interpretation. Strikingly, however, when 1 Kgs 6:23–28; 8:7; 1 Chr 28:18; 2 Chr 3:10–13; 5:7–8 describe the Griffins, the term *kissē'* 'throne' never appears. Moreover, the statues are not said to raise their wings vertically in the manner of throne Griffins. Rather, they "spread" *(prś)* them horizontally to "shelter" *(skk)* the Chest. It sounds more like a canopy, as 1 Kgs 8:7 makes explicit. Many Israelites, and probably the Temple's Phoenician architects, surely assumed that the Temple Griffins flanked or supported Yahweh's invisible throne, and poetic references to God's throne may well have the Temple Griffins in mind. But the Deuteronomistic Historian apparently wished to obscure this connotation. The reason is not difficult to divine. Dtr's ambivalence toward monarchy and its trappings (Deut 17:14–20; 1 Samuel 8, etc.) extends even to denying Yahweh some of the accoutrements of royalty.

We may now return to Exodus, written for an audience familiar with Solomon's Temple, aware of poetic references to Yahweh's Griffins and engaged with contemporary debate as to their significance (on P's date, see p. 732). When one reads in Exodus of two golden Griffins in the Tabernacle's inner chamber, one initially brings to bear a preconceived image: Yahweh's invisible throne (cf. Ramban). But this interpretation the Priestly Writer immediately undermines. P's Griffins stand face to face, not side by side, and so conform even less than their cousins in the Temple to Near Eastern throne iconography. When depicted face-to-face in art, Griffins generally flank not a god but a tree (e.g., 1 Kgs 6:29–35; 7:36; Ezek 41:18–19, 25; see de Vaux 1967: 238–42; Keel 1978: 142–43; Metzger 1994). Whether some Israelites imagined the Tabernacle *kappōret* as a throne is moot. The Priestly Writer clearly did not *(pace* Haran 1978: 251, 254).

THE PLACE OF MY FEET

What has all this to do with a tablet box? We have omitted an important complement to the throne. While today we generally sit in low chairs with our feet on the ground, ancient monarchs and gods sat in elevated seats exalted above their courtiers. But their feet did not dangle ludicrously; they rested on low stools.

Like any aspect of a god, divine feet bear a theological significance. In the Bible, Yahweh's feet represent his presence in the terrestrial realm, manifest in the sound (Gen 3:8) or sight of his footsteps (Ps 68:25; contrast Ps 77:20, "your footprints were not known") (cf. Wolfson 1992; Eilberg-Schwartz 1994: 124). Israelites may not defecate in the camp, since that is where Yahweh treads (Deut 23:13–15). In Isa 60:13 and Ezek 43:7, God explicitly calls the Temple "the place of (the soles of) my feet," Ezekiel adding that holiness is therefore imperative. Exod 24:10 describes the clear/pure (ṭhr) blue sky as supporting Yahweh's feet (see NOTE, "clarity"). And Isa 66:1 offers a still more exalted image of the divine throne: "The heavens are my chair and the earth my footstool." At the eighth-century B.C.E. Syrian shrine at 'Ein Dara, huge footprints graphically portray the deity's entry into the sanctuary (Abū Assāf 1990). Mesopotamians even wore foot-shaped fetishes, presumably for good luck (van Buren 1945: 9–10). Closer to the Bible, Ugaritic mythology depicts 'Ilu, i.e., "God," delightedly wriggling his toes on his footstool at the advent of the great goddess 'Aṯiratu (*KTU* 1.4.iv.29–30), whose own name may mean "footprint" (Ugaritic *'ṯr* 'march,' Arabic *'aṯar* 'track, trace'; see NOTE to 34:13). (For footstools as a prominent motif in Ugaritic myth, see also *KTU* 1.3.ii.22, 37; 4.i.34; 5.vi.13; 6.i.60, iii.15; [7.i.5–6]; 17.ii.11.)

Among the contexts in which Egyptian literature mentions divine feet is the deposition of magical texts and treaties (de Vaux 1967: 257–58). The relevant example comes from a letter of Ramesses II concerning his pact with the Hittites: "See: the writing of the oath which I have made to the Great King, the king of Hattu, my brother, is placed beneath the feet of the god (Teshup?) . . . and beneath the feet of the Sun god (of Heliopolis)" (de Vaux 1971: 148). These deities guarantee the royal signatories' fidelity. (Other texts, too, were supposedly deposited beneath a deity's feet, e.g., Egyptian medical texts [*ANET* 495].)

Here at last, we find the connection with the Israelite Testimony Chest. Not according to the Book of Kings, but according to popular belief and royal ideology, the giant Griffins of Solomon's Temple created a space where God was invisibly enthroned. Where better to store the document whereby Yahweh became Israel's sovereign than beneath the symbol of his sovereignty? Thus the Chest came to symbolize, in some circles, Yahweh's *footstool* (Isa 60:13; 66:1; Jer 3:16–17; 14:21; 17:12; Ezek 43:7; Ps 99:5; 132:7–8; Lam 2:1; 1 Chr 28:2) (see Metzger 1970, esp. p. 156; Mettinger 1982: 23).

Just as the Deuteronomistic Historian and the Priestly Writer never call the Griffins the upholders of God's throne (*kissē'*), so they never mention a footstool (*hădōm*). Indeed, whereas a footstool is by its nature ancillary to a throne, the Bible in general and P in particular accord far more attention to the Chest than to the Griffins above or around it. In Exodus, this is apparent even in the relative sizes of the Chest and the *kappōret*. Unlike the Temple, where monumental Griffins dwarf the Chest beneath and between them, the Tabernacle Griffins cannot be much larger than the Chest and might be far smaller.

SPECULATION: Scholars generally assume that the Chest in Solomon's Temple is *not* surmounted by little golden Griffins, since they are redundant with the great wooden ones. The redundancy would be lessened, however, if we could find distinct functions for the two pairs of Griffins. If the large ones support or flank Yahweh's invisible throne, the little ones may cover his feet, just as the Seraphim of Isa 6:2 may cover God's feet with their wings (although the interpretation is uncertain). This assemblage might even be the inspiration for Ezekiel's vision of *four* Griffins.

The Priestly Writer rejects the notion that Yahweh's presence is automatically bound to the Chest. But some non-Priestly texts imply the contrary. In Num 10:33–36 (JE), for example, the raising and lowering of the Chest is equivalent to Yahweh's rising and resting. A similar equation between the Chest and Yahweh's presence is suggested in Numbers 14:42–44; Joshua 3–6; 1 Samuel 4–6; 2 Sam 6:14, 16, 21; 2 Kgs 19:14–15 (de Vaux 1971: 146). In contrast, P never speaks of "Yahweh's Chest" or "the Deity's Chest," expressions found 112 times elsewhere in the Bible (Seow 1984: 186–87). Nor does P associate the Chest with Yahweh's name (contrast 2 Sam 6:2). Although P calls the Tabernacle's interior *lipnê yahwe(h)* 'before Yahweh, to Yahweh's Face,' the author still attempts to downplay the concrete link between the Chest and the divine presence. He would probably agree with Nathan the prophet that Yahweh is one who quintessentially "moves about *(mithallēk)* in a tent," requiring no permanent place to sit or reside *(yāšab)* (2 Sam 7:5–8; cf. Terrien 1978: 170–71). This theology is particularly significant if, as Seow argues, P was written in an era when the Chest and/or Temple no longer existed. Just as Ezekiel envisioned Yahweh's presence deliberately leaving the Temple (Ezekiel 1), so the Priestly Writer emphasized that the disappearance and presumed destruction of the Chest imply no diminution of Yahweh's power and presence (see further below, p. 732).

The Priestly Writer probably also wished to downplay the royal legitimation and mythos implicit in portraying Yahweh as monarch. P refers only vaguely to Israelite kings (Gen 17:16; 35:11; Lev 4:22–26 [?]) and never calls Yahweh "king" *(melek)*. Similarly, the author reserved the term *ṣabā'ōt* 'armies' not for Yahweh's heavenly host but for *Israel's* masses (NOTE to 6:26). In short: the Priestly Writer repudiated the theology of King Yahweh enthroned in Zion, the city of David (Mettinger 1982: 80–115). For P, not just the king but all humankind is Yahweh's "image and likeness" (Gen 1:26–27; cf. Mettinger 1974; Kutsko 2000). The very term *kappōret*, connoting ritual purification (NOTE to 25:17), implicitly exalts the priest rather than the king as the sole medium of Clearing and atonement *(kippūr)*.

This concludes our guided tour of the Tabernacle. To approach any closer to God, we would have to ascend to Heaven itself (see further pp. 674–94).

I WILL CLOTHE HER PRIESTS IN
RIGHTEOUSNESS: THE SACRED VESTMENTS
(ordained in chap. 28, made in 39:1–31)

Naked, we all look rather alike. But expensive, elaborate clothing can highlight and even create social distinctions. Houtman (2000: 466–67) cites various biblical verses to prove that, for Israelites as others, "the clothes make the man."

This applies most obviously to the clergy. Upon the death of his predecessor, each successive heir of Aaron must assume the vestments of priesthood, long ago anointed by Moses with consecrating oil (Utzschneider 1988: 172–73). In Roman times, the Jews' foreign rulers would even keep the Great Priestly garments under lock-and-key, dispensing them to favored pretenders (see 1 Macc 10:20–21; Josephus *Ant.* 15.403–8; 18.90–95; 20.6–7).

While the Priestly Writer admits that one function of the priestly costume is "for glory and for splendor" (28:2, 40), he stresses another aspect as well. Sacred service is a risk undertaken by the house of Aaron and the tribe of Levi on Israel's behalf (cf. Leviticus 10; Numbers 16, 18). Woven of the same stuff as the Tabernacle and like it adorned with gold, sewn together by a similar technique *(ḥbr)* and sanctified by a similar ritual, the priestly uniform shields its wearer from Yahweh. The bells on his skirt (28:35), the linen underwear (28:43) and, by implication, the golden diadem (NOTE to 28:38) all protect the Great Priest when he encroaches on Yahweh's domain. Otherwise, the impurities he bears both for himself and vicariously for the Israelites would bring about his annihilation (see below). Based upon Ezek 42:14; 44:19, Haran (1978: 177) supposes that priests wear their regalia only in the shrine, lest they mix the Holy and the impure. But, according to Lev 21:12, the Great Priest may not leave the sacred precinct for any pretext because of his anointment. (How and where he sleeps, defecates and propagates are not addressed.)

All priests share four basic garments: the hat *(migbaʿat)*, shift *(kətōnet)*, sash *(ʾabnēṭ)* and underpants *(miknāsayim)*. To these the Great Priest adds four more: the Ephod *(ʾēpôd)*, the pectoral pouch called *ḥōšen*, the Robe *(məʿîl)* and the Blossom *(ṣîṣ)*. His hat, moreover, is called not *migbaʿat* but *miṣnepet* 'Turban,' presumably a more elaborate affair. Like the Torah, the following exposition will focus mainly on the Great Priest's ensemble, following the order of robing in 29:5–6; Lev 8:7–9. (For variety's sake, I shall use the terms "Aaron" and "Great Priest *[kōhēn gādôl]*" interchangeably.)

After washing, the priest dons linen undergarments *(miknāsayim)* (Exod 28:42–43; Lev 6:3). Because these sometimes go unmentioned (Exod 29:8–9; Lev 8:13) and are not consecrated with blood (Exod 29:21; Lev 8:30), many infer that they stand apart from the sacred vestments proper (e.g., Milgrom 1991: 385). Sarna (1991: 185, 187) plausibly supposes that, unlike the heavier and more complicated outer garments, the priest dons his *miknāsayim* unassisted (28:42; Lev 6:3; 16:4); i.e., they are not part of the robing ritual. (According to *m. Tamid* 5:3, only the priests' underpants ever leave the Tabernacle precinct; the other priestly vestments remain within the Tabernacle.) Although the stated purpose of the priests' underwear is modesty (28:42), one would think that the Great Priest scarcely needs such coverage because of his long Robe (see NOTES to 28:4, "robe," 42, "underpants"). Evidently, all priests wear underwear whether they need it or not. And if the Great Priest is robed in a public ceremony, modesty will still be an issue.

Next comes the white Shift (kətōnet), a short linen robe bound with the Sash (ʾabnēṭ). This, plus a hat (migbaʿat), completes the cool and practical wardrobe of the ordinary priest.

The Great Priest, however, must endure two more layers. Aaron's blue, woolen Robe (məʿîl) reaches from neck to feet (see NOTE to 28:4, "robe"). Its lower hem is adorned with alternating woolen pomegranates and golden bells, apparently an elaboration of the tassels characteristic of ancient Near Eastern fancy dress (for Israelites, see ANEP figs. 351–55 [Black Obelisk]). Over this Robe goes the Ephod, a skimpier garment (NOTE to 28:4) fastened with two "shoulder-pieces" (kətēpōt; see NOTE to 28:7) ornamented with one gem each. The Ephod is made of mingled gold thread and dyed wool and linen; in fact, as much as half of its substance may be golden (Haran 1955: 383). Fastened on its front is a woven pouch called ḥōšen 'Beauty (?)' (see NOTE to 28:4). It is adorned with twelve gemstones and contains the Urim and Thummim, probably sacred lots (see below and NOTES to 28:30).

The priestly image of Aaron's ḥōšen appears to fuse several originally distinct concepts. On one level, it is a wallet pouch such as might contain aromatics (Cant 1:13) or, presumably, valuables. But it is simultaneously a rectangular, jeweled pectoral ornament (for parallels, see Maxwell-Hyslop 1971: 217–18; also NOTES to 28:17, 30). Because it is associated with justice, the ḥōšen particularly recalls the image of Truth (i.e., the goddess Maat) worn by Egyptian judges upon their breasts, at least in Hellenistic times (see Van Dam 1997: 69–70 for references). But, because its twelve jewels are inscribed with individual tribal names, the pectoral may also be regarded as a composite signet, a personal seal hung by a cord around the neck (cf. Gen 38:18).

Within the ḥōšen are the Urim and Thummim, the priests' alternative to prophetic spirit possession as a means to determine the divine will (cf. 1 Sam 28:6, "Yahweh did not answer him, not by dreams, not by Urim, not by prophets"). As in other cultures, the Israelite priest is simultaneously sacrificer and diviner. So we read in Deut 33:8, "Give to Levi your Thummim / And your Urim to the man, your faithful one" (cf. LXX and 4QTestim; for the textual reconstruction, see Propp 1987a: 54).

Lastly, the Great Priest dons special headgear: the Turban (miṣnepet) with its Blossom (ṣîṣ) inscribed "a Holiness of Yahweh."

Although I have made no experiments, so many layers of wool and gold may have been extremely uncomfortable. (Holzinger [1900: 139] proffers an illustration in which Aaron appears most wretched.) By Vg's understanding of lō(ʾ) yaḥgərû bayyāzaʿ, lit. "they shall not gird on in sweat," Ezek 44:17–18 mandates all-linen vestments precisely to remedy the problem of perspiration (see, however, Zimmerli 1983: 449–50). Haran (1978: 211) comments, "Under the weight of such splendid apparel, the high priest is certainly incapable of anything more than a slow, stately walk and the performance of tasks that do not necessitate bending down." (My fig. 16 [p. 434] offers a lighter, cooler image of the priestly garb.) If the Great Priesthood was an uncomfortable job, it carried a compensatory prestige enhanced by the elaborate, weighty getup. In any case, multilayered garments were not unusual in the Middle East. Although the Egyptians and Sumerians always dressed lightly, we find Syrians routinely depicted wearing layered attire (*ANEP* 15–19, 156–59 nos. 45–56, 58, 62, 452, 455, 460–61), and the kings of Assyria dressed heavily, too (*ANEP* 151–55 nos. 441–451). Like Aaron, Syrian priests wore purple robes and a golden crown (Pseudo-Lucian *Syrian Goddess* 42). The Great Priestly vestments particularly recall those of the Persian king, as described by Xenophon *Cyropaedia* 8.iii.13: a sleeved purple tunic, a tiara with a fillet, a purple robe with a white stripe and scarlet trousers (cf. Mordecai's garb in Esth 8:15; on possible implications for the date of P, see pp. 454, 732). As for Aaron, perhaps it was felt that several layers should insulate his body from the *ḥōšen* on his chest, and from the surrounding holy Tabernacle (below, p. 528).

In all, twenty-five names are inscribed on Aaron's costume: the twelve ancestral names engraved twice, in groups of six on the two shoulder stones (28:9–12) and singly on the pectoral stones (28:21), and then Yahweh's own name on the golden Blossom (28:36). Both sets of gems are called *zikkārôn* 'Memorial' (28:12, 29; see NOTE to 28:12); the priestly diadem, too, is called a "Memorial" in Zech 6:14 but not in Exodus (but cf. *zikkārôn* in Exod 13:9 apropos of a head circlet). The head, heart and shoulder (connected to the arm) may symbolize perception, thought and agency (cf. the command to wear words of instruction on forehead, heart and arm in Exod 13:9, 16; Deut 6:6–8; 11:18–19; Jer 31:33; Prov 6:20–22; 7:1–3 (see vol. I, pp. 423–25).

SPECULATION: Various explanations might be proposed for the redundancy of twelve tribal names worn on both shoulders and chest. Perhaps, assuming the inscribed carnelians are perched precisely atop the priest's shoulders, the shoulder stones are for God to read in Heaven, the breast stones for Israel on Earth (Cassuto 1967: 376–77). Since, however, Tabernacle worship is directed both horizontally, toward Yahweh's Presence within, and vertically, into the sky (see pp. 686–88), the names on the breast might rather be for Yahweh-on-Earth, while the shoulder names are readable by Yahweh-in-Heaven (cf. Houtman 2000: 505). It is also possible that the *kətēpōt* 'shoulder-pieces' cover the upper back, in which case the priest bears a "sandwich board" legible from front and back (see, however, NOTE to 28:12, "put . . . on the Ephod's shoulder-pieces").

We could even derive an edifying moral from the fact that the names appear twice, singly and grouped. By covenant and cult, the Israelites are related to Yahweh both as individuals and as a collective (cf. Ehrlich 1969: 191).

As for the twenty-fifth name, the head inscription *qōdeš ləyahwe(h)* 'a Holiness of Yahweh' is a kind of label of ownership, marking Aaron as Yahweh's property and thus as a sort of living human sacrifice (see NOTE to 28:36, "a Holiness of Yahweh," and below pp. 528–32). The head plaque reminds both Aaron and the people that the Great Priest bears upon him the Tabernacle's dangerous aura. And, because the priest represents the entire people whose names he carries, the inscription simultaneously marks all Israel as Yahweh's sanctified property (cf. Durham 1987: 388).

The plaque is more than an identity tag. According to 28:38, it makes Israel's offerings more pleasing to Yahweh, inasmuch as Aaron "shall Bear the Transgression of the Holinesses that Israel's Sons shall make holy, for all their holy gifts." In some fashion, the Great Priest reconciles Yahweh to the people. Thanks to Aaron's offices, in particular the recurrent Sin-offering and the annual Clearing Day, Yahweh ignores or annuls Israel's inadvertent transgressions (see NOTE to 28:38; pp. 700–701).

If Aaron offers sacrifices to Yahweh and effects expiation on Israel's behalf, what does he do on God's behalf? Exod 28:30 implies that he judges the people by virtue of the Urim and Thummim over his heart (see NOTES to 28:4, "Ephod," 15, 30). Whether he is supposed literally to cast these lots or merely to absorb their potency by osmosis, the Urim and Thummim represent the Great Priest's prerogative to judge by divine wisdom, so that Israel may live in maximal conformity with God's wishes. Elsewhere in the Bible, judgment is usually considered the province of the *šōpēṭ* 'judge' or *melek* 'king,' but unlike JE and D, the Priestly source makes no explicit provision for monarchy or a lay judiciary (admittedly, Gen 17:6; 35:11 presuppose kingship, while Lev 19:15 assumes a judicial process). According to Deut 33:8–10, the Urim and Thummim are Yahweh's gift to the Levitical priests, who "teach your judgments to Jacob and your direction(s) to Israel." (On the priest as judge, see also Deut 17:8–9; 21:5; Ezek 44:24; 2 Chr 19:8–11.)

His access to divine wisdom and his fancy clothes make the Great Priest in some sense tantamount to a king. After all, once Moses is dead, Aaron's son Eleazar takes precedence over the general Joshua, since Eleazar wields the Urim and Thummim (Num 27:21). (On the common inference that P was written in an era of theocracy, when priesthood had superseded monarchy—i.e., the Persian period—and that Aaron's robes are kingly in origin, see recently Gosse 1996 and also APPENDIX A, p. 732.)

SPECULATION: In the ancient Near East, kings wore impressive garments and were often said to posses a divine aura (Akkadian *melammu*; see Oppenheim 1943; Cassin 1968), even to be gods themselves (for a general discussion, see Frankfort 1978). The Bible hints that some Israelites considered the Davidic king in some sense divine (see p. 770).

Was the Great Priest similarly godlike? Surely the Priestly Writer did not hold Aaron in such esteem. For P, all humanity is Yahweh's flesh-and-blood portrait (Gen 1:26–27; Mettinger 1974; Kutsko 2000). And yet there is a divine aspect to the Great Priest, the holiest of all humans (below, pp. 688–89). By clothing Aaron in the same fabric that tents over the divine Presence, by dressing him in a golden Ephod with possible idolatrous overtones (cf. Judg 8:24–27; 17:5;

18:14–20; Hos 3:4), the Priestly Writer created an implicit equation between priest and God. The vestments give him "glory" and "splendor" (kābôd, tip'eret)" (28:2), divine attributes that Yahweh receives from both the lesser pantheon and from humanity (Ps 29:1–2, 9; 96:6–8). Similarly, Ps 132:9 proclaims that Yahweh's "priests wear Righteousness (ṣedeq)," elsewhere a quality both of Yahweh himself and of kings. The Great Priest's appearance to bless the people (Num 6:22–26) may have been a religious act analogous, mutatis mutandis, to viewing the cult image (theophaneia) in other religions (cf. Sir 50:5–20; Terrien 1978: 399–400). After, he bears Yahweh's name (see SPECULATION, p. 448).

Further, an important act of religious service in the ancient world, alongside sacrifice, was clothing the divine image in sumptuous garments. (In its own way, Judaism continues the tradition, providing special garments for Torah scrolls.) In Israel, one fed both Yahweh and the priest with sacrifices, and one clothed the priest with splendid robes. Moreover, the closest parallel to the golden rosette on Aaron's brow comes from the attire of Mesopotamian gods and kings (NOTE to 28:36, "Blossom"). Lastly, although the analogy is limited (Van Dam 1997: 46–53), the pectoral containing Yahweh's Urim and Thummim recalls the "Tablet of Destinies" (ṭuppi šīmāti), worn upon the breast, that gave the Mesopotamian high gods power over fate (Holzinger 1900: 138). Possibly related, too, is Yahweh's "Life Pouch" (ṣərôr haḥayyîm) mentioned in 1 Sam 25:29. Note that Ezek 28:13–14 implicitly associates the gemstones adorning the ḥōšen with a divine Griffin inhabiting "Eden, Deity's Garden."

Thus some may have regarded the Great Priest, like the king, as a quasi-god (cf. Hubert and Mauss 1964: 23). An emissary from Israel to Yahweh, he is the counterpart of the divine mal'āk 'Messenger' dispatched from Heaven to Earth. Compare Mal 2:7, "A priest's lips conserve knowledge, and they seek Direction (tôrâ) from his mouth, for he is Yahweh of Brigades' Messenger (mal'ak yahwe[h]-ṣəbā'ôt)." The Dead Sea scrolls even call the Great Priest ml'k pnym bm'wn qwdš 'the Face Messenger (i.e., angel of Yahweh's Presence) in the Holiness Habitation' (1QSb 4:25). According to Sir 50:5–6, the priest shines like the astral bodies that serve God (on the correlation of priests and angels, see also Philo Spec. Leg. 1.66). The mythologization of the priesthood will culminate in the Letter to the Hebrews, which identifies Jesus as God's heavenly Great Priest, one who is not just like God's sons but is the very Son of God.

The Priestly Writer continually wrestles with a paradox so excruciating it verges on the comic. Israel and Yahweh crave nearness, yet can scarcely tolerate one another's company (see further pp. 682–704). Just as Deuteronom(ist)ic literature speaks of Yahweh's Name inhabiting the Temple—his full essence is too vast and holy to be so confined (e.g., Deut 12:5, 11, 21; 14:23–24; 16:2, 6, 11; 26:2; 1 Kgs 8:20, 41–44, 48)—in P, Aaron bears Yahweh's name on his head among the people. Moreover, according to Num 6:27, he is to put Yahweh's holy name on the people through the priestly benediction. (Excavated Judean amulets bearing the text of the blessing [Yardeni 1991; Barkay 1992] suggest that "put" is meant literally.) Conversely, Aaron bears into the Tabernacle Israel's tribal names because the actual people is too numerous and impure to enter. The priest's office, in a word, is to mediate between Yahweh and Israel (McNeile 1908: lxiv); see 27:21; 29:28. Aaron is Israel's ambassador to Yahweh, and Yahweh's ambassador to Israel (Houtman 2000: 468).

One Latin term for priest, *pontifex*, etymologically means "bridge-maker." While the significance for the ancient Romans is a subject of dispute, this would be a most appropriate description for Aaron the Great Priest.

A SONG OF DEGREES: GRADUATED HOLINESS

Although the general pattern has always been obvious, Haran (1978: 158–165) deserves credit for explicating in the greatest detail the Tabernacle's concentric zones of graduated holiness (see also Jenson 1992). As one would expect, the areas of greatest sanctity are furnished with the most expensive materials, while the areas of least sanctity have the cheapest. Thus there is no bronze inside the Holiness of Holinesses and no gold in the Plaza (Jenson 1992: 101).

For metals, the ranking by descending value is pure gold, gold, silver, bronze. For fabrics it is blue wool, purple wool, worm-crimson wool, linen, goat hair, leather. For techniques of weaving and embroidery, it is *ḥōšēb* (weaving of figures), *rōqēm* (weaving with a pattern or embroidery), *'ōrēg* (monochrome weave) (see NOTES to 26:1, "webster's work," 36, "embroiderer's work"). Haran also posits that when several components are listed, they are in order of descending proportion—e.g., the Tabernacle curtains of "linen, blue and purple and worm-crimson" (26:1) are mostly white linen, whereas the Veil of "blue and purple and worm-crimson and twisted linen" (26:31) is mostly dyed wool. While this assumption cannot be proved, it does lend elegance to Haran's analysis. By varying the materials's value and proportions, the Priestly Writer expresses subtle gradations of holiness.

Befitting their extreme sanctity, the objects within the Tabernacle are made of pure gold (chap. 25). In contrast, the Tabernacle frames, the Veil posts and the Screen posts are plated in ordinary gold (26:29, 32). For the textiles, the Veil is holiest, as it is primarily blue and decorated in *ḥōšēb* work (26:31), whereas the curtains are *ḥōšēb* but primarily linen (26:1). Also of lesser sanctity is the Tabernacle Screen, mostly blue, but mere *rōqēm* work (26:36). Still less sacred is the outer curtain of goat hair (26:7), and least holy of all is the leather roof cover (26:14). In accordance with Haran's scheme, the inner tent has gold clasps (26:6), while the outer tent has bronze (26:11).

It is a general principle that the vertical components of gold-plated wood stand on pedestals of less valuable metal, presumably because they touch the ground. The bases of the Tabernacle frames and the Veil posts are silver (26:19, 25, 32), while the Screen posts rest in bronze bases (26:37).

As for the outer Plaza, even the most holy Altar is only of bronze (27:2). The wooden posts have silver fixtures at the top but stand in bronze bases (27:10, 11, 17). While the sheets are simple linen (27:9), the Plaza Screen is mostly blue and of *rōqēm* work (27:16).

By their composition, the three textile barriers—the Veil inside the Tent, the Plaza Screen and the Tabernacle Screen—stand out from the fabrics that surround them. The Veil is mostly wool, polychrome, worked in *ḥōšēb* technique and thus superior to the Tabernacle curtains. Similarly, the Plaza Screen is dyed wool and linen, finer than the flaxen sheets of the Plaza. Between comes the Tabernacle Screen, made of the most precious dyed wool and linen, yet hung on posts standing in bases of mere bronze. Thus the Tabernacle Screen shares aspects of both Tabernacle and Plaza.

Haran (pp. 165–74) applies a similar analysis to the priestly garments, which are like an inside-out Tabernacle. The cheapest, most profane item, linen underpants, lie closest to Aaron's skin (28:42). The Tunic is finer linen (28:39); the Sash is basically linen, mixed with dyed wool in *rōqēm* style (28:39; 39:29); then the Robe is all of blue, but only in *'ōrēg* technique. Finally, farthest from Aaron's skin and exposed to the air of the Tabernacle, is the Ephod-*ḥōšen* ensemble, mostly cloth-of-gold in *ḥōšēb* work (28:6, 15). Like the Tabernacle curtains, Aaron's garments are consecrated by anointment, lending them immunity to Yahweh's potentially lethal sanctity (Haran, p. 177).

Finally, we should note that not just space but time may possess graduated sanctity. The week-long purification and consecration of Tabernacle and priesthood (chap. 29) ensures that the totally pure, i.e., Yahweh, does not contact profane, earthly matter without proper preparation (see further pp. 675–703).

WHO SHALL STAND IN HIS HOLY PLACE? THE PRIESTLY ORDINATION
(ordained in Exodus 29; fulfilled in Leviticus 8)

Anthropologists devote considerable attention to the rituals by which individuals modify their social status (van Gennep 1960; Turner 1967). Worldwide, rites of passage follow a set sequence: (a) designating the initiate; (b) his/her separation from the community; (c) a series of symbolic acts, often arduous, imparting new status and powers; finally, (d) reintegration into the community in an altered position. We have already seen how Yahweh, Moses and Israel go through their own narrative rites of passage in the Exodus story (vol. I, pp. 32–36, 239–40). Now the text describes the procedure whereby previously ordinary Israelites, i.e., Aaron and his sons, are elevated and sanctified. No less than the Tabernacle or the Sabbath, the clergy must be "made" and consecrated (cf. Utzschneider 1988: 168).

Unlike other ancient Near Eastern priesthoods, but like the Brahmins of India, the Aaronic priesthood is strictly hereditary. Even if one undergoes special training and initiation, the basic qualification is descent—hence the Rabbinic dictum that the unlearned priest is no less a priest (*m. Hor.* 3:8; *m. Yoma* 1). In P, the priesthood is Yahweh's gift and burden to the House of Aaron (on rival priesthoods, see vol. I, pp. 284–86; vol. II, pp. 567–74). It is not exactly a covenant of grant like the Davidic monarchy (cf. Weinfeld 1970). For, although Aaron is arbitrarily elected, his grandson Phinehas later *earns* the eternal priestly covenant when he saves Israel by promptly punishing and atoning for the crime of Baal

Peor (Num 25:11–13; on priesthood as a covenant, see Num 18:19; Jer 33:21–22; Mal 2:4–8; Neh 13:29; Sir 45:7, 15, 42).

Why is Aaron selected? On one level, the answer is obvious: the Priestly Writer advanced the interests of a priesthood claiming Aaronic descent (p. 732). But we must inquire again at the literary level: by what virtue is Aaron chosen? Initially, one might think that Moses just wants to keep the holy business in the family. Upon reflection, however, one remembers that Yahweh originally promoted Aaron as Moses' prophetic *spokesman* to Pharaoh (6:30–7:2), since Moses was disqualified on account of his lips' "uncircumcision," connoting both physical impairment and ritual impurity (see vol. I, pp. 273–74). In contrast, Aaron's facility made him the ideal go-between. As prophet he helped Moses and Israel communicate with their temporary, illegitimate sovereign, Pharaoh; as priest he will mediate between Israel and their eternal, true sovereign, Yahweh.

The inherent paradox of the Tabernacle—a sacred space resting on the impure Earth amid an impure people—is paralleled by the paradox of priesthood (see below, pp. 675–703). How can an ordinary man subject to ritual uncleanliness through death, disease, bodily emissions and moral transgression approach Yahweh? Will he not be instantly struck down? And if he should attain temporary purity and sanctity, how can he then go among the people without compromising his holiness and again incurring death (cf. Ezek 44:19)?

P's answer is to single out a specific family from all Israel. Then, through the step-by-step rite of *millū'îm* 'Filling,' the House of Aaron is raised to a higher level of sanctity and empowered to mediate between God and Israel. While he falls short of the quintessential "Holiness of Holinesses" that characterizes the inner sanctum, Aaron at least possesses the lesser "Holiness" of the Tabernacle as a whole. Washed in water, purified by blood, consecrated with oil and garbed in protective gear, the priest can survive contact with the Divine and safely pass back and forth between Yahweh and Israel. But the privilege of serving God naturally entails many restrictions. Priests may not bury the dead or engage in ritual mourning. They may not wed previously married women and are excluded from service by various physical impairments (Leviticus 21; Ezek 44:20–22, 25).

Assuming one is of the correct lineage, how exactly does one become a priest? According to Exodus 29 and Leviticus 8, the ritual of Filling proceeds as follows (the minor discrepancies between the accounts will not concern us). First the candidates present a bull, two perfect rams and a basket of three different types of bread. They are washed and then dressed in their ceremonial garments, and oil is poured upon Aaron's head. (This differs from ordinary toilet, when oil would be applied between bathing and dressing [2 Sam 12:20; cf. Ps 109:18].) The bull is offered as a Sin-offering, and its blood is applied to the Altar to effect Clearing (*kpr*). As for the rams, the first is a wholly burnt Ascending-offering (*'ōlâ*) dispatched as a "Soothing Scent" straight to Yahweh in Heaven. The second is the Filling Ram proper, whose purpose is further to purify the priests by Clearing (29:33). The fatty parts are burnt for Yahweh, along with some bread. The rest will later be eaten by Moses as the officiant, and by the priests as the initiates.

We now come to the most striking part of the ritual: the Filling Ram's blood is applied to the priests' right ears, right thumbs and right big toes, and then to the Altar. The emphasis on the right side probably reflects a universal prejudice, although Hebrew is far less dextro-centric than, say, English. But why these body parts in particular? First, the practical explanation: the face, hands and feet are the only skin not covered by the sacred vestments; thus, they may need independent purification. Second, the symbolic: it is through the *ears* that the priest is instructed in God's will (this is still a semiliterate society); it is with his *feet* that he goes about his holy business; it is with his *hands* that he executes his sacred office. In other words, the Filling blood purifies the priests' faculties of understanding, locomotion and manipulation (cf. Philo *Moses* 2.150; Dillmann 1880: 465). A problem with these interpretations, however, is that the blood rite is not unique to the priesthood. A person purified from the skin disease ṣāra'at undergoes a similar ritual, with both blood and oil applied to ear, thumb and toe (Lev 14:14, 17). It seems, therefore, that the rite simply raises one's state of purity, making the impure pure and the already pure super-pure (cf. Ehrlich 1969: 193). But, again: why ear, hand and foot?

By definition, the Filling ritual falls under the rubric of rite of passage (Milgrom 1991: 566–69, 889; Gorman 1990: 103–39). Milgrom poses a provocative question: where is the ordeal that is a virtual *sine qua non* of such ceremonies? Several answers are possible. First, spending a solid week—on pain of death—in the sacred precincts dressed in oily and bloodied garments might be slightly unpleasant (Lev 10:7). More seriously, Leviticus 9–10 in effect describes an ordeal by fire: Aaron safely sacrifices and is not harmed by the "fire from before Yahweh" (Lev 9:24), whereas Nadab and Abihu (Lev 10:2) and later some presumptuous Levites (Num 16:35) will transgress and be consumed by that same fire. But there is another, more immediate test, at least symbolically.

A common type of initiatory ordeal is mutilation. Overall, our best ancient Near Eastern parallel for the biblical Filling ritual comes from Late Bronze Age Emar (Syria): the consecration of a special priestess is built around a seven-day festival, with daily animal sacrifices and ritual anointment (cf. Fleming 1992: 63–69). But, in addition, the Emar priestess has her hair cropped (Sigrist 1993: 390, 400), like priestly initiates in Egypt (Sauneron 2000: 36–37) and particpants in many rites of passage (Olyan 1998)—but unlike Israelite priests (cf. Lev 21:10; Ezek 44:20).

For anthropologists, the haircut in the context of rites of passage is classed as a symbolic mutilation, the scarification or severing of a non-essential body part— e.g., an earlobe, finger, toe, hair lock, foreskin—first as an ordeal and then as a sign of changed status upward or downward (Van Gennep 1960: 71–72; Propp 2004a). The mutilation can also represent vicarious self-sacrifice (*pars pro toto*) and submission to a higher power (Burkert 1996: 34–55). Thus, in the Bible, the slave-for-life undergoes ear-piercing (21:6), and captives' thumbs and big toes are severed (Judg 1:6–7) as permanent tokens of degradation and dependence. These, like circumcision, are actual injuries. But some initiatory wounds are purely symbolic, more like the knightly dubbing in lieu of decapitation.

The symbolic wound *par excellence* is the application of blood to one who is uninjured (see vol. I, pp. 33, 35–36, 233–40, 434–39, 443–44, 452–54, apropos of circumcision and the *Pesaḥ*). The ordeal by pain is vicarious, undergone by the blood donor but transfered to the initiate. Rites of passage often dramatize the candidate's death and resurrection. With an initiatory sacrifice, the death is real — but it is not the initiate's. In Israel, the Filling Ram must die so that Aaron and his sons may be born again to priesthood.

Once we recognize the Filling Ram's blood as representing the priests' own blood, the symbolism of 29:20 is fairly clear. A priest must be sound in body, and yet, by the rite of passage complex, he must sustain at least a token injury to show his submission to God. At Emar, it is a haircut; in Israel, it is daubing certain extremities with ram's blood. The bloodied finger, toe and ear are *symbolically severed*, which in turn symbolizes the priests' death. That the same blood is then spattered around the Altar and returned to the candidates implies that, by undergoing symbolic mutilation, the priests themselves have become *living sacrificial victims* (cf. Romans 12:1) (Knight 1976: 177). P in fact regards the entire tribe of Levi as donated to Yahweh as ransom for Israel's firstborn sons (Num 3:12–13, 40–51; 8:16–18; cf. Judg 17:5, 10–13), who are at least theoretically subject to human sacrifice (NOTE to 22:28, "sons"; vol. I, pp. 454–56). With the Filling blood, the priests are branded as Yahweh's own and placed under his protection (cf. Milgrom 1991: 529). Once they are purified and marked for God, the initiates and their garments are sprinkled with the special oil that confers sanctity.

Although Exodus is not quite explicit (see NOTES to 29:35, "likewise," 36, "Sin bull"), apparently the entire ritual is repeated each day for a week (following 11QTemple XIV–XV, partly reconstructed). And concomitant with the priests' ordination is the Altar's sanctification. Again, one senses a paradox: priests cannot be consecrated without a functioning Altar; the Altar cannot be consecrated without a functioning priesthood. In a future generation, the senior priests would presumably consecrate initiates (so 11QTemple XV:18; see below). But who can make the first priests? In this regard as in others, Moses stands apart as a once-in-history phenomenon (or perhaps as a royal figure; see Milgrom 1991: 556–57). As if to explain his temporary role in the cult, later Jewish legend will celebrate Moses' sexual abstinence and freedom from bodily defilement (e.g., Ginzberg 1928: 3.472), and the Torah already implies Moses' extraordinary purity, since he survives close contact with Yahweh unscathed (cf. 19:10–15; 24:11) or nearly so (see pp. 620–23).

SPECULATION: Because they share blood and oil with the Altar, the priests may be regarded not just as living sacrifices but as living altars. How so? When the people make the Sin-offering, the animal's fat and blood are sent to the Altar, which absorbs the offerer's inadvertent sin or impurity. The rest of the animal is eaten by the priests, who symbolically absorb the people's offenses (see pp. 699–700). Both priesthood and Tabernacle are cleansed once a year on Yom Kippur (Leviticus 16).

And the Great Priest is like an altar in yet another respect. His living body affords protection for the manslayer (Num 35:25,28; Josh 20:6), just as accidental killers may seek protection at the Altar's horns. See further NOTE to 21:14, "my altar."

Not only space but also time can possess graduated Holiness. Throughout the week of Filling, the sanctity levels of both priesthood and Altar rise. Each day, the sacrifices, offered by the nonpriest Moses upon an unconsecrated Altar, would be technically invalid, at least for future generations. But each day they are more efficacious. Finally on the eighth day, Aaron is sufficiently holy to take over, and the Altar is sufficiently holy to attract and sustain Yahweh's fire. (The Rabbis are divided on whether Moses surrenders the priesthood to Aaron or maintains his unique prerogatives until death [*Exod. Rab.* 37:1]; the latter seems more likely [note, e.g., 34:34–35].)

SPECULATION: Elsewhere we have seen P both accepting deviant traditions and implying that they are superseded: the divine name *'ĕlōhîm* (6:2), the domestic *Pesaḥ* rite (vol. I, pp. 448–51), the Griffin throne (above, p. 519). Moses' officiating at the Tabernacle may be P's solution to the existence of a rival Levitical priesthood antedating the Aaronid clergy (cf. vol. I, pp. 284–86). P admits that Levitic (i.e., Mosaic) sacrifice was indeed formerly legitimate—for only seven days!

The text does not state clearly whether the priests' ordination is for all time or must be reinstated in every generation. Milgrom (1991: 520) understands the ordination ritual of Exodus 29 as eternally valid, requiring no reenactment. Once Aaron and his sons are consecrated, their descendants inherit their status automatically, along with their robes. Thus, when Eleazar succeeds Aaron, there is no special sacrifice; the garments are simply transferred (Num 20:22–29). But Eleazar had already undergone ritual consecration alongside his father. What about future generations?

According to 29:29–30, future Great Priests undergo a seven-day ordination and anointment to "fill their hand" (NOTES to 28:41). Lev 4:3, 5, 16; 6:15; 16:32, and especially 21:10; Num 35:25 also envision future Great Priests who are anointed (*b. Ker.* 5b; *Lev. Rab.* 10:8; against Jub 31:3–4; 11QTemple XIV:15–17 [Delcor 1986]). But what else is involved? Are they daubed with blood and oil on head, hand and foot? Is there a Sin-offering? Who presides: the prior Great Priest before his death, some other senior priest or the king (cf. Milgrom 1991: 556–57)? What happens during the intersacerdocy? All we know is that inadvertent murderers are released from their internment (Num 35:25, 28–32; Josh 20:6).

A *priori*, there must have been some ritual of consecration whereby a young man of priestly heritage, after a special education, was elevated to actual priesthood. Some living ceremony must underlie that described in Exodus 29. The mention of *millū'îm* as a regular offering in Lev 7:37 suggests its periodic reenactment (according to 11QTemple XV:3, it was repeated annually [see Milgrom 1991: 558–66]). Ezekiel 44:26–27 also envisions a future seven-day inauguration *cum* Sin-offering, but it is unclear whether this is a perennial or a onetime event. (Maimonides *Sēper 'Ăbôdâ* 2.12–13 opines that *either* donning the garments *or* being anointed repeatedly for seven days would suffice to install a Great Priest.)

A HOUSE OF MERCHANDISE:
THE TABERNACLE AS FACTORY

The Book of Exodus describes Israel's rise out of bondage. Finally free to work for themselves and their god, the people explode into artistic endeavors, as if to rival their Egyptian contemporaries. Moreover, the biblical authors and other Israelites probably suffered from a cultural inferiority complex vis-à-vis Phoenicia—witness Solomon's importation of Tyrian craftsmen and his imitation of Phoenician architecture (Dever 2001: 144–57). The chauvinism of the original audience would have been gratified by the notion that Yahweh first inhabited not a Phoenician palace–temple but a sumptuous nomad's tent, built not by foreigners but by native Israelites with archaic-sounding names redolent of a tent-dwelling past, according to a model provided by God himself (NOTES to 31:2, "Bezalel," 31:6, "Oholiab").

The Priestly Source has little use for kings and prophets (NOTE to 7:1; vol. II p. 521). Its heroes instead are priests and artisans. The very terms *tərûmâ* 'Donation,' *tənûpâ* 'Elevation' and *ʿăbōdâ* 'work' connote both sacrifice and the amassing and working of materials. No less than sacrifice, construction is indispensable to bringing Yahweh to Earth and keeping him here. Like the burnt offering, Tabernacle-building is literally "sacri-fice," i.e., making the profane Holy.

As the Tabernacle was abuilding and as it was afterwards maintained, the sacred precinct would have been a hustle of activity. If the erection of the Tabernacle were a documented, historical event, we would mark the economic stimulus provided by broad employment and foreign trade—e.g., the exotic gems and spices—and the negative effects of wealth removed from circulation. For, however Jesus and his followers deplored the intersection of worship and commerce (Matt 21:12–13; Mark 11:15–17; John 2:14–17), ancient temples, no less than medieval monasteries, were hubs of industry and exchange. Stager and Wolff (1981: 97–98) list the economic activities archaeologically associated with Palestinian cult sites: metallurgy (see also Torrey 1943; Oppenheim 1947), oil production, pottery-making, textile manufacture and the sale of sacrificial animals. Writes Zaccagnini (1983: 245): "The emergence and spread of specialized crafts in the ancient Near East are strictly bound to the organization of the temple and palace economic structure and are a direct consequence of the process of surplus accumulation. . . . [The crafts] appeared or were given a thoroughly new dimension, both in terms of quality and the number of items produced, as soon as a class of specialized craftsmen existed who worked full time in the temple or palace ateliers." Berlejung (1996) even calls such artisans a type of "theologian."

Regarded with jaundiced cynicism, opulent public edifices are a waste of resources. Viewed from another angle, however, such projects not only symbolize but create that which they represent: Society. This is the religion's very essence (cf. Durkheim 1915).

THE SOUL'S RANSOM: THE CLEARING SILVER
(ordained in 30:11–15; fulfilled in ?)

The most mystifying section of the Tabernacle instructions may be 30:11–15. Why count the Israelites? Why conduct a census by a mandatory tax, rather than count the people directly? Why must the counted ransom their lives from Yahweh? If considerable silver was already donated, why now give more? When is the census conducted? Who is included in the count? Is this census onetime or perennial? What has the census to do with its literary context? I shall address these questions separately.

Why a census? Complex organizations must keep accounts, whether to provide for the common welfare or just "for the record." Literacy arose in the Fertile Crescent alongside bureaucracy. The scribes' main role was economic bookkeeping.

Land allotment and military conscription in particular require accurate headcounts (cf. Kupper 1950: 107; Speiser 1967; Weinfeld 1991: 293–94; Fales 1992); the Priestly Source conceives of Israel as an army about to take possession of land (vol. I, pp. 281, 405). Of all the pentateuchal sources, P is the most concerned with genealogical statistics: family relationships, age at reproduction, age at death, the population of each clan and tribe. It would be natural for the Priestly Writer to describe how such information was actually collected.

Why not count directly? Many cultures display a taboo on counting people or possessions. For example, to this day a traditional Jew will not enumerate the tenman quorum required for public prayer *(minyān)* but will instead recite a tenword prayer while pointing at each eligible worshiper (cf. *b. Yoma* 22b). And every ten years, the U.S. Census Bureau struggles vainly to obtain an accurate count of the American citizenry. There are at least three basic motives underlying our seemingly instinctual aversion to being counted. First, resisting the census may be a form of political protest. To be counted is to be taxed, conscripted and controlled. To remain uncounted is to remain free. Second, while most of us no longer actively believe in personified malefic forces, we frequently act as if we do. A census evidently makes people uneasy, lest the spirits grow jealous and prune back the population through disease or warfare. This taboo stems from unfocused paranoia based upon a very realistic sense of the precariousness of human existence, specifically the fact that a burgeoning population is liable to attract predators (see further below). Third, societies differ in the extent to which people identify themselves as individuals or as members of a family or clan. We Americans occupy one end of the spectrum, but the Israelites fell closer to the other (Robinson 1967), as did primitive humans. Arguably, something about headcounts violates our innate tribalism. (D. N. Freedman [privately] offers a fourth reason not to count: "It was an observation about the Black Plague of the Middle Ages in Europe, that it spread 'as a man walks . . . , ' from village to village and town to town; and it coincided with census-taking."

Why a ransom? The half-shekel tax is described as *kōper nepeš* 'ransom for each individual life' and as *kesep kippūrîm* 'Clearing Silver' (30:12, 16). How have the Israelites become so estranged from Yahweh that they must literally buy back their lives?

As 30:12 makes clear, it is the very act of counting that necessitates *kippūrîm*. Similarly, in Num 31:48–50, after enumerating the troops, the military officers dedicate to Yahweh jewelry taken in battle *ləkappēr ʿal-napšōtênû* 'to effect Clearing for our *souls*.' The exception that proves the rule is the Levitical census in Numbers 3–4. Since the entire tribe of Levi is donated to Yahweh as Israel's ransom for their firstborn (Num 3:40–51; 8:14–22), they need not ransom themselves.

As we have seen, to count is to control. Knowing the name and number of the stars (Ps 147:4) and everything under Heaven is Yahweh's sovereign prerogative. Further: the root for conducting a census, *pqd*, frequently describes acts of recompense, whether reward (e.g., Gen 21:1; 40:4; 50:24–25) or punishment (e.g., Exod 20:5; 32:34). Many commentators suggest that in Priestly theology, counting is tantamount to usurping divine knowledge and authority (e.g., Speiser 1967: 183–84; Clements 1972: 194; Houtman 2000: 562)—just as, for J, eating the fruit of Knowing Good and Bad is the primordial act of hubris (Genesis 2–3).

More precisely, in P the census is both offensive to God and yet permitted by him (rather like the kingship according to 1 Samuel 8; 10:18–19). It is an act of lèse-majesté for Israel to count Israel, but the priests can counteract Yahweh's vengeance by effecting *kippūrîm* 'Clearing.' Similarly, at Mari and Chagar Bazar in ancient Syria, the periodic census was called *tēbibtu* 'purification' and carried out by officers called *ebbu* 'pure,' presumably as a euphemism. In fact, a census creates ritual *im*purity (cf. Kupper 1950).

To count people is to attract malefic influences. True, like virtually all the biblical sources, the Priestly worldview makes no room for demonology (cf. vol. I, pp. 240–241, 434–37). Yet P's wording seems strangely vague. Yahweh does not quite command Moses to take a census. He says, "When you *lift the head* of (i.e., count) Israel's Sons. . . ." He does not say, "lest *I* harm them," but instead "lest there be against them harm." Like the paschal blood, the mandatory half-shekel appears to appease Yahweh's semiautonomous violence, the Destroyer (*hammašḥît*), who may ultimately be demonic in origin (vol. I, pp. 434–39). In both cases, P treads gingerly around a sensitive subject: God's responsibility for misfortune. Whether by the paschal blood or by the "Clearing Silver," Yahweh protects Israelites from himself.

Highly illuminating is comparison with David's calamitous census, reported in both 2 Samuel 24 and 1 Chronicles 21. The accounts basically agree in substance and even wording, the latter being a postexilic rewriting of the former. As we are told, David feels moved to conduct a census, despite the warnings of his general Joab. The author does not explain what is wrong with a census; this is regarded as self-evident. Immediately after the count is concluded, David is struck with contrition and prays that Yahweh forgive him his sin. God offers him a choice among three punishments: a seven-year famine, military defeat or a three-day plague. Somehow, the population will be cut back. David chooses the last option, and Yahweh's "Destroying Messenger" (*hammalʾāk hammašḥît*) is dispatched to effect the plague. Then there is another tally—of the dead. But just when the plague threatens Jerusalem itself, Yahweh decides that Israel has had enough and stays the angel's hand. The place where the Destroying Messenger stands will one day become the site of Solomon's Temple.

Both accounts exculpate David for this fiasco, but in different ways. 2 Sam 24:1 explains that Yahweh, in his anger against Israel, incited David to count them. In other words, the king is God's tool against his own people. 1 Chr 21:1, however, imputes the incitement to *śāṭān*, which may be understood either as "an adversary" or as "Mr. Adversary," i.e., Satan. Whether this supernatural opponent acts on his own initiative or at Yahweh's behest we cannot tell. But he is well on his way to becoming the Christian God's diabolical Enemy.

From David's experience, we may learn what sort of threat the half-shekel payment of Exod 30:11–16 is meant to avert. The antidote to supernatural "harm" is atonement and purification, afforded by the sacrificial cult and, in Exodus, by the "Clearing Silver" (on this use of *kpr*, cf. Ps 78:38, "But he is merciful; he Clears [*yəkappēr*] sin and does not destroy [*yašḥît*].") Yahweh takes the Israelites' money instead of their lives. (Similarly, according to Ramban, David's real fault was neglecting to pay the *per capita* half-shekel to Yahweh in the first place.)

As observed above, the sense of danger associated with a head-count is not unique to Israel. Dillmann (1880: 318) compares the Roman quinquennial census called *lustrum* 'purification,' wherein each citizen contributed a coin to facilitate an indirect computation of the population. The census was accompanied by expiatory offerings and prayers for well-being (Dionysus of Halicarnassus *Roman Antiquities* 4.22; Livy *Ab Urbe Condita* 1.44; for discussion and additional cross-cultural parallels, see Frazer 1919: 2.555–63; Weinfeld 1991; Githuku 2001).

What is the silver used for? The answer seems obvious: for the pedestals of the Tabernacle's frame and Veil, and for the pedestals and capitals of the Plaza (38:27–28). Similarly, in 2 Kgs 12:5–17; 2 Chr 24:5–14, the nation's silver goes toward maintaining and restoring the Temple (Fishbane 1995: 108–9). The problem is that much silver has already been donated (Exod 25:3; 35:5). Unless we impute inconsistency to P, we must assume that the first freewill Donation, in which the rich gave much and the poor little or nothing, was either inadequate (Abarbanel) or else formed the basis of the Tabernacle treasury and went to buy sacrifices (*y. Šeqal.* 1:1; on the funding of religion, see Torrey 1943; Oppenheim 1947; Hurowitz 1986). But it is equally possible that 25:3; 35:5 in fact have in mind the silver tax, carelessly included among the freewill offerings.

When is the census conducted? One would think at once. And yet, as we have observed, in 30:12 Yahweh assumes rather than commands that Moses will conduct a census (Abarbanel). In theory, it could take place at any time.

But is it not obvious that the census is immediate? Apart from counting Israel, its second purpose is to amass silver for the Tabernacle's components (38:25–28), and the Tabernacle is completed by the beginning of the first month of the second year (40:2, 17) (Rashi; Houtman 2000: 565). Accordingly, Rashbam infers that the tax is collected and the people counted when Moses assembles them in 35:1.

In Numbers 1, however, dated to the *second* month of the second year, Yahweh explicitly ordains a census: "*Lift the head* of all the community of Israel's Sons. . . ." Is this a second head-count? Even though Numbers 1 does not mention the half-shekel tax (Abarbanel), and even though Numbers excludes the Levites (Ramban), the censuses in Exodus and Numbers yield the *identical total*: 603,550 adult males (Exod 38:26; Num 1:46). Only two explanations are possible: either P inconspicuously recounts a miraculous violation of actuarial probability—i.e., during the intervening month, the number of those passing their twentieth birthday equaled the number of deaths plus the population of Levites (Ramban)—or else the two censuses are one and the same, with the Levites omitted both times (Wellhausen 1899: 139; Noth 1962: 236; Hyatt 1980: 293; Milgrom 1990: 338). The former is an interesting theory that might deserve elaboration, given the Levites' status as a ransom for the people (Num 3:45–51; 8:16–18; see below). But the latter solution seems simpler, especially since Exod 30:12 merely predicts a future census, whose results may be anticipated in 38:26 (see also NOTE to 30:13, "son of twenty year"). Such chronological displacement is frequent in P and often generates minor exegetical difficulties (see pp. 691–93).

How can we make temporal sense of the census? Clearly, by the beginning of the *first* month, the silver half-shekels have been smelted and reused in the Tabernacle. This is before, according to Numbers 1, the census is taken in the *second* month. The only possible resolution is Bekhor Shor's (on 38:28): the silver is in fact collected in the first month and used immediately. But the receipts are tallied a month later, when the population is officially announced. This delay is not surprising; any census is obsolete by its publication date. (Cassuto [1967: 470–71] similarly supposes that although the total is known in the first month, the figures continue to be processed [e.g., broken down by clan] for a month longer.)

Who counts; who is counted? We have already seen the likelihood that the census excludes the Levites. While only Numbers makes this explicit, their omission may be hinted at already in 38:21, where Ithamar and the Levites are entrusted with the census. Apparently, the counters do not include themselves, since they will not ransom themselves from Yahweh.

How often a census? Is the census a onetime event to gather silver for the Tabernacle components (Abarbanel) or a periodic head-count? Because Yahweh does not actually command Moses to take a census in Exodus, one might infer that a census is a perennial necessity, as if to say, "*Whenever* you count Israel's Sons" (Ramban). Admittedly, P never specifies that this ordinance is "for your generations," but perhaps it was obvious to the original audience, who were probably funding regular worship through periodic taxation. For example, in 2 Kgs 12:5–17; 22:3–7, the king directs the Temple's income toward refurbishment, and 2 Chr 24:6 refers specifically to *maśʾat mōše(h)* 'Moses' oblation' as a sacred donation.

I would draw two tentative conclusions from the fact that a second census is taken at the end of the wilderness wanderings, preparatory to allotting the tribal territories (Numbers 26). First, the census is envisioned as recurrent. Second, it is not held annually, but at the discretion of the religious authorities. In Roman times, however, as an innovation, the half-shekel was collected yearly from throughout the Jewish Diaspora (Josephus *War* 7.218; cf. *Ant.* 18.312; Matt 17:24–27; *m. Šeqal.*). Neh 10:33, curiously, mandates an annual *third*-shekel contribution, without citing Mosaic authority (Holzinger 1900: 145).

Relation to context? Overall, the contents of chaps. 30–31 seem most heterogeneous, as if the Priestly Writer were tying up loose ends. With the census, the author makes several points.

At the most superficial level, before the cult can become operational, it must have a means to raise future funds. Second, at this crucial juncture in history, a stocktaking is required; for the record, the historian must report the adult male population. Third, the Levites' role as census-takers foreshadows and complements their future status as hierodules.

Lastly, the silver amassed during the first census does not just go into the Tabernacle treasury. Rather, it is built into the structure of both the Tabernacle and its Plaza, the people's court accessible to any Israelite (38:25–28). The donors do not really lose access to their wealth; instead, they reap a great benefit. By purchasing their lives back from God at a nominal price, the Exodus generation obtains the periodic purification and reconciliation with God that should permit them to abide in his Presence — if only they can remain faithful to his Law.

PART VI. THE COVENANT BROKEN AND RESTORED (EXODUS 32–34)

◆

XX. *These are your deity, Israel* (32:1–35)

32 $^{1(E?)}$And the people saw that Moses had delayed to descend from the mountain, and the people assembled around Aaron and said to him, "Get up, make us deity that they may go before us, for this one, Moses, the man who took us up from the land of Egypt, we do not know what happened to him."

^{2}So Aaron said to them, "Strip off the gold rings that are in your *women's*, sons' and daughters' ears, and bring to me." ^{3}And all the people stripped off from themselves the gold rings that were in their ears and brought to Aaron. ^{4}And he took from their hand and bound it in the bag and made it a metal calf. And they said, "These are your deity, Israel, who took you up from the land of Egypt."

^{5}And Aaron saw/feared and built an altar before it, and Aaron called and said, "Tomorrow is a festival for Yahweh."

^{6}And they got up early the next day and *sent up* Ascending-offerings and presented Concluding-offerings. And the people sat down to eat and drink, and they got up to revel.

$^{7(D\text{-like})}$And Yahweh spoke to Moses, saying, "Descend, for your people whom you took up from the land of Egypt has corrupted, ^{8}they have quickly departed from the way that I commanded them. They have made themselves a metal calf and bowed to it and sacrificed to it and said, 'These are your deity, Israel, who took you up from the land of Egypt.' "

^{9}And Yahweh said to Moses, "I have seen this people, and, see: it is a hard-necked people. ^{10}And now leave me alone, that my *nose* may flare against them and I may finish them off and make you into a great nation."

^{11}But Moses placated Yahweh his deity's *face*, and he said, "Why, Yahweh, should your *nose* flare against your people whom you took out from Egypt with great strength and with a strong limb? ^{12}Why should Egypt say, saying, 'For bad he took them out, to kill them in the mountains and to finish them off from the earth's surface'? Turn back from your *nose* flaring and repent about the bad to your people. ^{13}Remember for Abraham, for Isaac and for Israel, your slaves, to whom you swore by yourself and spoke to them: 'I will mutiply your *seed* like the heavens' stars, and all this land that I said, "I will give to your *seed*," and they will possess to eternity.' "

¹⁴⁽ᴱ⁾⁾And Yahweh repented concerning the bad that he spoke to do to his people.

¹⁵Then Moses turned and descended from the mountain, and the two Testimony Tablets in his hands, tablets written from their two sides, *on here and on here* they were written; ¹⁶and the tablets, they were Deity's work; and the writing, it was Deity's writing engraved on the tablets.

¹⁷And Joshua heard the people's sound in its shouting, and he said to Moses, "A *sound:* war in the camp."

¹⁸And he said, "Not the sound of ʿănôt of strength, nor the sound of ʿănôt of conquest; the sound of ʿannôt I am hearing."

¹⁹And it happened, as he approached to the camp and saw the calf and dances, then Moses' *nose* flared, and he threw the tablets from his hands and smashed them at the mountain's bottom. ²⁰And he took the calf that they had made, and he burned with fire and ground till fine and sprinkled onto the waters' surface and made Israel's Sons drink.

²¹And Moses said to Aaron, "What did this people do to you that you brought upon it a great sin?"

²²And Aaron said, "My lord's *nose* should not flare. You, you know the people, that it is in bad; ²³and they said to me, 'Make us deity that they (cf. 32:1) may go before us, for this one, Moses, the man who took us up from the land of Egypt, we do not know what happened to him.' ²⁴So I said to them, 'Whoever has gold, strip it off yourself,' and they gave to me; and I threw it into the fire, and this calf came out."

²⁵And Moses saw the people, that it was wild—for Aaron had made them wild, for contempt among their *uprisers*—²⁶and Moses stood at the camp's gate and said, "Whoever is for Yahweh, to me!" And all Levi's Sons gathered to him.

²⁷And he said to them, "Thus has Yahweh Israel's deity said: Put, (each) man his sword upon his thigh, and cross and return from gate to gate in the camp and kill, (each) man his brother and (each) man his fellow and (each) man his relative." ²⁸And Levi's Sons did according to Moses' word. And about three thousand man of the people fell on that day. ²⁹And Moses said, "Today, your *hand has been filled* for Yahweh, indeed (each) man through his son and through his brother, even to place a blessing on yourselves today."

³⁰And it happened on the next day, and Moses said to the people, "You, you have sinned a great sin. And now, I will ascend to Yahweh; perhaps I can Clear for your sin."

³¹And Moses returned to Yahweh and said, "Ah now, this people has sinned a great sin, and they made for themselves a gold deity. ³²And now, if you will *lift* their sin . . . but if not, erase me then from your Document that you have written."

³³And Yahweh said to Moses, "Whoever has sinned against me, I will erase him from my Document. ³⁴But now go, lead the people to where I spoke to you. See: my Messenger, he will go before you. And in the day of my accounting, then I will account their sin against them."

³⁵ And Yahweh harmed the people, inasmuch as they had made the calf that Aaron made.

ANALYSIS

TEXTUAL NOTES

32:1. *Get up, make.* LXX interposes a conjunction.

† *took us up.* LXX has "took us *out*," as if reading **hôṣî'ānû*, vs. MT-Sam *he'ĕlānû.* This looks to be incidental, not evidence of a variant *Vorlage,* but LXX is extremely consistent in translating *hôṣî'* with *exagein* and *he'ĕlâ* with *anabibazein.* Most likely its *Vorlage* differed from MT-Sam. Between the two variants, *he'ĕlānû* is somewhat more likely to be original, as it is the rarer term both in the Bible and in Exodus (*hôṣî'* appears 23 times in Exodus, 72 times in the Bible; *he'ĕlâ* appears 10 times in Exod, 37 times in the Bible). In any case, only *he'ĕlâ* is securely attested in 32:1. See also TEXTUAL NOTES to 32:4, 7, 23; 33:1.

the land of Egypt. LXX^BFM has simply "from Egypt."

32:2. *sons'.* Syr inserts "and." The sons are entirely absent from LXX and some MSS of Syr. The most obvious explanation is parablepsis due to homoioteleuton with the preceding word and overall similarity to the following word, whether in Hebrew (*nšykm <bnykm> wbntykm*), in Greek (*tōn gynaikōn hymōn <kai huiōn> kai thygaterōn*) or in Syriac (*dnšykwn <wdbnykwn> wdbntkwn*).

† 32:3. *gold.* The metal is missing in Syr. In older witnesses, we would consider this the superior reading; the reconstructed *Vorlage* would be **hnzmym,* against MT-Sam *nzmy hzhb.* While Syr is not given to streamlining in the manner of Vg, however, it is prone to haplography. Therefore, it is more likely that an original Syr **qdš' ddhb' d'yt* was reduced to *qdš' d'yt* due to homoioarkton (*d . . . d*) or homoioteleuton (*' . . . '*).

† 32:4. *And they said.* So MT, Sam, Syr, *Tgs. Onqelos* and *Ps.-Jonathan* and LXX^AM. LXX^B, however, has "and *he* said," which Wevers (1990: 519) regards as the original LXX; coincidentally or not, it is supported by Kenn 103, 109. The difference is crucial: did Aaron's complicity go so far as to acclaim the calf as Israel's liberator? If so, one can easily imagine the other Versions pluralizing the verb in exculpation. On the other hand, since Aaron is the grammatical subject of the general context (see TEXTUAL NOTE to 32:6), one can also imagine LXX^B unconsciously making the verb singular. In any case, Yahweh's summary in 32:8 (even in LXX^B) credits the people, not Aaron, with these words. We find analogous ambiguity in the matter of who made the calf (TEXTUAL NOTE to 32:35).

took you up. Tg. *Ps.-Jonathan* has "took you *out.*" In the parallel 32:8, however, *Tg. Ps.-Jonathan* agrees with MT-Sam "took you *up.*" Cf. TEXTUAL NOTES to 32:1, 7, 23.

† 32:5. *saw/feared.* The consonants *wyr'* are ambiguous and allow two equally possible readings. MT, LXX, Vg, *Samaritan Tg. A* and *Tg. Onqelos* all read *wayyar(') 'and . . . saw*'; Syr and *Samaritan Tg. J* read **wayyīrā(') 'and . . . feared.'* *Tgs. Neofiti I* and *Ps.-Jonathan* have it both ways: "And Aaron saw . . . and feared."

† 32:6. *they*. In LXX, the subject of all verbs in vv 4–6 is Aaron not Israel, and its *Vorlage* presumably read *wyškm . . . wyʿl . . . wygš* (cf. TEXTUAL NOTE to 32:4, "And they said"). Although my translation follows the MT-Sam reading, since it is actually attested in Hebrew, it is easy to imagine an original text portraying Aaron as the chief idolater, as in LXX.

Concluding-offering. Syr continues: "and they sacrificed sacrifices."

†† 32:7. *saying*. I tentatively read *lʾmr* with 4QpaleoExodᵐ, Sam, LXX and Vg; it is absent from MT. We cannot be certain, however. While inserting "saying" would be a typical expansion (cf. TEXTUAL NOTE to 32:13, "to them"), its loss before *lk* would be a typical scribal error (homoioarkton). And *lk* itself may be secondary; cf. next TEXTUAL NOTE.

†† *Descend*. Reading *rd* with 4QpaleoExodᵐ, which offers the shortest text (Sanderson 1986: 55–56). MT and Sam have *lek-rēd* 'Go, descend,' possibly borrowed from 19:24 (see also TEXTUAL NOTE to 32:34, "go, lead"). And LXX, borrowing from Deut 9:12, reads: "Go quickly, get down from here," as if reading *qûm rēd mahēr mizze(h)* (see also *Bib. Ant.* 12:4). Finally, Syr partly synthesizes MT-Sam and LXX: "Descend, go you from here," as if reading *rēd lek-ləkā mizze(h)*.

took up. Again, LXX has "took *out*," this time with the support of Syr and *Tg. Neofiti I*; cf. TEXTUAL NOTES to 32:1, 4, 23. The source of this variant, here and throughout chap. 32, may be assimilation to Deut 9:12, where we find *hôṣē(ʾ)tā* 'you took *out*.'

land of Egypt. Kenn 69 and Syr lack "land of."

† 32:8. *I commanded them*. The standard MT-Sam consonantal text is ambiguous. *Ṣwytm* might be vocalized either *ṣiwwîtîm* 'I commanded them' (standard MT, *Tg. Onqelos*) or *ṣiwwîtām* 'you commanded them' (LXX, Syr [over-dot], Vg, Kenn 160). We find an explicitly first-person plene spelling *ṣwytym*, in Kenn 5, 9, 13, 17, 69, 75, 80, 81, 108, 109, 193, 196, 244, 260, 603, Rossi 18, 248, 503, 611, 669, 766 and Soncino Bible (1488); the same variants also obtain for the parallel in Deut 9:12. One might prefer the first person as the more difficult reading, since it is defectively spelled in standard MT-Sam. More important, MT "I commanded them" is confirmed by Deut 9:16, "You have quickly departed from the way that *Yahweh* commanded you."

They have made. Kenn 69 and Syr insert a conjunction.

† *a metal calf*. LXX has simply "a calf." This deserves consideration as the shorter reading, although it is unattested in Hebrew MSS. If MT-Sam is expansionist, the source is Deut 9:12, where MT-LXX reads "they made themselves a metal thing *(massēkâ)*" and Sam inserts "calf *(ʿgl mskh)*."

SPECULATION: If we systematically favor the shortest reading, the most likely scenario is that Exod 32:8 originally read "a calf" (LXX) and that Deut 9:12 originally read "a metal thing" (MT-LXX). In Exod 32:8, MT-Sam combined these variants, while Sam did the same in Deut 9:12. (We find analogous variation in the phrase "metal thing/calf" within the LXX tradition for Deut 9:16.)

† 32:10. *And now.* Exod 32:9 is wholly absent from LXX. One might argue that MT-Sam have imported the verse from Deut 9:13. We indeed find a repeated tendency to expand Exodus on the basis of parallels in Deuteronomy—admittedly, primarily in Sam not MT (for chap. 32, see TEXTUAL NOTES to vv 7, "Descend," "took up"; 8, "a metal calf," 10, "nation"; 11, "with great strength and with a strong limb"; 13, "stars"; 15, "tablets written"). Moreover, in MT-Sam, the sequence "And Yahweh spoke . . . and Yahweh said" in vv 7, 9 might strike one as awkwardly redundant. Still, this type of redundancy is well attested in passages whose textual integrity is not in question; see vol. I, pp. 192–93, and note especially Deut 9:12–13. Moreover, Israel's "hard neck" is a theme elsewhere in Exodus (33:3, 5; 34:9). More likely, v 9 dropped from LXX simply because both vv 9 and 10 begin "and." For further discussion, see Sanderson (1986: 101–2).

nation. Sam and 4QpaleoExod^m and three LXX MSS continue with words adapted from Deut 9:20: "And against Aaron Yahweh was very enraged, to destroy him; but Moses interceded on Aaron's behalf." This sort of harmonization is typical of Sam and 4QpaleoExod^m.

† 32:11. *Yahweh his deity.* LXX^B and Kenn 69 (first hand) have "Yahweh the God."

†† *Egypt.* So Sam and Syr; MT has "the land of Egypt."

†† *with great strength and with a strong limb.* Following the unique *lectio difficilior* of 4QpaleoExod^m *[bkwḥ gdwl w]bzrwʿ ḥzq[h].* The expression *bizrôaʿ ḥăzāqâ* 'with a strong limb' is paralleled only in Jer 21:5: *bəyād nəṭûyâ ûbizrôaʿ ḥăzāqâ* 'with an extended arm and with a strong limb,' inverting the familiar formula *bəyād ḥăzāqâ ûbizrôaʿ nəṭûyâ* 'with a strong arm and with an extended limb' (Deut 4:34; 5:15, etc.). Assuming 4QpaleoExod^m is original, this cliché probably inspired MT Exod 32:11 *bəkōaḥ gādôl ûb(ə)yād ḥăzāqâ* 'with great strength and with a strong *arm.*' Sam *bkḥ gdwl wbzrwʿ nṭwyh* 'with great strength and with an *extended* limb' represents the alternative accommodation to the norm and also more closely resembles Deut 9:29: *bəkōḥăkā haggādōl ûbizrōʿăkā hannəṭûyâ* 'with *your* great strength and with *your extended* limb' (but note also Deut 9:26). LXX Exod 32:11 copies Deut 9:29 even more closely ("with great strength and with *your extended limb*"), while Syr and *Tg. Neofiti I* adapt Exod 32:11 to Deut 9:29 *verbatim.* Still, we cannot discount the possibility that either MT or Sam is correct, and that 4QpaleoExod^m is an attempt to combine them. For further discussion, see Sanderson (1986: 145–47).

† 32:13. *Remember.* LXX renders with the participle *mnēstheis* 'remember*ing*' (see Wevers 1992: 219). This is doubtless free translation—to vocalize *zkr* as the participle **zōkēr* would be most unnatural—but it might reflect the infinitive absolute **zākōr*, against the MT imperative *zəkōr.*

† *Isaac.* Kenn 109, LXX, Syr and *Tg. Ps.-Jonathan* (Rieder 1974: 131 n. 10) prepose "and" (*w*). Although conjunctions randomly come and go, it is worth observing that the first letter of "Isaac," yodh, was often identical to waw in Greco-Roman era script (Cross 1961a; Qimron 1972). So this could be counted as dittography.

Israel. Sam and LXX have "Jacob," the more expected and hence less likely reading.

to whom. Lāhem is not reflected in LXX[B]; perhaps it was dropped as redundant.
to them. To clarify where the quotation begins, LXX adds "saying."

† *I will multiply.* The unique LXX *polyplēthynō* 'I will *much* multiply' probably follows Sam *hrbh 'rbh* 'multiplying I will multiply,' a cliché paralleled in Gen 3:16; 16:10; 22:17. On the one hand, the reduction of *hrbh 'rbh* to just *'rbh* might be a slightly irregular haplography. On the other hand, the expansion of *'rbh* to *hrbh 'rbh* would be a typical harmonization, to which Sam especially is prone.

stars. LXX adds "for multitude," as if reading **lārōb*, inspired by Deut 1:10; 10:22; 28:62.

I said, "I will give to your seed." LXX MSS present two variants, neither equal to MT-Sam: "*you* said to give to *their* seed" (LXX[A]) and "*you* said to give to *them*" (LXX[B]). Both probably are paraphrases of a slightly awkard *Vorlage* that is the same as MT-Sam.

† *and they will possess.* So MT (*wənāḥălû*). Sam, 4QpaleoExod[m], LXX, Syr, Vg and Tg. Neofiti I add "it" (*wnḥlwh*).

SPECULATION: Although we do not expect waw-yodh confusion in Sam, I cannot help wondering whether the correct reading is not *ynḥlw*, without the superfluous conjunction.

† 32:14. *spoke.* LXX, Syr and Tg. Neofiti I may reflect *'āmar* 'said,' against MT-Sam *dibber.* *'Āmar* would be the more expected reading, since the verb often connotes thought or purpose.

32:15. *the two Testimony Tablets.* Tg. Neofiti I has simply *wtryn lwḥy* 'and two tablets.' This *lectio brevior* probably resulted from error committed during translation: Hebrew *wšny l(w)ḥ(w)t h'd(w)t* became *wšny l(w)ḥ(w)t* due to homoioteleuton.

†† *his hands.* I follow the unique reading of LXX; all other Versions have "his hand." The source of confusion is that *ydw* is "his hands" (*yādāw*) in earlier Israelite orthography but "his hand" (*yādô*) in later spelling (Andersen and Forbes 1986: 62). Either reading, then, might be correct (*pace* Wevers 1990: 527). In v 19, MT and LXX agree that Moses was using two hands (Syr and Vg, however, have the singular). It is probably to relieve a similar ambiguity that the parallel in Deut 9:15, 17 specifies *štê yādāy* 'my *two* hands,' lest one read **yādî* 'my hand.' Cf. TEXTUAL NOTES to 32:19, "from his hands," 34:4, "and he took in his hand," 29, "in Moses' hand."

tablets written. LXX expands: "*stone* tablets written"; cf. 24:12; 31:18; 34:1, 4; Deut 9:11, etc.

32:17. *its shouting.* Samaritan tradition (e.g., *Samaritan Tg.*) and *Fragmentary Targum* midrashically interpret *br'h* as "in its evil' (*bərā'ōh*, vs. MT *bərē'ōh*).

32:18. *And he said.* Syr expands: "And Moses said *to him*" (also various witnesses to LXX).

† *'ānôt . . . 'annôt.* Except for Aquila and Theodotion, all ancient translations somehow reflect the MT distinction between these enigmatic words; see further NOTE. Against MT *'annôt*, some Sam MSS (von Gall 1918: 185; Baillet 1982:

34) read ʿwnwt 'iniquities' (ʿăwōnôt), and such is the interpretation of *Samaritan Tg.* and *Syr.* (If this reading is correct, it creates an opportunity for the English translator: "I hear not *singing* but *sinning*.")

32:19. *and dances.* Sam and LXX have w't hmḥlwt 'and *the* dances,' against the shorter and more difficult MT wmḥlwt.

the tablets. LXX expands: "the *two* tablets."

from his hands. So MT (Qere)-Sam-LXX-Tgs; the plural is confirmed by Deut 9:17, "my *two* hands." But Syr and Vg have the singular with MT Kethibh; cf. TEXTUAL NOTES to 32:15, "his hands"; 34:4, "and he took in his hand," 29, "in Moses' hand."

† *the mountain's bottom.* Against MT taḥat hāhār, Sam has a synonymous bthṭyt hhr, as in 19:17. Some or all of the Aramaic witnesses possibly but not necessarily follow this reading (BHS).

† 32:20. *burned . . . ground . . . sprinkled . . . made . . . drink.* In MT, these verbs lack explicit direct objects. LXX inserts "it" after each, and Syr does the same for the first three. This would normally be dismissed as paraphrase, but in fact Sam supplies pronominal objects for the first two verbs (wyśrphw . . . wyṭḥnhw). In any case, the MT *lectio brevior* is preferable.

For MT-Sam wyzr ʿl pny hmym, LXX has kai espeiren auton epi to hydōr 'and he sowed it upon the water.' It is true that zry 'sprinkle' and zrʿ 'sow' are semantically akin (Loewenstamm 1962b), and that Greek speirein also means "scatter," but Exod 32:20 and Num 17:2 are the only cases of Greek speirein corresponding to Hebrew zry. Here, at least, there is a strong possibility that the LXX *Vorlage* actually read *wyzrʿ ʿl pny hmym.* If LXX is correct, MT-Sam is haplographic; if MT-Sam is correct, LXX is dittographic. MT-Sam is probably original; it is semantically closer to Deut 9:21 wāʾašlīk 'and I cast.'

† 32:22. *Aaron said.* Kenn 181, LXX and *Tg. Neofiti I* add "to Moses." This is probably a clarifying expansion, since Aaron's calling Moses "my Lord" (Hebrew ʾădōnî, Greek kyrie) might mislead readers into thinking that *God* is the addressee. On the other hand, the shorter MT-Sam reading might be the result of parablepsis (ʾl . . . ʾl), with *wydbr ʾhrwn ʾl mšh ʾl* reduced to wydbr ʾhrwn ʾl.

You, you know. LXX begins with "for."

† *the people, that it is in bad.* For the difficult MT hāʿām kî bərāʿ hûʾ, LXX paraphrases: to hormēma tou laou toutou 'this people's impulsiveness.' Sam features a *lectio facilior* that might be correct: hʿm ky prwʿ hwʾ 'the people, that it is *wild*' (this may indeed be the LXX *Vorlage*). The root prʿ recurs in 32:25, which could be the source of Sam's variant. On the other hand, MT brʿ could be influenced by brʿh 'in its shouting' in 32:17. Whichever is correct, the source of the error is presumably the similarity of p and b in shape and sound in all periods.

32:23. *the man.* Missing in *Tg. Neofiti I*, perhaps because of the resemblance to the preceding and following words (mšh <hʾyš> ʾšr).

took us up. LXX has "took us *out*" (also *Tg. Neofiti I*); cf. TEXTUAL NOTES to 32:1, 4, 7.

from the land of Egypt. LXX^BFM omits "the land of."

32:27. *he said.* Syr specifies: "*Moses* said."

†† *and cross.* Reading *w'brw* with 4QpaleoExod^m, Sam, Kenn 181, Syr and LXX; MT lacks the conjunction (also *Tgs.* and Vg). MT is attractively short and difficult, but perhaps too awkward. Whichever is original, that the previous word ended in waw created an opportunity for haplography or dittography, especially assuming continuous writing.

32:28. *three thousand.* A few LXX MSS and Vg have "*twenty*-three thousand," followed in 1 Cor 10:8. Wevers (1990: 535) explains this as a corruption of *eis* 'about' into *eikosi* 'twenty.'

of the people. These words are missing in Vg. Jerome is admittedly given to deliberate compression, but this would be an unusual omission. Vg 32:28 contains a high concentration of deviations from MT, as if the Saint's attention were wavering.

32:29. *And Moses said.* Most Syr MSS omit "and," but that cannot be original. LXX and Syr add "to them."

today (first time). This is missing from *Tg. Ps.-Jonathan*, perhaps due to homoioteleuton, whether in Hebrew *(ydkm hywm > ydkm)* or in Aramaic *(*lkwn ywm' dyn > lkwn).*

† *Your hand has been filled.* 4QpaleoExod^m, Sam, LXX, Vg, Syr, *Tgs.* and Kenn 4, 9, 69, 84, 101, 125, 150, 153, 186, 686, Rossi 197, 668, 766 all read *ml'w ydykm* 'your hands have been filled,' against standard MT *ml'w ydkm.* I follow MT, because the idiom for priestly consecration is to "fill the hand," always in the singular (the only exception in MT is Ezek 43:26 [Qere]). Admittedly, many Levites are addressed, but in such cases Hebrew still prefers the singular.

MT vocalizes the verb as *mil'û*, either a Qal imperative (so *Tgs. Ps.-Jonathan* and *Neofiti I*) or an impersonal Pi'el perfect (*Tg. Onqelos* MSS are divided between the perfect and the imperative). See further NOTE.

for. Not reflected in LXX, Syr and Vg, probably because it is hard to understand *kî* here.

† *even to place.* Kenn 181, LXX, Syr and Vg lack the conjunction *w*, perhaps rightly. Since the previous letter is also waw, either dittography to produce MT-Sam or haplography to produce LXX-Syr-Vg is possible, especially in continuous writing.

† *today* (second time). Missing in LXX and Vg, presumably dropped in the interest of economy or by homoioteleuton *('lykm hywm > 'lykm).*

SPECULATION: A more devious approach would regard LXX-Vg as original. In MT-Sam, the double presence of *hywm* in v 29 is indeed suspicious. Since each time *hywm* follows another word ending in mem *(ydkm, 'lykm)*, perhaps it dropped from its original position, whichever that was, and was reinserted twice, once rightly and once wrongly.

† 32:30. *Yahweh.* LXX has "the God."

† 32:31. *Ah now.* Instead of MT *'nh*, Sam has *hnh* 'see,' possibly correctly; cf. TEXTUAL NOTE to 18:6, "I." LXX supports MT but adds "O Lord"; Syr expands "O Lord, God."

† 32:32. *lift their sin. . . .* Sam, LXX and *Tg. Ps.-Jonathan* continue with the ex-

pected *š* '(then) lift.' Since there is no obvious cause for scribal error, I follow the difficult and short MT; Aejmelaeus (1987: 81–82), however, considers MT too difficult to be correct. See further NOTE to 32:32.

† *then.* Sam and LXX lack *nāʾ*, perhaps correctly. It could be a quasi-duplication of the preceding suffix *-nî*.

32:34. go, lead. LXX[B] has "go, *descend and* lead," as if reading **lk rd wnḥḥ*, similar to MT 19:24; 32:7 (see TEXTUAL NOTE, "Descend"). Similarly, Kenn 107 has *lēk ʿālē(h) nəḥē(h)* 'go, go up, lead,' influenced by 33:1. Other LXX MSS and Vg agree with MT but insert a conjunction. MT-Sam is preferable as the asyndetic, shortest reading: *lēk nəḥē(h).*

the people. Kenn 1, LXX, Syr and Vg have "*this* people."

to where. LXX and *Tgs.* expand "to *the place* where," as if reading **ʾel-hammāqôm ʾăšer*, in diction reminiscent of Deuteronomy (12:5, 11, 26, etc.) and possibly also exploiting the cognate relationship between Hebrew *ʾăšer* 'where' and Aramaic *ʾatrā* 'place.' Rossi 16 (first hand) has *ʾel-māqôm ʾăšer* 'to *a* place where.' Sam is closer to MT, but replaces *ʾl* with *ʿl* 'upon.'

† *I spoke.* LXX and Syr have the more expected "I *said*"; cf. TEXTUAL NOTE to 32:14.

See. Sam, Kenn 69, 132, MT Sebhirin and Syr insert "and."

32:35. they had made. Syr *plaḥû* 'they had *worshiped*,' *Tg. Ps.-Jonathan gəhanû* 'they had *bowed*' and *Tg. Onqelos ʾištaʿ(ă)badû* 'they had *subjugated themselves*' obviate the ambiguity of MT-Sam—did Aaron or all Israel make the calf?—through a complicated chain of bilingual associations: Hebrew *ʿāśû* = Aramaic **ʿăbadû* 'they made,' then interpreted by Syr and *Tg. Ps.-Jonathan* as if Hebrew **ʿābədû* 'they worshiped.' *Tg. Onqelos* follows a similar interpretation but goes a step farther, associating Aramaic *ʿbd* with the Hebrew noun *ʿebed* 'slave' and the Aramaic Shaphʿel *šaʿbēd* 'enslave.'

SOURCE AND REDACTION ANALYSIS

See pp. 148–53.

NOTES

32:1. delayed. While the identification of *bwš* II 'tarry' with *bwš* I 'be ashamed' is belied by comparative Semitic evidence—their respective Proto-Semitic roots are **bwš* and **bwt*—at the folk etymological level, Ehrlich's (1908: 389; 1969: 198–99) explanation is quite reasonable: the Polel *bōšēš* means "to cause shame, discomfort."

around Aaron. One could also translate *ʿal-ʾahărōn* as "*before* Aaron" or "*against* Aaron," since *niqhal* 'assemble' plus *ʿal* always implies a threatening confrontation (Num 16:3; 17:7; 20:2) (Ehrlich 1908: 389).

What happened to Hur, deputized to be Aaron's coleader (24:14)? According to legend, he was killed resisting the apostates (*Exod. Rab.* 41:7). This would be the sound of violence that Joshua hears (32:17).

and said. What follows is a surprise. Logically one would expect the people to say, "Where is Moses?" or "What shall we do?" or "You, Aaron, lead us to Canaan." Instead, they propose a religious innovation.

Get up. The verb *qûm* often describes initiating an action, as we use "go" in English ("Go make us a breakfast," "He went and died," etc.).

make. From the aniconic perspective, assumed to be shared by narrator and reader, the people's demand is nonsensically self-undermining (Jacob 1992: 936). How can one "make" God? Compare Hos 14:4, "We shall no longer say 'deity (*'ĕlōhîm*)' of our hands' work (*ma'ăśē[h] yādênû*)," and Jer 16:20, "Shall a man make himself gods, and they are no-gods?"

deity . . . they. It is unclear whether *'ĕlōhîm* is better translated as singular ("a deity") or plural ("gods" [LXX, Syr, Vg]). On the one hand, only one image is fashioned. On the other hand, all the verbs and adjectives attached to *'ĕlōhîm* in vv 1, 4, 8, 23 are plural, so that, reading v 1 alone, we would naturally assume that the people are requesting that Aaron make several idols. Given the ambiguities, I have striven to make my translation as incongruent as the original. See further below, NOTE to 32:4, "These are your deity."

Bekhor Shor registers an extraordinary exculpation of Aaron and Israel that impresses for its novelty if not its cogency. The people are requesting a *judge* (cf. NOTE to 21:6), i.e., a new leader. To forestall the rebellion, Aaron essentially proposes a communal art project as a *pastime*, which Israel never mistakes for an idol (cf. also Ramban).

go before. Rather than trust in Yahweh's promise of a guiding Messenger (23:20), the people propose to construct their own (cf. Mann 1977: 155). Of course, the statue will not "go"; it will have to be carried (cf. Isa 46:1–2). But the people are already fluent in the language of idolatry.

this (one), Moses. The syntax may convey derision.

the man who took us up. The *man* Moses did not take the people up from Egypt; the *god* Yahweh did. But the Israelites' memory and understanding of the mighty events four months earlier have been evolving. As described in Exodus 7–15, Israel's liberation was wholly miraculous. And in chap. 20, they heard the speaking voice of "Yahweh your deity who took you out from the land of Egypt," whose first demands were that Israel worship no other gods and make no graven images. But in 32:1, they no longer believe that their emancipation was Yahweh's doing. Having turned their human leader into a god, the people are more than halfway to idol-worship. Yahweh will ironically mimic their words in 32:7; 33:1, describing Israel to Moses as "the people whom *you* took up from the land of Egypt." God even threatens truly to abandon Israel to Moses' leadership (33:1–6, 12) but eventually relents (33:14).

we do not know. Although it was at the people's behest that Moses had ascended the mountain (20:18[15]–21[18]), the Israelites' concern seems quite reasonable. But they should pray or solicit an oracle, not take matters into their own hands.

32:2. *women's, sons' and daughters' ears.* "Women (*nāšîm*)" are wives. Why does it not say, "in *your* ears"? Did adult men not wear earrings? Did a scribe omit a word? (Hypothetically, the original could have been **b'znykm wb'zny nšykm bnykm wbntykm* 'in your ears, in your women's, sons' and daughters' ears.') Judg

8:24 implies that Israelite men did not wear earrings, or at any rate wore less jewelry than desert nomads (cf. also Job 42:11). The *nezem* is explicitly worn by women also in Gen 24:22, 30, 47; Isa 3:21; Ezek 16:12; Hos 2:15; implicitly in Prov 11:22. See further NOTES to 32:3; 33:4.

Some commentators think that, by asking for materials, Aaron is just stalling for time (cf. Saadiah *apud* ibn Ezra). If so, perhaps he imagines that there will be a delay while the men cajole or compel their families to surrender their finery. It may (or may not) be overreading to suggest that the donation of earrings, rather than nose-rings or arm bands, is deliberately ironic. The ear is the organ of obedience. The very ears that heard Yahweh's voice ban the worship of graven images are to provide the materials for an idol. Sarna (1991: 203) notes that Gideon's idolatrous ephod, too, is made from earrings (Judg 8:24–27).

Aaron's collection of the people's gold makes perfect sense: he intends to fashion a golden image. But there is an element of implied irony, too. Elsewhere in the Bible, removing one's finery is an act of ascetic repentance associated with the *repudiation* of idolatry (Gen 35:2, 4; Exod 33:4–6). And the next time the people collect their earrings, it will be for making God's Tabernacle (35:22 [P]).

32:3. *all the people.* Although Aaron demanded only women's and children's ornaments, it seems that, in their enthusiasm, the men complied, too (Jacob 1992: 938).

stripped off from themselves. To explain the slightly anomalous use of the direct object marker with a reflexive Hithpaʿel verb *(wayyitpārəqû . . . ʾet-nizmê hazzāhāb)*, Rashi appears to understand ʾ*et* as ʾ*ēt* II, here equivalent to *min* 'from.' Better, I think, to recognize a double accusative: i.e., the jewelry is the logical direct object of *prq* 'strip off,' alongside the people themselves (Luzzatto).

32:4. *bound it in the bag.* Three interpretations have been proposed for the clause *wyṣr ʾtw bḥrṭ.* LXX has "formed it with the burin," after the ordinary meaning of *ḥrṭ* 'incise' and reading the verb *ṣwr* 'fashion, shape.'

To this, some object that one should engrave the calf only after it has been cast. Thus ibn Janaḥ, ibn Ezra and Saadiah, followed by Eissfeldt (1937) and Torrey (1943: 300–1), infer that here *yṣr* means "cast" and that *ḥrṭ* must mean "mold" (see also Syr *twps*ʾ). This fits the context very well, but, pending new discoveries, is hard to defend linguistically. Still, it is possible that Aaron carves a mold of some sort with his *chisel*; cf. Knobel's suggestion *(apud* Dillmann 1880: 226–27) that he digs out a mold in the sand.

An alternative, very attractive interpretation reads a defectively spelled *ḥārīṭ* 'bag' and the root *ṣrr* 'bind up,' which in Deut 14:25; 2 Kgs 12:11 refers to bundling silver (Luzzatto; Gevirtz 1984). The scene in Exodus thus parallels Judg 8:25, where gold collected for sacral purposes is wrapped in a garment *(śimlâ)*. And see also 2 Kgs 5:23: "And he bound *(wayyāṣar)* two talents, silver, in two bags *(ḥārīṭîm)*." (Another term for a bundle of gold or silver is *ṣərôr* [Gen 42:35; Hag 1:6; Prov 7:20], related to the verb *ṣwr/ṣrr* 'bind.')

SPECULATION: I do not know whether anyone has suggested that the Gold Calf is a two-dimensional image on a gold plaque. If so, *ḥeret* can bear the expected meaning "burin." Ezek 8:10–11 describes Israelite leaders venerating the incised images of animals. Note, too, that, in postbiblical Hebrew, Aramaic and Arabic, the root ṣwr can connote *painting*.

Somewhat similarly, Jacob (1992: 938–39) proposes that the text describes only the first and last stages of manufacture. The last step is "he made it a metal calf." The first step is "he sketched it with a stylus," presumably by scratching a design onto a hard surface.

Most likely, however, the Gold Calf is really a gold-plated, *wooden* object, though v 4 does not say so (Dillmann 1880: 340; Cassuto 1967: 412; next NOTE and NOTE to 32:20). In that case, though elliptical, v 4 makes perfect sense: Aaron collects gold, carves a wooden Calf with a chisel and creates a golden image. (Cassuto, however, thinks the burin is for incising details afterward.) Finally, we must note the obscure Punic term *ḥrṭyt*, which describes a cult object, possibly a statue made in the same manner as the Gold Calf (*KAI* 81.2).

metal. I do not think that the conventional translation "molten" is quite right for *massēkâ* (< *nsk* 'pour'). "Metal" is more appropriate. (Later Hebrew *matteket* 'metal' reflects an analogous derivation from *ntk* 'pour.') Thus the term *massēkâ* need not imply that the Calf is wholly gold. The best I can offer as a prooftext is Isa 30:22, "And you shall defile the plating of your silver idols and the covering (?) of your gold metal-image (*'ăpuddat massēkat zəhābekā*)." Luzzatto (on Exod 20:4) expresses a similar understanding, noting that in Isa 25:7 the root *nsk* and the noun *massēkâ* appear to connote a covering. (Dillmann [1880: 336] also compares Isa 40:19.) The method of the Gold Calf's destruction also makes the most sense under the assumption that it is gold-plated wood, not solid gold (NOTE to 32:20, "burned . . . ground . . . sprinkled").

calf. Rather than a gangly calf, we might have expected a more impressive animal, such as a lion or a horned bull. When calves appear in ancient art, they are in a dependent posture, suckled by cows (Keel 1980). One might infer that the biblical authors deliberately *disparaged* the idol by calling it "calf" (Noth 1962: 248), just as, arguably, Hosea uses the feminine "heifer" as an insult (Hos 10:5 [MT]; probably corrupt). But an ostracon from Samaria yields the Israelite name *'glyw*, apparently meaning "Yahweh is (my) Calf" (*AHI* 3.041). And Palmyrene inscriptions feature a comparable name *'glbwl* '(the god) Bol is a/my calf' (Stark 1971: 43–44, 104).

Perhaps Hebrew *'egel* denotes a more mature creature (Cassuto 1967: 412). Admittedly, an *'egel* can be a prancing (Psalm 29:6), untrained (Jer 31:18) one-year-old (Lev 9:3; Micah 6:6; also *KTU* 1.4.vi.42–43; 22.i.13). On the other hand, the feminine counterpart *'eglâ* can denote a three year old heifer (Gen 15:9), trained (Hos 10:11) for plowing (Judg 14:18) or threshing (Jer 50:11 [translation uncertain]). The Hittite Laws define a bull, as opposed to a calf, as a two-year-old and up. So, too, many argue, *'ēgel* denotes a young bull in its prime. (For humans, we encounter a comparable confusion over the meaning of *na'ar* 'youth, infant, servant'; see NOTES to 24:5, "youths"; 33:11, "youth.") Referring to the Gold Calf affair, Ps 106:19–20 recalls, "They make a calf (*'ēgel*) at Horeb, and bowed to metal *(massēkâ)* / And they exchanged their glory (i.e., their jewelry? their god?) for the image of a grass-eating bull *(šôr)*."

Bull or calf, the iconography is surprising. Since Aaron seems to identify the god in question as Yahweh (v 5), we might have expected a *humanoid* image. But that may be farther than Aaron is prepared to go. By producing an animal, he keeps his options open. He can argue that the animal does not represent the Deity but only supports his presence. See further below, pp. 580–83.

These are your deity. Ostensibly, given the plural modifiers *'ēlle(h)* 'these' and *he'ĕlûkā* 'brought you up,' one would take *'ĕlōhîm* simply as the plural "gods." But what "gods"? There is only one calf. Is Aaron trying to moderate the people's apostasy by refusing to make more than one image? Does he point to the calf and scoff, "Here are the gods you requested"? Are the gods in question Yahweh and the Calf *(Exod. Rab.* 42:3)? Is the Calf a semblance of several divine, bovine creatures?

True, sometimes Hebrew uses *'ĕlōhîm* of a single god, even Yahweh, as a true plural (possible examples include Gen 20:13; 31:53; 35:7; Exod 22:8; Deut 5:26[23]; 1 Sam 17:26, 36; 2 Sam 7:23; Jer 10:10; 23:36; Ps 58:12; see further below). But Exod 32:4 remains strange. It was plainly felt to be incongruous already in late biblical times, for Neh 9:18 rewrites Aaron's words in the singular: *zeh 'ĕlōhe(y)kā 'ăšer he'elkā mimmiṣrāyim* 'This is your Deity who brought you up from Egypt."

SPECULATION: The Bible may depict idolaters in particular as using *'ĕlōhîm* in the plural, even with a singular intent. Our passage is one case. Another, closely related, is 1 Kgs 12:28. King Jeroboam, to wean the northern tribes from worshiping in Jerusalem, constructs two gold calves and proclaims, "See: your deity, Israel, those who brought you up from the land of Egypt."

At first glance, it seems clear that Jeroboam's plural refers to the two calf idols. But we must be careful. If Jeroboam really said this, he cannot have been claiming that his new gold calves had rescued Israel centuries before, nor that they depicted two gods who had saved their people from Pharaoh. As far as we can tell, Jeroboam was more monolatrous than Solomon (cf. 1 Kgs 11:1–10). He would have worshiped Yahweh alone. Thus the plural makes little more sense for Jeroboam than it does for Aaron. I therefore suspect that the writers attributed to Jeroboam a statement designed to make him seem more of an apostate than he was. The fact that two statues are present may be immaterial.

If that seems implausible, then consider Isa 42:17, "They will reel backward and be ashamed with shame, those who trust in an idol *(pesel* [m.s.]), who say to a metal image *(massēkâ* [f. s.]), 'You *('attem* [m. pl.]) are our *'ĕlōhîm.*" This is not quite clear either. Perhaps the idol and the metal image are distinct, and both are addressed; perhaps the singular terms *pesel* and *massēkâ* are used collectively. Nonetheless, it appears most likely that the worshiper addresses his singular metal image in the plural, just as in Exod 32:1, 4, 8, 23. We should also consider 1 Sam 4:8 (OG 4:7–8), where the Philistines speak of Yahweh as *hā'ĕlōhîm hā'addîrîm hā'ēlle(h) hēm hā'ĕlōhîm hammakkîm 'et-miṣrayim* 'these mighty gods, they are the gods who smote Egypt.' This is how an Israelite author imagined idolaters speaking.

The anomaly is so familiar, we do not even notice it. With very few exceptions, the Bible uses the plural noun '*ĕlōhîm* as a singular, an example of grammatical incongruity for which Hebrew manifests no real parallel. It is the unique way, we are to imagine, in which right-thinking Israelites wrote and spoke. Conversely, the Bible depicts idolaters and polytheists as reflexively addressing even single idols in the plural. Similarly, to a necromancer, a single ghost is '*ĕlōhîm* '*ōlîm* 'gods ascending' (1 Sam 28:13). In other words, in the Bible's imagined world, how one uses the word '*ĕlōhîm* is a cultural code. The monotheist always uses it as a singular, in defiance of grammar; the polytheist always uses it as a plural, even in defiance of logic. The polytheist cannot conceive of a single deity; the Yahwist cannot conceive of pluriform deities. See further APPENDIX C.

Aaron's cry '*ēlle(h)* '*ĕlōhe(y)kā* *yiśrā'ēl* '*ăšer he'ĕlûkā* *mē'ereṣ miṣrāyim* is notable for its repetition of the sound *l*, creating a celebratory ululation comparable to the Arabic *šahāda: lā 'ilāh illā 'allāh* 'There is no god but God,' and the Hebrew ejaculation *hallălûyâ* 'Praise Yah(weh)!'

who took you up. How could the people believe that the Calf, made before their eyes, liberated them from Egypt? Plainly, they understood it as a symbol of some god, either Yahweh (Rashbam) or his divine Messenger (14:19; 23:20, 23; 32:34; 33:2). Writes Fretheim (1991: 281–82), "Up to now the messenger has been understood as a living representation of Yahweh but not separable from Yahweh himself. . . . By imaging the messenger, they make a representation concrete and accessible, hence having a greater independence from Yahweh." In support of the notion that the deity of the Exodus possessed a taurine aspect, compare Num 23:22; 24:8, "God, who takes them/him out from Egypt; he has indeed (?) wild-ox prongs."

32:5. saw/feared. See TEXTUAL NOTE.

tomorrow. Aaron may be stalling for time (Rashi), or it may simply be too late in the day to begin a celebration. This appears to be a new holiday not on the biblical calendar, since we are now in the fourth or fifth month, both of which are vacant of festivals (cf. 19:1).

SPECULATION: As we shall see below, Exodus 32 is an ostensible parody of the cult of Jeroboam I. According to 1 Kgs 12:32–33, Jeroboam inaugurated a festival calendar with a holiday in the eighth month, competing with the seventh month festival of Judah. If all the northern holidays were a month later than those in Judah, Aaron might be calling for the observance of Pentecost, in accordance with northern practice.

festival for Yahweh. Aaron clearly intends the calf as a Yahwistic symbol, like the historical bulls of the Northern Kingdom (see below, pp. 574–80). Is he redirecting Israel's apostasy, or is the Calf cult entirely monotheistic from the start (so Luzzatto)?

32:6. *Ascending-offers . . . Concluding-offerings . . . eat . . . drink.* The people's activities parody the Covenant ratification in chap. 24, which also featured sacrifices and a sacred meal before a visible Deity.

revel. Glad celebration is an important part of sacrificial worship (see, e.g., *śmḥ* 'rejoice' in Lev 23:40; Deut 12:12, 18; 16:11, 14; 27:7; 1 Sam 11:15). It is uncertain, however, just what the root *ṣḥq* 'play, sport, laugh, mock' implies here. Since *ṣḥq* can interchange with *śḥq*, Luzzatto sees a reference to music and dance, citing Jer 31:4, "you will again take up (?) your drums and go out in the dance of *mśḥqym*" (see also 1 Sam 18:6–7; 2 Sam 6:5, 21; Jer 30:19; 1 Chr 13:8; 15:29). Thus some exegetes think that the people are just singing and frolicking, as the reference to dance in 32:19 suggests.

On the other hand, other interpreters find in 32:6 a reference to sexual activity, even an orgy (Rashi). They compare Gen 26:8, where Isaac's *ṣḥq*-ing with Rebecca convinces Abimelech that the pair are married. Similarly in Gen 39:17, Potiphar's wife unjustly accuses her slave Joseph of *ṣḥq*-ing with her, i.e., molesting her sexually. Sex, to be sure, was not a part of authorized Israelite worship. But Exod 34:15–16; Deut 7:2–4 and a host of other passages associate apostasy with intermarriage, simultaneously describing cultic infidelity as "whoring" *(zny).* The defining episode of the fornicaton = apostasy equation is Baal Peor (Numbers 25).

To capture the ambiguity, an adequate if colloquial paraphrase for *ṣ/śḥq* might be "fool around," for, in general, the root describes untrammeled behavior. In 32:6, at least upon first reading, the context does not suggest sexuality (see, however, NOTE to 32:18). But, as we learn from David's uninhibited dancing in 2 Sam 6:14–22, religious frenzy can lead to immodesty. (Compare also the women of Shiloh in Judg 21:19–23, abducted while dancing at a religious festival.) If there is a sexual aspect in Exodus, however, the problem is less fornication per se and more violating the requirement of celibacy while Yahweh is still present on the mountain (19:15).

Lastly, the Midrash (*Exod. Rab.* 42:1) finds in *śḥq* an implication of bloodshed, as in 2 Sam 2:14–17, where it serves as a euphemism for "fight." This, too, is not impossible; after all, to Joshua the camp sounds like a battlefield (Exod 32:17). This would presumably be the altercation in which Hur dies (NOTE to 32:1, "around Aaron").

32:7. *Descend.* Whether we read *rēd* or *lek-rēd* (see TEXTUAL NOTE), Yahweh's injunction seems irately curt, as perhaps also in 19:24. The parallel in Deut 9:12 adds "Get up, quickly." Ehrlich (1908: 391) paraphrases, "You may go, I no longer need you; nothing will come of our dealings; I do not give you the tablets, and no Tabernacle will be erected."

whom you took up. Like an angry parent exclaiming to a spouse, "Look what *your* child did!" Yahweh implies that Israel is Moses' responsibility, not his own (Friedman 2001: 281). He is also using against the people their own words from v 1, "Moses, the man *who took us up* from the land of Egypt."

has corrupted. The implied object of *šiḥēt* is probably "their way" (ibn Ezra [shorter commentary]).

32:8. *quickly.* It is just forty days since the people heard the Decalog.

from the way. As Luzzatto observes, since they are probably worshiping Yahweh (see COMMENT), God does not say, "They have departed from *me.*" Rather, they are disobeying his rules for proper worship.

32:9. *I have seen.* Yahweh may be quoting himself at the Burning Bush (3:7, 9). Formerly, his "I have seen" held a promise of salvation: having beheld Israel's suffering, Yahweh determined to save them and make them his own people. Now, seeing their incorrigibility, he determines to wipe them out and found a new nation.

this people. Yahweh's language is derisive. Buber (*apud* Leibowitz 1976: 563) imagines God pointing an accusing finger downward.

hard-necked. That is, insubordinate. Israel refuses to "bow its neck to accept a yoke around its neck" (Bekhor Shor). The prideful have, as it were, an "iron sinew" (Isa 48:4), whereas the meek "bows his head like a reed" (Isa 58:5).

32:10. *leave me alone.* Why does Yahweh beg to be left alone? Moses cannot really hinder Yahweh from working his sovereign will. God is virtually inviting Moses to intercede on the people's behalf (*Exod. Rab.* 42:9; cf. *b. Ber.* 32a; Sarna 1991: 204). And Moses complies, offering a deliberate rebuttal to God (Leibowitz pp. 569–78): "Why should your *nose* flare?" (v 11) vs. "leave me alone, that my *nose* may flare against them and I may finish them off" (v 10); "Remember about Abraham" (v 13) vs. "make you [Moses] into a great nation" (v 10). No wonder Jeremiah esteems Moses, alongside Samuel, as Israel's most effective intercessor (Jer 15:1).

nose. Hebrew *'ap* connotes "anger"; see NOTE to 34:6.

make you . . . a great nation. Yahweh's statement *wə'e'ĕśe(h) 'ôtəkā ləgôy gādôl* echoes almost *verbatim* Yahweh's promise to Abram, *wə'e'eśkā ləgôy gādôl* 'and I will make you into a great nation' (Gen 12:2; see also Gen 17:20; 18:18; 21:18; 46:3). The replacement of *wə'e'eśkā* by *wə'e'ĕśe(h) 'ôtəkā* may add emphasis: "I will make *you* (not them) into a great nation."

This moment is Moses' greatest temptation. Instead of fathering a somewhat obscure line of Levites (vol. I, pp. 284–86) but otherwise serving, so to speak, as Israel's midwife, Moses is offered the opportunity to supplant Abraham, Isaac and Jacob as the national ancestor. Moses is frequently portrayed as volatile. But here he proves to be "very humble, more than all humans that are on the earth's surface" (Num 12:3). He prudently declines what God offers in a fit of pique, knowing that Yahweh must of his nature be true to his promises. In many ways, Moses is the quintessential loyal counselor, bravely facing down his liege when the latter is bent upon foolishness. Moses' selfless dealings with God set into harsh relief Israel's recurrent ingratitude.

Exod 32:10 marks a pivotal change in Yahweh's relationship with humanity. At first, displeased with all mankind, he started again with Noah, the "new Adam" (Genesis 6–9). Then he contracted his interest to Abraham (implicitly rejecting all other peoples), then again to Isaac (rejecting Ishmael), then finally to Jacob (rejecting Esau). Why not start again from Moses? Would not the promise to Abraham, Isaac and Jacob be sufficiently satisfied, since Moses is their descendant (*Exod. Rab.* 44:10)? Apparently Yahweh has changed his *modus operandi.*

32:11. *placated . . . face.* Just as the word for "nose," *'ap*, also connotes "anger," appeasement is indicated by an unruffled brow, nonflaring nostrils and the face's return to its proper hue.

his deity. Yahweh has just proposed to enter into a unique relationship with Moses.

Why. Already in his very first word, Moses slickly implies, "Perhaps it's not such a big sin."

whom you took out. Moses reminds God who really liberated the people: not Moses (32:1, 7) but Yahweh himself (Rashbam). Moreover, God exerted some effort to do this: "with great strength and a strong limb." This is Moses' first argument: all God's labor will be for naught.

32.12. *Why should Egypt say.* Or "Lest Egypt should say" (LXX), a usage of *lāmmâ* more common in the Persian era (Cant 1:7; Qoh 5:5; 7:16–17; Dan 1:10; Neh 6:3; cf. Ezra 4:11; 7:23) but found already in 1 Sam 19:17. Syr and Saadiah, however, take *lāmmâ* as equivalent to *'al* 'let not' in vv 11–12.

Moses' second argument appeals to God's vanity. The victory over Egypt's gods (12:12) will be pointless if Yahweh fails of his purpose or betrays his own people. This is the time-honored method of courtiers cajoling their sovereigns; Moses uses the same device in Num 14:13–16. And Ramban cites as a parallel Deut 32:26–27, "I said I would destroy them, I would make their name cease from Mankind, except that I fear the enemy's anger . . . lest they say, 'Our hand is exalted, and it is not Yahweh did all this.' " This technique works because kings are by nature competitive. Despite his theoretically limitless might, the anthropomorphized Yahweh still worries about his reputation among the nations (see also Deut 9:28; Josh 7:9; Ezek 20:14; 36:22–23; Joel 2:17).

For bad. *Bərā'â* combines the notions of "with malicious intent" and "toward a bad outcome." Ehrlich (1908: 392) suggests it is short for **bə'ēt rā'â* 'in an unlucky season.' Deut 9:28 elaborates, "Lest they say . . . 'Due to Yahweh's inability to bring them to the land that he spoke to them, *and from his hating them*, he took them out to kill them in the desert.' "

turn back . . . repent. Pulling out all rhetorical stops, Moses resorts to poetic parallelism: *šûb mēḥărôn 'appe(y)kā / wəhinnāḥēm 'al-hārā'â lə'ammekā*. (The jingle effect is less pronounced in reconstructed Israelite pronunciation, where the rhyming words would have sounded more like **'appayka* and **'ammaka*.)

about the bad. Although it is not said explicitly, Yahweh's first act of repentance (*niḥam*) was to regret liberating Israel. Moses twists the idea—Yahweh should instead repent of his new resolve to abandon the people. Cassuto (1967: 416) detects wordplay between Moses' command *hinnāḥēm* 'repent' and Yahweh's command in v 10, *hannîḥâ* 'leave (me) alone.'

32:13. *Remember for.* Childs (1974: 556) understands the idiom *zākar lə-* as "remember to so-and-so's credit."

Israel. Perhaps Moses uses Jacob's other name to emphasize the eponymous Patriarch's relationship with his descendants. That is, the nation Israel is heir to Yahweh's promises to the man Israel (Jacob 1992: 946).

your slaves. Moses' stresses the Patriarchs' unswerving fidelity.

you swore by yourself. This is Moses' greatest argument, citing God's oath by his own immortal self (Gen 22:16–17; 26:3–4, etc.). For Yahweh to go back on his word would paradoxically be to negate his own existence (cf. NOTE to 20:7, "raise").

32:14. *repented.* This would appear to end the affair. But, while he is no longer resolved to eradicate the entire people, the Deity is not yet fully placated. On Yahweh's changes of mind, see Freedman (1997: 409–46).

his people. Now the pronoun refers to Yahweh, suggesting that he reclaims his ownership of Israel (Cassuto 1967: 417).

32:15. *Testimony Tablets.* On the term *'ēdūt,* see NOTE to 25:16.

two sides. Does this refer to the two tablets jointly, so that each bears half the Decalog (*Mek. baḥōdeš* 8)? Or is each tablet inscribed front and back, as two complete copies?

they. Jacob (1992: 946) notes in vv 15–16 the emphatic force of the superfluous pronouns *hēm . . . hēmmâ . . . hû*' 'they . . . they . . . it.'

32:16. *Deity's . . . Deity's.* One could also translate *'ĕlōhîm* as "supernatural" (cf. NOTE to 8:15). The text stresses the heavenly origin of the tablets, the tragedy of their loss and the shock of Moses' spontaneous action (Ramban; Holzinger 1900: 111).

engraved. The term *ḥārût* is not necessarily a misspelling or variant of *ḥārût* 'incised'; the letters *teth* and *taw* are rarely if ever confused. More likely, this is just another root with a similar meaning. Other Hebrew roots with *ḥr-* (< PS *ḥ/ḫr-*) referring to cutting or scratching are *ḥrk* 'pierce,' *ḥrm* 'slit,' *ḥrs* 'scratch,' *ḥrp* 'be sharp,' *ḥrṣ* 'incise,' *ḥrq* 'cut,' *ḥrr* 'dig,' and *ḥrš* 'plow.'

32:17. *Joshua.* Moses had probably left him somewhat lower on the mountain, closer to the tumult below.

shouting. Rēaʿ here is equivalent to the more common *tərûʿâ,* which can denote either the shouts and horncalls of battle or the noise of cultic jubilation. Joshua the warrior inclines toward the first interpretation. The reader and Moses, however, already know what is afoot. Quite likely, the author chose the rare lexeme *rēaʿ* as a homograph of *raʿ* 'bad,' which appears in v 22 (see NOTE, "it is in bad"), and used *bərēʿō(h)* as a wordplay with *prʿ* 'be wild,' which appears in v 25 and perhaps 22 (TEXTUAL NOTE, "the people, that it is in bad") (cf. Ehrlich 1908: 393).

A sound: war. One could also translate *qôl milḥāmâ* as "the sound of war" or "hark: war." Joshua fears a repetition of the Amalekite attack of 17:8–13, the repulsion of which would be his responsibility (Dillmann 1880: 339).

32:18. *And he said.* "He" could be either Joshua (Saadiah) or Moses (ibn Ezra). The latter is the usual understanding.

'ănôt . . . conquest . . . 'annôt. The meaning of these clauses is much disputed, in particular the words *'ănôt, ḥălûšâ* and *'annôt.*

Let us begin with *ḥălûšâ.* It stands in parallel to *gəbûrâ,* whose meaning "strength, heroism" is not in doubt. Normally, the root *ḥlš* means "to be weak." Thus by one reading, the words feature the antithetical parallelism of "strength" and "weakness" (so *Tgs.,* Vg). There exists, however, a homophonous root *ḥlš* 'to overpower, cut down' (17:13 [see NOTE]; Isa 14:12). Thus Moses may be speaking in synonymous parallelism of "conquest" and "slaughter" (Rashbam). The matter cannot be resolved; after all, on a battlefield, one can hear the shouts of both the conquering and the conquered.

As for the untranslated *ʿănôt* and *ʿannôt*: as vocalized in MT, the first is a Qal infinitive construct, the second a Piʿel infinitive construct, both from the root *ʿny*. This distinction is not reflected in the consonantal text, however, where both are written *ʿnwt* (see, however, TEXTUAL NOTE on Sam). To further complicate the discussion, there are several verbal roots *ʿny* with diverse meanings: "answer, speak up," "sing," "be humble" and possibly "have sexual intercourse" (for the last, see NOTE to 21:10). And there is also a Canaanite goddess of violence and sex, ʿAnat(u) (Edelman 1966; Delcor 1990: 160–75), whose name was regionally pronounced ʿAnot (e.g., Beth Anoth/Anath in Judah [Josh 15:59; 19:38]) (Whybray 1967).

Disregarding the Massoretic distinction between *ʿănôt* and *ʿannôt*, we might conclude that Moses advises Joshua not to jump to conclusions. The two are surely hearing *ʿnwt* of some sort. But its nature must await discovery at the mountain's base. If we accept the MT distinction, however, then we must see Moses as archly correcting his disciple: what they hear is not *ʿănôt* but *ʿannôt*.

Which meaning or meanings of *ʿny* best fit 32:18? We are told that, having sacrificed, eaten and drunk, Israel proceeded to revel (*ṣḥq*) (v 6). LXX infers that *ʿny* describes inebriation (*exarchontōn oinou*; see Wevers 1990: 529). The roots *ʿny* and *ṣḥq* may well overlap in meaning; Tg. *Onqelos*, for instance, translates both with *məḥayyəkîn* 'making sport.' But precisely what activity is described? The main possibilities are sexual intercourse (see also NOTE to 32:6) and singing. By the former interpretation, the people are sexually aroused by the victory of Yahweh, who led them from Egypt to Sinai-Horeb (cf. NOTES to 15:20; 32:6). This interpretation chimes with Hosea 2. Yahweh proposes to "seduce" Israel, i.e., regain their allegiance, by leading the nation into the wilderness, where she will *ʿny* "as in her youth-days, and like the day of her ascent from the land of Egypt" (Hos 2:17). Yahweh will then espouse Israel: "You will call me 'my man' (i.e., husband) . . . and I will betroth you to me forever. . . and you will *know* Yahweh" (both carnally and covenantally) (Hos 2:18, 21–22). This leads to an outbreak of fertility, also described by the root *ʿny* (Hos 2:23–24). Among those who find sexual license in Exod 32:18 are ibn Ezra, Herzberg (1979: 63) and Levine (1999: 146–47).

Overall, however, since it is not clear that *ʿny* has a sexual meaning; since it is not clear that sex would make that much noise; since Moses sees Israel dancing (v 19), and since *ʿannôt* in Ps 88:1 has a musical connotation—"singing" is the most probable understanding of *ʿannôt* in Exod 32:18 (cf. Vg *vocem cantantium*). As for preceding phrases *ʿănôt gəbûrâ* and *ʿănôt ḥălûšâ*, these may be "shouts" (< *ʿny* 'speak up, respond') or true songs (< *ʿny* 'sing'): hymns of victory and perhaps, depending on the meaning of *ḥălûšâ*, dirges of defeat.

If these are Moses' words, not Joshua's (see previous NOTE), why does he not just tell his acolyte what is going on? In some earlier version of the text, does he himself not know? Or is he still in denial? After all, he has been attempting to placate Yahweh. Would he have appeased Yahweh had he fully appreciated the people's crime?

SPECULATION: What sort of song do the people sing so discordantly that Joshua mistakes the din for a battle? A logical choice would be a reprise of the militaristic Song of the Sea (15:1–18), which begins in the depths but climaxes at a mountain. Moreover, according to 15:20–21, it featured a female antiphon (ʿny).

32:19. *and dances.* We might have expected *wəʾet-hamməḥōlōt* 'and *the* dances' (Sam). Possibly some text has dropped out.

nose flared. Having assuaged Yahweh's anger, now that he sees the people's apostasy with his own eyes, Moses is no less furious than God had been in v 11 (Cassuto 1967: 419).

smashed. On one level, Moses' act is a simple tantrum. But smashing the tablets also symbolizes rupturing the Covenant. In the ancient Near East, to destroy a contractual document was to nullify the contents (Sarna 1991: 207). The most graphic illustrations are the Assyrian vassal treaties which, after Nineveh's fall, were apparently ritually smashed before the empty Assyrian throne. Somewhat similar is Zech 11:10, where a broken staff represents an abrogated covenant.

Does Moses on his own authority cancel Israel's Covenant with God? Surely, if Israel has already broken the Covenant, Moses' action is superogatory and symbolic, intended merely to impress and frighten Israel (Luzzatto). With the tablets shattered, it would seem that Yahweh and Israel no longer have any responsibilities toward one another. (Bekhor Shor [on v 32] suggests that Moses *deliberately offends* by breaking the tablets so that God will make him share Israel's fate rather than elevate him above his people.)

mountain's bottom. Moses apparently casts down the tablets from a slightly elevated position, so that they crash spectacularly, right before the jubilant throng.

32:20. *burned . . . ground . . . sprinkled.* Many commentators object that one cannot burn (*śārap*), grind (*ṭāḥan*), pulverize (*daq*) and sprinkle (*zārâ*) pure gold. One conclusion is that the author used a stereotyped description for destroying forbidden cult objects generally; compare 2 Kgs 23:4, 6, where King Josiah "took the vessels made for the Baal and for the Asherah and for all Heaven's Army, and he burned them . . . and carried their dust to Bethel . . . and took the Asherah from Yahweh's House to outside Jerusalem to the Kidron Valley, and he burned (*śārap*) it . . . and ground (*hēdēq*) it to dust and cast its dust over the Cemetery of the People's Sons" (cf. also 2 Kgs 23:15, where an entire shrine is broken, burnt and pulverized). From outside the Bible, we may also compare the curses on Mesopotamian monuments against, e.g., those who "cast it [the monument] into a river, or put it in a well, or destroy it with a stone, or burn it in the fire, or hide it in the earth" (King 1912: 41).

Others see the language as rooted in Canaanite mythology, where destroying the god Death by cutting, winnowing, burning, grinding, scattering/sowing (*drʿ*)

and finally feeding his body to the birds leads to new life in the fields, a kind of ancient Near Eastern "John Barleycorn" myth (*KTU* 1.6.ii.30–37) (*pace* Loewenstamm 1962b). The Gold Calf, in other words, is suffering the fate of a defeated deity according to ancient conventions (Fensham 1966).

The problem may be most simply resolved if we assume that *massēkâ* does not really mean "molten" but rather "metallic," here, metal-plated (cf. Isa 30:22). An image of hammered gold leaf attached to a wooden understructure would be susceptible to burning, grinding and sprinkling; cf. Deut 7:25, "Their gods' idols you must bring into fire; do not covet the silver and gold upon them and take for yourself." (Admittedly, above I have rejected as arbitrary Meyers's [1976: 32–33] similar hypothesis that the Tabernacle Candelabrum is gold-plated wood [NOTE to 25:18, "gold; *miqšâ*"].)

SPECULATION: If we accept that the Calf is wholly molten, then we must imagine Moses as beating it with a hammer until it is flat, whereafter the sheets might be crumbled into flakes. As for burning, I would suppose this to be an act of *purification*, preparatory to the people ingesting the remains. Jacob (1992: 948) supposes that "burn" in this context really implies a melting down, so that the Calf returns to an ingot.

waters'. Despite the name *ḥōreb* 'dry waste' (?), Mount Horeb is said to be a source of waters in 17:1–7, probably Deut 9:21 and implicitly Deut 33:8–9 (Van Seters 1994: 307). On the symbolism of a mountain flowing with water, see vol. I, pp. 605, 610–13.

Deut 9:21 describes Moses' actions in slightly different language. "And your sin that you made, the Calf, I took and burned it in fire and I crushed it ground fine, until it crumbled to dust, and I cast its dust into the *naḥal* descending from the mountain." A *naḥal* is a normally dry ravine that sometimes runs with water (the Arabic term is *wādi*). In light of Exodus, one may envision the ravine of Deut 9:21 as a brook.

made Israel's Sons drink. This act has received many explanations, none fully convincing. It has even been interpreted as meaningless. According to Bekhor Shor, it was simply time for Israel to drink. That they imbibed the Gold Calf was merely incidental.

The most common understanding invokes by analogy the ordeal of the suspected adulteress, made to drink the dissolved ink of a written curse in order to ascertain her guilt or innocence and, in the former event, punish her (Numbers 5) (*b. 'Abod. Zarah* 44a; Saadiah; Rashi). Likewise in Exodus 32, supposedly, the calf-water sorts idolaters from the faithful, killing the former and sparing the latter. Even though the Bible often compares Israel's relationship with Yahweh to a troubled marriage (e.g., Hosea 1–3), this is a great deal to read into Exodus 32. (The adultery analogy would make more sense if Israel imbibed Covenant curses.) Vv 34–35 just speak vaguely of Yahweh punishing the people. (On water serving as a supernatural judge through immersion and drinking ordeals, see Smith 1927: 165–81; Bottéro 1981).

Others see not an ordeal but a cleansing ritual, since Moses will eventually propose to reconcile the people to Yahweh (32:30). One could compare the purification rites described in Lev 14:5-7, 50-51 and Deut 21:4. In Leviticus 14, bird's blood mixed with water and other agents is applied to a person or house that has been declared cleansed of the disease ṣāraʿat; in Deut 21:4, a young cow (ʿeglâ) is decapitated near a brook to atone for bloodguilt. Also in 1 Kgs 18:30-40, Elijah atones for Israel's sins by sacrificing a bull and slaughtering the prophets of Baal in the wādi Kishon (Kaufmann 1960: 106). Propp (1987a: 87-88) makes yet another comparison: the purification rite of the Red Cow (Number 19) like Exodus 32 involves a ruddy bovine whose charred remains are dissolved in water, which is then sprinkled to remove ritual defilement. Perhaps, if sprinkling this "Impurity Water" cleanses ritual defilement, so imbibing the dissolved ashes of an artificial calf might atone for idolatry. But it seems rather forced to explain Moses' act as parodying the Red Cow or any other purifying rite. Indeed, to do so undermines the vignette's dramatic effect.

The foregoing explanations assume that Moses' aim is to punish or purify the people. He might also wish to punish the Calf itself. As we have observed, in Ugaritic myth, the god Death is burnt, winnowed and scattered, becoming food for the birds (Loewenstamm 1967, 1975). In Exodus, Moses disperses the Calf's remains as widely as possible, so that it can never be reconstituted. One could say that he consigns the Calf to the fate of an ordinary domestic animal: being divided, burnt, sodden and consumed. The "slaughter" and "consumption" of the Gold Calf could then be viewed as a parodic sacrifice, evoking the image of the "totem" animal deity ritually eaten by its own worshipers.

Further: Ramban points out that the gold will eventually pass through the Israelites' bodies and reappear gleaming amid their feces. And about 3,000 Israelites will die with the gold still in their bodies (v 28). Thus, although gold is ordinarily reused time and time again, the gold of the Calf can never be recovered, without scavenging through cemetery and latrine.

Ultimately, I would just recognize that Moses is, as we say, rubbing Israel's nose in its own misdeed. The Bible itself yields examples of people being punished with drinking the consequences of iniquity: e.g., "Yahweh our deity has finished us and given us poison-water to drink, for we have sinned against Yahweh" (Jer 8:14; cf. 9:14; 23:15). Moses compels the people to repudiate the Calf by participating in its destruction (Jacob 1992: 950).

SPECULATION: Ancient Near Eastern covenants were actuated by ritual curses dramatizing the violators' fate: being melted like wax, disemboweled like a lamb, etc. This is the symbolism of Genesis 15, where Abram and Yahweh enter into a covenant between the corpses of cloven animals (see also Jer 34:18). In some cases, materials were ingested. "Just as bread and wine enter the intestines, so may they (the gods) let this oath enter your intestines and the intestines of your sons and daughters" (Vassal Treaties of Esarhaddon 72, ll. 560-62 [ANET³ 539]). Moreover, water drinking sometimes played a role in the actuating ceremony (D. J. McCarthy 1981: 150).

The whole Sinai-Horeb Covenant scene lacks a dramatized, sympathetic cursing ritual. It may vestigially appear in the blood aspersions of 24:6, 8 (see pp. 308–9). But the motif arguably appears also in Exodus 32, where an artificial calf is dismembered and ingested, along with water. Had this occured *prior* to the breach of covenant, we would immediately have understood it as a symbolic threat: if Israel disobeys Yahweh, they are fated to be scattered and swallowed by their enemies. Compare Hos 8:7–8, where, after an attack against Samaria's Calf, we read, "Aliens will swallow him/it; swallowed is Israel."

As we shall see, Exodus 32 is probably a homily on the demise of the Northern Kingdom of Israel, which worshiped before gold calves and eventually suffered conquest, deportation, dispersion and assimilation. The Israelites were, so to speak, digested by the peoples among whom they were settled, as a punishment for violating Yahweh's Covenant (see further COMMENT, p. 579).

32:21. *this people.* For Cassuto (1967: 419), the demonstrative adjective *hazze(h)* has a "compassionate sense: this hapless people."

you brought. Although the reader knows that Aaron made the Calf (v 4), Yahweh has told Moses only that the *people* made the Calf (v 8). Moses directly confronts Aaron, either because he now knows the full story, or because, as leader, Aaron bears final responsibility.

great sin. In the Bible and the ancient Near East, the "great sin" *par excellence* was infidelity: infidelity in marriage (Gen 20:9) or infidelity in worship (2 Kgs 17:21) (Rabinowitz 1959b; Moran 1959).

32:22. *nose . . . flare.* I.e., do not be angry.

You . . . know the people. Aaron vainly tries to enlist Moses' sympathy. His feeble efforts at placating Moses contrast with Moses' more efficacious intercessions with Yahweh.

it is in bad. That is what MT literally says: *bərāʿ hûʾ*. There is a slight chance we should interpret "when it is shouting" (cf. *bərēʿōʾ[h]* in 32:17) and a greater chance that the text is corrupt (see TEXTUAL NOTE).

32:23. *they said.* Rather like the characters in Eden (Gen 3:12–13), Aaron refuses to accept responsibility. It was the people's idea from the start. And, ultimately, it was Moses' own fault for being so long absent.

32:24. *and they gave.* The consonantal text *wytnw* is susceptible of two readings. Even the MT vocalization and trope arguably point in different directions. By putting the main stop after *wytnw*, the cantillation suggests a jussive *wəyittənû 'and let them give,' with Aaron quoting his own command to the people. The vocalization, however, has a converted imperfect *wayyittənû* 'and they gave,' with Aaron as narrator to Moses (so LXX, Vg), an interpretation reinforced by the pausal form *hitpārāḳû*, which is vocalized as if over a clause-ending *ʾatnāḥ*. It seems, in short, that the Massoretes were torn between two interpretations. And there is a third reading, which takes *hitpārāḳû* as a perfect verb: "So I said to them, 'Who has gold?' They stripped off and gave to me" (Rashi). This unnatural exegesis may have been developed to exculpate Aaron from actually demanding gold.

threw. Aaron denies any intentionality in the fabrication of the Calf (Dillmann

1880: 341 and many others). Conceivably, however, *hišlîk*, like its English synonym "cast," bore a special connotation of founding metal (cf. Rashbam).

this calf. Frankel (1994: 337–38) comments that, taken literally, Aaron's words imply that the Calf still exists.

came out. Aaron is probably not claiming that the Calf simply stepped out of the furnace. Rather, as Rashbam and Bekhor Shor observe, the verb *yāṣā(ʾ)* can refer to the completion of a manufactured item (Isa 54:16; Prov 25:4); compare English "come out, come off."

Some scholars find the background of Aaron's seemingly outrageous statement in the ancient Near Eastern theology of the self-begotten idol (cf. Hurowitz 2004). This is an overinterpretation, anticipated in the Rabbinic view that the Calf was manufactured by Satanic power. Since we have already caught Aaron attempting to pass the blame onto the people, it is more natural to read his disclaimer as a bald-faced denial of responsibility, such as a child might make: "It just broke."

Ideally, however, we would combine these two readings. The context makes it perfectly clear that the idol did not just emerge. But Aaron mouths a common ancient Near Eastern belief in a context that invites ridicule.

32:25. wild. The root *prʿ* presumably includes the activities denoted above by *ṣiḥēq* (v 6) and *ʿannôt* (v 18) (see NOTES). Friedman (2001: 284), moreover, perceives a wordplay with *parʿō(h)*: "Aaron has 'Pharaohed' the people; he has done something to them that Pharaohs had done: made them ignoble in the eyes of those who oppose them. . . . [H]e has brought them back to the condition in which they were before the Sinai revelation: in disarray, without the law." Perhaps, but the comparison would be more effective if Aaron had *enslaved* Israel. More likely, the similarity of words is incidental (contrast NOTE to 5:4).

contempt among their uprisers. *Šimṣâ* may literally mean "whispering" (cf. *šemeṣ* in Job 4:12); an "upriser *(qām)*" is an enemy. Only German affords a succinct rendering of *šimṣâ bəqāmêhem*: *Schadenfreude* (Dillman 1880: 341).

Moses has already displayed his concern for Yahweh's reputation (v 12). Now he is worried about Israel's. Apparently, the people's revelry contains something distasteful beyond Calf worship, which would have struck Israel's polytheistic enemies as perfectly normal. One thinks of the scene between David and Michal (2 Sam 6:14–22): she despises *(bzh)* him for his uninhibited celebration *(śḥq)* before Yahweh, during which he exposes his genitals (or, by another interpretation, behaves promiscuously). So perhaps there is a sexual aspect to Israel's revel after all (see NOTES to vv 6, 18). At any rate, Moses' words prove prophetic. The Gold Calf would become a prooftext in later Christian anti-Jewish polemic (Bori 1990).

32:26. gate. Presumably to prevent anyone from escaping.

Whoever. The word *mî* 'who' is a running theme in the aftermath of the Gold Calf. Aaron quoted himself as having said, *ləmî zāhāb hitpārākû* 'Whoever has gold, strip it off' (v 24); now Moses responds *mî ləyahwe(h) ʾēlāy* 'Whoever is for Yahweh, to me'; below Yahweh will warn Moses *mî ʾăšer ḥāṭā(ʾ)-lî ʾemḥennû missiprî* 'Whoever sinned against me, I will erase him from my Document.' The entire chapter is a homily on responsibility, in essence asking the reader, "Who are *you*? Which side are *you* on?"

One would think that, during a "festival for Yahweh" (v 5), if someone asked "Who is for Yahweh?" the response would be a unanimous cheer. But the Israelites know exactly what Moses means: "Who is for Yahweh as *I* have represented him to you?" The Levites stand forward, the rest shrink back in shame.

all Levi's Sons. Levi is Moses' own tribe (2:1). Aaron, too, is of their number (4:14). Does he himself possess the chutzpah to step forward at this point?

32:27. Thus has Yahweh . . . said. As in 5:1, Moses adopts the prophetic style (Holzinger 1900: 111; Jacob 1992: 954). Has he received a fresh message from Yahweh, which the text does not record?

Israel's deity. Moses ironically paraphrases the people's cry, "These are your deity, Israel" (32:4, 8) (Ehrlich 1908: 398), in turn a parody of the Decalog: "I am Yahweh your deity" (20:2).

cross . . . return. I.e., go back and forth.

kill. Moses and Yahweh appear to have ordained an indiscriminate slaughter of the entire nation, in accordance with 22:19 and similar proscriptions on apostasy. When will it stop? Will Moses give a signal? Or will the Levites go back and forth just once, killing as many as they can in a single pass? In the event, only about 3,000 of the two to three million Israelites die.

brother . . . fellow . . . relative. In context, this must mean fellow Israelites, exclusive of the Levites. As in Deut 13:7–12, the kinship language emphasizes the suppression of fellow-feeling requisite for the bloody task. Deut 33:8–9 describes this as the ordeal by which Levi earned its priesthood (see also COMMENT).

three thousand. Yahweh had intended to wipe out all Israel (v 10). Pressed by Moses, he relented but did not wholly forgive. So this slaughter may be Moses' desperate measure that he hopes will assuage Yahweh's wrath.

Were only 3,000 of the 600,000 adult men (or two to three million individuals) guilty? One has the impression that almost the whole people was implicated in the Calf worship. If so, then the death of a few is a *pars pro toto* punishment—with the potential of more deaths to follow. It is but the first stage of reconciliation to Yahweh.

32:29. Your hand has been filled. MT *mil'û yedkem* is difficult. The best explanation is that the verb is an impersonal Pi'el: "Someone has filled your hand, your hand has been filled" (Rashbam, Luzzatto).

SPECULATION: Another approach would be to take *mil'û* as a Qal plural imperative, here agreeing with the pronominal suffix on a body part, rather than the noun itself (see vol. I, pp. 271–72). If so, the translation would be something like: "Be full, O your hand" in the sense of "Be full in respect of your hand."

The idiom "to fill the hand" often refers to priestly inauguration (see NOTE to 28:41, "fill their hand"). Moses informs the Levites that they have earned the priesthood by standing up for Yahweh (on Levitical sacerdocy, see vol. I, pp. 284–86; COMMENT below). Similarly in P, Phinehas will earn his priesthood by violently punishing apostasy (Num 25:6–13). There could also be an implication that the slain Israelites are Filling-offerings (*millū'îm*) of priestly consecration (see below). But Jacob (1992: 954–55) may be correct to detect irony. On one level, "fill the hand" refers to ordination. But in this context, the Levites are to fill their hands—with the avenging sword and with their brethren's gore.

SPECULATION: Ehrlich (1908: 398–99) argues that here "fill the hand" is an idiom meaning to "do one's best for God," a usage found in 1 Chr 29:5. I find it quite believable that Exod 32:29 uses the phrase playfully in multiple senses.

indeed. The syntax seems fractured. My translation interprets *kî* as an asseverative "indeed," rather than as a conjunction: "Today, *your hand has been filled* for Yahweh, *for* (each) man through his son and through his brother. . . ." Cassuto (1967: 422) compares 18:11, where *kî* similarly precedes a fragment.

through his son and through his brother. There are at least three ways to take this. By one interpretation, the Levites are enjoined to perform some sort of initiatory ritual upon one another, since as yet there is no senior priest to consecrate them—just as, in the Priestly source, the Levite Moses ordains the house of Aaron (see above, p. 532). A second possibility is that "fill the hand" does not here refer to ordination but simply to sacrifice. If so, Moses is commanding the Levites to make atoning offerings for their sinful brethren, the Israelites *(Tg. Ps.-Jonathan).* Most likely, however, *bibnô ûb(ə)'āḥîw* simply means "with/ through one's fellow Israelites." The slain sinners play the role assigned to the "Filling Ram" of chap. 29, the priestly ordination, whose blood is applied to the new priests and their garments.

even. I have chosen an emphatic "even" over the ordinary meaning of *wə*- 'and,' simply to smooth the syntax. The entire verse is quite difficult.

to place . . . a blessing. The priests are both recipients of blessing and, according to P, conferrers of blessing (Num 6:22–27). Simply put, they are conduits of divine power.

32:30. *next day.* The narrative cliché may here imply that a cooling-off interval is required before Moses can seek reconciliation with Yahweh.

Clear. On the root *kpr*, see NOTES to 25:17; 29:33.

32:31. *Ah now.* '*Annâ*, not really translatable, lends Moses' speech a sense of formal entreaty. Full confession must precede reconciliation. Having exacted vengeance against Israel on God's behalf, now Moses represents Israel before the aggrieved Deity.

32:32. *if you will lift their sin.* The idiom *nāśā(')* *ḥaṭṭā(')t/ʿāwōn*, said of God, means to "forgive" (see NOTE to 28:38, "Bear the Transgression of the Holinesses"). Moses' first sentence trails off, at least in MT, in a diffident shrug. We might have expected "And now, if you *lift* their sin, *then lift*" (see TEXTUAL NOTE). That, at any rate, is the sense (Rashi). But Moses may be reluctant to press the Deity during this tense negotiation, and would rather let Yahweh finish the thought himself.

erase me. As a bluff, Moses may be asking for immediate death (Dillmann 1880: 342), like Elijah in 1 Kgs 19:4. For Jacob (1992: 955–56), this is the Clearing *(kpr)* Moses promised to effect: he offers his own life as ransom *(kōper).*

your Document. Yahweh keeps some sort of written record, perhaps a scroll of fate or a table of genealogies, in which names may be written or erased (Rashbam;

Ramban; Niditch 1996: 80–81; possible references include 17:4; Isa 4:3; 65:6; Jer 17:1, 13; Ezek 2:9–10; Zech 5:1–4; Mal 3:16; Ps 40:8; 51:3; 56:9; 69:29; 109:14; 139:16; Dan 7:10; Neh 13:14). In the New Testament, this becomes the "Life Book" of those destined for Heaven (Luke 10:20; Phil 4:3; Rev 3:5; 13:8, etc.). The Mesopotamians similarly held that the gods kept a "tablet of destiny" and also inscribed fate in sheep entrails and in the stars (Bottéro 1992: 97–102). Hyatt (1971: 311) and Sarna (1991: 209) suggest that the underlying image in Exodus is a citizens' roll, such as in Numbers 1–4; Ezek 13:9; Ezra 2:1–62; Neh 7:6–64.

32:33. *Whoever has sinned.* Yahweh cannot wipe out Moses, since Moses is innocent. Israel, however, is not innocent.

32:34. *go, lead.* Yahweh defers final settlement of the issue.

the people. They are no longer "your people" (32:7) but not yet "my people" either (Cassuto 1967: 424).

to where I spoke to you. The relative pronoun *'ăšer* may serve in its original, locative sense. I am more than half convinced, however, by Ehrlich's (1969: 200–1) contention that *'el* here is equivalent to *'al* 'on, about.' The sense would then be, "Lead the people *according to what* I spoke to you (namely): 'See: my Messenger, he will go before you.' " That is, Yahweh cites his own words from 23:23.

my Messenger. As becomes clearer in 33:1–5, the dispatch of an emissary may be as much a punishment as a blessing. The people sought a substitute for Yahweh, and now he gives them one. See below, pp. 397–98.

day of my accounting. When is this day? How far in the future? Does Yahweh envision a single punishment or a continual chastisement (cf. *b. Sanh.* 102a)? On the one hand, one could (and I would) take this as a threat for the distant future, when the Assyrians will deport the calf-worshiping Northern Kingdom in 722/21 B.C.E. (Hyatt 1971: 311; see below, pp. 574–80). But possibly the punishment, at least in its first stage, is exacted in Moses' own time, as the following verse suggests.

I will account. This tautological method of expressing indefiniteness has been labeled the *idem per idem* construction, i.e., defining a thing as itself. For discussion, see Luzzatto and Lundbom (1978); also vol. I, pp. 224–26.

32:35. *harmed.* Apparently unsatisfied by the death of 3,000 (v 28), Yahweh punishes the people further—when and to what extent is left ambiguous. *Pace* Noth (1962: 251), I doubt that this punishment is related to drinking the ashes of the Calf (see NOTE to 32:20).

they had made . . . Aaron made. The ambiguity as to who made the Calf continues (32:1, 4, 8, 21, 23–24). In truth, Aaron and the people were equally complicitous. The multitude provided the instigation, but Aaron organized the project and either made the Calf himself or superintended its construction.

COMMENT

THE GOLD CALF AS POLEMIC

Already at the Burning Bush, Moses foresaw that he would have trouble both gaining and retaining the people's faith (Exodus 3–4). At each setback—the intensification of their servitude (chap. 5), being hemmed in at the Sea (chap. 14), dire hunger (chap. 16) and thirst (15:22–26; 17:1–7)—the Israelites have despaired and rebelled. Like a melodrama, the Bible's plot is propelled by alternating scenes of alienation and reconciliation between a faithful if irascible God and a fickle Israel.

This is a difficult relationship for both parties. God interprets the people's repeated backslidings as plain stubbornness, symptomatic of a "hard neck" (32:9; 33:3, 5; 34:9; Deut 9:6, 13). A more sympathetic assessment would describe Israel, after centuries of enslavement, as pathologically insecure. Between humans, at least, such a relationship would be dysfunctional. It appears, however, to be the best that Israel and Yahweh can sustain, if only by the continual, soothing intermediation of Moses. No wonder the prophets will compare the Covenant to a bad marriage! God and his people cannot live together and yet cannot live apart. (On P's solution—the Tabernacle—see below, pp. 682–703.)

Exodus 32 describes Israel's archetypal apostasy at God's own mountain, scant weeks after ratifying the Covenant (chap. 24). Having brought them to Yahweh's abode in the wilderness, Moses disappears, perhaps as part of the "test" mentioned in 20:20(17) (see NOTE). True to form, the Israelites panic; *Exod. Rab.* 42:3 aptly compares the scenario to vassals rebelling in their suzerain's absence. As they have had difficulty maintaining faith in a hidden God, so they completely lose trust in their absent leader. Having triply affirmed, "All the words that Yahweh spoke we will do . . . and heed" (19:8; 24:3, 7), the people immediately violate the Decalog by making for themselves a metal god in a calf's likeness. An invisible Deity, *sans* human representative or graphic representation, is simply too abstract for them.

The joining of JE with P considerably sharpens the tragic irony (see p. 371). While Aaron is making the Calf, Yahweh is unveiling to Moses a plan for securing God's presence in Israel's midst. The Tabernacle is to be constructed from the people's treasures and ministered to by Aaron and his sons (chaps. 25–31). But Aaron is putting Israel's gold to other uses.

Like other biblical stories of rebellion, Exodus 32 appears to be addressed to later generations, displaying the firstfruits of Covenant violation. The argument is *a fortiori*: if the generation of the Exodus lacked faith, with Moses still alive and Yahweh a brooding presence on the mountain, and with the parting of the Sea a living memory—how much harder for later Israelites (i.e., the original audience) and their successors (us) to believe and obey! In other words, the people's predicament is really the reader's. We are not at Sinai, we have only heard of the Exodus and Moses, we may never have experienced the hand of Yahweh. Exodus 32 and numerous other passages make it clear that Yahweh will punish Covenant violators in every generation. But if he will not speak to us, how can we know his will and so please him?

The rebellion stories can be read as advocating obedience to some theocratic authority, a person or group that in future times stands in for Moses and Yahweh. Deut 18:15–19 will speak explicitly of a prophet (or line of prophets) like Moses whose word must be feared. In other contexts, the priesthood is held to be the definitive interpreter of God's will.

I would also read Exodus 32 as a homily on patience and faith. Viewed positively, the story is an inducement for hope — in doubtful times, one must tirelessly wait for God's rescue. Viewed cynically, the story is a ploy by religious authorities to show that one must not expect immediate results from sacrifices and prayers. Look what happened when Israel grew tired of waiting for Moses and Yahweh!

THE LEVITES VS. AARON

The Gold Calf was, so to speak, the first skirmish in an internecine, intergenerational battle over the priesthood that was fought within the tribe of Levi (for bibliography and discussion, see M. White 1990; Risto 1998). The Bible nowhere explicitly recounts this war. Instead, scholars have plausibly inferred its existence between the lines of the text. Rehearsing its vicissitudes in detail will shed considerable light on Exodus 32 as well as the literary evolution of the Torah, and I beg the reader's indulgence.

The final outcome of these holy wars is well known. In Second Temple Judaism and afterward, only those claiming Aaronic pedigree were considered legitimate priests (see below). The earlier situation was far more fluid. While the origins of the Israelite priesthood are irrecoverable (see, provisionally, Gunneweg 1965; Cody 1969), in protohistorical times, it seems that the entire tribe of Levi was the priestly caste. While others could serve, a Levite was preferred (de Vaux 1961: 358–71). (It is even possible that *lēwî* 'Levite, attached person' was a professional rather than a tribal designation; see vol. I, p. 128.) Judges 17 exemplifies the principle: upon founding a shrine, Micah/Micaiehu initially appoints his own son as priest. But when a wandering Levite later happens by, Micah hires him on the spot, commenting, "Now I know that Yahweh will bless me, for the Levite has become my priest" (v 13). In other words, while Yahweh accepts all offerings, he particularly enjoys those mediated by Levites.

How did the Levites and others justify their entitlement? Deut 10:8–9 briefly describes the Levites' ordination in the days of Moses at Horeb (not at Jotbah; vv 6–7 are an interpolation): "At that time, Yahweh separated out the Levite tribe to bear Yahweh's Covenant Chest, to stand before Yahweh to attend him, and to bless in his name until this day." The Elohist similarly traces the Levites' consecration to Horeb: the priesthood was their reward for executing idolaters (Exod 32:29). And a related text, Deut 33:8–11, awards to Levi priestly prerogatives in allusive poetic couplets. (MT may be damaged; on the following reconstruction based on LXX and 4QTestimonia, see Propp 1987a: 54, 74–75 n. 35. On my translation of tenses, see vol. I, p. 507.)

Give to Levi your Thummim,
And your Urim to your faithful man,
Whom you tried at Massah
You strive with him by Meribah Waters,
Who says to his father, "I have not recognized you,
And to his mother, "I have not known you."
And his brother(s) he did not acknowledge,

And his son(s) he did not know.
For they obeyed your command(s),
And keep your Covenant.
They teach your laws to Jacob
And your direction(s) to Israel.
They put incense in your nose,
Ascending-offering(s) upon your altar.
Bless, Yahweh, his force;
Be pleased by his hands' labor.
Smite his *uprisers* (foes) on the hips;
And his haters, who (among them) may stand?

The Urim and Thummim are the sacred oracles manipulated by the priests (Exod 28:30; 1 Sam 14:3, 18, 41 [OG]; 23:9–12; 30:7–8), in addition to their offices of making sacrifice, burning incense and teaching (above, pp. 442–43, 625). Massah and Meribah are the springs of Mount Horeb, in which the Calf's ashes are dissolved (17:6; 32:20; Deut 9:21; vol. I, pp. 605, 612–13). Thus Deut 33:8–11 appears to presuppose the reader's familiarity with the traditions now found in Exodus 17 and 32.

And yet, Deut 33:8–11 is both like and unlike Exod 32:26–29. As in Exodus 32, the Levites are tested; as in Exodus 32, they are ordained as priests; as in Exodus 32, they are warlike; as in Exodus 32, the scene is Horeb, at least implicitly. Unlike Exodus 32, however, the Levites are said to reject not just "brother" and "kinsman" but parents and children, perhaps implying that they kill some of their own number.

SPECULATION: This would explain the indication in Deut 33:8 that Yahweh not only tested but even strove against the Levites, a theme not patent in Exodus. The leader of the Calf cult, Aaron, is himself a Levite (Exod 4:14), and according to Deut 9:20, Yahweh nearly killed him on the spot for his weakness. I think it likely that in a version of the Gold Calf story more complete than that preserved in Exodus, Levite followers of Aaron also fell in the purge. (This reading of Deut 33:8–11 is unique to me and will strike some as idiosyncratic; the reader may consult commentaries for other views—e.g., that the oracle describes a process by which lay Israelites were converted into "Levites" by renouncing prior kinship ties.)

We find further evidence of Levi's priestly status in the expression, characteristic of Deuteronom(ist)ic literature, *hakkōhănîm hallăwîyīm*, to be rendered either "the Levite priests" or "the priests, the Levites." Either way, the precondition for a priest's legitimacy is his Levitic extraction. Deut 18:1–8 clearly asserts that all Levite males are potential priests (Cody 1969: 129–32; cf. Wright 1954):

The Levite priests, all the tribe of Levi, shall have no share or possession with Israel. Yahweh's offerings and his possession they shall eat. . . . And this shall be the priests' law: from the people, from those who sacrifice a Slaughter-offering, whether bull or sheep, then he shall give to the priest the limb, the jowls and the stomach, the first of your grain, of your wine and of your oil, and the first of your flock's shearing you shall give to him. For him Yahweh your deity chose from all your tribes, to stand to serve in Yahweh's name. . . . And when the Levite from one of your gates comes from all Israel where he sojourns there . . . to the place that Yahweh will choose, then he will serve in Yahweh his deity's name like all his brothers the Levites standing there before Yhaweh. Share for share they may eat. . . .

Deuteronomy was promulgated when King Josiah proposed to consolidate national worship in Jerusalem, the place "chosen" by Yahweh (Friedman 1987: 101–35). Attempting to decommission all other shrines, Josiah offered the rural Levites a compensatory incentive: the assurance of a livelihood in Jerusalem.

The first glimmerings of rivalry between priestly houses appear in the late premonarchic era, when our sources depict a national center at Shiloh in the North. The focus of the shrine was the Covenant Chest, guarded by the priest Eli and his sons Hophni and Phinehas. Yahweh's oracle to Eli mentions explicitly hereditary priesthood, but does not state clearly what is Eli's "father's house" (for text-critical details, see McCarter 1980: 87–89):

I revealed myself to your father's house when they were in Egypt, slaves to Pharaoh's house. And I chose him from all Israel's tribes to be my priest, to ascend by my altar, to cense incense, to bear an ephod before me; and I gave to your fathers' house all the offerings of Israel's Sons. . . . I had said, said, "Your house and your father's house shall walk about before me forever," but now — Yahweh's word: (it would be) defilement to me, for I honor my honorers but my contemners are demeaned — see: days coming, when I shall hew off your limb and the limb of your father's house, that there be no elder in your house . . . all the days. But a man I shall not cut off from you from by my altar to wear out his eyes and to afflict his soul. . . . And I shall raise me up a trustworthy priest, who will do according to what is in my heart and in my soul. And I shall build him a trustworthy house, and he will walk continually before my Anointed all the days. And it will happen: each one remaining of your house will come to bow before him for a silver piece and a bread loaf and say, "Attach me, then, to one of the priesthoods, that I may eat a bread morsel." (1 Sam 2:27–36)

What is Eli's "father's house," the clan once chosen but now rejected by Yahweh? Wellhausen (1885: 142) and Cross (1973: 195–215) find a reference to *Moses*, locating a Mosaic or "Mushite" priesthood at Shiloh. A better case might be made, however, for the house of *Aaron*. (On my misgivings concerning the Mushite hypothesis, see vol. I, p. 285.) 1 Chr 24:3, 6 traces the house of Eli back to Aaron through Ithamar, Aaron's youngest son (on the difficulties, see Propp 1992). Since there were still postexilic Ithamarites (Ezra 8:2; 1 Esdr 8:29), the Chronicler must have possessed living traditions or even written records. And why should P have mentioned Ithamar at all unless his descendants were of some importance? Moreover, Eli's descendant Abiathar will own land in Anathoth (1 Kgs 2:26), assigned to the house of Aaron in Josh 21:18; 1 Chr 6:45 (on the list and its date, see Boling 1982: 492–97; 1985). A final possibility is that Eli's "father's house" is the whole tribe of Levi, who claimed but eventually lost the right to serve as priests (see below).

The doom of Eli commences immediately when his sons Hophni and Phinehas are killed in battle (1 Sam 4:11). But the identity of the "trustworthy priest" remains obscure for many chapters, as the curse continues to work its effect. One at first suspects Samuel of being Eli's replacement (cf. Westphal 1906: 217). But events prove otherwise, for Samuel's sons are little better than Eli's and do not inherit their father's eminence (1 Sam 8:3).

Although Eli's sons perish, at least two grandsons survive: Ichabod (1 Sam 4:19–22) and Ahitub (1 Sam 14:3). Ahitub has two sons: Ahijah (1 Sam 14:3) and Ahimelech, the latter becoming priest at Nob (1 Samuel 22) (see Gunneweg [1965: 106–7], however, for doubts). Although Ahijah had been a supporter of Saul (1 Sam 14:18–19), Ahimelech allies himself with David, King Saul's courtier, son-in-law and rival (1 Samuel 21–22).

When David succeeds Saul, he sets up a national cult site in Jerusalem, importing the Covenant Chest and housing it in a temporary tent. He appoints two high priests: Abiathar son of Ahimelech, and Zadok son of Ahitub (2 Sam 8:17). Abiathar represents continuity with the past, especially for the Northern tribes. As for Zadok, despite his apparent affiliation with Eli's grandson Ahitub, which would make him Abiathar's uncle, commentators dispute Zadok's real pedigree (e.g., Wellhausen 1885: 126). While many have identified Zadok as a non-Israelite Jebusite, Cross (1973: 214–15) more reasonably surmises that he was a Levitical priest (so Ezek 40:46; 43:19; 44:15) from Hebron, David's first capital, perhaps the Zadok referred to in 1 Chr 12:29 (but see Olyan 1982). In David's United Kingdom, it seems Abiathar represented Northern interests and traditions, while Zadok may have represented the South (Cross pp. 207–15).

David's efforts to unite South and North proved only partially effective. Each side continued to mistrust the other and the king (e.g., 2 Sam 19:43–44). To judge from 2 Samuel 20, David may have increasingly favored Judah in his later years, as did his son Solomon, who accused the Northern priest Abiathar of sedition and banished him to Anathoth. This left Zadok in sole control of the Temple and the Chest (1 Kgs 2:26–27). Zadok, so it would seem, is finally revealed as the "trustworthy priest" whose advent was prophesied to Eli a century before. Solomon's reign is probably when the Zadokite claim to exclusive priestly prerogatives began to crystallize.

There is a problem however. The most natural reading of 2 Sam 8:17 is that Zadok and Abiathar are kinsmen, refugees from the dispersed house of Eli. But then the "trustworthy" priest cannot be Zadok, either, since he represents the *success* of the Elides. For this reason, Cross (p. 214) is inclined to distinguish Ahitub father of Zadok from Ahitub grandson of Eli.

SPECULATION: My impression is that Zadok is an Elide after all, as a superficial reading would suggest. I understand the curse of Eli as meaning not that

Eli's line would literally die out, but that Eli would be replaced by one of his descendants as lineage founder, just as Yahweh proposes to replace Abraham, Isaac and Jacob with their descendant Moses (Exod 32:10). No longer will the high priesthood be available to any heir of Eli. The "trustworthy priest" Zadok will father a new line, to whom the high priesthood will be restricted.

After Solomon, the Northern tribes seceded (see below). Our sources are divided as to the extraction of the Northern clergy: was it Levitic (Judg 17:7–13; 18:30) or common Israelite (1 Kgs 12:31–32)? To account for the confusion, we can easily imagine rival groups asserting their own and denying others' Levitic ancestry. Perhaps, too, the modern, scholarly debate as to whether *lēwî* originally indicated a profession or a tribal affiliation already raged in ancient Israel. The presupposition of Judg 17:1–7 may still have been widespread: while any man could be a priest, a Levite was preferred.

We know suprisingly little of the Judahite clergy from Solomon to the Exile; the Books of Kings busy themselves rather with political affairs. Barlett (1968) plausibly argues that the priesthood was more appointive than hereditary, and there may have been periods in which the Zadokites were ousted. It is possible, for example, that the house of Eli briefly regained control of the Temple in Josiah's day, when the priest Hilkiah "discovered" a scroll, likely a proto-form of Deuteronomy (2 Kings 22–23; Friedman 1987: 101–135), which endorses *Levitic* priesthood (Deut 18:1–8). If so, the Elides were probably displaced again after Josiah's death. This scenario would account for the bitterness of the priest-prophet Jeremiah from Anathoth, perhaps the son of the same Hilkiah, and the only prophet to mention Shiloh and its abandonment (Jer 7:12–14; 26:6, 9; cf. Friedman 1987: 125–27).

After 597 B.C.E., when the Babylonians exiled the Judean leadership including the priests (Jer 29:1; Ezek 1:1; cf. 2 Kgs 24:24–26), and especially after Nebuchadnezzar destroyed the Temple in 587/86, priestly rivalries should have subsided. But the Exile proved to be of short duration. At least one Zadokite, Ezekiel, was laying plans for a new order, in which the status of the Levites would be settled permanently, to their disadvantage. Henceforth, only the Zadokites would be true "Levite priests" (Ezek 40:46; 43:19; 44:15). The Levites would replace the gentile Temple slaves as menials (Ezek 44:10–14; 48:11).

How could Ezekiel justify restricting the priesthood to his own circle? Calling the Zadokites "Levite priests" seems an implicit confession that originally all Levites enjoyed the right of priesthood. But Ezekiel maintained that Yahweh had *stripped the non-Zadokite Levites of their prerogatives* because of their sins (Ezek 44:10–16). It is generally assumed that the crime in question is officiating at local shrines, not at the Jerusalem Temple (cf. 2 Kgs 23:8–9).

In 538 B.C.E., Cyrus released the Judean exiles of Babylonia. In time, they succeeded in rebuilding Jerusalem and its Temple. Of all of Ezekiel's detailed plans for the restoration (Ezekiel 40–47), only his program for the Zadokites and Levites was more or less realized. Backed by the authority of the Persian empire, the Zadokites of the Second Temple finally crushed the old Levitic clergy, whose sacerdocy was in time completely forgotten. It is symptomatic that during the Exile and afterward, an alternative phrase to "the Levite priests" came into vogue. Alongside *hakkōhănîm hallǝwîyīm* (now referring to the Zadokites), we find *hakkōhănîm wǝhallǝwîyīm* 'the priests *and* the Levites,' attested almost exclusively in exilic and postexilic texts. In the new order, the traditional phrase "Levite priests" usurps the Levites' ancient prerogative, while the neologism "the priests and the Levites" emphasizes the dichotomy between the two classes.

Not surprisingly, Zadokite supremacism hindered the recruitment of Levites to serve in the rebuilt Temple (Ezra 2:40 = Neh 7:43; Ezra 8:15–19; Neh 11:18). Many Levites probably rejected Zadokite claims and refused to participate at all. For the rest, Wellhausen (1885: 147–48 n. 3) envisions a complex accommodation whereby many Levites were reclassified as priests, and the lower Temple servants—*nǝtînîm*, gatekeepers, singers—were elevated into Levites. At any rate, as Ezekiel had prophesied, in the Second Temple the Levites were mere hierodules. History was even doctored to ascribe the entire set-up to David (e.g., 1 Chronicles 23–26). It is the literature of this period that first explicitly ties the house of Zadok to Aaron, through Aaron's eldest surviving son Eleazar (Ezra 7:1–5; 1 Chr 5:29–41; 6:35–38).

Where the Priestly source fits into these developments is unclear (on P's date, see below, p. 732). P, like Ezekiel, restricts the priesthood to one family from the ranks of the Levites. Unlike Ezekiel, however, P makes the election of the Aaronids (Exod 28:1–5; 29:9, 44; 40:15) anterior to the Levites' ordination (Num 3:6–9; 8:5–19; 18:2–6). In P, the non-Aaronic Levites are "given" to the Aaronids, though it is not clear what they do, apart from transporting the Tabernacle (Num 1:50–51; 4). There is scarcely a hint of the old Levitic priesthood (cf. Wellhausen 1885: 121–27). The issue comes up only when, under Korah's leadership, certain Levites protest against Moses and Aaron: "Enough for you! For all the congregation is holy, and Yahweh is in their midst. So why should you elevate yourselves over Yahweh's community?" (Num 16:3). Interestingly, Korah complains on behalf of all Israel, apparently espousing the cause of lay priesthood in order to win popular sympathy. But Moses assumes that Korah's true goal is a broad, Levitic priesthood (Num 16:9–11). At any rate, somewhat differently from Ezekiel, P describes non-Aaronic priesthood as a heretical innovation, scotched in its infancy. The ensuing trial of the budding staves (Num 17:16–26) makes clear what is implicit in Exod 6:14–27. Even if the lines of Levi and Kohath are not the eldest, Aaron's is nonetheless the chief family in Levi, and Levi is the chief family in Israel. Aaron's third son Eleazar is the head of Levi (Num 3:32) and *ipso facto* the national chieftain (Num 27:19–23). (The only other possible vestige of Levitical priesthood in P is the week during which Moses serves as priest of the Tabernacle [see above, p. 532].)

One seeming difference between P and Ezekiel lies in the group to which each limits the priesthood: P restricts the office to *Aaron*, especially the line of Eleazar and Phinehas, while Ezekiel limits it to the *Zadokites*. For P to mention Zadok would have been anachronistic. But it is surprising that Ezekiel never refers to Aaron, Eleazar or Phinehas. Given the extensive similarities between P and Ezekiel, one suspects that P's characters Eleazar and/or Phinehas simply represent David's priest Zadok (cf. Cody 1969: 171–74).

Naturally, the Levitic priesthood continually fought back against Aaronic supremacism, especially before the Exile. Deuteronomy, with its explicit claims for a Levitic priesthood, may be an attempt to reclaim turf lost to the Zadokites. D mentions Aaron in only one extremely pejorative context: Yahweh almost killed him for making the Gold Calf (Deut 9:20). (Other references to Aaron in Deuteronomy come from P [32:50] and a later hand, possibly R [10:6–7].) Even earlier than Deuteronomy, the Elohist calls Aaron Moses' "fellow Levite", i.e., a Levite like any other, perhaps in response to exclusivist Zadokite claims (Exod 4:14; see NOTE). In E, Aaron serves as priest only once: in the affair of the Gold Calf; but even here he is not called *kōhēn* 'priest' (Exodus 32). His apostasy is avenged by Moses and Levi's Sons (vv 26–29), who are consecrated on the spot (v 29). Aaron appears in a negative light also in Numbers 12 (E), the Snow-white Miriam episode. Note that E, a Northern document, accords some priestly functions to non-Levites as well: Joshua, probably an Ephraimite (cf. Num 13:8, 16 [P]; Josh 19:49–50; 24:29–30; Judg 2:8–9), ministers in Meeting Tent (Exod 33:7–11), and Moses' Midianite father-in-law Jethro serves as a priest—in Aaron's presence (Exod 18:12). Moreover, the Genesis narratives of both J and E describe lay sacrifice (Gen 4:3–5; 8:20 [J]; 22; 31:54; 46:1 [E]).

Another voice of protest against Zadokite claims was Jeremiah, "from the priests that are in Anathoth" (Jer 1:1; cf. 11:21; 32:7–15), i.e., the house of Eli and Abiathar. Like Abiathar, Jeremiah was faithful to the dynasty of David, although not necessarily to its individual representatives (Jer 23:5–6; 30:9; 33:14–26). Jeremiah deprecated both Solomon's Temple and the Covenant Chest (Jer 3:16–17; chaps. 7, 26), even though his ancestors had tended both. Jeremiah revokes, as it were, the Zadokites' curse upon the Shilonite priesthood of Eli's house, quoted above (1 Sam 2:27–36). Priesthood and kingship are still intimately connected (cf. 1 Sam 2:35), but now the king's true priest is Levitic:

Not one man of David will be cut off, sitting on the throne of Israel's House. And of the Levitic priests not a man will be cut off from before me, sending up an Ascending-offering and smoking a Tribute-offering and making a Slaughter-sacrifice all the days. . . . If my covenant (with) the day and my covenant (with) the night could be broken, so that there be no day and night at their proper time, then, too, would be broken my covenant with David my slave, so that he not have a son ruling on his throne, and with the Levite priests my attendants. As the heaven's Army (i.e., the stars) is innumerable, and as the sea's sand cannot be measured, so will I multiply the seed of David my slave and of the Levites serving me. (Jer 33:17–22)

Later in the passage (v 24), Jeremiah refers to "the two families that Yahweh chose." The first is clearly David; the second might be all Israel or only the Levites (note v 26).

After the Exile, the last champion of Levitic priesthood was "Malachi" (probably not a name but a title: "My Messenger"), who was possibly himself a priest (in Mal 2:7, he calls the priest God's *mal'āk* 'messenger') (see Hill 1998: 17, 213). Malachi excoriates the clergy of his day, almost certainly Zadokite (on the postexilic priesthood, see Hanson [1975: 209–79]). He accuses them of offering spoiled bread and maimed animals (1:6–9, 13–14) and of breaking "Levi's covenant" (2:1–9). Perhaps, too, the prophet's cry, "Have we not all one father?" (2:10), is addressed to the priests, referring not to the Heavenly Father but to the patriarch Levi. At any rate, in Mal 3:1–4 Yahweh proclaims,

Behold: me sending my Messenger (mal'āk̂i), and he will clear a way before me, and suddenly the lord [God? the king?] whom you seek will come to his palace/temple (hêkāl), and the Covenant Messenger (mal'ak habbərît), whom/which you desire — see: him coming. . . . But who that may endure the day of his coming, and who that can stand when he appears? For he is like a refiner's fire and like launderers' lye. And he will sit, refining and purifying silver, and will purify Levi's Sons and refine them like gold or like silver, and they will become for Yahweh those who present a Tribute-offering in righteousness. Then the Tribute-offering of Judah and Jerusalem will please Yahweh as in days of yore, and as in ancient years.

As perhaps in Exod 32:26–29 and Deut 33:8–11, "Malachi" envisions the tribe of Levi purged of its corrupt elements — presumably the Aaronids.

The Redactor of the Torah was a participant in the last days of the epic battle of the Levites (cf. Friedman 1987: 217–33). Though a Zadokite, his philosophy differed from that of the Priestly Writer and Ezekiel (cf. Levitt Kohn 2002). Rather than ignore JE and D and the Levitic priesthood they espoused, he coopted them. In the composite Torah, P's hierarchy of Aaronid priests, Levites and common Israelites overwhelms the scattered references to lay and Levitic priesthood. From the same era, the Chronicler's work gives the Levites a high degree of dignity, while making them forever inferior to the Zadokite Aaronids. The postexilic Levites are admittedly menials, but the Temple sheds its sanctity even upon gatekeepers and musicians.

As for Exodus 32, the story appears simultaneously to assert pan-Levitic priestly prerogatives and to disparage those of the Aaronic line. To maintain Covenant fidelity, it implies, future Israelites should follow Levitic dictates. The Elohist grants that the Aaronids, too, are Levites (4:14), but only of the most disreputable sort. Their esteemed ancestor was faithless to Yahweh and to his kinsman Moses. It took the ordinary Levites to clean up the mess.

This raises the question: who and where were the Aaronid priests that the Elohist attacks? Here we lack sufficient information. One obvious possibility is Jerusalem, although we do not know for certain that the preexilic Temple priesthood claimed Aaronic descent. Another possibility, for reasons to be seen shortly, is the priesthood of Bethel.

THE ELOHIST VS. JEROBOAM

After Solomon died and Rehoboam ascended the throne (c. 920 B.C.E.), the United Monarchy fissioned into the kingdoms of Israel in the North and Judah in the South. Under the spell of the Torah's twelve-tribe scheme, many historians regard this division as somehow unnatural, requiring a special explanation. But the union of Judah and Israel was probably doomed from the start, as three civil wars during David's reign amply attest (2 Sam 2:1–3:1; 15–18; 20). Even earlier, the archaic Song of Deborah (Judges 5, c. eleventh century B.C.E.) neglects the Southern tribes and focuses only on the Northern. Halpern (1983: 9–12, 118–20, 146–59, 173–77) traces the division between North and South back to the Late Bronze Age.

The inevitable rift may have been widened when Solomon "sold" Northern cities to Phoenicia and intensified Northern Israel's corvée duty, while perhaps exempting Judah (Halpern 1974: 528). Solomon also immured the sacred Chest, originally a Northern cult object, in his glorious new Temple. No longer a distinguished "guest" sojourning in David's tent, the Ark became a hostage through which Solomon retained Northern loyalties (see 1 Kgs 12:26–33).

As the Bible tells it, the prophet Ahijah of Shiloh, disenchanted with Solomon's relaxed attitude toward religious purity, picked out Solomon's officer Jeroboam son of Nebat, of the tribe of Ephraim, to lead a secession. Forthwith, Jeroboam prudently fled to Egypt, where he bided his time and was doubtless fostered by Pharaoh as a potential destabilizer of Judah's growing power (1 Kgs 11:27–40).

The Bible depicts Rehoboam as a spoiled youth, lacking the maturity to govern a nation. When Jeroboam returned from exile, ostensibly to arbitrate between the northern tribes and the house of David, he rode a wave of disgruntlement whose cry was: "What share for us in David / Nor possession in Jesse's son? / To your tents, Israel! / Now see your house, David!" (1 Kgs 12:16). Jeroboam was elected king of a new polity, constituted of the ten northern tribes. His first official acts are described as follows:

And Jeroboam built Shechem in Mount Ephraim and settled in it; and he went out from there and built Penuel. And Jeroboam said in his heart, "Now the kingdom may return to David's House. If this people goes up to make Slaughter-offerings in Yahweh's House in Jerusalem, then this people's heart will return to their lordship, to Rehoboam Judah's king, and they will kill me. . . . So the king took counsel and made two gold calves and said of them, "Enough for you of going up to Jerusalem! See: your deity, Israel, who took you up from the land of Egypt." And he put the one at Bethel and the one he put at Dan. . . . And he made the Height House(s) (local shrines) and made priests from the people's extremities (*qəṣôt* = aristocrats?) who were not from Levi's Sons. And Jeroboam made a festival in the eighth month on the fifteenth day of the month, like the festival that was in Judah, and he went up by the altar—thus he did at Bethel—to sacrifice to the calves that he had made; and he stationed at Bethel the priests of the Heights that he had made. And he went up by the altar that he had made at Bethel on the fifteenth day of the eighth month, that he had made up from his own heart. And he made a festival for Israel's Sons, and he went up by the altar to make smoke. (1 Kgs 12:25–33)

The similarities between Exodus 32 and the history of Jeroboam are striking (cf. Aberbach and Smoler 1967):

1. The disgruntled people nominate a leader.
2. The leader fashions gold calves.
3. The images are made to facilitate contact with Yahweh, perceived as distant or absent.
4. The leader identifies the calves as "your deity/gods, Israel, who took you up *(he'ĕlûkā)* from the land of Egypt," treating *'ĕlōhîm* as grammatically plural.
5. The calves are contrasted, at least implicitly, with the tablets in the Covenant Chest. (In Exodus, Moses smashes the tablets upon seeing the Calf; in Kings, Jeroboam makes calves so Israel will no longer resort to Jerusalem, where the tablets reside.)
6. The Levitical clergy are depicted as antithetical to calf-worship. (In Exodus, the Levites kill the apostates; in Kings, Jeroboam appoints non-Levitic priests.)
7. The leader ordains sacrifices and a festival *(ḥag)*.
8. The religious innovation is called *ḥăṭā'â gədōlâ* 'a great sin' (Exod 32:21, 30, 31; 2 Kgs 17:21).
9. God's vengeance is deferred (Exod 32:34; 1 Kings 17).
10. Aberbach and Smoler (1967: 134) point to another parallel, but I think it fortuitous. Aaron is associated with men named Nadab and Abihu—in P, they are his sons—while Jeroboam has sons named Nadab and Abijah (1 Kgs 14:1, 20). But the names Abihu and Abijah are merely similar, not identical: *'ăbîhû'* 'He is my father' vs. *'ăbîyâ* 'Yah(weh) is my father.' (There is some evidence, however, that the pronoun *hû'* 'he' may replace the name Yahweh; cf. de Vaux 1983: 57–58.)

There are various ways to interpret the connections between Exodus 32 and 1 Kgs 12:25–33. Tradition takes both stories as historically accurate, yielding the rather implausible impression that Jeroboam, to spite Rehoboam and Yahweh, deliberately reenacted Aaron's ancient crime.

Modern scholars instead regard one story as commenting upon the other, or as each commenting upon the same thing. Since the Books of Kings contain far more verifiable historical information than does Exodus, a common view is that Exodus 32 is an allegorical attack on Jeroboam, just as 1 Kgs 12:25–33 is a historiographical attack (e.g., Friedman 1987: 70–74).

This still leaves open the question of literary precedence. Exodus 32 could be a reponse either to the account in 1 Kgs 12:25–33 or to Jeroboam's actual deeds. In the latter case, Exodus 32 could well be older than 1 Kgs 12:25–33 and closer to the real events.

Assuming that the account in Kings is largely factual, what may we infer of the historical Jeroboam's motives and acts? Solomon had hoped to secure the northern tribes' allegiance by splendidly housing their ancient palladium, the

Covenant Chest. Jeroboam, in order to make the northern secession permanent, was forced to surrender the Ark to Jerusalem. In its place, he fashioned two calves that somehow represented Yahweh's presence (see below). To have foisted these upon the people as an innovation would probably have been counterproductive. Instead, Jeroboam may have appealed to an actual tradition of sacred calves associated with Yahweh's cult, a tradition that existed prior to and alongside the Temple's iconography. In Cross's (1973: 199) words, Jeroboam "attempted to 'outarchaize' David." If so, the relationship between Exodus 32 and 1 Kgs 12:25–33 becomes even more complex: Exodus 32 could have arisen as a polemic against the practice that Jeroboam revived, and hypothetically could even antedate Jeroboam's secession.

What did Jeroboam actually say before his calves, and what did he mean? Was he introducing new gods? On the one hand, 1 Kgs 12:25–33 never states unequivocally that the calves represent any god other than Yahweh. And all available evidence corroborates that the Northern kingdom worshiped Yahweh in much the same way as did Judah (Cross 1973: 74–75). Even the Yahweh-zealot Jehu left the calves undisturbed (2 Kgs 10:31).

There remains the matter of Jeroboam's use of the plural: *hinnē(h) 'ĕlōhe(y)kā yiśrā'ēl 'ăšer he'ĕlûkā mē'ereṣ miṣrāyim* 'See: your deity/gods, Israel, who took you up from the land of Egypt.' There is little likelihood that Jeroboam was urging the Northerners to forsake Yahweh. And yet the prophet Ahijah, speaking for the Deuteronomistic Historian, rebukes him, "You have not been like my slave David, who kept my commandments and who walked behind me with all his heart, doing only what was right in my eyes. But you have done more evilly than all who were before you, and went and made for yourself *other gods and metal images ('ĕlōhîm 'aḥērîm ûmassēkôt)* to enrage me; and me you cast behind your back!" (1 Kgs 14:8–9). That is, Ahijah, as depicted by the Deuteronomistic Historian, does not accept the calves as part of Yahweh's cult. But Jeroboam himself must have.

We face two alternative possibilities. Either Jeroboam did speak of gods in the plural, but did not mean to repudiate monolatrous Yahwism, or else his words have been deliberately misreported in 1 Kgs 12:28 (cf. Knoppers 1995: 100–1). In the latter event, Aaron's plural speech in Exod 32:4—said of a *single calf*—must be based upon the very account of Jeroboam we possess in 1 Kings. If, however, it was possible to use *'ĕlōhîm* in the plural with a singular meaning (NOTE to 32:4, "These are your Deity"), then the relationship between Aaron's words and Jeroboam's words remains moot.

It is rather odd, in any case, that Aaron should appear as Jeroboam's surrogate. If Exodus 32 is a polemical allegory against Jeroboam, we might have expected an Ephraimite elder to be held responsible. Why does *Aaron* make the calf? The simplest answer, perhaps too simple, is that Elohist wished to kill two birds with one stone, simultaneously criticizing a priesthood and a dynasty he found odious. As a Northerner, he despised the Aaronids of Jerusalem. As a reactionary, he abominated Jeroboam's calves (cf. Friedman 1987: 70–74).

Another possibility is that the Elohist was attacking not Jeroboam per se but his cultic establishment. That is, Aaron in Exodus 32 may represent the *priests* who sacrificed before the northern calves at Dan and/or Bethel. Admittedly, 1 Kgs 12:31 says Jeroboam's priests were not Levites. But must we believe the Deuteronomistic Historian? Even his own source in Judges 17–18 preserves a tradition that, until the northern exile, the priests of Dan were Levites (note Judg 18:30; for the theory that Micah's image was a silver *calf*, see Malamat 1970: 12 n. 2). Perhaps the priests of Bethel claimed to be Levites of Aaron's house, an assertion accepted but mocked by the Elohist and flatly rejected by the Deuteronomistic Historian (Cross 1973: 198–99). The Elohist may have preferred the older rite of Bethel, with its eponymous stone pillar (Gen 28:18–19; 35:7, 14; see NOTE to 34:13). (In that case, however, it is difficult to ascribe the anti-pillar polemic of Exod 23:24 to E.) At any rate, the priests of Bethel suffered a posthumous punishment: Josiah exhumed their bones and burned them upon the altar of Bethel in order to desecrate it (2 Kgs 23:16).

SPECULATION: We considered above the possibility that the Gold Calf account of Exodus 32 lambastes not Jeroboam but the older cult that he revived. If so, then we can accept the claim of 1 Kgs 12:31 that Jeroboam made new priests. Perhaps he ousted the Aaronids of Bethel, who fled to Jerusalem and eventually coopted the Zadokite lineage; alternatively, P's rejected Aaronids Nadab and Abihu, elder brothers of Eleazar and Ithamar (Leviticus 10), may represent the bull priests of Bethel. Slight support for the theory of Aaronids at Bethel may be found in Judg 20:26–28, which locates there Aaron's grandson Phinehas (cf. Cross 1973: 199).

As so often, our evidence fails us just when our speculations grow most intriguing. We may at least say that, just as Exodus 32 must be read in the context of ancient debates over who was a priest, so it also addresses the question of whether a gold calf is an appropriate Yahweh symbol and perhaps whether Jeroboam's secession from Davidic hegemony was legitimate.

The fate of Jeroboam's calves is unknown. They may well make their final appearance in Sargon II's boast that he captured Israel's "gods in whom they trusted" (Cogan 1974: 104–5), quite as Hos 10:5–6 had predicted in an obscure oracle:

For the heifers (*sic?*) of Beth-aven (= Bethel),
Samaria's populace is distraught;
For its people mourn over it,
And its (Assyria's? the people's? the idols'?) priests exult (*sic?*) over it,
Over its glory, for it was exiled from it.
It, too, shall be carried to Assyria,
Tribute for King Contentious (*sic?*).

Most likely, in Israel's final extremity, the images were brought onto the battlefield, where they were captured (cf. 2 Chr 13:8). Ironically, like the Deuteronomistic Historian, the Assyrian monarch cannot accept the calves as monotheistic symbols. They are just "gods."

EPHRAIM AS THE WAYWARD CALF

The destruction and dispersion of Northern Israel in 722/1 B.C.E. presented the Judahites with their first great theological crisis. Had not Yahweh entered into a Covenant with all the tribes? How could ten of them be eliminated?

Over time, surviving Jews accepted their status as sole remnant, while still fostering fantastic legends of their lost brethren. But in the centuries immediately following the catastrophe, with recognizable pockets of Israelite exiles scattered through the Assyrian empire (2 Kgs 17:6; 18:11), visionaries fostered desperate hopes that the entire people would somehow be reconstituted.

In its original form, Jeremiah 31 was one such optimistic prediction. Yahweh would recall the lost house of Ephraim (Jeroboam's tribe and the major tribe of the North), ominously likened to an undisciplined *calf* (Jer 31:18) but nonetheless Yahweh's darling firstborn (Jer 31:9, 20). One day, all the tribes of Israel and Judah would again serve Yahweh in Zion (Jer 31:6, 12, 23). This was not to be, but after the Southern kingdom, in its turn, was destroyed in 587/86 B.C.E., Jeremiah's oracles were reinterpreted (by the prophet himself?) to refer to Judah and its hoped-for restoration. (Deut 4:25–31, where idolatry leads directly to exile with the hope of reconciliation, may similarly reflect on the fate of northern Israel; but more likely it is Dtr[2]'s reaction to Judah's exile [Friedman 2003: 317].)

Before Jeremiah, the prophet Hosea had had much to say about the northern kingdom and its calves, described as of both gold and silver. As often in Hosea, the syntax is difficult to follow: "They made a king—and not from me—they made a prince—and I did not know. Their silver and their gold they made for themselves idols. . . . Your calf, Samaria, is rejected; my *nose* (anger) flares against them. . . . And it—a smith made it, and it is not Deity, but Samaria's calf shall be fragments. . . . Aliens will swallow him/it; swallowed is Israel" (Hos 8:4–8; see also 10:5; 13:2). In Hos 11:1–4, as in Jeremiah 31, Ephraim is likened to both a child and a *calf*: "I trained Ephraim, carried him in my arms . . . ; with . . . cords I pulled them, with ropes of love, and I was to them like those who place a yoke over his jowls" (*sic*—the text is nearly incomprehensible).

SPECULATION: The image of Ephraim as calf may be found already in Gen 49:22. In Jacob's Blessing (Gen 49:2–27), five of the tribes are compared to animals—a lion, an ass, a snake, a gazelle and a wolf. Joseph, father of Ephraim, is called *bn prt* (MT *bēn pōrāt*), which some take as an archaic form of **bēn pārâ* 'cow's son,' i.e., a calf. Although the rest of the verse is equally enigmatic, the final word, *šûr* (MT), could be read as **šôr* 'bull.' Note, too, that this passage later calls God *'ăbîr ya'ăqōb* 'Jacob's bull/stallion.' Here, too, we could find evidence that the Joseph tribes and their divine symbol were taurine.

If the Gold Calf of Exodus 32 can be read as symbolizing not just Yahweh but the Northern tribes themselves, then a new interpretation of its destruction emerges. Just as the remnants of Israel would be swallowed up by the surrounding nations (and also, no doubt, absorbed into Judah), so the Calf is shattered, dissolved and swallowed (cf. Hos 8:7–8).

THE NEW COVENANT

Especially in light of Jeremiah 31, we must turn again to Exodus 32:34. Israel has broken the Covenant by making an idol. Moses has symbolically annulled the Covenant by smashing the tablets. The moral: the Northern tribes have lost their relationship to Yahweh, who one day will punish the offenders (32:34) (Van Seters 1994: 300). But then, in chaps. 33–34, the tablets are restored and the Covenant renewed. The moral: the Northern tribes, after their due chastisement, will be welcomed back into Yahweh's fold.

It is extremely tempting to correlate the textual evolution of Exodus with the events of history. A common view is that, when the northern saga E was combined with the southern saga J after the demise of the north (e.g., Friedman 1987: 87–88), their respective Covenant scenes were made into the successive acts of a drama, separated by the Gold Calf debacle (see pp. 150–52). The very composition of JE represented an effort to renew the Covenant of all Israel, reuniting the sundered people literarily. In this light, consider Jer 31:31–34:

> See: days coming—Yahweh's speech—and I shall *cut* (make) with Israel's House and with Judah's House a new Covenant: not like the Covenant that I *cut* with their fathers on the day I grasped their hand to take them out from the land of Egypt, which they, they broke. . . . But this is the Covenant that I shall *cut* with Israel's House after those days . . . I shall set my Direction *(tôrātî)* inside them and on their heart I shall write it. And I will be for them as Deity, and they, they shall be for me as a people. And a man will no longer admonish his fellow, or a man his brother, saying, "Know Yahweh," but they all will know me, from their smallest and to their biggest . . . for I will forgive their fault, and their sin I will not remember any more.

In other words, part of the restoration of Israel's unity will entail a new Torah, embodying the New Covenant. Is this Jeremiah reflecting upon the composition of JE, as well as its recently-penned continuation in Deuteronomy?

YAHWEH AS THE CALF

The story of the Gold Calf is also a disquisition on the nature of idolatry. The Decalog opens by prohibiting the worship of gods other than Yahweh and banning graven images (20:1–6). The Bible does not distinguish clearly between polytheism and idolatry. The moment one makes a statue, even in the service of Yahweh, one is worshiping "other gods" (see further pp. 167–70, 778).

That is the view of the biblical authors, anyhow. What of ordinary Israelites? Specifically: in the official, Yahwistic cult of the North, what did Jeroboam's gold calves represent? And how do Aaron and the people think of their calf in Exodus 32?

In ancient iconography and myth, the wild male bovine in its maturity represents untrammeled masculinity and fecundity. The domestic bull represents masculinity civilized—powerful, potentially violent, but under restraint (see NOTE to 21:18, "bull"). For her part, the female bovine, wild or domestic, is a maternal figure, large and nurturant. The calf is generally depicted as suckling under its dam (e.g., van Buren 1945: 36–39; for images and discussion, see also Keel 1980; Hestrin 1987b).

Throughout the Near East, various gods and goddess are called "bulls," "cows" and "calves"; I shall cite only the most prominent examples. At Ugarit and presumably also in Canaan, the bull deity *par excellence* was the graybeard head of the pantheon *ṭôru 'ilu 'abūka* 'Bull, God, your Father.' Also, the Ugaritic warrior deity Ba'lu impregnates a cow who bears him a son (*KTU* 1.5.v.17–22; 10). In Mesopotamia, the young warrior god of Babylon was Marduk, whose Sumerian name *AMAR.UTUK* means "Bull-calf of the Sun." The Syro-Mespotamian storm god Adad was called "Bull" (Green 2003: 18–24, 54, 57), and the bull motif was prominent also in Hittite art (Green pp. 89–152, esp. 105–16). Gilgamesh's divine mother was Ninsun the "Wild Cow." In Egypt, the goddess of fecundity and love, Hathor, was a cow or cow-woman. Schroer (1987: 29–45) interprets the suckling cows of Levantine art as goddess figures.

Due to its dependent status, the calf makes for a somewhat unexpected divine figure (cf. Fleming 1999). But, as any Christian or Hindu knows, some gods are venerable even in their infancy, evoking the worshiper's nurturant love rather than submissive awe. Admittedly, it is hard to imagine the gangly suckling calf as a potent symbol of Yahweh the Liberator, quintessentially a self-reliant deity. We should probably, therefore, refine our understanding of the term "calf" to include not only babies but also animals up to three years of age (NOTE to 32:4, "calf"). "Young bull" may be a better translation.

But the calves of the Bible need not represent Yahweh himself. In addition to the high god, Bull 'Ilu, Ugaritic mythology briefly mentions a calf: *'gl.'il.'tk* 'Divine Calf 'Ataku' (*KTU* 1.3.iii.43–44; 108.11). This is a former adversary of the gods, now subservient to them. Because he is associated with the great Dragon Lītan (= biblical Leviathan), some hypothetically correlate this "calf" with Job's bovine Behemoth, who symbolizes the dry land, just as Lītan/Leviathan symbolizes the Deep (Pope 1965a: 321). However that may be, ancient Near Eastern art depicts assorted animals, among them bulls, supporting standing and seated deities (e.g., *ANEP* figs. 470–74, 486, 500, 522, 526, 534, 537); perhaps Ugaritic 'Ataku is one such character. Excavations have uncovered several bull figurines from Syria-Palestine: from Ugarit, from Hazor, from a site near Shiloh (Mazar 1982) and from Ashkelon (Stager 1991: 3). We do not find large statues, such as the Gold Calf must have been. Presumably, over time their metal was melted down and reused. It is unclear whether these images represented major deities themselves, or whether the gods were imagined to be standing on their backs.

Returning to the gold calves of the Bible, we face three basic possiblities:

1. *The calves of Aaron and Jeroboam represent a deity other than Yahweh.* This is an older view once prevalent in modern and premodern scholarship. Some have identified the calf as a Baal symbol; others think of the Egyptian Apis and Mnevis bulls, on whom see briefly Kessler (2001). But Cross and others have argued persuasively that the Northern calves were Yahweh symbols. And Aaron explicitly

puts his calf in the orbit of Yahweh-worship: "Tomorrow is a festival for Yahweh" (32:5). The biblical authors may have demurred—see esp. 1 Kgs 14:9, "You (Jeroboam) made *other gods* . . . and me (Yahweh) you cast behind your back!"—but Israelite calf-worshipers surely considered themselves to be orthodox Yahwists (see further above, pp. 574–78).

2. *Each of the calves represents Yahweh himself.* This is the surface interpretation of Exod 32:4, 8 = 1 Kgs 12:28. The worship leader points to the image and proclaims, "These are/see your Deity/gods who took you up from the land of Egypt" (on the plural, see NOTES to 32:1, "deity . . . they," 4, "These are your Deity"). Micah's image, which some identify as a calf, is also said to be "for Yahweh" (Judg 17:3). Num 23:22; 24:8 acclaims Yahweh as "God *('ēl)*, who takes them/him from Egypt, he has indeed (?) wild-ox prongs *(tôʿăpōt rəʾēm)*." That is, the god of the Exodus has bovine horns. Finally, on a Samaria ostracon we find a personal name *ʿglyw (AHI* 3.041), which may mean "Yahweh is the Calf" (Koenen 1994) (but it could also mean "Yahweh's Calf").

3. *Each of the calves represents Yahweh's mount or throne-support.* This understanding, perhaps the majority view today (cf. already Ramban), draws upon both ancient depictions of gods seated between or standing upon bulls and also the analogy of the Griffins, between which Yahweh sits enthroned or upon which he rides (see pp. 515–21). If so, the gold calves are divine servants, perhaps representing the calf ʿAtaku. According to *Exod. Rab.* 42:5, Aaron's Calf was inspired by a vision of Yahweh's chariot, which includes a divine ox (Ezekiel 1).

By this interpretation, both Aaron and Jeroboam, their plural grammar notwithstanding, are really pointing to the empty space above their calves when they acclaim the god of the exodus. Halpern (1991: 68–69) imagines that Jeroboam's two bulls, at the northern and southern extremities of his kingdom, symbolically define the space between them as Yahweh's colossal chair. (On Canaan as Yahweh's throne, see also vol. I, p. 567.)

SPECULATION: One could develop further the notion that the mountain country represents God's seat. In Hab 2:17, Mount Lebanon parallels the bovine Behemoth (cf. Job 40:15–24), and in Ps 29:6 Mounts Lebanon and Sirion (i.e., Hermon) dance "like calves . . . sons of wild oxen *(kəmô ʿēgel . . . ben-rəʾēmîm).* At Ugarit, Baʿlu appears to sit enthroned upon mountains *(KTU* 1.101.1–3). The Hittites venerated divine mountains in bovine form as Seri(su) and Hurri/Tella (Haas 1994: 319–23). Perhaps Jeroboam's bulls similarly represent two theriomorphized mountains on which Yahweh sits or stands.

In the end, I do not think that we can or should choose among these interpretations. Cross (1973: 73 n. 117) reasonly comments, "The young bulls were no doubt conceived as pedestals for the same god in the two national shrines. However, there were, we suspect, grounds for the accusation in Exodus 32:4 = 1 Kings 12:28 that the bulls of Dan and Bethel were worshipped. A god and his animal 'participate in each other,' and while the god may be conceived as enthroned or standing on the bull in Canaanite mythology and iconography, he also is immanent in his animal so that the two may be confused." Part of the perennial appeal of religious iconography—and its nonappeal for certain monotheistic religions—is the ease with which it sustains multiple interpretations.

XXI. *This nation is your people* (33:1–34:35)

33   ¹(E)And Yahweh spoke to Moses, saying: "Go, go up from here, you and the people that you took up from the land of Egypt, (D-like) to the land that I swore to Abraham, to Isaac and to Jacob, saying, 'To your *seed* I will give it'—²and I shall send before you a Messenger, and I will expel the Canaanite, the Amorite and the Hittite and the Perizzite, the Hivvite and the Jebusite—³to a land flowing of milk and honey—(E)although I will not go up in your midst, for you are a hard-necked people, lest I finish you off on the way."

⁴And the people heard this bad word and mourned, and they did not put, (each) man his finery, on himself. ⁵And Yahweh said to Moses, "Say to Israel's Sons, 'A hard-necked people are you; (if) one instant I go up in your midst, then I will finish you off. And now, lay down your finery from on you, and I will know what I will do with you.' " ⁶So Israel's Sons stripped themselves their finery from Mount Horeb.

⁷And Moses, he would take the tent and pitch it/for him outside the camp, far from the camp, and he would call it "Meeting Tent." And it would happen, any seeking Yahweh would go out to Meeting Tent that was outside the camp. ⁸And it would happen, as Moses' going out to the Tent, all the people would stand up and station themselves, (each) man at his tent's opening, and gaze after Moses until his entering into the Tent. ⁹And it would happen, as Moses' entering into the Tent, the Cloud Pillar would descend and stand at the Tent's Opening, and he would speak with Moses. ¹⁰And all the people would see the Cloud Pillar standing at the Tent's Opening, and all the people would *stand* and bow down, (each) man at his tent's opening. ¹¹And Yahweh would speak to Moses face to face, as a man might speak to his friend, and he would return to the camp. But his attendant, Joshua son of Nun, was a youth; he would not depart from inside the Tent.

¹²And Moses said to Yahweh, "See, you are saying to me, 'Take up this people,' but you, you have not let me know whom/what you will send with me,' yet you, you said, 'I know you by name, and also you have found favor in my eyes.' ¹³And now, if indeed I have found favor in your eyes, let me know your ways that I may know you, so that I may find favor in your eyes. And see, that this nation is your people."

¹⁴Then he said, "My Face, it will go, and I will make rest for you."

¹⁵And he said to him, "If your Face is not going, do not make us go up from here. ¹⁶And by what, then, will it be known that I have found favor in your eyes, I and your people? Is it not by your going with us? Then I and your people will be distinguished from all peoples that are on the earth's surface."

¹⁷And Yahweh said to Moses, "Even this thing that you have spoken I will do, for you have found favor in my eyes, and I have known you by name."

¹⁸⁽ᴶ?⁾And he said, "Show me then your Glory."

¹⁹And he said, "I, I shall make all my splendor pass before your face, and I shall call Yahweh's name before you: for I shall favor whom I favor, and love whom I love."

²⁰And he said, "You may not see my Face, for Man may not see me and live." ²¹And Yahweh said, "See: a place by me; and you will station yourself on the mountain. ²²And it will happen, in my Glory's passing, then I will put you in the mountain's crevice, and I will shelter my hand/skirt over you during my passing. ²³Then I will remove my hand/skirt, and you will see my backparts. But my Face may not be seen."

34 ¹⁽ᴶ?⁾And Yahweh said to Moses, ⁽ᴿᴶᴱ?⁾"Carve for yourself two stone tablets like the first, that I may write on the tablets the words that were on the tablets that you smashed, ²⁽ᴶ?⁾and be ready for the morning. And you shall ascend in the morning to Mount Sinai, and you shall station yourself before me there on the mountain's head. ³But no man may ascend with you; and also a man may not be seen in all the mountain. Also, the flock and the herd must not graze opposite that mountain."

⁴⁽ᴿᴶᴱ?⁾So he carved two stone tablets like the first, ⁽ᴶ?⁾and Moses got up early in the morning and ascended to Mount Sinai, as Yahweh commanded him, and he took in his hand two stone tablets. ⁵And Yahweh descended in the cloud. And he stationed himself by him there, and he called upon Yahweh's name.

⁶And Yahweh passed before his face, and he called, "Yahweh, Yahweh, a merciful and benevolent god, *long-faced* and great in trust and reliability, ⁷conserving fidelity to a thousandth (generation), *bearing* transgression and crime and sin — although he does not acquit, acquit, reckoning fathers' sins upon sons and upon sons' sons, upon a third and upon a fourth (generation)."

⁸And Moses hurried and prostrated himself on the ground and bowed down. ⁹And he said, "If indeed I have found favor in your eyes, my Lordship, let my Lordship go in our midst, although it is a hard-necked people, yet may you pardon our transgression and our sin and possess us."

¹⁰And he said, "See: me *cutting* a covenant. Before all your people I will work wonders that have not been created in all the world or among all the nations, so that all the people in whose midst you are will see Yahweh's deed, that it is so dreadful, what I am going to do with you.

¹¹⁽ᴰ⁻ˡⁱᵏᵉ⁾"Keep for yourself what I am commanding you today. See: me expelling from before you the Amorite and the Canaanite and the Hittite and the Perizzite and the Hivvite and the Jebusite. ¹²Be careful for yourself, lest you *cut* a covenant with the inhabitant of the land upon which you are coming, lest he become a snare in your midst — ¹³rather, their altars you must break, and their pillars you must smash, and his Asherim you must cut down; ¹⁴for you must not bow down to another god, for Jealous Yahweh is his name; he is a jealous god — ¹⁵lest you *cut* a covenant with the land's inhabitant, and they *whore* after their gods and sacrifice to their gods, and he call you and you eat of his sacrifice, ¹⁶and you take

from his daughters for your sons, and his daughters *whore* after their gods, and they make your sons *whore* after their gods.

17(J?) "Metal gods don't make for yourself.

18 "The Unleavened Bread Festival you must keep. Seven days you shall eat unleavened bread, which I commanded you at the occasion of the New Grain Month, for in the New Grain Month you went out from Egypt.

19 "Every *loosening* the womb is mine, and all your cattle you must 'male,' *loosening* of a bull or a sheep, 20 but an ass's *loosening* you shall redeem with a sheep/goat, or if you do not redeem, then you shall 'neck' it. Every firstborn of your sons you must redeem.

And my *Face must not be seen emptily.*

21 "Six days you shall work, but on the seventh day you must cease; in plowing and in harvest you must cease.

22 "And a Festival of Weeks you shall make for yourself, the firstfruits of the wheat harvest, and the Ingathering Festival (at) the year's *revolution.* 23 Three times in the year all your malehood must appear to the Face of the Lord Yahweh, Israel's deity. 24 Because I shall dispossess nations from before you and widen your border, then not *any man* will covet your land in your going up to appear to Yahweh your deity three times in the year.

25 "Don't slaughter my Slaughter-offering blood with leavened food, and the Pesaḥ festival Slaughter-offering must not abide till the morning.

26 "The first of your soil's firstfruits you must bring to Yahweh your deity's House.

"Don't cook a kid in its mother's milk."

27 And Yahweh said to Moses, "Write for yourself these words, for *by the mouth of* these words I have *cut* a covenant with you and with Israel."

28 So he was there with Yahweh forty day and forty night; bread he did not eat, and water he did not drink. And he wrote upon the tablets the Covenant words, (R) the Ten Words.

29(P/R) And it happened, in Moses' descending from Mount Sinai, and the two Testimony Tablets in Moses' hand in his descending from the mountain, and Moses did not know that his face skin had "horned" in his speaking with him. 30 And Aaron and all Israel's Sons saw Moses and, see: his face skin had "horned," and they were too frightened to approach him. 31 But Moses called to them, and Aaron and all the leaders in the congregation returned to him, and Moses spoke to them. 32 And afterwards all Israel's Sons approached, and he commanded them all that Yahweh spoke with him on Mount Sinai.

33 And Moses finished speaking with them, and he put a veil on his face.

34 And in Moses' entering before Yahweh to speak with him, he would remove the veil until his going out, and he would go out and speak to Israel's Sons what he would be commanded. 35 And Israel's Sons would see Moses' face, that Moses' face skin "horned," and he would return the veil over his face, until his entering to speak with him.

ANALYSIS

TEXTUAL NOTES

33:1. *spoke.* As if to compensate for the absence of the expected *lē(')mōr* 'saying,' LXX and Syr have "said"; see next TEXTUAL NOTE.

†† *saying.* Reading *lē(')mōr* with Sam, Kenn 69 and Vg; it is absent in MT, LXX and Syr (see previous TEXTUAL NOTE), probably lost due to homoioarkton before *lēk.* But that the longer reading is expansionistic is also quite possible.

Go, go up. Syr reverses the commands.

the people. LXX, Syr and Vg read "*your* people," as in 32:7.

took up. Kenn 84, LXX and Syr have "took *out*"; cf. TEXTUAL NOTE to 32:1, "took us up."

the land of. Absent in Syr.

Isaac. LXX and Syr have "*and* Isaac."

† 33:2. *a Messenger.* LXX and Kenn 4 (first hand) have "*my* Messenger," as if reading **ml'ky* (vs. MT-Sam *ml'k*), parallel to 23:23; 32:34; cf. TEXTUAL NOTE to 23:20. I have followed the shorter, more difficult reading of MT-Sam. Since in 33:2 (but not 23:20) the next word begins with waw, similar to yodh in Greco-Roman era script (Cross 1961a; Qimron 1972), this could be a simple graphic error, whichever reading is original.

† *I will expel.* So MT and Sam. Most LXX MSS and Syr have "*he* (i.e., the Messenger) will expel"—Dillmann's (1880: 244) preferred reading—while LXX[B] originally read "*you* (Moses) will expel." These variants are either free paraphrases or else aural variants, confusing **wəgērēšt* (hypothetical dialectal pronunciation for both first and second person) *'et* and **wəgērēš 'et.*

† *the Canaanite.* Absent in LXX[B] and probably the original LXX. Various Greek MSS insert the Canaanites in various places to complete the list (see Wevers 1990: 541). It may also have been absent from the original text (see next TEXTUAL NOTE). Whenever the list of pre-Israelite inhabitants of Canaan appears, the Versions and MSS are at odds with one another (cf. TEXTUAL NOTES to 3:8, 16).

† *the Amorite.* Sam, Kenn 1, 5, 109, 181, 200, 253, Rossi 15, 16, 262, 296, 443, 444, 543, 668, 766, a few MSS of *Tg. Onqelos,* Syr and Vg insert *w* 'and,' which we would indeed expect. Since the preceding letter is yodh, similar to waw in Hellenistic period script (Cross 1961a; Qimron 1972), either haplography or dittography would be conceivable, especially assuming continuous writing. The lack of a conjunction before "the Amorite" might also be taken as evidence that "the Canaanite" was a later addition (previous TEXTUAL NOTE). Or this could simply be random variation.

† *and the Hittite.* Kenn 223, *Tgs. Ps.-Jonathan* and *Neofiti I* omit "and"; cf. previous TEXTUAL NOTE. In Sam, "and the Girgashite" follows "the Hittite."

and the Perizzite. Kenn 4 and *Tg. Neofiti I* omit "and."

† *the Hivvite.* LXX inserts "the Girgashite," although MSS differ on its exact position (Wevers 1990: 540–41). Sam, MT MSS (Kennicott 1776–80: 179; de

Rossi 1784–85: 76), including a Genizah MS *(BHS)*, LXX, Syr, Vg and *Tg. Onqelos* insert "and."

33:3. *to a land.* There is little doubt that the short and difficult MT-Sam is original. To repair the ellipsis, LXX begins "he will lead you"; on the MSS variants "I will lead you" and "you will lead," see Wevers (1992: 223). Vg similarly supplies "and you will enter."

you are. Paraphrasing, *Tg. Neofiti I* has *"they* are" (cf. 32:9; 34:9).

33:4. *and they did not put . . . on himself.* Instead of describing what the Israelites did *not* wear, LXX reports: *katepenthēsan en penthikois,* which roughly means "they mourned, wearing what-is-appropriate-to-mourning." Wevers (1990: 542) discerns an attempt to correct a perceived incongruity: in MT-Sam, the people are commanded to put off the ornaments (33:5–6) they were not in fact wearing (v 4) (also Dillmann 1880: 344); see NOTE to 33:4, "did not put."

33:5. *said to Moses, "Say to Israel's Sons."* LXX has simply "said to Israel's Sons," almost certainly due to parablepsis in Hebrew, skipping from one *'el* 'to' to the next (Wevers 1990: 542). This verse seems to have suffered an unusual amount of corruption in the LXX stream, as if a particular early scribe had been temporarily distracted; see following TEXTUAL NOTE.

(if) one instant . . . finish you off. LXX has something quite different: *"Beware, lest I bring upon you another plague* and finish you off." It appears that the original reading, MT-Sam *rgʿ 'ḥd* 'one instant,' was miscopied as **ngʿ 'ḥr* 'another plague' (cf. Kenn 193 *rngʿ [sic] 'ḥr*), which necessitated reading *'lh* not as the Qal *'eʿĕle(h)* (MT-Sam) but as the Hiphʿil **'aʿăle(h)* 'I will *bring up.'* The initial "Beware, lest" probably was added to the Greek to make a smoother transition (Wevers 1990: 542).

And now. Syr omits the conjunction.

your finery. LXX doubly renders with *tas stolas tōn doxōn hymōn kai ton kosmon* 'your glorious robes and ornament(s).'

from on you. The main LXX tradition omits these words (see Wevers 1990: 543). Apparently, *mʿlyk* fell out after *'dyk* 'your finery' in the *Vorlage* (homoioteleuton).

† *I will know.* MT-Sam *wə'ēdəʿâ* must mean something like "so I can figure out (what to do)." LXX, however, has "I will make known to you," as if reading **wə'ōdīaʿ* 'and I will make known' or perhaps **wə'ōdīʿăkā* 'and I will make you know' (cf. Kenn 84 [first hand] *w'dʿk*), the latter reading probably influenced by *w'dʿk (wə'ēdāʿăkā)* in 33:13, 17. In 33:5, the Hiphʿil verb (LXX) makes good sense and is possibly correct.

33:6. *their finery.* LXX again contains a double rendering: "their ornament(s) and their garb."

from Mount Horeb. On the possibility that the end of v 6 is corrupt, see NOTE.

33:7. *the Tent.* LXX-Syr *"his* tent" follows a tradition that this is not the Tabernacle of chaps. 25–31, 35–40 but Moses' own domicile (see REDACTION ANALYSIS, p. 153).

† *it would happen, any seeking Yahweh.* Against MT *whyh kl mbqš yhwh yṣ',* Sam makes the plural explicit: *whyw kl mbqšy yhwh yṣ'w.* Either might be correct.

Ordinarily, I prefer singulars to plurals, but in this case Sam is the more unusual reading.

† *would go out to Meeting Tent that was outside the camp.* LXX is somewhat briefer: "went out to the tent (LXX^B: that was) outside the camp." (In the shorter LXX reading, "outside the camp" is where the people go, not where the tent is. But this is probably a corruption in Greek due to homoioteleuton: *skēnēn tēn* > *skēnēn.*) I take the excision of *mōʿēd* 'Meeting" as a desperate expedient to evade the problematic equation of this tent with the Tabernacle. But we cannot exclude the possibility that LXX preserves an original reading, *h'hl,* expanded into MT-Sam *'hl mwʿd.*

33:8. *going out to the Tent.* LXX^{BM} continues, "outside the camp," carelessly reduplicated from the previous verse.

station themselves. LXX has *skopeuontes* 'watching,' which would ordinarily correspond to the root *ṣpy,* hence the tentative *BHS* suggestion that LXX read **wṣpw,* against MT-Sam *wnṣbw.* An alternative would be to suppose that LXX recognized the "standing guard" implication of *niṣṣab* (cf. Moses' sister by the Nile [2:4]) and was influenced by the parallel with the following *wǝhibbîṭû* 'and gaze' rather than the preceding *yāqûmû* 'would stand.' In 33:21, however, LXX translates the verb *niṣṣab* literally as "stand," so perhaps LXX did follow a variant *Vorlage* here.

into the Tent. Influenced by the following clause, *Tg. Neofiti I* has "into the Tent's *opening.*"

33:10. *see . . . stand.* The verbs are singular in MT but plural in Sam, Vg and *Tgs.,* to match the final plural verb *wǝhištahǎwû* 'and bow down.'

† 33:11. *Joshua.* The main Syr reading is *hwšʿ,* i.e., Hoshea (cf. MT Num 13:8, 16; Deut 32:44; Syr Num 11:28). This is so strange, it could be correct. But note that, as in Deut 32:44, the preceding letter is waw, similar to yodh in certain Hebrew scripts (Cross 1961a; Qimron 1972); it is therefore possible that we have haplography: **wyhwšʿ > whwšʿ.*

depart. For MT *ymyš,* which is slightly difficult (see NOTE), Sam has the expected *ymwš.* The latter reading could be a correction, or MT could reflect waw-yodh confusion (cf. Cross 1961a; Qimron 1972). Or the root may always have had variant internal vowels.

33:12. *you said.* *Tg. Neofiti I* preposes "see," as earlier in the verse, while LXX adds "to me."

by name. Here and in v 17, LXX loosely paraphrases *para pantas* 'beyond all (others).' On the real meaning, see NOTE, "I know you by name."

33:13. *And now.* Syr omits the conjunction.

† *your ways.* Although the consonants *drkk* indicate a singular, in MT they are vocalized *dǝrākekā,* probably a plural (despite the lack of a Qere notation). Similarly, Sam and many MT MSS have an explicit plural *drkyk* (Kennicott 1776–80: 180; also *Tg. Neofiti I*). *Tgs. Onqelos* and *Ps.-Jonathan,* however, have the singular (on LXX, see NOTE). Decisive for me is Ps 103:7, which calls Yahweh's attributes of mercy (Ps 103:7; cf. Exod 34:6) *dǝrākā(y)w* 'his ways.'

And see. Against MT-Sam *wr'h,* LXX has *kai hina gnō* 'and so that I may know,' as if reading **w'dʿ(h)* as earlier in the verse.

this nation. LXX^B, Syr and *Tg. Neofiti I* have "this *great* nation," borrowing from Deut 4:6, *haggôy haggādôl hazze(h).*

33:14. *he said.* Syr, Vg and some LXX MSS specify: "*the Lord* said." The same LXX minuscules also add "to him," while Syr adds "to Moses."

My Face, it will go. Against MT-Sam *pānay yēlēkû,* Syr has "Go before me," as if reading **lēk ləpānay* or, less idiomatically, **ləpānay lēk (BHS).* More likely, however, Syr has deliberately avoided referring to God passing before Moses; cf. the supposed *tiqqûn sōpərîm* 'scribal correction in Gen 18:22 so that God does not stand before Abraham (cf. C. McCarthy 1981: 70–76).

33:15. *going.* LXX^A and Syr add "with us," imported from v 16; *Tgs.* similarly supply "among us."

make us go up. LXX has "make *me* go up," reading **t'lny,* against MT-Sam *t'lnw.* On the one hand, this may well be a scribal error (on waw-yodh confusion in the Greco-Roman period, see Cross 1961a; Qimron 1972). On the other hand, as Wevers (1990: 549–50) suggests, LXX may be a deliberate change to emphasize Moses' sense of identity with the people (see following).

33:17. *I will do.* LXX and Kenn 69 add "for you," emphasizing God's relationship with Moses; cf. previous TEXTUAL NOTE.

† *I have known you.* Reading with MT-LXX the converted imperfect *wā'ēdā'ăkā* (cf. 33:12), vs. Syr and *Samaritan Tg. *wə'ēdā'ăkā,* a cohortative/imperfect 'and I shall know you.'

by name. See TEXTUAL NOTE to 33:12.

† 33:19. *I, I shall make all my splendor pass.* LXX "I will pass *in* my splendor" might well be a loose rendering of MT-Sam *'ănî 'a'ăbîr kol-ṭûbî.* But it would correspond even more closely to a hypothetical **'ănî 'e'ĕbôr kol-ṭûbî* 'I, all my splendor, will pass,' possibly original. On the syntax, cf. NOTE to 6:3, "I, my name, Yahweh."

and I shall call . . . before you. This entire clause is absent from *Tg. Neofiti I,* dropped by parablepsis (homoioarkton) in Aramaic (*w'qry . . . w'hws*). Since the phrase is present in the *Fragmentary Targum,* also representative of the Palestinian Targum tradition, this would seem to be a peculiarity of this MS.

† *Yahweh's name.* LXX has "*my* name, Yahweh," reading **šmy yhwh,* against MT-Sam *šm yhwh.* Either LXX is dittographic or MT-Sam haplographic. (In all Versions, the parallel in 34:5 reads *šm yhwh* 'Yahweh's name,' not **šmw yhwh* 'his name, Yahweh.').

33:20. *see me.* LXX supplies "see *my Face.*"

† 33:22. *shelter. Śkk* as a by-form of *skk* 'shelter' is unique to this verse. Ehrlich (1908: 407) may be correct, in place of *wśkty* (MT-Sam), to read **wśmty* 'and I will *put.*'

over you during my passing. The end of the verse is absent from Vg, which, though given to streamlining, does not usually eliminate meaningful material. It seems that Jerome's *Vorlage* or Jerome himself skipped from *kpy* 'my hand' to *'bry* 'my passing' (homoioteleuton).

33:23. *I will remove my hand.* Syr has instead "I will make my Glory pass," as in 33:19, thus reducing the anthropomorphism.

seen. LXX adds "for you."

34:1. *like the first.* At this point, LXX adds "and ascend to me to the mountain," as if reading *w'lh 'ly hhrh*, probably borrowed from Deut 10:1 (cf. also Exod 24:12) to make the sequence of events clear: Moses is still with the people, he hews out the Tablets, he ascends, then God writes. But this creates redundancy with v 2. There is nevertheless a very slight chance that the LXX plus is original, dropped from MT-Sam by homoioarkton with the following *wktbty* 'and I will write.'

† *that I may write.* Bib. Ant. 12:10 appears to read **wəkātabtā* 'that *you* may write.' This is likely a harmonization with 34:27–28, which appear to say that Moses wrote on the tablets (but see NOTES).

†† *the Tablets.* So 4QpaleoExod^m and Vg. MT-Sam-LXX "the *first* tablets" is probably derived from Deut 10:1 (Sanderson 1986: 55).

34:2. *in the morning.* This is absent in LXX and one Syr MS, probably dropped on purpose to remove the redundancy with "for the morning" (Wevers 1990: 555). Cf. TEXTUAL NOTE to 34:4, "in the morning."

before me. Not reflected in Syr.

34:3. *and also.* Syr lacks "also." While this is the shorter reading, hence attractive, it may well be an assimilation to "But (no) man *(wə'îš)*" at the head of the verse.

Also. Sam, Kenn 84, 129, 181, 186, 674, 686, Rossi 274, 419 and a few Tg. Onqelos MSS and editions have *wgm* 'And also,' presumably inspired by *wəgam* previously in the verse.

34:4. *he carved.* Probably independently, Sam, one LXX minuscule (426) and the Arabic and Ethiopic Versions specify "*Moses* carved." Cf. next TEXTUAL NOTE.

† *Moses got up.* Sam has "*he* got up" (also Vg). Thus, while MT puts the subject "Moses" at the beginning of the verse, Sam puts "Moses" in the middle (previous TEXTUAL NOTE). Either could be correct, although it may be easier to imagine a scribe moving Moses forward than postponing his mention.

in the morning. This is dropped by LXX^B as redundant with Hebrew *hiškîm*/ Greek *orthrizein* 'rise early.' LXX^A, however, has *to prōi* to match MT-Sam, and this Wevers (1990: 555–56) considers to be the original LXX.

† *and he took in his hand.* So MT-Sam. LXX^B has instead "and *Moses* took" without reference to his hand. Somewhat closer to MT-Sam, we find in LXX^A and Vg "and *Moses* took *with him*." The latter Wevers (1990: 556) considers the original LXX, but I am not sure. The shorter LXX^B could be authentic and might even reflect a *Vorlage* superior to MT-Sam. If so, MT-Sam-LXX^A-Vg were expanded to resemble 32:15 and Deut 10:3.

SPECULATION: Given the uncertainty as to the number of hands with which Moses holds the Tablets, we should note that MT-Sam *ydw* might be vocalized **yādāw* 'his hand*s*.' Cf. TEXTUAL NOTES to 32:15, "his hands," 19; 34:29, "in Moses' hand."

† 34:6. *Yahweh, Yahweh.* So MT-Sam. LXX^B has simply *Kyrios*, as if there were only one *yhwh* (= Kenn 171). Thus, either LXX^B is haplographic or MT-Sam dittographic. (LXX^A supports MT-Sam.) See further NOTE.

34:7. *keeping trust.* So MT-Sam. LXX has "*and* keeping justice *and doing mercy.*" This double rendering seemingly attempts to combine *nōṣēr ḥesed* in 34:7 with *'ōśe(h) ḥesed* in 20:6 (Wevers 1990: 557).

acquit. LXX supplies the implicit object: "the guilty."

upon a third. Sam MSS (von Gall 1918: 189) and Kenn 9, 17, 109, 181, 686, Rossi 17, 419, 840 insert "and," to parallel the next phrase.

† 34:9. *my Lordship* (first time). Absent in LXX. While the Greek is most likely streamlining, it is possible that there were two ancient variants with *'dny* in different places, and that MT-Sam, where *'dny* appears twice, is a conflated reading.

my Lordship (second time). LXX^AM has simply "Lord," perhaps reflecting a reading **yhwh*, against MT-Sam *'dny* (also LXX^B *ho kyrios mou*).

† *transgression . . . sin.* All the ancient translations pluralize these nouns, which ordinarily we would dismiss as paraphrase. In fact, however, very many MT MSS and editions do read plurals *l'wnynw . . . lḥṭ'tynw* 'our transgressions . . . our sins' (Kennicott 1776–80: 182; de Rossi 1784–85: 76–77; *BHS*), as do Sam MSS. I generally regard singular collective language as more original and idiomatic than plural; here, however, there is greater ambiguity. For the first word, there is no difference in pronunciation between *'ăwōnēnû* (sing.) and *'ăwōnênû* (pl.); for the second, there is little difference between *ḥaṭṭā(')tēnû* (sing.) and *ḥaṭṭō(')tênû* (pl.).

† *and possess us.* Although supported in all witnesses, the conclusion of Moses' speech seems something of a *non sequitur*. Perhaps *wnḥltnw* is an ancient corruption. One would expect another noun for "sin" to parallel *la'ăwōnēnû* and *ləḥaṭṭā(')tēnû*, but none springs to mind.

SPECULATION: There are however, a few *verbs* that would fit rather well. Closest to MT-Sam *wnḥltnw* would be **wmḥltnw* 'and *forgive* us.' The letters mem and nun are easily confused in paleo-Hebrew script, and aural confusion could happen in any period. (Alternatively, we could regard the first two letters of *wnḥltnw* as originally a mem, which became *wn* by ink abrasion. This would yield a quasi poetic, though slightly awkward **wəsālaḥtā la'ăwōnēnû ûl(ə)ḥaṭṭā(')tēnû məḥaltānû* 'may you pardon our transgression, and for our sin may you forgive us.') The chief argument against this reconstruction is that the verb *mḥl* is first attested in postbiblical Hebrew. If we require a known Biblical Hebrew verb to achieve the same sense, we might also consider **wḥmltnw* 'and spare/pity us' (mem-nun confusion plus metathesis).

Ewald (*apud* Dillmann 1880: 388), however, thinks that the verb should refer to guidance. While his emendation **wnḥytnw* 'and lead us' is too radical, we could obtain a similar meaning by replacing MT-Sam *wnḥltnw* with **wnḥltnw*, i.e., *wənihaltānû* 'and give us hereditary land.' In the larger context, however, "possess us" does make a certain sense; it is preferable to drastic conjectural emendation (see further NOTE).

34:10. *he said.* Vg clarifies "*the Lord* answered," while 2QExod^b and LXX further expand: "*the Lord* said *to Moses.*"

a covenant. Most LXX MSS add "for you (sing.)"; LXX^A, however, supports MT-Sam.

Before all your people. By inserting a conjunction after these words, Syr joins "before all your people" to the preceding clause.

among all the nations. LXX has a singular "in any people," probably a loose translation to match more closely the preceding phrase "in all the world."

for you. The absence of "for you" in LXX^A might be explained in three ways. Perhaps, in the process of correcting the verse to MT (see above, "a covenant"), a scribe canceled both cases of *soi* 'for you.' Alternatively, *soi* might have accidentally dropped by homoioteleuton after *poiēsō* (*sō* closely resembles *soi* in Greek letters). Lastly, Wevers (1990: 559) cites possible "auditory confusion" in the sequence *poiēsō soi.*

34:11. *what I am commanding.* LXX has *"all* that I am commanding you," as if reading **'t kl 'šr,* against MT-Sam *'t 'šr.* This expansion is inspired by 6:29; 7:2; 31:6; 34:32; 35:10; 38:22, etc.

today. Absent in LXX. One might regard MT-Sam-4QpaleoExod^m *hayyôm* as an expansion based upon the expression "today" ubiquitous in Deuteronomy (e.g., Deut 4:40; 6:6; 7:11, etc.). But one can more easily explain LXX by haplography with the next word in the Hebrew *Vorlage: hywm hnh > hnh* (homoioarkton).

† *Amorite . . . Canaanite.* Sam and Syr reverse these vis-à-vis MT.

† *Hittite . . . Perizzite.* Sam interposes "and the Girgashite," also included in 4QpaleoExod^m. "Hittite" and "Perizzite" are reversed in LXX^B, vis-à-vis MT.

† *Hivvite . . . Jebusite.* Kenn 104 and Tg. *Neofiti I* lack "and the Hivvite." LXX interposes "and the Girgashite."

34:12. *upon which.* So MT (*'lyh*). Sam *'lyw* 'upon whom' refers to the "inhabitant," not the "land."

† *lest he become a snare.* Kenn 193, 686, Rossi 198, Syr and Vg insert "for you (sing.)," as if reading **pn yhyh lk lmwqš,* against standard MT-Sam *pn yhyh lmwqš* (also LXX^A). On the one hand, the shorter reading could be the result of haplography by homoioarkton *(l . . . l).* On the other hand, the longer reading may be an expansion derived from 23:33 *ky yhyh lk lmwqš* 'indeed it will become for you as a snare.' LXX^B also inserts "for you," but in the plural *(hymin),* even though the verse otherwise addresses Israel in the second person singular.

† 34:13. *and his Asherim.* So MT *(w't 'šryw)* and 4QpaleoExod^m *(w'šryw).* Sam, LXX, Syr and Tgs. have *w'šryhm* 'and *their* Asherim." This fixes the odd switch of suffix in MT—there is a tendency in the ancient translations, and even in Hebrew MSS themselves, to change collective singulars into plurals—and may be a harmonization with Deut 7:5 (also Deut 12:3; see next TEXTUAL NOTE). Still the incongruence within 34:13 is surprising. MT may be too difficult to be original.

cut down. LXX continues, "and the statues of their gods you shall burn in fire," derived from Deut 7:5, 25; cf. Deut 12:3.

34:14. *to another god.* Massoretic scribal tradition enlarges the final resh of *'ahēr* 'another,' i.e., *l'l 'hR,* lest one should read **l'l 'hD* 'to one God.'

Jealous Yahweh is his name. Curiously periphrastic is LXX *ho . . . kyrios ho theos zēlōton onoma theos zēlōtēs estin,* which probably means "the Lord God is a jealous name, a jealous God" (Wevers 1990: 562).

34:15. *the land's inhabitant.* LXX^B expands and clarifies, albeit awkwardly: "the land's inhabitants, *toward the Philistines*" (on *allophylous* 'aliens' = Philistines, see Wevers 1992: 250).

† 34:16. *and you take.* So MT-Sam. LXX and Syr are considerably fuller: "and you take from their (*sic*) daughters for your sons, *and from your daughters you give to their sons* and *your* (sing. in LXX; pl. in Syr) daughters whore after their gods, and they make your sons whore after their gods" (LXX[B] has "and your sons whore," likely to be an inner Greek corruption: *kai ekporneusōsin tous huious sou* > *kai ekporneusōsin hoi huioi sou*).

The most obvious Hebrew *Vorlage* for the longer reading would be **wlqḥt mbntyw lbnyk wmbntyk lbnyw ttn wznw bntyk 'ḥry 'lhyhn whznw 't bnyk 'ḥry 'lhyhn*, against MT-Sam *wlqḥt mbntyw lbnyk wznw bntyw 'ḥry 'lhyhn whznw 't bnyk 'ḥry 'lhyhn*. But there are no obvious grounds for parablepsis, apart from the ubiquitous sequence *w . . . w*. To facilitate corruption, we could instead reconstruct **wlqḥt mbntyw lbnyk wntt mbntyk lbnyw wznw bntyk 'ḥry 'lhyhn whznw 't bnyk 'ḥry 'lhyhn*, less elegant but more liable to haplography, a skip from *lbnyw to *lbnyk*. If this is indeed what happened, then the MT-Sam tradition subsequently "repaired" the damage by changing *bntyk* 'your daughters' into *bntyw* 'his daughters.'

I have followed the shorter MT-Sam reading, however, since it alone is actually preserved in Hebrew. LXX-Syr may be expanding to make the law more comprehensive, influenced by Deut 7:3–4, "Do not intermarry with them; your daughter do not give to his son, and his daughter do not take for your son. For he will divert your son from (following) after me and he/they will serve other gods" (cf. also Judg 3:6). There are other cases of LXX adapting Exodus 34 to Deuteronomy 7; see TEXTUAL NOTES to 34:13 above. Here, however, because the resemblance is slight, one could even argue that Deut 7:3–4, if originally based upon Exod 34:16, is further evidence for the *longer* reading.

34:17. *Metal gods.* LXX begins "And."

34:18. *The.* LXX begins "And."

† *which.* Against the standard MT *lectio difficilior* '*ăšer* (also most Tg. Onqelos witnesses), we find in Sam, LXX, Syr, Vg, Tgs. Ps.-Jonathan and Neofiti I, MSS of Tg. Onqelos and several MT MSS (Kennicott 1776–80: 182; de Rossi 1784–85: 77) the more expected *ka*'*ăšer* 'as,' possibly correctly.

† *in the New Grain Month.* Sam has a shorter *bw* 'in it,' probably borrowed from 23:15 — unless MT 34:18 has been harmonized to Deut 16:1, "for in the New Grain Month. . . ."

†† 34:19. "*male.*" So Sam, which is consonantally the same as MT, except that Sam MSS vary between *tzkr* and *tzkyr*, suggesting a Hiphʻil *tazkîr instead of the MT Niphʻal *tizzākār*. Tgs. Onqelos and Ps.-Jonathan paraphrase *taqdîš dikrîn/ dikrayyā*' 'sanctify (the) males,' perhaps also reflecting a Hiphʻil. See further NOTE.

It is not certain that the troublesome word is original, however. It is not reflected in Syr, which may well be paraphrasing: "Everything opening the womb is mine, and all firstborn of your cattle, of the bulls and of the sheep." More significantly, in LXX the verse reads, "Everything opening the womb is mine, the males, a (LXX^B: every) calf's firstborn [i.e., firstborn calf] and a sheep's firstborn." This would correspond to a *Vorlage* *kl pṭr rḥm ly hzkrym (kl) pṭr šwr wśh. Tg. Neofiti I similarly has "all your cattle, the males," as if reading *wkl mqnk hzkrym. *Hzkrym 'the males' instead of tzkr would definitely be *lectio facilior*, but possibly MT-Sam is too difficult to be correct. The parallel in 13:12, "you will make each *loosening* of the womb pass over to Yahweh, and each *loosening*, animal spawn, that may be for you, the males [hazzəkārîm], to Yahweh," could be taken either as support for LXX 34:19, or as the source of its reading (see also TEXTUAL NOTE to 13:12).

As an alternative LXX *Vorlage*, more remote from 13:12 and closer to the attested forms of 34:19, we could read a collective *hzkr 'the male(s)' (cf. Deut 15:19), synonymous to hzkrym in 13:12 and graphically similar to tzkr in 34:19, especially in the square script (so Knobel *apud* Dillmann 1880: 351). My intuition is that this is the original reading in 34:19, even though we would have to suppose that Sam's reading was at some point transmitted in non-Samaritan script. In paleo-Hebrew letters, he' does not resemble taw.

34:20. *ass's.* Syr has "cattle's." Exod 34:20 has probably been accommodated to 13:12, where "cattle" itself may be the result of scribal error (see TEXTUAL NOTE).

† *if you do not redeem.* Sam, Syr, Tg. Neofiti I, Vg and LXX^B have "if you do not redeem it (tpdnw)." Cf. TEXTUAL NOTE to 13:13.

you shall "neck" it. Unfamiliar with the root 'rp or regretting the waste of a good animal, LXX has *timen dōseis* (LXX^{AFM} adds *autou*) 'you will pay (its) value.' On the possibility that LXX is reading a form of 'rk 'estimate,' see TEXTUAL NOTE to 13:13.

† *Every.* Sam, many MT MSS (Kennicott 1776–80: 182; de Rossi 1784–85: 77; BHS), MT Sebhirin, Syr, Tgs. Neofiti I and Ps.-Jonathan and Tg. Onqelos in several MSS and editions begin with w 'and.' The previous letter is waw, and so, assuming continuous writing, either haplography to produce MT or dittography to produce Sam would be conceivable. The parallel in 13:13 begins with "and" (see, however, TEXTUAL NOTE to 13:13).

firstborn of your sons. So MT (bəkôr bāne[y]kā); Sam and Kenn 69 have 'human firstborn *among* your sons' (bkwr 'dm bbnyk), as in Sam Exod 13:13, 15. Tg. Ps.-Jonathan reads "firstborn of your *son*" in the singular, but this is evidently collective language, as is seen more clearly in Tg. Ps.-Jonathan 13:13: wkl bwkr' d'ynš' bbrk 'and every human firstborn among your *son* (sic).'

† *for.* LXX lacks a conjunction, perhaps rightly.

34:21. *the seventh day.* LXX^B lacks "day," which, if correct, would be a unique idiom. More likely, we simply have streamlining.

34:22. *for yourself.* LXX has "for *me*," as in 23:14.

† 34:23. *must appear.* On the proposed reading *yir'e(h) 'must see' (Qal) for MT-Sam yērā'e(h) "must appear (to)" (Niph'al), see TEXTUAL NOTE to 23:17.

the Lord Yahweh, Israel's deity. LXX and Syr have simply "(the) Lord, Israel's God," as if lacking either hā'ādôn or yahwe(h) (compare Deut 16:16). If this *lectio brevior* is original, then MT has conflated variants. But the alternatives, that LXX-

Syr either wished to avoid a redundant "the Lord, Lord" or harmonized with Deut 16:16, seem more likely. To complicate matters, Sam has "*the Chest of* Yahweh, Israel's deity," ungrammatically substituting *h'rwn* for MT *h'dn* (cf. TEXTUAL NOTE to 23:17).

† 34:24. *nations.* So standard MT (*gôyīm*). Rossi 198 has *gôyīm gədôlîm* 'great nations,' while Sam has a synonymous *gwym rbym.* (LXX "*the* nations" is presumably a loose translation of MT; see also TEXTUAL NOTE to 23:18.) Although parablepsis by homoioteleuton (*ym . . . ym*) is a possible explanation for MT, more likely the two longer readings assimilate to common expressions; for *gôyīm gədôlîm*, cf. Deut 4:38; 9:1; 11:23; Josh 23:9; Jer 50:9; for *gôyīm rabbîm*, cf. Deut 7:1; 15:6; 28:12; Isa 52:15; Jer 22:8; 25:14; 27:7, etc.

going up. For MT *ba'ălōtəkā*, Sam has *bh'lwtk*, ostensibly 'in your sacrificing,' which does not make sense in context. Most likely, the he' was imported from the following infinitive *lhr'wt* (*sic*; see next TEXTUAL NOTE).

† *appear.* On the conjectural emendation **lir'ôt* 'to see' (Qal), vs. MT *lērā'ôt* (Sam *lhr'wt*) 'to appear' (Niph'al), see TEXTUAL NOTE to 23:17.

† 34:26. *The first of.* This is not reflected in LXX, perhaps because of the redundancy with *prōtogenēmata* 'firstfruits.' But note that in 23:19, LXX has a literal *tas aparchas tōn prōtogenēmatōn* 'the first of the firstfruits.' It is thus conceivable that the LXX *Vorlage*, and the original text of Exodus, lacked *rē(')šît* in 34:26, and that in other Versions it has been imported from 23:19.

34:27. *Israel.* Syr expands: "*all* Israel."

34:28. *So he.* Uniquely, LXX specifies "and Moses."

with Yahweh. Sam, LXX and Tgs. have *lpny yhwh* 'before Yahweh,' probably derived from 34:34. Perhaps, too, this felt more seemly, to have Moses wait upon God.

and he wrote . . . the Covenant words. Against MT-Sam *wayyiktōb 'al-hallūḥōt 'ēt dibrê habbərît*, LXX has "and he wrote these words on the Covenant Tablets," as if reading **wyktb 'l lḥt hbryt 't hdbrym h'lh.* This solves a problem: are the "Covenant words" the contents of 34:10–26, as v 27 implies, or the Decalog (Wevers 1990: 569)? Syr follows MT-Sam but expands: "the *stone* tablets."

† 34:29. *from Mount Sinai.* Possibly correctly, LXX[B] (and presumably the original LXX) has "from the mountain." Thus MT-Sam "Sinai" may be a secondary gloss. On the other hand, the phrase "from the mountain" occurs later in the verse, and so LXX[B] may be harmonizing. Perhaps by coincidence, Kenn 109 (first hand) and 232 feature an awkward conflation of MT-Sam and LXX: *mn hhr syny* 'from the mountain, Sinai.'

† *Testimony Tablets.* LXX has simply "tablets," suggesting that MT-Sam *hā'ēdût* might be a gloss. Again, however, the shorter reading could be the result of corruption, in this case the loss of *h'dt* after *lḥt* due to homoioteleuton. On the importance of this variant and the preceding, see SOURCE ANALYSIS, p. 142.

in Moses' hand. So MT (*byd mšh*). LXX and Tg. *Neofiti I* have "in Moses' hands" (**bydy mšh*), while Sam has *bydw*, probably **bəyādô* 'in *his* hand' (so Samaritan Tg., LXX minuscule 126 and the Sahidic) but possibly **bəyādāw* 'in *his* hands.' On the number of hands with which Moses holds the Tablets, see also TEXTUAL NOTES to 32:15, "his hands," 19; 34:4, "and he took in his hand."

in his speaking with him. Syr MSS clarify: "when God spoke with him."

34:30. *and all Israel's Sons.* So MT, Sam and LXX^AFM: *wkl bny yśr'l.* LXX^B (here presumably the original LXX) has "all Israel's *elders*" as if reading **wkl zqny yśr'l* (cf. TEXTUAL NOTES to 3:18; 4:29; 12:21; 17:6). These would be the leaders mentioned in v 31. Vg ("Israel's Sons) and Syr ("all Israel") proffer the shortest readings, but are not our most reliable or oldest witnesses.

see. Hinnē(h) is not reflected in LXX.

34:32. *Israel's Sons.* A correction to LXX^A has "Israel's *elders*, against MT-Sam-LXX^B; contrast TEXTUAL NOTE to 34:30.

† *approached.* Sam, LXX, Syr and Vg all add *'lyw* 'to him.' On the one hand, we usually prefer the shortest reading, here MT, and "to him" could have been borrowed from vv 30–31. On the other hand, *'lyw* could have dropped due to homoioteleuton after *ngšw* 'approached.'

† 34:33. *Moses finished.* LXX^B and Kenn 99 have "he finished." In MT-Sam, "Moses" could be an explanatory gloss. Alternatively, LXX^B might be haplographic, with *mšh* having fallen out due to homoioarkton before *mdbr* 'from speaking.'

† 34:34. *Israel's Sons.* LXX "*all* Israel's Sons" may be a typical expansion, inspired especially by 34:32. But this might conceivably be the original text, assuming **'l kl* 'to all' > *'l* 'to' (homoioteleuton).

† *what he would be commanded.* Against the MT passive construction *'ăšer yəṣuwwe(h)* (also Syr-Tgs.), Sam has *kl 'šr yṣwhw* (*yəṣawwēhû) '*all* that he would command *him.*' Vg combines aspects of MT and Sam: "*all* that had been commanded *to him.*" Finally, LXX has 'what *the Lord* would command *him,*' as if reading **'šr yṣwhw yhwh.* The addition of "all" in Sam-Vg is likely a simple expansion to conform to a cliché (cf. 7:2; 25:22; 31:6; 35:10, etc.). As for the verb, the shorter and more difficult reading is MT, featuring the relatively rare Puʿal conjugation. Sam would be an adaptation to the more common Piʿel and perhaps a dittography of the following waw: *'šr yṣwh w* > *'šr yṣwhw w.* LXX then further expands Sam to explain who commanded whom.

SPECULATION: It is barely possible LXX preserves the original reading, progressively reduced in Sam and MT: **'šr yṣwhw yhwh w* (LXX) > *'šr yṣwhw w* (Sam [homoioteleuton]) > *'šr yṣwh w* (MT [haplography]).

† 34:35. *that Moses' face skin had "horned."* LXX has simply "that it had become glorified [the LXX paraphrase for 'horned']." On the one hand, one might regard MT-Sam as filling out a short text. But the LXX occasionally streamlines where MT-Sam seems redundant (Wevers 1990: 573). On the origin of the LXX paraphrase for *qāran,* see p. 620.

†† *he would return the veil . . . until his entering.* So Sam and Kenn 13, 18 (*whšyb 't hmswh*). I take MT "*Moses* would return the veil" (*whšyb mšh 't hmswh*) as a clarifying expansion. Unexpectedly, Syr assimilates to 34:33: "Moses would

remove [sic] the veil from his face *whenever* he would enter." LXX[B] equals MT, except that it reads "*a* veil," also carelessly adapting to 34:33. In MT '*et-hammaswe(h)* is clearly definite, and we expect the definite, inasmuch as the veil has already been mentioned.

SOURCE AND REDACTION ANALYSIS

See pp. 148–53.

NOTES

33:1. *Go, go up.* This command, prefatory to restoring the Covenant, reverses "Go, descend" in 32:7, which introduced the rupture of the Covenant (MT; but see TEXTUAL NOTE). Due to the large mass of intervening legislation, Yahweh's command to depart will not be fulfilled till the last word of Num 10:27, *wayyissā'û* 'and they set out.'

In the Torah's topography, Egypt is the lowest place on Earth, Canaan the highest. One always "descends" to Egypt and "goes up" to Canaan. The wilderness in which the people now camp, notwithstanding its mountainous terrain, occupies a middle territory (Rashi). Ibn Ezra, however, proffers a different understanding, probably anachronistic: "up" is north, "down" is south.

you took up. Initially, Yahweh seems angry; he again refers to the people as Moses' responsibility (cf. 32:7). But in mid-verse the tone changes. God remembers that he must help bring Israel to Canaan in order to keep his ancient promises (cf. 32:13).

33:2. *Messenger.* A *mal'āk* is any emissary, earthly or supernatural. In the Bible, Yahweh's Messengers are mostly divine. They are portions of God's essence dispatched to help the righteous and punish the wicked (on angels, see further vol. I, pp. 198–99; below, pp. 619–20).

In 23:23–31, Yahweh had promised the people that his Messenger would lead them to victory in Canaan. This promise was reiterated in 32:34: although Yahweh's wrath was not fully assuaged, he would still send the Messenger to go before Israel. And again in 33:2, Yahweh promises that his Messenger will lead the people. But he makes clear for the first time that, despite this guidance, God himself will not travel amid the Israelites. The people accordingly mourn when they hear "this bad word."

Who or what is the Messenger? Perhaps he is a minor deity, maybe "Yahweh's Army Captain" who meets the people in Canaan (Josh 5:14–15). Or is the Messenger Moses himself (cf. NOTE to 23:20)? Could it be the Midianite guide Hobab (Num 10:29–32) (cf. Holzinger 1900: 109)? Yahweh's mysterious *ṣir'â* "hornet(s)" (Exod 23:28; see NOTE)? Moses himself appears not to know, for in v 12 he protests, "You have not let me know whom/what you will send with me." Ehrlich (1969: 201) may be correct that Yahweh gradually draws Moses to the realization that he, Moses, is the Messenger, at least for now.

In context, Yahweh's promise of a Messenger in 33:2 may be read as part of his rebuke of Israel. As Spinoza (*Tractatus theologicus-politicus* chap. 2 [1951: 38]) observes, by granting his people a Messenger (understood as a guardian angel) rather than his own presence, Yahweh demotes Israel to the status of other nations (cf., e.g., Deut 32:8–9 [LXX; see vol. I, p. 122]). In v 16, Moses argues that it is precisely Yahweh's presence that will separate Israel from all other peoples of the world. Having lost this distinction, the people mourn in 33:4. But their spokesman Moses tries to remedy the situation, requesting a more immediate form of divine presence (vv 14–15) as well as visual proof (v 18).

Canaanite . . . Jebusite. On these peoples, see briefly below, pp. 746–53.

flowing of milk and honey. On this cliché for plenty, see Propp (1999).

33:3. *I will not go up.* In the composite text, this is tantamount to revoking the planned Tabernacle (Luzzatto).

lest I finish you off. In the Priestly Source, Yahweh's presence is inherently dangerous to Israel because of his extreme holiness (see below, pp. 689–90ß). In JE, however, Yahweh is just dangerously irascible.

33:4. *mourned.* Ever since 17:7 (E), the people have been concerned about Yahweh's presence in their midst (see vol. I, p. 606). Now, through their irresponsibility, they have driven Yahweh away, at least for the moment. Although the people have another reason to mourn—many have just died (32:27–28, 35)—this does not seem to motivate their grief. Ehrlich (1908: 401) may well be correct that *hit'abbēl* means not so much "mourn" as "don the accoutrements of mourning"—sackcloth, ashes, ripped clothes, etc., in contrast to their festive finery. At any rate, Moses cannot reconcile Israel to Yahweh single-handedly. The people must show signs of sincere repentance.

did not put . . . finery. This may be a case of hysteron proteron, since the people are commanded to take off their ornaments only in the next verse (cf. Rashbam). Saadiah, however, sees an ongoing process: the people *continue* to remove their ornaments throughout vv 4–6. To doff one's finery is an act of mourning (Rashbam); Dillmann (1880: 344) compares Ezek 24:17; 26:16; Jdt 10:3–4.

Did not the people already discard their jewelry to make the Calf? Perhaps only the women and juveniles contributed (NOTE to 32:2), and now the men follow suit. Or, one might explain, previously gold ornaments alone were donated; now all other fine jewelry and garments are put aside.

33:5. *one instant.* Like an exasperated parent, Yahweh has exhausted his patience. He needs a vacation from his chosen people.

lay down. Does the verb *hôrîd* 'lower' refer in particular to head gear?

and I will know. God has yet to make up his mind. There is still hope that he will relent and travel in Israel's midst.

33:6. *stripped themselves.* The root *nṣl*, here in the reflexive Hithpa'el, echoes the despoiling of Egypt in 3:22; 11:2–3; 12:35–36, denoted by the same root (Rashi; Cassuto 1967: 428; Van Seters 1994: 334). As they stripped the Egyptians, so they now strip themselves. If the evocation of Egypt is deliberate, is there an implication that these are ill-gotten or tainted gains? Or is Israel just entering into a temporary period of mortification and atonement? There is also a more proximate allusion:

the last time the people removed their jewelry, it was to fashion the Gold Calf (32:2–3, 24). And, in the composite text, there is also anticipation: the people will soon donate their valuables to fashion the Tabernacle (chaps. 35–40 [P]).

their finery. The reflexive verb *hitnaṣṣēl* has, so to speak, two objects: the people themselves and their ornaments (*pace* ibn Ezra, who takes 'ēt here as 'ēt II, tantamount to *min* 'from'). See also NOTE to 32:3, "stripped off from themselves."

from Mount Horeb. If the text is intact, then the implication may be "*starting at* Mount Horeb *and ever after*" (Luzzatto), or conceivably "*far from* Mount Horeb." But the language is peculiar. It is likely, as many have conjectured, that something like "And the people departed" fell out before "from Mount Horeb," whether in the course of redaction or afterward.

SPECULATION: It is not really certain that *hitnaṣṣēl* means to remove clothing or jewelry *from the body.* Exod 33:6 is easy to translate under the assumption that *hitnaṣṣēl* means "to take away *for one's own benefit.*" If so, the meaning is: having taken off their finery, the people carried it off from Mount Horeb, presumably for future use. But I still think that the verse is corrupt.

33:7. *the tent.* Why the definite article? Conceivably, it is a sign of indeterminacy—"a certain tent" (cf. Joüon 1965: 425–26 §m–o). More likely, however, the implication is "the famous tent of which you've heard, namely, Meeting Tent." But Cassuto (1967: 420), in line with Rabbinic tradition, thinks "the tent" is Moses' own domicile, last mentioned in 18:7.

pitch it/for him. In the phrase *wənāṭâ-lô*, what is the referent of *lô*? There are three possibilites: Moses, Yahweh and the Covenant Chest.

For Jewish tradition, the tent in vv 7–11 is Moses' own home (e.g., ibn Ezra). If we read the Torah as a whole, this cannot be the other Meeting Tent, i.e., the Tabernacle, because: (a) the Tabernacle has not yet been built (chaps. 25–40); (b) it will be lodged in the center of the camp (Num 2:17), and (c) it will be inaccessible to nonpriests such as Joshua (e.g., Num 3:5–10). Luzzatto, however, solves the problem, as indeed the Redactor must have understood matters. This Meeting Tent is a paltry substitute for the other Meeting Tent, to which Israel is no longer entitled. The referent of *lô* may still be Moses, assuming that he has erected this tent for his own use, to facilitate his communication with Yahweh.

It is also possible that *lô* refers to Yahweh (Dillmann 1880: 345). God has just declined to travel in Israel's midst, and so Moses finds a compromise, erecting a tent on the camp's outskirts. Now Moses and others must go out to meet God. The people see Yahweh descend, and their faith is gradually restored. Similarly in 2 Sam 7:1–1, Yahweh claims to have "traveled about in tent and in tabernacle."

Many, however, understand *lô* as "for it," referring to the Covenant Chest, comparing 2 Sam 6:17, "within the tent David had pitched for it *(nāṭâ-lô)*" (e.g., Holzinger 1900: 113; H. Davies 1967: 35–37; de Vaux 1971: 141). Friedman (2003: 11), however, denies that the E source reckons with the Covenant Chest at all.

he would call it. Alternatively: "one would call it, it was called" (Ehrlich 1908:

403; 1969: 201). Cassuto (1967: 430), however, takes the verb at face value: Moses called it "Meeting Tent," *precisely because it was not the real Meeting Tent*, now possibly never to be built (see also Sarna 1991: 212).

Meeting Tent. The implication in context is that Yahweh and Moses repair to Meeting Tent *(mô'ēd)* to confer *(y'd)*, so that God can make up his mind. The word *mô'ēd* also refers to a council, and in Ugaritic literature it denotes the divine assembly. On the term's transformation in the Bible, see NOTE to 27:21, "Meeting Tent," and pp. 691–94, 703–5.

seeking. To "seek Yahweh" or "seek Yahweh's face" means to establish communication, generally in order to obtain a favor (e.g., 2 Sam 21:1; Hos 5:15; Ps 27:8). Sacrifice is presumably involved, although no altar is mentioned here.

The text first envisions an anonymous person resorting to Meeting Tent for private purposes. Then, in greater detail, it describes Moses' ceremonious walk to the Tent. While Moses is one of many to make the trip, he is the only person whom the people watch carefully because his arrival at the Tent invariably elicits a theophany.

33:8. *gaze after.* In simple witness? Or "with respect and affection" (Cassuto 1967: 431)?

33:9. *Cloud Pillar.* In P and JE alike, the Cloud is Yahweh's vehicle that he parks either by the door of Meeting Tent (E) or on the roof (P) (NOTE to 40:38, "cloud . . . fire"; vol. I, pp. 549–50). Here, it is somewhat unclear whether Yahweh speaks to Moses from within the Cloud, or whether he gets out and enters the Tent along with Moses. Within E, the reference to "face to face" communication in v 11 supports the latter understanding. But Moses' request for a closer experience of God (vv 18–23 [J?]) may support the former, at least for JE and JEP.

stand. Note the assonance in *'ammûd he'ānān wə'āmad* 'Cloud Pillar . . . and stand,' evident also in v 10 *'ammûd he'ānān 'ōmēd* 'Cloud Pillar standing' (cf. Cassuto 1967: 432). The root *'md* 'stand' also chimes anagrammatically with the Tent's name: *mō'ēd* 'Meeting.'

Tent's Opening. In JE, all Israel witnesses Yahweh's conversing with Moses at Tent's Opening (Num 12:5; Deut 31:15). In P, however, Tent's Opening is what *bars* the average Israelite's access to Yahweh.

33:10. *stand and bow down.* Are they not already standing? Why stand up before bowing down? Sometimes *qām* 'stand' can mean "to initiate an action" rather than literally "stand up" (Ehrlich 1908: 403). The *locus classicus* is Gen 27:19, *qûm-nā' šəbâ* 'stand up, sit!' (Colloquial English would say, "Go and sit down," which makes as little sense.) See also NOTE to 31:2, "Get up."

Cloud Pillar standing. See NOTE to v 9, "stand."

33:11. *face to face.* In this direct encounter, Moses apparently differs from the average Israelite of v 7b, who may go to the Tent to speak to Yahweh but is not vouchsafed an audience. Ehrlich (1908: 403–4; 1969: 201) compares Oriental court etiquette, by which few are privileged to see the king's face (cf. 2 Kgs 25:19; Esth 2:14; see also Parpola 1980: 172).

his attendant. Although "his" probably indicates Moses (cf. Num 11:28, *məšārēt mōše[h]* 'Moses' attendant'), we cannot exclude the possibility that the suffix refers to Yahweh. We could also translate *məšārətô* as "*its* attendant," i.e., the Tent's.

son of Nun. Whenever Joshua is given his patronymic, "son of" has an unusual form: *bin* rather than *ben*. It seems that, because the father's name began with nun and was monosyllabic, Jews habitually pronounced *bin-nûn* as a single word **bin-nûn*, in which case the vowel ḥireq is expected.

For P at least, the sacred minister Joshua is a member of the tribe of Ephraim (Num 13:8), without any right to serve in Meeting Tent. Thus it appears that, in the composite text, along with the cancellation of the Tabernacle project, Aaron the Calf-maker has forfeited his family's intended elevation to the priesthood (chaps. 28–29). What role the Levites play (cf. 32:29) at E's Meeting Tent is unspecified, although Moses himself is a Levite.

youth. The exact implication of *na'ar* here is disputed. It can describe any human male, from a baby (e.g., 2:6; 1 Sam 1:22; 4:21) to a full-grown man of marriageable (Gen 34:19) or military age (1 Sam 21:3–6; 2 Sam 2:14; 1 Chr 12:29; cf. the Egyptian loanword *n'rn* 'soldiers' [Hoch 1994: 182–83]), or a servant of any age (e.g., Num 22:22; Judg 7:10). Joshua, described in 24:13; 32:17; 33:7–11 as Moses' acolyte, in 17:8–16 is the nation's warleader and clearly no child. And yet, Num 11:28 calls Joshua Moses' *məšārēt* "since his young-manhood" *(mibbəḥūrā[y]w)*, suggesting that he is still fairly young in Exodus. (Although I have ascribed both passages to E, it is a little hard to reconcile the hero of the Amalek battle with the servant of 33:7–11, who sounds as if he is being introduced for the first time.)

In 33:11, one possiblity is that *na'ar* and *məšārēt* 'attendant' are essentially synonyms, since there is no doubt that "youth" can mean "servant" (Ramban); compare especially 2 Sam 13:17, *na'ărô məšārətô* 'his attendant youth.' On the other hand, 33:11 is one of several passages describing "youths" as facilitating religious activity (see also NOTE to 24:5). Such personnel were probably the priests' assistants, whether cadet priests (1 Sam 2:13, 17) or the hierodules that in later Temple times would be called *nətînîm* 'the Donated.' This may even have been the original form of giving a firstborn son to Yahweh (Exod 22:28): donating him as a sacred "youth" (see vol. I, pp. 455–56).

SPECULATION: Given that sexual intercourse creates ritual defilement (see NOTE to 19:15), and given that Joshua lives alone in the tent, and given that tradition accords him no children, in this context *na'ar* may connote a bachelor (Ehrlich 1908: 404, comparing Gen 37:2) or a male virgin, just as the feminine *na'ărâ* 'lass' often describes an unwed female. (On a similar interpretation for *ṣōbə'ōt* in 33:8, see NOTE.)

The closest parallel to Joshua is Samuel, not a priest by birth but given by his mother into Yahweh's service. (Although he is her firstborn, he does not appear to be Yahweh's by right; instead, Hannah vows him to God.) As Joshua is *na'ar* 'youth' and *məšārēt* 'attendant' to Moses, so is Samuel to Eli (1 Sam 2:11, 18, 21; 3:18). As Joshua lives inside Meeting Tent, so Samuel sleeps in the shrine of Shiloh (1 Sam 3:2–18).

SPECULATION: Perhaps one function of the cultic "youth" was to serve as a medium, like Samuel. Blenkinsopp (1992: 195) observes that in the Egyptian "Voyage of Wen Amun" (*ANET* 29), the god Amun communicates via a possessed youth. This potentially illuminates Exod 33:7–11. When Moses needs to converse, Yahweh condescends to be present. But when ordinary persons wish to commune with God (v 7), their medium is Joshua (v 11).

If this is correct, the Priestly Writer's effort to "put Joshua in his place" is palpable. In Num 27:21 (P), Joshua must "stand before Eleazar the priest and inquire of him for the Urim's judgment before Yahweh; by his (Eleazar's) *mouth* (i.e., command) he (Joshua) must go out and by his mouth he must go in." In other words, Joshua, the former medium, may now divine only through the Great Priest.

Another possibility is that Joshua's role in Exodus 33 is simply to monitor the presence of the Cloud Pillar. Whenever it descends, he sends a message to Moses.

would not depart. Taken literally, this contradicts Joshua's later roles of spy (Numbers 13–14) and commander (Book of Joshua). Exod 33:11 should not be understood to mean that Joshua spent all his life's days in the tent. It was only his temporary albeit full-time job.

Ehrlich (1908: 404) parses the verb *yāmîš* (for the expected **yāmûš* [Sam]) as an impersonal Hiphʿil: "one would not make (him) leave." Either way, there may be an evocation of 13:22, "The cloud pillar would not depart (*lō[ʾ] yāmîš*) by day."

33:12. *you are saying.* The participle *ʾōmēr* is not temporally specific. We might have have expected **ʾāmartā* 'you have said.' The point is that Yahweh told Moses to lead Israel in 32:34, and this is still his desire. Following 33:7–11, the implication is that the present conversation takes place at Meeting Tent (Jacob 1992: 967).

To my ear at least, there is a tone of overfamiliarity in Moses' words, even disrespect. Such freedom is the sign and consequence of intimacy, and in this context a rhetorical strategy. Moses is establishing his right to hector Yahweh. Although he appears to speak querulously on his own behalf, he is really exploiting his grace with God to obtain a favor for Israel.

you have not let me know. Yahweh promised to send a Messenger "before you," to help Moses lead Israel to Canaan (23:23–31; 32:34; 33:2). But he did not name the Messenger. Would it be a human? A minor deity? An aspect of Yahweh himself? Moses will settle for nothing less than God's presence.

you said. Alluding to 32:34; 33:1.

I know you by name. For Cassuto (1967: 433), this is the language of election (cf. Isa 43:1; 45:3–4; 49:1). More precisely, the image is that of a royal court. A great king has many, many servants. It is a sign of his dignity *not* to know their names, save those of his favorites (Rosenmüller *apud* Dillmann 1880: 346). So "I know you by name" means the same as "you have found favor in my eyes."

Moses criticizes the imbalance in his relationship with God with some audacity. Yahweh knows the name of his servant Moses, yet Moses does not know the name of the servant whom Yahweh will send, nor does he fully know Yahweh himself.

SPECULATION: Another possible interpretation is that Yahweh and Moses *know each other* by name; they are not strangers. Recall that Moses has received special revelations about the name "Yahweh" in 3:13–15 (E) and 6:2–3 (P) and is about to receive another in 34:5–7 (J?). If so, "I have known you by name" means much the same thing as "Yahweh would speak to Moses face to face" (v 11). The two principal ways by which Yahweh is known to Israel are by his Name *(šēm)* and by his Face *(pānîm)* (see pp. 619–20).

33:13. *your ways.* The translation of *derek* is uncertain. Apparently out of perplexity, the ancient Versions render *derek* as "face, appearance" (Vg, Aquila), or they paraphrase "appear to me yourself" (LXX).

A minor problem is that we are not quite sure whether *drkk* is singular or plural (see TEXTUAL NOTE). More important, while Hebrew *derek* ordinarily means "way," its Ugaritic cognate bears the additional connotation of "power." (The semantic link is presumably the verb *drk* 'trample.') Some possible examples of this latter usage have been conjecturally identified in the Bible, our verse among them (J. Strugnell *apud* Smith 1990: 113 n. 133). In other words, Moses' request to know Yahweh's "power" is equivalent to his asking to see God's "Glory" in v 18. Notably, Num 14:17–18 associates Yahweh's attributes of mercy and vengeance, proclaimed in Exod 34:6–7, with his *kōaḥ* 'strength,' hypothetically synonymous with *derek.* (Deut 4:37, moreover, associates Yahweh's *kōaḥ* with his Face; cf. Exod 33:14–15, 20, 23.)

Nonetheless, "ways," the only surely attested meaning in Hebrew, makes better sense in context—in four respects. First, Moses cannot bring Israel to Canaan without guidance through the paths of the Sinai Desert; in fact, Yahweh promises below to guide Moses (NOTE to 33:14, "make rest for you"). He needs Yahweh to inform him of the *routes* the people must take (Rashbam). Second, Yahweh must make clear to Moses and Israel his own intended *movements:* will he travel with them on the way or not (Luzzatto)? Third, the people, if not Moses himself, need reminding of Yahweh's ways, i.e., the *behaviors* that he expects of them, from which they have "quickly departed" all too recently (32:7). Fourth, Moses requests clearer knowledge of God's own *characteristics* (Dillmann 1880: 346, comparing Deut 32:4; Ps 18:31), perhaps specifically his judicial principles (Cassuto 1967: 433).

so that I may find favor. This does not really make sense. Moses has established that he has already found favor with Yahweh (v 12). The point must be, "so that I may *continue to* find favor" or "so that I may find *even more* favor."

this nation is your people. Moses desires divine favor—but not, as he has already demonstrated, at the people's expense (32:9–14). It is as Israel's leader that Moses hopes to please Yahweh. His specific request is that Yahweh not abandon the nation to Moses' own human leadership. He is specifically rejecting Yahweh's implicit refusal to claim Israel as his people (32:7; 33:1).

33:14. *My Face. Pānîm* has the additional connotations of "presence" and "front side," which come to bear in what follows. Yahweh had said he would not travel in Israel's midst (33:3) but also implied that he would reconsider his decision (v 5). In addition, he promised to send a Messenger (v 2), an ambiguous and less intimate form of divine presence. It is unclear here whether, by sending his "Face," Yahweh compromises or capitulates. The latter seems more likely—note that LXX and Syr understand *pānay* as "myself," a usage that Rashi and ibn Ezra find also in 2 Sam 17:11 *(pāne[y]kā hōləkîm baqrāb* 'your *face* is going into battle') and that Ahituv (1997: 6*) detects in Deut 4:37 *(wayyôṣî'ăkā bəpānā[y]w* 'and he took you out with/as his *face).*

In fact, "face" is inherently ambiguous. Sometimes a part stands for the whole, so that "face" = "self," and sometimes a part is just a part. In my understanding, the Face is not Yahweh's full essence. It is, so to speak, an archangel, i.e., a Messenger fully empowered to represent God on Earth. Depending on the context, it can be regarded as equivalent or non-equivalent to Yahweh, just as, among idolaters, an idol both is and is not the god (Jacobsen 1987a; cf. above, pp. 167–70, 580–83).

As we now realize, Yahweh's promise of a Messenger was always Delphic. Originally, it seemed a gift, then a punishment. Urged by Moses, Yahweh clarifies his intention to send his Face, the greatest of all Messengers. In the context of 33:18, 22–23, "Face" appears to be equivalent to "Glory," the aspect of Yahweh's presence visible to humans (Ahituv 1997: 6*).

make rest for you. The clause *wəhănîḥōtî lāk* could be variously understood. On the most superficial level, it appears to mean "I will appease you"; compare Ezek 5:13; 16:42; 21:22; 24:13; Zech 6:8; Prov 29:17 (cf. Saadiah *apud* ibn Ezra; Ehrlich 1969: 202). Then again, particularly in Deuteronom(ist)ic literature, the expression refers to divine guidance and protection, bringing Israel into peaceful residence *(mənûḥâ)* in Canaan (e.g., Deut 3:20; 12:10; 25:19; Josh 1:13, 15; 22:4; Isa 63:14) (Rashbam; Dillmann 1880: 347). Moses will not make it all the way to Canaan, but at this point Yahweh still intends him to (contrast Num 20:2–13, 24; 27:13–14; Deut 1:37; 3:23–28; 4:21–22). Or the promise could be vaguer: I will bring you, after a life of toils, to a peaceful death and burial. Ahituv (1997: 5*) compares Isa 14:3, "on the day that Yahweh shall have made for you rest *(hānîaḥ)* from your pain and trouble."

Cassuto (1967: 434) catches a punning reference to 32:10. There, Yahweh told Moses, *hannîḥâ-lî* 'leave me alone.' Here Yahweh says, *wəhănîḥōtî lāk* 'and I will make rest for you.' The first statement was uttered in the rising flood of divine anger. The second marks its subsidence.

SPECULATION: Revocalizing and even rearranging the consonants *whnḥty lk* yield other potential meanings. In light of the subject under discussion, one could read **wəhinḥîtî lāk* 'and I will *lead* for you,' comparing 13:21, *lanḥōtām hadderek* 'to lead them the way' (Ehrlich 1908: 405). More radically, we could read **wəhannōtî lāk* 'and I will be *favorable* to you,' since Mose is jealous for his divine *ḥēn* 'favor,' and since the root appears verbally in 33:19, *wəhannōtî 'et-'ăšer 'āḥōn* 'and I will favor whom I favor.' At the least, these may be paronomastic allusions.

33:15. *If your Face is not going*. In other words, "Do not make us leave from here *unless* your Face is going. . . ." It would seem that, just as he earlier offered his own life (32:32), now Moses risks the entire people's fate. Better they should drop dead in the desert, at the foot of Yahweh's mountain, than traverse the wilderness and inhabit Canaan without the divine presence.

The conversational flow is tenuous in vv 12–17. It would be tempting, but I think misguided, to rearrange the contents as follows:

> [12]And Moses said to Yahweh, "See, you are saying to me, 'Take up this people,' but you, you have not let me know what you will send with me,' yet you, you said, 'I know you by name, and also you have found favor in my eyes.' [16]And by what, then, will it be known that I have found favor in your eyes, I and your people? Is it not by your going with us? Then I and your people will be distinguished from all peoples that are on the earth's surface. [15b]If your Face is not going, do not take us up from here."
> [14]Then he said, "My Face, it will go, and I will make rest for you."
> [15a]And he said to him, [13]"And now, if indeed I have found favor in your eyes, let me know your ways that I may know you, so that I may find favor in your eyes. And see, that this nation is your people."
> [17]And Yahweh said to Moses, "Even this thing that you have spoken I will do, for you have found favor in my eyes, and I have known you by name."

This is indeed the conversation's logical substructure (cf. ibn Ezra). But it is hard to see how the text could have become so disarranged, unless it were always so. One could regard vv 12–17 as a realistic depiction of the circuitous paths of genuine speech, as Moses tries desperately to wheedle, even bully Yahweh into a reconciliation with Israel. Closer inspection, however, reveals a structure more esthetic than logical. The discourse uses chiasm to focus our attention on the divine Face:

> A. [12]And Moses said to Yahweh, "See, you are saying to me, 'Take up this people,' but you, you have not let me know what you will send with me,' yet you, you said, 'I know you by name, and also you have found favor in my eyes.'
> > B. [13]And now, if indeed I have found favor in your eyes, let me know your ways that I may know you, so that I may find favor in your eyes. And see, that this nation is your people."
> > > C. [14]Then he said, "My Face will go, and I will make rest for you."
> > > C'. [15]And he said to him, "If your Face is not going, do not take us up from here.
> > B'. [16]And by what, then, will it be known that I have found favor in your eyes, I and your people? Is it not by your going with us? Then I and your people will be distinguished from all peoples that are on the earth's face."
> A'. [17]And Yahweh said to Moses, "Even this thing that you have spoken I will do, for you have found favor in my eyes, and I have known you by name."

33:16. *I and your people*. Most likely, Moses chooses this language in fear that Yahweh is still disinclined to take pains for Israel, whereas Moses himself still stands in God's graces. There might also, however, be a note of self-aggrandizement: God should make Israel unique among nations and Moses unique among Israelites (Rashbam). In response, Yahweh promises to restore Israel's Covenant and to exalt Moses personally (34:10; cf. also v 28). In the composite text, the sign of Moses's uniqueness is the transformation of his face in 34:29–35 (P/R) (Rashbam; Bekhor Shor). See also NOTE to 34:10, "with you."

distinguished. While this is a literal translation of *niplênû*, there is an additional connotation of being distinguished by a *miraculous sign (pele')* (cf. LXX, Vg, Tg. Onqelos). Israel's distinction is the immediate presence of Yahweh himself, not a minor patron deity (NOTE to 33:2, above). Cassuto (1967: 435), moreover, finds a reference to the Ten Plagues, whereby Israel was distinguished *(plyˀ)* from Egypt (8:18; 9:4; 11:7). In 34:10, Yahweh will promise to work further *niplāˀōt* 'wonders' on behalf of Israel and Moses.

33:17. *this thing*. Literally, "this word." In the redacted context, this could refer to P's Tabernacle (chaps. 25–31) (Sarna 1991: 213).

33:18. *And he said*. "Moses saw that it was an opportune occasion, and that his words were acceptable, so he went on to ask (God) to show him a vision of his Glory" (Rashi).

Show me. The man who could not look straight at the Burning Bush (3:6 [E]) now requests a full vision of Yahweh's Glory (although he already experienced a theophany in 24:9–11 [E]) (see above, pp. 151–152).

Moses' persistent desire to see Yahweh emblematizes a common human sense of alienation from the divine (see below, pp. 675–91; for a Freudian interpretation, see Eilberg-Schwartz 1994). Mythology is replete with cautionary tales of heroes who presume to obtain a full vision of a god: from Greece, the best known examples are Semele and Actaeon.

your Glory. Although the Hebrew noun is the same, this may not be quite the same as P's *kābôd*, the supernatural fire that *conceals* Yahweh (cf. also Ezek 1:27–28). That frequently appears to all Israel and so would not be a special favor (Exod 16:7, 10; 24:17; Lev 9:6, 23, etc.). Probably Moses is asking to see Yahweh in his *kingly splendor*, to demonstrate that God will guide Israel. Alternatively, *kābôd* may just mean "self," as apparently in Gen 49:6 (MT): *bəsōdām ˀal-tābō(ˀ) napšî / biqhālām ˀal-tēḥad kəbōdî* 'May my soul not enter their council / May my glory not consort with their assembly' (but contrast LXX and Sam) (cf. Rashi, ibn Ezra). Overall, Cassuto (1967: 435) is probably correct: said of Yahweh, *kābôd* essentially means "theophany" (cf. Aquila *opsis* 'appearance').

Following Rashbam, Luzzatto argues that Moses is asking specifically for a renewal of the Covenant. His case rests upon two parallels to the Abrahamic covenant in Genesis 15. First, "by what shall I know" in Gen 15:8 anticipates "by what will it be known" in Exod 33:16. Second, in Gen 15:17, a burning oven representing Yahweh "passes" before Abram; here, it is Yahweh's fiery Glory.

33:19. *make . . . pass*. Yahweh condescends to be inspected by Moses, like a flock before a shepherd or an army before a commander (cf. Ehrlich 1969: 202).

But Moses is not entitled to look long; he is granted only a glimpse (Cassuto 1967: 435).

splendor. Ṭûb means "goodness, sweetness, wealth, beauty." It is also a divine epithet, as in the names *'ăḥîṭûb* and *'ăbîṭûb* 'My Brother/Father is Splendor.' And in the present context, one thinks also of the nuance of covenantal benevolence (Gen 32:10, 13; Deut 23:7; Josh 24:20; 1 Sam 25:30; 2 Sam 2:6; 7:28; Jer 18:10; 33:9; see Fox 1973). Most important, in Ps 145:7 *ṭûb* appears to describe Yahweh's merciful attributes from Exod 34:6.

Another intriguing possiblity is that here *ṭûb* is collective and equivalent to Rabbinic Hebrew *ṭîb* 'quality, attribute' (Ehrlich 1908: 406; 1969: 203). If so, Yahweh is simply promising to reveal to Moses his personal characteristics.

I shall call. In the Rabbinic understanding, God is teaching Moses how to pray (Rashi).

Yahweh's name. Although this interpretation of *bəšēm yahwe(h)* seems the more natural (Luzzatto), the MT trope favors a translation, "I shall call Yahweh by name" or "I shall call by name: 'Yahweh' " (see also NOTE to 34:5). On the implications for understanding 34:6–7, see NOTE to 34:5, "Yahweh's name."

favor whom I favor. In the immediate context, Yahweh is reaffirming his loyalty to Moses. He is also implicitly threatening that he may or may not favor Israel when they pray (Rashi). That is, while allowing Moses to manipulate him, Yahweh saves his dignity by emphasizing his sovereign right to arbitrary judgment. (On the *idem per idem* formula, see vol. I, pp. 224–26.) Lastly, Yahweh adumbrates his contrasting attributes of judgment and mercy, to be proclaimed in 34:6–7 (Ramban).

33:20. *my Face.* In context, "Face" must be the same as "Glory" and "splendor."

see me. Although this passage denies that Yahweh's face may be seen, Moses is elsewhere known as the man "whom Yahweh knew/spoke to, face to face" (33:11; Deut 34:10), conversing "mouth to mouth" (Num 12:8). Conversation is different from actual sight, however (Jacob 1992: 975). On seeing Yahweh, see Smith (1997: 100–9); on seeing gods in general, see Eck (1985).

live. Ordinarily, Yahweh is deadly to behold (e.g., Isa 6:5, "Woe is me, for I shall die . . . because the King, Yahweh of Armies, my eyes have seen"). Yet many passages describe God's *concealing* his Face as a punishment (cf. Friedman 1995: 7–117). And in other contexts, to see Yahweh (or be seen before him) is the same as worship; see NOTES to 23:15, "must not be seen," 17, "appear." (On Yahweh's lethality, see also below, pp. 689–90.)

33:21. *place. Māqôm* is used in its etymological sense: "a place to stand *(qwm)*." It can also connote a cult site (Noth 1962: 257).

by me. As opposed to the Tent, which is with Israel. Yahweh is inviting Moses to his own home on the mountain (cf. Jacob 1992: 976).

33:22. *I will put.* Apparently, Yahweh picks Moses up in his hand and moves him (ibn Ezra).

crevice. Caves that pentrate the Earth's surface and lead to the underworld are places of mystic experience in many cultures, including the Near East (Smith 1927: 197–200). But this is a cave in a mountain, and its main function is to shelter (cf. Isa 2:10, 19, 21). One wonders whether the spot was pointed out to or visited by later pilgrims; it may well be the same as Elijah's grotto in 1 Kgs 19:9, 13 (Cassuto 1967: 437).

shelter. Spelled slightly differently, this term also describes the Griffins' wings canopying over the Covenant Chest in 40:3; see also NOTE to 25:20, "screening."

hand/skirt. As Yahweh approaches, he covers Moses with his *kap,* so that Moses cannot see his face. Then, as he departs, he allows Moses to glimpse his back. Normally, *kap* denotes the hand or its palm. Although Yahweh's "hand" is elsewhere a punishing agent (Roberts 1971; vol. I, p. 229), here as in Isa 25:10; 49:2; 51:16; 62:3, it protects and shelters (Dillmann 1880: 348; Aḥituv 1997: 6* n. 8).

One cannot imagine a human, even one of gigantic proportions, performing the contortion described in Exodus. Evidently, Yahweh can either extend his arm a great distance or fully detach his hand from his body, at least insofar as he is manifest on the human plane (see below, pp. 619, 687). Malul (1997), however, makes a very strong case that *kap* can also mean "skirt" (ordinarily *kānāp*). In that case, Yahweh is covering Moses with his own garment, as a man covers a bride (cf. Ezek 16:8; Ruth 3:9; on a Mari parallel, see van der Toorn 1995: 335).

during my passing. Or: "until I shall have passed (*'ad-'obrî*)."

33:23. *backparts.* This story qualifies others indicating that Moses obtained a full, frontal view of God (24:11; 33:11; Num 12:8; Deut 34:10). In this vignette, the divine Face may not be experienced. The fullest vision flesh and blood can sustain is of the divine *back,* still part of God's essence but a side less fraught with his dangerous aura than his Face or front side. The context suggests that Yahweh's Face is constituted by his attributes of mercy and punishment, through which he interacts with humanity (34:6–7). Bekhor Shor compares the sun: while one cannot look it in the face, one may comfortably admire its afterglow.

SPECULATION: Perhaps *'ăḥōrāy* does not describe part of Yahweh's anatomy but prepositionally means "after me," both in the sense of "in my train" and "after I have passed" (cf. Jacob 1992: 977). But more likely not; the term is clearly anatomical in 1 Kgs 7:25; Ezek 8:16.

34:1. *Carve for yourself. Ləkā* 'for yourself' probably has little force; the basic sense is "Go and carve" (ibn Ezra). There could, however, be a touch of pique in God's words (see below).

be ready for the morning. The language is similar to 19:11, 15, introducing the first Covenant. In fact, Ehrlich (1908: 408–9) suggests that, as in 19:15, the point is specifically that Moses must not cohabit with his wife. This could be; the word *nākôn* 'ready' parallels *ṭāhôr* 'pure' in Ps 51:12.

you shall ascend. Rather than receive tablets from Yahweh on the mountain, Moses must lug up a blank set. This creates a frame with his descent in 34:28–29.

you smashed. Is there a note of irritation in Yahweh's voice? God had made the original tablets, which Moses shattered on his own initiative. Now, like a stern parent, God insists that Moses perform some of the compensatory labor himself.

34:3. *no man . . . flock . . . herd.* The holiness requirements of 19:10–13, 21–24 are reiterated. But this time there is no Joshua, no Aaron and Hur, no elders—only Moses and Yahweh will be on the mountain.

34:4. *he carved.* Jacob (1992: 980) supposes that Moses spends an entire day preparing the Tablets. But it is routine in any case for acts in biblical narrative to be spread over at least two days.

34:5. *stationed himself.* In vv 5–6, it is notoriously difficult to tell whether Moses or Yahweh is the subject of the verbs. On the one hand, only Yahweh is named in v 6, so he is the natural subject (ibn Ezra [shorter commentary]; Rashbam; Ramban). Apparently, he emerges from his cloud-vehicle in order to be seen by Moses (Ehrlich 1908: 409). On the other hand, Moses had already been commanded "station yourself," so it is natural to see a tacit change in subject from Yahweh to Moses (Tg. *Ps.-Jonathan,* Vg). I favor the latter understanding, since in 33:21; 34:2, Moses is the subject, and since the following reference to Yahweh "passing ('*br*)" in v 6 implies a staionary Moses (Dillmann 1880: 349). See also following NOTES.

called. Again, the ambiguous subject is potentially either Moses invoking Yahweh *(Tg. Ps.-Jonathan)* or Yahweh proclaiming his own name (ibn Ezra; Rashbam; Cassuto 1967: 439). Because Yahweh had said he would pronounce his name to Moses (33:19), the latter understanding may be preferable. But is it possible for the subject to switch from Yahweh to Moses and back to Yahweh with no indication? Assuming that Moses is the subject of "stationed himself" (previous NOTE), perhaps he then calls out, "Yahweh!" (v 5), and Yahweh repeats and amplifies upon his own name in v 6.

Yahweh's name. One could also translate, "he called the name, Yahweh" (MT cantillation, Syr) or simply "he summoned Yahweh," assuming that the subject is Moses (previous NOTE).

It appears that vv 6–7 are Yahweh's full name, which, in the composite Torah, he has been progressively revealing to humanity and Israel. Thirty-two words may seem an impossibly long appellation, even for a god. But Isaiah in particular delights in bestowing long names, both upon his own children (Shear-yashub and Maher-shalal-hash-baz) (Isa 7:3; 8:3) and upon a newborn baby of probably royal parentage: *pele' yô'ēṣ 'ēl gibbôr 'ăbî'ad śar-šālôm* 'Miracle-counselor, Hero-god, Eternal-father, Peace-prince' (Isa 9:5). So, too, I imagine, we must read Exod 34:6–7 as one long divine name. It is also a description, so that the word *šēm* bears both its literal meaning, "name," and its extended meanings of "nature" and "reputation" (cf. Ehrlich 1969: 203). On the names of God, see below, pp. 757–62.

34:6. *before his face.* The author tantalizes the reader by describing not what Moses sees but instead what Moses hears. "Before his face," in the composite text, also sets up the transformation of Moses' visage in vv 29–35 (P/R).

and he called, "Yahweh, Yahweh." There are various ways to understand *wayyiqrā(') yahwe(h) yahwe(h).* By my translation, the subject could be either Moses or Yahweh (cf. previous NOTES). And one could also render "and Yahweh called, 'Yahweh . . .'" (Saadiah *apud* ibn Ezra). We can at least eliminate Moses as the subject by comparing Num 14:17–18, "As you [Yahweh] spoke, saying, 'Yahweh, *long-faced* and great in trust . . .'" (Ehrlich 1908: 409; 1969: 204).

That leaves two interpretations: "and he (Yahweh) called, 'Yahweh, Yahweh' " and "and Yahweh called 'Yahweh.' " But it is unidiomatic for the subject to be repeated at so short an interval: "And Yahweh passed . . . and Yahweh called." My inclination is to see Yahweh announcing his own name twice, the understanding imposed by the cantillation. As for why Yahweh would repeat his name, Bekhor Shor homiletically detects an allusion to his twofold nature: merciful and strict. More plausibly, Luzzatto finds emphasis, "Yahweh *and none other*," comparing redundant diction in Deut 32:39, "I, I am he, there is no deity with me." Most likely, however, repetition itself constitutes invocation, whether God calls Man (Gen 22:11; 46:2; Exod 3:4; 1 Sam 3:10) or Man calls God (Josh 22:22; Ps 22:2 [Rashi]; cf. 1 Kgs 18:39). God can also, as here, cultically invoke himself; compare 20:24(21): "in any place where I announce my name, I will come to you and bless you."

SPECULATION: There is a slight chance that Yahweh's full name is not all of vv 6–7 but just the reduplicated "Yahweh-yahweh." The first time Moses asked him his name, God answered redundantly: *'ehye(h) 'ăšer 'ehye(h)* 'I will be who I will be' (3:14) (cf. Jacob 1992: 983). This some scholars take as a version or distortion of Yahweh's real name (see vol. I, pp. 224–25). The name *yahwe(h) yahwe(h)* in 34:6 would be closest to Cross's (1973: 68–69) hypothetical reconstruction of 3:14, **yahwi ḏu yahwi* 'he creates what he creates.'

merciful . . . benevolent. While these are general descriptions of God that appear elsewhere in the Bible, in the composite account they also bear on the currently tense relationship between Yahweh and Israel. God promises to be merciful—up to a point—but also vengeful—up to a point.

Although Jewish tradition finds in 34:6–7 thirteen divine attributes (e.g., Roš Haš. 17b), there is no clear list structure such as we find in the Decalog. After compiling various reckonings, Luzzatto admits that the number thirteen, though sanctioned by tradition, is somewhat arbitrary. Cassuto (1967: 439–40) thinks that there are really seven attributes. But I do not believe that we are meant to count anything here.

SPECULATION: Variants or citations of 34:6–7 appear throughout the Bible—in 20:5–6; Num 14:18; Deut 5:9–10; Jer 30:11; 32:18–19; 46:28; 49:12; Joel 2:13, Jonah 4:2; Micah 7:18–20; Nah 1:2; Psalm 103; 145:8; Lam 3:32; Dan 9:4; Neh 9:17—as if the words were known to all (cf. Dozeman 1989b). Is Exod 34:6–7 Yahweh's revelation of a chant that Israel can use in future crises to remind God of his transgenerational mercy?

long-faced. 'Appayim 'face' is the dual of *'ap* 'nose, nostril.' Although it can literally mean "two nostrils" (e.g., Gen 2:7; Exod 15:8) *'appayim* more often by synecdoche describes the bilateral face as a whole, i.e, the two sides of the nose. As we shall see (COMMENT), the concept "face *(pānîm)*" is the theme of chaps. 33–34.

In this context, however, *'appayim* draws its primary meaning from the metaphorical sense of *'ap:* "anger" (think of a snorting, flaring, rubicund nose).

'Erek 'appayim 'long-angered' might theoretically mean "nursing a grudge," but the context and exegetical tradition favor "slow to anger"; its antonym is *qaṣar-'appayim* 'short-faced,' i.e., impatient (Prov 14:17) (ibn Ezra [shorter commentary]).

great in trust and reliability. Rab 'great' could also be translated "rich" (Jacob 1992: 984). *Ḥesed* and *'ĕmet*, both connoting long-term obedience, have legal overtones in a covenantal context (Sakenfeld 1978; Zobel 1986).

34:7. *conserving.* The verb *nāṣar* (as opposed to *šāmar* 'keep') is otherwise limited to poetry (Ehrlich 1908: 410). Its presence here lends a ceremonious aspect.

thousandth (generation). On this interpretation of *'ălāpîm*, see NOTE to 20:6.

bearing transgression. I.e., forgiving. On the idiom, see NOTE to 28:38.

although. Yahweh qualifies his merciful aspect by his vengeance, what 20:5 calls his "jealousy *(qn')*" (see NOTE).

acquit, acquit. The infinitive absolute is emphatic. Despite Yahweh's compassion, he will dispense *limited* punishment. But God's love and mercy last 250 times longer (a thousand generations) than his anger (four generations)—and possibly even longer, if *'ălāpîm* means "thousands (of generations)" (NOTE to 20:6).

third . . . fourth (generation). See NOTE to 20:5.

So familiar is the scene, it is easy to miss the surprise element, comparable to Elijah's experience at Horeb (1 Kgs 19:8–14). Exod 34:6–7 does not depict what one might expect of a full revelation of Yahweh: a beaming, armed, kingly figure, lauded as Creator, Conqueror and Administrator. Perhaps that apparition would be God's Face, which he conceals from Moses.

Instead of a visual image, we and Moses receive a *verbal* portrait of Yahweh's personality. He knows how to cherish a grudge, but is more inclined to reward than to punish. These are Yahweh's "backparts" i.e., his Covenant-governed characteristics that interact with Israel, better able than the deadly Face to cope with Israel's wavering fidelity. Now, after the Gold Calf fiasco, Yahweh realizes that he must make it clear that he both rewards and punishes.

34:8. *hurried and prostrated.* I.e., quickly bowed down. Moses' genuflection is a posture of both submission and supplication. He probably bowed as soon as Yahweh appeared (Rashi). If, however, Moses bows after Yahweh's speech (so ibn Ezra), his alacrity reflects his joy that Israel now has a chance to regain its favor with the merciful God, as in Num 14:17–19 (Ehrlich 1969: 204).

34:9. *I . . . our.* Moses tries to manipulate Yahweh through argument. If Yahweh favors Moses, then he must favor Israel with his presence—even though, taking Yahweh's side again, Moses admits that the people are incorrigible. Rashi, however, implausibly understands *kî* as "if." If so, it must go with what follows: *if* Israel is disobedient, then may Yahweh forgive them. (See further below.)

although. One could also understand *kî* in its ordinary sense: "because." (A less likely understanding is "if"; see previous NOTE.) Yahweh must himself travel with the people, rather than an angel, *because* Israel is by nature insubordinate and will respect no lesser authority (cf. Ramban).

Moses seems almost to trick Yahweh here, slipping in the idea that God must after all dwell in Israel's midst. (Compare my discussion of God revealing his name to Moses and Israel in vol. I, pp. 224–26.) In the composite text, this is the basis for the renewal of the Tabernacle project: there Israel can atone for its future derelictions (Luzzatto). In other words, God has pronounced himself to be merciful, and yet Israel remains sinful. Yahweh himself must admit the necessity of the Tabernacle.

possess us. Who is to possess what? Tg. Ps.-*Jonathan* paraphrases "and let *us* possess *the land* that you promised to our Fathers, that you would not exchange us for another people," thus reading *ûn(ə)ḥaltānû* as causative. (Tg. *Onqelos wtḥsynn'* and Tg. *Neofiti I wtʾḥsn ytn* are ambiguous; they could be translated "and possess us" or "and cause us to possess.") The difficulty with the Tg. Ps.-*Jonathan* interpretation is that nowhere else does the Qal *nāḥal* mean "cause to possess." Tg. Ps.-*Jonathan* is, in effect, reading the Piʿel *wəniḥaltānû*.

As for the MT Qal verb *ûn(ə)ḥaltānû*, it must mean "(O Yahweh,) take us as your property *(naḥălâ)*" (cf. Deut 4:20), with the double meaning that the people of Israel and the land of Canaan alike are Yahweh's legal property; cf. 33:16, "your people will be distinguished from all peoples" by belonging to God (Rashi). This would fulfill Yahweh's intention to make Israel his "treasure," distinct from all the peoples of the Earth (see NOTES to 19:5–6).

34:10. *cutting.* On this idiom for making a covenant, see briefly NOTE to 24:8, "cut." By becoming Israel's legal suzerain, Yahweh "possesses" Israel (v 9).

a covenant. With whom? Apparently with both Moses and Israel (v 27).

wonders. Rashbam understands *niplāʾōt* as "distinctiveness," the etymological meaning (root *plyʾ*). Thus Yahweh answers Moses' prayer to make him and Israel "distinguished" (33:16). In the fullest reading, *niplāʾōt* are the wonders by which Yahweh's chosen are singled out.

created. While his excision of a letter seems arbitrary, Ehrlich (1908: 411) is correct that the expected word would be **nrʾw (nirʾû)* 'seen,' not *nbrʾw (nibrəʾû)* 'created' (cf. Micah 7:15; Ps 78:11). Perhaps, rather than scribal error, this is playful creativity on the author's part. In fact, the following sequence is replete with similar sounds (bilabials, liquids, glottal stops): *niplāʾōt... nibrəʾû ... wərāʾâ* 'wonders . . . created . . . saw.' This chain is framed, moreover, by the quasi-symmetrical phrases *ʿamməkā ʾeʿĕśe(h) . . . ʿōśe(h) ʿimmāk* 'your people I will work . . . do for you.'

that it is so dreadful. Superficially, one would understand *kî nôrāʾ hûʾ* as "*for* it is dreadful." And this might be so, explaining just what is so wondrous about Yahweh's proposed deeds. But I have taken *kî* as the subordinating conjunction "that" after the verb *rāʾâ* 'see.' In other words, "see" takes a double object: "Yahweh's deed" and "that what I am going to do for you is dreadful" (cf. Ehrlich 1908: 411; 1969: 204, although I would not emend the text as he does); for a similar construction, see 32:25; 34:35. At the same time, at least to my ear, *kî* also retains its emphatic force, hence: "*so* dreadful."

with you. Who is "you (sing.)"? It could be Israel addressed collectively, as in the following verses. Rashbam and Bekhor Shor, however, think that "you" is Moses, as in "your people." Yahweh is hinting at the transformation of Moses' face in vv 29–35, by which Moses will be distinguished from all Israel, and indeed from all humankind. Just as here the promised deed is *nôrāʾ* 'dreadful' (< *yrʾ*), so the people will "fear *(yrʾ)*" upon beholding Moses (34:30). This wonder will be accomplished "before all your people." This is a plausible reading, particularly of the composite text.

34:11. *Keep for yourself.* Even though the second person singular is still used, the addressee is no longer Moses but all Israel. The language is redolent of Deuteronomy and also Exod 23:20–33 (see pp. 147, 726–29).

Amorite . . . Jebusite. On these nations, see below, pp. 746–53.

34:12. *cut.* I.e., make a covenant.

snare. The twin threats of intermarriage and consequent apostasy; see vv 15–16. In addition to Yahweh, Israel must do its part to keep itself *plyʾ* 'distinct' (33:16) (cf. Sarna 1991: 217).

34:13. *altars.* Altars to Canaanite gods may not be used in Yahweh's service, even if reconsecrated. They must rather be destroyed, lest people be confused which god is being honored. The simplest kind of Canaanite shrine is an altar accompanied by either a stone pillar or a wooden post (see next NOTE).

pillars . . . Asherim. Instead of surveying the voluminous literature on these cultic objects, I will just offer my opinion of what they represented.

In a hypothetical, animistic phase, ancient Semites were wont to conduct worship before boulders or stony outcroppings and trees (Smith 1927: 185–212; for Egyptian parallels to the latter, see Keel 1978: 186–87). In historical times, Northwest Semites called the stone fetish a **baytu ʾili* 'god's house' (Hebrew *bêt-ʾēl*) and the sacred tree an **ʾaṯiratu* 'after-evidence (of a theophany)' or '(sacred) site' (Hebrew *ʾăšērâ*). These were places where a spirit resided, perhaps one of limited power. Most likely, the sacred tree was particularly associated with divine feminity (cf. Hestrin 1987a, 1987b).

Over time, people began to manufacture substitute sacred loci that could be installed at will—stone pillars and wooden posts—and to associate them with the worship of the high gods of the regional pantheon. Sometimes they were prayed before and sacrificed to; sometimes they were just anointed with oil (for a Tyrian parallel, see Keel 1978: 183); sometimes they were besought for oracles. Du Mesnil du Buisson (1963: 133 n. 4) compares "the whispers/charms of tree/wood and stone" in Ugaritic (*KTU* 1.3.iii.22), and see also Hos 4:12: "My people, it inquires of its tree/wood, and its rod tells to him."

While wooden posts do not survive the millennia, the deserts of Canaan are dotted with stone monuments, dating back to the Neolithic (Avner 1993; 2001) and continuing through later eras (Mettinger 1995). Even one of our latest sources, Philo of Byblos' *Phoenician History* (c. 100 C.E.), records that the Phoenicians worshiped from ancient times "pillars and staves" (Smith 1927: 196, n. 5). He transcribes in Greek the native term for the pillar, *baitylos*, which he defines as an "en-souled stone" *(lithos empsychos)* (Eusebius *Praep. evangelica* 1.10.23; Attridge and Oden 1981: 52–53).

Already in the second millennium B.C.E., various peoples of the ancient Near East venerated a goddess called ʾAṯiratu, a consort of the high god. This figure was originally a personification of the sacred tree or post, though in some places the connection was completely forgotten. At Ugarit, for example, her attributes were marine rather than arboreal. Often ʾAṯiratu was equated with the deified abstraction Qudšu or "Holiness." Together with her spouse 'Ilu or "God" she subsumed the essence of the pantheon. In fact, she was sometimes called 'Ilatu or "Goddess," i.e., the goddess *par excellence* (Maier 1986). Analogously in the first millennium B.C.E., there is evidence that the stone pillar or betyl was receiving local veneration as an independent deity Bethel (cf. Dalglish 1992).

The Israelites retained a relatively primitive form of pillar and tree or pole worship. The pillar was called *maṣṣēbâ*, derived from the root *nṣb* 'stand up' and so meaning "upright thing" or perhaps "station." Gen 28:11–22, where Jacob erects a pillar at "Deity's House," i.e., Bethel, proves that, like the Phoenicians, the Israelites knew the original connotation of *bêt-'ēl* as baetyl. Also potentially relevant is Gen 49:24, where God is called *'eben yiśrā'ēl* 'Israel's Stone' (Smith [1927: 210] compares the idol of Abnil at Nisibis.) Some Israelites, including the Yahwist and Elohist, had no objection to a pillar, provided it was a simple physical feature serving as part of a Yahweh shrine, as in Exod 24:4. At most, it might be anointed or inscribed (e.g., Josh 24:26), but it must never be prayed to. Because, however, such artifacts smelled of idolatry and the pre-Yahwistic past, the most stringent biblical authors advocated smashing all pillars, as does our verse. (The simple documentary model suffers here, because J and E seem both to accept and ban pillars; see APPENDIX A.) For further bibliography on sacred pillars, see Fleming (1992: 76–77 n. 27).

As for the *'ăšērâ*, the Israelites knew all three manifestations: sacred tree, wooden pole, goddess. Some were relaxed about worship under a tree (Josh 24:26), provided not too much was read into the symbolism. The pole, too, might be regarded as "Yahweh's Asherah" (cf. "Yahweh . . . and his Asherah" in inscriptions from Kuntillet 'Ajrûd and Khirbet 'el-Qom [AHI 8.017; 25.003). However, because the Canaanites and possibly some Israelites knew of a goddess of the same name and perhaps represented by the same symbols, the Asherah, too, was put under the ban. Trees are important in Israelite and biblical symbology, and scholars have equated various shrubs, trees and poles with the Asherah—the trees of Eden (Genesis 2–3), the Burning Bush (Exodus 3–4), the Tabernacle Lampstand (Exod 25:31–39), Aaron's flowering rod (Num 17:16–28) and Moses' snake-pole (Num 21:4–9) (see also above, p. 551). It remains moot whether some Israelites entertained the possibility of a familial relationship between Yahweh and Asherah: as husband-and-wife, father-and-daughter or son-and-mother (the latter is suggested by the drawing of a cow suckling her calf that accompanies the Kuntillet 'Ajrûd inscription, assuming that the calf represents Yahweh).

In effect, the sacred stone pillar and the sacred wooden post/tree banned in 34:13 are twins. For example, they stand together at the shrine of Shechem (Josh 24:26). Particularly telling are two mocking passages from Jeremiah: "saying to wood (or: a tree), 'You are my my father,' and to stone (or: a rock) 'You birthed me' " (Jer 2:27); "she polluted the land and committed adultery with stone (or: the rock) and with wood (or: the tree)" (Jer 3:9). Even if these are sculpted idols, Jeremiah castigates them according to their substance, not what they depict, recalling the stone pillar and the wood Asherah.

For further discussion of Asherah as a goddess, see below, pp. 761, 771 n. 49.

34:14. *Jealous Yahweh is his name.* An alternative rendering of *yahwe(h) qannā' šmô* is "Yahweh, his name is Jealous." "Name *(šēm)*" here implies "essence" as well as "reputation." It is Yahweh's nature to demand Israel's exclusive veneration. As the following references to "whoring" suggest, he is like a jealous husband married to a wanton Israel (see below).

34:15. *lest you cut a covenant.* The repetition of these words from v 12 is a classic example of *Wiederaufnahme*, marking the intervening material as a digression or even possibly an interpolation (Kuhl 1952).

whore. Many biblical authors possess a characteristic mind-set, by which religious infidelity is associated with sexual impropriety on two levels. As Israel's "husband" (see especially Hosea 1–3), Yahweh cannot tolerate her dalliance with other gods. Simultaneously, individual Israelites must not have marital relations with Canaanites, which might lead to familial and national apostasy. The classic case is Solomon, whose connections with foreign women supposedly led to Israel's first national catastrophe, the division of the kingdom (1 Kings 11). The Torah admonishes against "whoring *(zny)*" in a religious sense also in Lev 17:7; 20:5–6; Num 14:33; 15:39; Deut 31:16; see further next NOTE.

34:16. *daughters . . . sons.* Exod 34:10–16 recapitulates and expands upon 23:23–33, explaining in just what way the Canaanites may prove a "snare": through intermarriage (cf. Genesis 24; 26:34; Deut 7:1–6; Josh 23:12–13; Judg 2:2–3; 3:5–6; 2 Kgs 11:1–6).

34:17. *Metal gods.* This prohibition probably covers gold-plated wooden idols as well as pure metal images; see NOTE to 32:4, "metal." Naturally, in the immediate context, one cannot but see a rebuke for the Gold Calf (Bekhor Shor).

34:18. *Unleavened Bread.* For extensive discussion of this holiday, see vol. I, pp. 427–59. Bekhor Shor suggests that the reiteration of the festival calendar implicitly chides Israel for making up a new feast in 32:5.

34:19. *loosening.* On the word *peṭer* as describing a woman's firstborn, see NOTE to 13:2.

'male.' Sam and MT both read a verb here: MT *tizzākār*. Although major Jewish commentators find a third feminine singular, the subject being either "your cattle" (ibn Ezra) or the unnamed mother (Rashi), it is more natural to see a second person masculine singular, addressed to Israel. If *tzkr* is not a corruption (see TEXTUAL NOTE), it must have a denominative meaning "consecrate as a male" (so *Tgs. Onqelos* and *Ps.-Jonathan*; cf. Deut 15:19) or "declare as a male." While this may seem an implausible formation, we have comparable delocutive verbs such as *bikkēr/hibkîr* 'declare as firstborn' and, more remotely, *qiddēš* 'declare as holy' (see Hillers 1967). (Ehrlich [1969: 204] explains MT's vocalization *tizzākār*, rather than the expected **tizzākar*, as intended to evoke *zākār* 'male'; more likely, however, the form is pausal.) One can imagine Deut 15:19, *hazzākār taqdîš* 'you must sanctify the male,' as D's clarification of *tzkr* in Exod 34:19. On firstborn consecration, see vol. I, pp. 454–56, vol. II, p. 695.

SPECULATION: The verbal usage of *zkr* may at least be alluded to also in 1 Sam 1:19. Although *wayyizkərehā yahwe(h)* is most naturally understood as "and Yahweh remembered her (Hannah)," one could find an alternative interpretation: "and Yahweh gave Hannah a firstborn son to consecrate."

34:20. *ass's loosening*. On this verse, see NOTES to 13:13.

'neck'. I.e., break the neck, decapitate.

Face . . . seen. "Seeing the (divine) Face" implies pilgrimage and sacrifice.

emptily. I.e., empty-handed. See NOTE to 23:15.

34:21. *six days*. The week must be defined at this point so that the Weeks Festival (v 22) can be performed.

work. Rashbam observes that, when not otherwise qualified, the root ʿbd connotes agricultural labor.

plowing. Even during the most intense agricultural activity, the Sabbath must be kept (ibn Ezra; Rashbam; Ramban). The festival context contains further implications: even if one plans to donate the crop to God, it must not be tended on the Sabbath. Probably, to do so would render it ritually unfit.

34:22. *Weeks*. Also known as Shavuot or Pentecost.

firstfruits of the wheat harvest. Something is elliptically omitted: *at the time* of the firstfruits of the wheat harvest (Saadiah) or *a festival* of the firstfruits of the wheat harvest.

year's revolution. Since Sukkot is the autumn harvest festival, *təqûpat haššānâ* could refer either to the midpoint of a Spring-based year or the beginning of a Fall-based year (vol. I, p. 385).

34:23. *must appear to*. A popular theory emends the text here and in parallel passages to read **yir'e(h) 'et-pənê hā'ādōn yahwe(h)* 'must *see* the Face of the Lord Yahweh.' For reasons discussed under TEXTUAL NOTE to 23:17, I favor the received Niphʿal vocalization, taking *'ēt* as *'ēt* II 'with, in the presence of.' Whoever may be seeing whom, the image is that of a royal audience.

34:24. *any man*. Here, *'îš* refers to each single foreign nation (Bekhor Shor), not to individual neighbors (vs. Hyatt 1971: 325). Israelites should not fear an invasion while they are busy with pilgrimage, because their borders will be extensive. Probably underlying this notion is an internal custom of suspended intertribal hostilities during pilgrimage time, as among the Arabs (*pace* Michaelis apud Dillmann 1880: 354). It is a perennial temptation to attack others while they are at a religious celebration, from the days of the Hasmoneans (1 Macc 2:32–38) and the Qumran community (1QpHab 11:4–8) to the Yom Kippur War of 1973.

covet. Initially, it appears that *ḥāmad* 'covet' has a special connotation of "steal" (Saadiah), a meaning some have also tried to read into the Decalog. But more likely *ḥmd* is an emotional state (see NOTE to 20:17[14]). In Gen 2:9; 3:6; Deut 7:25; Josh 7:21, covetousness leads directly to theft.

three times. The repeated references to appearing before Yahweh's Face three times in the year in vv 23–24 frame the intervening material as a digression (cf. Kuhl 1952). It addresses implicit objections to pilgrimage that must often have been voiced: what of the security of one's goods? Is it wise to leave the nation unguarded?

34:25. *slaughter*. *Šāḥaṭ*, which normally means "slaughter," here connotes sacrifice by fire on an altar, just as *zābaḥ*, which etymologically also means "slaughter," almost always refers to a burnt offering (for discussion, see pp. 420, 695–703). In fact, the parallel in 23:18 reads has *zābaḥ*. (Alternatively, one could read 34:25 in the Rabbinic mode: *by the time* one slaughters the paschal victim, there must be no leavened food anywhere [Rashi].)

leavened food. Representing minor impurity, leaven is the opposite of sacrificial blood, which purifies. On the incompatibility of leaven and holiness, see vol. I, pp. 429–34.

Pesaḥ festival Slaughter-offering. Exod 23:18 and 34:25 are variants of the same law. Many understand 34:25 to be a rewriting of 23:18, with Deut 16:1–17 a still later exposition (e.g., Levinson 1997: 53–97). In 34:25, the expression *zebaḥ ḥag happāsaḥ* is problematic. In my understanding, *Pesaḥ* is not a *ḥag* 'festival'; the proper name for the spring pilgrimage is *hammaṣṣôt* 'Unleavened Bread' (vol. I, p. 398). Moreover, the parallel in 23:18 reads *ḥēleb ḥaggî* 'my festival fat,' with *ḥag* understood as connoting a festival *offering*, not necessarily the pre-festival sacrificial meal of *Pesaḥ* (see, however, NOTE, "my Slaughter-offering"). In 34:25, therefore, the reference to *Pesaḥ* may be a gloss inspired by the reference to *ḥāmēṣ* 'leavened food' (see Haran 1978: 327–29). The word *zebaḥ* 'Slaughter-offering' could also be a secondary clarification of an unusual use of *ḥag* in 23:18.

cook a kid. See NOTES to 23:19.

34:27. *Write for yourself.* "For yourself." In this context, *ləkā* emphasizes the command: "Go, write down—for I shall not." Moses is to inscribe an unnamed surface, presumably parchment. See also NOTE to 34:1, "Carve for yourself."

by the mouth of these words. I.e., according to their import. But what are "these words"? As the text stands, they must be the contents of 34:10–26 (Rashbam). (It is not inconceivable, however, that 34:27 originally concluded chap. 23, the first Covenant.) In any case, "the words" are not the Ten Words of v 28; those are written by Yahweh himself (see NOTE below).

I have cut a covenant. To "cut *(krt)*" a covenant is to institute a treaty. V 27, together with 34:10, frames the intervening laws as the stuff of the Covenant with Moses and Israel.

34:28. *day . . . night.* Why not simply "forty day(s)"? Perhaps to preclude the impression that Moses fasted only during the daylight, as in minor Jewish fasts and the Muslim Ramaḍān.

bread. Leḥem can also be translated "food." Did Moses eat nothing? Was he sustained merely by God's presence? Did he eat divine food, perhaps snuffing up sacrificial vapors like a god? Was the flow of time altered, so that the forty days seemed to him but a day?

he wrote. Although the subject of the prior verbs is Moses, ibn Ezra, Ramban and Rashbam correctly take Yahweh as the subject here, since 34:1 and Deut 10:2, 4 credit God with writing on the Tablets (so also Dillmann 1880: 353). Less likely, the subject is Moses (Holzinger 1900: 119). Cassuto (1967: 448) suggests that the verb *wayyiktōb* may be impersonal, tantamount to a passive.

the Ten Words. The expression *ʿăseret haddəbārîm* creates a frame with 20:1–17(14), the Decalog proper (cf. Deut 4:13; 10:4), thus surrounding the entire Covenantal legislation.

Though some have sought *another* Decalog inside chap. 34, I cannot find it. Exod 34:1 and Deut 10:1–4 understand the "Ten Words" to be the same on the first and second Tablets. For further discussion, see above, p. 150.

34:29. *Testimony.* On the term *ʿēdūt,* see NOTE to 25:16.

"horned." There are three basic exegetical approaches to the verb *qāran.* All start with the primitive Semitic noun **qarnu* 'horn' (Hebrew *qeren*). The rival interpretations are that (a) Moses's face shone; (b) Moses' skin was made horny; (c) Moses' forehead sprouted horns. The matter will be discussed further under COMMENT. Here, suffice it to say that Moses comes down the mountain terrifyingly altered.

in his speaking. Bədabbərô implies "while speaking" and "ever since speaking," as well as "because of speaking" (for the last, see Ehrlich 1969: 205). The verb *dibber* 'speak' is the *Leitwort* of vv 29–35, with seven occurrences in all (Cassuto 1967: 451).

34:30. *too frightened.* Depending upon how we interpret *qāran* 'horned,' the Israelites flee either in holy dread or in instinctive revulsion. Leibowitz (1976: 635) compares the vignette in Gen 45:3–4, where Joseph's brothers, scarcely recognizing their lost brother, recoil and must be invited to approach. In Christianity's twofold Bible, this scene also foreshadows Jesus' tense reunion with his followers following the Resurrection (Matt 28:17; Luke 24:37–41).

34:31. *leaders.* First the chieftains approach cautiously and speak with the apparition. Then, reassured, all the people approach to hear what Moses has to say.

34:32. *all that Yahweh spoke.* Assuming that the context is Priestly (see p. 142), this must be the Tabernacle instructions (chaps. 25–31). In the composite text, however, it includes also the Decalog (chap. 20) and the miscellaneous laws and exhortations contained in chap. 34.

34:33. *veil.* The word *maswe(h)* is found only in this story, and its meaning is largely deduced from context. The root is probably *swy*, from which are derived Phoenician *swt* (*KAI* 11:2; 24:8) and *swyh* (*KAI* 76A.4) and Hebrew *sût* (Gen 49:11 MT), all meaning "garment.

We must assume that, for the rest of his life, Moses goes about veiled, unless he is communicating with God or Israel. Perhaps this is an ancient Semitic institution; Wellhausen (1897: 135) compares the veiled seers of the Arabs. In the composite text, it is striking that the man who once hid his face from seeing God at Horeb (3:6 [E]) becomes at Sinai one upon whom others cannot look (34:30 [P/R]).

34:34. *before Yahweh. Lipnê yahwe(h)* is P's technical term for the Tabernacle. Yahweh and Moses would periodically confer in the sacred tent, apparently renewing the altered condition of Moses' face.

In the context of P, 34:34 must be prospective: once the Tabernacle is built, this is what Moses will do. In the composite text, however, the immediate referent could be the temporary Meeting Tent of 33:7–11 (E), later replaced by the priestly Tabernacle.

what he would be commanded. One could also translate *'ăšer yəṣuwwe(h)* as "what would be commanded." But the Sam-LXX variant "he/Yahweh commanded him" (see TEXTUAL NOTE) favors making Moses the subject of the MT Pu'al.

34:35. *see.* Most likely Moses removes the veil simply to be better understood when speaking. The text stresses, however, that Israel continually beholds Moses' altered visage, which apparently reinforces their trust in him.

COMMENT

WHAT'S IN A FACE, WHAT'S IN A NAME?

Exodus chaps. 25–40 address basically a single topic: how will Yahweh be present among his people? As a Messenger? In the Tabernacle? Through the Covenant? As the Gold Calf? As Moses' face? As his own Face? The theme word of this section is *pānîm* 'face, front, presence,' sometimes referring to Israel—as when a Messenger goes before *(lipnê)* them—sometimes referring to Moses—as when contact with the Deity transforms his visage—and most often referring to Yahweh. Worship is conducted in the Tabernacle *lipnê yahwe(h)* 'before Yahweh,' literally 'to Yahweh's Face.' Although God denies that a human can survive a vision of his Face (33:20), Yahweh and Moses converse *pānîm 'el-pānîm* 'face-to-face' (33:11). Most important, Moses insists and Yahweh grants that the divine countenance will lead Israel (33:14–15).

Yahweh's Face is a hypostasis, i.e., a part of the divine being that stands for the whole. The idea is easy to grasp. If I offer to show you my sons, you are not surprised if I produce a photograph, rather than two flesh-and-blood boys. The image is an adequate substitute for the imaged. But if the photograph depicts their hands, or is taken from the rear, you would be nonplussed. You would not accept these as meaningful images. You would, however, accept a photograph of their *faces* or *front sides* (for this example, cf. Lakoff and Johnson 1980: 37). After all, with our natural sight we can only view one side of an object at a time.

So, too, Yahweh's Face or Front is a part of the Deity, one side of his reality. To use a metaphor I shall elaborate upon later, it is a projection of his anterior aspect into our three-dimensional realm (below, p. 687). Like the polytheist's idol, it can be regarded as either identical to or distinct from the Deity. In this respect, it is fully equivalent to an angelic Messenger, also a semi-distinct divine manifestation (see vol. I, p. 198). In fact, in recounting the events of the Exodus, Isa 63:9 calls the divine, saving agency *mal'ak pānā(y)w* 'his Face Messenger.' (In Mal 3:1, Yahweh may similarly equate *mal'ak habbərît* 'the Covenant Messenger' with *pānāy* 'my Face.') Later Jewish literature will name this entity Penuel ("God's Face"), Metatron (1 Enoch 40:9; 71:8–9; *b. Sanh.* 38b, etc.) or *śar happānîm* 'the Face Prince.' Gnostic Christians will identify him with Jesus Christ (Ahituv 1997: 10*).

If a face is a visible symbol, a pictogram so to speak, a name is an audible symbol. God is not the sound "Yah-weh," but these two syllables, or the four letters Y-H-W-H, in some contexts represent his presence. In Deuteronomic literature, it is Yahweh's Name that inhabits the Temple instead of an idol. Isa 30:27 graphically describes Yahweh's Name as a fire-breathing personification: "See: Yahweh's Name coming from a distance, its *nose* (anger) burning, its smoke heaviness, its lips full of wrath, and its tongue like a consuming fire, and its breath like a flooding stream." Pious Jews still call God "the Name *(haššēm)*." This language has old Canaanite roots; in Ugaritic myth, the goddess 'Attartu (Astarte) is called *šm.b'l* 'Ba'lu's Name' (*KTU* 1.16.vi.56).

The Priestly source, however, does not dwell on Yahweh's Name (but see Num 6:27) and does not mention supernatural Messengers at all. P's preferred terms to describe the divine presence are *kābôd* 'Glory' and *pānîm* 'Face,' as in the phrase *lipnê yahwe(h)* 'before Yahweh' and as in the priestly blessing "May Yahweh shine his Face at you" (Num 6:25–26). On one level, the Glory is an abstraction of Yahweh's ineffable majesty. But it is also reified as a fiery, flying vehicle, of which Ezekiel 1 provides, so to speak, the blueprint.

These currents in biblical theology—paralleled in Northwest Semitic writings from Carthage and Ashkelon (Cross 1973: 30; Aḥituv 1997: 7*–9*)—are synthesized in the complex transactions of chaps. 33–34. Though assured that Yahweh's Face will be present (33:14–15), Moses is permitted to glimpse only Yahweh's back—which, as we already commented, scarcely gives a sense of the entire personality. We are led to equate the divine back with Yahweh's anonymous Messenger (promised in 23:20, 23; 32:34; 33:2), his Glory (33:18), and his Name (34:5–6). (Significantly, while in cognate literatures "Baal's Face" or "Baal's Name" can be a goddess, the Torah does not acknowledge female hypostases. These will return in Lady Wisdom (Prov 8:22–31) and gain popularity in later Judaism, e.g., the Shekhinah [Patai 1967].)

MOSES THE MINOTAUR?

Having discussed the question of whether Yahweh's "Face" will accompany Israel in the wilderness, the Sinai-Horeb passage concludes with a description of Moses' own transformed visage (34:29–35). There is considerable uncertainty as to what process is denoted by the unique verb *qāran*, presumably related to *qeren* 'horn.' The three approaches worthy of consideration are that (a) Moses' face was made *glorious*; (b) his skin was *toughened*; (c) his forehead sprouted *horns*. (I do not consider at all likely the theory that Moses is described as wearing a horned *mask*; see Propp 1987d: 375 n. 1, 382–83.)

The oldest interpretation is that Moses' face was glorified (LXX, Syr, *Tgs.*). Underlying this interpretation, at least for *Tgs.*, is a deliberate exegetical misreading of *'ôr* 'light' for *'ôr* 'skin' (Propp 1987d: 377–79). This does not negate the possibility, however, that *qāran* really means "to be glorified."

In what does glorification consist? Most exegetes assume that it is the radiation of light (e.g., *Exod. Rab.* 47:6 "glory-horns"; Rashi, "the light was shining and projecting in the form of a sort of horn"). Horns are a symbol of power in the Bible and throughout the ancient Near East (Süring 1980); in Mesopotamian iconography, a stack of horns bears some relationship to the gods' radiant aura called *melammu*. The best biblical evidence for the horn = light equation is Ps 132:17, "There I shall cause a *horn* to sprout for David, I have trimmed a *lamp* for my anointed." Moreover, to demonstrate a connection between horns and shining, Bekhor Shor invokes the poetic image of the "dawn gazelle" (Ps 22:1), apparently a mythic creature below the horizon whose antlers are the rays of the rising sun (*b. Yoma* 29a). Greenfield (1959) has demonstrated that the Semitic languages as a whole tend to associate shining with the sprouting of plants; why not also the sprouting of horns?

Further, in Num 27:20, Moses is commanded to share his *hôd* 'splendor, authority' with Joshua, so that Israel will heed him (Haran 1984: 165–67). While this could refer simply to Moses' divine mandate, it could also imply a transfer of radiance.

Lastly, Hab 3:3–4 may equate "horn" specifically with radiant splendor (ibn Ezra):

> ³From Teiman Yahweh comes
> And the Holy from Mount Paran. . . .
> His splendor *(hôdô)* covered the sky,
> And his glory *(təhillātô)*, it filled the earth,
> ⁴And it will be brightness like light *(wənōgah kā'ôr tihye[h])*,
> Two horns from his hand for him *(qarnayim miyyādô lô)*,
> And there is the covert of his might *(wəšām ḥebyôn 'uzzō)*.

Few scholars would claim to understand v 4. Its parallel in Deut 33:2 is equally or even more enigmatic: *mîmînô 'ēšdāt lāmô* 'from his right hand *'ēšdāt* (?) to him.' (A Gordian-knot solution: *qarnayim* [cf. Amos 6:13] and *'ēšdāt* [= *'ašdōt*; cf. Deut 3:17; 4:49; Josh 12:3 (note Teiman!); 13:20]) are *places* near which Yahweh travels.) At any rate, in Habakkuk "horns" may parallel words for glory and light, one of which appears also in Num 27:20 *(hôd)*.

Why should Moses' face shine in Exodus? Elsewhere in the Bible, when a face is said to "shine" *(hē'îr)* it means something like smile (cf. English "beam"). While Moses might descend the mountain with a disconcerting rictus of ecstasy, it is hard to see why his *skin* receives such emphasis. If *qāran* means "shine," it must literally refer to luminosity.

SPECULATION: The human tendency to perceive powerful humans and gods as shining, especially from the head, is noteworthy. Needless to say, there is no real radiation. Do we just respond to the facial features, perhaps the gleam of sweat or the flush of passion?

I incline toward a different explanation. Our shiver-response to fear suggests that our ancestors possessed the ability to puff their hair like cats, perhaps especially a crest on the head, in order to appear larger (see Burkert 1996: 18; Lorenz 1966: 268–69). This ability may have been used in male competitive display. My hunch is that we also retain a vestigial ability to *perceive the crest*, to respond submissively to humans surrounded by a (now invisible) fuzzy aura. Hence the hallucination of the halo.

The averted gaze is also part of this evolution. To look someone in the face is to challenge them, which is why, e.g., ordinary people may not behold the King of Assyria's countenance (Parpola 1980: 172). (On the privilege of beholding the king, see also 2 Kgs 25:19; Esth 2:14). In Exodus, first Yahweh and then Moses, we are told, may not be stared in the face.

If this is the true meaning of *qāran*, the veiled, shining Moses may be regarded as a walking Tabernacle, manifesting and yet concealing Yahweh's splendor. Or he could represent Israel: "Moses alone stood in a relation to God close and intimate enough for such a transfiguration to be possible or bearable; the people durst not gaze even upon the reflexion. But Moses was the representative of his nation, and the glory upon his face was a pledge and symbol of the abiding of the divine glory upon the whole people" (McNeile 1908: cxxiii).

One's first impression may be that Moses' countenance is a mirror for Yahweh's own (cf. 2 Cor 3:18). We might compare Ps 34:6, "They gazed at him (Yahweh) and shone *(wənāhārû),*" and especially Isa 60:1–5 (cf. also Isa 58:8–10):

> Arise, shine *('ôrî),* because your light *('ôrēk)* came,
> And Yahweh's Glory, it shone *(zārāḥ)* on you.
> For, see: the dark covers the earth,
> And darkcloud the peoples;
> But on you Yahweh shines *(yizraḥ),*
> And his Glory, it appears on you.
> And nations will walk by your light *(lə'ôrēk),*
> And kings by the brightness of your shining *(lənōgah zarḥēk).* . . .
> Then you will see and shine *(wənāhart).*

Here the addressee shines in response to God's luminescence; for a Mesopotamian parallel, see Foster (1993: 587). In Exodus 34, the Israelites, who cannot see Yahweh directly, behold his appearance indirectly in Moses' visage, as we see the sunlight in the moon's face. Fretheim (1991: 311) writes in this vein: "Moses now functions as a divine messenger. . . . We are told in 33:11 that God speaks to Moses face-to-face. Yet it is twice stated that God's face cannot be seen in all its fullness, even by Moses (33:20, 23). One might then say that *Moses' shining face is the vision of the face of God which is available to the community*" (emphasis in original). In other words, Moses himself is the supernatural "Face" that leads Israel (33:14). Fretheim goes on to make the obvious comparison with Jesus, God incarnate, who appears as a man transfigured in Matt 17:1–9; Mark 9:1–9; Luke 9:28–36.

Again, this theory's main weakness is the text's emphasis on Moses' "skin *('ôr)*." Why not just say "his face shone"? Might the verb *qāran* mean something else entirely?

As I observed in Propp (1987d: 384–85), many languages associate skin with "horniness" in the sense of a toughened texture. The first to apply this meaning to 34:29–35 was the medieval heretic Ḥiwi of Balkh (confuted and anathematized by ibn Ezra): "Moses' face dried up like horn." Moderns of the same opinion are Eerdmans (1939: 20–22) and Albright (1950: 14 n. 1).

As for why and how Moses' skin became unusually hard, the answer is to be found in P's previous narrative vignette, where Moses penetrated Yahweh's fiery shield, the "Glory" (24:16–18a). 2 Enoch 37 (*OTP* 1.160–1) describes an angel "white as snow" cooling Moses' face to protect it from God's flaming presence. And according to Hekhalot Rabbati §159, the angels themselves serve God only for a day, "for their vigor has grown weak and their faces have turned black" (see Davila 2001: 139). The ancients commented on how forge-work in particular toughened a smith's skin (e.g., the Egyptian "Satire on the Trades" [*ANET*³ 433]; Sir 38:28; for the effect of heat on skin, see also Job 30:30; Lam 5:10). Moses thus may receive literally the imperviousness metaphorically granted to Ezekiel: "Like a stone harder than flint I made your forehead" (Ezek 3:9). By this theory, when the people flee in Exod 34:30, it is because they are revolted by Moses' ugliness (cf. Isa 52:14–15; 53:3). (Though affirming the traditional "shining" interpretation, Jacob [1992: 1005–6] sees a connection between *qrn* and the root *qrm* 'crust, scab,' and observes that in Job 16:15 *qeren* may mean "skin.")

Why would the Torah depict Moses as disfigured? Perhaps to show the price the Lawgiver paid to mediate the divine presence to Israel. One could even regard Moses' disability as another example of a symbolic wound incurred during a rite of passage (see pp. 308–9, 528–31; Propp 2004a). Further: assuming the vignette is P, the Priestly stratum is pervaded by a subtle denigration of Moses and the Levites, the better to elevate Aaron and his house (see further vol. I, pp. 283–86, 567–74). If the Priestly Writer could not deny Moses' pivotal role, he could at least describe him as of hideous aspect. (See also above, pp. 153–54.)

Some interpreters espouse the idea that Moses was literally horned (Sasson 1968; Batto 1992: 124), precisely as in Medieval and Renaissance art (Mellinkoff 1970). This is not so different from the first approach, since horns were a sign of divinity in the ancient Near East (Süring 1980). The effect in the composite text would admittedly be most striking. The people apostatized before a bovine god (chap. 32 [E]); now they get a bovine leader (cf. Sasson 1968). Moses the minotaur would stand alongside the horned bull gods and demigods of Ugaritic myth, offspring of Ba'lu (*KTU* 1.5.v.17–22; 10) and said to bear his *face* (*KTU* 1.12.33).

My objections are: why does the text not say that Moses' *head* or *forehead* sprouted horns? Why doesn't the text use the Hiph'il *hiqrîn*, which in Ps 69:32 means "to grow horns"? How can concealing his *face* hide Moses' horns? Why the emphasis on *skin*? I can just barely imagine that the author describes Moses' epidermis gathering itself into small calf's horns right above the eyes, as perhaps Aquila understood the text ("his face skin became horned"). But I consider this explanation the least likely.

As already stated, I reject as utterly fanciful the notion that Moses is described as donning a ritual mask (Propp 1987d: 383–84). Still, the theory is noteworthy. Consciously or unconsciously, this modern suggestion responds to the near-ubiquity of masks in religions worldwide. They were probably used by our common ancestors in shamanic rituals, back to the caves of Lascaux (Campbell 1976). Exodus does not depict Moses as masked. Rather, his face, branded by Yahweh — whether horned, beaming or hardened — becomes the Mask of God.

PART VII. BUILDING
THE TABERNACLE
(EXODUS 35–40)

◆

XXII. *And Moses completed the Task* (35:1–40:38)

35 [1](P)And Moses assembled all the congregation of Israel's Sons and said to them, "These are the *words* that Yahweh commanded to do them. [2]Six days a task may be done. But on the seventh day a Holiness shall be for you, a sabbatical Sabbath for Yahweh. Anyone doing a task on it must be put to death. [3]Do not burn fire in all your dwellings on the Sabbath day."

[4]And Moses said to all the congregation of Israel's Sons, saying, "This is the *word* that Yahweh commanded, saying: [5]'Take from with you a Donation-offering for Yahweh. Everyone noble-hearted shall bring it, Yahweh's Donation: gold, silver and bronze, [6]blue and purple and worm-crimson and linen and *goats* [7]and reddened ram skins and beaded skins and acacia wood [8]and oil for illumination and fragrances for the Ointment Oil and for the Spice Incense [9]and carnelian stones and *filling* stones for the Ephod and for the *ḥōšen*.

[10]'And every wise-hearted among you, they shall come and make all that Yahweh commanded: [11]the Tabernacle, its Tent and its cover, its clasps and its *qərāšîm*, its crossbars, its posts and its bases, [12]the Chest and its poles, the *kappōret* and the Veil screen, [13]the Table and its poles and all its implements and the *Face Bread* [14]and the Illumination Lampstand and its implements and its lamps and the Illumination Oil [15]and the Incense Altar and its poles and the Ointment Oil and the Spice Incense and the Opening Screen for the Tabernacle Opening, [16]the Ascending-offering Altar and the bronze mesh that is its, its poles and all its implements, the Basin and its Stand, [17]the Plaza's sheets and its posts and its bases and the Screen of the Plaza's gate, [18]the Tabernacle's tent-pegs and the Plaza's tent-pegs and their cords, [19]the Textile Garments for attending in the Holiness: the Holiness Garments for Aaron the priest and his sons' garments for priesting.' "

[20]And all the congregation of Israel's Sons went out from before Moses. [21]And every man whose heart ennobled him came, and everyone whose spirit ennobled him, they brought Yahweh's Donation-offering for the Meeting

Tent Task and for all its Work and for the Holiness Garments. ²²And the men came in addition to the women. Everyone noble-hearted brought nose-ring and earring and finger-ring and *kûmāz*, any gold item, and every man that elevated a gold Elevation-offering for Yahweh. ²³And everyone with whom was found blue and purple and worm-crimson and linen and *goats* and reddened ram skins and beaded skins, they brought. ²⁴Each donor of a silver or bronze Donation-offering, they brought Yahweh's Donation-offering. And everyone with whom was found acacia wood, for the Task of the Work they brought.

²⁵And every wise-hearted woman, with her hands they spun. And they brought spinning-stuff: the blue and the purple, the worm-crimson and the linen. ²⁶And all the women whose heart uplifted them, with wisdom they spun the *goats*.

²⁷And the chieftains, they brought the carnelian stones and the *filling* stones for the Ephod and for the *ḥōšen* ²⁸and the fragrance and the oil, for illumination and for the Ointment Oil and for the Spice Incense. ²⁹Every man and woman whose heart ennobled them to bring for all the Task that Yahweh commanded to do by Moses' *hand*, Israel's Sons brought largesse for Yahweh.

³⁰And Moses said to Israel's Sons, "See, Yahweh has called by name Bezalel son of Uri son of Hur from the tribe of Judah ³¹and filled him with a divine spirit in wisdom, in understanding and in knowledge and in every task, ³²and for planning plans, to make in gold and in silver and in bronze ³³and in stone carving for *fillings* and in wood carving, to do every planning task; ³⁴and to direct he has set in his heart. Him and Oholiab son of Ahisamach from the tribe of Dan, ³⁵he has filled them with heart-wisdom to do every task of carver and of webster and of embroiderer—in the blue and in the purple, in the worm-crimson and in the linen—and of weaver, doers of every task and planners of plans. 36 ¹And Bezalel and Oholiab will make, and every wise-hearted man in whom Yahweh set wisdom and understanding, to know (how) to do all the Holiness Work Task, for all that Yahweh commanded."

²So Moses called Bezalel and Oholiab and every wise-hearted man, in whose heart Yahweh set wisdom, everyone whose heart uplifted him, to approach to the Task to do it. ³And they took from before Moses all the Donation-offering that Israel's Sons brought for the Holiness Work Task to do it. But they, they brought him still more largesse *by morning by morning*.

⁴And all the wise doing all the Holiness Task came, *man (by) man* from his task that they were doing, ⁵and they said to Moses, saying: "The people are bringing more than enough for the Work in respect of the Task that Yahweh commanded to do it."

⁶So Moses commanded, and they *made a voice pass* in the camp, saying: "Man and woman must not do any more Task for the Holiness Donation-offering." And the people were restrained from giving. ⁷And the Task was enough for them for all the Task for doing it—and more!

⁸And every wise-hearted among those doing the Task made the Tabernacle, ten curtains: twisted linen, blue and purple and worm-crimson, Griffins, webster's work he made them. ⁹The one curtain's length eight-and-twenty by

the cubit, and breadth four by the cubit, the one curtain. One measure for all the curtains. [10]And he fastened five of the curtains one to one, and five curtains he fastened, one to one. [11]And he made blue loops on the one curtain's *lip*, on the edge on the *fastening*; so he made on the outer curtain's *lip*, on the second *fastening*. [12]Fifty loops he made on the one curtain, and fifty loops he made on the edge of the curtain that was on the second *fastening*, the loops aligning one to one. [13]And he made fifty gold clasps and fastened the curtains one to one with the clasps, so that the Tabernacle was one.

[14]And he made *goat* curtains to tent over the Tabernacle: eleven curtains he made them. [15]The one curtain's length thirty by the cubit, and four cubits the one curtain's breadth. One measure for the eleven curtains. [16]And he fastened the five curtains separate and the six curtains separate. [17]And he made loops fifty on the *lip* of the curtain outermost on the *fastening*, and fifty loops he made on the *lip* of the curtain, the second *fastening*. [18]And he made bronze clasps, fifty, to fasten the Tent, to be one.

[19]And he made a cover for the Tent: reddened ram skins and a beaded skins cover above.

[20]And he made the *qərāšîm* for the Tabernacle: standing acacia wood, [21]ten cubits the *qereš*'s length, a cubit and a half-cubit the one *qereš*'s breadth, [22]two *arms* for the one *qereš*, pegged one to one; so he made for all the Tabernacle's *qərāšîm*. [23]And he made the *qərāšîm* for the Tabernacle, twenty *qərāšîm* for the austral, southward side. [24]And forty silver bases he made under the twenty *qərāšîm*, two bases under the one *qereš* for its two *arms*, and two bases under the one *qereš* for its two *arms*. [25]And for the Tabernacle's second flank, for the north side, he made twenty *qərāšîm* [26]and their forty bases, silver, two bases under the one *qereš* and two bases under the one *qereš*. [27]And for the Tabernacle's *seaward* backparts he made six *qərāšîm*. [28]And two *qərāšîm* he made for the Tabernacle's corners at the backparts. [29]And they shall be twinning from below; together they shall be whole to its *head*, to the one ring. So he made for the two of them, for the two corners. [30]And there shall be eight *qərāšîm* and their bases, silver: sixteen bases, two bases, two bases under the one *qereš*. [31]And he made acacia-wood crossbars: five for the *qərāšîm* of the Tabernacle's one flank [32]and five crossbars for the *qərāšîm* of the Tabernacle's second flank and five crossbars for the Tabernacle's *qərāšîm* at the *seaward* backparts. [33]And he made the inner crossbar to bar amid the *qərāšîm* from end to end. [34]And the *qərāšîm* he plated gold; and their rings he made gold, housings for the crossbars; and he plated the crossbars gold.

[35]And he made the Veil: blue and purple and worm-crimson and twisted linen, webster's work he made it, Griffins. [36]And he made for it four acacia-wood posts and plated them gold, their Y-brackets gold, and he cast for them four silver bases.

[37]And he made a screen for the Tent Opening: blue and purple and worm-crimson and twisted linen, embroiderer's work, [38]its posts, five, and their Y-brackets, and he will plate their *heads* and their *ḥăšūqîm* gold, and their bases, five, bronze.

37 ¹And Bezalel made the Chest, acacia wood: two cubits and a half its length and a cubit and a half its breadth and a cubit and a half its height. ²And he plated it pure gold from inside and from outside. And he made for it a gold *zēr* around. ³And he cast four gold rings for it on its four *feet*, and two rings on its one flank and two rings on its second flank. ⁴And he made acacia-wood poles and plated them gold. ⁵And he inserted the poles into the rings on the Chest's flanks for carrying the Chest.

⁶And he made a pure gold *kappōret*: two cubits and a half its length and a cubit and a half its breadth. ⁷And he made two Griffins, gold: *miqšâ* he made them on the *kappōret*'s two ends; ⁸one Griffin on this end here and one Griffin on this end here; on the *kappōret* he made the Griffins on its two ends, ⁹so that the Griffins will be spreading wings above, screening over the *kappōret* with their wings, and their faces *one to one*, toward the *kappōret* the Griffins' faces were.

¹⁰And he made the Table, acacia wood: two cubits its length and a cubit its breadth and a cubit and a half its height. ¹¹And he plated it pure gold. And he made for it a gold *zēr* around. ¹²And he made for it a handbreadth's frame around. And he made a gold *zēr* for its frame around. ¹³And he cast four gold rings and set the rings on the four corners that belonged to its four legs. ¹⁴Aligned with the frame the rings were, housings for the poles for carrying the Table. ¹⁵And he made the poles, acacia wood, and plated them gold, for carrying the Table. ¹⁶And he made the implements that were on the Table: its bowls and its spoons and its rinsers and the dippers from which may be poured, pure gold.

¹⁷And he made the Lampstand, pure gold: *miqšâ* he made the Lampstand, its *thigh* and its *reeds*, its cups, its *kaptōrîm* and its *flowers*, they were from it. ¹⁸And six *reeds* going out from its sides—three Lampstand *reeds* from its one side and three Lampstand *reeds* from its second side—¹⁹three "almondized" cups on the one *reed—kaptōr* and *flower*—and three "almondized" cups on the one *reed—kaptōr* and *flower*—so for the six *reeds* going out from the Lampstand. ²⁰And on the Lampstand four "almondized" cups—its *kaptōrîm* and its *flowers*—²¹and a *kaptōr* under the two *reeds* from it, and a *kaptōr* under the two *reeds* from it, and a *kaptōr* under the two *reeds* from it, for the six *reeds* going out from it. ²²Their *kaptōrîm* and their *reeds*, they were from it, all of it one *miqšâ*, pure gold. ²³And he made its lamps seven and its tweezers and its fire-pans, pure gold. ²⁴A talent, pure gold he made it and all its implements.

²⁵And he made the Incense Altar, acacia wood: a cubit its length and a cubit its breadth—foursquare—and two cubits its height; from it its *horns* were. ²⁶And he plated it pure gold: its *roof* and its *walls* around and its *horns*. And he made for it a gold *zēr* around. ²⁷And two gold rings he made for it beneath its *zēr* on its two flanks on its two sides as housings for poles for carrying it with them. ²⁸And he made the poles, acacia wood, and plated them gold.

²⁹And he made the Ointment Oil, a Holiness, and the Herb Incense, pure, compounder's work.

38 ¹And he made the Ascending-offering Altar, acacia wood: five cubits its

length and five cubits its breadth—foursquare—and three cubits its height. ²And he made its *horns* on its four corners—from it its *horns* were—and he plated it bronze. ³And he made all the Altar's implements: the pots and the shovels and the bowls, the forks and the fire-pans—all its implements he made bronze. ⁴And he made for the Altar a mesh, lattice work, bronze, under its rim as far as its half. ⁵And he cast four rings at the four corners for the bronze mesh, housings for the poles. ⁶And he made the poles, acacia wood, and plated them bronze. ⁷And he inserted the poles into the rings on the Altar's flanks to carry it with them. Hollow-planked he made it.

⁸And he made the Basin, bronze, and its Stand, bronze, out of the mirrors of the *ṣōbǝʾōt*-women who *ṣābā(ʾ)*-ed (at) the Meeting Tent Opening.

⁹And he made the Plaza: on the austral, southward side, the Plaza's sheets, twisted linen, one hundred by the cubit, ¹⁰their posts twenty and their bases twenty, bronze; the posts' Y-brackets and their *ḥǎšūqîm*, silver. ¹¹And on the north side: one hundred by the cubit, their posts twenty and their bases twenty, bronze; the posts' Y-brackets and their *ḥǎšūqîm*, silver. ¹²And on the *sea* side: sheets, fifty by the cubit, their posts ten and their bases ten, the posts' Y-brackets and their *ḥǎšūqîm*, silver. ¹³And on the *forward, sunrise* side: fifty cubit. ¹⁴Sheets, fifteen cubit, for the *shoulder*, their posts three and their bases three. ¹⁵And for the second *shoulder*, from this (side) and from this (side) for the Plaza's gate, sheets, fifteen cubit, their posts three and their bases three. ¹⁶All the Plaza's sheets around, twisted linen; ¹⁷and the bases for the posts, bronze, the posts' Y-brackets and their *ḥǎšūqîm*, silver, and their *heads'* plating, silver, for they were *mǝḥuššāqîm* silver, all the Plaza's posts. ¹⁸And the Plaza's gate Screen, embroiderer's work, blue and purple and worm-crimson and twisted linen; and twenty cubit length, and height by breadth five cubit, corresponding to the Plaza's sheets. ¹⁹And their posts four and their bases four, bronze, their Y-brackets, silver, and their *heads'* plating and their *ḥǎšūqîm*, silver; ²⁰and all the tent-pegs for the Tabernacle and for the Plaza around, bronze.

²¹These are the accountings of the Tabernacle, the Testimony Tabernacle, that were accounted at Moses' *mouth* (as) the Levites' Work, *by the hand of* Ithamar Aaron's son, the priest. ²²And Bezalel son of Uri son of Hur from the tribe of Judah had made all that Yahweh commanded Moses, ²³and with him Oholiab son of Ahisamach from the tribe of Dan, a cutter and webster and embroiderer in the blue and in the purple and in the worm-crimson and in the linen. ²⁴All the gold worked for the Task in all the Holiness Task: and the Elevation-offering gold was nine-and-twenty talent and seven hundred and thirty shekel by the Holiness Shekel. ²⁵And the silver of the community's accountings: one hundred talent and one thousand and seven hundred, five-and-seventy shekel. ²⁶A beka per *skull*, the half-shekel by the Holiness Shekel, for each passing over the accountings, from the *son of* twenty year and upward, for six hundred thousand and three thousand and five hundred and fifty. ²⁷And the one hundred talent of silver was for casting the Holiness's bases and the Veil's bases: the one hundred bases for the one hundred talent, a talent per

base. ²⁸And the one thousand and seven hundred and five-and-seventy he made Y-brackets for the posts. And he will plate their *heads* and *ḥiššaq* them. ²⁹And the Elevation-offering bronze: seventy talent and two thousand and four hundred shekel. ³⁰And he made with it the bases of the Meeting Tent Opening and the Bronze Altar and the bronze mesh that pertained to it and all the Altar's implements ³¹and the Plaza's bases around and the bases of the Plaza's gate and all the Tabernacle's tent-pegs and all the Plaza's tent-pegs around.

39   ¹And from the blue and the purple and the worm-crimson they made Textile Garments for attending in the Holiness, and they made the Holiness Garments that were Aaron's—as Yahweh commanded Moses.

²And he made the Ephod: gold, blue and purple and worm-crimson and twisted linen. ³And they beat out the gold plates and cut threads to work amid the blue and amid the purple and amid the worm-crimson and amid the linen, webster's work. ⁴Shoulder-pieces they made for it, fastening; at its two sides it was fastened. ⁵And the woven-band for its ephod-binding that was on it, it was from it, like its work: gold, blue and purple and worm-crimson and twisted linen—as Yahweh commanded Moses.

⁶And they made the carnelian stones, set in gold plait-rings, engraved (with) seal engravings, by the names of Israel's sons. ⁷And he put them on the Ephod's shoulder-pieces, Memorial stones for Israel's Sons—as Yahweh commanded Moses.

⁸And he made the *ḥōšen*, webster's work, like an ephod's work: gold, blue and purple and worm-crimson and twisted linen. ⁹It was foursquare, doubled they made the *ḥōšen*; a span its length and a span its breadth, doubled. ¹⁰And they *filled* in it four rows of stone—a row: ʾōdem, piṭdâ and bāreqet, the one row; ¹¹and the second row: nōpek, sappîr and yāhǎlōm; ¹²and the third row: lešem, šǝbô and ʾaḥlāmâ; ¹³and the fourth row: taršîš, carnelian and jade; plait-ringed in gold in their *fillings*. ¹⁴And the stones, they were by the names of Israel's sons, twelve by their names, seal engravings, (each) *man* by his name, for twelve tribe. ¹⁵And they made upon the *ḥōšen gablūt* chains, rope work, pure gold. ¹⁶And they made two gold plait-rings and two gold rings, and they set the two rings on the *ḥōšen*'s two edges. ¹⁷And they set the two gold ropes on the two rings on the *ḥōšen*'s edges. ¹⁸And the two ropes' two ends they set on the two plait-rings; and they set them on the Ephod's shoulder-pieces, against its front. ¹⁹And they made two gold rings and put on the *ḥōšen*'s two edges, at its *lip* that is against the Ephod inside. ²⁰And they made two gold rings and set them on the Ephod's two shoulder-pieces, below, against its front, opposite its fastening, above the Ephod's woven-band. ²¹And they tied the *ḥōšen* by its rings to the Ephod's rings with blue cord for being over the Ephod's woven-band, so the *ḥōšen* would not slip from upon the Ephod—as Yahweh commanded Moses.

²²And he made the Robe, weaver's work: completely blue; ²³and the Robe's *mouth* in its midst like an anus *mouth*, a *lip* for its *mouth* around; it would not be torn. ²⁴And they made on the Robe's skirts pomegranates of blue and purple and worm-crimson. ²⁵And they made pure gold bells and set the bells amid

the pomegranates on the Robe's skirts around amid the pomegranates—²⁶a bell and a pomegranate, a bell and a pomegranate—on the Robe's skirts around, for attending—as Yahweh commanded Moses.

²⁷And they made the shifts: linen, weaver's work, for Aaron and for his sons, ²⁸and the Turban, linen, and the hump-hats, linen splendor-hats, and the linen underpants, twisted linen, ²⁹and the Sash, twisted linen, blue and purple and worm-crimson, embroiderer's work—as Yahweh commanded Moses. ³⁰And they made the Holiness Crown's Blossom, pure gold, and wrote on it seal-engraving writing: "a Holiness of Yahweh." ³¹And they set on it blue cord to set on the Turban above—as Yahweh commanded Moses.

³²And all the Work of the Meeting Tent Tabernacle was completed. And Israel's Sons did, as all that Yahweh commanded Moses, so they did. ³³And they brought the Tabernacle to Moses: the Tent and all its implements, its clasps, its *qərāšîm*, its crossbars and its posts and its bases ³⁴and the reddened skins cover and the beaded skins cover and the Veil Screen, ³⁵the Testimony Chest and its poles and the *kappōret*, ³⁶the Table, all its implements and the *Face Bread*, ³⁷the pure Lampstand, its lamps—the arrangement lamps—and all its implements and the Illumination Oil, ³⁸and the Golden Altar and the Ointment Oil and the Spice Incense and the Tent Opening Screen, ³⁹the Bronze Altar and the bronze mesh that pertained to it, its poles and all its implements, the Basin and its Stand, ⁴⁰the Plaza's sheets, its posts and its bases and the Screen for the Plaza's gate, its cords and its tent-pegs and all the implements of the Tabernacle Work for Meeting Tent, ⁴¹the Textile Garments for attending in the Holiness: the Holiness Garments for Aaron the priest and his sons' garments for priesting—⁴²as all that Yahweh commanded Moses, so Israel's Sons did all the Work.

⁴³And Moses saw all the Task, and, see: they did it—as Yahweh commanded Moses, so they did. And Moses blessed them.

40   ¹And Yahweh spoke to Moses, saying: ²"On the day of the first new moon, on the first of the month, you shall erect the Meeting Tent Tabernacle; ³and you shall put there the Testimony Chest, and you shall screen the Veil before the Chest, ⁴and you shall bring the Table and arrange its arrangement, and you shall bring the Lampstand and *raise* its lamps, ⁵and you shall set the Golden Altar for incense before the Testimony Chest and you shall put the Opening Screen for the Tabernacle, ⁶and you shall set the Ascending-offering Altar before the Meeting Tent Tabernacle Opening, ⁷and you shall set the Basin between Meeting Tent and between the Altar and set water there, ⁸and you shall put the Plaza around and set the Plaza gate Screen, ⁹and you shall take the Ointment Oil and anoint the Tabernacle and all that is in it, and you shall make it holy and all its implements, so that it will be a Holiness, ¹⁰and you shall anoint the Ascending-offering Altar and all its implements, and you shall make the Altar holy, so that the Altar will be a Holiness of Holinesses, ¹¹and you shall anoint the Basin and its Stand and make it holy, ¹²and you shall Bring Near Aaron and his sons to the Meeting Tent Opening and wash them with water, ¹³and you shall make Aaron wear the Holiness Garments and anoint him and make him holy so that he may priest for me, ¹⁴and his sons you

shall Bring Near and make them wear shifts [15] and anoint them as you anointed their father so that they may priest for me. And their anointment shall be for being for them as an eternal priesthood *to their ages*."

[16] And Moses did; as all that Yahweh commanded him, so he did.

[17] And it happened, in the first month, in the second year, on the first of the month, the Tabernacle was erected. [18] And Moses erected the Tabernacle, and he set its bases and put its frames and set its crossbars and erected its posts [19] and spread the Tent over the Tabernacle and put the Tent cover over it, above—as Yahweh commanded Moses—[20] and he took and set the Testimony into the Chest and put the poles on the Chest and set the *kappōret* on the Chest [21] and brought the Chest into the Tabernacle and put the Veil Screen and screened before the Testimony Chest—as Yahweh commanded Moses—[22] and he set the Table in Meeting Tent on the Tabernacle's northward flank, outside the Veil, [23] and arranged on it a bread arrangement before Yahweh—as Yahweh commanded Moses—[24] and he put the Lampstand in Meeting Tent opposite the Table, on the Tabernacle's southward flank [25] and *raised* the lamps before Yahweh—as Yahweh commanded Moses—[26] and he put the Golden Altar in Meeting Tent before the Veil [27] and censed Spice Incense on it—as Yahweh commanded Moses—[28] and he put the Opening Screen for the Tabernacle, [29] and the Ascending-offering Altar he put (at) the Meeting Tent Tabernacle Opening, and he *sent up* on it the Ascending-offering and the Tribute-offering—as Yahweh commanded Moses—[30] and he put the Basin between Meeting Tent and between the Altar and set there water for washing—[31] and Moses, Aaron and his sons would wash their hands and their feet from it, [32] in their coming into Meeting Tent or in their approaching to the Altar they would wash—as Yahweh commanded Moses—[33] and he erected the Plaza around the Tabernacle and the Altar and set the Plaza gate Screen.

And Moses completed the Task.

[34] And the cloud covered Meeting Tent, and Yahweh's Glory filled the Tabernacle. [35] But Moses could not enter into Meeting Tent, for the cloud tented upon it, and Yahweh's Glory filled the Tabernacle. [36(R?)] And at the cloud's lifting itself from over the Tabernacle, Israel's Sons would set forth upon all their settings forth; [37] but if the cloud would not lift itself, then they would not set forth until the day of its lifting itself. [38] For Yahweh's cloud (would be) over the Tabernacle by day, and a fire would be by night in it, to the eyes of all Israel's House, in all their settings forth.

ANALYSIS

EXCURSUS ON THE LXX TABERNACLE ACCOUNT

I wish to circumvent the quagmire that is the LXX version of the Tabernacle construction, and will content myself with describing the problem and referring the interested reader to detailed treatments.

In general, the Greek version of chaps. 35–40 differs from MT in the order of the parts fabricated, as well as in being shorter. Certain explanatory phrases are missing, and not all elements are included where expected, especially the Incense Altar. (On the problem of incense and the theory that the Gold Altar is a late intrusion, see pp. 369, 514.)

Here is the basic evidence in tabular form. (The hierarchy of Roman and Arabic numerals follows the order of the Hebrew, i.e., MT-Sam. Omissions in LXX vis-à-vis the Hebrew are indicated by * * *; pluses by < >. Verse numbers differ between MT and LXX, and among editions of LXX; for the latter, I have followed Wevers 1991.)

HEBREW	GREEK
I. Sabbath (35:1–3)	I. Sabbath (35:1–3)
II. Materials (35:4–9)	II. Materials (35:4–8)
1. Gold	1. Gold
2. Silver	2. Silver
3. Bronze	3. Bronze
4. Blue wool	4. Blue wool
5. Purple wool	5. Purple wool
6. Crimson wool	6. Crimson wool
7. Linen	7. Linen
8. Goat hair	8. Goat hair
9. Reddened ram skins	9. Reddened ram skins
10. Beaded skins	10. Beaded ram skins
11. Acacia	11. Acacia
12. Oil	12. * * *
13. Spices	13. * * *
14. Carnelian	14. Carnelian
15. *Filling* stones	15. *Filling* stones
III. Craftsmen (35:10)	III. Craftsmen (35:9)
IV. Projects (35:11–19)	IV. Projects (35:10–19)
1. Tabernacle	1. Tabernacle
2. Tent	2. * * *
3. Cover	38. Cords
4. Clasps	3. Cover
5. Frames	4. Clasps
6. Crossbars	6. Crossbars
7. Posts	5. Frames
8. Bases	6. * * *
9. Chest	7. * * *
10. Poles	8. * * *
11. *kappōret*	9. Chest
12. Veil	10. Poles
13. Table	11. *kappōret*
14. Poles	12. Veil
15. Table implements	32. Sheets
16. Bread	33. Posts
17. Lampstand	< Carnelian >
18. Lamp implements	24. Spice incense

19. Lamps
20. Illumination oil
21. Incense altar
22. Poles
23. Ointment oil
24. Spice incense
25. Opening screen
26. Altar
27. Bronze mesh
28. Poles
29. Altar implements
30. Basin
31. Stand
32. Sheets
33. Posts
34. Bases
35. Plaza screen
36. Tabernacle tent-pegs
37. Plaza tent-pegs
38. Cords
39. Aaron's garments
40. Aaron's sons' garments

V. Donors and Donations (35:20–29)
1. Nose-ring
2. Earring
3. Finger-ring
4. *Kûmāz*
5. Gold
6. Blue wool
7. Purple wool
8. Crimson wool
9. Linen
10. Goat hair
11. Reddened ram skins
12. Beaded ram skins
13. Silver
14. Bronze
15. Acacia
16. Blue wool
17. Purple wool
18. Crimson wool
19. Linen
20. Goat hair
21. Carnelian
22. *Filling* stones
23. Spices
24. Oil

23. Ointment oil
13. Table
14. * * *
15. Table implements
17. Lampstand
18. Lamp implements
19. * * *
20. * * *
26. Altar
27. * * *
28. * * *
29. Altar implements
21. * * *
22. * * *
25. * * *
30. * * *
31. * * *
34. * * *
35. * * *
36. * * *
37. * * *
39. Aaron's garments
40. Aaron's sons' garments

V. Donors and Donations (35:20–29)
1. Nose-ring
2. Earring
3. Finger-ring
4. *Kûmāz*
   < Bracelet >
5. Gold
6. * * *
7. * * *
8. * * *
9. Linen
10. * * *
11. Reddened ram skins
12. Beaded skins
13. Silver
14. Bronze
15. Acacia
16. Blue wool
17. Purple wool
18. Crimson wool
19. Linen
20. Goat hair
21. Carnelian
22. *Filling* stones
23. Spices
24. * * *

8. Reddened ram skin cover
9. Beaded ram skin cover
10. Veil
11. Chest
12. Poles
13. *kappōret*
14. Table
15. Table implements
16. Bread
17. Lampstand
18. Lamps
19. Lamp implements
20. Oil
21. Incense altar
22. Ointment oil
23. Spice incense
24. Opening screen
25. Bronze altar
26. Bronze mesh
27. Poles
28. Implements
29. Basin
30. Stand
31. Sheets
32. Posts
33. Bases
34. Plaza screen
35. Cords
36. Tent-pegs
37. Implements
38. Holy garments
XXI. Tabernacle assembly command
(40:1–15)
  1. Meeting Tent Tabernacle
  2. Chest
  3. Veil
  4. Table
  5. Lampstand
  6. Lamps
  7. Incense altar
  8. Opening screen
  9. Altar
  10. Basin
  11. Plaza
  12. Plaza screen
  13. Ointment oil
  14. Anoint Tabernacle
  15. Anoint Altar
  16. Anoint Basin and Stand

3. * * *
4. * * *
7. Bases
5. Crossbars
6. Posts
10. * * *
11. Chest
12. Poles
13. * * *
19. * * *
21. * * *
22. * * *
25. Bronze altar
26. * * *
27. * * *
28. Implements
29. * * *
30. * * *
20. Oil
23. Spice incense
17. Lampstand
18. Lamps
14. Table
15. Table implements
16. Bread
38. Holy garments
31. Sheets
32. Posts
33. * * *
24. Opening screen
34. Plaza screen
35. * * *
  8. Reddened ram skin cover
  9. Beaded ram skin cover
36. Tent-pegs
XXI. Tabernacle assembly command
(40:1–14)
  1. Meeting Tent Tabernacle
  2. Chest
  3. Veil
  4. Table
  5. Lampstand
  6. Lamps
  7. Incense altar
  8. Opening screen
  9. Altar
  10. * * *
  11. Plaza
  12. * * *

17. Wash, dress and anoint Aaron
18. Wash, dress and anoint priests
XXII. Tabernacle assembly execution
  (40:16–33)
  1. Tabernacle
  2. Bases
  3. Frames
  4. Crossbars
  5. Posts
  6. Tent
  7. Testimony
  8. Chest
  9. Poles
  10. *kappōret*
  11. Veil
  12. Table
  13. Bread
  14. Lampstand
  15. Lamps
  16. Incense altar
  17. Incense
  18. Opening screen
  19. Altar
  20. Basin
  21. Plaza
  22. Plaza screen
XXIII. Yahweh's descent (40:34–37)

13. Ointment oil
14. Anoint Tabernacle
15. Anoint Altar
16. * * *
17. Wash, dress and anoint Aaron
18. Wash, dress and anoint priests
XXII. Tabernacle assembly execution
  (35:15–27)
  1. Tabernacle
  2. Bases
  3. * * *
  4. Crossbars
  5. Posts
  6. Tent
  7. Testimony
  8. Chest
  9. Poles
  11. Veil
  10. *kappōret*
  12. Table
  13. Bread
  14. Lampstand
  15. Lamps
  16. Incense altar
  17. Incense
  18. * * *
  19. Altar
  20. * * *
  21. Plaza
  22. * * *
XXIII. Yahweh's descent (40:28–32)

In addition to the foregoing differences, the Greek of chaps. 35–40 differs subtly from that in LXX chaps. 25–31. The experts disagree on what this means, specifically on the question of whether the variation is deliberate effect (Gooding 1959; Aejmelaeus 1992) or evidence of a different author (Wevers 1992: 143–46).

Rather than make an argument here, I shall simply register my informed impressions, which are closest to the conclusions of the most recent and detailed study (Wade 2003):

1. In LXX chaps. 35–40, we have a different Greek writer from LXX chaps. 1–34.
2. The author of LXX chaps. 35–40 was no translator at all, for he was not working from a Hebrew manuscript. Rather, he was summarizing LXX chaps. 25–31.
3. This raises the question of why the first LXX translator stopped in chap. 34. Did he become incapacitated? Did he tire of his task? Did he die? Or did his *Vorlage* also stop there, perhaps concluding with something such as

"And Moses did; as all that Yahweh commanded him, so he did"? By the last theory, MT-Sam Exodus 35–40 and LXX Exodus 35–40 may represent parallel attempts to fill out the text. (One should here distinguish MT from Sam, since in the latter the command and execution accounts are slightly closer in diction than in MT; see TEXTUAL NOTES to 26:8, "and breadth four by the cubit, the one cubit," 10, "in the fastening," "and fifty loops," 18–20, "twenty frame," 26, "crossbars, acacia wood"; 28:20, "Plait-ringed in gold," 23, "two gold rings"; 29:5, "with the Shift and the Ephod's Robe and the Ephod," 21, "from the blood . . . from the Ointment Oil," "shall be holy," 28, "for Yahweh," 38, 41, "its libation"; 36:10; 38:12; 39:9, "doubled," 26).

In most of the following TEXTUAL NOTES, I have confined my efforts to accounting for the MT-Sam family. Any quest after an older form of the text based upon LXX, or based upon nothing, would be a different sort of enterprise, one even more speculative than our customary pursuit.

TEXTUAL NOTES

35:1. *to them.* This is absent from LXX[B] and perhaps the original LXX, presumably lost in the *Vorlage* by parablepsis: a skip from ’*l(y)hm* to ’*lh* (homoioarkton).

† *commanded.* LXX has the blander "said" *(eipen)*. This may reflect a variant *Vorlage* *’*mr*, against MT *ṣwh*, since LXX almost never renders *ṣiwwâ* as "say" (but see Lev 9:6; Josh 11:20). In 35:4, LXX has *synetaxen* 'commanded' and so is more varied in diction than MT-Sam.

† 35:2. *a task may be done.* Tentatively reading *tēʿāśe(h) məlā(’)kâ* with MT and *Tgs. Onqelos* and *Ps.-Jonathan.* Sam has *yʿśh (yēʿāśe[h]) mlʾkh*, as in MT-Sam 31:15, while LXX, Syr and *Tg. Neofiti I* read **taʿăśe(h) məlā(’)kâ* 'you (sing.) may do a task.' In that it is fully grammatical, MT is the easiest reading but hence somewhat suspect. Sam, in contrast, uses a masculine verb with a feminine subject, while LXX switches in 35:2–3 from second person plural to singular (remedied by Vg *facietis* 'you [pl.] may do'). See also TEXTUAL NOTE to 31:15.

on the seventh day a Holiness shall be. Syr and Vg have a simplifying paraphrase "and the seventh day shall be holy."

for you. "For you (pl.)" is absent in LXX and Syr, probably deleted to alleviate the incongruence introduced by reading **taʿăśe(h)* 'you (sing.) may do'; see TEXTUAL NOTE to "a task may be done" above.

† 35:3. *burn.* Where MT has a Piʿel *təbaʿărû*, Sam has a Hiphʿil *tbʿyrw*. Either could be correct; the meaning is unaffected.

Sabbath day. LXX concludes: "I am Lord," i.e., **’ny yhwh*; cf. esp. Lev 19:3, 30; 26:2 for this formula in the context of Sabbath legislation.

35:4. *saying . . . saying.* Kenn 128 and Syr omit the first *lē(’)mōr.* More surprisingly, Syr renders the second *lē(’)mōr* as if reading **laʿăśōt:* "the *word* that Yahweh commanded *to do.*" Apparently, Syr is influenced by 35:1, "the *words* that Yahweh commanded *to do.*"

† 35:5. *shall bring it.* So MT (*yəbî'ehā*). Sam, LXX, Syr and most MSS of *Tgs.* omit "it." My translation follows MT, which feels slightly awkward and yet is fully grammatical (ibn Ezra [shorter commentary] compares 2:6, "She . . . saw him — the boy"; see further Ramban).

†† *gold, silver and bronze.* So Sam (*lectio brevior*). MT, 4QReworked Pentateuch[c] and *Tgs.* put conjunctions before both "silver" and "bronze," while LXX lacks all conjunctions. See also next TEXTUAL NOTE and TEXTUAL NOTE to 25:3.

†† 35:6. *blue . . . purple . . . worm-crimson.* So Sam, Kenn 152, Rossi 503, 592 and a few *Tg.* MSS (de Rossi 1784–85: 78). MT begins with "and," while LXX omits all conjunctions. See also TEXTUAL NOTE to 25:4.

linen. LXX and Syr translate as if reading **šš mšzr* 'twisted linen'; cf. TEXTUAL NOTE to 25:4, "linen."

†† 35:7. *acacia.* Reading *šiṭṭîm* with a shin; *śiṭṭîm* with a sin in L is a careless error.

35:8. *and oil.* Here we begin to encounter major discrepancies between LXX and other Versions of Exodus 35–40, which grow more severe beginning in 36:8. For the most part, these are not to be explained by the mechanics of textual corruption; see EXCURSUS, pp. 631–37.

Like its parallel in 25:6 (see TEXTUAL NOTE), verse 8 is entirely missing from LXX. Oil and incense are also absent from LXX 35:14–15 (see TEXTUAL NOTES) but are included elsewhere (TEXTUAL NOTES to 35:13, "the Table," 19, "for priesting").

† 35:10. *shall come and make.* The subject of the sentence, *kol-ḥăkam-lēb* 'every wise-hearted,' is singular, yet in MT the verbs are the plural jussives *yābō'û wəya'ăśû.* Sam, LXX and Vg, however, read singular verbs *ybw' w'śh* (*yābô' wə'āśâ*). The MT, as it features incongruence in number, would seem to be original; the variant is probably a hypercorrection. We find a somewhat comparable situation in 35:25; see TEXTUAL NOTE to "spun."

† 35:11. *Tabernacle . . . Tent . . . and . . . cover . . . clasps . . . qərāšîm . . . crossbars . . . posts . . . bases.* In vv 11–19, MSS of MT, of Sam, of *Tgs.* and of LXX differ considerably in their deployment of conjunctions. It is not feasible to list all the variants; suffice it to note that virtually all possibilities are attested. For convenience, my translation follows *BHS.* To account for the variation, I would cite primarily the random distribution of conjunctions in lists, with perhaps a greater tendency to add than to subtract over time, and the fact that, in this particular case, most elements in the list end in waw, creating conditions for haplo-/ dittography in continuous writing.

qərāšîm . . . crossbars . . . posts . . . bases. Corresponding to four terms in MT, LXX has two: *mochlous . . . stylous. Mochlos* is a crossbar. *Stylos*, however, is ambiguous, as it can correspond to either *qereš* 'frame' or *'ammûd* 'post.' Since the Tabernacle features *qərāšîm* but not *'ammûdîm*, I assume that the former are intended here (*pace* Wevers 1990: 579); the posts of the Plaza will be mentioned below (TEXTUAL NOTE to 35:13, "the Table"). In short, vis-à-vis MT-Sam, LXX omits "posts and bases" and reverses *qərāšîm* and "crossbars."

35:12. *Chest.* LXX adds "of the Testimony."

Veil screen. LXX has only *to katapetasma*, possibly but not necessarily reflecting a *Vorlage* without the word *ḥmsk*. Alternatively, the original LXX may have read **to katakalymma tou katapetasmatos* 'the covering of the curtain' (= MT-Sam; cf. LXX 40:19), which by parablepsis and consequent correction became *to katapetasma*.

35:13. *the Table.* Before the Table, LXX inserts matter appearing (in different order) in MT 35:8–9, 15, 17: "*and* the Plaza's sheets and its posts and the carnelian stones and the incense and the anointing oil *and*." (The first and last conjunctions are not present in the standard MT.) On the differences between LXX and other Versions, see EXCURSUS, pp. 631–37.

and its poles. This is absent in LXX, which evidently subsumes the poles under "implements." (Also possible, amid the profusion of *w't/kai* 'and,' is haplography.)

and all its implements. Vg omits "all," whether in the interests of brevity or by Hebrew haplography *(kl klyw > klyw).* See also TEXTUAL NOTES to 30:27; 31:7, 8; 35:14, 16.

and the Face Bread. This is absent from LXX, whose list in general focuses on imperishable, solid structures. (Again, given the repetition of *w't/kai* 'and,' we must reckon with possible haplography.)

35:14. *and the . . . Lamp.* Before 35:14, LXX^A treats the burnt offering Altar (MT 35:16), minus various details (see TEXTUAL NOTES to 35:16). LXX^B, however, is closer to the order of MT.

† *its implements.* So MT *klyh* (also Syr, Vg and *Tgs.*). Sam, LXX, Kenn 253 and a Genizah text *(apud BHS)* read *kl klyh* 'all its implements.' We encounter this dilemma elsewhere (TEXTUAL NOTES to 30:27; 31:7, 8; 35:13, 16). On the one hand, the longer reading is ripe for haplography *(kl klyh > klyh);* on the other hand, the longer reading might be the result, not so much of dittography, but of harmonization and a natural tendency to expand and exaggerate. In MT 35:13–14, 16 we find *kl klyw . . . klyh . . . kl klyw,* while Sam *et al.* have a less diverse *kl klyw . . . kl klyh . . . kl klyw.*

and its lamps. MT *w't nrtyh* is absent in both LXX and Sam. Were the phrase missing only from the Greek, we would simply cite LXX's overall brevity vis-à-vis MT-Sam (see pp. 631–37). In this case, however, the common *Vorlage* of LXX and Sam probably did suffer corruption, due either to homoioteleuton with the preceding *w't (kl) klyh* or to homoioarkton with the following *w't šmn.*

and the Illumination Oil. This is absent in LXX, which seems to subsume the lamps and the fuel under "its implements" (Wevers 1990: 580).

35:15. *and the Incense Altar.* All of v 15 is absent in LXX. More precisely: the Incense Altar and its poles are missing, while the anointing oil and incense appear within 35:13, 19 (see TEXTUAL NOTES to v 13, "the Table," v 19, "for priesting").

If this were an isolated case of LXX being shorter than MT, we might explain LXX by a sequence of error and correction: first a scribal jump from v 15 to v 16 (both begin *[w]'t mzbḥ h* '[and] the Altar'); then reinsertion of the oil and incense—but not the Incense Altar—at the end of the list in 35:19; finally, a change of "the Ascending-offering Altar" to "the Altar" (first TEXTUAL NOTE to 35:16), since there is now only one. The scenario becomes far less plausible, however, when we consider LXX's thoroughgoing brevity and, in particular, its neglect of the Incense Altar (see TEXTUAL NOTES to 31:8, 9; pp. 369, 514–15).

35:16. *Ascending-offering Altar.* LXX, which omits the Incense Altar, here has simply "*the* Altar," since no confusion is possible.

bronze mesh . . . poles. LXX lacks both these items, which are apparently subsumed under "implements."

all its implements. Kenn 18, 80, 136, Vg and some MSS and editions of *Tg. Ps.-Jonathan* omit "all," presumably by haplography in the Hebrew *Vorlage*; cf. TEXTUAL NOTES to 30:27; 31:7, 8; 35:13, 14.

Basin . . . Stand. Both of these items are absent in LXX; Wevers (1990: 580) suggests that they are included in "all its implements."

35:17. *Plaza's sheets.* All of MT vv 17–18 is missing in LXX. More accurately: the sheets and posts are shifted to before 35:13 (see TEXTUAL NOTE), while the bases and front screen are simply not mentioned.

† *its posts . . . its bases.* Although the translation would not be affected, I am unsure whether to read '*mdyw . . . 'dnyh* 'his posts . . . her bases' with standard MT or '*mdyh . . . 'dnyh* 'her posts . . . her bases' with Sam, Kenn 4, Rossi 592, 656. Since *ḥāṣēr* 'Plaza' can be masculine or feminine, either would be correct (ibn Ezra). But MT is slightly more difficult, employing both genders in a single phrase (moreover, chap. 27 consistently treated *ḥāṣēr* as masculine). Sam is probably a later adjustment to harmonize the suffixes; see also TEXTUAL NOTE to 39:40.

SPECULATION: Actually, we would expect neither MT nor Sam, but instead *'mdyw . . . 'dnyhm* 'its posts . . . their bases' as in 27:10–11 (cf. 27:17–18). Accidental loss of mem from the second word could have produced MT, with Sam representing a later correction departing farther from the original.

35:18. *the Tabernacle's tent-pegs.* All of v 18 is absent in LXX, whether by '*t . . . 't* homoioarkton or because these components are too trivial and ordinary to mention.

35:19. *the Textile Garments . . . Holiness Garments for Aaron the priest.* Vis-à-vis the other Versions, LXX reverses these two phrases. Perhaps the cause was an old haplography from one '*t bgdy h* 'the garments' to the next, later remedied by the erroneous reinsertion of the lost matter. LXX also appears to interpret *haśśərād* and *ləšārēt* as synonymns (see TEXTUAL NOTE and NOTE to 31:10) and hence paraphrases "in which they shall attend."

† *for attending in the Holiness.* So MT-Sam *(ləšārēt baqqōdeš)*, a phrase paralleled in 28:43; 29:30; 35:19; 39:1, 41; Ezek 44:27. LXX has "they shall attend *in them*," with most MSS (LXX^A but not LXX^B) continuing "in the Holiness." Thus there are three variants, the relationship among which is unclear: "in the Holiness" (MT-Sam), "in them" (LXX^B) and "in them in the Holiness" (other LXX; also LXX 39:12 = MT 39:1).

SPECULATION: One could consider the longest reading of LXX^A et al. a conflation of the other two. The LXX^B reading *lšrt bhm* might be the original, first expanded in LXX^A into *lšrt bhm bqdš* and then corrupted in MT-Sam by *b . . . b* parablepsis into *lšrt bqdš*. Note that, wherever else P uses the phrase *šērēt bāhem*, it refers to the sacred vessels (Num 3:31; 4:9, 12, 14; also 2 Kgs 25:14 = Jer 52:18). In Ezek 42:14, however, the expression refers to clothing, as in LXX Exod 35:19.

† *for priesting.* LXX continues "and the ointment oil and the compounded incense," which in MT appears in 35:15 (see TEXTUAL NOTE to 35:13, "the Table"). Since these were already mentioned in the LXX version of 35:15 (see TEXTUAL NOTE), their inclusion here is redundant. Wevers (1990: 577) attributes the repetition to the fact that in chap. 30, anointing oil and incense follow the manufacture of the priestly garments (chap. 28).

† 35:21. *came.* While MT and Tgs. read the Qal *wayyābō'û* 'came,' Sam (*wyby'w*), LXX, Syr and Vg read a Hiph'il *wayyābî'û* 'brought.' We would in fact expect the Hiph'il, which recurs throughout vv 21–29, and Sam et al. are very likely correct, producing P's characteristic "short-circuit inclusio" (Paran 1989: 106 n. 107–8). Nevertheless, I have retained MT as *lectio difficilior.* See also TEXTUAL NOTES to 35:22, "came"; 36:4, "came."

† *and everyone.* Reading *wkl* with MT. Sam, Syr and probably Kenn 193 (erased) have a longer *wkl 'yš* 'and every *man.*' The case is difficult to decide. On the one hand, since the following word is '*šr*, one might explain MT as haplographic due to homoioarkton (' . . . '). On the other hand, since *kl 'yš* occurred earlier in the verse, Sam-Syr might be harmonistic. For a fuller discussion, see also TEXTUAL NOTE to 35:23, "and everyone . . . whom."

Task . . . Holiness Garments. Before these two items, LXX expands by inserting "all," to match "for all its Work." The converse inference, that MT-Sam twice lost *kl* 'all' by homoioteleuton after *l* 'for,' seems less likely.

† 35:22. *came.* My translation follows MT, despite considerable doubts. Again, Sam, LXX, Syr, Vg all read *wayyābî'û* 'brought,' this time surprisingly joined by Tg. Onqelos. See also TEXTUAL NOTES to 35:21, "came"; 36:4, "came."

† *brought.* In MT, the verb is plural (*hēbî'û*); in Sam, it is singular (*hby'*). Either might be correct; the phenomenon is paralleled in 35:10, 25 (see TEXTUAL NOTES).

† *and finger-ring.* The conjunction is absent in Sam and the Soncino Bible (1488). After (*wə*)*ṭabba'at*, Sam, LXX, Kenn 69, Rossi 543, 592; 199, 611 (first hand), a Tg. MS (de Rossi 1784–85: 80) and *Exod. Rab.* 48:6 add (*w*)'*gyl* (another type of round jewelry), perhaps correctly. If secondary, however, (*w*)'*gyl* derives from a similar list in Num 31:50.

† *any gold item.* Kenn 4, 18, 101, 111, 136, 158, 181, Rossi 10, 16, 17, 230, 262, 419, 656, 668, 669, 766, Syr, a few Tg. MSS (de Rossi 1784–85: 80), several witnesses to LXX and Tg. Ps.-Jonathan insert "and."

Syr and Rossi 10 (?), 17 (?), 529, 579, 683 agree with standard MT *kly*, but read not the singular *kəlî* but the plural *kəlê* 'items.' Either might be correct.

†† 35:23. *and everyone . . . whom.* This time, reading *wkl* with Sam, against MT *wəkol-'îš* (cf. TEXTUAL NOTE to 35:21, "and everyone"). My decision is admittedly arbitrary. In vv 21–24, MT has *kl 'yš 'šr . . . wkl 'šr . . . wkl 'yš 'šr . . . wkl 'yš 'šr . . . wkl 'šr*, while Sam has *kl 'yš 'šr . . . wkl 'yš 'šr . . . wkl 'šr . . . wkl 'yš 'šr . . . (w)kl 'šr.* My translation presupposes **kl 'yš 'šr . . . wkl 'šr . . . wkl 'šr . . . wkl 'yš 'šr . . . wkl 'šr,* the shortest reading possible, albeit hypothetical. (LXX, which never mentions "man" at all, might reflect a still shorter text, but is probably periphrastic.) The alternative would be to conflate MT and Sam, keeping *'yš* wherever possible and assuming it was lost by haplography before *'šr.*

† *blue . . . beaded skins.* While MT-Sam includes "blue and purple and worm-crimson and linen and *goat* and reddened ram skins and beaded skins," LXX has merely "linen and hyacinth (*hyakinthina* = Heb. *tāḥāš* 'beaded') skins and reddened rams' skins." Wevers (1990: 584) observes that MT appears self-contradictory: do the men (35:23) or the women (35:25–26) bring the woven stuff and goats' hair fabric (see NOTE to 35:25, "woman")? The fact that LXX lacks this tension could be a sign of a secondary correction.

† 35:24. *Each.* Perhaps correctly, Sam, LXX[B] and Kenn 6 (erased), 196 begin "and" (*w*). Notice that the previous word ends in waw, creating the occasion for haplo-/dittography in continuous writing.

†† *for the Task of the Work.* I follow Sam *lml'kt h'bwdh* (also a Syr MS). MT-LXX has *ləkol-məle(')ket hā'ăbōdâ* 'for *all* the Task of the Work.' This longer reading is likely inspired by the prevalence of *kōl* 'all' throughout this section, and in particular by *kol-(ham)məlā(')kâ* in vv 29, 31, 35 and *kol-məle(')ket* in vv 24, 33, 35. But it is also possible that MT is original and that *lkl > l* due to parablepsis.

† 35:25. *with her hands.* For MT *bydyh,* Sam and Kenn 84 have *bydh* 'with her *hand.*' But weaving is a two-handed job.

† *spun.* Where MT treats a collective reference to individuals as a plural (*ṭāwû* 'spun' [pl.]), Sam has a singular *ṭwh* (for expected **ṭwth;* see NOTE); cf. TEXTUAL NOTES to 35:10, 22, etc. Either might be correct. MT is grammatically *lectio difficilior* but might be influenced by *kol-hannāšîm . . . ṭāwû* in the following verse. LXX paraphrases the verb as an infinitive ("wise . . . to *spin* with her hands").

blue. According to BHS, a Genizah MS inserts "and."

the worm-crimson. Sam, LXX, Syr, Vg, Tgs. Ps.-Jonathan and Neofiti I and many MSS and editions of MT and of Tg. Onqelos (Kennicott 1776–80: 185; de Rossi 1784–85: 80) insert "and."

35:28. *the fragrance.* So MT (*habbōśem*). Sam and perhaps LXX have the more common plural *hbśmym* 'the fragrances,' as in 25:6; 30:23; 35:8. In Exodus, the singular *bōśem* appears otherwise only in 30:23.

and the oil, for illumination. So MT (*haššāmen ləmā'ôr*). Sam has *šmn hm'wr* 'the illumination oil' as in 35:14, but then the rest of the verse does not make sense, since the lighting oil is not an ingredient of the anointing oil.

LXX lacks entirely "the oil for illumination." Considering 35:28 in isolation, we would recognize a simple case of parablepsis, skipping from one "oil" to the next. But, as Wevers (1990: 586) observes, LXX also omits the lamp oil in 25:6; 35:8, 14.

† 35:29. *every.* Sam, LXX, Kenn 129, 152, 186, 232 and Rossi 549 insert "and."

† *whose heart ennobled them.* While MT has *nādab libbām 'ōtām,* Sam has *ndb 'tm lbm* (cf. Kenn 80). Either might be original.

to bring. LXX has instead "to come and do." This must be regarded as free paraphrase, but somewhat recalls the confusion between "come" and "bring" among the Versions in 35:21–22 (TEXTUAL NOTES).

35:30. *Yahweh.* LXX has instead "the God," perhaps borrowed from the following verse (Wevers 1990: 587).

† 35:31. *in wisdom.* Sam, Kenn 5, 69, 84, 110, 140, Rossi 262, 440, 500, 668, 789, LXX, Syr, Vg, Tg. Neofiti I and many MSS of Tg. Onqelos insert "and." See also TEXTUAL NOTE to 31:3.

† *and in knowledge and in every task.* For a speculative reconstruction of this odd phrase, see TEXTUAL NOTE to 31:3; on LXX, see the following TEXTUAL NOTE.

† 35:32. *and for planning plans.* For the end of v 31 and the start of v 32, against MT-Sam "and in knowledge and in every task, and for planning plans," LXX paraphrases "and with knowledge *of all,* to design according to *all* works of design."

† 35:33. *planning.* The MT consonants *mḥšbt* are ambiguous and find no parallel in 31:5. While MT has a singular *maḥăšābet* (also Tg. Neofiti I and Fragmentary Targum), Sam has the plural *mḥšbwt,* which appears in vv 32, 35 (also Tgs. Onqelos and Ps.-Jonathan). Either might be correct, but MT is *lectio difficilior,* because it is more diverse.

to do. Kenn 1, 17, Rossi 16, 592, 668 and Vg insert "and."

35:35. *heart-wisdom.* LXX *sophias kai syneseōs dianoias* 'wisdom and understanding, intelligence' must derive from 35:31, where Yahweh fills the craftsmen's hearts with *ḥokmâ . . . təbûnâ . . . da'at* (although there *da'at* is rendered by *epistēmē,* not *dianoia*).

† *every task.* Against standard MT *kl ml'kt,* Sam and very many MSS of both MT and of Tgs. read *bkl ml'kt* (Kennicott 1776–80: 186; de Rossi 1784–85: 81; vs. von Gall 1918: 193–94). The meaning is unaffected. LXX has a longer reading: "all the tasks *of the Holiness,*" as if reading **kl ml'kt hqdš.* The reference to "the Holiness" probably anticipates 36:1. See, however, next TEXTUAL NOTE.

† *of craftsman.* Although it is hard to be certain, MT-Sam *ḥārāš* appears to lack an equivalent in LXX. This omission might be related to the previously mentioned LXX variant: against MT-Sam *kl ml'kt ḥrš* 'every task of a craftsman,' LXX presupposes **kl ml'kt hqdš* 'all the Task *of the Holiness*' (in all periods, *h* closely resembles *ḥ,* and *d* closely resembles *r*). This reconstructed LXX *Vorlage* is unlikely to be original, however. First, it anticipates 36:1; second, it forces one to treat the following *ḥōšēb* and *rōqēm* as infinitives not participles. There is a slight chance, however, that behind MT-Sam and LXX lies an original **kl ml'kt hqdš ml'kt ḥrš,* variously reduced by haplography in the extant Versions.

in the blue and in the purple. Absent in LXX, on whose brevity see pp. 631–37.

† *in the worm-crimson.* Sam, many MT MSS (Kennicott 1776–80: 186; de Rossi 1784–85: 81), Syr, Vg, Symmachus, Theodotion, Tgs. Ps.-Jonathan and

Neofiti I and MSS and editions of *Tg. Onqelos* insert "and." Vis-à-vis other Versions, Syr reverses "worm-crimson" and "linen."

and weaver. This awkwardly placed word, conceivably a stray gloss, is not clearly reflected in LXX. Perhaps it was considered to be subsumed under the preceding near-synonymns *ḥōšēb* and *rōqēm.*

Syr has a *lectio facilior* that is probably an inner-Syriac development: *wbzqwr* 'and in cloth,' as if reading something like **ûbā*āreg* (cf. Kenn 69 [?], 104 *wb*rg*), against the MT participle *wə*ōreg* 'and weaver.' While Syr may be a paraphrase to resolve a perceived awkwardness, it is also possible that the original Syr had *wzqwr* (*wzāqûrā**) 'and weaver' (= MT-Sam), later "corrected" as *wbzqwr*.

doers of. So MT (**śy*). Sam **św* 'they did' (confirmed by *Samaritan Tg. *bdw*) makes no sense and must be the product of waw-yodh confusion in the Greco-Roman era (cf. Cross 1961a; Qimron 1972), even though the letters are distinct in Samaritan script. LXX, remote from MT-Sam throughout the verse, paraphrases the last part: "to do every task of design, embroidery."

† 36:1. *in whom.* While MT has *bāhēmmâ* after *ût(ə)bûnâ* (also Syr-*Tgs.*), Sam puts *bhm* after *yhwh.* Either could be correct, and the variation is probably random. But it could also be the result of a mistakenly repaired scribal omission (a few Sam MSS and Kenn 9, 129 lack *bhm* entirely [von Gall 1918: 194]). In both readings, the previous word ends in *he**, creating a conducive environment for loss of *bhmh* due to homoioteleuton. And if the original order was *wtbwnh bhmh* (MT), the visual similarity of *n* and *m* in paleo-Hebrew script could have been a further stimulant to error.

† *Yahweh gave.* LXX has instead "was given," making no reference to the Deity. This is a short, attractive variant, especially since MT-Sam could have borrowed "Yahweh gave" from the next verse. If so, the original text read ***ăšer nātan/ nittənâ ḥokmâ ût(ə)bûnâ bāhēmmâ* 'in whom one gave/was given wisdom and understanding.' In the absence of Hebrew evidence for the variant, however, conservatism favors MT-Sam. After all, LXX may represent a theological revision, a "divine passive" (D. N. Freedman, privately).

to know (how) to do. Tgs. Ps.-Jonathan and *Neofiti I* alleviate the slight awkwardness of *lāda*at la*ăśōt* by expanding: "to know *and* to do."

36:2. *every wise-hearted man.* The Faro edition (1487) of MT and *Tg. Neofiti I* omit "man," as in 28:3; 31:6; 35:10, 25; 36:8.

Yahweh. LXX has "the God"; cf. TEXTUAL NOTE to 35:30.

36:3. *the Task.* LXX preposes "all," probably under the influence of 36:1 and similar occurrences.

Holiness Work. Presumably paraphrasing, Syr has instead "Meeting Tent."

they, they brought him still more largesse. LXX has "they themselves still accepted* the Donation-offering(s) *from those who brought,"* perhaps a paraphrase.

36:4. *came.* Many Sam MSS read either *wyby*w* (also Kenn 69) or *whby*w* 'brought'; cf. TEXTUAL NOTES to 35:21, 22. Other Sam MSS support MT.

† *all the Holiness Task.* Perhaps correctly, Kenn 104, 225, LXX and Syr omit "all."

† 36:5. *said.* So MT; Sam has *wydbrw* 'spoke.' Either might be correct.

36:6. *man and woman.* Against MT 'yš w'šh, some Sam MSS (von Gall 1918: 194) and perhaps the Syr *Vorlage* read 'yš 'w 'šh 'man *or* woman.'

† *must not do.* Where MT has the plural ya'ăśû, Sam and Kenn 155 (?) have the singular y'šh. Either might be correct; for the phenomenon, cf. TEXTUAL NOTE to 35:10, 22, "brought," 25, "spun."

Task. "Task" is not reflected in LXX, perhaps dropped for ease of translation. In general, LXX has some difficulty translating məlā(')kâ; e.g., see TEXTUAL NOTE to 36:7.

† *were restrained.* Against MT wayyikkālē', Sam has wykl 'completed.' Since these variants are nearly synonymous, it is difficult to tell what underlies the ancient translations. LXX ekōlythē, Syr 'tklyw and Tg. Neofiti I 'tklw are closer to MT, while Vg *cessatum est*, Tgs. Onqelos and Ps.-Jonathan pəsaq and a marginal gloss to Tg. Neofiti I 'šlymw more resemble Sam. In MT overall, the verbal root kly is attested 206 times and kl' 18 times—thus sheer probability favors MT in 36:6.

On the other hand, Sam arguably yields the literarily richer text. The conjunction of waykal 'all,' məlā(')kâ 'task,' qōdeš 'Holiness' and 'āśâ 'do, make' throughout vv 1–7 sharpens the allusion to Creation. Compare Gen 2:2–3: waykal 'ĕlōhîm bayyôm haššiššî (so Sam, LXX, Syr) məla(')ktô 'ăšer 'āśâ wayyišbōt bayyôm haššəbî'î **mikkol-məla(')ktô** 'ăšer 'āśâ waybārek 'ĕlōhîm 'et-yôm haššəbî'î wayqaddēš 'ōtô kî bô šābat **mikkol-məla(')ktô** 'ăšer bārā(') 'ĕlōhîm la'ăśôt 'and Deity completed on the sixth (MT: seventh) day his task that he had done, and he ceased on the seventh day from all his task that he had done. And Deity blessed the seventh day and made it holy, for on it he ceased from all his task that Deity created in making.' (On Creation the Tabernacle account, see further pp. 675–76, 691–94.)

36:7. *for all the Task in making it.* Perhaps because the Hebrew is slightly awkward, LXX resorts to paraphrase: "for making the furnishings."

† *and more!* Where MT has the infinitive absolute wəhôtēr, it appears that LXX, Syr, Vg, Tgs. Ps.-Jonathan and Neofiti I read with Sam the unconverted perfect whwtyrw 'and they *had* more,' i.e., they had leftovers. The MT infinitive absolute might also be rendered in this manner, as if a finite verb (GKC §113z).

36:8. *every wise-hearted.* Against the MT singular kol-ḥăkam lēb, Sam, Syr, Vg and Tgs. have the plural kl ḥkmy lb, matching the plural verb wayya'ăśû. (Conversely, LXX puts the verb "made" into the singular.) In general, the other Versions tend to pluralize the original collective singulars retained in MT.

among those doing the Task. Syr has "*and* those doing the Task."

the Tabernacle. From this point, LXX diverges radically from other Versions, presenting the items in a different order and in an abbreviated fashion vis-à-vis MT-Sam. Accordingly, its testimony will be invoked less frequently. For discussion, see EXCURSUS, pp. 631–37.

† *ten.* Before 'śr, Sam inserts 'św 'they made.' Which reading is preferable? Assuming that MT is original, Sam's longer text reflects the frequency of the root 'śy in the verse (wayya'ăśû . . . bə'ōśê . . . 'āśâ) and maybe a quasi-dittography of the following 'śr 'ten.' (Note, too, that in the parallel 26:1, "ten" is preceded by the verb ta'ăśe[h].) Assuming that Sam is original, however, MT is haplographic (ho-

moioarkton). Ultimately, Sam is unidiomatic—we do not expect a verb here—and I judge its reading the less likely.

†† *blue.* So Sam, Syr, Tg. *Neofiti I* and Kenn 5, 186. MT, Vg and Tgs. *Onqelos* and *Ps.-Jonathan* have "*and* blue."

Griffins. Absent in Tg. *Neofiti I* and Vg; see TEXTUAL NOTE to 26:1.

† 36:10. *and five curtains.* So MT *(wəhāmēš yərî'ōt);* Sam and Kenn 69, 75, 157, 232 have *wḥmš hyry'wt* 'and five *of the* curtains.' On the problem, see also TEXTUAL NOTES to 26:3, 8; 36:15.

† 36:11. *on the edge on the fastening.* Against MT *miqqāṣâ bammaḥbāret,* Sam has *bqṣh bmḥbrt.* See also TEXTUAL NOTE to 26:4, "on the fastening."

so. With MT. Sam, Kenn 69 and Syr have "*and* so."

36:12. *Fifty.* The first part of this verse, up through "on the second *fastening,*" is missing in Vg. Apparently it was dropped by parablepsis, since the same words "on the second *fastening*" end 36:11.

the curtain. Syr reads an illogical "the *one* curtain," carelessly duplicated from earlier in the verse.

36:14. *to tent.* For this interpretation, derived from Syr and Tg. *Neofiti I,* see NOTES to 26:7; 36:14.

†† 36:15. *for the eleven curtains.* Tentatively reading with Sam *l'šty 'šrh hyry'wt,* vs. MT *lə'aštê 'ešrē(h) yərî'ōt* 'for eleven curtains.' While this is a general difference between Sam and MT (see TEXTUAL NOTES to 26:3, 8; 36:10), in this case the fact that the preceding letter is *h* might be an additional cause of scribal corruption, be it haplography to produce MT or dittography to produce Sam. See further TEXTUAL NOTE to 26:8.

36:17. *loops, fifty.* Syr "loops, fifty loops" conflates variants *ll't ḥmšym* and *ḥmšym ll't,* the former presumably original and the latter borrowed from later in the verse.

† *the curtain outermost.* Sam (Kennicott 1776–80: 188; de Rossi 1784–85: 81; vs. von Gall 1918: 195) and Vg have "the *one* curtain outermost," as in MT 26:10. This could well be correct—we expect "the one" before "the second"—and perhaps in MT *h'ḥt* fell out by homoioarkton before *hqyṣnh.* Cf. first TEXTUAL NOTE to 36:21.

† *the second fastening.* So MT-Sam: *haḥōberet haššēnît.* But what we would expect is either **baḥōberet haššēnît* or **bammaḥberet haššēnît* 'of the second fastening.'

† 36:21. *the qereš's length.* So MT. Possibly correct, however, is Sam-Syr-Vg "the *one* qereš's length," matching the following phrases, etc. (cf. also TEXTUAL NOTE above to "the curtain outermost" and TEXTUAL NOTE to 26:16). Still, MT is *lectio brevior et difficilior.* Tg. *Neofiti I* has a plural ("the *qərāšîm's* length"), presumably a careless error.

†† *a cubit.* So Sam and Kenn 75, 95; standard MT prefixes a conjunction. See also TEXTUAL NOTE to 26:16.

† 36:22. *arms.* Many Sam MSS read *ytdwt* 'pegs' for MT-Sam *yd(w)t.* See also TEXTUAL NOTES to 26:19; 36:24.

Here, but not in the parallel 26:17, Syr duplicates the first phrase of the verse, "two *arms* for the one *qereš*, two *arms* for the one *qereš*." It appears that a scribe simply jumped back to the end of v 21, which ends "the one *qereš*." The error escaped detection and correction, because such redundancy characterizes the Tabernacle pericope as a whole (e.g., 36:24, 26). Conceivably, however, Syr has preserved (or recreated) the original reading, which would indeed have been prone to haplography; see further below and SPECULATION under TEXTUAL NOTE to 36:30.

36:24. *its . . . arms.* Many Sam MSS read *ytdtyw* 'its pegs' for MT-Sam *ydtyw*. See also TEXTUAL NOTE to 36:22.

† 36:29. *And they shall be.* It is difficult to take *wəhāyû* as past, even though the context requires it (cf. GKC §112*pp-uu*). "And they shall be" plainly derives from the instruction in 26:24, where the future makes sense (GKC §112*ss*). To my knowledge, the only translation honestly to reflect the anomaly is the 1490 Ixar edition of *Tg. Onqelos: wyhwn* 'and they shall be.' My translation assumes that the autograph already contained this error; accordingly, I have declined to restore what the scribe doubtless intended: **wyhyw* 'and they *were*' (Sebhirin).

This reading also sheds light on 26:24, where Sam has *whyw* and standard MT *wəyihyû* (see TEXTUAL NOTE). There I preferred Sam, because, were the original reading *wəyihyû*, the copyist and subsequently the Massoretes would naturally have read in 36:29 a converted imperfect **wayyihyû*, avoiding grammatical difficulty. See further on "they shall be" below; also TEXTUAL NOTES to 36:30, "And they shall be," 38, "and he will plate," 37:9, "will be," 38:28 "will plate," 39:3, "and cut" and 40:31, "would wash."

†† *together.* So Sam; MT has "*and* together." See TEXTUAL NOTE to 26:24.

† *they shall be* (second time). I have again chosen the ultra-difficult MT *yihyû*, which makes the narrative future by carelessly duplicating 26:24 (see TEXTUAL NOTES to "And they shall be" above; also TEXTUAL NOTES to 36:30, 38; 37:9; 39:3; 40:31). The reading of Sam and many MT MSS (Kennicott 1776–80: 189; de Rossi 1784–85: 81–82) *hyw* 'they *were*' I take to be a correction. Syr lacks the troublesome word altogether; either it was deemed redundant with the initial verb or was dropped by homoioteleuton after *wyḥdw*. Other translations (apart from the 1490 Ixar edition of *Tg. Onqelos*) perforce follow Sam's past tense, since the sense of MT is unacceptable. Whichever reading is really original, a further consideration in v 29 is that the preceding word ends in waw, similar to yodh in Greco-Roman period Hebrew script. This created an opportunity for haplography to produce Sam or dittography to produce MT, assuming continuous writing.

† *whole.* So MT *(tammîm).* Sam and perhaps Kenn 686 have *t'mym* 'twinning' as earlier in the verse, creating a degree of redundancy. *Tg. Neofiti I (mt'myn . . . mt'myn)* supports Sam, as probably do other *Tgs.*; see further TEXTUAL NOTE to 26:24.

† *to its head.* Against MT-Sam *'l r'šw*, two Sam MS, Kenn 1, 4, 69, 111, 129, 155, 181, 193, 686 (?) and *Tg. Neofiti I* read *'l r'šw* 'up to its head' as in MT 26:24 (see TEXTUAL NOTE) (Kenn 109 conflates *'l 'l r'šw [sic]*). It is difficult to say whether MT or Sam is original.

† 36:30. *And there shall be.* MT, now with the support of Sam, reads *whyw.* Again, the ancient translations take this to be an unconverted perfect, but it is more likely a careless error in the autograph. Compare TEXTUAL NOTES to 36:29, 38; 37:9; 38:28; 39:3; 40:31.

sixteen bases. As in 26:25, Syr omits "bases," presumably in the interests of economy.

† *two bases, two bases under the one qereš.* So MT-Sam, but this impossibly implies *four* bases for each frame, not two. Kenn 4, 103, 150, 151, 189, 191, 193 and Tg. *Neofiti I* "two bases under the one *qereš*" is most likely a haplographic rendition of standard MT.

SPECULATION: The text should really say "two bases *under the one qereš and* two bases under the one *qereš*," as in MT 26:25 (see TEXTUAL NOTE). The error in 36:30 may go back to the autograph, assuming the author simply miscopied 26:25. Superficially, Syr "two bases *under the one qereš and* two bases under the *other qereš*" appears to preserve the hypothesized original. But this is a secondary elaboration of the difficult MT-Sam. "One . . . other" implies there are two of something; it does not mean "each."

† 36:31. *And he made.* I follow MT, even though Sam offers a more difficult *wyʿśw* 'and *they* made.' It is hard to imagine that, for this verb alone, Sam would use the plural. More likely, Sam reflects the beginnings of an exegetical tradition carried through rigorously in Syr, where all verbs in chap. 36 are plural.

† *one.* The number is masculine (*hʾḥd*) in Sam and several MT MSS (Kennicott 1776–80: 189), feminine in standard MT (*hāʾeḥāt*). *Ṣēlāʿ* 'flank' can be of either gender, but in this section of Exodus it is consistently feminine. Sam's masculine *hʾḥd* has been borrowed, I suppose, from MT-Sam 26:26 (see TEXTUAL NOTE).

† 36:32. *for the Tabernacle's qərāšîm.* So standard MT (*ləqaršê hammiškān layyarkātayim yāmmâ*). But Sam, many MT MSS (Kennicott 1776–80: 189; de Rossi 1784–85: 82), Tg. *Ps.-Jonathan* and MSS and editions of Tg. *Onqelos* (de Rossi; Sperber 1959: 156) have *lqršy ṣlʿ hmškn* "the *qərāšîm* of the Tabernacle's *flank*," as in MT-Sam 26:27. I have, however, corrected 26:27 on the basis of standard MT 36:32; see further TEXTUAL NOTE to 26:27.

he plated gold. After this, Vg inserts "having cast their bases from silver," apparently skipping down to v 36.

† 36:33. *barring.* Because the parallel in 26:28 MT-Sam has a Hiphʿil *mabrîaḥ*, one might consider in 36:33 revocalizing the MT Qal *librōaḥ* as a Hiphʿil **labrîaḥ* (cf. GKC §53q). But, as ibn Ezra remarks, many roots have the same meaning in more than one conjugation. See further TEXTUAL NOTE to 26:28.

† 36:35. *the Veil.* So MT (*ʾet-happārōket*). Sam, however, has simply *prkt* 'a veil,' as in 26:31.

twisted linen. Mšzr 'twisted' is absent from 4QReworked Pentateuch[c], lost due to homoioarkton before *mʿśh.*

he made it. Against the standard MT singular *ʾōtāh,* many MT MSS and a few

Tg. MSS (Kennicott 1776–80: 190; de Rossi 1784–85: 82) read an illogical *'ōtām* 'them,' derived from 36:8, 14.

Griffins. Not mentioned in *Tg. Neofiti I* and Vg; see NOTE to 26:1.

36:37. *for the Tent Opening.* LXX (37:5) has "for the doorway of the Tent *of Testimony.*" And 4QReworked Pentateuch^c reads *l['w]hl mw'd* 'for *Meeting* Tent,' omitting the doorway.

embroiderer's work. LXX (37:5) adds "Griffins" as in 36:35.

†† 36:38. *its posts.* So Sam and most Syr MSS. MT, LXX (37:6) and some Syr MSS insert a conjunction. 4QReworked Pentateuch^c and most witnesses to LXX (37:6), moreover, read "(and) *their* posts," a senseless assimilation to the following phrases (LXX^B = MT).

and their Y-brackets. Syr and some witnesses to *Tg. Ps.-Jonathan* add "five," matching the posts and bases.

† *and he will plate.* Against MT-Sam *wṣph*, we would expect the converted imperfect **wayṣap*. There are three possible explanations: (a) the true reading is an infinitive absolute **waṣappō/ē(h)*; (b) the tense is pluperfect ("he *had* plated"); (c) an early scribe, perhaps the author, unconsciously carried over the converted perfect from the command in 26:37 (*waṣippîtā*). My translation supposes the last explanation (compare TEXTUAL NOTES to 36:29, 30, 38; 37:9; 39:3; 40:31).

† 37:5. *carrying the Chest.* So MT-Syr-Tgs. But Sam, de Rossi 503, Kenn 107 (?) and perhaps LXX (38:4) add *bhm* 'with them.' This longer reading is probably derived from the parallel in 25:14 (cf. also 30:4; 37:27; 38:7); the shorter reading, without *bhm*, is paralleled in 25:27; 37:14, 15. Conceivably, however, MT is haplographic, since the preceding word *h'm* 'the Chest' ends in nun, similar to mem in paleo-Hebrew script.

37:6. *its . . . its.* The suffix is properly feminine in MT, as the antecedent *kappōret* is feminine. Sam has masculine suffixes, since that is more common throughout this section. (A contributory factor may have been that, in archaic Hebrew spelling, both suffixes *-ô* 'his' and *-āh* 'her' were written *-h*.)

†† 37:9. *will be.* I read *whyw* with Sam, Kenn 69, 80, 150, 152, 247 and a few MSS of *Tg. Onqelos* (Sperber 1959: 156), against the more logical MT *wayyihyû* 'were.' There is no doubt that the text *should* say *wyhyw* in the past tense and that the future *whyw* is a careless repetition of 25:20. The question is: how old is the mistake? My tentative assumption is that such lapses are quite old, perhaps original, since they are sometimes shared by MT and Sam, despite a tendency to correct them. See further TEXTUAL NOTES to 36:29–30, 38; 39:3; 40:31.

† *one to one.* So Sam (*'ḥd 'l 'ḥd*). MT has *'îš 'el-'āḥîw* '(each) man toward his brother,' as in 25:20 (see, however, TEXTUAL NOTE, "(each) man toward his brother"). The former is the norm in chap. 36 for both MT and Sam, and also for Sam in chap. 25; the latter is the norm in MT chap. 25. I have arbitrarily assumed that chap. 25 originally used "(each) man toward his brother" consistently, and that chap. 36 originally used "one to one" consistently. The two accounts have been harmonized to varying degrees in both Sam and MT.

37:11. *gold zēr around.* Syr has "a gold rim *on its frame* around," borrowed from the next verse.

†† 37:13. *cast.* So Sam-Vg. MT, Syr and *Tgs.* add "for it"; cf. MT-Sam 25:26. (Sam's omission of "for it" in 37:13 makes the shorter LXX-Vg variant in 25:26 more likely; see TEXTUAL NOTE, "for it.")

of. Against MT-Sam *lə-*, 4QpaleoExod^m and apparently Syr read '*l* 'on.'

37:15. *carrying the Table.* Syr adds "with them"; cf. TEXTUAL NOTE to 37:5.

37:17. *its thigh and its reeds.* See TEXTUAL NOTE to 25:31.

its cups, its kaptōrîm. Before each feature, Syr inserts "and."

37:19. *kaptōr and flower.* Both times this phrase occurs, Syr inserts "and" before each ornament.

and three "almondized" cups. Tg. *Neofiti I* omits the repeated material; cf. TEXTUAL NOTE to 25:33.

†† *on the one reed* (second time). I read with Sam and many MT MSS (Kennicott 1776–80: 192) *bqnh h'ḥd* to match both the first part of the verse and also 25:33. MT *bqnh 'ḥd* 'on one reed' is probably the product of *h . . . h* haplography. (Note, similarly, that many Sam MSS consistently drop the *h* before '*ḥd* in both 25:33 and 37:19 [von Gall 1918: 169, 197].)

37:20. *its kaptōrîm.* Syr inserts "and."

37:21. *and* (first time). Absent in Syr.

and a kaptōr. Tg. *Neofiti I* and Kenn 129 omit the third iteration; cf. TEXTUAL NOTE to 25:35.

for the six reeds. Kenn 129, 178 and Syr prepose "so," as in 37:19 (also Syr 25:35).

from it. Kenn 69 (marg.), 84, 129, 686, Rossi 17, 248, 262 (?) 503, 543, 592, 611, 656, 825 (some of the foregoing were later corrected) and *Tg.* MSS (de Rossi 1784–85: 82) have instead "from *the Lampstand*," while Syr has a composite "from it, *from the Lampstand.*"

37:22. *Their kaptōrîm and their reeds.* Syr preposes "And" and also reads "its . . . its," referring to the Lampstand rather than its branches; cf. TEXTUAL NOTE to 25:36.

one. While MT has the feminine '*aḥat*, Sam has the masculine '*ḥd*; see TEXTUAL NOTE to 25:36.

37:24. *A talent, pure gold.* Although standard MT *kikkār zāhāb ṭāhôr* must be taken as apposition, one might revocalize **kikkar zāhāb ṭāhôr* and translate "a talent *of* pure gold." See also TEXTUAL NOTE to 25:39.

37:26. *and its horns.* Absent in Tg. *Neofiti I*, presumably dropped by waw-waw parablepsis (*w't . . . wy'ṣ*).

38:1. *And he made.* Uniquely, 4QReworked Pentateuch^c has *[wy]'ṡw* '[And they] made.'

† *its length . . . its breadth.* Against MT-Syr-*Tgs.* '*orkô . . . roḥbô*, Sam has simply '*rk . . . rḥb* 'length . . . breadth,' without "its" (possibly also Vg). The case is difficult to decide. On the one hand, the Sam reading is more unusual; on the other, it matches 27:1, and so might be a harmonization.

† *foursquare.* The word *rābûaʿ* is absent in Sam and Kenn 9, 136, 170, 176. Its presence in standard MT-Syr-*Tgs.* might be a harmonization with 27:1; conversely, *rbwʿ* could have dropped from Sam due to a vague similarity with the preceding *rḥb(w)* (previous TEXTUAL NOTE).

38:3. *the bowls.* Syr uses two terms here, both equivalents to *mizrāq: qardālā'* 'cauldron' and *šaḥlā'* 'sparger.'

† *the forks.* Many MT MSS (Kennicott 1776–80: 193; de Rossi 1784–85: 82–83), Sam, Syr, Tgs. Ps.-*Jonathan* and *Neofiti I* and MSS of Tg. Onqelos (Sperber 1959: 158) insert "and."

all its implements. Kenn 69, 80, 129 and Syr insert "and."

38:9. *one hundred by the cubit.* Reading with MT-Sam *m'h b'mh.* LXX (37:7), however, reads **m'h bm'h* 'one hundred by *one hundred,*' a metathesis that is hard to make sense of (cf. Wevers 1990: 613). Cf. TEXTUAL NOTES to 27:18; 38:11.

† 38:10. *bronze.* This is missing in Sam and LXX (37:8), probably as a random omission. But conceivably Sam preserves the original text, MT having been expanded on the basis of 27:11. Cf. TEXTUAL NOTE to 27:12.

38:11. *one hundred by the cubit.* As in 38:9, LXX (37:9) reads **m'h bm'h* 'one hundred by *one hundred.*' Cf. TEXTUAL NOTES to 27:18; 38:9.

† 38:12. *by the cubit.* Against standard MT *bā'ammâ,* Sam has simply *'mh* 'cubit' (also Kenn 107, 129, 132, 152, 155, 160, Rossi 419, 503, 766). The parallel in 27:12 has *'ammâ* without the preposition.

38:14. *sheets, fifteen cubits.* Kenn 132 and Syr insert "and" before "fifteen cubits," thereby joining the previous word to 38:13: "fifty cubits (of) sheets."

38:15. *fifteen cubits.* Syr adds "for the *shoulder*" from the previous verse.

† 38:17. *the posts' Y-brackets and their ḥăšūqîm.* Instead of MT *wāwê hā'ammûdîm wahăšûqêhem,* Sam has simply *wwyhm* 'their Y-brackets.' In general, we find among the Versions variation between "the posts' Y-brackets" and "their Y-brackets" (see TEXTUAL NOTES to 27:10, 11). In the present case, Sam seems to reflect an earlier, unattested reading **wwyhm wḥšqyhm,* reduced to *wwyhm* due to homoioteleuton. Despite a general preference for the shortest reading and a suspicion that my reconstructed proto-Sam is the original text, I have followed MT.

† *all.* Against MT *kōl,* Sam has *lkl* 'for all,' as in MT 27:19 (but not in Sam; see TEXTUAL NOTE, "all the Tabernacle's implements in all its Work"). Either could be original.

38:18. *blue.* Tg. *Neofiti I* inserts "and."

and twenty. Kenn 181, Syr and LXX (37:16) omit the conjunction.

length, and height by breadth. To resolve the difficulty (see NOTE), Dilmann (1880: 364) suggests that *bərōhab* 'by breadth' is an addition. But it is the nature of secondary expansions to alleviate not create unclarity. If glossation has occurred, the more likely original is *bərōhab* 'in breadth' (which admittedly does not make sense), later glossed by *wəqômâ* 'and length' to restore the author's undoubted intent. Cf. ibn Ezra's (shorter commentary) paraphrase, "its width *which is* its height."

† 38:19. *And* (first time). The conjunction is absent from many Sam MSS and Kenn 13, 136, perhaps correctly. The parallel 27:16 lacks "and."

† 38:20. *the tent-pegs for the Tabernacle.* So MT *(haytēdōt lammiškān);* Sam has simply *ytdwt lmškn* 'tent-pegs for the Tabernacle.' Sam's omission of the definite article is somewhat surprising. It is as if the scribe had begun to write **ytdwt*

hmškn 'the Tabernacle's tent-pegs' before realizing that the reference to the Plaza precluded *status constructus* (see GKC §128a).

† 38:21. *the Tabernacle, the Testimony Tabernacle.* MT-Sam *hammiškān miškan hāʿēdūt* is suspiciously redundant and may conflate older variants: *hammiškān and **miškan hāʿēdūt.* In fact, LXX (37:19) has "the Tent of Testimony," as if its *Vorlage* had simply *miškan hāʿēdūt* (Cross 1994: 137).

38:24. *the gold.* Against MT *hazzāhāb,* Sam has simply *zhb* 'gold,' anticipating the following *zhb htnwph.*

seven hundred. Syr uniquely has "*four* hundred." In 38:28, however, Syr has "seven hundred" with the other witnesses.

twenty. LXX^B (39:1) has "thirty," as later in the verse. LXX^A, however, agrees with MT-Sam "twenty," which, as the most diverse text, is presumably original.

38:25. *And the silver.* Vg compresses v 25 into nothing; Jerome may have considered it redundant with v 28. But more likely the loss is accidental, a skip from *qdš* (v 24) to *qdš* (v 25).

†† *seven hundred, five-and-seventy.* So Sam; MT has "seven hundred *and* five-and-seventy." Either might be original.

†† *shekel.* So Sam and LXX (39:2), the *lectio brevior.* MT continues "by the Holiness Shekel," which, if secondary, was derived from the surrounding verses.

†† 38:27. *the one hundred bases.* So Sam; MT has simply "one hundred bases" without the definite article. Either might be correct.

†† 38:28. *seven hundred, five-and-seventy.* See TEXTUAL NOTE to 38:25.

will plate. The verbs *waṣippâ* and *wahiššaq* are ostensibly future tense. While one could translate them as disjunctive pluperfects, the problem is more pervasive; see TEXTUAL NOTE to 36:29, "And they shall be," etc. In any case, emendation to the expected *wayṣap and *wayhaššēq is not called for.

and hiššaq-ed them. Syr adds "silver."

38:29. *And the Elevation-offering bronze.* Instead of "And," Syr begins "All."

seventy. Although the original LXX probably supported MT-Sam-Syr-Tgs. "seventy," some MSS have 370 or 470, the latter figure importing 400 from the end of the verse (Wevers 1990: 636).

two thousand and four hundred. My translation follows MT-Sam-Syr-Tgs.-LXX^A. LXX^B (39:7) has 1,500 shekels but is probably secondary within the Greek tradition (Wevers 1990: 636; 1992: 205). Vg 72,040 is garbled, misreading MT-Sam *šbʿym kkr wʾlpym wʾrbʿ mʾwt šql* 'seventy talent and two thousand and four hundred shekel' as **šbʿym ʾlp wʾlpym wʾrbʿym šql* 'seventy *thousand* and two thousand and four hundred shekel.'

shekel. Tg. *Neofiti I* adds "by the Holiness Shekel."

† 38:30. *that pertained to it.* Sam explicates: "that pertained *to the Altar.*"

† 39:1. *worm-crimson.* Vg adds "and linen." Haran (1978: 173 n. 52) feels "there is no doubt" that linen originally appeared in the verse, since it was a major component of the vestments.

they made (both times). Vg has "*he* made."

for attending. *Lšrt* is absent in 4QReworked Pentateuch^c, probably lost due to overall similarity with the preceding *šrd* (Tov and White 1994: 282).

† 39:2. *And he made.* So MT-LXX^B (*wayyaʿaś*); Sam has *wyʿśw* 'and *they* made'

(also Kenn 69 and LXX^A [36:9]). My translation follows standard MT as the most diverse text.

twisted linen. Vg adds "webster's work," transferred from v 3.

39:3. *And they beat out.* Vg makes the verb singular, to match the following verb *wəqiṣṣēṣ* (cf. next TEXTUAL NOTE).

†† *and cut.* Against the MT-Vg singular *wəqiṣṣēṣ* 'and he (will?) cut,' Sam, Syr and Tgs. have the expected plural *wqṣṣw.* But the tense is still a problem, since we expect a converted imperfect. My translation follows Ehrlich's (1908: 422) emendation to an infinitive absolute **wəqaṣṣēṣ.* But cf. TEXTUAL NOTES to 36:29, 30, 38; 37:9; 40:31 for other tense errors.

the worm-crimson. Against MT *twlʿt ḥšny*, Sam, Kenn 69, 75 and 4QReworked Pentateuch^c have an ungrammatical *htwlʿt ḥšny* (on such constructions, see GKC §127f–g). The scribe was presumably influenced by the sequence *btwk h-* elsewhere in the list.

† 39:4. *they made.* This time, where MT and 4QReworked Pentateuch^c have the plural *ʿāśû,* Sam has the singular *ʿśh.* Sam may well be correct, given the propensity to pluralize throughout the Versions.

at. Kenn 84 and 4QReworked Pentateuch^c have *ʾl* 'to' as in 28:7, against MT-Sam *ʿl* (see TEXTUAL NOTE).

it was fastened. Kenn 69, 104, 129, 132, 136, 155, 264, 686 and 4QReworked Pentateuch^c insert a conjunction: *wḥbr,* as if reduplicating the preceding *waw.* Cf. TEXTUAL NOTE to 28:7, "it shall be fastened."

39:5. *woven-band.* Absent in 4QReworked Pentateuch^c, perhaps dropped due to the general similarity between *wḥšb* and *wḥbr* (v 4; see previous TEXTUAL NOTE).

that was on it. Unlike 28:8, Syr does not reflect *ʾšr ʿlyw.* Theoretically, it could have been either omitted for ease of translation or lost due to waw-waw homoioteleuton *(ʾpdtw . . . ʿlyw).* The phrase is absent also in 4QReworked Pentateuch^c, suggesting scribal error, since this work is not given to streamlining but does manifest carelessness.

blue. Syr and LXX (36:12) insert "and."

39:6. *And they made.* Kenn 107, Rossi 503 and Vg have "and *he* made." Vv 6–7 are absent from 4QReworked Pentateuch^c, presumably dropped due to homoioteleuton ("as Yahweh commanded Moses . . . as Yahweh commanded Moses") or homoioarkton ("and they made . . . and they made").

† 39:7. *And he put.* MT has the singular verb *wayyāśem,* Sam the plural *wyśmw.*

† *them.* Even though the antecedent *ʾăbānîm* 'stones' is feminine, MT and Sam have the masculine *ʾōtām* 'them' (cf. TEXTUAL NOTE to 28:9, "on them"). 4QExod-Lev^f, however, has the expected feminine in the archaic form *ʾwtnh* (cf. MT 35:26).

† 39:8. *And they made.* MT and LXX^A (36:15) have the singular *wayyaʿaś,* while Sam, 4QReworked Pentateuch^c, Kenn 69, 389B, Rossi 262, 265, 592 and LXX^B (36:15) have the plural *wyʿśw.* Either might be correct.

webster's work. 4QReworked Pentateuch^c originally transferred this phrase to the end of the verse. It was subsequently restored above the line to equal MT-Sam.

† *like an ephod's work.* Reading *kmʿśh ʾpd* with MT and 4QReworked Penta-

teuch[c], against Sam-LXX (36:15) *km'šh h'pwd* 'like *the* Ephod's work.' But either might be correct; see further TEXTUAL NOTE to 28:15.

blue. Syr and LXX (36:15) insert "and"; see also TEXTUAL NOTE to 28:15.

and purple. The conjunction is absent in 4QReworked Pentateuch[c].

† 39:9. *they made.* So MT ('*āśû*); Sam has the singular '*šh.* Either might be correct.

† *doubled.* With hesitation, I have retained the awkward MT. Sam lacks the final "doubled" without obvious grounds for parablepsis, and so may be preferable as *lectio brevior.* The parallel in 28:16 lacks the redundancy.

39:10. '*ōdem, piṭdâ and bāreqet.* For the list of stones in vv 10–13, I follow Sam and MT in the deployment of "and." Other Versions insert more conjunctions. See also TEXTUAL NOTE to 28:20.

39:14. *seal engravings.* Syr expands: "*engraved (with)* seal engravings" as in 39:6.

tribe. Paraphrasing, 4QReworked Pentateuch[c] has instead "Israel's Sons."

† 39:16. *two gold plait-rings and.* This phrase, which lacks a parallel in MT 28:23 (see TEXTUAL NOTE, "two gold rings"), might be secondary. But it appears in all Versions.

†† 39:17. *the two gold ropes.* Reading with 4QExod-Lev[f] and Sam (also MT-Sam 28:24) *štê 'ăbōtōt hazzāhāb.* The MT variant *štê hā'ăbōtōt hazzāhāb* (also Sam MSS) is ungrammatical. Presumably, the scribe began to write just **štê hā'ăbōtōt* 'the two ropes' as in the next verse, and never bothered to scratch out the extraneous definite article (for other examples, see GKC §127g).

the two rings. Influenced by 39:16, Kenn 84 and 4QReworked Pentateuch[c] omit the definite article.

on the ḥōšen's edges. Kenn 1, 19, 132, 200, 244 and Syr expand: "on the ḥōšen's two edges," as in 39:16 (see also TEXTUAL NOTE to 28:24).

† 39:18. *the two ropes' two ends.* Against MT's long construct chain *štê qaṣôt štê hā'ăbōtōt* (also Tg. Neofiti I), Sam employs apposition: *šty hqṣwt šty h'btwt* 'the two ends, the two ropes.' See futher TEXTUAL NOTE to 28:25, where the same situation obtains.

While in the parallel 28:25, Syr appears to be corrupt, here Syr and Tg. Onqelos resort to paraphrase, in effect reversing the two elements: "two ropes *that were on* two sides."

39:20. *below.* Syr carelessly has "inside," borrowed from the preceding verse.

39:21. *to the Ephod's rings.* 4QExod-Lev[f] continues "as Yahweh commanded Moses," an accidental anticipation of the sequence *h'pd k'šr ṣwh yhwh 't mšh* later in the verse.

on the Ephod's woven-band. 4QExod-Lev[f] adds an explicating *byth* 'inside,' derived from 39:19.

† *Moses.* 4QExod-Lev[f] and Sam continue *wy'św 't h'rym w't htmym k'šr ṣwh yhwh 't mšh* 'and they made the Urim and the Thummim as Yahweh commanded Moses.' Cross (1994: 139) thinks this could be original, having dropped by either homoioarkton (*wy'š[w] 't [h] . . . wy'š[w] 't [h]*) or homoioteleuton (*k'šr ṣwh yhwh 't mšh . . . k'šr ṣwh yhwh 't mšh*). But we find the same difference in 28:30 (see TEXTUAL NOTE), and so accident is not entirely to blame—especially given a propensity to harmonize and expand in both Sam and 4QExod-Lev[f].

† 39.22. *And he made.* So MT and *Tg. Ps.-Jonathan (wayya'aś)*. 4QExod-Lev[f] (reconstructed), Sam, Kenn 84, LXX (36:30), Vg and *Tgs*. *Onqelos* and *Neofiti I* have *wy'św* 'and *they* made,' as is more common in the immediate context.

†† *the Robe.* Reading with 4QExod-Lev[f] and Sam *hm'yl*; MT-Syr has * mə'îl hā'ēpōd* 'the Ephod's Robe,' as in 28:31. *Hm'yl* is the shorter and, because of the difference from 28:31, more difficult reading. See futher TEXTUAL NOTE to 28:31.

†† 39:24. *worm-crimson.* My translation follows neither MT nor Sam but rather MT 28:33 (see TEXTUAL NOTE). In 39:24, MT and *Tgs. Onqelos and Ps.-Jonathan* continue with a difficult *mošzār* 'twisted,' while Sam, Kenn 9, 69, 107 (?), 129, Rossi 10 (marg.), LXX (36:32), Vg, Syr and *Tg. Neofiti I* continue *(w)šš mšzr* (conjunction lacking in *Neofiti*). I conjecture that the originally short text (= MT 28:33) was expanded à la Sam, and that MT is a garbling of that expansion, perhaps a partial erasure.

† 39:25. *amid the pomegranates* (first time). This phrase is absent in Sam and LXX (36:33). One possibility is that MT conflates two ancient variants: *'l šwly hm'yl sbyb btwk hrmnym* 'on the Robe's skirts around amid the pomegranates' (Sam) and **btwk hrmnym 'l šwly hm'yl sbyb* 'amid the pomegranates on the Robe's skirts around' (unattested). But more likely MT is original, and Sam dropped "amid the pomegranates" either in the interests of economy or by homoioteleuton *(p'm[w]nym . . . rm[w]nym)*. We find a similar situation in 39:9, with Sam ostensibly alleviating redundancy in MT (see TEXTUAL NOTE, "doubled").

39:26. *a bell and a pomegranate, a bell and a pomegranate.* Sam expands and harmonizes with 28:34: "a *gold* bell and a pomegranate, a *gold* bell and a pomegranate." Subsequently, LXX (39:34) and Vg appear to have reduced Sam, either by deliberation or by haplography into "a gold bell and a pomegranante." Syr similarly has "*gold* bells and pomegranates." (The Versions are also at odds in 28:34; see TEXTUAL NOTE.)

39:29. *the Sash.* LXX (36:37) makes this plural, referring to all the priests' girdles, as in 28:40.

†† *blue.* So Sam, Kenn 151, 199, 615, Rossi 3, 419, 479, Syr and *Tg. Neofiti I.* Standard MT inserts "and."

worm-crimson. Syr adds the formulaic "and twisted linen."

† 39:32. *all the Work of the Meeting Tent Tabernacle.* My translation follows MT *kol-'ăbōdat miškan 'ōhel mô'ēd.* Sam (also Kenn 1, 109), as elsewhere, breaks up this phrase with *kl 'bdt hmškn 'hl mw'd* 'all the Work of the Tabernacle, Meeting Tent' (TEXTUAL NOTES to 40:2, 6, 29); this is also the understanding of *Tgs.: maškənā' maškan zimnā'.* (For Sam inserting an article to break up an extralong construct chain, cf. TEXTUAL NOTE to 39:18.) Sam may be original, however, and there is even a slight chance that Sam and MT conflate two still older variants: "the Tabernacle" and "Meeting Tent."

† *as all that.* So MT *(kəkōl 'ăšer)* and *Tgs. Onqelos* and *Neofiti I.* Sam and Rossi 17 *k'šr* 'as' (also *Tg. Ps.-Jonathan* and LXX [39:11]) might be preferred as the shorter, less hyperbolic reading, were it not the case that "as Yahweh commanded Moses" is ubiquitous in the preceding material. On the other hand, MT may anticipate "as all that Yahweh commanded Moses" in 39:42.

so they did. The redundant phrase is absent in Kenn 5, 109, 193, Rossi 185.

39:33. *its clasps.* In 39:33–41, MSS of MT (Kennicott 1776–80: 199–200; de Rossi 1784–85: 83–85), Sam and *Tgs.* are quite mixed in deployment of conjunctions; Syr inserts "and" before each item of the list. With one exception, I have not noted such variants below.

Syr also considerably augments v 33: "the Tent and all its implements *and its rings* and its clasps and its planks *(qərāšîm) and its tent-pegs and its crossbars* and its posts and its bases."

† 39:36. *all its implements.* Sam and a large array of MT MSS and *Tgs.* MSS (Kennicott 1776–80: 199; de Rossi 1784–85: 84) insert "and," perhaps correctly.

† 39:40. *its cords and its tent-pegs.* Against MT-*Tg.* Onqelos *'et-mêtārā(y)w wîtēdōte(y)hā* 'his cords and *her* tent-pegs,' Sam has *'t mytryh w't ytdtyh* 'her cords and *her* tent-pegs.' Cf. TEXTUAL NOTE to 35:17, "its posts . . . its bases."

39:42. *as all.* Syr and Vg lack "all," to match the following verse (and also 39:1, 5, 7, etc).

39:43. *Yahweh commanded.* Syr adds "to Moses" as earlier in the chapter.

† 40:2. *the Meeting Tent Tabernacle.* So standard MT *(mškn 'hl mw'd).* Sam and Kenn 1, 9 (?), 84, 109, 111, 129 read *hmškn 'hl mw'd* 'the Tabernacle, Meeting Tent.' Either might be correct; see TEXTUAL NOTES to 39:32; 40:6, 29.

40:3. *there.* MT-Sam *šm* is not reflected in LXX and is absent from Kenn 1; perhaps it was lost because of its similarity to the preceding *(w)śmt.* But LXX is not a close rendering of MT-Sam in this section.

† *Veil.* So MT-Syr-*Tgs.*-Vg: *prkt.* Sam and Kenn 1, 69, 129, 132, 136, 199 have the anagram *kprt* (also editions of *Tg.* Ps.-*Jonathan*; on the confusion, cf. TEXTUAL NOTES to 26:34; 30:6). The *kappōret* cover is mentioned in 40:20 and arguably might be expected here, too; moreover, the Griffins atop the *kappōret* are said to *skk* 'screen' the Chest in 25:20. Still, in the immediate context, it is the *pārōket* that "screens" (40:21) (Cassuto 1967: 479); thus, MT appears more likely than Sam. If so, "the Testimony Chest" in v 3 is understood to include the tablets, the box, the poles and the *kappōret* cover, as specified in 40:20.

SPECULATION: The discord between MT and Sam raises the possibility that originally v 3 treated both the *kappōret* and the *pārōket* 'Veil.' MT simply lost one and Sam the other (cf. Dillmann 1880: 368). Cf. TEXTUAL NOTE to 40:18.

40:4. *Incense. Tg.* Onqelos expands: "*Spice* Incense."

† 40:6. *the Meeting Tent Tabernacle.* Sam and Kenn 9 (?), 84, 157 have *hmškn 'hl mw'd* 'the Tabernacle, Meeting Tent.' See TEXTUAL NOTES to 39:32; 40:2, 29.

† 40:10. *and you shall make . . . holy.* In place of the MT-Sam converted perfect, 4QExod-Lev^f reads *wqdš*, either an imperative or an infinitive absolute. The meaning is unaffected.

† 40:12. *and you shall Bring Near Aaron and his sons.* So Sam-MT. 4QExod-Lev^f features inverted syntax, probably borrowed from v 14: *'t* (no conjunction)

’*hrn w’t bnyw tqryb* ‘Aaron and his sons you shall Bring Near.’ Either variant is possible.

† 40:14. *make them wear.* Sam, Kenn 196 and Rossi 825 have *wəhilbaštām* as in 29:8 (also Num 20:26), against the synonymous MT-4QExod-Lev[f] *wəhilbaštā ’ōtām* (also Exod 28:41).

shifts. 4QExod-Lev[f] has ’*t hktn[wt]* ‘the shifts.’

40:15. *their father.* Syr has instead "Aaron, your brother," an exegetical expansion.

† *shall be for being for them . . . priesthood.* So MT-Sam: *wəhāyətâ lihyōt lāhem mošḥātām likhunnat ʿôlām.* I wonder whether this awkward construction does not conflate two variants: **wəhayətâ lāhem mošḥātām likhunnat ʿôlām* ‘and their anointment shall be for them as an eternal priesthood’ and **lihyōt lāhem mošḥātām likhunnat ʿôlām* ‘for their anointment to be for them as an eternal priesthood.’

40:16. *so he did.* Absent in 4QExod-Lev[f]. Although Cross (1994: 142) favors this as *lectio brevior,* the fact that the preceding word is miswritten (’*wtm* for ’*wtw*) does not inspire our confidence in the scribe. For the phenomenon, cf. TEXTUAL NOTE to 39:32, "so they did."

† 40:17. *in the second year.* 4QExod-Lev[f], Sam and LXX add an explicating *lṣ’tm mmṣrym* ‘since their going out from (Sam MSS: the land of) Egypt.’

on the first of the month. Syr rearranges and augments the verse: "And it happened on *the first of* the first month, in the second year, on the first of the week. . . . "

40:18. *its frames.* Uniquely, 4QExod-Lev[f] inserts "and its clasps": *wyśm ’t qrsy[w w]’t qršyw.* This makes no sense — the clasps are part of the textile covering, not the solid substructure — and cannot be original (*pace* Cross 1994: 142).

40:19. *and spread.* 4QExod-Lev[f] uniquely has *wyntn* (*sic*) ‘and set,’ as elsewhere in the chapter.

40:20. *on the Chest* (first time). 4QExod-Lev[f] has ’*l h’rwn* ‘to the Chest’ as previously in the verse, against MT-Sam ‘*l h’rwn.*

†† *on the Chest* (second time). Kenn 4 and Rossi 699 have simply ʿ*ālā(y)w* ‘on it.’ More seriously, MT and Sam continue *mlmʿlh* ‘above,’ but this is absent from 4QExod-Lev[f], our oldest MS, and also perhaps from LXX (see Cross 1994: 142). I have followed the shortest reading. The MT-Sam plus might be inspired by the preceding verse, as well as by 25:20; 37:9.

40:21. *the Testimony Chest.* 4QExod-Lev[f] and Kenn 75, 80, 84, 129 have *h’rwn h’[dwt]* ‘the Chest, the Testimony’; for the phenomenon, see TEXTUAL NOTES to 39:3, "the worm-crimson," and 39:17, "the two gold ropes."

† 40:22. *and he set.* Against MT-*Tgs. wayyittēn,* Sam has *wyśm* ‘and he *put.*’ Each variant is equally likely. (Note that *wyśm* consistently appears in 40:21–30, with MT 40:22 being the sole exception.)

† *in Meeting Tent.* Against MT-Sam *b’hl mwʿd,* 4QExod-Lev[f] has ’*l ’hl mwʿd* ‘*into* Meeting Tent.’

† 40:27. *Spice Incense.* So MT. 4QExod-Lev[f] adds *lpnyw* ‘before him,’ while Sam adds *lpny yhwh* ‘before Yahweh,’ as in Lev 4:7.

40:29. *(at) the Opening.* In Sam, the preposition is explicit (*lpny ptḥ* '*before* the Opening'), as in 40:6. In MT, here followed, it is implicit (simply *petaḥ*).

† *the Meeting Tent Tabernacle.* On Sam-Kenn 109 *hmškn 'hl mw'd* 'the Tabernacle, Meeting Tent,' see TEXTUAL NOTE to 39:32. The word *miškan* is entirely absent in Kenn 4, 18, 107, 160, 223, Rossi 296, 419.

† 40:31. *Moses, Aaron and his sons.* So Sam (Kennicott 1776–80: 202; vs. von Gall 1918: 205). MT puts a conjunction between "Moses" and "Aaron."

would wash. I retain MT *wərāḥăṣû*, a converted perfect expressing future, iterated action (also LXX [38:27], Syr and Tgs). Sam, in contrast, has the singular converted imperfect narrating past activity: *wyrḥṣ . . . mšh* 'and Moses . . . *washed*' (also Vg). It goes against the narrative's logic, however, that the priests should wash at this point (NOTE to 40:2). Lev 8:6 will duly report their bathing.

† 40:33. *the Task.* Sam, Kenn 9 (?), 84, 615, LXX and Vg insert *kl* 'all,' as in 35:29; 36:7; 39:43.

† 40:37. *then . . . not.* Against MT-Sam-Tgs. *wəlō(')*, many Sam MSS and Kenn 129 have the more natural *l'*, without the conjunction. Ibn Ezra (shorter commentary) regards the MT conjunction as emphatic.

40:38. *Yahweh's cloud.* Rossi 18 (first hand) and LXX omit "Yahweh's."

†† *by night in it.* So Sam. MT has a slightly awkward *laylâ bô* (also Tgs.); Sam has the more natural *bô laylâ* (probably also Syr). While random metathesis is always a possibility, and MT is attractively difficult, in this case an original *bw lylh l'yny* (Sam) may have become **bw l'yny* (homoioarkton), whereafter *lylh* was erroneously reinserted, producing MT *lylh bw l'yny*.

all Israel's House. Kenn 129, 153 and LXX have simply "all Israel."

SOURCE AND REDACTION ANALYSIS

See pp. 365–71.

NOTES

35:1. *Moses assembled.* Moses addresses the people, so that they may know what to contribute (ibn Ezra, Bekhor Shor). Rashbam further suggests that at this time Moses collects the half-shekel census tax (see NOTE to 30:12, "When," and above pp. 534–38).

In the received composite text, *wayyaqhēl* 'assembled' chimes with *wayyiqqāhēl* 'assembled themselves' in 32:1, where the Israelites gathered to demand that Aaron replace Moses with an idol (Jacob 1990: 1012–13). For Calf and Tabernacle as alternative manifestations of Yahweh's presence, see pp. 151–53.

all the congregation of Israel's Sons. This might include the women, whose contributions are mentioned below (Ramban). But the reference to the men going to their women may imply that the men alone directly hear Moses' words (see further NOTE to 35:22).

These are the words. *Dəbārîm* 'words' bears the additional connotations of "affairs, instructions." Below, Moses will similarly introduce the Tabernacle ordinances with "This is the word that Yahweh commanded" (v 4).

One might think that the "words" in 35:1 are the Sabbath commands alone. In the larger context, however, Moses is actually introducing all his discourse in 35:2–36:1 concerning both the Sabbath and the Tabernacle. On the equivalency of Sabbath and Tabernacle as sacred time and sacred space, see pp. 691–94.

35:2. *task.* The word *malā(')kâ* is ambivalent, connoting either a single task or work in general. In commandments about the Sabbath, it typically describes ordinary domestic labor (20:9–10; 31:14–15, etc.). But in the broader context, *malā(')kâ* also refers to making the Tabernacle; indeed, it is a theme word of the Tabernacle account (below, p. 718). Any task, from plowing one's field to constructing Yahweh's earthly abode, is forbidden on the Sabbath. Lest one think otherwise, the first thing Moses must tell the people, before they consider how to build the Tabernacle, is that it will not override the Sabbath (Rashi). If God himself does not create on the Sabbath (Gen 2:2–3; Exodus 16; vs. John 5:17), neither should Israel.

35:3. *Burn . . . fire.* In 20:8–11; 31:12–17, Yahweh previously ordained a day of rest, without clearly defining the nature of labor. That cooking is forbidden on the Sabbath is implied already in 16:23: "Whatever you would bake, bake; and whatever you would cook, cook" on the sixth day (Cole 1973: 234; Childs 1974: 634; Durham 1987: 475). One might infer the same from the exemption for cooking on the Sabbath-like first and last days of Unleavened Bread (12:16) (ibn Ezra [shorter commentary]). Along the same lines, 35:3 limits the use of fire on the Sabbath. And Num 15:32–36 extends the ban even to gathering kindling.

Exactly what Exod 35:3 forbids, however, is not entirely clear and is the subject of a famous dispute between Rabbanite and Qara'ite Jewry. For the former, while no new flame may be kindled, fires lit before the Sabbath, e.g., Sabbath candles, are permitted (*m. Šabb.* 2–3). For the dissident Qara'ites and Samaritans, however, combustion itself is forbidden. During the Sabbath, there is no cooking, no light, no warmth (Schur 1995: 248–49). The Rabbinic Sabbath is a day of luxuriation; for the other sects, it is, at least in part, an ascetic discipline. Despite the ingenious arguments of medievals such as ibn Ezra (shorter commentary), I see no way to determine the Torah's intent. The injunction *lō(')* *taba'ărû/*tab'îrû* (see TEXTUAL NOTE) could be rendered as either "do not kindle" or "do not permit to burn" (see further next NOTE).

Of all sorts of work, why single out fire making? First, although the longer context refers to building the Tabernacle, 35:3 explicitly refers to the Israelites' home life (see next TEXTUAL NOTE). Perhaps, for them as for us, "hearth and home" were a natural pair, the former capable of representing the latter. Tending the fire would then be the domestic labor *par excellence*—though, admittedly, not all Israelite houses had hearths (Holladay 1992: 309).

Second, combustion may be inherently inimical to Sabbath rest. Fox (1986: 199) comments, "This prohibition perhaps reflects the anthropological use of fire as a transforming force in culture. . . . Since the Shabbat was apparently to be static in nature, or at least transformative of time alone, fire (which by its nature causes chemical changes) could not be employed."

Third, making light is the first and quintessential act of Creation. To desist from making light would then be the opposite of Creation, i.e., to rest (Jacob 1990: 1013). With the creation of light, time began. On the Sabbath, time stops.

your dwellings. From both the context in general and 35:2 in particular, one might get the misimpression that the Sabbath is meant only for the Tabernacle builders. Exod 35:3 reminds the reader that the requirement to rest one day a week applies to all.

But still the language is not quite clear. Does *mōšəbōtêkem* 'your dwellings' connote houses or settlements? By the first understanding, one could theoretically evade the commandment by making an outdoor firepit. More likely, however, the meaning is "settlements," as in 12:20 (see further NOTE to 20:23). But does this then include the Tabernacle? The shrine must be exempt, since burnt offerings are made on the Sabbath (e.g., Num 28:3–10) (*Mek. šabbətā'*; Dillmann 1880: 359; Ehrlich 1908: 413). This seems paradoxical: the Tabernacle builders must desist from labor on the Sabbath, but the priests, once worship is inaugurated, must continually make fire on the Sabbath. One solution would be to suppose that 35:3 originally prohibited *starting* a fire by friction. Feeding an existing flame, however, would be permitted.

35:4. *saying.* In context, *lē(')mōr* could also be rendered "to say [to you]" (Rashi).

This is the word. The ensuing Tabernacle instructions are one of the "words," i.e., commands, that Moses was given on Sinai (see NOTE to 35:1, "These are the words").

35:5. *Everyone noble-hearted. Kōl nədîb libbô* literally means "everyone noble of his heart." We might have expected simply **kōl nədîb lēb*, but the diction is evidently modeled after the fuller 25:2 *kol-'îš 'ăšer yiddəbennû libbô* 'every man whose heart ennobles him' (cf. ibn Ezra). See also NOTES to 25:2, "ennobles him"; 35:10.

gold . . . silver . . . bronze. The catalogue of the Tabernacle's components here conveys the great measure in which the people are expected to contribute (Ramban).

35:10. *wise-hearted.* The biblical writers often evince a sense of inadequacy vis-à-vis the wisdom and artistic skill of their neighbors. For example, Solomon imports Phoenician workers to design and build the Temple (1 Kings 5–7). Sometimes this inferiority complex is even veiled in contempt. Jer 10:7–9, for instance, mocks the supposedly wise nations who contribute silver, gold, blue and purple—the very stuff of the Tabernacle—to adorn a wooden idol. Exod 35:10 chauvinistically implies that the craftsmen who built the Tabernacle were more than a match for the artisans of Phoenicia, including Solmon's architects (see further p. 533).

The text describes two types of heart that together realize Moses' vision of the Tabernacle: the *generous* heart that donates supplies and the *wise* heart that can use them. While the artisan's skill is considered a divine gift (31:3, 6; 35:31, 34–36:2), the people's generosity is innate. We are reminded of Pharaoh's heart in chaps. 7–14. Both by nature and by Yahweh's interference, it was too "heavy" and "strong" to bow to the inevitable and release Israel (see vol. I, pp. 353–54). Unlike the wise and generous Israelites, Pharaoh was both foolish and grasping.

35:11. *Tabernacle . . . Tent . . . cover.* The first item *(miškān)* is the inner fabric of wool and linen; the second *('ōhel)* is the curtain of goat-hair; the third *(mikse[h])* is the leather roof cover. On these and other Tabernacle components, see above, pp. 405–10, 505–6.

35:19. *Textile Garments.* On the priestly vestments, see above, pp. 429–54, 522–28.

35:20. *Israel's Sons went out.* The somewhat superfluous narration of Israel's parting from Moses creates the impression of unanimous alacrity.

35:21. *every man whose heart ennobled him.* Although this might be interpreted as referring to the populace's generous initiative, ibn Ezra (shorter commentary) argues that the subjects are rather the wise-hearted craftsmen, "each whose knowledge made him superior to his fellows" (also Ehrlich 1908: 415). The proof is 35:25–26: "And every wise-hearted woman, with her hands they spun. . . . And all the women whose heart uplifted them, with wisdom they spun."

came. I.e., came back to Moses. From v 21 alone, one might think that the people instantly return with their valuables. But vv 22–29 detail, in reverse chronological order, how the materials are gradually assembled.

brought. The verb *hēbî'* serves as the Leitmotif of 35:21–29; 36:3–6 (see also TEXTUAL NOTES to 35:21, "came," 22, "came," 29, "to bring"). It creates an impression of person after person appearing to deposit valuables before Moses (Leibowitz 1976: 662–63; Jacob 1990: 1017).

Work. See NOTES to 27:19, "its Work"; 30:16, "Meeting Tent Work."

35:22. *came upon the women. Wayyābō'û 'al-hannāšîm,* if correct (TEXTUAL NOTE), is slightly obscure, due to the many meanings of the preposition *'al.* By one interpretation, the women have already returned to Moses, and now the men come "in addition" (Rashi; ibn Ezra; Ramban; Jacob 1990: 1017). The alternative, to which I incline, is that the men approach their wives to accept the women's jewelry (Bekhkor Shor) and spun stuff (NOTES to 35:25) for donating to Moses. In the composite text, 35:22 resonates with 32:2, where the women and children surrender their jewelry in order to make the Calf (cf. Ramban).

nose-ring. The meaning of *ḥaḥ* is clarifed by 2 Kgs 19:28 = Isa 37:29, "I will put my *ḥaḥ* in your nose."

earring. Nezem denotes either a nose-ring (Gen 24:47; Isa 3:21; Prov 11:22) or an earring (Exod 32:2–3; Prov 25:12). Parallel to *ḥaḥ* (previous NOTE), "earring" seems preferable here. (Ibn Ezra, however, concludes the opposite: in 35:22, *ḥaḥ* is an earring, *nezem* a nose-ring.)

kûmāz. We are unfamiliar with this item, mentioned only here and in Num 31:50. While ibn Ezra thinks of an armband, *b. Šabb.* 64a envisions a genital plaque and Saadiah a belt. As for cognates, Dillmann (1880: 360) cites Arabic *kumza* 'clump' < *kamaza* 'shape into a round form.' For further dicussion, see Houtman (2000: 351).

elevated a gold Elevation-offering. I.e., made a gift to Yahweh. The text appears to distinguish the gold "Elevation-offering" *(tənûpâ)* from the silver and bronze

"Donation-offering" (*tərûmâ*) in 35:24, but the terms are closely related (cf. 29:27, "that is elevated and that is donated") and may constitute a hendiadys (NOTE to 29:24, 27). Note that 38:29 calls the bronze *tənûpâ* not *tərûmâ*.

35:25. *woman*. By one reading, the text features hysteron proteron, jumping back in time to explain where the fabric came from. That is, the men approach their women (v 22) and commission them to spin the cloth (v 25), which they then present to Moses (v 23). Alternatively, v 23 refers to raw materials that the men bring to the women (I. Herzog in Spanier 1987: 98).

spun. In many cultures, cloth is a treasure produced by women, a symbol of the social texture created by marriage (see the essays in Weiner and Schneider [1989], esp. pp. 33–72). Spinning was specifically women's work in the cultures of the Mediterranean (Pliny *Natural History* 8.74) and Near East, including the modern Bedouin (Cassuto 1967: 347). In the Bible, the spindle is a sign of effeminacy (2 Sam 3:29; Prov 31:19). On techniques of spinning, see Vogelsang-Eastwood (2000: 271–74).

In contrast to spinning, the gender-specificity of weaving is less clear-cut. In Homer's world, weaving was women's work (e.g., Penelope at her loom); according to Josephus *War* 1.479, making men weave was a punishment. Yet Herodotus reports with surprise that in Egypt men wove (*Histories* 2.35), and the weavers of the Tabernacle are unambiguously male, denoted by the masculine participles *'ōrēg, rōqēm* and *hōšēb*. The Bible mentions women weavers only in 2 Kgs 23:7, as part of the Asherah cult.

Several interpretations are possible. First, in Israel, weaving may simply have been practiced by either sex. Second, perhaps women engaged in domestic weaving, men in industrial-scale weaving. Third, the Tabernacle may be atypical: the men signify their submission to God by engaging in feminine behavior (Dillmann 1880: 360; cf. NOTE to 15:1, "Israel's Sons" and Eilberg-Schwartz 1994, esp. pp. 137–62.)

Exod 35:25 features minor grammatical incongruity. While the subject is singular (*kol-'iššâ* 'every woman'), the verb is plural (MT *ṭāwû*), as if the subject were **kol-hannāšîm* 'all the women,' as in the following verse. Sam, however, has a singular *ṭwh* (we would expect **ṭwth*, but see GKC §76*i* for parallels).

they brought. The subjects of *wayyābî'û* (masc.) are the men, who convey the wool.

spinning-stuff. *Maṭwe(h)* may connote the fleeces, already dyed, from which the women spin threads, which in turn the men weave into fabric. Alternatively, it may describe the finished fabrics that the men present to Moses.

35:27. *chieftains*. The tribal leaders contribute the imported luxury goods: gems and spices.

filling stones. Perhaps each chieftain brings his own tribal gem for the Priest's pectoral (Bekhor Shor).

35:30. *See*. The command is now plural (*rə'û*), addressed to all Israel. Originally, Yahweh had commanded Moses alone (*rə'ē[h]*, 31:2) (ibn Ezra [shorter commentary]).

35:32. *planning plans*. Alternative translations of *hǎšōb mahǎšābōt* might be "crafting handicrafts" or "inventing inventions."

35:35. *to direct*. This deserves mention, because not all who are skilled can teach (ibn Ezra).

carver. As we learned from 31:5 (see NOTE, "stone carving . . . wood carving"), *ḥrš* can connote specifically gem- or wood-carving.

and weaver. *'Ōrēg* denotes the least skilled weaver (Haran 1978: 160).

36:1. *will make*. MT and Sam *wəʿāśâ* is a converted perfect, i.e., the future tense. But of all the ancient translations, only *Tg. Ps.-Jonathan* so interprets the verb. The others implausibly construe it as past tense (as if *wayyaʿaś), making 36:1 not the continuation of Yahweh's command but the beginning of its fulfill- ment. (Perhaps the ancient translators were influenced by the perfect verb *nātan* 'gave.') This misreading is why in our Bibles, the verse is detached from chap. 35, to which it properly belongs (Dillmann 1880: 361). We encounter less easily dispelled tense problems in 36:29–30; 37:9, 38; 39:3; 40:31 (see TEXTUAL NOTES).

for all that Yahweh commanded. *Ləkōl 'ăšer-ṣiwwâ yahwe(h)* could also be trans- lated "*in accordance with* all that Yahweh commanded" (Syr).

36:2. *called*. Having addressed the entire people, Moses turns to the craftsmen and their leaders.

to approach. The verb *qārab* refers to participation in religious rites, whether the *Pesaḥ* (12:48), Altar service (40:32) or censing before Yahweh (Lev 16:1). For further discussion, see Milgrom (1991: 577–78).

36:3. *they took*. The artificers carried away from the national hoard the materi- als necessary for their specific tasks.

36:4. *came*. Before Moses, perhaps to his tent (ibn Ezra).

man (by) man. Or "each man." Having divided up the labor, the workers are si- multaneously engaged in their specialties, supervised by Bezalel and Oholiab.

from his task. The job of carting off the people's donations impedes the crafts- men's progress.

36:5. *more than enough for the Work*. There is irony in the artisans' complaint. Once, the people complained about their forced servitude *('ăbōdâ)* to Pharaoh. Now, the craftsmen lament Israel's insatiable eagerness in Yahweh's Work *('ăbōdâ)*. Reading the redacted Torah, we naturally impute their generosity in part to guilt and fear after the Gold Calf incident (chap. 32).

36:6. *they made a voice pass*. The ancient translations correctly take this to refer to an anonymous herald or heralds.

task(s) for the Holiness Donation-offering. Sforno thinks that "task(s)" refers specifically to making fabrics and hewing wood. These were needed in precise, predetermined quantities, unlike the precious metals.

36:7. *the Task*. How should we understand *hamməlā(')kâ*? For Rashi, "Task" here implies the effort of bringing the Donation-offering. Ramban however, ob- serves (apropos of v 6) that *məlā(')kâ* can connote valuables as the fruits of labor, e.g., in Gen 33:14; Exod 22:7; 1 Sam 15:9 (also Ehrlich 1908: 418; 1969: 206). Fi- nally, ibn Ezra thinks the referent is the portion of the work already accom- plished—i.e., what had been done already was enough.

enough for them. Enough for whom? According to Rashi, for the artisans. But ibn Ezra (shorter commentary) adds the possibility "for each man and woman"—

i.e., each had contributed his or her share. And Rashbam thinks the mem of *dayyām* is adverbial and not to be translated at all; the meaning is simply "enough."

and more! Or "and they had a surplus" (Dillmann 1880: 362; cf. TEXTUAL NOTE). The entire convoluted verse might be paraphrased: "They had more than enough materials to work with in order to make the Tabernacle."

One might have expected Yahweh to set a fixed amount for the donation, or to ensure miraculously that the correct amount is given (cf. 16:18). Instead, he allows the people to demonstrate the full measure of their generosity. Perhaps this is why the Tabernacle instructions do not specify weights for metal objects such as the Griffins and the silver post-bases (but contrast 25:39, for the Lampstand). Ramban comments that Yahweh is depicted as less rapacious than the stereotypical tyrant, whose needs are limitless. As for the surplus, Bekhor Shor (on 38:25) plausibly conjectures that it is deposited in the Tabernacle's treasury (but see pp. 534–38).

36:10. *he fastened.* In v 8, the subject was plural, referring to the craftsmen; but from v 10 onward, through chap. 38, it is singular. Does Bezalel make the Tabernacle single-handed? Probably not. The third person singular is often used in an impersonal sense, tantamount to a passive (cf. GKC §144d). So we could paraphrase, "five of the curtains were fastened." See also NOTE to 39:1, "they made."

36:13. *the Tabernacle was one.* The text does not explain what is done with the excess fabric (contrast 26:9b, 12–13). Hyatt (1980: 273, 329) infers that the author of the Tabernacle execution texts (for him, a later hand) simply did not understand the instructions in chap. 29. More likely, the writer wished to be brief. In any case, the matter of the overhang will become relevant only once Moses spreads the Tabernacle on its frame (chap. 40). In chap. 36, the people are still assembling its components.

36:14. *to tent.* Understanding *l'hl* with Syr (contrast Syr 26:7); it could also be rendered "as a tent." Tg. *Neofiti I* (*ḥpyy lmyprs*) and Vg *ad operiendum tectum* 'covering as a tent' combine both understandings. See further NOTE to 26:7, "to tent."

36:19. *for the Tent.* Or: "to be a tent" (ibn Ezra).

36:29. *they shall be . . . they shall be.* On the tense, see TEXTUAL NOTES.

36:30. *two bases, two bases under the one qereš.* On the meaning and the likely original text, see TEXTUAL NOTE.

36:36. *their Y-brackets gold.* I.e., gold-plated (cf. NOTE to 26:32, "Y-brackets").

36:38. *and he will plate.* On the tense discrepancy, see TEXTUAL NOTE, "and he will plate."

their heads. In my understanding, each post is surmounted by a forked "head," also called a *wāw* 'Y-bracket.' These are plated in precious metal (see NOTE to 26:32, "Y-brackets").

37:1. *Bezalel.* His role is stressed only for the most holy Testimony Chest (ibn Ezra, Ramban). It is unclear whether Bezalel personally makes *all* the remaining sancta (ibn Ezra) or just the most important items (on the use of the third person singular, see NOTE to 36:10).

37:5. *he inserted the poles into the rings.* This seems redundant with 40:20, "And he . . . put the poles on the Chest" (cf. also Num 4:6). Ehrlich (1969: 206) infers that that in 37:5, Bezalel merely *fits* the poles to the rings (see also NOTE to 25:15).

37:9. *will be.* On the tense, see TEXTUAL NOTE.

37:25. *Incense Altar.* The commissioning narrative (chaps. 25–31) treated the Golden Altar apart from the other Tabernacle furniture (30:1–10). In contrast, the execution narrative includes it in its proper place (on the problem, see pp. 369, 514). Unlike 30:10, chap. 37 does not refer to the incense rite on Clearing Day (Yom Kippur), because it will be treated fully in Leviticus 16 (Childs 1974: 636).

37:29. *Ointment Oil . . . Herb Incense.* In the interest of brevity, the text omits the details of 30:22–38, contenting itself with "compounder's work" (Ramban). (On other material omitted in chap. 37, see Durham 1987: 484.)

Holiness . . . pure. On *qōdeš* and *ṭāhôr* in apposition, see also 30:35, apropos of incense (Ehrlich 1908: 420).

38:2. *plated it bronze.* This is an anachronism in P (cf. pp. 691–94). The Altar will not be plated till Num 17:1–5, when Korah's bronze censers are devoted for this purpose (unless Numbers simply describes a re-plating).

38:8. *mirrors.* In Antiquity, mirrors were made not of glass but of burnished metal, especially copper (which may be meant by *nəḥōšet* here). For photographs of mirrors, see *ANEP* 21, 23, figs. 71, 76, 78.

Is there any special significance to mirrors, as opposed to other objects of copper or bronze? There is a natural association between washing and mirrors, although the Basin is for cleaning hands and feet, not the face. A burnished inner surface would have enhanced the water's natural reflective properties.

Why do the mirrors come specifically from women—the mysterious *ṣōbə'ōt* (next NOTE)? The gift of valuable metal corresponds to other donations of women's finery (35:22) (Ramban). Comparing the catalog of fripperies in Isa 3:16–24, ibn Ezra detects an ascetic renunciation of vanity (see also next NOTE). And Bekhor Shor interprets the Basin as a silent admonition to marital fidelity, as it presumably supplies the water for the adultery ordeal (Num 5:11–31).

Other commentators take a suprisingly positive view of self-beautification. The Midrash regards the mirrors as already consecrated by the women's heroic cosmetic efforts, without which the people would not have so proliferated in Egypt (Ginzberg 1928: 3.174–75).

In addition to primping, the mirrors might have a sacred or magical function. Underlying 38:8 may even be a common belief that mirrors attract demons and ghosts (cf. Crawley 1961; Litvinski 1987). As the mirrors are converted into a vessel of purification, malefic spirits are deprived of a potential place of manifestation (as distorted human figures). (On Priestly rituals and demonology, see pp. 446, 535.)

The mirrors seem to stand apart from the greater bronze Elevation-offering, which may be why the Basin is omitted from the list of bronze furnishings in 38:29–31 (Rashi). It is made for the priests, whereas the other sancta are for Yahweh (Cassuto 1967: 467).

ṣōbə'ōt-women who ṣābā(')-ed. *Ṣōbə'ōt* is a much-discussed enigma. Tradition regards these women as "assembling" *(ṣb')* at the Tabernacle for religious devotions: e.g., fasting, prayer and study (ibn Ezra; cf. LXX [38:26], Syr, *Tgs.*). But ordinarily the root *ṣb'* refers to a *military* muster, as in the common noun *ṣābā'* 'army.' Might the *ṣōbə'ōt* be female guards (Vg)? Some official function, not necessarily warlike, is suggested by Num 4:23, 35, 39, 43; 8:24-25, where the same root connotes the Levites' service (Luzzatto); overall, P often applies military images to the Wilderness period. "Meeting Tent Opening" is frequently described as the site of religious observances, specifically sacrifice. Perhaps the *ṣōbə'ōt* are entrusted with examining women for ritual impurity, just as later Levites excluded the unclean from the Temple (2 Chr 23:19), or perhaps they assist with the sacrifices. Some, however, suppose that *ṣōbə'ōt* are simply female relatives of the priests and Levites, attending to such "women's work" as baking, cleaning, consorting with the clergy, singing and dancing (Dillmann 1880: 363); see SPECULATION below. If the *ṣōbə'ōt* are, in essence, female Levites, it is noteworthy that their donation of bronze is paralleled by another extraordinary bronze contribution: the consecration of Korah the Levite's censers and their recycling as plating for the Altar.

The foregoing explanations do not impute any special signficance to the mirrors, beyond the fact that any woman might naturally own one. But what if mirrors are particular to *ṣōbə'ōt*? That is, what if *ṣōbə'ōt* are especially alluring? Compare 1 Sam 2:22, where Eli's sons offend Yahweh by "lying with the *ṣōbə'ōt* women (at) Meeting Tent Opening" (although the key phrase is absent in OG-4QSam[a] and may be secondary [McCarter 1980: 81; Tov 2001: 273]). Some have supposed that sexual intercourse is the original purpose of *ṣōbə'ōt*—i.e., they are either sacred prostitutes (Morgenstern 1966: 97) or women seeking husbands (Ehrlich 1908: 420-21; 1969: 207; compare Judg 21:19-21; *m. Taʿan.* 4:8 for matchmaking in ritual contexts). As for etymology, Ehrlich divorces *ṣōbə'ōt* from *ṣb'* 'muster' (cognate to Arabic *ṣaba'a* 'to go forth'), invoking instead Arabic *ṣbw/y* 'to act foolishly or amorously,' presumably related to Aramaic *ṣəbā'* and Akkadian *ṣabû* 'desire' (cf. also Hebrew *ṣəbî* 'beauty, adornment'). By this approach, it would be natural for *ṣōbə'ōt* to possess mirrors (cf. Hyatt 1971: 330), symbols of love deities in Greece and elsewhere (for cultic mirrors in Egypt, see Görg 1984; on mirrors in general, Litvinski 1987: 558; on Israelite and ancient Near Eastern cultic sexuality, Wacker 1992).

Admittedly, 1 Sam 2:22 is hardly decisive. In fact, one might come to the opposite conclusion: the *ṣōbə'ōt* are essentially nuns, like the Roman Vestals and the Mesopotamian *enētu*. This would make the Elides' sex crime in 1 Sam 2:22 even more heinous. In Exodus, the women's donation of mirrors would betoken their renunciation of sex (cf. Houtman 2000: 572), since celibacy was required in Yahweh's presence (NOTES to 19:15).

SPECULATION: Although the text never says so, one assumes that the priests are celibate while the Tabernacle is standing. The Great Priest cannot even leave the sacred precinct (Lev 21:12). Might the *ṣōbə'ōt* be their wives, perforce also celibate until camp is broken?

(at) Meeting Tent Opening. From Exodus alone, it would be slightly unclear whether "Meeting Tent Opening" is where the women ṣābā(') (see previous NOTE) or where the Basin stands (cf. 30:18). The parallel in 1 Sam 2:22 (MT) suggests that the former is the intent.

Here we have another example of Priestly anachronism (see pp. 591–93): the Basin was made before there ever was a Meeting Tent Opening (Ramban)! In effect, the sense is "the ṣōbǝ'ōt-women who *would* ṣābā(') (at) Meeting Tent Opening" (Jacob 1990: 1030).

38:10. *Y-brackets . . . ḥǎšūqîm.* On these features, see NOTES to 26:32, 27:10.

38:18. *length, and height by breadth.* The wording is strange, as the Plaza Screen should possesses only two dimensions: twenty cubits long by five cubits high. What is the point of *wǝqômâ bǝrōḥab* 'and height by breadth?' Most likely the verse's continuation provides the answer: the Screen is composed of sheets like the Plaza's, which apparently measured five cubits square.

38:21. *These.* I.e., the following (Ramban, Rashbam; vs. Rashi, ibn Ezra).

accountings. No one translation suffices for the root pqd (see NOTE to 3:16, "acknowledge"; 30:12, "accountings"). Here *pǝqûdîm* combines notions of amassing, overseeing, taking on deposit and record-keeping. It refers not to the foregoing narration of manufacture but to the following tallies of materials. The section is rather like a final business accounting—specifying the parties, what they did and how much material they used. Amusingly, *Exod. Rab.* 51:2, 6 imagines the Israelites accusing Moses of embezzlement, and so Moses in effect produces the receipts (D. N. Freedman privately compares Samuel's self-exculpation in 1 Sam 12:3–5). For an illustration of Egyptian metalsmiths taking an inventory by weight, see *ANEP* 40, fig. 133.

Testimony Tabernacle. I.e., the Tabernacle housing the Chest housing the Testimony ('ēdūt) Tablets. There is also a play with the Tabernacle's other name, "Meeting (mô'ēd) Tent" (see p. 385).

the Levites' Work. This is generally taken (e.g., by Rashi) as a reference to the Levites' role in transporting the Tabernacle (Numbers 4; 7:1–8), but why bring that up here? Admittedly, P is prone to anachronism (see pp. 691–94), but this seems a rather trivial matter to merit anticipation.

The simpler explanation is that Ithamar and the Levites are here entrusted with *collecting* and *bookkeeping.* Although their "Work" would one day be caring for and transporting the Tabernacle, their first "Work" is as treasurers. The following numbers ostensively derive from their records.

38:24. *worked.* 'Āśûy presumably means "processed"—by smelting (Hurowitz 1986: 289 n. 1), casting, beating, etc. Vg, however, translates it as *expensum* 'weighed out.'

Elevation-offering. I.e., the gold was transferred from private to divine ownership. See NOTE to 29:24.

nine-and-twenty. Although often decried as exorbitant, the figure is not obviously fantastical (see next NOTE). Only slightly more gold (thirty talents) was sent by Hezekiah to Sennacherib (2 Kgs 18:14; *ANET* 288). Solomon was supposedly accustomed to receiving gifts of 120 talents of gold from friendly kings (1 Kgs 9:14; 10:10), while his own internal revenues yielded 666 talents (1 Kgs

10:14). Similarly, Ezra 8:26 claims to have brought back to Jerusalem golden vessels to the weight of 100 talents. According to 1 Chr 22:14; 29:4, 7, David bequeathed 100,000 talents (c. 3,780 tons) of gold to Solomon for the Temple (see also Dillmann 1880: 365; Kitchen 1997: 147–48)! We can also gauge the reality of the Tabernacle gold by comparing the almost two million troy ounces of gold (c. 68.5 tons/62,000 kg.) produced in California in 1850 (Boxall 2000). See further next NOTE.

talent. The *kikkār* is equivalent to 3,000 shekels. Thus the entire amount of gold is 87,730 shekels. Since we know from 25:39 that the Lampstand and its paraphernalia weigh a talent, all the other gold of the Tabernacle amounts to 84,730 shekels (c. 2,134 lbs./970 kg.). Some must plate the Incense Altar, Table, Testimony Chest and Tabernacle framework (including their gold rings) and also be made into threads woven into Aaron's vestments. The remainder, presumably the majority, may go to the *kappōret* atop the Chest. But a lid weighing over a ton would surely crush the wooden box beneath.

Holiness Shekel. See NOTE to 30:13, "Holiness Shekel."

38:25. *silver of the community's accountings.* Bekhor Shor asks: why are only the gold and bronze (vv 24, 29) but not the silver called a *tənûpâ* 'Elevation-offering.' The silver stands apart, he explains, as an obligatory tax. And yet 30:11–16 and 35:24 call the census silver a *tərûmâ* 'Donation-offering' (Cassuto 1967: 472), a term elsewhere associated with *tənûpâ* (e.g., 29:26–28). Thus that 38:25 does not call the silver an Elevation-offering may be mere happenstance.

38:26. *beka.* Inscribed limestone *bqʿ* weights from Judah weigh between 5 and 7 grams (Kletter 1998: 211–17 243).

per the skull. Per capita; see NOTE to 30:12, "lift the head."

passing. See NOTE to 30:13, "passing over the accountings."

six hundred thousand . . . and fifty. On the census and its result, see pp. 534–38. P's figure of 603,550 adult men correlates with E's "about six hundred thousand"; see NOTE to 12:37.

At a rate of a half-shekel per head, the total silver was 301,775 shekels (c. 7,600 lbs./3,447 kg.). Of this, 100 talents (300,000 shekels) went to the silver bases.

38:27. *one hundred bases.* There are forty-eight *qərāšîm* with ninety-six bases, plus four silver bases for the four Veil posts.

38:28. *plated their heads.* It is not clear whether "their" refers to the posts or the Y-brackets. My assumption is that the Y-bracket *is* the silver-plated post head (NOTE to 26:32, "Y-brackets").

Since the Plaza is framed by 56 posts, plus 4 posts for the Plaza screen, and assuming each post is associated with one Y-bracket and one *ḥāšûq*, then the combined weight of a bracket and a *ḥāšûq* is 1,775 divided by 60, i.e., 29.58 shekels (c. 11.9 oz./338 g.). This is consistent with the notion that silver plating adorns both the Y-bracket and the *ḥāšûq* (if it is a spar not a binding; see NOTE to 27:10).

38:29. *Elevation-offering.* According to 35:24, the bronze is classified as a "Donation-offering," but there may be little difference between *tənûpâ* and *tərûmâ* (NOTES to 29:24, 27).

38:30. *bases of the Meeting Tent Opening.* I.e., for the Tabernacle Screen. On the analogy of vv 28–29, we might suppose that the seventy talents go to the sixty bases, with the remainder used for the other objects, including the Altar. On the nonmention of the Basin, see NOTE to 38:8, "mirrors."

39:1. *they made*. Since 36:10, all the verbs of making have been singular. Now the narrator reminds us that it was not Bezalel alone who made the Tabernacle and the priestly garments. See also NOTE to 36:10.

worm-crimson. On the nonmention of linen, see TEXTUAL NOTE to 39:1 and NOTE to 31:10.

as Yahweh commanded Moses. This phrase is repeated seven times in the section treating the priestly garments (39:1, 5, 7, 21, 26, 29, 31), followed by three more emphatic formulations (39:32, 42, 43) for a total of ten. Jacob (1990: 1036) observes that "as Yahweh commanded Moses" is again repeated seven times for the Tabernacle's erection (40:19, 21, 23, 25, 27, 29, 32) and ten more for the priests' investiture (Lev 8:9, 13, 17, 21, 29, 36; 9:10). Presumably, this is a deliberate pattern. The formula refers back to 35:1, "These are the *words* that Yahweh commanded to do them," and its parallels in 35:4, 10; 36:1, 5; 38:22.

39:3. *gold plates*. Hebrew *paḥ* may be derived from Egyptian *pḥ3* '(stone) plate' (Ellenbogen 1962: 130; Muchiki 1999: 253). On this method of making wire from foil, see Ogden (2000: 165).

amid the blue. This might mean either that threads of wool and linen are intermingled with gold wire, or that each woven strand consists of wool, linen and gold; cf. *b. Yoma* 71b–72a. Which color predominates we cannot tell; Ps 45:10 and Cant 3:10 possibly refer to cloth of gold, and Haran (1955: 383–84) posits that gold is the main component of the Ephod.

39:6. *made the carnelian stones*. Obviously, the artisans did not "make" the stones. Rather, the reference is to the settings.

39:8. *ḥōšen*. It is no longer called the "Judgment *ḥōšen*" (28:15) because its function is not under consideration. Similarly, the Urim and Thummim contained within, used for adjudication, are omitted (Gray 1983: 183–84; Durham 1987: 494). In any case, these oracles are apparently not made by the craftsmen but obtained elsewhere (Dillmann 1880: 366).

39:27. *shifts*. For all the priests, not just the Great Priest.

39:28. *Turban*. For Aaron.

splendor-hats. For the lesser priests. The head-gear *pəʾēr* (also Isa 3:20; Ezek 24:17, 23; 44:18) is apparently so called because it glorifies *(pʾr)* its wearer. See also NOTE to 28:1, "glory and splendor."

39:29. *the Sash. B. Yoma* 6a records a disagreement as to whether this refers to all the priests' sashes or only to Aaron's. The difficulty is that 39:2–26 definitely refers to Aaron's vestments; vv 27–28 definitely refer to all the priests' garments; then vv 30–31 again refer solely to the Great Priest. Thus there is a question whether v 29 has already returned us to Aaron (R. Judah the Prince), or whether all priests, including Aaron, wear identical sashes (R. Dosa). To me, the latter seems more likely.

twisted linen. Since it is mentioned first, linen may be the main component.

39:30. *wrote*. I.e., engraved, as specified in 28:36 (ibn Ezra [shorter commentary]).

39:31. *set on it blue cord.* Rashi (on 28:37) makes much of the minor contradiction with 28:37, "And you shall put it on blue cord," the question being: is the ṣîṣ on the cord or vice versa? But Ramban (on 28:37) sees no difference, and neither do I.

39:32. *completed.* The verse features hysteron proteron. In reality, first Israel did as Yahweh commanded, then the work was finished (Alshikh *apud* Leibowitz 1976: 696).

Israel's Sons. Naturally, only the craftsmen make the Tabernacle. But (a) they represent the people; and (b) the entire nation donates the materials (see Leibowitz 1976: 698–99).

did, as all that Yahweh commanded Moses, so they did. In the present context, *'āśû* could be rendered as not "did" but "made."

This formula, paralleled in 12:28; 39:42; 40:16; Num 1:54; 17:26, emphasizes Israel's compliance, already stated seven times in this section (NOTE to 39:1, "as Yahweh commanded Moses"). Presumably the idiom was used whenever a subordinate reported to a superior. Compare Lachish Ostracon 4: *kkl 'šr. šlḥ 'dny. kn. 'śh. 'bdk* 'as all that my lord dispatched, so your servant did' (*AHI* 1.004.2–3).

39:33. *Tabernacle.* Here as in 26:1–6, *hammiškān* connotes the inner curtains (Ramban).

to Moses. The Tabernacle's components are essentially a "kit" awaiting assembly by Moses as per Yahweh's instructions.

39:37. *pure Lampstand.* See NOTE to 31:8.

the arrangement lamps. This probably means "the lamps arranged in a row"; see NOTE to 27:21, "arrange." But the root *'rk* may have a special association with lamps, conceivably meaning to fill a lamp with oil or trim the wick (cf. Lev 24:3–4; Ps 132:17).

39:42. *all the Work.* The phrase *kol-hā'ăbōdâ* in vv 32 and 42 frames vv 33–41, enumerating the Tabernacle's parts.

39:43. *saw.* Moses inspects the people's work. On the echoes of Creation, see pp. 675–76, 691–92. Unlike God, however, Moses does not pronounce the work "good"—perhaps this would have been presumptuous (Fox 1986: 217).

blessed. The verb *bērak* may be translated variously (see in general Scharbert 1975). Ehrlich (1908: 423; 1969: 208) suggests that "thanked" is most appropriate here. There is also a connotation of saying "farewell" (cf. Gen 24:60; 47:10; 1 Kgs 8:66). But the parallel in Lev 9:22–23, where first Aaron and then Moses and Aaron bless the people, suggests primarily a wish for or pronouncement of good fortune. In Leviticus, this blessing appears to inaugurate the sacrificial cultus by calling down fire from Heaven. Similarly, in Exodus, Moses' blessing is preparatory to erecting the Tabernacle.

40:2. *the day of the first new moon.* In my translation, both "new moon" and "month" correspond to Hebrew *ḥōdeš.* The phrase *bayôm haḥōdeš hārī(')šôn* is technically ambiguous: does *rī(')šôn* 'first' modify *yôm* 'day' or *ḥōdeš* 'month' (Ehrlich 1969: 208)? It must be the latter; otherwise, we would not know which month is meant. Moreover, the idiom *yôm haḥōdeš* refers to New Moon day (Ezek 46:1). Consequently, the verse is redundant (see next NOTE). We would rather expect *bahōdeš hārī(')šôn bə'ehād lahōdeš* 'in the first month on the first of the month,' as in 40:17, etc.

According to 40:2, 17, Moses erects the Tabernacle on the first day of the second year of freedom, nine months after the arrival at Sinai (19:1) and almost a year after the exodus from Egypt on the fourteenth of the first month (12:6, 18). Accordingly, the first festival observed in the Tabernacle will be *Pesaḥ* (Num 9:1–14).

The careful reader will notice a chronological difficulty, however. Exod 40:10–15 implies that, at this time, the Tabernacle is not just built but also consecrated, along with the priesthood (so Josephus *Ant.* 3.201). Similarly, Ezek 48:18–19 and 11QTemple XIV:9 put the Temple cleansing on Nisan 1.

The problem is that the consecration-ordination lasts an entire week (Exod 29:30, 35, 37). Thus, according to Rabbinic sources (see Ramban's lengthy discussion), there is a temporal jump here to the eighth day, and Moses really had erected the Tabernacle on the twenty-third day of the eleventh month—in fact, he had disassembled it and reerected it every day for a week! But this could hardly be the plain sense (ibn Ezra).

Rather, the reference to the priests' ordination in 40:12–15 must be *prospective* (Childs 1974: 637). This is why their consecration goes unmentioned in the execution account (vv 16–33) but is properly narrated in Leviticus 8. After all, the ordination sacrifices presuppose an existing Tabernacle. Presumably the priests are consecrated during the first week of the new year.

A great deal of the Torah is set during the Tabernacle's first days of operation, and Num 7:1 explicitly returns us to this very point in time: "And it happened, on the day Moses completed erecting the Tabernacle, and he anointed it and made it holy. . . ." According to Numbers 7, simultaneously with the priestly ordination, the tribal leaders begin to bring their offerings, one per day for twelve days (ibn Ezra). At least during the first week, the donated animals are presumably kept and not sacrificed, pending the priests' installation. On the fourteenth day of the month, the people observe the *Pesaḥ* (Num 9:1–14). Num 9:15–22 then resumes the matter of Exod 40:34–38—the fire-cloud over the Tent instructing Israel when to move on. Numbers 10 describes the silver trumpets that signal Israel's departure, and on the twentieth day of the second month of the second year they finally break camp. The Tabernacle is disassembled and loaded onto wagons, and the priests bear the Testimony Chest before the people. In other words, all of Leviticus and Numbers 1–6 is contained within a gigantic parenthesis between Exodus 40 and Numbers 7. Time seemingly stops as Israel inaugurates the cult (see further pp. 691–94).

on the first of the month. This redundant comment seems to be a gloss, whether secondary (Ehrlich 1969: 208) or by the Priestly Writer himself, clarifying "day of the first new moon" (previous NOTE). The first of the month is a minor holiday (e.g., Num 10:10; 28:11–15; 1 Sam 20:5–6, etc.) and presumably an auspicious time for new beginnings.

Can we determine the day of the week? Since new "Face Bread" (40:4, 23) is normally laid out on the Sabbath (Lev 24:8), one might infer that Moses erects the entire Taberacle on the day of rest (cf. ibn Ezra). While this hardly seems likely, one might well imagine that it is set up either just before or just after the Sabbath (see TEXTUAL NOTE to 40:17, "on the first of the month," apropos of Syr). But the question is probably frivolous. Num 9:19 implies that the Tabernacle service is irregular during Israel's wanderings. That is, the Tent is probably erected on any and every day of the week, depending upon the divine cloud's motions.

40:4. *arrangement.* In two rows (Lev 24:6); see p. 397.

raise its lamps. If "raise" here means "kindle" rather than "install" (NOTE to 25:37, "raise"), then it may be evening (cf. 27:21).

40:5. *before the Testimony Chest.* But outside the Veil, *pace* Heb 9:3–4.

40:7. *set water.* The Tabernacle is being readied for use: the Table is laid, the lamps are lit, the Basin is filled.

40:9. *anoint.* This is a new command, executed in Lev 8:10. Anointing the Tabernacle imparts the quality of "Holiness" (Exod 28:41). For a discussion of Moses' movement between different zones of Holiness as he consecrates the priesthood and shrine, see Klingbeil (1997).

all that is in it. I.e., the contents of the Tabernacle proper. V 10 will specifically mention the anointing of the Altar and the Basin, because they are not literally "in" the Tabernacle (Cassuto 1967: 479–80).

40:12. *Bring Near Aaron and his sons.* Not at once, but after the Tabernacle is constructed (NOTE to 40:2). "Bring Near" *(hiqrib)* implies "consecrate."

40:15. *their anointment shall be for being for them.* On whether future priests require re-anointment, see p. 532. On the awkward syntax, see TEXTUAL NOTE.

40:17. *second year.* In the ancient Near East, temples were generally built or said to have be built in a king's first year, demonstrating their sponsors' piety (Hurowitz 1992a: 226). The Tabernacle is erected in the second year since the Exodus, but in the first year since Yahweh assumed sovereignty over Israel at Sinai.

was erected. To the sequence *hûqam . . . wayyāqem mōše(h)* 'was erected. . . . And Moses erected,' Jacob (1990: 1045) compares Gen 2:1–2 (P): *waykullû . . . waykal 'ĕlōhîm* 'were completed . . . and Deity completed.' While this language is unlikely to be a conscious evocation of Creation (*pace* Jacob), it may be a stylistic trait of P.

40:18. *Moses erected.* Assisted by his fellow Levites (ibn Ezra)? Or solo, by dint of Samson-like strength (Ginzburg 1928: 3.178–79; Ehrlich 1908: 424)? Even the rationalist Ehrlich (1969: 208) insists that Moses set up the Tabernacle unaided—"although I don't know how [he] did this thing"—since only Moses was in a sufficiently high state of ritual purity and consecration to handle the sancta.

It any case, it is striking that the Israelite artisans do not complete their own labor. Elsewhere in the ancient Near East, craftsmen would ritually disassociate themselves from the fabrication of sacred objects—e.g., in Mesopotamia, by symbolically lopping off their hands (Jacobsen 1987a). In this case, Bezalel and company simply bow out. Moses' role as ultimate builder constitutes a kind of buffer, prior to the Tabernacle's full consecration. Thereafter, only the priests are entitled to manipulate its sacred utensils.

40:20. *put the poles.* This is a minor difficulty, perhaps a lapse on the Priestly Writer's part. According to 37:5, the poles are already in place (see NOTE). Num 4:6 again speaks of the poles' installation, and yet, according to Exod 25:15, the poles should be permanently installed (see NOTE to 25:15 for further discussion).

40:29. *and the Ascending-offering Altar.* The inverted syntax contrasts the Plaza Altar with the aforementioned Incense Altar (v 26).

he sent up. Moses officiates (29:38–42), because Aaron is not yet a priest (Rashi).

Ascending-offering and the Tribute-offering. I.e., the daily burnt offering and the grain offering (29:38–42).

would wash. I.e., Moses would wash during the week of priestly consecration; ever afterward, the priests would wash. *Pace* Rashi, *wərāḥăṣû* in MT must be prospective-habitual, not narrative past (see also TEXTUAL NOTE).

40:33. *And Moses completed the Task.* Between vv 32 and 33 should logically come the actual consecration of the structure and its personnel, described in Leviticus 8 (cf. Num 7:1). Here again we have anachronism in P (see further pp. 691–94). On allusions to Creation in the Tabernacle account, especially 40:33, see pp. 675–76.

40:34. *cloud . . . Glory.* Physically, the cloud envelops or rests upon the Tabernacle on the outside, while the Glory fills the inside (Ramban). Clements (1972: 243) compares Isa 6:3–4, where Yahweh's Glory is said to fill the Earth, as clouds of incense fill the Temple. Also in Ezek 43:5, Yahweh's Glory fills the Temple's inner court.

Exod 40:34–35 features parallelistic, quasi-poetic language (Beer and Galling 1939: 178; Cassuto 1967: 484), a characteristic of P (Paran 1989: 98–136). Cassuto further notes the numerous evocations of 24:15–17 (Yahweh's "Glory," the "cloud" that "covers," Moses "entering"), cumulatively implying that the Tabernacle is, in effect, Mount Sinai on the march (see also p. 688).

40:35. *could not enter.* Ehrlich (1908: 424) takes this literally: when Yahweh's Glory fills the entire Tabernacle, there is no room for Moses. But the point may simply be that Moses cannot survive contact with Yahweh's concentrated presence. In any case, this is why in Lev 1:1, Yahweh speaks to Moses "*from* inside the Tent." Moses cannot come in (cf. ibn Ezra; Durham 1987: 501).

It appears elsewhere, however, that Moses *can* enter (Exod 25:22; 33:9; 34:34–35; Lev 9:23; Num 7:89). And, of course, the priestly office will require that Aaron and his sons enter the Tabernacle daily. Rashbam sensibly infers that although Yahweh's Glory is ever-present in the Tabernacle, after the inauguration it is restricted to the zone over the Testimony Chest, just as in 1 Kgs 8:11, the cloud excluding the priests from the Temple is only temporary. (Num 9:15–23, too, reports that the cloud alit upon the Tabernacle the day it was erected, but does not mention the Glory inside.)

In the composite Torah, Milgrom (1991: 137) catches a cross-source allusion to 3:5–6 (JE), where Moses could not approach or behold Yahweh in the Bush. On Moses suffering bodily harm while inside the Tabernacle (34:34–35), see pp. 622–23.

40:37. *if the cloud would not lift itself.* The redundant language stresses Israel's total obedience. Num 9:15–23, just before the people's departure from Sinai (Num 10:11), explains in greater detail how the cloud's motions affect Israel and the Tabernacle service.

40:38. *cloud . . . fire.* Exod 40:38 caps the many references to cloud and fire in Exodus (3:2–3; 13:21–22; 14:19–20, 24; 16:10; 24:16–18; 33:9–10, 22; 34:5) (Durham 1987: 500; vol. I, pp. 36, 549–50). The cloudy-fiery pillar that protected Israel and led them through the wilderness, the same refulgence that was manifest at Sinai, now rests over and within the Tabernacle as a continuing guarantee of guidance and protection (cf. Num 14:14).

It seems that Exod 40:38 finally explains the nature of the cloud-fire pillar. The cloud is Yahweh's vehicle, while the fire is his Glory; compare 24:17, "the appearance of Yahweh's Glory was like a consuming fire." Once the Tabernacle is ready, God's fiery presence, as it were, parks its cloud vehicle on the roof (Num 9:15–23). After the Tent and clergy are purified and consecrated, the Glory leaves the cloud to fill the Tabernacle (Exod 40:34–35), igniting the wood upon the Altar to inaugurate worship (Lev 9:24) (and probably simultaneously incinerating Nadab and Abihu [Rashbam on Exod 19:8; Lev 9:24; 10:2]). When it is time to leave, the Glory reenters the cloud and together they take off (Exod 40:36; Num 9:15–23). Once again, the fire, i.e., the Glory, is visible only at night, shining through the cloud.

in it. "It" is more likely the cloud, less likely the Tabernacle (ibn Ezra [shorter commentary]).

to the eyes of all. As Num 14:14 *ʿayin bəʿayin* 'eye to eye' stresses, it is important that all Israel witness the cloud and interpret its silent commands. Cf. Exod 29:45–46: "And I will tent in Israel's Sons' midst, and I will be for them as a deity, and *they will know* that I am Yahweh their deity who took them out from the land of Egypt by my tenting among them—I am Yahweh their deity." This promise is now fulfilled (Driver 1911: 404).

Israel's House. The title *bêt yiśrāʾēl*, rare in the Torah (in Exodus, only 16:31; 40:38), was perhaps chosen to suit the context: Yahweh's "house" now stands within "Israel's House" (compare the more blatant play between "David's House" and "Yahweh's House" in 2 Samuel 7).

settings forth. Just as the final word of Genesis, *bəmiṣrāyim* 'in Egypt,' sets up the Book of Exodus, so the last word of Exodus, *masʿêhem*, denoting the stages of a long trek, anticipates what follows. The Books of Leviticus, Numbers and Deuteronomy will take Israel from Mount Sinai to the borders of Canaan. They do not know their way but must rely entirely upon Yahweh.

COMMENT

PROLEGOMENON

The following discussion of biblical religion combines the Bible's testimony with data from other ancient texts and artifacts. It also draws on the fruits of comparative ethnology and anthropological theory, including sociobiology. And it relies heavily on intuition.

For this I make only slight apology. We cannot observe and interview the Hebrew authors or other ancient Israelites. Biblical scholars are the ultimate armchair anthropologists, framing hypotheses and analyses based upon incomplete and possibly inaccurate reports. Should we desist entirely? After all, the Priestly Writer consistently declines to interpret or justify cultic practices, except to hammer home his Reason of Reasons: "You will be holy, for I, Yahweh, am holy" (Lev 19:2; cf. 11:44–45; 20:7, 26; 21:6–8; Num 15:40). The modern, anthropologically minded exegete, however, cannot refuse the challenge of the text's opacity. I agree with Jenson (1992: 67–68): "An outside perception is not necessarily a disadvantage. Indeed, it is often the anthropologist from another culture who is able to work out the logic of a world-view. For the 'natives', the underlying logic of the culture's beliefs and rituals may well be implicit and unrecognized."

Ultimately, after we sort through the facts, we have only informed empathy to connect us to the past. Every generation reconstructs Antiquity according to its own lights, and likewise every scholar. I know that my picture of biblical religion resembles at times Gnosticism or Kabbalah, at times science fiction. Anachronistic metaphors and analogies help me (and I hope you too) feel the power of a religious system long dead.

AT THE BEGINNING

In the prototypical ancient Near Eastern myth of Creation, having defeated his enemy, the storm god creates the cosmos and/or fashions his eternal abode, which is simultaneously celestial and terrestrial (Kapelrud 1963). In doing so, he recapitulates the career of a human chieftain, proving and consolidating his power, and then establishing a palatial residence (cf. Utzschneider 1988: 152–59). The Book of Exodus is a variation on this theme. Yahweh defeats Pharaoh and leads the Israelites to his holy mountain, where they build his abode (see further vol. I, pp. 34, 554–72, 608–13). Formally, it is a Creation story.

Creation myths are more than proto-scientific theories about the origins of matter and physical structure. They also account for social organization. In particular, they legitimate the hiero-political structures maintaining the temples where the myths are composed and recited (e.g., Clifford 1994). Consequently, *temple*-building and *world*-building are symbols of one another. The Bible often portrays God as a builder (cf. Isa 40:12–14; Ps 104: 2–3, 5; Prov 3:19–20; Job 38:4–6, etc.) (Hurowitz 1992a: 235–42), and even the language of Gen 1:1–2:4a, which we are about to examine closely, mimics a royal building inscription: "he made . . . when he completed . . . the task" (Hurowitz p. 94).

Commentators have noted the manifold ways in which the Tabernacle pericope in Exodus 25–31, 35–40 evokes P's Creation account in Gen 1:1–2:3 (e.g., McNeile 1908: 155–56; Kearney 1977; Blenkinsopp 1976; Leibowitz 1976: 696–98; Weinfeld 1981; Levenson 1988: 78–99; Weimar 1988; Blum 1990:

306–7; Coote and Ord 1991: 95–97; Buber and Rosenzweig 1994: 14–21; Klein 1996: 266). If P originally existed as an independent, coherent document, its prologue (Creation) would naturally foreshadow its climax (the Tabernacle) as well as its conclusion (Cities of Refuge); see further pp. 681–82 below.

How specifically does P's Tabernacle account recapitulate Creation? First, the Tabernacle is erected on New Year's day (Exod 40:2), the same date on which dry land reappears after the Flood (Gen 8:13) and presumably the date of Creation itself (Blenkinsopp 1976: 283).

Second, we have a pattern of sevens, evoking the seven days of Creation. (Admittedly, the Bible features the number seven in many other contexts [Pope 1962a].) The Tabernacle is ordained in seven speeches (25:1–30:10; 30:11–16; 30:17–21; 30:22–33; 30:34–38; 31:1–11; 31:12–17), and in 40:17–33, Moses "did as Yahweh commanded him" seven times (Gorman 1990: 48). As Creation culminates in the Sabbath (Gen 2:1–3), the Tabernacle instructions culminate in the Sabbath (Exod 31:12–17). Exod 31:17 explicitly recalls Creation: "[in] six days Yahweh made the heavens and the earth, but on the seventh day he ceased."

Third, there are extensive linguistic contacts between the two narratives. Here are excerpts from P's Tabernacle account: "I have **called** (qārā[']tî) by name Bezalel son of Uri . . . and filled him with a **divine spirit** (rûaḥ 'ĕlōhîm) . . . in **every task** (kol-məlā[']kâ)" (31:2–3; 35:30–31); my **Sabbaths** you must keep . . . , for **six days** Yahweh **made** ('āśâ) **the heavens and the earth**, but on the **seventh day** (bayyôm haššəbî'î) he **ceased** (šbt) and caught his breath" (31:13–17); "And all the Work of the Meeting Tent Tabernacle was **completed** (kly); and Israel's Sons **did** ('āśû), as all that Yahweh commanded Moses, so they **did** ('āśû)" (39:32); "And Moses **saw** (wayyar[']) **all the Task** (kol-hamməlā[']kâ). . . . And Moses **blessed them** (waybārek 'ōtām)" (39:43); "And Moses **completed** (kly) the **Task** (məlā[']kâ)" (40:33); "On the day Moses **completed** (kallôt) erecting the Tabernacle . . . then he **made it holy** (wayqaddēš 'ōtô)" (Num 7:1).

Now compare the following verses from Gen 1:1–2:3: "Deity created the **heavens and the earth**" (Gen 1:1); "And **Deity's breath/wind/spirit** (rûaḥ 'ĕlōhîm) fluttered over the the the waters' face" (Gen 1:2); "And Deity **saw** (wayyar[']) " (Gen 1:4, 10, 12, 18, 21, 25, 31); "And Deity **called** (wayyiqrā[']) " (Gen 1:5, 8, 10); "And Deity **blessed them** (waybārek 'ōtām)" (Gen 1:22, 28; cf. 2:3); "So the **heavens and the earth** and all their army were **completed** (kly). And Deity **completed** (kly) his **task** (məla[']ktô) that he had **done** ('āśâ) on the **sixth day**, and he **ceased** (šbt) on the **seventh day** (bayyôm haššəbî'î) from **all his task** (kol-məla[']ktô) that he had **done** ('āśâ). And Deity **blessed** (waybārek) the **seventh day** (yôm haššəbî'î) and **made it holy** (wayqaddēš 'ōtô), for on it he **ceased** (šābat) from **all his task** (kol-məla[']ktô) . . ." (Gen 2:1–3). (See also TEXTUAL NOTE to 36:6, "were restrained.")

Because we read the Bible forward, first Genesis and then Exodus, we naturally perceive the Tabernacle as recapitulating Creation. The reverse is equally true, perhaps even truer: Creation anticipates the Tabernacle. Thus *Pesiq. Rab Kah.* 1.4: "On the day that Moses completed erecting the Tabernacle, the world was erected along with it. . . . Before the Tabernacle was erected, the world wobbled; from the instant that the Tabernacle was erected, the world was made firm" (for other Rabbinic texts in this vein, see Schäfer 1974).

GOD'S WINGED WORD

As the following pages will show, these allusions to Creation are not just decorative. They provide the exegetical key for the entire Priestly Source and its image of the Tabernacle. To see how this is so, we must reconsider Gen 1:1–10 (for the underlying Hebrew text, see Hendel 1998):

> At the beginning of Deity-created-Heaven-and-Earth, when the Earth was disordered and chaotic and dark was upon Deep's *face*, and Deity's breath/wind/ spirit *(rûaḥ)* fluttered *(mərahepet)* over the waters' *face*: then Deity said, "Be light!" And light was.
>
> And Deity saw the light, how it was good, and Deity separated between the light and between the dark. And Deity called the light "Day," and the dark he called "Night." And evening happened, and morning happened. One day.
>
> And Deity said, "Be a plating *(rāqîaʿ)* in the waters' midst, to be a separator between waters and waters." And so it happened. And Deity made the Plating, and he separated between the waters that are under the Plating and between the waters that are above the Plating. And Deity called the Plating "Heavens." And evening happened, and morning happened. Second day.
>
> And Deity said, "Be pooled the waters from under the Heavens into one pool, so that the dry land may be revealed. And so it happened. And the waters were pooled from under the Heavens to their pools, so that the dry land was revealed. And Deity called the dry land "Earth," and the waters' pool he called "Seas." And Deity saw how it was good.

To paraphrase: according to Gen 1:1–2, our three tangible dimensions were originally filled with water. God, or some part of him, existed "above" the Deep, apparently in another dimension (see further p. 687). By calling light into being, God created time, the alternation of day and night. God next created space, i.e., a hemispherical bubble of air, bounded beneath by dry land and all around by water. This bell jar is the Heaven and Earth, or Universe, that we inhabit.

I wish to linger on the phrase *rûaḥ . . . mərahepet*, which is, like all the best images, a mixed metaphor. *Rûaḥ* is the common Hebrew term for moving air, be it a mighty tempest or a puff of exhalation. In the latter sense, *rûaḥ* is tantamount to the life force animating the body and may be rendered "spirit" (< Latin *spiritus* 'wind, breath'; compare also *anima*). Like any living being, Yahweh possesses his own *rûaḥ*, which he sometimes shares with Israel's leaders—e.g., judges, kings and prophets—giving them supernatural authority or influence.

Mərahepet is the Piʿel participle of the rare verb *rḥp* (only Gen 1:2; Deut 32:11; Jer 23:9). In Ugaritic, the cognate *rḥp* refers to avian flight *(KTU* 1.18.iv.20–21, 31–32; 19.i.32; 108.8), while in Syriac *rḥp* describes a hen sheltering her chicks. Although it is hard to decide which meaning better fits Deut 32:11, "As a vulture stirs its nest and *rḥp*s over its young," brooding seems more natural. In Jer 23:9, however, *rḥp* describes the tremor of a drunkard's limbs. In sum: *rḥp* denotes the extension and/or rapid motion of a wing (cf. Buber and Rosenzweig 1994: 15–17). What did the Priestly Writer understand by winged, moving air? Apparently, many things.

First, *rûaḥ . . . mərahepet* is God's own exhalation speaking his creative words (Coote and Ord 1991: 96). Compare Ps 33:4–11:

> For Yahweh's word is straight,
> And all his work is stable. . . .
> By Yahweh's word were Heavens made,
> And by his mouth's wind/breath *(rûaḥ)* all their *army*,
> Gathering the sea's waters like a heap (or: in a waterskin, reading *bənōd* for
>   MT *kənēd*),
> Putting Deeps into treasuries. . . .
> For he, he spoke, and it was,
> He, he commanded, and it stood firm. . . .
> Yahweh's plan will stand firm forever,
> His heart's thoughts for age (by) age.

But *rûaḥ* is also the personified wind on whose pinions Yahweh soars. Compare Ps 104:1b–13a:

> My deity Yahweh, you have been very great.
> You wore might and majesty,
> Garbed in light as a robe,
> Extending Heavens as a tent-curtain,
> Who ceils his upper chambers in the waters,
> Who appoints clouds (as) his mount *(rəkûbô)*,
> Who travels on wind's wings *(kanpê rûaḥ)*,
> Making the winds *(rûḥôt)* (as) his messengers,
> Flaming fire his ministers,
> Founding Earth on its foundations,
> So it may never wobble forever—
> Deep its covering like a garment;
> Over mountains stand waters;
> From your snort they [the waters] flee . . . ;
> They ascend mountains, they descend clefts
> To a place which you established for them;
> A boundary you set; they may not cross,
> May not return to cover the Earth—
> Who releases springs in the ravines,
> They meander amid mountains. . . .
> Who waters mountains from his upper chambers.

As many have noted, P's description of God's wind *(rûaḥ)* over the Deep in Genesis 1 recalls the myth of the storm god defeating the Sea and afterward sustaining life with the sweet waters of spring and shower (vol. I, pp. 608–10). But it has escaped notice that a specific image probably underlies God's flying wind/breath/spirit. The first clue comes from 2 Sam 22 = Ps 18:5–17, attributed to King

David and spoken in the royal persona (the following translation synthesizes the two versions):

When Death's breakers overwhelmed me. . . .
In my distress, I call (to) Yahweh,
And to my deity I plead.
From his palace/temple he hears my voice. . . .
Smoke went up from his nose,
And fire from his mouth consumes;
Coals burned from him.
And he distended Heavens and descended
With darkcloud under his feet.
And he mounted on Griffin *(wayyirkab ʿal-kərûb)* and took flight
And soared on wind's wings *(kanpê rûaḥ).* . . .
From his brilliant presence his clouds burned,
Hail and fire coals.
Yahweh thunders from Heaven,
And Highest gives forth his voice;
And he released his arrows and scattered them,
Lightning he shot and panicked them,
So that sea's channels were revealed.
World's foundations are exposed
By Yahweh's snort,
By the breath of his nose wind *(minnišmat rûaḥ ʾappô).*
He sends from on High; he takes me,
He draws me up from many waters.

The royal psalmist exults that, when the battle seemed lost, the God of the storm descended to rescue him and, according to the latter half of the psalm, instruct him in the martial arts. Now he can master his enemies as easily as Yahweh once mastered the sea. Crucially, the "wind's wings" on which Yahweh descends to part the waters are explicitly identified as a Griffin (or, if *kərûb* is collective, Griffins).

Second Samuel 22 = Psalm 18 is a royal hymn ideologically remote from the Priestly source. A similar image, however, is found in the Book of Ezekiel, which evinces many similarities to P (cf. Levitt Kohn 2002). In Babylonia, the prophet beholds a fiery storm approaching. It resolves itself into four winged monsters darting wherever the wind/spirit *(rûaḥ)* takes them. Their wings support the Plating *(rāqîaʿ)* of Heaven, where a man of fire, clad in irridescence, sits enthroned. A divine voice addresses Ezekiel, and *rûaḥ* enters his body. For good measure, since words may be either spoken or written, the prophet ingests a scroll. Now he is Yahweh's mouthpiece and scribe. Deprived of volition, he himself is like the flying creatures, driven hither and thither by the divine *rûaḥ* (Ezek 1:1–3:14).

What or who are these wind-swept, winged beings of the storm? Chapter 10 identifies them as the Griffins *(kərûbîm)* that flew down to pick up Yahweh when he abandoned his Temple to join his people in exile. Might this shed some light on the prologue to Genesis?

One supposed difference between P and Ezekiel is that Ezekiel's God is served by angels and Griffins, whereas P's Deity reigns in splendid solitude. There is some truth here, but the difference is more in emphasis than in theology. Ezekiel openly describes divine beings beside Yahweh, while P is oblique. But after all, why is P's Tabernacle ornamented with Griffins (25:18–20; 26:1) if not to depict Yahweh's heavenly servitors? (See further below.)

Bearing in mind the equation of the winged wind and the Griffins in 2 Samuel 22 = Psalm 18 and Ezekiel, if we ask why Gen 1:2 describes God's "wind/breath/spirit" as "fluttering" like a bird over the Deep, there can be but one answer. This is a Griffin conveyance like that described by Ezekiel, although whether it soars triumphantly or broods maternally remains moot.

Is there any further evidence that P reckons with divine beings beside Yahweh? In Gen 1:11–25, God proceeds to create all the living: plants, fish, birds, amphibians, insects, reptiles and mammals. Within this list, separating the plants from the animals, come the astral bodies, apparently living creatures, appointed to "govern" day and night (vv 14–18). This is probably meant literally, for the Israelites considered the stars to be minor deities (e.g., Gen 37:9; Deut 4:19; Judg 5:20; Ps 148:3; Job 38:7; Dan 8:10; see Halpern 1993b; above, pp. 510–11). In Gen 1:14–18, P alludes to such beliefs without endorsing them explicitly.

Finally comes Creation's culmination (Gen 1:26–27):

And Deity said, "Let us make Man in our image as our likeness, to rule over the sea's fish and over the Heavens' birds and over all the Earth's beasts and over all the walkers walking on the Earth."

So Deity created Man in his image; in Deity's image he created him; male and female he created them.

There should be no question to whom God says "Let us make Man." It must be to his heavenly servants, male and female. But P is still somewhat obscure, attributing humanity's creation to both the pantheon ("Let us") and to God alone ("So Deity created"). Even the Priestly Writer's decision to call God 'ĕlōhîm 'Deity,' admittedly conditioned by his theory of progressive revelation (see vol. I, pp. 50, 272, 283), creates ambiguity, for 'ĕlōhîm literally means "gods." Thus the phrase bəṣelem 'ĕlōhîm could be rendered as either "in Deity's image" or "in gods' image, i.e., male and female."

In P's indirectness, we may catch the dim echoes of a vigorous theological dispute within ancient Israel. As a whole, the Bible accepts the existence of divinities beside Yaweh. Only their *worship* is forbidden (see pp. 770–75). This distinction, still lost on most readers, was also lost on many Israelites, at least according to biblical polemics. This may be why P only implies the existence of Heaven's denizens. In particular, the Priestly Writer seems to have taken pains to reinterpret the old divine epithet *yahwe(h) ṣəbā'ōt yōšēb hakkərūbîm* 'Yahweh of Brigades, the Griffins-sitter,' describing Yahweh as the heavenly Storm King.

P declines to include the Griffins explicitly in its Creation account, and the Tabernacle Griffins, to judge from their stance, do not flank a throne or form a chariot (above, pp. 516–19). In P, Yahweh's armies (*ṣəbāʾōt*) are no longer the Host of Heaven; they are, on the one hand, all Creation (Gen 2:1); and, on the other, Israel's serried ranks (NOTE to 6:26). In other words, when treating the notion of Yahweh's divine servants, P consistently equivocates. (We find an analogous situation with regard to the dead: P's notion of *kārēt implies* a belief in the afterlife, but the doctrine is never explicit [Propp 1987b]).

In Gen 1:28–30, God authorizes the first humans to perpetuate their species by sexual reproduction ("bear fruit and multiply") and also to sustain themselves by eating. But they may not shed blood; they must subsist on plants alone. The animals, too, are to be vegetarian. Throughout the ancient Near East, such harmony among creatures typifies a state of primordial paradise (eg., Sumerian Dilmun [*ANET* 38; Jacobsen 1987b: 186; Clifford 1994: 36]) as well as the gods' temples (e.g., Hierapolis [Pseudo-Lucian *Syrian Goddess* 41]). The biblical analogue is Isaiah's vision of Eden restored, where wolf and sheep, lion and calf, adder and child abide in peace (Isa 11:1–10).

Last comes the orotund coda of P's Creation (Gen 2:1–3):

So the Heavens and the Earth and all their *army* were completed. And Deity completed on the sixth day his task that he had done, and he ceased (*šbt*) on the seventh day from all his task that he had done. And Deity blessed the seventh day and made it holy, for on it he ceased (*šbt*) from all his task that Deity created in making.

As Exod 20:8–11 and 31:12–17 make explicit, this is why Israel must keep the Sabbath (*šabbāt*): to imitate God, who himself rested on the seventh day and, if this is the correct translation, "caught his *breath (wayyinnāpaš)*" after so much taxing use of his creative *rûaḥ* (NOTE to 31:17). (For further discussion of Creation, the Sabbath and the Tabernacle, see below, pp. 691–94.)

THE GREAT RIFT

The upshot of Creation is that Yahweh eternally inhabits the sky amid his celestial servitors, while his creatures live out their short lives below (on God's exalted viewpoint, see Isa 40:22; 57:15; Ps 2:4; 33:13–14; 93:4; 103:19; 123:1). The heavenly and earthly realms are separated by the barrier of the "Plating (*rāqîaʿ*)." The equation Creation = separation is common to all ancient Near Eastern cosmogonies (Clifford 1994) and is paralleled in many other cultures (e.g., Lienhardt 1961: 28–55).

Though somewhat removed, God is still in sufficient contact with the lower regions to be mortally offended when humans (and presumably animals) resort to "violence (*ḥāmās*)," which I understand as including both murder and carnivorous behavior (Gen 6:11–13; see p. 689). With the Flood, God wipes the slate clean and begins anew with one pair of each species, including Man (so P; the tradition of *seven* pairs of clean animals comes from J [Gen 7:2]). Realizing that he cannot curb his creatures' meat lust, God now compromises. The animals are implicitly allowed to continue their predatory and scavenging ways. And Man is permitted to eat meat—with one priviso, whose convoluted syntax almost defies translation:

> However, flesh with its soul *(nepeš)*, its blood, you may not eat. And, however, blood for your souls I shall demand. From every animal's hand I shall demand it. And from all Man's hand, from the hand of Man (for) his brother, I will demand Man's soul *(nepeš)*. The shedder of Man's blood, by/for Man *(bā'ādām)* his blood must be shed, for in Deity's image he made Man. (Gen 9:4–6)

Nepeš 'soul, throat,' like *rûaḥ* 'breath/wind/spirit,' probably refers to the air animating the body. The Priestly source, as if intuiting the oxygenation of the blood, boldly equates blood and breath with each other and with life itself. Indeed, blood's tendency to clot outside the body suggests something holy and fragile, more ephemeral even than Manna in the sun (cf. vol. I, p. 600).

God decrees that henceforth any beast or man that kills a human incurs bloodguilt. How the animal's guilt is dealt with is not stated (see, however, NOTES to 21:28). But, then as now, many more humans fall to their fellows than to predators. P states unequivocally that every homicide is a sacrilege, an effacing of the divine image and a capital offense.

This compromise does not really eliminate the problems of bloodshed and bloodguilt. As we shall see, P later states that, once the Tabernacle is functioning, *all* animal slaughter is tantamount to murder and an affront to Yahweh (Lev 17:4)—with one crucial exception. Slaughter in the Tabernacle Plaza and sacrifice upon the Altar have the power fully to dispel bloodguilt, permitting Israel to live with God's Holiness and still eat meat. The dietary laws implicitly impose a further restriction: the few land animals licit to eat are all vegetarian (Leviticus 11; Deut 14:4–20). That is, while the carnivores and scavengers may continue their "violence," Israelites may not enjoy the fruits thereof. As for actual homicide, on the eve of Israel's conquest of Canaan, Yaweh reveals his grand plan for keeping the land free of bloodguilt: capital punishment for intentional murderers and cities of refuge for accidental manslayers (Numbers 35).

The prohibition of murder might reasonably fall within God's responsibility as society's guardian. But why should Yahweh care how his creatures feed themselves?

GODLINESS AND CLEANLINESS

Definitions of the "Holy" range from Rudolph Otto's (1936) celebration of the inherently scary-yet-fascinating to the smug sense of rectitude evinced by some modern religious communities. Words such as English "holy" and Hebrew *qādôš* really do not have any meaning, apart from that with which speakers and writers invest them.

For me, at least half of Holiness is fear—fear during a confrontation with a predator, fear upon viewing a corpse, fear upon exposure to the low and powerful sounds generated by storms and temblors (Tuzin 1984). Like pain, this self-preserving fear was favored by evolution, and indeed is found in many animal species.

There is also a lesser fear—call it respect—that contributes to the establishment of social hierarchy. This in its own way facilitated group and individual survival and likewise was favored by natural selection (Wright 1994: 236–63). Unremitting, reciprocal fear charges relationships in all social groups between the dominant and the dominated, between "alpha" and "omega," even if social posturings are rarely *à outrance*. Males in particular appear to experience this fear, hence their emphasis on asserting rank. Many human societies have developed rites to advance juniors in social prestige without threatening seniors, who instead intimidate younger candidates by threats, ordeals and noises. (On rites of passage, see Van Gennep 1960; Tuzin 1980: 55–78.)

Human societies are characterized by concentric circles of dominance/submission of varying complexity. The primal alpha male is either the father or the maternal uncle (so-called fratriarchy). Beyond the father or uncle may be a clan patriarch. Beyond the patriarch may be a chieftain or king. Beyond a king may be his overlord. And, for polytheistic societies, above mankind live the gods, with one alpha male typically at their head. In good primate fashion, this divine king may even have achieved his status by killing his ancestors and monopolizing the females, as in the theogonic myths of Greece, Hatti and Mesopotamia (Cross 1976). In Israel, there is no doubt who is alpha and who omega, who is feared and who fears, who receives and who pays homage in the form of prayer and sacrifice.

Qōdeš 'Holiness' I take to be Yahweh's *prerogative*, that which properly belongs to him and sets him above his Creation. (This fits the evidence better than the once popular theory that *qdš* means "to set apart" [cf. Rashi on Lev 19:2]; for counterarguments, see Jenson [1992: 48 n. 4]; also Emerton [1967: 235–36] on the view that that *qdš* properly refers to radiance). Yahweh is often called *qādôš* 'the Holy' or *qədôš yiśrā'ēl* 'Israel's Holy.' His Holiness is innate; God swears by it as if by his own essence or life (Amos 4:2; Ps 89:36) (Levine 1987: 252).

How does one approach the Holy? Only in a nonthreatening, submissive manner, prostrate and bearing gifts, in order to reap the benefits of intimacy without threatening Yahweh's dominance (cf. Burkert 1996: 80–101). Under no circumstances may one touch what is God's—also called *qōdeš* 'a Holiness'—without permission and precautions.

That *qdš* betokens a special property (in both senses) of the divine is a notion Israel shared with its neighbors. Canaanite polytheism, for example, calls the gods *qdšm* 'the Holy ones' (*KAI* 27.12; cf. 4.5, 7; 14.9, 22) and personifies "Holiness" as the chief goddess. No less than the high god "God" ('Ilu), the feminine Qudšu embodies the defining essence of divinity. This is why the Ugaritic pantheon is called both "Sons of Holiness" (*bn qdš*) and "Sons of God" (*bn 'il*). Thus, beside "Holiness," an equally satisfactory translation of *qōdeš* would be "Godliness."

In addition to social fear, the ancient sense of the Holy is conditioned by a related primal emotion/behavior: fastidiousness. Burkert (1996: 123) suggests that ritual purity is above all a matter of cleanliness, a naturally selected behavior for all species that bathe in water, sand or dust, or lick or groom themselves (see also Stowers 1998: 188).

For humanity, we know that individuals and cultures vary in the degree to which they are concerned with cleanliness, and that context makes a difference (cf. Freud 1918: 36–97). For a modern Westerner, for example, it would be pathological to perceive filth everywhere and to be constantly washing—unless one worked in a hospital. Anticipating the discoveries of microbiology, the ancient mind considered the terrestrial realm to be tainted by invisible agents of disease and death. Naturally, precautions were taken to minimize their presence: prophylactic purity taboos and therapeutic purification rituals.

There is also a natural human tendency, observable in many children and some obsessive-compulsive adults, to erect arbitrary schemes of classification, which may receive subsequent rationalization. At age one, an infant might be fascinated by thresholds, cultivating a sense of inside vs. outside. At two, the same child may conclude that white food is good, green food is bad. At three (s)he may provide complicated reasons why white food and green food must not be mingled. In this spirit, the Bible imposes restrictions on the mixing of crops (Lev 19:19; Deut 22:9), fabrics (Lev 19:19; Deut 22:11), animals (Exod 22:19; Lev 18:23; 19:19; 20:15; Deut 22:10; 27:21) and gender-specific attire (Deut 22:5). To what extent these reflect popular cultural taboos is unknown, but it is difficult to imagine a religious authority imposing them from above as innovations.

Even before Pasteur, a prudent person perhaps would not touch a rotten corpse without washing afterward. A thoughtful person might attempt to generalize about impurity, dividing everything in the world into categories of clean and unclean. And a philosopher might conjecture that, just as there is a state of absolute defilement—death—so there must be a state of absolute purity—a realm of unlimited vitality. This, too, is qōdeš 'Holiness.'

The Holy as an intellectual category I trace to a mental reflex to make distinctions and to objectify the Other, even to create an Other where none exists (cf. Durkheim 1915: 52–57, 356–65). This Other is unfamiliar and powerful, hence terrifying. And it is filled with life. It is so pure, it must exist someplace else. Although Eliade (1959: 13) speculates that, for earliest humans, Holiness was everywhere, by the time we get to ancient Near Eastern literate societies, the world has become largely de-charmed, depersonalized, secularized. Holiness lodges in Heaven and in certain places on Earth, no longer in every beast and every tree.

Even though gods are themselves resistant or immune to aging and disease, they evidently find death and putrefaction literally repulsive. We earthlings, despite having been made in their image, are sickly and short-lived, worms in the divine form, so to speak (Ps 22:7; Job 17:14; 25:6). Thus, in our natural state, Yahweh finds us disgusting (cf. Lev 26:11, 15, 30, 43, 44). It is striking that, in Hebrew and cognate languages, the same term denotes the Earth on which humanity lives and the underworld of the dead in which we are buried (Hebrew 'ereṣ), as if to say, "In the midst of Life we are in Death." In their self-loathing fastidiousness, the ancients suffered not so much from Romantic *Weltschmerz* as from a nauseating consciousness of *Weltschmutz*.

There is, admittedly, a biblical countercurrent glorifying humanity, not for our ritual purity but for our God-given authority. The classic text is Ps 8:4–7:

When I see your Heavens, your fingers' work,
Moon and stars you established—
What is Human that you remember him,
Or Man's Son that you reckon him?
But you made him fall little short of divinity *('ĕlōhîm)*
And crowned him with glory and splendor
And made him rule your hands' work.
Everything you set under his feet.

Somehow, cleanliness is related to godliness (cf. 2 Sam 22:21= Ps 18:20; 24:4; 73:13; Job 9:30; 22:30). Holiness *(qōdeš)* seems to be an active substance with properties recalling electricity (e.g., it can be transmitted between bodies; it can create fire). Profanity *(ḥōl)*, in contrast, is simply the absence of Holiness. For clean *(ṭāhōr)* and unclean *(ṭāmē')*, the situation is reversed: uncleanliness spreads like disease, while cleanliness is just sterility. The clean allows Holiness to enter; the unclean repels Holiness, often violently. E.g., in the Korah story, Yahweh's fire both consecrates bronze untensils and kills the men carrying them (Num 16:35–17:2). At least in our world, Holiness is fragile, while pollution is rampant; according to Hag 2:11–13, impurity is even more contagious than Holiness (Levine 1987: 247).

What produces uncleanliness? We are not suprised to find impurity associated with disease and death. But impurity is also associated with reproduction: vaginal blood and seminal fluid. This is not necessarily a contradiction. Birth and death both represent transitions between nonbeing and being (Maccoby 1999; see below, pp. 692–93). In many cultures, moreover, substances passing from within to without the body are inherently defiling (Douglas 1966). In addition, the blood of menstruation signifies the absence of new life; semen deposited anywhere other than in a vagina is also the opposite of new life—i.e., death. (Admittedly, this does not account for the defilement caused by ordinary sexual intercourse.) It is even possible that menstrual blood is regarded as a monthly miscarriage, and that the blood of parturition is regarded either as belonging to a dead twin or as nine-months' worth of stored menstrual blood, as in some New Guinea societies (cf. Gillison 1993: 11, 48, 202).

Impurity can also be produced by moral sin, for Yahweh finds human misbehavior literally repellent. If we bear in mind Durkheim's (1915) thesis that religion's purpose is to instantiate social cohesion (see also Turner 1968), we will not find P's intersecting terminology of atonement and purification surprising (see further pp. 698–703). That which separates God from Man and that which separates Man from Man are equally offensive to the system. Although P takes it to an extreme, in its essence this is common Near Eastern theology. For example, when

Gudea of Lagash (c. 2125 B.C.E.) builds a temple, he both performs ritual purifications and reconciles parents to children, masters to slaves (Jacobsen 1987b: 403–4).

There is no escaping our impure lot. Even were we perfectly righteous, we could not avoid the offense of bodily defilement. An Israelite's whole duty, therefore, is to *limit* not eliminate uncleanliness. We must avoid certain substances and behaviors; and, whenever purity is nonetheless compromised, we must make the Sin-offering to obtain Clearing before Yahweh (see below).

REPAIRING THE BREACH

The Tabernacle is dedicated to a paradoxical proposition. God and Israel both want to live together, yet Yahweh's attribute of Holiness is incompatible with earthly corruption. How can the Tabernacle "tent among them amid their impurities" (Lev 16:16)? Whenever the Holy and the impure touch, at least one of the two is inevitably eliminated: the Impure repels the Holy and/or the Holy annihilates the Impure. Therefore, any meeting of God and Man should result in Yahweh's retreat into Heaven and/or death for the humans. No wonder Epicurean philosophers envisioned no contact at all between the human and the divine realms.

To completely undo the primordial, creative separation that raised Heaven above Earth and created *Lebensraum* for all creatures would be neither possible nor desirable. The Universe has returned to pre-Creation Chaos only once, in the catastrophic Flood, which will never recur (Genesis 6–9). Mankind's attempt to reach Heaven by building a tower (Genesis 11) was rejected by God as hubris. The whole purpose of biblical worship, and ancient worship in general, is to bring the human and divine into *safe* contact. How is this accomplished?

The simplest method is to exploit *topography*, to situate shrines for celestial deities on mountains (Clifford 1972; Levi 1981; Iakovidis 1981) and for chthonian deities in caves. The flatlanders of Mesopotamia even built artificial mountains, the ziggurats that inspired the story of Babel.

Second, some spots on Earth possess *intrinsic sanctity*, perhaps as the purported center of Creation. The *omphalus mundi* 'world-navel,' a term proper to the Greek shrine at Delphi, links the Earth below to the font of life above. Thus Sumerian Nippur had its temple *Duranki* 'Bond of Earth and Heaven'; Babylon had *Etemenanki* 'House that is the Foundation of Heaven and Earth,' while Israel had *bêt-'ēl* 'God's House,' also known as "Heaven's Gate," where angels ascended and descended (Gen 28:11–22).

A third, more sophisticated technique is to *simulate* Heaven on Earth. For us, who regard metaphors as mere figures of speech, "sympathetic magic" seems a pathetic sham. But to understand ancient religion, we must accept that the temple is simultaneously the god's true abode and a symbolic representation of his heavenly home, just as an idol both is and is not the deity it depicts (Jacobsen 1987a; above, pp. 167–70, 580–83). This is why any temple can be referred to as "Heaven" (Metzger 1970; Cross 1973: 142–43; Levenson 1988: 90–91; e.g., 1 Kgs 8:30;

Ps 11:4; 68:34–36). In *Exod. Rab.* 35:6, God explains exactly how the Tabernacle-works: "If you make below like what is on high, I will forsake my (angelic) Counselors on high and settle my Presence among you below" (cf. also Josephus *Ant.* 3.123; Heb 9:22–24). P's Tabernacle is a simulacrum of Yahweh's true home, with celestial Griffins rendered in two and three dimensions, with light shining amid the pure, scented clouds, with utmost Holiness strictures maintained.

How the Tabernacle cult unites Heaven and Earth may be inferred by analogy from 1 Kings 8, particularly vv 12–13, 27–28, where Solomon describes his new Temple:

> Yahweh proposed to tent (*škn*) in darkcloud. I have built, built a princely house for you, a firm seat for your eternal sitting/throne/dwelling (on *mākôn ləšibtəkā*, see vol. I, pp. 542–43). . . .

> Shall Deity really dwell upon Earth? See: the Heavens and the Heavens' Heavens do not contain you, much less this house that I have built! But you turn to your servant's prayer . . . so that your eyes may be open toward this house night and day, toward the place of which you said, "My Name shall be there."

Part of God's essence is immanent in the Temple and Tabernacle. Instead of a tangible, man-made idol, the biblical authors refer to Yahweh's "Glory" (*kābôd*) or his "Name" (*šēm*), aspects of the divine perceivable respectively by the eye and ear (Terrien 1978: xxviii, 121). To rationalize these paradoxes and render them more palatable, I propose a geometric analogy inspired by Plato's cave (*Republic* 7.514–17, 532). Let us say that a god inhabits a polydimensional realm that here and there extrudes into our three-dimensional space as a *projection*, just as a circle is the two-dimensional projection of a sphere onto a plane. Each temple is a partial rendering and manifestation of a god's ineffable home; each idol is a projection of the god's transmundane form. While not comprehending the whole essence of divinity, these projections are nonetheless full manifestations within our frame of reference. As a consequence of this transdimensionality, a god or parts of his body can even appear in two places at once.

In a sense, the Tabernacle and Temple realize Babel's aspiration of repairing or rather vaulting the rift between God and Creation: not by storming Heaven but by *enticing* Yahweh to Earth. But this returns us to our dilemma: how can the Holy and the Impure coexist?

A SAFE CONTAINER

According to JE, Moses first encounters Yahweh at "Deity's mountain, Horeb" on "Holiness ground (*'admat qōdeš*)" (3:1, 5). When Yahweh descends again onto the mountain in fire and cloud (19:18 [J]; 20:18[15] [E]; 24:16–17 [P]; Deut 4:11–12), Sinai/Horeb is again a nexus between Heaven and Earth. The mountain is screened off, and the people are commanded to observe rudimentary ritual purity strictures: literal cleanliness and sexual abstinence (19:10–14). As the

Tabernacle moves through the wilderness bearing Yahweh's cloudy-fiery presence in the midst of a people observing purity requirements, the Tent is essentially a portable Sinai. Wherever it stands, it bridges the gulf between Heaven and Earth (Milgrom 1991: 142–43; for some qualifications, see Schwartz 1996: 123–24). The Tabernacle's function is to transport God's presence from Sinai to Canaan in a safe container.

P makes the parallel between Sinai and the Tabernacle nearly explicit. Compare 24:15–16 with 40:34: in both, God's "cloud *('ānān)*" "covers *(ksy)*," bringing down the "Glory *(kābôd)*" to "tent *(škn)*." When Moses "enters *(bw')*" the cloud on Sinai (24:18), he is perhaps harmed (34:29–35; see pp. 620–23); when Yahweh's concentrated Glory fills the Tabernacle, Moses cannot enter at all (40:35) (cf. Weimar 1988: 359–64).

To mitigate the stark confrontation of the Holy and Impure, P envisions a complex system of graduated sanctity (pp. 527–28). In Israel as throughout the ancient Near East, a shrine sheathes the divine presence within concentric circles of diminishing sanctity, insulating the Holy and the impure from one another. The Tabernacle's outer Plaza is accessible to any Israelite free of routine impurity. The Tabernacle itself may be entered only by a priest. The space behind the Veil is invaded but once a year by the Great Priest. Without these safeguards, Yahweh's Holiness could not exist at all on Earth.

A HOLY PEOPLE

Why is the common person denied a direct experience of Yahweh? One answer is obvious: the Priestly Writer represented a class whose interest lay in restricting access to God, a guild that lived off of Israel's donations. And yet, according to a non-Priestly text, Yahweh chose all Israel to be "a priests' kingdom and a holy nation" (19:6; see NOTES). P, too, explores in detail the relationship between the sanctity of God, clergy and people, and Israel's distinctiveness as a nation.

The priest, especially the Great Priest in his splendid regalia, represents Yahweh to the people (see pp. 525–26). As God primordially separated *(hibdîl)* light and dark, Heaven and Earth, the realms of purity and corruption, the priest must "separate *(hibdîl)* between the Holiness and between the profane, and between the impure and between the pure" (Lev 10:10; cf. 11:47; Ezek 22:26; 44:23). Like the Creator, he distinguishes and separates between the things of Heaven and the things of Earth.

The priest does not just separate; he also mediates by teaching. He instructs the people like him to make distinctions (Lev 10:11; Ezek 44:23), so that they will be distinct among peoples (Lev 20:24–26) and acquire Holiness secondhand (see below). The most ascetic laity may even voluntarily assume the Naziritic taboos, attaining maximal purity and sanctity (Numbers 6).

Lev 19:2 commands/predicts: "You will be holy, for I, Yahweh your deity, am holy" (cf. Lev 11:44–45; 20:7, 26; 21:6–8; Num 15:40–41). Israel must and will maintain its purity because Yahweh dwells within the camp (Num 5:3) and will one day reside in the land (Num 35:34). Failure to observe the necessary distinctions and separations will be stringently punished for the communal welfare (e.g.,

Lev 7:20–21; 19:7–8; 22:3, 9; Num 18:32 19:13, 20; Joshua 7). Thus the divine presence is no unmitigated blessing. Biblical passages extolling the benefits of proximity to God (e.g., Ezek 37:21–28; 47:1–12; Haggai 1:2–11; Ps 65:4) must be balanced against the fearsome "Day of Yahweh," when the sky darkens and all Creation trembles when he comes (Isa 2:12–3:15; 13:6–22; 34:8–15; 63:4–6; Jer 46:10–12; 47:4–7; Ezek 7:7–27; 30:3–5; 34:12; Joel 1:15–2:17; 4:14–15; Amos 5:18–20; Obadiah 15; Zephaniah 1:2–2:3; 3:8; Zechariah 12–14; Mal 3:19, 23; Lam 1:21), for "who can bear the day of his coming and who left standing at his appearance?" (Mal 3:2) (cf. Houtman 2002: 322). Much of this ambivalence arises from the image of Yahweh as a terrifying-yet-fructifying storm god (most recently, Green 2003). Freud, moreover, might drop a hint or two about our attitudes toward our parents and elders generally. It is common human experience that intimacy with the mighty, e.g., kings, confers special advantages as well as commensurate dangers. (The notion that temples are both beneficial and dangerous is not restricted to Israel; for Sumerian parallels, see Kramer 1988.)

The Priestly source spells out fully the potential benefits and risks of Yahweh's presence in Leviticus 26, a catalog of the blessings (good harvests, peace, military success, reproductive fertility, God's continued residence) and the curses (disease, defeat, drought, wild beasts, famine, cannibalism, exile, national dissolution—in short, *ḥāmās* 'violence' [pp. 681–82, 702–3]) that Israel may expect, depending upon their adherence to the Law. In keeping Yahweh's Torah imparted by the priests, Israel has the potential to fulfill the natural destiny of humanity, created *bəṣelem 'ĕlōhîm* 'in the image of Deity/deities' (cf. Mettinger 1974). In the redacted Torah, the priest and Israel channel Yahweh's blessing to all nations (Gen 12:3; 18:18; 22:18; 26:4; 28:14).

For the Torah, the wilderness in which the people find themselves symbolizes the whole hostile world. Israel is beset by hunger (chap. 16), thirst (15:22–27; 17:1–7; Num 20:1–13), nomad raiders (17:8–16), snakes (Num 21:6–9) and, potentially, disease (NOTE to 15:26). Their defense is Yahweh's presence—even though God kills more Israelites than any of the other dangers.

THE SACRED AND THE SCARED

Haran (1978: 187) writes that the Tabernacle possesses a "lethal aura." We note the many death threats associated with its rites—for the Great Priest (28:35; Lev 16:2, 13), for the priests in general (Exod 28:43; 30:20–21; Lev 8:35; 10:6–7, 9; 22:9), for the Kohathites (Num 4:15, 19–20), for the Levites (Num 18:3) and for all Israel (Num 1:53; 8:19; 17:25; 18:5, 22). Leviticus 10 and Numbers 16 are cautionary stories of people dying while attempting to serve Yahweh (compare also 1 Sam 6:19 and 2 Sam 6:6–7). Moses himself may suffer physical impairment from shuttling back and forth between the human and the divine realms (Exod 34:29–35; see pp. 620–23). No wonder the desperate people wail, "Look, we are perishing and lost, all of us lost! Anyone approaching, approaching to Yahweh's Tabernacle dies! Have we finished perishing (yet)?" (Num 17:27–28).

Due to the West's secular-scientific orientation, and Christianity's emphasis on deferred retribution in the Hereafter, nobody any more finds worship terrifying.

Churches and synagogues are not regarded as likely to spontaneously detonate. Instead, conceive the Tabernacle as a *nuclear power plant*, channeling cosmic power from Heaven to Earth (cf. Quirke 1992: 70; Hutton 1994: 147). It must be meticulously tended by specially trained personnel clad in protective garb, wearing special identity badges, who periodically deal with crises of contamination. The least breach of protocol can be disastrous, not just for the technicians but for the entire community.

The most dangerous moment for a temple is the instant when it is switched on. In a split second, the shrine ceases to be a human artifact and becomes Heaven-on-Earth. Incredibly, the Impure and the Holy almost touch. Just as the Tabernacle is insulated spatially within zones of graduated sanctity, so its term of operation is preceded by seven days of graduated sanctity. If Yahweh had tried to inhabit the Tabernacle when it was first erected, his Holiness would have destroyed it. Instead, the weeklong purification-sanctification of the clergy and the shrine (Exodus 29) prepares the Tabernacle to go on line with minimal risk of a meltdown.

When the Tabernacle's Holiness level finally reaches the maximal earthly setting, it is as if a circuit is closed. Attracted from holiest Heaven into the holiest inner sanctum, a portion of Yahweh's essence descends to Earth. Then, attracted to the holiest Altar, fire leaps through the Tabernacle to ignite the offering in the Plaza (Lev 9:23-24). And the sweet savor rises back to Yahweh in holiest Heaven. Thus Yahweh himself burns the first fully legitimate sacrifice to his own heavenly presence. The following chapters, Leviticus 10-17, deal with the precautions that Israel and the priests must observe to sustain the cycle, to keep Yahweh present among them.

GOD WHO HIDES HIMSELF

Prophets, Psalms and Job all speak of alienation from God. Modern theologians describe the divine presence as "elusive" (Terrien 1978) or even "disappearing" (Friedman 1995). In Exodus, the rescued people ask, "Is there Yahweh in our midst or not?" (17:7). When Moses himself vanishes, they make themselves a deity in the form of a sculpted calf (chap. 32), as if they cannot endure a few days without a tangible symbol.

Humans may crave contact with the divine for many reasons: sublimated longing for parents; nostalgia for a never fully superseded animistic mind-set; frustration with a bureaucratized society that limits our access to power, etc. But the overriding factor is general insecurity in a dangerously unpredictable world.

The Yahwist tells tragic tales of humanity's attempts to become godlike or to penetrate the divine realm: by attaining godlike wisdom, by seeking immortality, by mingling the human and divine races and by building a ramp into Heaven (Genesis 2-3; 6:1-4; 11). Each of these efforts is quashed as hubris. We never stop trying, though. For the sage, for example, it is his wisdom that affords *ersatz* immortality (Prov 3:18; 11:30).

In contrast, P's ideal is to approach God through *imitatio Dei:* "You will be holy, for I am holy." Precisely by observing scrupulous distinctions and separations, Israelites can minimize their own separation from Yahweh. In the Tabernacle precinct, God and Man are parted, not by the height of Heaven, but by the twenty cubits of the outer chamber. Only the Veil's thickness separates the ordinary priests from Yahweh (Exod 26:33). And on Yom Kippur, smoke alone stands between the Great Priest and the Divine (Leviticus 16).

HOLY COMMUNION

A sacred shrine is where separations are minimized, if not transgressed or erased. For the Tabernacle, this is most obvious when Aaron moves back and forth between Yahweh and Israel. But it is also part of the background of the seemingly trivial ša'aṭnēz regulation: the ordinary Israelite may not mingle linen and wool, the respective fruits of agriculture and animal husbandry (Lev 19:19; Deut 22:11)—but of precisely such stuff are the Great Priestly vestments and the Tabernacle curtains woven (Exodus 26, 28). Again: at Creation, God separated the various living things "each according to its kind" (Gen 1:11, 12, 21, 24, 25). Yet the Tabernacle is decorated with images of the hybrid Griffins, even though the ordinary Israelite is forbidden to make images of any animal species (Exod 20:4; Deut 5:8) (cf. Jenson 1992: 86–87).

The clergy's special role notwithstanding, ritual also minimizes social separations, and indeed the constitution of community is the fundamental function of religion (Durkheim 1915). Eliade (1954; 1959: 68–113) explains that worship unifies society by symbolically transporting participants back in time to some First Moment (illud tempus). Standing in the Tabernacle Plaza, in communion with Yahweh and one's fellows, performing ancient rites, one rejoins the common ancestors, i.e., the Exodus generation with whom Yahweh covenanted. One feels the presence of Aaron the Great Priest and Moses the liberator. Inside the Tabernacle, swathed in layers of fabric, one senses Yahweh's Griffin-flanked spirit lodged in clouds of incense, the ineffable Presence that fluttered over the uncreated Deep. The sense of Yahweh's unapproachable transcendence is replaced by awe at his precarious immanence (cf. Sommer 2001: 61–63). (On Israelites' emotional experience upon visiting Yahweh's shrine, see further Smith 1997: 52–80, 118–41.)

But seriously—did anyone believe this? We associate playacting with childhood, but many if not all aspects of human culture partake of play (Huizinga 1970; see further below). Less naive than many of us, so-called primitives may sometimes admit that their rites are an embarrassing sham (cf. Tuzin 1997) and frequently do not regard them as literally effective (cf. Douglas 1966: 1–2, 58–72). But shared cynicism, too, promotes social cohesion, provided it is covert. What connects individuals more strongly than secret shame?

THE TENT OF SINGULARITY

Scripture is rife with anachronism. Often, the Rabbis simply threw up their hands: "There is no earlier and later in the Torah" (b. Pesaḥ. 6b, etc.). Some of the Bible's temporal anomalies we now attribute to the combination of sources. But why was the editor himself so indifferent? It was because his sources themselves, P in particular, did not follow a strictly logical time-flow.

In the course of this commentary, I have occasionally noted anachronisms in the Priestly account that frustrate our efforts to make temporal sense of events (cf. vol. I, pp. 590–92, 594). Most are not to be considered as mistakes but as foreshadowings. Many have to do with the donation of materials for the Tabernacle. For example, according to 38:8, the Basin is plated with mirrors of women who frequented the portal of Meeting Tent (see NOTES)—but there is not yet any Meeting Tent. Similarly, according to Num 17:3, Korah's censers are used to plate the Bronze Altar—which, according to 27:2; 38:2, was already bronze-plated. Exod 25:3 and 35:5 refer to a freewill donation including silver, seemingly redundant with the half-shekel tax of 30:11–16 (see p. 536). The results of this census-tax are reported in 38:25–28, and the silver put to use—before the census is actually held (Numbers 1; see above, pp. 536–37). (For another possible anachronism, see NOTE to 35:25, "woman.")

Above all, the events surrounding the erection and consecration of the Tabernacle are disarranged chronologically and cannot be reconstructed with assurance. In the following chart, which represents my best guess, notice the lack of correlation between the order in which the Torah reports the events and the order in which they are assumed to have transpired.

P's anachronisms—of which further examples could be supplied—are so pervasive they cannot be the result of careless supplementation. We cannot say, either, that they reflect the Priestly Writer's apathy to chronology, for of all the pentateuchal authors he is the most generous with dates. As difficult as it is to accept, I think that the writer *deliberately slurred time*, collapsing all the events surrounding the building and consecration of the Tabernacle into an atemporal *illud tempus*, a first time beyond time. In this light, recall the language shared between the Creation and Tabernacle accounts (above, pp. 675–76). Consider, too, the relationship between Tabernacle building and the Sabbath in 31:12–17 and 35:1–3, which together constitute the hinge of P's two-paneled Tabernacle pericope. P implies the congruence between Sabbath observance and Tabernacle worship also in Lev 19:30; 26:2: "You shall keep my Sabbaths and fear my Shrine" (Sarna 1991: 156). What exactly is the connection between the Sabbath and the Tabernacle?

The key is the term *mənûḥâ* 'rest.' On the one hand, the Tabernacle and later the Temple are each the place of Yahweh's *mənûḥâ* (Num 10:33–36; Isa 66:1; Ps 132:8, 13–14; 1 Chr 28:2) and also the symbol of Israel's *mənûḥâ* (1 Kgs 8:56). And every Sabbath is the time for God's and Israel's *mənûḥâ*. What the Tabernacle and Temple represent in space, the Sabbath represents in time. Worship takes Israel back to the first Sabbath, when Yahweh rested, and even a week before to day 0, when God had not yet begun his labors, and time did not exist. If the Sabbath is a kind of Tabernacle in time (NOTE to 31:16, "doing the Sabbath"), no less is the Tabernacle a Sabbath in space.

The Tabernacle-Sabbath space/time locus represents primordial inertia, the blessed inactivity to which only a god is fully entitled, since the heavenly realm is timeless (Deut 11:21; Ps 72:5, 7, 17; 89:3, 29–30, 37–38; 119:89 [?]; Job 14:12; Sir

Chart 1. Tentative Reconstruction of the events of month 1, year 2

Day 1. The Tabernacle is assembled (Exod 40:1, 17); the cloud descends (Exod 40:34a; Num 9:15–23)

Day 7 (?). Moses is instructed concerning the Lampstand (Num 8:1–4) and the Levites are consecrated (?) (Num 8:5–19)

Day 8. The priests and the Tabernacle are fully consecrated (Lev 8:1–9:22); the Levites are consecrated (?) (Num 8:20–29); the Glory enters Tabernacle (Exod 40:34b–35); the first sacrifice is made (Lev 9:23–24); Nadab and Abihu are killed (Leviticus 10); the chieftains begin to bring dedication offerings (Numbers 7)*

Day 10 (?). The paschal animal is selected (implicit; cf. Exod 12:3)

Day 14. The paschal sacrifice (Num 9:1–14)

Day 15. The start of the Unleavened Bread Festival (implicit; cf. Exod 12:15–20; Lev 23:6–8)

Day 19. The chieftains finish bringing dedication offerings (Numbers 7)*

Day 21. The conclusion of the Unleavened Bread Festival

---

* This assumes that in Num 7:1, 10, 84, the "day" that the Altar is anointed is really the *last* day, since, according to Exod 29:36–37, it is anointed daily for an entire week. If the "day" is rather the *first* day, then the chieftains bring their offerings on days 1–12.

45:15). An Earth creature, in contrast, is time's thrall, subject not only to death and decay, but also to generation and birth. (Cf. Maccoby's [1999] thesis that transitions between nonbeing and being cause impurity precisely because they violate the timelessness of the divine realm.)

I would regard the Tabernacle pericope and Sabbath legislation as, among other things, P's response to the Yahwist. In J, Humanity was expelled from God's presence, condemned to labor outside Eden "by your brow sweat" (Gen 3:19), just as, according to Mesopotamian myth, humans were created to liberate the gods from toil (e.g., *Atra-Ḥasīs* [Lambert and Millard 1969]; for further ancient Near Eastern parallels, see Weinfeld 1981; Batto 1987; Levenson 1988: 100–20). For the pessimistic Yahwist, humanity can never be godlike, may never again approach God.

P proposes a solution, however. Inside the Tabernacle and on the Sabbath day, Adam's curse is lifted. Both rest and labor are redefined, so they are no longer opposites. *Məlā(ʾ)kâ* 'task' and *ʿăbōdâ* 'work' are not mere subsistence activity; they are also building the Tabernacle and worshiping there. Man's punishment becomes Israel's blessing.

The Tabernacle-Creation theme, while proper to the Priestly source, also plays in the entire composite Torah. Moses, whose mother "saw how he was good" (2:2 [J]; cf. Gen 1:4, 10, 12, 18, 21, 25, 31 [P]), imitates the Creator by building God's first earthly residence, where the divine presence abides beneath the Griffin's wings, just as before time it fluttered over the waters. And Yahweh as Israel's overlord is implicitly contrasted with Pharaoh, who also made Israel work and build— but never gave them rest (*mənûḥâ*). In fact, the evil king had presciently accused Moses and Aaron, "you are interrupting (*hišbattem*) them from their tasks," *malgre lui* setting the precedent for the Sabbath (*šabbāt*) (Deut 5:15; NOTE to 5:5).

Following Eliade, we might say that the Tabernacle cultus collapses time and space into one another, returning us to the moment of Creation. But is not the astrophysicists' notion of a Black Hole—for that is what we are talking about—utterly anachronistic for the Bible?

Certainly. And yet, Hebrew uses the same word for a point in time and a point in space: *mōʿēd*, from the root *yʿd* 'to converge, meet.' The Tabernacle's archaic name is *ʾōhel mōʿēd* 'Meeting Tent.' It is simultaneously at *illud tempus* and *ille locus*. Were the Priestly Writer still alive, if he attempted to align his worldview with ours, he would explain that, in Meeting Tent and on the Sabbath day, space and time meet in a singularity: a space without space and a time without time.

LOCUS AND LOGOS

The Priestly Stratum, some say, cannot have been an independent document, because it lacks a Covenant ceremony at Sinai like that described in 24:1–11 (E) (e.g., Cross 1973: 318–20). But why should a Covenant ratification narrative be necessary? More important is that there be a Covenant at all, and Leviticus 26 (P) makes it perfectly clear that at Sinai Israel and Yahweh reaffirmed their status as treaty partners (cf. Schwartz 1996: 130–32). P refers explicitly to covenants with humanity and all living creatures (Gen 6:18; 9:9–17), with Abraham and his descendants (Genesis 17; Exod 2:24; 6:4–5) and with Phinehas (Num 25:12–13). In no case is there a ratifying ceremony. What right, the author may have asked, did Israel have to accept or reject divine regulations?

Anyway, it is not exactly true that P lacks a Covenant ritual. It is just of a different nature from what JE and D describe. Consider: at the center of the Tabernacle's concentric zones of purity—inside the Plaza, within the Tabernacle, behind the Veil, inside the Chest—sits the "Testimony" (*ʿēdūt*), i.e., the Covenant document (see NOTE to 25:16). Every act of Tabernacle worship celebrates and reaffirms that Covenant. We may compare the Abrahamic covenant in J and in P: for the Yahwist (Genesis 15), the *one-time* dismemberment of animals activates the covenant; for the Priestly Writer (Genesis 17), the circumcision ritual of the Abrahamic covenant is an *ongoing* duty.

Although they are separate pieces, the Testimony Chest and the *kappōret* always appear together in the Tabernacle pericope. This duality reflects a deeper duality in the manner of Yahweh's communicating with Israel. Since the invention of writing, words have existed in two forms: the spoken and the written. The former are fluid and ephemeral but lodge in the heart; the latter are static and eternal but easily ignored. The semiliterate society of Israel esteemed both modes (see Niditch 1996). Accordingly, the Tabernacle enshrines two manifestations of God's word. Moses *hears* the divine voice from between the Griffins (25:22; Num 7:89; cf. Exod 30:6; Lev 16:2), although it presumably falls silent after Moses' death. Eternally valid, however, is Yahweh's *written* Covenant with Israel, engraved upon the tablets. Neither encompasses Yahweh himself, but each is divine in origin and partakes of his essence. Like Yahweh's "Name," "Face," "arm," "feet," etc., the Word is a part of the divine whole manifest in and interacting with the sublunary world, whether articulating a pact with Israel or calling light into being.

In this respect, Priestly theology continues directly into Judaism, which sets the Torah scroll, God's Word, in the central niche of the synagogue. Worshipers face the scroll; it is dressed in fine clothes and precious metals and paraded around. Although its parchment skin may not be touched, its garments may be kissed. In short, to outward appearances, Torah serves as a surrogate for God. To call Judaism "bibliolatry" or "nomotheism" would be worse than caricature, but the ancient instinct to care for the divine symbol is plainly redirected toward the sacred scroll. And Christianity, at least in its Johannine strain, might justly, if simplistically, be characterized as real "logolatry" (below, pp. 720–21).

That Israel's worship is directed, not just to the divine presence above the Chest but also to the Law within, is the key to Priestly theology: the convergence of sacred space and sacred word. The divine exhalation that spoke the world into existence and briefly conversed with Moses is captured in writing and stored beneath the *kappōret*, the holiest, purest place on Earth.

Cult and Covenant unite the Israelite tribes into a nation, overriding clan loyalties and personal interest (cf. Halpern 1991). Cult creates the *potential* for Yahweh's presence in Israel's midst; Covenant *guarantees* it, providing certain conditions are met. Cult and Covenant are each fraught with blessing and curse. Cult and Covenant, once ruptured, can be restored with rites of *kippūrîm* 'Clearing' and *ḥaṭṭā(ʾ)t* 'Sin-offering,' which in Priestly parlance connote both social reconciliation and ritual purification. In Priestly theology, Cult *is* Covenant; Covenant *is* cult.

THOUGHT FOR FOOD

However bizarre and outmoded it seems to many today, the burnt animal sacrifice is the most natural thing in the world. First: as omnivores, we like to enrich our basically vegetarian diet with flesh. Second: meat consumption betokens power (Fiddes 1991). We therefore wait until society's dominant male—the Deity—has eaten before partaking ourselves. Whether or not this creates "table fellowship," i.e., putative kinship or corporate identity among participants (cf. 18:12; 24:11; Deut 12:7), is a matter of interpretation (Smith 1927: 269–440; Jay 1992: 6–7). The basic fact is that it is mere courtesy, not to say prudence, to let the most powerful member of society dine first, particularly when he has power of life and death over us (cf. Burkert 1996: 150). (The same rationale—the Master eats first—also explains the widespread custom of offering firstfruits and firstlings to the gods; for further discussion, see vol. I, pp. 454–56.) Herein lies the symbolic essence of the sacrificial meal: by sharing at Yahweh's table, humans both exercise and celebrate their position alongside God at the apex of the food chain.

As for burning the sacrificial victim, very few cultures routinely consume their meat raw. After all, part of our distinction from the other animals is the control of fire (Levi-Strauss 1978: 478–95; Fiddes 1991: 87–93; cf. Müller 1891: 121 apropos of Vedic religion). Our stomachs are inferior to those of other carnivores, no longer suited to eating flesh unless it is cooked or extremely fresh.

So sacrifice is as natural as eating. It becomes somewhat odd only when we add the elements of guilt and *atonement*. Guilt per se is not strange; a kin group feeling a burden of reciprocal responsibility will thrive better than a group composed of entirely self-centered individuals—who would not really constitute a social group at all. Thus natural selection favors social responsibility. Our forebears' lives were poor, short and, from our perspective, nasty and brutish. But they were certainly not solitary.

The question is: if we are natural omnivores, why should eating meat make anyone feel guilty? Hunting societies characteristically perform rituals that articulate and dispel a feeling of guilt vis-à-vis their prey, regarded as a worthy adversary and the object of literal sym-pathy ("with-feeling") (cf. Burkert 1983: 20–21; Balicki 1970: 218–20; Serpell 1986: 141–49; Guenther 1999: 70–80; and, on modern ambivalence toward venery, Cartmill 1993). How much more guilt might we expect from pastoralists, who nurture the very beasts on whose flesh they subsist (on the Nuer, for instance, see Evans-Pritchard 1956: 248–86)?

Since the "Neolithic Revolution" some 11,000 years ago, the breeding of cattle has considerably demystified the procurement of meat. One need not pray for a lucky kill; the victim, plump, slow and trusting, is readily at hand. Slaughter becomes quite casual. And yet we know from Greek (Burkert 1983) and Israelite literature that some intellectuals, at least, felt discomfort at their society's carnivorous ways. Nathan's parable of the poor man's ewe lamb (2 Sam 12:1–4), for example, is intelligible only on the assumption that it is psychologically possible to humanize a domestic beast: one can raise a lamb "as a daughter," so that slaughtering and eating it would be tantamount to murder and rape. The requirement to permit animals to rest on the Sabbath (20:10; 23:12; Deut 5:14) and other humane laws similarly personify nonhuman animals (see further NOTE to 23:19, "mother's milk"), for "the righteous (man) knows his beast's spirit" (Prov 12:10). Eccl 3:18–21 even questions whether there is any meaningful difference between humanity and the other creatures (for comparable Bedouin beliefs, see Musil [1928: 673]):

> I, I said in my heart concerning Man's Sons: ". . . They, they are beasts. . . . The fate of Man's Sons and the fate of the beasts is one fate; this one's death is like this one's death; and each has one spirit, so that Man's advantage over the beasts is nothing. . . . Everyone goes to one place; everyone was from the dirt; everyone returns to the dirt. Who knows whether Man's Son's spirit is what ascends upward, or whether the beast's spirit is what descends downward into the earth?"

That humans and their beasts constitute a greater society is a subtext in both the Plagues Narrative of Exodus and the Book of Jonah. Not surprisingly, the Israelites and other ancient complex societies conceived of themselves as a flock, with the king or god as the Good Shepherd (Eilberg-Schwartz 1990: 120–21; vol. I, pp. 221–22, 532–33, 568–69).

For his part, the Priestly Writer considers vegetarianism the ideal and equates slaughter with taking human life. That killing an animal generates bloodguilt is implied already in the tortuous syntax of Gen 1:29–30; 9:2–6:

See: I have given you every seed-bearing herb. . . . and every tree in which is a seed-bearing tree fruit, they shall be food for you. And for every earth animal and for every sky fowl and every walker on the earth in which is a living soul: every green herb for food. . . .

And fear of you and dread of you shall be upon every earth animal and upon every sky fowl, on everything that walks on the earth and on all the sea's fish—in your hand they are given. Food for you shall be every walker that is alive; like green herbs, I have given you all. However, flesh with its soul *(nepeš)*, its blood, you may not eat. And, however, your blood for your souls I shall demand. From every animal's hand, I shall demand it. And from Man's hand, from the hand of Man (for) his brother, I will demand Man's soul *(nepeš)*. The shedder of Man's blood, by/for Man *(bā'ādām)* his blood must be shed, for in Deity's image he made Man.

Lev 17:3–4 spells out the implication of this principle:

A man, a man (i.e., anyone) from Israel's House who slaughters a bull or a sheep or a goat in the camp or who slaughters from outside the camp and to the Meeting Tent Opening did not bring it to offer an offering to Yahweh before Yahweh's Tabernacle—blood will be reckoned to that man. He will have shed blood. And that man will be Cut Off from his people's midst.

"Cut Off" is the penalty of *kārēt*, the divine severing of the lineage that punishes the worst offenses (vol. I, pp. 403–4).

I cannot offer more than speculations as to how and why guilt entered meat-eating, how predator came to identify with prey. To my knowledge, the phenomenon is unique to humans. That is, a domestic dog may behave in a manner reminiscent of human guilt when he has broken a household taboo. But, should he kill and eat a mouse—as I have seen—his demeanor will be one of pride not culpability. (I am not sure how the dog would act if the mouse were a fellow pet.) Some cultures justify vegetarianism on the grounds of metempsychosis—i.e., the transmigration of souls—but this seems a secondary rationalization, not the root cause of guilt. Perhaps the empathy is a side effect of our evolutionarily favored hunting prowess: to catch a gazelle, be the gazelle.

I simply take it as given that there is a human propensity to identify with the animals we eat—after all, their flesh becomes our own—and consequently to feel guilt over our carnivorous habits (see Serpell 1986: 150–70). Yet few if any cultures pursue a vegetarian diet, except by necessity or as the choice of some individuals or as a caste-related taboo (e.g., Indian Brahmins and Greek Pythagoreans; see briefly Burkert 1972: 124–26). Instead, societies use religious rituals to absolve the carnivorous majority, the most familiar examples in our culture being Jewish and Muslim ritual slaughter, both supposed to minimize the victims' pain. And, while the modern Christian and secular cultures provide no exact analogy, bloodless, odorless supermarket displays deliberately create the impression that meat naturally comes wrapped in plastic, not from a carcass. (French-derived culinary terms in English—"beef," "veal," "pork," and "mutton" for "bull," "calf," "pig" and "sheep"—could also suggest an aversion, but probably have more to do with the vicissitudes of Anglo-Norman history than carnivorous guilt.)

The Bible's tidy solution is the equation blood = life (Lev 17:11, 14; Deut 12:23). So long as one abstains from blood (Gen 9:4; Lev 3:17; 7:26; 17:10–14; 19:26), *one has not really taken life*. According to Deut 12:16, 23–24; 15:23; Jer 7:21, one need not even present the blood to God; as in P's pre-Sinaitic dispensation, it suffices merely to discard it. Because the animals they may eat are themselves vegetarians, Israelites are doubly insulated from culpability (Leviticus 11; Deut 14:3–21). Even an ox that has shed but not ingested blood is forbidden (Exod 21:28).

MAGNUM MYSTERIUM: LET US PREY

From here it is a short step to the notion that sacrifice and blood rites can remove other forms of guilt/impurity, and another step to a general principle that "without bloodshed there is no release [from sin]" (Heb 9:22). The identification of predator with prey makes each offering a vicarious self-sacrifice (cf. Evans-Pritchard 1956: 280; Hubert and Mauss 1964: 98; Eilberg-Schwartz 1990: 135–36, 249–50 n. 29). It is no coincidence that the J source makes sacrifice and murder coeval (Gen 4:1–16). One pays for offenses against society and/or the Deity not with one's own blood but with an animal's. In the words of a Punic stela from N'gaous (Algeria): "Spirit for spirit, blood for blood, life for life . . . a lamb as a substitute" (Alquier and Alquier 1931). This is the symbolism of the Akedah, when Abraham offers a ram in lieu of his own offspring (Genesis 22 [E]).

To judge from its etymology, the Northwest Semitic noun *maḏbaḥ (> Hebrew *mizbēaḥ* 'altar') originally denoted a place of *ḏbḥ* 'slaughter.' In Gen 22:9–10 and 1 Sam 14:32–35), preserving archaic tradition, we still find victims laid upon the altar alive; compare also 2 Kings 23:20: "And he slaughtered *(wayyizbaḥ)* the priests of the High Places . . . upon the altars *(hammizbᵊḥôt)*." Immediately after the killing, the meat was presumably cooked in a nearby firepit and then eaten. The altar was thus basically a slaughter block (cf. Judg 9:5; 2 Kgs 23:20); the main religious moment was the kill. (This may be why Egyptian priests wore panther skins, in memory of their prehistoric role as huntmaster [cf. Lorton 1999: 161].)

Over time, however, the notion developed that the victim was sent to Heaven by being burnt. The slaughter block then became a sacred hearth, an altar in our sense, and the actual slaughter was conducted nearby. (Cf. Ezek 40:39–42; 41:22; 44:16, where *šulḥān* 'table' connotes variously a slaughter block and the great Altar.)

Thus Israelite religion, particularly in its Priestly guise, largely de-sacralizes slaughter. Other cultures place great emphasis on the victim: it is named, pampered, adorned or, conversely, ritually abused (on later Jewish celebration of the sacrificial victim, see *m. Bikk.* 3). To insulate society from guilt, the beast is slaughtered with a special knife by a special person, either priest or pariah, according to a prescribed procedure (see, e.g., Burkert [1983: 3–7] on the Greek pratice; Hubert and Mauss [1964: 30–31, 33] on the Hindu; Lienhardt [1961:

292–93] for the Dinka). The kill is the sacrifice. For P, too, slaughter must be performed on a perfect specimen and within the Tabernacle precincts. But it is the owner who kills, not a ritual specialist. Even a woman, ordinarily excluded from ritual activities, may bring and presumably slaughter her own sacrifice (cf. Lev 12:6, 8; 15:29; Numbers 30; 1 Sam 1:25; Prov 7:14; b. Ḥag. 16b; see Gruber 1987: 46 n. 37; Braulik 1992). The priest steps in only to convey some meat and blood to the Altar, which thus becomes a *symbolic slaughter block*, and the priest a *symbolic slaughterer*. Only then is the killing a full *zebaḥ* 'sacrifice.' For alimentary offerings, the celebrants are now free to eat the rest without fear of bloodguilt.

We may now appreciate the importance of blood manipulation in Israelite sacrifices. While all sacrifices insulate celebrants from the guilt of life-taking, the most potent expiatory ritual, the *ḥaṭṭā(ʾ)t* 'Sin-offering,' cleanses the guilt and defilement caused by ritual impurity and other inadvertent offenses (Leviticus 4–5; 6:17–7:10). The victim's blood is not simply poured out or splashed against the Altar but divided into two parts. For ordinary, inadvertent violations, some blood is applied to the Bronze Altar's horns and the rest poured around its base (Lev 4:25, 30, 34). Various entrails are burned upon the Altar; the remainder is eaten by the priests. When the offender is the Great Priest or the whole community, however, more extreme measures are required: the blood is brought inside the Tabernacle.

Characteristically, P does not explain how the Sin-offering effects expiation. But the various manipulations involved—laying hands upon the victim, bloodying the Altar's horns, pouring out more blood at the base, disposing of the carcass outside the camp—must have some function, some meaning to those who actually performed the rites. Milgrom (1991: 253–92) claims that this blood purges not humans but the Tabernacle of human-caused impurities. Others more plausibly argue that the rite cleanses the offerer, too (e.g., Kiuchi 1987; Zohar 1988; Jenson 1992: 157–59; Maccoby 1999: 164–208). I think the most natural interpretation is that, by laying hands, the offerant transfers his sin/impurity to the victim (NOTE to 29:14, "Sin-offering"). Disposing of the carcass outside the camp banishes some of the offense. As for blood, a reasonable inference, confirmed by Lev 16:16, is that it *transfers sin/impurity to the Tabernacle or the Altar* (compare Jer 17:1: "Judah's *ḥaṭṭāʾt* 'sin' is written . . . on their heart's tablet and on their altars' horns"). And the blood libation puts some of the offense into the earth beneath the Plaza (on the ground's affinity for blood, see also Gen 4:10–11; Num 35:33; Deut 19:10; Ezek 9:9; 36:18; Joel 4:19; Ps 106:38; 1 Chr 22:8).

SPECULATION: In ancient Near Eastern religions, the supernatural powers reside not only in the sky but also underground. One strongly suspects, therefore, that the Sin-offering retains an atavistic vestige of chthonian rites appeasing the dead or other netherworldly powers (cf. Homer *Odyssey* XI), just as the Altar's horns point upward to the celestial realm. In this sense, too, cult reunites the long-sundered Heaven and Earth/Underworld (*ʾereṣ*)

The rest of the Sin-offering the priests eat (Lev 5:13; 6:10–11; 7:6–10; 10:17, 19; Ezek 42:13; 44:29; Hos 4:8). Here, too, the symbolism is not far to seek. The offerer's sin, transferred to the sacrificial victim, ends up partly inside the Tabernacle, partly inside the priests themselves (cf. Milgrom 1991: 637–39; *pace* Hutton 1994: 147). It appears that the Priestly Writer was leery about spelling this out, perhaps fearing satire like Hos 4:8, according to which priests may become as guilty and impure as those whose Sin-offerings they consume (see NOTE to 28:38, "Bear the Transgression of the Holinesses").

In sum, although the matter is too complicated for full analysis here, I understand that the Sin-offering transfers sins/impurities from Israel to the Tabernacle and its personnel, where they may be safely stored pending the annual catharsis on Yom Kippur (Leviticus 16). In a similar manner, the bloodguilt accumulated through ordinary slaughter is also centralized and neutralized by the Tabernacle (Leviticus 17).

But this raises an obvious question: are not the Holy and the Impure utterly incompatible? Ordinarily, they are. But it is precisely through the Sin-offering that a mediation is effected. For the normal Sin-offering, blood is applied to the Altar's extremities, top and bottom. (On the horns and bloodguilt, see also NOTE to 21:14, "my altar.") For more flagrant offenses, the blood is put upon the Golden Altar and the Veil, presumably because these have greater power to contain sin/impurity.

P's *magnum mysterium* is that impurity *is* compatible with Holiness, but only if properly transferred by the Sin-offering. The Tabernacle and its officers function like a filter. Throughout the year they grow more and more defiled, yet they continue to function. When too much sin/impurity accrues, it is discharged *en masse* on Clearing Day via the scapegoat and sent to Azazel, i.e., Death (?; see Tawil 1980) (see further below; also NOTES to 29:33).

SPECULATION: The ritual of Clearing Day assumes that the shrine's power to absorb sin is finite. The same may also be implied by the Tabernacle consecration ceremony (Exodus 29; Leviticus 8–9). For seven days, the House of Aaron is rapidly drained of impurities by multiple Sin-offerings. Presumably, all their offenses adhere to the Altar. Because they have never before been purged and yet must achieve a super-human purity, it follows that the accumulation must be considerable.

When, in Lev 9:24, Yahweh finally ignites the first fully valid holocaust with supernatural fire, it is generally understood as a sign of his favor (cf. Judg 13:15–20; 1 Kgs 18:22–38; 1 Chr 21:26; 2 Chr 7:1–3). And yet, elsewhere in P, Yahweh's fire "comes out" (*yṣ'*) to avenge purity *violations* (Lev 10:2; Num 16:35). Perhaps it is the Altar's being supercharged with sin/impurity that provokes God's cleansing fire. If so, among the goals of Yom Kippur is to ensure that Yahweh's fire need never again erupt.

BLOOD WILL HAVE BLOOD

The atoning, purifying virtue of blood, itself ritually unclean, is the sublime paradox that allows humans and God impossibly to dwell together. By virtue of the Sin-offering, transgression and impurity acquire a cleansing power. The very blood that would otherwise count as murder is applied to the ultra-holy Altar (29:37) without adverse consequences. Instead, the act discharges guilt. Girard (1977: 36) comments: "How can one cleanse the infected members [of society] of all trace of pollution? Does there exist some miraculous substance potent enough not only to resist infection but also to purify, if need be, the contaminated blood? Only blood itself . . . can accomplish this feat." Like snake venom, blood is a poison that is its own antidote. Here is another analogy: through the Sin-offering, the ultimate staining agent becomes the ultimate detergent. Rev 7:14 spells out the paradox explicitly, in a manner evocative of soap commercials: "They have washed and whitened their robes in the Lamb's blood."

SPECULATION: The Sin-offering rite may in fact be less paradoxical than the foregoing suggests. If the laying of hands transfers sin/impurity from offerer to victim, then killing the beast may not create bloodguilt at all, just as executing a murderer eliminates rather than generates bloodguilt (cf. Propp 1993). In other words, the Sin-offering may be a special procedure for converting blood from a defiling to a purifying agent. Compare Num 35:33–34: "And don't pollute the land . . . for blood, it is what pollutes the land. And the land cannot be Cleared of the blood that is shed in it, except by the blood of its shedder." In other words, to keep the land free of bloodguilt, one must shed blood.

What makes blood so defiling when it is outside a body? It is not just fluid out of its proper place, which by Douglas's (1966: 121) influential treatment would qualify it as defiling. Blood is evidence that violence has recently occurred and may recur. Not surprisingly, the color red produces anxiety in humans and even in rhesus monkeys (Humphrey 1992: 38–49).

Fear is good, not only because it protects us from harm but because it checks our impulses. The violence that continually threatens to rend society is controlled mainly by the potential for retribution. Again Girard (1977: 36): "The function of ritual is to . . . 'trick' violence into spending itself on victims whose death will provoke no reprisals," i.e., the animal sacrifice. Not that we reason this out so carefully. Killing is in our nature, hence Burkert's mock-Linnaean nomenclature *Homo necans* 'Killer Man.' But so is self-control in our nature. No less than lions, wolves and other social carnivores, our survival depends on our ability to direct our violence toward the common good.

In sum: many writers describe animal sacrifice, like the hunt and rites of passage, as discharging male aggression in ways beneficial to the group (e.g., Girard 1977; Burkert 1983; Jay 1992). The Priestly Writer himself holds such a view, advocating bloodless flesh eating as the solution to the general "violence" (*ḥāmās*) that obtained before the Flood and brought on universal obliteration (Gen 6:11–12; 9:4–6). Ritualized meat consumption, in contrast, has the power to stabilize and even create society. (Modern researchers' focus on *male* aggression, however, may be misplaced: when herding replaced hunting, slaughter ceased to be an all-male province.)

SHOULD I EAT BULLS' FLESH, DRINK GOATS' BLOOD?

The most difficult biblical sacrifice to explain is the holocaust, which, as Theophrastus carped (*apud* Porphyry *Abst.* 2.26), seems a colossal waste of meat. Still, while a hunting society must be parsimonious, pastoralists can afford profligacy. From the shepherd's viewpoint, the ostensive prodigality is really a far-sighted investment, an animistic Pascal's Wager. We give to Nature/the gods/God in proportion to our meager means in the hopes that it/they/he will feel obliged to return the favor in porportion to its/their/his infinite means (on the social networks created by giving, see the classic study of Mauss [1967], esp. pp. 12–15 on sacrifice as gift exchange with the gods; contrast Hubert and Mauss [1964]). The goal is an eternal, self-replenishing cycle of reciprocal obligation.

Moreover, the identification of predator and prey may again play a role. Burkert (1996: 30–31) argues that, like a trapped fox severing its own paw or a lizard surrendering its tail to a predator, humans will give up a part of their bodies (ritual mutilation), a part of their families (child sacrifice/consecration) or part of their wealth (sacrifice) to save themselves from a powerful, dangerous being: "Cult . . . means to avert danger by consenting to a tolerable loss, in this way manipulating the 'eater,' " i.e., the god. This is precisely the symbolism of the apotropaic paschal sacrifice: the "wounded" doorway fools the forces of destruction into thinking that a human has already died (on the *Pesaḥ* as P's transition to true sacrifice, see vol. I, pp. 445–51).

From P's perspective, what would happen if there were no sacrificial cult at all? Would Yahweh starve, like the Egyptian pantheon (cf. Shafer 1997: 24) or like the gods in the Mesopotamian Flood story (*Atra-Ḥasīs* III.iii.31; iv.21–22 [Lambert and Millard 1969: 95, 97]; cf. *Gilgamesh* XI.159–61 [*ANET* 95])? Presumably not, to judge from numerous passages disparaging the efficacy or necessity of sacrifice (1 Sam 15:22; Isa 1:10–17; Jer 6:20; 7:21–26; Hos 6:6; Amos 5:21–27; Micah 6:6–8; Ps 40:7–8; 50:7–15; 51:18–19; Prov 15:8; 21:3, 27). And yet we cannot be certain. P does imply that, in some sense, Yahweh subsists on Israel's offerings as his food (Gen 8:21; Exod 29:18; Lev 21:21; 22:25; 26:31; cf. Deut 4:28; 32:38; 1 Sam 26:19; Ezek 41:22; 44:16; Mal 1:7, 12; Ps 115:5–6).

As for humanity: without the sacrificial cult, Israel would see once again the "violence" that provoked the Flood, the ineradicable bloodguilt that the land absorbs but does not discharge (cf. Gen 4:10–11; 6:5–7 [J], 13 [P]). A new Flood there cannot be, by God's own oath (Gen 9:8–17 [P]). But should Canaan absorb too much blood, it will vomit out its inhabitants in communal *kārēt*, the ultimate curse upon Israel (Lev 18:24–28; 20:22–23; cf. Ps 106:38–41). Thus the Tabernacle and Altar serve to protect the land from defilement and Israel from exile. There are, admittedly, capital crimes for which ritual affords no expiation — idolatry, sex crime, deliberate homicide (Frymer-Kensky 1983: 407–9). But P's equation of slaughter and murder is clear in its implication. Without the Tabernacle, Israel's natural, carnivorous proclivities alone would bring about its ruin.

Because sacrifice provides not only food but also purification-atonement (*kippūrîm* 'Clearing'), the cult permits maximal proximity between God and humankind. By the terms of the Covenant, life flows back and forth between Earth and Heaven, as purification rites mitigate their natural antagonism (cf. Shafer's [1997: 24] description of Egyptian sacrificial theology).

HOMO NECANS ATQUE LUDENS

The Hebrew term for ritual is '*ăbōdâ*, literally "work." Worship, no less than farming, herding and building, is what Israel must do to survive. '*Ăbōdâ* may also be rendered "service," for ancient worship symbolically supplied all divine wants, the "care and feeding of the gods" (cf. Oppenheim 1964: 183).

And yet, unlike plowing a field or building a house, a ritual's connection to actual subsistence may be invisible to the outsider. In our terms, rather than "work," worship might be better regarded as a form of "play" (Huizinga 1970: 29–46), witness the oft-noted parallels between religious ritual and drama (e.g., Turner 1968). How different is worshiping an idol from playing house with a doll? Are gods imaginary friends for grownups? Play takes place in a restricted space for a defined time; it has esoteric rules, with social consequences for those who refuse to abide by them or would make their own; it creates an imagined, alternative world; it may be secret, with the sexes segregated or certain potential playmates excluded; special masks or clothes may be worn; there is a willing suspension of disbelief; there is a period of tension followed by release, once the game has been performed satisfactorily; it may be done over and over.

All this recalls religious ritual, and Huizinga even claims that what we call civilization is but an aspect of play—in which case, our work/play antinomy is illusory. At any rate, since animals exhibit ludic behavior, we may be sure that play is biologically fundamental, whatever its evolutionary purpose. Although Huizinga calls our species *Homo ludens* 'Man who plays,' a sense of fun is not our unique possession. But only for humans is play deadly serious.

THE PASTORAL MYSTIQUE

Why does the Bible record that Yahweh's first dwelling on Earth was a tent? The naive answer would be that this is the historical truth (see further below).

An equally naive answer would be that, in order to worship en route from Egypt to Canaan, the Israelites needed a tabernacle. Ordinary nomads can periodically visit fixed holy spots during their seasonal wanderings. But emigrating nomads would require a portable temple (Philo *Moses* 2.71–73; Josephus *Ant.* 3.103), pending their settlement in the land and the opportunity to construct a permanent structure (Luzzatto on 25:1).

Moreover, soldiers and their gods inhabit tents. P imagines Israel not just as migrants but as Yahweh's troops marching through the desert. This makes sense in narrative context—they are about to battle the Canaanites—and also reflects the Priestly Writer's aim to demythologize the divine title *yahwe(h) ṣabā'ōt* 'Yahweh of Brigades' (see vol. I, pp. 281, 405). Thus Kitchen (1993: 121*) and Homan

(2002: 111–16) find the closest parallel to the biblical Tabernacle in Ramesses II's battle tent.

The historian of religions comes up with yet another explanation of the Tabernacle, not at all incompatible with the foregoing. The Canaanites, to whom the Israelites were culturally akin (pp. 739, 743), maintained that some of their gods inhabited tents; the Israelites held similar traditions. Our main data come from a region technically north of Canaan, but with good reason scholars accept Ugaritic mythology as generically Canaanite.

In Ugaritic literature, two tabernacles, which may be one and the same (Clifford 1971: 35–57), stand out: (a) the tent in which the gods gather in "meeting" (m'd), and (b) the tent inhabited by the head of the pantheon, the deity "God" ('Ilu, El), a domicile also mentioned in a Canaanite myth preserved in Hittite (ANET 519). Other gods, too, live in tents (Homan 2002: 190). It stands to reason that the biblical 'ōhel mō'ēd 'Meeting Tent in which Yahweh resides on Earth draws from the wellsprings of Canaanite mythology, since in many other respects the figure of Yahweh is rooted in the imagery of 'Ilu (Cross 1961b: 224; 1973: 44–75; Smith 2002; see also p. 787). Other possible vestiges of the mythic tent of Canaan are biblical passages implicitly or explicitly likening Heaven to a tent (2 Sam 22 = Ps 18:10, 12; Isa 40:22; 42:5; 44:24; 45:12; 48:13; 51:13, 16; Jer 10:12; 51:15; Zech 12:1; Ps 19:5; 104:2; 144:5; Job 9:8; 36:29; see Houtman 1993b: 210–22). Centuries later, Rev 13:6; 15:5; 21 and 4QShirShabb[d] 1.ii.10–16 will combine the imagery of Tabernacle and Temple to describe Heaven (below, pp. 721–22; Koester 1989: 38–39).

But this elicits a further question: why did some Canaanites and perhaps other kindred peoples believe that their high gods inhabited tents? Neither the Ugaritians nor the Israelites were primarily nomadic when they produced their canonical literature, for literacy itself is a feature of urbanism. On the contrary, one assumes that the Ugaritic and Israelite scribes felt the city-dweller's characteristic disdain toward the nomad (cf. Gen 4:11–16; 16:12; 27:39–40).

The answer is that both the Ugaritians and the Israelites were the descendants of tent-dwelling nomads. The Bible claims as much, and linguistic and archaeological evidence (Finkelstein 1988: 244–50) suggests that the Canaanites and Israelites derive from the Middle Bronze Age seminomadic Syrian culture scholars call Amorite (Liverani 1973). We do not actually know whether the Amorites themselves pictured their deities as tent-dwellers, but a pastoral mystique might be expected to linger among their descendants. Analogously, while Mesopotamian culture traditionally despised the Amorite nomad as uncouth (Liverani, p. 105), the two mightiest kings of the eighteenth century B.C.E., Hammurapi of Babylon and Shamshi Adad I of Assyria, with perverse chauvinism boasted their descent from tribal tent-dwellers (Finkelstein 1966), as modern Arabs may boast a Bedouin heritage. Even as late as the reign of Cyrus in the sixth century B.C.E., the territory west (amurru) of Mesopotamia was still seen as the land of tent-dwelling kings (ANET 316; original text in Weissbach 1911: 6).

The Canaanites pictured their high god 'Ilu as an old man with a white beard sitting in a luxurious tent—what we would call a sheikh. It is instructive to compare the biblical model of a human nomad chieftain, Abraham, with Ugaritic 'Ilu (see Pope 1955; Miller 1973). Once capable of derring-do, each retains his placid authority even as those around him plot and act. His main weakness is a suceptibility to wheedling and intimidation from women. We easily detect a caricature of nomadic patriarchy from the standpoint of urban sophistication.

Whether Canaanite 'Ilu was actually worshiped in a tent is moot. The apparent absence of a temple to 'Ilu at Ugarit has led to speculations of a tabernacle cult. Kitchen (1993: 121*) observes that the legendary hero Kirta worships the gods in a tent (*KTU*. 1.14.iii.55; *ANET* 144). Scattered references to tent or hut shrines— e.g., among the Hittites (Kronasser 1963: 27), Carthaginians (Diodorus Siculus *Bibliotheca Historica* 20.65.1; Homan 2002: 70, 101–2), Arabs (Lammens 1928: 101–79) and at Hatra (Hillers 1972)—and the discovery of a sacred tabernacle at Timna (Rothenberg 1972: 151–52)—leave no doubt of the institution's reality in ancient Syria-Palestine (Fritz 1977: 109–11).

How can one both despise and idealize tent-dwelling? The explanation is simple. For peoples of Amorite extraction, the tent represented the primordial, the pure, the idyllic—so long as it was inhabited by literary characters out of the past, such as gods or ancestors. A contemporary tent-dweller, in contrast, was viewed as a savage. (The American attitude toward log cabins would not differ much.) The idealized tent can also exist in the future: compare Hos 12:10, "I will again make you dwell in tents, like the days of Meeting *(kîmê mō'ēd)*," simultaneously evoking camping out during pilgrimages (Deut 16:7) and the pentateuchal *'ōhel mō'ēd* 'Meeting Tent.'

Predictably, wherever they settle, former nomads recycle old words for tent. For instance, Old Turkic *yurt* 'tent' in Modern Turkish means "country, fatherland." Similarly, probably derived from proto-Semitic *'ahl* 'tent' (< *'hl* 'tie' [Akkadian *e'ēlu*]) are Akkadian *ālu* 'city' and Arabic *'ahl* 'family.' For its part, the Bible manifests frequent semantic overlap between *bayit* 'house' and various words for tent, particularly in poetry (Homan 2002: 16–27). For example, the terms *bayit* and *'ōhel* 'tent' are parallel in Ps 84:11; Prov 14:11; Job 21:28 (Avishur 1984: 158), and tent imagery can flow naturally into house imagery (Ps 104:2–3; 132:3). Often "tent" is simply a metaphor for habitation (Jer 4:20; 30:18; Zech 12:7; Mal 2:12; Ps 52:7; Job 5:24; 8:22, etc.). It seems that Meeting Tent and David's sacred tent were sometimes called *bêt yahwe(h)* 'Yahweh's House' (Josh 6:24; Judg 19:18 [?]; 2 Sam 12:20). Conversely, the Temple may be referred to as a "tent *('ōhel)*" or "hut *(śukkâ)*" (Ps 15:1; 27:5–6; 61:5; 1 Chr 9:19, 21, 23; 6:33; 23:32; 2 Chr 24:6; 29:6). In the case of the shrine at Shiloh, overlapping house and tent language creates confusion as to which sort of structure actually stood there (below, p. 708).

THE MOTHER TENT

One might expect a priori that for many post-nomadic peoples, the tent is a female symbol, representing the matrix from which domestic culture springs. Among the Bedouin, for example, the women erect the tents (Doughty 1921: 1.217; Dickson

1983: 60), to which they are largely confined. Similarly, the Bible associates men with exteriority—the field—and women with interiority—the tent—evoking both their respective anatomical structures and their social status (Seeman 1998). In Patriarchal times, the sphere of respectable women is the tent (Gen 18:6–10; 24:65–67); a man must enter *(bwʾ)* the one in order to enter the other. (Compare, too, the Rabbinic tradition that R. Yose understood both the words "tent" [*b. Moʿed Qaṭ.* 7b] and "house" [*b. Šabb.* 118b] to connote a wife.) The exception that proves the rule is the effeminate "mama's boy" Jacob, a "tent man" explicitly contrasted to the "field man" Esau (Gen 25:27–28). (Jacob's female antitype, in this sense, is his unfortunate, outgoing daughter Dinah [Genesis 34].) It is also possible that, like the Bedouin, Israelite women pitched tents; in Isa 54:2, Israel, personified as a childless widow, is exhorted to expand her tent in preparation for her fruitful marriage to Yahweh. Women may also be described as making tent-shrines in 2 Kgs 23:7 and Ezek 16:16, but the contexts are unclear.

Further evidence for the association of tents with women comes from female names containing the element *ʾōhel* 'tent': Oholibamah (Gen 36:2), Oholah and Oholibah (Ezekiel 23), plus epigraphic *ḥmy-ʾhl*, a woman (Hestrin and Dayagi-Mendels 1979: 51 [number 34]; *AHI* 100.412.1). The man's name Oholiab in Exodus is an exception, however. (Note, too, that in names such as *ḥmy-ʾhl* and Oholiab, the tent itself is masculine not feminine; see NOTE to 31:6, "Oholiab.")

Moreover, Homan (2002: 79–87) analyses in detail the tent's erotic overtones. The association is most overt in 2 Sam 16:22, where Absalom lies with his father's harem in a special tent. (Psalm 132:3 may refer to a bed within a tent, but the language is not quite clear.)

Might the Tabernacle somehow be a female symbol, at least for men who worship there? After all, the Arabic root *ḥrm* connotes both women's quarters *(ḥarīm, muḥarram)* and the sacred *(ḥaram)*, both of restricted access. And among the Canaanites, "Holiness" itself is personified as the great goddess Qudšu (see Maier 1986: 81–96; her other name, ʾAṯiratu, may also mean 'holy place' [NOTE to 34:13]). While Seeman (1998: 125) disassociates the Tabernacle from female associations, Cole (1973: 194) compares the Tabernacle to a nomad's tent as follows: the people's Plaza is the corral; the Holiness is the general quarters, and the inner sanctum concealing an inaccessible mystery is the *women's quarters.* The Tabernacle's perfumes are like those used by lovers (Ps 45:9; Prov 7:17; Cant 1:13; 3:6–7; 5:5; Ruth 3:3; Esth 2:12; 3 Macc 4:6), a connection made explicit in Sir 24:15. The Holiness of Holinesses is secret, not to be defiled by the eyes (Lev 16:2, 12–13; Num 4:18–20). Yahweh even kills the men of Beth Shemesh for peeping into his sacred Chest (1 Sam 6:19–20).

I know no evidence that biblical man viewed Yahweh as a *female lover* (cf. Eilberg-Schwartz 1994 on God as Israel's *male* lover). But *maternal* imagery would make considerable sense, since Yahweh is elsewhere compared to a mother (e.g., Isa 66:7–14; see further Trible 1978; Propp 1999). Unlike lover imagery, mother imagery would have an emotional effect for readers of both sexes.

In the course of time, the female associations of Tabernacle and Temple would be made explicit. Sir 24:8 portrays personified Wisdom pitching her tent, i.e., the Tabernacle, among Israel; and *b. Yoma* 54a compares the Chest's poles pressing the Temple veil to breasts straining against a blouse. Later Judaism, bereft of Tabernacle and Temple, would celebrate the female divine hypostasis Shekhinah (*šəkînâ* 'indwelling,' cf. *miškān* 'Tabernacle') who/which represents God's personified presence on Earth (see in general Patai 1967).

WOULD YOU BUILD ME A HOUSE FOR MY DWELLING?

The Ugaritic poem called "Of Ba'lu" (translation in *ANET* 129–42) describes the storm god's ascent to power. As the story begins, tent-dwelling 'Ilu is the source of divine authority. But in the end, the younger, more dynamic Ba'lu triumphs over his foes and, having built a palace atop Mount Zaphon, is acclaimed king of gods and men; an old order yields to a new. In this plotline, we can still hear reverberations of the ancient settlement of Ugarit by pastoral nomads, their conversion to an agrarian, urban economy, the growth of their military prowess and the centralization of political power culminating in a monarchy (see briefly Singer 1999: 608–21).

The Bible paints a comparable picture. Its literary genre is history, not myth, and it acknowledges only one deity. But as at Ugarit, divinity moves from tent to palace, from a textile Tabernacle to a Temple of stone and cedar. Here, too, we find the aftereffects of a somewhat later transition from seminomadism to sedentarism to monarchy (see APPENDIX B).

If Yahweh's transition from Tent to Temple recapitulated recent social developments in Israel, one might expect his change of domicile to have been controversial. For the biblical authors, the question was: is Yahweh better imagined as a nomad sheikh or as a well-housed king? According to 2 Samuel 7, when David first proposes to build a permanent Temple—"See, then: I am dwelling in a cedar house, but the Deity's Chest is dwelling inside the Curtain *(hayrî'â)*" (v 2)—the prophet Nathan reports Yahweh as remonstrating:

> Would you, you build me a house for my dwelling? No, I have not dwelt in a house from the day of my taking Israel's Sons up from Egypt and until this day, but I am one who goes about in tent and tabernacle. Wherever I went about among all Israel's Sons, a word did I speak . . . saying, "Why have you not built me a cedar house?"? (vv 5–7)

Although God goes on to promise that David's son will build the Temple, most scholars view Nathan's oracle as articulating a popular antipathy toward any permanent cultic establishment. Mendenhall (1973) simply continues in Nathan's tradition when he disparages Solomon's Temple as a sell-out to Canaanite Baalism, the importation of an alien, monarchy-legitimating cult into the tribal, egalitarian ethos of premonarchic Israel.

In a way, tent-worship and monarchy are inherently antagonistic. Monarchy means centralization—political, economic and religious. But the whole point of a tent is that it can be taken down and moved from place to place. When Northern rebels secede from the kingdom, their cry is "To your tents, O Israel" (1 Kgs 12:16;

cf. 2 Sam 20:1; see Homan [2002: 187–92] for a different reading). The royal Deity, eternally esconced in his heavenly palace-temple, is a type of the mortal king and his eternal dynasty, and the king is conversely the human image of God, at least according to royal ideology. For its part, the Priestly Source has no role for a king, eschews royal imagery for Yahweh (see pp. 478, 483, 533), celebrates all humankind as Yahweh's "image" and "likeness" and in accordance advocates worship in a tent.

There have been sporadic attempts to reconcile the antinomy between Tent and Temple by supposing that the former actually stood inside the latter. Samaritan tradition, for example, claims that Meeting Tent was placed within the sanctuary at Mount Gerizim (cf. Josephus *Ant.* 18.85). Since the Shiloh accounts speak of both a tent (Josh 18:1; 19:51; 1 Sam 2:22; cf. Ps 78:60) and a solid structure (Judg 18:31; 1 Sam 1:9, 24; 3:3), Cassuto (1967: 346) similarly envisions a temple surrounding a tabernacle, while Maimonides *Sēper ʿĂbôdâ* 1.1 conversely imagines a stone structure over which the Tent was draped. Most recently, Friedman (1987: 181–87) has suggested that the Tabernacle was erected in the inner sanctum of Solomon's Temple.

Despite many arguments in its favor, I do not think that Friedman's theory convinces. It is true that Ps 15:1; 26:8; 27:5; 43:3; 46:5; 61:5; 74:7; 76:2; 84:2 call the Temple "tent," "hut" and "tabernacle." It is true that Solomon is said to have brought Meeting Tent up to his newly built Temple (1 Kgs 8:4 = 2 Chr 5:5). It is true that Chronicles repeatedly identifies the Temple with the Tabernacle (1 Chr 9:19, 21, 23; 6:33; 23:32; 2 Chr 24:6; 29:6). It is true that Rev 15:5 speaks of the heavenly "temple of the tent of witness" (i.e., Meeting Tent). It is true that the Dura Europus frescoes show the Chest covered with a tent (Kraeling 1956: p. LVI; on Phoenician parallels, p. 104 n. 343). Nonetheless, I remain unpersuaded. First and foremost, the Tabernacle as I reconstruct it simply does not fit inside the Temple's adyton (on Friedman's measurements, see above p. 503–4). Second, the poetic passages must be speaking in metaphor, nostalgically calling the solid house a tent (cf. Homan 2002: 16–27), since the psalmists cannot literally be proposing to take shelter in the forbidden Debhir. Third, given the level of architectural detail, we might have expected 1 Kings 6–8 explicitly to situate the Tabernacle within the Temple, which it does not. Fourth, the evidence from Chronicles is suspect, since the author manifests a particular interest in demonstrating the continuity of tent worship (1 Chr 6:17; 2 Chronicles 1). In short, we must suppose either that 1 Kings deliberately suppresses the location of the Tabernacle, or that Chronicles forces an identification between Tabernacle and Temple. I find the latter more in keeping with the evidence, and regard the Tent and Temple as alternative not complementary loci of worship.

The tension between Tent and Temple would have a surprising afterlife. Jesus himself voiced hostility toward the Temple and was understood to have prophesied its destruction (Matt 12:6; 21:12; 26:61; 27:40; Mark 11:15–16; 14:58; 15:29; John 2:14–22; Acts 6:13–14). Upon his death, the Veil was supposedly rent, as if in partial fulfillment (Matt 27:51; Mark 15:38; Luke 23:45). As soon as the Second Temple was no more, however, the early Christians regarded Jesus as the Tabernacle *redivivus*, God's temporary, soft, mobile presence on Earth (see below, pp. 720–22).

THE TABERNACLE AS HISTORY

Despite some gaps, the Bible's history of the Tabernacle is straightforward. Built at the foot of Mount Sinai, the Tent accompanied Israel throughout their forty years' wandering. According to Judg 20:27, the Testimony Chest was kept for a while at Bethel; with or without the Tabernacle is unstated (cf. Noth 1960: 94–95). Eventually, the Tent was installed at Shiloh (Josh 18:1; 19:51; 1 Sam 2:22), although some passages appear to describe a true temple (Judg 18:31; 1 Sam 1:9, 24; 3:3).

We know both from excavations (Shiloh 1971) and from Scripture (Jer 7:12, 14; 26:6, 9; Ps 78:60) that Shiloh was destroyed in the eleventh century B.C.E. At this time, the Philistines are said to have temporarily captured the Chest (1 Sam 4:11). Of the Tabernacle itself there is no word. Conceivably, priestly survivors brought it to Nob (cf. 1 Samuel 21).

It is unclear whether the tent in which David stored the recovered Chest in Jerusalem was something new or a reconstitution of the old tent of Shiloh. Although it is never called *miškān* or *'ōhel mō'ēd*, David's tent, too, had a priesthood, the Chest, an altar and sacred oil (2 Sam 6:17; 1 Kgs 1:39; 2:28; 8:4). But if we accept the testimony of Chronicles, David's tent was definitely not the genuine Tabernacle, which at this time stood at Gibeon (1 Chr 16:39–40; 21:29–30; 2 Chr 1:3–6; cf. Josh 9:23, 26; 2 Sam 21:9; 1 Kgs 3:4). How it got there we do not know. (Was it brought by refugees from Nob?) At any rate, after Solomon built the Temple, the Tabernacle seems to have disappeared from history.

Since none of this is testable by archaeology, we are left with guesswork. First, is an archaic tent-shrine plausible? Yes, given the parallels alluded to above (pp. 703–5). But where in the desert did Israel find so much gold, silver, bronze, gemstones and dyed fabric? (According to *Exod. Rab.* 33:8, jewels descended from Heaven alongside the Manna!) Hyatt (1980: 260) estimates that the Tabernacle contained nearly a ton of gold (actually, it is slightly more; see NOTES to 38:24), 3.25 tons of silver and 2.5 tons of bronze. This sounds like a lot, but Enns (2000: 549) reminds us that it amounts to only 0.0225 lbs. of metal for each of the more than 600,000 adult males. The Tabernacle's more than twenty-nine talents of gold does not seem exorbitant compared with Solomon's purported annual income of 666 talents (1 Kgs 10:14; see further NOTES to 38:24). As for the source of Israel's wealth, we are told that they had "despoiled" the Egyptians of gold, silver and robes (3:22; 11:2; 12:35). But here we encounter more serious implausibilities, for dyed fabric was not valued in Egypt until the Hellenistic period, and, even then, all our classical references to purple are to small items such as garments, never to tents (Danker 1992: 558).

Most researchers find it credible that some sort of holy tent preceded the Temple but incredible that it was on the lavish scale of P's Tabernacle. They assume either that the Priestly Writer imaginatively transferred the decoration of the First or Second Temple to a tent, or that P accurately describes an actual tent shrine from a later, wealthier phase of post-Mosaic history. For the latter view, the prime contenders are the shrine of Bethel (Noth 1960: 94–95), the tent of Shiloh (cf. Haran [1978: 198–204], who still finds considerable elaboration based on Solomon's Temple [pp. 191–92]), David's tent in Jerusalem (Cross 1961b) and the sanctuary of Gibeon (Hertzberg 1929: 163–81; cf. Halpern's [2001: 293 *et passim*] theory that the Chest was a Gibeonite artifact). And, if P is postexilic (see APPENDIX A), another explanation recommends itself: the Tabernacle is modeled on the sumptuous war tents of the Persian royalty (cf. Houtman 1994: 110).

In the end, it all amounts to a grand shrug. Could the Israelites in some archaic period have served Yahweh in a tent? Certainly. Could it have been as lavish as that described in Exodus? Conceivably. Could the Priestly Writer and his sources have imaginatively reconstituted and elaborated an archaic form of the early cult? Definitely. Is the Priestly Source less a work of history and more a vision for a reformed cult, so that its Tabernacle is just a mirage? Quite likely (see further below, p. 732).

THE TABERNACLE AS LITERATURE

To say the least, the Tabernacle pericope (chaps. 25–31, 35–40) challenges our notions of literature. Why is it so boring?

This question, which has led critics to excise swatches of text as superrogatory, is simply misplaced. The real question is: why are *we* so bored? After all, as a dry inventory, the Tabernacle chapters do not stand alone in biblical or Jewish literature, let alone world literature. We find detailed Temple descriptions in 1 Kings 6–7; Ezekiel 40–48; Rev 21:9–22:9; 11QTemple and 4Q554. Homer, for his part, has his soporific catalog of ships (*Iliad* 2.484–759). Even in our times, works ranging from *Moby Dick* to ephemera such as military and medical thrillers and "hard" science fiction incorporate lengthy technical treatises that many readers skip—while, for others, they make the whole book worthwhile. List-like literature has a venerable history (Watts 1999: 37–45), particularly in works whose scope is "epic" (cf. Baentsch 1903: 286) or whose genre is monumental (see Hurowitz 1985; 1992a: 249–59). The narrative poems of Ugarit and Mesopotamia are full of verbatim repetitions that are essentially, like Exodus, narratives of command and fulfillment. These must have been as delightful to the original audience as they are tedious to us.

The real reason the Tabernacle chapters bore most of us is that most of us don't care about the Tabernacle. If we did, we would revel in the use of texture, color, scent and sound to make the Tabernacle seem real (Janzen 1997: 194). For most modern readers, a schematic drawing would be more than sufficient (cf. Blum 1990: 302). For a sensual experience, we turn instead to the Song of Songs. But neither our esthetics nor our values, not to mention our attention span, are those of the original audience, who must have cared deeply about the Tabernacle—whether because they mourned its loss or because they expected to build another one (see pp. 722, 732). Even so have Jewish scholars for two millennia pored over the laws of sacrifice—precisely because they can no longer make actual sacrifice (cf. Ehrlich 1908: 418–19). While I do not suppose that any amount of literary analysis will make the Tabernacle pericope palatable to most readers, we should at least acknowledge the substantial evidence of design and not seek to improve upon what has been handed down to us in order to alleviate our own boredom (see below).

Plainly, the author lingered lovingly over every opportunity for repetition, which are numerous: (a) Yahweh's initial instructions (25:1–30:38), (b) his summary of Bezalel's task (31:7–11), (c) Moses' instructions to the people (35:11–19), (d) when the people build the components (35:20–38:20; 39:1–31), (e) when they present the components to Moses (39:32–43), (f) when Yahweh commands Moses to assemble the Tabernacle (40:1–8), (g) when Moses is told to anoint the components (40:9–15) and finally (h) when Moses assembles the Tabernacle (40:17–33). (The consecration mandated in 40:9–15, although presupposed by 40:34–38, is not actually performed until Leviticus 8; Num 7:1.) This redundancy is probably original, not the result of literary accretion. It finds a parallel in the Old Babylonian Samsuiluna B inscription (eighteenth century B.C.E.), where first the god and then the narrator describe the temple (Hurowitz 1985; see also Hurowitz 1992a: 69 for a parallel in the annals of Tiglath Pileser I).

Apart from redundancy, another reason that commentators have suspected composite authorship for chaps. 25–31, 35–40 is their irregular structure. Surely the pristine text was more coherent, easier to diagram. Again, I find this assumption simplistic, even condescending.

The complexity—call it disarray, if you like—of the Tabernacle narative stems rather from the author's employing three incompatible organizational strategies. The first two are purely structural: AB/A'B' strict parallelism and AB/B'A' mirror parallelism (chiasm). The third principle is train of association, whether by subject matter or theme word (below, pp. 716–17). As we watch each principle interfering with the others, like ripples in a pond, we are privileged to glimpse into the Priestly Writer's creative mind.

Let us first consider ordinary AB/A'B' parallelism, which exists at the micro- and macro-levels. Micro-level parallelism is found in the following sentence (elements extraneous to the pattern are italicized):*

A. And the cloud covered Meeting Tent,
  B. and Yahweh's Glory filled the Tabernacle.
    But Moses could not enter into Meeting Tent
A'. for the cloud tented upon it,
  B'. and Yahweh's Glory filled the Tabernacle. (40:34–35)

A larger example of AB/A'B' parallelism is 26:1–11, describing the Tabernacle's two covers (McEvenue 1974: 8):

---

* N.B.: The reader may object that ignoring certain words in order to produce a pattern is illegitimate. But it is the *sequence* of the remaining elements that interests me. That I never alter. The parallel structures are simply the frame on which the Priestly Writer laid out his text; they are not the entire text.

A. And the Tabernacle you shall make, ten curtains: twisted linen, blue and purple and worm-crimson, Griffins, weaver's work you shall make them.

    B. The one curtain's length eight-and-twenty by the cubit, and breadth four by the cubit, the one curtain. One measure for all the curtains.

        C. Five of the curtains, they shall be fastening (each) *woman to her sister*, and five curtains fastening (each) *woman to her sister*. And you shall make blue loops on the one curtain's *lip*, on the edge on the *fastening*, and so you shall make on the outer curtain's *lip* on the second *fastening*.

            D. Fifty loops you shall make on the one curtain, and fifty loops you shall make on the edge of the curtain that is on the second *fastening*, the loops aligning (each) *woman to her sister*.

                E. And you shall make fifty gold clasps and fasten the curtains (each) *woman to her sister* with the clasps,

                    F. so that the Tabernacle shall be one.

A'. And you shall make *goat* curtains to tent over the Tabernacle: eleven curtains you shall make them.

    B'. The one curtain's length thirty by the cubit, and breadth four by the cubit the one curtain. One measure for the eleven curtains.

        C'. And you shall fasten the five curtains separate and the six curtains separate. And you shall double the sixth curtain against the Tent's front.

            D'. And you shall make loops fifty on the one curtain's *lip*, the outermost on the *fastening*, and fifty loops on the *lip* of the curtain, the second *fastening*.

                E'. And you shall make bronze clasps, fifty, and bring the clasps into the loops and fasten the Tent,

                    F'. so that it shall be one.

Macro-level parallelism may also be found whenever the command and execution accounts follow the same order: e.g., in both 25:10–40 and chap. 37, the order is Chest–Table–Lampstand. Other examples of this parallelism are too numerous to list.

If the Priestly Writer had been ruled by simple parallelism, the two panels of his Tabernacle account would have proceded in identical order, as in ancient Near Eastern poetic narrations of command and fulfillment (Cassuto 1967: 453). Biblical prose narrative, in contrast, shuns exact repetition and favors variety by abbreviation, amplification or reorganization (the great exception to this rule in P is the highly redundant Numbers 7, the chieftains' donations).

For the case at hand: the narrator does not just restate Yahweh's words to Moses, only changing "You shall make" to "And he made." Instead, as a whole, the Tabernacle pericope is characterized by AB/B'A' chiasm (cf. Paran 1989: 163–74). These are not crassly perfect chiasms, however, but structures subtly suggestive of chiasm. Again, certain elements must sometimes be chipped away to reveal the underlying pattern.

Mirror symmetries may be detected everywhere, from the micro- to the macro-levels. An example of micro-level chiasm would be P's characteristic rhetorical flourish, the "short-circuit inclusio," e.g., 25:11 "And you shall plate it pure gold, from inside and from outside you shall plate it" (see further McEvenue 1971: 43–44; Paran 1989: 47–97).

Here are some other examples of small-scale chaism:

A. And you shall insert the poles
   B. into the rings
      C. on the Chest's flanks for carrying the Chest by them.
   B'. In the Chest's rings
A'. the poles shall be (25:14–15)

A. and their faces
   B. (each) *man toward his brother,*
   B'. toward the *kappōret*
A'. the Griffins' faces shall be (25:20b)

A. The one curtain's length
   B. eight-and-twenty by the cubit,
   B'. and breadth four by the cubit,
A'. the one curtain 26:2 (26:8)

At the macro-level, we first notice the approximately mirror-image symmetry of Yahweh's commands in chaps. 25–31 and their execution in chaps. 35–39 (italicized episodes extraneous to the chaistic pattern will be considered separately):

Materials (25:1–9)
A. Sacred furniture (25:10–40)
   B. Tabernacle and Plaza (chaps. 26–27)
Priestly vestments (chap. 28)
Priestly inauguration (chap. 29)
Incense Altar (30:1–10)
Accounting (30:11–16)
Basin (30:17–21)
Spices (30:22–38)
      C. Election of craftsmen (31:1–11)
         D. Sabbath ordinance (31:12–17)
         D'. Sabbath ordinance (35:1–3)
Materials (35:4–29)
      C'. Election of craftsmen (35:30–36:1)
Materials (continued) (36:2–7)
   B'. Tabernacle (36:8–38)
A'. Sacred furniture (chap. 37)

B". Plaza (38:1–20)
Accounting (38:21–31)
Priestly vestments (39:1–31)
Assembling the Tabernacle (39:32–40:33)

Despite the broken symmetry in the sequence B'-A'-B", it is plain that at the center stands the all-important Sabbath command.

There are examples of mid-scale chiasm. Regarded with a sufficient level of abstraction, the first panel of the Tabernacle narrative displays considerable symmetry (cf. Steins 1989):

A. Six-day wait, revelation on seventh (24:16–17)
   B. Instructions for making the Tabernacle (25:1–27:21)
      C. Priestly garments (chap. 28)
      C'. Priestly consecration (29:1–37)
   B'. Preparing the Tabernacle (29:38–30:38)
Bezalel and Oholiab (31:1–11)
A'. Six-day week, rest on seventh (31:12–18)

Enveloping this chiasm in the redacted text are references to the stone tablets (24:12–15; 31:18).

We also find smaller examples of chiastic narration, for example in 25:31–39 (translation slightly modified to reflect Hebrew word order):

A. And you shall make a Lampstand
   B. pure gold:
      C. *miqšâ* the Lampstand shall be made,
         D. its *thigh* and its *reeds*, its cups, its *kaptōrîm* and its *flowers*, they shall be from it.
            E. And six *reeds* going out from its sides—
               F. three Lampstand *reeds* from its one side and three Lampstand *reeds* from its second side—three "almondized" cups on the one *reed—kaptōr* and *flower*—and three "almondized" cups on the one *reed—kaptōr* and *flower*—
               F'. thus for the six *reeds* going out from the Lampstand. And on the Lampstand four "almondized" cups—its *kaptōrîm* and its *flowers*—and a *kaptōr* under the two *reeds* from it, and a *kaptōr* under the two *reeds* from it, and a *kaptōr* under the two *reeds* from it,
            E'. for the six *reeds* going out from the Lampstand.
         D'. Their *kaptōrîm* and their *reeds*, they shall be from it,
      C'. all of it one *miqšâ*,
   B'. pure gold.
A'. And you shall make its lamps seven . . .

With a little goodwill, one might imagine the Priestly Writer chosing this rhetorical strategy to reflect the Lampstand's bilateral symmetry.

The literary structure of 31:13b–17 may also be laid out as chiastic (Van den Eynde 1996: 504 n. 7). The six flanking elements emphasize the seventh, crucial element, borrowed from the Decalog (G):

A. my Sabbaths you must keep.
   B. For it is a sign
      C. between me and between you
         D. *for your ages*, to know that I, Yahweh, am your sanctifier.
            E. And you shall observe the Sabbath. . . .
               F. Its desecrater must be put to death . . . for any doing a task on it . . . shall be Cut Off from its kins' midst.
                  G. Six days a task may be done. But on the seventh day: a Sabbatical Sabbath, Holiness for Yahweh.
               F'. Anyone doing a task on the Sabbath . . . must be put to death . . .
            E'. And Israel's sons shall observe the Sabbath . . .
         D'. *for their ages*, an eternal covenant.
      C'. Between me and between Israel's sons . . .
   B'. a sign for eternity;
A'. for six days Yahweh made the Heavens and the Earth, but on the seventh day he ceased and caught his breath.

Thus the first panel of the Tabernacle pericope finishes with marked oratorical flair. The words *šābat wayyinnāpaš* 'ceased and caught his breath' set a fitting stop to seven chapters of uninterrupted divine speech, supposedly uttered over forty days.

There are also symmetrical structures on various scales that are not really chiastic but feature inclusio, i.e., identical or similar beginning and ending material. In a complex example, the paragraph 35:21–29 is framed on either end by lengthy "short-circuit inclusio":

> And every man whose heart ennobled him came, and every whose spirit ennobled him, they brought Yahweh's Donation-offering for the Meeting Tent Task and for all its Work and for the Holiness Garments. . . . Every man and woman whose heart ennobled them to bring for all the Task that Yahweh commanded to do by Moses' *hand*, Israel's Sons brought largesse for Yahweh.

A broader macro-level inclusio is the frame created by 19:1 and 40:17, both date formulas surrounding the events at Sinai. And a still broader inclusio is formed by Exod 40:34–38 and Num 9:15–23, which both explain the motions of God's cloud over the Tabernacle in similar language, enveloping the laws in between (cf. Blum 1990: 302).

Many commentators are offended not only by the Tabernacle section's redundancy but also by its inconsistency. Although the text repeatedly lists the contents of the Tabernacle, the order is never the same (see Table 1, pp. 719–20), and neither is the level of detail. This should not occasion much surprise. After all, the articles were all under construction simultaneously. It is just a matter of in what order the author chooses to present them (Cassuto 1967: 462). And, as we have observed, whereas verbatim repetition is the hallmark of ancient Near Eastern epic, deliberate variation is the hallmark of biblical prose narrative. (I shall not treat the minor disprepancies between Exodus 29 and Leviticus 9 concerning the priestly ordination, but, *pace* Milgrom [1991: 545–49], I do not see evidence of distinct compositional layers.)

There is, to be sure, a degree of consistency: e.g., the sequence is always Chest, *kappōret*, Table, Lampstand; the Bronze Altar always precedes the Plaza, which always precedes the Plaza Screen. While it would be tedious to analyze each of the eight enumerations of the Tabernacle's components in further detail—for that, see Jacob's (1990: 1008–48) harmonizing overanalysis—one tendency stands out.

In lists B–G, the Tabernacle—i.e., the fabrics, skins, wood frame, bases, bars— always leads. This makes sense: in practical terms, one would install the sacred objects only after the Tabernacle is built. Levine (1965: 308–9) compares the Temple description in 1 Kings 6, which likewise moves from the outside inward. In list A, Yahweh's first instructions to Moses, however, the sequence is different: the Chest, Table and Lampstand precede the Tabernacle. This is not difficult to explain: the holy furniture is more interesting than the outer Tabernacle and receives first mention, even though, as a practical matter, the container must be made before its contents. For the differing sequence of command and execution, Jacob (1990: 1010) and Leibowitz (1976: 706–7) aptly compare Deut 10:1–5: "Yahweh said to me, 'Carve yourself two stone tablets like the first . . . and make yourself a wooden chest'. . . . And I made an acacia wood chest and I carved myself two stone tablets like the first . . . and I put the tablets in the chest that I had made." Similarly, chap. 28 describes the priestly vestments not in the order they are donned (contrast 29:5–6; Lev 8:7–9) but in order of descending importance, beginning with the Ephod, the outermost garment. (On the differing order of ritual lists, see also Rainey 1970.)

A few sequential anomalies in list A require further comment. As a whole, chaps. 28–30 disrupt the chiastic macro-pattern of the Tabernacle narrative (pp. 713–14), as the Priestly Writer neglects form for content and theme-word association. The matter of chap. 30 in particular seems miscellaneous and displaced. The Golden Altar of Incense, which should have been treated alongside the Table and Lampstand in chap. 25, is not introduced till 30:1–10 (see above, pp. 369, 514–15). Likewise, the Basin, which properly belongs in chap. 27 alongside the Bronze Altar, is not mentioned until 30:17–21. In lists B–G, these two items always appear in their proper places.

The received critical opinion is that the Incense Altar and Basin were secondarily inserted by a scribe who did not dare to interrupt the text before him, and so stuck them at the end alongside other heterogenous materials. I find it more believable, however, that the Priestly Writer had a reason for proceeding as he did, which it is our job to discover. Meyers (1996: 45–46), for instance, suggests that the Golden Altar acts as a boundary between the Inner and Outer Sancta; as belonging to neither realm, it requires separate, independent treatment. I am not convinced, however, because the same is true (according to Meyers) of the Bronze Altar vis-à-vis the Tabernacle and the Plaza, yet it is treated in its logical place. And what of the Basin?

I would start instead from Ramban's observation that the Incense Altar follows logically after 29:43–46, with its reference to Yahweh's Glory and his presence in the Tabernacle. It makes some sense first to describe the construction, purification and sanctification of the Tabernacle, and then the censing that lures the divine presence to Earth. Fumigation is the final stage in getting the Tabernacle operational; to begin before the shrine is fully prepared for Yahweh would be disastrous (cf. above, p. 690). Exod 30:10, moreover, which explicitly anticipates Leviticus 16, the great ritual of "Clearing" (*kippūrîm*), in turn introduces the census tax by which Israel ransoms itself (*kōper*) and attains purification and atonement (*ləkapper, kippūrîm*) (30:11–16). That is, 30:1–16 as a whole describes the means by which Yahweh may be attracted into the Tabernacle as well as the means by which the Israelites may protect themselves from his presence. The theme continues in 30:17–21, which provides a means for the priests to protect themselves from God by washing (Cassuto 1967: 395). The ingredients of the oil and incense that follow (30:22–38) then fall under the rubric of Unfinished Business. But even here there is a sort of logic. For Durham (1987: 402), the seeming miscellany at the end "amounts to the endowment of the upkeep of the place and equipment for worship." That is, in the future the ingredients for the incense and oil will be purchased with the people's half-shekel. (While I do not consider the foregoing analysis of the organization of chap. 30 quite satisfying, it is the best I can come up with.)

Beside structure, another sign of literary artistry is diction, i.e., choice and deployment of words. Although detecting wordplay is a subjective matter, Jacob (1992: 776) notes the following examples: *mōʿēd* 'Meeting'/*ʿēdūt* 'Testimony'; *qāṣâ* 'end'/*qāṣe(h)* 'end'; *kappōret*/*parōket* 'Veil'; *qərāšîm* 'frames'/*qərāsîm* 'clasps'; *tōʾămîm* 'twinning'/*tammîm* 'whole'; *məquṣʿōt* 'corners'/*miqṣāʿōt* 'corners'; *beśem* 'fragrance'/*bōśem* 'fragrance'; *qinnāmōn* 'cinnamon'/*qəne(h)* 'cane'; *śərād* 'textile'/*šārēt* 'attend'; note also *ḥōberet*/*maḥberet*/*ḥōbərōt* 'fastening.' In fact, much of P's Tabernacle lingo is peculiar, with a profusion of rare Puʿal and Hophʿal participles to describe manufacturing processes, whose nature is sometimes uncertain: *məʾoddām* 'reddened,' *məḥuššāq* 'bound, connected (?),' *mûsāb* 'surrounded,' *məputtāḥ* 'engraved,' *məṣuppe(h)* 'plated,' *məquṣṣāʿ* 'cornered off,' *məšubbāṣ* 'plait-ringed,' *məsullāb* 'pegged,' *məšuqqād* 'almondized' (cf. Jacob 1992: 783). These usages lend a certain stylistic consistency and special literary character, albeit that of a technical manual.

Moreover, we should note the prevalence of anatomical imagery, common in metaphor generally (on Semitic usage, see Dhorme 1920–23). The Tabernacle has *yarkātayim* 'flanks,' *ʾăḥōrayim* 'backparts,' *ṣəlāʿōt* 'sides, ribs,' *kətēpayim* 'shoulders' and a *pānîm* 'face, front.' The Lampstand has a *yārēk* 'thigh.'

While there is no evidence of the full-blown numerology of later Jewish exegesis, there is also evidence that the Priestly Writer was counting occurrences of key words and phrases, favoring the numbers seven and ten (see NOTE to 39:1, "as Yahweh commanded Moses"). (Again, a degree of subjectivity is inescapable— not in counting per se, but in the partition of pericopae and deciding what is significant.) For example, Paran (1989: 221) notes that ten main verbs describe the fabrication of the Table in 25:23–30, and that the Altar instructions of 27:1–8 contain ten verb-initial clauses (pp. 192–93). Similarly, in the framed paragraph 35:21–29, the word *kōl* 'all' and the root *bwʾ* 'come' occur ten times each (Paran, p. 153). A better example of phrase-counting plus chiasm may be found in the refrain of chaps. 39–40:

A. as Yahweh commanded Moses" (7x)
  B. as Yahweh commanded Moses, so they did
    C. as all that Yahweh commanded Moses, so Israel's Sons did all the Work.
  B'. as all that Yahweh commanded him, so he did
A'. as Yahweh commanded Moses (7x)

Seeking patterns can be dangerous, however. For example, although correctly identifying *qṭr* as the theme root in 30:1–10, Cassuto (1967: 392) miscounts its occurrences as seven rather than eight.

Various refrains lend cohesion and structure to the whole Tabernacle pericope: e.g., the *tabnît* 'model' shown on mountain; "an eternal rule *(to your ages)*"; "(Did) as Yahweh commanded Moses"; "And Yahweh spoke/said"; "This is/these are" (Utzschneider 1988: 211–17). Recurrent are the roots *kpr* 'be Clear' (29:33, 36–37; 30:10, 15–16) and *qdš* 'be holy' (28:3, 38, 41; 29:1, 21, 27, 33, 36–37, 43–44; 30:29–30; 31:13; 40:9–10, 11, 13), the noun *məlā(ʾ)kâ* 'task' (31:3, 5; 35:2, 21, 24, 29, 31, 33, 35; 36:1–8; 38:24; 39:43; 40:33) and a threat of death for improper procedure (above, p. 689).

Lastly, the Tabernacle's relationship to the Bible's macro-structure is also noteworthy. We have already rehearsed at length how the diction and structure point backward to Creation (above, pp. 675–76, 691–94). As we shall directly see, in Christianity's double Scripture, the Tabernacle and its personnel explicitly prefigure Jesus.

TABLE 1 The Order of the Tabernacle Construction

A. *Yahweh's initial instructions to Moses (25:10–30:37):*

1. donation of materials	10. Bronze Altar	18. Basin and Stand
2. Testimony Chest	11. Plaza	19. water
3. *kappōret*	12. Plaza Screen	20. Ointment Oil
4. Table	13. Illumination Oil	21. Spice Incense
5. Face Bread	14. priestly vestments	22. Bezalel and Oholiab
6. Lampstand	15. consecration of priests,	23. summary of task
7. Tabernacle	Altar and Tabernacle	24. Sabbath
8. Veil	16. Golden Altar	
9. Tabernacle Screen	17. census tax	

B. *Yahweh's summary of Bezalel's task (31:7–11):*

1. Tabernacle	5. Lampstand	9. priestly vestments
2. Testimony Chest	6. Golden Altar	10. Ointment Oil
3. *kappōret*	7. Bronze Altar	11. Spice Incense
4. Table	8. Basin and Stand	

C. *Moses presents the task to the people (35:1–19):*

1. Sabbath	8. Face Bread	15. Bronze Altar
2. donation of materials	9. Lampstand	16. Basin and Stand
3. Tabernacle	10. Illumination Oil	17. Plaza
4. Testimony Chest	11. Golden Altar	18. Plaza Screen
5. *kappōret*	12. Ointment Oil	19. priestly garments
6. Veil	13. Spice Incense	
7. Table	14. Tabernacle Screen	

D. *The people build the components (35:30–38:20; 39:1–31):*

1. Bezalel and Oholiab	7. *kappōret*	13. Bronze Altar
2. donation of materials	8. Table	14. Basin and Stand
3. Tabernacle	9. Lampstand	15. Plaza
4. Veil	10. Golden Altar	16. Plaza Screen
5. Tabernacle Screen	11. Ointment Oil	17. priestly vestments
6. Testimony Chest	12. Spice Incense	

E. *The people bring the components to Moses (39:33–41):*

1. Tabernacle	7. Lampstand	13. Bronze Altar
2. Veil	8. Illumination Oil	14. Basin and Stand
3. Testimony Chest	9. Golden Altar	15. Plaza
4. *kappōret*	10. Ointment Oil	16. Plaza Screen
5. Table	11. Spice Incense	17. priestly vestments
6. Face Bread	12. Tabernacle Screen	

F. *Yahweh commands Moses to assemble the Tabernacle (40:1–8):*

1. Tabernacle	6. Lampstand	10. Bronze Altar
2. Testimony Chest	7. Illumination Oil	11. Basin
3. Veil	(implicitly)	12. water
4. Table	8. Golden Altar	13. Plaza
5. Face Bread	9. Tabernacle Screen	14. Plaza Screen

G. *Moses is told to anoint the assemblage (40:9–15):*

1. Tabernacle	3. Basin and Stand
2. Bronze Altar	4. priests

(continued on next page)

H. *Moses assembles the Tabernacle: (40:16–33):*

1. Tabernacle	7. Lampstand	12. Bronze Altar
2. Testimony Chest	8. Illumination Oil	13. Basin
3. *kappōret*	(implicitly)	14. water
4. Veil	9. Golden Altar	15. Plaza
5. Table	10. Spice Incense	16. Plaza Screen
6. Face Bread	11. Tabernacle Screen	

THE FLESHLY TABERNACLE AND THE HEAVENLY TABERNACLE: TENT IMAGERY IN THE NEW TESTAMENT

According to Genesis 1, in the beginning, the divine exhalation (*rûaḥ*) was both with God and of God, spreading its wings over the Deep. Before God spoke, nothing was made. But then God's command created first the light and then all the living. Eventually, the divine word would become stone. The Testimony Tablets, together with the Glory above them, would constitute the focus of Tabernacle worship. Lodged in the gloomy Inner Sanctum, each symbolized Yahweh's presence among and relationship with the people.

To this précis, compare John 1:1–5, 14:

In the beginning was the Word,
And the Word was in front of/equivalent to (*pros*) the God,
And God was the Word;
This (word) was in the beginning in front of/equivalent to the God.
Everything came about through it,
And without it not one thing that came about came about.
In it was life,
And that life was men's light.
And the light shines in the dark,
And dark has not overwhelmed it. . . .
And the word became flesh and tabernacled (*eskēnōsen*) among us . . .
And we beheld his Glory.

The author of John understood P perfectly. For him, however, what restores communion between Earth and Heaven and brings down the Glory is neither a place of worship nor a document. Nor is it God's pre-Creation Wisdom, which, according to Sir 24:8–10, similarly "tabernacled" in Israel (for discussion, see Koester 1989: 24–26, 108–15). Instead, it is Jesus of Nazareth.

The notion per se of God's spirit putting on flesh is not John's invention; compare Judg 6:34, "Yahweh's spirit put on (as a garment) Gideon" (also 1 Chr 12:19; 2 Chr 24:20). This divine *rûaḥ* may be imagined as an independent being traveling between Heaven and Earth (1 Kgs 22:19–23). John's innovation is to identify a *dead man* as God's creative Reason personified.

That John likens Jesus to a tabernacle implies that his incarnation was but temporary, just as the Tabernacle moved from place to place and was ultimately lost (Terrien 1978: 418–19). According to John, Jesus claims to be equivalent to the Temple, implying that he will assume a more exalted and permanent state in the Hereafter, just as Solomon's Temple had succeeded Moses' Tabernacle (John 2:20–22).

Like John, Paul compares transitory human existence to living in a tent: "For we know that if our earthly tent habitation is destroyed, we have a building from God, a house not made manually, eternal in the heavens . . ." (2 Cor 5:1–4). Since Jesus existed with God before Creation, in him all things resume their primordial unity (Col 1:15–20).

Another New Testament allusion to Creation and the Tabernacle is Luke 1:35, the angel's prophecy to Mary that God's Holy Spirit will overshadow (*episkiasei*) her, thereby impregnating her. At the most literal level, the reference is to a man spreading his skirts (Hebrew *kanāpayim*, literally "wings") over a woman to signify marriage (Ezek 16:8; Ruth 3:9). But the language also evokes the Tabernacle's sweeping skirts (Terrien 1978: 416) and, beyond that, God's breath/wind/spirit fluttering its wings (*maraḥepet*) over the feminine Deep (*təhōm*).

We find another Tabernacle reference in Mark 9:2–9. When the apostles propose to make three booths for Jesus, Moses and Elijah (it is unclear whether they actually do so), a cloud overshadows the scene (*nephelē episkiazousa*). This alludes both to the hut on Mount Zion of Isa 4:5–6 and beyond that to the original Tabernacle at Sinai, sheltered by Yahweh's cloud and filled with his Glory (Terrien 1978: 426).

The Letter to the Hebrews in particular is permeated with Tabernacle symbolism (Koester 2001: 393–458). The Tent's outer chamber represents traditional Jewish worship, which the author regards as the superseded forerunner of the true faith (cf. Koester 1999: 166–67; 2001: 400–1). God really lives in a *heavenly* Tabernacle, with Jesus as Great Priest and co-regent "seated at the right hand of the throne of Greatness in the heavens, a minister in the sanctuary and true Tabernacle" (Heb 8:1–2; cf. 1:3–13; 2:17; 4:14–5:10; 7:20–8:2). Like the Great Priest on Yom Kippur, Jesus succeeded in penetrating the Veil separating God and Man. Indeed, his perforated human flesh *is* the Veil. As Great Priest, Jesus performs all the Torah's rites of purification. Sacrificing not animal blood but his own, he removes his followers' sins, for "without bloodshed, there is no release" (Heb 9:22). This remission needs no annual reenactment on Clearing Day; it is eternally valid. So purified, Christians can enter the true Tabernacle "through the curtain, that is, through his flesh" (Heb 10:19–20). The imagery is deliberately paradoxical, even totemistic, with Jesus simultaneously portrayed as God, priest–king and offering (compare above pp. 525, 531, 695–703 on the vicarious nature of animal sacrifice).

Rev 15:5, too, situates God in the heavenly "Temple (*naos*) of the Tent of Witness" (Greek *skēnē tou martyriou* = Hebrew *ʾōhel mōʿēd* 'Meeting Tent' via a spurious derivation from *ʿēd* 'witness'). This perpetuates an old tendency to equate Tabernacle and Temple (see above, pp. 707–9). Revelation seems to understand the *tabnît* 'model' beheld by Moses as none other than Yahweh's heavenly Tent

(NOTE to 25:9, "making you see . . . model"). (For further discussion of Tabernacle imagery in Revelation, see Koester 1989: 116–51.)

In the composite Old–New Testament, the Tabernacle of Exodus points backward to God's original removal of himself from his Creation, and forward to the temporary intrusion of his incarnate Word into Creation, and farther forward to the descent of his heavenly dwelling at the Eschaton, when disease, death and time itself will cease, dissolved into the primordial, atemporal One.

FOR LOVERS OF THE BIBLE

The biblical writers did not write either the first or the last word on bridging the gap between Heaven and Earth, between God and humanity. The theme has deep roots in ancient Near Eastern religion, and recurs throughout the long history of Jewish thought, particularly in its mythologized branches of Christianity and Kabbalah.

Some Israelites may have believed that their sacred structures had finally solved the problem of bringing Yahweh to Earth. With hindsight, their assurance seems pathetic. We know that any "eternal" building or city is doomed to decay. Shortly before the Second Temple's destruction, one Jew was understood to have predicted its demise, even claiming to replace the Temple. But he was destroyed before the Temple itself, whereupon his followers reinterpreted him as a divine presence temporarily "tenting" on Earth in human flesh, one day to return. The Rabbis, for their part, built a Temple of Law in which they denied God any active role (b. B. Meṣ. 59b), even while some pursued exotic exercises to send their souls to Heaven (Halperin 1988).

Modern Jews and Christians—and atheists like me who try to enter into the biblical spirit—can no longer visit the Tabernacle. All we have is an enigmatic, ancient text. Perhaps it, too, will one day disappear. But as long as it lasts, we have a privilege the Torah denies to laymen, Levites and ordinary priests. We may intellectually penetrate the curtains and behold the inner sanctum, where Yahweh's presence hovers between the Griffins and the Law. The act of reading becomes our pilgrimage, a rite of passage that imbues our lives with transformation and transcendence. The time we spend in reconstructing the Tabernacle is sacred time; the image held in our minds is sacred space. Scripture, so to speak, is a mandala (cf. Niditch 1986). Through its contemplation, the reader can leap from the Here-and-now to the There-and-then, back to Israel's first constitution as a nation and civilization—and even beyond to the First Time, when the only mind was God.

APPENDIX A
THE DOCUMENTARY HYPOTHESIS

◆

The Sources of Exodus

This section briefly surveys the hypothetical literary sources underlying the present Book of Exodus and highlights certain methodological problems.

Lyric Poetry

The oldest literary source preserved in Exodus may be the victory hymn of Exod 15:1b–18, the Song of the Sea (on its relationship to its context, see vol. I, pp. 482, 553–54). All students of the Song's syntax and morphology concur that they appear archaic (Cross and Freedman 1997; Robertson 1972; Freedman 1976; Russell 2002). Our first assumption should be that Exod 15:1b–18 is truly the oldest relic in the Bible, standing midway between the Ugaritic poetry of the Late Bronze Age and the flourishing of Hebrew literature in the ninth–fifth centuries B.C.E. If we can find convincing evidence that belies this dating, however, then we should reckon with competent forgery.

The latter possibility should not be dismissed out of hand. We know from the Tell Fekheriyeh inscription that a ninth-century B.C.E. scribe could convincingly fake eleventh-century script (Abū Assāf, Bordreuil and Millard 1982: 98–105). As for the language of Exod 15:1b–18, Robertson's study argues that the poetry of Job is equally archaic, and yet most critics date Job to the Persian era, considering the language to be pseudo-archaic and/or dialectal. (I agree that the prose framework is Persian era; the poetry could be much older, however.) Exod 15:1b–18 is suspiciously lucid for an ancient poem, especially in comparison with the supposedly coeval Song of Deborah (Judges 5).

Exod 15:1b–18, moreover, betrays similarities with works from the monarchic or possibly even later periods, especially Isaiah 12:1–6; Psalms 74, 77, 118 and, above all, 78 (see vol. I, pp. 565–67). Does this mean that they are contemporary works (so Brenner 1991)? Or did later writers draw inspiration from and create allusions to the Song of the Sea? The most recent study (Russell 2002) emphatically supports the latter position.

The Song of the Sea can have been composed no earlier than the twelfth century B.C.E., when the Philistines entered the region (15:14). The allusions to

Moab and Edom and the nonmention of Ammon (v 15) arguably indicate composition before the eleventh century; see Cross and Freedman (1997: 44 n. 42) and, on the date of Edomite settlement, Levy et al. (2004).

Lists and List-like Sources

Among the sources of Exodus may also be lists. By "list" I mean a literary genre: a repetitive, formulaic catalog of similar statements, sometimes intended to be counted. Exodus contains two likely examples of the pure list, plus considerable list-like material (Watts 1999).

The most obvious list is the Decalog (Exod 20:1–17[14]), which almost all scholars consider older than its current context. I agree that the Decalog probably circulated independently in an oral milieu, with variations in order and wording (see pp. 113, 146). I do not, however, assume that the Decalog is archaic, even Mosaic, as some would have it (e.g., Mendenhall 1954). The language shows not a single trace of archaic syntax or morphology. It is more a synopsis, like the later and pithier "golden" rules of Hillel and Jesus. The Decalog is intended to be a countable list with ten elements, although enumerating them is difficult (see pp. 302–4).

Another likely list source is the "Paschal Rule" of Exod 12:43–51, which contains seven formulaic, rhythmic clauses, at least in its implicit substructure (vol. I, p. 375). As with the Decalog, expansion appears to have blurred the underlying list.

The third list, possibly proverbial, is the eightfold sequence in 21:24–25: "life for life, eye for eye, tooth for tooth, arm for arm, leg for leg, burn for burn, wound for wound, stripe for stripe."

In the related category of *list-like* literature, we must include all the legislation in Exod 20:23(20)–23:19 and 34, and also the Tabernacle instructions in chaps. 25–31 (Watts 1999: 49–55). Even more list-like is the Tabernacle summary in chaps. 35–40 (above, pp. 710–20). Whether these corpora ever stood as independent sources is unlikely. The laws were probably derived from various legal and aphoristic catalogs such as are found elsewhere in the ancient Near East. As for the Tabernacle pericope, it is hard to imagine a context for it other than that which it now occupies.

Extended Narratives: the J, E and the D-like Strata

Next oldest, by conventional models, are the extended, reconstituted documents critics call J and E. I will not rehearse here all the reasoning that led nineteenth-century c.e. biblical scholarship to the "New Documentary Hypothesis," upon which I relied in the body of my commentary; its most lucid recent exponent is R. E. Friedman (1987, 1992, 2003).

One challenge to conventional wisdom is my argument that, using the methods and assumptions of conventional source analysis, the bulk of the pre-Priestly narrative in Exodus comes from E not J. Independently and simultaneously, Friedman (1998, 2003) reached the same conclusion. Here, however, I want to inject some doubts and qualifications, responding to alternative models that deny the existence of E altogether.

The Documentary Hypothesis, that the Torah consists of fragments stitched together, explains quite well why Scripture at times contradicts itself and at times repeats itself. Putting the pieces back together, however, is a more problematic task. Were the source materials few or numerous? Written by how many authors? The answers depend upon how we interpret *cross-references*. To one mindset, these demonstrate narrative continuity, proving that now discrete units once flowed together in lengthy documents. To another mind-set, they represent an editor's attempt to impose order upon and inject themes into chaotic raw materials. And to a third mind-set, seeming cross-references simply confirm that our documents relied upon common sources, whether oral or written. That is, when parallel, related documents were combined to form the Torah, the incidental and inevitable by-product was a web of allusions, certainly appreciated but not deliberately created by the editor. There is no doubt that we have all three types of cross-reference in the Torah; distinguishing among them, however, can be quite subjective.

I cannot undertake here a full-scale analysis of the cross-references in the pre-Priestly Torah, to which subject Kessler (1972) has devoted an entire dissertation (known to me only in summary). I shall instead illustrate the problem with two salient examples from Exodus.

First: in Exod 4:2–5, Moses' rod is turned into a snake. In 7:15, Yahweh commands him to take "the rod that turned into a snake" and strike the Nile with it. Then in 17:5, Yahweh commands Moses to take "your rod, with which you struck the Nile" and strike Mount Horeb with it. To me at least, these cross-references sound like a single author's voice emphasizing the wondrous versatility of Moses' rod, also called *maṭṭē(h) hā'ĕlōhîm* 'the divine rod' or 'Deity's rod.' To posit a special redactional layer strikes me as excessive, but others might differ.

In my second example, however, I find the editorial cross-reference model more attractive. At the end of Genesis, Joseph had adjured his clan one day to bury his mummy in Canaan. The Hebrew vizier's final promise: "Deity *('ĕlōhîm)* will acknowledge, acknowledge you *(pāqōd yipqōd 'etkem)* and take you up *(wǝheʿĕlâ 'etkem)* from this land to the land that he swore to Abraham, to Isaac and to Jacob . . . Deity *('ĕlōhîm)* will acknowledge, acknowledge you. . . ." (Gen 50:24–25). In Exod 3:15–17, "Deity" tells Moses, "I acknowledge, acknowledge you *(pāqōd pāqadtî 'etkem)* . . . I will take you up *('aʿăle[h] 'etkem)*." And again in Exod 13:17–19, we are reminded that Joseph had foretold, "Deity *('ĕlōhîm)* will acknowledge, acknowledge you *(pāqōd yipqōd 'etkem)*," and are assured that his sarcophagus left Egypt with Israel.

In the body of my commentary, I took the straightforward documentarian approach: since in the non-Priestly portions of Genesis, *'ĕlōhîm* is the sign of E, we can attach these passages and much of the basic story of the Exodus to the Elohist. The last half of the twentieth century, however, witnessed several challenges to the simple documentarian model, especially in regard to J and E. I will choose as my interlocutor David M. Carr (1996: 152–232), whose work on Genesis synthesizes much previous work (e.g., Rolf Rendtorff, Erhard Blum) and brings new rigor, clarity and frankness. Although staunchly defending P's status as a literary document (see below), Carr leans more to redaction as an explanation for the pre-Priestly Torah, along the way dispensing entirely with the Elohistic source. If he is correct, my source analysis of Exodus must be incorrect.

Carr begins his analysis with Gen 22:15–18, where, after a story using the divine name 'ĕlōhîm, we find a switch to yahwe(h) and other indications of a secondary insertion ("And Yahweh's Messenger called to Abraham *a second time*"). Even Friedman (2003: 65), who in general is disinclined to reckon with editorial intrusions, finds that something has been added here. In this passage, Yahweh promises to bless Abraham, multiply his offspring, give them a land and make them a source of blessing for other nations. These very themes reappear in Gen 26:3–5, which explicitly cites the promise to Abraham. Here, too, there is evidence of a seam, for v. 3 ("sojourn [gûr] in this land") is redundant with v 2 ("dwell [šəkōn] in the land") (cf. Carr pp. 153–54). Finding in these passages parallels to Deuteronomy and Deuteronomistic language and ideology, Carr (pp. 157–59) calls them "semi-Deuteronomistic"; in my terms, they are "D-like." Carr carefully explains: "[T]his pair of texts is certainly not the work of a strictly 'Deuteronomistic' editor. . . . Instead, they are the work of an author/reviser who creatively revised and extended the non-P Genesis tradition, while working in a context where Deuteronomistic themes and language are 'in the air' " (p. 159).

Carr finds more evidence of his semi-Deuteronomistic redaction in Gen 18:19, "For I have known him [Abraham], so that he may command his sons and his house after him, and they will keep Yahweh's way to do righteousness and justice, so that Yahweh may bring upon Abraham what he spoke to/concerning him." This verse could be lifted from its context without impairing the flow and is probably secondary. Another D-like passage is Gen 10:16–18a, a list of the Canaanite nations. (Carr also finds the D-like hand in Gen 9:25–27, the curse of Canaan.)

Carr further regards Genesis 14–15 as having undergone a thorough D-like revision of materials originally extraneous to the pre-Priestly Genesis narrative. Relevant to our present concerns is Genesis 15, which predicts the people's future enslavement and departure from Egypt (Gen 15:13–14) as well as the conquest of Canaan (Gen 15:18–21). For Carr (p. 165), the theme of "inheritance (yrš)" (Gen 15:3, 4, 7–8), the "Exodus-like description of God as the one who 'brought [Abraham] out of Ur to give [him] this land' " (Gen 15:7), and the concluding covenant (Gen 15:18), plus the list of peoples in vv 19–21, mark Genesis 15 as semi-Deuteronomistic.

Most important for us, the theme of Yahweh's oath to Abraham recurs in Gen 50:24–25:

> And Joseph said to his brothers, "I am about to die. But Deity will acknowledge, acknowledge you and take you up from this land to the land which he swore to Abraham, to Isaac and to Jacob." And Joseph adjured Israel's Sons saying, "Deity will acknowledge, acknowledge you, and you shall take up my bones from here."

The authorship of these verses is crucial because, as we have seen, they set off a chain of allusions in Exod 3:15–17; 13:17–19; Josh 24:32.

For Carr (p. 167), Gen 50:24–25 forms a unity:

> The first half of Joseph's speech points backward to YHWH's covenant promise to bring the Israelites out of Egypt (Gen 15:14–21) and to YHWH's oath to Abraham (Gen 22:15–18; 26:3bß–5), all texts that appear to be secondary extensions of the non-P material. The second half of Joseph's speech points forward to a series of texts extending into the Deuteronomistic history, from taking Joseph's bones out of Egypt (Exod 13:19) to burying them in Shechem (Josh 24:32; cf. Gen. 33:19). Neither Gen. 50:24 nor Gen 50:25 makes as much sense alone as it does with the other, and both are tightly linked with a layer of extended non-P materials, reaching . . . to the Deuteronomistic history itself.

Carr does not consider all these passages to have been written at one time in a single, systematic revision.[1] But he notes certain common characteristics (pp. 172–73): they are well worked into their immediate contexts; they are within direct speech, and they stress common themes across narrative units: the divine promise or covenant contingent upon human obedience and belief, the gift of the land and the duty to suppress the Canaanites.

What are the implications for the Book of Exodus? If Carr is correct in isolating a semi-Deuteronomistic stratum, then my attribution of much of Exodus to E is cast into doubt. There is much to be said for the view that Exod 3:15–18a is a D-like insertion into an original that ran "Then Deity said to Moses, 'I will be who I will be.' And he said, 'Thus you will say to Israel's Sons: "I-will-be" has sent me to you. And you will come, you and Israel's elders, to Egypt's king. . . . ' " The omitted material contains the cross-reference to Gen 50:24, an awkard *ʿôd* 'further, again,' a list of the nations of Canaan and the cliché "flowing of milk and honey," all arguably D-like. Likewise, we could remove from its context Exod 13:19, "And Moses took Joseph's bones with him, for he had adjured, adjured Israel's Sons, saying, 'Deity will acknowledge, acknowledge you, and you will take up my bones from here with you,' " without causing disruption.

Having established the likelihood of a D-like redactional layer in pre-Priestly Genesis, Carr (pp. 177–293) examines the underlying residuum. He concludes that it represents diverse cycles of material stitched together, but denies the existence of continuous J and E accounts. In particular, he argues that the E source is an illusion (pp. 196–202). Some of his arguments are strong, some are weak. Carr demonstrates apparent connections between so-called J and E stories that seem to presuppose one another and display similarities in theme and wording. For examples, compare the following:

> And Yahweh said to Abram, "Get you from your land and from your birthplace and from your father's house to the land that I will show you. And I will make you into a great nation, and I will bless you and enlarge your name. So become

---

[1] Other passages that Carr (pp. 168–72) considers possibly semi-Deuteronomistic need not concern us here.

a blessing! And I will bless your blessers, and your maligners I will curse, and all families of the earth will be blessed through you" (Gen 12:1–3, conventionally J).

And the Deity tested Abraham, and he said to him, "Abraham, Abraham [so Sam, LXX]," and he said "Here I am." And he said, "Take, then, your son, your only, whom you love, Isaac, and get you to the land of Moriah, and send up him there as an Ascending-offering on one of the mountains that I will say to you" (Gen 22:1b–2, conventionally E).

And Yahweh said to Jacob, "Return to your fathers' land and to your birthplace, and I will be with you (Gen 31:3, conventionally J).

I am the god (of?) Bethel. . . . Arise, go from this land and return to the land of your birthplace (Gen 31:13, conventionally E).

And Deity said to Israel in night visions, and he said, "Jacob, Jacob." And he said, "Here I am." And he said, "I am the God, your father's deity. Do not be too frightened to descend into Egypt, for I shall make you into a great nation there. I, I will descend with you into Egypt, and I, I will also take you up, up. . . . (Gen 46:2–4, conventionally E).

Old-style source criticism must simply shrug at the similarities and cite formulas for setting forth on a journey apparently shared by J and E, whether as part of common speech, common oral tradition, or documents upon which the Yahwist and Elohist both relied. But Carr makes a good *prima facie* case for the lack of distinction between J and E. He does not deny the obvious: some stories in Genesis prefer the name Yahweh, some *ʾĕlōhîm*. But he rejects the thesis that the latter can be read as a connected whole, i.e., a pre-Priestly, Elohistic source.

To cut a long discussion short, taking all the arguments, strong and weak alike, I find Carr's thesis compelling—*only as long as we ignore Exodus.*

What can Carr make of Exod 3:13, "Suppose I come to Israel's Sons and say to them, 'Your father's deity has sent me to you,' and they say to me, 'What is his name?'—what should I say to them?" Since Yahweh forthwith obliquely reveals his true name Yahweh in vv 14–15, it is apparent that Moses does not know it.

There are two ways to interpret this exchange (vol. I, p. 223). The less likely is that Moses is painfully aware that, unlike his fellow Hebrews, he does not know God's true name, having been raised in Pharaoh's court. The more likely is that *nobody* knows God's name until this moment. The ceremonious tone of Yahweh's speech in v 15 suggests a new proclamation: "Yahweh your fathers' deity, Abraham's deity, Isaac's deity and Jacob's deity . . . this is my name to eternity, and this is my designation age (by) age." We must reckon also with the testimony of the Priestly Writer in Exod 6:2–3: "I am Yahweh. Now, I appeared to Abraham, to Isaac and to Jacob in God Shadday, but I, my name Yahweh, was not known to them." In the Priestly Source, the name Yahweh hardly appears (Gen 17:1 is the exception) until this pronouncement. Where did the Priestly Writer get the idea that the name Yahweh was first revealed to Moses, if not from Exod 3:13–15? Is it just coincidence that a corpus of stories in Genesis exclusively uses *'ĕlōhîm* as the divine name, a corpus that parallels accounts preferring the name "Yahweh"? It is hard to conceive.

There are compromise positions, to be sure. Perhaps not a document but a stream of Israelite thought believed that the name Yahweh was first introduced to Moses. The final heir to this tradition was the Priestly Writer. Stories about the Patriarchs originating from this circle, whether or not they were ever bound into a transgenerational narrative, would have called God *'ĕlōhîm*. So we could satisfy both Carr and me by defining E not as a document but as a body of literature and tradition.

Even if we rule out of court my best evidence for E, i.e., the concatenation of *pqd*-statements in Gen 50:24–25; Exod 3:15–17; 13:17–19, and attribute them instead to an editor, I would still say that, by a hair, the texts I assign to the Elohist as a whole bear more resemblence to E in Genesis than to J: references to Messengers, testing, fear of God, a slight preference for the divine name *'ĕlōhîm* (in MT-Sam at least; the divergent divine names in LXX constitute a dilemma so far unaddressed). But I am not of fixed opinion on the subject.

Were we to apply Carr's methods and assumptions to Exodus, as he has not done so far, the semi-Deuteronomistic stratum might be found particularly in chaps. 3–4; 13–14; 15:24–26; 19–20; 24; 32–34, where we find evidence of multiple strands and/or D-like language. I am particularly puzzled by the parallel between Exod 23:14–33 (E?) and 34:10–26 (J?), which overlap in content and share D-like language. Why the redundancy, if we have an editor at work? The more obvious inference would be that J and E share a D-like source, which is contrary to the thrust of Carr's analysis and raises its own problem: if J and E quote material hostile to Canaanite pillars (23:24; 34:13), why do such installations feature prominently in the JE account (see above, p. 614)?[2]

My impression, which I cannot prove or even defend in detail, is that the Yahwist and Elohist drew upon a common D-like preaching tradition, a tradition that more strongly influenced the D-like supplementer of JE (= Redactor[JE]?), in addition to the Book of Deuteronomy and ultimately the Deuteronomistic History of Deuteronomy–2 Kings. That is to say, D-like language and ideas entered the text through diverse routes.

Dating the sources J and E is difficult. It is not as if we had original manuscripts, unearthed in datable archaeological contexts, subject to paleographical and linguistic analysis. We do not have documents at all, except those produced by the questionable source-critical method. If the J vs. E distinction is correct, it is indeed striking that no linguistic differences between them have yet been identified. This suggests that, just as Redactor[JE] felt free to trim his sources (see Friedman 2003: 13), he also reworded them to enhance their consistency. Naturally, this further reduces the chances that we can successfully and definitively disentangle E from J. So what *can* we say?

---

[2] A possible answer: *Canaanite* pillars are forbidden; *Israelite* pillars are quite acceptable.

Friedman (1998) argues that the pentateuchal J source is part of a larger work extending through Joshua, Judges and Samuel, ending in 1 Kgs 2:46. If this is true, or if the lesser claim that J and the Court History of David's reign are merely related texts is confirmed, then we may be able to date the Yahwist.

Here my prejudices confront the facts. My *feeling* is that the highly readable, often disreputable tales of David and Solomon were written in a period when the monarchy was long extinct, when ancient kings could be paraded as negative moral exemplars with impunity. My *judgment*, however, observes that there is no evidence of Persian-era language or content in these sections of the Bible. The latest detailed analysis, Halpern (2001), puts the Court History in the tenth century B.C.E., within living memory of the events. That is where I would provisionally situate J.

As for E, a plausible but unprovable view situates the Elohist in the North, in the eighth century B.C.E. or earlier, among Levitic circles hostile to the Aaronic priesthood (Friedman 1987: 61–88). After the fall of Northern Israel in 722/21 B.C.E., Redactor[JE] interwove the two documents to create a national history serviceable for Judeans and Israelite refugees alike, structuring the Sinai pericope with a pattern of Covenant rupture and renewal, in order to articulate his hope for a full national restoration (see pp. 151, 579).

The Priestly Work

Despite a broad consensus on what constitutes Priestly style and ideology (McEvenue 1971; Paran 1989), areas of dispute remain. Because of a few internal contradictions and redundancies within Priestly texts, some scholars, buoyed by the past achievements of source criticism, have tried to dissect P as well. The most successful is Friedman (1987), who isolates a Redactorial level combining JE with P, a stratum whose literary style resembles P but whose function is completely different. Building upon Cross (1973: 293–325), Friedman shows how the final Redactor deployed genealogies and itinerary notices ("and they set forth from X and they came to Y") to stitch together episodes from JE and P. Friedman thereby mediates in the debate between those who consider P a redactional supplement and those who consider it a coherent source (for the latter view, see Propp 1997 and more extensively Carr 1996: 43–140).

Also recently influential is the model of Knohl (1995), who partitions P into an older P(riestly) document and a younger H(oliness) revision. Much, perhaps most, of what was previously thought to be P, Knohl transfers to H, hinting that H may even be the pentateuchal Redactor.

For Knohl, H in Exodus would be:

a. Exod 4:21b; 9:35; 10:20–23, 27, the strengthening of Pharaoh's heart (Knohl p. 62).

b. Exod 6:2–7:6; 11:9–10, Yahweh's self-disclosure to Moses, the Levitic genealogy and the deputation to Pharaoh—i.e., the frame around the Plagues (pp. 61–62).

c. Exod 10:1–2, the introduction to the plague of locusts (p. 62).
d. Exod 12:1–20, 43–49, the Paschal legislation (pp. 19–23).
e. Exod 16:2–3, 6–13, 16–21a, 22–27, 31–35 (more or less), the "Priestly" Manna and Sabbath account (cf. pp. 17–18).
f. Exod 20:11, the expansion to the Sabbath command (p. 67).
g. Exod 24:12–18, Yahweh's descent onto Mount Sinai.
h. Exod 25:1–9, the Donation
i. Exod 27:20–21, an interjection into the Lampstand law (pp. 47–48).
j. Exod 28:3–5, the Tabernacle craftsmen (pp. 64–75, n. 15)
k. Exod 29:38–46 the Continual-offering (pp. 49, 63).
l. Exod 30:10, the annual purification of the Gold Altar (p. 32).
m. Exod 31:1–18; 35:1–3, the Sabbath commands that constitute the pivot of the Tabernacle account (pp. 15–16, 63–67).
n. Exod 32:15, an interjection into the Gold Calf story (p. 67).
o. Exod 34:29–35, Moses' altered visage (pp. 66–67).
p. Exodus 35–40, the building of the Tabernacle (p. 66).

For Knohl, the only truly Priestly passages of Exodus are:

a. Exod 2:23aß–25, Israel's enslavement (p. 60).
b. Exod 6:13 Yahweh's command to Moses and Aaron (p. 61 n. 4).
c. Exod 7:8–13; 8:12–15; 9:8–12, the Plagues of Egypt (pp. 60–61).
d. Exod 14:1–4, 8–9, 15–18, 21a,c, 22–23, 26–27a, 28–29 (more or less), the crossing of the Sea (cf. p. 62).
e. Exod 25:10–27:19; 28:1–2, 6–29:37; 30:1–9, 11–38, the commissioning of the Tabernacle (pp. 63–66).[3]

Although he has convinced many, when I read Knohl, I cannot avoid the uncomfortable feeling of circularity, of presupposing what is argued and arguing what is presupposed. How can his thesis be falsified? Any time we find vocabulary and themes from P present in H (or vice versa), Knohl supposes an insertion. This may have happened, but how can we prove it or even show the likelihood? May Knohl be guilty of reifying literary themes like Holiness as a redactional stratum? There may well be more to it, but Knohl's exposition is unsystematic and hard for me to follow.

Still, one cannot deny that there are some internal contradictions within the so-called Priestly matter. E.g., did a Levite's service begin at age twenty-five (Num 8:23–26) or thirty (Numbers 4)? Is the penalty for sexual intercourse with a menstruant seven days of impurity (Lev 15:24) or *kārēt*, i.e., the exile and/or eradication of one's entire lineage (Lev 18:19, 24–30)? Is the festival sacrifice for Weeks (Shavuot) one bull, two rams and seven sheep as the wholly burnt Ascending-offering, plus two sheep as an eaten Concluding-offering and one goat as a Sin-offering (Lev 23:18–19), or is it two bulls, one ram and seven sheep as the

---

[3] As far as I can tell, Knohl leaves unattributed Exod 7:7; 12:50–51; 16:36.

Ascending-offering, plus a goat as a Sin-offering (Num 28:27)? Plainly, the Priestly stratum adapts materials of diverse origin. Whether we can successfully reconstruct them I am less certain. The old JEDP hypothesis can be explained in about twenty minutes and has met with ready assent, since it accounts for dozens of problems immediately apparent to any attentive reader of the Bible. Not so the H theory, at least not for me, at least not yet. Someone must recast Knohl's argument in a more systematic form before it will be easy to understand and test.

Where did the Priestly document(s) originate? Like Wellhausen (1885, 1899), Friedman (1987: 161–216) sees P's origins in the Jerusalem Temple; unlike Wellhausen, he points to the First rather than the Second Temple. I have trouble with this, since I do not accept Friedman's complementary theory that the Tabernacle stood within the First Temple (see pp. 708–9). For me as for Fretheim (1968), P makes the most sense as a *protest* against the Temple hierocracy, continuing the argument of 2 Sam 7:5–6: "Would you, you build me a house for my dwelling? No, I have not dwelt in a house from the day of my taking Israel's Sons up from Egypt and until this day, but I am one who goes about in tent and tabernacle." P is implicitly antimonarchical (see p. 521) and anti-Temple, advocating instead worship in a tent as in days of yore. (Chronicles compromises, implying that the Second Temple *is* in some sense the Tabernacle; see pp. 708–9.) Because it is related to but slightly older than Ezekiel in both language (Hurvitz 1982) and content (Levitt Kohn 2002), I imagine that the Priestly materials originated in the late monarchic period, attaining their final form in the exile or early restoration (this later dating is based upon the likelihood that the Great Priest wears modish Persian-style leggings; see pp. 454, 524).

Moreover: P was the product of an outcast priestly group, rather like the Zadokites of Qumran centuries later. When Jerusalem fell, Yahweh himself seemed to have endorsed P's critique, and priests and prophets like Ezekiel began to assess what had gone wrong. They reread and assimilated Judahite religious literature and formulated diverse plans for a restoration. As Levitt Kohn shows, this was the context in which the final Torah was redacted to reconcile the competing strands of preexilic thought and tradition. Many have further argued that the whole project was sponsored by the Persian emperors, who supposedly fostered the canonization of law and custom throughout their diverse realm (e.g., Watts 1999: 138–43, but see now Fried 2004).

Who Wrote the Bible?

Greek epic graphically portrays the singer of heroic tales, such as Homer himself must have been (*Odyssey* 1.153–55, 337–44; 8.62–83, 254–369, 471–521; 22.330–53). In the Bible, the prophetic books both recount the activities of prophets and preserve their words, and the depiction is largely corroborated by the Books of Samuel and Kings. *But the Books of the Hebrew Bible never describe anyone making laws or writing history.* The biblical historians and legists masked themselves from posterity. Who were the Yahwist, Elohist, Priestly Writer and their two or more editors?

By definition, they were scribes. Despite the simplicity of the twenty-two-letter alphabet, I assume that few Israelites had the leisure or incentive to become literate. Scribes were hired mainly to record economic transactions. Only the ultra-elites of Palace and Temple would have employed them to write what we would consider fine literature.

Herein lies a paradox. The Bible, like all other works of ancient Near Eastern higher literature, was written by elites for elites. And yet it contains a pervasive, trenchant critique of kings, priests, prophets and the wealthy and influential in general. Overall, it appears to speak for the common man—the small-scale farmer "under his vine and fig tree." But that man was most likely illiterate.

In modernity, populist politicians—by definition elite—affect the common touch in their quest for an electoral majority. Although ancient Israel was no modern democracy, there are certain similarities. The monarchy, we are told, originated in acclamation (1 Samuel 8–10). For the Northern Kingdom, more culturally conservative than Judah, multigenerational dynastic rule was the exception not the norm (cf. Ishida 1977). A king had to retain his popular mandate, or at least control of the army, and so could never stray too far from populist concerns. In Israel and Judah, as in modern America, even belles lettres were tinged with populist themes. But their cultural consumers were, ironically, the powerful and leisured.

Who Read the Bible?

I think that many modern readers are liable to experience a sense of betrayal upon their first exposure to the fruits of source criticism. Has the pentateuchal Redactor tricked us all, for thousands of years? Yes and no. The humorless, hyper-rationalistic legacy of Christian exegesis did blind many readers to the playfulness of the Torah's compilation. More faithful to the Old Testament spirit is the Rabbinic mode, in which opinions are repeatedly proposed and rebutted, even as all are considered to be "the words of the living God." But traditional Judaism, too, missed the analogy between the Talmud and the Torah, instead occupying itself in explaining away all biblical contradictions.

The final Redactor, and before him Redactor[JE], did not deliberately perpetrate a hoax. True, the Torah's editors fooled Jews and Christians for two millennia and a half, but that is our fault, not theirs. Indeed, they let blatant contradictions and redundancies stand in their work, as if asking to be found out. Why? Were they heir to a premodern mind-set, steeped in an oral milieu comfortable with contradiction? That's a little condescending. Were they inept? That's worse than condescending. "The minor contradictions to be found in the Bible," wrote Heinrich Heine, "are for me an assurance that it has not been put together with some definite ulterior purpose. Bad faith is always careful about details" (quoted from Prawer 1983: 208–9). Amen.

The reason we look askance at the Redactor is that *only his work has survived*; its hypothetical constituents J, E, JE and P have long turned to dust, rendered obsolete by the Redactor's achievement. But when he produced the Torah in the sixth–fourth century B.C.E., some or all of the ancient sources were still lying about. He couldn't have fooled anyone, and wasn't trying to. He was playing a challenging *game*, to see whether parallel versions could be fitted together with minimum jarring. The ancient reader, who probably had already read at least P and JE, if not J and E separately, woud have admired the new Torah's cleverness and pardoned its flaws. Could he have known it, he might have applied Doctor Johnson's *bon mot* on women preachers and dogs walking on their hind legs, "It is not done well; but you are surprised to find it done at all."

Caveat Lector

For me, source criticism begins and ends with the question: "Why does the Torah contradict itself?" The modern answer: it is a pastiche of originally independent documents, none wholly preserved. Any further effort to comprehend the process of literary formation should be undertaken only with supreme circumspection. For the documents whose history we claim to trace cannot really be said to exist.

Pursuing a will-o'-the-wisp, our field risks falling into a bog. Generations of Bible students are taught that the goal of criticism is to find contradiction as a first not a last resort, and to attribute every verse, nay every word, to an author or editor. That is what we do for a living. But the folly of harmonizing away every contradiction, every duplication, is less than the folly of chopping the text into dozens of particles or redactional levels. After all, the *harmonizing* reader may at least recreate the editors' understanding of their product. But the *atomizing* reader posits and analyzes literary materials whose existence is highly questionable.

We cannot return to a precritical naiveté, and I would not wish to. But we must admit that subjectivity is inescapable. Each student must take pains, by searching introspection, to understand why and at what point (s)he puts down the knife of analysis. As Carr argues, reading the final text and speculating about its possible antecedents need not be mutually exclusive enterprises. But, at some point, each critic must cry "Enough!"

In this commentary, I have sought a middle ground. For some readers, my JE + P model will seem overly atomistic; others will find it simplistically harmonistic, ignoring real problems in the supposed sources. I like Wellhausen's (1885, 1899) version of the Documentary Hypothesis, or a refinement such as Friedman's, because it can be easily explained and grasped. I would compare the theory to Newtonian physics, which are certainly simplistic and, we now realize, fundamentally incorrect. But Newton's laws can be taught to a high school student, and they still get me all to work every day. So, too, source analysis will always serve a pedagogical purpose, and it even promises new insights. But we must disabuse ourselves of the conceit that we will ever know exactly how the Torah came to be.

APPENDIX B

THE HISTORICITY OF
THE EXODUS FROM EGYPT

◆

The Problem

"All history, so far as it is not supported by contemporary evidence, is romance." Samuel Johnson's pronouncement to James Boswell during their tour of the Hebrides is entirely apropos for the Exodus story.

It is instructive to contrast the Book of Exodus with the First and Second Books of Kings. After the division of the kingdom recounted in 1 Kings 12, we find frequent references to documentary sources such as as "The Daily Matters of Judah's Kings" and an analogous chronicle from the northern kingdom (1 Kgs 14:19, 29; 15:7, 23, 31, etc.; thirty-three references in total). It is no coincidence that many major events reported in 1–2 Kings—mainly wars and reigns—are confirmed by independent documentary evidence from Egypt and Mesopotamia, and also comport with the testimony of archaeology. It is also no coincidence that, during this period, we find increasing evidence of Israelite literacy in the form of Hebrew inscriptions. Most historians are comfortable making judicious use of the narratives in 1–2 Kings.

Conversely, the earlier chapters of the Old Testament, from Genesis through 1 Kings 11, which recount the lives of colorful characters ranging from Adam to Solomon, make almost no reference to written evidence. It is no coincidence that, to date, evidence of Israelite literacy prior to the eighth century B.C.E. is sparse. And it is no coincidence that the accounts of the early historical books square very poorly with the evidence from geology, Egyptology, Assyriology and Syro-Palestinian archaeology.

The narratives of 1–2 Samuel and 1 Kings 1–11, however, concerning the administrations of Samuel, Saul, David and Solomon, may contain considerable truth. Many of the accounts have a matter-of-fact tone and, instead of supernatural causation, focus on political and psychological motivation. The stories are laden with plausible historical, political and geographical content and context that cannot be dismissed out of hand. Although these chapters do not name documentary sources, one suspects that some existed and were utilized by the writers (for extensive discussion, see Halpern 2001).

But for the pre-monarchic accounts of Genesis through Judges we must reckon with the centuries that separate the purported events from their being written down sometime in the mid-first millennium B.C.E. (see p. 730). As we read backward from Kings through Genesis, the supernatural element predictably grows ever more prominent, the factual ever wispier (cf. Friedman 1995: 7–117). The Historical shades imperceptibly into the Romantic and the Romantic into the Mythic.

Exodus on Trial

According to the Bible, in the year 1446 B.C.E. (1 Kgs 6:1; see Dever 2003: 8), Moses led over 600,000 adult Hebrew men, that is, two to three million persons total, out of Egypt (Exod 12:37; Num 2:32; 4:48). With them left an unspecified number of fellow travelers from other nations (Exod 12:38; Num 11:4). After sojourning in the wilderness for forty years (Num 14:33–34; 32:13; Deut 2:7, etc.), Israel occupied Canaan by force, as recounted by the Book of Joshua.

Is this true? If we could travel backward in time, what would we would see? Lacking a time machine, how should we judge the evidence?

Everyone has his or her biases, which is why we empanel juries of twelve and allow for further judicial review. Since a trial's main purpose is to get at what really happened, the courtroom serves as a useful model for historical investigation. Here I shall expose my own prejudices as juror; perhaps you share some of them yourself.

For me, the Torah makes a most unconvincing witness on seven counts.

First, it talks too much, and indeed catches itself in contradiction. Imagine if we only had scattered, short allusions to Israel's Exodus from Egypt—how much more credible the tradition would be! I accept the claim in Amos 9:7 that the Philistines came to Canaan from Crete (cf. also Gen 10:14), precisely because it is brief and incidental. Had we an entertaining, quasi-Homeric narrative of the Philistines' migration, my skepticism would begin to mount, and I would be inclined, quite wrongly, to dismiss the whole affair.

Second, the Torah is just too good a storyteller. I have shown how closely the story of Israel's journeys from Canaan to Egypt and back again resembles a heroic "fairy tale," as per Vladimir Propp's classic analysis (vol. I, pp. 32–36). The Torah's formulaic plotline and high entertainment value inspire my immediate distrust. Of course, history can be fully as entertaining as fiction.

Third, the Torah is fuzzy on critical details. The Book of Exodus does not date the Israelites' departure from Egypt to external events (see, however, Exod 12:40). Nor does it name the three rulers of Egypt who play a role: Joseph's Pharaoh, the Pharaoh of the oppression and the Pharaoh of the Exodus. They are all just "Pharaoh." To be sure, this anonymity follows native Egyptian practice (Kitchen 1998: 105–6). But it troubles me.

Fourth, I expect to see a witness's face in a courtroom. But in the Torah, there is no "I," neither is there really a "you." Rightly or wrongly, the Book of Nehemiah inspires my confidence in its authenticity and substantial historical worth precisely because there is a first-person narrator taking responsibility. And the Deuteronomistic Historian (the editor of Deuteronomy–2 Kings), while keeping his anonymity, cites sources that imply an archivist possessing eyewitness accounts. The Torah, in contrast, never speaks in the first person and virtually never cites documents to corroborate its account (only Num 21:14, 27). It rather challenges the reader to accept the narrator's omniscience, which extends even into Yahweh's mind. I do not trust a chronicler who hides himself and claims to know more than he possibly could.

Fifth, although tradition ascribes the books of Genesis through Deuteronomy to Moses, who would have experienced the events of the Exodus directly, modern research has shown the extreme likelihood that the Torah enshrines the words of four authors who lived centuries later: first the Yahwist and Elohist, and then the Deuteronomist and Priestly Writer, who based their own versions upon J and E (vol. I, pp. 47–52; vol. II, APPENDIX A). In a legal sense, the testimony of J, E, D and P is hearsay, with evidence of collusion among the witnesses.

Sixth, the Torah is not an impartial witness. While telling its story, it also warmly advocates all sorts of behaviors and beliefs: kindness to animals, hostility to idolaters, avoidance of pork, etc. Presenting an accurate account of events is not the Torah's sole, probably not even its main, concern.

Seventh, the Torah describes unnatural occurrences so bizarre that, were they the testimony of a modern witness, I would unhesitatingly consider him/her to be schizophrenic or "under the influence." Because of the peculiar history of biblical research as a subdiscipline of theology, it is embarrassingly necessary to insist that the supernatural has no more place in academic scholarship than it has in the courtroom.

None of the foregoing means that the basic story of the Exodus is necessarily false—any more than a masked, overtalkative, ill-informed, polemical, self-contradictory, hallucinatory witness with delusions of omniscience can never be trusted. Maybe the story of Israel's departure from Egypt is historically accurate. But, given my biases, I would not be surprised if it fared poorly when tested against the material evidence.

What Really Happened?

THE PROBLEMS

To get at the historical, a seemingly sensible first step would be to strip the Torah of its supernatural events and examine what remains. So let us jettison the talking shrubbery, the reptilian rod, the incendiary ice storm, the walls of water, the loquacious Deity, etc. Can the residuum be called "historical"?

The truth content of the Exodus narrative has been assayed according to two basic approaches. James K. Hoffmeier (1996) and Baruch Halpern (1993a) have mainly tested *isolated details* in the narrative in order to build the case for its credibility, suggesting that it rests upon written records. Others test the *basic story* against known Near Eastern history (e.g., Dever 2003). If the events really happened, there should be no problem with either method; their results should jibe. But if they do not, then I feel that it is more important to test the general story. Confirming or confuting it by isolated details is obscurantist niggling.

If the story of the Israelite migration, minus the supernatural, were literally true, or at least as true as what passes nowadays for truth in journalism or historiography, what might we expect to find in the archaeological record? What discoveries could potentially validate the Bible's account? A full confession of Egypt's debacle would be too much to ask from the hieroglyphic record. And the alluvial mud of the Nile Delta affords scant chance of recovering Hebrew settlements in Egypt (see, however, Bietak 1992, 2003). But perhaps we could at least find an inscription in an official's tomb, lauding the occupant's effectiveness in quelling a slave revolt? A Pharaonic monument vaunting the king's fearless "rescue" of his troops in the face of a flood, or his "success" in "expelling" the vile Asiatics from his realm? In the deserts that the Israelites are supposed to have traversed with their herds, we might find stone circles indicative of fire pits, tent-peg holes or stone corrals. We should certainly detect ash layers and rubble at sites such as Jericho that the Bible reports as conquered and/or destroyed, ideally with some textual corroboration of what happened. We should find a new populace in the Canaanite high-lands manifesting Egyptian influence in their material culture and language. And, to fit the chronology of 1 Kings 6:1, we should find this in the Late Bronze Age (c. 1600–1200 B.C.E.). The discovery of any of the above would make for front-page news. But, of course, it is all fantasy.

Even de-supernaturalized, the story of the Exodus does not map well against the historical and archaeological record. In fact, it hardly maps at all. By the Bible's own chronology, the year of the Exodus fell during Egypt's heyday under the Eighteenth Dynasty, indeed during the imperium of the puissant Thutmosis III (c. 1490–1436 B.C.E.). It is simply "impossible"—so many have said—that the Hebrew slaves attained liberation at the very apex of Egyptian power.

Here I must register a *caveat*. The "impossibility" of a fifteenth-century B.C.E. Exodus is not the same kind of impossibility as trillions of water molecules rushing in opposite directions and staying in place for the space of half a day, or the emergence of a fast-acting virus lethal to all firstborn animals and humans, to which the Hebrews and their cattle possess congenital immunity. If tomorrow archaeologists were to recover a letter from one Moses to Thutmosis III requesting unpaid leave for a multitude of slaves, or even an embarrassed, official missive reporting the slaves' escape, Egyptian historiography would not be overthrown. Egyptologists would just slightly rewrite their chapters on the New Kingdom.

There are, however, some problems with a fifteenth-century Exodus that are true impossibilities. First is the mention of the store city of "Raamses" (Exod 1:11), a royal name only in the thirteenth–twelfth centuries B.C.E. (Egyptologists prefer the spelling "Ramesses" for the king.) A similar objection bars the reference to Philistines in Exod 13:17; 15:14; 23:31, since they entered Canaan only after Ramesses III's eighth year, c. 1178 (see below). Perhaps these are simple anachronisms, reflecting the date of the sources' composition but not impugning their essential veracity. A more serious problem is the absence of recognizable Israelites in the Amarna letters, tablets which describe in detail the conditions in four-teenth-century B.C.E. Canaan (Moran 1992)—unless they are the notorious 'Abiru, in which case there is little or no history in the Books of Joshua and Judges (see below). So we face a choice. In addition to all the miracles, we may drop these scattered awkward details and the image of Israel in Joshua and Judges. Or else we may drop the Late Bronze Age date, which is, after all, external to the Torah (1 Kgs 6:1).

The latter course is favored today. Most now would place Israelite origins in the late thirteenth century B.C.E., the beginning of the Iron Age. Starting in this pe-riod, we find hundreds of new settlements being founded in the hilly Israelite heartland (Finkelstein 1988; see further below). From exactly the same period, Pharaoh Merneptah's victory stele hyperbolically vaunts his "eradication" of a group called "Israel" (*ANET* 376–78). Merneptah also commissioned artists to depict his triumph on the walls of Karnak (Yurco 1990).

Assuming that the settlement of Canaan followed a generation after the Exodus, we might date the departure from Egypt to the early thirteenth century B.C.E. Here again we encounter problems, however. First, Ramesses II (c. 1290–1224) like Thutmosis III was a mighty king. Still, it is entirely possible that, the Pharaoh's boasts notwithstanding, a determined band of slaves escaped. A greater problem is that the new highland settlements of the thirteenth–twelfth centuries B.C.E. show little connection with Egyptian material culture (except for a taboo on pig con-sumption). Competent archaeologists consider these villages to be natural outgrowths from Canaanite culture (e.g., Dever 2003). Similarly, the Hebrew lan-guage is a purely Canaanite dialect, with the only Egyptian borrowings trade-words such as are found throughout the Near East (Lambdin 1953; Muchiki 1999).

I am not sure that the paucity of Egyptian cultural influence is all that impor-tant, though. First, the shared pig taboo is striking. Second, we have the earlier example of the Hyksos of Tell ed-Dabʿa (map 1), Asiatics in Egypt whose material culture is in many respects more Canaanite than Egyptian (Bietak 1981). If we could find settlements in Ramesside Egypt indistinguishable in layout and burial pattern from the highland villages of Canaan, we would probably have found the Hebrews in Egypt. (Bietak [1992, 2003] makes just this claim.) Third, as long as we're tossing out evidence from the Bible, who's to say that the Hebrews really spent several centuries in Egypt (see TEXTUAL NOTE to 12:40)? Maybe it was a single generation and their culture remained intact.

Moreover, *contra* Dever, the lack of evidence for the highland settlers' foreign origins does not necessarily indicate that they were indigenous. Hall (2002: 43) cites various migrations that are textually known to have occurred but are none-theless archaeologically invisible: the Celts into Asia Minor, the Slavs into Greece, the Vandals into Europe, the Mongols into China, the Tutsi into Rwanda and Burundi. Others have invoked the Gauls' migration into Galatia (Malkin 1994: 45), the Angles', Saxons' and later the Normans' invasions of England, and even the Arabs' conquest of the Levant (Isserlin 1983: 86). Absent inscriptions, archae-ology can tell only part of the story.

Another problem is the Bible's silence on Egyptian forays into Syria-Palestine in the late thirteenth–early twelfth centuries B.C.E. under Merneptah and Ramesses III. Had the Israelites forgotten these inconvenient facts? Was there a deliberate cover-up? Were the events relatively insignificant for the native populace? Or had Israel not yet arrived (cf. Rendsburg 1992)?

Redating the Exodus to the early Iron Age does not solve all our problems. We must also jettison some of the Bible's geographic tradition. Supposed settlements such as Kadesh Barnea, cities such as Gibeon, Heshbon and Dibon, and the kingdoms of Moab and Edom did not exist until well into the later Iron Age (Dever 2003: 18–35; on earlier Edomite antecedents, see Kitchen 1998: 93 n. 103 and Levy et al. 2004). The same sort of problems apply to Joshua's purported conquests: virtually none of the cities he is said to have taken shows any evidence of occupation in the appropriate period (see Dever pp. 37–71).

As we move backward through the biblical narrative, at some point we leave the Historic and enter the Romantic. What if there was an Abraham or a Moses who, like Arthur of Britain (an actual chieftain), lived but did not do a single thing tradition credits him with? Is he "historical"? What should be our minimal criteria for a historical Exodus? Might the story be wholly fictitious?

Here one may object: surely it was "common knowledge" in ancient Israel that Yahweh and Moses had liberated their ancestors from Egypt. Who would make up such a tradition?

I do not find this argument compelling. The rags-to-riches tale, or rather the riches-to-rags-to-riches tale, is popular worldwide and conforms to the Vladimiar Proppian archetype (vol. I, pp. 32–36). The deeper and longer the transitory degradation, the greater the ultimate exaltation. Asking "Who would falsely acknowledge slave ancestry?" is like asking "Who would falsely claim that their ancestors came to America with only their shirts on their backs?" Lots of people would. The biblical story's very popularity, from the post-Israelite period until today, only reinforces the point: everyone wants to attach themselves to the tradition of the enslaved Hebrews. The story has always possessed a universal appeal.

Moreover, while I do take seriously the Exodus as a popular Israelite tradition, attested in so many genres of biblical literature (see esp. Jer 16:14; 23:7), I will feel more confident when we find epigraphic evidence that any Israelites apart from the biblical authors believed that Yahweh had freed their ancestors from Egypt. For now, that the average Israelite believed in the Exodus is merely a reasonable assumption, not a fact.

Even if every Israelite knew a version of the Exodus story, I would still doubt its veracity. While orally transmitted tales can reflect actual events, often they do not. Sometimes an essentially true tale is transferred from the actual protagonist to a more famous hero, who may belong either to folklore or to real history; historical events may assume a mythic guise and vice versa (see the essays in Gazin-Schwartz and Holtorf 1999). To further confuse the matter, in a literate or semi-literate milieu, stories can move back and forth between the written and the oral—witness, e.g., the widely known "fact" that the Danish king offered to wear a Jewish badge during the Holocaust, a figment of novelist Leon Uris's imagination

(Gilbert 1997: 77–78). I would always treat oral traditions with the most extreme caution. Archaeology has verified some popular traditions, the parade example being Heinrich Schliemann's recovery of ancient Troy. But Schliemann's success in finding Ilium may be less significant than what he did *not* find: real evidence of the Trojan War as recounted by Homer. Whatever happens to be accurate in oral traditions about the past generally survives because of its contemporary interest, not out of a concern for accuracy (see further below).

What Really Happened?

POSSIBLE SOLUTIONS

The stronger or stricter one's hypothetical Exodus model, the more brittle. The fundamentalist's Exodus shatters against the hard evidence of monumental inscriptions and city walls. What about "softer" theories? Might they be able to slip around and between known facts?

A popular view among experts today is that the highland Israelites were immigrants not from Egyptian slavery but from lowland Canaanite serfdom, thus only indirectly under Egyptian oppression (Mendenhall 1962; Gottwald 1979; Dever 2003). As for the Exodus story, it may be the experience of a smaller but influential group who migrated from Egypt. But which group? One logical candidate would be the tribe of Levi, latecomers unable to claim a territorial patrimony, perhaps not a true tribe at all, but successfully asserting their prerogative as priests of their new god Yahweh. After all, most of the Bible's Egyptian names are found among the Levites: Phinehas, Hophni, Merari, Pashhur and, above all, Moses (see further p. 781, n. 107). Apart from Levi, other plausible candidates for an Egyptian sojourn are the "Joseph" tribes of Ephraim and Manasseh (Dever 2003: 229–32). Some scholars posit several sequential "exodi," as if, throughout the New Kingdom, Egypt positively leaked Hebrew slaves (see already *b. Sanh.* 92b). Moreover, to account for the patriarchal tradition and the general celebration of tent-dwelling, we could imagine that some elements of early Israel were recent seminomads, seasonally oscillating between the desert and the sown (on transhumance and the early Israelites, cf. Finkelstein 1988; Homan 2002).

The Exodus story might be a conflation, the experience of none of the Israelites and of all the Israelites. If so, the tradition's coalescence is part of Israel's formation into an ethnic group and nation (Hendel 2005: 59–62). This would explain why numerous elements of the biblical account do find resonances in the archaeological record—*but not in a single time and place.* Instead, they are spread across the entire Late Bronze–Early Iron Ages. Consider:

a. In the seventeenth century B.C.E., the Mediterranean volcanic island Thera/ Santorini massively erupted, perhaps causing a tsunami and shrouding the whole region in days of gloom—reminiscent of the ninth plague and the shifting of the Suph Sea (see vol. I, pp. 348–52).

b. C. 1550 B.C.E., there occurred a mass departure of Semites (the "Hyksos") from Egypt, after over a century of domination. As Donald Redford (1992:

395–429) has shown, the rise and especially the fall of the Hyksos was storied far and wide among both Levantine and Aegean folk. Josephus (*Ap.* 1.91–104) is the first among many writers to associate the Hyksos with the Hebrews.

c. Ramesside-era Egyptians recalled the Hyksos as fanatics "who ruled without Re" (i.e., without the Sun god's approval) and had worshipped only the god of violence, Seth. Taken literally, this would imply monotheism (de Moor 1997: 76, 102).

d. Egyptian sources contemporary with the Hyksos' expulsion mention unusual meteorological phenomena (Redford 1992: 420).

e. The Israelites' 400-year sojourn in Egypt (12:40 [MT]) recalls the Egyptian tradition that the god Seth ruled over Egypt for 400 years (*ANET* 252–53). Moreover, Num 13:22 proves that the Israelites possessed traditions about the date when the Hyksos metropolis Tanis (map 1) was founded.

f. One of the Hyksos rulers was named $y^c qbhr$; the short form of his name would be the same as biblical "Jacob." His seals have been found as far south as Kerma in Nubia and as far east as Gaza. It is hard to deny a connection with the biblical traditions of Jacob and Joseph as potentates revered in both Egypt and Canaan, but this Jacob of history was hardly a tent-dwelling sheikh.

g. The Hyksos maintained military alliances and trade relations with the Nubians. There is scant, tantalizing evidence that the Israelite Levites had Nubian associations or origins. The name of Aaron's grandson Phinehas is Egyptian for "the Nubian," and Moses' second wife was a "Cushite," i.e., Nubian (Num 12:1).

h. In the sixteenth–fifteenth centuries B.C.E., almost all of the fortified cities of Canaan, including Jericho, were destroyed—most by the Eighteenth-Dynasty Pharaohs. Thus, as the Middle Bronze Age ended in the Levant, a large-scale expulsion of Asiatics from Egypt was followed by an age of conquests.

i. Throughout the New Kingdom (c. 1558–1085), Asiatics were prominent in Egypt. Some were slaves, some were raised in Pharaoh's court, and some bore Egyptian names (Redford 1987: 144–48; 1992: 168–69, 198–99, 214–37; Kitchen 1998: 88–91).

j. Egyptian texts from the reigns of Amenophis III, Ramesses II and Ramesses III mention seminomads called the "Shasu of $yhw3$" located in the vicinity of Midian, east of the Arabah (Weinfeld 1987: 304–5; Redford 1992: 272–73). Although the Egyptians, at least, did not understand $yhw3$ as a divine name, it is hard to deny a probable early attestation of the name of Israel's god (see further below, pp. 757–58).

k. In the fourteenth century B.C.E., we find an iconoclastic monotheist, Amenophis IV = Akhenaten, on the throne of Egypt (see pp. 762–94).

l. In the fourteenth century, we also find an intrusive element in the interstices of Canaanite society. The cuneiform spelling of their name or title, *ḫa-bi-ru*, could well correspond to Hebrew '*ibrî* 'Hebrew' (see NOTE to 21:2). The 'Abiru are not a powerful confederacy of tribes or, so far as we can tell, an ethnic group. They are a diverse bunch of freebooters. Still, the 'Abiru bear a limited resemblance to the pre-monarchic Israelites as portrayed in the Book of Judges. If the 'Abiru of Canaan and the early Israelites are the same, both the contemporary

Amarna letters and the later Book of Judges show how little each side understood the other. For the urban, Late Bronze Age Canaanites, the ʿAbiru were a marginal nuisance; in Israelite memory, the same is true of the Canaanite city states.

m. Some textual evidence suggests an international epidemic in the fourteenth century B.C.E., reminiscent of the biblical Plagues (Hendel 2005: 64–67).

n. In the same period, the Egyptian cities of Pithom and Ramesses were built (cf. Exod 1:11).

o. The late thirteenth century B.C.E. saw massive movements of populations throughout the Mediterranean and ancient Near East, entailing the fall of kingdoms and the rise of new polities (Dever 2003: 175–76). (It is probably not relevant, but interesting nonetheless, that from this era comes a report of two slaves attempting to escape from Egypt into Canaan [*ANET* 259].)

p. In the thirteenth century also, we find major destruction levels at Tell Beit Mirsim, Bethel, Jokneam and Hazor, the last three said to be taken by Israel, according to the Bible (the ancient name of Beit Mirsim is uncertain). At Hazor, statues were even mutilated, as if images were anathema to the invaders (Ben Tor 1999). Many other sites of unknown ancient identity also show destructions between 1225 and 1175 B.C.E. (Apart from Hazor, however, almost all the cities said to be captured or burnt by Joshua and the Israelites show no evidence of destruction, many being uninhabited in the Late Bronze–Early Iron Age transition [Dever 2003: 26–71].)

q. In the thirteenth–twelfth centuries B.C.E., immigrants settled the Canaanite highlands, with the population approximately tripling from the thirteenth to the eleventh centuries B.C.E. The vast majority of settlements were new foundations (Dever 2003: 98). To judge from surviving artifacts, the newcomers were successful farmers and herdsmen, possibly tribally organized, producing a large agricultural surplus but maintaining a relatively even wealth distribution (Dever p. 175). They terraced the hillsides to create arable land, they dug cisterns and silos to collect water and grain. These settlers produced their own pottery on-site, employing a limited range of forms descended from Late Bronze Age prototypes. They did not create fine art, and they did not raise or eat pigs (Dever pp. 101–28). Whether and how these settlements communicated and cooperated are unknown. We know nothing of their religion. They probably spoke a Canaanite dialect.

Although the settlers' antecedents are disputed, there is little doubt that they evolved into Israel. Dever calls them "proto-Israelites" (p. 194) and sees their origin as a "motley crew" of "urban dropouts," "'Apiru and other 'social bandits'" and "local pastoral nomads," with refugees from Egyptian slavery possibly playing a role (pp. 181–82). Dever makes a strong case for the Israelite movement as a reaction against the difficult socioeconomic realities of Late Bronze Age Canaan (pp. 182–89).

r. In the late thirteenth century B.C.E., Pharaoh Merneptah encountered and claimed to have eradicated a group called "Israel." The hieroglyphic writing of the name shows that this "Israel" was a group of people, presumably tribal, not a city, nation or region.

s. In the twelfth century B.C.E., the Philistines settled along the Canaanite coast, where Exod 13:17 locates them (see below, p. 751).

Each of the foregoing facts bears some resemblance to the biblical record of the Israelites' origin. While some (many? most?) may be red herrings, others might constitute the kernel inside the Exodus legend. How shall we sift for the truth?

A "soft" version of the Exodus theory, i.e., one relatively unconcerned with conformity to the Torah, might attempt to embrace several or all of these facts. E.g.: perhaps some Asiatics entered Canaan from Egypt in the sixteenth century B.C.E. to become the urban Canaanites (Redford 1992: 412–13), as well as their unstable nemesis the ʿAbiru of Canaan and also the nomadic Shasu of the hinterlands. Other Semites stayed in Egypt, experienced Akhenaten's monotheism, were impressed into servitude, built Pithom and Raamses, and finally escaped. All these relics of the Hyksos reunited in the thirteenth–twelfth centuries B.C.E. to settle the uplands—and *voilà* the Israelites! (Such a theory would nicely explain Pharaoh's fear that Israel would "be added to our enemies . . . and go up from the land" [Exod 1:10; cf. Hoffmeier 1996: 122].) But it is sheer fantasy, and other equally (im)plausible scenarios could be improvised.

Before leaving the topic of the historical circumstances behind the Exodus, we should consider the possibility that no Israelite ancestors were ever in Egypt at all. Some who consider the Israelites wholly indigenous to Canaan suggest that they had indeed been slaves *to* Egypt, only not *in* Egypt. Rather, they were Canaanites who had borne Egypt's imperial yoke throughout the New Kingdom, until the Pharaohs lost control of Canaan in the twelfth century B.C.E. (e.g., Hendel 2005: 59–62). If so, the real Exodus is not Israel's departure from Egypt but Egypt's departure from Israel.

What Really Happened?

THE HISTORIOGRAPHY OF MYTHIC EVENTS

I hope to have shown that the question "Did the Exodus happen?" does not mean anything, or rather can mean almost anything. What do we mean by "Exodus"? What do we mean by "happen"? This indeterminacy is a liability of that peculiar field, the Historiography of Mythic Events, i.e., the critical assessment of narratives whose cultural signficance bears no proportional relationship to their truth content. Mytho-historical narratives may be entirely factual, albeit superladen with symbolism (the voyage of the Mayflower), entirely fictional (the Round Table) or something in-between (the Battle of Roncesvalles). Writes classicist I. Malkin (1994: 5):

In general, a myth may become historical either through the transformation of a real event into a myth or through the transformation of a myth into history. The need for myth is attested in the tendency of certain real events to slip into mythic roles: the Battle of Marathon, the death of Leonidas at Thermopylai, the siege of Massada, the Tonypandy massacre, the Boston Tea Party, the mutiny on the

Potemkin, and so on. An event which becomes mythic, functions significantly (and often symbolically) in the life of the community as long as it corresponds to some authentic need. It is useless, beyond the narrow circle of scholarship, for historians to point to contradictory "facts" or try to "demythologize" these events. . . . Conversely, myths may sometimes become historical "events."

Like all good stories, most mythic narratives are driven by conflict, the simpler the better, as in Good vs. Evil. Two ancient antinomies in particular freight the Exodus tradition with its symbolism. One derives from the myth wherein the storm god defeats the sea/river god to establish his kingdom over Mankind and all Creation. The primordial battle between Air and Water, Order and Chaos, for dominion over the Land is recapitulated in the Bible, as Yahweh's wind dries the Suph Sea to rescue his people and defeat his enemies; later, he will do the same to the Jordan River (for extensive discussion, see vol. I, pp. 554–61; below, pp. 795–96, 803).

The other ancient, mythic antinomy underpinning the Exodus tradition is the mutually perceived contrast between the Egyptian elites—wealthy, highly literate, militarily secure, culturally static, depending upon alluvial river water— and the peoples on their borders—seminomadic, poor, marginally literate, subject to incursions and cultural flux, dependent upon highland rainwater. Not surprisingly, texts from Egypt and Palestine bespeak each region's hostility toward the other: the vile Asiatic vs. the rapacious Egyptian. Even before the historical record begins, the complex relationship and conflicted attitude of the inhabitants of Canaan vis-à-vis the superpower to the West provided a continual stimulus to cultural change (cf. Joffe 1993), increasingly so during the Late Bronze–Iron Age transition (Bryan 1996; Higginbotham 2000).

In the era immediately preceding Israel's rise, the proximate representatives of Egyptian culture, more opprobrious than the Egyptians themselves, were the Canaanite city-state rulers. These princelings served the Pharaohs, sometimes nominally and sometimes in reality, enforcing their yoke upon the poorest denizens of the land, until, perhaps, the latter fled into the hills to become the Israelites (Dever 2003: 167–89, esp. 186–87). The Bible's most explicit critiques on the Egyptian-Canaanite connection are found in Gen 9:25–27, the curse of Canaan, and in Gen 10:6–19, which, against ethno-linguistic reality, makes the Canaanites kin of the Egyptians rather than of the Israelites.

Though mythic, the Torah is a crafted work of written literature, not a transcription of oral saga. Its mode of narration differs wholly from the world of classical or Near Eastern epic (Kawashima 2004). But it differs even more from modern historiography.

Immersed in a world of written, verifiable information, Americans may have difficulty imagining the transmission of narrative in an ancient milieu. Let me offer a familiar example of a proto-literate culture, one in which traditions are manipulated even as they grow organically, a culture in which information is constantly exchanged between the oral and the written. I am thinking of the society of the very young. For I cannot escape the queasy feeling that the biblical accounts of Israel's origins are analogous to the hilarious versions of American and world history produced by our schoolchildren. Everything flows. George Washington, Abraham Lincoln, Martin Luther King and Squanto—each commemorated in his own annual historical festival—become contemporaries, exchanging exploits and iconography. Imagine sifting that for history! But that may be precisely our enterprise, in the Historiography of Mythic Events.[1]

So What?

A good myth is mightier than history, immune to both evidence and analysis. I have no doubt that, the foregoing remarks notwithstanding, the Israelites' Exodus from Egypt will remain a historical fact for 99 percent of educated Americans. The story of triumph against impossible odds is narrated with the sequential, Vladimir Proppian elements that we are programmed to find most affecting (vol. I, pp. 32–36). The tale of "When Israel was in Egypt's Land," imbibed by all in childhood, fundamental to two world religions, inspirational to millions seeking deliverance from their trials, cannot be lightly laid aside. If, against all the evidence, we still go through life enveloped in such myths, they are probably good for us.

Peoples and Places

The following pages contain brief synopses, in alphabetical order, of what is known and thought concerning the various ethnic terms and geographic names that appear in Exodus. The reader should also consult the accompanying maps (pp. 755–56).

Amalekite. The linguistically rather odd name *'ămālēq* appears nowhere in ancient inscriptions. The Amalekites were regarded by the Israelites just as the Egyptians regarded the Shasu: as uncouth, nomadic raiders. More closely related to the Edomites, they were considered distant kindred of the Israelites (Gen 36:12, 26; 1 Chr 1:35–36).

Amorite. The Hebrew term *'ĕmōrî* etymologically derives from Akkadian *amurrû* 'westerner'; the name was probably borrowed from the Akkadian by the Amorites themselves. Beginning in the late third millennium B.C.E., Mesopotamian references to the tribal nomads of Syria abound. Eventually, many Amorites settled in Mesopotamia and established local dynasties; their most famous ruler was Ḥammurapi of Babylon (eighteenth century B.C.E.). In the Late Bronze Age, Amurru denoted a specific kingdom in the upper Orontes valley of Syria, originally owing fealty to Egypt but later going over to the Hittites.

Although we lack any texts in the Amorite tongue, Amorite personal names demonstrate an affinity with the later Northwest Semitic languages of Syria–Palestine (Huffmon 1965a). It is likely that the second millennium B.C.E. saw a

---

[1] For an even more surreal experience, one should read the anti-Jewish versions of the Exodus current among Hellenistic Egyptians and preserved by Josephus in *Against Apion*.

proliferation of Amorites in the region so that, in the Bible, "Amorite" functions as a synonym for Canaanite. Ezekiel polemically, but probably accurately, claims that Israel itself is the child of the Amorites (Ezek 16:3, 45).

Baal Zephon. *Ba'al ṣəpōn* is originally a divine name: "the (god) Baal of (Mount) Zaphon" in northern Syria. Assyrian annals call the mountain itself *ba'li ṣapuna* (e.g, Luckenbill 1926–27: 1.274–75; 2.13). Wherever Canaanites settled, they founded cities and shrines named after the Syrian storm god, just as Greeks would acknowledge multiple mounts Olympus, in addition to the original in Thessaly. There were at least three shrines to Baal Zephon in Egypt (see Houtman 1993a: 106), and even Mount Zion was considered an embodiment of Zaphon (Ps 48:3). Baal Zephon was evidently a god of mariners, reliant on his winds, and he had the particular ability to sink ships by storm (*ANET* 534) (Albright 1950). In his Egyptian guise, Baal directed the gods' celestial ship (Helck 1971: 447–50). It is striking that Yahweh's defeat of Pharaoh, by means of drying the sea with his wind, occurred by the city Baal Zephon. Was Yahweh of the Exodus originally an avatar of Canaanite Baal, or of Egyptian Seth, with whom Baal was identified? Or is this one-upmanship, as one could translate *lipnê ba'al ṣəpōn* (Exod 14:2) as "in (the god) Baal Zephon's *face*" (see NOTE). The location of the biblical city Baal Zephon remains uncertain (see below, pp. 753–54).

Canaanite. *Kəna'ănî* properly means "inhabitant of the land of Canaan," i.e., the modern territories of Israel, the West Bank and Lebanon. "Canaanite" in the Bible generally denotes the residents of Syria-Palestine, excluding the Israelites, Arabs, Edomites, Moabites, Ammonites, Arameans (i.e. the "sons of Eber" in Gen 10:21–30 [J]; 11:16–26 [P]) and the Philistines. The Canaanites were perceived as aborigines, affiliated with the dominant populations of Late Bronze Age Canaan (cf. Gen 10:15–19), rather than with the newly formed or newly arrived peoples of the Iron Age. In the Bible, but not in ancient Near Eastern documents, the term "Canaanite" overlaps semantically with "Amorite" and "Hittite." For a survey on ancient references to Canaanites, see Rainey (1996).

Edomite. Edom was the territory south and east of Judah. The Edomite kingdom coalesced out of tribal antecedents perhaps as early as the beginning of the Iron Age I (Levy et al. 2004). Examination of biblical genealogies discovers frequent overlaps among the clans of Judah, Edom and Arabia, suggesting that the fraternity of Israel (Jacob) and Edom (Esau) had a foundation in reality (Axelsson 1987: 66–83). Were the Judahites just Edomite clans who switched sides?

Elim. An oasis with palm trees, of uncertain location; contenders are the Wadi Gharandel, Wadi Tayiba and 'Uyun Musa, all south of Suez (Houtman 1993a: 103).

Etham. The name appears to reflect Egyptian *itm*, the solar creator god Atum, whose name appears also in biblical Pithom (cf. Görg 1992; below, pp. 753–54). The location is unknown.

Girgashite. Possibly a group that immigrated to Canaan from Asia Minor, where in the neighborhood of the Troad we find such geographical names as Gergis, Gergithion, Gargara and Gergitha (e.g., Herodotus 5.122.1.8; 7.43.1.2). The name *girgāšî* also seems related to Ugaritic *grgš*; a northern origin is further suggested by the Egyptian foreign toponym *qrqs* and Hittite *karkisa* (cf. Baker 1992).

Hebrew. I have devoted considerable discussion to the term '*ibrî* under NOTE to 21:2. Here, I will simply summarize my impressions. (For orientation and further detail, see Na'aman 1986; Lemche 1992; Rainey 1995; Cross 1998: 69.)

1. Throughout the second millennium B.C.E., thoughout the Middle East and as far afield as Anatolia and Iran, texts mention a group of mobile, disreputable persons called '*ab/piru*. (Because the term is generally written in Sumerian, however, we are rarely certain of the reading; Sumerian SA.GAZ or simply GAZ does not necessarily equal '*ab/piru.*) Egyptian and Ugaritic texts write the word consonantally as '*pr(w)*; cuneiform documents, however, suggest a pronunciation '*abiru.* Some 'Abiru were slaves in Egypt in the twelfth century B.C.E. (e.g. ANET 247, 261). At least in the Levant, most were presumably Northwest Semites.

2. The 'Abiru may have recruited impoverished peasants and led a movement to the highlands, establishing hundreds of new settlements. An Amarna letter even alludes to people "becoming" 'Abiru (EA 74).

3. Indifferent to the term's previously negative connotations, or perhaps defiantly proud of them, the newly forming Israelite culture called itself '*ibrî* 'Hebrew.' (For further discussion, see also pp. 742–43.)

Hittite. The biblical term *ḥittî* reflects a complex semantic development. Originally, *ḥatti* denoted a region in Anatolia; scholars generally call its aborigines "Hattians." Beginning in the seventeenth century B.C.E., however, Ḥatti was co-opted by an Indo-European-speaking people who established an empire, based in Turkey and reaching down into Syria. In modern parlance, these are the "Hittites" proper.

Reflecting the Hittites' southern sphere of influence in the Levant, Mesopotamian texts refer to Syria as *māt ḥatti* 'Ḥatti-land.' However, after the Hittite empire fell in the upheavals that terminated the Late Bronze Age, smaller states combining aspects of Canaanite, Aramean and Hittite culture persisted along the north Phoenician coastline until the seventh century B.C.E. These "neo-Hittite" principalities may have influenced the biblical usage of *ḥittî*. Often in the Old Testament, "Hittite" seems to be a synonym of "Canaanite" (e.g., Gen 10:15; Ezek 16:3, 45). Sometimes, however, it surprisingly appears to be a subgroup in the south (Genesis 23). In Josh 1:4; Judg 1:26; 1 Kgs 10:29; 2 Kgs 7:6; 2 Chr 1:17, however, the "Hittites" are specifically the neo-Hittites.

In the Torah, at least, Hittite infallibly means Canaanite. The usage has nothing to do with the Hattians and Hittites of Anatolia in the Middle and Late Bronze Ages, nor does it seem to describe the northern neo-Hittite city-states. Rather, the usage most resembles Mesopotamian terminology, in which Canaan was part of "Ḥatti-land." Similarly, the Torah's association of the terms Hittite and Amorite recalls Assyrian inscriptions, in which Ḥatti and Amurru are adjacent or overlapping regions of Syria (Luckenbill 1926–27: 1.262–63; 2.3).

Hivite. Hebrew *ḥiwwî*, describing some inhabitants of central Canaan, is not paralleled in ancient inscriptions. Possibly it is related to Hebrew *ḥawwâ* 'tent camp.'

Horeb. The noun *hōreb* appears to mean "waste." In E and D, it denotes Yahweh's special abode or "Deity's mountain." According to Deut 1:2, "It is eleven days from Horeb via Mount Seir to Kadesh Barnea"; according to 1 Kgs 19:3–8, Horeb is forty-one days' hard travel from Beersheba. Whether Horeb is the same mountain as Sinai is moot. Quite possibly, as in modern times, so in ancient days there were rival sites for the mountain of lawgiving. (See further below under *Sinai.*)

Horite. As the LXX transcription *chorraios* indicates, the ancient pronunciation of MT *hōrî* was *hurrī.* Although an association with the homonyms *hōr* 'hole' and *hōr* 'freeman' cannot be excluded (Knauf 1992), it is hard to escape the connection with Akkadian *hurru,* describing a people (the Hurrians) spread broadly throughout the Near East from the third to the first millennium B.C.E., from Anatolia through north Mesopotamia (Hoffner 1973a; Morrison 1992). In the Late Bronze Age, the Hurrian kingdom of Mitanni contested the rule of Syria and North Mesopotamia with Egypt, Assyria and the Hittites. Egyptian texts from the Nineteenth Dynasty refer to Asia in general, including Canaan, as Hurri-land. Some Amarna-era Canaanites bear Hurrian names.

Surprisingly, however, the Bible locates the Horites in the southern region of Seir (Gen 14:6; Deut 2:12, 22). Was this a pocket of Hurrians who fled south in the Late Bronze Age integration?

Jebusite. While the etymology of *yəbûsî* is unknown, it may be related to an Amorite name from Mari: *yabusum.* According to Josh 15:63; 2 Sam 5:6, etc., the Jebusites were the pre-Israelite inhabitants of Jerusalem who still survive "until this day." The name of one Jebusite, Araunah of Jerusalem (2 Sam 24:16, 18), is linguistically either Hurrian or Hittite *(HALOT).*

Marah. Possibly Ain Hawarah, forty-seven miles southeast of Suez, where in modern times the waters are proverbially brackish (Thompson 1992).

SPECULATION: As observed in vol. I, pp. 575–76, there is reason to think that Marah is situated on the *Egyptian* side of the Sea, and that an editor relocated it in the Sinai desert (Exod 15:22). Consider Num 33:6–11:

And they journeyed from Succoth, and camped in Etham that is on the edge of the wilderness. And they journeyed from Etham, and it turned back (and camped? [cf. LXX]) by Pi-hahiroth that is in front of Baal Zephon, and they camped in front of Migdol. And they journeyed from Pi-hahiroth [see *BHS* apparatus] and crossed in the midst of the Sea into the wilderness, and went a three days' way in the desert of Etham and camped in Marah. And they journeyed from Marah and came to Elim, and in Elim were twelve eye-springs of water and seventy date palms, and they camped there. And they journeyed from Elim and camped by the Suph Sea. And they journeyed from the Suph Sea and camped in the Sin Wilderness.

Why does the text break the pattern "and they journeyed from X and they camped in Y" that otherwise dominates Num 33:1–49? Why does Etham appear twice (vv 6–7, 8)? Why does Israel return to the Sea after leaving Elim (v 10)? A simpleminded reading would accept Num 33:6–11 at face value: Israel returned to the Sea after leaving Elim, even if Exodus makes no mention of this *volte-face*. Most critics, however, suspect a textual error in Numbers 33. But perhaps neither Exodus nor Numbers preserves the original tradition.

Num 33:1–49 seems a simple, monotonous list, secondarily expanded in vv 3–4, 14, 38–40 to incorporate material from the Exodus and Numbers narratives. What if the original form of vv 6–11 was the following:

> And they journeyed from Succoth and they camped in Etham. And they journeyed from Etham, and camped in Marah. And they journeyed from Marah and came to Elim. And they journeyed from Elim and camped by the Suph Sea. And they journeyed from the Suph Sea and camped in the Sin Wilderness.

This reconstruction, in contradiction to Exodus, puts Elim and Marah on the *Egyptian* side of the Suph Sea. It also reduces the number of way stations from forty-two to an even forty, not counting Raamses (cf. Cross 1973: 309).

Let us then suppose that a later scribe harmonized Numbers 33 with Exodus, subject to one restriction: he could only add, not subtract. The result would be Num 33:6–11 in its present form, with the double mention of Etham and the Suph Sea.

We have reconstructed an ancient contradiction between Exodus and Num 33:1–49. Which would be the older tradition? Perhaps that underlying Numbers 33. If we read the Exodus way-station notices sequentially, we discover a break: we last left Israel at Etham (13:20), but where is the expected "and they journeyed from Etham" (cf. Num 33:7)? It could have been deleted by an editor moving Marah and Elim across the Suph Sea, into the Shur Wilderness (15:22).

Who would do this, and why? The most obvious culprit is the final Redactor of JE with P. As for why—I imagine he wished not to break the tension of the pursuit narrative in 13:17–15:21, and also aimed to associate the themes of Murmuring, Water in the Wilderness, Lawgiving and Testing with Israel's desert wanderings. If so, however, then a still later hand must have expanded Num 33:1–49 to harmonize with Exodus. This lack of parsimony is a defect in the hypothesis.

If Marah originally lay on the Egyptian side of the sea, then we might revive the old idea that Marah is one of the Bitter Lakes (*murra*) (map 1) of Egypt, or a related feature (see Dillmann 1880: 162). (If so, however, the miraculous freshening of the waters was only temporary.)

Massah and Meribah. As I argued in vol. I, pp. 605, 612–13, these are the miracle springs of Mount Horeb.

Midian. A region in the northern Hejaz, east of the Gulf of Aqaba (see Knauf 1988a). Numerous Midianite towns arose suddenly during the Late Bronze–early Iron Age transition. Because of Moses' familial relationship with Jethro the priest of Midian, because of Midian's proximity to Mount Sinai (see below), because Yahweh is said to come from the south both in the Bible (Deut 33:2 Judg 5:4–5; Ps 68:8–9, 17–18; cf. Isa 63:1–6; Zech 9:14) and in an inscription from Kuntillet 'Ajrūd (*AHI* 8.021, "Yahweh of Teman"), and because the Egyptians encountered "Yahweh Shasu" (pp. 742, 757) in the deserts southeast of Canaan, a popular scholarly theory is that Israel learned to worship Yahweh from Midian (for a recent version, see Cross 1998: 53–70). Although favored by the J and E sources, the Midianites are viewed with hostility by the Priestly Writer (see further vol. I, p. 176).

Migdol. A common Delta region toponym in the New Kingdom; the name is Canaanite for "tower, fortress." One particular Migdol was prominent in the seventh–sixth centuries B.C.E., when on independent grounds we would date the composition of much biblical literature (Redford 1987: 143; Dever 2003: 19; see briefly below). Although this is probably the Migdol envisioned by the author and his readers, we cannot exclude the possibility that a different Midgol played a role in older traditions (Kitchen 1998: 78).

Moab. The region and kingdom east of the Dead Sea, contemporary with the Israelite kingdoms (see Bienkowski 1992). Moab's most famous king is Mesha in the mid-ninth century B.C.E., known both from the Bible (2 Kgs 1:1; 3:4–27) and his own monumental inscription (*KAI* 181).

Perizzite. The Perizzites do not appear in ancient Near Eastern sources. While some relate the name to a Hebrew term for village settlements (*pərāzî, pərāzôt*), more likely it is Hurrian (Speiser 1962: 242).

Philistine. The Philistines invaded Egypt and Canaan as part of the international convulsion that terminated the Late Bronze Age. After Ramesses III repulsed them c. 1178 B.C.E., they settled along the Canaanite coast (Dothan and Dothan 1992; Oren 2000). All the Pentateuch's references to Philistines are therefore anachronistic (Gen 21:32–34; 26:1, 8, 14–15; Exod 13:17; 15:14; 23:31). According to the Bible, the Philistines contested the control of Canaan with nascent Israel and continued to exist alongside the Israelite kingdoms. In time, they would bequeath their name to the land of Palestine.

Pi-hahiroth. Neither the name nor the location is certain. Against MT *pî haḥîrōt*, LXX suggests a reading of either **py hḥṣrt* or **py hḥwt* (TEXTUAL NOTE to Exod 14:2). Proposed Egyptian equivalents are *p3 ḫ3rti* in the eastern Delta region (Redford 1987: 142) and *p3 ḥr* (Kitchen 1998: 78). *P(r)-ḥtḥrt* 'Hathor's House' between Tanis and Bubastis is also potentially relevant, as is the noun *ḥnrt* 'fortress.'

Pithom. Egyptian *p(r) (i)tm* 'Atum's House' could denote either a city or a shrine. The exact location is disputed (see below).

Raamses. In MT, the name is spelled *ra'amsēs* and *ra'məsēs*, both reflecting Egyptian *r'mssw*. The Egyptian metropolis Piramesse ("Ramesses' House") (map 1) was the capital of the Nineteenth- and Twentieth-Dynasty Pharaohs. (Other cities of the same name were of relatively minor significance; see Kitchen 1998: 69–72.) According to Exod 1:11; 12:37, Raamses was a store city built by Hebrew slaves; it was also their later point of departure from Egypt. Anachronistically, Gen 47:11 refers to a region of the Delta as "the land of Raamses."

Rephidim. An unknown place in the wilderness, perhaps Wadi Refayid (Abel 1933: 2.213, 435), assuming that Horeb is in the (modern) Sinai desert; perhaps er-Rafid in Arabia, assuming that the mountain is east of the Gulf of Aqaba (see below).

Shur. A region or site in the north Sinai, between Canaan and Egypt (Gen 16:7;

20:1; 25:18; Exod 15:22; 1 Sam 15:7; 27:8). Some think that Shur is a fortress or a line of fortresses, since Hebrew *šûr* means "wall." More precision is not presently possible (Seely 1992), although Na'aman (1980:100–5) argues strongly for Shur = Tell el-Far'ah (south).

Sin, Sinai. Since the fourth century C.E., Christian tradition has identified Jebel Musa in south Sinai as the Bible's Mount Sinai; another contender is Jebel Serbal, c. twenty miles to the northwest. But the mountain's biblical association with Midian favor instead a location in northwest Arabia, perhaps Jebel al-Lawz, the highest peak in the region (see Kerkeslager 2000; map 2). We need not choose only one mountain, however, since tradition reckons with two names: Sinai (J and P) and Horeb/the Deity's Mountain (E and D). These could theoretically be distinct sites.

A perennial puzzle is the absence of Sinai from surveys of Israelite history such as Deut 26:5–9; Josh 24:2–13; Psalms 78, 105, 136. Was the Sinai tradition a later invention? Or was it an archaic tradition that became suspect because it was co-opted by the kings of Judah and applied to Zion? Or was it simply presupposed? For approaches to the problem, see Huffmon (1965b); Loewenstamm (1992: 31–38).

Succoth. The Hebrews' first stopover after leaving the Egyptian heartland is Succoth (Exod 12:37; 13:20; Num 33:5–6). Most scholars view *sukkōt* as a Hebraization of Egyptian *tkw/tkt* (or vice versa). *Tkw* was a city and region in the eastern delta, most likely Tell el-Maskhuta (Kitchen 1998: 73–76). The Hebrew name *sukkōt* means "huts" and may have motivated a pun apropos of the festival of Sukkot; see vol. I, p. 413.

Suph Sea. The Hebrew term *yam sûp* has traditionally been translated "Red Sea" but more recently "Reed Sea," since that is what the phrase literally means. We do not know why the Red Sea should have been called "Reed Sea," since reeds do not grow in or near its salt waters. Nevertheless, there is little doubt that in Exod 23:31; Num 14:25; 21:4; Deut 1:40; 2:1; Judg 11:16 [?]; 1 Kgs 9:26; Jer 49:21, the Suph Sea is the Gulf of Aqaba. In Exod 10:19; 13:18; Num 33:10–11, however, the Suph Sea appears to be the Gulf of Suez. In short, the Suph Sea is the Red Sea and its two northern arms (map 2). We cannot account for the name, except to cite the Israelites' limited knowledge of geography (e.g., Gen 2:10–14) and, apparently, littoral botany.

Some modern interpreters of the name, however, appear to be motivated by a peculiar combination of religiosity and rationalism. They assume, on the one hand, that the Exodus story is true or based upon truth. But they deny, on the other hand, that a sea can be split, and are understandably bothered by the fact that a reed-less sea should be called "Reed Sea." From these considerations, a case is built for the "Suph Sea" not being a sea at all, but a marsh in which the Egyptian cavalry was mired. The main evidence for the view is that fact that the Egyptian phrase (*p3*) *twf(y)*, which corresponds to Hebrew (*has*)*sûp*, describes a papyrus marsh — admittedly not a specific swamp. Comparable military mishaps are then cited, as if they were relevant to the historicity of Exodus (vol. I, p. 551).

I prefer to take the story "literally" — as fiction. According to Exodus, the people of Israel in their hundreds of thousands crossed the Gulf of Suez on dry land, with the Egyptians in hot pursuit (see Huddleston 1992; Houtman 1993a: 109–10 for more discussion and other possibilities).

The Route of the Exodus

Clearly, the Israelites did *not* take the only logical way from Egypt to Canaan: the brief trip (c. 180 miles) along the Ways of Horus in North Sinai—i.e., "the way of the land of Philistines" (Exod 13:17)—because it was fortified (Oren 1987). I consider it a waste of time to consider in great detail the route of the Exodus (on which see Davis 1990). Here's why:

1. We are unsure of the readings of two geographical names: Goshen (LXX *Gesem*), where the Hebrews had settled (Gen 45:10; 46:28), and Pi-hahiroth by which they passed (see TEXTUAL NOTE to Exod 14:12). Neither spot can be identified with an ancient name or located precisely.

2. We do not know in what century the accounts were written, or on what information they were based: archives, firsthand knowledge of Egypt, secondhand knowledge of Egypt, sheer guesswork? (See APPENDIX A.)

3. We can identify definitively almost none of the places mentioned in Exodus, with predictable results. Those predisposed to find the accounts to be factual advocate identifications that work for whenever they date the Exodus (e.g., Kitchen 2003: 254–63). Those convinced that the account is nonfactual bolster their case by identifying the sites primarily with places uninhabited when the Exodus supposedly occurred, but settled in later times, when they think the sources were written (e.g., Redford 1987). If there is a problem, one can always suppose that the true location is yet to be discovered, or that the archaeological record is incomplete.

4. The parade example of this phenomenon demonstrates that crucial information may already have been tainted in Antiquity. *If* Exodus is based upon factual information of the early Iron Age, the city of Raamses must be Piramesse. *If*, however, Exodus is a fabrication of the Saite period (664–525 B.C.E.), then, some argue, Raamses should be Tanis or Bubastis, to which Ramesside monuments were transported from Piramesse (Bietak 1981: 279; Wente 1992; but see Kitchen 1998: 83; 2003: 256).

Here I throw up my hands. I get a headache reading the conflicting reconstructions of the equally erudite but nakedly polemical Egyptologists Kenneth Kitchen and Donald Redford, who know far more than I and yet reach diametrically opposing conclusions (see chart below). For a biblical scholar, the only sensible recourse is agnosticism. (My instinct, for what it's worth, is to mediate between Kitchen and Redford, taking the Bible's geographical accounts as flawed, mid–first millennium refractions of authentic Late Bronze Age traditions.)

5. The whole thing may never have happened.

CHART 2. Kitchen vs. Redford: The Geography of the Exodus

---

1. Raamses
   Kitchen: Raamses = Pi-Ramesse = Qantir. Ramesside era remains.
   Redford: Raamses = Bubastis. Continuous occupation.
2. Succoth
   Kitchen: Succoth = Tkw = Tell el-Maskhuta. Ramesside era occupation.
   Redford: Succoth = Tkw = Tell el-Maskhuta. No Ramesside occupation.
3. Pithom
   Kitchen: Pithom = P(r)-(i)tm = Tell er-Retaba. Ramesside remains.
   Redford: Pithom = P(r)-(i)tm. Location unknown, but founded by Necho II
   (609–594 B.C.E.).
4. Pi-hahiroth
   Kitchen: Pi-hahiroth = unknown.
   Redford: Pi-hahiroth = unknown.
5. Baal-Zephon
   Kitchen: Baal-Zephon = unknown
   Redford: Baal-Zephon = Ras Qasrun (on Lake Bardawil, between Lake Sirbonis
   and the Mediterranean). Saite era.
6. Migdol
   Kitchen: Migdol = unknown
   Redford: Migdol = Migdol of Jer 44:1; 46:14; Ezek 29:10; 30:6 = Tell el-Ḥeir?
   Saite era.

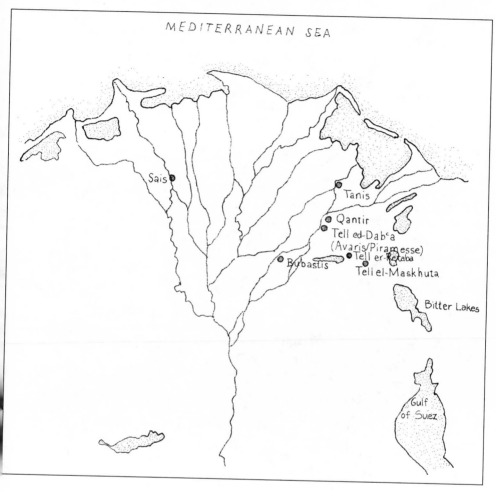

Map 1. Nile Delta

Map 2. The Israelites and their neighbors

Appendix C
THE ORIGINS OF MONOTHEISM

◆

The Divine Names

1. *Yahweh.* This is the proper name of Israel's god. Over time, pronouncing it became taboo, so that we are not entirely certain how to vocalize the written consonants *yhwh.* The process of avoiding *yhwh* began already in late biblical times, as we see from the relative frequency of "Yahweh" and "Deity" in the Books of Kings vis-à-vis the later Books of Chronicles. In the Bible-based faith communities, the name has been replaced with various terms meaning "the Lord" (Greek *kyrios*, Aramaic *mār[əy]ā'*, Latin *dominus*, Hebrew *'ădōnāy*) or "the Name" (Samaritan Aramaic *šəmā'*, Hebrew *haššēm*) as well as other circumlocutions. For further discussion, see Freedman and O'Connor (1986).

Yahweh is also found in other cultures. Before Israel, the *word* Yahweh first appears in Egyptian texts apropos of the Late Bronze Age nomads of Edom (Weinfeld 1987: 304–5; Redford 1992: 272–73). But there is no evidence that *yhw3* denoted a god; it seems rather to have been a geographical or tribal name (at least so far as the Egyptians knew). Contemporary with Israel, there is also evidence that the Syrian city-state Hamath venerated Yahweh (Dalley 1990; Zevit 1992).

If Semitic, the name *yahwe(h)* must be a verbal form of the root *hwy*, which in various cognate languages means "blow, fall, destroy" and, especially in Hebrew, "happen, become, be." In Israelite proper names, *yahwe(h)* contracts to *yāhû* (suffix), *yəhô* and *yô* (prefix). There is also a short form *yāh/yâ*, which can occur independently.

In Hebrew alone among the Semitic languages, the root *hwy* ordinarily takes the form *hyy*. One could take *yahwe(h)* as an archaic or dialectal Qal verb (proto-Hebrew **yahwiyu*), equivalent to normal Hebrew *yihye(h)* 'he is/will be' (for vestigial *hwy*, see Gen 27:29; Isa 16:4; Job 37:6; Neh 6:6; Eccl 2:22; 11:3). That the Israelites understood the divine name in this manner is suggested by Exod 3:14, *'ehye(h) 'ăšer 'ehye(h)* 'I will be who I will be' (see NOTE). (Some find evidence for divinities "He is" from Ebla [Müller 1981] and "I am" from Nabatean settlements in Sinai [Knauf 1984].)

Alternatively, *yahwe(h)* could be Hiph'il, a contraction of proto-Hebrew **yahahwiy(u)*, meaning "He will cause to be, he creates." Though morphologically unobjectionable, many feel discomfort with such an abstract statement serving as a divine name. It is also unclear whether the contraction **yahahwiyu > yahwe(h)* could have occurred early enough to be reflected in the Late Bronze Age Egyptian evidence cited above, which calls the nomads *yhw3* not **yhhw3*.

SPECULATION: A popular theory holds that the verb *yahwe(h)* was originally an element in a longer utterance. What was it? The first answer that springs to mind might be "Yahweh, Yahweh, a merciful and benevolent god, *long-faced* and great in trust and reliability, conserving fidelity to a thousandth (generation), *bearing* transgression and crime and sin—although he does not acquit, acquit, reckoning fathers' sins upon sons and upon sons' sons, upon a third and upon a fourth (generation)" (34:6–7). Another obvious candidate would be "I will be who I will be" (3:14) (see vol. I, pp. 224–25).

Some scholars, however, have nominated the phrase *yahwe(h) ṣəbā'ōt yōšēb hakkərûbîm* (Cross 1973: 60–71, 69–70). *Yōšēb hakkərûbîm* means "enthroned (upon) the Griffins," but what of the first two words? Although *yahwe(h) ṣəbā'ōt* is generally rendered "Yahweh of Hosts," Cross argues for "He creates the (heavenly) armies," acknowledging that the reference might simultaneously be to Israel's human fighters (see also Seow 1992). Among other parallels, Cross cites Haddu's epithet at Ugarit *'al'iyn* 'exalted, victorious,' short for *'al'iy.qrdm*, which may mean "I prevail over warriors" or "I am eminent among warriors."

For further insight, I would look to Exod 15:3, potentially our oldest Israelite explanation of the name Yahweh. To me, "*yahwe(h) 'îš milḥāmâ*, Yahweh is his name" implies that Yahweh is short for *yahwe(h) 'îš milḥāmâ*. But what does that mean? Against the usual understanding "Yahweh is a Man of War," we could take *'îš milḥāmâ* as the grammatical *object* of *yahwe(h)*. If so, two possible translations suggest themselves. First, following Cross, the verse may be rendered, "He creates the man of war; Yahweh is his name."

The context of Exod 15:3 points in a different direction, however. Although the Hebrew root *hw/yy* almost always means "be, become," the original Semitic sense "fall" survives in Job 37:6 and probably Eccl 11:3; compare also the nouns *hawwâ/hayyâ/hōwâ* 'downfall.' We might therefore translate Exod 15:3 as "He *throws down* the man of war," echoing v 1, "Horse and chariotry he hurled (*rāmâ*)," and anticipating v 4, "Pharaoh's chariots and his force he *cast* (*yārâ*)." And we could similarly understand *yahwe(h) ṣəbā'ōt* as "He casts down armies," whether terrestrial or celestial (on the rebel gods, see Gen 6:1–4; Isa 14:14–27; 24:21–23; 34:4; Ezek 28:1–19; Psalm 82; Job 15:15; 1 Enoch 6–11; Clifford 1972: 160–68; Forsyth 1987: 15, 83, 132–33).

The fact that we can find these and other plausible candidates for the full divine name suggests to me that, after all, the original name was simply "Yahweh," as the Egyptian evidence of the "Yahweh-Shasu" would suggest (p. 742). But, like later Jews, the biblical writers fostered a belief that God's true name was a longer utterance, which they delighted in reconstructing.

2. *Deity*. *'Ĕlōhîm* properly means "gods." Contextually, however, the term usually describes the one god Yahweh, in which case it takes singular modifiers (see,

however, pp. 246, 551–52 above). Cross (1973: 44) proposes that *'ĕlōhîm* originally indicated the cosmic unity represented by the various local manifestations of God *('ēl)*, what he calls the "plural of cult manifestations," just as we find references to "the Baals" and "the Ashtoreths (= Astartes)." I would understand *'ĕlōhîm* as a plural of abstraction meaning "divinity" (so already Bekhor Shor on Exod 32:4); more recently, Cross (1998: 50 n. 73) has similarly understood the epigraphic plural *'lhn* as "the Godhead."

This usage was probably inherited from Israel's polytheistic forebears, who called a high god "the gods" when praising him as subsuming the powers of the pantheon or as symbolizing their power. Thus, for example, the Canaanite vassals of the Amarna letters address Pharaoh as "my gods" (EA 281.2; 296.2, 7; cf. also 96.4; 97.3; 189. rev. 14 [?]). We find the same phenomenon sporadically in Mesopotamia (Johnson 1961: 26–27; Dalley 1989: 164). In Greece, too, the gods are spoken of in singular and plural, depending on whether one is stressing their diversity or unity (Vernant 1980: 98–99).

3. *Shadday.* Both the derivation and meaning of *šadday* are unclear. Equivalents in LXX, Symmachus, Aquila and Theodotion are *theos* 'God,' *hikanos* 'sufficient,' *epouranios* 'heavenly,' *ho theos tou ouranou* 'the god of heaven,' *kyrios* 'Lord,' *pantokratōr* 'almighty' and *axios* 'worthy' (*Gen. Rab* 46:3; see further Zorell 1927; Bertram 1959). The traditional English rendering is "Almighty," based on *pantokratōr.*

The Bible itself provides no clear explanation of Shadday, for the puns with *šôd* 'devastation' (Isa 13:6; Joel 1:15) and *šādayim* 'breasts' (Gen 49:25) may be just that—homophony not etymology (see below). Given the ambiguities of pre-Massoretic consonantal writing, the very pronunciation *šadday* is somewhat uncertain. The first consonant might be *śin* not shin, and the daleth could be single not double. And even if the first consonant is shin, it might go back to either Proto-Semitic *š or *t. The doubling of the daleth we can trace as far back as Late Antiquity, when the name is transliterated as *Saddai* in LXX[B] Ezek 10:5. Moreover, the Rabbinic interpretation "sufficient" assumes a derivation *šadday = ša + [d]day*, i.e., with shin and geminated *d* as in MT. (On the other hand, the name *šədē'ûr* [Num 1:5, etc.] lacks gemination.)

Further, the root of *šadday* might be either *šdy* or *šdd*, depending on whether we analyze the noun as a *qaṭṭal* or *qaṭlay* type. If the latter, is the suffix the same found in masculine names such as *yīšay*, *ḥaggay*, etc.? Or might it be the old Canaanite *feminine* suffix, as in Hebrew *śāray = śārâ* and more commonly in Ugaritic? (Cf. Lutsky's [1998] contention that Shadday was originally a goddess.)

The oldest biblical attestations of Shadday are in the archaic or archaistic poetry of the Torah: Jacob's Blessing (Gen 49:25) and Balaam's Oracles (Num 24:4, 16) (Cross and Freedman 1997; Freedman 1980: 85–90; see, however, Robertson 1972). In Gen 49:25, Shadday parallels "your father's god" (or "God your father"); in Num 24:4, 16, it parallels "God *('ēl)*" and "Lofty *('elyôn)*." The difficult Psalm 68, which also displays archaic traits, in v 15 speaks of Shadday spreading something, perhaps gold and silver wings (v 14), and causing snow to fall. Shadday appears also in Ps 91:1, a poem of unknown date: "dwelling in the

covert of Elyon, let him lodge under the shadow/protection of Shadday." A further example is Isa 13:6 (also quoted in Joel 1:15): "Wail, for the day of Yahweh is
near, like violence (*šôd*) from Shadday it comes." Ezek 1:24 and 10:5 associate
Shadday with loud sounds, most likely thunder.

Shadday appears most thickly (about thirty-one times) in the Book of Job,
which, like Balaam's oracles, is set east of Israel. The environment is quasi-
patriarchal (see Pope 1965a: 3–5), and the language is studiously archaistic or
simply archaic (cf. Robertson 1972). Shadday frequently parallels both *'ĕlôah*
'God' (Job 5:17; 6:4; 11:7, etc.) and *'ēl* 'God' (Job 8:3, 5; 13:3; 15:25, etc.). The
name "Yahweh" is avoided in the poetry of Job (except possibly 12:9), comporting
with the non- or pre-Israelite setting.

In P, God Shadday appears as the being who renews the promise of posterity
and land to the Fathers (Gen 17:1; 28:3; 35:11; 48:3). Gen 17:1 and Exod 6:2–3
equate him with Yahweh. In P, Shadday is also an element in three pre-Mosaic
names: *ṣûrîšadday* 'Shadday is my Rock,' *'ammîšadday* 'Shadday is my Kinsman'
and *šadê'ûr* ('Shaday [*sic*] is a Fire') (Num 1:5, 6, 12, etc.). This accords with the
Priestly theory that Yahweh was known only as *'ēl*, *'ĕlōhîm* or *'ēl šadday* before
Moses' time (see NOTE to 6:20, "Jochebed").

Shadday also appears once in JE (Gen 43:14). And in narrative, nonpenta-
teuchal prose, the name occurs again only in Ruth 1:20–21: "Shadday has greatly
embittered me . . . Yahweh has testified (*'ānâ*) against me (or "humiliated
[**'innâ*] me" [OG]), and Shadday has done me harm." As in Balaam's Oracles
and Job, the setting is Transjordanian (Koch 1976: 328).

We turn now to the sparse nonbiblical attestations of Shadday. The oldest to
date comes from an Egyptian statuette of the thirteenth century B.C.E. (Petrie
1890: pl. 24), where we find an Asiatic name written in syllabic orthography
as *ša-di-'-m-ì* (Cross 1973: 53–54). This is presumably an inversion of biblical
'ammîšadday 'Shadday is my Kinsman,' although an interpretation *šadday-'immī*
'Shadday is with me' cannot be ruled out. (On earlier possible references at
Ugarit, see Cross 1973: 54 n. 41; Loretz 1980.)

The Deir 'Allā plaster inscriptions from eighth-century B.C.E. Jordan contain
non-biblical oracles attributed to Balaam the son of Beor, known from Numbers
22–24 (Hoftijzer and van der Kooij 1976; Hackett 1980). Here the term *šdyn*
appears as a *plural* divine epithet paralleling *'l[h]n* 'gods,' just as, in the biblical oracles of Balaam, Shadday parallels *'ēl* 'God' (Num 24:4, 16). In the poorly preserved text, the *šdyn* are possibly commanded to send darkness and clouds.
Thamudian (Arabic) *'l šdy* and Palmyrene *šdy'* may be still later avatars from the
east and south.

Of the many etymologies proposed for Shadday, some assume the Massoretic
vocalization and normal Semitic phonetic correspondences, while others posit
various irregularities. That the Hebrew sibilants were pronounced differently in
different regions (Judg 12:6) only compounds our uncertainty. Among the viable
contenders are "the pourer" (cf. Smith 1881: 423–24); "the hurler" (Tur-Sinai
1957: 73); "the violent" (Noth 1928: 130–31; Baudissin 1929: 2.4, n. 2; Bertram
1959: 502–6); "the mountain" (Burrows 1940); "the mountain-dweller" (Albright

1935: 184; Cross 1973: 52–60); "the mountain wind, east wind, easterner" (borrowed from Akkadian *šad[d]û* of the same meaning; cf. *šdy'* in *b. Giṭ. 31b*); "the breast-fed" (cf. the Aramaic name tadday); "the breasted" (whether as a god or a goddess [Biale 1982; Lutsky 1998]); "the tent-dweller" (< Ugaritic *dd* 'tent [?]' [cf. Clifford 1972: 51–53]); "the savior" (Görg 1981b; cf. Egyptian *šd* 'save'); "the field-dweller" (Weippert 1961; Loretz 1980; cf. Hebrew *šāde[h]* 'field'), and "the spirit" (Nöldecke 1886: 736; cf. Hebrew *šēd* 'spirit, demon'). Not all of these fit well with both the evidence of the Bible and Deir 'Allā.

Relatively few scholars have advocated the interpretation that to me seems most likely, or, rather, least unlikely: derivation as a loanword from the Arabic root *šdd* 'to be strong' (cf. Renan 1859: 270; Baethgen 1888: 295). How else can we explain the Greek rendering *pantokratōr* 'almighty' and Syriac *ḥsyn'* 'mighty'?

Where do these rival derivations of Shadday leave us? Given their plethora, no one is likely to be correct. In other words, each individual proposal is outweighed by the cumulative probability of its rivals. Perhaps the Israelites themselves were not sure what the name meant.

Still, our study has not been entirely fruitless. We have discovered particular associations of Shadday with Transjordan-North Arabia, with the Patriarchs, with ancient times, with fertility, violence, mountains, snow, loud sounds and the storm. The natural inference is that Shadday was an ancient Transjordanian storm god identified with Yahweh. (For further discussion of Shadday, see Niehr and Steins 2004.)

4. *Asherah.* Some scholars believe that many (most?) Israelites, even those nominally monotheistic, acknowledged that Yahweh had a consort Asherah (see recently Dever 2005). Most likely, her name means "place." At least in Israel, she was known as *'ăšērat yahwe(h)* 'Yahweh's Place,' just as the Egyptian goddess Hathor's name means "House of Horus." (See also the deity *bêt-'ēl* 'God's House' [cf. Dalglish 1992].) Postbiblical Judaism perpetuated the tradition of referring to a god's "place" as if it were a divine name; compare *šəkînâ* 'Residence' (a female hypostasis) and *hammāqôm* 'the Place' (a circumlocution for God). See further above, pp. 613–14; below, p. 771 n. 49.

5. *Gods.* The Bible variously expresses Yahweh's superiority over other gods. Often, as in Exod 15:11, we have a claim of his incomparability (see Labuschagne 1966). Sometimes the celestial gods are called upon to worship or praise Yahweh, in an implicit act of submission (e.g., Ps 29; 97:7; 103:20–21; 148:1–3; Job 38:7). Elsewhere, however, Yahweh's superiority is simply asserted, as in Jethro's confession in Exod 18:11: "Now I know that Yahweh is greater than all the gods." Similarly, Ps 95:3 calls Yahweh *melek gādôl 'al-kol-'ĕlōhîm* 'great king over all gods/king greater than all gods' (see also Ps 97:9). Deut 4:34–35 specifies in what respect Yahweh is unique: "Has any deity tried to come to take for himself a people from the midst of a(nother) people with trials, with signs and with wonders and with war and with a strong arm and with an extended arm and with great frights . . . ? You have been shown, for (your) knowledge, that Yahweh is the deity; there is none other apart from him."

Are the "gods" to whom Yahweh is superior his vanquished rivals? Are they the angels of his court? Or are they the gods of other nations? The answer is probably all of the above, for it appears that the gods of other nations were conceived sometimes as Yahweh's retinue (see TEXTUAL NOTE to 1:3) and sometimes as dead gods (Ps 82:7). In a culture that eventually outlawed the veneration of Yahweh's celestial servants, while never denying their existence (see Halpern 1993b), statements of Yahweh's uniqueness would be apropos. And assertions of his superiority to foreign deities, whose worship was also forbidden, would serve the patriotic theme of Exod 15:1–18 and of the Book of Exodus as a whole. Deut 4:7; 33:26–29 and 2 Sam 7:22–23 chauvinistically associate Yahweh's divine incomparability with Israel's national incomparability (Labuschagne 1966: 149–53).

When first the northern and then the southern kingdoms of Israel and Judah were dispersed by the Mesopotamian powers, Yahweh-worshipers faced a crisis. They could either confess their god's powerlessness and adopt new religions, or else claim that even his people's degradation was part of Yahweh's plan. This theological readjustment was not unique to Israel. Babylonian thinkers, for example, understood the exile of their idol Marduk as *evidence* of his universal sway (Roberts 1977).

As sole, universal god of Israel, Yahweh had to play the several roles elsewhere apportioned among the entire pantheon: Creator, Warrior, Father, God of Storm and Springs, Craftsman, Healer, Sender of Plague, Bestower of Fertility. Only the Underworld appears to have been beyond Yahweh's bailiwick.

Reacting against past religious apologetics, many scholars nowadays regard Israelite monotheism as the culmination of a graduate evolution. The following essay, originally published in *Ugarit-Forschungen* 31 (1999) 537–75, makes the case for the sudden introduction of monotheism in Israel.

Monotheism and "Moses": the Problem of Early Israelite Religion

MONOTHEISM

It is popular knowledge that the Hebrew Bible forbids the worship of any god but Yahweh. Idols must be smashed and temples of other deities destroyed; the very names of foreign gods are taboo. Worship, conducted by God's chosen priesthood, is permissible only in the royal city of Jerusalem. Right or wrong, this is our common conception of biblical monotheism.

It is also widely known that, in the mid-fourteenth century B.C.E. (ca. 1377–1360),[1] Pharaoh Akhenaten (Amenophis IV) and Queen Nefertiti abolished the entire menagerie of the Egyptian pantheon. Temples were shut, idols were destroyed and sacred names were effaced. The seat of royalty was transferred to a newly founded city, Akhetaten (modern 'el-'Amarna). There Akhenaten, Ne-

---

[1] New Kingdom chronology is still slightly unsettled, with an error margin of up to thirty years. My dates come from D. B. Redford, *Akhenaten the Heretic King* (Princeton: Princeton University Press, 1984) 13.

fertiti and their court adored only the Aten, the solar disk whose light each day enlivens the world.[2]

The Bible itself records that the Hebrew ancestors came from Egypt, where they had sojourned either 430 or 215 years.[3] Israel's liberator and lawgiver was supposedly reared at the Egyptian court (Exod 2:10–11; cf. Acts 7:22), and he bears an Egyptian name.[4] The emergence, in roughly the same time and place, of history's first iconoclastic, monotheistic religious movements cannot be coincidence—or so some have claimed.

The most prominent exponent of this view is Sigmund Freud, of whose *Moses and Monotheism* (1939)[5] Y. H. Yerushalmi provides a helpful summary:

Monotheism is not of Jewish origin but an Egyptian discovery. The pharaoh Amenhotep IV established it as his state religion in the form of an exclusive worship of the sun-power, or Aton, thereafter calling himself Ikhnaton. The Aton religion, according to Freud, was characterized by the exclusive belief in one God, the rejection of anthropomorphism, magic, and sorcery, and the absolute denial of an afterlife. Upon Ikhnaton's death, however . . . the Egyptians reverted to their old gods. Moses was not a Hebrew but an Egyptian priest or noble, and a fervent monotheist. In order to save the Aton religion from extinction he placed himself at the head of an oppressed Semitic tribe then living in Egypt, brought them forth from bondage, and created a new nation. He gave them an even more spiritualized, imageless form of monotheistic religion and, in order to set them apart, introduced the Egyptian custom of circumcision. But the crude mass of former slaves could not bear the severe demands of the new faith. In a mob revolt Moses was killed and the memory of the murder repressed. The Israelites went on to forge an alliance of compromise with kindred Semitic tribes in Midian whose fierce volcanic deity, named Yahweh, now became their national god. As a result, the god of Moses was fused with Yahweh and the deeds of Moses ascribed to a Midianite priest also called Moses.[6]

---

[2] Studies on Akhenaten and his religion include J. Assmann, "Die 'Häresie' des Echnaton: Aspekte der Amarna-Religion," *Saeculum* 23 (1972) 109–26; Redford, *Akhenaten*; C. Aldred, *Akhenaten King of Egypt* (London: Thames and Hudson, 1988); E. Hornung, *Echnaton: Die Religion des Lichtes* (Zürich: Artemis, 1995), and Assmann, *Moses the Egyptian* (Cambridge, Mass.: Harvard University Press, 1997) 168–207. Akhenaten's motives are the subject of perennial speculation, the extreme views being that he was an abstracted philosopher-king and mystic, on the one hand, and that he was engaged in a naked power struggle with the Amun priesthood, on the other. See D. P. Silverman, "Divinity and Deities in Ancient Egypt," *Religion in Ancient Egypt* (ed. B. E. Shafer; Ithaca/London: Cornell University Press, 1991) 75–76; Hornung, "The Rediscovery of Akhenaten and His Place in Religion," *JARCE* 29 (1992) 43–49.

[3] See the commentaries on the variants in Exod 12:40.

[4] J. C. Griffiths, "The Egyptian Derivation of the Name Moses," JNES 12 (1953) 225–31; see also below, n. 138.

[5] *Standard Edition of the Complete Psychological Works of Sigmund Freud* (ed. J. Strackey; London: Hogarth Press and the Institute of Psycho-Analysis, 1953–74) 23.7–137.

[6] Y. H. Yerushalmi, *Freud's Moses* (New Haven/London: Yale University Press, 1991) 3–4. The last sentence is a bit misleading. For Freud, the Midianite priest's true name is unknown; tradition, how-

Among academic biblicists, *Moses and Monotheism* has met with kneejerk incredulity, even scorn.[7] And no wonder: the author clearly did not know what he was talking about! Freud was confecting fantastic pseudo-history, midrash if you like, both to legitimate a theory of religion's bloody origins[8] and to work out a lifelong conflict over his own Jewish heritage.[9]

Even by the standards of his time, Freud was just a learned amateur. But he is still worth reading. I shall argue here that at least one element in his hypothesis, i.e., that Atenism influenced Israel, remains viable. While I do not claim that it is correct, I insist that it is sufficiently plausible to be entertained by critical scholars, alongside or in conjunction with other possibilities.

The greatest liability of *Moses and Monotheism* and similar works[10] is overspecificity: Moses was Akhenaten's vizier, his high priest, or Akhenaten himself (no one has yet nominated Nefertiti), there were two Moseses, etc. These suggestions appear ludicrous to biblical scholars, who nowadays tacitly agree that, concerning the historical Moses, the less said the better.

In order to rescue Freud's thesis from its creator, we had best restate it as broadly as possible. Below we shall introduce elaboration and qualification, but let us begin with something sufficiently vague: *Israelite monotheism was somehow related to Akhenaten's Aten-worship.*

In defining this relationship, we confront two main alternatives: either Israel influenced Egypt, or Egypt influenced Israel (more complex scenarios are also conceivable). I would not dismiss the first out of hand; after all, the story of Joseph (Genesis 37; 39–50) ascribes to Israel's ancestors great influence at the Pharaonic

---

ever, has called him "Moses." Of course, *Moses and Monotheism* contains much more than historical speculation. H. Eilberg-Schwartz, *God's Phallus* (Boston: Beacon Press, 1994), is a recent effort to elaborate and refine Freud's psychoanalytic approach to monotheism. A more complete explanation of the phenomenon than I can offer here would ideally combine the historical, social and psychological dimensions.

[7] W. F. Albright's verdict is typically dismissive: "totally devoid of serious historical method . . . deals with historical data even more cavalierly than with the data of introspective and experimental psychology" (*From the Stone Age to Christianity*, 2d ed. [New York: Doubleday Anchor Books, 1957] 112). Ironically, compared to most biblical scholarship, Albright's position approaches Freud's relatively closely (see below, n. 24).

[8] The theory of the primordial parricide is expounded in *Totem and Taboo* (1912–13), *Standard Edition* 13.1–161.

[9] See D. Boyarin, "'An Imaginary and Desirable Converse': *Moses and Monotheism* as Family Romance," *Reading Bibles, Writing Bodies* (ed. T. K. Beal, D. M. Gunn; London/New York: Routledge, 1996) 184–202.

[10] On Freud's precursors, see Yerushalmi, p. 5; Assmann, *Moses, passim.* The correlation of Moses and Akhenaten has a surprisingly long pedigree; Hellenistic Egyptian writers had probably already confounded the two (Assmann, pp. 29–44). More recent writers associating Moses and Akhenaten in a fantastical manner include M. Haedrich (*Et Moïse créa Dieu* [Paris: Laffont, 1970]), P. Aziz (*Moïse et Akhenaton* [Les énigmes de l'univers; Paris: Laffont, 1980]), A. Osman (*Moses Pharaoh of Egypt* [London/Glasgow/Toronto/Sydney/Auckland: Grafton, 1990]), E. Bock (*Moses* [Worcester, U.K.: Floris, 1986]) and G. Greenberg (*The Moses Mystery* [Secaucus, N.J.: Carol, 1996]). Novelist Howard Fast (*Moses, Prince of Egypt* [New York: Crown, 1958]) even gives Moses an Atenist girlfriend! More sober is H. Haarman, *Religion und Autorität* (Hildesheim/Zurich/New York: Olms, 1998), but he, too, adheres to such improbabilities as Freud's Aten = Adonai connection (pp. 72–73).

court.[11] And historians ranging from Flavius Josephus to Donald Redford[12] have regarded the Israelites as, at least in part, relics of the Hyksos, the Semitic rulers of Egypt ca. 1665–1560 who worshiped the Asiatic storm god Baal in the guise of Egyptian Seth.[13] A Ramesside novel, *King Apophis and Sekenenre*, intriguingly reports that the Hyksos king Apophis (r. ca. 1595–1563) worshiped Seth alone.[14] One could argue that Akhenaten's relative indifference to the afterlife reflects Asiatic sensibilities.[15] As for iconoclasm, Tryggve N. D. Mettinger argues that early Semitic worship was largely aniconic, conducted before unsculpted stones, and thus at least latently iconoclastic.[16]

Admittedly, the Hyksos were supposedly thrust into Asia ca. 1560, two centuries before the Amarna interlude. But archaeological confirmation of this expulsion is elusive.[17] In any case, "ethnic cleansing" is rarely if ever fully successful; even if some were deported, there would have been many Hyksos "Marranos" who took or already bore Egyptian names and so became invisible to history. Moreover, multitudes of Asiatics were continually entering Egypt both voluntarily and involuntarily throughout the New Kingdom; some were presumably returning descendants of the Hyksos, or groups culturally akin to them. We know that Asiatics and Egyptians intermarried.[18] Egyptians and Semites in New Kingdom Egypt talked about all sorts of things, including theology; several foreign gods entered the Egyptian pantheon at this time.[19] Perhaps, one might suggest, among these Asiatic

---

[11] Cf. H. H. Rowley, *From Joseph to Joshua* (London: Oxford University Press, 1950) 116–22. For a ludicrous attempt to make Akhenaten's religious inspiration a Hebrew-Hyksos Moses, see J. Collier, *King Sun: In Search of Akhenaten* (London: Ward Lock, 1970) 97–98, 111, 231, 235–44.

[12] Josephus, *Contra Apionem* 1.91–104; Redford, *Egypt, Canaan, and Israel in Ancient Times* (Princeton: Princeton University Press, 1992) 408–29. See also B. Halpern, "The Exodus and the Israelite Historians," *Abraham Malamat Volume* (ed. S. Aḥituv, B. A. Levine; ErIsr 24; Jerusalem: Israel Exploration Society, 1993) 89*–96*.

[13] On the Hyksos' ethnicity, see C. A. Redmount, "Ethnicity, Pottery, and the Hyksos at Tell El-Maskhuta in the Egyptian Delta," *BA* 58 (1995) 182–90.

[14] Papyrus Sallier I; for a translation, see A. Erman, *The Literature of the Ancient Egyptians* (trans. A. M. Blackman; German orig. 1923; New York: Benjamin Blom, 1971) 165–67. While J. C. de Moor (*The Rise of Yahwism*, 2d ed. [Leuven: University Press, 1997] 76, 102) regards the Apophis tradition as evidence of Baalistic monotheism among the Hyksos, Assmann (*Moses*, 28) finds a retrojected memory of Akhenaten. And Redford discounts the story as pure fiction.

[15] But Hornung ("Rediscovery," 48–49) suggests that Akhenaten himself was Lord of the Underworld, replacing Osiris.

[16] *No Graven Images?* (ConBOT 42; Stockholm: Almqvist & Wiksell, 1995).

[17] J. Weinstein, "Exodus and Archaeological Reality," *Exodus: The Egyptian Evidence* (ed. E. S. Frerichs, L. H. Lesko; Winona Lake, Ind.: Eisenbrauns, 1997) 94–96.

[18] On "race relations" in New Kingdom Egypt, see Redford, *Egypt, Canaan, and Israel*, 229–33; also J. K. Hoffmeier, *Israel in Egypt* (New York/Oxford: Oxford University Press, 1997) 52–143.

[19] E.g., Ba'l, 'Anat, Qudš, Rašp, Ḥôrān, 'Aṭtart and others; see R. Stadelmann, *Syrisch-palästinensische Gottheiten in Ägypten* (Probleme der Ägyptologie 5; Leiden: Brill, 1967); W. Helck, *Die Beziehungen Ägyptens zu Vorderasien im 3. und 2. Jahrtausend v. Chr.*, 2d ed. (Ägyptologische Abhandlungen 5; Wiesbaden: Harrassowitz, 1971) 446–73. On the numerous Semitic loanwords in New Kingdom Egyptian, see J. E. Hoch, *Semitic Words in Egyptian Texts of the New Kingdom and Third Intermediate Period* (Princeton: Princeton University Press, 1994).

groups were monotheistic proto-Israelites, whose doctrine Akhenaten borrowed and adapted.[20]

Given, however, the lack of contemporary evidence for Hyksos monotheism and given that Israel cannot be documented extra-biblically before the thirteenth century,[21] nearly all critical historians concede Akhenaten's priority as the inventor of monotheism.[22] Anything else would be irresponsible at present. But we should not close the case completely, lest future discoveries make us appear foolish.

This returns us to Freud's thesis: Akhenaten influenced Israel. Despite the superficial plausibility and broad circulation of *Moses and Monotheism*, few books on the history of Israelite religion mention Freud, Akhenaten or the Aten.[23] This is particularly true of North American scholarship;[24] in some European works,

---

[20] On Asiatic mercenaries at Amarna, see R. Giveon, *Les bédouins Shosou des documents égyptiennes* (Documenta et Monumenta Orientis Antiqui; Leiden: Brill, 1971) 31–34.

[21] In the late thirteenth century, a stele of Merneptah mentions a group called "Israel," whose relationship to the contemporaneously burgeoning population of highland Canaan and to the later people of Israel is debated (N. Na'aman, "The 'Conquest of Canaan' in the Book of Joshua and in History," *From Nomadism to Monarchy* [ed. I. Finkelstein and N. Na'aman; Jerusalem: Yad Izhak Ben-Zvi and the Israel Exploration Society; Washington, D.C.: Biblical Archaeology Society, 1994) 247–49. For the text in translation, see ANET 376–78; for orientation on the archaeological profile of early Iron Age Canaan, see the essays in *From Nomadism to Monarchy*; Finkelstein, "The Great Transformation: The 'Conquest' of the Highlands Frontiers and the Rise of the Territorial States," *The Archaeology of Society in the Holy Land* (ed. T. E. Levy; London: Leicester University Press, 1995) 349–65, and the numerous studies cited therein.

[22] This raises the question: whence did Akhenaten derive *his* monotheism? The best answer, albeit not completely convincing, is that of J. H. Breasted (*A History of Egypt* [New York: Scribner's, 1909] 359): monotheism was the ultimate apotheosis of Egyptian kingship, the absolutism of which has rarely been equaled in human history; of all Pharaohs, Akhenaten was the most absolute, because he was God's sole ministrant. Cf. also Hornung ("Monotheismus im pharaonischen Ägypten," *Monotheismus im alten Israel und seiner Umwelt* [ed. O. Keel; BibB 14; Fribourg: Schweizerisches katholisches Bibelwerk, 1980] 84–85) and Aldred (*Akhenaten*, 240). H. Brunner ("Monotheismus," *Lexikon der Ägyptologie* [Wiesbaden: Harrassowitz, 1982] 4.199), however, voices the obvious objection: were not the Old Kingdom Pharaohs as absolute as Akhenaten? R. Gnuse ponders, from a different perspective, the links between monotheism and political autocracy throughout history (*No Other Gods* [JSOTSup 241; Sheffield: Sheffield Academic Press, 1997] 147–53).

[23] Few books, that is, by biblical scholars. Egyptologists, who may read the Bible more naively than do biblicists, but also are keenly aware that intellectual traditions survive for centuries undocumented (see n. 100), are more open-minded: e.g., Aldred, *Akhenaten*, 306; Assmann, *Moses*, 12; V. A. Tobin, "Amarna and Biblical Religion," *Pharaonic Egypt, the Bible and Christianity* (ed. S. Israelit-Groll; Jerusalem: Magnes, 1985) 268; H. A. Schlögl, *Echnaton-Tutanchamun* (Wiesbaden: Harrassowitz, 1983) 66; Brunner, "Monotheismus," 199–200. But, tellingly, two Egyptologists very well informed about the Bible, K. A. Kitchen (*Ancient Orient and Old Testament* [Chicago: Inter-Varsity, 1966]) and D. B. Redford (see n. 27)—the former positive and the latter negative on the Bible's reliability—respectively ignore and dismiss a possible connection. Another skeptic is Giveon ("Western Asiatic Aspects of the Amarna-Period: The Monotheism-Problem," *L'Égyptologie en 1979* [Colloques Internationaux du Centre Nationale de la Recherche Scientifique 595; Paris: Centre Nationale de la Recherche Scientifique, 1982] 2.249–51).

[24] A notable exception is Albright, *From the Stone Age to Christianity*, 12–13, 270; "Moses in Historical and Theological Perspective," *Magnalia Dei* (Fs. G. E. Wright; ed. F. M. Cross, W. E. Lemke and P. D. Miller, Jr.; Garden City, NY: Doubleday: 1976) 129. See also J. Bright, *A History of Israel*, 3 ed. (Philadelphia: Westminster, 1981) 160, and A. H. Silver, *Moses and the Original Torah* (New

Akhenaten still receives a sentence or two.[25] How can we account for Freud's oblivion?[26] Why has the Moses-Akhenaten connection, so appealing to amateur historians and novelists, seemed so far-fetched to professional biblicists? I will discuss in turn the following objections that have been or might be raised:

1. *The Aten-Yahweh connection is blasphemous.*
2. *The connection is so plain an amateur might see it.*
3. *Atenism and Yahwism were not identical.*
4. *Atenism was an arid, elitist faith.*
5. *Yahweh is an anthropomorphic deity.*
6. *Akhenaten was not really a monotheist.*
7. *The Israelites were not monotheists.*
8. *The biblical authors were not monotheists.*
9. *The biblical authors became monotheists, but were not so originally.*
10. *Israel was no more monotheistic than Moab, Ammon, Edom, Egypt and Mesopotamia.*
11. *Iconoclasm was a late development in Israel.*
12. *Atenism was confined to the court at Amarna.*
13. *There is no evidence of Israelites in Egypt.*
14. *Religious evolution is gradual and unidirectional.*

Each of these arguments requires discussion. While some are trivial, others bear weight.

1. *The Aten-Yahweh connection is blasphemous, impugning the originality and authenticity of the Mosaic creed.* Such considerations may account for Akhenaten's absence from religiously conservative works on Israelite and Egyptian interrelations. But covert theological prejudice has no place in academic discourse.

York: Macmillan, 1961) 30, both influenced by Albright. Ironically, this part of Albright's work has been rejected as religious apology because it affirms the antiquity of Mosaic Yahwism—even as it also implies that Mosaic Yahwism was partly derivative. Cf. B. O. Long, *Planting and Reaping Albright* (University Park: Penn State University Press, 1997) 43–44. A more recent English-language work of conservative bent, arguing for the Hebrews' presence in New Kingdom Egypt, passes over Akhenaten's possible influence upon Israel (or vice versa) in audible silence (Hoffmeier, *Israel in Egypt*).

[25] But rarely more. For example, a recent, massive anthology mentions Atenism only twice (W. Dietrich and M. A. Klopfenstein, ed., *Ein Gott allein?* [OBO 139; Freiburg, Schweiz: Universitätsverlag; Göttingen: Vandenhoeck & Ruprecht, 1994] 44, 172). A noteworthy exception is de Moor (*Rise of Yahwism*, 364–65), who writes in a vein similar to Albright's: "If there was one age in the history of the Ancient Near East favouring the emergence of the exclusivism that appears to be so characteristic of early Yahwism, it was the Amarna period" (cf. also P. Sanders, *The Provenance of Deuteronomy 32* [OTS 37; Leiden/New York/Köln: Brill, 1996] 75). But de Moor's theory, too, suffers from overspecificity: pre-Mosaic Yahwism, ultimately inspired by Akhenaten, was mediated by the Ramesside vizier Beya = Moses, whose religion was equally influenced by Amun theology, itself a counterreformation against Amarna (pp. 136–51) (see also n. 138 below).

[26] The Doctor himself might readily answer, "Repression." I.e., even after Freud's exposé, we cannot face up to Moses' murder!

2. *The connection is so plain an amateur might see it.* I would not underrate the unconscious force of this scruple.[27] We fancy ourselves a guild of virtuosi confidently extracting from minimal data information that would elude the less astute. That an idea is obvious does not make it wrong.

Having disposed of what scarcely deserves mention, we may now entertain more substantive objections. The first, however, is still fairly frivolous.

3. *Atenism and Yahwism were not identical.* Granted. All that they really share is "Thou shalt have no other gods before me. . . . Thou shalt not make unto thee any graven image." The question is, how significant is that?

The following objections concern specific differences between Atenism and Yahwism.

4. *Atenism was an arid, elitist faith without social conscience or comfort, relevant only for the semidivine Pharaoh, son of the Aten, and his immediate circle.*[28] *It little resembles Yahwism, whether in its popular or biblical forms.*[29] It is true that Akhenaten's scanty literary remains do not stress ethics. But, no less than Egypt's traditional gods, the Aten's earthly representative, Akhenaten, demands and lives by *m3ʿt* 'Rightness."[30] The Aten loves and labors for his Creation.[31] Atenism was not amoral; rather, it espoused most traditional Egyptian values. From our perspective, Atenism may seem an exclusively elite phenomenon divorced from day-to-day reality—but the same, according to many scholars, is true of biblical religion. As for the Pharaoh's unique relationship with his god, replace the Aten with Yahweh and Akhenaten with Israel and the analogy is striking: like the Aten vis-à-vis Akhenaten, Yahweh is concerned almost exclusively with his "son" Israel.[32]

5. *Yahweh is an anthropomorphic (specifically, andromorphic) deity, while the Aten possesses no human form.* Although this difference is real, the matter is somewhat more complicated. One cannot simply say that the Amarna concept of deity is more abstract than the biblical. After all, there is at least an icon for the Aten (the sun with rays ending in *hands*),[33] and his essence is visible to all every day in the sky. And the Aten did have an andromorphic manifestation: King Akhenaten

---

[27] Witness the sentiment and tone of Redford (*Egypt, Canaan, and Israel*, 377): "One 'discovery' that never ceases to fill the hearts of students and laymen with modest pride and their eyes with the light of recognition is the alleged similarity between the religion Akhenaten preached and 'Mosaic monotheism.' " Redford calls this resemblance "the classic 'red herring.' "

[28] E.g., J. Baines, "Society, Morality, and Religious Practice," *Religion in Ancient Egypt* (ed. B. E. Shafer; Ithaca/London: Cornell University Press, 1991) 189–91.

[29] Below, I shall distinguish carefully between "Israelite religion," i.e., the religion of the Israelite and Judean masses accessible primarily through archaeology, and "biblical religion," i.e., beliefs and practices described and advocated in the Bible. Each is a category of what I call "Yahwism."

[30] Freud, *Moses and Monotheism*, 75; Tobin, "Amarna and Biblical Religion," 271. For passages, see W. J. Murnane, *Texts from the Amarna Period* (SBLWAW 5; Atlanta: Scholars Press, 1995) 51, 52, 73.

[31] Murnane, *Texts*, 200, n. 10.

[32] There is also a resemblance between Akhenaten's doctrine and the Judean claim that the Davidic monarch was Yahweh's semidivine "son"; see below, n. 44.

[33] This was an innovation; Silverman ("Divinity and Deities," 83) notes that previously the sun had been represented as a simple disk, with neither rays nor hands.

himself, and before him Amenophis III.[34] In contrast, there are no certain Israelite representations of Yahweh.[35] The difference between the Aten and Yahweh is rather a matter of *literary* imagery: Yahweh attracts far more andromorphic language than does the Aten—after all, Mankind was made "in his image" (Gen 1:26–27; 5:1). But Yahweh is compared to beings and things other than a human male, including the sun (Ps 84:12).[36] Conversely, the Aten is said to possess "face," "heart," "mouth" and "limbs"[37] and is often called "father"—in one text, "father and mother"[38]—all anthropomorphisms. And the Aten receives trappings of human monarchy: the cartouche, the uraeus and the royal Sed festival.[39] Humans have always struggled with anthropomorphism when imagining the Divine.

The following objections deal with the nature of monotheism, a source of perennial semantic quibbling.[40] Against recent trends, I find the word too convenient to be abandoned in favor of such unfamiliar neologisms as "monolatry" and "henotheism."[41] For the ancient world, functional definitions of "monotheism"

---

[34] Akhenaten even had his own chief prophet and was paraded about like an idol (Silverman, op. cit.). See also Assmann, "Die 'Häresie,' " and, on Amenophis III's solar godhood, W. R. Johnson, "Amenhotep III and Amarna," *JEA* 82 (1996) 65–82.

[35] For discussion on whether the Kuntillet ʿAjrud pithos portrays Yahweh, see J. M. Hadley, "Some Drawings and Inscriptions on Two Pithoi from Kuntillet ʿAjrud, VT 37 (1987) 180–211, "Yahweh and 'His Asherah': Archaeological and Textual Evidence for the Cult of the Goddess," *Ein Gott allein?* (OBO 139; Freiburg, Schweiz: Universitätsverlag; Göttingen: Vandenhoeck & Ruprecht, 1994) 246–47, and J. A. Emerton, "'Yahweh and His Asherah': The Goddess or Her Symbol?" VT 49 (1999) 315–37. For statuary conceivably portraying Yahweh, see R. S. Hendel, "Aniconism and Anthropomorphism in Ancient Israel," *The Image and the Book* (ed. K. van der Toorn; Leuven: Peeters, 1997) 212–18.

[36] See n. 140.

[37] For examples, see Murnane, *Texts*, 110, 122, 144, 182, 187, 191.

[38] Murnane, *Texts*, 158. The same expression outside Amarna, however, describes Amun, who is definitely male (Assmann, *Solar Religion*, 84). Moreover, almost every other Atenist text calls the Aten Akhenaten's "father," not "mother." For further examples of ostensibly androgynous deities, see H.-W. Jüngling, "'Was anders ist Gott für Menschen, wenn nicht sein Vater und seine Mutter?' Zu einer Doppelmetapher der religiösen Sprache," *Ein Gott allein?* (ed. W. Dietrich and M. A. Klopfenstein; OBO 139; Freiburg, Schweiz: Universitätsverlag; Göttingen: Vandenhoeck & Ruprecht, 1994) 365–86. On Yahweh's own sporadic androgyny, see P. Trible, *God and the Rhetoric of Sexuality*, 3d ed. (Overtures to Biblical Theology 2; Philadelphia: Fortress, 1983). And for parallels apropos of human kings, see Mettinger, *In Search of God* (Philadelphia: Fortress, 1988) 206. Tobin ("Amarna and Biblical Religion," 253–54) finds evidence of the Aten's relative asexuality in its/his lack of a consort—but, in a sense, Nefertiti is the Aten's spouse.

[39] Silverman, "Divinity and Deities," 83.

[40] For general orientation on monotheism, see D. L. Peterson, "Israel and Monotheism: the Unfinished Business," *Canon, Theology, and Old Testament Interpretation* (Fs. B. S. Childs; ed. G. M. Tucker, D. L. Peterson and R. R. Wilson; Philadelphia: Fortress, 1988) 92–107; B. Lang, "Monotheismus," *Handbuch religionswissenschaftlicher Grundbegriffe* (ed. H. Cancik, B. Gladigow and K.-H. Kohl; Stuttgart/Berlin/Köln: Kohlhammer, 1998) 4.148–65. A helpful bibliography on monotheism through 1985, compiled by J. Scharbert, is available in E. Haag, ed., *Gott, der Einzige: Zur Entstehung des Monotheismus in Israel* (Quaestiones Disputatae 104; Freiburg/Basel/Vienna: Herder, 1985) 184–92. The most comprehensive and recent synthesis is Gnuse, *No Other Gods*, esp. pp. 62–128.

[41] These terms arose in nineteenth-century scholarship and have yet to enter general parlance. Admittedly, "monotheism" itself is a relatively recent coinage, first attested in the seventeenth century but not popular until the nineteenth (Lang, "Monotheismus," 150–51).

and "polytheism" are more useful than philosophical definitions: "monotheism" is monotheistic *behavior*, i.e., venerating a sole godhead (what others call "mono-latry").[42] "Polytheism" is the active worship of several godheads.[43]

6. *Akhenaten was not really a monotheist since he himself was a god; therefore, his religion differs from Israel's.* Akhenaten did not rescind pharaonic ideology *in toto*, and many inscriptions accord him divinity. Yet scholars increasingly recognize that his religion was radically monotheistic, even to the point of banning the word *nṯrw* 'gods.' If Akhenaten was divine, it was as the terrestrial incarnation of the Aten; his religion was exactly as monotheistic as Christianity. Moreover, on the Israelite side, there is considerable evidence that Judean kings, too, claimed divine sonship and quasi-godhood.[44] And we might compare Akhenaten's quasi-divine family, sole ministrants to the Aten, to another Israelite image: Yahweh's angelic court.[45] At any rate, as we shall directly see, the Israelites were even more equivocal monotheists than was Akhenaten.

7. *The Israelites were not monotheists.* The Bible admits, nay insists, that rulers and masses alike often strayed from a religious ideal, whether ritual, dogmatic or ethical. Many scholars take these polemics at face value,[46] citing in support archaeological discoveries of cult objects and local shrines unmentioned or condemned in Scripture.[47] For these scholars, the Bible's religious program is out of

---

[42] A perceptive reader has suggested that, since I use the term imprecisely, I put "monotheism" within quotation marks, as I shall do for "Moses." I see the point, but refuse to condone the prevalent sophistry that renders all general terms useless. Tellingly, in a recent anthology entitled *Aspects of Monotheism* (ed. H. Shanks and J. Meinhardt; Washington: Biblical Archaeology Society, 1997), each contributor on Israelite, Jewish and early Christian religion is at pains to establish that the religion under discussion was not purely monotheistic. Apparently, apart from the minds of philosophers and mystics, there is no such thing as monotheism; compare William James's *obiter dictum*, "[polytheism] has always been the real religion of common people, and is so still today" (*The Varieties of Religious Experience* [New York: New American Library, 1958] 396).

[43] A rigid dichotomy between mono- and polytheism may not be useful for describing human religions in general. Where does "animism" fit in? But for the textual religions of the ancient Near East, the distinction is real.

[44] Passages imputing a divine essence to the king (maximally) include Exod 22:27; 1 Sam 12:5; 2 Sam 7:14; 14:17, 20; 19:28; 1 Kgs 21:10, 13; Isa 8:21; 9:5; Jer 30:9; Zech 12:8; Ps 2:7; 45:7; 89:26–30, 37–38; Qoh 8:2. For a comparison of Israelite and Amarna conceptions of divine monarchy, see Tobin, "Amarna and Biblical Religion," 237–50.

[45] Cf. Hornung, "Monotheismus," 88.

[46] Within a few pages, H. Niehr asserts that we must on principle mistrust everything the Bible says about the Canaanites, and on principle accept everything it says about "idolatrous" Israelites ("The Rise of YHWH in Judahite and Israelite Religion," *The Triumph of Elohim* [ed. D. V. Edelman; Grand Rapids: Eerdmans, 1996] 48–51). Surely both groups are maligned by the sources; we cannot reconstruct a popular religion based solely on such aspersions.

[47] Most prolific on this subject is W. G. Dever: "Material Remains and the Cult in Ancient Israel," *The Word of the Lord Shall Go Forth* (Fs. D. N. Freedman; ed. C. L. Meyers and M. O'Connor; Winona Lake, Ind.: Eisenbrauns, 1983) 571–87, esp. 579; "The Contribution of Archaeology to the Study of Canaanite and Early Israelite Religion," *Ancient Israelite Religion* (Fs. F. M. Cross; ed. P. D. Miller, Jr., P. D. Hanson and S. D. McBride; Philadelphia: Fortress, 1987) 209–47; "Ancient Israelite Religion: How to Reconcile the Differing Textual and Artifactual Portraits," *Ein Gott allein?* (ed. W. Dietrich and M. A. Klopfenstein; OBO 139; Freiburg, Schweiz: Universitätsverlag; Göttingen:

touch with its larger social context. Yet uninscribed archaeological remains generally illuminate practice, not the interpretation of practice. Their personal names, at least, do not indicate that the Israelites were polytheists.[48] Archaeology has so far unearthed no god lists or mythology to definitively establish Israelite polytheism.[49]

Scholars who envision widespread Israelite polytheism necessarily posit a chasm between the "literate urban elite" that produced the Bible and the masses.[50] Granted, archaeology suggests that Israelite society, originally egalitarian, became increasingly stratified through the preexilic period.[51] Granted, literacy was probably restricted. But who are the "elite" whose idiosyncratic values the Bible supposedly articulates? Not the kings or the priests or the wealthy, all of whom incur frequent criticism. The Law and the Prophets more often address

---

Vandenhoeck & Ruprecht, 1994) 105–25. See also the scholars cited in n. 102. For a detailed study of Israelite popular religion in a specific period, see S. Ackerman, *Under Every Green Tree. Popular Religion in Sixth-Century Judah* (HSM 46; Atlanta: Scholars Press, 1992).

[48] J. H. Tigay, *You Shall Have No Other Gods* (HSS 31; Atlanta: Scholars Press, 1986); de Moor, *Rise of Yahwism*, 10–40. For some reservations on the utility of these data—many already voiced by Tigay himself—see Mark S. Smith, *The Early History of God* (San Francisco: Harper & Row, 1990) xxi.

[49] The best evidence for polytheism comes from the Kuntillet 'Ajrud inscriptions (*AHI* 8.015.2; 016.1; 017.1; 021.2), several of which mention "Yahweh . . . and his Asherah," a phrase that also appears in a Khirbet 'el-Qom text (*AHI* 25.003.3, 5, 6). Many scholars infer that, in popular belief, Yahweh had a consort, Asherah; e.g., D. N. Freedman, "Yahweh of Samaria and his Asherah," *BA* 50 (1987) 241–49; Dever, "Asherah, Consort of Yahweh? New Evidence from Kuntillet 'Ajrud," *BASOR* 255 (1984) 21–37. Others reject the notion, regarding the Asherah as a symbol of Yahweh himself; for discussion and bibliography, see Mark S. Smith, *Early History*, 80–114; Gnuse, *No Other Gods*, 69–71, 115–17, 184–85; Emerton, "Yahweh and His Asherah."

This is not a case in which more data are likely to solve the problem. Plainly, the Israelites themselves were in disagreement over what Asherah was and whether it/she was licit. Even if some Israelites did reckon with a goddess, her relationship to Yahweh is uncertain. It is not clear, even at Ugarit, that El and Asherah are married in the human sense—she has her own progeny independent of him—and still less is it clear that an Israelite Asherah would be Yahweh's wife, rather than his daughter or mother. Asherah might also be a feminine hypostasis of God comparable to various ostensibly masculine hypostases and angels—Yahweh's "Face" (*pānîm*), "Name" (*šēm*) and "Glory" (*kābôd*); God's "House" (*bêt-ʾēl*)—and anticipatory of later feminine hypostases such as *ḥokmâ* 'Wisdom,' *bat-qôl* 'Daughter-Voice' and *šəkînâ* 'Immanence' (see P. K. McCarter, "Aspects of the Religion of the Israelite Monarchy: Biblical and Epigraphic Data," *Ancient Israelite Religion* [Fs. F. M. Cross; ed. P. D. Miller, Jr., P. D. Hanson and S. D. McBride; Philadelphia: Fortress, 1987] 143–49). If *'ăšērâ* means "place," as its etymology suggests (cf. Aramaic *'atrā'*), then it is directly comparable to the common Rabbinic circumlocution for God: *hammāqôm*.

Another Kuntillet 'Ajrud inscription names in parallel Baal and *šm 'l* 'El's Name' (*AHI* 8.023.2–3). It is unclear whether these are two deities or one, and whether either is to be equated with Yahweh. Even at Kuntillet 'Ajrud, we find no lists of deities comparable to texts from Egypt, Mesopotamia and Syria.

[50] On the Bible as elitist, see (from very different perspectives) Dever, *Recent Archaeological Discoveries and Biblical Research* (Seattle/London: University of Washington Press, 1990) 7, and P. R. Davies, *In Search of Ancient Israel* (JSOTSup 148; Sheffield: Sheffield Academic Press, 1992).

[51] J. S. Holladay, Jr., "The Kingdoms of Israel and Judah: Political and Economic Centralization in the Iron II A–B (ca. 1000–750 BCE)," *The Archaeology of Society in the Holy Land* (ed. T. E. Levy; Leicester University Press, 1995) 368–98.

the interests of small farmers, whose settlements indicate a static egalitarianism throughout the period.[52] And I would not exaggerate the cultural gap between literate and illiterate.[53] All property owners, rich or poor, and even the destitute employed scribes to draw up contracts, record ownership, register complaints, etc.[54] Scribedom, the same institution that produced the Bible, was influential and omnipresent, over time unifying, codifying and communicating national culture, somewhat like our mass media. To judge from the Bible, some scribes were in turn strongly influenced by the prophets, or certain schools of prophecy, and by the levitical priesthood.

Regarded too narrowly, biblical polemics against heterodoxy and heteropraxis are liable to misinterpretation. First, it is widely recognized that some of these reflect intra-elite political rivalries over priesthood and kingship, not just disagreements over theology or ritual per se. An example would be the Golden Calf account (Exodus 32), widely read as an attack on Jeroboam I (1 Kgs 12:25–33).[55]

Second, we cannot forget that, although all societies profess an ideal of tranquility, disharmony is the norm. Why should Israel be different? Strife need not be imputed to class conflict; it is endemic in tiny, impoverished villages. In non-Western societies, allegations of neighbors' magico-religious maleficence are a constant social destabilizer, but also a means for coping intellectually with misfortune.[56] The Bible's analogy to witchcraft and taboo is the Covenant: if things are going wrong, someone, somewhere, knowingly or unknowingly, has violated the pact between Yahweh and Israel. Root out the malfeasant, and Yahweh *must* restore blessing. Thus the biblical notion of a compact binding not only Israel but also God has a distinctly magical aspect (*pace* Yehezkel Kaufmann [see n. 63]).[57]

---

[52] Ibid.

[53] On the role of writing in semi-literate societies, see several works by J. Goody: *The Domestication of the Savage Mind* (Cambridge, U.K.: Cambridge University Press, 1977), *The Interface between the Written and the Oral* (Studies in Literacy, Family, Culture and the State; Cambridge, U.K.: Cambridge University Press, 1987), *The Logic of Writing and the Organization of Society* (Cambridge, U.K.: Cambridge University Press, 1986) and Goody's edited volume, *Literacy in Traditional Societies* (Cambridge, U.K.: Cambridge University Press, 1968). On Israel in particular, see S. Niditch, *Oral Word and Written Word* (Library of Ancient Israel; Louisville: Westminster John Knox).

[54] Among many works on the subject, see A. Lemaire, *Les écoles et la formation de la Bible dans l'ancien Israël* (OBO 39; Fribourg: Éditions Universitaires; Göttingen: Vandenhoeck & Ruprecht, 1981); also M. Haran, "On the Diffusion of Literacy and Schools in Ancient Israel," E. Lipiński, "Royal and State Scribes in Ancient Jerusalem," and E. Puech, "Les écoles dans l'Israël préexilique: données épigraphiques," all published in *Congress Volume Jerusalem* 1986 (VTSup 40; ed. J. A. Emerton; Leiden/New York/Copenhagen/Köln: Brill, 1988) 81–95, 157–64, 189–203.

[55] E.g., M. Aberbach and L. Smolar, "Aaron, Jeroboam, and the Golden Calves," *JBL* 86 (1967) 129–40; F. M. Cross, *Canaanite Myth and Hebrew Epic* (Cambridge, Mass.: Harvard University Press, 1973) 73–75.

[56] Compare Burmese religion as described by M. E. Spiro, *Burmese Supernaturalism: A Study in the Explanation and Reduction of Suffering* (Englewood Cliffs, N.J.: Prentice-Hall, 1967).

[57] This description illuminates the Bible's virtual nonmention of demonic causality for misfortune and illness, a silence contrasting with both earlier ancient Near Eastern and later Judeo-Christian demonology. The connection is all but explicit in Exod 15:26: "If you listen carefully to the voice of Yahweh your god, and what is right in his eyes you do, and give ear to his commands and observe all his

In any case, taking biblical claims of rampant heresy literally is somewhat like envisioning a thriving coven at Salem, Massachusetts.[58]

Not to be misunderstood: I do not conceive of Israelite religion as monolithic. Quite the opposite, biblical religion itself represents a diverse intellectual movement existing in both symbiosis and tension with diverse popular religious traditions.[59] Still, as a whole, the Bible professes worship of Yahweh alone, without idols; Yahweh's creation of the world and his universal dominion; his wondrous liberation of Israel from Egypt; his gift of Canaan to Israel conditioned by the Covenant; the efficacy of sacrifice conducted by Levites, and the legitimacy of prophetic inspiration.[60]

And what about popular religion? I find it telling that advocates for widespread Israelite polytheism either leave its essential tenets unspecified, as if it were a simple fertility cult—if there is such a thing—or else assume near-identity with "Canaanite religion," whatever that might be. Similarly, they decline to locate the masses' religious leaders. And yet, in almost all societies, there are specialists to whom ordinary folk refer the inquisitive (i.e., children and visitors, including anthropologists) for information on practices and beliefs to which the laity devote little thought, or concerning which they do not feel entitled to an opinion. Most likely, surface appearances are correct: the diverse "elite" represented in the Bible was in fact Israel's recognized religious leadership, articulating and shaping common belief. Far from being socially isolated, Israel's "Little" and "Great Traditions"[61] must have been in constant interaction.

---

rules, all the disease that I set in Egypt I will not set upon you. Rather, I, Yahweh, am your healer." In other words, Israelites need no longer bind demons; God has bound himself to protect them, providing they keep the Covenant. Demons return to official Judaism only after the Exile, when the Covenant's efficacy had lost credibility, and works such as Job and Chronicles (1 Chr 21:1) again attribute misfortune to supernatural, malefic influence. Persian dualism and mythology doubtless contributed to the transfer of misfortune from God's agency to the demons', but the Covenant's apparent failure was the necessary precondition. (Despite its promising title, the *Dictionary of Deities and Demons in the Bible* [ed. K. van der Toorn, B. Becking, P. W. van der Horst; Leiden/New York/Köln: Brill, 1995] does not discuss demonology in its introduction [pp. xv–xviii]; among the relevant entries for Old Testament demonology, however, are "Azazel," "Deber," "Destroyer," "Evil Spirit of God," "Lilith," "Rabiṣu," "Satan" and "Satyrs.")

[58] I would, moreover, carry this argument to its logical conclusion. Just as witchhunting can actually preserve if not encourage witchcraft, so the Bible's polemics probably elicited heterodoxy in some quarters, if only as a protest (compare Julian the Apostate or modern Satanism).

[59] For a general methodological treatment, albeit somewhat different from my own approach, see J. Berlinerblau, "The 'Popular Religion' Paradigm in Old Testament Research: A Sociological Critique," *JSOT* 60 (1993) 3–26.

[60] One might attribute this homogeneity to selectivity during the canonization process (e.g., Morton Smith, *Palestinian Parties and Politics That Shaped the Old Testament* (New York/London: Columbia University Press, 1971] 1–14). Yet, on linguistic criteria alone, we cannot regard the whole Bible as a forgery of the Persian–Hellenistic period (*pace* Davies, *In Search of Ancient Israel*). The Old Testament evinces sufficient internal coherence and diversity to show that it represents, if not a "school," then a variegated tradition dating back to preexilic Israel and Judah, whatever the date of codification.

[61] See R. Redfield, *Peasant Society and Culture* (Chicago: University of Chicago Press, 1956) 40–59.

What, then, of the apparent hostility between the biblical authors and their addressees? Religious authorities never exercise absolute sway in their own communities. Prophets and shamans are often regarded as mad or outcaste. Rabbis, priests and imams have for centuries fulminated against their flocks' shortcomings—the faithful would not respect them if they did not—and yet their message is frequently ignored in practice. However vituperative their rhetoric, the holy personnel regard their people as wayward children, not as adversaries. This relationship is only superficially dysfunctional. If the commons did not fall short, they and their leaders would be hard pressed to rationalize inevitable human suffering; the system would collapse into "cognitive dissonance." Like engineers designing backup systems, societies generally evolve multiple, alternative ways to explain and control misfortune. Both masses and elites live comfortably with their "double think." [62]

Finally, the more we envision Israel's masses as polytheistic, i.e., less eccentric in their broader, Near Eastern cultural milieu, the more we make the monotheistic biblical authors eccentric in *their* immediate, Israelite cultural milieu. More is lost than gained. [63]

My image of Israelite religion squares with what we read in the Bible, is not contradicted by archaeology (to which the "Great Tradition" is largely invisible) and can be found duplicated in many better-attested cultures. Still, let us grant that the biblical authors, the "Yahweh-alone party" of Morton Smith and Bernhard Lang, were highly atypical of their own society, solitary cranks crying in the wilderness. We must then ask why *their* religion so resembles Akhenaten's. Or does it?

8. *The biblical authors were not monotheists*. In a strict philosophical sense, most were not—neither are Jews, Christians and Muslims who believe in a hierarchy of angels and saints ruled by God, and a "lowerarchy" of demons and ghosts ruled by Satan/Iblis. [64] Still, in contrast both to ancient Near Eastern religions (Atenism excepted) and to Rabbinic Judaism, Christianity and Islam, the Bible's monotheism seems relatively rigorous. [65] The principal exceptions are Yahweh's angelic retinue—sometimes called "God's sons" or "the gods," sometimes

---

[62] Compare the coexistence of Shinto and Buddhism in Japan, or the relationship between "official" Burmese Buddhism and "popular" practices chronicled by Spiro (n. 56), especially pp. 247–80. Burmese Buddhism is tinged with animism even among the urban elite; Burmese rural animism has pronounced Buddhist aspects. In Burma, according to Spiro, no one is more than mildly bothered by this confusion. What distinguishes the biblical tradition is its increasing attempt to define itself as the *sole* religious system: the "Great Tradition" at war with the "Little Tradition." One senses throughout the Bible that the average person just didn't understand the fuss, and this rings true, not just with modern Burma, but even more plainly with cultures recently converted to Christianity and Islam, religion systems less tolerant of contradiction than is Buddhism.

[63] Although badly needing qualification and updating (e.g., bringing to bear archaeology), Y. Kaufmann's defense of Israelite cultural uniformity is more pertinent than when it was written (*Tôlǝdôt hā'ĕmûnâ hayyiśrǝ'ēlît* [Jerusalem: Bialik Institute, 1937–56] esp. 3.589–623; *The Religion of Israel* [trans. M. Greenberg; Chicago: University of Chicago Press, 1960]) 122–49. See also R. Albertz, "Biblische oder Nicht-Biblische Religionsgeschichte Israels?" *"Und Mose schrieb dieses Lied auf"* (Fs. O. Loretz, ed. M. Dietrich and I. Kottsieper; AOAT 250; Münster: Ugarit-Verlag, 1998) 27–41.

[64] See n. 42.

[65] Kaufmann, *Tôlǝdôt*, 3.659–85; *History*, 122–49.

equated with the deities of foreign nations[66]—and the king, whose divinity remains a thorny issue.[67] Even the arch-monotheist Second Isaiah may acknowledge Yahweh's celestial retinue,[68] and the Song of Moses (Deut 32:1–43) finds no contradiction between Yahweh's absolute sovereignty (v 39) and the existence of the Nations' gods (v 8);[69] the point is that the foreign gods are relatively powerless. I would grant that Akhenaten was the purer monotheist. But the Bible, despite its internal variety, is overall much closer to monotheism than to polytheism.

Unlike Akhenaten, however, the biblical authors did not consciously reject polytheism per se as a theology. They rather rejected divine rivals to Yahweh for Israel's allegiance; Norman Gottwald's term is "mono-Yahwism."[70] Again, if the biblical authors were polytheists, where are their myths, god lists and prayers?[71] To claim that the Yahwist, Deuteronomist, Amos, Isaiah et al. honored many gods, but that their works were censored after the Exile, is to pile conjecture atop speculation.

A variant of the last argument is the following:

9. *The biblical authors became monotheists, but were not so originally; therefore, Atenism cannot have played a formative role.*[72] Scholars often regard the Exile as the turning point in the development of true monotheism. But that Yahweh's mastery of nature and history was sung more shrilly beneath the willows of Bab-

---

[66] See Halpern, "The Baal (and the Asherah) in Seventh-Century Judah: Yhwh's Retainers Retired," *Konsequente Traditionsgeschichte* (ed. R. Bartelmus *et al.*; Fs. K. Baltzer; OBO 126; Fribourg: Éditions Universitaires; Göttingen: Vandenhoeck & Ruprecht, 1992) 115–54. Note that, even when conceived as foreign gods, Yahweh's attendants lack names and personalities. We do not read of interactions between Yahweh and his servants Chemosh, Milcom, Asshur, etc. One has the impression that this line of thought was a half-hearted attempt to explain away or incorporate polytheism, and that it was not taken too seriously.

[67] See n. 44. Since I am now concerned with biblical, not Israelite, religion, and since the Bible never accords her a positive role, Asherah's possible status as Yahweh's consort is irrelevant (see n. 49).

[68] Maximally, Isa 35:3–4; 40:1–8; 48:20–21; 52:7–10; 62:10–12. See Cross, "The Council of Yahweh in Second Isaiah," *JNES* 12 (1953) 274–77. But Freedman argues with equal plausibility that Yahweh's addressees are the Nations ("The Structure of Isaiah 40:1," *Perspectives on Language and Text* [Fs. F. I. Andersen; ed. E. W. Conrad and E. G. Newing; Winona Lake, Ind.: Eisenbrauns, 1987] 167–93). These views are not necessarily incompatible, if Yahweh's angels are the foreign deities.

[69] Reading with LXX and 4QDt¹ *bny 'l(w)hym* 'sons of God' for MT *bny yśr'l* 'sons of Israel.' Compare also Deut 4:19–20. Sanders (*Provenance of Deuteronomy* 32, 193–200) finds further mythology in Deut 32:22, with reference to various plague deities.

[70] *The Tribes of Yahweh* (Maryknoll, NY: Orbis, 1979) *passim*.

[71] I discount the Combat Myth as proof of polytheism; Leviathan/Rahab/Serpent is not a god whom one might worship. Second Isaiah would not have evoked the Myth (Isa 51:9–11) had he felt it impugned God's exclusivity. (Among many studies on theomachy in Near Eastern myth, see most recently N. Wyatt, "Arms and the King," "*Und Mose schrieb dieses Lied auf*" [Fs. O. Loretz, ed. M. Dietrich and I. Kottsieper; AOAT 250; Münster: Ugarit-Verlag, 1998] 833–82.)

A better example of myth may be the Fall of Helel (Isaiah 14), where we find the breakthrough of true polytheism. Still, the tale is not recounted for its own sake; rather, it is a metaphor for a hubristic Mesopotamian monarch. It functions as a literary allusion, like classical pagan references in Renaissance Christian texts. Isaiah presumably did not venerate Helel, but his audience knew the myth well, and some probably did engage in astral worship. We approach mythology most closely in Gen 6:1–4, where the "sons of God" act contrary to Yahweh's wishes. Though anonymous, these divinities are more than faceless servants.

[72] E.g., Redford, *Egypt, Canaan, and Israel*, 378.

ylon, in the face of seemingly incontestable counterevidence, does not mean that these ideas were new. Where does preexilic biblical literature approvingly refer to gods other than Yahweh?[73] Is there the slightest similarity to the developed polytheisms of Egypt, Canaan and Mesopotamia? Israelite universalistic monotheism, if not explicit, is implicit on every page of the Bible. The Yahwist, for example, never outright describes the Nations' gods as nonentities. But his Creation account leaves room for no divine personality other than Yahweh, perhaps served by a faceless angelic court. J's primeval history is in a sense anti-myth: the chief god's interlocutors and rivals are not other divinities, but humanity.[74] And the preexilic prophets contain passages fully as monotheistic and universalistic as Second Isaiah (e.g., Isa 2:1–22; Jer 2:5–28; 10:2–16; 11:9–13; 51:15–19; Hos 2:4–15; 13:1–4; Amos 5:8; 9:5–8; Micah 4:1–4; Hab 2:14). Some of these passages could conceivably be later interpolations—any biblical text could be a later interpolation—but to impose a rigid evolutionary scheme upon the data is to enter a vicious circle with no escape. Yahweh's absolute mastery over nature and history is the presupposition of all biblical prophecy,[75] but contact with a wider world would bring these ideas to the fore.

Lacking evidence to the contrary, we must accept as at least plausible the tradition that Israel's monotheism dates back to the nation's origins, when the influence of Amarna is most expected. Postponing Israelite monotheism makes it harder, not easier, to explain historically.[76]

---

[73] The closest case might be Micah 4:5, "All the nations walk, each in the name of its god(s), but we walk in the name of Yahweh our god forever." But the tone is probably mocking, since the previous verses describe the eventual enlightening of the Gentiles. Deut 32:3 also concedes the existence of the Nations' gods (n. 69), but in a context emphasizing their incomparability to Yahweh.

Other texts usually cited in this connection come from the historical books. Because all fall in direct quotation, they do not necessarily represent the authors' or editors' viewpoint; indeed, the Deuteronomistic Historian, the compiler of Deuteronomy–Kings, is unequivocally anti-polytheistic. In Judg 11:24, when Jephthah rhetorically asks the Ammonites, "Should you not inherit that which Chemosh [sic! it should be Milcom] your god has given you?" is the author condoning foreign religion, or does he portray Jephthah as diplomatic or ironically condescending, addressing the Ammonites on their own level? Likewise, Naomi's speech to Ruth, "Your sister-in-law has returned to her folk and to her god(s)," implying Ruth should do the same (Ruth 1:15), adopts the supposed viewpoint of the addressee; it need not imply the author's endorsement of a pluralistic theology. Lastly, in 1 Sam 26:19, David chides Saul, "You have driven me this day from reliance upon Yahweh's domain, as if to say, 'Go, serve other gods.' " The author is not claiming that travelers and exiles are obliged to honor local cults. Rather, David is depicted as sulking histrionically: "All right, then, I'll go commit apostasy!" David evokes Saul's compassion by painting exile in the worst possible light: as in the underworld, so away from the sacred soil of Canaan one cannot fully serve Yahweh (cf. 2 Kgs 5:17).

[74] Cf. H. P. Müller, "Gott und die Götter in den Anfängen der biblischen Religion. Zur Vorgeschichte des Monotheismus, *Monotheismus im alten Israel und seiner Umwelt* (ed. O. Keel; BibB 14; Fribourg: Schweizerisches katholisches Bibelwerk, 1980) 99–142.

[75] See, however, J. D. Levenson, *Creation and the Persistence of Evil* (San Francisco: Harper & Row, 1988), for some qualifications.

[76] Cf. Halpern, " 'Brisker Pipes than Poetry': The Development of Israelite Monotheism," *Judaic Perspectives on Ancient Israel* (ed. J. Neusner et al.; Philadelphia: Fortress, 1987) 87: "Virtually no major component of Israel's later monotheism is absent from the cult at the turn of the millennium, with the introduction of the kingship. . . . Early Israelite religion is not self-consciously monotheistic; it defines itself in terms of loyalty to YHWH, in terms of YHWH's incomparability, but not in terms of

10. *Israel was no more monotheistic than were Moab, Ammon, Edom and, for that matter, Egypt and Mesopotamia, all of which, in the first millennium, focused worship on a single national god. Therefore, the similarity to Amarna religion is meaningless.*[77] Such an assessment is inaccurate. The Mesopotamian and Egyptian national religions were neither monotheistic nor monolatrous (and certainly not aniconic). True, worship might temporarily focus on a single god embodying the might of both the pantheon and the state ("henotheism"). But the existence of other deities, domestic or foreign, was never denied. Increasing assertions of a unity underlying the divine realm—all gods are aspects of Amun, Asshur, Marduk, etc.[78]—do not constitute monotheism, but pantheism of a type familiar from India and elsewhere.[79] Philosophically, pantheism and monotheism may be analogous efforts to integrate religion, but they attain their result by distinct means: one by the inclusion of all into One, the other by the exclusion of all save One (who must co-opt the excluded deities' traits in compensation). The true colleagues of the pantheists of Egypt and Mesopotamia were not the biblical authors, but other Israelites who apparently believed that Yahweh *was* Baal (Hos 2:18).[80] As for the kingdoms of Ammon, Moab and Edom, should they prove to have been monotheistic, as is not unlikely,[81] then we might imagine an international movement spreading from Amarna through Israel into Asia.[82] Phoenicia and Aram, at any rate, remained solidly polytheistic.[83]

YHWH's transcending uniqueness. It has as yet no developed notion that being monotheistic . . . is central to its identity." Mettinger (*No Graven Images?*, 135–97) suggests much the same for aniconism.

Second Isaiah may be the most eloquent biblical writer to dwell upon Yahweh's unique divinity *per se*, in which he reflects an international trend manifest in both Greece and Iran (N. Lohfink, "Gott und die Götter im Alten Testament," *Theologische Akademie* 6 [1969] 62–63; H. Vorländer, "Der Monotheismus Israels als Antwort auf die Krise des Exils," *Der einzige Gott* [ed. B. Lang; Munich: Kosel, 1981] 84–113, 134–39). But even Second Isaiah does not compare monotheism and polytheism as systems. Jeremiah, on the other hand, mocks the Judeans for the multitude of their gods (Jer 2:28; 11:13) and so has a better claim as Israel's first self-conscious monotheist.

[77] E.g., J. Wellhausen, "Israel," *Encyclopedia Britannica* (1883), reprinted in *Prolegomena to the History of Israel* (Gloucester: Peter Smith, 1973) 440. Cf. Cross, "The Epic Traditions of Early Israel," *The Poet and the Historian* (ed. R. E. Friedman; Chico, Calif.: Scholars Press, 1983) 36–37.

[78] See Hornung, *Conceptions of God in Ancient Egypt: the One and the Many* (Ithaca: Cornell University Press, 1981); T. Jacobsen, *The Treasures of Darkness* (New Haven/London: Yale University Press, 1976) 234–36; W. G. Lambert, "The Historical Development of the Mesopotamian Pantheon: A Study in Sophisticated Polytheism," *Unity and Diversity* (ed. H. Goedicke and J. J. M. Roberts; Baltimore: The Johns Hopkins University Press, 1975) 191–200.

[79] For a brief comparison of Hindu monism and biblical monotheism, see Gnuse, *No Other Gods*, 217–20.

[80] Mark S. Smith, *Early History*, xxv.

[81] Ibid., 24–26; A. Lemaire, "Déesses et dieux de Syrie-Palestine d'après les inscriptions (c. 1000–500 av. n. e.)," *Ein Gott allein?* (ed. W. Dietrich and M. A. Klopfenstein; OBO 139; Freiburg, Schweiz: Universitätsverlag; Göttingen: Vandenhoeck & Ruprecht, 1994) 127–58.

[82] The Edomites, however, produced andromorphic statuary unlike any found in Israel, and so may not have been iconoclastic monotheists. See I. Beit-Aryeh, *Ḥorvat Qitmit* (Institute of Archaeology Monograph 11; Tel Aviv: Tel Aviv University, 1995).

[83] R. J. Clifford, "Phoenician Religion," *BASOR* 279 (1990) 55–66; J. C. Greenfield, "Aspects of Aramaic Religion," *Ancient Israelite Religion* (Fs. F. M. Cross; ed. P. D. Miller, Jr., P. D. Hanson and S. D. McBride; Philadelphia: Fortress, 1987) 67–78.

Aside from monotheism, the other common trait of Atenism and biblical Yahwism is the abhorrence of sacred statuary. Could this be coincidence?

11. *Iconoclasm was a late development in Israel.* Even though idolatry is disparaged or banned by almost all biblical prophets and legislators,[84] some scholars attribute the idea first to the Deuteronomist, who supposedly rewrote the older sources.[85] But what pre-Deuteronomistic literature assumes or condones idolatry? (A possible example: the teraphim in Gen 31:19–35; 1 Sam 19:13–16.) Archaeologists have remarked on the relative absence, throughout the Israelite period, of male statuary.[86] Aniconism—not necessarily iconoclasm—may have a long prehistory in Semitic religion.[87] In short, there is no evidence that aniconism and iconophobia were late developments in Israelite history or in biblical thought.[88] If

---

[84] For the direct ban, see Exod 20:4–5, 23; 34:17; Lev 19:4; 26:1; Deut 5:8–9; 27:15. Cf. also Gen 31:19, 30–35; 35:2–4; Exodus 32; Lev 26:30; Num 33:52; Deut 4:25–28; 28:36; 29:16; 31:29; Judges 17–18; 1 Sam 5:1–5; 1 Kgs 12:28–30; 14:9; 15:12–13; 21:26; 2 Kgs 10:29; 11:18; 17:12, 16, 29–31, 41; 18:4; 21:7, 11, 21; 22:17; 23:11, 24; Isa 2:18, 20; 10:10–11; 19:3; 30:22; 31:7; 40:18–20; 41:6–7, 29; 42:8, 17; 44:9–20; 45:20; 46:1–7; Jer 1:16; 2:27–28; 10:2–16; 25:6; 44:8; 50:2, 38; 51:15–19, 47, 52; Ezek 6:4–6, 9, 13; 8:3–5, 10; 14:3–7; 16:36; 18:6, 12, 15; 20:7–8, 16, 18, 24, 31, 39; 22:3–4; 23:7, 30, 37, 39, 49; 30:13; 33:25; 36:18, 25; 37:23; 44:10, 12; Hos 4:12, 17; 8:4–6; 13:2; 14:4; Amos 5:26; Micah 1:7; 5:12; Nah 1:14.

[85] According to C. Dohmen, *Das Bilderverbot*[2] (BBB 62; Bonn: Hanstein, 1985), no bans on images antedate the fall of the North in 722. But many would deny we possess any extensive Israelite literature from before the eighth century anyway.

[86] E.g., Dever, *Archaeological Discoveries*, 157. Female statuary, in contrast, grows more popular, probably continuing the Neolithic veneration of the powers of reproduction.

[87] Aniconism *per se*, i.e., the avoidance of anthropomorphic or theriomorphic representations of the divine, is common worldwide (Mettinger, *No Graven Images?*, 28–29). Real iconoclasm, as in Amarna religion and the Bible, is far rarer (on Nabatean parallels, see Mettinger, 57–68). On Israelite aniconism as part of a broader Iron Age movement, see Hendel, "Aniconism and Anthropomorphism," 210. Other vital studies are S. Schroer, *In Israel gab es Bilder* (OBO 74; Freiburg, Schweiz: Universitätsverlag; Göttingen: Vandenhoeck & Ruprecht, 1987), a maximalist treatment of the role of visual art in Israelite culture and religion, and O. Keel and C. Uehlinger, *Göttinnen, Götter und Gottessymbole* (Quaestiones Disputatae 134; Freiburg/Basel/Wien: Herder, 1992) 149–98, which chronicles a decline in figurative representation of deities during the Iron Age. The same authors also argue that Israel's brand of aniconism owed a profound debt to the solar cult of pre-Israelite Jerusalem (Keel and Uehlinger, "Jahwe und die Sonnengottheit von Jerusalem," *Ein Gott allein?* [ed. W. Dietrich and M. A. Klopfenstein; OBO 139; Freiburg, Schweiz: Universitätsverlag; Göttingen: Vandenhoeck & Ruprecht, 1994] 269–306).

In an earlier paper, Hendel ("The Social Origins of the Aniconic Tradition in Early Israel," *JBL* 50 [1988] 365–82) sought a native origin for aniconism, arguing that Israel's ambivalence toward human monarchy discouraged representing a kingly Yahweh seated upon a cherub throne (cf. also W. W. Hallo, "Texts, Statues and the Cult of the Divine King," *Congress Volume Jerusalem 1986* [VTSup 40; ed. J. A. Emerton; Leiden/New York/Copenhagen/Köln: Brill, 1988] 54–66). This raises several questions, however. Why make a cherub throne at all, even an empty one, if monarchic imagery is offensive? Why does biblical literature constantly describe Yahweh as *melek* 'king,' if the very notion legitimates human monarchy? And what about the Amarna connection—Atenistic aniconism is hardly antimonarchic—and the evidence for early Semitic aniconism proffered by Mettinger? We could, however, modify Hendel's argument, suggesting that in Israel the empty cherub throne was a *compromise* between the kings and antimonarchists: Yahweh was both like and unlike the Davidic monarch (who contented himself with a throne of mere lions, not of cherubim [1 Kgs 10:19–20]).

[88] The Israelites, or at least the biblical authors, compensated for the absence of sacred images in various ways. The polytheist's idol is a concretized, partial theophany, a vessel into which a deity pours

they go back to the beginning, Amarna influence is plausible. In fact, the lack of distinction between polytheism and idolatry is a shared oddity of Atenism and biblical Yahwism.

Next come what may be the main objections to the Akhenaten-Israel connection:

12. *Atenism was a flash in the pan confined to the court at Amarna, lasting at most twenty years and leaving no legacy.*[89] This is not quite true. Granted, the religion flourished mainly at Amarna.[90] But Atenism had a prehistory in the solar cult of the Eighteenth Dynasty, as the sun's visible disk was increasingly venerated as the sole source of life. The Aten was associated in particular with Amenophis III, Akhenaten's predecessor and progenitor.[91]

Second, aspects of Atenism outlived Akhenaten; indeed, Egypt was never the same.[92] The next three (or four)[93] Pharaohs began as Atenists, and Assmann demonstrates the abiding influence of Amarna in the pantheistic Amun theology of Ramesside Thebes, wherein the godhead is absolute, cosmic and yet personal.[94] Under Ramesses III, part of Akhetaten was briefly resettled, and Ramesside officials were well acquainted with the Amarna fiasco, dubbing Akhenaten the "Enemy from Akhetaten."[95] In visual art, a degree of Amarna style survived, while some post-Amarna funerary texts replace the solar barque with the Aten. Akhenaten permanently legitimated Late Egyptian as a literary language.[96] Even royal burial practice was changed by the Amarna interlude.[97] A thousand years later,

---

a measure of his/her spirit; like any artwork, it is and is not that which it depicts (cf. Jacobsen, "The Graven Image," *Ancient Israelite Religion* [ed. P. D. Miller, Jr., P. D. Hanson, S. D. McBride; Fs. F. M. Cross; Philadelphia: Fortress, 1987] 15–32). The most obvious biblical analogues are Humanity itself, created as God's image (see J. F. Kutsko, *Between Heaven and Earth* [Biblical and Judaic Studies from the University of California, San Diego, 7; Winona Lake: Eisenbrauns, 2000]), and the Covenant Ark, throne of the invisible Deity. Other quasi-theophanies are the human prophet, filled with Yahweh's spirit and speaking in the divine persona; the angel, which many texts equate with the Deity himself, and God's various hypostases—his "Face," "Name," "Wisdom," "Arm," etc.—which attain a quasi-independent divine status (cf. n. 49).

[89] E.g., H. M. Orlinsky, *Ancient Israel*, 2d ed. (Ithaca, NY: Cornell University Press, 1960) 35; C. H. Gordon and G. A. Rendsburg, *The Bible and the Ancient Near East* 4th ed. (New York/London: Norton, 1997) 85.

[90] Even at Akhetaten, however, Silverman ("Divinity and Deities," 87) finds evidence of Egypt's traditional religion being practiced outside the palace.

[91] Aldred, *Akhenaten*, 239; Redford, *Akhenaten*, 170–72. Redford out-Freuds Freud, suggesting that Akhenaten's fanaticism mirrored his veneration of his late royal father, known as the "Dazzling Sun-disk" (p. 234). (For a precursor to this view within early psychoanalytic circles, see Eilberg-Schwartz, *God's Phallus*, 42–43.) For Amenophis III as the Aten, see Murnane, *Texts*, 20–22, and Johnson, "Amenhotep III and Amarna" (n. 34 above).

[92] Hornung, *Conceptions of God*, 220.

[93] On the confusing post-Akhenaten succession and Horemhab's brief Atenistic period, see Murnane, *Texts*, 10, 12, 34.

[94] *Egyptian Solar Religion in the New Kingdom* (London/New York: Kegan Paul, 1995) 10, 290–310. On Amun's uniqueness, transcendence, incorporeity and undepictability, see also de Moor, *Rise of Yahwism*, 52–56.

[95] Murnane, *Texts*, 12, 240–42.

[96] Hornung, "Monotheismus," 88.

[97] Hornung, "Monotheismus," 95; Schlögl, *Echnaton-Tutanchamun*, 66.

Hellenized Egyptians still retained garbled reminiscences of Akhenaten's short-lived revolution.[98] Thus, even if Akhenaten's faith flowered but briefly, his revolution survived long in infamy.

One astonishing fact is sufficient proof that, directly or indirectly, Atenism affected Israel. Egyptologists and biblicists alike acknowledge that Psalm 104, especially vv 20–30, somehow depends upon Akhenaten's Hymn to the Aten.[99] Might Akhenaten's legacy to Israel not have been more extensive than a single poem?[100]

13. *There is no evidence of Israelites in Egypt. They were rather an indigenous people of pastoral-nomadic and/or peasant background*[101] *whose culture and religion were wholly Canaanite. Yahweh was simply a "merger" of Canaanite El and Baal.*[102] Admittedly, no Egyptian inscription mentions Moses or the Israelite

---

[98] On the allusions in Manetho and others, see E. Meyer, *Aegyptische Chronologie* (Abhandlungen der königlich preussischen Akademie der Wissenschaften; Berlin: Reimer, 1904) 92–95; Redford, "The Hyksos Invasion in History and Tradition," *Or* 39 (1970) 1–51; Assmann, *Moses*, 29–44. Albright raises the interesting possibility that even Philo Byblius' report of ancient Phoenician (sic!) solar monotheism dimly reflects Amarna religion (*Yahweh and the Gods of Canaan* [Garden City, New York: Doubleday, 1968] 229).

[99] E.g., F. Crüsemann, *Studien zur Formgeschichte von Hymnus und Danklied in Israel* (WMANT 32; Neukirchen-Vluyn: Neukirchener Verlag, 1969) 287–88, n. 3; E. von Nordheim, "Der grosse Hymnus des Echnaton und Psalm 104," *Studien zur altägyptischen Kultur* 7 (1979) 227–51; P. Auffret, *Hymnes d'Égypt et d'Israël* (OBO 34; Fribourg, Schweiz: Éditions Universitaires; Göttingen: Vandenhoeck & Ruprecht, 1981) 176–302; P. Dion, "YHWH as Storm-god and Sun-god. The Double Legacy of Egypt and Canaan as Reflected in Psalm 104," *ZAW* 103 (1991) 43–71; J. D. Levenson, *Creation and the Persistence of Evil*, 59–63. Even Redford (*Egypt, Canaan, and Israel*, 387–88), who otherwise discounts Akhenaten's influence upon Israel, acknowledges a relationship. Among the few who doubt any affinity between Psalm 104 and the Aten Hymn is C. Uehlinger ("Leviathan und die Schiffe in Ps 104,25–26," *Bib* 71 [1990] 499–526); see also E. Bille-De Mot (*The Age of Akhenaten* [New York/Toronto: McGraw Hill, 1966] 171), who culls various parallels from the Ṛg Veda. The Aten Hymn itself is available in translation in Murnane, *Texts*, 112–16, and in most of the works on Akhenaten cited throughout this article. For a list of parallels to Psalm 104, see the appended Chart.

[100] As Dion observes (op. cit.), the relationship between Psalm 104 and the Aten Hymn is almost incredible, but also undeniable. He compares the survival of Ugaritic/Canaanite mythology in postexilic Israel. Many other examples could be cited, including Karaite preservation/excavation of Qumran literature, and the presence of Late Bronze Age mythology in Philo of Byblos. The only full telling of the primordial Egyptian myth of Isis and Osiris is Plutarch's. And, for Egyptian-Israelite borrowings, there is the manifest genetic relationship between Psalm 20 and the Horus prayer preserved in Papyrus Amherst 63; see most recently Z. Zevit, "The Common Origin of the Aramaicized Prayer to Horus and of Psalm 20," *JAOS* 110 (1990) 213–28. The Egyptian influence on biblical Wisdom is well known; see n. 176. Psalm 104 is evidently not based directly upon Akhenaten's Hymn; rather, there probably were several now-lost intermediary texts in Egyptian and/or Northwest Semitic, especially Phoenician (note the exiguous evidence for Phoenician solar monotheism cited by Albright [n. 98]).

[101] E.g., I. Finkelstein, *The Archaeology of the Israelite Settlement* (Jerusalem: Israel Exploration Society, 1988); Dever, "Archaeology and the 'Conquest,' " *ABD* 3.545–58; T. L. Thompson, *Early History of the Israelite People* (Studies in the History of the Ancient Near East 4; Leiden/New York/Köln: Brill, 1992) 301–39, 401–15; Gnuse, *No Other Gods*, 23–61.

[102] Among the many scholars to classify Israelite religion, especially early Israelite religion, as a subspecies of Canaanite or Syro-Palestinian religion, are Morton Smith, *Palestinian Parties and Politics*, 27–29; Lang, *Monotheism and the Prophetic Minority* (Sheffield: Almond Press, 1983) 20–26; M. D. Coogan, "Canaanite Origins and Lineage: Reflections on the Religion of Ancient Israel," *Ancient Israelite Religion* [Fs. F. M. Cross; ed. P. D. Miller, Jr., P. D. Hanson and S. D. McBride; Philadelphia:

slaves; admittedly, the bulk of Israelite population may have been indigenous to Canaan, only gradually differentiating itself ethnically.[103] But even many skeptical historians find a kernel of truth in the Exodus tradition,[104] citing the presence of numerous Asiatics at various levels of Egyptian society in the New Kingdom: kings, princes raised at court, freemen and slaves.[105] Some were called ʿprw, which may or may not be the origin of the term ʿibrî 'Hebrew.'"[106]

Significantly, several members of the tribe of Levi, Israel's dispersed hereditary clergy, bear Egyptian names.[107] These Levites are the most promising suspects if one seeks a vehicle for getting Amarna theology into Canaan.[108] While an exodus of millions of slaves would probably be reflected at least obliquely in Egyptian sources, a smaller escape of, say, a few hundred Levite workers would not necessarily receive mention. Arriving after tribal boundaries were established, these latecomers infiltrated where they could and popularized the religion of Yahweh.

Do we really need Levites out of Egypt to explain Israelite or biblical religion? Many would say not. But, in our enthusiasm for Canaanite–biblical parallels, I fear we neglect the lesson of our own scholarly history. Once, everything in the

---

Fortress, 1987] 115–24; Mark S. Smith, *Early History*, 4–5 (with qualifications); G. Ahlström, *Who Were the Israelites?* (Winona Lake: Eisenbrauns, 1986) 83; Niehr, "The Rise of YHWH," and Gnuse, *No Other Gods*. On the merger of El and Baal, see Mark S. Smith, 21–22, and for further bibliography, Gnuse, 121–22.

[103] Dever, "Cultural Continuity, Ethnicity in the Archaeological Record and the Question of Israelite Origins," *Abraham Malamat Volume* (ed. S. Aḥituv, B. A. Levine; ErIsr 24; Jerusalem: Israel Exploration Society, 1993) 22*–3*; "Ceramics, Ethnicity, and the Question of Israel's Origins," *BA* 58 (1995) 200–13. On the problematic issue of ethnicity reflected in the archaeological record, see also Finkelstein, "Pots and People Revisited: Ethnic Boundaries in the Iron Age I"; D. Small, "Group Identification and Ethnicity in the Construction of the Early State of Israel: From the Outside Looking In," and B. Hesse and P. Wapnish, "Can Pig Remains Be Used for Ethnic Diagnosis in the Ancient Near East?" all in *The Archaeology of Israel: Constructing the Past, Interpreting the Present* (ed. N. A. Silberman and D. Small; JSOTSup 237; Sheffield: Sheffield Academic Press, 1997) 216–37, 238–70, 271–88.

[104] E.g., Gottwald, *Tribes*, 35–41; Dever, "Cultural Continuity," 31*.

[105] On Semites in Egypt, see Redford, *Egypt, Canaan, and Israel*, 198–99, 214–37; Hoffmeier, *Israel in Egypt*, 142–43.

[106] See O. Loretz, *Habiru-Hebräer* (BZAW 160; Berlin/New York: de Gruyter, 1984), and the works cited therein.

[107] Moses' name comes from Egyptian *mose* 'born' (see n. 4). Other Levitic names from various eras with certain or likely Egyptian derivation are Phinehas, Pashhur, Hophni and Merari (see Albright, *Yahweh and the Gods of Canaan*, 165). Moreover, Moses has an anonymous Nubian wife (Num 12:1), a fact possibly related to the etymology of Phinehas: *p3-nḥsy* 'the Nubian.' The Levite Hanamel apparently bears a half-Egyptian name ("Khnum is El/God"), as does Putiel (*p3 dy 'l* 'Given of El/God'), Phinehas's maternal grandfather—but Putiel is not certainly a Levite. In Exod 17:10, 12; 24:14 (JE), Hur probably has an Egyptian name ("Horus"), but he, too, is not necessarily a Levite (cf. the Judahite Hur in Exod 31:2 [P]). It is most striking that Hanamel and Pashhur (the latter name also attested epigraphically) are not ancient figures, but contemporaries of Jeremiah. Are these traditional family names, or was there an ongoing connection between Egypt and the Levites (see below)?

[108] This does not necessarily contradict other models for the Exodus. We would simply have to envision several "exoduses," as has often been conjectured (most recently by A. Malamat, "The Exodus: Egyptian Analogies," *Exodus: The Egyptian Evidence* [ed. E. S. Frerichs, L. H. Lesko; Winona Lake, Ind.; Eisenbrauns: 1997] 15–26.

Bible, indeed all world literature, was blithely derived from Mesopotamian prototypes, especially the Gilgamesh Epic.[109] The field has now outgrown its "pan-
Babylonian" phase—only to fall headlong into "pan-Canaanitism." The Bible
seemed thoroughly Mesopotamian, until Canaanite texts were recovered. Perhaps it seems thoroughly Canaanite now, but will it always? While some Canaan-
ite-biblical parallels may reflect the indigenous origins of some or most of the
Israelite populace, others may stem from a common Amorite background, or be
the result of Canaanite-Israelite interactions in later periods.[110] In particular, the
name "Yahweh" is so far not known from Canaanite sources (see below).

But let us nevertheless grant that the Israelites were, so to speak, self-hating
Canaanites, their popular religion merely an organic outgrowth of Late Bronze
Age Canaanite custom and belief. Let us grant that the Egyptian derivation of
Levitic names is meaningless—no one at all was ever a slave in Egypt. We still
must not forget that Egypt had ruled Canaan throughout the New Kingdom, including the Amarna episode, until the reign of Ramesses VI.[111] Egyptian solar religion in general—not necessarily Atenism per se—spread throughout the Near
East.[112] The Amarna correspondence from Canaan may show some familiarity
with the new protocols at Akhenaten's court: the vassals seem to omit reference
to Amun soon after Akhenaten's accession, without endorsing the Aten.[113] The
best evidence that Canaan was familiar with Atenism is EA 147 (Tyre), which
Assmann compares both to Akhenaten's Great Hymn to the Sun (ll. 111–14) and
to Ps 104:29–30:[114] "My lord is the Sun who comes forth over all lands day by day,
according to the way (of being) of the Sun, his gracious father, who gives life by his
sweet breath and returns with his north wind; who establishes the entire land in

---

[109] J. Rogerson, *Myth in Old Testament Interpretation* (BZAW 134; Berlin/New York: de Gruyter,
1974) 43–51; K. Johanning, *Der Bibel-Babel Streit* (Europäische Hochschulschriften 23; Frankfurt
am Main/New York: Lang, 1988).

[110] There is also the question of how much we know about Canaanite religion. The usual assumption is that Northwest Semitic inscriptions, particularly those from Ugarit, shed light on the popular religion of Syria–Palestine. But, unlike the Hebrew Bible, these sources undeniably articulate the
concerns of a privileged, urban elite. Thus, if the Israelites really were Canaanites, the Bible may be a
better source on popular culture than the extant Canaanite inscriptions—few of which come from
Palestine proper, in any case.

[111] See de Moor (*Rise of Yahwism*, 64–71) for a maximalist assessment of Egypt's influence upon
Canaan during this epoch.

[112] Mark S. Smith, *Early History*, 118. Giveon (*The Impact of Egypt on Canaan* [OBO 20;
Freiburg, Schweiz: Universitätsverlag; Göttingen: Vandenhoeck & Ruprecht, 1978] 13), however,
minimizes the influence of Egyptian religion in Canaan.

[113] De Moor, *Rise of Yahwism*, 68. Admittedly, the evidence is scant. Amun is mentioned in EA 1
(from Babylon), 19, 20, 24 (Mitanni), 71, 77, 86, 87, 95 (Byblos), 164 (Amurru), 369 (Egypt), all to (or
from) the court of Amenophis III. The exception that proves the rule is EA 27:87, a letter to Akhenaten, not from a vassal, but from Tushratta of Mitanni. The great king, not necessarily *au courant* with
the vicissitudes of the Egyptian cult, mentions Amun—but this letter deals with old business from the
days of Amenophis III, and may fall as early as Akhenaten's second regnal year (E. F. Campbell, *The
Chronology of the Amarna Letters* [Baltimore: The Johns Hopkins University Press, 1964] 25). Ultimately, de Moor's argument rests on the five vassal letters from Byblos and the one from Amurru.

[114] *Moses*, 192.

peace, by the power of his arm."[115] So, even without direct contact in Egypt, Akhenaten could have influenced Israel, either during his own reign or through the Amun-Re theology of the succeeding epoch, itself inspired by Amarna.

14. *Religious evolution is gradual and unidirectional.* This assumption, often unvoiced, underlies most modern reconstructions of Israelite religion. True, incremental development may explain the native religions of Egypt, Mesopotamia, Greece and India, so-called "primary religions." But it is not a realistic explanation for biblical Yahwism, which bears the earmarks of a "counter-religion,"[116] i.e., one that defines itself by opposition to another.[117] Such religions and philosophies are generally established in a brief time: Atenism, Buddhism, Confucianism, Christianity, Islam, Mormonism, Baha'i, to name the most prominent.[118] That scientific progress, at least, is spasmodic has become a cliché: the "paradigm shift" occurs due not only to blind social forces, but also to the insight and persuasive force of individuals.[119] The same can be true of religion.[120]

Moreover, long-term religious development, whether gradual or sudden, is never unidirectional. Various archaic folk elements may achieve the sanction of the elite; and, conversely, we find violent reformations, archaizings, iconoclasms, fundamentalisms, etc. For the case at hand, I do not envision a unilinear evolution of Yahwism into Judaism. Rather, aspects of the "Little Tradition"—superstition from the authorities' perspective—eventually attained sufficient respectability to be assimilated into the "Great Tradition," just as Mishnaic Hebrew, the presumed offshoot of a rustic dialect, attained legitimacy as a literary language.[121] In truth, the

---

[115] Translation from W. L. Moran, *The Amarna Letters* (Baltimore/London: The Johns Hopkins University Press, 1992) 233. On the continuation of the text, see below.

[116] I borrow the term from Assmann (*Moses*, 3), who regards Egyptian religion as the Other against which "Mosaic" religion defined itself. This requires considerable qualification, however, for the Bible has much to say about the "abominations" of Canaan and Mesopotamia, too.

[117] Israelite popular religion, insofar as it deviated from official religion, might be described as a "counter-counter-religion." Such religions may (e.g., neo-Paganism) or may not (Satanism) perpetuate or recreate archaic forms.

[118] Cf. R. Pettazzoni, *The All-knowing God* (Italian orig. 1956; New York: Arno, 1978) 2. Zoroastrianism, often included in this list, is a special case. If anything, its origins are murkier than those of Yahwism. For a brief discussion, see M. Boyce, *Textual Sources for the Study of Zoroastrianism* (Textual Sources for the Study of Religion; Chicago: University of Chicago Press, 1984) 1–16.

[119] T. S. Kuhn, *The Structure of Scientific Revolutions* (Chicago: University of Chicago Press, 1962).

[120] Cf. A. H. Silver, *Moses*, 1–5.

[121] For example, in postbiblical Jewish literature (including the early Christian), personalized angels and demons are prominent, whereas they are absent from most of the Old Testament. S. M. Olyan (*A Thousand Thousands Served Him* [Texte und Studien zum Antiken Judentum 36; Tübingen: Mohr (Siebeck), 1993]) stresses the role of elite biblical exegesis in the development of detailed angelology. This may be so, but do not all peoples believe in numberless spirits, both kindly and malefic? We also find in later texts numerous evocations of the old Combat Myth and the fall of the astral gods, a phenomenon Cross calls "the recrudescence of mythic themes" (*Canaanite Myth*, 343). With Kabbalism, Judaism will segment its Godhead and readmit the feminine (R. Patai, *The Hebrew Goddess*[3] [Detroit: Wayne State University, 1990]). In Christianity, we even find the divine triad and sacred marriage motifs reasserting themselves: God the Father, God the Son—but now a human mother. Jesus in fact incarnates several venerable mythic archetypes: the semidivine king, the deity who descends from

balance between monotheism and polytheism may have changed but little as Yahwism developed into Judaism. It is the textual sources that adapted themselves.

Reacting against past trends, particularly in the last century, our *Zeitgeist* finds more significance in gradual social development than in the impetus of Great Men.[122] With appropriate if unthinking mistrust of 'foundation' legends, the unconscious (il)logic runs something like this: since the texts about Israel's break with the past at Sinai under Moses' leadership are historically dubious, i.e., written long after the supposed events and full of anachronisms and improbable phenomena, we may be certain there was no founding movement at all. Given the axiom of unidirectional change, since Yahwism slowly evolved into (more or less) monotheistic Judaism, it must have begun as something entirely its opposite: Canaanite polytheism.[123] Is this realistic? Too often the axiom of the "ancient Near Eastern cultural continuum" has authorized reconstructing an Israel maximally resembling its neighbors (and *vice versa*); then the reconstruction is cited to prove the continuum.[124] We must rather steer between Scylla—the claim that Israelite popular religion was identical to its Northwest Semitic matrix—and Charybdis— the claim that it was identical to later Judaism. By definition, the truth lies somewhere in the middle.[125]

"Moses"

A counter-religion requires a personal catalyst: a charismatic individual to articulate popular frustration and envision ways beyond. The Founder does not finish the work. Paul, Ali and Abu Bakr, and Brigham Young are almost as important for their respective traditions as Jesus, Muḥammad and Joseph Smith. Generally, the creative period lasts two generations, while the Founder's aura lingers on his disciples. Then doctrine begins to ossify.

Among American and Israeli scholars educated fifty years ago, it seemed self-evident that Yahwism fit this profile perfectly. "The events of exodus and Sinai require a great personality behind them. And a faith as unique as Israel's demands a

---

heaven through earth to the underworld (a role played by both Christ and his antitype, Lucifer-Satan), the storm god who controls the winds and seas and feeds the masses, the chthonian healer god and the passive dying-and-rising god of vegetation.

[122] Cf. Levenson, *Creation and the Persistence of Evil*, 60. For an extreme description of the collective's supposed inability to form a culture unless guided by a Great Man, see J. G. Frazer, *Folk-Lore in the Old Testament* (London: Macmillan, 1918) 3.97.

[123] Cf. Dever, "Material Remains," 578–79: "I propose, *as a working hypothesis* [emphasis added], that early Israelite religion developed gradually out of the Late Bronze and early Iron Age fertility cults of greater Canaan. . . . 'Normative Judaism' . . . is a construct of the late Judean Monarchy and in particular of the exilic period."

[124] For a classic example, see R. Ratner and B. Zuckerman, " 'A Kid in Milk'?: New Photographs of *KTU* 1.23, Line 14," *HUCA* 57 (1986) 15–60. R. Rendtorff, too, cautions against "leveling" the differences among the religions of Syria-Palestine ("El, Baʿal und Jahwe," *ZAW* 78 [1966] 277–92).

[125] Our sister field of New Testament studies grapples with a comparable dilemma: to what extent should we Judaize Jesus and his disciples? Here, extremism is more warranted, since the earliest Christians *were* Jews, whereas Israel's Canaanite origins are hypothetical.

founder. . . . To deny that role to Moses would force us to posit another person of the same name!"[126] Today, after the demise of Albrightian optimism, we are less sanguine. Even to propose that a Moses might have done something important—leading a minor exodus or instituting the Covenant or establishing monotheism or writing small parts of the Torah—would smack of reactionary apologetics.[127]

Instead, the majority (or loudest) view today is that, after an early period in which Yahwism was indistinguishable from Canaanite religion, Israel's peculiar theologies of monotheism and Covenant were invented during the reigns of Hezekiah (ca. 715–687) and Josiah (ca. 640–609) by radicals wrapping themselves in the false mantle of Mosaic authority.[128] Although the J and E sources already ostensibly describe Moses as a liberator, lawgiver and super-prophet who espoused a Covenant-based monotheism, these sources, if they existed at all, are either exilic or postexilic;[129] they shed no light on early beliefs. The Torah was compiled and attributed to Moses to buttress the claims of postexilic Judah's hierocracy and landowners.[130]

It is poor method, however, dogmatically to judge all traditions as late as possible and as inauthentic as possible, on the (indisputable) grounds that all nations exaggerate the antiquity and veracity of their traditions. After all, according to the most radical skeptics, the Bible does not contain any ancient Israelite texts;[131] the more moderate skeptics hold that nothing antedates the eighth century. How then can we say what inhabitants of Iron Age Palestine did or did not believe and practice?

Quite apart from *a priori* skepticism, Moses' negligible historical role is said to be apparent in his relative absence from biblical hymnody and prophecy (only Deut 33:4; Isa 63:11–12; Jer 15:1; Hos 12:14; Micah 6:4; Mal 3:22; Ps 77:21; 99:6; 103:7; 105:26; 106:16, 23, 32).[132] Since the Bible's historiography, where Moses is ubiquitous, is supposed to be an elite, literary product, whereas the prophets presumably interacted with ordinary folk as well as with the powerful, Moses must have been a nonentity to the masses.

I am unconvinced by this argument. I doubt that the Primary History (Genesis–Kings) is essentially romance, unrelated to common Israelite belief and tradition.

---

[126] Bright, *History of Israel*, 127.

[127] On the scholarly image of Moses through the 1960s, see E. Osswald, *Das Bild des Mose in der kritischen alttestamentlichen Wissenschaft seit Julius Wellhausen* (Theologische Arbeiten 18; Berlin: Evangelische Verlagsanstalt, 1962). A broader, popular treatment is D. J. Silver, *Images of Moses* (New York: Basic Books, 1982).

[128] Morton Smith, who most influentially posited a chasm between Israelite and biblical religions, traced the "Yahweh-alone party" as far back as Elijah in the ninth century (*Palestinian Parties*, 34). Today such an early date sounds conservative.

[129] E.g., J. Van Seters, *The Life of Moses* (Louisville: Westminster/John Knox, 1994); Davies, *In Search of Ancient Israel*.

[130] On the Torah's Persian-era social matrix, see F. Crüsemann, *Die Tora* (München: Chr. Kaiser, 1992) 381–423.

[131] E.g., Davies, *In Search of Ancient Israel*.

[132] Moses is credited with the authorship of Exod 15:1–18; Deut 32:1–43; 33:2–29 and Psalm 90, but these works do not actually mention Moses.

How could it have commanded the respect of its intended audience if it violated much that they knew or believed? And how are we to explain Moses' occasional presence in poetry—including preexilic poetry—if he was of no importance? Unless these are postexilic insertions, Moses must have been a known figure, albeit of marginal interest to poets and ecstatics.[133]

We must, of course, regard critically Moses' centrality as cultural founder in J, E, D and P. These are only four voices, and interrelated to boot; they are not independent eyewitnesses.[134] And we possess them only in a heavily edited form. But to impute all references to Moses, monotheism and Covenant to later editors is sorry method. It may not be wrong, but it cannot be proven right.

Because I, too, am skeptical that Moses was quite the hero the Torah makes him out to be, I have put his name within quotation marks. "Moses" might be a single man, but he might also be a succession of leaders.[135] Much (most?) of Yahwism could have been established within two generations. As with any religion, we may assume "Mosaic" religion underwent considerable change and accommodation, including schismatic tendencies, among both the elite leadership and the masses. But when did "Moses" live? And what exactly might he have done?

The Origins of Israelite Religion

The Bible dates Moses to the period before Israel's occupation of Canaan. Some modern scholars find a substantial nugget of veracity in this tradition.[136] Perhaps our "Moses" led some Levites from Egypt;[137] he could also have been the transmitter to Israel of Egyptian iconoclastic monotheism, perhaps received secondhand from the reformed cult of Amun-Re.[138] But, having banished pan-Babylonianism

---

[133] Moses, we should note, is still largely absent in *post*exilic poetry, when the Mosaic tradition was supposedly growing in importance. The situation is surprising, but not inexplicable. As an offshoot of Canaanite poetry, biblical hymnody is inherently mythopoeic, deemphasizing the historical arena, celebrating God as Protagonist and rarely mentioning human tools like Moses. And the prophets, for all their insistence on Covenant, show little interest in history proper; current events are their passion. With a direct channel to God, they do not need traditions from the past. Thus, although Moses' near-invisibility in poetic sources might be taken to reflect his popular insignificance, the reverse could be true. J, E, D and P might preserve popular historical tradition, of little concern to singers and visionaries.

[134] On the sources' interdependency, see R. E. Friedman, *Who Wrote the Bible?* (New York: Summit, 1987).

[135] I am less inclined to see him as simply personifying a "Moses group" or an office within that group, positions entertained by Gottwald (*Tribes*, 35–41), though he remains open to Moses as a historical individual.

[136] A reconstructed "primitive" or "Mosaic" Yahwism fairly similar to later biblical religion was widely visualized among a past generation of scholars, including Albright and Kaufmann; Mendenhall ("Covenant Forms," 72), too, speaks of "the rediscovery of Moses" under Josiah. A recent exponent is Albertz, *Religionsgeschichte Israels in alttestamentlicher Zeit* (Grundrisse zum Alten Testament 8/1; Göttingen: Vandenhoeck & Ruprecht, 1992) 68–104.

[137] For R. B. Coote, however, Moses and his circle were Egypt-bred Canaanites who administered the highlands for Pharaoh (*Early Israel* [Minneapolis: Fortress, 1990] 89–90).

[138] If the historical Moses appears anywhere in the extra-biblical record, he might be the Asiatic vizier who served several Ramessides, Beya or Rʿ-ms-sw-ḫʿ-m-nṯrw, as proposed by Knauf (*Midian*

and pan-Canaanitism, I would not fall into the remaining heresy, pan-Egyptianism.[139] We cannot explain Yahwism simply as a transplanted Egyptian solar sect. For one thing, Yahweh is only occasionally compared to the sun.[140] And the Canaanite connection is too strong. Indeed, despite my foregoing strictures, I think Yahwism's debt to Northwest Semitic religion is generally *underestimated*. It is well established that Yahweh evinces striking parallels to both El and Baal of Canaan.[141] But it is less often remarked that pre-Israelite Northwest Semitic religion, at least in its urban form, was already *latently monotheistic*. By this I mean that among the gods was one named "God" ('Ilu/El) who embodied the pantheon's power and divinity.[142] Cananite language was thus pre-equipped with terminology and concepts that could theoretically express monotheism, if needed—as Christian and Muslim missionaries have repeatedly experienced with other polytheist and animist cultures throughout the world (see below, n. 168). I would describe biblical Yahwism as the elite manifestation of a syncretistic counter-religion, expressing an Egyptian concept in Northwest Semitic terms. An Egyptian monotheist like Akhenaten would inevitably find in the Sun and the king the most expressive symbols of divinity. But "Moses" had to restate this idea for Syro-Palestinians. His godhead was andromorphic,[143] essentially a combination of two divine types: the Divine Patriarch and the Battling Storm God.[144]

[Abhandlungen des deutschen Palästinavereins; Wiesbaden: Harrassowitz, 1988] 97–99, 135–46) and de Moor (*Rise of Yahwism*, 214–27). But, until we know Beya's ultimate fate, this must be considered a remote conjecture. Even the name is not quite right, for Hebrew *mōše(h)* is Egyptian *ms* 'born,' not *ms-sw* 'begot him' (contrast Hebrew *r'mss*, with *two* sibilants).

[139] Of which the classic example remains A. S. Yahuda, *The Language of the Pentateuch in its Relation to Egyptian* (London: Oxford University Press, 1933).

[140] Ps 84:12; possibly Deut 33:2; Isa 60:1; Hos 6:3. See J. G. Taylor, *Yahweh and the Sun* (JSOTSup 111; Sheffield: Sheffield Academic Press, 1993); O. Keel and C. Uehlinger, "Jahwe und die Sonnengottheit von Jerusalem"; Mark S. Smith, *Early History*, 115–24.

[141] Mark S. Smith, *Early History*, 1–79.

[142] Hence perhaps his title *il bn il* 'God of divinities,' i.e., quintessential god (CAT 1.65.1; for Near Eastern parallels, see O. Loretz, *Des Gottes Einzigkeit* [Darmstadt: Wissenschaftliche Buchgesellschaft, 1997] 59, n. 263; on divine All-Fathers in general, see Pettazzoni, *All-knowing God*). I do not claim that any Ugaritites or Canaanites were practicing monotheists or pantheists—although the latter would not suprise me. M. H. Pope (*El in the Ugaritic Texts* [VTSup 2; Leiden: Brill, 1955]) makes the best case against El-pantheism, but he relies largely on myths in which El's power and authority appear circumscribed (see also Loretz, pp. 58–58, 124–25). In any culture, we must distinguish between mythology, where gods' powers are limited for plot purposes, and cult, where gods are lauded as virtually omnipotent. (Though elaboration would take us too far afield, I also conceive the goddess Asherah/Qudšu/Elat as embodying the holiness of the entire pantheon, called both *bn 'il* 'sons of God' and *bn qdš* 'sons of Holiness.')

If there is anything to the Bible's tradition of the Patriarchs—which scholars still debate—then Israel's pre-Yahwistic forebears, whether within Canaan or outside it, may also have been latently monotheistic El-worshipers; cf. Cross, *Canaanite Myth*, 3–75, esp. 13–43; Freedman, *Pottery, Poetry, and Prophecy* (Winona Lake, Ind.: Eisenbrauns, 1980) 77–178.

[143] Or sometimes tauromorphic, as perhaps in the Golden Calves (Exodus 32; 1 Kgs 12:25–30) and Num 24:8.

[144] Other divine characters play a lesser but not insignificant role in Yahweh's composite persona: the Sun God, the Plague God, even the Mother Goddess. As N. P. Lemche notes, such fusion was not unique to Yahweh (*Ancient Israel* [The Biblical Seminar; Sheffield: Sheffield Academic Press, 1988] 228–29).

Psalm 104 is a fine example of syncretism. On the one hand, it exhibits close parallels to Akhenaten's "Hymn to the Sun" (see chart). On the other hand, its motifs of the Storm God expelling the waters and sitting enthroned in heaven are purely Northwest Semitic, as are various stylistic features.[145] No one would date this Psalm to the "Mosaic" period.[146] Rather, it attests to Amarna's long-lived influence upon Israel, whether received directly in Israel or mediated by Canaan. Already in the Late Bronze Age, EA 147, quoted above, combines Atenistic solar imagery with Canaanite storm imagery:[147] "My lord is the Sun who comes forth over all lands day by day, according to the way (of being) of the Sun, his gracious father, who gives life by his sweet breath and returns with his north wind;[148] who establishes the entire land in peace, by the power of his arm . . . who gives forth his cry in the sky like Baal, and all the land is frightened at his cry." Here is an early example of the solarized Storm God, an ancient type more common in the Iron Age (Asshur, Marduk, Baal Shamem, Zeus Heliopolis, Yahweh).[149]

How did "Moses" express the concept of monotheism? Perhaps by the Covenant. Whereas Akhenaten was the literal son of God, Israel could be God's metaphorical son, i.e., his covenanted vassal.[150] But here we collide with another conclusion of recent biblical scholarship: Covenant theology is an invention of the Assyrian period and specific to Deuteronomic literature.[151] Admittedly, Deuteronomy may well use Assyrian treaties as its model[152]—but that reflects the date of

---

[145] Von Nordheim, "Grosse Hymnus"; Dion, "YHWH as Storm-god and Sun-god."

[146] I have no opinion on the date of Psalm 104. It mostly lacks the linguistic archaisms typifying the Song of the Sea, the Song of Deborah and other works; see F. M. Cross, Jr., and D. N. Freedman, *Studies in Ancient Yahwistic Poetry* (SBLDS 21; Missoula, Mont.: Scholars Press, 1975); D. A. Robertson, *Linguistic Evidence in Dating Early Hebrew Poetry* (SBLDS 3; Missoula, Mont.: Society of Biblical Literature, 1972). On the other hand, except perhaps for the reference to ministering angels in v 4, Psalm 104 also lacks the characteristics of late biblical poetry found in its neighboring psalms; see A. Hurvitz, *Bên lāšôn ləlāšôn* (English title: *The Transition Period in Biblical Hebrew*; Jerusalem: Bialik Institute, 1972) 173.

[147] De Moor, *Rise of Yahwism*, 162–63.

[148] The expression "sweet breath . . . north wind" is originally Egyptian (C. Grave, "Northwest Semitic ṣapanu in a Break-up of an Egyptian Stereotype Phrase in EA 147," *Or* 51 [1982] 161–82). In a Canaanite context, however, one cannot but think of Baal's abode, Mount Zaphon, as the continuation makes explicit.

[149] See Mark S. Smith, *Early History*, 44, 115–25. Smith's earliest example is Sumerian Ningirsu.

[150] See F. C. Fensham, "Father and Son as Terminology for Treaty and Covenant," *Near Eastern Studies in Honor of William Foxwell Albright* (ed. H. Goedicke; Baltimore/London: The Johns Hopkins University Press, 1971) 121–35.

[151] Most influentially, L. Perlitt, *Bundestheologie im Alten Testament* (WMANT 36; Neukirchen-Vluyn: Neukirchener Verlag, 1969).

[152] R. Frankena ("The Vassal Treaties of Esarhaddon and the Dating of Deuteronomy," *OTS* 14 [1965] 140–54) displays an impressive list of parallels. But even here there is room for doubt. It is true that the extended curses of Deuteronomy 28 sound rather Assyrian; see H. U. Steymans, *Deuteronomium 28 und die adê zur Thronfolgeregelung Asarhaddons* (OBO 145; Freiburg: Universitätsverlag; Göttingen: Vandenhoeck & Ruprecht, 1996). But the direction of influence is not completely clear. On the one hand, the Assyrians had been the Israelites' overlords from the mid-eighth century and doubtless imposed written covenants upon them, replete with gory threats. On the other hand, the Assyrians' own term for treaty, *adê*, is borrowed from Aramaic '*dy*. Thus, it is possible that the

Deuteronomy, not necessarily the date of the Covenant. Before Deuteronomy, Hos 6:7 and 8:1 (cf. 2:20; 10:4) know of a Covenant between Yahweh and Israel, and other prophets and poets employ the genre we call "Covenant lawsuit."[153] And JE describes the Covenant in detail,[154] unless we invoke Deuteronomic retouching. The word *bərît* does not always appear in contexts that presuppose a binding, exclusive relationship between Yahweh and Israel, but the term is old, already present as a Semitic loanword in Ramesside Egyptian.[155] Thus the idea and form of Covenant, as Mendenhall and Baltzer originally proposed, could well be rooted in the Late Bronze Age, whether in political treaties between the Hittites and their Syro-Palestinian vassals, or perhaps more broadly in common international law.[156] To be sure, their strongest argument, that treaties containing historical reviews are exclusive to the Late Bronze Age, now needs minor qualification—there are two later counter-examples[157]—but the theory retains its essential cogency.

The hypothesis that "Moses" invented the Covenant in the Late Bronze or Early Iron Age may sound suspiciously Deuteronomic and hence anachronistic.[158] Certainly, *we* recognize Deuteronomy as the secondarily adapted charter of Josiah's seventh-century reformation.[159] But Deuteronomy itself purports to be Moses' final testament from centuries before. It is a tendentious version of what some Israelites—ultimately, many Israelites—could conceive a Moses as having said. It is closed-minded to insist that, precisely because Deuteronomy purports to embody Moses' teaching, *ipso facto* it has nothing to do with that teaching.[160] We

---

Assyrian treaties are based upon Syro-Palestinian prototypes, rather than *vice versa;* cf. H. Tadmor, "Assyria and the West: the Ninth Century and its Aftermath," *Unity and Diversity* (ed. H. Goedicke and J. J. M. Roberts; Baltimore: The Johns Hopkins University Press, 1975) 42–43.

[153] E.g., Deuteronomy 32; Isa 1:2–3; 3:13–14; Jer 2:4–13; Micah 6:1–8; Psalm 50. See H. B. Huffmon, "The Covenant Lawsuit in the Prophets," *JBL* 78 (1959) 285–95; J. Harvey, *Le plaidoyer prophétique contre Israël après la rupture de l'alliance* (Bruges/Paris: Desclée de Brouwer; Montreal: Éditions Bellarmin, 1967).

[154] Exodus 19–24, 33–34 (non-P sections). Cf. D. J. McCarthy, *Treaty and Covenant*[2] (AnBib 21A; Rome: Pontifical Biblical Institute, 1981) 256–73.

[155] Hoch, *Semitic Words*, 108–9. *Bərît* may also appear in a Hurrian hymn from Ugarit in the divine title *ilbrt* 'God of the Covenant' (?); see Cross, *Canaanite Myth*, 39.

[156] G. E. Mendenhall, "Ancient Oriental and Biblical Law," "Covenant Forms in Israelite Tradition," *BASOR* 17 (1954) 27–46, 50–76; K. Baltzer, *Das Bundesformular*[2] (WMANT 4; Neukirchen-Vluyn: Neukirchener Verlag, 1964); G. E. Mendenhall and G. A. Herion, "Covenant," *Anchor Bible Dictionary* (New York: Doubleday, 1992) 1.1179–1202; cf. E. Bickerman, "Couper une alliance," *Archives d'histoire du droit oriental* 5 (1950–51) 133–56. It is true that nowhere does the Bible present the full text of the Covenant between Yahweh and Israel (*pace* Mendenhall). But that bits and pieces of the covenant formulary pervade the Bible, especially Deuteronomy, indicates an older tradition of Covenant used secondarily to impose literary structure.

[157] McCarthy, *Treaty and Covenant*, 119, 147–48.

[158] But Gottwald, no fundamentalist, considers it "at least possible, conceivably probable, that notions of covenanting between god and people and of divine law-giving were introduced in some form among that same group . . . in which Moses was a leader" (*Tribes*, 36).

[159] See, e.g., Friedman, *Who Wrote the Bible?*, 101–35, for a reformulation of W. M. L. de Wette's classic theory.

[160] A comparison: our extant written records of the Buddha's doctrine are a millennium later than the man himself. Yet critical scholars do not doubt they preserve the essence of Siddhartha's teaching,

know that the Deuteronomistic Historian respected his sources' integrity—else he would have expunged the less reputable exploits of Samuel, David and Solomon, especially "high place" worship (1 Samuel 9–10; 1 Kgs 3:4–5). Scholars often associate the composition of Deuteronomy with a "neoclassical" or "archaizing" movement throughout the ancient Near East.[161] The terms "neoclassical" and "archaizing" imply an antecedent tradition. In Egypt and Mesopotamia, we know that ancient records were scrutinized, copied and collected, as well as imitated in new compositions. But only for Israel does one assume the "revival" was wholly fraudulent.

In distinguishing the various theological streams that converged into Israelite Yahwism, we have omitted one crucial element: the name "Yahweh." At least since F. W. Ghillany (1862), scholars have found in the Jethro tradition evidence that Moses (I would say "Moses") owed a profound debt to the Midianites.[162] For Freud, as we have seen, Yahwism was simply a synthesis of Atenism with a Midianite cult, mediated by the two Moseses. There was no positive evidence in Freud's day beyond the location of Horeb/Sinai near Midian (Exod 3:1) and the tradition of Moses' Midianite in-laws (Exod 2:16–22; 3:1; 4:18–19; 18; Num 10:29–32; Judg 1:16; 4:11). Now we can add another datum: Egyptian texts from the reigns of Amenophis III, Ramesses II and Ramesses III[163] mention semi-nomads called the "Shasu of yhw3" located in the rough vicinity of Midian, east of the Arabah.[164] This is the very time and place in which one might place "Moses."

One might object that this sounds all too artificial: Egyptian monotheism + Midianite Yahweh + Canaanite Divine Patriarch and Battling Storm God types + Hittite Covenant form + Iron Age national god theology = Yahwism. But thereby we summarize a century of biblical scholarship. Throughout history and prehistory, the cultures of Syria–Palestine have been quintessentially synthetic, adapt-

---

albeit subject to considerable elaboration (e.g., Mahayana sutras). On Buddhist textual sources from Asoka onward, see G. Schopen, "Two Problems in the History of Indian Buddhism: The Layman/ Monk Distinction and the Doctrines of the Transference of Merit," *Studien zur Indologie und Iranistik* 10 (1985) 9–47.

[161] E.g., McCarter, "The Religious Reforms of Hezekiah and Josiah," *Aspects of Monotheism*, 57–58.

[162] For older bibliography, see Rowley, *From Joseph to Joshua*, 149–56. Freedman (*Pottery, Poetry*, 177–78) also regards the name "Yahweh" as introduced to Israel by the historical Moses, who learned it from desert tribes.

[163] Giveon, "Toponymes ouest-asiatiques à Soleb," *VT* 14 (1964) 244. For brief discussions with bibliography, see M. Weinfeld, "The Tribal League at Sinai," *Ancient Israelite Religion* (Fs. F. M. Cross; ed. P. D. Miller, Jr., P. D. Hanson and S. D. McBride; Philadelphia: Fortress, 1987) 304–5; Redford, *Egypt, Canaan, and Israel* 272–73.

[164] De Moor (*Rise of Yahwism*, 124–26) argues that the Egyptians, rightly or wrongly, took Yhw3 to be an ethnic name. He also tentatively identifies these Yhw3-folk with the *Ia-we* of EA 154:7—but this is effectively refuted by R. S. Hess, "The Divine Name Yahweh in Late Bronze Age Sources," *UF* 23 (1991) 183–86. De Moor further observes that Yahweh may originally have been the tribe's deified eponymous ancestor, later becoming the familiar biblical God (pp. 323–69). For Knauf (*Midian*, 42–60), however, "Yahweh" probably denoted a mountain in Arabia. Whatever his origin, it is possible that in the Iron Age Yahweh was worshiped, not only in Israel, but also in Syria; see S. Dalley, "Yahweh in Hamath in the 8th Century BC: Cuneiform Material and Historical Deductions," *VT* 40 (1990) 21–32.

ing artifacts, styles, words and concepts from Egypt, Mesopotamia, Hatti, Greece and the desert. All counter-religions are "artificial," produced by deliberate creativity. They spread by persuasion and example, a role for which the dispersed Levites, heirs of "Moses," were ideally suited. "Moses" may not have achieved his synthesis in a coup, but perhaps he accomplished enough to become the embodiment, for later generations, of all that characterized Israelite religion.

Here is a historical analogy to the origins of Yahwism as I have sketched them. Pre-Islamic Arabia was, like Canaan, latently monotheistic, venerating among other deities a high god named '*al-'ilāh* 'the God,' later Allah, whose cult was centered at Mecca.[165] One man, Muḥammad, having encountered the necessary-but-not-sufficient stimulus of Jewish and Christian monotheism, as well as certain native monotheistic Arabian sects, recast the indigenous faith, expressing an adapted concept in Arab terms.[166] Certain compromises were necessary, and "polytheistic" vestiges survived—angels, demons, saints, "Allah's Daughters"[167]— but the resulting counter-religion was a true paradigm shift, a radical but not absolute break with the past.[168]

One problem potentially undermines this picture of earliest Israelite religion and the "Mosaic" contribution. When did Israel become literate? Radical monotheism, whether espoused by Akhenaten or by the Deuteronomist, is a parade example of the "either/or" thought-style characteristic of the literate.[169] I have

---

[165] It is unclear whether Allah before Muḥammad was a fully active or an otiose deity; possibly there was regional variation. On pre-Islamic Arabian religion, see M. Höfner, "Die vorislamischen Religionen Arabiens," *Die Religionen Altsyriens, Altarabiens und der Mandäer* (Die Religionen der Menschheit 10,2; Stuttgart/Berlin/Köln/Mainz: Kohlhammer, 1970) 354–402; F. E. Peters, *Muḥammad and the Origins of Islam* (Albany: State University of New York Press, 1994) esp. pp. 105–32.

[166] On possible native antecedents to Muḥammad's monotheism, see Peters, *Muḥammad*, 94–99, 117–18, 122–28.

[167] On the revoked "Satanic Verses" of Sura 53, which recall the Israelite Asherah dispute, see Peters, *Muḥammad*, 160–62.

[168] Cf. the comments of R. Finnegan and R. Horton: ". . . moves toward greater emphasis on the supreme being, occurring in situations either prior to or outside the range of Muslim and Christian proselytizing, open up fascinating possibilities for an understanding of the so-called 'conversion' of pagan peoples to these two great monotheistic religions. . . . The move toward a more monotheistic religion can be seen as an inherent possibility of the pre-existing system, actualizable in specific social and political circumstances. Islam and Christianity are catalysts, hastening reactions all of whose necessary ingredients were already 'in the air'. Indeed, the horde of scholars now concerning themselves with the impact of world religions on Africa and elsewhere might do well to start their reflections, not with the Koran and the Bible, but with [E. Evans-Pritchard's] *Nuer religion* and [G. Lienhardt's] *Divinity and experience*; not with Ibn Yasin and Bishop Crowther, but with Arianhdit and the Aro Chukwu oracle operators" (*Modes of Thought* [ed. R. Horton and R. Finnegan; London: Faber & Faber, 1973] 47). R. Pettazzoni writes in a similar vein, "Behind the one omniscient God of a monotheistic religion we glimpse the figure of the omniscient chief god of a polytheism, as behind that in turn there confronts us the all-seeing Supreme Being of a primitive worship" (*All-knowing God*, 437). These animadversions are relevant for both the emergence of Islam and the emergence of Yahwism.

[169] See the various works of Jack Goody (n. 53); Halpern ("Jerusalem and the Lineages in the Seventh Century BCE: Kinship and the Rise of Individual Moral Liability," *Law and Ideology in Monarchic Israel* [ed. B. Halpern and D. W. Hobson; JSOTSup 124; Sheffield: JSOT, 1991] 11–107); H. Shanks, "Frank Moore Cross: an Interview III," *BRev* 8.6 (1992) 25–26.

trouble envisioning an unlettered "Moses" conceiving and transmitting his teachings in an illiterate milieu. Of course, for both tradition (e.g., Acts 7:22) and Freud, this is not necessarily a problem: Moses would have been fluent in hieroglyphics! For the more sober, the fact that Israelite inscriptions from before the ninth century scarcely exist might seem near-proof that "Moses" did not invent Israelite religion in anything like the form we have it.[170]

Few inscriptions are not *no inscriptions*, however. We have student texts such as abecedaries dating back to the twelfth–eleventh centuries ('Izbet Ṣarṭah), close to Israel's origins. These alone suffice to prove the existence of early scribal culture. Indeed, the alphabet itself is a legacy from the Late Bronze Age; even so trivial a matter as the spelling of *rō(ʾ)š* and *ṣō(ʾ)n* with an aleph that had quiesced by the fourteenth century bespeaks the ancient roots of Hebrew scribal tradition.[171] True, inscriptions do not become numerous until the eighth–seventh centuries; true, we possess no autographs of ancient Hebrew *belles lettres*.[172] But the sad fact is that, apart from the odd monument, Israelite scribes in all periods set their most important words to perishable papyrus and parchment, leaving to posterity only ephemera. Who can say what ancient records were available to the biblical authors? That the expansion of literacy in the eighth–seventh centuries coincides with the flowering of monotheism need not imply that monotheism is the creation of this period. More likely, expanding literacy simply fueled the ambition and effectiveness of the increasingly jealous intellectual elite, conveyors of the "Mosaic" tradition.

There is little in the Bible that sounds "Mosaic," i.e., that is couched in a proto-Hebrew dialect. At most, we have Exod 15:1–18, the "Song of the Sea,"[173] which makes no unambiguous monotheistic claim—although v 11 vaunts Yahweh's incomparability.[174] Because my main interest is in defending the plausibility of a connection between biblical Yahwism and Atenism, less in reconstructing the

---

[170] On Hebrew inscriptions, see J. Naveh, *Early History of the Alphabet* (Jerusalem: Magnes, 1982) 65–78. In defense of early monarchic Israelite literacy, see N. Na'aman, "Sources and Composition in the History of David," *The Origins of the Ancient Israelite State* (ed. V. Fritz and P. R. Davies; JSOTSup 228; Sheffield: Sheffield Academic Press, 1996) 71–86.

[171] Z. Harris, *Development of the Canaanite Dialects* (New Haven: AOS Series 16, 1939) 26, 42.

[172] It has been argued that, in any society, writing is first used for mundane record-keeping, and that widespread literacy is a precondition for the development of fine literature. This is quite true for the autochthonous scripts of Mesopotamia and Egypt. The tablets of Ugarit prove, however, that in the Late Bronze Age, alphabetic writing was quickly adopted for literature. After all, hieroglyphic and cuneiform literature had already existed for millennia; the concept did not require invention *de novo*.

[173] Contrast the Gathas, apparently by Zoroaster himself, although they may have been transcribed almost two millennia later (Boyce, *Textual Sources*, 1–2). But it is precisely their extreme archaism that warrants dating the Gathas so early. Several scholars, most notably Freedman, have attempted to extract information about early Israelite history and religion from linguistically archaic biblical poems (*Pottery, Poetry*, 77–178). But the corpus is tiny and cannot be dated as reliably as inscriptions excavated *in situ*. Moreover, the most thorough linguistic study to date, while confirming the antique style of Exod 15:1–18, also places Job far earlier than any exegete had ever dared to (Robertson, *Linguistic Evidence*—but now see de Moor, *Rise of Yahwism*, 131–62).

[174] On the relationship between Yahweh's uniqueness and monotheism, see C. J. Labuschagne, *The Incomparability of Yahweh in the Old Testament* (Pretoria Oriental Series 5; Leiden: Brill, 1966).

historical "Moses," I would even consider the possibility that Akhenaten's teaching reached Israel, not in earliest days, but during the monarchy, in time to influence Deuteronomic theology.[175] Scholars agree that, in some fashion (via Phoenicia?), the Egyptian "Instruction of Amenope" (first half, first millennium) influenced Proverbs, particularly 22:17–24:22.[176] Perhaps the same stream bore the legacy of Amarna.[177] As we have seen, few scholars deny the Atenist roots of Psalm 104, yet none dates it to the Late Bronze Age.

Inconclusion (sic!)

I would here invoke and exorcize one more scholarly axiom: *We are obliged to adopt as provisional truth the most likely and parsimonious reconstruction, based on the evidence available.* No doctrine could sound more innocuous but be so pernicious. What obliges us? Who? Given the gaps in our knowledge, the complexity of historical processes and our inability to conduct proper experiments, we should aim rather for multiple, parallel hypotheses, as complex as the events they purport to explain. We can and must take into account the 95 percent of information hidden from our view, the sea bottom connecting solitary islands of data. The only sensible response to fragmented, slowly but randomly accruing evidence is radical open-mindedness. A single, simple explanation for a historical event is generally a failure of imagination, not a triumph of induction.

For the case at hand: the notion that the Bible owes a debt to Amarna, directly or indirectly, is not ludicrous and is yet to be disproved. Granted, the trail of parchment, papyrus and potsherd can no longer be followed. Archaeologically speaking, the Israelite intelligentsia remain as "invisible" as the much-discussed early Hebrew nomads. Under such conditions, to deny Akhenaten's influence absolutely, or to assert it confidently, would equally be academic hubris. We must dare to equivocate, eschewing the absolute answers demanded by our monotheistic cultural heritage.[178]

---

[175] Recall, in this context, the strange fact that seventh-century Levites bear previously unattested Egyptian-Hebrew names (n. 107).

[176] N. Shupak, *Where Can Wisdom Be Found?* (OBO 130; Fribourg: University Press; Göttingen: Vandenhoeck & Ruprecht, 1993). On the general question of Egyptian influence upon Israel, see Redford, *Egypt, Canaan, and Israel*, 365–94.

[177] Admittedly, "Amenope" is wholesome material ideal for scribal training, whereas Akhenaten's doctrine had been anathema for centuries.

[178] I thank Susan Ackerman, Daniel Arovas, Shannon Burkes, Richard S. Cohen, David Noel Freedman, Richard Elliott Friedman, David M. Goodblatt, Ronald S. Hendel, Bernhard Lang, Thomas E. Levy, Peter Machinist, John A. Marino, Shawna Dolansky Overton, James G. Propp, Melford E. Spiro, Jeffrey H. Tigay and Donald F. Tuzin for their help at various stages of this research.

CHART 3. (from Dion, "YHWH as Storm-god and Sun-god," p. 60)

Psalm 104:20–21 You set darkness—it is night; then all the beasts of the forest are creeping about Lions are roaring for prey, seeking their food from God	Aten Hymn 24–33 When you set in the western lightland, Earth is in darkness as if in death; Every lion comes from its den. All the serpents bite; Darkness hovers, earth is silent, as their maker rests in lightland.
Ps 104:22–23 The sun rises—they retire, in their dens they lie down.	Aten Hymn 34–41 Earth brightens when you dawn in lightland, When you shine as Aten of daytime; As you dispel the dark As you cast your rays, The Two Lands are in festivity. Awake they stand on their feet, You have roused them; Bodies cleansed, clothed, Their arms adore your appearance, The entire land sets out to work.
Man goes out for his job, for his labor until the evening.	
Ps 104:24 How numerous are the things you made, YHWH! All of them, you made wisely.	Aten Hymn 68,93 How many are your deeds, How excellent are your ways, O Lord of Eternity!
Ps 104:25–26 There are found creeping things without number, beasts both small and great; There do ships move about, Leviathan that you formed to play with.	Aten Hymn 49–52 Ships fare north, fare south as well, Roads lie open when you rise; The fish in the river dart before you, Your rays are in the midst of the sea.
Ps 104:27–28 All of them, they depend on you to give them their food in its season. Give it to them—they gather it up. Open your hand—they are well sated.	Aten Hymn 76–78 You set every man in his place, You supply their needs; Everyone has his food.
Ps 104:29 Hide your face—they are thrown into disarray. Take back their breath—they expire and to their dust they return.	Aten Hymn 121–122 When you have dawned they live, When you set they die.

APPENDIX D
THE THEME OF EXODUS IN THE BIBLE

◆

The Cycle of Renewal

The story of Israel's flight from Egypt is the most important in the Hebrew Bible. It must be retold in every generation, as evidence of Yahweh's might and fidelity. In Exod 10:1–2, God explains that he had made Pharaoh obdurate "in order to set these my signs in his core, and in order that you may tell into the ears of your son and of your son's son how I lorded it in Egypt, and my signs that I set among them, that you may know that I am Yahweh." In the seventh century B.C.E., Judeans still swore, "As Yahweh lives, who brought Israel's Sons out of the land of Egypt" (Jer 16:14; 23:7). And later still, in Ezra's time, the singers chanted: "You set signs and wonders upon Pharaoh and upon his slaves and upon all the people of his land . . . and made yourself a name as of this day" (Neh 9:10). Ever since, readers of the Bible have drawn inspiration and hope from the tale of Israel's liberation from Egypt and subjugation to God—whatever its historical veracity (see AP-PENDIX B).

A previous generation of American biblical scholars claimed to have isolated the Bible's uniqueness vis-à-vis the ancient world in its linear, historical consciousness (e.g., Wright 1964). Athwart this aspect, however, runs the annual cycle of festivals, tracking the sun, moon and seasons. And history itself, as recounted in the Old Testament, displays cyclical aspects.

In vol. I, pp. 554–62, we saw how the basic plotline of Exodus—a god of storm and groundwater dries the Sea, fertilizes the desert and establishes his kingdom at his holy mountain—recapitulates Israelite and pre-Israelite myths of cosmogony. Later in the Bible, the Exodus itself becomes a template for future reenactments of God's great, creative act *in illo tempore* (cf. Eliade 1954; Fishbane 1979: 121–40).

The first Exodus encore is when Israel crosses into Canaan. In fact, one could call Joshua 3–5 an "anti-Exodus," since the events occur in reverse order from those in the Torah:[1]

---

[1] The chart fudges by omitting the cessation of Manna in Josh 5:12, which corresponds to Exodus 16.

A. Angelic vision (Exodus 3–4)
  B. Paschal celebration (Exodus 12:1–42)
    C. Requirement of circumcision (Exodus 12:43–49)
      D. Sea crossing (Exodus 13:17–15:21)
        E. The wilderness (Exod 15:22–Joshua 2:24)
      D'. River crossing (Joshua 3:1–5:1)
    C'. Requirement of circumcision (Josh 5:2–9)
  B'. Paschal celebration (Josh 5:10–11)
A'. Angelic vision (Josh 5:13–15)

Later, the prophets invoke the Exodus tradition (e.g., Amos 2:9–10; 3:1–2; Micah 6:1–5). Finding Israel to be corrupt, some imagine a return to the wilderness, a new Exodus and a covenant renewal, rather like an unhappy couple taking a second honeymoon to reinvigorate their relationship (Hos 2:16–22; cf. Jer 2:1–7; Ezekiel 16) or an estranged father and son making a road trip (Hos 11:1–4). Going farther, Hos 9:3; 11:5 predicts a return to Egypt, as well as exile in Assyria.

With the deportation of the northern Israelites in 722/21 B.C.E., the fantasy of a second Exodus achieved a new specificity and urgency. Surely, if Yahweh took Israel out from Egypt, he could gather them from the earth's four quarters and lead them back to Canaan (Isaiah 10–12; Jer 16:14–15; 23:1–8; 31:1–22). Conversely, if Judah, too, proved disobedient, among her punishments would be a return to Egypt (Deut 28:68).

The need for a second Exodus became even more pressing, when the remnant of Judah, too, was deported to Babylon. Again, seers envisioned a restoration, a passage to Canaan not through the Sea but across the Desert (Jer 31:23–33:26; 50:4–8, 19–20, 33–34; Ezek 20:33–44; 34; Zechariah 10). In particular, Second Isaiah envisioned the journey to be accompanied by ecological wonders: the transformation of the wilderness into paradisiacal fertility and *a fortiori* the regeneration of the land of Israel (Isa 41:17–19; 43:16–21; 48:20–21; 60:7–19). This salvation would recapitulate both the Exodus and the primordial, creative battle, only this time Yahweh would make the dry into wet to save his people (Isa 44:27; 50:2–3; 51:9–11; see further vol. I, pp. 606–13).

Above, I have compared the Exodus story to a rite of passage, wherein the initiate leaves his home and status, undergoes a harrowing rebirth, and returns in a new capacity (vol. I, pp. 35–36). The quintessential communal rite of passage is the pilgrimage (Turner 1974). Each time Israel is potentially or actually exiled from its land, an opportunity is created for regeneration and ascent to new glory. In the Jewish context, the final reenactment of the Exodus will be the Ingathering of the Exiles in the Messianic Age. (Already in the Bible, the transforming pilgrimage need not be for Israelites alone; Isa 19:19–25; 23:10–11; Ezek 29:1–16; Amos 9:7 envision foreign nations, too, undergoing their own versions of Exodus [cf. Fishbane 1979: 128–29].) Moreover, individuals can have their own regenerative experiences that anticipate or echo the Exodus (Zakovitch 1991: 46–98; Geoghegan 2004).

The Plagues Tradition in the Bible

Several passages in the Bible are related to or perhaps based upon the Plagues narrative of the Torah. As none follow Exodus precisely, scholars have often speculated on whether they have before them a variant version, perhaps even one of the pentateuchal sources prior to its redaction. If so, this would afford striking confirmation of the Documentary Hypothesis. Closest to the received text is Ps 105:26–36:

> [26] He sent Moses his slave,
> Aaron, whom he had chosen;
> [27] They [LXX, Syr "He"] set among them the words/matters of his signs
> And his wonders in the land of Ham [i.e., Egypt].
> [28] He sent darkness and it darkened,
> But they indeed [?] rebelled against his word(s).
> [29] He turned their waters to blood
> And killed their fish.
> [30] Their land swarmed with frogs
> In the rooms of their kings.
> [31] He said, and ʿārōb came [or: and he brought ʿārōb],
> Lice in all their territory.
> [32] He made hail their rains,
> A fire of flames in their land.
> [33] And he smote their vine and their fig
> And smashed the tree(s) of their territory.
> [34] He said, and locust came [or: and he brought locust],
> And grasshoppers innumerable;
> [35] And it ate all the herbage in their land
> And ate the fruit of their soil.
> [36] And he smote every firstborn in their land,
> The first of all their strength.

Here we find the following sequence: darkness, blood, frogs, ʿārōb-lice, hail, locusts, firstborn (Loewenstamm 1992: 82). It is highly likely that Psalm 105 has before it our composite Torah. V 24, for example, combines Exod 1:7 (R/P) and 1:9 (J): "And he made his people very fruitful (wayyeper), and made him more mighty/numerous (wayyaʿămīṣēhû) than its foes (miṣṣārā[y]w, punning with miṣrayim 'Egypt')." Similarly, the joint reference to ʿārōb (E) and kinnîm 'lice' (P) strongly suggests that the present text lies before the author.

And yet, like the Priestly source (vol. I, pp. 315–17), Psalm 105 tells of only seven Plagues, and the order differs from the Ten Plagues of Exodus. It may not be too troubling that the insect plagues of ʿārōb and lice are reversed. Less expected is the omission of murrain and šəḥîn. And most surprising is the location of darkness: in Exodus, it comes between locusts and firstborn and is something of a climax; in Psalm 105, darkness is the first plague, more of a preparation. Since the darkness is essentially harmless, in some ways Psalm 105 makes more sense than Exodus.

SPECULATION: Recall that the Elohistic plague of darkness seems truncated (see vol. I, pp. 310–21). One might hypothesize that darkness originally stood first as in Psalm 105, but was later for some reason shifted to its present position, along the way losing its introduction. If something of this sort occurred, however, it was in a pre-Elohistic form of the tradition. As E stands, 10:21–23 is necessary to its context; moreover, only the later Plagues in E feature the separation of Israel and Egypt.

Assuming that the psalmist knew the narrative in its current form, three possible explanations for his divergences from Exodus suggest themselves: (a) the poet freely reorganized; (b) he knew another, non-Elohistic, tradition that put darkness first; (c) the text is corrupt, and v 28 originally stood between vv 35 and 36. (The fact that eight of the eleven verses quoted here end in the same letter affords ample opportunity for error.) My guess is that the author knew both the version we have, i.e., JEP, and the original Priestly account, which featured only seven Plagues (vol. I, pp. 315–16). His original effort is a reconfigured synthesis of the two versions.

It appears that Ps 78:44–51 also knows only seven Plagues:

44 And he turned their "niles" to blood,
and their streams they cannot drink
45 He sends against them *'ārōb*, and it ate them,
And frog(s), and it destroyed them.
46 And he gave to the grasshopper their harvest,
And their labor to the locust.
47 He killed with hail *(bārād)* their vine,
And their sycamores with *ḥănāmal* ["hail" ? "fire"?].
48 And he delivered to the hail *(bārād)* their livestock,
And their cattle to the flames/diseases *(rəšāpîm)*
49 He sends against them his *nose-flaring* (anger),
Rage and fury and trouble,
A mission of messengers of ill;
50 He smooths a path for his anger.
He did not spare from death their life/living beings *(napšām)*,
And delivered their life/beast(s) *(ḥayyātām)* to the plague.
51 And he smote every firstborn in Egypt,
The *first of strength* in Ham's tents.

Scholars disagree on how to enumerate the Plagues of Psalm 78. Before reaching a conclusion, we must comment on three controverted points.

First: in v 45 do we have two plagues or a single, combined plague of frogs and *'ārōb*? Loewenstamm (1992: 80) takes the latter position, maintaining that, if we did not know Exodus, we would not distinguish separate incidents in v 45. He argues that, just as in v 46 ḥāsîl and ʾarbe(h) 'locust, grasshopper' are one plague, so in v 45 are frogs and lice. The counterargument, however, is simple: whereas ḥāsîl and ʾarbe(h) really are the same creature, frogs and insects are not. Also, although he never says so explicitly, Loewenstamm seems to feel that each plague should receive one bicolon. But since in vv 84–50 one of the Plagues has been expanded, it is easy to imagine that frogs and ʿārōb have each been restricted to a single colon. I and the majority of commentators would therefore count frogs and ʿārōb as two plagues.

The second problem arises in v 48, where Loewenstamm (1992: 80–81) emends brd 'hail' to *dbr 'plague.' While such a metathesis is credible, the only textual support is the relatively late Greek translation of Symmachus. The parallel colon cannot help us choose between bārād and deber, for rəšāpîm can denote arrows (Ps 76:4), fire (Cant 8:6) or plague (Deut 32:24; Hab 3:5 [parallel to deber]); compare the eponymous Resheph, the Canaanite god of archery and disease. The conservative course is to follow the MT and the large majority of Versions, in which two bicola are devoted to the plague of hail.

The third difficulty pertains to the last bicolon of v 50. Loewenstamm (1992: 81–82) distinguishes this death from the preceding death of the cattle and from the following death of the firstborn. He understands napšām in its normal sense as "themselves, their life" and takes ḥayyātām as a rare term for "their life, their living" (cf. Ps 143:3; Job 33:22; one could also read the infinitive *ḥăyōtām). Loewenstamm would accordingly render, "He did not spare from death them/ their life, and delivered their life to the plague."

In this bicolon Loewenstamm discovers a plague of death against Egyptians in general, hinted at but not described in Exod 9:14: "For this time I am going to send all these my afflictions against you and against your slaves and against your people" (see Loewenstamm, pp. 92–93 n. 44). But it is difficult to accept such a reading. Exod 9:14 is rather vague, and, as Loewenstamm himself admits, the next verse contradicts his interpretation: "For now, I could have sent forth my arm and smitten you and your people with the plague"—but I did not. More likely, then, deber 'plague' in Ps 78:50 refers either to the following death of the firstborn or to the death of cattle by murrain, whether or not we emend bārād to *deber in v 48. Admittedly, napšām would ordinarily mean "their life, themselves." But since ḥayyâ generally means 'beast(s)' (so OG), we could interpret napšām as "their living thing(s)," i.e., domestic animals. The parallelism nepeš//ḥayyâ would then be a poetic breakup (cf. Melamed 1961: 115–53) of the familiar phrase nepeš ḥayyâ 'living soul,' often connoting animals (e.g., Genesis 1 passim, etc.).

In short, like most commentators (e.g., Lauha 1945: 49–51), I count the following seven Plagues in Psalm 78: blood, ʿārōb, frogs, locusts, hail, murrain, firstborn. Loewenstamm also finds seven, but he combines ʿārōb with frogs and adds a plague against Egyptians in general. By either analysis, the absence of the uniquely Priestly Plagues (lice, šəḥîn) affords important support for the Documentary Hypothesis.

Although Psalm 78 is quite close to E, they do not agree precisely. Various details lacking in E are supplied to fill out the poetic parallelism, making the description more graphic. The river channels are called *nōzəlîm* as well as *yə'ōrîm*, the locusts are called *ḥāsîl* as well as *'arbe(h)*, the hail is perhaps called *ḥănāmal* as well as *bārād*, the fire is perhaps called *ḥănāmal* or *rəšāpîm* instead of *'ēš*, the firstborn are called *rē(')šît 'ônîm* as well as *bəkôr*, Egypt is called *ḥām* and *śədē(h) ṣō'an* as well as *miṣrayim*. Psalm 78 specifies that the plants smitten by the hail were the grapevine and the sycamore fig, whereas Exodus is more vague. Such additions need not arise from a variant text or tradition. Similarly, the reversed order of frogs and *'ārōb* in Psalm 78 vis-à-vis Exodus is trivial within a poetic bicolon; compare the order of *'ārōb* and lice in Ps 105:31.

A more substantial difference is that E contains eight Plagues—blood, frogs, *'ārōb*, murrain, hail, locusts, darkness, firstborn (vol. I, pp. 315–16)—whereas Psalm 78 lacks darkness and thus has only seven. Many have been struck by the peculiar treatment of darkness in Exodus and in Psalms 78 and 105: it is truncated in Exodus (10:21–23), moved to the fore in Psalm 105 and omitted entirely in Psalm 78. Some assign Exod 10:21–23 to P or a third source to explain this confusion (see SOURCE ANALYSIS to 7:8–11:10). I instead infer that the Redactor trimmed E's episode to conform to P's pattern (REDACTION ANALYSIS to 7:8–11:10). As for the omission of darkness in Psalm 78, if eight events are to be reduced to the more stereotypical seven (Pope 1962a), something must go.

The most important disagreement between E and Psalm 78 is that, while Psalm 78 has the order locusts-hail-murrain, E has murrain-hail-locusts. One possibility is that, if Psalm 78 is based upon E, Psalm 78 reflects the original sequence, and E has suffered disarrangement. There are in fact slightly problematic redundancies in these Elohistic Plagues: locusts and hail alike destroy vegetation, and hail and murrain alike destroy cattle. The Elohist explicitly deals with the former by referring to the agricultural calendar (9:31–32; 10:5, 15)—the hail and locusts destroy different crops—but the problem with the cattle is left unresolved (see, however, NOTE to 9:6). Reversing hail and locusts in E as *per* Psalm 78 would solve certain problems: the locusts would eat only the greenery, and then the hail would destroy the plants completely (9:25; cf. Loewenstamm 1992: 97–98). By this scenario, the cross-allusions and calendrical references in Exod 9:31–32; 10:5, 15 would be later additions, subsequent to the inversion of locusts and hail. While such a development is possible, we must ask: why would a copyist or editor go to the trouble of rearranging E and inserting harmonizing notices?

Similarly, that murrain and hail formerly stood in reversed order in E is possible but problematic. Apropos of Exodus, many have observed that, if all the Egyptian cattle die from murrain (9:1–7; see NOTE to 9:6), how are any left to be killed by hail (9:19–21, 25) or to die during the paschal night (11:5; 12:12, 29)? Reversing the two plagues eliminates the problem, since the hail kills only some cattle. The seemingly gratuitous comment about the pious Egyptians sheltering their cattle (9:20) would then serve an important function: to save the beasts for the next episode, the plague of murrain.

But such a radical reordering of Exodus would raise a new problem (only the *pious* Egyptians' cattle would then die of murrain) without solving an old one (the death of firstborn cattle during the paschal night). Moreover, as the murrain episode is far shorter than the hail, the overall tendency toward greater detail as the Plagues progress would be violated. And, again, we must wonder why a scribe would have shifted the Elohistic episodes. We had better not adjust Exodus on the basis of Psalm 78. It is easier to imagine a psalmist using his poetic license to re-order the Plagues than to posit an extremely invasive copyist shuffling episodes in Exodus.

In sum, the similarities and differences between Psalm 78 and E have several possible explanations. One, as we have just seen, is that Psalm 78 is based upon a variant version of E; another is that Psalm 78 is a loose retelling of E. Yet another possibility is that Psalm 78 is based not upon E but upon a hypothetically similar J account, either eliminated by Redactor[JE] or so thoroughly combined with E that it can no longer be reconstituted. Finally, the Psalmist might have used an otherwise unknown source, whether written or oral.[2]

In addition to Psalms 78 and 105, other probable biblical allusions to the Plagues of Egypt are Exod 15:26, "any of the disease I laid upon Egypt" (R?); Deut 28:27, "Yahweh will smite you with the *šəḥîn* of Egypt," and Deut 28:60, "He will turn against you all the illness of Egypt before which you dreaded." But, while Deut 28:27 seems to allude to P's plague of *šəḥîn*, it is possible that Deut 28:27, 60 refers not to the Plagues but to illnesses considered characteristic of Egypt. 1 Sam 6:6, on the other hand, adverts specifically to E, especially to Exod 10:2: "And why should you make firm *(təkabbədû)* your heart as Egypt and Pharaoh made firm their heart? When he [Yahweh] lorded it *(hit'allēl)* over them, then he released them and they went." Note, too, that the Philistines' specific ailment, *'ŏpālîm* 'tumors, buboes, pustules' (1 Sam 5:6, 9, 12; 6:4 [Kethibh]) is otherwise mentioned only in Deut 28:27, adjacent to the "*šəḥîn* of Egypt"; thus, there may be a connection with P as well.

Ezekiel, too, may allude to the Priestly and Elohistic Plagues. Consider the following oracle against Egypt (Ezek 32:2–8):

Son of Man, raise a lament over Pharaoh king of Egypt and say to him, ". . . you are like the Serpent (read **tnyn* for MT *tnym*) in the seas. And you splashed in your rivers and muddied the water with your feet, and you fouled their rivers. . . . And upon the surface of the field I will cast you . . . and I will put your flesh upon the mountains and fill the valleys with your rottenness (?). And I will water the land with your effluent, with your blood, up to the mountains, and the channels will be full of you. And I will cover . . . the heavens, I will darken their stars. And the sun, I will cover it with cloud, and the moon will not shine its light. All the luminaries of light in the heavens I will darken over/on account of you, and I will put darkness over your land.

---

[2] The fluidity of the Plagues tradition lingered into the early postbiblical era. 4QParaphrase of Genesis and Exodus, which seems to harmonize Exodus with Psalms 78 and 105, omits *šəḥîn* and for the rest has the order: blood, frogs, lice, *'ārōb*, murrain, darkness, hail, locusts, firstborn.

Pharaoh is likened to a serpent (cf. Exod 7:8–12), a river creature who will die on dry land (cf. 7:26–8:10) and fill the channels of Egypt with its blood (cf. 7:14–25). Yahweh will also send darkness (cf. 10:21–23), and, in Ezek 32:13, he kills the cattle of Egypt (cf. Exod 9:1–6) (Fretheim 1991: 121). These resemblances to the Plagues tradition are so subtle, however, as perhaps to be incidental, reflecting the shared idiom and mind-set of the Priestly Writer and Ezekiel (cf. Levitt Kohn 2002).

It is likely, at least, that the Plagues cycle has influenced Ezekiel's prophecy of Yahweh's battle against Gog (Ezek 38:22–23): "I will enter into judgment with him, with plague (*deber*) and with blood; a pouring rain and hailstones; fire and sulphur I will rain upon him. . . . I will make myself known in the eyes of many nations, and they will know that I am Yahweh." Most striking of all is Ezek 30:1–18, where Yahweh kills the Egyptians, sets fire to their land, dries up the Nile, destroys their idols, darkens the day and works "judgments" (cf. Exod 6:6; 12:12) against Egypt, "that they may know that I am Yahweh" (cf. Exod 7:5, 17; 8:18; 10:2; 14:4, 18).

Ezek 9:1–8, moreover, evokes the final plague, the Death of the Firstborn, and the sparing of those whose houses are marked with the paschal blood.

> And he [Yahweh] called in my ears, a great voice, saying, "Bring near the city's punishments, and (each) man, his destruction tool (*kəlî mašhētô*) in his hand."
> And behold: six men coming from the way of the upper gate, which is turned northward, and (each man), his shattering tool in his hand, and one man in their midst dressed in linens, and the scribe's kit on his hips. And they came and stood by the Bronze Altar. . . . [Yahweh] called to the man dressed in the linens with the scribe's kit on his hips, and Yahweh said to him, "Pass (*ʿăbōr*; cf. Exod 12:12, 23) in the midst of the city, in the midst of Jerusalem, and cross a '*t*' on the foreheads of the men who groan and moan over all the abominations done in its midst. . . . The old and youth and virgin and child and women you must kill with destruction (*ləmašhît*), but do not approach against any man on whom the '*t*' is." . . .
> And once they had struck (*kəhakkôtām*; cf. Exod 12:13), and I was left, then I fell on my face and shouted and said, "Ahah, my Lord Yahweh, are you going to destroy (*mašhît*) all Israel's remnant in your spilling your wrath upon Jerusalem?"

These avenging "men" are really angels. One of them, a scribe, puts a saving sign on the foreheads of the righteous, comparable to the blood of the paschal lamb/kid. The other six are Destroyers proper. Thus Ezekiel 9 occupies an intermediate position between E (Exod 12:23) and P (12:13): like P, it uses the term *ləmašhît* impersonally, but like E it envisions supernatural beings who are quasi-independent of Yahweh (see vol. I, pp. 401–2).

In Joel 3, it is barely possible that the oracle on "Yahweh's day" in vv 3–4 has been influenced by the Plagues and Exodus traditions:

> And I will set wonders in the heavens and in the earth,
> Blood and fire and smoke columns;

The sun will be turned to darkness,
And the moon to blood.

Although the Passover Haggadah associates this verse with the Plagues, the imagery may be generic.

If we emend Amos 4:10, we can find another allusion to the Plagues. In the midst of a list of approximately seven calamities (Amos 4:6–11), mostly quite different from those of Exodus (note, however, locusts in v 9), Yahweh obscurely proclaims, "I sent against you disease on the way of/to/from Egypt *(deber bəderek miṣrayim)*." Some such emendation as **deber kədeber miṣrayim* 'disease like Egypt's disease' or simply **deber miṣrayim* 'Egypt's disease' *(BHS)* would yield a clear reference to the Plagues tradition—but this is conjectural (note that the phrase "way of Egypt" occurs also in Isa 10:24, 26). As the text stands, the most likely referent is Yahweh's chastisement of *Israel* in the desert.[3]

Lastly, the seven-Plagues tradition attested in P, Psalms 78 and 105, and obliquely in the seven-plus-one Plagues of E, is paralleled in the Roman period. Revelation 16 describes seven bowls of misfortune to be poured out upon the wicked, producing (1) skin disease, (2–3) sanguification of waters, (4) heat, (5) dark, (6) drying of the Euphrates and (7) thunder, lightning and earthquake. But this more likely reflects the visionary's penchant for sevens than the anomalous survival of the pre-Redactional Plagues tradition (see Pope 1962a, 1962b).

In Short

The biblical authors were inclined to consider the great happenings of Exodus chaps. 12–40, which are spread over almost a year (NOTE to 40:2), as a single event. Yahweh's taking Israel out from Egypt, the Exodus proper, is associated with various subsequent events: the gifts of water and Manna and above all the establishment of the Covenant (Exod 16:32; Deut 4:45–46; 29:24; 1 Kgs 8:9; Jer 7:21–23; 11:3–4; 31:31–32; Ps 81:5–8) (see Loewenstamm 1992: 31–32). Such telescoping is most pronounced in Psalm 114, which, lauding Yahweh's mastery over water, overleaps the years and the miles between the Suph Sea and the River Jordan (see vol. I, p. 560–61):

In Israel's going out from Egypt,
Jacob's House from a foreign-tongued people,
The Sea saw and fled,
The Jordan turns backward. . . .
Before the Lord, dance, O Earth,
Before Jacob's god,
Who converts the mountain into a water pool,
The hard-rock to a water font.

---

[3] The *deber* of Egypt may also be mentioned in 1 Sam 4:8, if we read with McCarter (1980: 104) **ûb(ə)mô dāber* 'and with plague' for MT *bammidbār* 'in the desert.'

What does the story of the Exodus purport to teach? That Yahweh is the source of cosmic power, the singular Godhead. That he has a special, covenantal relationship with Israel. That, as Creator, he directs both natural forces and the course of human events in order to accomplish his will; this he has demonstrated in the past and will continue to demonstrate in the future. That, although Israel itself may frequently disobey Yahweh, no man, not even the god-king of Egypt, can successfully defy him. That he makes and keeps his promises faithfully, but may still change his mind. That the annual cycle of commemorative festivals provides opportunities for historical education, promoting ethical indoctrination. That Yahweh relates to Israel and humanity in two ways: as a presence in the Tabernacle or Temple, and through the medium of Covenant. That God is one and Israel is one (cf. Sarna 1986: 2–4).

In Deut 4:32–34, Moses himself offers a succinct and eloquent summary:

Ask, then, about earlier days that were before you, from the day that Deity created a human upon the earth, and from the (one) edge of the heavens to the (other) edge of the heavens. Has there happened like this great thing, or has its like been heard? Has a people heard the voice of a living deity speak from the midst of fire . . . or has a deity assayed to come to take him (one) nation from the midst of a(nother) nation with trials, with signs and with wonders and with war . . . as all that Yahweh your deity did for you in Egypt, before your eyes?

APPENDIX E
AFTERTHOUGHTS

◆

These reflections follow the structure of the Commentary: Translation, Textual Notes, Source Analysis, Redaction Analysis, Notes and Comment.

Translation

Bible translators take themselves far too seriously. Too often, they feel the oppressive weight of a sacred mission (see the fascinating translators' Preface to the King James Version). But, really, there is no ideal translation or style of translation. For ancient works, we need *alternative* versions, ranging from those truest to the language of translation, that make the text most comfortable, to those truest to the original, that make the text most strange. Mine falls clearly into the latter category.

In retrospect, I am not sure that my English version of Exodus ought to have been called a "translation" at all. It might more accurately have been described, after John Dryden, as a "metaphrase" (Kerr 1900: 1.237). Unlike a conventional translation, a metaphrase inclines to betray its "target" language for its source language, yielding peculiarities that range from non-idiomatic syntax to the coining of neologisms.

Biblical metaphrase is nothing new. Hyperliteral translation dates back to Aquila's Greek version (c. 125 C.E.). In English, metaphrase was first exemplified by John Wyclif's fourteenth-century rendering of the Vulgate. From 1862, we have Robert Young's *Literal Translation of the Bible*, which goes so far as to be incomprehensible in its treatment of verb tenses; the same is said to be true of Julia E. Smith's *The Holy Bible* (1876) (not seen by me). The twentieth century has seen revived interest in this medium: in German by Buber and Rosenzweig (1934), in French by Chouraqui (1975) in English by Fox (1986, 1995), Korsak (1992) and me.

There is a difference between translating modern and ancient works. Whether written in German, French or Hindi, all twenty-first-century literature shares a certain sociohistorical context. While it might be interesting to produce metaphrases of contemporary writings, I doubt their utility outside of the elementary language classroom. On the contrary, we require elegant translations fully as readable as the originals. Rendering ancient works, especially those written in poorly understood languages from alien cultures, is quite another matter—all the more in the Bible's case, where the marketplace already provides many rival, fluid translations, and most of all in a philological commentary such as this.

Some biblical metaphrases claim an esthetic motivation. The Buber-Rosenzweig version brilliantly demonstrates what effects may be reproduced—in particular the "theme word" *(Leitwort)*—when translators follow the restricted lexicon of Biblical Hebrew and eschew more varied diction. Beyond this clear benefit, Buber-Rosenzweig and Fox aspire to imbue their renderings with the spontaneity of the oral performance that they feel characterizes the original. Here we find the lingering influence of Johann Gottfried Herder (1744–1803) and the Romantic and nationalist movements of the nineteenth and twentieth centuries.

My motives for metaphrase are somewhat different. Partly, I am attempting to redress the power imbalance inherent in all translation. I am trying to de-Anglicize and un-Westernize the Bible, and combat the misimpression that this masterpiece can be appreciated fully in any tongue other than the original. (Having access to the Hebrew, I find the celebrated King James Version excruciatingly dull!) I would make few artistic claims for my version of Exodus. If anything, I see it as "punk" art, intended to shock the reader into a new consciousness by making the overly familiar unfamiliar, even grotesque.

I also have altruistic reasons for metaphrase. I frequently meet lovers of the Bible who wish they could have learned Hebrew. I thought, would not such persons appreciate metaphrase as a means to glimpse the back, if not the face, of the Hebrew original?

Trivial as it sounds, I think my greatest stylistic contribution to Bible translation is my war against "of," which usually does not correspond to any Hebrew morpheme. "Of" is a common English word of honest, Anglo-Saxon ancestry. But it did not become a fixture in statements of possession, alongside the genitive, until after 1066 C.E. The overuse of "of" in formal English usage, imitating French "de," is the bastard spawn of Anglo-Norman bi-lingualism, to be excised from Bible translation wherever feasible. By minimizing "of," we can better reflect both spoken English and ancient Hebrew, and return to the native style of our earliest Old English Bible translations. In Aelfric's version (tenth century C.E.), for example, *'ereṣ šin'ār* 'the land of Shinar' is *Sennaar-lande; ben-'ādām* 'the son of Man' is *Adames bearn.* When it comes to translating Hebrew, Beowulf affords a better model than Shakespeare.

Textual Notes

I did not originally set out to produce an in-depth text critical edition of Exodus. After all, the text is extremely well preserved. What changed my mind, however, was the long-awaited publication of the Dead Sea scrolls of Exodus. These called for a fresh, comprehensive treatment.

What to include and what to exclude? The enormous mass of biblical MSS in Hebrew and many other languages from over two millennia creates quite a methodological challenge. When does the information cease to be relevant? My approach has been to present a broad variety of ancient sources, confident that, however slim the chances, here and there old readings survive.

Within the family of Hebrew MSS we call the "Massoretic Text"—the currently preferred spelling, incidentally, is "Masoretic"—I have made an unsystematic effort to convey its variety of readings, rather than simply equate MT with a single MS. The degree of variation is tiny, to be sure. But I wished to correct a common misperception in the general public. With due respect to their perennial diligence, Jewish scribes did *not* work with superhuman accuracy. The immutable Hebrew text, transmitted with word-for-word, nay letter-for-letter accuracy, is a myth of modern orthodox Judaism, now widely disseminated in the form of a best seller (Drosnin 1997) but perfectly false. Anyone who needs convincing to the contrary should spend five seconds with a copy of Kennicott's (1776–80) collation of medieval manuscripts. For those who cannot find this collector's item, my textual apparatus will give a sense of the actual situation.

A minor but rankling problem is the random presence or absence of the conjunction *wə-* 'and' in our Hebrew MSS. In the interests of completeness, I have recorded this trivial variation. Following standard text critical method, whenever possible, I have blamed the inconsistency on haplography or dittography, often preferring the shorter reading. But the real cause is perfectly clear. Scribes just did not think that conjunctions mattered much, and inserted or deleted them at whim. (Naturally, this further dooms the enterprise of letter-counting.)

A special subcategory of the foregoing issue is when the letter waw stands close by a yodh, since these two letters temporarily resembled one another in the Roman era square script (Cross 1961a; Qimron 1972). In vol. I, perhaps I should have given more credence to Sam than to MT in adjudicating these variations, since its version of the paleo-Hebrew alphabet differentiates more clearly between these two letters. (But, even here, we cannot eliminate the possibility that behind Sam lay manuscripts in the square letters, with waw and yodh indistinguishable.)

To explain some textual variation, I have often invoked the possibility of continuous writing, i.e., ancient texts lacking word divisions. I doubt that these actually existed, however; all our inscriptional evidence suggests that the Israelites regularly employed word dividers. Still, because these dividers are not used with total consistency, and because written words sometimes can be impacted when space grows scarce, we can never ignore the possibility of isolated continuous writing. No doubt I have overemphasized the phenomenon.

I think that I was right to give only limited credence to readings restored from LXX and other ancient translations, and instead to privilege MT, Sam and the Qumran scrolls. When we speak of the LXX *Vorlage* as containing such-and-such Hebrew reading, we are really describing what lay in the translator's *mind*; whether it also lay on the table before him is another matter. And when it comes to Hebrew MSS, i.e., the families of MT, Sam and the Dead Sea scrolls, compared to other textual critics I have slightly de-privileged MT, to redress a historical imbalance, i.e., a bias toward MT. But I do share the consensus view that, among all textual streams, the most conservatively transmitted is the Massoretic.

The textual criticism of the Tabernacle pericope (chaps. 25–31, 35–40) is among the most vexed problems in the discipline. In weighing variants, should one attempt to make the two panels agree to the extent possible, or disagree to the extent possible? Since neither method, rigorously pursued, produces plausible results, I have been unabashedly subjective in many of my text-critical choices.

In the future recording and organizing of text-critical evidence, the computer should prove far more convenient than the book. For each word, one should be able to click from reading to reading or to summon parallel versions of entire passages. But still, as anyone who has engaged in this labor knows, the amount of information approaches infinity, the large majority meaningless. Critical discretion will always be necessary.

Source Analysis and Redaction Analysis

It would also be useful to apply computer technology to presenting the Documentary Hypothesis in all its variations. One could actually watch the text coalesce according to the model of this or that critic. However, as discussed in greater length APPENDIX A, I feel that scholarship is approaching the limit of what can be known about the Torah's textual antecendents.

Like two source critics whose work I greatly admire, Richard Elliott Friedman and David M. Carr, I do not regard the analysis of the whole text as incompatible with the quest for its constituents. Quite the contrary. From Friedman in particular—for over two decades, my colleague at the University of California, San Diego—I have learned the value of reading the Torah as a collage, whose striking effects are the result of conscious and unconscious editorial juxtapositions. I found this part of my work in many ways the most congenial, as it challenged the atomizing tendencies of modern pentateuchal criticism in general and my own inclinations and training in particular. I enjoyed stepping into the editors' shoes, often consulting medieval commentaries to obtain a better understanding of the composite whole.

Notes and Comments

Of these sections, which are the meat of the commentary, I have but little to say. I regard as my most important contributions the treatment of the paschal ritual (vol. I, pp. 427–61), the analysis of the Song of the Sea (vol. I, pp. 502–72) and the interpretation of Tabernacle–Temple theology (vol. II, pp. 495–583, 674–709). In the last, I have tried to rehabilitate the supposedly dry-as-dust Priestly source as predicated upon a viable religious system that offered both intellectual satisfaction and emotional pathos. I am proud that, unlike most commentaries on Exodus, mine pays as much attention to the Tabernacle as does the Book of Exodus itself.

The End

Alas, the latter-day burgeoning of commentary writing may be a sign of intellectual decadence. After the mid-twentieth century, the flow of new ancient Near Eastern texts relating to the Old Testament has dried to a trickle. To keep itself busy, recent scholarship has been reworking and refining older ideas, scouring away certain "positivistic" tendencies that have supposedly blemished past work, and importing language and concepts from other disciplines into biblical studies, with mixed results. (For a critique of some recent trends, see Dever 2001.)

Positivism fails us most when it aims for single, simplistic answers. For me, the truth is more often an array of options. Scholarship consists of weighing their merits fairly, and then possessing the self-discipline *not* to judge among them. This, at any rate, has been my *modus operandi*, in both my brief Notes and lengthy Comments.

Being judicious makes one feel virtuous, but also rather dull—hence my occasional forays into the speculative. My fondest hope for the field is that we will discover new caches of Near Eastern documents and become headlong positivists once again, a little wiser than before.

I wish you joy in your researches. *Valete,* ἔῤῥωσθε, לכו לשלום!

INDEX OF AUTHORS

◆

INDEX OF SUBJECTS

◆

INDEX OF SCRIPTURAL AND ANCIENT SOURCES

◆

SCRIPTURAL SOURCES